Date Due

HANDBOOK OF INNOVATIVE THERAPY

SECOND EDITION

HANDBOOK OF INNOVATIVE THERAPY

SECOND EDITION

Edited by

Raymond Corsini

John Wiley & Sons, Inc.
New York • Chichester • Weinheim • Brisbane • Singapore • Toronto

Library of Congress Cataloging-in-Publication Data:
Handbook of innovative therapy / [edited by] Raymond Corsini.—2nd ed.
    p. cm.
    Rev. ed. of: Handbook of innovative psychotherapies. c1981.
    Includes bibliographical references and index.
    ISBN 0-471-34819-8 (cloth: alk. paper)
    1. Psychotherapy—Handbooks, manuals, etc. I. Corsini, Raymond J. II. Handbook of innovative psychotherapies.
    [DNLM: 1. Psychotherapy—methods. WM 420 H23155 2001]
  RC480.5 .H2765 2001
  616.89′14—dc21
                                                00-043434

Printed in the United States of America.

10 9 8 7 6 5 4 3 2 1

To Kleo, again

Contents

Preface

This is the second edition of this book, which in its first edition had sixty-six summaries of innovative psychotherapies. Sixteen summaries were removed, twenty were added, and four of the older ones were brought up to date, in this edition. The word *innovative* is not used as a synonym for *new*, but rather as meaning *different* or *unusual*, although most of the systems detailed here were not in existence twenty years ago.

Each of the psychotherapists are psychologists or psychiatrists. All are aware that there are other systems in existence, such as the big three of Sigmund Freud, Alfred Adler, and Carl Jung, as well as the more modern methods of Carl Rogers, Albert Ellis, and others, but each of the authors in this book believes that he or she has something to say that is new and valuable. As an ex-practitioner, I believe that the world in general and psychotherapists in particular should read and understand the novel conceptions of these individuals. Psychotherapy, although now over one hundred years old as a specific speciality, is still in the process of growth and development, with the general tendency of therapists moving more and more from the limitations of older systems to the explorations of new methods.

It is evident that people suffer from a variety of hidden illnesses, conditions about which, to a great extent, no one but themselves know. Conditions like stress and tension, feelings of unworthiness, inabilities to adjust, inadequacies to survive or to have friendships, and family and work maladjustments are common, and more and more such people seek help for improvement of their lives from practitioners of psychotherapy. Psychotherapy is an art based on a theory which these practitioners and their followers have tested by actual practice. Each therapist is certainly familiar with other, more popular psychotherapies, and probably has used them. But each one has decided that their own new system or variation of an older system had passed the test of experiment and now each has offered his or her insights to the world at large.

Mental treatment at the present time keeps growing not only in numbers of therapists and patients, but also relative to kinds of treatments used—with the intent of finding faster, cheaper, and more effective modes of treatment.

The people in this book have been selected because they have had the courage and the wisdom to strike out in new directions, and their work is presented here in the hope that what they have done and what they have written is read with care and concern. My intent and that of the authors is to advance the field of psychotherapy. No therapist should miss reading this collection of the best of what is new in this field.

Raymond J. Corsini
Honolulu, Hawaii

Chapter 1

ACTUALIZING THERAPY

EVERETT L. SHOSTROM and DAN MONTGOMERY

One of my long-term and long-held goals is to write the definitive book on psychotherapy. In this book I will combine everything that I know from both my own experience and the experience of others to generate the final system of psychotherapy. Everett Shostrom and Dan Montgomery beat me to it in their chapter on Actualizing Therapy.

Actualizing Therapy is intended to be the final therapy, combining all theories of known value—a synthetic supersystem, if you will, of the best of all known theories and procedures. Such a therapy is not a mere piecing together of unrelated elements but is a true creation, in the same sense that an artist assembles into meaningful patterns unrelated items.

I believe an eclectic system of this type will eventually be the therapeutic system of the future. At the present time we are all like the blind men of Hindustan, each clearly seeing a part of the elephant; eventually, I expect, the elephant will be put together, and there will be one final system of psychotherapy—and of personality theory. This position will, of course, be rejected by proponents of single-mode theories and therapies, but in my judgment Actualizing Therapy is a step in the direction that we must eventually go to really become a profession based on science.

Actualizing Therapy employed in an individual or group setting is a system for helping people to get in touch with themselves. A basic tenet of Actualizing Therapy is that most people are other-directed rather than inner-directed (Riesman, 1950). They look to the outside—to authorities and people they respect—for "shoulds," "have tos" and "musts," not realizing that they could better learn to live from within: to trust their own thoughts, feelings, and bodies. Experiencing one's self within and expressing one's self without: This is the process of actualization.

Actualizing Therapy incorporates a creative synthesis from many schools of theory and practice in psychotherapy that focus on body, mind, and feelings. From Buber (1951) and Allport (1937, 1961) comes the emphasis on achieving one's "particularity." From Maslow (1954) comes the emphasis on self-actualizing as a reasonable goal of psychotherapy. From Leary (1957) and Satir (1966) comes the emphasis on the feeling polarities of anger–love and strength–weakness as core structures in the personality.

The goal of Actualizing Therapy is to restore a client's trust in his own being, and to aid him to become rhythmic and expressive on the feeling polarities in verbal, feeling, and bodily ways. Replacing survival tactics with actualizing growth responses enables the client to handle problems of living with creative self-expression, interpersonal effectiveness, commitment to values, and choice of one's mission in life.

HISTORY

Actualizing Therapy emerged through the close friendship of Everett Shostrom, the senior author of this chapter, and Abraham Maslow. Maslow (1954) proposed self-actualization as a reasonable goal of therapy. Shostrom (1976) designed a system of concepts and techniques capable of assisting a client along the journey of actualizing.

The theoretical underpinnings of Actualizing Therapy came from research at the Institute of Personality Assessment at Berkeley by Leary, Barron, MacKinnon, and Coffey (Leary, 1957). Factor analysis of personality traits on a sample of over 5000 cases showed that two dynamic polarities form the core of personality: anger–love and strength–weakness. Other polarities, such as masculinity–femininity, dominance–submission, and independence–dependence, were also found to be significant. For simplicity and to provide key reference points of latitude

1

and longitude in the domain of feelings, anger–love, strength–weakness were chosen by Shostrom to be the core elements of Actualizing Therapy.

These "compass points of the self" correspond to Maslow's classic research on personality (1954), where he found that actualizing people express tender love and anger with ease, and that they are competent and strong, yet keenly aware of weaknesses.

In 1962 Shostrom collaborated with Maslow to produce the Personal Orientation Inventory (POI; Shostrom, 1963), the first assessment procedure for measuring actualizing tendencies. The POI introduced a scientific research orientation to Actualizing Therapy, and research over the past 16 years has shown that persons completing Actualizing Therapy are more synergistically balanced on the four polarities.

An important dimension to the historical evolution of theory and technique of Actualizing Therapy is the close personal association of Shostrom with founders of other schools of psychotherapy. This association came about primarily through a series of films Shostrom produced on each of the following persons and their theories: Abraham Maslow, Rollo May, Carl Rogers, Victor Frankl, Albert Ellis, Fritz Perls, Alexander Lowen, and Arnold Lazarus. In addition to these films, Shostrom produced several films of a more philosophical nature with Paul Tillich, Alan Watts, and Ashley Montague.

Actualizing Therapy is a creative synthesis. From Rogers (1951) comes the focus on a client's feelings and the importance of nonjudgmental warmth between client and therapist. From Perls (1969) comes the focus on the client's awareness in the here and now. From Ellis (1962) comes the view of therapy as the process of revising assumptions about life. And from Lowen (1975) comes the focus on the client's body as a primary tool for diagnosis and therapy.

Taken together, the creative synthesis puts equal importance on thinking, feeling, and bodily aspects of being.

In 1976 Shostrom's most comprehensive work, *Actualizing Therapy: Foundations for a Scientific Ethic,* was published. The book includes verbatim transcripts, lists of films on Actualizing Therapy, therapeutic techniques, and a full range of tests known collectively as the Actualizing Assessment Battery.

In 1979 the Growth Process Inventory (GPI) was published. The GPI measures survival patterns taken from Lowen's bioenergetic character types, and also reveals actualizing growth tendencies on the dimensions of anger, love, strength, weakness, and trust. The GPI represents Shostrom's latest efforts to build a system that reveals actualizing tendencies as well as pathology, and that supports healthy intra- and interpersonal functioning.

CURRENT STATUS

Shostrom was director of the Institute of Actualizing Therapy in Santa Ana, California, where he and Dan Montgomery were engaged in research, writing, and therapy. Shostrom was Distinguished Professor of Psychology at the United States International University, where Actualizing Therapy is a part of the professional psychology curriculum.

The roots of Actualizing Therapy are found in two publications, the *Personal Orientation Inventory* (Shostrom, 1963) and *Therapeutic Psychology* (Brammer & Shostrom, 1977). The POI has generated many published studies and is currently being used in therapeutic, educational, industrial, and religious settings.

The most comprehensive book available for studying Actualizing Therapy is *Actualizing Therapy: Foundations for a Scientific Ethic* (Shostrom, 1976b).

With its emphasis on normal human growth, Actualizing Therapy has also found expression in popular literature. *Man, the Manipulator* (Shostrom, 1967) was a best-seller, having sold nearly 2 million copies. *Healing Love* (Shostrom & Montgomery, 1978) integrated actualizing principles with religious thought.

In addition to books and tests, Shostrom has produced two historically significant films on psychotherapy. The first, *Three Approaches to Psychotherapy I* (the "Gloria" film), features Rogers, Perls, and Ellis working with the same client, and received worldwide attention. Another film, *Three Approaches to Psychotherapy II* (the "Kathy" film), features Rogers, Shostrom, and Lazarus working with the same client. The film received the American Personnel and Guidance Association award for the most outstanding film of 1979.

THEORY

Actualizing Therapy is based on a model of becoming an actualizing person rather than curing a state of illness or merely solving immediate life problems.

The central model of Actualizing Therapy (Figure 1.1), is systematically explained throughout this section. For a more comprehensive treatment of the model, the reader is referred to Shostrom's *Actualizing Therapy* (1976b).

Traditionally psychotherapy has steered away from the suggestion of universal values. However, the polarities of anger–love, strength–weakness seem to us to come close to a concept of universal values that support personal growth and interpersonal fulfillment through the journey of life.

The advantage of the actualizing model in Figure 1.1 is that it shows how growth is arrested and how growth

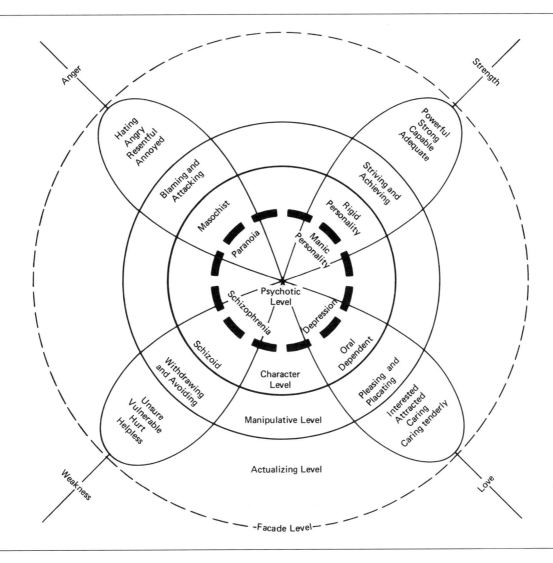

Figure 1.1   The actualizing model.

can be restored: The model joins a system of malfunction with a system of healthy functioning.

Notice that the thickness of the circles changes as one moves from the outer, actualizing level into the inner, progressively more constricted rings of manipulation, character disorder, and psychoses. The broken line of the outermost circle shows that the facade or "public self" of the actualizing person functions as a semipermeable membrane, allowing the person to be in constant touch with his own core (the area inside the circle) and to express himself freely along the polar vectors of anger–love, strength–weakness. The arrows form figure eights between the opposing polarities, showing that the actualizing person is not only expressive of his core self but also sensitive to emotional, intellectual, and physical information received from others. The person takes these inputs into his core for consideration of a genuine response.

A good analogy for an actualizing lifestyle is the human heart. The constant movement of expansion and contraction suggests the dynamic rhythm of the polarities. A person dies physically when the heart stops pulsating. A person dies emotionally when the polarities of anger, love, strength, and weakness are constricted. Without vivid, pulsating feelings, the person becomes insensitive to his own core as well as to the needs and feelings of others.

Bleuler (1940) has said that schizophrenia is the inability to modulate affect. Actualizing Therapy holds that actualizing includes the *ability* to modulate affect fully. If schizophrenia is the major mental disorder— and it allegedly accounts for 90 percent of the people in mental hospitals—then it is logical to define actualizing as the opposite of schizophrenia. Indeed the data of Fox, Knapp, and Michael (1968), based on the POI, demon-

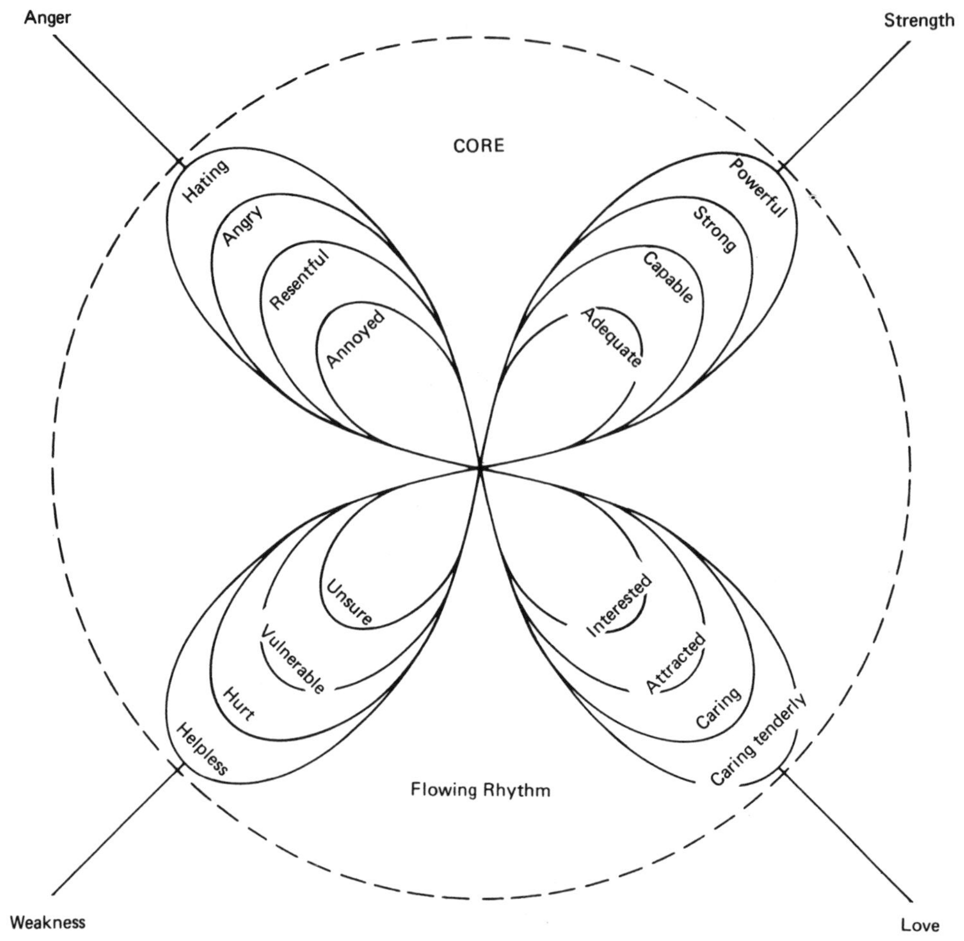

Figure 1.2   The actualizing spectrum.

strates that hospitalized schizophrenics are extremely low on all scales of actualizing. The actualizing person, in contrast, develops the capacity for a full feeling repertoire, as shown in Figure 1.2.

Actualizing does not mean arriving at a final state of full emotional awareness and perfect self-expression. Rather, it connotes an attitude of openness to what one is feeling, coupled with a willingness to express those feelings in actualizing ways. One learns compassion for one's limitations and takes comfort in one's manipulative tendencies, knowing that growth is a process that requires commitment, patience, and self-acceptance. "Effortless effort" describes the paradox of actualizing growth. In the actualizing spectrum of Figure 1.2, the ability to modulate affect enables a person to sometimes move in a "maxi-swing" to points of intense feeling at the very ends of the polarities, but more often to be sensitive to more subtle, milder levels of emotional expression shown as "mini-swings."

The journey of life involves enhancing emotional sensitivity. As one becomes more at home with one's self and

more in touch with others, there arises a new and more accurate picture of reality. From this vantage point options become visible that were once obscure; elasticity and flexibility increase one's satisfaction in living. Actualizing behavior emerges out of being finely tuned to one's own and others' needs, desires, and feelings.

Grace and trust are interlocking concepts at the heart of Actualizing Therapy. The experience of grace—of knowing that we are loved and lovable—allows us to lay down our defenses, come out of our hiding places, and be what we are. The experience of grace generates trust. When trust energizes the core of our being, we are able to risk expression of natural feelings that come spontaneously with involvement and interest in living. We are able to be on the outside (public self) what we feel within (core). But trust in our cores does not always prevail. Emotional traumas, deprivations in childhood, wrong teachings about life, and limitations placed on us by circumstances can result in fear, not trust, dominating our inner cores.

Fear brings resistance to experiencing and expressing feelings. Fear causes us to constrict our feelings, rigidify our behavior, and lose our sensitivity. Increasing amounts of fear make a person more defensive, more desperate, and more emotionally numb. Fear is similar to cold; too much fear causes our cores to freeze and become inactive.

In Actualizing Therapy we seek to invite a distressed person back into the warmth of human encounter to "thaw out" his or her core. We do this through vigorous action techniques that mobilize the person's core feelings and that move him or her from indifference to caring, from apathy to full feeling. Psychopathology may be understood in terms of limited or distorted attempts to actualize. Manipulative behavior, character disorders, and psychotic states (see Figure 1.1) represent survival tactics for trying to get along in the world when one has been hurt and frightened. Therapy is a system of rebirth where the individual reexperiences fears and finds the strength to trust his or her core in spite of negative influences from life.

We define the core as an untouched, perfectly preserved sense of self. The core may be threatened, resulting in core pain, but it can never be destroyed. Individual therapy enables the client to make contact with repressed core pain. The client expresses intense feelings of rage, terror, shame, or longing that reside in the core as residue from past betrayals or rejections. In time the person is invited into group therapy, where he or she has a laboratory for interpersonal relationships. In a group the client works through ancillary feelings of embarrassment or guilt by learning to admit his or her manipulations. The client becomes free to experiment with experiencing and expressing the feeling polarities in the "here-and-nowness" of the group. *Dependence* in asking for help becomes *independence* as the client becomes more expressive at the core level. Finally, the client understands what it means to be *interdependent:* to be strong and yet vulnerable; to be autonomous and yet surrender to one's feelings of love for others.

Levels of Psychopathology

As shown in Figure 1.1, we seek to understand pathology against the background of healthy functioning. Healthy functioning is based on trust in one's core; pathology is based on fear.

To understand how fear works to constrict the core, we use the analogy of the amoeba, a tiny one-celled organism. If the amoeba is repeatedly pricked by a pin, it permanently contracts itself to survive the attack. If a person is threatened psychologically or physically, especially early in life when basic character is being formed, he or she learns to contract bodily musculature and constrict awareness and expression of feeling. Control rather than trust comes to characterize the person's behavior. The stronger the inner fear and accompanying

core pain, the more rigid and defensive the lifestyle. Core pain is defined as a person's reaction to the denial of his fundamental right to exist and to express his being in satisfying ways. At the deepest level of the core, there is hurt and pain reflected in the feelings: Why wasn't I loved, given freedom to be, the right to exist?

Unresolved core pain yields defensive, survival-oriented behaviors that can be understood as the person's creative, yet self-defeating, attempts to get along in a world that is perceived as basically hostile. The behaviors can be predicted for each level of fearful constriction by understanding the specific way in which the person was invalidated by physical or psychological threats, early in life. Efforts to control his organismic responses to life (feelings, thoughts, and bodily responses) as well as fearful calculation in relationships to others are the basis for his immobility ("stuckness") and problems. The *manipulative level* of behavior is common to everyone. Manipulative patterns are based on a more normal level of fear and occasional calculating rather than feelingful responses to others. Persons stuck at the manipulative level are usually not suffering enough to seek professional psychotherapy, but they can benefit from principles of Actualizing Therapy presented in an educational or religious context.

At the *character level* the person is more tightly walled from life. There is a greater use of defense mechanisms to ward off inner core pain. Perception, affect, and cognition are more rigid. The person does not learn from experiences in life, and tends to respond to new events or relationships in stereotypic ways that reflect contamination from unresolved childhood conflicts. The person stuck at the character level is the one most likely to seek psychotherapy. Although he may have little or no insight into his problems (usually construing them as the work of fate, bad luck, or some other party), he knows that he is suffering. This suffering may be understood as a positive force that compels the person to get out of the straitjacket of survival tactics and surrender to the rhythm of growth and actualizing available to everyone.

The *psychotic level* of fearful constriction is the drastic "Custer's last stand" of a person who is being torn to pieces by unresolved core conflicts. The feelings of terror, rage, longing, or apathy finally overwhelm the person's rigid ego control, and the personality disintegrates. The process is symbolized by the thick, broken line at the center of Figure 1.1.

It must be emphasized that only certain character traits or psychotic behaviors (those most exemplary of behavior on the anger–love, strength–weakness continuum) are described here. While actualizing theory does not purport to account for all character or psychotic behavior, it does explain much pathological behavior as abortive attempts at actualizing: It joins a theory of malfunction with one of healthy functioning.

In actualizing theory it is assumed that energy is present at all personality levels, energy that provides the motivational force impelling the person to action. The more energy invested in fortifying the facade, repressing core pain, and utilizing survival behavior tactics, the less is available for actualizing growth. Repressed feelings require energy investment in chronically tensed musculature.

The actualizing process, then, consists of aiding the person to become aware of core pain, to express feelings that have been rigidly held back, to experiment with actualizing behaviors, body awareness, and feeling expression on the four polarities, to develop a sense of core trust in being oneself, and to use newfound energies for effective and satisfying living.

METHODOLOGY

General Techniques

Therapy is as much an art as it is a science. The artistic dimension comes from the therapist's ability to orchestrate the client's awareness in feeling, thinking, and bodily aspects of being, so as to transform rigidity to movement, defensiveness to growth. The following techniques are therapeutic tools for facilitating awareness and change: (1) reflection of feeling; (2) reflection of experience; (3) therapist self-disclosure; (4) interpretation; (5) body awareness; and (6) value clarification.

Reflection of Feeling. This is the reexpression, in fresh words, of the essential attitudes (not so much the content) expressed by the client. To reflect different dimensions of the total gestalt of the client's feelings, the therapist may focus on the client's self-feelings, the client's feelings toward others, or the client's feelings about the situation(s) in which he finds himself.

Reflection of Experience. This involves observing the posture, gestures, tone of voice, breathing, facial expression, and eye contact of the client *while* he is expressing himself, and feeding certain information back to him as it happens in order to expand his awareness of what his body is doing. This technique is effective for focusing on contradictions between what the client says he feels and what the therapist sees his total organism saying. For example, the person who says he is not angry yet shortens his breath and doubles his fists can benefit from experiential feedback.

Disclosure of the Therapist's Feelings. The client is thus provided with a real human encounter. The therapist needs courage to express his own percepts of the client, as well as to discuss his own weaknesses and defenses candidly. In so doing he models a basic tenet of Actual-izing Therapy: Owning your weaknesses is a precursor of actualizing your strengths.

Interpretation. This is an attempt by the therapist to present the client with a hypothesis about relationships or meanings for the client's consideration. Interpretation brings a fresh look at behavior, a new frame of reference, or a revised outlook on life. Other uses of intellectual interpretation include clarifying the client's problems, gathering relevant information, exploring alternative solutions in order to set therapeutic goals, clarifying values, trying out a therapeutic plan with periodic reevaluation in light of new information and changing circumstances, providing the client with cognitive understanding of therapeutic experiences, and generalizing growth processes in the client to new life situations. Further techniques for the intellectual approach to therapy can be found in the works of Krumboltz and Thoresen (1969), Brammer and Shostrom (1977), and Lazarus (1971).

Body Awareness Techniques. Such techniques involve giving attention to the body and what it is expressing at the moment. To be able to feel fully requires that one get in touch with the body. Actualizing Therapy focuses on three aspects of body work: learning to breathe fully from the diaphragm, learning to relax body musculature, and learning to express oneself bodily on the feeling polarities. The following are ways in which body exercises help people to develop contact with the polar dimensions of anger, love, strength, and weakness.

To facilitate expression of *anger,* the therapist can engage the client in role playing a "family argument." The therapist says "yes," and the client is asked to say "no" while reflecting on past experiences of being required to do something he did not want to do. The technique is to go back and forth, gradually increasing volume and bodily participation. The client has a safe opportunity to experience the bodily dimensions of anger, and to become more comfortable in self-assertion and interpersonal confrontation. A second technique is to allow the client to beat a couch with a tennis racket. This desensitizes the person's fear of angry self-expression and facilitates an integrated expression of anger through the body-feelings-mind. It also allows for the release of rage or other strong negative feelings stored in body musculature from painful past experiences.

Feelings for the *love* polarity can be elicited through two exercises. In the first exercise the therapist and client work together to feel their caring for one another by warmly saying "yes" instead of "no." The therapist may be himself or he may role play a person to whom the client wants to evoke tender feelings, for instance, the client's mother or father. The exercise may bring a desire to touch or hug, which is appropriate in that it helps the client express caring in a physical way. The second exercise is "facial touch." The therapist role plays a mother or father and the client surrenders to feelings of being a child once again. The therapist says, "I'd like you to close your eyes now and I'm going to touch your face. I'd like you to feel that I'm your father (mother)." With that the therapist begins gently touching and outlining the brow, eyes, nose, cheeks, mouth, and chin. While tracing the client's face the therapist makes positive comments typical of those parents make when they are gazing tenderly at and gently touching their children. This physical and verbal expression of tenderness can be a very meaningful demonstration of the importance of caring. The exercise often brings tears to the client's eyes and awakens strong caring feelings.

On the *strength* polarity we have found that stamping one's feet firmly into the ground gives a real sense of feeling one's strength. By stamping his feet until he begins to feel the muscle strain in calves and thighs, the client will enhance his feeling of self-support. A second exercise, helpful for demonstrating strong resistance to being manipulated by one's environment, is to lie on a couch with both knees up, pounding the couch with both fists and saying, "I won't give up!"

A technique for getting into touch with one's *weakness* is to stand in front of a couch, bent forward, with all weight on one's feet. The feet should be about 15 inches apart, with toes turned slightly inward. The fingers touch the floor out in front for balance. The knees are bent forward and then slowly brought back so that they begin to tremble. The vibration brings a tingling sensation in the feet and legs. Respiration begins to deepen. When standing this way becomes painful, the client is told to fall backward onto the couch. The point of the exercise is to experience falling (which represents one's weakness dimension, or "fall-ability") and surrendering to one's weakness. In a second exercise to get in touch with one's vulnerability the client is asked to stand with feet about 30 inches apart and hands on hips. The therapist then grasps the client's arms at the elbow and pushes him forward and down. As the client slowly lets himself down to the floor, he experiences deep feelings of vulnerability and surrender. The ability to surrender to one's feelings of weakness and vulnerability is central to Actualizing Therapy. To surrender is to accept one's losses. The fear of falling is related to the fear of surrendering to another, especially parents and others who have manipulated one. As individuals overcome their fear of falling, they give in more readily to their bodies and their feelings.

These and other body-awareness techniques can be found in Lowen (1975), Schutz (1973), and Shostrom (1976b).

Value Clarification. This involves prioritizing one's values. Priorities are statements of one's needs, wants, and desires at any one moment. Priorities also involve a wide perspective of future goals and past learning experiences. A practical method of choosing priorities is asking the client to periodically arrange the concerns and commitments most important to his life. A "priority recital" enlightens the client as to how to invest himself and as to what changes he needs to make to act on future goals or present desires. The actualizing person eventually develops a system in which he or she is constantly aware of priorities and changes, ready to act in terms of committed values. Operating from core values brings creativity, flexibility, and joy.

Manipulative Analysis

In addition to general techniques, analysis of manipulation is an important part of Actualizing Therapy. Manipulations are patterns of survival by which people adapt to their environments without having to feel. As the client talks, the therapist begins to see a pattern emerging in which the individual is utilizing one or more manipulative patterns (see Figure 1.1, Manipulative Level). Once the pattern becomes clear, the manipulations are analyzed from the standpoint of short-term and long-range effects. For example, manipulations are most often used for controlling, exploiting, or seducing others, for avoiding situations, or for structuring time. These tactics provide short-term gains. However the long-term effect can be shown to be self-defeating in that the manipulative behaviors alienate the individual from others and keep him or her immature and dependent.

A second method to explore the client's manipulative patterns is for the therapist to role play the client and to ask the client to role play significant other people in his or her life. In this way the client sees mirrored back to him the particular ways in which he seeks to control others. He also experiences the frustration, confusion, and hurt that he normally dishes out to others. This technique can provide an experience of surprising self-discovery as well as lead to greater empathy and understanding toward people clients have formerly manipulated.

Actualizing Therapy helps the client develop a sense of worth by showing him that his manipulative behavior was a creative but self-defeating attempt to survive in a world that has manipulated him. He discovers that manipulative tactics can be transformed into actualizing behavior. For instance, blaming and attacking can be changed into the more healthy expressions of anger: asserting and confronting. Withdrawing and avoiding can be changed into feeling vulnerable and empathizing. The therapist encourages the development and practice of the new actualizing behaviors, and gently points out when the client regresses to former manipulative patterns.

A further technique of manipulative analysis is based

on Perls's (1973) approach of "gestalt shuttling." A person whose personality is fragmented by polarization operates in an either/or manner. He plays nice guy or bully; he is weak or strong. In Actualizing Therapy the client learns to encompass both ends of his polarities in more direct and satisfying ways. In the shuttling technique the therapist places an empty chair in front of the client and has the client project onto the empty chair the parts of his own personality that he tends to disown and deny. By switching back and forth between chairs and expressing himself through a dialogue between the polarities, the client establishes better contact with both ends of the continuum. He learns to appreciate each of the polarities: to be both caring *and* assertive, vulnerable *and* strong.

Character Analysis

When the therapist sees that a client's problems are deeply rooted in historical experiences, character analysis becomes an appropriate technique. Character styles, which are complex systems of negative muscular defenses, are originally adopted to withstand early manipulations by parents and other significant people.

Each level of personality (see Figure 1.1) has significant feelings associated with it, and these feelings become the focus of psychotherapy at the character level. It should be noted that feelings are avoided at the level of manipulation, whereas they become defensive or hostile at the character level. Feelings expressed at the character level have become lodged in the muscle structure as masochistic spite and rage, oral longing and bitterness, schizoid terror and hostility, and rigid betrayal and rejection.

To facilitate expression of these significant core feelings locked into each character style, we use an approach derived from Lowen (1975). The client lies on a couch, mattress, or pad, and assumes the passive role characteristic of a child in a crib.

The therapist, through the technique of character dialogue, plays the role of parents or significant others who manipulated the client earlier in life through discounting the client's feelings: rejecting, abandoning, or making excessive demands. This dialogue causes angry, hurt, and rageful feelings—character feelings—to be loosened and expressed openly. The client lies on the couch, kicks his legs, pounds his hands, and shouts "no!" many times in refutation of such parental patterns:

SCHIZOID CLIENT: I AM! (core need: to feel his existence).

THERAPIST (leaning over client and expressing the original parental response):   You are nothing! (or) We don't want you! (or) I wish you weren't here! (or) I wish you were never born!

SCHIZOID CLIENT: No! No! No! I hate you!

ORAL CLIENT: I NEED YOU! (core need: to feel wanted)

THERAPIST: Your needs don't matter! (or) There are other people around here besides you! (or) Forget it, you're not important!

ORAL CLIENT: No! No! No! I don't need you!

MASOCHISTIC CLIENT: I WANT TO BE FREE! (core need: to feel free)

THERAPIST: We understand. (or) Don't worry about us. (or) Just remember all we've done for you. (or) Respect your parents!

MASOCHISTIC CLIENT: No! No! No! Get off my back!

RIGID CLIENT: I WANT YOUR LOVE! (core need: to feel love)

THERAPIST: Of course, you know I love you. (or) Stop pestering me! (or) Don't sit so close! (or) Don't touch yourself there (genital area)!

RIGID CLIENT: No! No! No! I don't need your love!

In the above character dialogues it is important for the client to take a stand against parental demands by saying "no." Being able to stand up for one's self breaks the pattern of dependence and generates feelings of self-confidence. In later sessions, as the client becomes more independent, he is directed by the therapist to a new character dialogue that focuses on the fulfillment of client needs. This time the client stands on his own two feet, face to face with the therapist (who is role playing the parent figure), and asks for what he needs. The therapist, as he hears the genuine expression of need in an adult fashion, responds to the request for fulfillment by the client.

SCHIZOID CLIENT: Please believe in me. I need you.

THERAPIST (reaching toward client):   I believe in you. I support you.

ORAL CLIENT: Please help me.

THERAPIST: I want to help you.

MASOCHISTIC CLIENT: I want to be free. Please respect me.

THERAPIST: I want you to be free. I do respect you.

RIGID CLIENT: Please love me.

THERAPIST: I do love you. I do care.

The power of this exercise is the emotional bond that is re-created between the client and a parent figure. In this way the client reestablishes trust in his or her core needs for self-affirmation, support from others, freedom to be, and love.

As the client gives in to the spontaneous body movements that express original core needs, integration of body and feelings takes place. This process takes time, however, and may require repeated attempts. After integration of body and feelings, realistic acceptance of losses takes place. At the character level the schizoid person accepts his aloneness and the reality of his existence. The oral person accepts that his longing will never be fully filled. The masochist gives up his feelings of hostility and spite and accepts limited freedom. The rigid person accepts his betrayal and heartbreak, and surrenders to his need for love. All become more lovable and loving in spite of their hurt and losses. By understanding their historical development, by accepting losses as well as strengths, and by becoming genuinely expressive of thoughts, feelings, and body, clients find a new harmony within and a courage to grow in the world rather than merely survive.

APPLICATIONS

A study by Shostrom and Riley (1968) confirms the hypothesis that experienced, seasoned therapists tend to be creative synthesizers. Creative synthesis means that a therapist may use a combination of techniques, or different single techniques, for different clients. For example, the psychologist might choose to use several different approaches with one client. Or the therapist might use one model (such as Gestalt Therapy, Rational-Emotive Therapy, or Behavior Modification) throughout the duration of one client's therapy, but use a different approach with another client.

The strength of Actualizing Therapy is its creative synthesis of many therapeutic systems around the central framework of self-actualization as the comprehensive goal of psychotherapy.

Those who choose therapy are more often people who are hurting inside even though they are not "sick" in the old-fashioned psychiatric sense. In fact, Actualizing Therapy has been used most successfully with normal or mildly disturbed persons [referred to in the American Psychiatric Association's *Diagnostic and Statistical Manual* (1980) as those with character disorders]. Actualizing Therapy has not been used extensively with psychotics or strongly neurotic populations.

When used for individual or group psychotherapy in the clinical setting, the Personal Orientation Inventory provides an objective measure of the client's level of actualizing as well as positive guidelines for growth during therapy. In a study relating changes in POI scores to stages of Actualizing Therapy, Shostrom and Knapp (1966) found that all POI scales significantly differentiated a sample of psychiatric outpatients beginning therapy from those in advanced stages of the psychotherapeutic progress.

The technical instruments of Actualizing Therapy are a set of psychological inventories known as the Actualizing Assessment Battery (AAB; Shostrom, 1976a). These instruments measure the dynamics of *intra-* and *inter-*personal functioning. The recognition of patterns in the person's historical development, coupled with an understanding of the major survival or growth systems that he or she presently uses, is important in launching Actualizing Therapy and in suggesting directions that clients can take in their personal journey of actualizing. In addition to its usefulness in individual therapy, we believe that the AAB is an important research tool for exploring the positive effects of therapy. Inventories from the AAB, including the newly developed *Growth Process Inventory* (Shostrom, 1979), are used to measure survival and actualizing patterns in a wide variety of populations including college students, church congregations, delinquents, alcoholics, teachers, hospitalized psychotics, and nominated actualizing persons.

Many psychologists and clergymen have been conducting "marriage enrichment workshops" (Bustanoby, 1974), in which they use the AAB as a basis for discussion of the health or wellness of the marriage partners. The AAB is particularly suited to workshops of this kind because it provides a quick evaluation of the actualizing status of the individuals themselves, by means of the Personal Orientation Inventory (Shostrom, 1963), and of the actualizing status of the relationship, as measured by the Caring Relationship Inventory (Shostrom, 1966) and the Pair Attraction Inventory (Shostrom, 1970).

Actualizing Therapy has potential for broad use, even though it is an eclectic system, because the basics can be taught in a two- or three-week workshop to clinicians, counselors, pastoral counselors, and teacher counselors who have had a minimum of formal training in psychotherapy.

CASE EXAMPLE

Joe comes to the office of an Actualizing Therapist from a crisis that developed the night before. His fiancée, Karen, has broken their engagement. Joe expresses fear of losing Karen. He says that an on-again, off-again pattern has characterized his dating relationships in adolescence and now as an adult. He feels sure that he could persuade her to come back, but knows that this would not really change the pattern. What he hopes to gain in therapy is deeper insight into the roots of his problem and some kind of genuine change in his relationships with women.

In exploring the historical roots to Joe's problems, the therapist asks him about the relationship between his mother and father. Immediately a clue jumps out as Joe responds: "Mother was always disappointed in Father. He never lived up to her demands; she complained a lot about him."

The therapist senses that Joe may have become the mother's substitute husband—that her frustrated marital energies may have been displaced into heavy yokes to be born by Joe.

The therapist explores how Joe's mother related to him. Joe replies, "She always told me that I was her good little soldier. I tried to make her happy by pleasing her with my achievements. I didn't rebel because she always made me feel guilty if I disappointed her. It was as though I had to be the good boy that my father wasn't."

The therapist suggests to Joe that perhaps he felt betrayed by his mother's lack of love and resentful at her many demands. Joe gets more in touch with core feelings of fear and anger.

"I didn't realize it then," he says, "but I was a childhood Dr. Jekyll and Mr. Hyde. I felt so much pressure to be a good little boy that I had to deny anything that didn't fit the picture—especially sexual feelings, which were taboo to mother. I busied myself trying to do everything she wanted. I wanted her love, but she never really gave it to me."

The therapist asks if Joe sees a connection between his past relationship with his mother and his present problems with Karen. Joe makes a discovery. "I guess I start out being afraid of every woman I date. Then I try to impress them with my achievements. And I always feel guilty and uncomfortable with my sexual feelings. Most of all I'm afraid that she will somehow get control of me like Mother had." The therapist zeroes in on the obvious: "Joe, your on-again, off-again pattern with Karen and with other women you have dated has been your way of keeping distance in your relationships. No woman scores a home run with you because you keep sending her back to first base. When you feel the threat of too much intimacy, you call 'foul.' So you constantly keep the woman off balance and achieve your need to control and limit the depth of the relationship."

In terms of actualizing theory, the therapist sees Joe's problems as having to do with getting stuck on the strength polarity in early childhood. Joe's survival tactics for coping with a demanding, smothering mother involved learning to strive and achieve in order to meet her expectations for perfection. Joe now complains of rheumatism in his spine, which is probably related to having too much "backbone"—stiffening his back in order to appear responsible. Joe avoids the other polarities of anger, love, and weakness, because he would have to give up his tactic of controlling others by making them admire him because of his achievements. Most of all he avoids surrendering to tender, loving feelings. Having been controlled by his mother in childhood, he is determined to control women (i.e., Karen) by avoiding genuine intimacy and by striving to impress them instead.

Joe's present behavior is a creative but misdirected attempt to avoid the pain of betrayal. The therapist helps Joe to see how he can form a more satisfying bond with Karen by learning to affirm his freedom yet risk *yielding* to loving feelings. This is the basis for transforming manipulative coping patterns into actualizing growth patterns.

In the second and third sessions the therapist focuses on different aspects of Joe's problems by taking the part of Joe's mother, by playing Karen, and by representing warring factions of Joe's own personality. The explorations are done through psychodramas, gestalt shuttling techniques, and guided fantasy. Joe makes more and more progress in working through the impasse that has blocked his actualizing development. He realizes that getting a doctorate, becoming a professor, and writing seven books have not enabled him to break free of his fear of rejection and betrayal by women. He is glad for his professional development, yet he realizes that it was in part a compulsive attempt to find love and approval in safe ways that excluded his emotions and his sexuality. He could get the praise of students and readers, while keeping them at arm's length. The full impact of Joe's growing awareness comes when he says during a fourth session: "I have really succeeded in getting people's attention, but I find that I'm a very lonely person because I never commit myself to anyone. I've overdeveloped my intellect in order to keep in control. And I've left my feelings and my body out in the cold."

Indeed, Joe's body becomes a vital part of therapy during Sessions 4 through 8 because his body reflects the conflicts he is wrestling with. Bioenergetic techniques are used to mobilize his breathing and to enhance his sensitivity to sexual feelings. A series of exercises is repeated for several weeks to help break down muscular tension in his back, jaw, shoulders, and pelvis. These exercises release a flood of new vitality and bodily excitement. Joe comments week by week that he has more energy than ever before.

Joe reports several dreams of an erotic nature, but feels less threatened by them. Because the therapist views sexual feelings, fantasies, and dreams as normal, Joe's embarrassment and self-consciousness begin to change to a sense of adventure and enjoyment in regard to his sexuality. The mind is finally being connected to the heart and genitals—a process that has been severely blocked by a stern mother and a demanding superego.

In his relationship with Karen, Joe feels less concerned with always pleasing her and more concerned with expressing his needs, desires, and values. Yet, ironically, it is through his newfound freedom to assert himself that he finds the ability to surrender to genuine loving feelings for Karen.

The therapist accentuates new experiences with Karen by having Joe become more aware of all the feeling polarities, getting personal experience in surrendering to each one. Especially in group therapy, which he joins in his fourth week, Joe has ample opportunities to experience and express love, anger, strength, and weakness at different times and in various combinations. The group members persist in not accepting his controlling and distancing tactics, expressing instead their desire that he be more vulnerable and involved.

The therapist augments Joe's learning in group therapy by helping him finish working through the unfinished business with his mother in individual therapy. In a later session the therapist asks Joe to stand with his back against a door, knees bent forward, and to surrender to the feeling of weakness that develops in his legs. This position helps recapture the original feelings of helplessness that Joe had in the early years of his life. But it gives him an opportunity to choose a new, more actualizing response in place of the old tactic of cutting off his feelings and stiffening his back. The therapist coaches Joe: "Tell your mother that you want her to love you for yourself. Tell her that you're not a god, but that you're human too—that you have sexual feelings and desires. Tell her that you have the right to make mistakes—to be "fallible"—and that you are not going to feel embarrassed about it any more. Tell her that you love her but you are not going to bow down to her. Let yourself express whatever you feel."

As Joe surrenders to the bioenergetic process, he begins to cry. The second time through he gets very angry. The third time he gets in touch with his own strength, and feels a deep relief in just being able to be himself—whatever that may be. The therapist has Joe go through the exercise one last time, this time addressing Karen instead of his mother. As the integration of past and present, and of body and feelings, is being accomplished, the therapist gives Joe more homework: "I want you to think about some good things about your father and I want you to think of some bad things about your mother." The therapist is seeking to break down the stereotypic perception that made a goddess out of mother and a devil out of father.

Further sessions with Joe involve a greater awareness of the constrictions in his body, particularly in the pelvis, where chronic muscular tension has cut off the flow of sexual feelings, just as his mother had wanted it to. At one point the muscles of the chest are massaged while Joe leans backward over a breathing stool. The tensed chest muscles have been a part of Joe's armor to defend himself against his own tender feelings from the heart. Learning to loosen up and feel sensations in the areas of heart and solar plexus helps Joe be in better contact with his core, and to establish more trust in the "Inner Supreme Court" that supports him in making choices from his whole being.

Another assignment the therapist gives Joe is designed to help him work through his perfectionism. The therapist says, "Did you ever experience yourself as a student getting nine out of ten questions right on a test, and still feeling like a failure?" Joe answers that he did. The therapist says, "On a scale of one to ten, how do you rate yourself as a human being?" Joe replies, "Well, before I started therapy I guess I rated myself about nine—always better than other people, but never good enough to be perfect. But now I'm starting to think of myself as more of a six or seven."

The therapist gives Joe the following homework: "Keep thinking all week about yourself as a six or seven and think of everyone you meet as about the same. This will help to 'humanize' your perception of people. It will help you break the old pattern of seeing authority figures as nines and tens and everyone else as twos and threes. You need to get rid of more of your fear of people and feel more at home with them instead."

Joe is giving up the rigid protective shell of his survival orientation from childhood. The first fruits of actualizing are in the warm and positive responses he gets from others when he comes across as more human and vulnerable. This change in attitude comes as a surprise to Joe, because he has spent his life trying to get people to like and respect him but has consistently failed because no one likes a showoff and a prude.

Joe feels that he has worked through his most troublesome problems after eight individual sessions. The therapist agrees, but reminds him that growth comes slowly and he will need to further develop his actualizing orientation to life. The therapist suggests that Joe continue to attend group therapy for several more months to consolidate his gains and to support his growth.

SUMMARY

In Actualizing Therapy we believe that the most effective way to aid clients in making wise and satisfying choices is to work through core conflicts and core pain that block awareness and growth.

Since the core is the center of one's existence, a key process is to enable clients to get acquainted with their core characteristics. This includes accepting that they are to some extent disabled by painful childhood experiences, and learning to surrender to the feelings of terror, rage, longing, or betrayal that they have formerly denied. When clients let go of their rigid defense strategies and give in to painful core feelings, they move through the impasse from manipulating to actualizing.

The presence of a supportive therapist or group makes it safe for the clients to experience strong negative feelings without constricting themselves or distorting reality. In experiencing core pain in an honest and direct way, clients find that it passes through them (emotional catharsis) and that they lose their fear of feeling. Releasing strong negative feelings from the core results in the emergence of strong positive feelings such as trust, harmony, and confidence. Thus clients come to be more at home with all that they are, the good and the bad, the negative and the positive, the manipulative and the actualizing. They learn compassion and the ability to forgive themselves and others for inevitable mistakes that occur in living.

In individual Actualizing Therapy, the emphasis is on the bodily and the intellectual dimension of each client's personality and value system. Group therapy is a miniature society in which interpersonal expression of emotion becomes a primary focus. Individual therapy is analogous to a lecture-discussion in college; group therapy is the laboratory session. Each is necessary for total learning.

In the laboratory of the group clients are afforded the opportunity to try out a new stance in life, to express values to which they are committing themselves, and to expand their awareness and expression of the feeling-polarities.

Individual and group work also seek to uncover a person's deepest needs at the core level and satisfy those needs. Most people have their physiological and safety needs met, but their love needs have been ignored or exploited. Fear can be replaced by trust in one's core as individual or group therapy helps a person to surrender to needs for love and to have these needs satisfied in direct, realistic ways. As this happens, the person becomes more free to move on to esteem needs and self-actualizing needs. Actualizing needs are nurtured by developing a style of emotional expression and interpersonal trust based on honesty, awareness, freedom, creativity, and mission.

A basic tenet of Actualizing Therapy is that energy released from core conflicts becomes immediately available for growth and creative living. Availability of energy for growth, coupled with learning to express oneself along the feeling polarities, offers clients a wide spectrum of actualizing possibilities. Being what you are (awareness of character structure) and becoming all you can be (trust in the core and self-expression along the polarities) are the heart and soul of Actualizing Therapy.

REFERENCES

Allport, G. W. (1937). *Personality: A psychological interpretation.* New York: Holt.

Allport, G. W. (1961). *Patterns and growth in personality.* New York: Holt.

American Psychiatric Association. (1980). Diagnostic and statistical manual of mental disorder (3rd ed.). Washington, DC: Author.

Bleuler, E. (1940). Cited in J. F. Brown, *Psychodynamics of abnormal behavior.* New York: McGraw-Hill.

Brammer, L. M., & Shostrom, E. L. (1977). *Therapeutic psychology: Fundamentals of actualizing counseling and therapy* (3rd ed.). Englewood Cliffs, NJ: Prentice-Hall.

Buber, M. (1951). *The way of man.* Chicago: Wilcox and Follett.

Bustanoby, A. (1974, August 30). The pastor and the other woman. *Christianity Today, 7–10.*

Ellis, A. (1962). *Reason and emotion in psychotherapy.* Seacaucus, NJ: Lyle Stuart.

Fox, J., Knapp, R. R., & Michael, W. B. (1968). Assessment of self-actualization of psychiatric patients: Validity of the Personal Orientation Inventory. *Educational and Psychological Measurement, 28,* 565–569.

Krumboltz, J. D., & Thoreson, C. E. (1969). *Behavioral counseling: Cases and techniques.* New York: Holt.

Lazarus, A. A. (1971). *Behavior therapy and beyond.* New York: McGraw-Hill.

Leary, T. (1957). *Interpersonal diagnosis of personality.* New York: Ronald Press.

Lowen, A. (1975). *Bioenergetics.* New York: Coward.

Maslow, A. H. (1954). *Motivation and personality.* New York: Harper & Row.

Perls, F. S. (1969). *Gestalt therapy verbatim.* Lafayette, CA: Real People Press.

Perls, F. S. (1973). *The gestalt approach and eyewitness to therapy.* Ben Lomand, CA: Science and Behavior Books.

Riesman, D. (1950). *The lonely crowd.* Garden City, NY: Doubleday.

Rogers, C. R. (1951). *Client-centered therapy.* Boston: Houghton Mifflin.

Satir, V. (1966). *Conjoint family therapy.* Palo Alto, CA: Science and Behavior Books.

Schutz, W. C. (1973). *Elements of encounter: A bodymind approach.* Big Sur, CA: Joy Press.

Shostrom, E. L. (1963). *Personal orientation inventory.* San Diego, CA: EdITS/Educational and Industrial Testing Service.

Shostrom, E. L. (1966). *Caring relationship inventory.* San Diego, CA: EdITS/Educational and Industrial Testing Service.

Shostrom, E. L. (1967). *Man, the manipulator.* Nashville, TN: Abingdon.

Shostrom, E. L. (1970). *Pair attraction inventory.* San Diego, CA: EdITS/Educational and Industrial Testing Service.

Shostrom, E. L. (1976a). *Actualizing assessment battery.* San Diego, CA: EdITS/Educational and Industrial Testing Service.

Shostrom, E. L. (1976b). *Actualizing Therapy: Foundations for a scientific ethic.* San Diego, CA: EdITS/Educational and Industrial Testing Service.

Shostrom, E. L. (1979). *Growth process inventory.* San Diego, CA: EdITS/Educational and Industrial Testing Service.

Shostrom, E. L., & Knapp, R. R. (1966). The relationship of a measure of self-actualization (POI) to a measure of pathology (MMPI) and to therapeutic growth. *American Journal of Psychotherapy, 20,* 193–202.

Shostrom, E. L., & Montgomery, D. (1978). *Healing love.* Nashville, TN: Abingdon.

Shostrom, E. L., & Riley, C. (1968). Parametric analysis of psychotherapy. *Journal of Consulting and Clinical Psychology, 32,* 628–632.

Chapter 2

ALLO-CENTERED PSYCHOTHERAPY

DAN MOTET

Dan Motet came to Hawaii from Romania after training at the University of Washington. He wrote to me, as had a number of people who had wanted to be in Hawaii, and I received his letter at a particularly difficult time for me, and I first threw it away. But then I retrieved it, wrote on the same sheet and sent it back. Within a week he was here in Hawaii, the land that he had often wanted to see. I employed him for a while doing an encyclopedia of psychology. He eventually got settled, married, and is now the father of two daughters. According to my belief that one's theory is an extension of one's personality, Dan is a most generous and loving person. Motet's thesis fits well with mine, because I am an Adlerian. What he has written, as he indicates, is a universal technique seen in apparently conflicting systems such as Encouragement Therapy and Provocative Therapy, stressing the power of love for others as the essence of psychotherapy.

DEFINITION

Allo-Centered Psychotherapy (ACP) is basically a new philosophical approach to therapy. Its name derives from the Greek word *allos,* meaning *other.* Its purpose is to redirect the patient's orientation from self to others with the assumption that in this way a better understanding of both self and others can be achieved. To introspection, this therapy adds "extrospection" and "interspection," meaning an increased focus on others, including those who live with us, and on the interactions between others and between ourselves and others. The emphasis is changed from self and introspection, to others and empathy.

A problem of many schools of psychology is a tendency to describe what is in reality a particular limited culture at a certain time as a general human condition. As that situation changes, such ideas lose validity. In a larger sense, the positions of such schools are a reflection of an egocentered and ethnocentered point of view. The allo-centered view strives to understand things in a more universal and historical context and to differentiate what is generally human from what is a cultural historical snapshot. This therapy recognizes the value of other therapeutic approaches and builds on them, seeking to shift the balance from the naturally prevalent self-centeredness to allo-centrism. The allo-centered personality is an ideal to aim for, however few people actually reach it fully. However, in the process of becoming more allo-centered the patient develops into a more healthy, accepted, and liked person.

HISTORY

The proliferating abundance of self-help literature has put some powerful psychological techniques into the hands of the public. When used indiscriminately, these techniques can backfire. Many responsible authors have used this type of self-help to make people aware of the need for qualified help, or to teach them generally useful skills such as communication and relaxation. Unfortunately, others, by using catchy labels and serial publications, have given the public the false impression that anyone can delve into their psyche without careful training. As a result, countless individuals have engaged in introspection, self-diagnosis, and attempts for self-change. Especially since the 1960s and 1970s, this trend, grafted on our Zeitgeist, has contributed to the increase of the general focus on self, already prevalent in our highly individualistic society.

Psychological theories and practice tend to focus on self. It is enough to look into a dictionary of psychology to see the abundance of concepts revolving around the self:

Self-abasement, self-accusation, self-actualization, self-alienation, self-analysis, self-appraisal, self-awareness, self-blaming, self-confidence, self-consciousness, self-consistency, self-concept, self-control, self-criticism, self-cueing, self-debasement, self-deception, self-defeat, self-derogation, self-desensitization, self-destructiveness, self-determination, self-development, self-differentiation, self-discipline, self-disclosure, self-discovery, self-efface-ment, self-efficacy, self-esteem, self-examination, self-expression, self-fulfillment, self-gratification, self-hate, self-help, self-ideal, self-identity, self-image, self-love, self-management, self-maximization, self-observation, self-perception, self-preservation, self psychology, self-realization, self-reference, self-regulation, self-reinforce-ment, self-respect, self-stimulation, self theory, self-understanding, self-worth.

During my graduate study and internship years I was impressed by the frequency with which such introspection becomes neurotic in predisposed individuals. As the current prevailing mood is toward negative thinking, the introspectionists will tend to gravitate around problems, weaknesses, and failures. This frequently leads to depression, poor self-image, low self-esteem, hypochondria, and so forth. The mechanism through which such problems develop is discussed in the theory section that follows.

I soon realized that the tendency toward self-centeredness also has cultural roots. English is the only major language in which the pronoun I is exclusively capitalized, while the pronoun thou, reflecting an intimate close relation with another human being, is practically eliminated. It does not even exist in the dictionary of my 1998 top-of-the-line word processor. It is still used in relationship with God, but, as the Bible translations started using modern language, it disappeared even from there. Martin Buber describes the situation beautifully in his discussion of the I-thou versus the I-it relationship (Buber, 1958/1970).

At the same time there was a concern about the development of what was called the Me Generation or the Narcissistic Generation. People failed to give help to others in distress, thinking that it was not their job to do so or that they did not want to invade others' privacy. As this came more and more to the attention of the public, people wondered with dismay whether ours was becoming a nation of callous, selfish individuals who do not care for anyone but themselves. As a relative newcomer to America and not contaminated by the self-flagellating tendency stirred up by the Vietnam War protest, I was struck by the contrast between the apparent lack of concern toward people in distress and the unsurpassed tendency of Americans to help, no matter where in the world a need arose. People responded generously and spontaneously to the plea of a child needing care on the other side of the globe, or to the distress of a family whose house has burned in a neighboring state. I realized then that the problem was not selfishness or callousness, but rather a lack of awareness of the other: Once aware of the need, most Americans were ready to respond with an unsurpassed generosity or even self-sacrifice.

The need for an increased awareness and understanding of others became obvious to me, and the idea of Allo-Centered Psychology and Psychotherapy germinated.

First, there were my university lectures during which I was introducing, now and then, elements of Allo-Centered Psychology, submitting them to the keen and bright scrutiny of my students at Seattle Pacific University. My profound thanks to them!

Allo-Centered Psychology and Psychotherapy was presented in a few papers at conferences, but I soon became aware that people, although listening with interest, were not yet ready to accept such a radical change in focus against what they have been told for generations: "Know Thyself," or "You have to love yourself first in order to be able to love others." Allo-Centered Psychology was also running against the training of generations of therapists to focus on self-esteem, self-actualization, self-awareness, self-help, self-improvement, and not much on the *other*.

I continued to use Allo-Centered Psychotherapy in my therapy practice with good results for over 25 years. I shared a few aspects of ACP with others, without labeling them as such, and some applied them successfully, but not systematically. Allo-Centered Psychotherapy was also included in the *Baker Encyclopedia of Psychology* (Motet, 1985) and in Corsini's *Dictionary of Psychology* (1999). During the last several years the public has become more ready for ACP. Witness the success of the best selling Chicken Soup series that features numerous stories of allo-centered people and actions.

My move to Hawaii in 1981 was prompted not only by the love for the islands and their beautiful people, but also by the desire to test ACP in a most diverse cross-cultural environment. I chose to work in three areas of the island of Oahu that presented remarkably different cultural, educational, economic, and ethnic populations. This experience allowed me to confirm the universal applicability of Allo-Centered Psychotherapy. In turn, ACP was enriched by what I learned from the interactions with a variety of cultures, and especially with the Hawaiian culture, whose Spirit of Aloha is most compatible with allo-centrism.

Concerning the historic roots of Allo-Centered Psychology, I have already mentioned Buber's I-thou concept. Existentialism introduced three concepts indicating modes of the world: *Umwelt* (the world around, the environment), *Mitwelt* (the with-world, the world of relationships), and *Eigenwelt* (own world, inner world, relationship with self). Buber focused on the I-thou relationship, included in the *Mitwelt.* Allo-Centered Psychology also focuses on the I-thou, but with the greatest emphasis on the thou, the presently most neglected part of the dyad. In addition, ACP considers the interdependence of the I-thou relationship with the social and natural environment in which it develops. Allo-Centered Psychotherapy shifts the currently prevalent emphasis on *Eigenwelt* onto *Mitwelt* and also, to a degree, on the *Umwelt.*

Adler's social interest (Adler, 1939) is also an important root, with the difference that in Allo-Centered Psychology, social interest is seen as learned rather than inborn. In addition, less emphasis is placed on childhood, though its importance is affirmed. Similarly, in Allo-Centered Psychology, individuals are seen as having choices and therefore as being responsible for their actions. We could say that Adler remains the most important influence on ACP.

Another important precursor is Gordon Allport (1955), through his emphasis on values, on the uniqueness of each individual, and on *becoming* (the self makes choices and can influence its own development, which is continuous; the individual is not victimized by the past). I discuss these kinships in more detail in the theory section of this essay.

An important source from which ACP derives information is my own experience during my teenage and young adult years in Romania. Under the Nazis and the Communists, I could see people function under great stress, revealing behavioral and cognitive aspects difficult to see in more normal situations. This experience makes me feel a strong kinship with Viktor Frankl (1962/1980) who, in the even more stressful environment of a concentration camp, came to discover the importance of *meaning in life* that is also stressed in Allo-Centered Psychology.

CURRENT STATUS

Being a solo psychotherapy provider, somewhat restricted by the advent of managed care, I did not develop a group to study Allo-Centered Psychology and Psychotherapy. Currently, Allo-Centered Psychotherapy is basically the result of my work with over a thousand patients in diverse environments. For over 25 years, of which 18 were in full-time clinical therapy work, I developed and confirmed in practice the theoretical basis of ACP. I have no doubt that, though it has not always been labeled as such, ACP has been of value to many of my patients. This is understandable as ACP is more a distinct philosophical approach to therapy rather than a new school. It utilizes, in addition to specific techniques, already proven methodologies, thus having a rather eclectic look as seen from without. Nevertheless, if one were to analyze what is happening within the therapy, its allo-centrism would become evident. During these years I not only developed the ACP but also defined its limitations and pitfalls.

I do not expect that Allo-Centered Psychology and Psychotherapy will become popular, because it runs against the narcissistic and self-centered tendencies of our time. What I hope is that some therapists who have allo-centered beliefs and philosophies of life themselves, will study this approach and try it in practice so that their patients will benefit from its potential.

In the service of developing allo-centrism in patients, it was important to find out which of the existing therapeutical techniques are useful for different patients, in specific situations, and at certain times. In addition, some techniques specific to allo-centered therapy were developed.

THEORY

Terminology

I chose the term *allo-centered* because I could give it a more complex meaning than *other-centered* would have had. Common words, frequently used, tend to become degraded, distorted, or stereotyped. For instance, important words such as *love* and *hate* get devalued: "I love God," "I love my wife," "I love my children," "I love cheese"; or "I hate dictatorships," "I hate cold weather." Love and hate come to mean no more than "I like" and "I dislike," and it is up to the receiver of the message to unravel the meaning, a task which is not always easy.

For the opposite of allo-centered I chose the term *self-centered*. This term is more precise and less likely to be confused with other meanings than *narcissistic* (also used in psychoanalysis and as a type of personality disorder), *selfish* (implying intent and a shade of antisocial trend), or *ego-centered* (used by Jean Piaget to describe the behavior of young children).

Causes of Self-Centeredness

We live in a quite affluent society. Even welfare recipients in the United States live at a standard above that of the majority of the world's population. Affluence leads to striving for self-sufficiency (actually a myth; we do not make our clothes or grow our food, etc.) and results in the notion "I do not need anyone; I have the means to succeed and grow on myself and by myself." Materialism causes a preoccupation with things rather than people. The materialistic person is more concerned about an I-it (car, house, money) relationship than about an I-thou relationship. Hedonism, so prevalent in our society, focuses the attention of the individual on the satisfaction of his own desires rather than on other people. Paradoxically, both pampering and abuse of children result in self-centered individuals: Pampered children tend to grow into adults who think that the world revolves around them; abused children, forced to focus on their own survival, tend to grow into adults with a protective shell that keeps others out. Insufficient training for empathy in our families and education is another significant cause of self-centeredness. The emphasis on *self-*

love also leads to self-centeredness. According to Allo-Centered Psychology the idea that one has to love oneself first, before one can love another, is fallacious. In the allo-centered view one becomes a loving person by first being loved and then returning the love. Is not the baby of a loving mother more loving than that of an unloving one?

In the late twentieth century, it became very fashionable to delve into Eastern philosophies and, more frequently than not, misuse them. Meditation, involving emptying one's mind, does not lead to care for others, but rather to focus upon self and self-enlightenment. Few in our society would spend the time to get the training necessary to reach the stage of meditation at which the remaining motive is selfless service. It is more helpful for a Westerner to focus in meditation on sceneries, desired actions, or prayer.

The cheapening of the concept of *love* and *friendship* leads also to an illusion of closeness to others where actually little or no closeness exists. We frequently hear people saying "I love everybody" or calling simple acquaintances "friends." This last behavior creates serious problems in relationships. For example, in the context of a relationship between immigrants and their hosts, this can lead to the false stereotype that "Americans are not to be trusted as friends." The typical scenario runs something like this: A foreign visitor arrives in the United States and is introduced to an American connection who not long after that introduces him as "my friend X from Y country." Hungry to make connections in a foreign country, the newcomer takes the word *friend* to mean what it should, and is impressed by the friendliness of the host. Soon his expectations of friendly behavior lead to disappointment when he sees that such expressions as "see you soon" or "we should keep in touch" do not have the literal meaning he gives to them. The visitor's initial elation can turn to bitterness.

Consequences of Self-Centeredness

Poor Social Adjustment

Self-centered people tend to be poorly adjusted. Having little interest in others, they do not get to know them well. Consequently, they have inadequate reactions to others, eliciting negative responses from them, which in turn justifies their further detachment, uneasiness in relating, and fear of rejection. Such people are also prone to misattributions that lead to further miscommunication, misunderstanding, and conflict. To them, others are not only unknown, but also unpredictable. This leads to insecurity. As self-centered people share with the narcissistic personality a sense of entitlement, they will also have a low frustration tolerance. Lacking an understanding of others' sensitivities and needs, they frequently hurt, alienate, or even turn others against them. This deprives them of true friends. Similarly, they have a poor understanding and acceptance of social rules, which are devised to protect the interest and well-being of the society as a whole. As a consequence, the self-centered person is more prone to develop such problems as shyness, avoidance, isolation, loneliness, depression, frustration, anger, anxiety (even paranoia), and anti-social behavior.

Impaired Growth

Excessive preoccupation with self-analysis leads, paradoxically, to a poor self-image. People often perform self-analysis to find out not what is good, but what is wrong with them. This trend is also reflected in media, focusing on what is negative rather than on what is nice, noble, and beautiful. The media might answer, "That's what people want and that's what we deliver."

Whenever I ask people to list their strengths and weaknesses, invariably negatives prevail. When friends are asked to make similar lists about the patient, the list of positives is much longer and the list of negatives much shorter. You end up with a better self-image if you are allo-centered and pick up feedback from others than if you go by your own, often negatively biased, assessment.

Self-centered people deprive themselves of feedback from others by not creating opportunities for such a feedback when they do not focus outward, on others, and also by discouraging the feedback through their self-centered, defensive attitude. Even when feedback is provided, they tend to misinterpret it. This way they remain with their fault-seeking introspection without reference validation.

Another problem that tends to develop in self-centered people is a lack of group identity. When asked to make a list describing themselves by filling in sentences starting with "I am," they deliver few such statements as: "I am a student," "I am a son/daughter," or "I am an American." Lacking collective identification, self-centered individuals have difficulty finding an identity. They are most likely to say "I am trying to find out who I am" and show insecurity and anxiety. Extreme cases may generate a "me against the world" attitude that may contribute to paranoia or antisocial behavior.

Self-centered persons also have more difficulty growing because they have a tendency not to seek professional help. This may be due to pride, a false sense of self-sufficiency, shyness, or uneasiness about revealing themselves to others.

The Allo-Centered Personality

The allo-centered personality is an ideal to aim toward. It is a lifetime process of development. It leads to self-growth, social adjustment, and better health. The increased awareness of others enlarges a person's horizon to encompass others' way of thinking and perceiving. It also helps improve the knowledge of self, both by making it possible to receive and correctly interpret feedback from others, and by enabling recognition of characteristics in others that defensiveness would not have let us see in ourselves. The better we come to know ourselves, the better we are equipped to know others. Allo-centered people are involved in a process of knowing others in order to know themselves, and knowing themselves in order to know others.

Altruism, once developed, is a powerful motivational force. Defined as an unselfish concern for the welfare of others, it is a natural consequence of the development of an allo-centered personality. It may even be considered an essential trait of allo-centrism.

Allo-centered altruism requires that help be tailored to the needs of the assisted one; otherwise it may be a false altruism, more of a power trip. An example occurs in the joke about a Boy Scout who was late because he helped an unwilling old lady cross the street.

Allo-centered persons have meaning in life because their energy use is expanded to include others. Their horizon is enlarged and their life becomes more interesting and purposeful, as Frankl has very well described it (1963). There are three types of values through which meaning is expressed (Frankl, 1962/1980): *experiential* (attained by being receptive in the world to what others have created), *creative* (attained through our action), and *attitudinal* (represented by our stance toward what happens). Allo-centered personalities striving for growth seek to attain all these values. Lack of meaning can lead to existential neurosis and depression. It is hard to plow through difficulties in life when you do not have a "why," a motivator.

Allo-centered persons are aware of others' needs, and they care. They are not passive observers of others, but active agents of progress and growth. They are optimistic, positive, action-oriented. Their lifestyle seeks to maximize gains rather than minimize losses.

Allo-centered persons are not obsessed by the fear of depending on others. They are rooted in a good self-image and are strong enough to allow a certain amount of dependency without fear of losing their freedom of choice beyond what they voluntarily surrender in the service of allo-centrism. They are sought as friends and can form deep, intimate, reliable relations.

Another characteristic of the allo-centered person is a benign, healthy humor. They can have the self-detachment needed for honest self-appraisal and can poke fun at themselves. An allo-centered person's self, validated by relationships with others, is not fragile nor easily threatened.

Allo-centered people have an investment in others, and therefore are involved and committed. Being nondefensive, they do not hesitate to take responsibility for their actions, not with the intent of self-castigation, but for learning and growth. They put a greater focus on self-improvement rather than lingering on introspection. They do not ask themselves "Who am I?" but rather "Who am I becoming, for whom, and for what?" They continuously seek purposeful and meaningful growth so they can become more useful and needed for the benefit of others; as a result, they also become more self-fulfilled. In order to grow, they seek feedback. They gladly engage in discussions meant to improve their knowledge and test the correctness of their opinions. Conversely, self-centered people often avoid discussing important issues in our society, as well as giving feedback to others. They are afraid of being found wrong and project that fear onto others. One day I left in a hurry from home with one black and one brown shoe. Although I met over 20 persons that day, and I sat down and talked nearly an hour with eight of them, nobody made any observation about my shoes, although they later admitted seeing them. Many years ago, as a new immigrant to the United States, I asked all my "friends" to correct my pronunciation so that I could speak a better English, something much needed for my profession. In spite of my insistence, not a single one did. They confessed that they were projecting their own uneasiness about being corrected. This makes us live in a society without feedback, where we easily become like boats navigating in darkness, without map, compass, or radar. It is no wonder that so many are sinking.

The issue of self-image is an interesting one to debate. For instance, how good should a good self-image be? At what point does it become self-conceit? And could it be that some people who complain of poor self-image are in reality fishing for compliments from people who try to help them restore their self-image? In Allo-Centered Psychology, therefore, the term *realistic self-image* is preferred. The best way to achieve this realistic self-image is to check it against the perception and feedback of others. The Allo-centered person achieves this by more efficiently consulting reference groups and persons.

Allo-Centered Psychotherapy has cross-cultural validity. On the dimension individualism–group orientation, the American Anglo-Saxon culture is on the individualism end, while such cultures as Asian, Pacific Islander, and Latin American are toward the group-oriented end of the spectrum. The allo-centered approach takes a moderate position by encouraging the individual to be oriented toward other individuals instead of either the group or the self. This way it creates a good meeting ground for people of different cultures living in our pluralistic society.

Allo-Centered Psychology also has to analyze, be

aware of, and counteract the dangers involved in pseudo-allo-centrism. True allo-centrism does not mean letting others' expectations lead your life. Allo-centered individuals are free agents, unique persons who choose to invest their freedom in benefiting others. We also have to beware of false allo-centrism exhibited for different personal gains: glory, election, winning someone's admiration and love, and so on. It can never be emphasized too much that allo-centered people are not busybody "helpers" taking over others' lives; rather, they act in the interest of the other, with the other's consent, and, as much as possible, in an unobtrusive way. They are never psychological Peeping Toms interested in others out of pure curiosity, for the purpose of gossip or, even worse, for the pursuit of self-centered goals.

METHODOLOGY

Allo-Centered Psychotherapy can use any technique that seeks to develop allo-centrism. It addresses behavioral, affective, cognitive, and spiritual aspects. It is easier to develop allo-centrism by encouraging the patients to focus first on a person who is important to them and who is likely to respond with positive feelings. To bring about attitudinal changes that will last and will generalize, the therapy has to take into consideration all four dimensions: behavioral, affective, cognitive, and spiritual.

Allo-Awareness Technique

One technique specific to this kind of psychotherapy is the *allo-awareness technique.* It includes analysis of the patient's interaction with a significant other whose behavior, feelings, and cognitive style are analyzed, first as perceived by the patient, then considering all alternative possibilities. The purpose is to focus the patient's attention on the significant other and refine the accuracy of the patient's perception of that person.

Whether we start working with the behavioral, affective, or cognitive aspect depends on the patient's style. An individual talking mostly in terms of action will be more open to an awareness of the other's behavior. Another person, using feeling-related concepts, will be more sensitive to an affective approach. Similarly, a patient employing cognitive terms will be more comfortable starting with an analysis of the cognitive reactions of the significant other.

The allo-awareness technique includes three phases presented here in alphabetical order: *affective phase, behavioral phase,* and *cognitive phase.* These phases are not rigidly delimited nor mechanically applied. The therapist's skill is needed to blend allo-awareness development smoothly into the therapy, for instance by using a Socratic approach.

Affective Phase

Explore with the patient what the significant other may have felt in a certain situation in which both were involved. It is important to insist that the patient consider, with the least amount of help possible from the therapist, all the potential alternative feelings. This minimizes the possibility that the patient will oversimplify, project, or get committed to a specific perception of the significant other and thus become defensive about changing it.

Behavioral Phase

List with the patient the possible behaviors that would support each of the hypotheses that were made about the other's feelings. The question to ask is: What would the other have done if she had felt that way?

After listing the possible behaviors, ask which of these behaviors were actually displayed by the significant other. At this stage, some of the conceivable feelings attributed by the patient to the other are eliminated, others are validated, and others are maintained as feelings that may have not resulted in behaviors observable to the patient.

Cognitive Phase

On what cognitive basis may the significant other operate in that specific situation? Is that cognitive base true, false, or incomplete?

At this point we may introduce analysis of the patient's part in the interaction. What did the patient actually say to the other and what does he infer that the other knows? If the significant other's cognitions are false or incomplete, what could the patient do to change them? Did the patient lack the skills to communicate? If so, we teach them.

Now the cycle is repeated from the patient's point of view.

Affective

What are the patient's feelings in response to those of the significant other? Here we connect the patient's feelings with the other's feelings and behaviors.

Behavior

What could the patient do? Which are all the potential actions? How may the significant other interpret, in response, each of the patient's behaviors (cognitive aspect), how may the other feel about them (affective aspect), and react to them (behavioral aspect)?

This approach tends to break the self-centered cycle of blame and deferred responsibility in which the patient is usually engaging. For instance: "When the other is doing this to me, I feel . . . , because I am . . . , due to the fact that when I was a child, my parents (or society, or school) did . . . to me." The intent is to replace the self-focused attitude with an allo-centered one. The patient becomes more and more aware of how the other's behavior, feelings, and thinking may be influenced by his behavior. The patient can influence the relationship. He is not powerless in a situation determined by the past or by vaguely defined events and forces about which he can do nothing.

Cognitive Check

Did the patient learn something new about the other? How will this new understanding affect his feelings and behavior toward the significant other?

Assignment

The patient is urged to test, through the interaction with the other, the insight gained in the previous session(s). It is helpful to take some notes and discuss them in future sessions.

This description of the allo-awareness technique is not a mold but a flexible model that has to be adapted to the patient and presenting situation. The analysis may start with the behavioral or cognitive phase. The depth of the analysis is tailored to the patient's ability to understand and utilize the insights it generates. As the patient's awareness of the other increases, these steps may be repeated at an increasingly deep level. It is left to the skill of the therapist to make the interplay between affective, behavioral, and cognitive phases run smoothly at the patient's pace.

Developing Love

Another method can be used when a patient wishes to develop warm, loving feelings toward a person whom he thinks is worthy of those feelings, but for certain reasons, has difficulty experiencing them. This technique does not preclude dealing with the causes that may block the patient's ability to develop or express such feelings. The patients to whom we now refer are not sociopaths, but relatively healthy individuals who do not feel as much warmth or love toward a child, a spouse, a parent, or a good friend as they would like to feel. A large number of candidates for this method are spouses who feel that their relationship has cooled off and their marriage is threatened. It is important that the persons toward whom the patients are to develop warm feelings be individuals likely to respond to them. This prevents the patients from being hurt and thus having even more difficulty developing warm, loving feelings toward others. The technique was developed after an intensive anal-

ysis of the subjective feelings experienced by people in deep, lasting love. The focus of these feelings is apparently located at about the middle of the sternum, where a special sensation, close to warmth, is experienced. Indeed, if we look at a mother holding her baby, or a child holding a stuffed animal, a puppy, a doll, or a security blanket, the same middle of the sternum point is most frequently chosen. The importance of hugs points to the same anatomical area. Maybe that's why the heart, the organ closest to that "magic" point, is considered the organ of love.

The technique involves several steps based on guided imagery. Although there is flexibility within these steps, this sequence of the steps is recommended, as experience shows it to be the most efficient.

Relaxation is induced with the use of any rapid method. A deep muscular relaxation is not so important here. The focus is on an active mental relaxation, which is based not on emptying the mind or focusing on a single object, but on filling the mind with a relaxing scenery associated with a warm sensation. For example, the patient may visualize a beautiful beach, with a deep, relaxing, blue sky on which a few white, round, fluffy clouds are drifting carelessly, carried by the wind. Beneath, there is a coconut tree with long, arched leaves swaying in the wind. The ocean is clear, greenish close to the beach, turning darker and darker blue until it becomes purplish toward the horizon. Round waves are rolling one after another, bringing in peace, calmness, and serenity; as they wash off, they take away stress, leaving the patient more and more relaxed. Other possible types of imagery include lying comfortably in an armchair in front of a fireplace, with other relaxing details in the room, or a meadow with a calm, beautiful lake and wildflowers, trees, birds, and the like.

Whichever relaxing scenery is used, it is followed by guided fantasy on familiar cues related to sensations of warmth, such as lying in the sun or being close to a fire. The patient is then guided to focus on this experience of warmth, internalizing it and localizing it in the chest area, especially on the "magic" spot. At this point, the feeling of warmth is associated with linguistically significant concepts such as "a lovely sensation."

Next, the feeling is generalized. The patient is guided to expand this feeling as a bubble or a cocoon of warmth generated from the chest and expanding to create a pleasant, comfortable environment. Once the patient becomes able to develop this feeling with relative ease, we expand this experience to include the image of the significant other. It is interesting that in practice this frequently happens spontaneously. If not, we proceed gradually, having the patient fantasize the person walking by at a certain distance, concomitant with an increase in that warm, pleasant feeling. Little by little the feeling of closeness is increased, and so is the warmth, until the other person is included in the cocoon. If the patient experiences any anxiety, the distance is increased for a while and the patient refocuses on the warm, pleasant feeling. Then, the approach is tried again. If the anxiety reappears, the dynamics will be analyzed with the patient, and dealt with.

In more severe situations, when the patient has great difficulty achieving an allo-centered approach, a more indirect technique is called for. The therapist can choose a suitable card from a TAT-like projective test, or any other appropriate picture or drawing, and ask the patient to tell a story about the picture, giving instructions similar to those for a TAT test. In the story, the patient will most frequently identify with one of the persons from the picture. The therapist then chooses another person from the picture, one as closely identifiable as possible with a significant other from the patient's life. The process continues as in the first described technique, with the therapist asking the patient to talk about this other person's feelings, behavior, and cognitions, then to discuss what the person with whom he identified would do, feel, and think in response, and so on.

Another technique is to ask the patient to role play the part of the significant other while the therapist acts as a counselor using active listening, confrontation, clarification, and so on to help the other attain better self-knowledge. As a result, the patient is at least in some measure identifying with and better understanding the other.

Relationship Cycles

Allo-Centered Psychotherapy methods are also useful in breaking negative relationship cycles and enhancing positive ones. Relationship cycles develop when the behavior of one of the dyad evokes in the other an enhanced similar (positive or negative) behavior to which the first one responds with an even stronger behavior, and so on. Such cycles develop most frequently among people who are close to each other, especially between family members, neighbors, and coworkers. Such cycles need attention because they can have significant consequences.

Most negative cycles are built on an initial misperception of the other's intent or a misattribution of his actions. Whenever a negative cycle starts developing, or as soon as possible, it is useful to apply allo-centered methods to correct the perception of the intent or the attribution of motives.

Other Techniques

Another powerful method, the two chairs Gestalt technique, can also be used with more stable patients. A milder technique is the story completion technique. In this the therapist presents an incomplete story about a person identifiable with the significant other and asks the patient to finish it. In the process, the therapist and patient analyze the feelings, behaviors, and cognitions of that person. Practically any legitimate and ethical methodology can be used, but the philosophy of ACP does not allow the therapist to "pull psychological tricks" on the patient, who needs to be informed of the goals and methodology. The therapist is like a trainer of a behavioral, emotional, and cognitive athlete striving to improve his performance. By definition, the therapist has to have respect, empathy, care—in a word, an allo-centered attitude—toward the patient.

An important part of ACP is the skill training in which the patient is taught skills needed in interaction with others, such as active listening, I-messages, conflict resolution, problem solving, and non-verbal cues reading.

APPLICATIONS

Allo-Centered Psychotherapy is appropriate in treating problems related to self-centeredness or interpersonal issues. It is especially useful when there are difficulties with the primary support group or with the social environment. Cases of anxiety, depression, social withdrawal, loneliness, avoidance, marriage and family problems, parenting problems, adjustment disorders, work-related tension, conflict resolution and anger management and the like benefit from the use of ACP methods. It is important to emphasize that ACP does not replace other proven methods of therapy (i.e., Cognitive-Behavioral Therapy) but supplements them in all of the situations described above.

Anxiety is alleviated when the world becomes more predictable, less threatening. This is achieved when others are better known and we become aware what to avoid, and whom we can trust.

Depression and social withdrawal are associated with a lack of enjoyment and a sense of hopelessness related to a negative view of the world and distrust in others' willingness to give support and care. After building an allo-centered attitude, it is easier for the patient to eliminate this negative view and identify those who would be supportive and caring. This will make it easier to work on past experiences or other problems that made the patient depressed.

Loneliness and avoidance are characterized by a desire to have company, thwarted by a fear of rejection. It is obvious here how the better knowledge and therefore predictability of others, as gained through allo-centered therapy, would be beneficial to the treatment.

Marriage and family problems are frequently created either by misperceptions and misattributions, or by an inability or unwillingness to deal with a difficult personality. Power struggle is often a cause of conflict in families. Yet power struggle never benefits anyone in the family, not even the "winner." A family in which there is a power struggle is like a wooden boat in which the crew is fighting with axes: Sooner or later the boat will be sunk by its own crew. A family fight for domination leads to accusations, hunting for faults and errors, and defensiveness. The stronger personality is often labeled domineering, even when that strength is actually put in the service of the family. In all these cases, a better understanding of others, achieved through ACP, is essential for any conflict resolution or attempt to improve communication.

In parenting, a certain child may be incorrectly labeled, and then treated according to that label. An unnatural, artificial identity is frequently forced on the child. It is well known that some adolescents tend to view adults as out of touch with the present times and therefore unable to provide guidance. Adolescents may also misread adults' attempts to shield them from dangers as overbearing and restrictive. The much discussed adolescent rebelliousness is not an inevitable developmental stage, but a failure to develop allo-centrism in one party or the other. Self-centered parents may fail to recognize that their children are growing up and dread the moment when their children will grow up into independent adults. The empty nest syndrome would not take such a dramatic dimension in allo-centered parents who, although they would miss their children, would feel pride in their emancipation. On the other hand, allo-centered adolescents would empathize with the parents, who care for them, and would appreciate their experience and knowledge and use it to their advantage. Even when they disagree with their parents' point of view, they will give it thorough consideration before deciding whether or not it is of value for them. Allo-centrism facilitates the understanding of both parents and children. There is no longer a power struggle, but a cooperation to find the best course of action in each situation. In this way, not only can adolescents receive good advice from parents, but adolescents can also become valuable consultants to parents.

Repeated situations in which students have shot peers and teachers in U.S. schools have evoked horror and invited questions about how that could happen, even in otherwise peaceful communities. All kinds of theories and explanations have been offered, but can one imagine allo-centered students murdering colleagues and teachers in cold blood? If such isolated, alienated, and enraged children were to develop at least some allo-centrism, they would better understand others and would care about them. Even with potential murderers quite beyond reform, other, allo-centered students would be able to perceive their violent intent and thwart it.

The preceding discussion leads to another issue of importance in our society: anger, which is a reaction to frustration, fear, hurt, or humiliation. Frustration is reduced when people understand each other and have empathy. Fear is less likely to develop when we understand the people around us. Misreading each other is a frequent cause of hurt, but caring people tend to have a more correct perception and understanding of each other. An allo-centered attitude avoids or deals more readily with the development of these four roots of anger and therefore with anger itself.

CASE EXAMPLE

G. H. was a 46-year-old woman living with her parents in a modest three-bedroom house with a 1,000-square-foot yard around it. She came with her father, who said he was afraid that she might commit suicide if her parents died. She was so dependent on them that she did not feel that she could survive alone.

G. H. was quite withdrawn and uncommunicative. She insisted that her father stay in session with her, and it was clear that without him she would not say a word. In fact, he was quite helpful in gathering, over about three sessions, the information that normally would have constituted the initial interview. This time was also used to start indirectly establishing some rapport with G. H. by doing active listening to her father's statements.

As a child, G. H. seemed to be developing within normal parameters. Because both parents were employed, she was practically raised by her paternal grandmother, who lived across the street. G. H. did well in school and had a few friends. When she was 11, her grandmother died suddenly of a heart attack, and her mother quit working to stay with G. H., although she was in school most of the day. From this time on, G. H. started to complain that school was hard for her and that other children were teasing her. Her grades started dropping and her mother and father had to help her do her homework. By the time G. H. was finishing intermediate school, she started missing more and more classes, claiming that she was ill. She frequently complained that she was teased by her peers. This assertion was not confirmed by the teachers, but was believed by her mother. Although mother and daughter stayed home together, alone, for many hours, there was little communication between them beyond what was necessary for everyday life. The TV was on all the time and was the focal point of attention in the house.

When G. H. finally completed intermediate school and had to enter high school, the situation reached a point of crisis. With difficulty G. H. agreed to go to school, mostly at the insistence of her father that she give it an honest try. She went, but kept finding all kind of motives to stay home. The school counselor had several sessions with her, but when she tried to put her into group counseling, G. H. stopped going to counseling. By this time her grades had deteriorated greatly. G. H. complained of peer teasing, and that the school was too difficult for her. Finally, the parents and the school decided that it would be better for her to be home schooled with the help of a retired teacher.

G. H. finished school but became more and more homebound. One former schoolmate tried to maintain some connection with her by visiting her now and then, but gave up after a while, as there was not much interaction during her visits. G. H. became more and more reclusive, visited only now and then by a few of her close relatives. She was spending most of her time in the house and stopped going out of the yard by herself. She rarely even went with her mother to shop or to get a haircut. Her parents also, and especially her mother, tended to be rather homebound. Not only did their family become isolated from the outside world, but family members also became isolated from each other.

G. H. never married nor even dated anyone. By the time she was brought in for therapy, she was depressed, sleeping most of the day. She was eating often and was quite obese, and continuing to gain weight. Lately, she had lost interest even in reading and TV and had become quite lethargic. She had frequent crying spells. A deep sense of hopelessness and worthlessness were prevailing, and she hoped that one day she would just lie down and die. She thought frequently of suicide but felt that it would take too much effort. In an attempt at irony, she commented that she did not have the energy to kill herself and even if she had, she would probably bungle the attempt, "like everything else." She also added that whatever values she retained from her childhood Sunday school stopped her, at least for the time that her parents were alive. She was terrified by the idea that they would someday die and repeated that she deeply wished that she would die before them.

There was no history of substance abuse. In addition to her obesity, G. H. complained of stiffness and numerous muscular pains. Her physician attributed these pains to her weight, tension, and lack of exercise.

The father, 78 years old, seemed to be the most functional member of the family, although he was quite soft and noncommittal. He had worked until the age of 65 in the same governmental clerical position he had held since the age of 18, climbing modestly through the ranks as he gained seniority. G. H.'s mother, 76 years old, had met her husband when she was 24, while working as a typist at the same institution. A cautious, shy romance developed and at the age of 27, she consented to marry him, mostly out of a need for security. She continued to work in the same institution in a small, rather isolated cubicle, which suited her just fine. The mother did not like going to the cafeteria for lunch, so the father brought in food that they shared, mostly in silence. At the age of 29 she gave birth to G. H.

At the age of about 40, the mother was granted a medical early retirement and stayed home to take care of her daughter G. H. She seldom went out alone. She shopped only at hours when there were very few people in the store. She also went for a walk on a nearby, mostly deserted little beach.

Except for the mother's depression, both parents seemed healthy and without any significant medical problem.

Assessment.   This woman (G. H.), living in a family environment conducive to depression, was herself severely depressed and withdrawn. The healthiest person in the family was the father, who although rather passive and unassertive, could be counted on to bring G. H. to therapy. The patient was living in a world of her own, with little reaching out, in a quite self-centered life. She, like her mother, and perhaps influenced by her, adamantly refused any medication. She gave clear signals that she would quit therapy if medication was suggested. Complicating the situation was a clear avoidance tendency that was going beyond what a social withdrawal due to depression would show.

The diagnosis was Major Depressive Disorder, Recurrent, Severe, Without Psychotic Features, and Avoidant Personality Disorder.

Treatment Plan.   This patient seemed a good candidate for ACP. In addition, when the patient would become more trusting, careful motivational approaches for pharmacotherapy would be attempted. Other methods, such as Cognitive-Behavioral Therapy and Stress Management, were also included, but the following description will focus especially on ACP, which constituted the foremost and most efficient form of therapy in this case.

Treatment.   After five sessions, the patient seemed to have started building some confidence in the therapist, although she was still quite defensive and nonverbal. At that point indirect allo-awareness methods were used. The mother and father were also brought in session and I suggested that G. H. should get a puppy. Suddenly G. H. started sobbing, and the father explained that she had a puppy when she was about 12. Somebody left the gate open, the puppy went out in the street, and a car hit and killed it. She refused to get another puppy because none could replace Bobbie. I finally knew that there had once existed a significant other that could be used in ACP. The discussion started around what Bobbie did, what must she have felt, what she might have been thinking, and so on. Bobbie was quite anthropomorphized. The dog was a good subject for an indirect allo-awareness technique, and G. H. was coming to life when talking about Bobbie. Did Bobbie love her? "Of course!" Did she love Bobbie? How did she feel when she loved Bobbie? Did she feel warmth? In what place? Did she ever feel like that with anyone else? "Maybe with Grandmother," but she was not sure. Would Bobbie want her to feel the same? Then maybe Bobbie would want her to have another puppy to remind her of the feelings she had with Bobbie. When after two more sessions it became conceivable that she could get another puppy, we again convened the whole family to discuss getting another puppy for G. H. A note was made about what she said concerning her feelings about her grandmother, although the uncertainty and the fact that the grandmother wasn't around any more made her not yet a suitable significant other for ACP.

When I met again with the whole family and brought up the issue of getting a puppy, the mother came out of her silence and with a surprisingly assertive tone said: "We need to get a purebred dog." A surprisingly strong and even hostile reply from G. H. came almost instantly: "No way! Purebred puppies are snobbish; they would not like me!" We made note of this statement also and moved on to find arguments for getting a "poi dog," the Hawaiian term for a mongrel: cheaper, less chance of having birth defects, a chance to save a dog from being put to sleep by the humane society, needing more love, being more likely to be grateful, and so on. (The latter arguments were intended to focus on allo-centered qualities.)

A trip to the humane society was planned, and I decided to accompany the family, foreseeing a chance for important therapeutic events. We passed by the enclosures where adult dogs were kept to stop in front of those with puppies. G. H. passed relatively fast by the first such enclosure to stop at the second, looking intently at a group of five or six puppies. "I want that one," she said pointing toward the runt of the litter who was staying quiet, cowering in the far corner while the others were competing for people's attention at the front. "Why that one?" "They are laughing at him because he is smaller!" The analogy with her past experience in school was striking, so I pleaded with the parents to get that dog. It was difficult in the beginning, especially with the mother who, after conceding to renounce a purebred, wanted at least a strong, presentable dog. Fortunately the father joined us and the mother grudgingly acquiesced. The ominous remark of a kennel volunteer that the puppy probably would not be there for long because it would be hard to find someone to want her, speeded up the decision. G. H. asked that she hold the dog for a while before leaving it for preparation until the next day. The dog was not very responsive and looked half scared, half content.

The dog got the name of Bobbie-Two with numerous nicknames, including Bob. Through allo-centered techniques we came to clarify together that Bob wasn't actually laughed at by the other puppies. She was just not assertive enough to compete for attention, although she was quite a nice and lovable dog. We also delved into what feelings the other puppies might have had about Bob, for instance: Maybe she wanted to be left alone and didn't like them if she was staying aside all the time. We found unfortunate this misunderstanding of Bob, and we speculated on what would have happened to Bob if she had continued to live in these conditions. "She would have become a fat dog who would have never come out of her doghouse," blurted G. H., and before I could say a word she added in tears, "Just like me." This was the turning point in therapy, and from then on we could mix the indirect approach, using Bob, with the direct approach, talking about G. H.

We started to alternate individual therapy sessions with family sessions where the father came to life and became a catalyst of the therapeutic process. He admitted that he had lost hope, himself not being too outgoing, but now, seeing the progress, he wanted to change and help his family too. The mother also asked for individual therapy sessions. A complex case herself, she provided a better understanding of the dynamics, which further helped the therapy with G. H.

An interesting rivalry developed between the mother and G. H. for Bob's love and attention, which was "therapeutic" for Bob, but created problems for G. H. I explained to them the true understanding of love. Love for a person is not like the content of a bag, where the more you give to someone, the less remains for others. Love for a person is like a tree that develops independently of the love for another. Only when those trees try to grow in the same place—like a threesome relationship in a marriage—and one tree tries to dislodge the other, only then there is a problem. Otherwise, as the trees grow in a grove, they grow stronger than a lonely tree on a mountain ridge would: They protect each other from the wind, they keep warmer during the winter frost, and they actually help each other grow. In the same way, a person in love becomes more loving toward others. We had to work on this for several sessions. During these sessions G. H. asked what love really is and how do you come to love people. I asked her if she really wanted to experience stronger love for someone, and she said, "For Dad and Ma." The time was obviously right for the love-developing technique previously described. We used as the starting point the feeling she had when she was holding Bob. After several sessions she surprised her father with a hug and after several more she startled her mother with one. We started the same training with the mother and things gradually warmed up in the family.

In the meantime Bob was growing beyond expectations and what the family had planned as a lapdog became a good-sized beautiful, loving, and playful dog.

This in turn activated the energy level in the family but also made evident the need for Bob to be taken out of the yard for exercise. The father started taking the dog out, but one day the mother, surprisingly, performed this tour of duty. G. H., jealous, ran to accompany her. Some rivalry soon developed on who would hold the leash. This dispute didn't last long because Bob proved to be too much of a challenge for the duo, so mother and daughter returned home exhausted and very disappointed, feeling inadequate to handle Bob. I suggested that they use both a leash and a choke collar and cooperate to master the challenging moments when they passed by a tree or hydrant. We did not miss the chance to talk about Bob's need for friendship with her peers even though she was neutered. The main problem turned out to be that at the other end of the leash of the dogs that Bob wanted to befriend was usually a human being with whom neither G. H. nor her mother were eager to interact, much less befriend. "For the sake of Bob's happiness" we started to work on the awareness and recognition of non–family members and to learn small talk and techniques to politely conclude the interaction when wanted, in order to provide them with the security of a way out. An old lady, "mother" of a handsome Labrador, became their first "dog-friend," and very slowly and cautiously their circle of interactions enlarged.

By now, I had, most of the time, the whole family in session. I suggested that Bob should attend an obedience school to become more manageable and less likely to run in front of some car. This was another landmark, and the father had to accompany the ladies of the house for the first few training sessions, after which they took over themselves. The "dog-talk" made them develop some acquaintances at the obedience school, and I worked on their anxiety, arguing that dog-lovers cannot be such bad people, and they deserve a chance to be noticed. We introduced more and more humor into our therapy and they learned to poke fun at themselves. Although the interactions with the "dog-people" were not evenly balanced in both directions, there was interaction, and this was good progress.

Another important turning point occurred when the mother, ill with a severe flu, could not get out of bed and G. H. alone took Bob, by now well trained, for a walk to the park.

G. H. and her family continued to improve. Even today they are not the most outgoing family, but they function well and have a few dog- and non-dog-friends, or more precisely, acquaintances. The saga continues, and at times I wonder whether I or Bob was their true allo-centered therapist. I like to think that Bobbie-Two was just my first disciple in Allo-Centered Psychotherapy. It helps my self-image.

SUMMARY

Allo-Centered Psychotherapy (*allos* = other in Greek) is a different philosophical approach to therapy. With applications in all areas of psychotherapy and counseling, except for psychosis, ACP changes the emphasis on self, common in most of the present psychotherapies, to an emphasis on others. In the allo-centered approach to psychology and psychotherapy it is considered that the focus on self and on introspection is a contributing factor to a series of psychological problems. Self-absorption leads to a poor knowledge of others and in consequence to a deprivation of the mostly positive feedback that we receive from others. On the other hand, introspection is seldom used to find a person's strengths and qualities, but rather focuses on weaknesses and problems. This is due partially to our nature as well as to the influence of the negativistic spirit of our times. At the same time, self-centered people, having a poor understanding of others, find them unpredictable, and expect the worst from them. The self-centeredness may lead to isolationism, loneliness, depression, anxiety, and so on.

Allo-Centered Psychotherapy works to transform self-centeredness into other-concern, which leads to a better understanding of others and an increased ability to deal with them. It also produces a positive, supportive response, especially from significant others.

Allo-Centered Psychotherapy does not reject any other legitimate approaches, but rather builds upon them. Most of the commonly employed therapeutic methods can be used, some directly, and some in modified form. In addition, some methods specific to ACP have been developed, certain of which have been presented in this chapter.

REFERENCES

Adler, A, (1939). *Social interest: A challenge to mankind.* New York: Putnam.

Allport, G. W. (1955). *Becoming: Basic considerations for a psychology of personality.* New Haven, CT: Yale University Press.

Buber, M. (1970). *I and thou.* New York: Scribner. (Original work published 1958)

Corsini, R. (1999). *Dictionary of psychology.* Philadelphia: Brunner/Mazel.

Frankl, V. E. (1980). *Man's search for meaning: An introduction to logotherapy.* New York: Simon & Schuster. (Original work published 1962)

Motet, D. (1985). Allo-Centered Psychotherapy. In D. Benner (Ed.), *Baker encyclopedia of psychology* (p. 45). Grand Rapids, MI: Baker Book House.

Chapter 3

ART THERAPY

MYRA LEVICK

We humans, in our basic wisdom about ourselves, tend to find ways to "cure" ourselves when we are troubled. One of the most common of ways to divert ourselves from problems, to get relaxed and in touch with others, to express our feelings, is through aesthetic productions. Just as music and dance and poetry have been employed consciously by professionals in therapeutic fields, so too art has been used for psychotherapeutic purposes.

In the following chapter, Myra Levick explains how the production of art becomes psychotherapy. Experts in Art Therapy are able to use this means of expression for release, for understanding, and for greater adjustment to life.

Art has a diagnostic as well as a curative value. Surely one who has problems of adjustment is likely to show evidence of this through imaginative creative productions. As a matter of fact, a clever and well-trained art therapist may be able to understand the nature of a troubled person's difficulties through examination of his or her projections. As this chapter demonstrates, we can see progress through paintings.

Naturally, for this therapy—as well as for all other forms of therapy—the quality of the treatment is a function of the sensitivity of the therapist and the nature of the client's problems.

Art Therapy as a discipline has been growing rapidly over the last 30 years, and its definition has evolved over the years. Fink, Goldman, and Levick (1967) define Art Therapy as "that discipline which combines elements of psychotherapy with untapped sources of creativity and expression in the patient"; Levick (1967) a "prescribed substitution of creative activity to replace neurotic symptoms and to strengthen defenses successfully by the patient before illness becomes acute, and establish a prescribed relationship with the therapist."

The current definition as described by the American Art Therapy Association is as follows: Art therapy provides the opportunity for nonverbal expression and communication. Within the field there are two major approaches. The use of art as therapy implies that the creative process can be a means both of reconciling emotional conflicts and of fostering self-awareness and personal growth. When using art as a vehicle for psychotherapy, both the product and the associative references may be used in an effort to help the individual find a more compatible relationship between his inner and outer worlds.

MISSION STATEMENT OF THE AMERICAN ART THERAPY ASSOCIATION

The American Art Therapy Association, Inc. (AATA) is an organization of professionals dedicated to the belief that the creative process involved in the making of art is healing and life enhancing. Its mission is to serve its members and the general public by providing standards of professional competence in, and of, the field of Art Therapy.

DEFINITION OF PROFESSION

Art Therapy is a human service profession that utilizes art media, images, the creative art process, and patient/client responses to the created products as reflections of an individual's development, abilities, personality, interests, concerns, and conflicts. Art Therapy is based on knowledge of human development and psychological theories that are implemented in the full spectrum of models of assessment and treatment, including educational, psychodynamic, cognitive, transpersonal, and other therapeutic means of reconciling emotional conflicts, fostering self-awareness, developing social skills, managing behavior, solving problems, reducing anxiety, aiding reality orientation, and increasing self-esteem.

Art Therapy is an effective treatment for the developmentally, medically, educationally, socially, or psychologically impaired, and is practiced in mental health rehabilitation, medical, educational, and forensic institutions. Populations of all ages, races, and ethnic backgrounds are served by art therapists in individual, couples, family, and group therapy formats.

Educational, professional, and ethical standards for art therapists are regulated by the American Art Therapy Association. The Art Therapy Credentials Board, Inc. (ATCB), an independent organization, grants postgraduate registration (ATR) after reviewing documentation of completion of graduate education and postgraduate supervised experience. The Registered art therapist who successfully completes the written examination administered by the ATCB is qualified as board certified (ATR-BC), a credential requiring maintenance through continuing education credits (Summer 1999, *AATA Newsletter*).

HISTORY

Precursors

Ernest Harms, founder and former editor of the *International Journal of Art Psychotherapy,* traced the healing effects of the arts (in this case, music) back to biblical sources that describe how David tried to cure King Saul's depression by playing the harp (Harms, 1975). Emil Kraeplin, in 1912, and Eugen Bleuler, in 1918, also suggested that drawings of patients be considered in making diagnosis. Hans Printzhorn, in the early 1970s, spurred well-known psychopathologists to use the art expressions of their patients to diagnose their pathological conditions. Emanuel Hammer states: "From these causal diagnostic beginnings, a great number of systematic diagnostic methods have been developed which today we call tests; and the method has been designed as a projective technique" (in Harms, 1975, pp. 241–244).

In 1925 Nolan D. C. Lewis began to use free painting with adult neurotics (see Naumburg, 1947). Max Stem described free painting in psychoanalysis with adult neurotics and stated that one of the reasons that this modality has not been generally adopted may be due to part to a lack of understanding in the use of this technique and results (see Fink, Goldman, & Levick, 1967). Art Therapy, however, emerged out of the personality theories of Freud, Jung, and others and was particularly influenced by the technique of psychoanalysis. The concept of the unconscious, as presented by Freud, along with the idea that individuals express memories and thoughts through symbols, eventually provided a major theoretical base for Art Therapy. Jung further expanded on this when he gave psychological meanings to forms inherent in artwork, such as the mandala. The growing interest in the late nineteenth century in developmental psychology, influenced by the work of Jean Piaget, Maria Montessori, and John Dewey, led to research that identified the development of children's drawings. The impact of art educators like Viktor Lowenfeld, Florence Cane, and Franz Cizek on developing new techniques based on this new understanding is significant in the early definitions of Art Therapy theory (Junge, 1994).

Beginnings

"Art Therapy as a profession was first defined in America in the writings of Margaret Naumburg" (Levick, 1973). Naumburg dates her awareness of the relationship between children's drawings and psychotherapy to her early years of experience as director and art teacher of the Walden School, which she founded in 1915. She became convinced that the free art expression of children represented a symbolic form of speech basic to all education. As the years passed, she concluded that this "form of spontaneous art expression was also basic to psychotherapeutic treatment" (Naumburg, 1966, p. 30).

Under the direction of Nolan D. C. Lewis, she initiated an experimental research program in the use of spontaneous art in therapy with behavior-problem children at the New York State Psychiatric Unit. The results of the study were first published in 1947. In 1958 graduate courses in the principle and methods of her concept of dynamically oriented Art Therapy were instituted at New York University. Her prolific writings, lectures, and seminars throughout the country spearheaded growing interest in the field and stimulated mental health professionals and educators to question and explore the possibilities of a broader conceptual framework in the application of art as a diagnostic and therapeutic tool.

Subsequent art therapists, some trained by Naumburg, added significant impetus to the development of this modality and should be mentioned briefly. Eleanor Ulman originally defined her profession as art teacher. She received some training in art education through lectures and seminars at the Washington School of Psychiatry and a series of lectures on Art Therapy by Naumburg. In the early 1950s she took a position in a psychiatric clinic. She later worked at the District of Columbia General Hospital where Bernard Levy, chief psychologist, taught her the principles of diagnosis (Ulman, 1966). In 1961 she published the first issue of the *Bulletin of Art Therapy,* which has continued to be a major publication in the field.

Ben Ploger was both an art teacher and art therapist. He began teaching art in 1935, and became professor and chairman, Department of Fine Arts, Delgado College, New Orleans, Louisiana. In the early 1960s he was persuaded by a psychiatric nurse to volunteer to teach art to mentally disturbed nuns cloistered in the religious unit of the De Paul Hospital. He soon began to introduce and implement his own particular expertise throughout the hospital and was made director of art psychotherapy there in 1966 (personal communication).

In 1950 Edith Kramer initiated and for nine years conducted an Art Therapy program at Wiltwick School for Boys, New York City. Her first book, *Art Therapy in a Children's Community,* was written in 1958. Kramer is widely known as a lecturer and teacher in the field.

During World War II, Don Jones, a conscientious objector, volunteered for duty at Marlboro State Hospital, New Jersey. In a letter to me he stated, "Having had an art background before, I immediately became intrigued by the many graphic productions and projections of patients which literally covered the walls of some rooms and of passageways between different buildings." In 1950, a number of psychiatrists and social workers from the Menninger Clinic were his students in painting classes at Kansas University. He was soon introduced to Karl Menninger and shared with him a manuscript and paintings reflecting his wartime experiences. This resulted in his being employed as an art therapist at Menninger's Foundation, and marked the beginning of the Art Therapy program at the institution. Jones remained there until 1966, when he became director of the Adjunctive Therapy Department, Harding Hospital, Worthington, Ohio. He is a past president of the American Art Therapy Association.

I received a bachelor of fine arts degree in painting in 1963 and was planning to pursue training in art history. However, I answered a provocative job advertisement for a trained artist to work with mental patients in the first open inpatient unit in a general hospital in Philadelphia and spent the next five years in intensive in-service psychiatric training with the staff under the direction of the late Morris I. Goldman. An Art Therapy program was implemented, and in collaboration with Goldman and Paul Jay Fink, I wrote several papers about experiences with Art Therapy. During that time I also attended graduate school and in 1967 received a master's degree in educational psychology from Temple University. That same year Goldman became director of the Hahnemann Community Health Center, Philadelphia, and within a few months he and Fink, then director of education and training, Department of Psychiatry, Hahnemann Medical College and Hospital, initiated the first graduate training program leading to a master's degree in Art Therapy in the world. I was appointed director.

In 1968 Hahnemann Medical College and Hospital hosted a lecture series in Art Therapy and a reception for practicing art therapists throughout the country. At that meeting an ad hoc committee was elected to develop guidelines for the organization of the National Art Therapy Association. The committee members were Elinor Ulman; Don Jones; Felice Cohen, a well-known art therapist at Texas Research Institute in Houston; Robert Ault, an art therapist at the Menninger Foundation, who had been trained by Don Jones and who replaced Jones when he left Menninger; and this writer. In 1969 the American Art Therapy Association (AATA) was officially launched into existence at Louisville, Kentucky.

The art therapists mentioned here reflect only a small number of the highly competent men and women who were ultimately responsible for establishing Art Therapy as a profession in the United States and abroad. For an in-depth description of the history of Art Therapy the reader is referred to *A History of Art Therapy in the United States* (Junge, 1994).

CURRENT STATUS

The AATA has designated professional entry into the field at the master's or graduate level training in institute or clinical programs. Graduate training must include didactic and practicum experience, but the emphasis may vary depending on the facility in which the student is trained. A master's degree from an academic institution or a certificate of completion from an institute or clinical program is supported by the AATA as professional qualification for entry into the field.

Undergraduate programs that provide basic areas of fine arts and the behavioral and social sciences in preparation for graduate training are also supported by the AATA. These two areas are prerequisites for specialized Art Therapy training, which includes a knowledge of history, theory, and the practice of Art Therapy itself. Guidelines and criteria for Art Therapy training and clinical training are available from the American Art Therapy Association, Mundelein, Illinois. Numerous academic institutions, clinics, and institutes currently train art therapists, and other institutions provide undergraduate coursework in preparation for graduate training. A list of available programs and whom to write to for information is available upon request from the AATA.

Procedures for program approval were instituted in 1978, and the first group of programs meeting these requirements was announced in November 1979. As of 1999 there were 31 approved graduate programs in Art Therapy. Other educational opportunities listed by AATA include four university graduate programs and one undergraduate degree program. The names of these programs and their contact persons can be obtained through the AATA office in Mundelein, Illinois. Principles of conduct and standards of practice have been evolving since the field was organized in 1969. There have been many revisions to these documents, but there is now a published Code of Ethics and a General Standards of Practice Document, published in 1989. All of these documents are available through the AATA office.

Initially there were three classifications of members in the association: (1) active membership, which is open to all persons "who are or have been actively engaged in the therapeutic use of art" (AATA pamphlet, 1970); (2) associate membership, which is available to volunteers or individuals who "may or may not be engaged in the therapeutic use of art, who wish to support the program of the Association" (AATA pamphlet); (3) student membership for students involved in Art Therapy training.

Early on, as standards for training were developing, the association also established specific criteria for registration; art therapists who have met those standards receive a certificate of registration by the AATA and may use the initials ATR. The question of also providing a certifying examination similar to that of other health professionals was hotly debated for a number of years. The prevailing argument for such a process was the fact that certification will help strengthen the Art Therapy community and support licensing. In 1993 the Art Therapy Certifying Board (ATCB) was established as a separate organization for the purpose of supporting and protecting the community of art therapists and the public (Carolan, former president of ATCB, 1999). There are now nine categories of membership: ATR, professional, associate, life member, honorary life member, contributing and retired ATR, professional and associate. As of 1999, there were 4,342 members, of which 2,812 are ATRs and 1,060 of which are board certified.

In 1974 Linda Gantt and Marilyn Strauss Schmal prepared a comprehensive, annotated bibliography of literature in the field of Art Therapy from 1940 to 1973 through a grant from the National Institute of Mental Health. The body of Art Therapy literature has grown considerably in the last 25 years. More and more practicing art therapists are documenting their work, publishing articles, and writing books. There are four major publications in the field: *Art Therapy: The Journal of the American Art Therapy Association; Newsletter: American Art Therapy Association, Inc.; The American Journal of Art Therapy* (previously *Journal of Art Therapy*); and *The Arts in Psychotherapy: An International Journal.* In addition to references there is a limited bibliography at the end of this chapter.

THEORY

Not all practicing art therapists view human beings' behavior as a product of unconscious thoughts and feelings. Current training in the field embraces many orientations; therefore, it follows that the philosophy of art therapists coming from theoretical frameworks such as Behavior Modification, Gestalt, Client-Centered, Humanistic, and so forth, would be different from that originally put forth by Naumburg. "Most drawings of the emotionally disordered express problems involving certain polarities, e.g., life-death, male-female, father-mother, love-hate, activity versus passivity, space rhythm, color, some being specialized and others being generalized in composition" (Naumburg, 1947, p. v). The psychoanalytic approach to ego mechanisms of defense is the basis for treatment methods in Art Therapy (Naumburg, 1966). Naumburg maintains that spontaneous art expression releases unconscious material; the transference relation between patient and therapist plays an important role in the therapeutic process. Further, the encouragement of free association in pictures closely allies dynamic Art Therapy to psychoanalytic therapy (Ulman, 1961).

More recent proponents of Naumburg's original premise maintain that the patient's artistic productions, like the dream brought to the analyst, cannot be interpreted without the patient's associations. Condensation, displacement, symbolism, and secondary elaboration, components of dreams and graphic productions, plus the patient's associations, provide more information than is often observable in the clinical setting (Fink, 1967).

In 1958 a second theory of Art Therapy was formulated by Edith Kramer. While recognizing the unconscious as a determinant for the human being's behavior, she believes that the very act of creating is healing; that the *art* in therapy provides a means of widening the range of human experience by "creating equivalents for such experiences" (Ulman, 1961, p. 13). Kramer places great emphasis on the process of sublimation and feels that the arts are to be highly valued in the treatment process of the mentally ill. She clearly identifies her role with patients as different from that of the art teacher, in that in teaching art to patients the process takes precedence over the product (Ulman, 1961).

The art therapists who have adopted the Naumburg ideology are viewed as psychotherapists by the followers of the Kramer ideology; the art therapists who, like Kramer, place emphasis on the healing quality of the creative process are viewed as art teachers (Ulman, 1961). The current literature, which consists primarily of case studies, reflects a wide variety of theoretical concepts somewhere between Naumburg and Kramer. Many of these theoretical formulations and methodologies have evolved as the result of the many graduate training programs that have been established throughout this country in the past eight years. As was suggested previously, a number of pioneers in the field developed their own unique Art Therapy theories based on years of experience rather than on a single theoretical frame of reference. There are no longer just two accepted, divergent viewpoints, but many valid frames of reference that lead to as many valid goals.

For those dynamically oriented art therapists, the goal is to allow a transference relationship to develop so that through the patients' associations to their spontaneous drawings insights into conflicted areas of the psyche may be uncovered. In the process of making verbal what was nonverbal, conscious what was unconscious, the art psychotherapist makes connections and clarifications in an effort to help the patient interpret his or her own symbolic images.

In placing emphasis on the healing aspect of the creative process, the goal of Art Therapy is to provide a means, according to Kramer, "wherein experiences can be chosen, varied, repeated at will" (Ulman, 1961, p. 13). It also provides an opportunity to reexperience conflict and to resolve and integrate the resolution.

I was primarily trained in a psychoanalytic milieu. As a pioneer in educating art therapists, I soon discovered that while this theoretical construct is critical in understanding developmental stages, learning other approaches was necessary in order to help Art Therapy students develop successful therapeutic skills. This was strongly reinforced by doctoral studies that focused on learning and behavioral theories and six weeks of my sabbatical spent working as an "art person" at the clinic in Hampstead, England, under the supervision of Ms. Anna Freud and her staff. These experiences as a therapist, educator, and student have repeatedly demonstrated that the most valid goal is that which is consistent with the needs of the patient/client regardless of theoretical orientation.

While written many years ago, the following remains consistent with the current definition of Art Therapy. A list of goals all art therapists should keep in mind includes: (1) providing a means for strengthening the ego, (2) providing a cathartic experience, (3) providing a means to uncover anger, (4) offering an avenue to reduce guilt, (5) facilitating a task to develop impulse control, (6) introducing an experience to help develop the ability to integrate and relate, and (7) helping patients/clients use art as a new outlet during an incapacitating illness (Levick, 1967).

METHODOLOGY

The clinical application of Art Therapy encompasses the hospitalized child and adult, psychotic and neurotic populations voluntarily seeking some form of psychiatric intervention or treatment, prison populations, mentally retarded populations, learning disabled chil-

dren, troubled couples and families, and, more recently, those individuals manifesting emotional problems resulting from physical illnesses such as chronic kidney disease, cancer, hemophilia, asthma, diabetes, and neurological diseases.

Art Therapy sessions may be conducted on a one-to-one basis, in small or large groups, and with families. They may be held in the art therapist's office, the classroom, the dining room of an inpatient unit, or the basement of a general hospital. The locale is contingent on the needs and ideology of the director or administrator of the institution that employs an art therapist or the orientation and style of the art therapist in private practice.

Specific methods and techniques necessarily vary. However, it is generally accepted within the profession that the art therapist must have a sound knowledge of and considerable experience with all art media to carry out treatment goals in the Art Therapy session. For example, fingerpaint, oil paints, and clay are tactile media that foster the compulsion to smear. If the treatment goal is to provide structure toward helping the patient gain internal controls, these supplies would be detrimental. A more productive choice of media might be felt-tip markers or crayons.

Patients who need to be encouraged to communicate with others but cannot do so verbally often benefit from some form of group mural activity. For the child who is withdrawn or who has a behavior problem because of a specific learning disability, the first drawing accepted and valued by the art therapist/teacher may be the first step toward self-acceptance. For troubled families, Art Therapy may dispel family myths and uncover denied scapegoating. Unhealthy alliances can be confronted and changed, and healthy separation of generations and consequent individuation can be reinforced. Drawings done by chronic, long-term, inarticulate patients often serve as the only means of evaluating prognosis, establishing treatment goals, and determining discharge procedures. For all patients/clients, Art Therapy, a nonverbal form of communication, provides a way to gain distance from disturbing thoughts and feelings. For the psychotic patient, it often helps to separate fantasy from fact; for the severely neurotic patient, it may help connect feelings and thoughts. The length of therapy varies according to the setting in which it is conducted and the orientation of the therapist. For example, in a short-term hospital unit, Art Therapy would be consistent with the treatment goals of the milieu. In a one-to-one situation where the art therapist has a therapeutic contract with the patient, the length of therapy would reflect both the needs of the patient and the therapist's particular clinical orientation.

With the establishment of the ATCB and maintaining certification through continuing education, art therapists continue to learn and grow, designing innovative interventions to meet the demands of limited insurance coverage and managed care. It has also become incumbent upon us to learn more about assessments. Graphic images are not easily quantifiable and many art therapists have relied on known psychological tests. A list of art therapists who have developed Art Therapy assessments is included in the bibliography and the reader is referred to a most recent and comprehensive work, *The Art and Science of Evaluation in the Arts Therapies* (Feder & Feder, 1998). The Feders have written a number of books and articles on the arts therapies. They stress the difficulty in trying to quantify not only graphic images, but movement and music as well. As a brief example, and because it is discussed in the Feders' book, I will describe briefly my own efforts in this area.

As a result of my doctoral studies and work in England with Ms. Freud, my first book, *They Could Not Talk and So They Drew* (1983), looked at the relationship between cognitive and emotional development in the drawings of normal children and using Piaget's stages and psychoanalytic defense mechanisms of the ego developed criteria for identifying normal cognitive and emotional development. Several years later, in collaboration with art therapists at the Miami-Dade County School District, the Levick Emotional and Cognitive Art Therapy Assessment (LECATA) was designed and integrated into the evaluation procedures for children with special needs at that school district. In addition, training seminars have been held around the country over the last 10 years for those interested in utilizing such an instrument. Considerable reliability has been established, and this test is currently being administered to hundreds of children in the Palm Beach School district to collect data for norming this test. This assessment has also served as a useful evaluation in custody cases, and for this writer, who has been qualified as an expert witness in four states, in murder trials and alleged sexual abuse cases. Because of these efforts, Art Therapy has been declared as valid as psychology and psychiatry in a judicial position paper (Levick, Safran, Levine, 1990). A growing number of art therapists around the country have since been qualified as an expert witness in a variety of criminal cases.

APPLICATIONS

In this writer's experience, Art Therapy has demonstrated its efficacy with a variety of populations diagnosed with a variety of mental disorders. The most prevalent of these is schizophrenia, probably because the schizophrenic patient, suffering an acute episode, is usually in a severe state of regression and "seems compelled to express himself compulsively and continually through any art media" (Levick, 1975). Spontaneous drawings

and associations are elicited and used to gain a better understanding of areas of conflict. "The art therapist offers the patient clarifications, connections, confrontations, and interpretations depending on the patient's capacity to handle the material being expressed" (Levick, 1975).

There is a need for caution in providing oil paints for the older adult schizophrenic patient. This medium may foster regression and thus overwhelm the patient. The following, however, is a case in which the therapist devised a method to prevent regression for the schizophrenic patient and yet provide a safe and productive way for him to use this medium:

> A man in his early 30s, who had previously demonstrated some artistic talent, communicated that he wished to paint in oils. On his own, he obtained the medium and was later observed in great distress. He had stopped painting with the brush and had begun painting with his fingers directly on the canvas and seemed unable to stop. In reviewing the situation with him, it became clear that to refuse to allow him to use this medium would only create more frustration and reinforce his feelings of inadequacy. Therefore, it was suggested that he conceptualize his ideas first in pastels on paper, then copy his own drawing in oil paint. In this way, he established some structure thus avoiding regression and fulfilling his wish to progress to a more difficult medium. (Levick, 1975)

Many mental patients who have been hospitalized for years have learned that "doing something is good for them." Art Therapy can provide an activity that may alleviate anxiety, and is useful in situations where verbalization cannot be elicited—in fact, it is not necessary. Patient gratification is obtained in the act of participating in the creative process. Art Therapy also provides a form of resocialization for the chronic patient who often feels isolated from society.

The mid-life-depressed patient usually resists any request to perform a task that might reflect his feelings of helplessness and inadequacy. The art therapist must be cognizant of this and not offer any activity or project that would cause frustration or anxiety. The art therapist must keep in mind too that if electroconvulsive therapy (ECT) is given, there will be a transitory memory loss. Therefore, to engage such a patient in any activity, the goals must be tasks that will foster ego enhancement. One such patient who was encouraged to draw or paint anything he wanted with the art therapist acting as teacher obtained considerable gratification from his experience. Though he had no conscious awareness of hostile feelings, he projected these onto a painting of a ferocious fish, which he proudly carried home with him when he was discharged from the hospital (Levick, 1975).

Obsessive-compulsive neurotic patients rely heavily on their ability to intellectualize and often resist involvement in an activity, particularly a nonverbal one, such as drawing or painting. Here too the art therapist must be skilled in therapeutic techniques in order to establish a therapeutic relationship. With this type of patient it is sometimes helpful to draw projecting thoughts and ideas onto the same piece of paper in a shared experience. Mirroring as a means of confrontation can be particularly useful here. For example, a young woman reported a dream. When asked how she felt upon awakening, she said she was very depressed. The art therapist asked her to draw these feelings; the patient took brush in hand, dipped into the paint, and furiously put strokes of vivid color across the paper. The art therapist proceeded to mirror this demonstration and then asked the patient to describe the therapist's actions and product. The patient could not avoid recognizing that this reflected anger, not depression, and recognized her own anger, even though it was still somewhat removed from conscious awareness. These kinds of interactions cut through lengthy obsessive verbalizations and facilitate the ability of the obsessive-compulsive patient to get in touch with feelings that can then be expressed in an acceptable way.

There are numerous articles in the literature describing work with alcoholics, prisoners, and physically and emotionally handicapped children. A great deal of work has been done with families using the Art Therapy evaluation designed by the late Hanna Kwiatkowska. This evaluation is used widely throughout the country by art therapists working with various kinds of populations, both child and adult. Family evaluation consists of six tasks (Kwiatkowska, 1967) and provides a considerable amount of data about individual ego strengths and weaknesses and family interactions. Often data elicited through the Art Therapy evaluation will provide direction for future therapeutic interventions.

This writer was asked to evaluate a family who was facing the real problem of dealing with the terminal illness of their 19-year-old son. This young man, whose illness had first been discovered when he was 14, had had his leg amputated and wore a prosthesis, which he handled very well. In the evaluation, the parents and children (including a daughter aged 23) were asked to draw family members. The father, who had originally protested that he could not draw, finally proceeded to draw family members—all without completed lower limbs. During this evaluation, this and other sensitive issues were not pointed out. However, after the family recognized the need for therapy and reviewed their evaluation with the therapist, the father's drawing of the family suggested the direction, not just for the father, but for the entire family in the therapeutic process. It soon became obvious that one way of denying their son's illness was to act as if they too had physical problems; this was initially manifested in the father's representing all family members with incomplete lower limbs.

Greater awareness on the part of educators of learning disabled students has reinforced early writings by Kramer (1958) and Naumburg (1966) regarding the knowledge that can be gained of developmental sequences and intrapsychic conflicts from children's drawings. Kramer, Naumburg, and other well-known art therapists have demonstrated that spontaneous drawings of both children and adults reveal normal and pathological evidence of fears, fantasies, thoughts, and affects stimulated by internal and external pressures, ego strengths, and weaknesses, id derivatives, and normal and abnormal defensive mechanisms (Levick et al., 1979).

The trained art therapist can, by studying children's drawings, "guide the therapeutic team in pinpointing developmental, motoric, perceptual, or emotional problems that may interfere with learning" (Levick, Dulicai, Briggs, & Billock, 1979, p. 364).

The literature is limited regarding the use of Art Therapy with the learning disabled and including children with ADD and ADHD. Levick et al., (1979) provide a list of unpublished theses that address this problem from several different viewpoints. These references are cited in a book on learning disabilities (Levick et al., 1979). The reader is referred to the references listed at the end of this chapter and particularly to *Art Therapy—A Bibliography, January 1940–June 1973* (Gannt & Schmal, 1974) for further information.

CASE EXAMPLE*

The following case example reflects this writer's training in dynamic and psychoanalytic theory. Naumburg (1966, p. 8) states that "in Art Therapy, transference is not only expressed verbally but also projected in many pictures." She concludes that this transference relationship in Art Therapy is more easily dealt with through the use of spontaneous images associated to the patient, who then can more readily understand original "objectification of his conflicts which may have begun in his earliest family relationships" (Naumburg, 1966, p. 8).

The following case is followed over a period of two years through examples of transference and countertransference manifestations in drawings. Naturally, these specific drawings are taken out of context of the therapeutic process. Most of these drawings represent the patient's spontaneous graphic therapy. Some, done jointly by the patient and this writer, were precipitated by crisis situations in the therapeutic process and were invaluable in quickly bringing into consciousness transference and countertransference feelings. Hopefully this

---

*Part of this case example was taken from Levick (1975b).

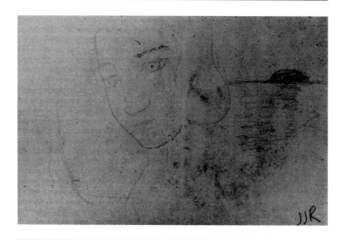

Figure 3.1

will not interfere with perceiving how the drawing facilitated the therapeutic process.

Figure 3.1 is introduced to demonstrate that C from the beginning used a tree to represent primarily father–male, water–mother. Struggling at that time with his own self-concept, he said the face was both mother and himself with a "blind man's stare." At that early session he recalled "hiding in a tree watching people" and that "he loves to be in water" (Levick, 1975).

For this therapist, the picture and the associations suggested that the patient could intellectually and graphically identify male versus female, but emotionally could not identify himself. As these symbols, in many different combinations and variations, continued to appear, this became obvious to the patient and he recognized them as the real issue of therapy, which was initially described as "fear of going back to college."

Four months into therapy the patient was manifesting resistance by relating the fantasy that to "be close to a woman stimulated his fear of hurting a woman, which made him think of wanting to hurt his mother." Finally, his interpretation was that "not revealing too much in therapy was a way of sparing me his rage." My understanding of this (not interpreted then) was that as he spared me (mother) his rage, he also spared me (mother) the love that he was even more fearful of expressing. So I suggested we draw each other, to provide us both with the opportunity to obtain distance from feelings while sharing a "safe" experience. Figure 3.2 is his drawing of me, which we both recognized bore a greater resemblance to Botticelli's madonna than to me. I pointed out that the madonna of that period represented the "good" and "bad" woman—mother and prostitute (Canaday, 1958). He quickly recognized that his mixed feelings for mother were being projected onto me. My drawing of him (Figure 3.3) also surprised us. I drew him as a boy of about eight to ten years of age with closed eyes and tight

Figure 3.2

Figure 3.3

mouth. He did not like being seen as a "little boy who wouldn't look"; but I had to recognize that perhaps I did not want to "see" that the "hurt little boy" was also a grown man. The following month he was in the process of winding up his affairs at work prior to starting college and was concerned about his capacity to maintain a re-

Figure 3.4

Figure 3.5

Figure 3.6

lationship with a female coworker whom he really liked. I suggested he draw her. Figure 3.4 reveals a much older looking person than his friend, one who "had done a lot of living." Her hair (naturally dark) is depicted as red-brown (like mine). The ice blue in the picture is a color he had associated with his mother. This picture represents the parataxic distortions discussed above, those people in our everyday lives to whom transferential feelings are connected. C had sexual fantasies about the coworker but also wanted to think of her as a sister: Therefore in his mind the fantasies were bad. It was pointed out that in fact he had not permitted himself to really know her. After this had been brought into consciousness, he was able to maintain the friendship of this young woman without letting his fantasies or fears interfere. This drawing technique was successfully employed several times to help him deal with a few other people in social and work groups he obviously had strong ambivalent feelings about.

During a session a month later, he became aware he was "being very resistant." It must be remembered the young man was very sophisticated in psychological terminology. He decided to "draw his resistance." Figure 3.5 is a picture that became very significant and one we both referred to in later sessions. Although he had planned to draw a representation of his avoidance of important matters, he was momentarily stunned when he recognized that what he had drawn was like a cross-section of a cavern with a little figure trying to get in. It took little interpretation on my part for him to see that his "resistance" was indicative of his fear of getting close, and in his words "the wish to be born from me." At that time he was very depressed and asked for another session several days later. He experienced a frightening dream about a nun he remembered from his childhood. She had actually been very nice to him, but in the dream she was trying to seduce him. Figure 3.6 is his drawing of the nun (as in the dream). After many associations, including the nun representing me, and reviewing the last sessions and drawings manifesting his "fighting me," we concluded that "therapy" was the seduction; the white face with red eyes and red mouth was like a newborn baby taking its first breath of air. He recalled being told his own birth was a difficult one and that his mother was very ill "because of him." He then equated getting well with being born and being rejected.

During the next month he reported a dream in which he said I was realistically represented for the first time. In one of the dream sequences he said I was standing on a veranda with a German soldier in civilian clothes and my dress changed from salmon color to white. There were many aspects to this dream, but in terms of transference he made the following associations: His maternal grandmother had insisted on being buried in a salmon-

Figure 3.7

Figure 3.8

color dress; his mother had worn a salmon-color dress to his high school graduation and he had danced with her; he once wanted to be like Siegfried, the German hero. I asked him to draw me and the man in the dream. Unconsciously he drew the couple in the exact position of himself and his mother in a photograph taken at the time of his graduation. (He had shown me this picture along with several others in an early session of therapy.) When I pointed out this obvious connection, he readily acknowledged it, but added that he thought changing the color of my dress (in his dream) was the beginning of his efforts to "separate me from mother."

Several months later he was again very depressed and resistant. Finally, feeling very frustrated, I suggested we draw together. He agreed and he began to draw a "yellow" island (Figure 3.7). (In the past C had reported a fantasy of taking me to the "Canary Islands" and had dreamed of being on a "yellow island.") It should also be noted here that the rug in my office is a yellow shag rug. I put in a tree and three houses. He placed a man in a boat in the water and a small indistinct figure on the ground. He stopped, said "we were finished" and that "he felt good about the picture." He realized that both figures were him representing his uncertainty about transferring to a school abroad for the coming winter and interrupting therapy. In that session he decided if he went he would find a "substitute" for me (a "good mother"). I realized that in the drawing I provided both mother (houses) and father (tree) symbols for him to relate to and identify with.

During the following months C vacillated between progression and regression, exhilaration and depression. In the spring, 15 months after he had started therapy, he decided not to go abroad to school and met someone from another state who invited him to move there and attend college. He completed the first year of college with high grades, gave up all current plans to transfer to another local college, and informed me he was moving away within two weeks. The last session was so acutely painful for both patient and therapist that I again suggested a joint drawing to try to aid, at least nonverbally, his separation anxiety (Figure 3.8). He drew a bridge with three arches underneath. I converted the arches into houses with open doorways. He placed an object at each end of the bridge, perched there precariously, and said one was himself, the other me. In the center he placed a rose. The rose had appeared in pictures before and at that time we understood it to represent a male symbol presented to a woman. He told me he liked the picture, and he left therapy and the city—again taking flight from mother (therapist) and seeking refuge with another substitute. I realized that I had graphically left the doors open for him to return.

C wrote to me during the next nine months, first describing how happy he was. Finally realizing that this represented another flight, he became very depressed and returned to the city. He asked if I would resume therapy. Since I had certainly "left the doors open," we had our first session several weeks after his return. He was obviously at a loss for words, so from past experience I quickly suggested a joint drawing "to see where we both were." Figure 3.9 shows two figures. I had started the one on the right. It was very clear to me as soon as I drew it that while I extended my hand I did not know what role I was to assume. He drew himself, and, as he described it, "he was holding on but turning away from me and closing his eyes."

A month later, depressed and anxious about plans to get an apartment and to reapply to college in the fall, he spontaneously drew two heads that he said represented himself, consciously aware of the split. To him it repre-

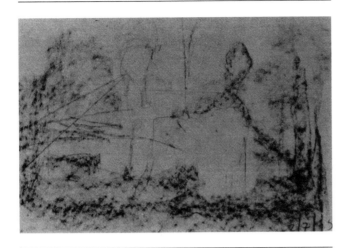

Figure 3.9

Figure 3.10

sented the fear of what he must now do in therapy—define his identity. The barren tree underneath, he said, was the mother he could no longer look to for support. He must now control his feelings about the past and his behavior in the future. In discussing this with my supervisor, we concluded it also represented his awareness of having to deal with me as a woman and his rage toward his mother. Intellectually and to some degree emotionally he had separated me from mother.

In the next several months he made considerable progress in therapy that was primarily reality oriented, dealing with problems at work, new acquaintances, getting in touch with old friends, and preparing for college in the fall. In May 1975 he asked me to draw with him. Unlike previous times we both began at the same time—he on the left side, I on the right (Figure 3.10).

I wanted to do a thatched hut, but instead found myself doing the outline of a house and an incomplete figure next to it. He drew the palm tree, moved in front of me and completed my figure with hair, hands, and running feet. He then put a figure climbing his tree. Together we put coconuts in, and I put two more incomplete figures in. He finished the figures, making them look scared, and put a chimney and smoke on my house, which he decided looked more like an island church. Finally, while I put in the green background, he put in the path connecting the tree and my figure, excluding the other figures. Both C and I were pleased with this picture. For him it implied he could now determine his own relationships. He could accept or reject people and places and even "add" to them, as he had the chimney on my house. While I did not make the interpretation, his subsequent pictures indicated he knew he now had to act on his new awareness. He was obviously as afraid of this as he was excited, and began to talk about termination. Picking up on his need to control the course of termina-

Figure 3.11

tion, I confronted him with his fears about the future, and he admitted he was "afraid of continuing in therapy, but not sure why." It seemed clear he was again resisting, and it was agreed we would meet once a month for the next few months. Pictures done during two of these sessions represented C at a crossroad, not sure which road to take. In one picture in which he placed me facing him (Figure 3.11), it is difficult to determine whether he is saying good-bye or hello.

In August, just four days prior to the time I was to leave for vacation, C learned of the death of his father. I saw C, at his request, spoke to him before I left, and he made an appointment for several days after my return. C did not wait until I returned. He had again taken flight, unable to deal with the real loss and the symbolic counterpart—termination of therapy, as manifested in Figure 3.11.

I did not hear from C for two and one half years following this flight. Then I received a call from him announcing that he was back in the city briefly and asking whether I would see him. This visit took place shortly thereafter in my office. C reported that the past two and one half years had been filled with many gratifications, many anxieties, and even some acute depressive periods. He also reported that he had made up his mind, when he recognized that his leaving reflected another flight, that he needed to begin to deal with some of his problems on a more mature level and "use what he had learned in therapy through our long relationship."

In summary, the patient did begin to cope during his two-and-one-half year absence from therapy, had enrolled in another university, and was preparing for graduation. He also had applied for a scholarship in a master's degree program at a well-known eastern college and had been accepted. Since that time, he has communicated with me through letters and an occasional visit. He completed his graduate work in painting, traveled abroad, wrote, taught and for the last seven years has made his home in a rather sophisticated city in the South. For the past two years, he has been a successful exhibiting artist. He acknowledges that he still has many moments of self-doubt but also knows that he now has the insight to, in his words, "get past them and go on."

The material presented here graphically demonstrates the utilization of Art Therapy to facilitate the awareness of transference and countertransference feelings and their connections to early childhood experiences through associations to the drawings. In dealing with such issues as fear of closeness and separation, I found my own spontaneous drawings communicated therapeutic distance and support more quickly than any verbal expressions. In training art therapists, bringing these transferential feelings to consciousness through drawings facilitates the student therapists' awareness of their own responses and sharpens their recognition of these manifestations in their patients' drawings.

SUMMARY

Although tremendous strides have been made in this field in the last decade, Art Therapy is still a young profession in terms of a body of literature and scientific documentation. However, many scholarly books and articles written by art therapists are now being reviewed and published in journals representing other disciplines. And art therapists, independent of psychiatrists and psychologists, present papers at national and international conferences of related disciplines.

"The similarity between this methodology of Art Therapy and psychoanalytic psychology provides the art therapist with an enormous amount of clinical information which implies a greater appreciation for this modality as a diagnostic and therapeutic process" (Vaccaro, 1973).

As stated previously, true scientific documentation has not been forthcoming, and I must question whether such documentation is possible in a profession that deals with human thoughts and feelings. The most valid documentation, however, is found in the pictures made by the patients/clients, appropriately translated by the trained and skilled Art Therapist. The therapist can then help the patient/client to see, to understand the meaning of these graphic productions, own them and either accept the discovered emotional content or change it toward self-awareness and growth.

REFERENCES

Agell, G., Levick, M., Rhyne, J., Robbins, A., Rubin, J. A., Ulman, E., Wang, C., & Wilson, L. (1981). Transference and countertransference in Art Therapy. *American Journal of Art Therapy, 21,* 3–24.

Canaday, J. (1958). Metropolitan Museum of Art Series, N.Y.

Coles, R. (1970). *Erik H. Erikson, the growth of his work.* Boston: Little, Brown.

Feder, B., & Feder, E. (1998). *The art and science of evaluation in the arts therapies.* Springfield, IL: Charles C. Thomas.

Fink, P. J. (1967). Art as a language. *Journal of Albert Einstein Medical Center, 15,* 143–150.

Fink, P. J., Goldman, M. J., & Levick, M. F. (1967). Art therapy, a new discipline. *Pennsylvania Medicine, 70,* 60–66.

Gantt, L., & Schmal, M. S. (1974). *Art therapy—A bibliography. January 1940–June 1973.* Maryland: National Institute of Mental Health.

Harms, E. (1975). The development of modern Art Therapy. *Leonardo, 8,* 241–244.

Harris, D. (1963). *Children's drawings as measures of intellectual maturity.* New York: Harcourt, Brace, & World.

Junge, M., & Asawa, P. (1994). *A History of Art Therapy in the United States.* Mundelein, IL: The American Art Therapy Association.

Kramer, E. (1958a). Art therapy at Wiltwyck School. *School Arts, 58,* 5–8.

Kramer, E. (1958b). *Art therapy in a children's community.* Springfield, IL: Charles C. Thomas.

Kwiatkowska, H. (1967). The use of families' art productions for psychiatric evaluation. *Bulletin of Art Therapy, 6,* 52–69. [With discussion by N. L. Paul, 69–72.]

Kwiatkowska, H. Y. (1978). *Family therapy and evaluation through art.* Springfield, IL: Charles C. Thomas.

Landgarten, H. (1993). *Magazine photo collage: A multicultural assessment and treatment technique.* New York: Brunner/Mazel.

Levick, M. (1998) *The Levick Emotional and Cognitive Art Therapy Assessment (LECATA).* Unpublished manuscript.

Levick, M. F. (1967). The goals of the art therapist as compared to those of the art teacher. *Journal of Albert Einstein Medical Center, 15,* 157–170.

Levick, M. F. (1973). Family Art Therapy in the community. *Philadelphia Medicine, 69,* 257–261.

Levick, M. F. (1975a). Art in psychotherapy. In J. Masserman (Ed.), *Current Psychotherapies.* New York: Grune & Stratton.

Levick, M. F. (1975b). Transference and countertransference as manifested in graphic productions. *International Journal of Art Psychotherapy (U.S.A.), 2,* 203–224.

Levick, M. F. (1983a). Resistance: Developmental image of ego defenses, manifestations of adaptive and maladaptive defenses in children's drawings. *Dissertation Abstracts International, 43,* no. 10.

Levick, M. F, (1983b). *They could not talk and so they drew: Children's styles of coping and thinking.* Springfield, IL: Charles C. Thomas.

Levick, M. F. (1984). Imagery as a style of thinking. *Art Therapy, 1,* 119–124.

Levick, M. F. (1986). *Mommy, Daddy, look what I'm saying: What children are telling you through their art.* New York: M. Evans & Co.

Levick, M. F. (1998). *See what I'm saying: What children tell us through their art.* Dubuque, IA: Islewest.

Levick, M. F., Dulicai, D., Briggs, C., & Billock, L. (1979). The creative arts therapies. In W. Adamson & K. Adamson (Eds.), *A Handbook for specific learning disabilities.* New York: Gardner Press.

Levick, M. F., Saffron, D. S., & Levine, A. (1990). Art therapists as expert witnesses: A judge delivers a precedent-setting decision. *The Arts in Psychotherapy, 17,* 49–53.

Malchiodi, C. (1990). *Breaking the silence: Art therapy with children from violent homes.* New York: Brunner/Mazel.

Naumburg, M. (1947). *Studies of free art expression in behavior of children as a means of diagnosis and therapy.* New York: Coolidge Foundation.

Naumburg, M. (1966). *Dynamically oriented Art Therapy: Its principals and practice.* New York: Grune & Stratton.

Rubin, J. A. (1973). A diagnostic interview. *Art Psychotherapy, 1,* 31–44.

Silver, R. A. (1988). *Draw-a-story: Screening for depression and emotional needs.* Mamaroneck, NY: Ablin Press.

Silver, R. A. (1989a). *Developing cognitive and creative skills through art* (3rd ed.). Mamaroneck, NY: Ablin Press.

Silver, R. A. (1989b). *Stimulus drawings and techniques: In therapy, development, and assessment* (4th ed. rev.) Mamaroneck, NY: Ablin Press.

Silver, R. A. (1990). *Silver drawing test of cognitive skills and adjustment.* Mamaroneck, NY: Ablin Press.

Ulman, E. (1961). Art therapy: Problems of definition. *Bulletin of Art Therapy, 1,* 10–20.

Ulman, E. (1966). Therapy is not enough—The contribution of art to general hospital psychiatry. *Bulletin of Art Therapy, 6,* 13–21.

Vaccaro, V. M. (1973). Specific aspects of the psychology of Art Therapy. *International Journal of Art Psychotherapy (U.S.A.), 1,* 81–89.

Wilkerson v Pearson (1985). NJ Super. 333 (Ch. Div.)

Wohl, A., & Kaufman, B. (1985). *Silent screams and hidden cries.* New York: Brunner/Mazel.

Zwerling, I., Podietz, L., Belmont, H., Shapiro, M., Ficher, I., Eisenstein, T., & Levick, M. (1984). Engagement in families of holocaust survivors. *Journal of Marital and Family Therapy, 10,* 43–51.

Chapter 4

AUTOGENIC TRAINING

HEIDE F. BRENNEKE

Autogenic Training is a procedure that most psychotherapists have heard about but don't quite understand. I was lucky to find Heide Brenneke, who was willing to explain the process in this book.

As the perceptive reader will note, this procedure has many elements in common with a variety of other systems, such as Biofeedback, Psycho-Imagination, and Stress Management; but at the same time it adds some new elements.

Autogenic Training is used much more in Europe than the United States, and so far it has not penetrated too deeply into the understanding of American therapists. Some of the concepts may be difficult to understand at first, but essentially Autogenic Training seems to seek to establish a state somewhere between full consciousness and the oblivion of sleep and hypnosis. In this intermediate state, one's unconscious is more accessible—according to the theory.

Another important element of Autogenic Training is that after one has learned the process, the therapy itself is and should be independent of a therapist. In effect, one enters this altered state of consciousness to let the growth force within get to work to rectify the various insults the body and the mind have suffered in the past, to attain self-healing.

Autogenic Training is a psychophysiologic form of psychotherapy that works with the body and the mind simultaneously. Through passive concentration on autogenic formulas the trainee self-induces an altered state of consciousness in which he or she learns to manipulate the bodily functions through the mind, resulting in the normalization of both bodily and mental states.

In other words, self-regulatory mechanisms, such as homeostasis and recuperative and self-normalizing processes, are promoted through the concentration of autogenic formulas. These results are diametrically opposed to stress.

Autogenic Training is often used in conjunction with medical forms of treatment in psychophysiologic illnesses such as chronic constipation, bronchial asthma, peptic ulcers, hypertension, and sleep disorders.

Behavior disorders and motor disturbances such as anxiety, insecurity, neurotic reactions, stuttering, cramping, and nervous twitching are effectively treated through the practice of Autogenic Training.

HISTORY

Autogenic Training is based on studies of sleep and hypnosis as conducted by Oskar Vogt, neuropathologist of

the Berlin Neuro-Biological Institute during the years from 1894 to 1903. Vogt observed that many of his patients were able to put themselves into a state similar to a hypnotic one after they had experienced his hypnosis treatment. They learned to control stress, tension, and fatigue in this manner and were also able to eliminate symptoms such as headaches, backaches, and so forth.

In 1905 J. H. Schultz began to explore a method that could enhance the therapeutic values of hypnosis without causing unfavorable passivity and dependence on the part of the patient. Schultz observed the sensations patients would experience under hypnosis—such as relaxation, warmth, and heaviness in the limbs or in the entire body—and based his standard formulas on these findings. Corresponding effects observed by patients were added to the training formulas to influence heart and breathing rates and to control warmth to the solar plexus and coolness to the forehead.

Most research in Autogenic Training has been done in Germany. Beginning in 1960 much research has been published in the English language by Wolfgang Luthe, probably the foremost authority in Autogenic Training today.

In recent years interest in Autogenic Training has increased in the United States; however, this interest is still mostly confined to the medical arena and strongly emphasizes stress reduction.

CURRENT STATUS

Many practitioners today, like myself, are not members of the medical profession. The use of Autogenic Training has become the basis for an eclectic approach to psychotherapy, with practitioners drawing from Western as well as Eastern disciplines. It is becoming more and more apparent that Autogenic Training is not confined to the body and the mind alone. There have been many reports of spiritual experiences while in the autogenic state.

This writer is not aware of any training center in the United States where interested persons could study. A great number of practitioners are of German background, and most of the training happens on a one-to-one basis. The International Committee on Autogenic Therapy is based in Canada.

The most comprehensive book on Autogenic Training to date is Wolfgang Luthe's *Autogenic Therapy* (1969a).

THEORY

Stress and tension are necessary for effective living and survival. However, when stress becomes more powerful than the ability to handle it, it becomes a danger to health. The human body reacts to stress in a manner that is useful to primitive living, where a balance between stress—fight or flight—and restoration is assured.

Not only are there today pressures for survival, jobs, human relationships, and structuring of time, but for many individuals there is also constant sensory overstimulation. In addition many people ingest chemicals such as caffeine, alcohol, drugs, and food additives, which affect the autonomic nervous system, on a regular basis. Addiction to many of the sensory stimulants and/or chemicals is based on physical dependencies they generate.

Autogenic Training is based on the fact that the autonomic nervous system can be voluntarily controlled, and stress therefore reduced at command. The autonomic nervous system is divided into the sympathetic and the parasympathetic nervous systems, which have opposing functions. In general, the sympathetic nervous system is concerned with energy expenditure, while the parasympathetic nervous system is concerned with restorative processes. For example, while under sympathetic nervous system control, there occurs vasoconstriction of the lacrimal, parotid, and submaxillary glands, copious sweating, increased heart and breathing rates, secretion

of epinephrine and norepinephrine by the medulla of the suprarenal gland, and so forth. Blood pressure increases and digestion is decreased due to contraction of the stomach and inhibition of glandular secretions in the stomach, intestines, and pancreas.

When under parasympathetic nervous system control the processes are reversed: The lacrimal, parotid, and submaxillary glands are stimulated to produce copious secretions high in enzyme content, sweating stops, the heart and breathing rates slow down, there is no known effect on the suprarenal gland, blood pressure decreases due to vasodilation in the peripheral blood system, and digestion is increased due to secretion of enzymes and increased peristalsis (Jacob & Francone, 1974).

All relaxation and all meditative states increase the functions of the parasympathetic nervous system, with the rare exception of paradoxic phenomena resulting from autogenic discharges (Luthe, 1962; Luthe, Jus, & Geissmann, 1962).

Through the continued practice of Autogenic Training, a state of parasympathetic nervous system control can be induced on command and stress levels reduced so that the basis for psychophysiologic illnesses such as hypertension, ulcers, colitis, headaches, migraines, backaches, and so forth, is weakened or eliminated.

The preceding description covers stress reduction. Though valuable, the benefits of Autogenic Training only begin here. Through passive concentration the trainee pays attention to internal processes to the exclusion of outside stimuli, generating a kind of stimulus deprivation similar to hypnosis. He or she can enter an altered state of consciousness in which consciously held beliefs can be explored, set aside, and the mind can be allowed to expand beyond its accustomed limits.

The trainee, working on his or her own at this point, can have spontaneous access to various experiences from the unconscious and can possibly have spontaneous spiritual experiences. Examples are visualizations of colors, faces, objects, memories of possibly unresolved past events, feelings of pleasure and contentment based on either body sensations or verbal concepts, and so forth. From this point the trainee can enter what Schultz calls the *interrogatory attitude* in which answers from the unconscious can be expected to problems that the trainee may or may not be aware of. Schultz also discusses Nirvana Therapy (Schultz, 1932; Schultz & Luthe, 1962), applied in situations of stimulus deprivation, desperate situations, or in clinically hopeless cases.

If the trainee works with a therapist, the process becomes admittedly less autogenic. Based on the theory that the creativity of a trainee in an altered state of consciousness is greatly increased, and that information produced is less inhibited than when the individual is in a fully conscious state, the therapist will ask questions for the purpose of clarification in problem areas. The therapist will also encourage the directing of self-healing energy to areas of disease or stress, will prompt visualizations, and will attempt to establish new behavior and/or thinking patterns.

Autogenic Training is still limited by the assumptions of the therapist and his or her insights into the areas in need of exploration and change. But due to the lack of verbal interaction between therapist and client, the trainee's conscious mind does not act as censor and the unconscious has free play to bring new experiences into conscious awareness.

As it is easier to receive answers from the unconscious in a meditative state, so is it easier to teach the unconscious new patterns in an altered state of consciousness. The unconscious often retains patterns long after they are needed, sometimes limiting the client's potential to a paralyzing degree. The autogenic state can be used to explore these beliefs and to abandon those of no further purpose.

Beliefs that limit a person and cause problems are often those not consciously acknowledged because they are "unbelievable"—that is, archaic, unevolved, embarrassing—or they are beliefs a person has adopted from an outside source without checking their relevance to personal essential understanding.

Problems are kept alive through selective negative memory about how "things are and always have been and therefore always will be." In a meditative state the unconscious can be encouraged to focus on selective positive memories and to visualize alternative behaviors and feelings, thus gradually training a new set of expectations.

Affirmations should follow new understanding, provided that they evolve from an exploration and take into account the state of the present reality so as not to overextend credibility.

METHODOLOGY

The room used for Autogenic Training should be pleasantly warm and quiet. Metabolism slows down in deep relaxation and trainees often begin to feel cold. If the training lasts for more than three to five minutes a light blanket will assure comfort. If the horizontal position is assumed, a pillow under the knees for people with lower back problems or a small pillow for general comfort is recommended.

A calm, pleasant voice and proper timing by the practitioner greatly improve the success for the relaxation response.

Three different positions are recommended for clients in Autogenic Training:

1. The horizontal posture, not recommended if the trainee has a tendency to go to sleep.

2. The armchair posture.
3. A simple sitting or cabbie posture.

In the first two postures the legs are kept slightly apart, the arms on the side of the body or resting separately on the armrest, the head in alignment with the spine. In the third posture the legs are separate, the forearms are resting on the thighs, hands hanging without contact, the neck is relaxed with the head hanging slightly forward. The weight in this posture is in the pelvis.

As the concept of passive concentration and voluntary manipulation of body functions, essential to Autogenic Training, is foreign to many people in Western cultures, a few preliminary exercises are used to establish that experience. Passive concentration is non-goal-oriented, is not concerned with outcome or performance.

There are an endless variety of exercises to familiarize the trainee with the experience of passive concentration and voluntary control over functions often believed to be not controllable.

The following are a few examples of directions and information given in Autogenic Training.

Breathing Exercise. Become aware of your breathing. Do not change anything, just notice the parts in your body that are affected by your breath and allow yourself to be carried by that breath. Become aware of any changes that may occur, and follow these changes without value judgment and censoring. Then begin to change your breath in the following manner. On your next inhalation first fill your abdomen, then your chest; as you exhale deplete your chest first and then your abdomen. Now a wavelike motion occurs, up on inhalation, down on exhalation.

Now concentrate on the exhalation, making sure that every amount of air is expelled, allowing a natural pause at its termination. You will notice that your next inhalation becomes automatically deeper. Now with each exhalation allow the tensions and pains to drain from your body. With every inhalation take in all the feelings you would like to experience, such as happiness, relaxation, contentment, joy. Now if indeed you were able to evoke these feelings, become aware of doing that by just thinking about them.

Cancellation: Then allow your breath to become more natural again—more shallow.

Body Inventory. Without looking for it, actively allow that part of your body that is the most tense or painful at any given moment to come into your awareness. Then explore it. Notice its size, shape, depth, the kind of pain or tension it is—sharp or dull. Look at its color, its texture, and notice its emotional content. Often the pain or tension will disappear and a new place will come into your awareness. Then proceed with the same exploration in another area.

Left-Right Balance. Become aware of your left side and compare it with your right side. Notice any differences. If one side is shorter than the other, pretend that you are made of some elastic material and that without any actual movement you can stretch this material to the extent that it will match the other side. If one side is lower than the other, imagine that you are filled with some liquid and then allow that liquid to swish around in your body until the level is equalized.

The trainee is once more reminded of his active participation in the use of the Autogenic Training method and at this point the peace formulas may be introduced, such as:

1. I am calm and quiet.
2. Nothing around me is of any importance.
3. My thoughts pass like clouds in the summer sky.

When on occasion the discrepancy between the actual state of mind of the trainee and the statement is too great, a process formula should be adopted, such as: "As I am lying (sitting) here I am getting calmer and quieter." The peace formulas are designed to:

1. Trigger a relaxation response.
2. Acknowledge the fact that there are outside interferences, but that at this moment they are of no consequence.
3. Acknowledge that there are thoughts coming through the awareness at all times, but that the trainee chooses not to pay active attention to them for the moment.

Luthe (1969a) suggests that subjects need to practice the standard formulas for four to ten months, advancing to each consecutive step only after mastery of the preceding one. Many practitioners today introduce all basic formulas at the very beginning, and experience has proven that most subjects will accomplish the different states within a very short time.

As Luthe (1969a) points out, "a sensation of heaviness may or may not occur, and . . . many changes of bodily functions occur which one cannot feel." It is also important for the patient to know that according to experimental observations, the exercises are effective as long as they are performed correctly, even if one does not feel anything at all.

The six standard autogenic exercises are introduced:

1. My right hand is heavy. (Left-handed persons begin with their left hand.)
2. My right hand is warm.[1]
3. My heartbeat is calm and regular.
4. My breathing is calm and regular. It breathes me.
5. My solar plexus is flowingly warm.
6. My forehead is light and cool.[2]

The practice session may be interrupted at this point or any time the therapist or client sees fit, or the autogenic state may be used for further work.

The following are a few suggestions of explorations that are likely to occur in subsequent training sessions.

To Train Visualization

1. In front of your inner eye allow a color to appear and then observe this color, watch its possible changes. After several minutes the therapist will suggest that this color recede and disappear (the procedure to follow to cancel all suggestions).
2. In front of your inner eye, without deciding who it is going to be, allow the face of someone you love to appear. Then observe the face, experiencing it in every detail possible.

Both visualization explorations can be taken further by asking questions as to emotional content, symbolism, and dialogue.

To combine a visualization with "reframing and anchoring," the following exercise may be introduced.

The therapist tells the client, "In front of your inner eye (awareness), without deciding what it is going to be, allow the memory of a beautiful experience to emerge and relive it in every detail possible. See it, hear it, feel it, smell it, allowing as much information to surface as possible, including parts that you are now experiencing for the first time." After a few minutes the therapist asks the client to extract the basic feeling from this experience and to describe it with one or two concepts. Concentrating on these concepts, retaining the feeling, the client is then asked to make contact between his left (right for left-handed persons) thumb, index, and middle fingers in order to anchor the feelings in the body. The exercise is terminated at this point with the suggestion that at any time in the future when the feeling that was just experienced is desired, the trainee can trigger it by making the contact in his or her hand.

---

[1] After the second formula a generalization phenomenon occurs in which all limbs become warm and heavy on a regular basis. At times it may be indicated for the therapist to help this generalization process along by suggesting each limb's heaviness and warmth specifically. This is especially useful in a group session where verbal feedback is inappropriate.

[2] Vascular dilation in the head leads to headaches. This formula assures vascular contraction.

To use the above as a basis for reframing, the exercise can be continued by suggesting that the trainee in the imagination move ahead in time to an event anticipated with some anxiety and go back and forth between the pleasant past experience and the future one until he or she can move through the entire anticipated event without feelings of anxiety, drawing power and positive feelings from the past event whenever necessary.

Toward Healing of Physical Problems.

The trainee is asked to become aware of an area in the body that he or she is concerned about. The therapist might say:

> In front of your inner eye (awareness) allow an image to appear that shows you the cause of onset of this problem. Then look at the sequence of events that have kept this problem alive until today. Now entertain the possibility that on occasion—and maybe only very rarely—there is something good that comes out of having this problem. On occasion you may get something either from yourself or from someone else that you would not receive if you did not have this particular physical problem. Allow an image or a thought to come into your awareness that will show you the payoff. Now ask your unconscious to show you an alternate way, a more constructive way to receive the same payoff. Find another alternative, and another. Follow this with an affirmation.
>
> Now for the moment, knowing that you have this problem, set it aside and imagine that it does not exist— just for the moment. Then go back into your past and remember the times that you were free from this concern. Continue to look back and focus on all the times that you were free of any complaint regarding this area. Feel it, see yourself in the circumstances, and hear yourself.
>
> Now visualize yourself without it today—what you would do, what there would be instead. See yourself very clearly, hear yourself talking about yourself, feel yourself with that new-found health.
>
> Then concentrate on the area in your body that you have had the concern about and allow all your energy to merge there for a moment, allow all your concentration, all your love to concentrate in this one place. Notice the warmth and the energy expanding the area, clearing it of all restrictions and pain. Allow a white light to surround that part of your body, imagining it to heal you. Now allow the white light to expand and surround your entire body. Retain a feeling of health and well-being.

Behavior and Emotional Pattern Changes.

A similar process is followed in relationship to behavior and emotional patterns that are no longer useful to the person. The trainee is clued in to the feeling that precedes the behavior, and alternative behavior responses are explored. When the emotion itself is the problem, the underlying belief is explored as well as the reaction that follows, which is the attempt at regaining balance.

After several sessions in which processes similar to the above have been used, the therapist encourages spontaneous problem solving without step-by-step guidance. This is accomplished by asking the trainee to focus on a problem area and to ask the unconscious to bring up new ways of dealing with it. The client is encouraged to access information in as many modes as are available (visual, auditory, or kinesthetic). Some persons are able to recall the process of exploration after the session, others will be aware of some solution without remembering the actual process, and a third group will not remember anything but will realize sometime later that the problem no longer exists or has changed significantly enough that it can be handled.

This is a time when the therapist reminds group participants once more not to make comparisons: Every person's process is unique. There is no right or wrong and there is no goal; each and every process is an expansion of the conscious mind, valid in itself.

Each session ends with a general visualization and with general affirmations. Participants are asked to visualize themselves the way they want to be and with what they want to have in their lives. For the moment all known reality is set aside.

This kind of visualization can be viewed as an affirmation in itself. However, verbal affirmations seem to work well with many clients. In contrast to affirmations used as part of the process of specific explorations, these ending affirmations are expansive, such as:

1. I have the wisdom to know what is right for me.
2. With every day that passes I am getting a greater feeling of well-being, safety, and security.
3. I am learning to say good-bye to. . . .
4. Every time that I relax I go deeper, faster.
5. I am learning that I have a perfect right to all my feelings.
6. I am learning to picture myself the way I want to be.
7. I am learning to replace _____ with _____.
8. I love myself unconditionally.
9. I am prosperous and happy in my work.
10. I live a full and rich life.

It needs to be stressed that affirmations will (1) change spontaneously and (2) lose their impact because the process of change is already underway.

To conclude a session and to cancel the autogenic state the practitioner asks participants to:

1. Give a thought to coming back.
2. Increase the breathing rate.
3. Move and stretch your body.
4. At your own pace open your eyes and come back to the room.

Proper cancellation of the autogenic state is important before moving about. Sudden interruption tends to induce an anxiety state.

When practicing alone the trainee follows the same procedure. With the help of a timer set for one or two minutes longer than the planned session the client can train his or her own internal clock to conclude the session after a predetermined interval.

Frequency and Procedure of Practice.   Students are instructed to practice the six standard exercises (see above) a minimum of three times a day for between 5 and 20 minutes. Frequent practice allows the student to reach the autogenic state more quickly and therefore benefit from it even at sudden demand. Frequent practice also encourages a more natural interchange between conscious and unconscious processes.

Ideal times for practice are early in the morning before leaving the house; in the middle of the day, even when there appears to be no time to practice or when there is a shift in activity; and in the evening before going to sleep.

If the evening session is done in bed it should not be terminated in the usual fashion by stretching and moving around to get back into muscle control and breathing. The trainee should just allow himself or herself to go from the autogenic state directly to sleep.

The following structure is recommended should the trainee wish to use Autogenic Training as a problem-solving technique:

In the morning session the trainee looks ahead to the day by allowing priorities to emerge or programming the kind of day he or she would like to experience, thus programming events to fit the expectation.

In the middle of the day at a time of need for rest or where there is a shift in activity, the session is extended to a longer period of time and concentrates mostly on relaxation, allowing anything to emerge that occurs spontaneously, using an interrogatory attitude.

The evening session is used to review the day and to look at any unfinished business, either positive or negative.

All three sessions should include a brief, positive visualization and affirmations that seem relevant.

Autogenic Training can be practiced under adverse conditions once one is firmly established in quiet surroundings.

APPLICATIONS

Autogenic Training can be practiced by any person who is suggestible, has the motivation to be helped, and has established trust with the practitioner.

To the extent that Autogenic Training is used with the six standard exercises alone it will benefit anyone, since it reduces stress and allows the trainee to induce parasympathetic nervous system control. In practicing Autogenic Training with the first six standard exercises the trainee will spontaneously achieve other benefits in terms of problem solving, clarity of direction, and overall better access to the unconscious.

Autogenic Training is especially indicated in cases of psychophysiologic illnesses such as headaches, migraines, ulcers, colitis, and aches and pains that have no apparent organic origin, and for clients who suffer from states of anxiety and insecurity. This latter group reports the most rapid positive results.

If trainees use Autogenic Training mostly as a tool for personal development, physiological benefits still occur, and the spontaneous benefits mentioned above are easily evoked and increased through the interrogatory attitude. Autogenic Training is less effective if the client has strong dependency needs and is not yet willing to take responsibility for his or her own life and health.

Psychotic states and certain heart diseases are contraindications for Autogenic Training. It is advised that anyone with a heart problem have permission of the attending physician to participate.

On occasion either the heart or breathing formula is contraindicated and deleted if it produces anxiety in the trainee. It may then be assumed that the remaining exercises and the generalized relaxation reponse will automatically reduce the heart and breathing rate.

CASE EXAMPLE

My work with Autogenic Training has mostly been with groups and experiential with the exception of occasional blood pressure readings. Therefore, I am restricting myself to reporting verbal feedback on the changes participants experience after they have practiced Autogenic Training over a period of time (anywhere from two weeks to several years).

Most of the persons I have worked with have had previous psychotherapy treatments and use Autogenic Training as a self-help tool for stress management, general well-being, mind expansion, for continued personal development. The results of using Autogenic Training are expressed most frequently as follows:

1. A generalized sense of peace even when the training is not actually being practiced.
2. A greater awareness of body tensions developing and a more rapid way of letting go of them even though the trainee may at that point not choose to practice Autogenic Training.
3. An increase in frequency and vividness of remembered dreams, and sudden insights that seem to

come from the unconscious while the trainee is in a waking state. These insights may occasionally be spiritual in nature.

4. Problems are solved with less anxiety and, to a certain extent, automatically, with more relaxation and more trust attributed to the belief that the unconscious mind will lead to the resolve of the problem, by drawing from previously unavailable information.

5. Frequency of headaches, pains, aches, and migraines is greatly reduced and in some cases eliminated. Sufferers from colitis and ulcers report a decrease in symptoms.

6. Blood pressure frequently drops 10 to 25 percent systolically, 5 to 10 percent diastolically (Luthe, 1960; Schultz & Luthe, 1959).

To summarize the results of extended practice of Autogenic Training: Trainees sense a greater power to cope with both their physical and their emotional problems and find easier access to their mental processes as they train their unconscious to participate and interact increasingly with their conscious minds.

Marie B., age 33, summarizes what is possible with the Autogenic Training method.

Initially she came to learn Autogenic Training to help her cope with the stress resulting from her PhD program in nursing. She was an easy subject to work with as she thoroughly enjoyed the autogenic state and, after being introduced to the standard formulas, was able to induce it quickly.

In the process of working with her over a period of two months, one session per week, the following problems emerged and were subsequently successfully worked through.

Four months prior to her mentioning it she was diagnosed as having a breast lump. The attending physician was not sure whether it was malignant, and based on her age assumed that it was not. However, neither was the lump clearly a fibro-adenoma. It was irregular in shape and had characteristics of several different kinds of lumps. He decided to wait for another two months before taking a biopsy or excising it.

Marie was frightened that it was cancer. She was asked to set her fear aside each day for a few minutes while practicing autogenics and to imagine herself and her health to be stronger than the lump: to imagine dissolving it through the powers of her mind and to have the cells be absorbed by her bloodstream and destroyed by her immune system. Then she was asked to visualize herself healthy, without the breast lump, to hear herself talking to her friends about no longer having it, to feel her breast without the lump, and to bathe herself in a white light.

The lump disappeared within three days. This was confirmed by her physician. Marie was convinced that her practice dissolved the lump, although there is clearly no proof that this indeed was the case.

After one of the sessions Marie reported the following:

I saw myself in my relationship with my husband the way I have experienced my mother: using withdrawal of affection as punishment for not receiving the kind of attention that I wanted. This has been a problem for a while. I have been feeling out of touch with my ability to be a loving person. I have tried very hard to be loving and it has not felt sincere. During this session I visualized myself being loving and then began to experience that love and caring.

The following week she reported that her love had stayed with her for the entire time and that her husband had commented on the difference in her and in their relationship. A couple of months later, Marie had continued to stay in touch with her own lovingness, apparently having eliminated her punitive behavior of the past. She said that even though the awareness was not new, her ability to change her behavior was something that she had not experienced before the internal process during the Autogenic Training session. She felt that she now re-owned a part of herself.

Asked for some general comments about the results of her practicing Autogenic Training, in addition to many of the points listed at the beginning of this section, Marie listed the following:

1. Using the white light around my body whenever needed makes me feel less vulnerable physically.
2. It is easier for me to focus on my work.
3. I feel that I have found a structure for a more positive approach to my life that I did not find in the more traditional therapy that I have had.

SUMMARY

Autogenic Training differs from other therapies in that it is intended as a self-help tool. It is healing to the body, calming to the mind, and plays a major role in disease prevention. Through health affirmations and visualizations it concentrates on well-being and the ability to heal oneself, taking the focus away from Western preoccupation with symptoms.

The unconscious mind is a teacher with limitless resources. It is neither restricted to form nor education. There is no way to ever outgrow this teacher.

In the last analysis each person needs to find the answers to his or her own problems. Often the way to resolve one's problems is blocked by consciously held barriers. Autogenic Training removes these barriers; the only skills necessary are those of questioning and attentive observation.

Autogenic Training uses a holistic approach and is easily and quickly learned because it utilizes processes that are natural and innate to humans. Last but not least, it is reinforcing because it is a pleasant and painless way to personal development.

REFERENCES

Jacob, S. W., & Francone, C. A. (1974). *Structure and function in man.* Philadelphia: W. B. Saunders.

Lindemann, H. (1973). *Relieve tensions the autogenic way.* New York: Wyden.

Luthe, W. (1960). Physiological and psychodynamic effects of autogenic training. In B. Stokvis (Ed.), *Topical problems of psychotherapy.* New York: S. Jarger.

Luthe, W. (1962). The clinical significance of various forms of autogenic abreaction. In *Proceedings of the Third International Congress of Psychiatry.* Toronto, Ontario, Canada: University of Toronto Press.

Luthe, W. (1969a). *Autogenic therapy.* New York: Grune & Stratton.

Luthe, W. (1969b). Autogenic training: Method, research, and application in medicine. In C. T. Tart (Ed.), *Altered states of consciousness.* New York: Wiley.

Luthe, W., Jus, A., & Geissmann, P. (1962). Autogenic state and autogenic shift: Psychophysiologic and neurophysiologic aspects. *Acta Psychotherapeutica et Psychosomatica, 10.*

Schultz, J. (1932). *Das Autogene Training.* Stuttgart, Germany: Thieme Verlag.

Schultz, J., & Luthe, W. (1959). *Autogenic Training: A psychophysiologic approach in psychotherapy.* New York: Grune & Stratton.

Schultz, J., & Luthe, W. (1962). Autogenic training. In *Proceedings of the Third International Congress of Psychiatry.* Toronto, Ontario, Canada: University of Toronto Press.

Chapter 5

BIOFEEDBACK THERAPY

ALBERT G. FORGIONE and REED HOLMBERG

If, assuming a holistic position relative to psychology, we agree that individuals are essentially unitary and that there is not body and mind, but rather body/mind, the two being aspects of the same thing, then we are monists, and we are forced to say that the mind is the body and the body is the mind. In my judgment, most of us in the field of psychotherapy philosophically are monists but practically are dualists—a contradiction that probably deserves fuller explanation, but this is not the time or place.

One of the most important theoretical advances in psychology and medicine has to do with feedback generally and biofeedback specifically. As Forgione states, it is doubtful that Biofeedback will emerge as a full therapy on its own, but there seems to be no question that in the eventual eclectic psychotherapy of the future, when practitioners will be properly trained (as none are today), Biofeedback will be an essential procedure. Eventually also, the doctor of the mind will be a hybrid, knowledgeable about many more things than current practitioners—and much less knowledgeable about things that most practitioners study nowadays.

Biofeedback is a therapeutic method of forming information loops that allows the patient, the therapist, or both to observe and modify internal psychophysiological events while they are in process. Every biofeedback application involves the amplification (usually electronic) of a physiological event followed by the processing of the amplified signal and the presentation of this information to sense receptors and associated central nervous system networks originally designed for detection of stimuli in the external environment (Figure 5.1). According to demand characteristics of the therapeutic situation or instruction, the perceived information is either directly modified by the patient or used as a guide for other mediational activity, such as relaxation training, to recondition reactive patterns of physiological activity.

HISTORY

Precursors

Self-regulation, the practice of voluntary modification of one's own physiological activity, motor behavior, or conscious processes, has been an endeavor of human beings for ages. It is impossible to date the origin of Zen and yoga meditation. But in this country, biofeedback may be traced to an almost humorous beginning. Bair, in

1901, found that subjects acquired the ability to wiggle their ears only if they received feedback information. His biofeedback instrument was a system of levers and a kymograph (Stoyva, 1978).

In Europe a movement had begun that was to merge years later with this insignificant beginning. In 1879 Romain Vigouroux, a disciple of Charcot, commented on the changes in skin resistance in insensitive areas of hysterics. Ten years later Charles Féré reported that the resistance of the skin to the passage of electrical current would vary as a function of cognitive activity and sensory stimulation. Almost simultaneously it was observed that the skin exhibited electrical potentials to mental and external stimulation. This electrodermatological response was initially known as the Tarchanoff reflex after its discoverer, and later, the skin potential response (SPR). However, Féré's method was adoped by American psychologists and was labeled the galvanic skin response (GSR). Only lately has it been appropriately termed the skin resistance response (Venables & Christie, 1973). These early observations of physiological parameters varying in relationship with a psychological condition initiated the emergence of psychophysiology as a discipline of its own.

The turn of the century was a time of great excitement and discovery, relating mental events to body processes on the one hand and to unconscious processes on the other (Ellenberger, 1970). By 1933 Hans Berger reported

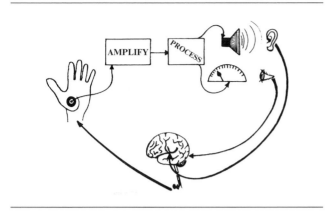

Figure 5.1 Bioinformation Feedback Loop

that the alpha rhythm was blocked by startle. The electroencephalogical investigation of emotion began (Lindsley, 1970). Armed with these tools, psychologists began to add to the body of knowledge relating physiological activity to dimensions of experience. The discipline of psychophysiology had been established.

As early as 1917, Edmond Jacobson (1967) began to apply a technique called progressive relaxation to insomnia and other tension states. Jacobson, a researcher in muscle physiology, proceeded from the point of view that the reduction of proprioceptive impulses from the muscles was associated with and could result in a systemic condition of relaxation. This concept was to later be the rationale for electromyographic (EMG) Biofeedback.

Beginnings

Biofeedback seemed to burst on the scene in the mid-1960s. Its appearance, however, resulted from the convergence of three directly related disciplines: electrical engineering, learning theory, and psychophysiology. Moreover, Behavior Therapy, as a more active mode of therapy demanding objective validation of behavioral change, was challenging the established, interpretive psychoanalytic therapies. There developed a tendency to more actively involve the patient in his therapy rather than to wait passively for insight to occur. The far-reaching impact of psychophysiology was that private physiological correlates of emotion and mental events were becoming social events with the aid of electronic instrumentation. The therapist could now record and interpret internal events of the patient with a more objective eye and intervene immediately with reinforcement not possible with the more interpretative techniques. The facility of the consciousness of both the patient and the therapist to deny emotional content (due to the crude human interoceptive sensory system [Gannon, 1977] in combination with motivational distortion of perception)

was bypassed. Relevant physiological information could now be objectively presented to the finely sensitive exteroceptors. With correlates of emotion being perceived as external events, they were more difficult to deny and more directly subjected to cognitive and conscious strategies.

Before Biofeedback, the attainment of self-knowledge of psychophysiological events and their modification by self-regulation were available only to the yogi who devoted years of self-discipline and meditation to develop interoceptive sensitivity. By combining his technology and knowledge of conditioning, modern humans have extended their potential capabilities beyond those of even the most sophisticated yogi. For example, Basmajian (1963) showed that single motor units could be differentially controlled by EMG feedback.

Following the publication of Basmajian's work, Thomas Budzynski (1979) and Johann Stoyva (1979) developed a technique using EMG feedback for inducing relaxation in the treatment of tension headache. In the middle 1960s the results of operant cardiovascular conditioning experiments with animals appeared in the literature. At the same time correlations began to be published between emotional set, consciousness, and the amount of alpha waves in the electroencephalogram (EEG) of human subjects (Basmajian, 1979). By 1979 there were so many workers in the field that the Biofeedback Research Society was formed (later renamed the Biofeedback Society of America).

In retrospect, probably the first biofeedback device was the human being himself. The early mesmerists were convinced that a magnetic field emanated from the hands to influence cures and induce the crisislike trance. Neurohypnology, later to be known as hypnosis, was a more respectable label for the same phenomenon, albeit that the trance was more somnolent. In these interactions the hypnotist conveys a set or expectancy to the subject, then proceeds to reinforce successive approximations to the posture and relaxed states approaching "sleep" that constitute the definition of "hypnotic state." The hypnotist, subtly and at times unknowingly, is guided in his administration of suggestions, tone of voice, and challenging by the overt motor responses and physiological indicators (breathing rate, muscle tonus, eye roll) that the subject emits. In a similar tradition, a technique called Autogenic Training was developed in which statements of body condition are repeated over and over as the patient searches his body for interoceptive feedback of approximation to the suggested condition (Schultz & Luthe, 1959). Although these two trends in psychology are not directly related to the development of Biofeedback as it is known today, they represent the tradition of behavioral control by reinforcement from which Biofeedback emerged.

CURRENT STATUS

With the present emphasis on relaxation training and skill training in psychology, Biofeedback in various forms is finding increasing use by psychologists in private practice and hospital settings. The applications are not restricted to those of the Behavior Therapy tradition. Adler and Adler (1979) reviewed its use in general psychiatry from a tradition of psychodynamic therapy. More medically oriented workers are increasingly applying Biofeedback to cardiovascular disorders, rehabilitation, spasticity control, and psychosomatic disorders (Basmajian, 1979). In the 1970s, dental applications of EMG Biofeedback began to appear in the literature (Carlsson, Gale, & Ohman, 1975), and dental school curriculum now includes classes in Biofeedback (Forgione, 1979).

The premature flurry of interest and publicity that alpha feedback caused in the late 1960s has all but died. Although alpha feedback is still used by some clinicians in combination with other techniques to achieve relaxation, other biofeedback techniques find more general use. Listed in order of popularity, electromyographic, electrodermal, thermal, and cardiovascular feedback are used today.

There are numerous state biofeedback societies affiliated with the Biofeedback Society of America. *Biofeedback and Self-Regulation* is the official journal of the society. The society offers numerous courses for professionals at various locations throughout the country each year. Currently, Biofeedback is a topic of increasing interest in Europe. The Annual European Congress of Behavior Therapy offered extensive biofeedback training courses in 1979 for the first time.

A wide variety of books are available for those wishing to learn about Biofeedback. Since 1972, Aldine Publishing Company (Chicago) has published an annual, edited by leaders in the field. The title is *Biofeedback & Self-Control.*

THEORY

Because Biofeedback only recently emerged from its laboratory background, functional relationships are being established in the field. The behavior therapeutic orientation tends to emphasize *that* a technique works and the *degree* to which it works rather than *how* or *why* it works. For example, statements such as "The biofeedback instrument is symbolically in a very special relationship with the patient; it can be seen as a nurturing or withholding mother, connected by an 'umbilical cord' (electrode leads) and responding sensitively to his every shift in feeling" (Adler & Adler, 1979) may allow Biofeedback to be integrated into psychoanalytic theory, but they add little to the knowledge of change on a behavioral or physiological level.

In order to facilitate understanding of the theoretical bases of biofeedback applications, we first relate its use to shape lowered arousal states to the established relaxation techniques. Next we outline the uses of Biofeedback to clarify its meaning. We then comment upon the theoretical issues that biofeedback use must recognize and the challenge it presents.

From the moment of conception, the cells of the body develop according to a tripartite design: the ectoderm into the neurological system, the mesoderm into the muscles of movement, and the endoderm into the gut and associated glands. This tripartite design is reflected in many ways as one studies psychology. In social psychology, for example, an attitude is defined as an interrelated system of three components (see Schwartz & Shapiro, 1973).

1. *The Cognitive Component:* Beliefs of the individual (evaluative) that attribute good and bad qualities to an object; beliefs about the appropriate or inappropriate ways of responding to an object; and perceptual sets that orient the individual in particular ways to external and internal information such as memory and feelings.

2. *The Action Tendency Component:* Behavorial readiness is associated with the cognitive component: to attack or flee an object associated with a negative attitude, to affiliate with, orient to, reward, and support an object associated with a positive attitude.

3. *The Feeling Component:* Emotions or body-marshaling responses of the automatic nervous system are elicited by the object or thoughts of the object.

Lang (1971), recognizing the three body systems, captured the importance of direct, multimodal therapy and the indicated points of application for Biofeedback.

We will need to confine ourselves to measurable behaviors in all systems, and discover the laws that determine their interaction. The data suggest that we must deal with each behavior system [on] its own terms. Thus, a patient who reports anxiety, fails to cope or perform effectively under stress, and evidences autonomic activity that varies widely from the practical energy demands of the situation, needs to receive treatment for all these disorders. He should be administered a treatment directed simultaneously at shaping verbal sets (so as to reduce reported stress over the variety of situations in which it appears), assisted in building effective coping bahaviors and practicing them in appropriate contexts, and finally, administered a program for attenuating autonomic arousal and excessive muscle tonus, with the goal of reducing the distraction and interference of peripheral physiological feedback. In short, psychotherapy should be a vigorous multisystem training program tailored to the unique behavioral topography presented by the patient. (p. 109)

In agreement with Lang, it is fortunate that frequently success in the control of one system eventually appears to result in change throughout the other systems of response. Either by insight, relief from aversive feedback from the autonomic system, or the learning of a new active coping behavior such as assertion, changes in the presenting complaint may occur. However, reinforcement of appropriate levels of functioning in the other two systems may be necessary to ensure durability for the psychological change. In cases where resistance to change occurs, direct modification of the interfering system may be productive. It is an error to assume that the three systems of every patient always act as a coordinated whole.

A concept that influences many treatment strategies in learning-based therapies (and many others as well) is that reduction in the motive state underlying (or consistently evoking) a behavior will facilitate a change in that behavior.

Anxiety is a motive state that does any of the following:

1. Causes discomfort in its physiological expression.
2. Results in dysfunction of organ systems (psychosomatics).
3. Disrupts or distorts cognitive and perceptual functions.
4. Consistently triggers inappropriate sets of overt behaviors or inhibited behaviors (tension).

Any or all of these consequences leave the patient feeling powerless in the face of the emotion. Over the years, psychologists have employed relaxation techniques to assist in behavorial change or reduce anxiety levels in patients.

The major relaxation techniques are classified in the tripartite scheme in Figure 5.2. The basis for classification is the principal target of the relaxation technique. All central techniques involve the focus of perception in a single noncritical way. In this fashion, conflicting thought patterns and emotional tendencies are diminished. Generalized, systemic patterns appropriate to the relaxing suggestion, mantra, or image are then reinforced (Patel, 1977). With the autonomic techniques, the breath patterns are employed to modify emotional reactive patterns both directly (physiologically) and indirectly by focusing the consciousness on maintaining paced patterns as in diaphragmatic breathing or engaging in breathing rituals as in the yogic pranayama (Harris, Katkin, Lick, & Habberfield, 1976; Scholander &

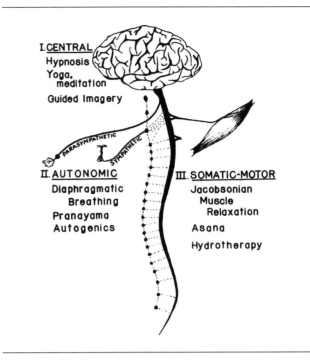

Figure 5.2

Simmons, 1964). Autogenic training employs focused concentration on suggestions of autonomic modification (the hands warm, the stomach calm) and the concentration of the awareness upon interoceptive sensations of change in the desired direction. Autogenic training has been applied to the other systems (Luthe & Blumberg, 1977). The striated muscles of the somatic-motor systems are the principal focus of modification for the Jacobsonian muscle relaxation, yogic body positions (asanas), and hot bath and massage techniques.

Biofeedback applications are classified according to this scheme in the applications section of this chapter.

As a psychophysiological method, Biofeedback is particularly suited to assist in emotional change or to help modify the resultants of emotional discharge. It has, however, been employed in at least three different ways by therapists. It will be helpful to outline these uses so that we can focus upon only the important theoretical issues at this stage in its development.

First, as a psychophysiological technique, it can provide a *diagnostic baseline* (Fair, 1979) from which improvement or failure can be measured. In the establishment of the diagnostic baseline, the unique behavioral topography of the patient to stressful events is analyzed. The differential loading of central process (i.e., obsessional thoughts of panic), somatic-motor (tension, muscle spasm, and related symptoms such as dizziness resulting from temporomandibular joint syndrome), or autonomic (racing heart, hyperventilation, sweatiness, hot flashes) systems can be determined by verbal report and correlations with autonomic and EMG readings. The monitoring of the SPR or GSR concurrent with the administration of a standard fear inventory or a stimulus hierarchy will also reveal the degree of concordance between subjective report and physiological arousal (Katkin & Deitz, 1973).

The second use of Biofeedback is for the benefit of the therapist. Objective physiological data obtained over the period of psychological or behavioral intervention serves as important feedback *to the therapist* in determining the course of analysis or the efficacy of treatment. The therapist can integrate biofeedback information with verbal reports by the patient and his own inference. Because the data are objective, Biofeedback can reduce biased observations of the patient and the therapist. In short, it can provide additional data to make interpretations more robust. The most common application of Biofeedback as a guide to the therapist is in relaxation training. A cue function for the patient is a variation of this second use. As a reinforcement for task performance, feedback information is invaluable *to the patient* in relaxation training either with a specific relaxation technique or in the shaping of low arousal states by sequential criteria (Stoyva, 1979). With more traditional psychotherapy, Sedlacek (1975) and Toomim and Toomim (1975) have reported on the GSR's value in guiding *both therapist and patient* to relevant content and reducing resistance to threatening material.

The third use of Biofeedback is most familiar to the public: either as a relaxation technique itself or as a method modifying a specific body function directly or indirectly. When the biofeedback application itself is employed as the relaxation technique, it is assumed that reduction of physiological activity in the targeted area and system will result in "relaxation" of the other systems of the body. For example, it is currently common to employ frontalis placement EMG in training of relaxation. Muscle feedback relaxation alone shows some promise in treatment of conditions such as chronic anxiety (Raskin, Johnson, & Rondestvedt, 1973; Townsend, House, & Addario, 1975). It is reasonable to expect, however, that results would be superior if an autonomic response were employed in addition to EMG in these studies.

There are two major theoretical issues that must be dealt with in biofeedback training.[1] The first is *what is being trained,* and the second is how the learned controls are to be transferred to the patient's everyday life without the benefit of the feedback instrument. The two issues are necessarily intertwined, but it is not necessary to

answer the first to establish the necessary and sufficient conditions for the second.

Lazarus (1975) proposed that the self-regulation of somatic disturbances cannot be isolated from the larger context of the person's adaptive interaction with his environment. This adaptive interaction is constantly being mediated by social and psychological processes. In short, Biofeedback should be viewed as one facet in the treatment of the total person. What mediates biofeedback effects will be an open question for some time. Lazarus reviewed some of the possibilities:

1. The relaxation process could serve as a means of developing attention strategies incompatible with those fixating on the stress-producing sources of tension.
2. The trained, relaxed psychological state is simply incompatible with tension or chronic arousal.

It is not easy to define relaxation. Often relaxation is operationally defined as a low reading on the one psychophysiological dimension modified. This practice can be misleading since individuals as a group show both stimulus-response *specificity,* the tendency for different stimuli to produce unique patterns of autonomic activity, and response *stereotypy,* an idiosyncratic response pattern to all stimuli (Sternbach, 1966). The use of multiple measures to define relaxation and anxiety states is strongly indicated (Tyrer & Lader, 1976). Using our tripartite scheme, an operational definition of relaxation would have to include an EEG criterion such as the presence of alpha waves, an autonomic criterion such as spontaneous SPR activity within an envelope ±0.3 mV, and an EMG criterion such as frontalis activity below 3μV.

Out of recognition of a need to train all body systems in a pattern of relaxation, most recent suggestions for biofeedback training in the clinic include at least two peripheral psychophysiological responses in addition to cognitive strategies (Fair, 1979; Stoyva, 1979).

Epstein and Blanchard (1977) have pointed out that recently emphasis has shifted from the factors that mediate the observed changes in behavior to the factors that are important in continued control. Although a strategy may be learned when feedback is available, it is most important that the patient continue control of the physiologic response when feedback is removed. It has been proposed that feedback training sensitizes the patient to detect sensory changes associated with the criterion values of the physiologic response, but few studies test for this possibility. Self-control is not automatically produced when feedback is removed. Epstein and Blanchard state that self-maintenance is dependent on three factors. First, the patient must be able to discriminate when to implement self-control procedures. Second, he

---

[1] For the reader interested in the detailed anatomical and physiological basis for Biofeedback, Wolf's discussion (1979) provides information beyond the scope of this section.

or she must be able to discriminate changes in physiological activity that indicate success and serve as self-reinforcements; and third, the choice of reinforcer should be appropriate to maintain self-control over long periods of time.

Another issue often neglected in biofeedback research is the higher order learning that contributes to a sense of mastery over emotion or pain. As the patient views a physiological process varying according to some coping strategy he or she employs, the former sense of powerlessness diminishes. In addition, the patient learns that there are degrees to physiological processes and emotion, and that it is possible to discriminate differences in degree. Whether these factors act as organizing influences in the behavioral changes effected by Biofeedback Therapy is yet to be determined. Lazarus (1975) suggests that biofeedback studies provide a powerful tool to resolve the basic psychological questions concerning the modes of self-regulation of emotion that are available to individuals under different environmental contexts. A review of the advances in biofeedback research 10 years hence will determine whether this tool was, in fact, wisely used.

An excellent paper by Meichenbaum (1976) discusses the possible role of cognitions in each of the various phases of biofeedback training. The interested reader will find his discussion an excellent amplification of the points made in this chapter.

METHODOLOGY

There are three critical points in the biofeedback loop pictured in Figure 6.1 at which artifact or other confounding variables may intrude. The first is the interface between body surface and electrode. This point poses little problem in EMG and the majority of biofeedback applications, but is of major consequence in GSR and SPR applications (see Venables & Christie, 1973). With dry electrodes common in less expensive GSR devices, for example, special care must be taken because pressure variations against the electrode lead to variable contact area, causing resistance to vary independent of skin physiology.

The second point of artifact is the type of electronic instrument used and the processed signal displayed. Again, the electrodermal applications have been the source of some problems. As mentioned earlier, American psychologists opted for the GSR rather than the SPR in their early research. This has led to some confusion. The traditional application of electrodermal monitoring in clinical settings is to use the tonic (base-level) GSR as an index of emotional level so that in relaxation training, the goal is to raise the tonic resistance. However, GSR fluctuates (phasic activity) on this base level

either spontaneously or to specific stimuli. Phasic drops in resistance may occur to a number of stimuli or to mental events that are not aversive. It was only recently proposed that the recovery wave of the phasic GSR was diagnostic of aversiveness. Former studies using only the magnitude of the drop in resistance had found mixed results. This led some workers to suggest that electrodermal phasic responses were of little value in the study of anxiety. In light of the recent analysis of the recovery limb of the GSR, these suggestions must be reevaluated along with the earlier negative findings. Had the SPR been used, this confusion might not have resulted.

The SPR is composed of a negative and a positive component. The positive component is monotonically related to increases in noxious stimulation and aversiveness (Forgione, 1972; Raskin, Kotses, & Bever, 1969). Some biofeedback instruments, such as the SPR by Cyborg Corporation, allow the clinician to immediately distinguish between positive and negative components of the SPR. Tonic levels, then, are easily monitored by a simple GSR device. Frequency of response (another index of arousal) may also be measured with this type of instrument. To draw inferences from phasic activity, however, the SPR or laboratory-quality GSR with paper record must be used. The type of instrument, then, affects the information available and the inferences that may be drawn. Another typical problem encountered in the area of what is being monitored and the type of feedback used appears with EMG feedback. Alexander, French, and Goodman (1975) have shown that different effects can be obtained if frontalis EMG feedback is trained with auditory or visual signals. It seems that if the eyes are used, interaction from the muscles of this system can render frontalis area muscle control difficult. With auditory feedback, these muscle systems are not active and feedback signals are more representative of relaxation. This type of research clarifies many methodological issues. For example, Shannon, Goldman, and Lee (1978) compared three feedback techniques in training blood pressure control. They found the technique that provided the maximal information with the shortest latency to be superior.

The third point of possible artifact in the biofeedback loop, the detection of signal variations and processing of the signal by cortical activity, is most difficult to define and control. In this step, expectancy, set, patient motivation, and instructions are critical variables that can be controlled only in part by the skills of the therapist. For example, Meyers and Craighead (1978) found that instructions significantly affected GSR base level. It is within this domain that clinical judgment must be exercised as to whether Biofeedback is to be used as the principal form of therapy or as an adjunct to a broader psychological approach.

The most common psychological biofeedback operation is aimed at modifying chronic states of elevated emotional tone, aversive sensory consequences of the elevated emotional condition in a particular body area (tension headache or racing heart), or the physiological resultant of these states (high blood pressure). Medical operations aim at either rehabilitation of a body function impaired by trauma such as muscle reeducation or modifying neurological states such as epilepsy (see Basmajian, 1979).

Regardless of the instrumentation, the setting requires a comfortable reclining chair in a sound-attenuated room with constant temperature and lighting. A therapist is always present in the early sessions for instruction and coaching. Once patient instruction has occurred, the patient can usually manage his own sessions or be minimally surpervised by a technician. Obtained values are always charted so that an objective record of progress is available. Response rates may also be tallied in an automated fashion with more sophisticated systems. With the advent of more inexpensive GSR and EMG portable devices, home practice with instruments on loan is finding greater popularity. Home care offers many advantages, not the least of which is that it requires the patient to take the time out of his or her day to practice in a setting that may have many cues of arousal.

During the first office session, it is customary to give the patient a rationale for using relaxation training in the treatment program. The therapist then usually explains the role of Biofeedback, applying the instrument to himself to demonstrate its use and desensitize the patient to electronic instrumentation. The first session usually ends with an audiotape being made for the patient to use to practice relaxation at home before the next scheduled session.

Because of variations in the physiological expression of response to stress among patients, the second session is usually devoted to obtaining a physiological profile (Fair, 1979) to assess stability or lability of at least two response systems under rest and moderate stress. Some individuals, for example, show maximum response to stress in the somatic-motor system while others show predominantly autonomic responsivity. Still others will show combined somatic-motor and autonomic responses. Based upon this information, the therapist will select a sequence of instrument applications to teach the patient control of his or her response to stressors (Stoyva, 1979). To assist in the assessment of somatic-motor tension locations in the body, the Davicon Corporation has developed a dual-channel EMG device. Rather than requiring electrode paste and adhesive discs, the electrodes themselves contain miniature amplifiers. This innovation allows instantaneous readings to be taken with dry electrodes and permits multiple test sites to be measured in a short period of time. Often,

guided by EMG feedback, the patient can be shown that simple postural changes will significantly reduce tension levels in the body.

Although it has been customary to employ only one feedback instrument to one body system (either GSR or EMG frontalis), the use of multiple instruments providing feedback for at least two body systems is finding greater popularity (Naliboff & Johnson, 1978). For example, one technique that has been employed at our facility over the past five years is SPR-contingent EMG biofeedback training. Temporomandibular joint patients are treated for facial pain resulting from tension in the muscles of the jaw, a common source of headache also called the myofascial pain dysfunction syndrome (Laskin, 1969). The technique was devised to allow immediate detection of those patients who "do combat" with the EMG device. This technique is based upon the assumption that sympathetic arousal both impedes the learning process and blocks fine internal perception. It later became apparent that the technique facilitated EMG training even in those patients who were positively motivated. The patient is instructed to reduce SPR until responses of less than ±0.5 mV occur. The trigger of the feedback device is set to produce silence for responses of this magnitude. As long as the SPR feedback is silent, attention can be devoted to frontalis EMG reduction. If GSR feedback is employed, EMG training occurs only in the presence of decreasing conductance levels (increasing resistance). In this manner arousal states that might interfere with relaxation training are immediately brought to the patient's attention.

EMG feedback training continues until the patient can reliably maintain frontalis muscle tension at or below 2μV for extended periods of time. At that time attention is usually devoted to strengthening coping behaviors to extend the gains made in the clinic to real life and protect the new levels of emotional behavior.

APPLICATIONS

Specific biofeedback applications are classified in Figure 5.3 according to the tripartite scheme used for relaxation techniques discussed earlier. The principal forms of EEG feedback for central process modification are alpha, theta, and sensorimotor rhythm (Ancoli & Kamiya, 1978; Brown, 1977; Sterman, MacDonald, & Stone, 1974). For autonomic modification, SPR and GSR are the electrodermal applications while heart rate (HR) and blood pressure (BP) are general cardiovascular applications. Blood volume (BV) and the longer delayed skin temperature (TEMP) are autonomic applications that may be used for relaxation or in the treatment of migraine (head and hand locations) and Raynaud's disease. Since the autonomic system affects numerous body sites,

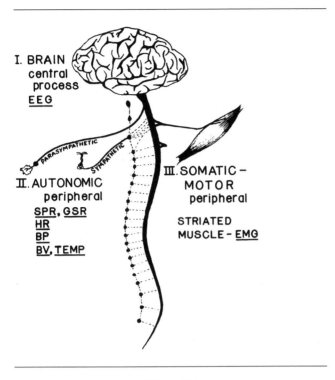

I. BRAIN
central
process
EEG

PARASYMPATHETIC

SYMPATHETIC

II. AUTONOMIC
peripheral
SPR, GSR
HR
BP
BV, TEMP

III. SOMATIC –
MOTOR
peripheral

STRIATED
MUSCLE - EMG

Figure 5.3

a variety of biofeedback applications may be used to monitor its activity. Generally, the electrodermatological instruments are used in relaxation training for short delay of reinforcement applications, and finger temperature is used for longer delay applications. For general relaxation training, frontalis EMG feedback is the most popular (Budzynski, 1979). It must be remembered that the frontalis placement of feedback electrodes provides an index of numerous muscle groups of the head (e.g., temporalis, corrugator, and eye muscles among others).

Biofeedback has been applied to so many specific problems that they cannot be exhaustively summarized herein. We will only highlight the most successful applications that have received the bulk of research attention in the past several years. The order of our review will be determined by our evaluation of frequency of clinical application during this period.

In 1974 Blanchard and Young critically reviewed the clinical applications of Biofeedback to that date. The reviewers were impressed with the rapid results of direct muscle feedback in the treatment of hemiplegia, which was refractory to traditional neuromuscular rehabilitation. The evidence at that time also strongly supported the use of EMG feedback for the elimination of tension headache and of subvocal speech while reading. By 1974 only one study using EMG to assist relaxation training (Raskin, Johnson, & Rondestvedt, 1973) was worthy of note by these reviewers. Interestingly, in that study reports of anxiety were not diminished, but relief of anxi-

ety-mediated symptoms such as tension headache and insomnia did occur. The negative finding substantiates Lang's statement, cited earlier, that the perception of anxiety and the verbal patterns of reporting must also be given therapeutic attention. All systems do not necessarily spontaneously change with change in one body system.

By 1976 Hutchings and Reinking reported that EMG-assisted relaxation procedures were the method of choice for the treatment of tension headache when compared to autogenic relaxation training. Currently, in the treatment of tension headache, EMG feedback is the most firmly established of all biofeedback applications for problems that involve a psychological etiology (Budzynski, 1978, 1979; Scott, 1979). Direct muscle Biofeedback is also firmly established in physical medicine and rehabilitation (Basmajian, 1979; Fernando & Basmajian, 1978).

The Biofeedback Society of America published a series of reports in 1978 (Stoyva, 1978) to address the issues of accountability and a sound research basis for clinical applications. In this series of reports are summarized the principal applications of Biofeedback: (1) psychophysiologic disorders, (2) vasoconstrictive syndromes, (3) gastrointestinal disorders, (4) vascular headache, (5) muscle-contraction headache, and (6) dysfunctions in the domain of physical medicine and rehabilitation.

The general findings of these reports (tension headache was cited above) were that for vascular headache, temperature and EMG feedback alone or in combination may be more therapeutic than EEG alpha feedback. Research, however, is still needed to ascertain how biofeedback and relaxation techniques can be most effectively combined. Peripheral vasoconstrictive syndromes have received some attention using blood volume and temperature feedback. A review article published after the task force reports will be of value to the reader interested in Raynaud's disease (Sappington, Fiorito, & Brehony, 1979).

An area of intense current research is heart rate and blood pressure feedback. Although it does not seem to be a widely used application among clinicians, it may soon be as demand from the medical community increases. There are many complex issues in this area of Biofeedback. Williamson and Blanchard (1979), in a pair of articles, review these issues and the results of research published since 1972.

An application gaining increasing interest from psychologists is temporomandibular joint pain (Carlsson, Gale, & Ohman, 1975; Fernando & Basmajian, 1978; Laskin, 1969; Rugh, Perlis, & Disraeli, 1977). The diagnostic classification is misleading because pain arising from the interaction of personality style, stress, and occlusal disharmony can cause a variety of physical reactions other than jaw-joint pain (unilateral head pain, dizziness, nausea, neck pain, arm and upper back pain, for example) that are stress related and may reinforce neurotic behavior patterns. EMG and relaxation training are the principal behavioral treatments. It is interesting to note that Schwartz, Greene, and Laskin (1979) found the Minnesota Multiphasic Personality Inventory (MMPI) profile of patients suffering from temporomandibular joint pain to be similar to the MMPI profile of low back pain patients. Patients with significantly elevated scores were nonresponsive to treatment. Gessel (1975) had predicted that with increasing severity of the pain syndrome, broader therapeutic approaches would be necessary to treat associated depression. Nouwen and Solinger (1979) found that in the EMG feedback treatment of low back pain patients, improvement with feedback must be protected by training self-control in daily life.

In the majority of biofeedback applications, control of targeted physiological processes and relief from discomfort have been clearly demonstrated. Workers in the field must now apply their attention to integrating their treatment with existing therapies or devising treatment strategies of their own to promote self-control outside the clinic. In addition, attention must be given to treating other emotional states. Although anxiety and related behaviors have been found to be very responsive to feedback applications, depression has been found to be rather refractory. For example, Biofeedback has been effective with sleep-onset insomnia, but early-waking insomnia, consistent with depression, has not been successfully treated. Depression often accompanies stress-related disorders of long standing. It was seen early as a complicating factor in the treatment of temporomandibular joint pain (Gessel, 1975) and migraine. Often drug dependency is also a factor in disorders of long standing. Diamond and Franklin (1975) treated 119 drug-habituated patients with combined TEMP and EMG feedback and found improvement in only 48 patients. Multimodal therapy may hold promise for these more severely afflicted, resistant patients. For the present, however, Biofeedback has the advantage that, as a short-term, specific therapy, it can be applied to a large number of patients. Patients refractory to this initial screening may then be assigned to the more time-consuming therapeutic approaches.

CASE EXAMPLE

A single, 28-year-old female nurse presented complaints of constant unilateral headache that at times involved her neck, shoulder, and upper back. There were periods of nausea and excessive pain while chewing, which seriously affected her diet. Repeated medical examinations produced negative findings. She reported being tense and almost constantly frustrated with her inability to express herself. She was quiet and constantly avoided eye contact during the first three hours of assessment. She had been treated with Valium (15–25 mg/day) with some success after a dentist had ground her teeth down in an attempt to treat her. Paper-and-pencil tests verified the clinical impression that the patient was hypersocialized, hypervigilant, obsessive, and compulsive about ordering her environment. She was both anxious and depressed. She lived in an apartment, one floor above her controlling mother and explosive, alcoholic father. The fear of social contact with males interacted with her nausea, severely limiting her social life. Superficial muscular observations revealed that the muscles of the right side of her face, jaw, and shoulder were painful to touch. Bilateral EMG analysis with surface electrodes showed disproportionately elevated readings on the right side. Episodes of day and nocturnal teeth clenching followed difficult days at work or with the family. These episodes led to sharp increases in pain upon awakening.

The treatment strategy was formulated to aim initially for relief of the pain resulting from her temporomandibular joint problem. The nausea was tentatively seen as being related to her oral problem. It was expected that once this diminished, her eating habits would improve. When these basic problems were under reasonable control, it was planned that the broader issues could be approached therapeutically.

A soft vinyl night guard was fabricated by a dentist to minimize the traumatic effects of her nocturnal clenching behavior. (The dentist was discouraged from grinding down her dentition further, since equilibration of dentition with muscles in spasm might have further complicated her conditon.)

Five 20-minute sessions of bilateral EMG feedback of masseter muscle activity combined with training in diaphragmatic breathing resulted in a 50 percent reduction of pain intensity ratings. Working in cooperation with the dentist, a plastic mouthplate was then constructed (Gelb, 1977) and equilibrated with the aid of bilateral EMG feedback to give balance to the muscles of jaw closure.

At that time relaxation training, guided by GSR feedback, was initiated. It immediately became apparent that the patient would allow herself to relax only to a point at which she could still maintain awareness of her environment. As the GSR base level (resistance) increased, there would occur immediate drops in resistance. In an almost stepwise fashion, the increase in resistance would occur to a point, followed by a large drop. Upon questioning, the patient revealed that she was afraid to "let go and relax." She was then assured that she could use the GSR as a guide to let go in little steps to prove to herself that she would not lose control.

With this titrated approach, she gradually desensitized herself to relaxation. Interestingly, once she was assured that she had some control and had demonstrated it to herself using the GSR signal, she abreacted feelings of anger at her father. The resurgence of muscular pain that followed subsided over the next two weeks with the help of EMG biofeedback training. Thereafter, pain reports reflected a reduction to 25 percent of original levels and the nausea did not reoccur. With changed diet and increasing involvement in relaxation exercises, her interpersonal communication skills improved. Assertion training was then combined with the relaxation training to protect her gains. Bilateral EMG levels were stabilized at low equal levels and pain-free days began to occur two months into treatment. Within six months she had moved from her parents' house, pain free. She was referred to a psychotherapist to obtain support during her transition to independent life and to further resolve her conflicting feelings about her parents and herself. A one-year follow-up indicated that she was dating and profiting from her psychotherapy. The mouthplate was worn only when she felt tension beginning in her jaw muscles (one hour per week on the average). She remained pain free with the exception of two minor episodes of pain, which were of short duration.

SUMMARY

The case example reveals the interdisciplinary nature of Biofeedback Therapy. Although not all applications are as complex as the case reported, it should be clear that a great number of patients seeking psychotherapy or medical treatment present a complex of interrelated problems that may not be adequately treated by one discipline alone. It is doubtful that Biofeedback will emerge as a therapy on its own, but its influence may result in expansion of existing therapeutic approaches. At present it is most comfortable in the camp of the behavior therapies that gave it birth, but the dynamic and phenomenological therapies may soon find uses for this new modality. It holds a promise of contributing a dimension of objectivity to those more traditional therapies forced by lack of technological advances at the time of their development to rely mainly upon inference and verbal analysis.

Biofeedback carries a message that has far-reaching, implications for psychotherapy. The therapist and the patient must recognize and deal with the body and its involvement in thought and emotion. The body processes, once the domain of medicine, have already begun to be subsumed under the disciplines of behavioral medicine and psychology. Hopefully, cooperation rather than territorial confrontation will take place as psychology and medicine converge with the advancement of knowledge.

REFERENCES

Adler, C. S., & Adler, S. M. (1979). Strategies in general psychiatry. In J. V. Basmajian (Ed.), *Biofeedback—Principles and practice for clinicians.* Baltimore: Williams & Wilkins.

Alexander, A. B., French, C. A., & Goodman, N. J. (1975). A comparison of auditory and visual feedback in biofeedback assisted muscular relaxation training. *Psychophysiology, 12,* 119–123.

Ancoli, S., & Kamiya, J. (1978). Methodological issues in alpha biofeedback training. *Biofeedback and Self-Regulation, 3,* 159–183.

Bair, J. H. (1901). Development of voluntary control. *Psychological Review, 8,* 474–510.

Basmajian, J. V. (1963). Conscious control of individual motor units. *Science, 141,* 440–441.

Basmajian, J. V. (1979). Introduction: Principles and background. In J. V. Basmajian (Ed.), *Biofeedback—Principles and practice for clinicians.* Baltimore: Williams & Wilkins.

Blanchard, E. B., & Young, L. D. (1974). Clinical applications of biofeedback training: A review of evidence. *Archives of General Psychiatry, 30,* 573–589.

Brown, B. B. (1977). *Stress and the art of biofeedback.* New York: Harper & Row.

Budzynski, T. H. (1978). Biofeedback in the treatment of muscle-contraction (tension) headache. *Biofeedback and Self-Regulation, 3,* 409–434.

Budzynski, T. H. (1979). Biofeedback strategies in headache treatment. In J. V. Basmajian (Ed.), *Biofeedback—Principles and practice for clinicians.* Baltimore: Williams & Wilkins.

Carlsson, S. G., Gale, E. N., & Ohman, A. (1975). Treatment of temporomandibular joint syndrome with biofeedback training. *Journal of the American Dental Association, 91,* 602–605.

Diamond, S., & Franklin, M. (1975). Autogenic training and biofeedback in treatment of chronic headache problems in adults. In W. Luthe & F. Antonelli (Eds.), *Therapy in psychosomatic medicine.* Proceedings of the 3rd Congress of the International College of Psychosomatic Medicine, Rome.

Ellenberger, H. F. (1970). *The discovery of the unconscious.* New York: Basic Books.

Epstein, L. H., & Blanchard, E. B. (1977). Biofeedback, self-control and self-management. *Biofeedback and Self-Regulation, 2,* 201–211.

Fair, P. L. (1979). Biofeedback strategies in psychotherapy. In J. V. Basmajian (Ed.), *Biofeedback—Principles and practice for clinicians.* Baltimore: Williams & Wilkins.

Fernando, C. K., & Basmajian, J. V. (1978). Biofeedback in physical medicine and rehabilitation. *Biofeedback and Self-Regulation, 3,* 435–455.

Forgione, A. G. (1972). Human discriminated avoidance and associated electrophysiological behaviors under schedules with different contingency probabilities. *Dissertation Abstracts, 33* (4) (order no. 72–25273; 398 pages).

Forgione, A. G. (1979). Psychology and psychostomatology. Paper presented at the Ninth European Congress of Behavior Therapy, Paris.

Gannon, L. (1977). The role of interoception in learned visceral control. *Biofeedback and Self-Regulation, 2,* 337–347.

Gelb, H. (1977). *Clinical management of head, neck and TMJ dysfunction.* Philadelphia: W. B. Saunders.

Gessel, A. H. (1975). Electromyographic biofeedback and tricyclic antidepressants in myofascial pain-dysfunction syndrome: Psychological predictors of outcome. *Journal of the American Dental Association, 91,* 1049.

Harris, V. A., Katkin, E. S., Lick, J. R., & Habberfield, T. (1976). Paced respiration as a technique for the modification of autonomic response to stress *Psychophysiology, 13,* 386–391.

Hutchings, D. F. & Reinking, R. H. (1976). Tension headaches: What form of therapy is most effective? *Biofeedback and Self-Regulation, 2,* 183–190.

Jacobson, E. (1967). *Biology of emotions.* Springfield, IL: Charles C. Thomas.

Katkin, E. S., & Deitz, S. R. (1973). Systematic desensitization. In W. F. Prokasy & D. C. Raskin (Eds.), *Electrodermal activity in psychological research.* New York: Academic Press.

Lang, P. (1971). The application of psychophysiological methods to the study of psychotherapy and behavior modification. In A. E. Bergin & S. L. Garfield (Eds.). *Handbook of psychotherapy and behavior change.* New York: Wiley.

Laskin, D. M. (1969). Etiology of the pain-dysfunction syndrome. *Journal of the American Dental Association, 79,* 147.

Lazarus, R. S. (1975). A cognitively oriented psychologist looks at biofeedback. *American Psychologist, 30,* 553–561.

Lindsley, D. B. (1970). The role of nonspecific reticuothalamocortical systems in emotion. In P. Black (Ed.), *Physiological correlates of emotion.* New York: Academic Press.

Luthe, W., & Blumberg, S. R. (1977). Autogenic therapy. In E. D. Wittkower & H. Warnes (Eds.), *Psychosomatic medicin: Its clinical applications.* Hagerstown, MD: Harper & Row.

Meichenbaum, D. (1976). Cognitive factors in biofeedback therapy. *Biofeedback and Self-Regulation, 1,* 201–216.

Meyers, A. W., & Craighead, W. E. (1978). Adaptation periods in psychophysiological research. *Behavior Therapy, 9,* 355–362.

Naliboff, B. D., & Johnson, H. J. (1978). Finger pulse amplitude and frontalis EMG biofeedback effects of single- and two-system training. *Biofeedback and Self-Regulation, 3,* 133–143.

Nouwen, A., & Solinger, J. W. (1979). The effectiveness of EMG biofeedback training in low back pain. *Biofeedback and Self-Regulation, 4,* 103–111.

Patel, C. H. (1977). Biofeedback-aided relaxation and meditation in the management of hypertension. *Biofeedback and Self-Regulation, 2,* 1–41.

Raskin, M., Johnson, G., & Rondestvedt, J. W. (1973). Chronic anxiety treated by feedback-induced muscle relaxation. *Archives of General Psychiatry, 28,* 263–267.

Raskin, D. C., Kotses, H., & Bever, J. (1969). Autonomic indicators of orienting and defensive reflexes. *Journal of Experimental Psychology, 80,* 423–433.

Rugh, J D., Perlis, D B., & Disraeli, R. I. (Eds.). (1977). *Biofeedback in dentistry: Research and clinical applications.* Phoenix, AZ: Semantodontics.

Sappington, J. T., Fiorito, E. M., & Brehony, K. A. (1979). Biofeedback as therapy in Raynaud's disease. *Biofeedback and Self-Regulation, 4,* 155–169.

Scholander, T., & Simmons, R. (1964). A conditioning procedure to increase the influence of the respiratory cycle upon electrodermal activity. *Journal of Psychosomatic Research, 7,* 295–300.

Schultz, J. H., & Luthe, W. (1959). *Autogenic training.* New York: Grune & Stratton.

Schwartz, G. E., & Shapiro, D. (1973). Social psychophysiology. In W. F. Prokasy & D. C. Raskin (Eds.), *Electrodermal Activity in Psychological Research.* New York: Academic Press.

Schwartz, R. A., Greene, C. S., & Laskin. D. M. (1979). Personality characteristics of patients with myofascial pain-dysfunction (MPD) syndrome unresponsive to conventional therapy. *Journal of Dental Research, 58,* 1435.

Scott, D. S. (1979). A comprehensive treatment strategy for muscle contraction headaches. *Journal of Behavior Therapy and Experimental Psychiatry, 10,* 35–40.

Sedlacek, K. (1975). GSR biofeedback in clinical practice (Tape T23). (Biomonitoring Applications, 270 Madison Avenue, New York, NY.)

Shannon, B. J., Goldman, M. S., & Lee, R. M. (1978). Biofeedback training of blood pressure: A comparison of three feedback techniques. *Psychophysiology, 15,* 53–59.

Sterman, M. B., MacDonald, L. R., & Stone, R. K. (1974). Biofeedback training of the sensorimotor electroencephalogram rhythm in man: Effects on epilepsy. *Epilepsia, 15,* 395–416.

Sternbach, R. A. (1966). *Principles of psychophysiology.* New York: Academic Press.

Stoyva, J. (1978). Editorial. *Biofeedback and Self-Regulation, 3,* 329.

Stoyva, J. M. (1979). Guidelines in the training of general relaxation. In J. V. Basmajian (Ed.), *Biofeedback—Principles and practice for clinicians.* Baltimore: Williams & Wilkins.

Toomim, M. K., & Toomim, H. (1975). GSR biofeedback in psychotherapy: Some clinical observations. *Psychotherapy: Theory, Research and Practice, 12* (1), 33–38.

Townsend, R. E., House, J. F., & Addario, D. A. (1975). A comparison of biofeedback-mediated relaxation and group therapy in the treatment of chronic anxiety. *American Journal of Psychiatry, 132,* 598–601.

Tyrer, P. J., & Lader, M. H. (1976). Central and peripheral correlates of anxiety: A comparative study. *Journal of Nervous and Mental Disease, 162,* 99–104.

Venables, P. H., & Christie, M. J. (1973). Mechanisms, instrumentation, recording techniques and quantification of responses. In W. F. Prokasy & D. C. Raskin (Eds.), *Electrodermal activity in psychological research.* New York: Academic Press.

Vigouroux, R. (1879). Sur le rôle de la résistance électrique des tissus dans l'électrodiagnostic. *Société de Biologie comptes rendus des séances, 31,* 336–339.

Wickramasekera, I. (Ed.). (1976) *Biofeedback, behavior therapy and hypnosis: Potentiating the verbal control of behavior for clinicians.* Chicago: Nelson-Hall.

Williamson, D. A., & Blanchard, E. B. (1979). Heart rate and blood pressure feedback I. A review of recent experimental literature. II. A review and integration of recent theoretical models. *Biofeedback and Self-Regulation, 4,* 1–50.

Wolf, S. L. (1979). Anatomical and physiological basis for biofeedback. In J. V. Basmajian (Ed.), *Biofeedback—Principles and practice for clinicians* Baltimore: Williams & Wilkins.

Chapter 6

BODY THERAPIES

BARRY GREEN

My own biases are such that I have trouble accepting Body Therapies as psychotherapies except through indirection. Here's what I mean: If someone massages me, and if I am convinced that that person is acting because of his or her feeling about me, then it is my perception of the actions that can affect me rather than the actions themselves. Thus, if we could imagine a robot that would give exactly the same manipulations that Body Therapist Dr. Milton Trager would do, the person being massaged would feel good because of the manipulation; however, if a human performed the massage, the recipient would feel good as well as cared for, important, valuable. I was given a short "Tragerizing" session and realize that it was the intimacy of the contact rather than the mere physical contact that was important to me.

I believe that the beneficial effects of Body Therapies are not completely explained by contact of body to body. In the case example, in Barry Green's excellent chapter, we find that the first five sessions were a kind of "icebreaker" through massage, but in the sixth conventional cognitive psychotherapy took over.

Instead of using this fact—that conventional psychotherapy eventually played a major part in Body Therapies—to negate the utility of Body Therapies, it should be recognized that perhaps they are important because they may defeat the common enemy all we therapists have—resistance. It may be that the laying on of hands works to break through the patient's resistance. If so, these body contacts have value.

Body Therapy is a process for creating a clarification of the body-mind-emotions-spirit through techniques applied to or learned by the body. Body Therapy encompasses both ancient Eastern traditions of spirituality and cosmology along with contemporary Western neuromuscular and myofascial systems of skeletostructural and neuro-skeleto reorganization. Body Therapy recognizes that the entire body is the vehicle for the perfect being that lies within all. This is the meaning of the Chinese concept *su wen* ("perfect channel")—when there is no trauma in the body or the psyche, then the Being that is the human birthright manifests itself. Body Therapy postulates that the traumas absorbed by the psyche from "false understanding" are simultaneously absorbed as traumas in specific areas of the body. Body Therapy works to facilitate clarification of these traumas through the use of physical manipulations, movement awareness training, energy-flow balancing, and emotional release techniques.

HISTORY

The history of Body Therapy dates back to the formation of Eastern culture. There are records of the ancient Chinese and Mongolians using body-oriented therapies for achieving physical and psychological well-being. Ancient Indians and Tibetans practiced numerous forms of "yogas" for the purification of the body-mind-emotions-spirit. The Japanese and Chinese developed the martial arts for both defense and for personal evolution of the inner self. These body-psyche disciplines and "yogas" such as tai chi, Zen, Taoism, Tantra, and samurai that have existed for more than 400 years are still an integral part of the societies and cultures from which they arose.

The Eastern traditions put forth the concept that the human being is a reflection, a mirror, of the cosmos. The macrocosm seen outside man is the same as the microcosm found inside of man. Just as the ancient scientists and sages plotted out the external natural phenomena, they also plotted out the internal natural phenomena. The Chinese described this internal map as the acupuncture system of energy paths known as meridians of *chi* energy. The Tibetans and Indians described another flow of internal energy they call *kundalini* that rose up in two channels on either side of the spine and activated focal points of body-psyche energy called *chakras*. All the ancient systems described the effects of balance or imbalance, flow or restriction; they all prescribed techniques, exercises, and therapeutic methods for achieving the optimal condition of body-mind-emotions-spirit. This optimal condition would achieve total harmony for the individual, total unity within himself and with his surroundings, nature. The ancients saw this optimal condition as the state of enlightenment, self-realization. They called this state *samahdi, nirvana,* the *tau,* and *fana.*

This concept as the body being the vehicle for the body-mind-emotions-spirit reached the West with the Hellenistic Greeks. "Sound mind, sound body" was the axiom for the Hellenistics. Though not as internally oriented as the Orientals, the Greeks paid homage to the body and its unity with the mind. The body was recognized as a part of the being until the coming of the Victorian era, when the body was viewed as being disgraceful. It was covered, considered immoral, and discarded as a vehicle for awareness and growth.

It was not until the age of science that the body was again used as a method for unifying the being. In the beginning of the twentieth century Wilhelm Reich observed that clinical patients with emotional disturbances all demonstrated severe postural distortions. His observations uncovered more connections between the body-psyche and led to the development of the Reichian school of Body Therapy. Reich's observations were the foundation for his system of character analysis and therapeutic method known as Vegetotherapy. The muscular holding patterns Reich called *character armor.* The armor was manifest in one or more of seven rings occurring in horizontal planes from the head to the pelvis. Every armored area blocked the flow of vital energy, or *orgone.* To break up the armoring would directly affect and change the neurotic character and body structure.

Following Reich came another pioneer in the field of Body Therapy, Moshe Feldenkrais. Feldenkrais postulated that the human organism began its process of growth and learning with only one built-in response, the "fear of falling." All other physical and emotional responses were learned as the human organism grew and explored. As the child grew he learned how to function physically and learned any concomitant emotions that accompanied the event or the physical learning. As Feldenkrais (1949) stated:

> Thus many of our failings both physical and mental need not be considered as diseases to be cured, or as unfortunate traits of character. They are acquired from faulty learning. Actions repeated habitually for a number of years mold even the bones. (p. 152)

To attain the full potential of the body-mind-emotions-spirit there must be, according to Feldenkrais (1949), "re-education of the kinesthetic sense and resetting of it to the normal course of self adjusting improvement of all muscular activity" (p. 155). This would "directly improve breathing, digestion, and the sympathetic and parasympathetic balance, as well as the sexual function, all linked together with the emotional experience" (p. 156). For Feldenkrais, reeducation of the body and its functioning was the essence for creating unity of the being.

Following the work of Reich and Feldenkrais came the contemporary schools and systems of Body Therapy. These include the deep fascial tissue manipulations performed by those of the Rolf school, the emotional release work of Primal Therapy and Rebirthing, and the movement work of Matthias Alexander, Judith Aston, Milton Trager, and Oscar Aguado.

CURRENT STATUS

Body Therapies are now a rapidly growing system. There are an indeterminate number of practitioners in the varying special schools and combined approaches. What was once a New Age approach to health and well-being of the body-psyche is now becoming a part of the mainstream. Rolfing has become a nationally known system; the Eastern body-psyche disciplines such as yoga, aikido, and tai chi chuan are increasingly more popular; and acupuncture is now a part of many Western medical practices.

Many schools of varying size and prominence exist, as well as many publications in the four areas of Body Therapy: physical manipulation, movement awareness training, energy-flow balancing, and emotional release techniques. This chapter will describe the current status of some of the major institutes in these four areas.

In the area of physical manipulations, the Rolf Institute operates its only training facility out of Boulder, Colorado. The Rolf process has been described in the two books by Ida Rolf, *Rolfing* (1977) and *Ida Rolf Speaks* (1978) and in Don Johnson's book, *The Protean Body* (1977). A quarterly bulletin, *The Bulletin of Structural Integration,* is available along with cassettes, films, and magazine reprints from the Rolf Institute. Other schools offering deep tissue physical manipulations are Postural Integration, the Soma Institute, Orthasomatics, the Institute of Psycho-Structural Balancing, the Lomi School, and the Arica Institute, Inc.

In the area of movement awareness training, the Feldenkrais technique has approximately 75 practitioners trained by Moshe Feldenkrais. The theoretical foundations of the work are explained in Feldenkrais's book, *Body and Mature Behavior* (1949), and techniques of the system are given in his *Awareness Through Movement* (1972). Other publications include *The Case of Nora* by Feldenkrais (1977), and *Somatics Magazine.* The main school is located in Israel; the American branch, the Feldenkrais Guild, is located in San Francisco. For information about trainings or certified practitioners, contact the Trager Association. The Aguado system of movement awareness, known as "the form," is taught by Oscar Aguado and a small staff of qualified teachers at various locations throughout the country. Teacher training began in the fall of 1980. Two books co-authored by Aguado are available, *The Form* (1977) and *Gravity, the Nether Side of Paradise* (1978).

In the area of energy-flow balancing, two of the major schools associated with Chinese and Indian systems of energy balancing are the New England School of Acupuncture and the Polarity Institute—Alive Fellowship. In this country, the oldest licensed school teaching Chinese systems of energy balancing is the New England School of Acupuncture. The Indian system of energy balancing is taught by the Polarity Institute—Alive Fellowship. The fellowship offers residential programs of one, seven, and nine weeks along with individual and group trainings in Santa Barbara, San Francisco, and Seattle. The fellowship utilizes the three main works of its founder, Dr. Randall Stone: The *Energy, Vitality Balance,* and *Polarity Therapy.*

In the area of emotional release the International Bioenergetics Institute, with its headquarters in New York City, lists many certified practitioners. Besides the main headquarters, numerous training facilities are located throughout the country and abroad. Numerous books on Bioenergetics have been published by Alexander Lowen. These include *Bioenergetics* (1975a), *Depression and the Body* (1972), *The Language of the Body* (1958), *Pleasure* (1970), *The Betrayal of the Body* (1969), and *Love and Orgasm* (1975b). Another method of emotional release is the Rebirthing process. The Theta House of San Francisco offers Rebirthing training at three levels. Rebirthing is described in the work of Leonard Orr and Sandra Ray, *Rebirthing in the New Age* (1977).

In addition to the various training courses listed above, a state-approved degree program emphasizing Body Therapy is now available through the University for Humanistic Studies in San Diego. This program meets the marriage, family, and child counseling license requirements for the state of California. This program is held in conjunction with the Institute of Psycho-Structural Balancing, also in San Diego.

THEORY

The following theory of personality is taken from the eclectic Body Psychology program known as Psycho-Structural Balancing, taught by the writer. Psycho-Structural Balancing recognizes personality as the development of ego states from the initial state of pure essence. According to the Eastern traditions, at approx-

imately the seventh month of gestation, the spirit (the essence, the soul, the divine) enters into the organism and the human being is present. In this state there is total bliss, total purity, no ego, no negativity, no personality. In this state the new being repeats internally the sound *so' ham,* a mantric repetition that means "That I am" (Muktananda, 1978). As birth occurs, the new being begins to repeat internally another mantric phrase, *ko ham,* which means "Who am I?" Now out of the womb and into the world, the baby begins a learning process to discover its identity. Continually repeating its internal mantric phrase, *ko ham,* it seeks through experience to learn how to do, how to love, and how to be. Having no predetermined patterns or knowledge, it adopts from external inputs. Mainly these external inputs come from the two main role models, mother and father.

Let us stop at this point and reconstruct the above graphically. As the spirit enters the new baby, it achieves that state of pure awareness and bliss and declares "That" to itself as it repeats internally "So' ham," "That I am." This we consider the state of essence, pure being. We will call this Level 1 and represent it as pure diamond. (See Figure 6.1.)

As birth occurs, the new baby changes its internal mantric phrase and asks, "*Ko ham?*" "Who am I?" Here it begins a learning process, taking in information from, in the early years, the key role models, mother and father. If the parents are blessed with clarity, purity, and unconditional, real love, then the child remains in Level 1, the state of pure being. If the parents pass on wrong understanding and negative love to the child, then the child develops another system of being that we call Level 2, shown as encircling the diamond level. (See Figure 6.2.)

Level 2 begins to cover the diamond level with false knowledge and negative love. False knowledge we will call the ego states, the *maya* or illusions of reality. Negative love is the ego love, such as giving to get, or "seesaw"

Figure 6.1

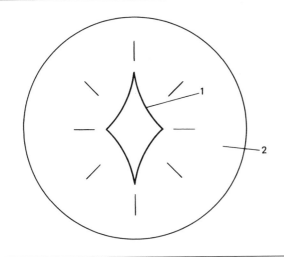

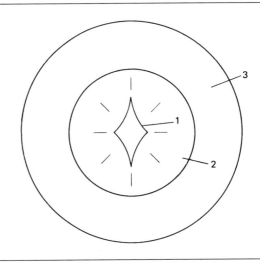

Figure 6.2

Figure 6.3

love (I love you, I hate you, I love you . . .) or guilt-motivated love. The child, in its need for love and acceptance, adopts the patterns and traits of the parents and/or surrogates. When these patterns and traits are not "true knowledge," *viveka* in the Indian terminology, the child develops a second layer that is the state of the ego personality, Level 2. The ego begins to cover the essence, to hide and obscure it from awareness. As the false knowledge is acquired, it creates a trauma in the psyche, and at the same time it creates a concomitant trauma in the body. The trauma is stored in the psyche as the Level 2 state of being, and it is stored in the body as tension and blockage of the flow of life energy.

The maps of "body psychology" have given correlations of which area of the body stores the different emotional traumas. For instance, the Arica Chua K'a map describes the knees as storing the fear of death and the perineum storing the fear of insecurity. Thus as the false knowledge creates a trauma in the psyche, it creates a corresponding trauma in the body.

To summarize Level 2, as the new being enters the world at birth it is not certain of who it is, it is not certain of its birthright, its essential being. The child has lost contact with the true knowledge of the mantra "*So' ham,*" "That I am." As it enters the world it asks, "Who am I?" As the child questions and receives answers, all of the false knowledge causes trauma in the psyche and the body, and the ego personality begins to develop and operate. This is the level of all the negative traits, programs, and admonitions that are basically imprinted from the mother and father.

The final level of personality is the social front, or the second ego personality level. Graphically this is a second ring around the diamond. (See Figure 6.3.) This level begins to develop between the ages of four and seven. Here the child realizes that the negativity of Level 2 is socially unacceptable and adopts a social front, a mask to cover the negativity.

Thus the personality is a process of learning and adapting the learned negative traits. To change is not to get better. In this model divine perfection is always present, but it is covered, hidden by layers of wrong understanding, negativity. Each person needs to be in the state of Level 1, the level of the diamond. All the clarity, brilliance, radiance, strength, beauty, and preciousness of the being is there in the diamond level. Remove the obstacles, the blocks in the psyche and the body, and the diamond being that lies within will be present and manifest. There will then be no blocks in the psyche; pure love and pure wisdom will manifest. There will then be no blocks in the body; pure energy will manifest.

METHODOLOGY

This section gives a brief description of four categories of Body Therapy methods and then focuses on this writer's eclectic system.

The four systems include physical manipulation systems, such as the connective tissue work of the Rolf school, and the deep tissue release systems, such as the Arica Chua K'a; energy-balancing systems, such as Chinese Acupuncture and Acupressure, Polarity, and Jin Shin Jystu; emotional release systems, such as Bioenergetics, Primal, and Rebirthing; and movement awareness systems, such as Aston, Feldenkrais, Trager, and Aguado. Many of the systems overlap and encompass aspects of the others. The categorization is based on the main feature of the method.

Under the aspect of physical manipulation, a number

of systems, including the school of Ida Rolf, employ connective tissue manipulation to posturally reintegrate and align the body. In a typical format the client undergoes a series of sessions, each lasting approximately one hour, in which the practitioner uses his or her fingers, knuckles, fist, or elbows to stretch, lengthen, separate, and organize the connective tissue planes of the body. The practitioner has the client move various areas as the stroke or pressure is applied. This assures that the intergration and organization occurs at a functional as well as a static level. The connective tissues being worked with are the fascial tissue, the encasing tissue of the various muscles, muscle groups, and compartments of the entire body. The other major form of therapeutic physical manipulation focuses on the muscle tissue. As the muscle tissue experiences trauma, it binds up and develops waste deposits within the tissue. Through the application of direct compression or by deep strokes, the tissue can be opened and the particles broken up to be removed by the blood flow. The practitioner applies pressure with the hand, fingers, knuckles, fist, elbow, and feet to accomplish the release of tension and holding patterns.

The energy-balancing systems recognize various patterns of energy flow in the body and seek to balance and harmonize these flows. The Oriental systems, such as Acupuncture and Jin Shyn, use the system of 12 major pathways called *meridians* with trigger points located on those pathways, the acupuncture points. These and other systems based on the meridians test for the excess or deficiency of energy in each of the major pathways. They then utilize various techniques to balance each meridian and the entire system of meridians. The meridians can be tested by reading the 12 different pulses located above the radial artery of both wrists, testing the strength of various muscle groups associated with each meridian, and checking correspondences to the Chinese Five Element Theory. These correspondences include the client's preference in tastes, colors, weather, time of day, emotional condition, sound of voice, and so forth. When the imbalances are determined, the practitioner manipulates the various points separately or in combination to balance the meridian flows. This manipulation can consist of the use of needles, sound, heat, color, moxabustion (burning of an herb near the point), or hands to create a circuit, or flow, between two points. The Indian systems such as Polarity and Arica Vortex work with another set of energy channels. These channels include the different levels of the body, such as the gross, the subtle, and the astral, and the psychic channels of the body, the *nadis.* The Vortex system presses on various pressure points that open up the flow in the *nadis,* and the Polarity system holds areas of the body to promote a flow or circuit.

The emotional release systems such as Bioenergetics, Primal, and Rebirthing utilize control of breath to promote an emotional release. Often the practitioner will also apply pressure to different areas of the body to facilitate the emotional release, such as on the sides of the neck or throat. The Bioenergetics system utilizes different exercises or movements to facilitate an opening of one or more areas. The Primal system may utilize an acting-out, or psychodrama, approach to facilitate emotional release. And the Rebirthing method utilizes immersion in water to simulate the womb for promoting emotional release.

The movement awareness systems work with reeducating the body and the nervous system. All involve various movements, both gentle and conscious, to allow an experience of correct body functioning. The Trager system utilizes gentle shaking, stretching, and rocking to allow a release and a relearning. In the Feldenkrais system, which is a training, educational system, there is no hands-on application by the practitioner or the trainer; it is also a client system, with the practitioner performing the subtle movements. The Aston and the Aguado systems are also training systems wherein the client is taught correct movement. The Aguado system differs from the previously described systems in that it is a dance form as well as a movement awareness system. In all the systems the new knowledge releases the old patterns of physical and emotional learning and replaces them with right functioning of the body and psyche.

The following is a detailed description of an eclectic system of Body Therapy, Psycho-Structural Balancing, taught and practiced by the writer. Basically the system is designed to clarify and open the body-psyche so that the image and concept of a "clear channel" is present.

Physically this means relating to the body as a mechanical structure and as a living system of energy. As a mechanical structure the body is seen as the skeletal frame supporting, moving, and protecting the life support systems within. The body is evaluated for proper gravitational alignment, and the joints are checked for freedom and range of movement, elasticity, binding, and material buildup. Also evaluated are the relative proportions of body parts, that is, shin to thigh, limbs to torso, head to body, top to bottom portions of body, front to back, and so on. The other major evaluation of the physical body is intrinsic to extrinsic. This is checking the balance between the deep subtle movers of the skeleton and the gross external movers of the skeleton. Evaluation of the final extrinsic layer of the body, the skin, also occurs.

The body is then evaluated for its organization and development of three major areas relating to body-mind connections. The first area is the legs and pelvis, from the feet to the solar plexus. This area is important to the concept of being connected to the ground. The pelvis is the foundation upon which the support system, the legs, is attached. The practitioner utilizes an appropriate combination of physical manipulations and/or movement awareness systems to release the holding patterns in the belly, pelvis, and legs to achieve a self-supporting lower center. This could include techniques from the circulatory massage systems, such as Swedish or Esalen; deep tissue compression releases, such as the Arica Chua K'a; fascial tissue releases, such as the Ida Rolf system; skin releases, such as the Arica techniques; martial arts exercises, such as from tai chi; and movement awareness techniques, such as from Feldenkrais, Trager, Aguado, or Trepidations.

The second area relates to the chest and diaphragm regions, including the arms and shoulder girdle. This is seen as the area involved with reaching out and connecting with the world. The ability to fully breathe and have full and free movement of the arms and shoulders is the goal of working with this area. Along with the previously mentioned techniques would be Arica Psychocalisthenics, deep breathing exercises, and chanting.

The third area relates to the head and shoulders. This area corresponds to the proper plane of physical reference for the head, or intellect. The metaphor of having one's head sit squarely on one's shoulders applies. All of the aforementioned technologies for manipulations apply to this area.

Methodology for dealing with the psyche includes discharging the trauma, the emotional charge, by understanding how the false knowledge was learned and then replacing the false knowledge with "right understanding." Understanding how the false knowledge was acquired is the first step. This requires a remembering of the event(s) in which the pattern and programs were learned. A memory of the first learning of the trait is the desired goal. Then the release of the emotional charge is facilitated. The breathing releases from Primal and Rebirthing processes are used along with verbal facilitation. When the recollection of the learning process and the discharge of the trauma associated with the trait are accomplished, the client replaces the false knowledge with its opposite, right understanding. This is done through the writing of the affirmative opposite that corresponds to the negative pattern. A self-support regime is developed so that the client can be aware of when the negative trait is operating, can witness without the emotional charge formerly associated with the trait the mind as it brings the trait up. The final operation is a remembering of the basic goal of the process, the right understanding of the diamond state, the "I am That" awareness. For example, should the trait "You'll never make anything of yourself" come up, the process would be for the client to understand that this is the pattern operating, remember where the pattern came from (father repeated it from ages 4 to 20), and to then focus on the awareness of "I am not that," but rather "I am That," "I am a reflection of That which created me"—that is, "Who I am is always perfect." The connecting of the body and the

psyche occurs by having the client prepare for each of the coming sessions. The client is informed at the end of each session what the next session will deal with in the body and psyche. Clients should spend the time between sessions recalling their childhood and the earliest occurrences of negative programs associated with the area to be worked on. Then at the beginning of the session they can give feedback on their memory and report their feelings. From there the physical manipulations and/or movement awareness work proceeds. If emotions begin to surface during the course of the physical work, the practitioner facilitates their release. At the end of the session the practitioner and client discuss what has occurred, and the practitioner suggests exercises, breathing, meditation, or a combination of these to enhance further opening and/or maintenance of the area. Along with work on the specific areas, a regular regimen of conscious exercises, such as Arica Psychocalisthentics, tai chi, Feldenkrais, Aguado, or yoga, plus meditation and chanting, is recommended for the positive nourishment and growth of the body and psyche.

APPLICATIONS

The systems of Body Therapy are applicable to those who are willing to undergo the process. With voluntary acceptance, Body Therapy is applicable to all. Many practitioners in the different schools of Body Therapy deal with the incurably ill, the psychotic and mentally disturbed, alcoholics, the elderly, and infants. Yet the largest area of participants in Body Therapy are not in the high-pathology categories. Up to this time, most people seek Body Therapy as a self-development process.

Body Therapy is especially dynamic and recommended when mental therapies are at an impasse, for it is very powerful in creating movement and opening in the psyche. The deep physical manipulation systems and the emotional release systems are suggested for this purpose. However, those with heart conditions are excluded from these two Body Therapy systems. Those with heart conditions can benefit from the energy-flow systems, such as acupuncture, Polarity, Jin Shyn, or Arica Vortex. All of the systems directly relate to the cause of the impasse, and work to break up the blockage and restore the flow of energy to the psyche and the body.

Depression, despair, rage, and anger are worked with dynamically in the emotional release systems, the deep body manipulations, and the energy-flow systems. Discharging the emotional energy around these conditions can often bring immediate relief and resolution.

Since the therapist and the client are in physical contact with each other, Body Therapy is especially applicable for those needing to be touched lovingly. This holds true particularly in the system of Rebirthing and the hands-on movement awareness systems such as Trager, Alexander, or the table work of Feldenkrais.

As already mentioned, for someone to receive full benefit from the Body Therapy, he or she must accept the treatment voluntarily. The psyche must be willing to change. Without the permission of the psyche, the body will not be receptive. This is not to say that results will not occur. They will. Work such as the Rolfing process or the Acupuncture system will definitely have an effect without total agreement from the client. Yet the full effectiveness will be a function of the psyche and the body opening, receiving, and desiring to change.

This writer believes that when the obstacles of creditability are removed from the professional community of psychology, Body Therapy will be as widely utilized as the Freudian slip. It is direct, effective, immediate, long lasting, and grounded in the sciences of anatomy, physiology, spirituality, and mechanics.

CASE EXAMPLE

The following is a case history of a male, X. X participated in 20 sessions over an eight-month period. The first eight sessions focused primarily on deep tissue physical manipulations; the remaining 12 combined physical tissue work with emotional release and processing work.

X was 32 at the time of therapy. He was employed as a night-shift security officer. X was 6 feet 3 inches tall, 225 pounds, and considerably top-heavy. His postural deviations included a collapsed chest, head pushed forward, lordosis, holding in the right quadratus lumborum, holding in the gluteals and rotators of the femur, holding across the groin and pubis, lack of skeletal support from the legs, and elevation of the left shoulder. Movement at the pelvis and hip socket was severely limited. X described his energy level as "very low," and he had difficulty relaxing. Sexually, X's energy had been decreasing, and he had difficulty with maintaining an erection. X was in a period of "confusion, disorientation, and stuck." Relations were reported as "sour" with both friends and lovers. His work environment created an attitude of hostility. He reported frequent use of drugs and alcohol. Fear of others' judgment, criticism, and general paranoia were also reported. Insecurity was often reported during session feedback, along with accompanying frustration.

X's family history included a violent, alcoholic father in the law enforcement field. The father, self-righteous, highly judgmental, critical, and lacking in sensitivity or warmth, administered numerous physical beatings along with verbal abuse. The mother was physically absent, occupied with work. She was permissive to the ex-treme, in contrast to the father's rigid, authoritarian discipline. The older sister was physically and mentally antagonistic. X had few friends and was often harassed by peers and elders. He did poorly in school and operated in a fantasy world through adolescence, wanting escape.

The first five sessions of therapy dealt with opening the physical blocks and increasing the flow of energy and vitality. The Chinese Acupuncture meridians were evaluated through pulse reading, muscle testing, and the Five Element Theory correspondences. Acupuncture points and reflex points were palpated to increase energy flow and balance. These five sessions also included deep tissue release and strokes in the chest, feet and legs, pelvis, lumbar, and back areas.

In Session 6 specific work with negative programs and traits began. In this session X reported decisions to stop alcohol and drug abuse and that he had given notice of his resignation from work. He reported awareness of and dissatisfaction with role playing along with more physical strength and vitality. He expressed a desire to take care of himself and that his attitudes were changing. The diamond and two levels of ego personality were described to X. Deeper physical work was begun, including the abdomen and ribs.

Sessions 7 and 8 focused on negative childhood programming. X brought to the sessions memories of how traits were taught along with how he demonstrated these same traits in his adult life. X was aware of his adoption of his father's self-destructive traits and hostilities, as well as of his adoption of his mother's "poor me" martyrdom. More deep tissue work was done, along with skin "rolling," consisting of a lifting and rolling of the skin. Though X squirmed and winced, he did not vocalize. The *Om* mantra was suggested for daily practice.

It was then agreed that a period of assimilation would occur. X returned to therapy eight weeks later. At this time it was agreed that more work with the psyche was necessary. For the following 12 weeks X remembered scenes from childhood dealing with his major negative emotional traits that corresponded to his major body tension patterns. He wrote out the traits and scenes from childhood that demonstrated how he learned the traits. He then compared his childhood programming with his adult behavior. This created awareness of his adoption of the traits. Several of the sessions dealt with use of psychodrama for the release of the emotional charge. Throughout the 12 weeks X was on a daily routine of tai chi chuan, Arica Psychocalisthenics, meditation on the *Hamsa* mantra, and chanting of the *Om Namah Shivaya* mantra. Besides the two psychodrama sessions for releasing anger, there were also two primal-type emotional release sessions that included deep tissue work to encourage emotional release. After release of the anger and resentment, X went through a process of recycling the negative emotional traits into positive affirmations. He then examined how he could be his own positive "parent" and nourish himself and his psyche with positivity.

Male X has stopped his use of drugs and alcohol to anesthetize his emotions. He has broken off with a previous circle of friends and is involving himself with nourishing relationships. Currently in a master's level university program in order to acquire skills for a professional career, he has begun a search for work that is satisfying and nourishing financially, physically, and emotionally. He has created a routine of maintenance for his body and psyche and is vital and enthusiastic about his future.

X has greatly diminished his tendency to "head trip" and now expresses his emotional reactions more openly. The physical blockage at the pelvis has noticeably opened, as demonstrated by X's ability to maintain a half-lotus sitting posture, formerly an unbearable task.

SUMMARY

The writer believes that Body Therapies contribute many unique features and benefits to the field of psychotherapy. To begin with, Body Therapies seek to integrate the body-mind-emotions-spirit, dealing with each aspect as well as the whole being. This is particularly true in the holistic systems of Body Therapy such as Psycho-Structural Balancing, Polarity, and Acupuncture. These holistic systems believe that the health and well-being of the individual is a function of the health and well-being of the balanced body-mind-emotions-spirit, not just the elimination of psychopathological traits. Just as an iceberg shows only a fraction of its total, the holistic Body Therapies believe that the psychological and/or emotional pathologies and imbalances are only a symptom or part of the entire problem and imbalance. Thus I believe that the Body Therapies are a more thorough and complete process for the achievement of well-being and realization of the human potential.

The second aspect that Body Therapies contribute to the field is the principle and concept of energy. Acupuncture and the energy-flow systems most utilize this concept. Einstein proved to the Western world what the Eastern world had known for thousands of years: Energy and matter are interchangeable. The body is energy manifesting as matter. Emotions are energy, the mind is energy, the spirit is energy. Energy can be worked with. It can be measured and correlated, as in the Acupuncture and Five Element Theory work. Thus in the Body Therapy systems the various disciplines often utilize the principles of energy (the modern quantum ideas) for dealing with the achievement of well-being. Though this perhaps ventures into the field of parapsychology, I believe that

this dealing directly with the *prima mater* of life, the very energies that make up our being, is a powerful contribution to the field. The insertion of an acupuncture needle to balance a flow of energy, the connecting of two energy-flow points with the hands, the releasing of an emotionally charged tension pattern in the body—all these are powerful and direct methods of facilitating the growth and therapy process.

This leads into the aspect that is perhaps the most powerful contribution of the Body Therapies. The Body Therapies are very direct, producing immediate and often dramatic results. The outcomes of Rolfing, Primal Therapy, Rebirthing, Bioenergetics, and others certainly attest to this. Additionally, the duration of the Body Therapy systems is relatively short. Very few body system treatments continue for as long as a year.

The last factor is probably the most significant feature of Body Therapies; the therapists place their hands on the body. The act of touching is sorely lacking in many therapies, but it is the mainstay of most body systems. This direct connection, the act of touching, in whatever modality or approach it may take, may be the ingredient that leads to the wonders of the personal unfolding.

REFERENCES

Aguado, O., & Zucker, D. (1977). *The form.* South Laguna, CA: The School of the Form.

Aguado, O., & Zucker, D. (1978). *Gravity, the nether side of paradise.* South Laguna, CA: The School of the Form.

Connelly, D. (1975). *Traditional Acupuncture, the law of the five elements.* Columbia, MD: The Center for Traditional Acupuncture.

Dychtwald, K. (1978). *Body-mind.* New York: Jove.

Feldenkrais, M. (1949). *Body and mature behavior.* New York: International Universities Press.

Feldenkrais, M. (1972). *Awareness through movement.* New York: Harper & Row.

Feldenkrais, M. (1977). *The case of Nora.* New York: Harper & Row.

Ichazo, O. (1976). *Arica psychocalisthenics.* New York: Simon & Schuster.

Johnson, D. (1977). *The protean body.* New York: Harper & Row.

Kurtz, R., & Prestera, H. (1976). *The body reveals.* New York: Harper & Row.

Lowen, A. (1958). *The language of the body.* New York: Collier.

Lowen, A. (1969). *The Betrayal of the Body.* New York: Collier.

Lowen, A. (1970). *Pleasure.* New York: Penguin.

Lowen, A. (1972). *Depression and the body.* New York: Pelican.

Lowen, A. (1975a). *Bioenergetics.* New York: Penguin.

Lowen, A. (1975b). *Love and Orgasm.* New York: Collier.

Mann, W. E. (1973). *Orgone Reich and eros.* New York: Simon & Schuster.

Muktananda, S. (1978). *I am that.* Oakland, CA: S.Y.D.A. Foundation.

Orr, L. & Ray, S. (1977). *Rebirthing in the New Age.* Millbrae, CA: Celestial Arts.

Reich, W. (1949). *Character analysis.* New York: Orgone Institute Press.

Rolf, I. (1977). *Rolfing.* Santa Monica, CA: Dennis Landman.

Rolf, I. (1978). *Ida Rolf speaks.* New York: Harper & Row.

So, J. T. Y. *A complete course in acupuncture* (Vols. 1–3). Unpublished manuscript.

Stone, R. *Energy.* Unlisted.

Stone, R. *Vitality balance.* Unlisted.

Stone, R. *Polarity therapy.* Unlisted.

Chapter 7

BRIEF PSYCHODYNAMIC THERAPY

STANLEY B. MESSER and C. SETH WARREN

It is likely that psychoanalysis has had more print space than all other forms of psychotherapy combined. In this adaptation, therapy is made time-efficient in part by preestablishing a time limit. Sigmund Freud might have considered brief psychodynamic therapy "wild psychoanalysis" in that it calls for much more active participation of the therapist, early decision about the problem and the setting of goals—all elements eschewed in classical psychoanalysis. The authors' formulations depend in part on the thinking of Otto Rank, Sandor Ferenczi, and Franz Alexander who unlike Freud allowed for much more interaction between therapist and patient.

INTRODUCTION

Brief Psychodynamic Therapy (BPT) applies the principles of psychoanalytic theory and therapy to the treatment of selected disorders, typically within a time frame of 10 to 25 sessions. A time limit is usually determined at the outset of therapy that sets in motion psychological expectancies regarding when change is likely to occur. In this way, BPT takes advantage of Parkinson's Law that completion of a task is a function of the time allotted to it. BPT employs major concepts of psychoanalytic theory to understand clients, including the enduring importance and impact of psychosexual, psychosocial, and object relational stages of development; the existence of unconscious cognitive, emotional, and motivational processes; and the reenactment in the client's relationship to the therapist of emotion-laden issues from the past.

Principal techniques include reflection, clarification, interpretation, and confrontation of maladaptive interpersonal patterns, impulses, conflicts, and defenses along the axes of the "triangle of insight." This triangle consists of the interpersonal context of (1) important current figures in the client's life, (2) the transference, or perceived relationship to the therapist, and (3) childhood relationships, typically with parents and siblings. Links are made connecting various combinations of past, present, and transferential relationships. In addition to enhancing insight, the therapy provides a corrective emotional experience in which old and current traumas, "shameful" secrets, and other warded-off feelings and memories are brought to light in the benign pres-

ence of the therapist. In the broadest sense it is the therapist's creation of a caring, empathically attuned relationship that allows therapy to bring about insight, healing, and growth in a receptive client.

BPT involves more active dialogue and challenge than long-term psychoanalytic therapy. There is an early formulation of a therapeutic focus that is expressed in psychodynamic terms, such as core intrapsychic conflicts, maladaptive interpersonal patterns, or chronically endured psychic pain. Feelings that arise around termination, such as sadness, guilt, anxiety, and anger, receive special attention. Possible goals might include conflict resolution, a changed interpersonal pattern, greater access to feelings, more freedom of choice, as well as symptom remission.

HISTORY

Sigmund Freud

As with all matters psychoanalytic, the history of brief therapy starts with Freud. We know that Freud's treatments tended to be short by today's standards, rarely lasting more than a year. He also conducted some very brief treatments, notably with the conductor Bruno Walter for a partial paralysis of his right arm (six sessions), and with Gustav Mahler for impotence (one four-hour session). Originally Freud relied on the cathartic method designed to release strangulated affect attached to traumatic memories. This involved a frontal attack on the resistance, a technique still employed in those current brief dynamic therapies derived from Freud's drive/structural theory. Freud eventually abandoned the cathartic method in favor of free association in order to foster the development of a transference neurosis in which the patient's thoughts and feelings are directed to the analyst. With this change, the therapist became less active, less challenging, and less focused, thus ending the early version of Freudian brief therapy.

Otto Rank

There were psychoanalysts, however, who were impatient with Freud's turn to the passivity of the free association method and who introduced ideas subsequently incorporated into modern brief treatments. Chief among these were Otto Rank and Sandor Ferenczi. Rank (1929/1978) posited that we constantly move between emotional attachment and dependency, on one hand, and the opposite pole of separation and independence, on the other. Human beings are driven not just by a fear of attachment and separation, but by the will to individuate, grow, and develop. Rather than viewing resistance as the force arrayed against patients' own experiencing and understanding, Rank saw it as their unwillingness to accept the assertion of the therapist's will against their own. His objective was to free his patients by allowing them the experience of "willing" in therapy, and in this way becoming more responsible for themselves.

Rank advocated an emphasis on the present experience of the relationship rather than on past events; on the transference as an effort to reestablish the biological tie to the mother rather than its sexual manifestations; and the setting of an announced endpoint to therapy as opposed to allowing an open-ended venture. He encouraged the expression of feelings in the interaction with the therapist, as well as an analysis of patients' wish to deny and avoid them.

The most obvious link of Rank's innovations is to James Mann's time-limited psychotherapy. Like Rank, Mann (1973, 1991) emphasizes the process of engagement, attachment, and eventual loss, through which the patient learns to deal with separation from an ambivalently loved object. Oedipal issues are not at the forefront as they are for the drive/structural therapists who follow Freud. To promote this focus, Mann sets a time limit from the start so that the necessity for separation serves continuously as a catalyzing background factor. Like Rank, he regards time-limited therapy, for at least some patients, as the treatment of choice insofar as it requires them to deal with the dread of time and its implications for loss.

Sandor Ferenczi

Ferenczi (1921/1980) also objected to psychoanalysts' increasing passivity and their excessive reliance on intellectual explanations of associations, dreams, symptoms, and complexes. To aid the recovery of memory he advocated provoking affective experience in the transference, either through frustration or gratification. He encouraged patients to face their phobic objects or situations in order to mobilize anxiety, which could then be analyzed. To expose their unconscious conflicts, he also had patients fantasize about specific topics—akin to maintaining a focus. The purpose of these maneuvers was to enhance the emotional experience of psychoanalysis, leading to a briefer therapy. Modern brief dynamic psychotherapies can be viewed as continuing the work of Ferenczi. The high level of emotional involvement through therapist activity and the guiding of patient associations along the lines of a focus clearly characterize current approaches. Ferenczi and Rank (1925/1986) also had in mind the potential utility of combining techniques from different psychotherapies, a precursor to the eclectic and integrative brief therapies of today.

Franz Alexander

Best known among Alexander's concepts is the *corrective emotional experience,* which shifts the balance of curative elements of psychoanalysis from insight, based on interpretations, to the re-experiencing of emotional conflicts in the therapeutic relationship. Alexander and French (1946) wrote:

> Because the therapist's attitude is different from that of the authoritative person of the past, he gives the patient an opportunity to face again and again, under more favorable circumstances, those emotional situations which were formerly unbearable and to deal with them in a manner different from the old. (p. 67)

More important than the similarity between the venue of the old conflict and the transference situation, said Alexander, were their differences, in which lay the therapeutic value of the analytic procedure.

In retrospect, it is apparent that Alexander—and Ferenczi and Rank before him—presaged a shift from Freud's one-person, intrapsychically oriented psychology to the two-person psychology of modern psychoanalytic schools, especially object relations and interpersonal psychoanalysis. Although they did not articulate it as such, these pioneers were shifting from the intrapsychic, drive-oriented emphasis of Freudian psychoanalysis to the more relational, interpersonal psychology developed by Balint, Guntrip, Fairbairn, Winnicott, and Bowlby in England, and Sullivan, Thompson, Fromm, and Fromm-Reichmann in America (Aron, 1990; Mitchell, 1984).

Consider, in this connection, the concept of transference. In the Freudian view, it takes place in the mind of the analysand undistorted by the personality of the analyst, who is technically neutral and anonymous. This is so even if it unfolds in the presence of the analyst: It is an intrapsychic phenomenon. In the relational view, transference unfolds in relation to the personality and behavior of the analyst and the patient's associations are, in part, determined by them. It is an interpersonal phenomenon. The time-limited dynamic psychotherapy of Strupp and Binder (1984) for example, illustrates the way in which the patient reacts to the current behavior rather than to the silence or shadowy presence of the therapist, and how this becomes fodder for examination of their developing relationship and its problems.

The commonality between Alexander and the modern relational therapies lies in their emphasis on the patient's real experience of the therapist. By highlighting the centrality of that relationship for the patient's improvement, Alexander was setting the stage for viewing the relationship as other than a projection screen for patients' fantasies of the therapist. Ferenczi's experiments with gratifying or frustrating patients, and Rank's stress on patients' working out their separation/individuation problems with the therapist, pointed in a similar direction.

Alexander also stressed the need to formulate a comprehensive dynamic understanding of the patient in the first few interviews and to use it to plan the treatment. Goals should be established from the outset and potential complications anticipated. He also warned against promoting dependency in the patient by allowing regression beyond the point of origin of the problem. To prevent such undue dependency, and what he viewed as the unnecessarily long analyses of the time, he proposed that treatment be interrupted for time periods to allow the patient to actively work on life problems. His stated intention was to make therapy as brief as possible.

Recent History

Freud, Ferenczi, Rank, and Alexander, whose work was carried out in the first half of the twentieth century, have been referred to as the first generation of brief dynamic therapists (Crits-Christoph, Barber, & Kurcias, 1991). Starting in the 1960s, three psychiatrists—David Malan (1963), Habib Davanloo (1978), and Peter Sifneos (1972), working in London, Montreal, and Boston, respectively—established a foothold for brief dynamic therapy based on traditional models of drive/defense constellations and their confrontation by the therapist. These clinicians, who constituted the second generation, all worked in public clinics. Consequently, they recognized the pressing need for brief therapy and were willing to swim upstream against the prevailing view that psychoanalytically based therapy, to be effective, required several sessions a week over a long time period.

(Malan's work took off from the approach to brief therapy started by Michael Balint at London's Tavistock clinic.) Their therapies were emotionally intensive, highly confrontative, and often Freudian in their embrace of Oedipal pathology. They established selection criteria, which were fairly restrictive, and the need for a psychodynamically based focus. Patient responses to trial interpretations offered in the initial sessions were an important selection criterion.

Another figure who constituted part of this generation was James Mann (1973). Although he, too, was influenced by the drive/structural theory, he incorporated object relations and developmental theory into his time-limited treatment. Under the topic of object relations, he stressed the impact of environmental failure on psychopathology, including deprivation and loss. The developmental issue of separation/individuation and the related factor of time became cornerstones of his strictly time-limited 12-session therapy. Thus, it was particularly in the termination phase of therapy that issues of loss, separation, sadness, and anger were taken up and related to a central issue or focus discussed at the outset with the patient.

All of these therapies continue to be practiced and taught even while therapists of a third generation have developed treatments that reflect ongoing changes in psychoanalytic theory and practice. In our book, *Models of Brief Psychodynamic Therapy* (Messer & Warren, 1995), we referred to them as following the relational model characterized by Mitchell (1988) as follows:

> We are portrayed not as a conglomeration of physically based urges, but as being shaped by and inevitably embedded within a matrix of relationships with other people, struggling both to maintain our ties to others and to differentiate ourselves from them. In this vision the basic unit of study is not the individual as a separate entity whose desires clash with an external reality, but an interactional field within which the individual arises and struggles to make contact and to articulate himself. (p. 3)

Four prominent dynamic therapies that we see as representative of this model are (1) the supportive-expressive psychotherapy of Lester Luborsky and the Penn Psychotherapy Project; (2) the short-term dynamic model of Mardi Horowitz and the Center for the Study of Neuroses; (3) the control-mastery therapy of Joseph Weiss, Harold Sampson, and the San Francisco Psychotherapy Group; and (4) the time-limited dynamic psychotherapy of Hans Strupp, Jeffrey Binder, and the Vanderbilt research group. All four groups set out to develop and research general approaches to psychoanalytic therapy, rather than brief therapy in particular. However, along the way they developed brief therapies that are a substantial contribution to the theory and practice of interpersonal and relationally oriented therapy in which psychopathology is conceptualized as recurrent patterns of interpersonal behavior that are maladaptive, as discussed later in this chapter.

Other approaches to brief dynamic therapy are based on Kohut's self psychology, or pragmatically integrate techniques or concepts from nonpsychoanalytic orientations. The former stress an empathic perspective: the therapist's accurate grasp of what the patient is experiencing; the concept of the selfobject as someone (or something) that is experienced and used as if it were part of one's self; the primary role of the self in motivating behavior; and the notion that symptoms are a patient's efforts to restore the cohesion and continuity of the self. The major differences between long-term psychoanalytic self therapy and brief self therapy is that in the latter case the therapist focuses on a few particular issues and on interactions outside the therapy relationship (known as self-selfobject relations) as much as on the transference (Baker, 1991). In addition to Baker, authors who take Kohut's self psychology as a starting point for brief therapy include Gardner (1991), Basch (1995), and Seruya (1997).

Eclectic and integrative approaches have developed alongside the third-generation models. The object has been to improve the efficacy and range of applicability of any one theory of therapy. There are three major forms of integration and eclecticism: common factors, technical eclecticism, and theoretical integration. Proponents of the common factors approach believe that what moves therapy forward are not the variables that are unique to each therapy but those that cut across the separate domains (e.g., Garfield's [1989] brief therapy). Bellak (1992) developed a technically eclectic brief dynamic therapy that combines different techniques such as advice giving, family sessions, and medication. Seruya (1997) employs cognitive-behavioral interventions in a primarily self psychological approach. Gustafson (1986) proposed a theoretically eclectic therapy which draws on systemic theory to understand the patient in relation to his or her family. Incorporating elements of all three in a mixed model is McCullough's (1993) anxiety-reducing brief therapy.

CURRENT STATUS

Managed Care

The advent of managed care and new forms of health care delivery have given considerable impetus to the development of brief therapy, including its psychodynamic varieties. Managed care developed chiefly because of the rapidly rising cost of health care and the threat to the competitiveness of American business, which supports health care through employee benefits. Chrysler corporation, for example, estimated that health care benefits were adding $600 to the cost of producing each car (Broskowski, 1991). Thus, managed care is about cost containment and cost-effectiveness, with accountability the watchword. The advent of the dual-career family and the associated decrease in leisure time has also affected the preference of many consumers for brief therapy. To meet the challenge of cost containment policies and the integration of services occasioned by the health care revolution, providers have been encouraged to develop their skills in brief, planned therapy (e.g., Broskowski, 1995; Kiesler & Morton, 1988).

Even while advocating the utility and effectiveness of brief therapy, we are critical of many current practices of managed care with which it is often associated. Such practices include the use of less skilled case reviewers to supervise the services of more skilled and better trained clinicians, significant intrusions into patient privacy, and the dictation of services to providers who will feel compelled to conform more to cost factors than to the needs of the patient. Burdensome record keeping is also associated with these practices. Perhaps most important to acknowledge is that certain patients with chronic and severe dysfunctional conditions need long-term (even lifelong) mental health services, including supportive psychotherapy. In brief, we and others (e.g., Cummings & Cummings, 1997) believe that short- and long-term therapy should be available as choices for patients according to professionally judged and documented need.

Even before the current push for briefer therapies by managed care, surveys found that patients typically remained in therapy between five and eight sessions only (e.g., Garfield, 1989). About 70 percent of public clinic patients stop treatment before the tenth session. The modal number of sessions is 1, the median is 3 to 5, and the mean varies from 5 to 8 in different studies (Phillips, 1985). The National Medical Expenditures survey found that of those who utilized psychotherapy 34 percent had 1 to 2 visits, 37 percent had 3 to 10, 13 percent had 11 to 20, and only 16 percent had over 20 visits (Olfson & Pincus, 1994). Thus, if we define brief therapy as 20 sessions or fewer, fully 84 percent of patients fall within its purview. Phillips (1985) found that this distribution exists regardless of diagnosis, age, sex, presenting complaints, ethnic features, and whether the therapy started out as time limited or unlimited.

These results suggest that clinicians should be attending to brief therapy not for economic purposes alone but because it is what most patients opt for, whether clinicians prefer it or not (and psychodynamic therapists often do not; Bolter, Levenson, & Alvarez, 1990). It is also interesting to note that patients will remain longer in a time-limited therapy with the number of sessions specified in advance than they will remain in open-ended therapy (Sledge, Moras, Hartley, & Levine, 1990). One can presume, then, that a planned brief therapy such as BPT—with a focus and goals—will tend to decrease the general dropout rate and may increase patient satisfaction.

Empirically Supported Treatments

Another factor on the current psychotherapy delivery scene likely to affect the practice of BPT is the proliferation of practice guidelines for specific psychiatric disorders based strictly on the empirical evidence supporting each treatment. The advent of these empirically supported treatments, or ESTs, is an effort to introduce standards of care that are based on the best available scientific research. A committee of the Division of Clinical Psychology of the American Psychological Association (Task Force, 1995) recently published a report listing those therapies that it viewed as effective for various psychological disorders, as supported by empirical research. The impetus for this task force, whose recommendations continue to evolve (Chambless & Hollon, 1998), was to provide balance to similar reports published by more biomedically oriented groups (e.g., the American Psychiatric Association and the Agency for Health Care Policy and Research).

It is not surprising that the vast majority of the therapies that have been empirically tested are behaviorally oriented and brief. A scientific orientation to practice has been a hallmark of behavioral approaches from early on. Conducting research on long-term therapy is exceedingly difficult due to the dropout problem, and there are the questionable ethics of maintaining an untreated control group. Because of the way in which psychopathology and treatment goals are conceptualized in the nonbehavioral therapies (e.g., the importance of unconscious factors) research in these domains is challenging as well. The nonbehavioral therapies tend to place less emphasis on traditional outcome criteria than the behavioral treatments, in part because their definition of change is not solely symptom- or *DSM*-focused. All forms of psychoanalytic therapy, including BPT, may include some or all of the following outcome criteria, which are often difficult to capture in traditional research designs: attainment of insight, an enhanced sense of freedom and agency, a firmer sense of identity, raised self-esteem, greater ability to recognize and handle feelings, and greater pleasure and serenity (McWilliams, 1999).

The Task Force guidelines require randomized, controlled designs or a series of quantitative single-case studies. The subject sample and nature of problem must be specified and a treatment manual employed. Those therapies passing a more stringent set of requirements of proof are referred to as *well-established* and those with lesser standards of proof, as *probably efficacious*. Never-

theless, BPT is one of the few nonbehavioral treatments listed as probably efficacious for the treatment of depression. If one considers Interpersonal Therapy to be a psychodynamic treatment, BPT can be considered well established since Interpersonal Therapy is so considered. It is also regarded as probably efficacious for treating opiate dependence. There are other important kinds of data, however, that bear on the efficacy of BPT to which we now turn.

Outcome Studies of BPT

Meta-analysis

In the most recent of three meta-analyses, Anderson and Lambert (1995) reviewed 26 studies of the effectiveness of BPT. Relative to wait-list controls and minimal treatment groups, BPT was found to be substantially superior. However, BPT was not superior or inferior to other forms of psychotherapy at posttreatment, although it evidenced slight superiority at long-term follow-up. Studies employing manuals and therapists trained in BPT produced larger effects.

Short-term Versus Long-term Psychoanalytic Therapy

How does BPT compare to long-term psychoanalytic therapy? We are aware of only one such study, and this type of research is seldom attempted, due to the difficulty of conducting research on long-term therapy as noted above. Piper, Debbane, Bienvenu, and Garant (1984) compared four types of psychoanalytically oriented therapy: short-term individual (STI), long-term individual (LTI), short-term group (STG), and long-term group (LTG). The patients suffered from different degrees and combinations of anxiety, depression, low self-esteem, interpersonal relationship difficulties, and mild-to-moderate characterological problems. The two long-term forms of therapy averaged 76 sessions; the short-term forms, 22 sessions. Patients were matched on various criteria and assigned to the four groups. Outcome measures included traditional psychiatric symptomatology, interpersonal functioning, and personal target objectives.

There was a significant interaction between type of therapy (individual vs. group) and duration (long vs. short). From the therapist's perspective STI was rated best, followed closely by LTI and LTG, with STG therapy a distant fourth. From the patient's perspective, LTG therapy was rated best, followed closely by STI. LTI therapy was third and STG a distant fourth. Patients in all four forms of therapy evidenced improvement over pretherapy status. On six-month follow-up, patients either maintained their gains or showed additional improvement in all four therapies.

Piper and his colleagues then conducted a cost-benefit analysis and concluded that "In terms of cost-effectiveness and the quality of therapy process as viewed by the therapists LTG therapy and STI therapy were regarded as superior" (p. 278). We view these findings, as did Piper and colleagues, as very supportive of the value of brief, individual psychoanalytic therapy even when compared to long-term psychoanalytic therapy.

Dose-effect Relationship

Howard, Kopta, Krause, and Orlinsky (1986) set out to determine the form of the relationship between the dose of therapy, using the session as the unit of exposure to the active ingredients of therapy, and the effect of therapy expressed as a percentage of patients improved at any particular dosage. Based on session-by-session patient reports of their emotional well-being and researcher ratings of the closed charts, they found a rapid rise in the percentage of patients improved in the early sessions according to both patient and researcher ratings. By 13 sessions, roughly 55 to 60 percent of patients were considered improved. By 26 sessions, about 80 percent of the depressives and anxiety patients were improved but only 38 percent of the borderlines, according to researcher ratings.

Based on these and many other studies, we conclude that time-limited therapy is helpful to a substantial proportion of patients, and is often as helpful as time-unlimited therapy. Its effects seem to be as lasting as those of time-unlimited treatment. However, these global conclusions must be qualified in several ways (Messer & Warren, 1995). First, the dose-effect studies suggest that although time-limited therapy is helpful to a substantial percentage of patients, that percentage increases the longer that therapy continues. Second, BPT is not clearly superior to other forms of brief therapy or to medication. Neither, however, can we say that longer term psychoanalytic therapy is superior to brief psychoanalytic therapy. Third, patients diagnosed as depressed or anxious improve faster than do borderline patients. Reasonable proportions of the latter, however, also make gains in a relatively brief period (two to six months depending on the source of measurement). Fourth, measures of well-being and symptoms show earlier improvement in general life functioning, including interpersonal relationships. Fifth, and finally, patients in time-limited psychotherapy tend to maintain their gains.

Emotional Challenges in Conducting BPT

Brief psychodynamic therapy engages the student or practitioner in a learning process with emotional challenges that are worth facing honestly so they can be managed in an optimal way.

Guilt and Anger

Perhaps the most common feeling aroused in practicing BPT is guilt over shortchanging the patient. One imagines that if only one had a few more sessions, a few more months or another year, the cure would be complete. One might then get angry at a clinic, managed care company, or society that does not provide sufficient resources for healing psychological problems. At such times, it may be reassuring to recall that research supports the value of BPT, and that there is no conclusive evidence that it is inferior to long-term therapy.

Perfectionism and Grandiosity

A therapist may believe that in setting out to practice psychotherapy it is possible to cure all comers categorically and completely. To recognize the limitations imposed by intractable human nature, by our own all-too-limited human capacities, and by the inevitable strictures of work settings or other circumstances can be experienced as a narcissistic blow. The practice of BPT can be especially sobering in this regard. Such feelings can compromise brief therapy from the start. The therapist will convey dissatisfaction to the patient, who will view the therapy as second rate at best. To help mitigate these concerns, therapists need to recognize that the standard to which they may be comparing BPT is overly perfectionistic and hardly ever realized in practice.

Affects Concerning Separation and Termination

The many emotions aroused by the termination phase of BPT are frequently problematic for brief dynamic therapists, because leave taking comes about so quickly and, for therapists with several short-term patients, so frequently. A therapist may feel sad at the prospect of losing an intense and satisfying relationship; may mourn at being no longer needed by the patient; may feel guilty for "rejecting" or "abandoning" the patient; or may feel disappointed that there will not be time to explore other facets of patients' problems and personality in order to contribute to their amelioration. In spite of these difficulties, often some important issues have been addressed in therapy, immediate appearances notwithstanding. There may be a changed developmental trajectory, a partial internalization of a healthy therapist-patient relationship, and a degree of working through after termination. As Mann (1991) pointed out, termination presents important opportunities for affectively charged exploration and growth.

Power and Authority

Most forms of BPT require a more active stance by the therapist than does long-term psychoanalytic therapy, in order to channel treatment along the lines of the dynamic focus. Techniques employed by the drive/structural therapists include direct confrontation of patient defenses, which requires a rather bold show of therapist authority and assertiveness. Too great a need by therapists to express their power can lead either to more activity than the patient can comfortably tolerate or to excessive passivity as a way of guarding against the exertion of authority. Ability to modulate their legitimate power and authority and awareness of the potential for the abdication and misuse of both are therapists' major assets in mitigating such negative effects.

Feelings of Inadequacy

In learning BPT, therapists may be concerned about their diagnostic skill, both in selecting suitable candidates and in formulating a focus correctly. There is the threat from defining goals of therapy in advance, which more readily confronts the therapist with success or failure than typically would be true for a more open-ended therapy. Carrying out a new therapy brings inevitable anxiety over the adequacy of one's therapeutic skills as well. In such circumstances, it is important for therapists to maintain a sense of themselves as "good enough," to borrow Winnicott's phrase, in spite of errors or not accomplishing it all. Meeting with a group of therapists to discuss cases can lend confidence to the therapist in the correctness of the focus, and can help in discerning blind spots.

THEORY

It is difficult to discuss concisely the theory that underlies brief psychodynamic treatment because it is diverse and varied, with differences quite as essential as similarities. However, as noted earlier, we have attempted to organize the theory and practice of brief therapy by resorting to a categorical scheme that groups such therapies according to their reliance on particular underlying psychoanalytic models (Messer & Warren, 1995). In this section we describe in some detail the essential theoretical underpinnings of the major brief psychodynamic therapies. We emphasize the two major theoretical approaches—drive/structural and relational. We also note the influence of eclecticism and integration in the actual application of brief dynamic psychotherapy.

Drive-Structural Influences

We have previously characterized the work of Malan (1963, 1976), Sifneos (1972, 1979), and Davanloo (1978, 1980) as primarily representing the drive/structural approach to BPT. These and authors treating related topics have drawn on the concepts of classical psychoanalysis as well as their later revisions by the school of Ego Psychology and structural theorists such as Charles Brenner and Jacob Arlow.

Central to this approach is the concept of a drive, or wish. Following Freud's articulation of a dual-instinct theory, these authors all assume that sexual and aggressive impulses arise as bodily and physical instincts seeking expression and satisfaction. Such impulses inevitably bring the individual into conflict with external reality in the form of the physical, social, and cultural world that limits their expression. In addition, Freud posited that the individual gradually internalizes social mores and thus comes to feel conflict with regard to the unrestrained expression of sexual and aggressive urges.

The notion of conflict, in fact, is crucial to the theorizing of the drive/structural approach. The individual is understood to suffer psychological symptoms that are the disguised expression of unacceptable, and therefore repressed, impulses. Symptoms can be understood as deflections of the drive energy of an unacceptable wish transformed into a less objectionable (though often debilitating or self-defeating) form, with the original sexual or aggressive content hidden from view. For example, stuttering may be a way of simultaneously expressing, and not expressing, an aggressive impulse.

This modulation of drive energies is accomplished by the ego, a psychological structure that arises as the result of the individual's early interactions with the external world. The ego can be thought of as a set of functions that mediate between the drives and external reality, allowing for at least partial satisfaction of the drive impulses. The ego is understood also to perform the function of defenses, psychological structures that protect the individual from the subjective experience of danger, or anxiety. Anxiety is the experience that signals the overwhelming of the ego by unconscious sexual or aggressive impulses, and thus catalyzes further defensive activity on the part of the ego. Personality structure in this model consists of characteristic and enduring patterns of relationship between impulses or wishes, the defenses which are characterologically utilized to manage and contain these impulses, and the experience of anxiety, signaling the failure of the defenses. Symptoms can be thought of as the outcome of the dynamic interrelationship of drive, defense, and anxiety, representing the partial and somewhat unsuccessful attempt at adaptation, tending to include infantile or regressive components reflecting a return to developmentally earlier modes of adaptation (e.g., stuttering as immature speech).

One particular situation of importance to the drive/structural theorists, as it was to Freud before them, is the Oedipal complex. Each of these current theorists emphasizes the particular configuration of sexual impulses and the efforts by the ego to master them during the developmental period of three to five years of age.

Freud believed that all children wish to possess the parent of the opposite sex, and feel rivalrous with the parent of the same sex. The set of feelings arising in this love triangle includes passion, murderousness, guilt, and inadequacy, and forms the basis for much future conflict. Just as the Oedipal situation came to be central for Freud, this early love triangle and its later replications in the lives of neurotic adults forms the clinical focus of much of the drive/structural brief therapists.

For the drive/structural brief therapists the active interpretation of these intrapsychic conflicts is the basis for all therapeutic activity. It is the articulation of these central conflicts, and the patients' deep and emotionally meaningful realization of the impact of such conflicts on their lives, that enables them to become freed from the emotional traps and pitfalls that have stymied them and brought them into treatment. In particular, these conflicts are interpreted in the context of the relationship with the therapist, which is understood in the light of the psychoanalytic concept of transference. Freud used this term originally to describe the repetition in the psychoanalytic situation of a relationship with a developmentally early significant other, usually but not always a parent. The repetition for Freud represented the activation of early infantile sexual and aggressive impulses that had been frustrated. The transference repetition thus reflects the seeking after satisfaction in the present of unsatisfied wishes in the past. This clinical concept came to be central to psychoanalytic theorizing, and is relied upon by the drive/structural brief psychotherapists as well. The therapist articulates patterns in the current patient-therapist dyad and is thus able to identify important clues to the patient's central emotional conflicts. As these come to light, they can be interpreted by the therapist and taken in by the patient, enabling significant modifications in the relationships among wishes, defenses, and anxieties, and thus in the symptoms that arise from them.

Relational Influences

We have described the other major grouping of brief psychodynamic psychotherapies as relational (Messer & Warren, 1995). This group, a third generation, has been influenced substantially by the expanding and evolving body of psychoanalytic theory that has accompanied the development of psychoanalysis itself beyond its classical bounds. We have described as exemplary of this approach the work of Luborsky's Penn Group (Luborsky, 1984; Luborsky & Crits-Cristoph, 1990), Weiss and Sampson's Mt. Zion Group (Weiss, Sampson, & the Mount Zion Research Group, 1986), Horowitz (1988), and Strupp's Vanderbilt Group (Strupp & Binder, 1984).

The relational conception of personality is broadly psychoanalytic, drawing on Sullivan's interpersonal psy-

chiatry (1953); the interpersonal tradition in psychoanalysis as developed by Erich Fromm, Karen Horney, Erik Erikson, and others (Erikson, 1950; Fromm, 1944, 1947; Horney, 1950); Melanie Klein's object relations theory (Klein, 1950) and its further developments by Fairbairn (1950), Winnicott (1965), Guntrip (1961), Edith Jacobson (1964), Kernberg (1976), and other object relations theorists; John Bowlby's attachment theory (Bowlby, 1969) and the research it has stimulated; aspects of Kohut's psychoanalytic self psychology (Kohut, 1971, 1977) and its recent developments (Stolorow & Atwood, 1992); and finally, current research into the development of internalized representations of self, other, and self-other interaction by infant researchers such as Beebe (1994) and Stern (1985). Central to this approach is a shift away from the concept of drives and instinctual wishes as the primary or sole motivational construct, and a movement toward the idea of intrinsic motivations arising from the vicissitudes of human relating.

What we are calling a relational approach is thus actually a synthesis of several important, relatively independent traditions that have evolved out of traditional psychoanalytic views. The glue to this conglomeration of theories and models is the emphasis on internalized representations of self and other as the core of personality structure. Relational approaches, while diverse, stand together in contrast to the drive-structural view of mind in which the fundamental structures of personality are drives and the defenses against their direct expression, with anxiety signaling the failure of defense structures to contain unacceptable impulses. The relational models instead rely on some notion of primary, original, and independent structures of mind that provide for the mental representation of self, others, and relating.

Each of the brief relational therapies views psychopathology in terms of recurrent patterns of interpersonal behavior that are maladaptive. From this point of view the patient inevitably construes and constructs relationships in the context of his or her past interpersonal experience, with an emphasis on the particularly powerful shaping effects of early experience. Conflict is seen as arising in the context of interpersonal relationships as the result of conflicting wishes in relation to others. Conflict need not be related to infantile sexual impulses or primary libidinal or aggressive drives, but can instead include a wide range of affects, wishes, intentions, and subjectively experienced needs in relation to others (Sandler & Sandler, 1978). In this view, psychological conflict can arise in any developmental stage, and may be related to issues of separation, dependency, autonomy, and self-integration, as well as sexual or aggressive impulses (Stern, 1985). Deemphasizing instinctual drives as the engine of intrapsychic conflict tends to increase attention to the actual failures of the environment (e.g., Kohut, 1977; Winnicott, 1965). Greater weight is given to the role of real experience (rather than wish-fulfilling fantasy) in the development of object relations that forms the basis of personality and psychopathology. There is also a much greater emphasis on the adaptive aspects of apparently pathological relationships, again with reference to the original developmental situation and its requirements. From this point of view defenses are understood to function as adaptive mechanisms employed to minimize the experience of anticipated unpleasant affects, to control relationships so as to avoid traumatic or painful outcomes, and to attempt to bring about desired states of relatedness. This contrasts with the drive-structural view of defenses as primarily safeguards against the expression of unacceptable instinctual wishes or against anxiety, which signals the imminent appearance of such impulses in consciousness.

In addition, there tends to be more emphasis on the current maintaining factors in psychopathological transactions, with systemic notions like cyclical and self-perpetuating dynamics, as opposed to strict causal linkages to the past (e.g., Wachtel, 1985, 1993). In this sense, psychopathology is understood to be a dynamic, self-fulfilling process in which feared and anticipated relational events tend to be enacted by the individual in interactions with others, who will then tend to respond in ways complementary to the interpersonal actions of that individual.

Theory and Eclecticism

In describing the drive/structural and relational approaches, we have tended to emphasize their theoretical coherence in order to highlight essential features and to differentiate the groups. However, in actual clinical practice there is much diversity. In our book (Messer & Warren, 1995) we discuss the work of James Mann, an influential therapist and proponent of a highly specialized technique in BPT (Mann, 1973; Mann & Goldman, 1982) that cannot be readily categorized in our schema. We describe his approach as integrative, because he draws on elements of classical drive theory, ego psychology, attachment theory, object relations theory, and self psychology. Rather than being notable for a specific theoretical point of view, Mann's approach is of interest for his use of diverse theoretical concepts to form a singular and original approach to brief psychotherapy that arises from his integrative use of psychoanalytic theory. The pluralistic approach of theoretical integration seems appropriate to our field's current epoch, in which diverse theories even within the narrower domain of psychoanalysis all make claims for truth or utility. Perhaps ours is a time in which either/or theorizing makes less sense than both/and, in which therapists form their own therapeutic approach, drawing on what they perceive to be the valuable or strong elements of a wider range of theory.

In recent years efforts have been made to incorporate therapeutic techniques from different therapeutic traditions within and beyond psychoanalytic therapy, an approach known as eclecticism. In adding elements of other therapies, the object has been to improve the range of application and efficacy of brief psychotherapy. The movement toward eclecticism and integration has arisen in the context of a number of salient factors. First, there has been increased interaction across mental health disciplines and subdisciplines, leading to exposure to diverse clinical approaches, including behavioral and cognitive therapies, family systems therapies, and the influence of biological and somatic approaches to treatment. Second, the climate of mental health practice, as noted earlier, has been increasingly concerned with efficacy and cost. These pragmatic considerations have tended to deemphasize theoretical contributions while valuing more problem- and technique-oriented aspects of treatment. Third, there is the influence of psychotherapy research, which over the years has been unable to point clearly and definitively to the unique therapeutic advantages of any one theoretical approach. That is, most studies suggest generally that psychotherapy is effective, but have tended not to discriminate between various psychotherapeutic systems in terms of outcome. Some authors have taken this to mean that underlying factors common to all therapies, rather than specific therapeutic techniques, constitute their effective ingredients (Beitman, Goldfried & Norcross, 1989).

These pluralistic inclinations, including theoretical integration, technical eclecticism, and the common factors approach, form the basis of a number of brief therapy approaches. We have described some such models previously (Messer & Warren, 1995), including Garfield's common factors approach (Garfield, 1989), Bellak's technical eclecticism (1992), and Gustafson's approach to theoretical integration (Gustafson, 1986). In fact, we would suggest that the majority of clinical work done in real-life clinical settings is more of the eclectic and integrative sort, as it is primarily researchers who value testing out highly specified treatment approaches. Most clinicians are inclined to use what suits them, relying on models for new ideas and general orientation, but developing their own sets of techniques that they can adapt to their own particular style, clinical setting, and patient population.

METHODOLOGY: THE MAJOR TECHNIQUES OF BRIEF PSYCHODYNAMIC TREATMENT

Although they differ in their emphases and details, all approaches to brief psychoanalytic treatment rely on a number of common technical characteristics. First, patients are selected for their suitability for the treatment modality, as discussed in the next section (applications). Second, an individualized central clinical focus is developed for each case. Third, a time limit is set, whether explicitly or not. Fourth, and related to the use of a time limit, is the relative emphasis on termination and its special role in treatment. Fifth, all approaches to BPT typically rely on specific active techniques to accomplish therapeutic goals within the time limits. And last, most brief dynamic treatment approaches utilize some form of goal-setting.

Use of a Central Focus

Employing a clinical focus is a hallmark of all brief dynamic therapies. This involves the formulation of a central clinical theme to be developed in the early sessions, which serves to organize clinical observation and to guide interpretation and other clinical interventions. The central focus is an individualized statement of the therapist's understanding of the patient's presenting problems as an expression of an underlying dynamic central issue or conflict. Such an understanding seeks to incorporate as much of the current situation and relevant history as can be rapidly obtained. This central focus may be verbalized directly to the patient as a form of a working contract or used to engage the patient and increase motivation and interest in the therapy process. Some therapists do not state the central focus explicitly, but instead use it as a heuristic device to organize the ongoing flow of clinical information and to guide their interventions.

Although the central focus is sometimes presented in the brief therapy literature as a highly formalized statement or set of statements made to the patient in a set format and language, we do not think such formality is necessary. Instead, the articulation of the focus can take the form of interpretations made to the patient from the first interview based on an implicit clinical focus formulated by the therapist. When this goes well one would expect the patient to feel understood, and to become less anxious, more motivated for further exploration, and more interpersonally engaged.

Even though all psychodynamic treatment approaches rely on clinical formulations, in short-term therapy the central focus tends to be more circumscribed in scope, limiting the therapeutic inquiry so that clinical goals may be achieved within the time frame. In addition, the focus is generated more rapidly at the outset of treatment and is used more actively in brief psychotherapy than in open-ended treatment.

Use of a Time Limit

"Depend on it, Sir, when a man knows he is to be hanged in a fortnight, it concentrates his mind wonderfully."
—*Samuel Johnson*

All brief psychodynamic treatments operate within time limits. One author, James Mann (1973), makes the time limit a central theoretical and clinical construct, organizing his approach to brief therapy around the effects on the clinical process of an explicit and fixed number of sessions. He advocates the use of a 12-session time limit with a clear termination date to be set in the first or second session. Mann relies on the universality and poignancy of the experience of loss, and its impact at termination, to make the time limit a central technical feature of his brief treatment. It is understood that termination issues are activated subliminally from the beginning of treatment with the statement of a termination date. The patient's ambivalent responses to the issue of loss and separation are utilized therapeutically throughout the treatment but especially at termination. The theoretical emphasis is on the use of the time limit to enable the patient to address unresolved issues of loss, separation, and differentiation.

Other approaches make use of an explicit time frame, but do not emphasize the theoretical centrality of the intertwining of the clinical focus and the time limit. Still others do not make use of an explicit time limit, but instead emphasize principles of affective engagement, focused work, and the provision of a corrective experience. Although time is not made a central issue, it is utilized by the therapist to organize therapeutic activities and aims. In this latter view, while there is an implicit treatment contract for a time-limited therapy, patient and therapist negotiate the exact number of sessions in an abbreviated version of the usual psychotherapy termination process. In all psychodynamic approaches to brief treatment the time limit is understood to accelerate the process of psychotherapy by increasing the sense of urgency, immediacy, and emotional presence of the patient in order to accomplish therapeutic goals in the shortened time frame of brief therapy. There is no doubt that the effect of the time limit is as much an influence on the therapist as it is on the patient, and is likely in and of itself to increase therapist activity.

Role of Termination

Termination has historically been seen as a crucial phase of psychoanalytically oriented treatment. It is understood as the phase of treatment in which the clinical gains of the therapy thus far can be consolidated, and in which the issue of loss, separation, and individuation can be addressed directly within the here-and-now context of the ending of treatment. It is given a heightened importance in brief psychotherapy, which is in many respects a termination process from its outset.

Thus, brief therapy is particularly well-suited to addressing termination issues. Since the time limit is present from the beginning, the process of termination is activated at the start of the treatment. Both patient and therapist work throughout under the influence of termination-induced feelings, tending to focus attention on themes of loss, death, and limitations. Both patient and therapist are forced to deal with the impact of termination issues during the full course of the treatment. Resistances to termination can appear early in brief therapy, and can be addressed throughout the treatment. The brevity of treatment means that the pain of separating cannot be postponed to an indistinct and distant time and place. The time-limited treatment inevitably becomes a metaphor for the time-limited nature of human life, and thus such treatment is a convenient vehicle for dealing with forms of suffering that arise in the context of human mortality.

Active Stance of Inquiry

The concept of *active technique* (Ferenczi, 1921/1980) derives its meaning in contrast to the traditionally lesser role of therapist activity in long-term psychoanalytic therapy. It refers to any of a variety of techniques aimed at accelerating the therapeutic process to make it possible to accomplish goals of psychodynamic importance in the more limited time frame of brief therapy. Historically, psychoanalysts have been wary of intervening in ways that were thought to interfere with the development of transference, either by offering direct suggestions, disclosing personal information and feelings, or by directly gratifying transference wishes. On the other hand, brief therapists have long experimented with ways to modify the stance of analytic neutrality to increase therapeutic efficacy (Alexander & French, 1946; Ferenczi, 1921/1980; Rank, 1929/1978). These modifications have typically involved the use of time limits as already mentioned (Mann, 1973; Rank, 1929/1978), direct suggestions (Ferenczi, 1921/1980), the active confrontation and interpretation of defenses and resistances (Davanloo, 1980; Sifneos, 1972, 1979), and early and active interpretation of transference (Davanloo, 1980; Malan, 1976).

The use of confrontation and active interpretation of resistances and defenses is especially characteristic of drive/structural brief therapists, and is intended to accelerate the emergence of unconscious conflicts, permitting their more rapid resolution. Advocates of such techniques tend to relentlessly point out to the patient where he or she is avoiding feelings, leaving out significant information, or being vague. Defenses may be interpreted in rapid-fire succession, with the therapist in persistent pursuit of the patient's authentic emotional experience. Such persistence is justified on the basis of the unconscious relief patients are said to feel when forced to recognize the emotional truths—often unacceptable sexual or aggressive feelings—they have avoided and defended

against. Breakthroughs are followed by the emergence of significant new clinical material, and the cycle of resistance, interpretation, and breakthrough is repeated again and again.

Some of the third generation of brief dynamic therapies do not emphasize such confrontational techniques, but instead follow more in the tradition of Sullivan's (1953) *detailed inquiry*. This form of activity refers to a persistent curiosity on the part of the therapist which takes the form of ongoing clarification, questioning, seeking after more detail, and pointing out gaps or inconsistencies in the patient's narrative. These brief therapists also actively use their awareness of developing and ongoing interpersonal patterns in the patient-therapist relationship, and come to focus on these as a major source of clinical information. Such interpersonal transactions are thought to be indicative of enduring relationship patterns, and their active identification and clarification forms the basis of more relationally oriented brief therapy technique.

The following brief example illustrates the here-and-now focus on patient-therapist transactions. The therapist uses his own experience in the context of active transference interpretation linking past relationship patterns to the current therapeutic relationship.

T:　Each time I notice and comment that you are looking attractive or that you're doing well in your work you get tearful and cry.

P:　(crying) I feel I am not attractive. I feel I will be rejected. Father could never stand it. I won a ribbon in a race and he only could say the competition was not too great. Dad did the same restricting with Mother. She even had to limit her vocabulary for him.

T:　I see, so you feel you have some well established old reasons for feeling that way with me. (Luborsky, 1984, p. 96)

Goal Setting

The brevity of short-term psychotherapy, with the accompanying constraints on what can be accomplished, requires the setting of clinical priorities so that the time available is used most effectively. Thus, goal setting is linked to the use of a central focus, as well as to the time limit and the centrality of termination. Goal setting thus reflects the therapist's acceptance of limitations on what can be accomplished, and embodies an individualized approach to the aims of psychotherapy, as well as providing the means for assessing therapy outcome in an individualized and dynamically informed fashion.

Brief therapy makes greater use of explicit goal setting than does time-unlimited treatment. While not necessarily a formal feature of all brief dynamic psychotherapies, the use of goal setting is at least implied in the brief therapeutic project. This concept reflects the greater degree of problem solving and symptom focus that is characteristic of time-limited treatments. While sharing some features of the medical model found in many psychological treatments, including the emphasis on diagnosis (or clinical formulation) and symptom reduction, the brief dynamic psychotherapies add a further dimension to treatment goals. These include psychoanalytically informed ideas about emotional health and the aims of psychoanalytic treatment, which extend beyond, but include, the symptom focus. Such aims might include an increase of the following: insight into personal conflicts, emotional maturity, capacity for intimacy in relationships, and serenity, as well as a lessening of anxiety and depression. Such goals can be set with an individual patient in mind and directed at those problems that are of most immediate concern.

Summary

Some of these techniques are not necessarily specific to BPT, but taken together they form its essential characteristics. The selection of patients, use of time limits, a central focus, an active clinical stance, and goal setting are requisite to developing a psychodynamically sophisticated clinical formulation and providing the means of resolving some of the patient's central emotional problems. Although the goals of such treatment may not be as ambitious as those of longer term psychotherapies, they are nonetheless aimed at lasting personality changes along with amelioration of current symptoms and dilemmas.

APPLICATIONS

In this section, we will take up two important applications of brief psychodynamic therapy: to whom it applies, that is, the diagnostic and selection criteria; and its special relevance to children, adolescents, and the elderly.

Selection Criteria

In general, brief dynamic therapists rule out those patients whose severity of disturbance precludes their ability to engage in an insight-oriented therapy, or who need more time to work through their problems. However, it is difficult to generalize, as the different models set narrower or wider criteria. The drive/structural therapies, for example, set stricter suitability criteria, whereas the relational brief therapies are more inclusive; thus, we discuss both.

Drive Structural Therapies

Contraindications. These include: serious suicide attempts or potential; a history of alcohol or other drug addiction; major depression; poor impulse control; incapacitating, chronic obsessional or phobic symptoms; some psychosomatic conditions such as ulcerative colitis; and poor reality testing. With reference to *DSM,* this would encompass major depressive syndrome, schizophrenia, sociopathy, and paranoia, as well as the more severe personality disorders such as the borderline and narcissistic. Although the latter two syndromes can be treated in this form of brief therapy, they require modifications in focus, technique, and goals. We have discussed these at length elsewhere, along with the treatment of other "difficult" patients (Messer & Warren, 1995). For example, such patients may require a more adaptive, here-and-now focus, auxiliary modalities such as group therapy or family sessions, medication, or a more flexible approach to termination, such as the gradual tapering-off of therapy.

In addition to the psychopathological or diagnostic exclusionary criteria, Malan (1976, p. 69) adds the following rejection criteria:

1. Inability to make contact
2. Necessity for prolonged work in order to generate motivation for treatment
3. Necessity for prolonged work in order to penetrate rigid defenses
4. Inevitable involvement in complex or deep-seated issues that there seems no hope of working through in a short time
5. Severe dependence or other forms of unfavorable, intense transference
6. Intensification of depressive or psychotic disturbance

Indications. In terms of *DSM,* those included as suitable for drive/structural BPT are the adjustment disorders; the milder personality disorders such as avoidant, dependent, obsessive-compulsive, and histrionic; and the less severe anxiety and depressive disorders. Davanloo considers his ISTDP (Intensive Short-Term Dynamic Psychotherapy) suitable for patients with long-standing neurosis or maladaptive personality patterns with a focus on either Oedipal or loss issues or both (Davanloo, 1980; Laikin, Winston, & McCullough, 1991). He makes specific mention of patients with obsessional and phobic neurosis as suitable due his willingness to confront the defenses relentlessly.

Many of the diagnostic criteria are descriptive, static, or structural, and are based largely on the patient's history garnered from the psychiatric interview as well as the interviewer's observations. The three drive/structural therapists—Malan, Davanloo, and Sifneos—however, also stress the process of the interview to gauge a patient's likely response to the active, frequently confrontational techniques of this model of BPT. Davanloo in particular refers to the importance of making trial interpretations in the initial interviews. He then notes whether the patient responds with deepened involvement or with some form of decompensation such as severe anxiety, confusion, or even paranoia. If one of the latter reactions occurs, he becomes more supportive, and would consider the patient unsuitable for ISTDP.

Relational Therapies

Whereas the drive/structural model of brief therapy places considerable emphasis on the issues of patient selection and suitability, the relational model does not concern itself as much with these. The relational therapies in general are less demanding of the patient, particularly in their lesser emphasis on the use of confrontation of resistances and defenses. Instead, they put more weight on the therapist's personality characteristics, as well as the unique interpersonal and intersubjective field that emerges in the therapeutic relationship. Thus, they deemphasize patient characteristics taken in isolation. Nonetheless, Strupp & Binder (1984) list the characteristics that they associate with a successful brief treatment:

1. Emotional discomfort. The patient is sufficiently uncomfortable with his or her feelings and/or behavior to seek help via psychotherapy.
2. Basic trust.
3. Willingness to consider conflicts in interpersonal terms.
4. Willingness to examine feelings.
5. Capacity for mature relationships. The patient evinces sufficient capacity for relating to others as separate individuals so that identifiable relationship predispositions, no matter how painful and conflict ridden, can be enacted in the therapy relationship and then collaboratively examined.
6. Motivation for the treatment offered. The assessment of motivation is reflected in the judgments reflected in Criteria 1 through 5.

We can readily see from this list that more medically oriented diagnostic categories such as those of *DSM,* or even more dynamically conceived categories such as hysterical, obsessional, neurotic, and character pathology, are not viewed as relevant to the expectations for the patient's success or failure in relational brief therapy. "The object relations capacities sought in potential TLDP [time-limited dynamic psychotherapy] patients may be detected across a broad range of formal diagnostic syndromes. Therefore, neither a presenting symptom nor the diagnosis of a specific personality disorder will itself justify exclusion from this form of treatment" (Binder & Strupp, 1991, p. 139). The criteria are principally interpersonal and psychological, and can be assessed only from within the therapeutic situation. This is a form of interpersonal diagnosis, with the therapist's use of self as a crucial ingredient.

The Penn Group also tends to take a broad psychodynamic approach to the issue of patient suitability, noting that short-term supportive-expressive psychotherapy "is suitable for many kinds of patients" (Luborsky & Mark, 1991, p. 112). They, too, recommend screening out most borderline or psychotic patients, noting that patients with personality disorders may often require longer treatment. They rely on the supportive-expressive dimension to address the issue of degree of psychopathology, allowing for a greater measure of supportive techniques in the treatment of relatively sicker patients, and a greater measure of expressive techniques for healthier patients.

Applications to Children, Adolescents, and the Elderly

Developmental concepts form a basis for understanding the predictable or expectable challenges, crises, or transitions an individual is likely to face at various stages of life. For each population—children, adolescents, and the elderly—there are specific developmental factors that can be taken as the basis for a brief, focal treatment. That is, one can treat the person with respect to a particular life stage transition or crisis. In this way the developmental context is a vital part of the clinical assessment process, with problems identified not only in terms of symptoms and long-standing personality structures, but also in terms of a failure to meet developmentally determined challenges.

In a developmental life span approach to psychotherapy, the patient's problem is defined in terms of an adaptive failure, usually in the face of new demands from the patient's total life situation. These demands may be accidental, such as illness or other losses, or they may result from the developmental process itself, such as graduating from high school. The natural emphasis of a developmental framework is on situational factors in psychopathology and emotional crisis, rather than on the intrapsychic structure of personality. The latter, usually central to psychoanalytically construed work, is understood more as a background variable in terms of predispositions and previous efforts at adaptation. Such a crisis intervention model identifies the disparity between adaptive resources and situational demands, with the change process primarily aimed at reducing or eliminating the gap. This may or may not require specific psychodynamic change. Other interventions may suffice, such as modifying the environment, or simply enabling the patient to better utilize existing psychological resources. The goal of such an approach is to enable the patient to attain new and stable adaptive structures, which ideally will result in an improved ability to manage life stresses. At a minimum, the goal is to foster a return to a level of functioning that existed prior to the crisis or developmental challenge.

Children

Studies indicate that children are seen in outpatient psychotherapy for six sessions or fewer, on the average, in a variety of private and clinic settings (Dulcan & Piercy, 1985; Parad, 1970). Yet the literature on time-limited psychotherapy with children is remarkably meager (Warren & Messer, 1999). It would therefore appear that much psychotherapy of children is time-limited by default and not by plan. Children may be available only for a relatively brief period of time because of limited financial resources, minimal family motivation, or a clinic mandate. Given these realities, there is a pressing need for planned, time-limited psychotherapy to maximize the usefulness of psychotherapeutic intervention.

There are other developmental reasons for the use of time-limited models. Children have greater plasticity than adults. Important issues of character structure have not yet been settled. Children are much more in the process of becoming who they are than their adult counterparts. The therapist thus has every reason to count on the force of the developmental process itself to be a potential ally of the treatment process. For many children—usually those with the least severe psychopathology—a brief intervention might suffice to remove an obstacle to development, permitting the resumption of the developmental process. Thus, an effective psychotherapeutic intervention at the right time may have a disproportionately large effect on the rapidly developing child.

Adolescents

Because development continues at a rapid pace into and through adolescence, long-term models of psychotherapy can be problematic in some respects. The moving target of child and adolescent development makes the goals and purposes of treatment different from that of adults. The developmental process is still continuing rapidly, and the formation of personality structure is in progress. The adolescent is usually living with his or her family of origin, so much of the clinical material worked with in psychotherapy deals not solely with internalizations of parental objects but also actual ongoing transactions within a developmental, systemic family context.

Brief models of treatment are particularly suitable for adolescents for a number of reasons. First, this is a frequently uncooperative patient population that is difficult to work with. The use of an explicit time frame makes the adolescent more willing and motivated to engage in the psychotherapeutic process. Second, as a matter of practical necessity, much treatment with adolescents is time-limited as the ongoing transitions and life changes that we expect to take place between the ages of 14 and 20 often preclude long-term commitments to psychotherapy. Certainly for older adolescents, the central task of leaving home makes ongoing psychotherapy difficult to arrange. Finally, the clinical importance of separation and individuation is underscored by the setting of a time-limited framework. Short-term work is congruent with the natural tendency of adolescents to "push off" attachment objects and to struggle for autonomy and separate identity.

The Elderly

There has been insufficient attention to the place of psychotherapy with older adults. In the psychoanalytic tradition, there is an explicit bias against the treatment of the elderly, beginning with Freud (1905/1958), who wondered whether the substantial resources of psychoanalysis would not be better applied to the younger person, with more of life ahead and less entrenched psychopathology. Others have pointed out the negative countertransferences therapists tend to have in their work with older patients, including distaste for the physical and cognitive limitations of the elderly, pessimism about the possibilities for change, and the anxieties about one's own mortality stimulated by contact with an older person (Busse & Pfeiffer, 1972; Sparacino, 1978–79; Zinberg, 1965).

However, we believe that brief forms of psychotherapy are particularly suited to the older patient. Not only do such models address the pragmatic need for a briefer treatment in the context of aging, but some of these deal explicitly with the issues of time and loss so important to this developmental epoch. In a sense, the time-limited treatment setting precisely recapitulates the central dilemma of old age—mortality and loss. This may permit a reworking of the story of the patient's life to enable him or her to see life in a new light, to embrace in a fresh way the sum of his or her existence, to mourn, and to accept. Difficulties such as loss, illness, loneliness, and so forth can be a focus of treatment as they are manifested in an older person's problematic functioning. For example, retirement may leave a person with diminished self-esteem, which can be discussed in the context of the meaning of the loss of satisfactions of work and the possibility of substitute gratifications. Interpersonal relations have been found to bring many older people to therapy (Knight, 1996). In this connection, Nordhus and Nielsen (1999) have illustrated how older clients' problems can be conceptualized and treated in terms of their maladaptive interpersonal patterns.

CASE ILLUSTRATION

This case vignette is intended to illustrate some aspects of BPT that have been presented in previous sections. In particular, we wish to emphasize those aspects that characterize a psychodynamic approach, as well as the modifications required by time limitations. In this case the patient presents with psychiatric symptoms but little psychological insight about them. It illustrates working with overt symptoms while developing a clinical focus that is specifically psychodynamic in the context of externally imposed time limits.

At the time of the initial contact Jennifer was 27, married, and living in a city far from her place of origin. She presented for treatment after seeing a psychiatrist following the occurrence of two panic attacks. The doctor had prescribed the antidepressant Prozac, along with Klonopin, an antianxiety medication, and had suggested psychotherapy. She contacted one of the present authors, who was on a list of panel providers for her managed care contract. She had had no previous psychological or psychiatric treatment or preconceptions as to what psychotherapy would be like.

Jennifer's husband made the initial phone contact, described the problem, and set up the initial appointment for his wife. He accompanied her to the initial visit, and when she was invited into the consulting room, came in with her. With no prompting from the therapist, Jennifer made a little joke at the outset of the session implying that her husband's presence at the interview was why she was there, but glossed over this as the two of them discussed her panic disorder. While the therapist noted the psychological importance of the husband's involvement, he also felt that, given the nature of the referral and Jennifer's vulnerable condition, his involvement was an understandable protective attitude toward his spouse. At the same time, these events provided the first clues to a possible dynamic formulation of the patient's symptoms.

The treatment was time-limited by reason of the limitations of the patient's insurance contract. This was discussed at the outset, so the patient was aware that the number of sessions covered by her plan would be no more than 20. (She was seen twice weekly after the first consultation.) It was determined that she would be suitable for an active brief psychodynamic treatment in accordance with the diagnostic criteria described earlier in this paper, by virtue of her emotional availability, interest and motivation, and response to trial interventions in the first sessions. Her responses to early interventions included increased motivation, expression of a range of affects, emotional flexibility, and engagement with the therapist. Of special note was her willingness to consider psychological explanations for her somatic (panic) symptoms.

Her symptoms were fairly circumscribed, of recent onset, and relatively mild severity. A dynamic formulation could be readily constructed based on her presentation and history. It took into account her current symptoms and current and past relationships, including the therapeutic relationship. It also addressed issues of intrapsychic and characterological importance while remaining circumscribed in scope.

Jennifer's emotional flexibility, level of affective engagement, and tolerance for negative affects made it possible to utilize the active techniques previously outlined. She was able to make use of here-and-now transference interpretations linking different relationships and periods in her life. Likewise, she could tolerate active interpretation of resistances and defenses, responding to such interventions with increased insight, and contributing additional interpretations of her own. She was able to use the time limit and termination to mourn previous losses in her life, especially the loss of idealized parents that she came to understand she could not ever have.

In the early sessions there was some discussion of the details of her panic attacks, with an assessment of their severity, frequency, and the circumstances in which they occurred. The two panic attacks were the first Jennifer had ever experienced. They included thoughts of being completely out of control, or being in a situation from which she could not escape. As with her comment about her husband, she showed from the outset an interest in the emotional context of her symptoms. She appeared curious and interested to know more about her emotional life, and was prepared to consider the possibility that her anxiety had interpersonal and psychological meaning. While she felt willing to take the medication that had been prescribed, and was very concerned about having more panic attacks, she also expressed a reluctance in general to take medication, and was hopeful that our sessions would help to reduce or eliminate the need to take it.

Jennifer's history revealed significant early and continued disruptions in her attachment to her mother. Her mother had immigrated to the United States from Central America, though she was of Asian ethnicity. Her father was also an immigrant, but from a Middle Eastern country. Thus, there were complicated ethnic and cultural issues in the life of Jennifer's family. Her mother became ill immediately following Jennifer's birth, and returned to her home of origin in Central America, leaving Jennifer with her father for the first several months of her life. This loss was echoed again later in Jennifer's childhood (at six years of age) when her parents divorced, and her mother left the home, leaving Jennifer and her brother with their father. Although Jennifer had continued contact with her mother after this time, she was taken care of primarily by a housekeeper who came from the same town as her mother. Jennifer reports that this housekeeper was unkind and at times abusive to her and her brother. While she felt cared for by her father, she also experienced him as weak in some ways, and unable to understand her needs and protect her. She identified very much with his extended family, taking on the religious and ethnic identity of her father, and finding significant social support in the extended paternal family.

Jennifer reported feeling lonely throughout her childhood, and complained that she had difficulty maintaining relationships with friends. She noted that she did not have any significant friendships in the area in which she currently lived. Jennifer married her childhood sweetheart, with no other prior relationships. Her husband likewise had never had any other relationships.

In the early sessions Jennifer elaborated on the joke about her husband that was the first thing she had said in the treatment. She described feeling overly dependent on him, and found herself at times resenting his control over so many aspects of her life. Yet she also felt that she could not identify her own preferences, but relied on her husband to provide direction to her life.

The central formulation devised for this case emphasized the two linked themes that appeared in the patient's history, namely, the lack of developmentally adequate emotional support during most of her childhood, and a conflict between her dependency needs and her need to define and assert an autonomous self. Her panic attacks were understood and explained as symptoms of these deep and fundamental conflicts reaching a particularly critical moment in the context of her adult development, as she was just then beginning to face decisions with her husband about settling down and having children of her own. She also felt dissatisfied with her work situation, and felt unable to develop a sense of purpose in her vocational life, mirroring the conflicts she experienced in the domain of her personal relationships.

A number of clinical features were prominent from the beginning of treatment. While Jennifer was clearly bright, engaging, and personable, often joking and playful, she experienced herself as flat, boring, and without imagination. She immediately made herself comfortable with the therapist, seeming to relax and open up. Yet there was often a heavy and depressive atmosphere in the office that was at odds with her more outgoing and cheerful exterior. As the sessions continued this darker mood began to predominate, and she would tend to fall silent for longer periods of time, expressing feelings of hopelessness and despair. Along with these increased depressive symptoms there appeared the theme of ambivalence about the therapist, as Jennifer began to tease the therapist and complain that he was not doing enough. While Jennifer modulated the teasing at first, her feelings became more pronounced and clearly ambivalent, mirroring similar feelings toward her husband: "I like you and I hate you." As these feelings were explored, Jennifer struggled with deep feelings of inadequacy. She longed to be told what to do, directed, and taken care of. These wishes were clarified in the context of her marriage to her husband, who in many ways offered such care and protection. At the same time, she also acknowledged her frustration with his tendency to "take over," be in charge, and make all the couple's plans.

Her feelings of inadequacy and deep dependency longings were thus linked to the current evolving relationship with the therapist, to her relationship with her husband, and to her earlier familial relationships in which her developmentally appropriate dependency needs were unmet or disrupted by losses. The therapist clarified that she seemed unable to form a clear sense of herself and her needs because her early needs for safety, protection, and reliability had not been sufficiently met, leaving her with a superficial, "false self" adaptation. Her feelings of loss, abandonment, and loneliness were not addressed by her overly self-involved mother or preoccupied father, and so she was left to her own devices from too early on.

One last clinical theme can be noted. Her playful aggressiveness was a striking feature, and while her attacks on the therapist tended to escalate as time passed, her ability to function more assertively in work and with her husband was apparent. It was understood that her need to assert herself had been thwarted early in her development because of the lack of emotional safety in her environment. One can easily imagine that a mother who is so tenuously available is not a mother one can safely resist, rebel against, or defy, all essential components of the process of separation and individuation. Thus, Jennifer struggled with her aggressiveness, keeping it mostly to herself or avoiding it altogether. Her need for separateness, as well as connection, was clarified in the context of her blossoming ambivalence in the therapy relationship. It appeared that the therapist's willingness to accept and tolerate her hate, as well as her love, enabled Jennifer to express her autonomous strivings, and to feel that a new kind of relationship was possible based not so much on unquestioning dependency but on a more mutual, give-and-take mode of relating.

In summary, Jennifer's treatment illustrates various aspects of brief psychodynamic treatment. While it would not be correct to say that Jennifer resolved all of the issues pertaining to this focus by the end of her treatment, it did appear that she had experienced substantial improvement in a number of areas. She was entirely free of panic attacks without the use of any medication. Her relationship with her husband showed some improvement, with increased assertiveness on her part, and increased pleasure in her own separateness. This assertiveness also manifested itself in relationships at work. While depressive symptoms remained (and may likely remain as a permanent feature of Jennifer's experience), she seemed clearer about their origins, and felt better able to cope with them. She had made significant strides in clarifying her relationship with her mother, and had come to understand more realistically her mother's limitations, both in the past and presently. She realized how unrealistic her hopes were for her relationship with her mother, and, as she mourned the loss of the kind of mother she had yearned for, she felt less disappointment and bitterness.

It seemed clear to both patient and therapist that Jennifer could benefit from further treatment at some point in the future. At the same time, she also felt that she had traversed a crisis, made important strides in her emotional growth and feeling of well-being, and had improved her relationships significantly, while becoming free of her presenting symptom.

SUMMARY

Brief psychodynamic therapy has become an increasingly important mode of treatment in the current climate of cost accountability and crowded life schedules. Although it is not suitable for all patients, it fits the needs of a reasonable percentage and variety of clients seeking treatment. This therapy is best learned in the context of courses in clinical methods, psychopathology, and psychoanalytic theory. The conduct of BPT benefits from a therapist having learned and conducted long-term psychoanalytic therapy in which there is time for a fuller unfolding of interpersonal and intrapsychic issues along with their manifestations in the transference relationship.

Another important source of understanding people in depth is the therapist's own psychoanalytic therapy. This helps put therapists in touch with their countertransferential issues, which they can both guard against and use in a maximally helpful way. In a sense, it is more difficult to conduct BPT than traditional forms of therapy, because it requires the therapist to arrive rapidly at a focus and formulation by being alert to the different sources of clues and inferences the patient presents. It is a rewarding kind of therapy to employ insofar as it brings issues into relief in a relatively short time period, dipping beneath the surface of presenting complaints and symptoms to expose and treat underlying issues. At its best, it represents a fruitful compromise between a

therapy focused only on the symptom and/or problem presentation and one that surveys the personality in full depth and breadth. Thus, it has an important role in sustaining the values of psychoanalytic treatment, which is to understand and treat people's problems in the context of their current situation and earlier life experience.

REFERENCES

Alexander, F., & French, T. M. (1946). *Psychoanalytic therapy: Principles and application.* New York: Ronald Press.

Anderson, E. M., & Lambert, M. J. (1995). Short-term dynamically oriented psychotherapy: A review and meta-analysis. *Clinical Psychology Review, 15,* 503–514.

Aron, L. (1990). One person and two person psychologies and the method of psychoanalysis. *Psychoanalytic Psychology, 7,* 475–485.

Baker, H. S. (1991). Shorter-term psychotherapy: A self psychological approach. In P. Crits-Christoph & J. P. Barber (Eds.), *Handbook of short-term dynamic psychotherapy* (pp. 287–322). New York: Basic Books.

Basch, M. F. (1995). *Doing brief psychotherapy.* New York: Basic Books.

Beebe, B. (1994). Representation and internalization: Three principles of salience. *Psychoanalytic Psychology, 11,* 127–165.

Beitman, B. D., Goldfried, M. R., & Norcross, J. C. (1989). The movement toward integrating the psychotherapies: An overview. *American Journal of Psychiatry, 146* (2), 138–147.

Bellak, L. (1992). *Handbook of intensive brief and emergency psychotherapy,* (2nd ed.). Larchmont, NY: C.P.S., Inc.

Binder, J. L., & Strupp, H. H. (1991). The Vanderbilt approach to time-limited dynamic psychotherapy. In P. Crits-Christoph & J. P. Barber (Eds.), *Handbook of short-term dynamic psychotherapy* (pp. 137–165). New York: Basic Books.

Bolter, K., Levenson, H., & Alvarez, W. (1990). Differences in values between short-term and long-term therapists. *Professional Psychology: Research and Practice, 21,* 285–290.

Bowlby, J. (1969). *Attachment and loss: Vol. 1. Attachment.* New York: Basic Books.

Broskowski, A. (1991). Current mental health care environments: Why managed care is necessary. *Professional Psychology: Research and Practice, 22,* 6–14.

Broskowski, A. T. (1995). The evolution of health care: Implications for the training and careers of psychologists. *Professional Psychology: Research and Practice, 26,* 156–162.

Busse, E. W., & Pfeiffer, E. (1972). Mental disorders in later life. In E. W. Busse & E. Pfeiffer (Eds.), *Mental illness in later life* (pp. 107–144). Washington, DC: American Psychiatric Association Press.

Chambless, D. L., & Hollon, S. D. (1998). Defining empirically supported therapies. *Journal of Consulting and Clinical Psychology, 66,* 7–18.

Crits-Christoph, P., Barber, J. P., & Kurcias, J. S. (1991). Introduction and historical background. In P. Crits-Christoph & J. P. Barber (Eds.) *Handbook of short-term dynamic psychotherapy* (pp. 1–16). New York: Basic Books.

Cummings, N. A., & Cummings, J. L. (1997). The behavioral health practitioner of the future: The efficacy of psychoeducational programs in integrated primary care. In N. A. Cummings, J. L. Cummings, & J. N. Johnson (Eds.), *Behavioral health in primary care: A guide for clinical integration* (pp. 325–346). Madison, CT: Psychosocial Press.

Davanloo, H. (Ed.). (1978). *Basic principles and techniques in short-term dynamic psychotherapy.* New York: Spectrum Publications.

Davanloo, H. (Ed.). (1980). *Short-term dynamic psychotherapy.* New York: Jason Aronson.

Dulcan, M. K., & Piercy, P. (1985). A model for teaching and evaluating brief psychotherapy with children and their families. *Professional Psychology: Research and Practice, 16,* 689–700.

Erikson, E. H. (1950). *Childhood and society.* New York: Norton.

Fairbairn, W. R. (1950). *Psychoanalytic studies of the personality.* London: Tavistock.

Ferenczi, S. (1980). The further development of an active therapy in psychoanalysis. In J. Suttie (Ed.), *Further contributions to the theory and technique of psychoanalysis* (pp. 189–197). London: Karnak Books. (Original work published 1921)

Ferenczi, S., & Rank, O. (1986). *The development of psychoanalysis.* Madison, CT: International University Press. (Original work published 1925)

Freud, S. (1958). On psychotherapy. In J. Strachey (Ed. and Trans.), *The standard edition of the complete psychological works of Sigmund Freud* (Vol. 7, pp. 257–268). London: Hogarth Press. (Original work published 1905)

Fromm, E. (1944). Individual and social origins of neurosis. *American Sociological Review, 9,* 380–384.

Fromm, E. (1947). *Man for himself.* Greenwich, CT: Fawcett Books.

Gardner, J. R. (1991). The application of self psychology to brief psychotherapy. *Psychoanalytic Psychotherapy, 8,* 477–500.

Garfield, S. L. (1989). *The practice of brief therapy.* New York: Pergamon Press.

Guntrip, H. (1961). *Personality structure and human interaction.* London: Hogarth Press.

Gustafson, J. P. (1986). *The complex secret of brief psychotherapy.* New York: Norton.

Horney, K. (1950). *Neurosis and human growth.* New York: Norton.

Horowitz, M. (1988). Introduction to psychodynamics: A new synthesis. New York: Basic Books.

Howard, K. I., Kopta, S. M., Krause, M. S., & Orlinsky, D. E. (1986). The dose-effect relationship in psychotherapy. *American Psychologist, 41,* 159–164.

Jacobsen, E. (1964). *Self and the object world.* New York: International Universities Press.

Kernberg, O. F. (1976). *Object relations theory and clinical psychoanalysis.* Northvale, NJ: Jason Aronson.

Kiesler, C., & Morton, T. (1988). Psychology and public policy in the "health care revolution." *American Psychologist, 43,* 993–1003.

Klein, M. (1950). *Contributions to psychoanalysis.* London: Hogarth Press.

Knight, B. G. (1996). *Psychotherapy with older adults* (2nd ed.). Thousand Oaks, CA: Sage Publications.

Kohut, H. (1971). *The analysis of the self.* New York: International Universities Press.

Kohut, H. (1977). *The restoration of the self.* New York: International Universities Press.

Laikin, M., Winston, A., & McCullough, L. (1991). Intensive short-term dynamic psychotherapy. In P. Crits-Christoph & J. P. Barber (Eds.), *Handbook of short-term dynamic psychotherapy* (pp. 80–109). New York: Basic Books.

Luborsky, L. (1984). *Principles of psychoanalytic psychotherapy: A manual for supportive-expressive treatment.* New York: Basic Books.

Luborsky, L., & Crits-Cristoph, P. (1990). *Understanding transference: The CCRT Method.* New York: Basic Books.

Luborsky, L., & Mark, D. (1991). Short-term supportive-expressive psychoanalytic psychotherapy. In P. Crits-Christoph & J. P. Barber (Eds.), *Handbook of short-term dynamic psychotherapy.* (pp. 110–136). New York: Basic Books.

Malan, D. (1976). *The frontier of brief psychotherapy.* New York: Plenum.

Malan, D. H. (1963). *A study of brief psychotherapy.* New York: Plenum.

Mann, J. (1973). *Time-limited psychotherapy.* Cambridge, MA: Harvard University Press.

Mann, J. (1991). Time limited psychotherapy. In P. Crits-Christoph & J. P. Barber (Eds.), *Handbook of short-term dynamic psychotherapy* (pp. 17–44). New York: Basic Books.

Mann, J., & Goldman, R. (1982). *A casebook in time-limited psychotherapy.* New York: McGraw-Hill.

McCullough, L. (1993). An anxiety-reduction modification of short-term dynamic psychotherapy (STDP): A theoretical "melting pot" of treatment techniques. In G. Stricker & J. R. Gold (Eds.), *Comprehensive handbook of psychotherapy integration* (pp. 139–149). New York: Plenum.

McWilliams, N. (1999). *Psychoanalytic case formulation.* New York: Guilford Press.

Messer, S. B., & Warren, C. S. (1995). *Models of brief psychodynamic therapy: A comparative approach.* New York: Guilford Press.

Mitchell, S. A. (1984). Object relations theories and the developmental tilt. *Contemporary Psychoanalysis, 20,* 473–499.

Mitchell, S. A. (1988). *Relational concepts in psychoanalysis.* Cambridge, MA: Harvard University Press.

Nordhus, I. H., & Nielsen, G. H. (1999). Brief dynamic psychotherapy with older adults. *Journal of Clinical Psychology, 55,* 935–947.

Olfson, M., & Pincus, H. A. (1994). Outpatient psychotherapy in the United States, II: Patterns of utilization. *American Journal of Psychiatry, 151,* 1289–1294.

Parad, L. G. (1970). Short-term treatment: An overview of historical trends, issues, and potentials. *Smith College Studies in Social Work, 41,* 119–146.

Phillips, E. L. (1985). *Psychotherapy revised: New frontiers in research and practice.* Hillsdale, NJ: Erlbaum.

Piper, W. E., Debbane, E. G., Bienvenu, J. P., & Garant, J. (1984). A comparative study of four forms of psychotherapy. *Journal of Consulting and Clinical Psychology, 52,* 268–279.

Rank, O. (1978). *Will therapy.* New York: Norton. (Original work published 1929).

Sandler, J., & Sandler, A. M. (1978). On the development of object relationships and affects. *International Journal of Psychoanalysis, 59,* 285–296.

Seruya, B. B. (1997). *Empathic brief psychotherapy.* Northvale, NJ: Jason Aronson.

Sifneos, P. E. (1972). *Short-term psychotherapy and emotional crisis.* Cambridge, MA: Harvard University Press.

Sifneos, P. E. (1979). *Short-term dynamic psychotherapy.* New York: Plenum.

Sledge, W. H., Moras, K., Hartley, D., & Levine, M. (1990). Effect of time-limited psychotherapy on patient dropout rates. *American Journal of Psychiatry, 147,* 1341–1347.

Sparacino, J. (1978–1979). Psychotherapy with the aged. *International Journal of Aging and Human Development, 9,* 197–220.

Stern, D. (1985). *The interpersonal world of the infant.* New York: Basic Books.

Stolorow, R. D., & Atwood, G. E. (1992). *Contexts of being: The intersubjective foundations of psychological life.* Hillsdale, NJ: Analytic Press.

Strupp, H. H., & Binder, J. L. (1984). *Psychotherapy in a new key.* New York: Basic Books.

Sullivan, H. S. (1953). *Interpersonal theory of psychiatry.* New York: Norton.

Task Force on Promotion and Dissemination of Psychological Procedures (1995). Training in and dissemination of empirically validated psychological treatments: Report and recommendations. *The Clinical Psychologist, 48,* 3–23.

Wachtel, P. L. (1985). *Action and insight.* New York: Guilford Press.

Wachtel, P. L. (1993). *Therapeutic communication: Principles and effective practice.* New York: Guilford Press.

Warren, C. S., & Messer, S. B. (1999). Brief psychodynamic therapy with anxious children. In S. W. Russ & T. H. Ollendick (Eds.), *Handbook of child psychotherapies with children and families* (pp. 219–237). New York: Plenum.

Weiss, J., Sampson, J., & The Mount Zion Research Group (1986). *The psychoanalytic process: Theory, clinical observations, and empirical research.* New York: Guilford Press.

Winnicott, D. W. (1965). *The maturational process and the facilitating environment.* New York: International Universities Press.

Zinberg, N. E. (1965). Special problems of gerontological psychiatry. In M. A. Berezin & S. H. Cath (Eds.), *Geriatric psychiatry: Grief, loss and emotional disorders in the aging process* (pp. 147–159). New York: International Universities Press.

Chapter 8

BRIEF THERAPY[1]

LYNN SEGAL

Some people see Brief Therapy (perhaps because of its name) as a somehow abbreviated and therefore superficial version of existing techniques, or as a first aid or stopgap measure based on the principles of some existing major school of therapy, employed only when circumstances do not (or not yet) permit real, long-term therapy.

In the following contribution, Lynn Segal presents the basis of a therapeutic approach, as developed by the Mental Research Institute (MRI) in Palo Alto. The approach's brevity is not due to the simplification of an established form of therapy but is based on a different conceptualization of problem formation and problem resolution, that is, on a different scientific paradigm.

The MRI takes an interactional rather than an intrapsychic view, in contrast to some of the older therapies. It investigates problems within the interpersonal context in which they occur and perpetuate themselves. Brief Therapy emerges as the technique of choice within the systems-oriented frame of reference of Family Therapy—a field approach of the gestalt variety.

Nothing in this approach denies the importance of past experience as the cause of present attitudes, expectations, problems, and the like, but Brief Therapy sees insight as an epiphenomenon rather than a necessity for change.

Brief Therapy shares some important concepts with Ericksonian hypnotherapy, Behavior Therapy, and the work of strategic family therapists—Salvatore Minuchin, Jay Haley, and Mara Selvini; but nevertheless it is a complete, unitary system with its own well-developed rationale.

Brief Therapy (BT) is a generically based system for solving human problems, especially the kind brought to psychotherapists and counselors. While BT is most recognized in the field of family treatment, it has been used successfully with individuals, couples, and larger social organizations.

BT represents a new way of conceptualizing human problems and a different set of therapeutic techniques based upon this conceptualization (Watzlawick & Weakland, 1977). Most often short-term treatment is associated with crisis intervention or some type of "holding action" until long-term treatment can begin. By contrast, the brief therapist assumes that the goals of psychotherapy can be reached more quickly and effectively as a consequence of the premises he or she holds regarding human problems—how they arise and what is necessary to resolve them.

HISTORY

Precursors

The seminal ideas underlying BT were originally introduced into psychiatric thinking by Ruesch and Bateson (1951). Together, they began sketching the outline of a new epistemology based on the theories of cybernetics, communication, and systems research.

In 1956 the Bateson group—including John Weakland, Jay Haley, and Don Jackson—published the well-known article "Toward a Theory of Schizophrenia" (Bateson, Jackson, Haley, & Weakland, 1956). Although this publication is primarily known for the double-bind theory of schizophrenia, it also stands as a landmark for viewing psychiatric problems as communicative behavior, maintained and structured by social interaction, rather than disease entities that reside inside a person.

The Mental Research Institute (MRI) was formed by Don Jackson in 1959 for the purpose of exploring how these new interactional insights might be applied to psy-

---

[1] Although this chapter represents the work of the Brief Therapy Project, Mental Research Institute, Palo Alto, the author is solely responsible for its presentation.

chiatric treatment. Joined by Haley, Weakland, and other notables in the family therapy movement, including Paul Watzlawick and Virginia Satir, the California Family Therapy Movement got its formal start. Although there were many differences between institute members, they all agreed on a number of basic assumptions: (1) while one family member—the identified patient—exhibited pathology, the problem underlying these symptoms resided in the way the family functioned as a group; (2) this group behavior was understood as a rule-governed system, exhibiting homeostasis, feedback, redundancy, and other cybernetic principles; and (3) treating the family meant changing their interactive behavior, that is, changing their patterns of communication.

Beginnings

MRI's Brief Therapy Project began in 1967 for the purpose of seeing what might be done to alleviate patients' presenting complaints, limiting treatment to 10 one-hour sessions. All the project members were practicing family therapists with a special interest in the work of Jay Haley (1963) and Dr. Milton H. Erickson (Haley, 1967), known for his unique treatment techniques and rapid cures.

Our research design incorporated a number of features still in use today. We work as a team. One member does the interviewing while the rest look on from an observation room equipped with a sound system, one-way mirror, and audiotape recorder. The two rooms are connected by a telephone, permitting observers to phone in suggestions and corrections to the identified therapist while the interview is in progress.

Patients are not screened prior to treatment, and each case is seen for a maximum of 10 sessions. Following each hour of treatment, time is spent discussing the pros and cons of the interview and the best way to proceed during the next session. Follow-up questions are formulated immediately after the last interview, and presented to the patient(s) 3 and 12 months after the last session by a project member other than the identified therapist.

CURRENT STATUS

The Brief Therapy Project is now in its 33rd year of operation, and interest in our work continues to grow. We have presented our approach at conferences, workshops, and seminars across the United States, South America, and the major cities of Europe. The Introductory Brief Therapy Workshop, given three times a year at the Mental Research Institute, Palo Alto, California, continues to draw an international attendance. In September 1979, the first intensive, nine-month workshop in BT was of-fered; 10 participants were accepted to treat their own cases in front of the class as part of their training.

The major written presentation of our theory, *Change: Principles of Problem Formation and Problem Resolution* (Watzlawick, Weakland, & Fisch, 1974), has stirred quite an interest in the international psychiatric community and is now published in nine languages, including Japanese and Hebrew.

BT is now used in a wide variety of settings: psychiatric hospitals and clinics, corrections and protective services, social service agencies, and educational and physical health services. It is probably safe to say that one can find BT used in most settings that deal with human problems.

THEORY

Being pragmatists, we assume that theories are neither truth nor even the approximation of truth. A theory is merely a set of assumptions or working hypotheses that have heuristic value—in the case of therapeutic theories, to facilitate the solving of human problems. From this perspective, theories are like different human languages. Although most, if not all, do an equally good job as representational systems, some languages are better than others for solving a specific problem. "Street language" may be better in a hostage negotiation situation, while proper English would be more useful for a scientific presentation. However, it makes no sense to say that any one language is closer to the truth or reality than any other (Weakland, 1976).

Basic to the Brief Therapy viewpoint is the belief that behavior—"normal" or problematic—is maintained and structured by interaction with other people, usually family members. But interaction could also include friends, colleagues, or other professional helpers.

Human problems develop by mishandling of normal life difficulties that are predictable occurrences in the course of a person's lifetime. Such difficulties include accidents, loss of work, natural disasters, disturbances in one's usual routines, and transitions in the family life cycle: courtship to marriage, birth of the first child, children starting to attend school or reaching the teen years, all the children leaving home, and loss of a spouse through death or divorce.

There are three basic ways difficulties are mishandled: (1) by ignoring or denying that anything is wrong and not taking action; (2) by attempting to resolve difficulties that need not or cannot be solved, only endured until they pass; and (3) by taking action, but the wrong kind—the most common form of mishandling observed in our clinical practice.

Difficulties are not generally mishandled on purpose or for some unconscious gain. Rather, when people or families have a problem, they go about attempting to deal with it in a manner that is consistent with their frame of reference, that is, their view of reality and what they believe to be the right way to behave. Their attempted solutions are maintained because they are considered logical, necessary, or the "only thing to do." When such problem-solving efforts fail, the patient and his or her family are most likely to interpret the failure as confirmation of the problem's severity. This is then followed by more-of-the-same solutions, creating a self-perpetuating system of interaction. The patient is like a man caught in quicksand. The more he struggles, the more he sinks; the more he sinks, the more he struggles.

Although there are many different ways people take "wrong action" to solve a problem, four basic patterns have been repeatedly observed in our clinical practice (Fisch et al., 1975).

Attempting to Be Spontaneous Deliberately.

This pattern is found in cases involving sleep disorders, sexual difficulties, substance abuse, blocks in creative endeavors, and persons trying to force themselves or others to have a particular emotional feeling.

It is assumed that most people will occasionally have difficulty with bodily functioning or performance, and feelings wax and wane. If such difficulties are seen as normal life difficulties that self-correct with time, all would be well. But once a person sets about deliberate correction, he or she risks the possibility of getting caught in the paradoxical predicament of attempting to force spontaneous behavior. The patient-to-be may try to force himself to sleep, be potent, or cheer himself up and feel happy. When such methods as willpower, reasoning, or positive thinking fail to bring about the desired response, more of the same is tried, setting the stage for a full-fledged problem.

Seeking a No-Risk Method Where Some Risk Is Inevitable.

This inappropriate way of solving problems is often found in the areas of work and dating. For instance, the shy single male may try to avoid the risks of rejection or failure when attempting to make new female friends. He becomes so concerned with finding the perfect opening gambit that he never begins a conversation with someone of the opposite sex. Similarly, the single, the salesman, or the job seeker can all run into another variation of this pattern by *trying too hard* to make a good impression. In doing so, they only alienate the very people they are trying to impress.

Attempting to Reach Interpersonal Accord Through Argument.

The popularization of psychology and the human potential movement has led to the erroneous belief that all problems can be solved by discussion and sharing of one's feelings. Many families with marital or child-parent problems come to treatment presenting their problem as "we can't communicate." Many of these marital problems arise when one or both partners define the normal fluctuations of closeness or comfort they feel with each other as evidence of a relationship problem. This is then discussed, and their therapeutic chat degenerates into an argument, which is then interpreted as confirmation of their false assumption—something is wrong with the marriage. This leads to further discussion accompanied by a heightened awareness of the relationship, which makes their interaction even more awkward and uncomfortable. They create the very "reality" they wish to avoid.

Attracting Attention by Attempting to Be Left Alone.

Many problems defined as paranoia arise from this solution. A person gets started in this problem when he defines some teasing or harassment by others as insidious, indicating a lack of esteem that others have for him. The attempted solution may range from emotional or physical withdrawal to inquiry about the "persecution" or counterattacks. In either case, these solutions are likely to bring on more attention from others. If the person withdraws, others may seek him out to find out what is wrong. If the patient retaliates, this just sets off a pattern of escalating hostilities.

In short, the theory and techniques of Brief Therapy rest on two major assumptions.

> regardless of their basic origins and etiology—if, indeed, that can ever be reliably determined—the kinds of problems people bring to psychotherapists PERSIST only if they are maintained by ongoing current behavior of the patient and others with whom he interacts. Correspondingly, if such problem-maintaining behavior is appropriately changed or eliminated, the problem will be resolved or vanish, regardless of its nature, origin, or duration. (Weakland, Fisch, Watzlawick, & Bodin, 1974, p. 144).

METHODOLOGY

Given our view of problems and *how* they persist, the tasks of treatment become clear: (1) obtain an operational definition of the problem and the behavior that maintains it; (2) devise a plan to interdict the attempted solution; (3) implement the plan, revising or proceeding as necessary; and (4) termination.

Case Management

Most therapists would agree that warmth, empathy, trust, and patient involvement are important elements in a good therapeutic relationship. The brief therapist is also concerned with an additional set of relationship issues that permit him or her to exercise the best clinical judgment throughout the course of treatment.

More specifically, the therapist needs room to maneuver—the freedom to ask questions and obtain necessary information, choose which family members will be interviewed, select interventions, and gain the necessary leverage to see that they are carried out.

Given the limitations of space, it is impossible to begin explaining how this is carried out. The following list simply outlines some of the therapist's main procedures for maximizing his or her maneuverability: obtaining clear, specific information from the patient; using qualifying statements to avoid being pinned down until he or she decides what is the best position to take vis-à-vis the patient; taking time and not being pressured into intervening prematurely because of patient pressure; and using the "one-down" position, explained later in this chapter.

Data Collection

Treatment begins by simply asking the patient "What brought you in today?" Related questions focus on the referral source, why treatment was sought at this time, and how the problem is getting in the way of the patient's life, that is, what the problem is stopping the patient from doing or making him do unwillingly. This last question serves as a useful barometer of patient distress and provides additional clarification of the presenting complaint.

Next, an assessment is made of the problem-maintaining behavior. The therapist asks how the patient and others have been dealing with the problem and how they have deliberately attempted to solve it—what exactly do they say and do?

Last, the goal of treatment is clarified, emphasizing minimal change on the grounds that there are only 10 sessions in which to work. The therapist might say: "What, at the very least, would you like to see accomplished as a result of our efforts, and what concrete indicators might serve as signposts to indicate this?"

When collecting data, the brief therapist will phrase questions and clarifying remarks with an eye to obtaining descriptions of interaction that resemble the script of a stage play. For instance, if the patient says, "I really let her have it," the therapist will ask, "What exactly did you say? Then what did she say or do?"

Data collection usually takes from one to three interviews. During this period, other family members might be interviewed, alone or with the identified patient, asking them the same basic questions. This permits the therapist to assess which family member is a "customer" for treatment—the one who really wants to get down to the business of problem solving—and what positions the

family members hold about the problem and its treatment, *positions* denoting their beliefs, opinions, and feelings. Since BT utilizes a systems perspective, we have the option of working with family members other than the identified patient to change the attempted solution (see case example).

Case Planning

The first task of planning is determining the logic, rule, or basic thrust of the attempted solutions. By studying the various individual solutions, the therapist seeks to derive their common denominator as seen from the next higher level of abstraction. In this sense, the goals is to uncover the rule underlying the system of problem solving, for it is here that change usually needs to take place.

For example, a person who becomes anxious when speaking in public may try any or all of the following solutions: practicing in front of a mirror, practicing relaxation exercises, making extensive notes and outlines, or taking medication. While each solution is different, they share the common denominator of trying to make a perfect presentation.

The basic solution serves as a guide, telling the therapist what in general might be done to resolve things, and, more important, what to stay away from: what remarks or directives are the "minefield"—those comments or directives that are simply a variation of the same basic solution. In the case of the anxious public speaker, the minefield would be any intervention that implies it would help him make a perfect presentation.

The easiest way to avoid the minefield is to select an intervention 180 degrees away from the basic solution. With the anxious speaker, many different behaviors fulfill this condition. The patient could: (1) announce to the audience that he is nervous; (2) make a mistake on purpose; (3) act as if he forgot what he was saying and ask the audience for help; or (4) drop his note cards in the middle of his talk. Each of these behaviors represents a 180-degree shift from the attempted solution.

Obviously, getting the patient to carry out such assignments is not easy. From his perspective, this advice would appear to only make things worse. Therefore, the therapist must frame directives in a way that makes sense to the patient, and the information for such framing is derived from what has been learned from the patient's positions. Any of the following framings might be suitable for having a patient make a mistake on purpose: (1) as a method of in vivo desensitization; (2) exaggerating a problem as a way of learning how one does it; or (3) as a special exercise designed to stimulate insight. Some patients are simply intrigued with the question "Do you know how to give a really bad presentation?" And with some cases, we might use an intervention called "the devil's pact." The patient must agree to follow the therapist's assignment without knowing the basis for it or discussing it once it has been presented. The assignment is either carried out or treatment is terminated.

Ideally, the new therapeutic assignment seeks two objectives: to influence the patient to carry out a new solution that is not a variation on the basic solution, and, in doing so, to give up solutions that perpetuate the problem. For example, Erickson is reported to have cured an insomniac by convincing him to wax the kitchen floor during bedtime hours. From our perspective, this assignment fulfills both BT objectives: It stops the patient from trying to force himself to sleep by making himself stay up and wax the floor.

Although much time and effort goes into case planning, such a formulation is not treated as sacred or irreversible. The treatment plan is simply a working hypothesis for bringing about change, and it will be pursued, modified, or replaced, depending on its usefulness.

Interventions

It is assumed that the therapist is always influencing the patient as a consequence of the communication process and the context in which it takes place. However, there are points in treatment when the therapist makes a deliberate and concerted effort to use his or her influence to reach a particular objective of treatment.

Changing the Patient's View.   Although brief therapists don't believe insight is useful in resolving problems, if a patient's view of his or her problem is changed—not brought into line with reality—trying out a new solution can become easier. Similarly, a different view of the problem can make it *more difficult* for the patient to continue using the same old solutions that are perpetuating the problem. This technique is called *reframing*—"to change the conceptual and/or emotional setting or viewpoint in relation to which a situation is experienced and to place it in another frame which fits the 'facts' of the same situation equally well or even better, and thereby changes its entire meaning" (Watzlawick, Weakland, & Fisch, 1974).

For instance, if a husband who resorts to physical abuse during marital fights accepts the reframing that he is making a loyal sacrifice for his wife by meeting her unconscious need for punishment, it puts him in a dilemma that is therapeutically useful. Since his abuse is defined as a positive gift, he must find new ways to retaliate. The therapist can capitalize on this by suggesting that he "kill her" with kindness.

Similarly, a salesman who came to treatment because he felt his stuttering impeded his work performance benefited greatly when his speaking difficulty was reframed as an advantage, distinguishing him in a positive fashion from the stereotype of the fast, smooth-talking salesman who usually turned off many prospective customers. His acceptance of this new view left him more relaxed about his impediment, resulting in less effort to inhibit it and an improved ability to speak without stuttering. As Shakespeare wrote, "There is nothing either good or bad, but thinking makes it so."

Putting the Patient at Ease.   Patients are more likely to accept new ideas, try out assignments, and give more complete information if the treatment ambience is lowkeyed. At the beginning of the first interview, it will be suggested that everyone use first names. Traditional therapeutic techniques, such as the pregnant pause and requesting that the patient verbalize his affect, are rarely used, so that the treatment interview is more likely to resemble a normal conversation. All of these notions stem from the basic idea of "one-downmanship," with the therapist using a number of tactics to diminish the implied distance between himself and the patient. Rather than seeming to be a person with no problems and total understanding, the therapist portrays himself as another human being with frailties and limitations of his own.

When collecting information, the one-down position is used for clarification purposes. The therapist is likely to say, "Would you please go over that again? Unfortunately, I am one of those people who have to hear things about five times before I get it. Please bear with me."

In the later stages of treatment, when new ideas or directives are presented, they are framed as "not very important" or "just some small thing that might be of some help." At times one of the most useful therapeutic comments is instructing the patient to "go slow." If the patient returns for a session reporting progress, the therapist may comment that while he shares the patient's satisfaction, it would be wise not to move too rapidly because change always makes waves.

Motivation.   There are many ways of motivating the client to behave differently, depending on his or her opinions, beliefs, and attitudes. The angry and frustrated parent can be given assignments that allow him to harmlessly and therapeutically vent his feelings, while caretakers will be instructed to be even more helpful and sacrificing. The curious and insight-oriented can be motivated to try out novel ideas, to see what new things they can learn, while the resistive patient will be encouraged not to change.

Homework.   Assuming that therapeutic change takes place between sessions, many of our interventions are in the form of homework assignments that instruct the patient to take new action vis-à-vis the problem. Directives are in the form of small, concrete, specific tasks to be carried out once or twice before the next session. During the early stages of treatment, the patient's homework might be to formulate a goal of treatment or to decide which of his or her problems needs the most attention.

One of the most interesting classes of directives is called the *paradoxical injunction,* more commonly known as *symptom prescriptions.* These are particularly appropriate in cases where the attempted solution takes the form of attempting to force spontaneity. In trying to force his or her symptom, the patient must give up all the solutions used to eliminate it. Dr. Richard Fisch rapidly resolved a patient's complaint of premature ejaculation by instructing the marital couple to return home with a stop watch; the wife was told to time the speed of her husband's ejaculation so that, ostensibly, Dr. Fisch could have the necessary data needed to formulate a diagnosis. (The request for additional information was simply a cover story to make the assignment seem reasonable to the couple.) By attempting to carry out the assignment, all problem-engendering solutions were dropped, and much to the couple's surprise, the husband no longer ejaculated quickly. From the patients' perspective, treatment was over before it really began.

Termination

The brevity of patient contact and emphasis on action rather than insight or expression of feelings make for a relatively simple termination process. In most cases, the subject is not even broached until the last session or the one just preceding it. Basically, the therapist looks for three criteria in the patient's report that would indicate that he or she is ready to terminate: (1) a small but significant dent has been made in the problem; (2) the change appears durable; and (3) the patient implies or states that he can handle things on his own.

When wrapping up a case, the course of treatment is briefly reviewed, giving the patient credit for what has been accomplished. Patients are also cautioned against believing that the problem is solved forever. We predict that they will face this or a similar life difficulty again, and that how things go will depend upon how they deal with it.

Some patients are hesitant about terminating treatment, and in these cases we are likely to frame termination as a necessary vacation from treatment, giving them time to digest and incorporate the gains made into their daily lives. They are warned that any further change would be counterproductive, and that the best thing to do now is to "put things on the back burner and let them simmer." In three months they will be contacted for a progress report.

Finally, with resistive or negative patients, any improvement will be challenged as inconsequential or temporary, and the therapist will predict that things will probably get worse. As in all our work, every phase of treatment utilizes therapeutic strategy based upon the needs of the particular case.

APPLICATIONS

Given the generic nature of this approach, Brief Therapy can be applied to a wide variety of problems. Thus it makes little difference if the presenting complaint is a family problem, a classical psychiatric symptom, a behavior difficulty, or some physiological difficulty such as the nausea that accompanies chemotherapy. In each case the therapist will seek to interrupt the vicious cycle of problem-solution interaction and bring about useful and desirable change.

BT can be particularly useful in dealing with economically disadvantaged clients. Historically, this population has not taken to long-term treatment, analytic approaches, and nondirective therapists. These clients also prove difficult for the family therapist who insists that all family members attend each therapeutic interview. By its very nature and design, BT circumvents many of these problems: Treatment is of a short duration; the therapist speaks the language of the clients; directives and suggestions are a large part of the therapeutic procedure; and family problems are addressed without treating the entire family.

In institutional settings, many of the therapeutic problems stem from the fact that the patients are involuntary. Since BT is basically concerned with interaction between people, it is adaptable to such settings by focusing on how to change the staff's behavior (the staff, in this sense, is the customer for treatment) in order to change the behavior of the patient. For instance, a local juvenile holding facility was having a discipline problem with a 13-year-old boy who broke regulations. The usual procedure for this was confinement to his room and loss of privileges. In this particular case, however, the boy would tear apart the room, yelling, banging, and disrupting the rest of the unit. The staff had tried a number of things to quiet him, including putting him in an isolation cell, but he continued to make a disturbance that stirred up the rest of the boys. The staff decided that something was terribly wrong with the boy and called Dr. Fisch to make a psychiatric consultation. Dr. Fisch suggested the following BT type of solution, which worked quite well with this case. The next time the boy was confined to his room and started yelling, the counselor, in a loud, clear voice, called all the other boys to the door outside his room and said, "Johnny is banging and yelling again. I know it's disturbing, but there is nothing we can do to stop it. But since he is doing it, we might as well have a contest. I'm going to pass out slips of paper and pencils, and I want each of you to write your name and guess how long Johnny will bang. The winner gets a Coke." (On this unit, a Coke was a fairly good prize.) The unit counselor reported that the banging only lasted 10 minutes instead of two or three hours. Also, although it wasn't suggested but certainly was made to order, one of the boys had gone to the door and asked Johnny if he would bang for another five minutes so he could win the Coke. This really put an end to things. Subsequently, it was reported that the banging had stopped and Johnny was making a better adjustment to his stay.

One of the most common problems in medical work is patient compliance and cooperation. As illustrated in institutional work, the interpersonal framework allows one to intervene in such problems without necessarily interviewing the identified patient. The author and a colleague, as part of a doctoral thesis, treated five families where the husband had had a major heart attack but continued to engage in high-risk behavior—smoking, poor diet, overwork, and no exercise. Furthermore, each of these identified patients had so irritated their cardiologists and rehabilitation workers that, for the most part, they had given up on these patients. In some cases the men would have nothing more to do with any physician. Taking advantage of our interactional model, we worked with the wives of these patients. Although our cases were limited to five interviews, we were successful in changing the behavior of these women vis-à-vis their husband's high-risk behavior with small but significant positive results.

Finally, BT is seen as a skill or craft that can be passed on to others. Teaching and supervision are enhanced by the close translation of theory into practice, clearly defined tasks of treatment, a consistent way of evaluating the data, and specific techniques for influencing the client to change. Supervision, using BT theory as a way of understanding the treatment problems faced by the supervisee, lends itself to a process where the supervisee can become more responsible for evaluating his own treatment problems, how he has been handling them (his solutions to the problems), and what he might have to do differently to get the case moving.

CASE EXAMPLE

Problem

Mr. and Mrs. Jones entered treatment because their 15-year-old daughter, Jan, was misbehaving. She was cutting classes, staying out late at night, refusing to do things with the rest of the family (which included three siblings—14, 12, and 11 years of age), and making constant demands for money, clothing, and a variety of other things. Both parents emphatically agreed that she "had a knack for breaking you down" with her constant demands, which led to their giving in to her requests.

Attempted Solutions

The parents had dealt with her misbehavior in a variety of ways, primarily by reasoning and by restricting her to the house. They had tried sending Jan to live with her uncle who "was good with kids," but her misbehavior persisted and she was sent home. On one occasion Mr. Jones had her picked up by the police and kept in juvenile hall overnight, but this had no positive effect on her behavior.

Interventions

Session 1.   Since the parents gave such clear information and seemed quite united about their goals and methods, the therapist felt more secure about intervening even more rapidly than is our custom. He ended the first session by taking the position that they might "give her some of her own medicine" by acting unreasonable themselves when she began nagging them. Not wanting to commit himself fully, he suggested they think about this during the next week but *not* put their thinking into action. This assignment subtly suggests that they continue reasoning with her, even though it was identified as unworkable. However, if they were to think about what else they might say in the midst of struggling with her, they could not really deal with her in the same old way. What they did with this directive would also indicate their compliance to therapeutic directives and how such action affected the family system.

Session 2.   During the first half of the second interview, the daughter (the identified patient) was seen with her parents. The therapist concluded his contact with her by explaining that she had an amazing power over her parents by nagging them until they gave in to her wishes. She would be foolish to give this up, even if it meant "walking around in a chronic state of rage, or taking an occasional trip to juvenile hall. You'll get used to this." She was sent to the waiting room on the note that the only thing left for the therapist to do was to teach her parents to get used to this.

The therapist's statements to Jan simultaneously accomplished three objectives: (1) It aversively suggested that she continue misbehaving no matter what the cost; (2) the manner in which this was said implied that the therapist was in a coalition with the parents, increasing their compliance with treatment; and (3) the message also implied that Jan's main strategy was to break down the parents by nagging, which only works because they try to reason with her unreasonableness and eventually give in to her demands.

The remainder of the session was devoted to working with the parents. Mrs. Jones still seemed to be operating from a position of power she could not enforce. However, she did report backing off from her usual solution of trying to reason with Jan. Given her positive response to the suggestions made in Session 1, we decided to take things a step further.

It was explained to Mrs. Jones that words were her weakest weapon in dealing with Jan, and that much more could be accomplished by teaching her a very important lesson in life—one hand washes the other. To do this, the therapist explained the technique of *benevolent sabotage*. Any requests made of Jan were to be made as follows: "There is something I would like you to do. I can't make you do it, but I wish you would." This would only be said once. If there was no compliance, benevolent sabotage was to be employed. For example, Mrs. Jones could be late in picking Jan up for an important appointment or could somehow put her favorite white blouse in with the colored wash. When confronted about any of this, Mrs. Jones was to apologize and say, "I'm sorry, I don't know what's wrong with me." To make this behavior even more believable, Mrs. Jones was instructed to tell Jan that in the remaining part of the interview, she learned about some of her own personal problems and was feeling depressed. Her own self-absorption would now implicitly explain some of the mistakes she made that affected Jan's well-being.

Benevolent sabotage served two purposes. It harmlessly channeled Mrs. Jones's anger and frustration into an avenue that did not escalate hostilities, while implicitly steering her away from her usual way of dealing with the problem: reasoning and threats.

Session 3.   Parents reported that Jan was "in tears all week because no one would fight with her." Mrs. Jones had made one request in the prescribed manner, and Jan complied, so there was no need to use benevolent sabotage. However, the assignment had made the parents realize that they were continuing to make life easy for Jan on a noncontingent basis.

During this session, they asked for advice concerning Jan's birthday. They could not decide if they should buy her a present, especially the $35.00 pair of leather boots she had been requesting. Earlier in treatment, Mrs. Jones had complained that Jan would not wash her bras out by hand, resulting in frequent replacement at considerable cost. After a bit of figuring in the observation room, the following intervention was offered. They were to purchase four $8.00 bras, have them gift-wrapped, and present them to Jan for her birthday. If she balked at this, they were to apologize and explain they thought she had wanted them.

Mrs. Jones said that Jan's nagging was on the decline. But, at times, she would attempt to get her back into the same old game of arguing. This was dealt with by instructing the parents in another technique called *collusion*. The next time Jan attempted to engage her mother

in an argument when her father was home, he was to enter the room, pull a nickel out of his pocket, and give it to her. If she asked what the nickel was for, he was simply to say, "I felt like it." Then both parents were to leave the room without saying another word.

Collusion is similar to benevolent sabotage in distracting the parents from their usual verbal responses, which are not working, thereby breaking the redundancy of the system. Since the parents complained that "Jan was just too damn sure of herself," the assignment was *framed* as a way of "injecting her with a healthsome dose of insecurity."

Session 4.   The parents continued reporting improvement. Mr. Jones laughingly told how he gave Jan a nickel and the experience left her bewildered. They also presented the bras to her, and when she opened the present she said in a faint, disappointed voice, "Four bras, that would have been the same price as the boots I wanted." The parents apologized immediately, explaining that they thought she would have liked them because now she wouldn't have to wash them out by hand. Jan said, "Thank you," and quietly left the room.

During the last week they reported that Jan was more relaxed, taking her time eating at the dinner table and watching television with the family. Mr. Jones told how she had used her allowance to buy her mother some candy and warned the other children not to eat it. The parents couldn't get over the change in her. The therapist warned them—dangers of improvement—that if they continued dealing with her successfully, they would find it difficult to see her leave the home in a few years. He suggested that they might want to reverse her progress and directed them to bring about a *planned relapse* by taking one occasion to deal with her in their old way: reasoning and threats.

Session 5.   Mr. and Mrs. Jones found it difficult to bring about a relapse (a desired outcome from the fourth session). Jan continued to improve, staying at home more and showing a renewed interest in her sewing. Mrs. Jones: "She's a much happier person; I can't believe it."

Three-Month Follow-Up Interview.   The parents reported that Jan's behavior was "much better." There was less fighting and arguing, and she complied with simple requests. The parents had felt sufficiently confident to take a weekend trip, leaving her in charge of the other children. Everything had gone well. Mrs. Jones reported no need to act helpless or to use benevolent sabotage. There was no further treatment.

Twelve-Month Follow-Up Interview.   Jan's behavior continued to improve. She has acted more considerate, giving up her room to visiting relatives. She has shown more concern and respect for her siblings, and, in return, they have done small favors for her. Her school grades have risen from the F–D range to C's and B's. The parents socialize more on their own, and there was no further treatment.

SUMMARY

The psychotherapy industry is in the midst of a real crisis. Both practitioners and researchers are discouraged by the poor results of psychotherapy outcome studies; third-party payers are beginning to protest the spiraling cost of mental health services, while the demand for treatment continues to rise; and rumor has it that a national health insurance plan would not be financially feasible if it included psychiatric coverage.

Brief Therapy will not solve all of these problems, but the implications and consequences of our work do point in the right direction. Short-term treatment is cost effective, allowing the therapist to treat a greater number of patients within a given time frame. The generic nature of Brief Therapy permits the therapist to treat a wide variety of problems without devoting time, energy, and money for unnecessary, specialized training—Marital Therapy, Child Therapy, and so forth. The nature of the interviewing process and the directive stance make BT highly appropriate for the economically disadvantaged patient, who wants to discuss his or her presenting complaint and expects some concrete, understandable advice. Finally, BT is more easily and quickly taught to others. It utilizes a minimum of theory, which translates directly into a key number of practice principles and techniques. Supervision would also become a more efficient enterprise, defined as a professional relationship where the supervisee learns to refine the skills of the craft rather than working on his or her personal problems or mental health.

REFERENCES

Bateson, G., Jackson, D., Haley, J., & Weakland, J. (1956). Toward a theory of schizophrenia. *Behavioral Science, 1,* 251–264.

Fisch, R., Weakland, J., Watzlawick, P., Segal, L., Hoebel, F., & Deardorff, M. (1975). *Learning brief therapy: An Introductory manual.* Unpublished training manual, Mental Research Institute, Palo Alto, CA.

Haley, J. (1963). *Strategies of psychotherapy.* New York: Grune & Stratton.

Haley, J. (Ed.). (1967). *Advanced techniques of hypnosis and therapy: Selected papers of Milton H. Erickson, M.D.* New York: Grune & Stratton.

Ruesch, R., & Bateson, G. (1951). *Communication. The social matrix of psychiatry.* New York: Norton.

Watzlawick, P., & Weakland, J. (Eds.). (1977). *The interactional view.* New York: Norton.

Watzlawick, P., Fisch, R., Weakland, J., & Bodin, A. (1971). On unbecoming family therapists. In A. Ferber et al. (Eds.), *The book of family therapy.* New York: Science House.

Watzlawick, P., Weakland, J., & Fisch, R. (1974). *Change: Principles of problem formation and problem resolution.* New York: Norton.

Weakland, J. (1976). Communication, theory and clinical change. In P. Guerin (Ed.), *Family therapy, theory and practice.* New York: Gardner Press.

Weakland, J., Fisch, R., Watzlawick. P., & Bodin, A. (1974). Brief therapy: Focused problem resolution. *Family Process, 13,* 141–168.

Chapter 9

COGNITIVE BEHAVIOR THERAPY[1]

JOHN P. FOREYT and G. KEN GOODRICK

In the early years of psychotherapy there were three major trends: therapies based on (1) instincts (Freud), (2) mysticism (Jung), and (3) common sense (Adler). For quite a while, various innovators of psychotherapies modified one of these three approaches, combining them, altering them, and so forth. In 1924, Mary Cover Jones introduced something brand new in psychotherapy when retraining a fearful child: conditioning. Since then a considerable number of psychotherapeutic researchers and clinicians have become behavior modifiers, bringing with them various concepts and procedures from the laboratory. Among the major individuals in this trend have been Andrew Salter, Hans Eysenck, and Joseph Wolpe.

While these procedures, if they are strictly employed, are excellent for symptom removal from the "mindless"—from infants who ruminate, the mentally ill, or the very young, these procedures are not feasible in dealing with intact adults. And so was born what is a semantic and possibly a logical contradiction: Cognitive Behavior Therapy. Behavior modifiers began to consider the mind—they had to assume the existence of and to deal with cognition, and so they attempted to bring their strict laboratory-type thinking to general psychotherapeutic problems.

Cognitive Behavior Therapy refers to a set of principles and procedures that share the assumption that cognitive processes affect behavior and that these processes can be changed through cognitive and behavioral techniques. It is different from traditional insight therapy in that specific here-and-now cognitions are targeted for change through specific procedures, such as modeling or imaginal techniques, rather than emphasizing the past as a cause for current difficulties. *Cognitions* include beliefs and belief systems, thoughts, and images. *Cognitive processes* include ways of evaluating and organizing information about the environment and self, ways of processing information for coping or problem solving, and ways of predicting and evaluating future events.

HISTORY

Behavior Therapy has always claimed conditioning and learning theories as its theoretical underpinnings. Results of many of the early behavior case studies published in the 1960s in *Behaviour Research and Therapy*

and the *Journal of Applied Behavior Analysis* were attributed to respondent and operant conditioning. As more and more graduate students began to experiment with behavioral techniques, it became readily apparent that many patients' problems were far more complex than earlier studies implied. The conditioning models seemed inadequate to explain complex human learning.

Interest in self-control and self-regulatory processes in the late 1960s within Behavior Therapy helped shift behavior therapists' beliefs in environmental determinism (i.e., one's life is primarily shaped by one's external environment) to one of reciprocal determinism in which a person is not a passive product of his environment but an active participant in his development (Mahoney & Arnkoff, 1978). Also in the 1960s many behavior therapists began to investigate more fully their clients' thoughts. The work of Joseph Cautela in particular served to increase research interest in covert processes. Cautela's technique of covert sensitization was particularly important because of its use of aversive imagery for effecting behavioral change.

Albert Ellis's (1979) Rational-Emotive Therapy, based on the assumption that specific cognitions (irrational beliefs) were the cause of maladaptive behavior and negative affect, began to be read and discussed within the behavioral field. Aaron T. Beck's (1976) Cog-

[1] Supported by the Heart, Lung, and Blood Institute, National Institute of Health, Grants no. HL17269 and 1T32 HL09258-01A1.

nitive Therapy, which focused on cognitive styles associated with depression, was also influential with many behavior therapists.

The publication in 1969 of Albert Bandura's *Principles of Behavior Modification* was a significant event for many behavior therapists searching for more integrative models, in that he presented theoretical interpretations of the mechanisms of both operant and classical conditioning along with emphasizing the importance of cognitive mediational processes in the regulation of behavior. With the publication of Bandura's book, interest in thoughts and feelings increased. Conditioning models of human behavior began to give way to models emphasizing cognitive mediational processes. This trend was evident in the reinterpretation of systematic desensitization, originally conceptualized by Wolpe as a counterconditioning procedure, but now viewed by some as involving cognitive mediational processes such as expectation, coping strategies, and imagery. The cognitive interpretation of desensitization led to such specific therapies as covert modeling (Cautela, 1971), coping skills training (Goldfried, 1971), and anxiety management training (Suinn & Richardson, 1971).

A number of influential books have followed Bandura's. One of his students, Michael Mahoney, has been a major force in the Cognitive Therapy movement. Several of his books, including *Cognition and Behavior Modification* (Mahoney, 1974), have helped define the field. He was also editor of the movement's journal, *Cognitive Therapy and Research.* The first issue was published in March 1977.

CURRENT STATUS

The focus on cognitive mechanisms in therapy, formerly explained by simple classical and operant conditioning principles, is not a passing fad. However, to ensure its durability, Cognitive Behavior Therapy must continue to maintain a scientific approach in terms of strategy and methodology, as Behavior Therapy has tried to do. Its evaluation must rely on careful observation, hypothesis testing, and replication.

The major tasks facing Cognitive Behavior Therapy include:

1. The development of more reliable methods for assessing cognitive phenomena;
2. The refinement and extension of knowledge regarding the causal impact of cognitive phenomena on other categories of experience (behaviors, feelings, etc.);
3. The identification of parameters that influence the development, maintenance, or change of particular cognitive patterns;

4. The incorporation of those parameters into pragmatic therapy procedures; and
5. A continuing reappraisal of the assumptions and adequacy of the perspective. (Mahoney, 1977a, p. 10)

If Cognitive Behavior Therapy can successfully deal with these issues, it will undoubtedly become a major force within clinical psychology. However, despite its acceptance among many therapists, not all behaviorally oriented researchers welcome this hybrid. For example, Eysenck (1979), a staunch S-R theorist, warned that "Although cognitive theories seem fashionable at the moment among some behaviour therapists who should know better . . . being fashionable is not the same as being correct, or useful, or in line with the evidence." He felt that "Cognitive theory, *per contra,* does not even exist as a 'theory' that could meaningfully be criticized or tested; it is an aspiration, born of mentalistic preconceptions, in search of hypotheses."

Wolpe (1978, p. 442) pointed out that "Behavior therapists have deliberately influenced their patients' thinking ever since formal behavior therapy of the neuroses came into existence"; because of this he felt that cognitive approaches to therapy had always been integrated with the behavioral techniques. "Thought," wrote Wolpe, "obeys the same 'mechanistic' laws as motor or autonomic behavior" (p. 438). The principles of conditioning are sufficient to account for cognition, and overt behavior is a sufficient indicator of this conditioning.

Despite its critics, judging from its rapidly growing popularity (cf. Kendall & Hollon, 1979), the current status of Cognitive Behavior Therapy is healthy indeed.

THEORY

When behavior therapists began to apply laws of animal learning to humans, several discrepancies became apparent. Reinforcement or punishment could be applied before or after the target behaviors; the timing was not found to be critical as with animals. In some cases the undesirable behaviors could be "rewarded" and yet the result of therapy was a reduction in their frequency (Meichenbaum, 1976). All the counterconditioning models for systematic desensitization failed to explain why none of their components seemed essential (Murray & Jacobson, 1978). In war some very powerful contingencies have been applied without success to change the behavior of POWs, and it is doubtful that traditional Behavior Therapy techniques could be used to make a fashion model put on 40 pounds if such a gain would jeopardize her career. The reason for all this is that, according to social learning theory (Bandura, 1969, 1977), behavior is not automatically under the control of external contingencies. Rather, humans learn how to satisfy their primary and acquired needs by using contingency information to select behaviors that they expect will lead to desired outcomes based on past experience. According to this theory, therapeutic techniques must produce in the patient an expectation that change will occur and a clear understanding of goals. This expectation is a function of the patient's belief in his or her own ability to perform the required behaviors necessary for therapeutic change, and the belief that the therapeutic procedure will be effective (Bandura, 1977).

Thus the critical processes in therapy are viewed as cognitively mediated. In the same way, social learning theory posits that the critical processes maintaining maladaptive behavior are also cognitive. A person behaves in a maladaptive fashion because, through an abnormal learning process, one expects one can't change, or cope, or avoid feelings of anxiety or depression. The goal of therapy, then, is to change the patient's faulty evaluation of future outcomes, either by changing the way environmental information is processed or by training the patient in skills that will allow him or her to expect desired behavioral outcomes, or by doing both.

Mahoney and Arnkoff (1978) have noted that the cognitive learning perspective includes a wide variety of principles and procedures that have not been tied together into an integrative model. They do feel that there are some common assumptions used by cognitive learning theorists:

1. Humans develop adaptive and maladaptive behavior and affective patterns through cognitive processes (selective attention, symbolic coding, etc.).
2. These cognitive *processes* can be functionally activated by *procedures* that are generally isomorphic with those of the human learning laboratory (although there may be other procedures which activate the cognitive processes as well).
3. The resultant task of the therapist is that of a diagnostician-educator who assesses maladaptive cognitive processes and subsequently arranges learning experiences that will alter cognitions and the behavior and affect patterns with which they correlate. (Mahoney & Arnkoff, 1978, p. 692)

Some claim that cognitions play a primary or even an exclusive role in the formation of maladaptive processes. They argue that therapeutic change can be achieved solely through cognitive change. However, given that the relationships among cognition, behavior, and affect are not and may never be well understood, and that the critical factors in successful therapy remain largely unspecified, it is of little use now to try to develop anything more than preliminary hypotheses. What may be ulti-

mately important in theory development in this area is how the theory determines the way the therapist communicates the cognitive explanation of the presenting problem to the patient. The explanation must make sense to the patient and obviously lead to strategies for change that make sense and are feasible in terms of the patient's perceived self-efficacy. Fortunately, the ways theorists are now viewing cognitions and their therapeutic methods can be easily understood and accepted by patients since the approach does not deviate from commonsense notions of the relations among thoughts, feelings, and behaviors.

From various conceptualizations of the role of cognitions in the development of maladaptive behaviors (Meichenbaum, 1976) have come at least 10 cognitive learning therapies. These have been categorized by Mahoney and Arnkoff (1978) into therapies involving *cognitive restructuring, coping skills,* and *problem solving.* These therapies are summarized in Table 9.1.

The three cognitive restructuring therapies conceptualize cognitions as either part of a behavioral chain, as a thinking style, or as a belief system, depending upon the therapeutic approach. Rational-Emotive Therapy has been around for over 40 years, and is well known to most readers. It therefore will not be discussed in this chapter. For an excellent review of the therapy, one of the first and probably the most popular of the Cognitive Behavior Therapies, see the chapter by Ellis (1979).

Self-Instructional Training (Meichenbaum, 1977) views cognitions as self-instructions used in the development of response patterns. These cognitions verbally encode the information storage for stimulus saliency, proper sequence, and the topology of the behavioral sequence. If the encoding process was faulty, the learned behavior will be maladaptive. This theory derives from developmental studies of children who use vocal self-instructions to help themselves develop skills. It follows that new instructions provided by the therapist can be used to develop more appropriate skills.

As the skill is acquired, the self-instructions fade from awareness; the skill is performed "automatically," or without conscious verbal processes. However, the person behaves *as if* he were following instructions. This is an important distinction, since the current treatment methodology stresses to the patient that he is behaving *as if* there was a cognitive distortion or deficit, rather than stressing assessment of these distortions or deficits, which may or may not be part of the patient's awareness. This issue will be discussed in the methodology section.

Cognitive Therapy (Beck, 1976) sees the cause of depression and other mood disorders as the result of an irrational thinking style that leads the patient to interpret reality in a way that reflects negatively on both his self-evaluation and expected outcomes of behavior. The pa-

Table 9.1   Cognitive Therapies

Therapy	Theoretical Basis	Diagnosis/Assessment	Treatment	Applications
		COGNITIVE RESTRUCTURING		
Rational-Emotive Therapy (RET) (Ellis, 1979)	Cognitions comprise an irrational belief system. Problems stem from preoccupation with what others think about patient. Deviations from perfection and total love are interpreted as terrible catastrophes.	*Cognitive:* Irrational beliefs inferred from patient's reported affective response to life situations.	*Cognitive:* Persuasion, rational modeling, thought monitoring.	Has been used for depression, phobias, assertiveness.
		Affective: Negative affect due to irrational evaluation of personal outcomes. *Behavioral:* Behaviors restricted to limit negative affect (depression, anxiety).	*Behavioral:* Behavioral performance assignments.	
Self-Instructional Training (SIT) (Meichenbaum, 1977)	Behavior and emotions are controlled by self-instructional speech, which is internalized in childhood. Idiosyncratic thought patterns may develop, which are maladaptive. Cognitions are viewed as part of the response chain leading to behavior, which later leave awareness as behaviors become automatic.	*Cognitive:* Cognitions leading to maladaptive behavior have become automatic and unconscious.	*Cognitive:* Learn new self-instructions for new coping skills. Use appropriate imagery for problem solving.	Promising results with impulsive children, test anxiety, creativity enhancement. Some work with schizophrenics.
		Affective: Performance anxiety.	*Behavioral:* Practice coping skills with modeling, desensitization.	
		Behavioral: Aggression, hyperactivity, impulsiveness.		
Cognitive Therapy (Beck, 1976)	Cognitions comprise irrational thinking styles. Distorted thinking causes selective attention to and inaccurate prediction of consequences. May lead to distorted imagery of consequences.	*Cognitive:* Patient makes arbitrary inferences that reflect on himself negatively, exaggerates importance of events, disregards essential features of life situation. Dichotomous reasoning, overgeneralization of failures, distorted images.	*Cognitive:* Recognize and monitor cognitions. Self-examine thinking style while performing homework tasks. Practice adaptive thinking.	Promising results with depression. Possible use with psychiatric population.

Table 9.1   (*continued*)

Therapy	Theoretical Basis	Diagnosis/Assessment	Treatment	Applications
		Affective: Depression caused by negative view of self and opportunities for improvement due to distorted thinking style applied to problems.	*Affective:* Test relation between cognition and affect.	
		Behavioral: Restricted behavior characteristic of depression, anxiety.	*Behavioral:* Homework assignments, graded tasks.	

COPING SKILLS

Therapy	Theoretical Basis	Diagnosis/Assessment	Treatment	Applications
Covert Modeling (Cautela, 1971)	Mentally rehearsing target behaviors allows patient to learn sequence of events and train his affective responses to develop ability to act in stressful situations. Allows forming of adaptive self-statements (as in SIT) while practicing being relaxed.	*Cognitive:* Anticipated anxiety and stress prevents careful cognitive planning needed to cope with situation.	*Cognitive:* Rehearse target performance mentally.	Promising results for phobias, unassertiveness. May not be so effective as behavioral rehearsal.
		Affective: Phobias and unassertiveness.	*Affective:* Relaxation induced during mental rehearsal.	
		Behavioral: Restricted behavior characteristic of anxiety avoidance.		
Coping Skills Training (Goldfried, 1971)	Patient can learn to regulate anxiety by imagining increasingly threatening events, attempting to cope with the anxiety, and relax it away: similar to systematic desensitization but with active coping imagery.	*Cognitive:* No cognitive skills to cope with anxiety.	*Cognitive:* Patient goes through hierarchy of threatening imagery of problem situations, tries out coping strategies that may decrease anxiety, SIT.	Test anxiety, indecisiveness.
		Affective: Unable to cope with situations due to excessive anxiety.	*Affective:* Relaxation during cognitive learning.	
		Behavioral: Stress avoidance.	*Behavioral:* Role play threatening situations.	
Anxiety Management Training (Suinn & Richardson, 1971)	Patient learns to apply relaxation training as an active coping skill in various imaginary scenes. Training generalizes to problem situations.	*Cognitive:* No cognitive skills to cope with anxiety.	*Cognitive:* Relaxation and other coping skills applied during anxiety-causing imaginary scenes. A variety of scenes is used to promote generalizability of skills.	Anxiety control. Too few studies to evaluate effectiveness.

(*continued*)

Table 9.1   (*continued*)

Therapy	Theoretical Basis	Diagnosis/Assessment	Treatment	Applications
		Affective: Unable to cope with situations due to excessive anxiety.		
		Behavioral: Stress avoidance.		
Stress Inoculation (Meichenbaum, 1977)	Patient's inability to cope with stress caused by inaccurate appraisal of situation, lack of specific skills (relaxation, cognitive self-statements), lack of experience in dealing with stressful situations.	*Cognitive:* Lack of realistic evaluation of stressful situations.	*Cognitive:* Patient educated about the causes of his anxiety reaction: maladaptive self-statements replaced with adaptive ones.	A few promising studies. May help cope with anger, pain, performance anxieties.
		Affective: Anxiety under stress; excessive anger.	*Affective:* Learn physiological responses to stress. Relaxation training.	
		Behavioral: Inappropriate behavior under stress or stress avoidance.	*Behavioral:* Learn coping behaviors. Rehearse coping skills in stressful situation.	
		PROBLEM SOLVING		
Behavioral Problem Solving (D'Zurilla & Goldfried, 1971; Spivak, Platt, & Shure, 1976)	Emotionally disturbed and deviant persons are deficient in problem-solving ability, perceive fewer alternative behavioral responses to situations that are often antisocial. They have inaccurate expectancies about the results of their behaviors.	*Cognitive:* Poor problem-solving ability. Lack means-end imagery.	*Cognitive:* Learn how to specify problems, generate alternate solutions, and select best solution.	Some early work with emotionally disturbed children, psychiatric patients, disruptive children.
		Behavioral: Disturbed and antisocial behaviors.	*Behavioral:* Test and verify selected solution.	
Personal Science (Mahoney, 1977a, 1977b)	Personal problems are viewed as scientific problems. Skills taught parallel scientific research skills such as problem specification, data collection and interpretation, selecting hypothetical solution, experimenting, analyzing results, and revising or replacing hypotheses.	*Cognitive:* Poor problem-solving skills.	*Cognitive:* Self-monitoring means-end thinking, evaluation skills.	Paucity of empirical studies.

tient makes arbitrary inferences, exaggerates the importance of events, disregards essential features of a life situation, overgeneralizes failures, and may see things as either all good or all bad, with no middle ground. His imagery of expected outcomes may be distorted; the image may involve unrealistically negative or threatening events. The goal of therapy is to encourage more adaptive thinking through self-examination of cognitive style.

Covert Modeling Therapy (Cautela, 1971) assumes that persons are unable to cope with the anxiety and stress of certain situations because the anticipated anxiety or stress blocks adaptive, cognitively mediated strategies for coping. According to this theory of coping skills, a person can be helped to develop strategies for coping by rehearsing mentally the target behaviors he or she will need for an adaptive performance. While this therapy was originally theoretically couched in terms of covert conditioning, Mahoney and Arnkoff (1978) view it as a Coping Skills Therapy, since the images produced by mental rehearsal provide a vicarious learning experience, with the patient serving as his own model. During an imaginal sequence, the patient can try out and evaluate coping strategies before being faced with a real situation. Thus this therapy is similar to self-instructional training, in that the patient develops a plan of action that is verbally encoded while at the same time learning stress-coping techniques such as relaxation and meditation.

Coping Skills Training (Goldfried, 1971) is similar to Covert Modeling: The patient imagines a stressful situation and imagines coping with the anxiety. However, in Coping Skills Training the imaging occurs in a hierarchical sequence of events according to increasing anxiety, as is done in systematic desensitization. At each stage more anxiety is tolerated through the use of relaxation techniques to cope with the arousal caused by the images.

Anxiety Management Training (Suinn & Richardson, 1971) theorizes that anxiety responses to stressful situations can also serve as discriminative stimuli, and that these can be used in turn as cues for using coping strategies such as relaxation or altered cognitions of success or competency feelings. In this way coping skills become a response to anxiety as they are presumed to be in well-adjusted persons. As in Covert Modeling and Coping Skills Training, imagination of anxiety-arousing events is used. Again, the theory is that learning of skills can take place during imagined sequences. This theory was developed in part on the notion that people imagine future events in daydreaming, dreaming, fantasizing, or purposeful planning in order to predict how best to behave and what to expect.

Meichenbaum's (1977) *Stress Inoculation Training* is based on the theory that a fear or anxiety reaction in-volves a person's awareness of heightened physiological arousal and a set of anxiety-engendered thoughts and images. The anxiety state can therefore be alleviated by training in relaxation and changing the anxious thoughts and feelings. These coping techniques are rehearsed and then tried out in actual stressful analogue situations, such as unpredictable electric shock. These activities are supposed to result in the development of a cognitive set to resist stressors. This development occurs in controlled clinical settings so that the person can develop skills without being overwhelmed by stressors. The use of small doses of stress to build resistance is similar to disease immunization.

The *Problem-Solving Therapies* are based on the idea that problem solving requires a battery of cognitive skills, such as being able to see means-ends relationships to generate alternative solutions and to predict the results of possible solutions. Abnormal behaviors or emotional disturbance are viewed as resulting from inadequate problem-solving skills (D'Zurilla & Goldfried, 1971), especially as applied to social skills. Antisocial behavior may result from either inadequate appreciation for what is socially acceptable or an inability to find a solution that has an acceptable outcome. Problem-solving skills differences have been found between "normal" and "deviant" populations of preschoolers, emotionally disturbed children, adolescents, and institutionalized psychiatric patients, (Spivack, Platt, & Shure, 1976).

Another therapy based on problem-solving theory is Mahoney's (1977b) *Personal Science* approach. It posits that there are seven subskills needed for successful adjustment through problem solving:

1. Specify general problem
2. Collect information
3. Identify causes or patterns
4. Examine options
5. Narrow options and experiment
6. Compare data
7. Extend, revise, or replace

Theoretically the learning of these generalizable skills will allow a patient to select an appropriate and uniquely individual solution to his or her personal problems.

METHODOLOGY

The methodology of cognitive learning theory involves identifying and changing specific cognitive processes as they relate to problems of affect and behavior. Cognitions are now seen to play an important or essential role in behavior therapy (Bandura, 1969, 1977; Wolpe, 1978), but are largely left labeled as nonspecific factors. Cognitive Learning Therapy made these cognitive processes specific. The emphasis in therapy is to deal with here-and-now, goal-oriented cognitions in a systematic fashion using the social learning principles of modeling and rehearsal with self-awareness and relaxation training.

Whereas there are several different theoretical conceptualizations of how cognitions play a role in behavior and affect, the current trend in the study of psychotherapy is to explain how a methodology as applied elicits a common set of cognitive processes that are thought to be necessary for successful change. Table 9.2 depicts the four cognitive processes associated with change, along with the general procedures of Cognitive Learning Therapy that are thought to elicit them. The concepts depicted can be found in greater detail in Murray and Jacobson (1978) and in Meichenbaum (1976).

The first goal of therapy is to develop an expectation that help is available and that treatment will be effective. In Cognitive Learning Therapy this is achieved by helping the patient develop an awareness of maladaptive cognition-behavior-affect patterns. This can be done by having the patient self-monitor the thoughts, feelings, and behaviors that occur before, during, and after particular problem situations or moods. A self-monitoring recording sheet can be provided to the patient for this purpose. Through therapist interpretation and the patient's own analysis, an agreement can be reached on an explanation of the patient's problems in terms of the inappropriate cognitions associated with them. This mutual understanding provides the patient with a tangible reason for his problems. Rather than thinking he is going crazy, the patient now can identify the problem and see what needs to be changed. Together with his feeling of confidence in the therapist, this leads to an expectation that a successful outcome is possible. This in turn provides the motivation to continue treatment.

There are many techniques available to bring out cognitive information. Direct and indirect questions, correct or purposefully incorrect paraphrasing, or repeating the last words of a sentence may help the patient talk about cognitions. If these methods seem inadequate, additional anxiety-reducing, rapport-establishing techniques may be needed. The patient's cognitive self-awareness can be enhanced if the therapist can recognize recurring themes and point these out frequently.

If the patient fails to report a self-awareness of the kinds of maladaptive cognitions the therapist is looking for, then an alternative strategy is to tell the patient that the maladaptive cognitions associated with his problems have become automatic. It is explained that the maladaptive thinking that led to present patterns has faded from consciousness in the same way that thinking associated with tying a shoe no longer occurs past childhood. Thus the patient is viewed as behaving *as if* he were still guided by cognitions. This sets the framework and rationale for Cognitive Therapy, and gives meaning to the presenting problem. Some therapists may be more forceful in imposing their ideas about which kinds of cognitions need to be involved in therapy, as do rational-emotive therapists (Ellis, 1979), while others allow the patient to take an active role in selecting critical cognitive patterns and directions for change, as do cognitive therapists such as Beck (1976). The crucial criterion for

Table 9.2   Cognitive Learning Therapy Methodology

Therapeutic Process	Therapeutic Procedure	Procedural Examples
Expectation of help	Develop awareness of maladaptive cognition-behavior-affect patterns. Patient and therapist agree on a cognitive explanation of the problem that gives meaning to maladaption and prospect of a modality for change.	Self-monitor thoughts, feelings, and behaviors. Therapist offers interpretations, cognitive modeling.
Correction of maladaptive cognitions	Develop set of cognitions and behaviors that will replace the maladaptive ones.	Therapist guides patient in generating new cognitions and behaviors or suggests them.
Developing competencies in dealing with social living	Practice using new cognitions as they apply to social situations.	Patients uses imagery to practice dealing with situations. Analogue situations or in vivo experience in controlled situations serve as training episodes.
Changes in cognitions about self	As a result of new cognitions and training, patient reassesses *self-efficacy* in dealing adaptively with cognitions and situations.	Patient self-monitors behaviors and cognitions during practice sessions and is helped by therapist to interpret practice as evidence of increased self-efficacy to deal with former problem areas.

a successful assessment of cognitions is that their role seems plausible to the patient in explaining his problem (Meichenbaum, 1976).

Once the patient and therapist agree upon a set of maladaptive cognitions as explanatory of the maladaptive patterns, it remains to develop a new set of cognitions that can be understood to predispose the patient to change. It is assumed that the patient is rational enough to distinguish, with the therapist's help, between healthful and unhealthful patterns in cognition, affect, and behavior. The therapist can guide the patient using examples and by reinforcing constructive suggestions from the patient. The goal is to develop a new set of cognitions that the patient can readily perceive as leading to more adaptive patterns.

The third common process in therapeutic change is the development of the competencies needed to overcome the patient's limitations. In Cognitive Therapy, this involves practice in using the new set of cognitions. This practice is achieved either through imaginal performance, analogue situations, or in vivo experience. In some therapies (e.g., Anxiety Management Training), the new adaptive cognitive techniques are developed and tested during imaginal experience. Since heightened anxiety is thought to interfere with cognitive processes, practice usually occurs under conditions of relaxation. The goal is for the patient to report adequate cognitive control through a sequence of behaviors and feelings associated with former problem situations. This means that at each stage he is telling himself how to cope, what to do, and how to evaluate his behavior and its consequences.

While the results of cognitive practice may allow the patient to recite a complete sequence of adaptive, cognitive coping strategies, it may be necessary for the patient to acquire actual experience in using these new cognitive powers. This can be understood in terms of the last process necessary for therapeutic change: a change in the patient's cognitions about himself. The most important change is a sense of self-efficacy in dealing with his problem areas. Recent research in Cognitive Behavior Therapies tends to support Bandura's (1977) theory of self-efficacy, which states that treatments using direct behavioral intervention should be more effective in increasing self-efficacy than methods using purely cognitive techniques. In self-instructional training, rehearsal of self-instructions alone was found to be less effective than rehearsal with an opportunity to use the practiced cognitions in an actual stress situation (Meichenbaum, 1976). The methodology may thus need to include direct behavioral experience, with an emphasis on using new cognitions as a guide but not as a cause for therapeutic change. The patient must not only realize that he knows *how* to perform (cognitively), but that he actually *can* perform (behaviorally). The therapist can help the pa-

tient interpret his performance as evidence of his increased self-efficacy to deal with problems.

These general methodological principles have been applied to a number of therapeutic techniques (shown in Table 10.1). These techniques can be roughly categorized in terms of the types of target problems they address. Cognitive Learning Therapies deal with three broad areas: anxiety-stress reactions, depressive mood disorders, and social competencies. The methodologies for Stress Inoculation and Cognitive Therapy, two of the more promising techniques, are given here as examples.

Stress Inoculation

The procedures used in Stress Inoculation Training have been described by Meichenbaum (1977). He has divided the therapeutic sequence into three phases. In the educational phase the therapist and client conceptualize the client's stress problem. The second phase involves training the client in various coping skills. The third phase finds the client practicing these skills during exposure to actual stress. These three phases incorporate the four processes for therapeutic change discussed previously (Table 9.2).

In the educational phase the therapist must explain to the client, in lay terms, how his stressful reaction is the result of easily understood processes. A behavioral assessment is taken to discover the extent to which behavior is restricted by stress reactions, such as a particular phobia. The client describes his thoughts and feelings when placed in a stressful situation; to help in this, the client can close his eyes and imagine going through a typical stressful episode. The therapist then describes the anxiety reaction to stress in terms of a Schachterian model of emotional arousal. According to this model, the client's fear is caused both by perceived increases in physiological functions associated with fear, such as rapid heart rate, sweaty palms, and bodily tension, and by a set of anxiety-causing thoughts reflecting helplessness, panic, embarrassment, or fears of becoming insane. Meichenbaum (1977) points out that the scientific validity of such a model is less crucial than its plausibility for the client, since the important goal of the educational phase is to lay the conceptual groundwork for intervention.

In the last part of the educational phase, the therapist instructs the client to view the stress problem as a series of manageable phases rather than a single overpowering gestalt. This series includes preparation for stress, confrontation with the stressor, the possibility of being overwhelmed, and self-reinforcement after coping successfully. The possibility of being overwhelmed is included so that it is an expected possibility, a battle lost, but not the war.

In the rehearsal phase, the therapist trains the client

in coping techniques involving direct action or in cognitive techniques. Direct actions the client can take include becoming knowledgeable about stressful situations or phobic objects, planning alternative escapes, and relaxation induction. Increased knowledge should minimize any misconceptions and reduce the overwhelming perception of the stressor. Knowing that escape routes are available should make confronting the stressor less frightening. Relaxation allows fear reaction reduction through control of physiological responses.

In the assessment, maladaptive cognitions are pointed out to the client. These thoughts now become the cues for the use of coping techniques. Cognitive coping involves learning self-statements that help adaptively to assess the situation, control negative thoughts and images, and to recognize and relabel physiological arousal. Self-statements also include convincing oneself to confront the stressor, to cope with the fear, and to self-evaluate performance. Self-statements in each of these categories are generated by the client for his particular problem.

In the third phase of Stress Inoculation Training, the direct action and cognitive coping skills are applied in actual stress situations. The therapist exposes the client to ego- or pain-threatening stressors. These stressors do not include the phobic situation but may include unpredictable electric shock, imagined stress sequences, or stress-inducing films. During these stress situations, the client is urged to try out a variety of coping techniques learned during the rehearsal phase. The client will eventually develop an armamentarium of coping skills suited to his perceived needs and abilities.

Cognitive Therapy of Depression

One of the founders of Cognitive Therapy, Beck (1976) has described his approach to the treatment of depression. Depressed patients see themselves as "losers"; therapy is designed to make them feel like winners. The therapist will first select several target problems, which can be emotional, motivational, cognitive, behavioral, or physiological. Each target problem is formulated at three levels: in terms of abnormal behavior, such as inertia; in terms of motivational disturbances, such as wanting to escape; and in terms of cognitions of hopelessness and defeat.

For inertia, the patient is told that keeping busy will make him feel better. The therapist and patient can design a daily activity schedule to fill up each day. These behaviors should not be challenging. However, *graded task assignments* are made so that the patient is motivated to perform a series of tasks of increasing difficulty, which are related to the alleviation of a target problem. If difficulty is increased slowly, the patient should meet with a series of successes. The therapist can provide feedback about success to ensure that the patient is coming to

think of himself as a winner. This cognitive change is really more important than the behavioral change, since it is thought to be the critical factor in reversing the depressive cycle of failure and negative self-evaluation.

The patient can keep an account of all his daily activities, and put an "M" by the ones he feels he has mastered and a "P" by the ones that give some pleasure. Beck (1976) feels this *self-monitoring,* and *self-evaluation* procedure is useful in helping depressed persons realize their success potential and to focus on the pleasurable aspects of their lives, which they may fail to perceive as such.

For *cognitive reappraisal,* the patient and therapist review the relations between depressive cognitions and symptoms. The patient self-monitors thoughts, feelings, and behaviors that occur before, during, and after problem situations. In order to change maladaptive cognitive processes, the therapist can have the patient consider alternative explanations of experiences to show that there are other ways to interpret events besides those that reflect negatively on the self. Alternative strategies for problem solving are suggested since a depressed person may have become rigid in using unsuccessful techniques. The closed belief system involving negativism toward the world and the self is challenged; the therapist questions the reasons for such beliefs, and debates the patient, bringing out evidence to the contrary where applicable. Cognitive rehearsal involves having the patient imagine experiencing a sequence of events related to a problem area. Perceived obstacles and conflicts are thus brought up for discussion, and cognitive reappraisal and problem-solving techniques are used to work through them.

This brief description of two modes of Cognitive Learning Theory gives a general idea of the procedures used. While more structured and specific than traditional insight therapies, Cognitive Learning Therapies require more interpersonal perception skills than does strict Behavior Therapy. These skills are more an art than a science, since cognitive assessment and theory are not developed to the point of easy replication. The techniques and theory may never become a science due to the epistemological problems associated with discerning others' thoughts and the relation between thoughts and observable behavior.

APPLICATIONS

The Cognitive Learning Therapies represent a broad array of procedures that can be applied to virtually all psychological problems. However, treatments have thus far been fairly limited in populations and extremely limited in terms of demonstrated successes. Table 10.1 outlines some of the applications for each type of Cognitive Learning Therapy.

Self-Instructional Training (cf. Meichenbaum, 1977) has been used with hyperactive and impulsive children to help them perform more slowly and accurately. It has also been used with some successes for children who are socially withdrawn, schizophrenics (see the methodology section), and for increasing the problem-solving ability of college students.

Beck's (1976) Cognitive Therapy has shown preliminary promise with severely depressed patients when compared with tricyclic medication (Rush, Beck, Kovacs, & Hollon, 1977). In this study, the Cognitive Therapy group improved more rapidly and had less dropout from treatment. Three fourths of the cognitive group showed marked or complete remission of symptoms; less than one fourth of the drug group did. Beck (1976) claims that procedures that change cognitions and behaviors are more effective in alleviating depression than nondirective and supportive treatments.

Covert Modeling has shown some promise in the treatment of phobias and unassertiveness, but doubts have been expressed about its efficacy compared with therapies using actual motoric rehearsal (Mahoney & Arnkoff, 1978).

Coping Skills Training has been used with test anxiety and to reduce indecisiveness (Goldfried, 1971). Anxiety Management Training (Suinn & Richardson, 1971) has not yet received enough critical scrutiny to evaluate its effectiveness with various populations. Stress Inoculation appears promising for dealing with anger, pain, and performance anxieties (Meichenbaum, 1977).

Behavioral Problem Solving (D'Zurilla & Goldfried, 1971) has been used successfully with preschool students, emotionally disturbed children, adolescents, psychiatric inpatients, and delinquents. Finally, the Personal Science approach (Mahoney, 1977b) has been used with obese adults.

CASE EXAMPLE

Barbara was a 29-year-old white female referred by her minister because of increasing depression. On the first visit she appeared so distraught and unkempt that she was asked to see a psychiatrist, who admitted her to a hospital. There she was first given a psychological evaluation to assess the nature and degree of her depression. Testing was also initiated in order to assess possible organic components since she complained of constant headaches and dizziness.

She described her depression as being the result of several traumatic incidents that occurred during the previous year. She interpreted these events as having a catastrophic effect on her ability to cope. Included were the birth of her second child, her husband's involvement in a near-fatal accident, and the death of her father. She eval-uated the circumstances of the accident and death in a way that caused her to have deep guilt feelings. She used alcohol to help control her nerves, but she believed she had become too dependent upon it and wanted to give up its use altogether. Apparently she had depressive reactions following the births of both of her children. She never worked, dropping out of college in her junior year to get married and become a housewife. Her husband was a conductor for a railroad. Prior to his accident he was rather demanding and domineering with his wife.

She reported a considerable degree of sleep disturbance. She also reported having little or no appetite. Her libido had been below average since the birth of her second child approximately one year ago. During the testing she was depressed and anxious.

Test results showed her to be functioning in the average range of intelligence. The errors she made were nonspecific and seemed more closely related to motivational or attentional deficits than to organic factors. Scores on tests measuring her concentration and memory were below average. Apparently she was unable to concentrate on those tasks that involved some form of information processing. The deterioration of her performance toward the end of each task seemed due to her inability to concentrate.

The most significant affect expressed in her test productions was a pervasive sense of depression. Her Minnesota Multiphasic Personality Inventory profile indicated substantial psychopathology. *T*-scores were elevated above 70 on 6 of the 10 clinical scales, with peaks on *D, Pt,* and *Hy.* Her score on the Beck Depression Inventory was 35, suggesting severe depression. Her projective test productions suggested a sense of apathy and a profound lack of energy in dealing with environmental situations. She also showed a tendency to withdraw from others even on an informal basis. Associated with her apathy and lack of energy were ruminations and preoccupations. It was as if all of her energy was directed toward a ruminative train of thought in which she was preoccupied with the things she felt she had done wrong in her life. The latter particularly related to her husband's accident and her father's death. Along with the feelings of guilt were poor self-esteem and low feelings of self-worth.

Her ruminations also indicated a considerable amount of concern about her own bodily functioning and a preoccupation with death. It seemed that her recent situational experiences had focused her attention on her own frailty. Her ruminations about these matters had drained her emotionally to the point where she was no longer able to carry out her normal routine. Test results indicated that her bodily preoccupation was focused upon dysfunction rather than wholeness. These concerns seemed almost obsessional in that they represented a significant investiture of energy and occupied much of her time. She tended to perceive even harmless events in such terms.

Her affective productions appeared to be related to strong dependency needs. In particular, she viewed males as being able to cope with most situations, being strong and capable. The recent traumatic events had served to point out to her the fragility of human nature in general and her confidence in men in particular. Her faith in a strong, domineering father figurehead had been shaken to the point that she felt insecure and helpless. In fact, she reported that since his accident, her husband had been more open rather than demanding and domineering. She had, in a sense, lost the strong father figure that she had in her husband as well as having lost her own father. This insecurity that she felt in relation to those upon whom she was dependent was apparently heightened by her own perceptions of her inability to cope with normal routine. Not only did she feel helpless in coping with the situation, but she also had no one upon whom she could depend. Believing that one must "make one's own future," she had little or no hope of obtaining her expectations or goals for the future.

Associated with and probably secondary to her depression was a complete lack of trust in others. She experienced interpersonal relations as being particularly demanding in terms of the effort and energy required of her. Her ruminations and preoccupations with her own insecurity and helplessness precluded her expending the necessary energy to maintain satisfactory interpersonal relationships.

At the time of her hospitalization, Barbara's condition in terms of inability to cope with her conflicts had progressively deteriorated. She was at the point where she wanted to be alone and not have much to do with other people. She spent most of her time in ruminative thoughts that were destructive in the sense that they simply fed her depressed affect. Her sense of helplessness and hopelessness precluded any efforts on her part to cope with her situation. Test results suggested that her somatic complaints represented a psychophysiological reaction to the tension she was experiencing in her life. Her test productions of depression, helplessness, and dependency were consistent with those involved in a psychophysiological process. Diagnoses were: depressive neurosis, psychophysiologic disorder, and habitual excessive drinking.

During Barbara's two weeks in the hospital, her therapy involved attempts at restructuring her thinking and behavior in a systematic manner. Although the traumatic episodes of the past year were discussed and dealt with, the primary focus was on the here and now. The primary goal of the patient sessions was a transformation of Barbara's distorted thinking patterns. Each session consisted of discussing her feelings, thoughts, and attitudes, pointing out that her current behavioral patterns were a direct consequence of her mental set. Considerable time was spent demonstrating the irrationality of many of her beliefs.

After discharge she was seen in therapy twice a week for the next two months. She was asked to keep comprehensive records of the thoughts that went through her mind in response to events that upset her. Sessions were spent going over her records, discussing in detail the interrelationship of her thoughts to the events, determining whether they were realistic and reasonable. Faulty cognitions were analyzed, and Barbara was taught to restructure her thoughts in more reasonable ways.

Barbara was then seen weekly for 11 months. Each session dealt with Barbara's faulty beliefs, substituting more correct interpretations of her experiences. Her guilt over the death of her father required considerable discussion and restructuring. For example, her father had quietly been seeing another woman for at least one year when Barbara accidentally found out about it. She told her mother about her father's affair and firmly believed that this disclosure was the cause of her father's death. The illogic of this belief was pointed out to her. First, she had no real evidence that her mother had told her father that she knew of his affair. Second, her father had had a long history of serious heart trouble. Third, the affair occurred several years before her father's death, so it was doubtful that Barbara's disclosure to her mother would have an effect on her father years later.

About six months into therapy, she joined Alcoholics Anonymous. As her negative view of herself lessened, her poor relationship with her husband became clearer. A letter she wrote to him illustrates her feelings.

Dear Bill,

Let me tell you about *me*—as a person. Two years ago I was a poor, pitiful (no sympathy, please) alcoholic. I had drunk myself completely out of reality and my mental state was almost completely insane. During the last year of my drinking we had Tommy, more responsibility for me (I couldn't handle what I already had). I started drinking morning, noon, and night. Then came your near-fatal accident, and Daddy's death.

I knew I could stand no more drinking after being in the hospital, but knew nothing of the hell to follow. By "hell" I mean what I have had to go through in order to grow and learn these past two years trying to rebuild my life, facing reality, becoming a *whole* person again (really for the first time). God has given me this second chance to live again soberly and I pray everyday for the will to live each day sober and trying to do His will for me, trying to do the right things. I'm not trying to sound like a saint. I fail a lot; I simply pray for the will to keep on trying, even with my faults to keep on honestly trying for a better life, the right kind of life.

I have come a long way, with a long way to go. Don't we all have to keep on trying to live a better life? If not, what would be the purpose of living?

I know I'm still confused about many things. But one thing is clear to me now. I have my life to live (faults, failures, whatever), you have your life to live. I want to live my life *with* you, but not *for you.* I used to have no life (my fault), and lived completely trying to please you. Only I've never really pleased you very much. No wonder, for in trying to be what you wanted, I made myself completely miserable, and grew to resent you terribly. I was your doormat, but I let myself become this; in lots of ways you are not to blame. If I had been a stronger, more independent person when we married, I would never have let this happen, but I was basically insecure, very dependent, and yes, had even then a drinking problem which of course I never admitted then. Then we got married and I had to try to deal with this, and with a man who has a "large ego" (as you put it).

Several weeks ago I was not trying to hurt you when I asked if you wanted to separate. It was because you seemed so miserable with everything I did or said. I am what I am—a person with faults, and whether you can take me as I am with faults and ideas that may conflict with yours is up to you. I am willing to grow, try to understand you, and to change, even when I may not agree with your feelings; in other words, to respect your feelings and you as a person, but you must be willing to do this same thing for me.

Eventually the couple divorced. Barbara is still seen in therapy once a month. She has recently purchased a home for herself and her two children, and has taken a job as secretary-receptionist for a small oil exploration firm, her first job. She has not had a drink of alcohol for two years; she goes to AA at least once a week. She is dating but does not feel she is ready for marriage at this time.

At the time of this writing it has been almost three years since Barbara began treatment. She is continuing to function fully, no longer experiencing significant depression, and on the whole seems to be enjoying her life.

SUMMARY

Cognitive processes have become scientifically respectable within Behavior Therapy. Learning is no longer being seen as solely the result of conditioning; rather, cognitive, emotional, and social learning processes are being emphasized. There has been a shift from a position of environmental determinism—one's life is primarily shaped by our external environmental to one of a reciprocal determinism—one's life is the result of a continual interaction between organism and environment. The person is not a passive product of his environment but rather an active participant in shaping his development. Cognitive processes allow persons to analyze current environmental information, compare it with the past, make predictions, and plan and evaluate strate-

gies in accordance with their current and long-range needs. Cognitive Therapy tries to correct deficits and errors in these processes, using a wide variety of persuasive and behavioral techniques.

Since Cognitive Behavior Therapy is based on social learning theory, it is amenable to experimental validation. Techniques used by cognitive behavior therapists have their roots in basic research, and they are specific enough that their effectiveness can be empirically tested. Cognitive behavior therapists emphasize the importance of an operationally and methodologically sound approach to treating clients. The ultimate goal of Cognitive Behavior Therapies is to provide clients with the skills for regulating their own behaviors. Although cognitive processes are important mechanisms of human functioning, cognitive behavior therapists rely on behavioral and emotional procedures to effect change. While arguments concerning the primacy of cognitions over emotions or behavior persist, the future may find therapy directed at global life skills, which involve cognitive, emotional, and behavioral skills in interaction. Therapies that emphasize cognitive processes may be at an advantage since therapist-patient communication for effective problem solving takes place essentially in a cognitive (verbal) domain. Behavioral problems may require behavioral practice, emotional problems may require emotional practice, and cognitive deficits may require cognitive practice. But all problems will require a cognitive understanding of the therapeutic process on the part of the patient.

Whether Cognitive Behavior Therapy will continue to grow and prosper will ultimately depend on the empirical evidence and the refinement of cognitive assessment techniques. The next few years will undoubtedly be exciting ones for the Cognitive Therapy approach.

REFERENCES

Bandura, A. (1969). *Principles of behavior modification.* New York: Holt.

Bandura, A. (1977). Self-efficacy: Towards a unifying theory of behavior change. *Psychological Review, 84,* 191–215.

Beck, A. T. (1976). *Cognitive therapy and the emotional disorders.* New York: International Universities Press.

Cautela, J. R. (1971). Covert conditioning. In A. Jacobs & L. B. Sachs (Eds.), *The psychology of private events: Perspectives on covert response systems.* New York: Academic Press.

D'Zurilla, T. J. & Goldfried, M. R. (1971). Problem solving and behavior modification. *Journal of Abnormal Psychology,* 107–126.

Ellis, A. (1979). Rational-emotive therapy. In R. Corsini (Ed.), *Current psychotherapies* (2nd ed.). Itasca, IL: F. E. Peacock.

Eysenck, H. J. (1979). Behavior therapy and the philosophers. *Behaviour Research and Therapy, 17,* 511–514.

Goldfried, M. R. (1971). Systematic desensitization as training in self-control. *Journal of Consulting and Clinical Psychology, 37,* 228–234.

Kendall, P. C., & Hollon, S. D. (Eds.). (1979). *Cognitive-behavioral interventions: Theory, research, and procedures.* New York: Academic Press.

Mahoney, M. J. (1974). *Cognition and behavior modification.* Cambridge, MA: Ballinger.

Mahoney, M. J. (1977a). Reflections on the cognitive-learning trend in psychotherapy. *American Psychologist, 32,* 5–13.

Mahoney, M. J. (1977b). Personal science: A cognitive learning therapy. In A. Ellis & R. Grieger (Eds.), *Handbook of rational-emotive therapy.* New York: Springer.

Mahoney, M. J., & Arnkoff, D. B. (1978). Cognitive and self-control therapies. In S. L. Garfield & A. E. Bergin (Eds.), *Handbook of psychotherapy and behavior change: An empirical analysis* (2nd ed.). New York: Wiley.

Meichenbaum, D. (1976). Toward a cognitive theory of self-control. In G. E. Schwartz & D. Shapiro (Eds.), *Con-sciousness and self-regulation: Advances in research: Vol 1.* New York: Plenum.

Meichenbaum, D. (1977). *Cognitive-behavior modification: An integrative approach.* New York: Plenum.

Murray, E. J., & Jacobson, L. I. (1978). Cognition and learning in traditional and behavioral therapy. In S. L. Garfield & A. E. Bergin (Eds.), *Handbook of psychotherapy and behavior change: An empirical analysis* (2nd ed.). New York: Wiley.

Rush, A. J., Beck, A. T., Kovacs, M., & Hollon, S. (1977). Comparative efficacy of cognitive therapy and pharmacotherapy in the treatment of depressed outpatients. *Cognitive Therapy and Research, 1,* 17–37.

Spivack, G., Platt, J. J., & Shure, M. D. (1976). *The problem-solving approach to adjustment.* San Francisco: Jossey-Bass.

Suinn, R. M., & Richardson, F. (1971). Anxiety management training: A nonspecific behavior therapy program for anxiety control. *Behavior Therapy, 2,* 498–510.

Wolpe, J. (1978). Cognition and causation in human behavior and its therapy. *American Psychologist, 33,* 437–446.

Chapter 10

COMPREHENSIVE RELAXATION TRAINING

ALAN C. TURIN and STEPHANIE N. LYNCH

A considerable number of dimensions or modalities could be considered when one attempts to classify the various psychotherapies. Thus, for example, Psychoanalysis could be seen as a method that concentrates on the intellect, the cognitive functions, with insight being a primary goal; Client-Centered Therapy could be seen as primarily relating to feelings, with self-acceptance as a major goal; and Psychodrama could be seen as a system relating to behavior, with assertiveness as a goal.

However, in all systems, one major goal is relaxation, calming down, reducing tension. This is a primary reason for the enormous number of pills prescribed for tension reduction, and a primary reason for smoking, alcohol consumption, and drug taking, licit and illicit.

One common method of relaxation is to do something (or nothing, as the case may be) with the body to attempt to achieve peace through body work of some kind. In the following chapter, Alan Turin and Stephanie Lynch explain a systematic system of relaxation, which can be a primary method of treatment or which can be used along with any other method of psychotherapy. Relatively simple, having commonsense principles, CRT is a technique all psychotherapists should know.

Comprehensive Relaxation Training (CRT) is a unique "package" approach to relaxation training developed by Alan C. Turin. A CRT program includes prerecorded relaxation cassettes for home use, brief relaxation exercises, and abstinence from a variety of substances in common foods, beverages, and medicines that can increase stress and work against relaxation.

CRT is useful in the treatment (or prevention) of a variety of stress-related problems, including migraine and tension headaches, anxiety, and insomnia. In addition, some patients report spontaneous improvement in areas such as personal relations, mood, and general feelings of being able to cope. CRT may also be helpful to some individuals in reducing the risk of heart attack and stroke.

CRT may be employed as a primary therapy or used adjunctively, incorporated into other psychological or medical therapies. The entire CRT system can be taught by mental or medical health professionals to patients with no prior experience in relaxation training within four to six hours.

HISTORY

There is now a large body of research on behavioral techniques developed for or adapted to the treatment of stress-related disorders such as headache, anxiety, insomnia, and hypertension. A common thread running through many of these techniques is that some form of relaxation training is the major therapeutic element. The symptoms are often thought to be triggered by hyperarousal of the sympathetic branch of the autonomic nervous system or of the musculoskeletal system. In relaxation training, the individual is trained to lower his or her arousal level either on a short-term basis, to modify response to stressful situations, or to maintain lower physiologic arousal throughout the day.

Perhaps the oldest of the relaxation methodologies is meditation, and the most popular branch of this teaching is Transcendental Meditation. Here the individual is instructed to sit in a quiet environment and to repeat a brief phrase or word to himself, thus reducing external and internal stimuli and allowing relaxation to occur. Herbert Benson (1976) modified this technique by asking the learner to repeat the word *one* to himself, to sit comfortably, and to allow intrusive thoughts to pass by. Autogenic Training, as developed by Schultz and Luthe (1969), uses more elaborate phrases and essentially self-hypnotic suggestions for relaxation.

Jacobson (1938) and Wolpe (1969) have each developed active methods for relaxation training and for helping individuals to identify excessive levels of muscle tension through deliberate relaxation or tension and then relaxation of muscles. Hypnotic and self-hypnotic techniques often employ relaxation suggestions, taking advantage of both the relaxing effects of the trance induction and the individual's heightened suggestability while in the trance. Biofeedback, which measures physiologic parameters associated with arousal, presents information about these physiologic responses to the learner in the form of lights, sounds, or meter readings. Persons can then learn to control highly subtle musculoskeletal and autonomic responses if given moment-by-moment feedback to aid their learning.

The parameter chosen for measurement usually corresponds to the nervous system thought to be most highly correlated with the symptom (i.e., muscle relaxation biofeedback for individuals with muscle tension headaches). Feedback of other parameters is also often provided to assist the individual in learning general relaxation. Many practitioners use more traditional relaxation training methods such as relaxation tapes in addition to biofeedback, and a recent review of research suggests that relaxation training alone is as effective as the combination of relaxation training plus biofeedback (Silver & Blanchard, 1978). This strongly suggests that the induction and maintenance of low arousal (relaxation) is the primary therapeutic ingredient in biofeedback training for stress-related problems.

Caffeine, once felt to be a safe, mild central nervous system stimulant, has come under increasing suspicion as an agent in anxiety neurosis (Greden, 1974) and other stress-related disorders. Recent findings (Robertson et al., 1978) suggest that in many people, ingestion of even small amounts of caffeine leads to a dramatic increase in adrenaline and noradrenaline levels in the body, producing physiological effects similar to those caused by severe external stressors.

Sympathomimetic drugs also produce the effects of increased adrenaline levels, by introducing chemicals that act like adrenaline into the body. Careful examination of chemical components of drugs, particularly those with reported side effects such as "nervousness," reveals a surprising amount of caffeine and sympathomimetics among those drugs commonly prescribed for individuals with stress-related symptoms. Caffeine, for example, which is present in many pain-relieving drugs, may be useful when taken during individual migraine or tension headache attacks. However, it is often prescribed at daily maintenance levels. This can increase arousal on a long-term basis, often inducing stress-related problems such as anxiety, insomnia, irritability, and, at times, even more headaches, in a truly vicious circle.

The CRT program is designed, in part, to take into account the fact that no relaxation program can function at maximum effectiveness if trainees are ingesting caffeine, sympathomimetics, or other substances in foods, beverages, and medicine that work against relaxation.

CURRENT STATUS

The CRT system was developed in the context of Turin's group practice of clinical psychology. In that practice the system has been used with over 400 patients either as a primary therapy or as an adjunct to individual, marital, or family psychotherapy.

(CRT is a service mark of Alan C. Turin, PhD. However the letters CRT are used in this text to simply indicate any program organized along similar lines.)

Much of the empirical support for the combination of relaxation training with abstinence from stimulants is set forth in a review paper (Turin & Sawyer, 1979) on the antagonistic effects of caffeine and relaxation training.

A systematic (controlled) case study (Turin, Nirenberg, & Mattingly, 1979) shows some of the effects of CRT on one patient's mood. In this study the patient's anxiety and depression decreased.

A thorough exposition of CRT methods, theory, and practice is presented in the book *No More Headaches!* (Turin, 1981).

THEORY

The human organism's stress responses are influenced by many factors, including environment, internally generated cognitions, chemicals ingested or breathed, genetic and social history, and personality dynamics. The stress-related disorder and its attendant physical and/or psychological pain, effects on self-esteem, and interference with accustomed lifestyle and social relationships can be self-perpetuating. As the patient begins to feel increasing helplessness, the seeking of secondary gain becomes more important as a primary coping strategy, and it becomes more and more difficult for the patient to operate effectively on the environment. As disability from a stress-related disorder continues, several processes may occur. For example, pain or anxiety, with attendant depression, exhaustion, and other effects may preclude continuation of work and activities so that the patient faces reduced sources of self-esteem and gratification. Interpersonal relationships often deteriorate as the patient becomes increasingly helpless and preoccupied with symptoms. Reactive depression may reach clinical proportions and fuel further difficulties. Certain medications' side effects, such as depression, irritability, and drowsiness, may further preclude maintenance of lifestyle. Narcotic and analgesic prescriptions are particularly dangerous in that relief from pain and escape from difficulties are highly desirable to many patients, and dependence is likely to occur with some. Caffeine provides a temporary subjective lift, although its long-term effects may exacerbate many symptoms.

Any or all of the above problems may have the effect of producing anxiety and its physiologic correlates, leaving the individual in a heightened state of arousal, where even relatively mild situational occurrences may cause or exacerbate symptoms. The goals of the CRT program are to bring the patient into a lower, healthier state of arousal and to teach him on her to modify responses to stress.

Acute and chronic stress are directly or indirectly related to a broad variety of physical and psychological ills, ranging from headaches and anxiety to nervous breakdown and perhaps even stroke and heart attack. Relaxation training generally, and CRT specifically, provides a way to reduce, counteract, or prevent some of the negative effects of stress and stress-related problems.

In many cases, CRT can function as a primary therapy.[1] Many anxiety neurotics, headache patients, insomniacs, and so forth, have been so improved with CRT alone that they have felt no need for further medical or psychological help. In many other cases, however, CRT is not sufficient as a total therapy unto itself, but can be helpful in the context of ongoing medical or psychological treatment. For example, many patients are referred for CRT only, while their other medical and/or psychological needs are attended to by the referring professional.

The dynamics and severity of stress-related disorders vary tremendously. One way to examine these disorders is to note the degree to which psychological dysfunction determines the nature and severity of symptoms. In the case of tension headache, for example, CRT alone (after medical screening) might provide sufficient relief. However, a more complicated case of tension headache might require not only CRT but also individual, couple, or family psychotherapy and medication.

CRT is utilized not only to teach lowering of arousal and modification of responses to stressful events, but also to boost mood and self-esteem by training individuals to modify the symptoms directly by themselves. For example, use of relaxation techniques, review of arousal-increasing foods, drinks, and medications, and consultation with patients' physicians regarding the use of these substances often results in a rapid, at times dramatic, change in symptom frequency and severity. Such direct symptom relief often brings additional benefits since the patient can begin to resume his or her accustomed activities and interpersonal roles. The vicious circle of despair, isolated social contacts, preoccupation with symptoms, and reactive depression and anxiety may be reversed. Finally, psychotherapy can shift from a focus on stress-related symptoms to helping the patient regain the skills and attitudes necessary for development of a more satisfying, less stressful life style.

A basic theoretical thrust of the CRT program is that in order to treat a stress-related symptom, one must first help the patient to reduce the stress itself.

METHODOLOGY

Typically, administration of the entire CRT program involves about four to six sessions, each about 50 minutes long. Patients are educated as to the general role of stress in symptom development and maintenance; it is made explicit that hyperarousal of nervous system functioning can be responsible for or involved in the production of various stress-related problems (i.e., tension headaches, insomnia, migraine).

It is explained that with CRT, persons are helped to maintain generally relaxed levels of arousal, so they are less likely to experience symptoms. They are also provided with techniques to relax on an as-needed basis to handle various specific, perhaps unpredicted, stressors as they occur. As with any acute stressful situation, the emergence of the symptom may be handled by relaxation, in order to blunt or abort the effect of the episode and prevent it from leading to full-blown symptom formation.

For these purposes, individuals are trained in relaxation techniques and taught to avoid ingesting substances that can increase stress and work against relaxation. A complete explanation is given about these substances and their effects of increasing adrenaline and noradrenaline levels and increasing muscle tension. It is also explained that medications are adjusted only by consultation with the patient's physician.

Patients listen to a series of two prerecorded relaxation techniques, playing one of the tapes at least twice per day. The timing of the tape playing is to some extent dependent on the nature and timing of the occurrence of symptoms. The second step in relaxation training consists of brief relaxation exercises that can be used at any time without a tape recorder. These exercises can be used either to augment general relaxation or to combat specific stressors or episodes of symptom eruption. The brief relaxation exercises are to be practiced several times throughout each day, and, as with the tapes, are to be used regardless of symptom occurrence, since a major purpose of such a program is to provide the maintenance of a state of generalized low arousal as a method of prevention rather than simply to correct or alleviate symptoms once they occur. Systematic reviews are made of progress during the program, and brief relaxation exercises are tailored to the needs of the individual patient. A detailed review of a typical course of treatment is as follows:

During the first session, a review is made of the symptom(s), past and current, and whatever earlier therapeu-

---

[1] CRT is never to be used instead of necessary medical treatment.

tic efforts have been made. Patients are referred for medical consultation if appropriate, often to rule out possibilities such as brain tumor, temporomandibular joint dysfunction syndrome, or borderline hypoglycemia, but to screen other physical problems as well. The role of stress in producing and maintaining symptoms is explained, as well as the role of CRT in reducing stress and stress-related problems. The patient is given a form for keeping a daily record of symptom activity, medication, and relaxation practice sessions at home. In addition, the patient is to keep a three-day diary of all foods, drinks, and medications ingested.

During the second session, a complete review is made of foods, drinks, and medications containing substances that can increase arousal and interfere with relaxation. These substances include (but are not limited to) caffeine in commonly recognized sources such as coffee, tea, and cola drinks as well as in less commonly recognized sources such as pain, diet, and other medications, and coffee- and chocolate-flavored products such as coffee ice cream. It is explained that sympathomimetic substances, which act like adrenaline to increase stress, are found in a variety of common prescription and nonprescription medications, such as many asthma, sinus, weight-loss, and allergy medications, as well as in some common headache and pain medications. All current foods and medications are evaluated in this light, and the patient is urged to abstain from these substances, with the physician's consent.

During the third session, the patient is introduced to the first CRT tape, which is a 15-minute muscle tension-relaxation exercise plus passive relaxation imagery. The trainee is shown the various physical movements required (i.e., how to tense the various muscles involved) and informed that this is the first of many approaches to relaxation, that it may not be particularly effective when played in the office during the session due to the newness of the experience and the inhibiting presence of the therapist. He or she is further advised that the best way a person can help himself or herself to relax is not to worry about relaxing successfully, but to simply experience the tape noncritically. For example, when the tape says "your arms feel heavy," one is to imagine that one's arms feel heavy, rather than worrying whether the arms actually feel heavy or not. The patient is instructed to play the tape at least twice daily, at appropriate times and in appropriate settings, and to record the times of practice and levels of relaxation achieved pre- and posttape.

During the fourth session, the patient is introduced to the second 15-minute relaxation tape, which is more passive and "hypnotic" in nature, and rich with relaxation imagery. In some cases, tapes are first experienced in the office so that in the unlikely event that problems arise, they will occur in the presence of a trained therapist. This tape is used at home in the same manner as the first tape.

During the fifth session, progress is reviewed and the patient is introduced to brief relaxation techniques. Several techniques may be offered for the individual to experiment with, with an eye toward continuing regular use of the technique or techniques found easiest and most relaxing.

During the sixth session, all techniques, procedures, and therapeutic results are reviewed. The treatment is terminated or recommendations are made for continued or additional therapeutic efforts if and as appropriate.

APPLICATIONS

CRT may be useful in four major areas:

1. As a primary treatment for mental and physical stress-related problems such as nervous tension, anxiety, migraine and tension headaches, insomnia, and other conditions where either physical or mental stress is a known or suspected factor, and medical causes have been ruled out by a physician.
2. As an adjunct conducted concurrently with medical or individual, marital, group, or family therapy.
3. As a method of prevention for individuals at risk of either the stress-related problems mentioned above, or the more ominous problems such as heart attack and stroke.
4. As a tool for healthy individuals to maintain and enhance a relaxed lifestyle with all its attendant benefits.

As a primary treatment for stress-related problems, CRT can fill a substantial void in most present medical and psychological treatments. Typically, a medical approach to stress-related problems involves prescriptions for medications such as tranquilizers and painkillers. Oftentimes, the medications bring as many problems—such as depression, drowsiness, and dependence—as they resolve. Also, physicians often advise patients to "slow down and take it easy," an action many patients find difficult or impossible to implement without training in specialized techniques such as CRT. Typical psychological approaches, on the other hand, ignore the physiological underpinnings of stress-related problems by focusing almost exclusively on cognitive and emotional intra- and interpersonal issues. A person whose system is "speeding" needs help in slowing down that aspect of his or her physiology that is triggering stress-related symptoms. In the absence of such an approach, the patient is often left feeling personally inadequate for being unable to achieve adequate insight or psychological growth to shed his or her headaches, anxiety, and so forth. In addition to providing the symptom relief and improved mood that come with naturally induced relaxation, CRT enables the patient to change from being essentially a passive victim ministered to by others to a person who actively employs techniques to accomplish his or her own therapeutic results. A patient who can exert some direct control over the results of his or her own treatment not only gains in terms of symptom relief but in the invaluable and therapeutic sense of control over one's own life.

As an adjunct to individual, couple, group, and family psychotherapy, CRT is useful in a variety of ways. Since most individuals in psychotherapy are under at least some intra- and interpersonal stress, CRT can relieve that component of such stress that is amplified and intensified by excess physiological arousal. For example, the patient who drinks coffee to "calm his nerves" as a result of conflict with his or her spouse is more likely to overrespond and be quick to misinterpret anything said by his or her partner in a negative way. With relaxation comes the perspective of tempered and considered judgment. An opportunity to interrupt what would otherwise become a vicious circle of ever expanding conflict thus arises.

As a method of prevention for individuals at risk of stress-related symptoms, CRT has considerable, possibly even lifesaving, potential. CRT is not only useful in preventing everyday stress-related problems such as headache and anxiety, but it may also prove useful in preventing heart attack and stroke. Individuals who exhibit the so-called Type A behavior pattern (urgent time sense, competitive, etc.) are at increased risk of coronary artery disease and heart attack (Friedman and Rosenman, 1975). Individuals are also at increased risk of stroke from either sustained or transient upward surges of blood pressure. By slowing down one's physiological and emotional levels of general arousal, and providing techniques to maintain or reintroduce low arousal in the face of sudden arousing stimuli, CRT may ultimately help decrease the mortality and morbidity associated with these two major problems.

Finally, CRT can be used as a tool for healthy individuals to maintain and enhance a relaxed life style. Millions of perfectly healthy people have benefited from relaxation training, meditation, and so forth. Millions of others would benefit from abstinence from substances in foods, beverages, and medications that cause them to be nervous, "hyper," or otherwise overaroused without knowing why. CRT combines the best of each of these elements with the effect of a more relaxed, less pressured lifestyle.

CASE EXAMPLE

Jenny was referred to Turin by her physician for biofeedback and psychotherapy for multiple functional problems. At the time of referral, Jenny was 35, married, and a housewife with three young children. Jenny suffered both muscle contraction ("tension") and migraine headaches. The tension headache was always with her, and it was experienced as a dull "band" around her head, accompanied by constant neck pain. Superimposed on her tension headaches were migraine headaches, quite severe in nature, that occurred for about one week every two months or so. The throbbing migraine pain was felt in and behind her right eye and at her right temple. The stabbing pain and its attendant nausea, vomiting, and malaise drove Jenny to her bed during these attacks, and a housekeeper had to be hired to attend to the children.

Jenny also suffered what she referred to as "little heart attacks and angina." These were experienced as almost constant pains in her ribcage and left collarbone, neck, shoulder, arm, and wrist. In addition, she frequently experienced a "bulging, pressure" sensation in her abdomen. She was extremely nervous and subject to terror in a variety of circumstances. For example, she would frequently begin to go shopping, panic, and drive straight home as quickly as possible. She described herself as someone who always went at full speed: "It seems like all day I go—go—go. I never stop. I never get enough done."

Her typical method of dealing with her symptoms was to speed more. She would race around the house with her vacuum cleaner, cleaning frantically. She attempted to be so busy that she would forget her symptoms, stopping only to drink coffee so that she could "calm my nerves and prevent headache."

Jenny drank 6 to 10 cups of coffee a day and received additional caffeine in some of her headache medications. Since she initially refused to discontinue her coffee drinking, CRT training began with the relaxation tapes and brief exercises. Her response to this component of the program included diminished headache and chest pain. She commented that the tape had

> really kind of changed my whole life. I even had people waiting for me twice. I never do that. While I'm listening to the tape, I can diminish all pain. It feels like the effect stays with me for hours. I've been very successful at slowing down and taking things more calmly. Like my kid had a football accident, and for once I didn't rush him off to the hospital for X rays.

Encouraged by this initial response, Jenny agreed to gradually phase her coffee drinking down to zero. At the next session, she commented: "What a difference! My insides have been jumping up and down all the time, and now they're sleeping. I didn't dust as hard, and I didn't kill the bed so hard while I was making it. Now I can finally sit in a chair without moving."

Jenny experienced a futher reduction in symptoms, often going for days with no pains of any kind at all. Her "little heart attacks and angina" were now described as occasional "twinges." There was a visible, qualitative change in her appearance as she sat quiet and composed in the chair.

The possibility of further psychotherapy was explored, but both Jenny and the therapist agreed that it did not seem necessary. A year later, a postcard from Jenny informed the therapist that things were going fine, all headaches and pains were well under control, and that she never intended to touch caffeine again.

SUMMARY

Traditionally psychological and medical therapies for patients with present or potential stress-related problems have ignored the therapeutic possibilities of naturally induced and maintained states of reduced physiological arousal. In behavior therapy, techniques such as relaxation training and biofeedback training have provided methods to begin filling that gap. However, several problems limit the power and availability of such techniques as generally practiced, including:

1. Need for expensive equipment.
2. Need for specialized training and knowledge over and above general training in psychology, psychiatry, medicine, and so forth.
3. Variation in training techniques (i.e., some systems emphasize either general relaxation or relaxation in the face of specific stressors, but not both. Also, some employ either muscle tense-relax methods or "hypnotic" imagery, but not both).
4. Failure to consider the effects of substances that increase stress and prevent or disrupt relaxation. These are present in hundreds of common prescription and nonprescription medications, foods, and beverages, and can easily sabotage an otherwise elegant relaxation program.
5. Limited availability to those who could benefit, due to requirements for specialized training for treatment providers.

The CRT program is designed as a package, easily integrated into the practices of professionals who are already competent in fields such as psychology, psychiatry, medicine, social work, and nursing. The combination of tape and nontape, tense-relax and "hypnotic," extended and brief relaxation exercises, as well as abstinence from the many common foods and medicines that work against relaxation, provides a complete "package" approach to low-arousal therapeutics.

Biofeedback and relaxation training have already produced a burgeoning literature documenting their successes in the treatment of stress-related problems, including nervous tension, anxiety, insomnia, migraine and tension headaches, hyperactivity, hypertension, and Type A (coronary-prone) behavior pattern.

CRT combines and extends the main therapeutic ingredients of biofeedback and relaxation training, and adds the neglected component of abstinence from substances that increase stress and work against relaxation. Results with over 400 patients suggest that the method may equal and exceed the demonstrated results of biofeedback and relaxation training as generally practiced.

CRT is a brief-therapy package, which can be taught in four to six sessions. It can be easily learned and taught by professionals who are already competent in their own health/mental health profession, but have no special training in low-arousal therapy methods.

CRT can be used as a primary treatment or prevention method for stress-related problems. It can be comfortably integrated into or used adjunctively with other psychological or medical therapies. Finally, CRT can bring the benefits of a quieter, more relaxed lifestyle to perfectly healthy individuals.

REFERENCES

Benson, H. (1976). *The relaxation response.* New York: Avon.

Friedman, M., & Rosenman, R. (1975). *Type A behavior and your heart.* Greenwich, CT: Fawcett.

Greden, J. F. (1974). Anxiety or caffeinism. A diagnostic dilemma. *American Journal of Psychiatry, 131,* 1089–1093.

Jacobson, E. (1938). *Progressive relaxation.* Chicago: University of Chicago Press.

Robertson, D., Frolick, J., Carr, R., Watson, J., Hollifield, J., Shand, D., & Oates, J. (1978). Effects of caffeine on plasma renin activity, catecholamines and blood pressure. *New England Journal of Medicine, 298* (4), 181–186.

Schultz, J., & Luthe, W. (1969). *Autogenic Therapy: Vol. 1. Autogenic methods.* New York: Grune & Stratton.

Silver, B. .V., & Blanchard, E. B. (1978). Biofeedback and relaxation training in the treatment of psychophysiological disorders: Or are the machines really necessary? *Journal of Behavioral Medicine, 1*(2), 217–239.

Turin, A. (1979). *Comprehensive Relaxation Training (CRT).* Cassettes, patient manuals, and therapist manuals. Lexington, MA: Author.

Turin, A., & Sawyer, D. *Physiological and psychological effects of caffeine and relaxation training: Implications for the treatment of stress-related problems.* Submitted for publication, 1979.

Turin, A. C. (1981). *No more headaches!* Boston: Houghton Mifflin.

Turin A. C., Nirenberg, J., & Mattingly, M. (1979). Effects of comprehensive relaxation training (CRT) on mood: A preliminary report on relaxation training plus caffeine cessation. *The Behavior Therapist, 2*(4), 20–21.

Wolpe, J. (1969). *The practice of behavior therapy.* New York: Pergamon.

Chapter 11

CONDITIONED REFLEX THERAPY

ANDREW SALTER

Andrew Salter occupies an unusual position in the history of psychotherapy. While he is one of the most gifted writers in the field and one of the pioneers—indeed, the pioneer of modern behavioristic psychotherapy—the literature has generally accorded him a low-key position relative to the development of behavioristic psychotherapy. For example, in a book I edited,[1] the only mention of Salter is by Albert Ellis in Ellis's chapter on his own system of Rational-Emotive Therapy.

Salter, in his youth, was strongly affected by the writings of Jacques Loeb, the eminent physiologist, having been introduced to these writings by Paul de Kruif, the author of the classic Microbe Hunters *and* Hunger Fighters, *De Kruif's admiration of Salter's work is noted in a quote in the chapter summary, as well as by the fact that de Kruif dedicated his book* The Male Hormone *to Salter.*

For a broad philosophical understanding of the meaning of the behavioristic position, stretching beyond the more limited writings of current authors, the reader is invited to an intellectual treat by a seminal writer of landmark publications in psychotherapy.

Maladjustment is a learning process, and so is psychotherapy. Maladjustment is malconditioning, and psychotherapy is reconditioning. The individual's problems are a result of his social experiences, and by changing his techniques of social relations, we change his personality. Experience is not only the best teacher, it is the only teacher. We are not especially concerned with giving the individual stratified knowledge of his past—called "probing." What concerns us is giving him reflex knowledge for his future—called "habits." (Salter, 1949, p. 316)

Conditioned Reflex Therapy is based on the laboratory findings of Pavlov, Bechterev, Watson, and their successors. Of particular interest are Pavlov's conceptions of inhibition, excitation, and disinhibition. Mental health is based on a balance between inhibition and excitation, and psychotherapy is a process of disinhibition. *Assertion* is the term that has become attached to certain aspects of excitation.

Conditioned Reflex Therapy has a broader conception of maladaptive symptoms than its behavioral descendants, and has found that the removal of many subtle manifestations of inhibition results in a posttreatment patient who is truly happy, and not just phobia-free or more socially adept.

HISTORY

I majored in psychology at college, and when I discovered hypnotism I was fascinated by it—the unconditioned response of all psychology majors. The thoroughly behaviorist approach of Clark L. Hull (1933) in *Hypnosis and Suggestibility* made complete sense to me, and still does. In essence, Hull held that words spoken by the hypnotist are conditioned stimuli that result in ideomotor reactions in the hypnotic subject.

Influenced by Hull I wrote "Three Techniques of Autohypnosis" (1941). This explained three autohypnotic techniques in a self-control paradigm, and is the pioneer paper in the field (see Goldfried & Merbaum, 1973). These techniques were applied to such problems as stage fright, overeating, insomnia, and smoking.

From Hull it was a short step for me to Watson, Pavlov, and Bechterev. Hypnosis was essentially a manifestation of Pavlov's *second signal system,* that is, words. Just as sounds associated with meat came to produce salivation in Pavlov's dogs even when there was no meat present, so are words verbally conditioned bells waiting to be rung in human beings. When the appropriate word

---

[1] Corsini, R. J. (Ed.). (1979). *Current Psychotherapies.* Itasca, IL: F. E. Peacock. (Original work published 1973)

bells ring, the subject responds with "heavy" or "light" feelings, for instance. This theoretical position was developed in my *What Is Hypnosis* (1944).

Extremely early in my professional career it struck me that on the human level Pavlov's *inhibition* could well be the holding back of emotional reactions; and Pavlov's *excitation* on the human level, could be called *assertion.*

Here is a verbatim extract from the diary a young female patient kept for me. The entry is dated January 3, 1942.

> When I left your place on Saturday I was wondering just what I could do the following day along the lines you suggested. I arrived at the subway entrance, and the stairs were blocked by a crowd of people saying goodbye to each other. Some were going to go down the stairs, and the others had come with them as far as the subway to see them off. I knew they wouldn't be standing there long, and my first thought was to wait until they were through. But then I thought, "Why wait until tomorrow to start asserting yourself. Here's a perfect set-up for you." So I just said "Excuse me," and poked my nose right into the crowd. The people broke apart and I proceeded on my way. (Score 1.)

Why my interest in Pavlov? It must be relevant that when I was a child, my parents (whom I loved very dearly) would speak Russian to each other when they didn't want me to understand, and that I was brought up three houses away from a Russian Greek Orthodox church.

From my writings it is clear that besides being influenced by Pavlov, Bechterev, Hull, and Watson, my thinking was also affected by W. H. Gantt, E. R. Guthrie, N. R. F. Maier, Jules E. Masserman, and O. H. Mowrer.

But there is another person whose work affected me profoundly, even though my writings contain only a single reference to him. This person was Jacques Loeb, the great physiologist. One of his researchers at the Rockefeller Institute had been Paul de Kruif, later the author of the classic *Microbe Hunters.* De Kruif became my dear friend and Dutch uncle, and would often lecture me on Loeb. I listened with delight and read, and reread, a great deal of Loeb.

Jacques Loeb lives on as Dr. Max Gottlieb in Sinclair Lewis's *Arrowsmith*—a book for which de Kruif was Lewis's scientific adviser, and in which de Kruif's wife, Rhea, was the model for Leora, the heroine. Years later, de Kruif dedicated his book *The Male Hormone* to me.

CURRENT STATUS

In 1959 Eysenck (p. 67) listed the 10 criteria that differentiate behavior therapy from psychoanalysis. My *Conditioned Reflex Therapy* (1949), which had appeared 10 years earlier, was the first book or article in any language to embody Eysenck's 10 criteria, some of which are that Behavior Therapy:

1. Is "based on consistent, properly formulated theory leading to testable deductions."
2. Is "derived from experimental studies. . . ."
3. "Considers symptoms as unadaptive conditioned responses" that are "evidence of faulty learning."
4. "Treatment of neurotic disorders is concerned with habits existing at *present.* . . ."
5. Interpretation of symptoms, dreams, acts, and so forth "is irrelevant."

Because *Conditioned Reflex Therapy* was the first and pioneer work on Behavior Therapy, its ideas, perspective, and techniques were almost completely absorbed into the mainstream of Behavior Therapy—operant approaches excluded. The influence of *Conditioned Reflex Therapy* is visible, for instance, in the second book ever written on Behavior Therapy—Wolpe's *Psychotherapy by Reciprocal Inhibition* (1958).

In Patterson's (1966, p. 173) astringent words, "Wolpe's psychotherapy by reciprocal inhibition appears to be a more sophisticated application of the approach used by Salter."

Or as Reyna said:

> Despite differences in theory, there are many practical similarities between Wolpe's methods and those of Salter (1944, 1949) who earlier applied conditioning principles to the full spectrum of neurotic behaviors. . . . Salter's case studies show a wide range of techniques, which include "excitation" and the external instigation of a variety of assertive and relaxation responses incompatible with previous behaviors. (Wolpe, Salter, & Reyna, 1964, p. 174)

In Fensterheim and Baer's (1975, p. 23) clear words: "Andrew Salter . . . founded modern behavior therapy."

It may well be that Hullian theory can explain why I have never felt the drive to give courses or felt the goal gradient acceleration as I sped from city to city evangelizing for Behavior Therapy. In any event, I have contented myself with watching the growth of Behavior Therapy, and with the footnotes and mentions of my work that I have encountered.

Kazdin's classic work, *History of Behavior Modification* (1978), includes a thorough review and evaluation of my work and its historical setting. In Kazdin's words:

> Cases reported in *Conditioned Reflex Therapy* include applications of techniques closely resembling systematic desensitization, self-control, behavioral rehearsal, and covert conditioning based upon imagery. . . . Fuller versions of techniques initiated by Salter are still being em-

ployed by contemporary practitioners of behavior modification. (p. 174)

The interested reader will find fuller explanations of Conditioned Reflex Therapy in *Conditioned Reflex Therapy* (Salter, 1949) and *The Conditioning Therapies* (Wolpe, Salter, & Reyna, 1964; see Chapter 2).

THEORY

The personality of the individual is the result of the interaction of heredity and environment. Heredity provides the organism with such instinctual patterns as may exist, but these instincts soon become modified by the individual's experiences.

The individual learns an elaborate collection of emotional responses to people and things, and develops elaborate rationalizations for his or her attitudes and behaviors. The individual sees the new through the glasses of the old, and distorts the new accordingly, and proceeds to integrate it into his or her nervous system.

Heredity provides the phonograph, but environment builds the record library of the brain. Not only is it impossible to choose your relatives, but you cannot even choose yourself.

Just as Pavlov's dog learned to salivate when the bell rang, so does the baby learn that certain behavior on his part brings certain responses from those around him, and he gets conditioned quite as involuntarily. If each act of the child is met with a motherly "don't," equivalent to punishing the dog when he salivates, the child will inhibit his emotions, and withdraw into himself. In Pavlovian terms, the flow of saliva when the bell was rung to signal the appearance of meat is an example of an *excitatory reflex*. But if the bell is rung again and again, and not followed by meat, or the dog is punished, the saliva stops flowing, and this is an *inhibitory reflex*.

The newborn infant's behavior is excitatory. It acts without restraint. If we were not to interfere in any way except to gratify its physical needs, it would continue in its excitatory path. But we begin early to inhibit the child, and that is how the trouble begins.

People are surprised that babies learn when so young. The question is "Are babies stimulus receivers?" If they are, then learning has to take place. In fact, the child is the megaphone of his training, and he never does anything to his parents that they didn't do to him in the first place.

The basis of life is excitation. The creatures that survive in the jungle are those that slink and jump and kill. The polite and inhibited ones crouch behind a tree and are soon dead. The human species could never have survived if it were inhibited.

This is not palatable to most of us. Man, the talking primate, insists on clinging to his illusions despite overwhelming evidence to the contrary. We do not like to be reminded that, evolutionarily speaking, we are merely stomachs that grew more complicated.

But the human animal, intelligent as it may be, can no more think its way out of an emotional problem than the monkey in the zoo. Man can only be trained out of it. We are no better than our equipment, and our equipment is primitive. There is nothing objective about an animal's reactions. The human being is bounded by the human body. We are composed of jungle stuff, and ours is a monkey culture. Our troubles are caused by deviations into civilization, which is a fraud perpetrated on evolution. *Homo sapiens* has convinced himself that he is a dancing bear. Consequently, he can only lose his balance.

In the beginning was the gut, and the gut was law, and it is still so. It is the dog part of the human being that gets out of order, the part we keep telling ourselves we should be a little above, but we never are. The dog part runs by the dog rules. Everything is natural, under the circumstances. The twisted, unhappy person is normal, based on what happened to him. No one does what he should. He only does what he can, because that is what he has been conditioned to do. People are no more naturally one way or another than a piece of marble is naturally the Venus de Milo. Early environment is the sculptor's chisel.

Nothing is ever wrong in the individual's "should" department. It is the "able to" department that causes the difficulty. We live up to our conditioning, not our ideals.

I am always suspicious of the words "like to" or "don't like to." The inhibitory person does not "like" to talk, and the excitatory one does not "like" to keep quiet. An individual's philosophy of life is the product of his feeling-training. His philosophy changes with his emotional reeducation.

Only the drilling into the human tissues of healthy habits will yield "good" thinking and feeling. We are meat in which habits have taken up residence. We are a result of the way other people have acted to us. We are the reactions. Having conditioned reflexes means carrying about pieces of past realities.

We do not control ourselves. We are constantly being controlled by our habit patterns. What we deprecate as present irrelevancies are the imprints of past relevancies. We think with our habits, and our emotional training determines our thinking. Consciousness is like a moving picture. The emotional patterns of infancy are projected into awareness. We sit in the audience, and insist we're in the projection booth.

We have only the volition given by our habits. Where there is a conditioned reflex, there is no free will. Our "willpower" is dependent on our previously learned reflexes. If they are inadequate, the individual will bemoan his lack of "guts" and deprecate himself, though he is not at all to blame. Everybody is a carpenter using the only tools he ever had.

We feel by doing, and we do by feeling. We do not act because of intellectual reasons. Our reasons grow from our emotional habits. The important point about conditioning is that it is not at all an intellectual process. Whether we like it or not, the braincase has been permeated by the viscera. Life would be impossible if we had to think in order to breathe, feel, digest, blink, and keep our hearts beating.

Personality is not a question of logic. It is a question of feeling. Many bright people are as dull as dishwater. It is their emotional training that makes the difference.

Children are interesting because they are emotionally outgoing. A childish childhood is a happy childhood. The baby is born free, but his parents soon put him in chains. The tragedy of the drama of psychology is that all of the villains have friendly faces.

Excitation is a basic law of life, and neurosis is the result of the inhibition of natural impulses. I have also said, as can only be obvious in our daily life, that much of our activity is not logically motivated.

When we pause to consider what we have done when we felt happiest, we will recognize that we spoke without thinking. We expressed our innermost feelings. We did not waste time and energy percolating. We acted in an excitatory fashion.

People ask, "What are the roots of my troubles? How did I get this way?" They really mean, "How, in my childhood, was I robbed of my natural excitation? Where and how was this emotional component dwarfed, twisted, misdirected, or minimized?" *Hundreds of different causes produce the same fundamental deprivation of excitation.*

Causes such as the following are easy enough to determine, but they do nothing except satisfy our intellectual curiosity. I take them at random from my files:

1. Excessively well-mannered English family.
2. Unhappily married parents. A drunken father.
3. "Both my parents are quiet and reserved."
4. A mother-bound only child.
5. A psychopathic father. Great love one moment, overwhelming rage the next.
6. A more able older brother.
7. Brought up in an orphanage.

Finding and exploring the situations that have caused the psychological difficulty do nothing to facilitate the cure. A judge is interested in who is to blame for an automobile accident. The physician is concerned with healing the wounds of the injured. Psychiatry and psychoanalysis play the part of the judge, although they insist they are cast for the role of the physician.

Man's physical and emotional equipment is the same as it was ages ago. Yet modern man finds himself enmeshed in a web of constraining social forms with which he has more and more been required to conform, belying his essential nature, and denying that the human is, now as then, an animal—predatory, sadistic, craving, and emotional. From here springs conflict between artificial and natural, which overlooks the fact that man is a talking primate.

Living in society necessitates inhibition, but modern training goes too far when it teaches children to be polite at all times, not to contradict others, not to interrupt, not to be selfish, and always to consider other people's feelings. A well-adjusted person is like a housebroken dog. He has the basic inhibitions to permit him to live in society, but none extra to interfere with his happiness.

It will be objected that even the animals have their inhibitions. Doesn't the tiger crouch quietly before he leaps? If he went through the underbrush in an excitatory fashion wouldn't the other animals run away? True. Nevertheless, excitation is the meat of the jungle, while inhibition is the salt and pepper.

Following a set pattern, bowing to artificial vogue, conforming to a standardized mold, smothers excitation. This characterizes the inhibitory types—gentlemen-of-the-old-school, chivalrous colonels, well-brought-up boys, "officers and gentlemen," stoics, and ascetics. Every chink in their emotional armor, with a few approved exceptions, is plugged with a socially originated inhibition.

At first thought it might appear that a return to excitation would produce a world inhabited by undisciplined brutes, yet nothing could be further from the truth. Only the predominantly inhibited person is selfish, since he is constantly preoccupied with himself. The inhibitory person's consideration for others is merely a burned child's dread of the fire. He has no thought for others, because he does not have the ability to look outwardly upon those around him. He doesn't love, although he wants to be loved. There is no love without involvement, and he remains in his own shell. He has been conditioned against expressing the emotions of love. He is afraid of other people; he is afraid of responsibility; he is afraid to make decisions. His fears may express themselves in a show of aggression, egocentricity, and a lack of consideration. This type of inhibited person also worries constantly, and he is as maladjusted as his overpolite and shy brother. His suffering is equally intense.

A person has feelings of frustration and conflict when his psychological skills are inadequate to solve the problem that confronts him. It is as if he were trained to open doors, and it is not so much that the emotional lock before him is a new one as that the keys of inhibition are made of putty.

As we modify *behavior,* we modify the self-concept of the individual and the individual's emotional status. Behavior change precedes the change in the self-concept.

To change the way a person feels and thinks about himself, we must change the way he acts toward others. In short, just as the individual's private feelings of low self-esteem, shyness, and inadequacy were caused by earlier social experiences, so will new social experiences alter these personal feelings. Through Conditioned Reflex Therapy the individual is taught to interact socially in an excitatory fashion and not in an inhibitory fashion. Altering the individual's behavior alters the individual's self-image. One is a reflection of the other.

And, simultaneously, the individual's feelings of self-worth and social adequacy rise.

METHODOLOGY

The primary purpose of Conditioned Reflex Therapy is to alter the patient's psychological tilt from inhibition to excitation. Inhibitory feelings and inhibitory behavior are neurotic. Excitatory behavior is healthy.

Six techniques will do much to increase the individual's level of excitation. They are so interdependent and commingled that by practicing any one of them, the individual is, in effect, learning all of the others.

The first discipline (for that is what it is) I have called *feeling-talk*. It means the deliberate utterance of spontaneously felt emotions. "Thank heavens, today is Friday and the weekend is here" illustrates feeling-talk. However, saying merely "Today is Friday" would be dry fact-talk, and would do nothing to help emotional reconstruction. Man is the word-using animal, and his basic means for excitation is through speech. In a sense, feeling-talk means only to be emotionally outspoken, and is an aspect of small-talk.

My techniques of feeling-talk, rebaptized *assertion,* have attained much professional—and popular—acceptance. All too often I have found that calling feeling-talk *assertion* has resulted in an emphasis on the negative and the critical, and a soft-pedaling of the many other notes on the feeling-talk keyboard. And I must say that I have found too many of the advocates of assertion to be rather brassy, which is not the point of assertion at all.

Here are some examples of the side of assertion that I have found has been neglected by many of its advocates.

Remark	Type of Feeling-Talk
1. I like the soup.	Like
2. I like that snow scene. It makes me feel cool to look at it.	Like
3. That shade of green is perfect for you.	Praise
4. You did a marvelous job, Miss Jones.	Praise
5. Today is Friday. I thought it would never get here.	Relief
6. I can hardly wait until he gets here.	Impatience
7. My feet hurt.	Discomfort
8. What a wonderful time we had.	Enjoyment
9. The desk set was just what I needed.	Appreciation
10. I cleaned out the poker game.	Self-praise
11. I wonder what happens in the next installment.	Curiosity
12. It was the most extraordinary thing I had seen in a long time.	Amazement
13. Say it again. I like it.	Desire for approbation
14. I'm just dying to meet him.	Anticipation
15. There's nothing to it. I'll take care of it right away.	Confidence
16. This was a real good meal.	Contentment
17. I think the dessert was a mistake.	Regret
18. Darling, I love you with all my heart.	Love
19. Good grief, I feel terrible about that!	Anguish
20. Today is Friday. The week went fast.	Surprise
21. Now, that was stupid of me!	Self-criticism

Our golden rule is emotional truth, even if it means risking expediency. There is no harm in honoring social amenities and ethical conventions when they do not oppose our feelings. But we must forgo premeditated utterances and say what we feel when we feel it. When a cat feels happy, it purrs. When a dog has its paw stepped on, it howls. Let the inhibitory go and do likewise.

Animals also show emotion on their faces. The inhibitory person need not snarl like a tiger nor grin like a Cheshire cat that has read Dale Carnegie. However, he should furrow his brow when he is vexed, and wear a long face. "Be emotionally Gallic" is my counsel. I have named this second practice *facial talk.*

Our third rule of conduct is to *contradict and attack.* When you[2] differ with someone, do not simulate agreeability. Instead, externalize feeling, and contradict on an unprovable emotional basis. At first blush, this would seem to obstruct intelligent controversy. Actually, it only means interspersing emotional content among bare facts.

The next, and fourth, technique to keep in mind is the *deliberate* use of the word *I* as much as possible. "I like this. . . ." "I read that book and. . . ." "I want. . . ." "I heard. . . ." This will not make you appear priggish. It will sound natural. Somebody told one of my patients who was practicing this: "You know, you're conceited, but somehow I don't mind it from you."

The fifth discipline is to *express agreement when you are praised.* When someone says, "That's a fine suit you're wearing," do not remain expressionless. Do not shrug your shoulders and say, "It's nothing." Nor be satirical and say, "Of course, I'm wonderful." Instead, if

---

[2] I have retained some of my across-the-desk language.

you believe the compliment at all, say something like, "Thank you. It's my favorite suit. Gives me big shoulders, doesn't it?"

When Dr. Smith congratulates me on my success with Jones, I answer, "Thank you, Doctor. You know, he may consider himself fortunate that you were wide-awake enough to have sent him to see me." Notice that I have praised not only myself but also the physician. When you reflect praise like a mirror, the giver of the compliment will not deny it. The recipient, finding his self-praise accepted by the environment, develops increased emotional freedom. This is excellent self-conditioning. *Praise of self should also be volunteered,* and with straightforward naivete.

Improvisation is our sixth and last rule of conduct. Don't plan. Live for the next minute, and that's 59 seconds too long. This applies to what you are going to buy, where you are going to visit, and what you are going to say. Daydreaming is a sign of incomplete doing, and improvisation stops it. In order to build this spontaneity do not waste time Monday thinking about Tuesday and Wednesday. Live *now,* and tomorrow will take care of itself, even though we need more foresight than the grasshopper in the fable.

There are six typical procedures used in Conditioned Reflex Therapy.

The first series of procedures is addressed to increasing the excitatory level of the patient. These techniques were discussed above. In the words of Davison and Neale (1978, p. 497), Salter is "the originator of assertion training."

Another important technique introduced in *Conditioned Reflex Therapy* (1949) has been termed *behavior rehearsal.* This simply means going over with the patient future social encounters and discussing what to do and say if "they" say or do this—or, more probably—that. The therapist can play either the patient's role or that of the other participant in the projected encounter.

Behavior rehearsal is an important technique because of the *social* orientation of Conditioned Reflex Therapy. We view the patient's *social interactions* as the *primary source* of the patient's current inhibitions. And this is true despite the individual's having learned his or her inhibitions in the remote past.

The third technique used in Conditioned Reflex Therapy has become known as *systematic desensitization.* It was introduced in Case 3 in my *Conditioned Reflex Therapy* (1949). The patient

> listened with interest to my explanation of verbal conditioning, and next I told him to practice turning his feeling of claustrophobia on and off, and conditioning relaxation to it. . . .
>
> . . . My plan was for him to establish a link between controlling his senses and feeling good. I also told him to take care not to make his claustrophobia stronger than his feelings of well-being, or the conditioning would increase his discomfort.

Systematic desensitization, of course, is now one of the most widely used Behavior Therapy techniques. I did not intend desensitization only for use in phobias, but also for use as a technique of anxiety reduction in social and sexual relations.

From my "Three Techniques of Autohypnosis" (1941) to its attenuated and varied forms described in my *What Is Hypnosis* (1944) and *Conditioned Reflex Therapy* (1949), techniques of *self-control* are an important factor in Conditioned Reflex Therapy. As long as increasing the excitatory level of the patient remains our primary concern, teaching the patient techniques of self-control will be "getting at the roots" and will be quite helpful.

Teaching the patient to relax through *self-verbalizations* before entering (or while in) uncomfortable situations is another point emphasized in Conditioned Reflex Therapy. While this now seems a rather obvious point, as concern with self-instruction training and self-verbalization is now an important area of Behavior Therapy, historically it was not always thus.

I conclude this list of the primary techniques of Conditioned Reflex Therapy by mentioning the use of *covert conditioning based on imagery.* Imagery, as a provider of stimuli for use in conditioning, of course, is the essence of what has come to be called *systematic desensitization.* It is worth mentioning that elaborate lists of stimuli are quite unnecessary in teaching desensitization. Regulating the *duration* of the patient's imagery, and regulating the imaginary *distance* the patient is from a *single* high anxiety stimulus, is usually satisfactory.

Covert conditioning in the therapist's office (or the patient's home) to imagined anxious stimuli produces important benefits to the patient. And mobilizing covert conditioning in the presence of the actual anxiety-inducing stimuli—in an awkward social situation, for instance—is also extremely helpful. What is particularly interesting is that there is laboratory evidence that bona fide conditioning can take place as a result of a subject's juxtaposition of two imagined stimuli.

APPLICATIONS

Conditioned Reflex Therapy has shown excellent results with the entire spectrum of neurotic disorders. The phobias, anxiety, shyness, obsessive-compulsions, most insomnias and psychosomatic disorders—including migraine and *psychosomatic* coronary conditions—respond excellently to Conditioned Reflex Therapy. As for insufficient assertiveness in interpersonal relations, Conditioned Reflex Therapy should be considered the treatment of choice.

Long before Masters and Johnson, Conditioned Reflex Therapy was using most of their methods in the successful treatment of varied sexual dysfunctions. As

Fensterheim (1975, p. 16) wrote, with historical precision and a graceful pun: "We can trace the beginnings of these treatment methods to the seminal work of Salter . . . (1949)." The successful treatment of impotence is often a simple achievement via Conditioned Reflex Therapy. The treatment of poor orgasmic function in women calls for somewhat more effort, but here too the prognosis is usually excellent.

I have found that Conditioned Reflex Therapy is extremely efficacious in overcoming the work blocks of the creative, and I have some remarkable case histories of writers, musicians, and actors and actresses.

Particularly interesting to me have been patients with clusters of symptoms that are clearly neurotic but that defy easy categorization.

Before considering the limitations of Conditioned Reflex Therapy, I should mention that I have noticed that in recent years my caseload includes many fewer alcoholics, stutterers, and homosexuals. My explanation is simply that there has been a tremendous development of different therapies for alcoholism and stuttering, and that most—not all—homosexuals now consider themselves to be quite normal.

The limitations of Conditioned Reflex Therapy are essentially as follows:

Neither the highly defensive (I call them "yes, but-ers,") nor the highly paranoid will respond to Conditioned Reflex Therapy. Nor will such persons respond to any other forms of psychotherapy. Such persons can be spotted in a session or two, and certainly with the help of the Minnesota Multiphasic Personality Inventory.

Mild depressions are quite amenable to Conditioned Reflex Therapy, but as I have written elsewhere:

> Assertion trainers should be extremely cautious with depressed clients. In a way, treating depressed clients is an "orange sorting" problem. We have a conveyor belt with holes, and certain sizes of oranges can fall through the holes and larger sizes move on. We can handle certain kinds of clients. Certain other kinds of oranges have to go to people who can give medication and who can use biochemical approaches in treatment. As you talk to a client, and you see, quite correctly, the things that are making the person so depressed ("If she only realized thus and so about her husband," or "That situation with her mother isn't really thus and so"), you may be absolutely correct in your explanation. Nevertheless, your skills will not necessarily keep this person from going into an even deeper depression which really needs institutionalization. The fact that you can correctly see the psychogenesis of the situation does not mean that it can be treated by anybody's assertive, psychotherapeutic, or behavioral techniques." (Salter, 1977, pp. 35–36)

Any therapist who treats unmedicated schizophrenics should be aware that a core of the symptomatology will remain inaccessible until the patient is appropriately medicated.

I have done fairly well with sociopaths if their pathology is relatively mild and if their histories are not malignant.

In general, then, Conditioned Reflex Therapy is well-suited for all of the problems psychoanalysts believe they can treat and many of the problems analysts do not treat.

And Conditioned Reflex Therapy is so much faster and efficacious than arthritically crippled psychoanalysis! Now Conditioned Reflex Therapy and Behavior Therapy in general have reached such a level of acknowledged successful results that only the psychiatrically illiterate would dismiss them as being good only for phobias and mild neuroses.

As Charles Kettering once said to Paul de Kruif, "Remember, Paul, there is no such thing as an incurable disease. The disease has no objection to being cured."

CASE EXAMPLE

Mrs. R. H. is a blonde, attractive woman of 34. She tells me she is a professional pianist, and recites a series of formidable credits. Now, however, she plays the piano poorly. She was in an automobile accident, and has had surgery on both shoulders and on her arms. After a year of recuperation and physiotherapy she is playing the piano again, but her skill is as a shadow of her former self. In addition, the third finger of her right hand is uncontrollable. It feels numb and she cannot use it at will.

She has recently consulted two eminent neurosurgeons, considering neurosurgery to be the only solution for the problem of the third finger of her right hand. Intensive workups resulted in the same conclusion from each of the neurosurgeons: "I can't find any physical basis for this malfunction."

"Do you mean it's all in her head?" her husband asked the second neurosurgeon.

"I don't know" was the answer. "Perhaps she should see a psychoanalyst."

Her husband did not have a high opinion of psychoanalysis and holed himself up in a nearby university library. In the course of his reading he ran across my writings. I was the person to see. My brand of hypnotism would solve his wife's problem, and he particularly liked my book on psychoanalysis (Salter, 1952).

Before commencing physiotherapy, Mrs. R. H. had been very hopeful about its results, and some months earlier had signed contracts for a series of recitals. Could I restore sensation and control to her numb, uncontrollable finger in time for her first concert, which was four weeks away?

"Maybe," I said, "if the doctors you saw are right. But wouldn't you run out of here without bothering to open the door and go out through the wall like a Mickey

Mouse character if I promised you that I could help you? And in four weeks at that?"

She laughed weakly.

I advised her to cancel all of her scheduled concerts. "If everything goes as well as I hope, you'll have all the concerts you want. Your credentials are quite impressive."

My reason for telling her to cancel her schedule was simple. I felt that the achievement pressure of her schedule could seriously inhibit our therapy. Mrs. R. H. agreed to do as I advised.

While I could have immediately gone to work on efforts to restore her finger function, I felt that this would have been superficial treatment. If we succeeded, that would have been the end of the matter. But this would have been unfair to Mrs. R. H., when the repertoire of Conditioned Reflex Therapy has so much more to offer. Besides, more thorough treatment would maximize the possibilities of success in the treatment of her finger condition—which in itself is reason enough for taking such an approach. Borrowing a pharmacological term from Arnold Lazarus (which he uses in another connection), I would say that I advocate "broad spectrum" *personality changes.*

I shall discuss my treatment of the numb-fingered pianist in four parts, as follows:

1. The use of the Minnesota Multiphasic Personality Inventory (MMPI).
2. Preliminary phases—getting the history, particularly the present circumstances of the patient's life.
3. Deciding on the goals of treatment.
4. Carrying out the goals of treatment.

I like to have my patients take the MMPI after the first session with me so that I have the scores waiting for their second session. The significant scores of this patient were as follows: depression, 90th percentile; psychopathic, 90th percentile; paranoid, 80th percentile; masculinity-femininity, 15th percentile; hypochondria, 33rd percentile.

In short, the patient was somewhat depressed, somewhat rebellious (not amoral), and hypersensitive. The literature considers the low score on masculinity-femininity to be a sign of almost masochistic passivity. There were no signs whatever of any psychotic tendencies.

These scores correlated fully with my clinical impressions. What was also interesting and encouraging was that her "hypochondria" score was in approximately the 33rd percentile, verifying my clinical impression that she was not at all hypochondriacal. No "secondary gain" nonsense here.

My second concern was getting the patient's history,

particularly the present circumstances of her life. I also asked details about the accident and about her ruminations regarding music and her malfunctioning finger. All this helped me to determine the third phase, the goals of treatment. These were: (1) restoration of function in her finger; (2) restoration of a feeling of relaxation about music; (3) increasing the patient's level of excitation (i.e., assertion) in her personal and professional life.

In *carrying out the goals of treatment* I often mixed objectives in my consultations with her. But it is possible to describe my techniques separately.

"Forget hypnotism," I told her. "My first task with you is to get you out of the trance you've been in for years." She found my comment quite amusing, and not inaccurate.

The reader will recall that the third finger on the patient's right hand was both numb and without any control. The difficulties, therefore, were both sensory and motor in character. Relaxation, self-control, and covert conditioning were used to attack the problems of the finger. I taught the patient how to induce relaxation of her arms and fingers. I also queried her on her personal experiences with warmth and cold in her hands, and had her imagine these actual experiences (covert conditioning) in her fingers. She also practiced this (quite well) at home. In addition, to try to get at the motor aspects of her finger difficulty, I had her practice (successfully) imagining lightness and heaviness in her hands and fingers—more covert conditioning.

I did not tell her that I had done this exact type of covert conditioning with another woman some years before my pianist patient was born. In that case we were also dealing with the sequelae of an automobile accident, but then the woman's feet were like thin sticks that were completely paralyzed and did not respond to lit matches or ice cubes. By having that patient, for instance, recall childhood memories of her family gathered around a roaring, crackling fire, she was able to summon up feelings of warmth in her feet. Her thrill when we first achieved this is one of the most exciting moments of my professional career. I did not mention this patient to my pianist patient because I did not want to suggest any new symptoms to her.

At the same time I was teaching my patient to relax her entire body and to "feel relaxed about music." I felt that music was a source of excessive pressure to her, just like the need to perform successfully is to a man with impotence. This process of desensitization to the pressure to practice and to concertize could only help her finger.

I devoted a great deal of effort to increasing the patient's level of excitation in her personal and professional life. These areas included:

1. Her marriage. This was the second marriage for both the patient and her husband.

2. The problems caused by the admixture of her children, her husband's children, and their children.

3. Her mother—a tough, driving woman. Her father—important for his nonimportance.

4. Her husband's ex-wife, the mother of the patient's stepchildren, who lived in a nearby community and was a chronic source of frustration.

5. Her musical career.

What was particularly helpful was that the patient's remarriage was a happy one.

I taught the patient the six assertive disciplines mentioned at the beginning of my section on methodology, some simple behavior rehearsal and densensitization techniques, and that completed the strategies.

After four sessions the patient's finger—and her attitude—were fine. Her finger had recovered completely, with no additional physiotherapy, and her emotional level had become completely transformed for the better.

The point may well be raised that covert conditioning alone might have solved the finger problem and that the broad spectrum personality changes were a result of the improvement in the finger. If not, they were not that necessary.

However, I think that not to give a patient the maximum improvement that is possible through Conditioned Reflex Therapy is cruel and unfair, and gives support to psychoanalytic criticisms of behavioral treatment.

To respond to any possible criticism of my belief that each patient is entitled to as much improvement as possible, I shall quote from a review written by a music critic.

After her fifth session with me my patient decided to go on a tour as the piano accompanist of a famous violinist. She had been playing perfectly for some weeks, and I wanted her to get her feet wet in a subordinate position before venturing to resume her solo concertizing.

After her first appearance on this tour, a review of the concert appeared in a local paper, one of the most important newspapers in the country. The review had a four-column head: PIANIST OUTSHINES SOLOIST. Then the review went on to say:

> "The norm for concerts featuring instrumental soloists is for the piano accompanist to be far beneath the level of accomplishment of the soloist. Yesterday's ——— Hall recital was an exception. William A——— played with pianist R——— H———. Although A——— was the soloist, H——— [the pianist] provided the backbone as strongly as an orchestra does in a concerto. . . .
>
> H——— played with the piano fully open and used the instrument with imagination, tapping its resources expertly.
>
> She is definitely a soloist in her own right. Her ability to shape long movements and independently *assert the character of the music is beyond that of even the greatest*

accompanists living. . . ." (Italics added. Note the word "assert".)

I find it difficult to believe that this review ever would have been written if I had "only fixed my patient's finger." It was my total therapy that elicited Mrs. R. H. greater expressiveness, and that greater expressiveness in turn elicited this review and the incredible headline.

My pianist's employer, of course, was most unhappy—but it worked out well and besides, that's another story.

SUMMARY

I would be less than candid not to admit to a feeling of pride that my book *Conditioned Reflex Therapy* has been called "a landmark of the order of Darwin's *Origin of Species*" (de Kruif, 1949); one of the "landmarks in the history of psychology" (Sahakian, 1968); one of the "landmarks in the history of clinical psychology" (Nawas, 1972). And at more length, it has been said: "The books by Salter, Wolpe, Keller and Schoenfeld, and Skinner are landmarks in the history of behavior modification" (Kazdin, 1978). And the thinking and techniques of *Conditioned Reflex Therapy* certainly permeate Behavior Therapy, which gives me a great deal of satisfaction.

But what gives me the greatest professional satisfaction is one detail that distinguishes Conditioned Reflex Therapy from its descendants. Since Conditioned Reflex Therapy has a broader conception of maladaptive symptoms than its behavioral descendants, its objective is not just to eliminate the, for instance, claustrophobia or agoraphobia that brought the patient to treatment, but also to teach the patient to become a *broadly functioning* and *broadly feeling* human being.

The efforts of therapy should indeed be directed toward symptom removal, but with Conditioned Reflex Therapy's broader conception of symptoms, the removal of many of the subtle manifestations of inhibition results in a posttreatment patient who is truly happy, and not just phobia-free or more socially adept.

The result of behaviorally oriented therapy has too often been to rid the patients of the distressing symptoms that brought them to treatment—which is fine— but the behavior therapist should realize that patients almost always also suffer from debilitating symptoms with which they are not particularly concerned.

The Pavlovian concepts of inhibition, excitation, and disinhibition need refurbishing in the light of newer neurological findings. Nevertheless, the fact that I have eliminated claustrophobia and agoraphobia *solely* by increasing the patient's level of excitation (read "assertion") certainly calls for serious reflection.

This means, clearly, that excitation (or assertion) is by

no means indicated solely for problems of defective social interaction—a misapprehension that still clouds the perceptions of the vast majority of behavior therapists.

The historical record now shows that Behavior Therapy has advanced far beyond psychoanalytic therapy. The time has come to make Behavior Therapy still more liberating and self-fulfilling to the patient than it now is, and this, I believe, is the promise of Conditioned Reflex Therapy.

REFERENCES

Davison, G. C., & Neale, J. M. (1978). *Abnormal psychology* (2nd ed.). New York: Wiley.

de Kruif, P. (1949). Jacket copy of *Conditioned reflex therapy,* by A. Salter. New York: Farrar, Straus.

Eysenck, H. J. (1959). Learning theory and behaviour therapy. *Journal of Mental Science, 105,* 61–75.

Fensterheim, H. (1974). Behavior therapy of the sexual variations. *Journal of Sex and Marital Therapy, 1,* 16–28.

Fensterheim, H., & Baer, J. (1975). *Don't say yes when you want to say no.* New York: Dell.

Goldfried, M. R., & Merbaum, M. (Eds.). (1973). *Behavior change through self-control.* New York: Holt.

Hull, C. L. (1933). *Hypnosis and suggestibility.* New York: Appleton.

Kazdin, A. E. (1978). *History of behavior modification: Experimental foundations of contemporary research.* Baltimore: University Park Press.

Nawas, M. M. (1972). Landmarks in the history of clinical psychology from its early beginnings through 1971. *Journal of Psychology, 82,* 91–110.

Patterson, C. H. (1966). *Theories of counseling and psychotherapy.* New York: Harper & Row.

Sahakian, W. S. (1968). *History of psychology.* Itasca, IL: F. E. Peacock.

Salter, A. (1941). Three techniques of autohypnosis. *Journal of General Psychology, 24,* 423–438.

Salter, A. (1944). *What is hypnosis: Studies in auto and hetero conditioning.* New York: R. R. Smith.

Salter, A. (1949). *Conditioned reflex therapy: The direct approach to the reconstruction of personality.* New York: Farrar, Straus.

Salter, A. (1952). *The case against psychoanalysis.* New York: Holt.

Salter, A. (1977). On assertion. In R. E. Alberti (Ed.), *Assertiveness: Innovations, applications, issues.* San Luis Obispo, CA: Impact Publishers.

Wolpe, J. (1958). *Psychotherapy by reciprocal inhibition.* Stanford, CA: Stanford University Press.

Wolpe, J., Salter, A., & Reyna, L. J. (Eds.). (1964). *The conditioning therapies: The challenge in psychotherapy.* New York: Holt.

Chapter 12

COVERT CONDITIONING

JOSEPH R. CAUTELA and AVIS K. BENNETT

Cautela and Bennett present a rather interesting paradox in this chapter. As behaviorists, if they agree with J. B. Watson and B. F. Skinner, they essentially deny the importance of (but not the existence of) what we ordinarily call "the mind"—that is, thoughts and feelings. Indeed they write, "both [Watson and Skinner] felt that scientific quantification of covert behavior was unreliable and unnecessary."

Yet what do we find? These two avowed behaviorists (Cautela was head of the doctoral program in Behavior Modification at Boston College) essentially stress exactly what Watson and Skinner attempted to eliminate—covert behavior! In short, the chapter is about phenomenology—the mind—imagination!

The importance of this may not be apparent at first. To call this paradoxical behavior or to label these authors phenomenologists rather than Behavior Modifiers (with capital letters, since all therapists are behavior modifiers with small letters) misses the point. Cautela realizes that a true psychotherapy of intact adults requires an admission that there is a mind, that people can and do think, that they can visualize, and that they can imagine; he also understands that in the battlefield of the mind important changes can occur that will later manifest themselves in overt behavior, so that thought and emotion, rather than simply being an epiphenomenon, must be given status of independence.

This is one of the most scholarly of the chapters and well worth close reading.

Covert Conditioning involves both a concept and a set of procedures. Broadly defined, Covert Conditioning is the modification of covert processes in a manner similar to the way in which overt behavior is modified by operant conditioning techniques. In the covert conditioning procedure, the client is asked to imagine performing a behavior that is considered undesirable. The client is then asked to imagine a consequence designed to increase or decrease the probability of that behavior. These procedures are labeled covert sensitization (Cautela, 1967), covert reinforcement (Cautela, 1970a), covert extinction (Cautela, 1971), covert negative reinforcement (Cautela, 1970b), covert response cost (Cautela, 1976), and covert modeling (Bandura, 1970; Cautela, 1971, September). They are analogous to the operant conditioning procedures of punishment, positive reinforcement, extinction, negative reinforcement, response cost, and modeling (conceptualized within the operant framework).

Through the use of Covert Conditioning, an individual can learn to take responsibility for changing unwanted habits, learn new strategies to enhance future interactions, and generally increase adaptive functioning through the use of his or her creative imagination. Covert Conditioning facilitates the resolution of conflict

through change in the environment (covert and overt) rather than through resolution of intrapsychic conflicts underlying the problem behavior.

HISTORY

The human capacity to produce imagery has excited people throughout the millennia. From the earliest expression of imagination in cave drawings, human imagery has inspired the ages. Certainly the Renaissance could be viewed as the origination of the written word designed to evoke imagery, for masters such as Shakespeare, Spenser, and Chaucer seemed to display consummate psychological skill in kindling the imaginations of the world at that time (Singer, 1974).

Although early Christianity negated the importance of imagery, religious figures such as St. Theresa of Avila and St. John of the Cross viewed imagination as a bridge to knowledge of the essence of God (Peers, 1951). That kind of thinking seemed to emanate directly from the philosophy of Plato, who espoused a theory of forms, that is, he felt that innate ideas led to a higher realm where intelligible beings gained true knowledge (Watson, 1971). The influence of innate ideas, or inner experience, and the development of psychology as a separate field followed from that philosophical position.

With the advent of European psychology, the awareness of one's imaginative creativity and its inherent resource as a purveyor of behavior had a profound impact on psychoanalytic practice. Applying their analysis of imagery to the assessment of psychological processes, Freud and Jung wove symbolic interpretation into the core of European and early American psychology (Kazdin, 1978). However, the use of imagery in behaviorism has developed independent of the European tradition.

The origin of behaviorism was characterized by the development of an objective psychology based essentially on precise definitions of stimulus and response. Indeed, Watson (1919) led American psychologists far away from the study of inner experience by labeling thinking as subvocal speech. Skinner (1953) agreed with Watson that mentalistic concepts had no value in the scientific study of psychology and what psychologists needed to investigate were overt behavioral reactions such as speech and physical movements. Neither Watson nor Skinner denied that people have thoughts and images, but both felt that scientific quantification of covert behavior was unreliable and unnecesary (Watson, 1971).

The major impetus for the widespread introduction of imagery in American psychology was the emergence of Wolpe's (1958) systematic desensitization. Wolpe sanctioned the investigation of covert processes when he conceptualized systematic desensitization as a therapeutic procedure to modify phobic behavior. It was the first imagery-based procedure that embraced the tenets of behaviorism; that is, the method itself was sufficiently precise and repeatable so that it lent itself to experimental investigation.

Since Wolpe's initial contribution, which can be explained via a Pavlovian or respondent conditioning model, other psychologists from various theoretical orientations within a learning theory framework have investigated the process of imagery manipulation.

Stampfl and Levis (1967) developed implosive therapy (a procedure designed to flood a person with aversive imagery) based on Mowrer's (1960) two-factor theory of fear. Bandura's (1970) social learning theory of modeling stems from a mediational-contiguity model, while Homme's (1965) coverant control therapy, in which specific thoughts are made contingent upon the performance of target behaviors to be increased or decreased, and Cautela's (1973) Covert Conditioning are aligned with an operant orientation.

Still other behaviorists such as Meichenbaum (1974) and Mahoney (1974) subscribe to a somewhat different conceptual model in which faulty cognitive patterns (e.g., talking to oneself), problem solving, and imagining are viewed as mediators of behavior. These investigators label themselves cognitive behavior modifiers rather than learning theorists.

While systematic desensitization emerged in 1958 as a technique designed to eliminate *avoidance* behaviors (e.g., phobias), no parallel technique was advanced to eliminate maladaptive *approach* behaviors (e.g., addictive behaviors, socially inappropriate sexual behaviors). Covert Conditioning began to take shape in 1966 both as a vehicle for therapy and as a research instrument to investigate the elimination of maladaptive approach and avoidance behaviors. At that time, evidence was accumulating that punishment procedures utilizing shock could supress behaviors such as stealing, sexually deviant behavior, and addiction (Kuchner & Sandler, 1966). Cautela (1967) reported that the sequential pairing of a behavior a client wished to eliminate (alcoholism) with an aversive event (vomiting) in imagination led to a decrease in the overt behavior of drinking. Cautela labeled that procedure *covert sensitization*. The term *covert* was used because both the undesirable response and the aversive stimulus took place only in the imagination. The word *sensitization* was used because the purpose was to build up an avoidance to the undesirable response. The conceptualization of covert sensitization as an operantly based imagery procedure followed after the development of covert reinforcement. From that beginning, several imagery-based techniques (utilizing the underpinnings of operant conditioning) were developed by Cautela and have been applied to diverse behavioral disorders and populations.

CURRENT STATUS

A search of literature (McCullough, 1978, November) indicated that the years 1966 to 1978 yielded more than 400 studies investigating the effectiveness of covert conditioning procedures either through single-case design methods, group studies, or anecdotal case reports. Of these studies, 70 experiments and 49 dissertations were sufficiently rigorous to allow analysis of outcome data. These studies compared covert conditioning techniques to theoretical strategies that stemmed from other than an operant base—for example, hypnosis, positive self statements, expectancy instructions. The majority of studies reviewed focused on three procedures: covert sensitization, covert reinforcement, and covert modeling. However, additional studies on other procedures (covert extinction, covert negative reinforcement, and covert response cost) were included in the final evaluation.

The effectiveness of covert sensitization on maladaptive behaviors including alcoholism, smoking, overeating, and socially censured sexual behaviors was investigated. Research in covert modeling and covert reinforcement was reported in areas of phobia, attitude change, test anxiety, and pain reduction. An overall analysis of the research revealed that 52 percent of the studies demonstrated significant differences. Thirty-three percent of the results were in the expected direction, while 15 percent showed no differences between control groups and covert conditioning groups (McCullough, 1978, November).

A cogent review of Cautela's covert modeling as one of many imagery-based techniques has been presented by Kazdin (1978). While Kazdin reported a number of therapy outcome studies demonstrating the efficacy of covert modeling in reducing "subphobic" fears of college students (e.g., fears of rats or harmless snakes), he suggested that future research should emphasize more serious clinical problems.

In reviews and evaluations, the efficacy of Covert Conditioning is usually granted but there is some question about the adequacy of theoretical underpinnings. Investigators suggest further delineation of precise variables affecting behavior change.

Two studies (Bennett & Cautela, 1979, January) investigated the forward conditioning procedure, covert reinforcement, and a backward conditioning procedure, reciprocal inhibition, on the modification of a pain response. This was done by reversing the order of presentation of the reinforcement scene and a cognitive strategy; for example, in forward conditioning reinforcement followed presentation of the cognitive strategy and in backward conditioning reinforcement preceded the cognitive strategy. Each treatment procedure was effective in relieving pain. However, in a group design, subjects utilizing the covert reinforcement procedure reported significantly reduced pain when compared to subjects practicing the reciprocal inhibition procedure. Similarly, in the single-case designs, the operant procedure seemed more effective since people tolerated the pain for longer periods of time. These results suggest that when the response to be modified is an anxiety response, such as pain, an operant interpretation may be parsimonious as a reciprocal inhibition explanation. In a test where the response to be modified was not an anxiety response but the modification of pronoun usage (Ascher, 1973), the effectiveness of covert reinforcement may have been due to operant principles only.

In a survey of behavior therapists conducted to determine what behavioral treatment procedures are commonly used, covert conditioning procedures were often mentioned (Wade, Baker, & Hartmann, 1979). Compared to 13 other behavioral strategies, covert conditioning techniques were reported to be the sixth most frequently used.

Covert Conditioning has also been reported to be a paradigm that can be utilized along with other treatment modalities. In an anecdotal report, Singer (1974) described the effectiveness of covert sensitization as an adjunct to a psychoanalytic approach. Since the tendency toward voyeurism in Singer's client persisted despite considerable insight about his lifestyle, covert sensitization was introduced. Singer noted that within a few days of practice, instances of voyeurism had declined and within a few months had completely disappeared.

Covert Conditioning has been described in many standard texts on Behavior Therapy. A detailed elaboration of the procedures and how to use them can be found in *Covert Conditioning,* by Upper and Cautela (1979). Further, most college-level courses in Behavior Modification include material on Covert Conditioning.

THEORY

Within the covert conditioning model, three general categories of behavior must be considered: covert psychological behavior (thoughts, feelings, and images), covert physiological behavior (heart rate, pulse, and brain waves), and overt behavior. These categories are not mutually exclusive but are interactive and interdependent processes.

A number of important assumptions underlying these categories of behavior form the basis for the efficacy of Covert Conditioning. The first major assumption is that of homogeneity. The concept of homogeneity assumes a functional equivalence in overt and covert behavior; that is, overt and covert processes are similarly important in the explanation, maintenance, and modification of behavior. The second assumption may be called the interaction hypothesis. It states that covert and overt behaviors influence each other—for example, a visual cue signals the thought "I am afraid" and heart rate increases, or a person leaning over notices blood rush to the head and says, "I feel dizzy." The third assumption is that all categories of behavior obey the same laws of learning; that is, all covert levels of behavior, thoughts, images, and physiological responses may be reinforced or punished in the same manner as overt behavior. While in a broad sense generalizations and empirical findings concerning all learning apply to Covert Conditioning, an operant learning framework was chosen because of evidence indicating that all three categories of behavior respond to operant conditioning techniques (Cautela & McCullough, 1978).

The theoretical position of Covert Conditioning depends on the aforementioned assumptions. Since Covert Conditioning is based on a learning theory paradigm, therapeutic effectiveness depends on strict adherence to the model. The operant methodology underlying each covert conditioning technique is presented in Table 12.1. Integral to the theory is the necessity of the individual to

Table 12.1   Covert Conditioning Methodology

Covert Positive Reinforcement

| (R) imagine making a response | → | (S) | imagine a reinforcing event | → | (R) | increase in response rate |

Covert Negative Reinforcement

| (S) imagine aversive events | → | (R) | terminate S by imagining R to be increased | → | (R) | increase in response rate |

Covert Sensitization

| (R) imagine making a response | → | (S) | imagine an aversive event | → | (R) | decrease in response rate |

Covert Extinction

| (R) imagine making a response | → | (S) | imagine the reinforcing stimulus-maintaining behavior is withheld | → | (R) | decrease in response rate |

Covert Response Cost

| (R) imagine making a response | → | (S) | imagine the removal of a positive reinforcer | → | (R) | decrease in response rate |

Covert Modeling

| (R) imagine a model making the response | → | (S) | imagine the model is receiving pleasant or aversive consequences | → | (R) | decrease or increase in response rate, depending on consequences |

achieve and perform qualitative imagery. Factors such as image quality—for example, level of pleasantness or aversion, emotional arousal, clarity of imagery, and the amount of practice—all contribute to therapeutic improvement. The covert conditioning procedures could be impeded for some individuals if tension level is high or if they have interfering images. Relaxation training (Jacobsen, 1938) is taught to help reduce this interference.

The theoretical underpinnings of Covert Conditioning demand that a certain level of aversion be experienced with covert sensitization and covert negative reinforcement and a certain level of pleasantness be experienced with covert reinforcement. At least a minimum level of clarity and sufficient practice are needed to ensure conditioning effects. If the ability to use imagery is deemed inadequate for conditioning, clients are given practice in the office as well as assigned more practice at home.

Central to the efficacy of therapeutic progress and inherent in the covert conditioning system is the notion of a general level of reinforcement. Cautela has described the general level of reinforcement as being directly related to the number and quality of reinforcing and aversive situations a person experiences per unit of time. The writers' experience in clinical practice and use of the daily reinforcement survey schedule (Cautela, 1977b) indicates that the lower the level of reinforcement, the more susceptible one is to the effects of aversive stimulation.

The theoretical position of Covert Conditioning encourages the removal of a reinforcer in maladaptive approach behaviors, such as cigarette smoking and alcoholism. Since the elimination of reinforcing experiences is highly resistant to change, the implementation of

covert and overt reinforcement must be increased prior to and along with treatment. Covert reinforcement varies along a continuum that includes: (1) anticipation of a reinforcing event; (2) experience of that event; (3) retrieval of the event through the memory or use of memory aids, such as snapshots of the events.

Adherence to the theoretical system of the covert operant paradigm can lead an individual, through the production of his or her imagery, to countercondition old behavior, learn new response patterns, and gain self-control.

In order to optimize the use of covert conditioning procedures as a therapeutic system, an understanding of operant technology is necessary. The following examples represent the methodology described in Table 13.1.

Since Covert Conditioning assumes that covert behavior follows the same laws as overt behavior, response frequency is affected by the sequential pairing of the response and consequence. The probability of any covert behavior occurring again is influenced by the covert or overt behavior that follows it; for example, if the consequence is reinforcing, the behavior will increase in probability; if the consequence is punishing, the behavior is likely to decrease.

The underlying assumption across all the techniques is that a decrease in imagining a behavior will decrease the probability that the behavior will be performed overtly. Concomitantly, a decrease in overt behavior should decrease the covert behavioral component.

Experimental investigations of covert conditioning procedures have included presenting the response to be acquired in vivo (overtly) and in imagination. Acquisition of a new response was possible under both conditions when followed by imagination of the consequence.

In the following paragraphs, the clinical approach to Covert Conditioning will be summarized and examples of scenes employed in therapy will be presented.

The clinical implementation of covert conditioning procedures must be preceded by a behavioral analysis in order to determine the antecedents and consequences of the behavior to be changed (Cautela, 1968). Further information can be gleaned and a baseline measure taken by asking the client to record the frequency of occurrence, duration of the response, level of intensity, and location where the behavior takes place. This baseline is important because some clients report, "I'm *always* in pain," or "I *never* sleep." Clients are asked to complete the reinforcement survey schedule (RSS; Cautela & Kastenbaum, 1967) in order to determine which reinforcers are considered the most pleasant to the client. The following rationale is given to clients:

> Your behavior occurs because it is maintained by the environment. Whenever you perform that behavior, it is rewarded or punished by other people. There are many studies that indicate that if the consequences of behavior can be manipulated, then the behavior can be increased or decreased in frequency. We have found that just by having people imagine they are performing certain behaviors and then imagine particular consequences, behavior can change in a similar manner. I am going to have you imagine certain scenes, and ask you to imagine you are really there. Try not to imagine that you are simply seeing what I describe; try to use your other senses as well. If in the scene you are sitting in a chair, try to imagine you can feel the chair against your body. If, for example, the scene involves being at a party, try to imagine you can hear people's voices, hear glasses tinkling, and even smell the liquor and food. Now remember, the main point is that you are actually there experiencing everything. You don't see yourself there but are actually there. First let's determine if you can imagine the scene clearly. Close your eyes and try to imagine everything I describe. Ready? Raise your right index finger when the scene is clear.

After patients signal, they are asked if the scene was clear and how they felt about it. If the scene was clear and they could imagine the consequences as described, they are then asked to imagine the scene by themselves. (If there is any difficulty, the scene is repeated by the therapist, with modified or elaborated instructions, depending on what was difficult for the patient to imagine.)

Patients are told that whenever they finish imagining a scene by themselves, they are to indicate this to the therapist by raising the right index finger. At that point the therapist may say "Shift" or "Reinforcement" to signal the next scene to be imagined. Patients are then asked to practice the scene at least 10 times a day at home.

Types of scenes and covert conditioning strategies to be used are determined by situations that are discovered through the behavioral analysis. Examples of scenes that have been applied to specific behaviors using specific strategies follows.

Covert Sensitization (CS)

When a client wishes to change a maladaptive approach behavior, such as smoking, overeating, or alcoholism, the treatment of choice is CS. In treating obese clients, the client is asked to imagine:

> You have just had your main meal and you are standing around a dessert table with your friends. You reach for your favorite dessert and as you do you notice an unpleasant feeling in your stomach. You start to feel nauseous and sick all over. As you reach for the fork, food particles are welling up in your throat. You try to swallow them back down. Your throat is burning. You place your fork in the dessert and more undigested food comes up in your mouth. It tastes terrible. As you raise the fork to your mouth, you vomit all over your hands, the fork, the pie. Stinking vomit splashes on your friends. Your friends look horrified. You feel even sicker and vomit again. You run away from the table and go wash up. You feel so relieved to be away from the desserts.

Covert Reinforcement (CR)

Covert reinforcement has been used to modify both maladaptive approach behaviors and maladaptive avoidance behaviors. Consider the preceding example presented in CS in which punishing consequences (vomiting and social disapproval) followed the response to be decreased (dessert eating). A CR procedure could be used to increase the target behavior of not eating dessert:

> Imagine you are standing at the dessert table with your friends. As dessert is passed you politely refuse, and feel good about staying on your diet.

Since the procedure is covert reinforcement, the response to be increased is followed by a pleasant scene:

> Imagine you are your ideal weight. You look really slim in your favorite color and style. Someone you like says to you, "Gee, you've lost weight. I've never seen you look so good."

Clinical practice has indicated the need for treatment of "urges" to drink or overeat. A covert reinforcement self-control scene is presented:

> You are walking toward the refrigerator; as you open the door, you say, "No. I'm not going to snack between meals," and you feel really good about yourself as you walk away from the refrigerator.

Covert Negative Reinforcement (CNR)

When clients label themselves depressed, they often have difficulty imagining anything pleasurable. If aversive imagery can be imagined more vividly or realistically, therapy may begin by using escape from an aversive situation as a reinforcement for increasing certain behaviors. In CNR, a client is asked to first imagine an aversive situation. When the client signals the imagery is clear, the therapist says, "Shift." It is important that the noxious scene be terminated immediately by imagining the response to be increased. For example, to increase appropriate sexual behavior:

> Imagine that you are walking downtown when all of a sudden an unruly mob storms down the street in your direction. People are yelling and pushing and you're being carried along with the crowd. You can smell sweaty bodies. Your own body is being battered from all sides. You feel trapped. There is no way to escape. SHIFT. You are lying on a bed beside your wife. You feel relaxed and comfortable. You're beginning to feel aroused.

Covert Extinction (CE)

The covert extinction procedure removes the positive reinforcer maintaining the undesirable behavior. In the treatment of chronic cough:

> You are eating in a restaurant with friends. The waitress brings your favorite food to the table. It smells and tastes right. You start a coughing spell. Everyone continues to eat and talk as before. No one even notices you are coughing. Your cough subsides and you resume eating.

Covert Modeling (CM)

Covert modeling can be applied to the modification of a wide gamut of behaviors, but it has been especially useful in the area of assertiveness training.

> Imagine you see someone you admire standing in line at the theater. Someone cuts in line in front of him. He looks relaxed and calm as he steps up to the person and says, "This is my place in line." You see him smile and he looks like he feels good about himself as the intruder goes to the back of the line.

Covert Response Cost (CRC)

In employing covert response cost, a client is asked to imagine the behavior to be decreased followed by the imaginary loss of a positive reinforcer, such as money, jewelry, or a favorite possession. In the treatment of exhibitionism:

> Imagine that you are walking toward a group of people. As you get ready to expose yourself, you reach for your wallet and notice it is gone. You feel sick in the pit of your stomach. You don't know what to do since you have no more money.

It must be reemphasized that successful application of the covert conditioning procedures depends on many factors, including (1) increase in general level of reinforcement, (2) composite presentation of procedures, (3) practice in and out of the office, (4) continuing behavioral assessment, and (5) use of other behavioral procedures such as behavioral rehearsals, relaxation training, and contingency contracting.

In clinical practice, more than one procedure is usually presented to each client. For example, in the treatment of drug addiction, the therapist may want to introduce CE ("Imagine you are injecting yourself and there is no rush or high"). CS might be used to reduce the urge to take drugs, and CR could be used to increase alternative behaviors. In addition to these covert conditioning procedures, the client could be taught relaxation to reduce tension, a contingency contract could be developed to enhance reduction in drug taking, and self-control scenes could be an important variable in maintaining the desired behavior ("You are about to shoot up; you change your mind and feel really good about yourself as you throw the needle away").

Self-Control Triad (SCT)

Cautela has recently developed another therapeutic strategy, the self-control triad (SCT), to be used in conjunction with the covert conditioning procedures. The SCT can be viewed as an important mechanism in empowering the client with strategies for coping and self-control. That is, the triad is useful in altering an established behavior, maintaining a newly learned behavior, and preventing development of another maladaptive behavior.

A composite of three behavioral techniques is comprised in the SCT: thought stopping, relaxation, and covert reinforcement. While the procedure has not been verified experimentally, it has been found effective in private practice. First, a rationale is presented to the client that explains how the use of the SCT prior to, during, or after any anxiety-provoking situation could reduce stress and increase one's capacity to respond appropriately intellectually or emotionally. The procedure is practiced with the therapist as follows:

Clients are asked to close their eyes and to imagine the thought that is distressing them. When the thought is clear, they signal with the index finger. At that signal, the therapist yells, "Stop." Clients usually report that the thought disappeared, and they are then asked to imagine the thought and yell "Stop" to themselves while visualizing a big red stop sign. Next clients are asked to take a deep breath and exhale, feeling a wave of relaxation spread over their whole body. That sequence of imagining the negative thought, yelling "Stop," and then relaxing is paired and practiced by each client.

The third component is CR, imagining a pleasant scene selected from the RSS. When clients are able to "see" and feel the pleasantness of the scene, the whole triad is practiced together: (1) the client imagines the thought to be decreased and yells "Stop" covertly while imagining a red stop sign; (2) the client takes a deep breath and says the word "Relax"; and (3) the client imagines a pleasant scene. Practice usually continues with the client utilizing the imagery both with the eyes open and closed. (One advantage of this procedure is that it can be utilized with no infringement of privacy when others are around.) Homework practice of two sessions a day—for example, 10 trials with the eyes open and 10 trials with the eyes closed—is suggested to each client. Since satiation can occur on any scene, clients are asked to use a different reinforcer for every 20 trials. A useful suggestion is that upon waking each morning, the client choose his or her favored reinforcer for the day. That also ensures the ready availability of a scene and precludes the necessity of searching for a reinforcer when an anxious situation occurs.

The SCT can be used in many situations, such as driving in traffic, at the office, and at home, and is applicable to maladaptive approach behaviors as well as maladaptive avoidance behaviors. For example, if tension is associated with maladaptive eating habits, yelling "Stop" distracts one from the thought "I need a snack" and reciprocally inhibits the tension through the relaxation and pleasant scene. The pleasant scene reinforces the thought stopping and relaxing, thereby increasing the probability that new behavior will occur in a variety of situations.

Finally, covert conditioning procedures are employed in the daily behavioral assessment of successful and unsuccessful interactions. Clients are asked to review the day's events. If a situation arose when they should have asserted themselves and they didn't, they are asked to imagine they are handling the situation appropriately and then to imagine a pleasant scene (CR).

All the procedures as previously defined and described can now be used by the individual to change, maintain, or develop the desired response in any situation.

APPLICATIONS

When originally conceived, the covert conditioning procedures were applied mostly to adult clientele in private practice or in outpatient settings. Currently, the procedures are being extended to other populations, such as children, adolescents, and the elderly in a variety of situations, including residential institutions, schools, and hospitals.

The therapeutic intervention of various covert conditioning procedures, both individually and as a composite package, has been applied to cases of dental fear in children, sibling aggression, to increase social interaction in the autistic, and to curb maladaptive behaviors such as hand flapping and inappropriate hitting in the retarded. Covert Conditioning has been reported to reduce the urge to set fires in an adjudicated delinquent (Cautela, 1966), to enhance children's self-concept (Krop, Calhoun, & Verrier, 1971), and has been applied to the modification of organic dysfunction, for example, epilepsy (Cautela, 1973, May–June).

Adolescent problem behaviors such as poor study habits, test anxiety, obsessive sexually deviant thoughts, and inadequate social skills have all been successfully treated by both writers in Cautela's practice.

Recently the procedures were presented in an attempt to enhance physical rehabilitation in special needs children. In some cases, covert reinforcement was practiced to increase level of participation in treatment and to desensitize antecedent stimuli that appeared to increase frequency of handicapped behavior—for example, with a child with a club foot who was more apt to drag the foot when criticized.

Adult populations have experienced many and varied applications of Covert Conditioning. The presentation of a composite package of covert procedures successfully alleviated heroin addiction in a client who had used 20 bags per day for three years (Wisocki, 1973). A Synanon-type treatment had been unsuccessful and the client had felt his chances for rehabilitation were slim. However, the desire to use drugs began to be reduced as the client practiced imagining the various strategies. Gradually the habit of drug addiction was eliminated; a one-year follow-up indicated that treatment gains were maintained and no evidence of addiction was reported.

An unusual application of Covert Conditioning was in the treatment of life-threatening self-injurious behavior (Cautela & Baron, 1973). The client was hospitalized with a diagnosis of schizo-affective. During the time spent planning a behavioral intervention, the client had completely lost the sight in both eyes by poking them and had bitten off a considerable portion of upper lip tissue and some lower lip tissue. After a one-year treatment with Covert Conditioning, including training the hospital staff to reinforce appropriate behaviors while extinguishing inappropriate behaviors, the client showed no further self-injurious behavior. During a recent 10-year follow-up, the client reported that he is now married, has graduated from college and law school, and is currently employed as a lawyer for a state agency. There has been no reoccurrence of self-injurious behavior.

As mentioned, Covert Conditioning has been successfully applied in many maladaptive approach behaviors such as overeating (Brunn & Hedburg, 1974), alcoholism (Ashem & Donner, 1968), and sexual deviance (Barlow, Leitenberg, & Agras, 1969). A new area to receive the attention of Covert Conditioning has been the institutionalized elderly. Cautela (1981) has recently developed an elderly reinforcement survey schedule. Theoretically, an increase in the level of reinforcement should contribute to a reduction in depression. Nursing homes and housing areas for the elderly may be able to incorporate covert reinforcement as a self-control measure in a general therapeutic plan, thereby enhancing institutional efficiency and increasing quality of life for the elderly in general.

Covert conditioning procedures now are being applied in the field of behavioral medicine. Besides treatment of persistent cough, epilepsy, and asthma, Cautela (1977b) has described the effectiveness of Covert Conditioning in reducing pain associated with rheumatoid arthritis. A two-year follow-up indicated that the client has remained free from pain or been able to control pain whenever it occurred. There is growing evidence that the interaction of psychological and physiological factors influences susceptibility to and the course of cancer (Cautela, 1977c).

The writers' approach in treating organic dysfunction, such as seizures, has been the same as our approach in treating psychological disorders: A behavioral analysis operationally defines the dysfunction, measures the frequency, duration, and intensity of the disorder, and identifies the antecedents and consequences. Cautela suggests that every client with an organic dysfunction, regardless of type, should receive both a behavioral analysis and treatment as well as a medical diagnosis and treatment.

The authors recently treated a hospitalized client who was stricken with amyotrophic lateral sclerosis, a syndrome marked by muscular weakness leading to paralysis due to degeneration of motor neurons of the spinal cord, medulla, and cortex. The client was completely paralyzed but retained the motor ability to make an eye-blink response as well as some slight thumb movement. Goals in this case were to reduce fear and frustration in the client, family, and the hospital staff. The client was trained to practice calm, healing imagery designed to increase level of reinforcement and demonstrate that he still retained some control over his bodily processes. In order to reduce fear, covert reinforcement was used on the reliability of equipment functioning—for example, a respirator would continue to breathe for him—and thought stopping was introduced to control negative thinking. Compliance to medical regimen was increased by training the staff in principles of reinforcement and extinction. The client was also taught to reinforce the

family and staff whenever possible on a nonvocal communicator. The use of CR prior to the introduction of a portable respirator may have aided the client's successful transition in using it. What had originally appeared to the client, family, and hospital staff as an impending terminal illness was gradually reassessed. As the environment became less hostile and more reinforcing, alternatives for living began to be explored. Currently, with assistance from hospital staff and family, the client has been able to make visits home (using the portable respirator) and to attend occasional public functions.

Since the writers' advances in the field of behavioral medicine have been reported anecdotally, good research data is needed to support Cautela's behavioral/medical treatment regimen.

A major consideration and value in the application of covert conditioning procedures to any type of disorder is the idiosyncratic nature of the techniques.

Limitations in effectiveness could result from lack of practice during the session, lack of practice at home, or therapist failure to obtain adequate feedback on imagery assessment. Clients experiencing any difficulty pertaining to practice or those unable to develop appropriate and effective imagery have not in the past been able to achieve successful intervention. In the hospital setting, particularly if the staff is trained to encourage practice of covert conditioning strategies and to follow the principles of reinforcement as indicated by the behavioral/medical assessment, the probability of success should be increased.

CASE EXAMPLE

The following example details the successful application of covert conditioning procedures to the treatment of hacking cough and acute dysphonia (hoarseness).

History

Mary, the client, was a 16-year-old Caucasian female. She was referred by the university hospital for a persistent cough and acute dysphonia.

Mary was first seen early in 1973 by a physician. At that time she reported symptoms and a persistent cough (two weeks' duration). In April the cough appeared again. She was treated with Prednisone and relieved of her symptoms. In September another flare-up began and although for a while she improved greatly with medication, gradually a "deep, barking, brassy" cough developed and her speech was reduced to a "hoarse whisper." Subsequent treatments of various medications for allergies had no effect. On November 12, when symptoms had failed to respond to any treatment, it was decided the problem was not allergic and, after consultation with other physicians, Mary was admitted to the hospital. All tests during a six-day admission were normal. Mary was then referred to a hospital center for children, where she was hospitalized between November 30, 1976, and December 10, 1976, and again from March 4 to 7, 1977. She was tested extensively both times, and no organic basis was established to explain the continuing cough and dysphonia. She was referred to the hospital's psychosomatic unit but chose to see a private psychiatrist. After a number of sessions, Mary felt she wasn't being helped and reported back to the hospital center, where she was referred to these writers for "psychogenic cough."

Initial Visit

Mary and her mother, Mrs. Y, appeared for the initial consultation with the writers, who were cotherapists. Initially Mary's mother reported that Mary developed symptoms at the same time the mother and Mary's brothers were experiencing allergy attacks that required them to spend time away from work and school. (Mrs. Y works full time on the 11 to 7 A.M. shift as a registered nurse.) Mrs. Y felt Mary's cough was due to an undiscovered organic problem, but was upset by Mary's missing school and family difficulties with facing Mary's whispering and coughing. Mrs. Y reported that Mary's sister thought Mary was faking. However, Mrs. Y also reported hearing Mary cough during the night every night while she was sleeping. When Mary coughed or whispered, Mrs. Y paid a lot of attention to her (e.g., they watched soap operas together when Mary missed school, which was a frequent occurrence, and Mrs. Y kept telling Mary to talk louder and to repeat what she said).

During Mary's interview she reported that her father didn't get along with her mother and didn't participate in their lives even though he lived with them. She was very angry with him and reported that he asked about her cough only once a month. Mrs. Y was concerned about Mary's reported weight loss of 10 pounds, but Mary liked her thin self. She saw her mother as a martyr who had to work all night to keep the family going. Mary didn't get along with her high-achieving sister and had a chronically ill (asthmatic) brother who still wet the bed at the age 13. She reported becoming a "hermit" since her coughing began; she had tutors and no longer attended school, didn't go out with friends, and couldn't talk on the phone much due to the dysphonia. Further, wherever she went, people asked her if she had a cold, and that made her feel uncomfortable. The physical symptoms Mary reported were headaches, cough, whispering, itchy eyes and nose, generalized pain, dry throat, and wakefulness at night. Mary was convinced her cough was not psychological, but she reported wanting to be rid of it.

Assessment

It was hypothesized that Mary's coughing was being maintained by the medical and social attention paid to it and by the avoidance of anxiety associated with her entry into high school. The home environment further added to Mary's symptoms since she was unable to relate assertively with her siblings. Also there was apparently a lot of modeling of illness behavior by observing the asthmatic brother and frequent respiratory infections of the mother.

While one therapist interviewed Mary, her cough was being monitored by the cotherapist. Mary coughed 10 times per minute during a 15-minute interval.

Intervention

Based on the initial assessment, the therapists decided to use the following procedures:

1. Progressive relaxation (Jacobsen, 1938) and relaxation coupled with imagery:

   You are lying on a blanket at the beach. The sun is shining and you feel warm and comfortable. As your fingers slowly sift the sand you feel the warmth of the sun baking into your body. The warm sand is like a comfortable mattress and you feel peaceful and calm. Smell the salt air. Hear the gulls overhead. All the tension is flowing out of your body and you feel more and more relaxed. You can hear the waves lapping at the shore and you feel warm and wonderful, so peaceful, better than ever before.

2. Self-control triad (as previously described): Mary used this procedure in various situations that caused her tension to increase; for example, when her parents would argue, when her brother would tease her, and before, during, and after exams.

3. Covert sensitization on coughing: After every cough, Mary would imagine an aversive scene. Since Mary had indicated on the covert conditioning aversive scene survey schedule (Cautela, 1976) that she found bees to be very aversive, she was asked to imagine bees swarming all over her face, especially in her nose and ears, as soon as she began to cough.

4. Covert reinforcement and covert modeling on not coughing in public places and for increasing social activities. In covert reinforcement, Mary would imagine she was at the movies with friends, not coughing, feeling relaxed and calm and not even having an urge to cough, followed by a pleasant scene. In covert modeling, Mary would imagine her ideal self was at the movies with friends and she looked happy, peaceful, and calm as she noticed herself smiling because she wasn't coughing. For

increasing social activities utilizing covert reinforcement, Mary would practice 10 times a day imagining she was at a public place or talking on the telephone with friends and then imagining a pleasant scene. When covert modeling was the behavioral strategy being practiced, Mary would imagine the same scene by watching her ideal self in a similar situation.

5. Assertiveness training, which was originally formulated within a learning theory framework by Andrew Salter (1949), combined with covert modeling to increase assertive behavior. Covert procedures consisted of instructing Mary to imagine she was in a previous situation where she had failed to speak up but this time she saw herself speak up and then receive a compliment for having asserted herself.

6. Covert extinction on attention paid to her cough at home and in public places: For example, Mary would imagine she was at home in the midst of her family watching television (a regular family occurrence) and when she coughed, no one paid any attention to her.

7. Desensitization to her parents and siblings by covert reinforcement by having her imagine situations in which she usually felt anxious and overreactional, while she remained relaxed and calm and/or asserted herself appropriately, followed by a reinforcing scene.

8. Health sweep imagery to try to offset her perseveration on physical symptomology. Mary was asked to try to stifle the urge to cough, followed by imagining a soothing, healing liquid moistening her throat, seeping deeply into the tissue, penetrating and relaxing the muscles, leaving her throat feeling relaxed and calm, with no urge to cough, feeling healed.

It was not possible to interview the father and siblings. Therefore, special emphasis was given in training the mother in therapeutic procedures that would extinguish attention to the cough and reinforce family relationships and activities with Mary that didn't center on her cough.

Goals

The goals agreed upon by Mary and the therapists were that Mary would gradually return to school with a goal of full-time attendance, resume social activities, and be free of the cough.

Mary was seen twice a week, once by the female therapist and once by both therapists. Mary was trained in the use of imagery, given specific procedures as enumerated, and encouraged to keep records. Apparently she practiced consistently for the first few months and kept good records that included counting (using a wrist counter) the number of times she coughed, listing the number of scenes she did on CS, CR, CM, and CE, and rating her relaxation for comfort. Within four weeks, Mary's cough was timed at three per minute, and she was increasing her social contacts through telephone conversations. Then in November a plateau was reached and the writers began assertiveness training, healing imagery (e.g., health sweep and reinforcement of a healthy body), and use of the self-control triad whenever she felt tense in any situation.

In December Mary practiced less, her sister was home from school, her brother and mother were home sick, and her therapy sessions were reduced to once a week because of family illness. In January her visits decreased to one in three weeks and her cough increased to four to five times per minute when timed. Also in January Mary returned to the referring physician; it was suggested that she continue with the behavior therapist since she showed some evidence of "rehabilitation."

A consultation with Mary and her mother at that time about consistently attending therapy and practicing seemed to produce positive results. With resumption of support and practice, Mary's cough decreased to two per minute and persisted at that level until August, when she was specifically asked how she could be close to a boy (e.g., holding and kissing) if she coughed in his face. Two weeks later Mary reported she just "miraculously" stopped coughing one day while she was cleaning the family room with her brother. Coughing symptoms did not reappear. In September she began school on a full-time basis and in October was dismissed from formal treatment but encouraged to continue relaxation. A follow-up in January showed no coughing and an increase in the loudness of Mary's voice.

During another follow-up six months later, Mary reported she was doing well in school, had a boyfriend, and had resumed a schedule of social activities. Mary spoke in a normal tone of voice and reported she rarely coughs, even though she still has allergies.

SUMMARY

In summary, Covert Conditioning involves theoretical assumptions and a set of specified procedures that can modify both overt and covert behaviors in a manner similar to operant technology. Covert Conditioning has the advantage over some other theoretical systems such as cognitive behavior modification in that the operations are more specifiable. Also, conceptualization within an operant model allows for the investigation and utilization of findings from the vast body of literature in operant conditioning.

The research on the efficacy of Covert Conditioning has as much empirical support as any other set of therapeutic procedures, including Behavior Therapy. Current data indicate that the use of covert conditioning procedures in a wide variety of situations is increasing. Only a few investigations concerning process variables have been conducted.

The results thus far have been equivocal, especially when the dependent variable has been some measure of anxiety.

However, the writers see no inherent limitations of the assumptions or procedures that would preclude the utilization of Covert Conditioning for the modification of any behavior. As long as one is able to follow instructions, any individual is capable of benefiting from covert conditioning procedures whether applied by therapists or when used individually for self-control. In our experience, clients who have learned to use and practice the covert conditioning procedures gain a self-control technology that can be used for the rest of their lives for stress management and the control of any response they feel is undesirable.

While this may appear presumptuous, preliminary explorations into such areas as relaxation, autism, and organic dysfunctions have been encouraging thus far. It is perhaps better to be overly optimistic about the possible utilization of Covert Conditioning than to avoid its application due to some a priori perceived limitations.

REFERENCES

Ascher, L. M. (1973). An experimental analog study of covert positive reinforcement. In R. Rubin, J. Brady, & J. Henderson (Eds.), *Advances in behavior therapy: Vol. 4.* New York: Academic Press.

Ashem, B., & Donner, L. (1968). Covert sensitization with alcoholics: A controlled replication. *Behavior Research and Therapy, 6,* 7–12.

Bandura, A. (1970). Modeling theory. In W. S. Sahakian (Ed.), *Psychology of learning: Systems, models, and theories.* Chicago: Markham.

Barlow, D. H., Leitenberg, H., & Agras, W. S. (1969). The experimental control of sexual deviation through manipulation of the noxious scene in covert sensitization. *Journal of Abnormal Psychology, 74,* 569–601.

Bennett, A. K., & Cautela, J. R. (1979, January). *The use of covert conditioning in the modification of pain: Two experimental tests.* Paper presented at the meeting of the Association for the Advancement of Behavior Therapy, San Francisco.

Brunn, A. C., & Hedberg, A. G. (1974). Covert positive reinforcement as a treatment procedure for obesity. *Journal of Consulting Psychology, 2,* 117–119.

Cautela, J. R. (1966). *Behavior therapy and its implications for treatment of the delinquent child.* Paper presented to the Division of Youth Services, Boston.

Cautela, J. R. (1967). Covert sensitization. *Psychological Reports, 20,* 459–468.

Cautela, J. R. (1968). Behavior therapy and the need for behavioral assessment. *Psychotherapy: Theory, Research and Practice, 5,* 175–179.

Cautela, J. R. (1970a). Covert reinforcement. *Behavior Therapy, 1,* 33–50.

Cautela, J. R. (1970b). Negative reinforcement. *Behavior Therapy and Experimental Psychiatry, 1,* 272–278.

Cautela, J. R. (1971). Covert extinction. *Behavior Therapy, 2,* 192–200.

Cautela, J. R. (1971, September). *Covert modeling.* Paper presented at the meeting of the Association for the Advancement of Behavior Therapy, Washington, DC.

Cautela, J. R. (1973). Covert processes and behavior modification. *Journal of Nervous and Mental Disease, 1,* 157.

Cautela, J. R. (1973, May–June). Seizures: Controlling the uncontrollable. *Journal of Rehabilitation,* pp. 34–40.

Cautela, J. R. (1976). Covert response cost. *Psychotherapy: Theory, Research and Practice, 13,* 397–404.

Cautela, J. R. (1977a). The use of covert conditioning in modifying pain behavior. *Journal of Behavior Therapy and Experimental Psychiatry, 8,* 45–52.

Cautela, J. R. (1977b). *Behavior analysis forms for clinical intervention.* Champaign, IL: Research Press.

Cautela, J. R. (1977c). Toward a Pavlovian theory of cancer. *Nordisk Tidskrift for Behteendeterapi, 6,* 117–147.

Cautela, J. R. (1981). The behavioral treatment of geriatric patients with depression. In J. F. Clarkin & H. I. Glazer (Eds.), *Depression: Behavioral and directive intervention strategies.* New York: Garland.

Cautela, J. R., & Baron, M. G. (1973). Multifaceted behavior therapy of self-injurious behavior. *Journal of Behavior Therapy and Experimental Psychiatry, 4,* 125–131.

Cautela, J. R., & Kastenbaum, R. A. (1967). Reinforcement survey schedule for use in therapy training and research. *Psychological Reports, 20,* 1115–1130.

Cautela, J. R., & McCullough, L. (1978). Covert conditioning: A learning theory perspective on imagery. In J. R. Singer & K. S. Pope (Eds.), *The power of human imagination.* New York: Plenum.

Homme, L. E. (1965). Perspectives in psychology: XXIV. Control of coverants: The operants of the mind. *Psychological Record, 15,* 501–511.

Jacobsen, E. (1938). *Progressive relaxation.* Chicago: University of Chicago Press.

Kazdin, A. E. (1978). *History of behavior modification.* Baltimore: University Park Press.

Krop, H., Calhoun, B., & Verrier, R. (1971). Modification of the self-concept of emotionally disturbed children by covert reinforcement. *Behavior Therapy, 2,* 201–204.

Kuchner, M., & Sandler, J. (1966). Adversion therapy and the concept of punishment. *Behavior Research and Therapy, 4,* 179–186.

Mahoney, M. J. (1974). *Cognition and behavior modification.* Cambridge, MA: Ballinger.

McCullough, L. (1978, November). *The efficacy of covert conditioning.* Paper presented at the meeting of the Association for the Advancement of Behavior Therapy, Chicago.

Meichenbaum, D. (1974). *Cognitive behavior modification.* Morristown, NJ: General Learning Press.

Mowrer, O. H. (1960). *Learning theory and the symbolic process.* New York: Wiley.

Peers, E. A. (1951). *Handbook to the "life and times of St. Theresa and St. John of the Cross."* London: Burns, Oates, & Washburn.

Salter, A. (1949). *Conditioned reflex therapy.* New York: Farrar, Strauss.

Singer, J. R. (1974). *Imagery and daydream methods in psychotherapy and behavior modification.* New York: Academic Press.

Skinner, B. F. (1953). *Science and human behavior.* New York: Macmillan.

Stampfl, T. G., & Levis, D. J. (1967). Essentials of implosive therapy: A learning-theory based psychodynamic behavioral therapy. *Journal of Abnormal Psychology, 23,* 375–412.

Upper, D., & Cautela, J. R. (1979). *Covert conditioning.* New York: Pergamon Press.

Wade, T. C., Baker, T. B., & Hartmann, D. P. (1979). Behavior therapist: Self-reported views and practices. *The Behavior Therapist, 2,* 3–6.

Watson, J. B. (1919). *Psychology from the standpoint of a behaviorist.* Philadelphia: Lippincott.

Watson, R. I. (1971). *The great psychologists* (3rd ed.). New York: Lippincott.

Wisocki, P. A. (1973). The successful treatment of heroin addiction by covert techniques. *Journal of Behavior Therapy and Experimental Psychiatry, 4,* 55–61.

Wolpe, J. (1958). *Psychotherapy by reciprocal inhibition.* Stanford, CA: Stanford University Press.

Chapter 13

CRISIS MANAGEMENT

JAMES L. GREENSTONE and SHARON C. LEVITON

This is perhaps the most "out of line" chapter in the book, yet it is, paradoxically, the one that every reader should study most carefully, since the management of crises is something that no practicing therapist can avoid, and is a skill as useful as first aid for those who deal with people's problems.

As Greenstone and Leviton indicate, even experienced therapists sometimes fall apart when faced by crises. When faced with a situation that could provoke panic, knowing what to do and when to do it is a most important skill. Understanding the basic principles of Crisis Intervention and Management is a valuable asset to all, especially therapists, since any client or set of clients might go into a crisis period at any time.

In addition, the writers of this chapter include a valuable note regarding the dangers of crisis intervention to the professionals involved—a note that has general applicability to all of us who practice the art and science of psychotherapy.

Crisis Management, or Crisis Intervention, is the skillful intrusion into the life of an individual at that time in the person's life when, because of unusual stress and tension brought on by unexpected and disruptive events of life, the individual is not able to direct his or her life in the way that he or she would normally under noncrisis conditions. This intrusion is for the purpose of defusing a potentially destructive situation before such physical and/or emotional destruction occurs.

A crisis occurs when unusual stress is present in an individual's life that temporarily renders him unable to direct his life as he usually would. Such a level of stress may be reached as the result of a single event, many stressful events occurring at the same time, or from stressful events occurring serially. Crisis-producing events seem to occur for no apparent planned reason. They occur without warning, and usually in a sudden manner.

Crises are self-limiting and will abate without intervention. However, because of the disorganizing and destructive effects on personal functioning that could occur as a result, immediate and skillful intervention is required. Intervener survival addresses the personal needs and concerns of the crisis intervener. Successful and effective intervention into the crises of others may well depend on the degree to which the intervener is prepared to handle his or her own stress, tensions, safety, nutrition, and personal life. Failure to attend to these areas often results in injuries, physical illness, emotional problems, and a high burnout rate among professionals.

HISTORY

Crisis intervention theory was developed by Gerald Caplan (1964) and Erich Lindemann (1944) in the early 1940s. Their purpose was to study persons in actual crisis situations. These included the parents of those who were killed during World War II and of those who were the victims of the Boston Coconut Grove fire. Their work emphasized that individuals under great personal stress could be assisted in regaining their ability to function as they usually did through the skillful intervention of a third party. Since that time, much emphasis has been placed by various authors, theorists, and mental health professionals on providing immediate help to those individuals who are experiencing great distress in their lives (Farberow, 1967; McGee, 1974; Stratton, 1976). Private and community clinics have been established to provide such care on a walk-in basis, with no fixed appointment required. Concern in such intervention centers is on that which can be done at the critical time to help the person in crisis to return to his former level of precrisis functioning (Jacobson, 1971). If such assistance is available, the likelihood that the crisis victim will need subsequent psychotherapy due to prolonged maladjustment is reduced (Langsley & Kaplan, 1968).

The phenomenon of crisis has been defined from various aspects. These relate disruptions in a person's life to an increase in experienced stress and tension that does not allow personal functioning to occur as usual

(Burns & Dixon, 1974). According to Caplan (1964), life changes that alter usual living patterns can result in states of crisis for those involved. The categories of situational crises and maturational crises have been found useful in understanding these critical times (Aguilera, Messick, & Farrell, 1970).

Crisis intervention and conflict management procedures for police officers have been of major concern for Bard and Zacker (1976). Because the police officer is often the first line of response during crises such as domestic disputes, training was developed to assist the responding officer in providing skillful and immediate aid before such situations could deteriorate into violence and self-destruction (Bard, 1975).

Greenstone and Leviton (1979, 1980) and Rosenbluh (1974) have provided the crisis intervener, regardless of professional or paraprofessional background, with practical how-to procedures in a wide range of crisis situations. National training conferences sponsored by the Southwestern Academy of Crisis Interveners in Dallas, Texas, and the American Academy of Crisis Interveners in Louisville, Kentucky, also provide this type of interdisciplinary training and approach to Crisis Management.

CURRENT STATUS

Crisis Management and intervener survival is advocated and taught at the National Training Conference for Crisis Intervention. This conference is sponsored by the Southwestern Academy of Crisis Interveners and the University of Dallas. Both are located in Dallas, Texas. Courses taught by the American Academy of Crisis Interveners in Louisville, Kentucky, also offer this approach or modifications of it. To date interveners from a wide variety of professional backgrounds and concerns, including helping agencies, police departments, volunteer crisis centers, private practice, probation departments, and schools, have been trained.

The Southwestern Academy of Crisis Interveners and the American Academy of Crisis Interveners jointly publish, semiannually, *Emotional First Aid: The Journal of Crisis Intervention,* the only journal currently in print that deals exclusively with Crisis Management. It is abstracted by the American Psychological Association and appears in *Psychological Abstracts.* The journal is available on a subscription basis or as part of yearly membership in the academies.

THEORY

Regardless of the crisis, management requires special skills and the adaptation of skills unique to such situations. The skills involved, while based on current psychotherapeutic thought, may in their application vary significantly from the ways that they are employed in routine, weekly counseling sessions. Time becomes the critical difference. In weekly counseling sessions over a long period of time, or even in short-term counseling, it may be possible to work with an individual extensively to achieve problem resolution. The crisis intervener, however, may have only minutes or perhaps seconds to accomplish his or her purpose. To the degree that the crisis is managed, the need for subsequent psychotherapy is reduced. If the intervener is able to prevent additional personality disorganization and deterioration from occurring and to help the victim of crisis effectively mobilize the personal resources possessed during noncrisis times, those usual life-coping skills can take over and effective functioning can be reestablished, at least to the level of precrisis behavior. While some additional psychotherapy and/or support may be needed after successful intervention, it is usually much less intensive and lengthy than if there was no intervention or if it was mishandled. While much is done in most reputable training programs to develop highly skilled psychotherapists, little attention is paid to the importance and the skills of Crisis Management. While related to basic psychotherapeutic intervention, and adaptable to most theoretical approaches, Crisis Intervention constitutes a skill area all of its own, one to which attention must be focused.

In attempting to study a crisis, Rosenbluh (1974) noted that it does not go on forever, and as a result is self-limiting. The individual in crisis will eventually find a solution to the problems experienced, that solution being effective to a greater or lesser degree. Initially there is a marked increase in the state of tension present relative to a particular problem. It is at this time that usual problem-solving methods are attempted. Since these methods have been ineffective and continue to be so, the stress that the victim is under will again increase and serve to exacerbate the crisis. The victim is often unable to make effective choices about his life or to evaluate the situation. Disorganized behavior often results as inner tensions compete for expression. Bodily complaints may develop, and the victim may react to the situation by violence, at one end of the behavior continuum, or by complete withdrawal, at the other end. Violence may be directed either inwardly or toward others.

The intervener in crisis situations has two major objectives. First, trauma must be reduced wherever and whenever possible and as quickly as possible. Additionally, the intervener can make use of the situation not only to manage the current difficulties, but also to assist the victims of crisis to master future difficulties by the use of more effective and more adaptive coping mechanisms (Parad, 1965).

Crisis Intervention is an immediate attempt to deal

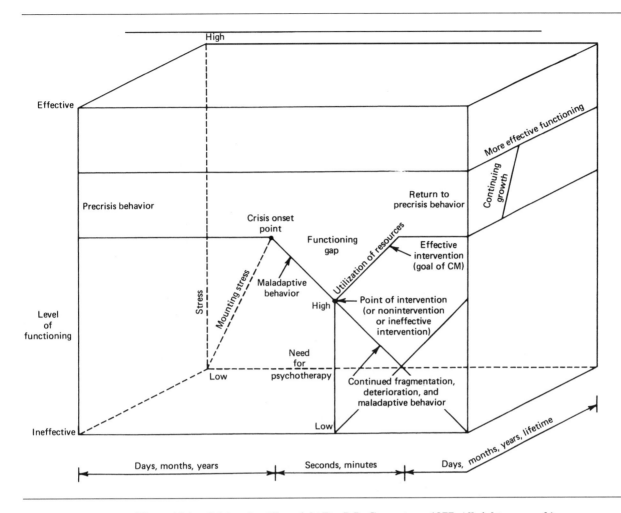

Figure 13.1   Crisis cube. (Copyright Dr. J. L. Greenstone. 1977. All rights reserved.)

with immediate problems. The major emphasis is to reestablish precrisis functioning and to assist the victim to achieve higher levels of functioning as appropriate and possible within the allowed time frame. The practice of elaborate history taking is deemphasized in Crisis Management. While some history is gathered, the primary emphasis is on the immediate past that surrounds the current crisis. Time, once again, dictates the extent of this exploration. In any event, some historical assessment must occur not only to establish the basis for the crisis, but also to make the most accurate determination regarding disposition and subsequent needs for therapy. Throughout, however, the emphasis of the intervener will be on the immediate situation and the management thereof.

In many other forms of psychotherapy and counseling, the role of the therapist may be nondirective or indirect at best, and there are few time restrictions. Yet in Crisis Management, the role of the intervener may be quite direct and active and the intervention may last only a few minutes. This rapid assistance in helping the victim to regain his precrisis efficiency may take the form of both emotional and physical support as needed and as judged to be beneficial. While effective and immediate Crisis Intervention and Management may reduce the need for additional psychotherapy, if further help is needed, the transition to most types of psychotherapy or other treatment is easily accomplished. The value in the use of intervention techniques as an adjunctive mode with most other psychotherapeutic systems can be readily seen. Crisis management procedures can be utilized prior to entrance of the victim into psychotherapy in order to better prepare the individual for the therapeutic relationship. These same procedures are valuable for the patient already involved in ongoing treatment who may experience subsequent crisis that may be detrimental if not immediately and effectively handled.

METHODOLOGY

The intervener in a crisis situation must ask himself several questions. These include: (1) What problem is the crisis victim experiencing now? (2) What is precipitating the crisis in his life at this particular time? (3) Of the several problems that may surface at this time, which need to be of immediate concern to me, and which can be dealt with later? (4) Which of the problems presented will be most physically or psychologically, damaging if not immediately dealt with? (5) Which problems can be most immediately and easily managed? (6) Are there problems that must be managed before other problems can be dealt with? (7) What resources are available both to me and to the victim of crisis that I can utilize as crisis management is attempted? (8) What variables or extraneous factors will hinder the intervention and what can be done to reduce their interference? and (9) What can be done to implement the most effective Crisis Management possible to defuse a highly volatile situation, and to do it in the shortest realistic amount of time?

The approach to a crisis situation is guided by the need for *immediacy*. The intervener must act *now*. The intervener's aim is to prevent further confusion and disorganization, to relieve the heightened state of anxiety as quickly as possible, and to see that the crisis victim does not hurt himself or others. To this end, intervention begins at the time that the crisis is encountered. The intervener must be ready to act, or in some situations make a decision not to act, at the moment he or she is faced with a person who is experiencing crisis. Little time is available for reflection or discussion of possible approaches. The full measure of the intervener's skill will come to bear at that moment, and the degree to which the intervener is prepared will be reflected in the efficiency of the intervention. Additionally, the intervener needs to know which situations he or she is not willing to enter or is prevented by lack of training from entering. Knowing one's limitations is as important to successful intervention as knowing one's skills.

The second major factor is *control*. Because the victim of a crisis is often not in control of his life at that moment, the intervener must assume control of the total situation to the fullest extent possible, and as circumstances dictate. This may be accomplished by nothing more than the physical presence of the intervener, which conveys a sense of security and structure, while at other times it may be necessary for the intervener to take control in a more insistent manner. The victim of a crisis is out-of-structure in his life, and he seeks the structure that he lacks. By taking control, the intervener temporarily provides the needed structure. Specific ways of gaining control of a crisis situation will vary depending on the skills and abilities of the particular intervener. Interveners can utilize their own creativity to develop those methods that are effective within the situations with which they are faced. However, regardless of the methods chosen, the attitude of the intervener is of paramount importance. Interveners must convey

through being as well as through behavior that control is centered in them. If this is not conveyed, control will not be gained regardless of the specific methods chosen. Persons in crisis will respond to structure and to those who represent it if they sense that it is sincere and not just a manipulative technique.

Assessment is the third major factor to consider. An on-the-spot evaluation must be performed. It must be quick while at the same time accurate. It must cover as many critical areas surrounding the crisis as possible to give the intervener as much useful information as possible in the shortest amount of time. The circumstances surrounding the particular crisis will dictate the nature of the assessment. Time, privacy, and other critical factors are some of those influencing circumstances. Simple and direct questions that avoid jargon and complicated verbiage will best serve the intervener and ultimately the victim. Identify, as soon as possible, the precipitating events in the crisis victim's life. Find out how the victim feels; if he or she is afraid; if there are thoughts of harming self or others. Note what actually happened and what the victim's perception is of what happened. Individual perception triggers crisis more often than do facts. Observe what the victim does and does not do; what is said and what is not said. Consider what would be expected under similar circumstances that is not occurring in this situation. Avoid judgment and attend to the nonverbal cues as a source of critical information that can be utilized quickly and efficiently. Such is usually done in regular counseling or therapy. However, under crisis conditions, this must also be done quite rapidly, and what is learned applied with equal speed.

Throughout, the personal attributes of the intervener will often affect the outcome of the intervention as much as any other single factor or combination of factors. A person in a state of crisis will usually respond to someone who seems to be approachable. The warmth, empathy, concern, supportiveness, calmness, steadiness, attentiveness, caring, and willingness to reach out to the victim emotionally, and even physically as needed, will demonstrate the intervener's approachability. Questions economically stated, and an ear willingly lent, will enhance the cause.

The next step for the intervener is that of *management*. The victim of crisis needs assistance in reestablishing effective methods of handling life in general and the particular problems that specifically led to this crisis episode. Maladaptive behavior must be replaced with more adaptive behavior. Because the goal here is management rather than problem resolution, the regaining of precrisis-level functioning efficiency is sufficient. Once this is attained, referral or longer term psychotherapy may be considered. Attempts at counseling or therapy prior to successful Crisis Management would meet with little success. This cannot be overemphasized in its importance to ongoing treatment. In Crisis Management, mobilization of personal resources and the resources of significant others in the life of the victim is the central function of intervention.

The intervener can be quite specific in terms of what must be done to accomplish the desired purpose. Reduction of anxiety and diffusing the intensity of the situation can be accomplished first. Sometimes removal of the victim from the crisis scene helps here. Let the victim know that you are there to assist, and to inform the person what can be and is being done to help. Remain confident and self-assured during contacts with the victim. While it is usually not helpful to hold out false hope or to lie to a victim, realistic optimism is generally well received. Allow the victim to talk and to tell what happened as desired. Interrupt sparingly, and then only to clarify. Usually, it is best to wait until the victim is finished ventilating to gain clarification. For the purpose of Crisis Intervention, the intervener will be most useful if the short-term nature of the intervention is remembered and emphasized. Concentrate on conveying to the victim how temporary the crisis is rather than dwelling on what may appear to be a chronic situation. If your intervention is successful, the victim will likely be more willing to trust your suggestion for getting help for the ongoing difficulties.

Throughout, maintain a sense of structure and certainty that the victim can hold on to. Give the victim information that he needs to again begin securing his personal life. Repeatedly let the person in crisis know that you believe in his personal ability to control his life, while at the same time, indicate your willingness to provide the necessary support over this short period of chaos. Additionally, seek out, as possible, those significant others who can assist you and the victim to reestablish the control that has been lost. Distinguish those significant others who will aid in your intervention efforts from those who will be unhelpful or even harmful. Consider also those community and individual resources on which you may call if you decide to refer the crisis victim for ongoing care. Certainly, if the victim is currently or has been in psychotherapy, contact the therapist. Such a contact may provide helpful information, while at the same time it will give the therapist useful details if therapy is continued. At this time, medications and the like can also be checked.

The last stage of intervention is that of *referral and follow-up.* Many skillful interventions have been lost at this point. What is done with or for the crisis victim, postcrisis, and how efficiently it is done may mark the difference between the person who lives from crisis to crisis, learning nothing, and the person who utilizes the crisis as a stepping-stone to a higher level of functioning efficiency and to the reduced likelihood of repeated crisis episodes. If you plan to continue personally with the victim in long-term psychotherapy, you can use the crisis experience to promote greater insight into the unresolved difficulties that result in this personal stress and chaos. If you intend to refer the victim for treatment, send him or her to someone with whom you have had personal contact or you know is able to work with those who have just experienced crisis. Do all that is necessary to arrange for the smooth transfer from yourself to the receiving therapist. Anticipate difficulties of the crisis victim and try to avoid anything that would keep him or her from getting the additional help needed. Subsequent to the referral, check with the victim and with the new therapist to be sure that successful transition has been accomplished. If there are problems, attempt to resolve them as quickly as possible in order to avoid losing any of the original momentum to get help.

APPLICATIONS

Crisis Management can be seen as a system that stands alone, or as an adjunct or a preparatory phase to psychotherapy. As a separate system, Crisis Intervention is directed toward those individuals who, because of the unusual stress experienced in their lives at a particular time, cannot direct their lives in the ways that they normally do. Included are those who experience sudden and unexpected disruptions in their usual life routine because of events such as rape, suicidal gestures, domestic disputes, spouse abuse, child abuse, and the like. Also included are those who experience crisis because of certain life changes that they may not be able to handle efficiently, such as marriage, divorce, separation, death or loss of a significant other, encounters with the legal system, promotions or demotions on the job, pregnancy, changes in school status, accidents with or without injury, and job loss. Intervention becomes an immediate aid during these times. The goals of such intervention may be limited. Support, guidance, and assistance is given only to the point that precrisis functioning is reestablished, and at that point the intervention is completed. Additional counseling or assistance may or may not be required. Often there is no such need. When there is the intervener then makes a referral to the appropriate resource or handles postcrisis therapy himself. While the goals of Crisis Management as a system are limited, they are directed to assist the crisis victim to regain the structure in his life that has been temporarily lost, and to be able again to exercise effective choice regarding available alternatives.

As an adjunct or preparatory phase to psychotherapy, Crisis Management may be used to redirect those critical instances that may be disruptive to the usual course of counseling or therapy. An individual who experiences crisis resulting ostensibly from a singular event, but in reality as the culmination of many unresolved events, clearly may evidence the need for subsequent treatment. Such deep-rooted problems may be seen during the intervention into the immediate situation. Because the victim of a crisis is out-of-structure with life, and because he may be particularly vulnerable during these times, much information regarding previously unresolved crises may be disclosed. In addition, the victim's vulnerability during these times may make him more receptive to suggestions for subsequent psychotherapy. The key to positive outcome seems to be the degree to which the intervener is successful in helping the victim to manage his crisis and the trust level that has been developed. Such success and trust may be related to the recognition on the part of the intervener that the crisis encountered requires a different approach than that usually used in therapy.

Prior to seeking psychotherapeutic treatment, many individuals undergo a crisis. However, by the time of their first appointment, they are usually no longer in a crisis state. Subsequent to beginning the therapeutic process, they may again experience a crisis due to life changes or as a result of awarenesses gained during the therapeutic process. The therapist's recognition of such occurrences, and efficient responses to them, may mean the difference between losing all that has been gained, or being able to continue effectively from that point once the crisis has been managed.

Certain individuals seem more prone to experience crisis in their lives than others. Recognition of such individuals as potential high risks can aid us in working with clients. Those who fall into this category can be noted and some preparation made so as not to be caught off guard should a crisis occur. Individuals who may be somewhat more prone to experience crisis in their lives than others are usually seen as feeling alienated from real and meaningful relationships. They may be the cause of such alienation, and even though social supports may be available, the crisis-prone person is either unable or unwilling to use them. Provocativeness, low self-worth, and difficulty learning from previously made mistakes are also characteristic of the crisis-prone. Their history may reflect ongoing emotional problems that have not been treated, difficulty on the job, marginal income, impulsiveness, marital problems, drug abuse, physical accidents and injuries, and frequent problems with the police or legal system. Lasting bonds are obviously absent for the individual prone to experience crisis, and such a person will sometimes be transient and without a permanent place to live.

Crisis intervention procedures are limited; they focus on the immediate rather than on the long-term problems the individual may experience. In Crisis Management there is no attempt to move beyond the current disruptive and disorganizing event or events experienced. All people who are upset are not necessarily experiencing crisis. The need for accurate recognition is critical to the system. Such limited focus and accurate recognition can be the cornerstone to any additional support services, or therapy that may be subsequently given.

Intervener Survival

Intervener survival addresses the needs and concerns of the intervener as he or she prepares for or actually performs intervention into a crisis situation. It is not sufficient to learn crisis management procedures without also attending to those specific sources of stress and tension that may impinge on the intervener and thereby affect his or her ability to perform the intervention efficiently and effectively. The intervener who experiences a personal crisis while attempting to assist others who are also in crisis is of no help to anyone, least of all himself. Sometimes it is assumed that the trained professional has mastered the areas of concern that may plague less trained nonprofessionals. This does not seem to be the case at all. Intervener and victim alike are subject to the same or similar stressors; both may fall prey to them.

If we are to be helpful, we must remain truly effective. In our roles as interveners in the crises of others, we may neglect our own needs, our own health and nutrition, our own safety, and our own responsibility for self-direction. We may become so involved in the lives of others that we fail to attend to ourselves. If this occurs, and we fail to place the same value on ourselves that we place on those we want to help, we may soon lose our effectiveness as interveners and cause harm to ourselves. If we neglect concerns for personal safety during interventions into crisis situations, or if we fail to recognize our own experience of stress, allowing it to go unchecked, our productivity and effectiveness will suffer. Conversely, if we are aware of these areas, have spent the necessary time and energy attending to them, and then have taken necessary steps to reduce the intensity of the problems in our own lives, we are better prepared to focus attention on the crises of others.

One aspect of this personal concern for self is the area of goal setting. All crisis interveners must ask themselves: What are my goals today? What am I doing to accomplish these goals? Have I set realistic goals for myself today? Given the "givens" of my situation, what are my chances for accomplishing these goals? When goals are prioritized within the framework of the present setting, chances of success are increased. Conversely, when goals are set based on what you would like a situation to be, or on what you wish conditions were, then the chances of accomplishing those goals are greatly diminished. Further, when unattainable goals are not recognized as such based on present circumstances, and responsibility for altering immediate goals is not taken, frustration, stress, and a sense of failure is likely to result both for the intervener and for the crisis victim he or she is trying to assist.

If frustrations are allowed to continue unchecked, stress levels rise as productivity falls. If, however, a decision is made to utilize the givens of the situation and thereby to set goals that are realistic to that situation, much energy is freed that can then be used in more effective ways. Sometimes this process is difficult, because we often set goals higher than we or others can achieve. Alteration of goals may then be seen as a symbol of failure. At that point, it may become easier to blame our feelings of frustration and tension on some outside source. This scapegoat may be the intervener's department, family, or even the crisis victim.

The bottom line is that regardless of how we attempt to disavow ownership for our feelings of frustration, anger, stress, and tension, they remain our personal responsibility. Further, the responsibility for lowering the effect of these stressors also remains ours. Seen in this way, the risk of taking charge in all areas of our lives for our own actions becomes an exciting challenge. The givens of the situation remain the same. What we can change is our assumptions.

CASE EXAMPLE

Mr. and Mrs. Jones arrived at the therapist's office with their 10-year-old daughter, Lisa. The appointment was suggested by the school counselor, who requested that Lisa be evaluated. The presenting problem is Lisa's disruptiveness in the classroom as demonstrated by her refusal to participate when called on, her constant moving about and chattering at inappropriate times, and her constant arguing with her classmates. This pattern began a year ago, and the school's attempts to effect changes in Lisa's behavior have failed. The teacher can no longer manage the situation.

Phase 1

As Dr. G. receives the family, he notices that Mr. Jones keeps fumbling with his watch and seems to be quite angry. Mrs. Jones seems harassed but apparently is in control. Lisa is sullen. As Dr. G. greets each family member, Mr. Jones clearly and angrily announces that the session is unnecessary, that the school is at fault for Lisa's problems, that he sees nothing wrong with what Lisa is doing in school, and that he feels imposed upon both by the school and by having to come to this session. The only reason that he has kept this appointment, he points out, is to pacify his wife's constant nagging. When Dr. G. suggests that the family sit down, Mr. Jones insists that he would prefer to stand since he would not be there very long. While Mrs. Jones sits, Lisa remains standing with her father and cuddles him. She glances at her mother with disdain.

Dr. G. recognizes that the stage is now set for impending crisis that could prevent any type of problem resolution if not managed properly. Mr. Jones is preoccupied with his own agenda, while Mrs. Jones seems caught in a struggle between her daughter and her husband. Lisa is also experiencing some difficulty in relating effectively to her parents. However, attention to Lisa's problems both at home and at school may well be affected by the way in which the crises of her parents are handled. This family is experiencing the effects of previously unresolved personal and marital problems, and cannot focus on current concerns until the tension is reduced and their crises managed.

At this point Dr. G. has several options. He could terminate the session, acquiesing to Mr. Jones's insistence that he does not want to be there anyway. He could suggest that termination will occur unless all sit down and discuss Lisa's problems. Or he could explain that because the school has made a referral, the focus of the session must be on school-related problems. While all three possibilities are related to the family and its problems in various ways, all three miss recognizing that this family is either already in crisis or about to experience crisis. This crisis situation, if recognized as such, can be managed, and at the same time provide inroads to the other, more extensive problems that require ongoing attention. Attempts to proceed therapeutically without first managing the existing crises may be met with little or no success.

Dr. G. attempts to intervene immediately upon recognizing the current situation, and he realizes that Mr. Jones needs immediate attention. He also notices that Lisa will probably take her cues from her father. While Mrs. Jones needs to be acknowledged, she can wait to be heard.

Dr. G. assures Mrs. Jones that he will attend to her shortly. He then returns and stands by with Mr. Jones and Lisa. Mr. Jones explodes his frustration and his anger. He pursues his same theme. Dr. G. knows that until these feelings are dealt with, there can be no constructive discussion, and he attends to Mr. Jones and notes several recurrent key phrases that reflect Mr. Jones's concerns. "I care about my little girl," "I want to do what is right for my child," "I am a good father" are some of the most obvious. Dr. G. works specifically with these concerns and reflects understanding of them and reassurance as to their validity. He builds on these concerns as a way of encouraging Mr. Jones to discuss his daughter's problems in school. The apparent threat to his parenting ability is used to encourage good parenting and problem solving on Lisa's behalf. Mr. Jones has been heard. His integrity as a parent is no longer being questioned. Now he may be more receptive to other concerns.

It is obvious that Dr. G. took immediate control by being willing to utilize the momentum of the situation as it was presented rather than trying to restructure it, as might have seemed appropriate at first glance. The session could have easily aborted without this immediate control and intervention.

Phase 2

Now that Mr. Jones is more agreeable to moving on, Dr. G. suggests that they all be seated. At this point he becomes attentive to Lisa. Having observed that Lisa and her father seem very close, and as a result of that closeness may appear to be conspiring against Mrs. Jones, seating is strategically structured with Lisa next to her mother.

Lisa begins to protest. She will either sit beside her father or she will not stay. She begins yelling, and as she does Mrs. Jones, who has been passive until now, accuses Mr. Jones of spoiling the child. She states that he always lets her have her way and is the source of Lisa's present problems at school. She continues that Mr. Jones cares more about what Lisa wants than he does about her. She becomes emotionally distraught and retorts that in the last year, he has spent all of his free time and energy with Lisa. Lisa then rushes to her father and begins laughing.

Dr. G. must act quickly to take control again. Where is the greatest need? Because a reasonable degree of trust has already been developed with Mr. Jones, perhaps it can be utilized. Mrs. Jones is becoming progressively more upset, crying and screaming. Lisa continues to laugh at her mother.

Dr. G. addresses Lisa first. Feeling that Mr. Jones will support his actions, Dr. G. calmly and firmly commands Lisa to return to her seat. Lisa looks at her father, and Mr. Jones tells her to do as told. Dr. G. tells Lisa that while he is very interested to hearing about her and her problems, this could best be done in a separate session. He suggests that she wait in the outer office while he talks with her parents, and then an appointment will be set for her. Mr. Jones gives support to this proposal and Lisa is taken out of the office by Dr. G.

Attention must now be given to Mrs. Jones. Expression of her feelings and of her concerns are allowed. Subsequent to this ventilation, Dr. G. asks for an agreement from both Mr. and Mrs. Jones that they will listen to the concerns and the problems of the other without interruption. Once this setting for dialogue has been established, Dr. G. asks one party and then the other to express fully the concerns that each has. Interruptions are prevented as per the agreement. Dr. G. serves as the clarifier of what is said, and helps each party to understand specifically what the other has said. When he feels it appropriate, Dr. G. begins removing himself from the dialogue, suggesting that Mr. and Mrs. Jones speak to each other without a mediator. Dr. G. continues to press for the need for clarity. Additionally, he directs their exploration of possible ways in which to handle the problems that exist between them currently in order to be able to work together to assist Lisa. Just as problems are sharpened to clarity, so are the possible ways of managing them that would thereby allow positive interaction between Mr. and Mrs. Jones on matters of joint concern.

It is apparent that even though the appointment was arranged primarily to examine Lisa's behavior in school, the total family is experiencing crisis. As an attentive, effective intervener, Dr. G. begins zeroing in on each person's particular crisis or impending crisis as soon as recognized. For Mr. Jones, the fact that he might be seen as a bad parent by the school, by the counselor, or by his wife precipitated a crisis for him. For Mrs. Jones, the fact that she felt she was constantly competing with her daughter for the attention of her husband, while being mocked by her daughter, created her crisis. For Lisa, the tensions within her family and the power struggles in which she found herself produced constant stress, which she handled alternately through withdrawal and aggressive behavior.

Phase 3

Dr. G. returns control of the situation to Mr. and Mrs. Jones as soon as they seem to be having some success in working with each other. He suggests that the family use the concerns about Lisa as a foundation for further exploration of the problems expressed during this session. An appropriate appointment is set for Lisa concerning her school problems, and parental cooperation is requested. While nothing has been done yet to resolve Lisa's problems, it is clear that because the crises that existed in this family have been managed, the likelihood that Lisa can be helped is greater than if such intervention had not been made. Additionally, while the crisis management procedures did not solve the ongoing problems between Mr. and Mrs. Jones, the possibility that the Joneses will continue with additional therapy is enhanced.

SUMMARY

Crisis Intervention involves entering into the life situation of the person who is experiencing crisis, as well as into the lives of significant others (individuals or groups), in order to diminish the effect of that problem or difficulty that has caused the perceived heightened state of tension or stress. In doing so the intervener will attempt to assist the victim in activating those sources of aid, both personal and social, that can help remove the sense of hopelessness and helplessness that accompanies crisis.

Crisis Intervention has different meanings to different people, depending on the service they offer and their par-

Table 13.1   Comparison of Psychoanalysis and Short-term Psychotherapy with Crisis Intervention

Areas	Psychoanalysis	Short Therapy	Crisis Management
Focus	Past and the unconscious	Past as related to current situation, unconscious	Present. Restore precrisis levels of functioning
Role of therapist	Exploratory; Nondirective, passive observer	Indirect, passive observer	Direct, active participant
Control	Shared	Shared	Intervener
Awareness	Unconscious	Mixed	Conscious
Goals	Restructuring the personality	Removal of specific symptoms	Management of immediate crisis situation
Range	Limited	Varied	Limited
Indications	Neurotic personality patterns	Acute emotional pain and disruptive circumstances	Sudden loss of ability to handle life situations in way usually handled
Average length of treatment	Indefinite	One to twenty sessions	Usually only a few sessions, may be no more than one

ticular professional frame of reference. Table 13.1 will clarify the specific area of concern addressed herein. As should be quite clear, a distinction is made between psychotherapy, regardless of form, and what is referred to as Crisis Management. It has been the writers' experience that regardless of academic training, most people can be trained to be effective crisis interveners. This includes those with limited or no prior formal professional training. The importance of every therapist's developing these skills and abilities, however, cannot be overemphasized. While most already possess the theoretical background and the capabilities for effective intervention, Crisis Management as an adjunct to the therapeutic function requires a rethinking and an adapting of already acquired skills. To do so may not only save, but also enhance, what might otherwise be a lost therapeutic attempt.

REFERENCES

Aguilera, D. C., Messick, J. M., & Farrell, M. A. (1970). *Crisis intervention: Theory and methodology.* St. Louis, MO: Mosby.

Bard, M. (1975). *The function of the police in crisis intervention and conflict management: A training guide* (U.S. Department of Justice, Law Enforcement Assistance Administration, National Institute of Law Enforcement and Criminal Justice). Washington, DC: U.S. Government Printing Office.

Bard, M., & Zacker, J. (1976). *The police and interpersonal conflict: Third-party intervention approaches.* Washington, DC: Police Foundation.

Burns, J. L., & Dixon, M. C. (1974). Telephone crisis intervention and crisis volunteers: Some considerations for training. *American Journal of Community Psychology, 2,* 120–125.

Caplan, G. (1964). *Symptoms of preventative psychiatry.* New York: Basic Books.

Farberow, N. W. (1967). Crisis, disaster and suicide: Theory and therapy. In E. S. Schneiderman (Ed.), *Essays in self-destruction.* New York: Science House.

Greenstone, J. L., & Leviton, S. (1979). *The crisis intervener's handbook* (Vol. 1). Dallas, TX: Crisis Management Workshops.

Greenstone, J. L., & Leviton, S. (1980). *The crisis intervener's handbook* (Vol. 2). Dallas, TX: Rothschild Publishing House.

Jacobson, E. (1971). *Depression: Comparative studies of normal, neurotic and psychotic conditions.* New York: International Universities Press.

Langsley, D. G., & Kaplen, D. M. (1968). *The treatment of families in crisis.* New York: Grune & Stratton.

Lindemann, E. (1944). Symptomatology and management of acute grief. *American Journal of Psychiatry, 101,* 141–148.

McGee, R. (1974). *Crisis intervention in the community.* Baltimore: University Park Press.

Parad, H. J. (Ed.). (1965). *Crisis intervention: Selected readings.* New York: Family Service Association of America.

Rosenbluh, E. S. (1974). *Techniques of crisis intervention.* Louisville, KY: Behavioral Science Services.

Stratton, J. (1976). Law enforcement participation in crisis counseling for rape victims. *The Police Chief, 43,* 46–49.

Chapter 14

DANCE/MOVEMENT THERAPY

DIANE DUGGAN

My general attitude toward psychotherapy is that it is an artificial, undesirable, and awkward way of getting "straightened out" and that in a perfect world people would be able to take care of their own problems or, if they needed assistance, they would get it from friends and family. In short, I see psychotherapy as practiced today as a necessary evil, a purchase of friendship.

How much better would it be to solve one's psychological problems by thinking on one's own, or by discussions with others, or by physical activities, or by social interactions rather than going to a stranger for help. Yet, for many people, professional assistance is the best solution to their problems.

In this chapter we can see how a natural form of therapy, dance, can be adapted in a formal manner. Undoubtedly, the reasons for the therapeutic value of dance are complicated. To some extent I imagine that therapy occurs from the physiological effects alone; but probably the more important factor is the interaction with the dance partners, relationships with the therapist, and new disclosures about one's body and one's self. Consequently, the psychotherapeutic values of dance come from several modalities, and while dance, like music, poetry, and other aesthetic procedures, may help because of the pleasure of participation, it has additional, important physiological benefits.

Dance/Movement Therapy is psychotherapeutic use of movement as a process to further the cognitive, social, and physical integration of the individual (American Dance Therapy Association, 1999). It is a holistic approach that, in recognition of complex body/mind interaction, deals with disturbances of emotional, cognitive, and physical origin through intervention on a body movement level. Movement is the therapeutic modality that provides a diagnostic tool for assessment and the material for exploration. It also serves as a mode of relationship between client and therapist and is the medium for change.

The dance/movement therapist focuses on expressive, adaptive, and communicative behaviors as manifested by the client's muscle tension, breathing, posture, movement dynamics, and interactions. Through movement experiences the client becomes aware of these behaviors and explores their significance. The movement process aids the client in developing alternate ways of coping with inner impulses and environmental demands, and integrates affective, cognitive, and somatic aspects of being.

The profession is known as Dance/Movement Therapy in recognition of the importance of both dance and body movement in the therapeutic process, as well as the

profession's roots in the creative arts. The combined title encompasses a range of orientations and techniques. Some dance/movement therapists do not use music or dance per se, but focus on inner sensing by the client. Other dance/movement therapists utilize elements of dance such as the integrative aspects of rhythm in their work.

HISTORY

Dance/Movement Therapy has roots in both dance and psychology. In dance its roots extend back to ancient times, when dance was used in religious ritual as a means of expressing profound emotion in times of hardship, transition, and celebration. In many cultures dance served a transcendent function, a means of achieving ecstatic communion with the spirit world in an effort to understand and cope with the forces of nature. It figured prominently in healing ceremonies in which shamans danced to exorcise evil spirits.

Dance served a preventive, regulative function as well. Traditional dances affirmed community identity and values through reinforcing cultural movement styles and patterns of interaction. Within the structure of the dance, individuals were afforded a means of releasing tension in a socially accepted manner and of coming to terms with their experience in the larger context of community values.

From the Dark Ages until the twentieth century, dance in Western culture became increasingly formalized and performance oriented, and its expressive, transcendent, and participatory aspects were often ignored. This began to change when Isadora Duncan and the dancer/choreographers who followed her moved away from formalized conventions of ballet toward a modern dance whose style drew on inner feelings for choreographic inspiration. Proponents of modern dance, such as Mary Wigman, influenced the development of many dance/movement therapists.

Rudolf Laban (1960) had a significant impact on the development of Dance/Movement Therapy through his Effort/Shape system of movement analysis and observation. Effort/Shape provided a systematized and consistent tool for dealing with movement behavior. It describes not what is done in movement but *how* it is done, thereby emphasizing individual variation in performing the same movement activity. Irmgard Bartenieff brought this system to the United States and trained many dance/movement therapists in movement observation and correctives.

Theoreticians, clinicians, and researchers in psychology also contributed to the field of Dance/Movement Therapy. Much of their work was published concurrently with the development of the field. Wilhelm Reich (1949) was particularly influential. In developing the analysis of resistance into character analysis he proposed a functional identity between psyche and soma, relating posture, breathing, and movement to characteristic coping style. He saw psychological defenses manifested physically in the character armor, chronic patterns of muscular tension that attempted to bind energy flow and deaden areas of conflict.

Lowen (1958) furthered Reich's theories in attempting to correlate topological patterns of tension with diagnostic categories. He also developed techniques of intervention that combined verbal analysis with movement activities designed to evoke emotional response and discharge tension.

Schilder (1950) wrote on the body image and the reciprocal interrelationship between psyche and soma. His work gave support to the conception of intervention on a body level in the treatment of emotional problems. Condon's (1968) findings of interactional synchrony and its importance in interpersonal communication have profound implications for the use of rhythmic dance as a therapeutic modality for individuals with severe interpersonal disturbances. Davis (1970) focused on intrapsychic aspects of body movement in her study of the movement patterns of hospitalized psychotic individuals. With Dulicai and Climenko she also studied nonverbal interactions in the therapeutic process (1977).

Marian Chace is generally acknowledged as the originator of Dance/Movement Therapy in the United States. A former Denishawn dancer teaching in the Washington, D.C., area, Chace began to gear her classes toward personal expression through movement rather than technique. Psychiatrists in the area heard of her skills and, after referring private clients to her, invited her in 1942 to use dance as a form of therapy with patients at St. Elizabeth's Hospital. Chace's work proved so successful in reaching and motivating nonverbal patients that Dance Therapy, as it was then called, was integrated into the regular treatment program at the hospital. After her retirement from St. Elizabeth's, Chace worked at Chestnut Lodge with Frieda Fromm-Reichmann and Harry Stack Sullivan.

Another seminal figure in Dance/Movement Therapy was Mary Whitehouse. In the 1950s she combined her extensive dance training with Jungian analysis to develop an approach to dance as a means of self-discovery and growth for higher functioning individuals. Whitehouse was particularly influential in the development of the profession on the West Coast. Liljan Espenak and Blanche Evan also developed techniques for dance as therapy with the "normal neurotic," while Trudi Schoop used dance in the treatment of hospitalized psychotic individuals.

These pioneer clinicians developed into teachers as students sought them out for training and apprenticeships. A growing need for communication and professional development resulted in the formation of the American Dance Therapy Association in 1966. The infant organization had 73 charter members, and Marian Chace was elected the first president.

CURRENT STATUS

The American Dance Therapy Association (ADTA) is the recognized professional organization for dance/movement therapists, and the great majority of practitioners are members. In 1999 the ADTA had a membership of slightly over 1,203 in the United States and 29 foreign countries. The association promulgates standards for clinical practice and education. A two-level registry procedure was developed that includes entry and advanced levels of professional practice. Therapists with the title Dance Therapist Registered (DTR) have a master's degree and are fully qualified to work in a professional treatment system. Therapists with the title Academy of Dance Therapists Registered (ADTR) have met additional requirements, including supervised professional practice, and are fully qualified to teach, provide supervision, and engage in private practice.

In addition to these formal training programs, courses and workshops are given throughout the country by dance therapists. These are listed in the ADTA's *Newsletter,* published bimonthly. The ADTA also publishes a free brochure on educational opportunities, listing programs and other ongoing training.

The ADTA holds an annual conference in the fall and encourages regional workshops and conferences throughout the year. The association also publishes literature on the field, including conference proceedings, monographs, the collected papers of Marian Chace, and the *American Journal of Dance Therapy.*

The growing professionalism in the field of Dance Therapy has resulted in its increasing recognition by governmental agencies and the mental health community. Dance/Movement Therapy is included in the 1975 Education for All Handicapped Children Act (PL94.142) as a related service. This has resulted in a growing number of dance therapists working in special educational settings. At this time the majority of dance therapists work in mental health settings such as psychiatric hospitals and community mental health centers.

THEORY

Movement is a fundamental fact of life; all observable human behavior consists of body movement. Movement has intrapsychic, adaptive, and interpersonal significance. A primitive and relatively uncensored expression of inner states, movement is a means of coping with the environment and a communicative link to others. Fundamental, pervasive, and multifaceted, movement lends itself to use within a variety of conceptual frameworks. Bernstein (1979) compiled eight different theoretical approaches written by leading dance therapists. Among these were Jungian, psychoanalytic, gestalt, and transpersonal orientations.

Fundamental to the work of all dance therapists, whatever their theoretical orientation, is a holistic philosophy that recognizes the complex interaction and interdependence of mind and body. Psychological states are manifested somatically in muscle tension, breathing, posture, and movement dynamics. The mind/body relationship is reciprocal, so not only does the mind influence the body, but experience on a body level has an impact on the psyche. The body reflects and affects an individual's feelings of the moment, history, characteristic attitude toward life, and even cultural identity. There is no simple one-to-one body/mind correlation; the relationships are complex and influenced by many variables.

Dance therapists are likely to view development according to their theoretical orientation, but all would agree on the importance of movement in the developmental process. In the earliest stages of development movement is one of the infant's most significant means of acquiring information about the self and the environment. Both the infant's own reflexive and random, undifferentiated movements and the handling the child receives provide sensory input. At this stage all learning is body learning.

Movement stimulates the kinesthetic sense, which, along with touch, is crucial in the development of the body image, the individual's mental representation of his or her body. The influence of the body image is considerable. Its early renditions are thought to provide a basis for the development of the ego (Fisher & Cleveland, 1968). The body image influences perception of the environment by acting as a basic frame of reference for spatial judgments, and it influences acquisition of motor skills through affecting the individual's ability to differentiate, control, and coordinate body parts.

Since human beings are capable of reflexive movement response to tactile stimulation as early as the seventh week after conception, it is not surprising that individual differences in movement have been identified in infants. Kestenberg (1965 a and b) describes these differences in terms of rhythms of tension flow and looks at them longitudinally, in relation to psychosexual stages, and in the mother-child interaction.

Movement has a profound role in emotional development. The infant's first relationship is based primarily on touch and movement. This relationship forms the prototype for subsequent relationships and affects the individual's self-concept and attitude toward life. In this relationship the infant learns to sense and relate to another through patterns of touch, movement, and bodily rhythms. The infant internalizes aspects of these patterns from the mother and learns to respond, accommodate, and assert, all on a movement level. Deprivation of movement and tactile stimulation at this stage has devastating effects on the individual's ability to relate and to perceive the self positively.

During this preverbal period, all experience is linked to body sensation and movement. Dance/movement therapists believe that the body is a repository of memories of this period and seek to tap them directly through the body. S. Chaiklin (1975) points out that while all existing psychiatric theories acknowledge preverbal levels of development, the techniques for intervention on this level are very limited. Dance/Movement Therapy has the advantage of connecting directly with this level through movement and making preverbal material available to the individual without first filtering it through language. In dealing with severely impaired individuals, language may be totally ineffective. Dance/Movement Therapy provides a means of establishing a relationship with these individuals on their level, so that work toward higher levels of functioning can begin.

In normal development, patterns of movement, interacting with the environment, are internalized over time, and they integrate with affective and cognitive processes. This integration results in a moving, feeling, thinking being capable of experiencing the full range of human emotions. The individual is aware of inner feelings, able to cope creatively with the demands of the environment, and able to engage in satisfying relationships with other people.

There is no one particular healthy style of movement. It is recognized that each individual has movement preferences that reflect his or her unique personality and also that different cultures value and encourage specific styles of movement. Emphasis in Dance/Movement Therapy is placed on awareness of and comfort with one's movement style and on a range of adaptive movement with which to meet the demands of the environment. It is not adaptive, for example, to move loosely, with free flow all the time. At times bound flow is required, as when carrying something extremely fragile.

Many dance/movement therapists see in emotional disturbance a pathological split between mind and body that cuts the individual off from his or her body and inner feelings. This split is accomplished through the body, with muscle tension and breathing patterns used to defend against unacceptable internal impulses or environmental threats. Patterns of chronic tension restrict blood flow and sensation in body parts that are related to the source of conflict. This limits body functioning and the amount of energy available to the individual as well. Traditionally psychologists have approached emotional disturbance through verbal intervention. Dance/movement therapists work through body movement to effect awareness and change on a body level and consequently on feeling and cognitive levels as well.

A major focus in Dance/Movement Therapy is deepening the individual's ability to experience the self. One aspect of this experiencing occurs on a body level. The dance/movement therapist helps the individual to get in touch with blocked areas and dysfunctional breathing patterns. These may be explored in movement to clarify their significance and the way in which they work for and against the individual. The distortions often speak eloquently of the individual's maladaptation in dealing with inner impulses and environmental demands. The feelings that these distortions attempt to block are also examined, both in movement and verbally, and related to other aspects of the individual's life.

Through inner sensing, the individual also experiences inner dynamics and states. Ideally, the individual does not direct his or her movement. The movement seems to simply unfold by itself. This unplanned movement may be limited, but if it is inevitable, authentic movement (Whitehouse, 1979), it reveals to the individual inner dynamics as they emerge in direct experiencing.

Alperson (1977) points out that an advantage of the body movement approach to self-awareness is that it does not demand definition prior to expression and therefore potentially limit the experience, as verbalization might. The individual can explore him- or herself directly in a state of flux. From this dynamic state emerge new ways of behaving and perceiving the self and others. The insights resulting from the movement experience are processed verbally to further clarify their personal meanings. Moving before talking prevents the client from being limited at the outset by accustomed ways of thinking about one's self and one's relationships.

The moving person feels him- or herself in the moment as a result of immediate multisensory feedback produced by the movement itself. Such kinesthetic, tactile, vestibular, visual, and auditory stimulation helps to strengthen the body image and develop a clearer, more stable sense of self. Movement also promotes physical well-being. Relaxation and corrective techniques reduce muscle tension and bring awareness to deadened areas, diminishing feelings of physical discomfort and increasing vitality. The development of control of the body increases feelings of worth and competence. All of these increase positive feelings about the self, giving the individual a stable base from which to undertake the difficult tasks of self-exploration and change.

Dance is an intrinsically pleasurable activity for most people, especially when there is no pressure to perform or compete. Rhythmic aspects of dance are particularly important. Snyder (1972) cites research findings that reveal that the body tends to synchronize internal rhythms, such as heartbeat and respiration, with motor activity and with outside rhythms. Rhythmic activities then can produce internal harmony and self-synchrony through synchronizing body rhythms. Rhythm facilitates interaction by creating a feeling of unity among people. The propensity for self-synchronization enables group members to relate to each other in an indirect but intimate and compelling manner as they move together to a common beat. This moving together parallels the interactional synchrony found in normal conversation, and Condon (1968) equates it with communication. For severely disturbed individuals it can provide an experience of belonging and connection with others.

Movement is not only a means of enhancing self-awareness and communication; it is also a medium for organizing and managing internal impulses. Severely disturbed persons may be all too painfully aware of internal impulses, to the point of being overwhelmed by them. Chace (H. Chaiklin, 1975) felt that dance was a powerful means of structuring and reintegration for the individual because it is a way of organizing expressive movement. The actual forming of expressive movement in Dance/Movement Therapy involves exercising a degree of mastery over impulses and can enable the severely disturbed individual to make some order of the chaos of his or her feelings.

Movement experiences in the Dance/Movement Therapy session can further aid the individual in managing impulses through the bodily expression of emotion in a safe and supportive environment, which can dispel some of the pain and panic associated with the feelings. This makes emotionally laden situations more manageable and can be a real step toward clarifying feelings, issues, and choices.

Dance/Movement Therapy supports change through enhancing the capacity for adaptive response and supporting development of more appropriate coping behaviors. The dance/movement therapist, starting with the individual's movement style and utilizing movement affinities and other techniques, seeks to enlarge his or her movement repertoire, thus affording a greater range of adaptive response to the environment. Opportunities for trying out alternate means of coping and conflict resolution are provided in the sessions. New adaptive behaviors are identified and supported until they are integrated and available to the individual in everyday life.

METHODOLOGY

Methodology in Dance/Movement Therapy varies according to the theoretical orientation of the therapist, the setting, and the type of client. There is considerable variation in the therapist's role as active participant or observer and the amount and type of structure provided. Although many decisions are made on the basis of training and personal style, the most important variable in determining methodology is the type of client. The needs of psychotic individuals are far different from those of higher functioning persons. Dance/Movement Therapy is flexible enough to adapt to both, emphasizing in some instances formalized structures and in others creative improvisation and inner sensing.

A feature common to the work of all dance/movement therapists is the process orientation. Dance/Movement Therapy is not a set of techniques to be used according to the client's diagnostic category, and there is no preset prescription for a Dance/Movement Therapy session. The dance/movement therapist responds to the client's movement behavior in the moment, seeing it as a continuous process of unfolding of the self.

The dance/movement therapist relates movement behavior on the level of intrapsychic and/or interpersonal functioning to the client's history and general therapeutic goals. The therapist may facilitate nondirective exploration of inner sensations or provide structures that support the individual and develop perception of the environment and adaptive response. He or she takes cues on how to proceed from the ongoing nonverbal and verbal feedback of the client. Sometimes methodology will change during the course of therapy as the client's needs change.

Movement, a concrete phenomenon, is transitory and exists only in the moment. To identify discrete and relevant dimensions from the continuous stream of movement behavior, the dance/movement therapist needs a systematized approach to movement observation. For the majority of dance/movement therapists, Laban's (1960) system of Effort/Shape fulfills this need.

In Effort/Shape, movement is viewed as efforts, dynamic qualities that relate to exertion of energy, and shape, which relates to body form in space (Dell, 1970). Effort qualities are seen on continuums between extremes of dynamic qualities in tension flow (free to bound), weight (light to strong), time (sustained to sudden), and space (indirect to direct). Shape is composed of shape flow (relation to the body itself), directional movement, and shaping (creating or adapting to forms in space).

The use of Effort/Shape gives the dance/movement therapist a language based on movement behavior rather than on psychological constructs. It facilitates observation, analysis, and comparison between individuals and over time of the qualities that give movement its expressive coloration.

Not all dance/movement therapists move with the client. Some take the role of observer, interacting with the client through words rather than active movement. Their decision not to participate in the movement reflects a belief that they may unduly influence the client and distract him or her from awareness of inner impulses. However, many dance/movement therapists function as participant observers, and gear their level of movement involvement to the situation at hand. They may participate in movement while working on interactional issues or when the client needs that support, then function as observer only when the client works on inner sensing.

Other dance/movement therapists, especially those working with severely disturbed persons, nearly always move with their clients. Their focus is often on facilitating connection with the environment rather than inner sensing. They use their body movement to reflect and respond to the client's movements and to engage the client in a nonverbal relationship.

For those dance/movement therapists who move with their clients, the Chacian technique of mirroring is an important therapeutic tool. Mirroring entails picking up and reflecting back to the client essential, characteristic elements of movement behavior. Mirroring serves several functions. First, it establishes a connection between the therapist and the client. The dance/movement therapist literally meets the individual on his or her level by sharing in the actual movement. The client may perceive the therapist as relating to him or her or as an actual part of him- or herself. Mirroring also develops an empathic bond between therapist and client. The dance/movement therapist gains some insight into the individual's feelings because the movement affects the therapist on a feeling level and calls forth associations that the client may or may not share. Finally, the therapist is able to facilitate the development of the specific movement to its fullest expression by picking it up. This development is aimed at increasing the individual's awareness of his or her movement behavior and establishing a connection between the movement and internal states. It also provides a release of energy and, at times, resolution of conflict on a movement level.

The development of movement themes is a major methodological process in the dance/movement therapy session. Here the client experiences him- or herself directly, with meaning and associations unfolding through the movement process. The first step in this process is identifying significant themes. With higher functioning clients this can be done by facilitating inner sensing, having the client listen to his or her own body, not moving until the impulse to do so becomes clear. If the impulse is to remain still, this too has meaning and is worked with. Themes can also emerge from suggestions for movement exploration made by the therapist. Exploration of movement polarities, body parts, or entities such as the kinesphere can reveal personal associations for the individual. Such explorations can have significance for the client in clarifying long-standing conflicts and characteristic modes of being in the world.

If at all possible, the development of the movement themes is accomplished by the client, with suggestions and feedback as necessary from the therapist. The purpose is to explore the issue and its meanings for the individual. The direct experience of movement, as opposed to simply talking about it, gives the issue immediacy and brings up associations that may have been forgotten. There is also an opportunity to explore different aspects of the issue and find a resolution on a movement level.

With clients who need more structure and connection to external reality, the therapist picks up recurrent themes as they are manifested in movement. Here the therapist is likely to guide the development through his or her own movement, calling on improvisational skills, a knowledge of the client, and an ability to observe and analyze the movement response. Although the therapist guides this process, the response of the client determines its direction. As they move, the therapist encourages the client to associate thoughts and feelings with the movements to aid in integrating these facets of the experience and to come to terms with the experience.

The amount of structure in sessions depends largely on the client's ability to structure him- or herself. Music provides structure, as do regular group rituals, such as greetings and warm-up exercises. Spatial formations are another way of providing structure. The circle is a favored formation because it allows a continuous unbroken contact among participants, provides unobstructed vision, and gives everyone a potentially equal standing. Sometimes spatial formations may be used to elicit responses or explore certain issues, as when the therapist structures dyads or small groups to work on interactional themes. The individual's awareness of his or her response to the situation is highlighted, and he or she receives immediate feedback on the impact on others of his or her characteristic style of relating.

Props are another means of structure available to the dance/movement therapist. A prop such as a stretch rope or piece of fabric can be used to keep a group of severely disturbed individuals together. A ball or other object might be used in greeting rituals or improvisations to direct focus and connect individuals. Props can be especially useful in work with autistic children, who may be able to relate to an object but not to another person. Here the prop serves both as a bridge to facilitate contact and as a defense for the child against contact that is too direct.

The use of music by dance therapists varies greatly. Some use no music at all, emphasizing internal rhythms and self-awareness. Other dance therapists do use music, but with varying aims. Some look at transference relationships to the music, whether the client fights the music, is dominated by it, or needs it to organize his or her response. Other dance therapists use music specifically to evoke emotional and movement responses and, with severely disturbed clients, to organize movement behavior.

In group work music has a powerfully cohesive effect, especially if it has a clear, definite rhythm. Group rhythmic movement is a means of engaging the total being. The beat promotes a deeply satisfying synchrony, both in terms of the organization of the individual's own internal rhythms and his or her movement in relation to others. This can provide a much-needed experience of contact and unity for persons with severe disturbances in interpersonal relations.

Verbalization plays a role in Dance/Movement Therapy in the form of providing suggestions, feedback, support, sharing, and, in some cases, interpretations. Verbal processing of the movement experience is important in aiding the individual to make sense of what has gone on in the session. The therapist uses words carefully, aware that excessive verbalization can dilute the movement experience, while not enough verbalizing may isolate the experience and prevent its application to other aspects of the client's life. Talking in Dance/Movement Therapy sessions engages the cognitive processes and helps to integrate thought, feeling, and action.

Many dance therapists have had training in systems

such as progressive relaxation, massage, yoga, and Feldenkrais technique. These techniques are used adjunctively, to supplement the dance therapy process as needed. They do not in themselves constitute dance/movement therapy methodology.

APPLICATIONS

Dance/Movement Therapy lends itself to use with a wide range of client populations because it is based on the fundamental, universal phenomenon of movement and because its methodology is flexible and responsive to the needs of the client. It has been used successfully with clients as diverse as profoundly retarded, multiply handicapped children with minimal voluntary movement and articulate neurotic individuals whose verbal defensiveness had stymied their progress in more traditional forms of psychotherapy.

While there are no apparent limitations to its applicability in terms of client population, Dance/Movement Therapy is best used in conjunction with a verbal modality when working with verbal clients. Some dance/movement therapists have had advanced training in psychotherapy. They act as primary therapists, combining verbal and movement techniques in their work. When practitioners have not had advanced training in psychotherapy, Dance/Movement Therapy is best used as an adjunctive modality. The dance therapist and verbal therapist should work closely together in this case to maximize their effectiveness.

There seem to be no contraindications for the use of Dance/Movement Therapy. As S. Chaiklin points out, the methodology changes to serve the purpose. The dance therapist may be nondirective in working with clients with strong, intact egos, but can structure sessions with formal, nonemotional patterns for clients with superficial controls who may be frightened by the intensity of feeling. Dance/Movement Therapy can be used to stimulate depressed clients or to relax agitated, tense ones. Goals and techniques vary according to its uses.

Dance/Movement Therapy has great value in the treatment of autistic children. Much of the work with them occurs on a one-to-one basis. The dance therapist relates to the child on a movement level, mirroring characteristic movements to establish a relationship based on the child's own repertoire. This approach shows an implicit acceptance of the child as he or she is and permits the child the security and gratification of familiar movements in the initial stages of contact. The dance therapist facilitates the child's meaningful exploration of the self and the environment, attempting to establish a coherent body image and enlarge the movement repertoire to develop adaptive coping skills.

Children with learning disabilities benefit from Dance/Movement Therapy on several levels. The tactile and kinesthetic stimulation derived through movement activities aid in strengthening the body image and integrating sensory input from other modalities. Movement activities are pleasurable and engage the total child, helping him or her to focus and sustain attention and to control impulsive behavior. The creative, process approach in Dance/Movement Therapy emphasizes each child's uniqueness as an asset rather than a liability, and helps to heal self-concepts that have been damaged by repeated failure. Children are helped to work through emotional issues in an atmosphere of support and trust.

Chace's original application of Dance/Movement Therapy was with hospitalized psychotic adults, and it is in this context that the treatment has gained perhaps the greatest recognition to date, Dance/movement therapists working with severely disturbed individuals seek to draw them out of self-absorption and fantasy into a greater connectedness with other people and the environment. They typically use music, the circle formation, and other organizing structures to bolster inadequate coping abilities and support meaningful contact. Movement activities directly enhance body awareness and integration as a prerequisite to clearer perception of the environment. Movement structures organize inner impulses and help to mobilize the emotional and physical resources of the clients.

In work with higher functioning clients the Dance/Movement Therapy process is useful in enhancing sensitivity to inner states and personal movement styles. The creative act in movement improvisation provides a means of tapping unconscious feelings and personal imagery, making them available for further exploration. Movement also serves as a medium for developing themes to clarify their meanings and evaluate their impact on adaptive and interpersonal functioning.

Dance/Movement Therapy is also being used with good results individually or in groups to treat people with conditions such as chronic pain, traumatic brain injury, developmental disabilities, and sensory impairments, including blindness and deafness. Dance therapy can be used with people of all ages, from infancy to old age. Those without disabilities may also participate in Dance/Movement Therapy to enhance self-knowledge and personal growth.

CASE STUDY

Maria, a slender 25-year-old woman, referred herself to a private Dance/Movement Therapy group for higher functioning adults. She chose Dance/Movement Therapy because she felt little connection with and control over her body. Maria wore thick glasses, and the corners of her mouth were downturned in what appeared to be a perpetual frown. Although verbal sharing was an important part of the group, Maria was reluctant to reveal herself in this way at first. Much of the information on her came from the initial interview and her movement. After a movement experience, however, Maria was able to share brief but meaningful reactions to her experience.

In movement it became clear that Maria disliked her body. In an exploration of the kinesphere, the area of personal space around the body, she moved almost exclusively in far-reach space, extending her limbs but not drawing them back in recovery. She explored the space close to her body only at the suggestion of the therapist, and then only briefly. She reported afterward that she had a great deal of trouble moving close to her body and did not want to touch herself.

Nor did she want anyone else to touch her. In neck and back massage activities, which other group members requested, Maria would tirelessly massage her partner but, after enduring a massage in an early session, steadfastly declined to let herself be massaged. She reported that touch was unpleasant for her.

Maria's movements in structured improvisations tended to be large and abrupt, with a sharp, aggressive quality. At one point when the group members were slowly and gently touching hands, she became uncomfortable and initiated a light but sharp slapping. In an attempt to engage her aggressiveness through pushing, it became clear that Maria was not connected with her center of weight. She held her pelvis stiffly behind her and gave way almost immediately, unable to mobilize her strength.

In free improvisation the fragility of Maria's control became obvious. She careened wildly through space, making sudden and reckless changes of level with no attempt to protect herself. Her interactions with others were characterized by abrupt beginnings and endings. No matter who had initiated the contact, it was she who controlled and ended the interaction. She showed no accommodation to the shapes or movement dynamics of her partners. After moving in this way she would become tense and withdrawn. She soon admitted that she felt out of control and frightened.

It was clear that Maria had very little sense of her body, and this contributed to her inability to engage her strength and control her movements. She began to concentrate on control in the structured corrective exercise portion of the session. While others in the group focused on awareness, she worked on developing slow, sustained movements, without holding her breath, and gradually began feeling a sense of control.

Free-movement improvisations were resting on the floor and sensing the center of weight. After a while Maria began to move in a primitive amoeba-like fashion, growing and shrinking from her newfound center. She returned again and again to this, even when the structure was loosened somewhat to give others in the group more options. At one point she reported that she did not need her eyes because she could explore the space around her with her body. In verbal sharing she began to talk about her negative feelings about her body and her food and cigarette binges. She also spoke of her inability to deal with and even bring up some of these issues in verbal therapy. It had taken her six months to reach this point.

In the next four months Maria developed rapidly. Although she usually began improvisations on the floor to center herself, she came up and gradually began to interact with others. At first she was directly aggressive, beginning to feel and mobilize her strength. This gave way to testing out support from others and then to working out feelings of frustration and rage against her parents. By the summer break she was beginning to move in a dyad with sensitivity and accommodation to her partner.

After the two-month break Maria continued to work in self-initiated dyads, sharing leadership and achieving moments of heightened interactional synchrony, which she reported as being very pleasurable. She reported to the group that she was making progress in her verbal therapy and had controlled her eating, although she had somewhat of a relapse over the Christmas holidays. Maria continued working on mobilizing her strength in movement and began to explore her emerging feelings of sensuality and sexuality.

Maria terminated therapy after a total of 18 months. She was moving out of her parents' house and out of the city. In terms of her movement, she was very much in touch with her body and literally standing on her own two feet. Her relations to others were more genuine and characterized by a real recognition of and accommodation to the other as well as a developing ability to hold her own. Maria's progress in therapy had paralleled the normal sequence of development and provided material for the issues she was dealing with in her verbal therapy: developing a positive sense of self, dealing with aggression, interacting genuinely with others, independence, and sexuality. Dance/Movement Therapy was particularly well suited for Maria because of her fundamental lack of connectedness with her body and her difficulty in verbalizing her feelings.

SUMMARY

Dance/Movement Therapy is a powerful and versatile therapeutic modality that lends itself to the treatment of a wide range of client populations. Virtually all people are capable of movement, no matter how limited, and their movement reflects and affects their internal processes. The dance/movement therapist uses the medium of body movement to make a therapeutic relationship and to enhance functioning in emotional, cognitive, and physical areas.

Dance/Movement Therapy has a profound impact on the individual because it involves direct experiencing rather than simply talking about experience. Movement taps primitive levels of experience and enables the individual to express feelings that defy words. Personal imagery and repressed feelings that are made available in Dance/Movement Therapy provide the basis for further therapeutic exploration verbally and in movement.

Dance is a communicative as well as an expressive modality. Aspects of rhythmic synchrony, spatial formation, and touch create connections among participants in the Dance/Movement Therapy session and foster feelings of contact and belonging.

Body movement is the mode of experience and growth at basic levels of development. Through the recapitulation of normal sequences of development, Dance/Movement Therapy promotes behavioral change. It facilitates expansion of the movement repertoire, providing a greater range of adaptive responses. It also provides support for new adaptive behaviors until they can be fully integrated and available to the individual.

Through its use of body movement to facilitate emotional growth, Dance/Movement Therapy engages the total person and provides an experience of integration and wholeness. Whether used as a primary or adjunctive treatment modality, Dance/Movement Therapy is a compelling and universally applicable treatment approach. It fosters self-awareness and provides a medium for self-expression, communication, and growth.

For further information on the field of Dance/Movement Therapy, contact the American Dance Therapy Association (ADTA), 2000 Century Plaza, Suite 108, 10632 Little Patuxent Parkway, Columbia, Maryland, 21044-3263, or visit their web site at http://www.adta.org.

REFERENCES

Alperson, E. D. (1977). Experiential movement psychotherapy. *American Journal of Dance Therapy, 1*(1), 8–12.

American Dance Therapy Association. Dance therapy (1999). Web site. http://www.adta.org.

Bernstein, P. L. (Ed.). (1979). *Eight theoretical approaches in dance/movement therapy.* Dubuque, IO: Kendall/Hunt.

Chaiklin, H. (Ed.). (1975). *Marion Chace: Her papers.* Columbia, MD: American Dance Therapy Association.

Chaiklin, S. (1975). Dance Therapy. In S. Arieti (Ed.), *American Handbook of Psychiatry.* Vol. 5, (pp. ••–••). New York: Basic Books.

Condon, W. S. (1968). Linguistic-kinesic research and dance therapy. *ADTA Combined Third and Fourth Annual Conference Proceedings* (pp. 21–42). Columbia, MD: American Dance Therapy Association.

Davis, M. A. (1970). Movement characteristics of hospitalized psychiatric patients. *ADTA Fifth Annual Conference Proceedings* (pp. 25–45). Columbia, MD: American Dance Therapy Association.

Davis, M. A., Dulicai, D., & Climenko, J. (1977). Movement researcher and movement therapist: A collaboration. *American Journal of Dance Therapy, 28*–31.

Dell, C. (1970). *A primer for movement description.* New York: Dance Notation Bureau.

Fisher, S., & Cleveland, S. (1968). *Body image and personality* (2nd rev. ed.). New York: Dover.

Kestenberg, J. (1965a). The role of movement patterns in development: I. Rhythms of movement. *Psychoanalytic Quarterly, 34,* 1–36.

Kestenberg, J. (1965b). The role of movement patterns in development: II. Flow of tension and effort. *Psychoanalytic Quarterly, 34,* 517–563.

Laban, R. (1960). *The mastery of movement* (2nd rev. ed.). L. Ullmann (Ed.). London: MacDonald and Evans.

Levy, F. (Ed.). (1995). *Dance and other expressive art therapies: When words are not enough.* New York: Routledge.

Lowen, A. (1958). *The language of the body.* New York: Macmillan.

Reich, W. (1949). *Character analysis.* New York: Farrar, Straus.

Sandel, S., Chaiklin, S., & Lohn, A. (Eds.). (1993). *Foundations of dance/movement therapy: The life and work of Marian Chace.* Columbia, MD: American Dance Therapy Association.

Schilder, P. (1950). *The image and appearance of the human body.* New York: International Universities Press.

Snyder, A. F. (1972). Some aspects of the nature of the rhythmic experience and its possible therapeutic value. *ADTA Writings on Body Movement and Communication: Monograph 2.* (pp. 128–149). Columbia, MD: American Dance Therapy Association.

Whitehouse, M. S. C. G. (1979). Jung and dance therapy: Two major principles. In P. Bernstein (Ed.), *Eight theoretical approaches in dance/movement therapy.* Dubuque, IO: Kendall/Hunt.

Chapter 15

THE DEEP PSYCHOBIOLOGY OF PSYCHOTHERAPY

ERNEST ROSSI

This is one of the chapters that I did not understand. The inclusion of Rossi in this book was inevitable. He started as a Jungian, then became a follower and collaborator with Milton Erickson and now has "found his own voice" with the production of this article. There is much in life that I do not understand, including Einstein's theory of relativity, and this is another area that is well beyond my understanding. Despite this, the chapter is well written, has what I suppose are meaningful illustrations, and has a sufficiency of references by the author and others. Apparently Rossi is convinced of the validity of his ideas, which essentially assert a direct link between psychological factors (such as thoughts and emotions) and biological factors (extending even to genes). In the first paragraph he asks "How do we facilitate our daily work of synthesizing the organic structure of our brain to optimize relationships with ourselves and our neighbors in harmony with the evolutionary informational dynamics of consciousness and cosmos?" and he attempts to give an answer.

This is an article that requires close reading, best with a dictionary at hand for the typical reader. What it all comes down to as I read this chapter is that there exists something called immediate-early genes (IEG) that mediate between nature and nurture, making proteins that optimize neurogenesis and encode new memory and learning.

Rossi admits that "It will probably require a millennium of research to document the facts and fallacies of mind-body communication and healing in a scientifically acceptable manner."

DEFINITION

The Deep Psychobiology of Psychotherapy may be defined as the exploration of mind-body experience, communication, and healing at all levels from the cultural and psychosocial to the cellular-genetic-molecular and the quantum. It is a highly integrative approach that greatly expands the traditional domains of phenomenological, analytical, and cognitive-behavioral psychology to include new insights into creativity, consciousness, and the human condition as they are continually updated by research in biology, physics, and mathematics. It seeks to break through the Cartesian dualism between mind and body by exploring questions such as: How is it possible for thoughts, emotions, imagination, and personal experience to influence physical health and vice versa? We know that our genes are expressed in our behavior, for example, but to what extent can we have a "psychobiological dialogue" with our genes to modulate how their information is expressed in self-creation and the process of physical healing? How do we facilitate our daily work of synthesizing the organic structure of our brain to optimize relationships with ourselves and our neighbors in harmony with the evolutionary informational dynamics of consciousness and cosmos?

HISTORY

The history of the Deep Psychobiology of Psychotherapy began with the author's exploration of the implications of early research in the 1960s and 1970s that documented how the psychological experience of novelty and enriched environments was encoded as new memory and learning in the organic structure of the brain on a molecular level (Rossi, 2000). This led to the formulation of the dream-protein hypothesis: "Dreaming is a process of psychophysiological growth that involves the synthesis and modification of protein structures in the brain that serves as the organic basis for new developments in personality."

Within this perspective the essence of psychotherapy becomes a process of facilitating "creative moments" that are encoded in new proteins and neural networks in the brain. But what is a creative moment? Such moments have been celebrated as the exciting "hunch" by scientific workers and as inspiration by people in the arts. The creative moment occurs when a habitual pattern of association is interrupted. There may be a spontaneous lapse or relaxation of one's associative process. There may be a psychological shock, an overwhelming sensory or emotional experience; it may be due to a psychedelic drug, a toxic condition, or sensory deprivation. Yoga, Zen, and spiritual and meditative exercises may likewise interrupt habitual associations and introduce a momentary void in awareness. In that fraction of a second when the habitual contents of awareness are knocked out there is a chance for pure awareness and an experience of new awareness or heightened consciousness. This fraction of a second may be experienced as a mystic state, satori, a peak experience, or an altered state of consciousness. It may be experienced as a moment of fascination or falling in love when the gap in one's awareness is suddenly filled with the new that has been created in a semi-autonomous manner within the deep psychobiology of our being.

From this perspective the new that appears in creative moments is the basic unit of original thought and insight as well as personality transformation. Experiencing creative moments is the phenomenological correlate of a critical change in the molecular structure of proteins within the brain associated with the creation of new cell assemblies, memory, and learning. Molecular transformations in the brain in response to psychological shock, arousal, and novelty were now recognized by the author as the deep psychobiological basis of psychopathology as well as the educational, constructive, and synthetic approach to healing and psychotherapy that had its roots in the early work of pioneers such as James Braid in Scotland, Pierre Janet in France, Maurice Bucke in Canada, Carl Jung in Switzerland, Rolando Assagioli in Italy, and Milton Erickson in America. James Braid, one of the fathers of hypnosis, for example, attributed the therapeutic effects of trance induction to the "psychophysiology of fascination" now regarded as a special state of psychobiological arousal and focused attention. Maurice Bucke described the most heightened state of psychobiological arousal as "cosmic consciousness." He attributed mental illness to a breakdown in the natural process of evolving consciousness. Borrowing from the work of the religious scholar Rudolph Otto, Carl Jung described heightened states of consciousness in the creative breakthroughs of spiritual innovators, artists, and U.S. scientists as an experience of the *numinosum* (an overwhelming experience of fascination with the mysteriousness and tremendousness of life and the universe).

Some of the most intriguing, innovative approaches to hypnosis and psychotherapy based on psychological shock, emotional arousal, and creative moments were pioneered by the late Milton Erickson and described as follows.

The induction and maintenance of a trance serve to provide a special psychological state in which the patient can reassociate and reorganize his inner psychological complexities and utilize his own capacities in a manner in accord with his own experiential life . . . therapy results from an inner resynthesis of the patient's behavior achieved by the patient himself. It is true that direct suggestion can effect an alteration in the patient's behavior and result in a symptomatic cure, at least temporarily. However, such a "cure" is simply a response to suggestion and does not entail that reassociation and reorganization of ideas, understandings and memories so essential for actual cure. It is this experience of reassociating and reorganizing his own experiential life that eventuates in a cure, not the manifestation or response behavior [to hypnotic suggestion] which can, at best, satisfy only the observer [and stage hypnotist]. (Erickson, 1948, p. 38–39)

CURRENT STATUS

The fundamental question, for a deep psychobiology of psychotherapy: "How do we integrate the many levels of mind-body communication and healing from the psychosocial to the cellular-genetic?" Is it possible to use the concept of *information* and the *transformations of information* to do this? Is it possible to create a new science of *information transduction* that explores how information experienced as human cognitive behavior (thoughts, words, images, emotions, meaning, etc.) is transformed into other forms of information expressed as the physical structure of our genes and proteins and vice versa? A major mission of this new science of information transduction is to trace the pathways by which human cognition and emotional experience modulate biological processes in health, sickness, and the dynamics of mind-body healing.

An interesting step in the creation of this new science of information transduction was pioneered by the biologist Thomas Stonier (1990). A visual summary of his ideas was illustrated by the author (Rossi, 1993) in Figure 15.1. From the broadest perspective the informational dynamics of the evolution of the physical universe as well as living systems is currently described as "getting its from bits" (Wilczek, 1999). That is, how can "its" (the apparently physical, molecular, and biological structures of the universe) evolve out of "bits" (binary information) from the quantum flux of the Big Bang origin of the universe? Information is regarded as the mathematical common denominator that brings together physics, biology, psychology, human consciousness, creativity, and culture. Is the information that organizes the energy and physical dynamics of nature the same as the information contained in thoughts, words, feelings, images, and imagination? If so, how do we facilitate the trans-

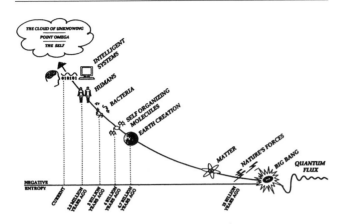

Figure 15.1   The evolution of information transduction from the Big Bang to the Self.

duction of information from one modality to another in creative experience and healing?

The French mathematician Henry Poincaré, the originator of nonlinear dynamics (currently called chaos theory or adaptive complexity theory), first described the four-stage creative process about 100 years ago at the same time that Sigmund Freud and Carl Jung were originating psychodynamics. This four-stage creative process is illustrated in the inner circle of Figure 15.2. The middle circle of Figure 15.2 illustrates the breakout heuristic as a model of psychotherapy (Rossi, 2000) that

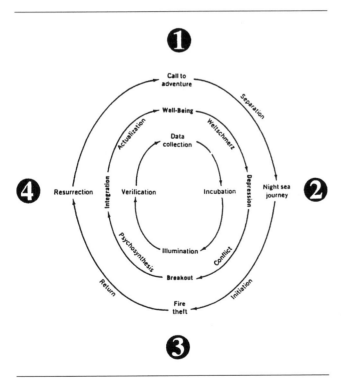

Figure 15.2   The breakout heuristic in psychotherapy.

corresponds to Poncaré's creative cycle. The outer circle is a condensation of Joseph Campbell's monomyth of the cultural dynamics of the hero that corresponds to the same four-stage creative process. The outer labels of Figure 15.2 illustrate how sociopolitical identity follows the same four-stage paradigm. Let us now focus on the dynamics of mindbody communication (also called information transduction) in this four-stage creative process as it is manifest in current theory of the deep psychobiology of psychotherapy.

THEORY

Figure 15.3 illustrates a four-stage outline of the complex field of mindbody communication and healing that corresponds to the creative cycle of Figure 15.2. Let us review these four stages as a foundation for a new understanding of what is actually going on between patient and therapist at the deepest levels of mind-gene communication (Rossi, 1993, 1996, 2000, 2001).

Stage 1: Mindbrain Information Transduction

The limbic-hypothalamic-pituitary system is currently recognized as a major information transducer between the brain and the body. Cells within the hypothalamus transduce (transform information from one form into another) the essentially electrochemical neural impulses of the brain that encode the phenomenological experience of "mind" and emotions into the hormonal "messenger molecules" of the endocrine system. These messenger molecules then travel through the bloodstream in a cybernetic loop of information transduction in Figure 15.3, where the four major stages of interest for psychotherapy are numbered.

The complex loop of mindbody communication illustrated in Figure 15.3 modulates the action of neurons and cells of the body at all levels from the basic pathways of sensation and perception in the brain to the intracellular dynamics of gene transcription and translation. It has been proposed that the molecular messengers (also called informational substances) of the endocrine, autonomic, and immune systems mediate stress, emotions, memory, learning, personality, behavior, and symptoms (Rossi, 1993, 1996). This communication loop is a two-way street by which (1) mind can modulate physiology of the brain and body and (2) biology can modulate mind, emotions, learning, and behavior.

Stage 2: Immediate-Early Genes in Creative Adaptation

A generation ago it was believed that genes were simply the units of physical heredity that were transmitted from

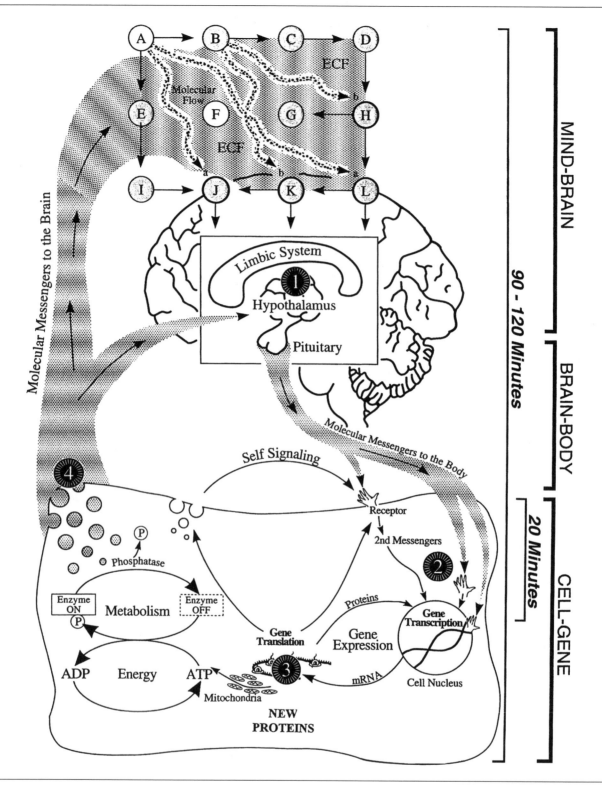

Figure 15.3   The Complex Loop of Mind-Body Communication and Healing in Psychotherapy. (1) Information from the outside world encoded in the neurons of the cerebral cortex of the brain is transformed within the limbic-hypothalmus-pituitary system into the messenger molecules that travel through the blood stream to signal receptors on all cells of the brain and body. (2) The receptors on the surface of cells transmit the signal via 2nd messengers to the nucleus of the cell where immediate-early genes signal other target genes to transcribe their code into messenger RNAs (mRNA). (3) The mRNAs serve as blueprints for the synthesis of proteins that will function as (a) the ultimate healing structures—the *material dynamics* of the body, (b) enzymes to facilitate *energy dynamics* and (c) receptors and messenger molecules for the *informational dynamics* of the cell. (4) Messenger molecules function as a type of "molecular memory" that can evoke state-dependent emotions, mood, memory, learning and behavior in the neural networks of the brain (illustrated as the rectangular array of letters A to L on the top).

one generation to another through sexual reproduction. Today we know that genes have a second major function: a major class of genes, immediate early genes (also called primary response genes or third messengers) are continuously active in responding to the hormonal messenger molecules signaling the need for creative adaptation to important changes in the environment. Everything from novelty, shock, surprise, touch, sexual stimuli, maternal behavior, and psychosocial stress to temperature, food, physical trauma, and toxins in the environment can be signaled to the genes via the hormonal messenger molecules that arrive from the limbic-hypothalamic-pituitary system (Merchant, 1996).

Immediate-early genes (IEGs) are the newly discovered mediators between nature and nurture. Immediate-early genes act as information transducers, allowing signals from the external environment to regulate genes within the internal matrix of the nucleus of life itself. Many researchers now believe that memories along with new experiences are encoded in the central nervous system by changes in the structure and formation of new proteins within the synapses between neurons (Eriksson et al., 1998). IEGs function as transcription factors regulating the "housekeeping genes" that make the proteins within the neuron that encode new memory and learning (Tölle, Schadrack, & Zieglgansberger, 1995). More than 100 immediate-early genes have been reported at this time. While many of their functions still remain unknown, neuroscientists are exploring the interrelated biological and psychological functions that immediate-early genes such as c-Fos and c-Jun are already known to serve, as illustrated in Figure 15.4. Most arousing psychosocial stimuli can induce immediate-early genes within minutes, and their main effects are mediated

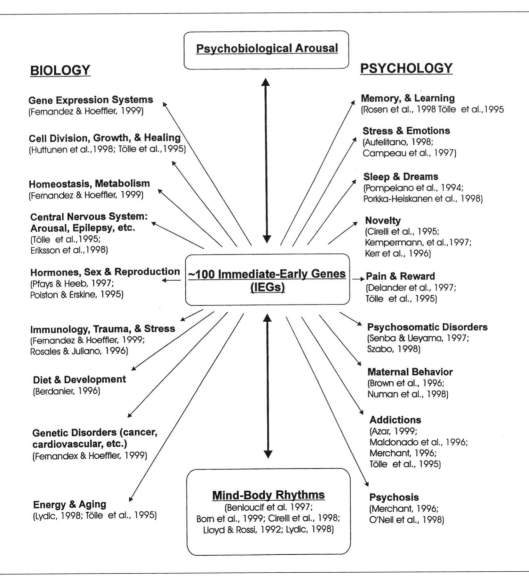

Figure 15.4 The central role of immediate-early genes (IEGs) in the Deep Psychobiology of Psychotherapy.

within 20 minutes to an hour or two. A more detailed discussion and complete citation of all the references of Figure 15.4 have been published previously (Rossi, 2000).

Stage 3: Protein Synthesis in Memory, Stress, and Healing

The third stage in the mind-gene communication loop is the process of gene translation that leads to the production of new proteins shown in Figure 15.3. The time required to make new proteins in response to psychological arousal and physical stress as illustrated on the right side of Figure 15.3 provides an important window into the informational dynamics of new approaches to psychotherapy. The domain of psychological time in minutes and hours as illustrated in Figure 15.3 relates the basic rest activity cycle of human behavior to the processes of mindbody communication. This is in sharp contrast to the more recent evolutionary form of more rapid mindbody communication mediated by the central nervous system in small fractions of a second that are briefer than the usual phenomenological span of consciousness.

Detailed research on the genetic, neuroendocrinal, and psychosocial levels suggests that the 90–120–minute ultradian rhythm (Lloyd & Rossi, 1992), originally described as the basic rest-activity cycle by Kleitman, is a more fundamental work cycle of life than the circadian cycle (the 24-hour rhythm). Ultradian in this context means any rhythm faster than the 24-hour circadian cycle; this chapter emphasizes only the major 90–120 ultradian rhythms on the genetic, endocrine, and cognitive-behavioral levels during sleeping, dreaming, and creative waking states that have important implications for psychotherapy.

Stage 4: Messenger Molecules and State-Dependent Memory

Stage 4 of Figure 15.3 illustrates how messenger molecules (such as hormones, neurotransmitters, growth factors, etc.) that have their origin in the processing of the larger protein "mother-molecules" in Stage 3 may be stored within the cells of the brain and body as a kind of molecular memory. These molecular messengers are released into the bloodstream where they can complete the complex cybernetic loop of information transduction by passing through the "blood-brain barrier" to modulate the brain's neural networks and psychological experience as illustrated by the block of letters A through L at the top of Figure 15.3. Such localized neuronal networks of the brain are modulated by a complex field of messenger molecules that can reach the limbic-hypothalamic-pituitary system as well as certain areas of the cerebral cortex. This is a new model of how the

sexual hormones, stress hormones, immune system cytokines (messenger molecules like IL-1 and IL-2) and growth factors of the body can modulate mind and emotions and visa versa.

If we are willing to grant that communication within the neuronal networks of the brain modulates changes in the strengths of synaptic connections, then we could say that meaning is to be found in the complex dynamic field of messenger molecules that continually bathe and contextualize the information of the neuronal networks in ever changing patterns. It is truly amazing to learn, for example, that most of the sexual and stress hormones that have been adequately tested have state-dependent effects on our mental and emotional states as well as on memory and learning.

Recent research indicates that most forms of learning (Pavlovian, Skinnerian, imprinting, sensitization, etc.) are now known to involve these hormonal messenger molecules from the body that can reach the brain to modulate the neural networks that encode mind, memory, learning, and behavior. Insofar as these classical forms of learning use messenger molecules, they ipso facto have a state-dependent component (Rossi, 1993, 1996) .

METHODOLOGY

The methodology of the deep psychobiology of psychotherapy expands traditional psychological research to include all the new approaches of neuroscience. Current research on state-dependent memory, learning, and behavior is a clear example. When subjects are given memory and learning tasks while under the influence of stress hormones such as adrenocorticotropic hormone (ACTH), epinephrine, or sex hormones (or even psychoactive drugs that mimic these natural hormonal messenger molecules), there is a varying degree of amnesia when the stress hormone or drug has been metabolized out of the system. That is, when memory is encoded under conditions of high emotional arousal, novelty, sex, stress, or trauma, it tends to become state-dependent or state bound to that psychobiological condition. Memory and learning is state-dependent on the original psychobiological conditions when it was first encoded. This state-dependent memory becomes dissociated or apparently "lost" after the person apparently recovers when the stress or sexual hormones are metabolized and return to normal levels. Reactivating stress or sex in another context, however, has a tendency to reestablish the original encoding condition with varying degrees of emotion and memory of the trauma. This is the psychobiological basis of much psychopathology related to early sexual and stressful life events as uncovered by classical psychoanalysis. This illustrates how state-dependent memory, learning, and behavior (SDMLB) bridges the Cartesian dichotomy between mind and body.

From a psychotherapeutic perspective, what is most interesting about these experiments is that they enable us to study the parameters of "reversible amnesia," which have been important criteria in understanding the phenomenology of psychoanalysis and therapeutic hypnosis (Rossi, 1993, 1996). Most experiments in state-dependent memory and learning demonstrate that this reversible amnesia is only partial. That is, there is usually some memory and learning available even in the dissociated condition after the stress hormones return to normal levels, so most of the hypnotic literature documents that hypnotic amnesia is usually fragile and partial in character. A full amnesia that is completely reversible is relatively rare in state-dependent memory and learning experiments as well as in psychoanalysis and therapeutic hypnosis. In the historical literature of hypnosis and psychoanalysis this same fragile and partial character of reversible amnesia may have been responsible for many of the puzzling and paradoxical features of memory that remain the source of continuing controversy that challenges the validity of the various theories of depth psychology. Since the earliest days of psychoanalysis it has been noted that a sudden fright, shock, trauma, or stress could evoke "hypnoidal states" that were somehow related to amnesia and dissociated and neurotic behavior. We now know they can activate the dynamics of mind-gene communication and state-dependent memory, learning, and behavior (Rossi & Cheek, 1988).

Psychoimmunoloqy and the Mindbody Connection

The most comprehensive demonstration of how psychosocial stress can modulate gene transcription was demonstrated by the research team of Ronald Glaser (Glaser, Kennedy, et al., 1990; Glaser, Lafuse, Bonneau, Atkinson, & Kiecolt-Glaser, 1993) at Ohio State Medical School. His research traces the effects of psychological stress (experienced by medical students during academic examinations) on the transcription of the interleukin-2 receptor gene and interleukin-2 production. These researchers documented the path of information transduction illustrated in Figure 15.3 from (1) the limbic-hypothalamic-pituitary system's hormones (primary messengers) that trigger (2) cell receptors to initiate (3) a cascade of secondary messengers (cyclic adenosine monophosphate, cAMP) that mediate gene transcription, which leads to messenger ribonucleic acid (the mRNA "blueprint" of the gene) production and the synthesis of new proteins that leads to the formation of (4) other hormonal messenger molecules that in turn flow back to the brain to modulate mind, memory, emotions, and behavior in a state-dependent manner.

A major challenge for fundamental research in psychobiologically oriented psychotherapy is to document how a positive psychotherapeutic intervention designed to reduce psychosocial stress could lead to a facilitation of the transcription of the interleukin-2 receptor gene and its translation into the interleukin-2 protein that functions as a messenger molecule in the immune system. This is a new paradigm of mindbody healing (Castes et al., 1999). It has profound significance for a general theory of mindbody communication and healing when we realize that other medical researchers (Rosenberg & Barry, 1992) have found that interleukin-2 is a messenger molecule of the immune system that signals white blood cells (cytotoxic T-cells) to attack pathogens and cancer cells. Thus, the traditional medical model of research represented by Rosenberg finds the same foundation of mindbody communication at the level of gene expression as the new field of psychoimmunology represented by Glaser. I propose that this will become the new criterion for evaluating all forms of mindbody healing in the future—biofeedback, body therapies, massage, meditation, imagery, active imagination, hypnosis, prayer, ritual, or whatever. Whatever the holistic method of mindbody healing, we can test whether it really facilitated mindbody communication and healing simply by taking a blood sample to determine whether a healing gene transcription actually took place with the very easy and reliable tests to determine whether immediate-early genes and mRNA have been made so that new proteins and hormones could be synthesized for growth, healing, and new phenomenological experiences of consciousness (Rossi, 2000; 2001).

APPLICATIONS

Unfolding the 90–120 ultradian cycle of mindbody communication of Figure 15.3 over time yields graphs of the alternating ultradian rhythms of activity and rest on the genetic, endocrine, and cognitive-behavioral levels as illustrated on the lower part of Figure 15.5. This coordination of the diverse systems of traditional psychobiology via their time parameters has been called the unification hypothesis of chronobiology (Lloyd & Rossi, 1992). This new understanding of the chronobiology from the molecular-genetic to the cognitive-behavioral levels may be taken as a new database for understanding the dynamics of mindbody communication and healing in psychotherapy.

The lower part of Figure 15.5 summarizes the alternating 90–120–minute ultradian rhythms of the awake and sleep states that have their ultimate foundation in gene expression in a simplified manner. The ascending peaks of rapid eye movement (REM) sleep characteristic of nightly dreams every 90–120 minutes or so are il-

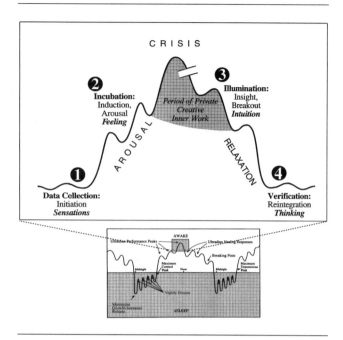

Figure 15.5   The four stages of the creative process in psychobiologically oriented psychotherapy. The lower diagram summarizes the alternating 90–120–minute ultradian rhythm of waking and sleep states of two days. The upper part of the diagram illustrates the four-stage creative process of psychotherapy as the utilization of one of the natural 90–120–minute ultradian rhythms illustrated in the lower diagram.

lustrated along with the more variable ultradian rhythms of activity, adaptation, and rest in the daytime. Figure 15.5 also illustrates that many hormonal messenger molecules of the endocrine system, such as growth hormone, the activating and stress hormone cortisol, and the sexual hormone testosterone, have a typical circadian peak at different times of the 24-hour cycle. Because the nonlinear chronobiological release of many of these hormones is recognized as having profound state-dependent effects on memory, learning, emotions, and behavior throughout the day, it is important to consider their relevance for psychotherapy.

An interesting example of the theoretical and practical implications of such chronobiological relationships between hormones and behavior is the "human alarm clock" effect. It has been found that people who are able to awaken in the morning at a specific time experience a greater release of cortisol and adrenocorticotropin in their blood stream just before their alarm clock rings (Born, Hansen, Marshall, Molle, & Fehm, 1999). As illustrated in Figure 15.5, however, there is a normal peak in cortisol just before awakening in the morning. This implies that the conscious intentionality to awaken at a specific time in the morning is able to utilize a normally involuntary circadian hormonal rhythm to control the

desired behavior of awakening at a certain time. We have long known that body processes can modulate conscious experience and behavior; the human alarm clock effect clearly documents the reverse: A conscious intentionality can modulate a normally involuntary circadian hormonal rhythm of messenger molecules throughout the body. It is precisely this reciprocal relationship between mind and body that is the deep psychobiological basis of information transduction, mindbody communication, and healing in psychotherapy (Rossi, 2001).

The upper part of Figure 15.5 illustrates my conjecture that the natural unit of psychobiologically oriented psychotherapy may be a utilization of one natural 90–120 ultradian cycle of activity and rest. Research has documented how the ultradian peaks of cortisol secretion that lead to psychophysiological states of arousal every 90–120 minutes or so throughout the day (labeled ultradian performance peaks in Figure 15.5) are typically followed after about 20 minutes by ultradian peaks of beta-endorphin that lead to rest and relaxation labeled ultradian healing responses (Rossi & Nimmons, 1991). It appears that nature has built in a natural but flexible and highly adaptive ultradian rhythm of activity, rest, and healing, the work cycle of life mentioned previously, every 90–120 minutes.

What, exactly, is the "work" that is done in each 90–120–minute ultradian cycle? I propose that the essence of such work is the formation of new proteins for a creative response to changing environmental conditions, stress, and healing. The basic implication of the deep psychobiological dynamics of new protein formation and healing in psychotherapy is that what has been traditionally called counseling or therapeutic suggestion may be, in essence, the accessing, entrainment, and utilization of ultradian/circadian processes that respond to psychosocial cues. Within this framework, the classical phenomena of hypnosis may be conceptualized as extreme manifestations and/or perseverations of time-dependent psychobiological processes that are responsive to psychosocial cues (Rossi, 1996). What the biologist calls the "entrainment of ultradian and circadian rhythms on all levels from the cognitive-behavioral to the cellular-genetic by physical and psychosocial stimuli" is the deep psychobiological basis of what psychotherapists call "suggestion to facilitate creativity and mindbody healing." This leads us to the formulation of new mathematical models of therapeutic hypnosis and psychotherapy (Rossi, 1996, 2000).

Table 15.1 outlines the four stages of the creative process as it is typically experienced every 1.5 to 2 hours in everyday life (Rossi & Nimmons, 1991). Throughout the day, particularly during the low phase of the ultradian rhythm. We all have a choice as to how we shall proceed with our natural psychobiological phases of consciousness, creativity, performance, and healing. We can heed

Table 15.1   The Ultradian Healing Response and the Ultradian Stress Syndrome as They Are Experienced in Everyday Life.

THE ULTRADIAN HEALING RESPONSE	THE ULTRADIAN STRESS SYNDROME
1. *Recognition Signals:* An acceptance of nature's call for your need to rest and recover your strength and well-being leads you into an experience of comfort and thankfulness.	1. *Take-a-Break Signals:* A rejection of nature's call for your need to rest and recover your strength and well-being leads you into an experience of stress and fatigue.
2. *Accessing a Deeper Breath:* A spontaneous deeper breath comes all by itself after a few moments of rest as a signal that you are slipping into a deeper state of relaxation and healing. Explore the deepening feelings of comfort that come spontaneously. Wonder about the possibilities of mind-gene communication and healing with an attitude of dispassionate compassion.	2. *High on Your Hormones:* Continuing effort in the face of fatigue leads to the release of stress hormones that short-circuits the need for ultradian rest. Performance goes up briefly at the expense of hidden wear and tear so that you fall into further stress and a need for artificial stimulants (caffeine, nicotine, alcohol, cocaine, etc.).
3. *Mindbody Healing:* Spontaneous fantasy, memory, feeling-toned complexes, active imagination, and numinous states of being are orchestrated for healing and life reframing.	3. *Malfunction Junction:* Mistakes in performance, memory, and learning; emotional problems become manifest. You may become depressed or irritable and abusive to self and others.
4. *Rejuvenation & Awakening:* A natural awakening with feelings of serenity, clarity, and healing together with a sense of how you will enhance your performance and well-being in the world.	4. *The Rebellious Body:* Classical psychosomatic symptoms now intrude so that you finally have to stop and rest. You are left with a nagging sense of failure, depression, and illness.

nature's call to take a healing break to experience what I call the ultradian healing response. This is often the best time to practice a natural form of self-hypnosis, meditation, deep self-reflection, and holistic healing. If we persistently choose to ignore nature's call for rest and restoration at such times, however, we will fall into the ultradian stress syndrome, where we are prone to experience the genesis of psychosomatic symptoms and the typical dynamics of Freud's psychopathology of everyday life.

CASE EXAMPLE

Examples of how a deep psychobiological model of the four-stage creative process may be utilized in practical psychotherapy have been described in detail (Rossi, 1993, 1996, 2000). In the case example presented here I propose a highly speculative outline of how the four stages of mind-body information transduction and healing illustrated in Figures 15.2, 15.3, and 15.5 may be experienced in the four stages of the Deep Psychobiology of Psychotherapy. It will probably require a millennium of research to document the facts and fallacies of this view of mindbody communication and healing in a scientifically acceptable manner.

Stage 1: Initiation

A woman in her 30s experiencing a period of emotional transition and stress suddenly begins to experience un-

usual and uncomfortable sensations of heat in her vagina. Medical examination indicates that she is having an outbreak of vaginal herpes for the first time in her life. She claims she has had no new sexual partners for over three years and her current partner has apparently been faithful. She is emotionally overwhelmed by this unexpected symptom that has the numinous effect of focusing her consciousness inward in an entirely natural manner. Recognizing this, the therapist initiates her into the symptom path to enlightenment (Rossi, 1996) by introducing her to symptom scaling: "On a scale of 1 to 10 where 10 is the worst you have ever experienced that heat and 5 is average, just how strong is your sense of heat in your vagina right now?" She replies that the heat is "Seven right now," and crosses her legs with a grimace of distaste. The therapist asks her, "Do you have the courage to really receive honestly just what you are feeling right now so you can fully experience what it leads to next?" This seemingly simple but numinous question focuses her attention on her symptoms as mindbody signals that will eventually be transduced into healing and emotional insights as we shall soon see.

Stage 2: Incubation and Arousal

She responds with her impression that the symptom of herpes is the source of the heat she is feeling and it seems to be getting worse by the minute as she focuses on it with growing fascination. The therapist supports this development by slowly and quietly murmuring an incomplete sentence, "I wonder if you can allow that to continue until . . . ?" Her eyes close as she apparently focuses inward. Her body tenses and she leans forward slightly over the next 20 minutes or so as she hesitantly becomes engaged in an active imagination wherein she whispers the following series of apparently spontaneous symptomatic transformations (that is, mindbody information transduction) and free associations with many pauses, "Now the heat is shifting around a little to my butt on the left cheek . . . now heat is moving through my body everywhere . . . it's like a burning allergy . . . my head hurts . . . feels like an outbreak of psoriasis on my scalp . . . I feel like I should confess it all to my mother like I did as a kid . . . my right shoulder aches . . . Why is my right side trembling? . . . Why am I starting to cry? . . . Why do I still try to get approval from my mother even when she never gave it but only punished me instead? . . . I'm burning up with heat all over!"

From a psychobiological point of view the heat she is experiencing indicates that she is going through a rather intense state of sympathetic system arousal as she experiences what has been traditionally called an emotional catharsis or crisis. This is the state of arousal illustrated as Stage 2 in Figures 15.2, 15.3, and 15.5. The hormonal stress messenger molecules of the limbic-hypothalamic-pituitary-adrenal system are being released into the bloodstream and traveling to cells of the brain and body where they trigger receptors and initiate cascades of secondary messengers to signal the activation of immediate-early genes (IEGs). These IEGs activate certain target genes to send their mRNA blueprints to the cell's protein factories where stress and healing proteins are made. Many of the stress proteins and hormones produced at this time are the same as those that were released during previous real life trauma when they were responsible for encoding memories in a state-bound form. This new release of these stress hormones in the context of psychotherapy reactivates the woman's original traumatic state just enough to reawaken the apparently lost state-bound memories with tears and the potential for a creative moment with a fresh perspective on her life.

Stage 3: Illumination and Insight

For a few tense minutes she continues with, "Burning! Burning! I know . . . I know I have to leave [her current boyfriend]. I always knew it was only temporary, really, but now I really do have to leave . . . He punishes me too, even when he doesn't know it . . . my left knee is twitching uncontrollably . . . Can't you make it stop? . . . Oh, I'm tired of all this . . . I will leave . . . I'm getting sleepy . . . I feel warm . . . just warm now . . . I really have to leave [boyfriend]." Her body sags back and she remains silent for about three or four minutes as her face gradually becomes calm, smooth and relaxed.

A profound psychobiological transition is now taking place; it is indicated by the two-line break just past the crisis peak in the upper diagram of Figure 15.5. At this time no one really knows what is happening in this period of private creative inner work at the moment of a creative cognitive-emotional breakthrough (as verbalized above when she realizes that she must leave her boyfriend). The author originally proposed the neuropeptide hypothesis of consciousness and catharsis to describe the dynamics of such creative moments: From the psychobiological perspective, the arousal and relaxation phases of inner work are mediated by the release of messenger molecules such as ACTH and beta-endorphin. More recent research suggests that immediate-early genes such as c-Fos and c-Jun are activated in brain cells during emotional pain and arousal of the crisis of transition between stress and the release of relaxation hormones (Lydic, 1998). This arousal may lead to the synthesis of new proteins that will connect synapses bridging neural networks. These proteins will become the cellular-molecular basis of a new psychological insight and healing as illustrated in Stage 3 of Figures 15.2, 15.3, and 15.5.

Stage 4: Verification and Reintegration

The therapist looks at the clock and with a mild sense of concern notices the session will end in 10 minutes. He clears his throat and murmurs, "Yes, and is that still going well?" After a moment the woman shifts her feet, nods her head yes, adjusts her posture to a more normal sitting position, blinks a bit, and finally opens her eyes as if awakening from a trance. The therapist then asks, "And I wonder what number describes what your level of comfort is now?" Somewhat surprised, she acknowledges that her symptoms are now at a level of "1 or 2 or maybe zero," that is, very close to complete comfort. She explains it is no longer a feeling of heat in her vagina, but rather a feeling of warmth, or is it a slight pressure, or a knowing somehow? From a psychobiological point of view she has moved past her state of arousal and catharsis in Stage 2 and emotional insight in Stage 3 to a state of comfort and parasympathetic relaxation in Stage 4 that is so characteristic of what people typically feel when a job is well done.

The therapist asks if she now knows what she has to do and she nods yes. She makes a few remarks about how she experiences a sense of relief in knowing that she now can make up her own mind with confidence about the important things in her life. She will leave her boyfriend and later she will tell others about it. By the next session a week later she reports that she has navigated the separation well. The herpes and burning sensations are apparently gone. At this time we can only speculate about how the shifts in the hormonal and immune system messenger molecules may have modulated the psychobiological state of her vagina mucosa so that her symptoms and the virus go into remission. A year later she remains symptom free and all available evidence indicates that her life was effectively "turned around" in this session.

SUMMARY

This chapter outlines currently evolving views of how complex, self-organizing systems of communication across all levels from the molecular-genetic to the psychosocial could lead to a unified theory of mindbody communication and healing in psychotherapy. Research in the areas of immediate-early genes, psychoimmunology, and state-dependent memory is integrated with the chronobiology of ultradian rhythms as a new window into the psychobiology of creativity, stress, and healing. A deep psychobiological perspective on psychotherapy that is consistent with much of the classical theory of psychoanalysis and psychosomatic medicine as well as the modern neuroscience of memory and learning at the cellular-genetic level is proposed. This new integration of theory and research leads to a psychobiological model of how we may utilize the creative process to facilitate mindbody healing in a manner that may seem visionary to some. Such a visionary ideal, however, may be what we need to develop truly new and inspired approaches to psychotherapy in the new millennium.

REFERENCES

Born, J., Hansen, K., Marshall, L., Molle, M., & Fehm, H. (1999). Timing the end of nocturnal sleep. *Nature, 397,* 29–30.

Castes, M., Hagel, I., Palenque, N., Canelones, P., Corano, A., & Lynch, N. (1999). Immunological changes associated with clinical improvement of asthmatic children subjected to psychosocial intervention. *Brain & Behavioral Immunology, 13,* 1–13.

Erickson, M. (1948). Hypnotic Psychotherapy. In E. Rossi (Ed.), *The Collected Papers of Milton H. Erickson* (Vol. 4, pp. 35–48).

Eriksson, P., Perfilieva, E., Björk-Ericksson, T., Alborn, A.-M., Nordborg, C., Peterson, D., & Gage, F. (1998). Neurogenesis in the adult human hippocampus. *Nature Medicine, 4,* 1313–1317.

Glaser, R., Kennedy, S., Lafuse, W., Bonneau, R., Speicher, C., Hillhouse, J., & Kiecolt-Glaser, J. (1990). Psychological stress-induced modulation of interleukin 2 receptor gene expression and interleukin 2 production in peripheral blood leukocytes. *Archives of General Psychiatry, 47,* 707–712.

Glaser, R., Lafuse, W., Bonneau, R., Atkinson, C., & Kiecolt-Glaser, J. (1993). Stress-associated modulation of proto-oncogene expression in human peripheral blood leukocytes. *Behavioral Neuroscience, 107,* 525–529.

Jung, C. (1960). The Transcendent Function. In R. F. C. Hull (Trans.), *The Collected Works of C. G. Jung: Vol. 8. The Structure and Dynamics of the Psyche* (pp. 67–91). Princeton, NJ: Princeton University Press.

Lloyd, D., & Rossi, E. (1992). *Ultradian rhythms in life processes: A fundamental inquiry into chronobiology and psychobiology.* New York: Springer.

Lydic, R. (Ed.). (1998). *Molecular regulation of arousal states.* New York: CRC Press.

Merchant, K. (1996). *Pharmacological regulation of gene expression in the CNS.* Boca Raton, FL: CRC Press.

Rosenberg, S., & Barry, J. (1992). *The transformed cell: Unlocking the mysteries of cancer.* New York: Putnam/Chapmans.

Rossi, E. (1993). *The psychobiology of mind-body healing* (Revised ed.). New York: Norton.

Rossi, E. (1996). *The symptom path to enlightenment: The new dynamics of hypnotherapy.* Phoenix: Zeig, Tucker & Theisen, Inc.

Rossi, E. (2000). *Dreams, consciousness and the human spirit: The New dynamics of self-reflection and co-creation* (3rd ed.). Phoenix: Zeig, Tucker & Theisen, Inc.

Rossi, E. (2001, In Preparation). *The psychobiology of gene expression: Neuroscience, neurogenesis and numinosum in psychotherapy and the healing arts.* New York: W.W. Norton Professional Books.

Rossi, E., & Cheek, D. (1988). *Mind-body therapy: Ideodynamic healing in hypnosis.* New York: Norton.

Rossi, E., & Nimmons, D. (1991). *The twenty minute break: Using the new science of Ultradian rhythms.* Malibu, CA: Palisades Gateway Publishing.

Stonier, T. (1990). *Information and the internal structure of the universe.* New York: Springer.

Tölle, T., Schadrack, J., & Zieglgansberger, W. (1995). *Immediate-early genes in the CNS.* New York: Springer.

Wilczek, F. (1999). Getting its from bits. *Nature, 397,* 303–306.

Chapter 16

DIRECT PSYCHOANALYSIS

JOHN N. ROSEN

Many years ago, while still an undergraduate and already interested in psychology, I learned that a neighbor, a woman in her mid-50s, had a daughter in a state mental hospital. I went along with her to visit her daughter several times. She was a beautiful young woman who talked on and on about "flies buzzing on the window." With a mixture of pity, excitement, wonder, and eventually discouragement, I attempted in all the ways I could think of to draw her out, to get her to communicate, even to just look at me. I never succeeded, never saw or heard of her since, and have often wondered what ever happened to that "crazy" girl.

Over the years, I have had, from time to time, in various capacities, the opportunity to deal with those who are frankly insane. Eventually I came to believe that they are *helpless and hopeless. But then I would hear of the work of Dr. John Rosen. He was always spoken of in wonder by those who saw what he accomplished, and when I began this book I wrote to him, never really expecting him to accept my invitation to contribute.*

The reader is now in for a thrilling experience—what follows is a chapter that should be read carefully by all those who wish to understand psychotherapy in its fullest.

Direct Psychoanalysis utilizes the insights and dynamics established by Freud and his coworkers, but modifies them in an effort to enhance their therapeutic value with a greater emphasis on treatment rather than investigation. It holds that the manifest content of mental illness is analogous to the cry of a baby, which indicates that something is wrong. With the baby, if the disturbance is corrected, the cry stops and the baby regains peace of mind. With the sick patient, if the disturbance is corrected, the symptoms stop. If the mother simply makes observations of the crying baby—for instance, the loudness of the cry, the redness of the baby's face, the writhings of the baby's body, and so forth—it might be excellent research but it would hardly stop the baby's crying. On the other hand, if the mother discovers the reason for the crying and does what has to be done about it, the crying will stop. In order to listen to the communications of a disturbed person in a meaningful way, a special kind of knowledge is required. The responsibility of the direct psychoanalyst is to understand the meaning of the manifest content. To that end he must spend endless hours listening to and observing his patient.

A direct psychoanalyst assumes the attitude of a benevolent, protecting, and controlling parent to discover the reasons for the disturbance. No drugs, shock, group, or other therapies are used in Direct Psychoanalysis.

HISTORY

Early in my medical career I was called upon to do a postmortem examination on two patients who presumably died suddenly of coronary thrombosis. The examination revealed no evidence, either grossly or microscopically, of anatomical pathology that could possibly explain their deaths. Although a pathologist classified these deaths as an "act of God," it was not a satisfactory answer to me at that time. Some colleagues who were working in the field of psychosomatic medicine mentioned the concept of psychological death when I discussed these autopsies with them. They suggested that I read Freud's monograph, *Totem and Taboo*. From that work I learned that anthropologists were familiar with the hysterical death that occurred among primitives when they violated a taboo by either looking at or touching a taboo object.

My interest in psychological medicine mounted rapidly, and I learned much from reading texts on psychosomatic medicine written by Eduardo Weiss, O. Spurgeon English, Flanders Dunbar, George Daniels, and others. Likewise, I noted that the majority of patients in my internal medicine practice showed no evidence of organic pathology but nevertheless were very ill. It was a real challenge to explain why the mind could do this to an individual. My previous attitude in clinical pathological conferences was one of "show me," and the presenter had to be prepared to demonstrate specific pathological changes in the tissue. In this new psychological field of medicine there were no specific pathological changes to be found. Could my two "coronary" deaths be explained on the basis of these new theoretical psychodynamic concepts? I applied to the New York Psychoanalytic Institute for admittance and was granted permission to take courses in psychosomatic medicine and certain other courses based on Freud's teachings. So much of the material dealt with the unconscious that I felt it necessary to explore my own unconscious, and at that point I undertook a personal analysis.

My own analysis, which I consider indispensable, lasted 11 years. The length of time was as much my decision as that of my analyst. My analysis, my reading of Freud and his coworkers, my study at the Psychoanalytic Institute, and listening to patients convinced me of the importance of understanding the unconscious. In this way one could become familiar with the meaning of the unconscious as manifested at various levels of regression, down to and including the deepest neoinfancy of the schizophrenic.

It became apparent to me and my analyst that I had a special ability to understand manifest psychiatric content and dream material. This was further verified when I successfully treated acute catatonic patients at Brooklyn State Hospital who had hitherto been treated with no results, and who when in the exhaust status would die. From the manifest content of what the patients shouted in their catatonic excitement I was able to understand the nature of their early childhood experiences and could interpret this back to the patients in such a way that they would begin to feel understood. After a considerable amount of this interpreting there came a point when the patients' temperature began to drop, they would break into a profuse sweat, and over the next few days would recover from the severity of the illness and start to function in ways that indicated they were more in touch with reality than before—they were able to take food, have natural sleep, and so forth.

This took place in the early 1940s when the standard treatment was shock therapy, lobotomy, and drugs. I found these procedures interfered with my kind of treatment because they hid the manifest content or made patients so changed by brain damage that they were unreceptive to the kind of communication required for direct psychoanalytic therapy. Although my work was ridiculed by many of my colleagues, I went my own way and compiled my own results, continuing to learn more and more about the nature of schizophrenia and all emotional illness from the point of view of etiology.

In 1945 I wrote a paper titled "The Treatment of Schizophrenic Psychosis by Direct Analytic Therapy," in which I reported on 37 patients. The findings were incredible from the point of experience of psychiatry at that early date. The results were verified by a member of the Massachusetts Psychiatric Society; as a result of the favorable reaction of the psychiatric profession to my work, I was called upon by many institutions and societies to lecture and/or demonstrate my method. When I presented my paper, one of the discussants was Dr. Paul Federn. In his review, he coined the phrase "direct psychoanalytic," from which the name *Direct Psychoanalysis* originated for this method of treatment.

CURRENT STATUS

The various techniques of treatment employed in Direct Psychoanalysis are fully documented in the textbooks I have written (1953, 1962, 1968). There also exists a 22-page bibliography of the articles and books available, not only about Direct Psychoanalysis but also about how we deal with countless manifest behavior patterns that emotionally disturbed patients evidence.

At the present time, Direct Psychoanalysis and the enthusiasm of all those involved is the basis for an attack against the futility of shock, drugs, and lobotomy. If the enthusiasm existing at this time continues undiminished, there is reason to hope for progress along these lines.

THEORY

The theory of Direct Psychoanalysis is more a matter of philosophy than physiology in the sense that psychotherapy is much closer to the teachings of the church than it is to the methods embodied in ordinary medical teaching and practice. The mind becomes distorted and distressed through malfunction rather than organic changes. I like to think of the analogy of a child banging on a concert grand piano, which normally produces beautiful music. Under no stretch of the imagination would one think that because the piano is thus "malfunctioning" something is wrong with the instrument. It is not that there is anything wrong with the mind, but for various reasons, which are our responsibility to discover, the mind in some cases ceases to function the way it is supposed to.

In Direct Psychoanalysis the brain is viewed as neither being damaged nor having hereditary influences that doom it to failure. Our approach, therefore, is seriously weakened by giving the patients "somatic therapy" such as drugs, electric shock, or brain surgery. Drugs interfere with the manifestations of any kind of mental activity, even the psychotic. The manifest content of the illness is viewed as an appeal for help. To respond to this plea we formulate a psychological approach that then becomes the treatment plan. The material uncovered in observing the psychotic patient follows along the lines of the original formulations laid down by Sigmund Freud,

Karl Abraham, Paul Federn, Victor Tausk, Bertram Lewis, and others. These concepts have to do with the existence of the id, the ego, and the superego, and with the levels of psychosexual development: namely, the oral, anal, and genital phases, in that order. In psychosis, the degree of maturity achieved in the direction of genital psychosexual level is weak. Considering the genital psychosexual level of development to be evidence of proper maturity, there is a tendency, because of this weakness, for the patient to regress to earlier oral or anal levels. The oral level essentially is demonstrated by deep schizophrenic manifestations, and the anal level is more at the manic-depressive level of regression. In psychotic regression, regression is to the pregenital level. That is, the patient regresses to the age where the infant is not yet aware of its gender. It knows nothing about sexual development at those very early oral and anal stages.

A tentative prognosis can be reached when evaluating a new patient by taking note of the degree of maturity and success achieved by him prior to the collapse into psychosis. Those patients who were underdeveloped prior to psychosis are the hardest cases to treat and become the least valuable functioning citizens if they recover. However, patients who graduated from college and had become professionals or who were significant members of their community present the best prognosis in terms of reestablishing a mature state from the present state of regression.

Based on the idea that the psychotic becomes a baby again, we have formulated the governing principle of Direct Psychoanalysis: "The therapist must be a loving, omnipotent protector and provider for the patient." Expressed another way, the therapist must be the idealized mother who now has the responsibility of bringing the patient up all over again. We believe that the cause of schizophrenia is that the individual was raised in an environment in which the maternal instinct was perverted, in the same sense that any other instinct can be perverted. The first mother figure (the real mother or a maternal surrogate) affects the child in the earliest neonatal period. The influence of this person determines the degree to which a healthy ego can develop. There are, however, also genetic factors that must also be taken into consideration. Some patients can withstand psychic trauma better than others. Little is known about these genetic factors. Since they have not given us any clues as to therapeutic progress in clinical experience, we cannot say more about genetic factors than to recognize that they probably exist. But to direct psychoanalysts they exist in the sense that some people can run faster than others, can play tennis better then others, and so forth, depending upon their endowments at birth.

We see no great difference between the dream and the psychotic material. Freud referred to the dream as a psychosis and referred to it as "the royal road to the unconscious." The psychotic process is perhaps a more regal road to the unconscious in the sense that it is relentless and does not end upon awakening. But if awakening can be brought about, so the psychosis can evaporate, like a dream that evaporates in the morning.

We place great store in the concept of the unconscious, being quite convinced that that portion of the mind has lost no memory of early events, both salutory and pathological. The earliest developmental years are recorded in the unconscious part of the mind even if there is little or no hope of recovering consciousness of these memories. We believe that the schizophrenic is reliving memories that the ordinary person cannot recapture. However, we all had a day when we first dressed ourselves or took our first steps by ourselves. We do not have to relearn these experiences because they are indelibly recorded in the unconscious portion of the mind, but to recover these memories is impossible.

We have found that the superego is not derived from the resolution of the Oedipus complex, as the current Freudian theory states. Rather, the superego (ego-ideal?) is formed from the earliest relationships with the mother through the processes of imitation, introjection, incorporation, and identification, much as Freud declared, and it consists of a continuing identification with the early maternal environment. It became apparent to me in the treatment of a schizophrenic patient that "taking in" is not only an oral "taking in," in relation only to the mother, but every symbolic equivalent of orality is the means for "taking in." I saw an example of this when a psychotic patient once took her lipstick from her pocketbook during a therapeutic dialogue and painted her eyes as if they were her lips. When I asked her what she was doing, her response was "I'm taking in a stage show." The "stage show" was the breast in the sense of Bert Lewin's description of the breast as the dream screen.

In a psychosis the patient often suffers frustration and even murderous rage directed against himself or the environment. Mainly this rage is a matter of the superego killing the ego or the ego killing the superego as they are locked in a relentless combat for the possession of the psychotic. If the superego cannot tolerate the ego, and vice versa, voices and sights are hallucinated by the psychotic patient. This hallucinatory process is really part of the patient himself, but it seems external and foreign to him. The superego is like a plague of vermin that create an intolerable itch. The psyche attempts to extrude and get rid of this toxic part of itself. This psychological attempt at healing cannot succeed, and as a result the psychosis goes on and on. It is from this understanding of what takes place that we have come to realize that the therapist must adhere to the governing principle of Direct Psychoanalysis.

Further, in our theoretical concept we believe that no person wakes up one morning psychotic, or even neurotic. Rather, the development of any severe mental illness consists of a gradual process that starts at birth in an attempt to struggle with an unincorporable maternal environment. As a result there never occurs a comfortable union between the various components of the psyche, namely the ego, the superego, and the id. Since there is never a union of these forces, the individual never has the strength that would result from this union. In union there is strength. This situation has been described as being like an individual who grows leaning like the Tower of Pisa. The Tower of Pisa remains at a point consistent with not collapsing, but the human being goes on and on in his weakend state, being confronted again and again with unmanageable social demands, as he encounters the demands of mature social living. The demands of puberty, adolescence, dating, mating, matrimony, parenthood, and so forth, are chronologically increasing ones made on the psyche that was weak to begin with. And ultimately one of these demands will bring about a partial or total collapse of the psyche; it seeks a haven in regressing to earlier, less demanding years of life. But there again, in this earliest level of life, which regression seeks to achieve, there still is no peace.

Therefore, since the demands of life are an ongoing experience, there comes a point at which the foundation is so overcome by sufficiently traumatic experiences that the individual collapses. We believe that no one is immune to developing a mental illness and that even the strongest person cannot withstand constant and intolerable psychic pain. In the state of regression that exists in schizophrenia, the unmet needs of the earliest formative years create a developmental vacuum. And as nature abhors a vacuum, it returns to perilous and defeating situations that it now hopes in some way to master but cannot.

Implicit in the story the patient tells us is an idea that might be best described as seeking the mother he once knew. One wonders why the patient invariably deals with a perilous and self-defeating situation created in his mind. It is almost as though he is conditioned to exist just this way. Whereas the healthy mind can construct pleasurable and enjoyable mirages with Garden-of-Eden-like gratifications immediately available (such as these required for a newborn baby), the sick mind will construct terrifying mirages such as mountainous waves in the ocean falling down upon him, causing suffocation and engulfment. Why can't psychotics fantasize pleasure instead of disaster? Through our studies we have been led to believe that they are seeking the rejecting mother they knew; this self-defeating situation is implicit in all psychotic patients.

METHODOLOGY

Before undertaking treatment a determination must be made of where the patient is on the psychological scale of being healthy to being utterly incapacitated. We believe that the patient goes downward from some neurotic form of defense—such as hysteria, perverson, psychopathy, and so forth—through various levels of regression at various rates of speed in terms of time, depending upon the patient's, genetic characteristics. This regression phenomenon goes down to the beginning of the psychosis, which direct psychoanalysts consider to be the manic-depressive phase. From there it goes further down through the levels of schizophrenia, namely, paranoid, hebephrenic, and finally catatonic withdrawal, in that order.

We require an understanding of where the patient is regressed to because for each patient we set up a treatment unit that can be likened to an individual mental hospital, created for the patient's individual needs. We rent a house and staff it with trained assistant therapists who are usually psychologists, sociologists, or those with equivalent academic background. These assistants have personal warmth and a feeling about psychotherapy as a way of life and are not interested in the number of hours per day that they work. These people, like the therapist, become the patient's foster family. They understand that the patient, since he is like a baby, now requires the same kind of care that a mother must supply for the newborn infant, which means 24-hour-a-day, seven-day-a-week care. In these treatment units, daily therapeutic dialogue takes place in which the patient and the therapist listen to each other in the presence of assistant therapists. The assistant therapists can then be instructed and made aware of what the therapist sees and is aiming toward. Also, the assistant therapists are able to continue along the lines that the therapist has established for the balance of the 24 hours, so that treatment is continuous and consistent. Like a baby, the psychotic has regressed to earliest infantile levels. He might wet, soil, and be unable to feed or clothe himself. Like a baby, the patient must be cared for night and day.

The therapeutic dialogue uncovers the fact that transference phenomena and intense resistance dominate the scene. This, as in conventional analysis, follows the pattern of repetition compulsion. If transference and resistance are successfully managed, the patient develops a childlike dependence on the therapist, and at this positive phase of therapy, education and discipline can begin.

It is not to be thought that therapeutic dialogue brings about rapid response. Sometimes endless hours of work result in simply a crumb of improvement, but one is not to be discouraged by this slow improvement. If one has patience over the long run, the patient eventually shows improvement and will begin to assert himself. This sign of growth will give added impetus toward the continuation of therapy. Sometimes five years go by before a patient is at the point where education and discipline can begin.

In contrast to the conventional 50-minute hour of orthodox psychoanalysis, we spend as much time as the patient seems to require in terms of understanding of the productions. I have spent as much as five or six hours continuously with one patient. On the other hand, I have spent as little as two minutes with a patient if it appeared that he was unable to tolerate any further revelations or insights concerning himself. In other words, the treatment is tailored to meet the needs of the individual patient.

Therapeutic dialogue is not ordinary conversation, but rather a highly specialized kind of communication that requires endless concentration and attention on the part of the therapist. All manner of details of the patient's speech and behavior require this attention. Further, the therapist must have the ability to understand the symbolic meaning of what the patient is saying and what the patient requires from the environment. The patient talks in primary-process language such as is employed in dreams or acts as one acts in dreams. This communication simply disguises the latent content, which tells the true story of what is wrong. Some therapists are more artful and understanding of this type of material than others. Even though a person may not have a particular gift for understanding psychotic communications, a personal analysis will provide 95 percent of what he needs to improve his ability to understand. Therefore, a prerequisite for the therapist to understand the dynamic meaning of what the patient is communicating is a deep personal analysis. The assistant therapists' work is also helped if they also have had a personal analysis. Two of the most useful assistants that I have employed for this type of therapy were young women who had gone through a psychotic episode themselves, had recovered, and were then exposed to further psychoanalysis.

If the therapist grasps quickly the meaning of what the patient is saying and is able to convey such information to the patient in such a way that the patient can comprehend it—and this requires considerable ingenuity on the part of the therapist—then the patient can express an enormous relief. The therapist, in fact, becomes to the patient the heavenly mother originally required or the witch who tortures him constantly. The patient will see the therapist in the light of his needs. In the case of intense negative transferences it is important, very often in self-defense, to remind the patient again and again, "I am not your mother, I am ————." Unwary therapists who are not able to understand the nature of the patient's transference or response—or transference psychosis, as it is more aptly labeled—may become the undeserved victim of what the original parents deserved. It is ill-advised to force treatment on a patient when the patient's behavior becomes aggressive and uncontrolled. There is always the danger of an attack against the therapist.

There are those who feel that success in treatment depends on the personality of the therapist, and that it does not make any difference what he says. I have found this an absolutely false concept. It is necessary to say pertinent things to get the patient to pay attention and to accept the therapist, to incorporate him for the purpose of ultimate identification with the therapist as the benevolent exponent in the governing principle of Direct Psychoanalysis rather than the "mother he knew." To do this it is not possible to keep suppressing the patient's cry for help; rather, it is necessary to comprehend it and do what is required. This does not mean doing specific things for the patient in terms of meeting conscious demands. What it does require is the utilization of such techniques as will satisfy whatever it is the patient is crying for.

The way to get the patient to understand that you know what his needs are is through direct interpretations. The patient does not consciously understand why he is crying but will appreciate that you understand him when you convey the correct interpretations to him. I have found that wrong interpretations are immaterial. Right interpretations produce the emotional confirmation that we seek.

Correct interpretations lead to understanding and gratification of needs. Mutual understanding and gratifications are probably the basis of all good human relationships. With this newly developed therapeutic relationship comes a parental responsibility on the part of the therapist, who in transference is first the mother and then the father and sometimes either, depending upon circumstances. Having achieved this relationship, the therapist must then teach the patient socially acceptable behavior, as any parent should.

Assuming that all goes well in the matter of understanding the patient's cry, a new kind of relationship develops between the patient's ego and the superego. The superego no longer is telling the patient "You are evil," "You are unworthy," "You should be dead." The environment no longer seems to be noxious to the patient, but if it pursues the governing principal of Direct Psychoanalysis it now hopefully includes all that one experiences from a "good mother." The patient begins to feel loved, cared for, and protected. The deadly schizophrenic nightmare beings to subside and indications of maturing behavior become apparent, much to everyone's gratification.

If a patient is properly and adequately treated, he recovers from his psychosis and now has a kind of psychological integrity that withstands those life events that he could not have tolerated prior to treatment. Such significant events could be the loss of a spouse, parent, or sibling, or a traumatic social event. Ordinarily such events will now produce depression or mourning, which is a healthy reaction, rather than pathological mourning, or psychosis. I find that my treated patients have weathered such occurrences with no more than the usual emotional reactions.

APPLICATIONS

Direct Psychoanalysis is useful in treating all kinds of emotional disturbances. For the psychotic, we consider the hospital setting the least advisable way to treat. The optimum way to treat a psychotic is to carry out a 24-hour-a-day, seven-day-a-week program under the direction of the therapist who conducts the therapeutic dialogue. The therapeutic dialogue is witnessed by the psychological assistants who themselves are being or have already been analyzed. From the insights obtained from the therapeutic dialogue in terms of understanding the manifest verbalizations, as well as nonverbal communications, they are guided in the continuing therapeutic experience provided for the patient. The assistants must always bear in mind the governing principle of Direct Psychoanalysis, derived from the Christian ethics of brotherly love. Although Christ preached it 2,000 years ago, up until the present time it has never really taken hold of the human race. The governing principle requires benevolent, loving, caring, providing, protecting behavior on the part of the therapist.

Drugs, shock therapy that dulls the brain and makes one forget, and lobotomy are interferences in this type of therapy. Some patients who have had more than a thousand electroshock and insulin shock treatments show absolutely no signs of improvement. Patients have been brought to us in such a state of numbness from tranquilizing drugs that they were unresponsive to any therapeutic efforts on our part.

After several years of ingesting a drug such as Valium, even if one discontinues the drug, the detrimental effects can continue. This indicates that the brain is now fixed, and one cannot reverse the process. If a patient is brought to us before any drug, shock, or lobotomies are used as treatment, their psychosis can sometimes be relieved within as short a time as two weeks.

Neurotic patients, particularly those suffering from anxiety hysteria, are the easiest to treat. We have found that hysterics, agoraphobics, claustrophobics, and those suffering from various forms of psychosomatic fixations can also sometimes be quickly resolved.

For the conventional analytic case, the analyst, instead of acting like an observer and a researcher, is required to do two things when he understands the meaning of the patient's complaint—the pathological, psychological material that the symptomology covers up—if the patient is sufficiently amenable: (1) educate the patient along the lines of insights uncovered and (2) train the patient in the exercise of discipline. For instance, in treating an alcoholic, if the meaning of the

"bottle" is understood in terms of orality, and so forth, the influence of the therapist in the matter of discipline that the patient will ultimately have to exercise is of paramount importance. There is no cure without discipline.

In the conventional training of a psychoanalyst, the student must do no more in relation to the patient than remain a mirror reflecting the patient's behavior back to the patient. When hoping to bring about a recovery from mental illness, this is an exercise in futility.

CASE EXAMPLE

M. S. B. came to this writer after 16 years in a state hospital, where he had been treated with the usual shock therapy and drugs. His paranoid delusional system, where he had become God, was very well organized and his behavior certainly carried out the concepts of God that fundamentalists would hold to.

He would spend his days marking down the names of countless people, either fictitious or people he had actually known. In beautiful handwriting he would describe them as good, bad, better, best, and under "good" he would give them eternal salvation, under "bad," eternal damnation, and so forth. These long written lists went on endlessly year in and year out.

Although I went into his background history carefully, there was nothing I could find that explained why he had to defend himself by becoming the most powerful personality that the human mind can conceive of, namely, God. As long as he was God he was safe from whatever terrors may have existed in life. But nothing in his history shed any light on the advent of his psychosis, which began with obsessive-compulsive behavior and manic-depressive manifestations at the age of puberty. By the time he was 18 he had developed a full-blown psychosis. The only possible influence found in the history of his background was the separation of his father and mother.

While I believe that a broken home is a devastating experience for a young child, I would not go so far as to state that divorce is sufficient explanation for the development of psychological defenses. Many children of divorced parents, although usually emotionally troubled, can survive this event and become healthy adults.

M. S. B. had a remarkable talent for painting and was given painting materials to occupy himself with. He would create a beautiful scene and then work over it until it was meaningless. He did this again and again and could never finish anything. Some of his paintings were so beautiful that it was a pity that he did not finish them.

The obsessive-compulsive neurosis that he developed was analytically fixated at the anal level. A sublimation of anality would be beautiful paintings or sculpting like those of children's finger paintings, mud pies, and sand castles. The fact that he never could finish his paintings could have been a refusal to supply what his mother wanted, namely, the completion of a bowel movement. Also, if he did it improperly, he would have been the victim of severe punishment, which would also lead to his fear of completion.

It is to be understood that this patient was free from anxiety. There is no doubt that his Godlike defense successfully protected him. All attempts to induce anxiety in him with threats of burning at the stake, as was done to Joan of Arc, or casting aspersions on his belief that he was God by means of logic, ridicule, or various other methods over several years of treatment brought little results. Finally I conceived the idea that perhaps it would be rewarding to shake his paranoid delusion in the hopes of inducing anxiety that might cause him to show some progress—either becoming more psychotic or moving upward to a more mature level.

In order to do this I now acted toward him as though I accepted the fact that he was God. After a period of several weeks of this acceptance, I had occasion to do the following: In a naive way I asked him to demonstrate some of his powers, such as walking on air, which he claimed he could do. When I asked him to show me how he walked on air, he got up on a chair and started to walk, and the force of gravity overcame his powers. He then got up on the table and violently tried to walk off the table on to air, which also failed. At this point it was clear that he was beginning to be very anxious about his belief in himself. The outcome of this was almost a hysterical state of terror. He turned white as a sheet and stood trembling. He pointed to various assistant therapists, claiming that they were "throwing harms in his way." He finally attacked one of them violently.

From this occasion onward, his belief in his delusional system began to come apart. For periods of time he became more and more reasonable and spent more time in reality. He ceased to proclaim "good," "bad," "better," "best," "eternal damnation," and "salvation." He began to show some understanding, although not much, as to why he thought he had to be God. Whereas at first, when threatened if he again said he was God, he found a clever way to counteract my threat. Now when I said that if he said he was God again I would punish him and I then asked him who he was, he replied, "I am who I am," which indicated that he was beginning to develop some common sense.

About six months after the first occasion that he felt he had lost his power, he became well enough to return to his home for visits with his family. After a period of testing in this way, he was allowed to rent an apartment of his own and to continue his career in painting. Within a year after leaving our hospital he had a show of his art that was so spectacular that it was written up in the *New York Times*. To this date, although he had traveled to Paris and has been living on his own, there has been no recurrence of his delusional system. On a few occasions when he was seen again it was hard to recognize any remnants of his psychotic status. There is every reason to believe that there will be no recurrence.

SUMMARY

Direct Psychoanalysis is a method of treating seriously disturbed patients, even those generally considered hopelessly insane. Developed by this writer in the early 1940s, the method depends on the insights gained through psychoanalysis as presented by Sigmund Freud. It consists essentially of attempts to communicate with highly disturbed patients by making direct interpretations of their various verbal and nonverbal communications. This writer saw, as did Freud, that psychosis is a withdrawal from reality of seriously psychologically wounded individuals who now have their own logic and who want to avoid relationships with others. They have regressed to various infantile levels of development.

Direct psychoanalysts differ from Freud in that instead of simply making observations, as he did, we introduce ourselves into the equation forcefully in order to make the patient aware of someone in the real world who may become a bridge back to reality. A direct interpretation aids this process, because it is the way in which the patient gathers that you understand him in the way that he does not understand himself. To quote from a recovered patient's letter, describing his feelings when he was ill: "My mind kept saying, why won't someone listen? Why can't anyone understand me?"

It is not to be inferred that Direct Psychoanalysis is applicable only to deeply regressed psychotics. It has proven most valuable many times in patients suffering from neurosis as well.

The hope of Direct Psychoanalyis is to counter the disarray that the psychoanalytic institutes are in at present. It is tragic that the writings of Martin L. Gross, (1978) in *The Psychological Society* and such severe critics as Andrew Salter (1972) in *The Case Against Psychoanalysis* are presently the vogue. This leads to the probable criminal abuse of human beings by those who agree with them in advocating drugs, especially lithium carbonate, which could easily prove fatal, as well as Valium and other tranquilizers. The continuing use of shock therapy, although it has proven again and again not only to be useless in curing a patient with a mental problem but to be harmful, to say nothing of lobotomy, is to be deplored. These methods, extreme examples of man's inhumanity to man, can be countered by showing the rapidity in which knowledgeable therapeutic dialogue can bring about far better results with no physical harm to the patient.

It is heartening that after 40 years of research and treating and teaching there is an ever-increasing flow of colleagues using Direct Psychoanalysis. I do not deny that the critics of conventional psychoanalysis have made out a sound case for their hostility. I do feel, however, that throwing out the concepts and contributions of Freud is analogous to throwing out the baby with the bathwater.

I am as critical of my psychoanalytic colleagues who sit by and do nothing more than become a mirror reflecting the patient's behavior as I am of those who use the physical therapies so thoughtlessly and uselessly. While at this point in my life I cannot take on the huge task of training that is required, I envision a future in which psychoanalysts are trained to do the things that are possible for them to do and a psychoanalytic peace corps of assistant therapists is also trained. They could then perhaps undertake the herculean task of dealing with the problems that exist in state hospitals, where 12,000 patients become the responsibility of a handful of doctors who themselves are hardly equipped to treat even one patient.

In Direct Psychoanalysis, we consider man's humanity to man to be a medicine.

REFERENCES

Bibliography of the literature on direct psychoanalysis. Doylestown, PA: The Direct Psychoanalytic Institute.

English, O. S. (1960). Clinical observations on direct analysis. *Comprehensive Psychiatry, 1,* 156–163. Abstracted by D. Prager (1961). *Psychological Abstracts, 35,* 510. Reprinted with revisions (1961) in O. S. English, W. W. Hampe Jr., C. L. Bacon, & C. F. Settlage (Eds.). *Direct analysis and schizophrenia.* New York: Grune & Stratton.

Gross, Martin L. (1978). *The psychological society.* New York: Random House.

Rosen, J. N. (1945). The treatment of schizophrenic psychosis by direct analytic therapy. *Psychiatric Quarterly.*

Rosen, J. N. (1953). *Direct analysis: Selected papers.* Doylestown, PA: The Doylestown Foundation.

Rosen, J. N. (1962). *Direct psychoanalytic psychiatry.* New York: Grune & Stratton.

Rosen, J. N. (1968). *Selected papers on direct psychoanalysis, Vol. 2.* New York: Grune & Stratton.

Salter, A. (1972). *The case against psychoanalysis.* New York: Harper & Row.

Scheflen, A. E. (1961). *A psychotherapy of schizophrenia: Direct analaysis.* Springfield, IL: Charles C. Thomas.

Chapter 17

EIDETIC PSYCHOTHERAPY

ANEES A. SHEIKH and CHARLES S. JORDAN

I suppose that I overuse the word unique *in reference to the various systems in this book, but all of the chapters are unique. There are other unique systems that I have not considered including; an example is Past Lives Therapy, the premise of which seemed to me to be absurd. However, a good many of the chapters are very different from anything that the typical, well-trained, eclectic, conservative therapist (as I view myself, incidentally) has experienced. Among these are Focusing, Holistic Education, Interpersonal Process Recall, Morital Naikan, Natural High, and Primary Relationship. Eidetic Psychotherapy joins this distinguished list.*

The report by Anees Sheikh and Charles Jordan is based on a truly unique conceptualization of what is wrong with people who are maladjusted and how to make readjustments. This chapter should be read in conjunction with Shorr's Psycho-Imagination Therapy and Iberg's Focusing. In each case, the emphasis is on the inner experience, the inmost aspect of the individual, and the therapists' behaviors are directed to helping the individual cure himself from within. I believe that most people new to the concept of Eidetics will be gratified to learn about this truly innovative method of psychotherapy.

Eidetic Psychotherapy is based on the elicitation and manipulation of eidetic images that are posited to act as the self-organizing nuclei in the psyche, to direct personality development, and to restore mind-body wholeness. They are a self-motivated, affect-laden imagery phenomenon with a visual core to which somatic and meaning components are attached. This tridimensional unity displays certain lawful tendencies toward change. The behavior of eidetics is purported to have specific meaningful relations to psychological processes. Every significant event in the developmental course of individuals implants an eidetic in their system. Eidetics are considered to be bipolarly configurated, involving ego-positive and ego-negative elements of the experience. It is believed that among other things, a quasi separation of the visual cue from other components, fixation on the negative pole of the eidetic, or repression of a significant experience can lead to a variety of symptoms. Eidetic therapists mainly aim to revive the tridimensional unity, shift attention to the neglected pole, and to uncover appropriate healthful experiences through eidetic progression. When original wholeness of the psyche has been mobilized, the therapeutic goal set by Eidetic Therapy is achieved.

HISTORY

Precursors

The early work on eidetic imagery was done largely at the Marburg Institute of Psychology in Germany under E. R. Jaensch in the early 1900s. The Marburg eidetic theory was developed out of experiments in which actual single external objects were presented through single exposures and the subjects projected the resultant images on an external background, usually a gray screen.

The eidetic, as defined by the Marburg School, consisted of a vivid visual image of a presented figure, which usually lingered on for a duration, localized in a space in front of the eyes, positive in color, and usually on the plane where the original figure appeared. The capacity to project such an eidetic was considered to be a rare quality possessed by some children but only a few adults with "photographic" memories. These *eidetikers* could scan the figure they projected continuously during inspection without any interference with the production of an eidetic image. Scanning was considered necessary to generate an image of the entire figure. Upon removal of the actual figure, they could continue to scan their image without loss of details (Ahsen, 1977a; Jaensch, 1930).

In contrast to this type of eidetic imagery, which has been labeled *typographic,* Müller (1826), Allport (1924), and Ahsen (1965) discussed a form of eidetic imagery that has been termed *structural.* It is internal and spontaneously evoked in all individuals. This type of image had also been reported in the Hindu tradition of Vedas and Tantras (Avalon, 1913; Müller, 1888). The internal eidetic is defined as

> a normal subjective visual image which is experienced with pronounced vividness: although not necessarily evoked at the time of the experience by an actual situation, it is seen inside of the mind or outside in the literal sense of the word, and this seeing is accompanied by certain somatic events as well as a feeling of meaning; the total experience in all its dimensions excludes the possibility that it is pathological. (Ahsen, 1977b, p. 6).

Allport's (1924) account supports this position. He stated that this category of images "should be understood to exclude both pathological hallucinations and dream images, and to admit those spontaneous images of phantasy which, though possessed of perceptual character, cannot be said to be literally revivals or restorations of any specific previous perception" (Allport, 1924, p. 100).

Beginnings

Akhter Ahsen was the first to apply the concepts of internal eidetics to a system of psychotherapy. Allport (1924) had laid the groundwork by restoring recognition of the central role of internal eidetics as a normal developmental phenomenon in all children rather than an ontogenetically archaic precursor of memory. However, he failed to recognize the continuing importance of eidetics in adults, perhaps because of his lack of clinical experience with an adult population. Ahsen filled in this important gap. He arrived at an understanding of the role of internal eidetics in consciousness through predominately three avenues: first, via mythic imagery of an eidetic nature that served as a guide in his own personal life; second, through his scholarly knowledge of the role of internal imagery in the evolution of human consciousness as reflected in the psychological, anthropological, and literary works of the East and West; and third, through his observations of the role of the naturally occurring eidetic imagery in symptom formation and resolution in his patients. Ahsen began formulating the concepts of Eidetic Psychotherapy in the late 1950s while in Pakistan. His first systematic presentation of the concepts appeared in 1965. This was followed by a more comprehensive presentation in 1968. In these first two publications Ahsen outlined a theory of personality development and therapeutic change. At the center of this system stand eidetic images, which he claims to have both a genetic and a developmental origin. The genetic eidetic will be discussed later.

The developmental eidetic image is affect-laden, vivid, repeatable, and universally present. This image pertains to key memories and fantasies associated with basic growth and conflict situations. When this image is elicited, it spontaneously progresses in an independent fashion beyond the bounds of voluntary control. Repeated evocation of this image leads to bypassing resistances and directing the image toward core problems in a self-organizing fashion (Ahsen, 1972, 1974).

The developmental eidetic represents an organismic event made up of a *visual* component—the image (I); a *somatic* pattern—a set of bodily reactions (S); and a *meaning,* including feelings (M). Ahsen refers to this tripartite structure as the eidetic complex, or ISM. The ISM is a semipermanent structure representing developmental events of highly positive or negative emotional value.

While this eidetic is vulnerable to the distortions of the memory process, that is, to fragmentation and overlay of several images, it can be made to regain the clarity through repeated evocation. The eidetic is not necessarily isomorphic with any external event, but is rather a representation of an experience, inclusive of the event and the individual's full-scale reaction to it.

Wilder Penfield's (1959) neurological work lends evidence for internal mental images that function in the same manner as Ahsen's ISM. During the course of brain surgery, Penfield observed that there were areas in the cerebral cortex from which a record of the past could be retrieved when stimulated by an electrode. The patients, under local anesthesia, were able to report with full consciousness and high fidelity details of recorded events within the brain. Penfield stated: "It is as though a wire recorder or a strip of cinematographic film with sound track had been set in motion within the brain. The sights and sounds, and the thoughts, of a former day passed through the man's mind again" (Penfield, 1959, p. 1719).

Both Ahsen and Penfield appear to be describing the same phenomenon: Both deal with internally evoked experiential pictures; both rely on repeated evocation of the problem experiences for elucidation, progressive evolvement, and understanding of the experience; both consider interpretation and change a natural and inalienable part of the reported experiential pictures; both stress the vividness of the image; both have observed that the image has somatic components and attributed meanings, including feeling states; both report the repeatability of the image and the progressive clarity of the image upon repetition. Also, both Ahsen and Penfield agree that the reports of internal images do not necessarily correspond to actual external events; rather, they represent a hybrid produced by a combination of the external events and the psychic events. Both men appear to be interested primarily in the function of the image for the individual rather than in trying to separate fact from fiction on the basis of rationality or irrationality.

CURRENT STATUS

In late 1960s and early 1970s practitioners of diverse persuasions (see Sheikh, 1978) began to herald Ahsen's Eidetic Psychotherapy as a truly innovative, new approach. G. E. W. Scobie (1974, p. 16) referred to Eidetic Psychotherapy as "one of the most significant developments yet to emerge in psychotherapy since Freud's psychoanalysis," and A. A. Lazarus (1972, p. vii) called Ahsen's work "a milestone in the evolution of a truly integrative and comprehensive system of effective psychotherapy." He further observed that "compared to Akhter's penetrating analysis of imagery formation and eidetic processes, all other clinical uses of imagery appear singularly embryonic" (1972, p. v). More recently, Thomas Hanna stated that eidetic psychotherapy is "a major innovation in the traditions of psychotherapy that is as neurologically informed as it is humanistically and holistically conceived." Eidetic psychotherapy, he continued, "is emphatically *not* a new wrinkle in psychotherapy. It is in fact, a new psychotherapy" (Hanna, 1979, p. 48).

Ahsen outlined the theory and technique of Eidetic Psychotherapy in three major books, *Basic Concepts in Eidetic Psychotherapy* (1968), *Eidetic Parents Test and Analysis* (1972), and *Psycheye: Self-Analytic Consciousness* (1977a). In addition, numerous articles and books by Ahsen and others, published in various parts of the world, review or extend the theory and application of Eidetic Psychotherapy.

THEORY

Origins of Personality

Ahsen's eidetic theory of personality is based upon the assumption that within the individual there is a "biolatent" or genetically endowed tendency toward wholeness. The eidetic image is posited as the synthesizing nucleus within the mind that preserves the encoded descriptions of positive life impressions. Ahsen states: "When a life activity has been traumatically mutilated its original is still available whole and complete in the encoded cell in the form of an arrested picture . . . which can be rejuvenated" (Ahsen, 1977a, p. 51). Hence, the eidetic theory of personality development is based on a biological model of encoded holograms that comprise a library of internal eidetic images. The eidetic image, whether of a genetic or an acquired origin, becomes the transforming lens through which the processes of image object relations, memories, sensations, feelings, and meaning are transmuted, synthesized, and encoded.

Ahsen's notion of the innate biolatent potential of the ISM resembles the concepts of innate releasing mechanism (IRM) and innate motor patterns as defined by ethologists. In discussing the concept of an innate releasing schema in the central nervous system, Konrad Lorenz states: "The term schema is misleading, to the extent that it easily gives the false impression that the organism innately possesses an overall picture of an object or situation, whereas in reality, the releasing mechanism never gives rise to more than one quite specific response" (1971, p. 127). Lorenz implies that some visual cue, though not a complete pictorial representation of an external object, may be involved in the IRM. The IRM is triggered by a "releaser" or orienting response in a particular sensory modality, which serves as a stimulus–transmission mechanism. In regard to the importance of visual releasers in humans, Lorenz states:

> They are more interesting because the innate releasing mechanisms which respond to them are by far the most differentiated among those so far known. Nowhere is the function of the innate releasing mechanisms as single lock of the response and that of the releaser as the appropriate key so clearly analyzable. (Lorenz, 1971; p. 141).

The selectivity of the IRM serves to ensure a biologically appropriate response for a given time, place, and species.

While Ahsen's ISM is not necessarily dependent on external stimuli for evocation, there are many similarities in the internally selective nature of the ISM and IRM. Both the ISM and IRM, when paired with an appropriate external stimulus, result in positive social and evolutionarily adaptive behavior. The ethologists, as well as Ahsen, believe that many social behaviors are guided by the innate parallel processing of the central nervous system and somatic cue functions. The notion of a necessary and sufficient external stimulus to evoke an innate central nervous system and paired somatic response, which occurs, for instance, in the smiling responses in human infants, also is part of both theories. A single visual cue or movement may trigger a complex instinctual response in animals, and it may also do so in humans; Ahsen cites many examples where a familiar object or gesture leads the individual to operate as if the part were the whole.

There are two major differences in Ahsen's and the ethologists' theories: First, the innate ISM in eidetic theory serves as both the IRM and releaser, while these two mechanisms are defined as independent processes by ethologists; second, the internal image has primacy in the ISM, while external stimuli and innate somatic patterns called releasers have primacy in triggering the IRM.

Image Object Theory of Object Relations

Normal development, according to eidetic theory, is a product of the interaction between innate biological images and the historical images.

> In eidetic theory of object relations, it is assumed that an intrapsychic image object is constitutionally present in the organism and experientially present in the consciousness of the child. Even when not seen explicitly by the child, the image object is latently present and becomes accessible when the potential matures with time. When the "reality" ministration or the external mother performs an activity in conformity with the genetic code (e.g., nursing at the breast), it confirms the original image effect, giving it a memory counterpart which then appears in the historical context. Thus, within this theory, the parental images are treated as a paradigm of primary image objects. (Dolan, 1977, p. 221)

Ahsen's "image object" theory of object relations diametrically opposes the analytical view of "object image" and mental functions. Psychoanalytical object relations theory proposes that the infant starts from chaos and requires parental introjects to establish reality orientation; Ahsen (1977a), conversely, emphasizes the importance of inner structures over the outside stimuli.

Psychical Dialectics and Personality Change

Personality development, according to Ahsen, involves a dialectical interaction between the forces of equilibrium and disequilibrium around the bipolar features of mental life. In normal development, the ISM exhibits a bipolar nature that creates "psychical dialectics" between a distinctly positive image and an associated negative image. As time passes, the favorite interpretation of the percept becomes confirmed and emotionally cathected, while the other pole is "dessociated." This dialectical nature of the eidetic is the pivotal point for a healthy development as well as the basis for symptom formation. Dessociation implies a temporary and retrievable loss, while the analytical concept of dissociation implies that the material is repressed and unavailable.

The explanation for image bipolarity and a dialectical process leading to a semipermanent monopolar configuration lies in psychic economics that serve both the equilibrium and nonequilibrium needs of the individual. To maximally utilize the available psychic energy and to accomplish memory storage in an efficient manner, the mind reduces the bipolar configuration of the ISM to a monopolar visual image temporarily dessociated from the somatic and meaning elements in the original ISM and stored as a point of light. This eidetic image reduced to a point of light can be repeatedly evoked to retrieve the unity of the ISM.

Ahsen believes that the avoidance tendencies of the ego, guided by the reality principle, possibly lead to symptom formation and rigid character structure. Psychically, the development and preservation of self-concepts and identity generated by the ego require that the image pole creating the most cognitive dissonance within the existing personal constructs be ignored or actively rejected. Therefore, confirming one of the poles leads to identity formation through the clustering of internally consistent images. These clusters become the basis of the individual's constructs, or traits, that lead to the modus operandi for selective attention, ego defenses, and more complex patterns of personality. While personality development guided by the rational decisions of the ego has tremendous adaptive value, the costs of linear rationality, used to excess, can be great in terms of lost flexibility and creativity. The adaptive functions of the linear, equilibrium-fixated ego need to be balanced by a nonlinear, nonequilibrium mechanism of self-renewal.

Nonequilibrium forces favor a transition state between the two stable states: the monopolar eidetic image associated with semipermanent personality structures on the one hand, and the bipolar eidetic image associated with the original experience on the other. In close parallel with the nonequilibrium thermodynamics of Prigogine and Nicolis (1972), it is suggested that the dynamic eidetic nucleus has properties that "perturbate" these transition states and result in higher levels of organization within the personality. Thus, the eidetic image may serve as Prigogine's "dissipative structure" that results from "order through fluctuations" and cannot be explained by an equilibrium-seeking tendency of the individual alone.

Thus the "dissipative" nature of the eidetic image may answer the question posed by Panagiotou and Sheikh (1974): How are old ISMs broken up and new ones created, to avoid inflexible stereotyped generalization of old response patterns? Futhermore, a new ISM created by this process progresses to a stimulation of the dissipative creative properties of a whole sequence of other meaningfully related eidetic images. The orderly progression of this sequence results in the creation of numerous new ISMs and a reordering of existing ones. Through this nonlinear, nonrational process, personality structures are rendered flexible and free to respond to the ever changing new demands of a dynamic flow of life within and without the individual.

Pensinger and Paine (1978) suggest that Karl Pribram's neural holograms may be dissipative structures that account for J. H. Schultz's "autogenic discharge" activity, which leads to deautomization of the automotized or semipermanent structures of the personality. While Pribram's neural hologram (1971) seems to explain the manner in which eiditic images are stored, ordered, retrieved, and reordered, Ahsen is careful to avoid a reductionistic neurological view of the eidetic image's structure and function. The concept of the retrieval of the entire hologram from a part of it seems to best correspond to one of Ahsen's "magical laws" of the psyche—that is, *part is whole*. Ahsen gives preeminence to these magical laws of the mind at the expense of rational and reductionistic approaches to understanding the manner in which personality change occurs.

Magical Laws of the Psyche

Ahsen arrived at a group of magical laws of the psyche on the basis of his clinical experience, his anthropological study of magical thinking, and his study of superstition in various cultures. These magical laws of the psyche are: (1) part is whole; (2) contact is unification; (3) imitation is reality; and (4) wish is action. The last three laws are subcategories of the first. Ahsen offers the following brief examples of how these magical laws operate symbolically in everyday activity: (1) I press a switch to put on electricity in the whole house—part is whole; (2) I hold my friend close to me to express my feelings of union—contact is unification; (3) I consult the road map when I go on a drive—imitation is reality; (4) I cannot punish somebody physically, but I wish he would drop dead—wish is action.

Personality Multiples

Ahsen gives every significant ISM the status of a minipersonality, which he calls a "personality multiple": "Under the magical principles every significant state turns out to be active in its own right, seeking its own direction and destiny" (1968, p. 32). Thus, one's identity is not viewed as a rationally and logically organized whole.

> It is Mr. X's one image at a particular time when he was feeling or doing something bearing relevance to his problems of existence. As he was virtually involved tens of thousands of times, he has generated an equal number of personality multiples along this line of action. All these personality multiples are now living, feeling and breathing in him, contending toward the same old aims they completed or left unfinished. They variously live the lives they once incarnated while something in this individual tries to force an illusory unity among them. (Ahsen, 1968, p. 141).

The millions of personality multiples that make up the personality are shaped out of self and others as viewed through parents, brothers and sisters, relatives, animals, and inanimate objects. According to Ahsen, the individual

> formulates these personality multiples, first of all in a relationship to the mother. Her various significant aspects are welded with relevant visual cues. The personality multiple formed in brothers and sisters usually represents themes of jealousy and death. Significant dresses worn by brothers and sisters under typical situations come to represent these themes. . . . Personality multiples projected in the father usually deal with themes of protection and discipline or his relationship with mother and problems of weaning and transition to his liberating image in the psyche. . . . Personality multiples may also be found projected in various space settings meaningful to the individual. They can be detected in various rooms of the house where the individual lived during early and late childhood. (1968, pp. 142–143)

The personality multiples continue to function unless they are resolved through growth experience or therapy. As discussed above, the eidetic image serves as the "dissipative structure" leading to transition states between bipolar and monopolar states that promote the discharge of both the positive and the negative emotions associated with a personality multiple, or ISM. This results in the neutralization of the emotion of the old personality multiple and the creation of a higher level of organization or a more expansive personality multiple around a new nuclear eidetic.

Ahsen states that the form of identity based on personality multiples "has no enemies in the repressed to fear and no rationalizations to defend constantly, it being a manifestation of release and openness. It is powerful and dynamic, fearless and all-embracing; it honors categories of living above categories of reasoning" (1968, p. 34). As a therapeutic focus, these personality multiples are excellent vehicles for analysis, communication, and catharsis.

METHODOLOGY[1]

In eidetic analysis the diagnostic and therapeutic procedures are inseparably intertwined. Eidetic analytic methods help not only in understanding the underlying dynamics but also in drawing up the therapeutic plan.

Eidetic analysis by Ahsen and by others who have followed his system indicates that symptoms are largely

---

[1] This section is a slightly modified version of a portion of "Eidetic psychotherapy," by Anees A. Sheikh, 1978, in J. L. Singer and K. S. Pope (Eds.), *The Power of Human Imagination,* New York: Plenum. Included with the permission of the publisher.

caused either by dessociation of components, by fixation on the negative pole, or by a partial or complete repression of a significant positive or negative experience. Consequently, the aim of Eidetic Therapy is achieved mainly by the revival of the tripartite unity, by a shift of the ego's attention to the neglected positive pole, which brings about a more balanced and realistic appraisal of the experience, or by the uncovering of the repressed experience through progression of eidetic imagery. Since Ahsen considers an eidetic event in its full intensity to be the psychic equivalent of the corresponding actual event, to reexperience personality multiples in the form of eidetics is to reexperience the individual's history, which thus becomes available for change through eidetic methodology.

There are three main levels in the eidetic psychotherapeutic process. The first level deals with symptoms of a psychosomatic, hysterical, or phobic nature. Next is the developmental level, which pertains primarily to the widespread problems developed in early life with reference to parents. Ahsen has developed two major eidetic tests, the Age Projection Test (1968) and the Eidetic Parents Test (1972), that form the basis for diagnosis and therapy at each of the first two states respectively. Ahsen also reports a third universal symbolic level of analysis that may help individuals to attain a deeper understanding and integration of meanings of psychic contents. However, as he has not yet presented this third level of analysis in detail in his published works, it will not be discussed herein.

Eidetic Psychotherapy begins with symptom composition, which is accomplished through a structured interview during which time the therapist tries to determine the exact nature of the physical (e.g., "I ache all over") as well as the psychological (e.g., "I can't think straight") elements of the symptom complex. The patient is also questioned about the worries or concerns that he or she may entertain about the symptom (e.g., "I am afraid of going crazy"). Worries and concerns about various parts of the body are also recorded. The symptom is composed completely in the language of the patient. Subsequent to the symptom composition, the therapist is ready to administer the Age Projection Test.

The Age Projection Test

The therapist asks the patient to give his first, middle, and last names, nicknames, and any other names by which he or she has been called since childhood, for these names are assumed to refer to an individual's various identities. Next the patient is asked to pay relaxed attention to what the therapist says. The patient is informed that when the therapist repeats certain words over and over again, he will see an image of himself somewhere in the past:

The salient features of the symptom discovered during symptom composition are now reiterated to the patient in his own words in a repetitious manner. In the course of this repetition, the patient is addressed by his various names alternately. This repetition artificially activates the symptom to an almost unbearable acuteness. At this point five seconds of total silence are allowed to elapse. Suddenly the therapist starts talking about the time when the patient was healthy and happy. As the therapist talks about health in those areas where the symptom now exists, the patient spontaneously forms a self-image subliminally. The patient is now suddenly asked to project a self-image and describe the following: (a) the self-image itself; (b) the clothing on the self-image; (c) the place where it appears; (d) the events occurring during the age projected in the self-image; (e) the events occurring during the year following the age projected in the image. (Dolan & Sheikh, 1977, p. 599)

This procedure usually uncovers an event that precipitated the symptom or that began a series of events that eventually led to symptom formation. Once the self-image related to this event is formed, the patient is asked to project it repeatedly until it becomes clear, and then he is interrogated further about the critical period.

If no relevant event is discovered, the last portion of the test, called "Theme Projection," is administered. The patient is told to see the self-image standing before the parents, crying to provoke pity and love. Then the self-image takes off one article of clothing and throws it down before the parents, saying, "Take it away, I don't want to wear it." The image proceeds: One of the parents picks the clothing up and deposits it somewhere. The patient sees where it has been placed, what objects appear to surround it, and what objects stand out. He is then asked to report any direct impressions or memories concerning the object that stands out most in his image.

Alternatively, an important image may evolve spontaneously during the dialogue on imagery between therapist and patient. Ahsen reports, however, that when the Age Projection Test is administered, the meaning and origin of a somatic or quasi-somatic symptom usually become evident. Based on information revealed by the test, a therapeutic image is then constructed, and the patient is asked to project the new image repeatedly. This therapeutic image may work in a variety of ways. It derives its therapeutic effectiveness from the four principles of magical functioning. Through these symbolic mechanisms, the image may prompt the release of repressed responses, lead to catharsis of accumulated affect, symbolically satisfy unfulfilled wishes, or correct an imbalanced ego interpretation of events by focusing on hitherto neglected aspects of the experience (Panagiotou & Sheikh, 1974).

In the area of psychosomatic and hysterical symptoms, stunning successes in an astoundingly brief period have been reported using the Age Projection Test. Numerous case histories are now available (Ahsen, 1968; Dolan & Sheikh, 1977; Sheikh, 1978). As these cases demonstrate, the symptom frequently is dispelled during the first session. Even when this occurs, further analysis of basic developmental trends may be undertaken through another important imagery test developed by Ahsen (1972), the Eidetic Parents Test.

Eidetic Parents Test

In Eidetic Therapy special significance is attached to the patterns of interaction between the patient and his or her parents and the patient's perception of polarities that existed in their relationship. The Eidetic Parents Test (EPT) is designed specifically to uncover eidetics in these areas. The test has been shown to reveal to a significant extent the quality of the familial relationships and their predominant positive and negative themes. This test is central to eidetic procedure and provides not only the means for identifying areas of conflict, but also the format for therapeutic procedure. The test involves a systematic scrutiny of features of the parental images to determine the exact nature of the interparental and parent-child patterns of interaction. The entire EPT consists of a total of 30 situation images in which various aspects of the parents and the parental relationships are visualized. The first item on the test proceeds in the following manner:

> Picture your parents in the house where you lived most of the time, the house that gives you feeling of home.
>
> Where do you see them?
>
> What are they doing?
>
> How do you feel when you see the images?
>
> Any reactions or memories connected with the picture? (Ahsen, 1972, p. 52)

The test includes standard verbatim instructions for presenting the stimuli. Ahsen has left nothing unspecified regarding the administration of the EPT, nor about the constitution of acceptable responses. After the participant has been introduced to eidetics with a brief practice image, the test is administered in a "piecemeal, phrase by phrase enunciation of each item."

Every image is to be repeatedly projected until its essential elements are sharpened and separated from its vague or changing aspects. The participant is encouraged to acquaint himself thoroughly with the eidetic image before he is asked to describe it. It is essential to the effectiveness of the EPT that the participant see the image over and over again, and describe his visual experience thoroughly. The participant is instructed not to force any aspects of the image, but to allow it to grow without any interference. He is encouraged to describe the image in "positive declarative statements."

It should be noted that eidetic responses, unlike dreamlike reveries, are not narrative. The repetitious, piecemeal projection of segments of the response is an important methodological feature in handling eidetics. It helps to construct the rigid sequence of what defines an eidetic area. Any attempt to project in a smooth, narrative fashion leads to a fictional response; the true eidetic, however, is not fictional. It is real: a true projection.

Verbal EPT stimuli are highly structured. The initial presentation of each stimulus permits only a brief response. Repeated projections allow no more latitude in responding; the image unfolds only under the guiding questions of the therapist. This limiting nature of the stimuli and the directiveness of their presentation have afforded Ahsen a rigid basis for comparison between individuals and the possibility of using comparative data for establishing interpretive guidelines.

The faithful reporting of eidetic responses is aided by the fact that they are repeatable to the last detail. The reporting by the patient, however, is complicated by a number of items, and the first response is rarely a pure eidetic. Ahsen has given the name *eidetic matrix* to the group of phenomena elicited during EPT administration. These include (1) the first response, (2) the primary response, (3) the secondary response, (4) the interjected response, (5) the underlying primary response, and (6) the overt behavior.

The first response reflects the participant's initial reaction to the instruction. This may take a variety of forms, including resistance, and, of course, will not always be an eidetic image. The primary response is the true eidetic. It never fails to be repeatable and tends to recur in an almost mechanical manner. It is usually bright and clear, rich in emotional accompaniment, and has a meaning or set of meanings that the individual can usually recognize with some certainty. Any portion of the primary response may be repeated for elaboration or detailed examination. When repeated, it elicits feelings and memories, and after many repetitions, which may be punctuated by resistances and other types of behavior, it may spontaneously be replaced by a new primary that, in turn, through repetition, may give rise to still another primary. The primaries arising out of repetition of the first primary are termed *underlying primaries*. The secondary response, interjected response, and overt behavior are types of reaction that frequently occur between primaries. After a few repetitions, the primary response may suddenly be replaced by material only superficially related to it, such as elements of the individual's ordinary fancy. Such responses are termed *secondary* and are usually used as a defense. Sometimes the individual punctuates the primary response with significant verbal or fantasy material. Ahsen calls this behavior an interjected response and points out that it occasionally contains important depth material of use in structuring therapy. Overt behavior refers primarily to the individual's facial expressions, postures, and other acts that express his attitude toward the imagery experience: For example, he may appear interested, indifferent, or irritated.

Repeated projection of the primary response along with the resultant affective elaboration and eventual replacement of one primary eidetic by another and then another is the crux of the full-length diagnostic-cum-therapeutic technique. It is through this process that actual therapeutic progress is made. The reader will recall that the primary eidetic is accompanied by somatic patterns and affective significations. Repetition of the primary eidetic image results in a fuller experience of these somatic and affective aspects along with the visual component; this process implies the acquisition of a degree of conscious recognition of the connections involved, as well as a rather thorough working over of the affective reactions. Only when this process has been carried to completion for one eidetic does the therapist begin with another. Thus, each progression or change represents a step forward, a deepening and broadening of understanding and assimilation, an illumination of another aspect of the complex problem that the individual is now prepared to examine.

The experience that emerges in the eidetic treatment often is at variance with the patient's conscious views. For instance, his experience of a parent via the eidetic imagery may differ radically from his conscious opinion of this parent. Generally, this consciousness-imagery-gap (C-I-G), or distortion, is caused by the patient's need to repress a painful experience. Or the distortion may be the result of the parent's brainwashing of the patient.

Once the C-I-G has been uncovered, the next step is to challenge the patient's beliefs and attitudes by confronting him with the contrary perceptions revealed in his eidetics. It is vital to take note of the patient's reactions to this procedure. *Does he deny the existence of a gap, and thus reject change?* If he resists, *what is the form of his resistance? Does he make an effort to bridge the gap? Is he eager to learn more about the unknown within himself?* The nature of the patient's reactions to the C-I-G clarifies the problem under investigation (Ahsen, 1972).

Recent developments in Eidetic Therapy include Ahsen's (1977a) positive group methods, which can be applied to couples and families. The group methods have been used for inpatients and outpatients (Twente, Turner, & Haney, 1978). Basically this procedure involves a group empathy process by which all members simultaneously work on their own eidetic experiences and offer empathetic responses to the other members' images based on the adoption of the others' content.

There are numerous other eidetic procedures that are beyond the scope of this chapter. Interested readers are referred to Ahsen's books.

APPLICATIONS

Eidetic diagnostic and therapeutic procedures can be utilized with all individuals who possess a minimum capacity to form eidetic images. They are best prepared for eidetic work by being exposed to positive images of parents or parent surrogates; for it is important that they are assured they were loved and accepted when they were children, before exploring negative images. Individuals who persistently resist eidetic images are usually those who are phobic of inner life and emotions. To prepare them for eidetic work, relaxation training and positive nature images have proven to be beneficial.

Patients who report no images can be aided in image formation by image sculpturing (Jordan, 1975, February), a process based on recruitment of sensory data from various sensory modalities. One patient who reported no images showed nystagmus of her eyes when closed, a symptom characteristic of individuals who are fearful of their internal states. To aid her in image formation, she was instructed to visualize the activity she enjoyed most. She chose making love to her husband. Instructed to relive any sensory experience involving contact with her husband, she reported first the tactile sensation of her hands on her husband's hairy chest and then the smell of his body. After repetition of these sensory experiences, an image of her husband's face appeared spontaneously, but in tunnel vision. She saw only a vague round image of his nose and eyes and part of his mouth. After further repetition and after she had been instructed to attend to details, the face appeared whole and clear, and this image became progressively richer.

According to the eidetic diagnostic classification system, symptoms often represent a disordered ISM, that is, MIS, MSI, SIM, and SMI. With patients for whom words and meanings (MIS, MSI) or somatization and impulsive discharge of bodily tensions (SIM, SMI) have primacy over images, the therapist enhances the defensive structures and then allows images to appear spontaneously. Once the image grows out of an ooververbal description or a somatic response, it is repeated many times, and the therapist points out the simultaneity of image, bodily response, and meaning, and the primacy of the image.

Individuals who are acutely psychotic are usually not capable of sustained focusing on eidetic images, and require supportive care and structure before beginning eidetic work on their own. Eidetic images have been used successfully in treating the extreme splitting and associational problems of schizophrenics, who are known to lack the ability to regenerate experience (Ahsen, 1977a).

A continuous series of developmental eidetics over a fairly long period of time often reconstructs a schizophrenic's emotional life and stops and reverses the general splitting process (Sheikh & Panagiotou, 1975). When introduced in a timely manner, Eidetic Psychotherapy can be used successfully with almost all individuals to reevoke the natural flow of eidetic images.

The therapist encourages autonomy and merely serves as a guide in the patient's self-exploration. Initially, while teaching the dialectical method of eidetics, the therapist is quite directive, but the content for therapy flows directly from the patient's consciousness. Excessive transference and dependency are thwarted by the autocatalytic nature of eidetic work, which greatly accelerates therapy.

CASE EXAMPLE

Mr. Smith, a 34-year-old merchant seaman, suffered from panic attacks characterized by pains in his left shoulder and chest that radiated down his left arm, extreme palmar sweating, and hyperventilation. Frightening hypnagogiclike hallucinations and nightmares also plagued him. These symptoms had begun two years ago following an incident on board ship, in which he had attempted to rescue the first mate, whom he considered to be his closest friend. The rescue attempt was quite heroic: He entered the hull of the ship where his friend had been overcome by gas fumes and attached a harness for hoisting his friend. As he was losing consciousness himself, he heard a loud thud, which upon exploration turned out to have been caused by the falling of the mangled body of his friend. At this point he panicked and ran, but soon he was overcome by gas fumes and lost consciousness. He was rescued after a nearby ship furnished gas masks. After regaining consciousness, he and the body of his friend were removed by helicopter. He was hospitalized in a foreign port for a mild brain syndrome, attributed to the gas intoxication and his traumatic reaction. By this time, he had begun to blame himself for the death of this friend, even though he was told that the rope hoisting his friend had become snagged and severed during the attempt to pull him to the deck, and that he was in no way responsible for the unfortunate development. After a week's rest, he was flown to the United States where he underwent further hospitalization for his worsening traumatic reaction of quasipsychotic proportions, marked by nightmares, hallucinations, panic attacks, and self-blame.

While in the hospital, he also began having intrusive daytime reveries. He attempted to relive the accident and particularly to piece together his gas-induced semiconscious moments in the hull of the ship. His failures to reconstruct the accident led to an exacerbation of symptoms and the fixed resolution that he was responsible for his friend's death.

Over the next two years, he consulted three different psychiatrists and two physicians who prescribed muscle relaxants and antianxiety and antipsychotic medication; but none of these reduced his symptoms. During this period, he had tried to return to work on another ship, but he became phobic and incapacitated by panic attacks and was consequently removed from the ship. It is important to note that the panic attacks occurred not only in connection with the phobic stimulus of the ship, but also in other situations.

In the first session of Eidetic Therapy, his symptoms were defined by eliciting eidetic images associated with the accident. Relaxation training was implemented to reduce the extreme tensions, sweating, and hyperventilation episodes associated with his current panic state. Initially his effort was only partially and transiently successful in reducing the symptoms.

In the second session, the Age Projection Test was administered: First the symptoms around his phobia of being on board ship were exacerbated and then he was taken back to a time before the symptoms occurred. He recalled being at home in Jamaica when he was 15 years of age with his mother, combing her hair and pulling out her gray hair for her. When focusing on this image, he became deeply relaxed and the sweating subsided. When associated memories were elicited, he recalled his mother being driven from home by his father and his continuing loyalty to her. Subsequently he commented that he felt responsible for his mother's death. Although he had instructed the shipping company not to inform his mother of his accident, they had ignored his request. He felt certain that the bad news had hastened her death two months later. However, his wife related that his mother had been ill for a year before the accident and that she died six months after his accident. The patient also felt guilty because his extended hospitalization had prevented him from visiting his mother before her death. Although he experienced considerable guilt in regard to his mother, in this session he strongly denied that she had anything to do with his present symptoms. He missed his third appointment due to the increase of his somatic symptoms and the fear that he was going to have a heart attack. It was clear to the therapist that these worsening symptoms represented resistance to admitting the painful core problem: his guilt over his mother's death.

In the third session, the patient's resistance was directly interpreted for him, and he was challenged to experiment further with the positive calming image of combing his mother's hair and pulling out her gray hair. Upon the administration of this image, he again began to have symptom relief: His hands stopped sweating and his muscles began to relax, but the pain in the left side of his chest and in his left shoulder and arm continued. He then reported the image of visiting his mother's grave and talking with her, and in so doing, he developed the conviction that she forgave him for not being at her deathbed. Immediately another vague image appeared to him from a recurring dream in which he saw his mother standing at the foot of his bed, saying, "Keep up the good work, son, God loves you." He was asked to repeat this image and these words, but to see his real mother standing in front of him rather than the vague dream image. Upon doing so, all of the pain left first his chest, then his shoulder, arm, and hand, and he felt thoroughly relaxed. He was encouraged to repeat this image in order to see the connection between the positive image of his mother and the disappearance of his symptoms. After he had resolved his guilt over his mother's death, he was able to work through the guilt associated with the death of the first mate and the phobic images related to the ship. He was encouraged to use these positive images if the symptoms recurred. Several weeks later, none of the symptoms that had plagued him for two years had returned.

In this case, as in other cases of the treatment of phobias (Dolan & Sheikh, 1976), and psychosomatic problems (Ahsen, 1968; Sheikh, 1978), a follow-up one or two years later revealed no recurrence of symptoms.

This case graphically illustrates the speed with which the nonlinear process of eidetics identifies the core themes and leads to resolving phobic and panic reactions or other neurotic symptoms. It is to be noted that the patient's earlier attempts at self-treatment through distorted memories and reverie images had failed (Jordan, 1979). It is only through focusing on the eidetic image standing clearly alone or extracted from dreams, hallucinations, memories, and reveries that lasting symptom relief is achieved.

SUMMARY

Eidetic Psychotherapy represents the most systematic and precise use of the natural images of consciousness in rapidly resolving conflict and promoting creative changes in the personality. Eidetic methods have been successfully employed to treat a wide variety of problems. Psychosomatic disorders seem to respond particularly well to this approach (see Ahsen, 1968; Jordan, 1977; Sheikh, 1978; Sheikh, Richardson, & Moleski, 1979).

Individual and group eidetic therapy methods have also been used extensively by people for their own personal growth. Ahsen's book *Psycheye: Self-Analytic Consciousness* (1977a) represents the extension of his work in the direction of self-analysis and self-education. He states that "the center of creative and renewal activity in the individual is always his own self, and no high priest of any sort should be allowed to stand between him and that light" (p. vi).

At the core of this process of self-renewal is the eidetic image, which serves as a dissipative structure to promote higher levels of organization and creativity. The eidetic image serves not only to restore the unity of experience seen in the ISM (Image–Somatic pattern–Meaning), but also to dissipate and neutralize the old frozen structures, freeing the individual to respond to the here-and-now demands of life as directed by higher levels of consciousness. While unity is not found among the numerous personality multiples, it is found within the creative experience of the eidetic, which is a reflection of the total unity of consciousness at an ego-transcendent level. This represents the essence of Eidetic Therapy. The eidetic image is a stepping-stone to higher consciousness, a symbol in the service of transcending symbols.

REFERENCES

Ahsen, A. (1965). *Eidetic psychotherapy: A short introduction.* Lahore, Pakistan: Nai Mat Booat.

Ahsen, A. (1968). *Basic concepts in eidetic psychotherapy.* New York: Brandon House.

Ahsen, A. (1972). *Eidetic parents test and analysis.* New York: Brandon House.

Ahsen, A. (1974). Anna O.—Patient or therapist? An eidetic view. In V. Franks and V. Burtle (Eds.), *Women in therapy.* New York: Brunner/Mazel.

Ahsen, A. (1977a). *Psycheye: Self-analytic consciousness.* New York: Brandon House.

Ahsen, A. (1977b). Eidetics: An overview. *Journal of Mental Imagery, 1,* 5–38.

Allport, G. W. (1924). Eidetic imagery. *British Journal of Psychology, 15,* 99–120.

Avalon, A. (1913). *Tantra of the great liberation.* London: Luzac.

Dolan, A. T. (1977). Eidetic and general image theory of primary image objects and identification processes. *Journal of Mental Imagery, 2,* 217–228.

Dolan, A. T., & Sheikh, A. A. (1976). Eidetics: A visual approach to psychotherapy. *Psychologia, 19,* 210–219.

Dolan, A. T., & Sheikh, A. A. (1977). Short-term treatment of phobias through eidetic imagery. *American Journal of Psychotherapy, 31,* 595–604.

Hanna, T. (1979). Review of Ahsen's books. In *Somatics, 6,* 10–11.

Jaensch, E. R. (1930). *Eidetic imagery.* New York: Harcourt.

Jordan, C. S. (1975, February). *Image sculpturing.* Paper presented at the Eidetic Analysis Institute, Yonkers, NY.

Jordan, C. S. (1977). *The assertive person: Assertive training through group eidetics.* Paper presented at the American Group Psychotherapy Association Meeting, San Francisco.

Jordan, C. S. (1979). Mental imagery and psychotherapy: European approaches. In A. A. Sheikh & J. T. Shaffer (Eds.), *The potential of fantasy and imagination.* New York: Brandon House.

Lazarus, A. A. (1972). Preface. In A. A. Ahsen, *Eidetic parents test and analysis*. New York: Brandon House.

Lorenz, K. (1971). *Studies in animal and human behavior*. Cambridge, MA: Harvard University Press.

Müller, J. (1826). *Ueber die phantastischen Gesichtsercheinugen*. Coblenz, Germany: Holscher.

Müller, M. (1888). *Natural religion*. The Gifford lectures delivered before the University of Glasgow.

Panagiotou, N., & Sheikh, A. A. (1974). Eidetic psychotherapy: Introduction and evaluation. *International Journal of Social Psychiatry, 20*, 231–241.

Penfield, W. (1959). The interpretive cortex. *Science, 129*, 1719–1725.

Pensinger, W. L., & Paine, D. A. (1978). Deautomatization and the autogenic discharge. *Journal of Altered States of Consciousness, 3*(4), 325–335.

Pribram, K. H. (1971). *Languages of the brain: Experimental paradoxes and principles in neuropsychology*. Englewood Cliffs, NJ: Prentice-Hall.

Prigogine, I., & Nicolis, G. (1972). Thermodynamic theory of evolution. *Physics Today, 25*(11), 23–28.

Scobie, G. E. W. (1974). Book review Ahsen, A. Eidetic parents test and analysis, 1972. *Glasgow Journal of Psychology, 12,* 16.

Sheikh, A. A. (1978). Eidetic psychotherapy. In J. L. Singer & K. S. Pope (Eds.), *The power of human imagination*. New York: Plenum.

Sheikh, A. A., & Panagiotou, N. C. (1975). Use of mental imagery in psychotherapy: A critical review. *Perceptual and Motor Skills, 41*, 555–585.

Sheikh, A. A., Richardson, P., & Moleski, L. M. (1979). Psychosomatics and mental imagery. In A. A. Sheikh & J. T. Shaffer (Eds.), *The potential of fantasy and imagination*. New York: Brandon House.

Twente, G. E., Turner, D., & Haney, J. (1978). Eidetics in the hospital setting and private practice: A report on eidetic therapy procedures employed with 69 patients. *Journal of Mental Imagery, 2*, 275–290.

Chapter 18

ENCOURAGEMENT THERAPY

LEW LOSONCY

Several times I have indicated that there is a connection between a person's manifest personality and his theory of therapy. This is certainly the case with Lew Losoncy, who just bubbles with enthusiasm and who views the whole world with excitement.

According to Adlerian theory (and Losoncy, as well as myself and several contributors of this book, is an Adlerian), psychotherapy is mainly a matter of encouragement. Think of it. Is it not true that most people who come for psychotherapy are discouraged, disspirited, defeated, unsure of themselves? Is not fear the common enemy that all psychotherapists face? And is it not courage that we attempt to give people—courage to face life more bravely, to see things as they are, to measure themselves accurately?

The essence of this system of therapy is to give clients courage to take an optimistic stance. How Losoncy suggests it be done follows.

Encouragement Therapy is an optimistic and practical approach to developing responsible, confident, and courageous clients. The main hypothesis is that regardless of which approach therapists use, when all is said and done, the major reason why people change is because *they themselves* are motivated to change. The primary task in therapy then is to encourage the client's own willingness and determination to change. The raw material for therapy already exists in the client's assets, strengths, resources, and potentially positive life outlook; reorganization is what is required. *Reorganization is achieved through developing the client's perceptual alternatives.* With fresh perceptions of self, others, and reality, clients begin to recognize the relationship among 1) what they think; 2) what they tell themselves; 3) how they feel; and 4) how they act. This powerful discovery gives them a sense of internal unity, personal control, self-power, and motivation for positive movement. Encouragement Therapy incorporates elements from various schools of humanistic psychotherapies applied in unique ways in each phase of the therapeutic process.

HISTORY

Precursors

Bertrand Russell suggested that in the vast realm of the alive human mind there are no limitations. This panoramic vision of human possibilities inspires the thought that somewhere within the client's universe exists a most effective and efficient perceptual and behavioral alternative, regardless of current life circumstances. The therapist, or encourager, continually conveys the theme that the mere fact of being alive represents hope and the possibilities for courageous living. Courageous living reflects the personal belief "I will determine myself to accept those things that I *choose* not to change, to move toward changing those things I choose to change, and to choose my directions with efficiency and courage." This, of course, is recognized as a variation of a popular creed. "Choose" is more accurate than can or can't.

The value of courageous living has been addressed for centuries. The Stoics, about 2,000 years ago, set the stage for recognizing the importance of the "human viewer" in what has become known as the philosophy of phenomenology. The Stoic Epictetus concluded that "No man is free who is not master of himself." Discouraged people are not free, but rather are slaves to their own perceptual myopia. Encouragers help their clients to regenerate their perceptual and behavioral life alternatives to overcome their discouragement. Alternatives are the gifts of being human, yet these gifts are rarely appreciated by discouraged people who choose to function as part-time humans. The unlimited power of the courageous person to overcome current circumstances was further supported by Epictetus in his comment that "Men are not disturbed by things, only thinking makes it so." Later this theme was echoed by the Roman emperor Marcus Aurelius, who concluded that "No man is happy who does not make himself so."

The strongest voice for phenomenology appeared 18 centuries later in philosopher Immanuel Kant. Kant discussed the differences between noumena and phenomena. Noumena are things that exist on the outside of the mind. Phenomena, however, are what the mind eventually brings home from this complex arrangement of noumena. Thus, while an optimistic and a pessimistic perceiver may be exposed to the same noumena, each brings home a different phenomenon. And while both may be in error, it is ultimately the perceiver's phenomenology that influences behavior. It is this phenomenology that stimulates the interest of Encouragement Therapy.

Indebted to the contributions of the phenomenologists, Encouragement Therapy turned toward those writers emphasizing active self-determinism and personal responsibility. Alfred Adler, the most important precursor to Encouragement Therapy, wrote to a pupil:

> Do not forget the most important fact that not heredity and not environment are determining factors. Both are giving only the frame and the influences which are answered by the individual in regard to his styled creative power. (Ansbacher & Ansbacher, 1956, p. xxiv)

Encouragement Therapy also drew on the work of the existentialists. On this issue of personal responsibility, Sartre wrote that "Man is nothing else but what he makes of himself" (1957, p. 15). People are viewed as responsible creators of their feelings, thoughts, actions, and life meanings. The best guess of where a person really wants to be in life is where that person *is;* the final proof that the person wants to be somewhere else occurs at the moment that the person sets foot on the new ground (Losoncy, 1981). As Sartre asserted, "There is no reality except in action" (1957, p. 32). Courageous living is ultimately measured by action toward stated goals.

Beginnings

Personality theorist Robert White saw encouragement as the essential ingredient in any efficacious therapeutic process. This comment perhaps was influenced by Alfred Adler, who was the first to recognize the significance of encouragement as a therapeutic tool (1959). Even today the emphasis on encouragement in relationships maintains deep respect in the growing Adlerian following.

One of Adler's pupils, Rudolf Dreikurs, further detailed the techniques and process of encouragement (Dreikurs, 1968; Dreikurs & Grey, 1968; Dreikurs &

Soltz, 1967). Dreikurs continually spoke of the importance of encouragement. The first book devoted totally to encouragement was *Encouraging Children to Learn,* co-authored by Don Dinkmeyer and Rudolf Dreikurs in 1963. This book shows how the techniques of encouragement can be applied to enhance learning. Walter O'Connell writes, lectures, and conducts workshops on encouragement, providing some empirical support for its use (O'Connell, 1975; O'Connell & Bright, 1977). O'Connell concludes that encouragement is a lifelong process of expanding self-esteem and social interest. This writer wrote two books devoted solely to encouragement: *Turning People On: How to Be an Encouraging Person* (2000) and *What Is, Is: How to Accept What You Choose Not To Change* (1997) with Diane Losoncy. In essence, I explicated that the process of encouraging others and encouraging oneself is essentially the same. Dinkmeyer and I combined efforts to co-author *The Skills of Encouragement.* (1997), a phase-by-phase and skill-by-skill breakdown of the encouragement process.

Encouragement Therapy incorporates elements from different humanistic schools of psychotherapy. The first phase of encouragement is heavily steeped in the ideas of Carl Rogers (1961), and uses relationship-building skills such as empathy, genuineness, respect, and unconditionality. The second phase of encouragement, or client perceptual expansion, shows the influence largely of Alfred Adler (1959), Albert Ellis (1962), and Charles Zastrow (1979). The third, or action phase of encouragement, can be recognized as being similar to Reality Therapy (Glasser, 1965). The final phase of encouragement is client self-encouragement.

The complete roots and beginnings of encouragement are too numerous to mention, and perhaps even to be aware of. Encouragement Therapy's biggest contribution may be in putting elements of many therapies together in a way that is believed to lead most effectively to client responsibility, confidence, courage, and motivation to change.

CURRENT STATUS

The Center of Encouragement in Wyomissing, Pennsylvania is committed to: (1) the scientific study of encouragement; and (2) the teaching and practice of encouragement with individuals, groups, and ultimately, the total community.

Encouragement Therapy has grown out of the Encouragement Training Program offered at the institute. Encouragement Training is a skills approach to encouraging self and others.

One focus of Encouragement Training (ET) is on the many groups in the community that, despite touching many lives every day, have not been viewed as helping professions. As of this writing, for example, tens of thousands of hairstylists throughout North America have received Encouragement Training. In fact, Matrix Essentials, a beauty manufacturing company, has all of its employees learn encouragement. Other groups such as bank tellers, bartenders, secretaries, waitresses, and volunteers have experienced ET as well.

In those professions that are more traditionally viewed as helping professions, ET has recently received widespread popularity. In schools, for example, thousands of teachers, administrators, board members, students, custodians, and cafeteria workers have received ET.

In the criminal justice system, administrators, police officers, guards, caseworkers, social workers, and counselors, as well as prisoners, have been trained.

Encouragement therapists believe that, to have an impact, any program ultimately needs the involvement of the total community.

> If our ultimate goal is an encouraging society which will tap everyone's best—and to be encouraging means to be willing to give and take the best in human relationships—then everyone needs to be included, and no longer do the behavioral scientists have a right to hoard all of the human nourishment. (Losoncy, in development).

Encouragement Therapy is a more in-depth extension of Encouragement Training and is limited to those individuals who already have a background in education, counseling, social work, and related areas. Therapeutic training is conducted in conjunction with an agency, school, or organization.

THEORY

Discouraged people are viewed as being unmotivated to change rather than being incapable of change. The encouragement therapist recognizes that this immobilization makes sense in light of the client's total phenomenology. How can discouragement possibly make sense? First of all, there are many fringe benefits to immobilization, including the comfort found in routine. Change provokes uncertainty and is thus anxiety producing (May, 1977). A second fringe benefit includes social rewards, such as attention and sympathy that the discouraged person receives (Losoncy & Losoncy, 1998). Third, the client has been busy, perhaps for years, selectively gathering beliefs about self, others, and reality, both consciously and unconsciously to support his or her discouragement. It is these personal beliefs that play the song to which the person's emotions and actions dance.

To remain discouraged, the client needs to keep two themes alive. The first is "I am not responsible for my life." The second is "I am a worthless and incapable person who has no assets, strengths, or resources."

This first theme, *irresponsibility,* is seen when the client continually blames other people, the world, or the past for his or her current life. We (1998) distinguish four types of blame: group blame (e.g., the Russians, Society, the Americans); person blame (e.g., "He hit me first"); thing blame (e.g., "This weather makes me miserable"); and self-blame (e.g., "Because I did a rotten thing, I am a rotten person"). Responsibility, as opposed to blaming, involves taking the position that "I am responsible for moving in a task-involved way to accept or change those things in my life that I choose. It is up to me! What is my first step?"

Irresponsibility might be revealed in the client's talk, emotions, or actions. Encouragement Therapy uses a model such as Table 18.1 to demonstrate the role of beliefs in life functioning. While each of these components functions interdependently and perhaps simultaneously, Encouragement Therapy takes the position that directly changing beliefs is the most efficient and effective approach. Imagine the impact of a person's courage when he or she starts dancing to the song of responsible as opposed to irresponsible beliefs!

The other discouraging belief is "I am a worthless and incapable person who has no assets, strengths, or resources." This person has chosen a rigid negative identity of self (e.g., "I'm the kind of person who always . . .") as well as finalized generalizations about other people and the world (e.g., "It's a dog-eat-dog world"). In their liability-oriented identity, discouraged people believe they have no chance to win a battle, solve a problem, find a solution, or even move toward a possible solution. They lack confidence in their own abilities (Dinkmeyer & Losoncy, 1997). Instead of focusing on the constructive steps they could take toward reaching their goals, their energies are consumed contemplating the hazards of failure.

Table 18.1   Role of Beliefs in Life Functioning

Components of Self	Beliefs (Talk)	Emotions	Actions
Irresponsibility	If only it weren't for . . .	Anger, depression	Immobilization or retaliation
Responsibility	It's up to me, wherever I am, to move ahead	Anxiety of possibilities, exhilaration	Courageous movement toward goals

The confident person, contrarily, concludes that "I am a complex bundle of talents and possibilities. I have many resources within me and it is up to me to energize these strengths. I always have the ability to perceive any given situation in many different ways and choose the best one for me." People with this rich vision of life have "perceptual alternatives" (Losoncy, 2000). It is at that exact moment when people are generating new perceptual alternatives that their humanness is fully validated. When responsibility and confidence are present, courage, which is risk-taking movement toward stated goals, is more likely to occur. Courage is witnessed at that moment when people hold their nose and jump with total commitment into a fuller self. On this note, French philosopher Jacques Maritian concluded that "a coward flees backward away from new things while a man of courage flees forward in the midst of new things."

How does this backward movement or discouragement occur? Are humans born discouraged, or do they become discouraged through life experiences?

Origins and Dynamics of Discouragement

Humans are born partly courageous and partly discouraged. They are courageous to the extent that they willingly take risks to move in new ways within their physiological limitations. Their courage, however, is indiscriminate and irresponsible. They lack responsibility because their needs must be ministered to by others if they are to survive. So it is impossible for the young child to feel that "It's up to me." Despite the fact that they lack responsibility, newborns have the potential of developing confidence through perceived mastery over their environment. The ideal encouraging atmosphere is one that "invites"[1] the development of responsibility and nourishes the potential for confidence, without destroying the original energy toward courageous movement.

Encouraging Responsibility

The most powerful invitations for the development of client courage come from the social environment. Thus, while newborns are incapable of assuming responsibility ("It's up to me"), they have the potential of slowly developing a more responsible outlook. In an environment where children are dominated, are rarely allowed to make decisions, aren't given appropriate responsibility, and don't perceive that their actions can have a di-

rect and positive impact on anything, they feel powerless.

By the same token, children may become irresponsible when they believe that the world revolves around them. Parents symbolically represent what children begin to expect from the world. The more inaccurately parents represent reality, the more likely children will develop discouraging beliefs.

> Much discouragement is a result of two basic mistaken beliefs about self, other, and life. The first error is in the failure of people to face and accept reality as it is and the second major mistake is in the failure of people to realize all of the possible alternatives available to them once they face and accept that reality. (Losoncy, 1980)

Responsibility is encouraged by helping people to realize "It's up to me to accept those things I choose not to change, to change those things I select, and to choose courageously and efficiently." The encouragement therapist is a healthy representative of reality who shows how new beliefs, talk, emotions, and actions "make sense."

Encouraging Confidence

The primary material to encourage already exists within the client's assets, strengths, resources, and potentially positive life outlook. Confident people move forward by vigorously generating fresh perceptions of their possibilities. However, discouraged people, believing that they can't change, focus on their liabilities. Yet, as John Dryden said, "When there is no hope, there can be no endeavor."

Newborns have the potential for confidence through perceived mastery over their environments. Observe the young child's expression the first time he or she successfully uses a spoon without anyone's help! Through their experiences, children begin to conclude "I'm capable at this" or "I'm no good at that." Their identity begins to emerge from their perception of these experiences.

There are numerous ways for children to begin to see themselves as incapable rather than as capable. When they perceive that they are worthwhile only when they perform well and succeed, they begin to lose confidence and shy away from those areas where they see themselves as incapable. This discouraging trend is especially noted at the onset of school, where the focus is on the number of wrong answers rather than the effort made. When heroes, successes, and perfection are valued, the only way to avoid a humiliating defeat is to choose discouragement and give up. The child concludes "I am incapable and have no assets," often generalizing this discouraging conclusion to other areas of life. And how does someone who is incapable act? They don't! Any thought of risking change provokes anxiety and fear of failure. The person buys safety at the cost of life.

---

[1] Encouragement Therapy refers to external factors as invitations rather than causes, to be consistent with what we (1998) call S–You–R Psychology. That is, in the end, people's responses are determined by their choice at "You" and are not automatically the result of the stimulus.

Confidence is the feeling of complexity and personal effectiveness and comes from a personal reservoir of perceived past successes. As people become sensitive to all of their vast potential to behave in new ways, they are impressed with the personal power constantly within their grasp (Dinkmeyer & Losoncy, 1997).

Through perceptual alternatives offered during therapy, the client develops a new vision of self, others, and reality. The client begins looking at life through new eyes. Consequently, all events are viewed more productively. With the combined feeling of responsibility ("It's up to me") and confidence ("I am complex, capable, and have many strengths, assets, and resources"), the client becomes self-motivated to change.

Process of Encouragement

As mentioned earlier, Encouragement Therapy incorporates ideas from various schools of humanistic psychotherapy. The therapist's approach changes according to the phase of the process. Phase 1 of Encouragement Therapy places emphasis on understanding the client's emotions. Since emotions are viewed as the servants to a person's beliefs, understanding how the client feels helps the therapist to identify the underlying discouraging beliefs. In Phase 2, cognition focusing, clients are invited to recognize the effects of their beliefs on their emotions and actions. This is accomplished by developing their perceptual alternatives, thus enriching their view of self, others, and reality. With these new perceptions, clients become more responsible and confident. When clients internalize these two conclusions of responsibility and confidence, the process moves to Phase 3, action focusing.

In Phase 3, the therapist is interested only in action toward stated goals. Here the client explores possibilities, develops plans, makes a commitment, sets goals, acts, and evaluates the action.

The final phase is holistic focusing. With their new feelings, thoughts, and actions, clients recognize the relationship between what they think, say, feel, and do. This powerful discovery gives them a sense of internal unity, personal control, self-power, and motivation for courageous action. They are independent, even of the therapist, and experience what John Mierzwa (personal communication, August 15, 1979) calls the ultimate gift of therapy, "freedom."

METHODOLOGY

The attitudes of encouragement therapists are as important in inviting client change as are the techniques they use. So, before proceeding to a discussion on the skills and techniques of the therapist and the phases of the encouragement process, a few comments on how the encourager views clients are in order.

Attitudes of the Encouragement Therapist

Psychotherapy is done by therapists who are, beyond everything else, people themselves. Just as the beliefs of clients effect their talk, emotions, and actions, so do the beliefs of therapists effect the encouragement process. So important are the attitudes of the encourager that it is doubtful that one could be successful in motivating clients without a positive view of life. In general, the main difference between clients and therapists is that therapists have more perceptual alternatives, or a richer vision of self, others, and reality. When the perceptual field of the therapist is constricted and closed, the needs of the client are shunted aside. Consequently, much of the work of the therapist is in living life in an open, responsible, and confident way. What are those therapist attitudes that tend to invite client courage?

1. Clients are viewed as discouraged rather than as suffering from psychopathology (Mozak & Dreikurs, 1973).
2. Whenever possible, therapists avoid data about clients that may limit their perceptual alternatives, regarding their possibilities (Losoncy & Losoncy, 1998).
3. The therapist's job is to make clients stronger and independent, as opposed to weaker and dependent (Rogers, 1961).
4. The therapist's beliefs or expectations about the client play an important role in therapeutic outcome (Losoncy, 2000).
5. While clients are viewed as being responsible for their behaviors, they are not blamed for them (Dinkmeyer & Losoncy, 1997).
6. The therapist's reactions play an important role in inviting or disinviting further client exploration (Festinger, 1954).
7. When therapists are imperfect and vulnerable human beings, clients are given permission to be the same (O'Connell & Bright, 1977).
8. Clients have many strengths, assets, and resources that need to be recognized and communicated to them to develop their confidence (Dinkmeyer & Losoncy, 1997; Losoncy, 2000).
9. The client's interests are important sources of motivation to be used in the therapeutic process. The task is to make the connection between these interests and the client's strengths, assets, and resources (Losoncy & Losoncy, 1998).

Process of Encouragement

Encouragement Therapy incorporates elements from various schools of psychotherapy, each employed in different phases of the process. Each phase focuses on certain components of the client, uses specific therapist skills, and demands unique approaches to achieve the desired therapeutic outcome for the phase. The client's pace determines movement through the various phases.

Phase 1. This phase consists of relationship building and exploration (affect focusing). The initial phase of Encouragement Therapy draws largely from what has become known as Person-Centered Therapy as developed by Carl Rogers (1961, 1977). The therapist focuses primarily on the emotions of the client in an accepting, nonjudgmental manner. Through empathic understanding, respect, and warmth, the therapist seeks to create a relationship in which the client can be who he or she really is. Total acceptance or unconditional positive regard enables the client to explore nondefensively his or her real underlying concerns. Since the client's first stated problem is often only the tip of the iceberg, attempts to solve this problem are often naive. If the client is understood, and not judged, with this initial problem, he or she is likely to conclude that there is a green light to explore further.

Encouragement therapists also are enthusiastic about the concerns and interests of their clients. If the therapist understands—really understands—what clients are feeling when they proudly present their new idea or their good news, the therapist can hardly be anything but enthusiastic. The encouragement therapist is not afraid of his or her positive emotions and can express them (Dinkmeyer & Losoncy, 1997).

Some approaches used in Phase 1 include reflection of feeling, encouraging clients to turn what they have just said into feelings, focusing on the client's interests, and looking for client's claims to fame.

Encouragement Therapy moves from the focusing on affect to the second phase, or cognition focusing, when the therapist concludes that the client feels accepted, understood, and ready to take on the challenges of looking at self, others, and reality in new ways. This second phase has been influenced by Rational-Emotive Therapy as developed by Albert Ellis (1962) and by Self-Talk Therapy as discussed by Charles Zastrow (1979).

Phase 2. This phase consists of expanding client perceptions (cognition focusing). Focusing initially on the client's emotions serves two purposes. First, it helps the client feel understood and accepted. Second, through an understanding of the client's emotions, the therapist gains insights into the client's beliefs. Beliefs—talk—emotions—action. So while the therapist empathizes with the emotions of the client, the goal of Phase 2 is to help the client to reach a new, higher level outlook on these self-defeating negative emotions, such as hurt or anger. Personal responsibility and confidence develop as clients begin to realize that they play a role in creating their misery and they can play a role in pulling themselves out of misery. Personal power is experienced as they come to conclude that their view of life affects how they feel about life.

Perceptual alternatives are the different ways of looking at and giving meaning to any situation (Losoncy, 2000). The therapist invites the development of the client's perceptual alternatives by focusing on the client's strengths, assets, and resources. Both the client and the therapist identify client assets, resources, and potentials. This is the primary material used to develop client confidence to change. Even those characteristics that are at first glance viewed as liabilities can be turned into assets. For example, a stubborn person might also be seen as persistent or determined. Encouragement therapists are similar to talent scouts who are able to envision the potential of clients and who then try to motivate them. They search for "talents in the raw" or "diamonds in the rough." As clients begin to feel that they are complex and have many assets, they are more likely to develop the confidence and courage to change (Dinkmeyer & Losoncy, 1997).

After assets have been internalized and the client's perceptual alternatives are developed, the therapist raises questions to encourage personal responsibility. The therapist asks, "Who or what are you currently blaming that is holding you back from taking personal responsibility for your life?" Other questions might include: "How much of your immobilization is related to how you look at your current circumstances? How many other ways do you think you could look at that? Which way is the most productive? What are your assets? How can you use your assets to overcome your current circumstances to reach your goals?" And, of course, the bottom-line question is, "Is your current situation something you choose to change, or do you choose to accept it?" This is the question that brings the client to the crossroads (Losoncy & Losoncy, 1998).

When clients develop responsibility ("It's up to me") and confidence ("I am a complex and capable person with many assets"), they are ready for Phase 3 of the encouragement process.

Phase 3. This is the phase of planning, commitment, and movement (action focusing). The client has been understood and accepted and has developed a richer vision of self, others, and reality. With this new-found responsibility and confidence, the client is brought to the insight that he or she can only be known by actions. A universe of well-intended thoughts, words, and feelings is not equal to one step in a positive direction (Losoncy & Losoncy, 1998).

Drawing from Reality Therapy (Glasser, 1965) during this phase the therapist focuses on the actual behavior rather than thoughts or feelings. The therapist keeps asking the questions: "What are you going to do?" and "When will you do it?" The encouragement therapist goes through nine stages in this action phase of the process: (1) exploring all of the perceptual and behavioral alternatives; (2) encouraging the client to develop a plan; (3) encouraging a total client commitment; (4) setting specific goals, which include times and places whenever possible; (5) reaffirming client responsibility and confidence; (6) encouraging client action through effort rather than focusing on success or failure; (7) nourishing client pride or "celebrating" the action (in the case of no action, starting again in an earlier phase); (8) task-involved evaluation of action; and (9) commitment to new action.

Phase 4. This is the freedom phase (holistic focusing). The ultimate goal of Encouragement Therapy is client responsibility and confidence. While this outcome is achieved through the assistance of the therapist, in the end the process is successful only when the client becomes self-encouraging. It is at this point that the client concludes "It's up to me and I can do it!"

Freedom is the feeling of personal control over one's life. To accomplish this, the therapist focuses on the total person (holism) and helps the client to recognize the relationship between what he or she thinks, says, feels, and does. This enlightening realization gives the client a sense of internal unity, personal control, self-power, and motivation for positive movement. When this goal is achieved, the condition of the central hypothesis of Encouragement Therapy has been met: In the end, the major reason why people change is because they themselves are motivated to change.

APPLICATIONS

Encouragement Therapy agrees with Gordon Paul's comment on treatment applications. Paul (1967, p.111) asked, "What treatment, by whom, is most effective for this individual with that specific problem, under which set of circumstances?"

Encouragement procedures might be justified for most nonorganic problems if one's starting point is "Where are you now and what is your next reasonable step?" Yet it may not be the most effective and efficient approach. The encouragement therapist is advised to be knowledgeable in many schools of psychotherapy. Keeping in mind Paul's basic question, the encouragement therapist is well aware that no single form of treatment can claim a monopoly on client improvement. Research from emotive, cognitive, and behaviorally oriented approaches has affected Encouragement Therapy, and has become what could be called a school with primary cognitive emphasis but with strong emotive and behavioral components (Phases 1 and 3).

In general, Encouragement Therapy is not the most efficient treatment with properly diagnosed, seriously disturbed clients. In this category are included: (1) organic problems; (2) disorders with accompanying hallucinations; and (3) severe depression that leads to an unbending morbid life outlook and failure to internalize resources. Even in the last instance, however, Encouragement Therapy proceeds with the first-line hypothesis that movement is possible.

Encouragement Therapy is most effective with the discouraged person who lacks positive motivation. People suffering from what is currently called "existential neurosis," or problems in living, can be assisted to develop meaning and goals in life. Discouraged people who are faced with major life adjustments (return to school, divorce, loss of loved ones) can be helped to develop courage to face these challenges. People lacking confidence in their own abilities can be given new ways of looking at themselves, others, and life that are more productive. Encouragement Therapy has potential for use in the schools with underachievers and timid students. Even school phobics have been successfully treated with this therapy. As a matter of fact, Encouragement Therapy groups have been used with students, teachers, administrators, and school board members.

Clients traditionally classified as "psychopaths" have been taught more responsible attitudes and action through encouragement. Clients with drug-related problems as well have been encouraged to develop self-confidence and responsibility to become dependent on self, rather than peers and drugs.

In general, Encouragement Therapy has promise as a treatment procedure in most cases where the client needs responsibility, self-confidence, and more positive and productive ways of looking at self, others, and life.

CASE EXAMPLE

Eugene was a 16-year-old high school junior with above-average intelligence, but a history of near school failure and repetitive discipline problems. His peers viewed him as the class clown who would take on any illegal challenge in school. His frequent classroom disruptions had his teachers at wits' end, and much of his time was spent in the disciplinarian's office. He was on the verge of being expelled several times, but his charm managed to keep him in school. An excellent football player, if Eugene managed to remain in school for his senior year, he would probably be elected captain of the football team. Eugene had a poor self-concept, referring to himself as an "idiot." He talked freely of being in the bottom fifth of his school class and, at grade time, he would flash his report card to everyone, revealing his failure.

The first therapist who saw Eugene described him primarily as an "attention getter" with psychopathic tendencies. Eugene told the therapist that he had no problems and didn't see why he had to go to a therapist since he wasn't insane. (Before you allow some of the information to limit your perceptual alternatives of Eugene's possibilities, review the list of therapist attitudes in the methodology section. This will provide a background for understanding the handling of the case.)

Another school therapist, F, was aware of his colleague's difficulties in dealing with Eugene and felt he would like to try a new approach in working with the difficult teenager. F felt that to be effective in treating Eugene, he needed to initially win the boy over. (The encouragement therapist believes that to be an effective therapist you need to have the presence and the willingness and cooperation of the client.)

Passing Eugene in the hallway, F enthusiastically patted him on the shoulder, congratulating him on his touchdown the previous weekend. He encouraged Eugene to talk about how it felt, how he accomplished it, and what the coach and the other players said to him about it (empathy, claims to fame). F pointed out to Eugene what a positive contribution his accomplishment made to the school (focus on contribution). F closed the conversation by asking Eugene if he had ever thought of playing college football. Eugene looked astonished at this thought and quickly responded, "Me, go to college? You must be kidding." F empathically answered, "Sounds like you have ruled college out for yourself. I hope whatever you do, Eugene, that you make full use of that unlimited brain that you have. If you'd ever combine your brains with your leadership talents, watch out world!" (empathy, respect, confidence, enthusiasm). F concluded by inviting Eugene to his office if he wanted to talk more about next week's game.

The seeds for an encouraging relationship were planted with the early relationship skills of empathy, warmth, respect, enthusiasm, and claim-to-fame focusing. It was no surprise that Eugene arrived two days later to see F. Part of the dialogue of this first session is included to demonstrate F's use of perceptual alternatives.

F: You sure have the ability to influence people.

E: Me? What do you mean?

F: Well, the other day, for example. You had two of your teachers so upset they lost control of themselves.

E: (Not sure how to respond) Oh? That's a talent?

F: Sure is. I mean, I believe that if you wanted to, you could probably amass the forces to put this school in a state of attack alert. That's what I mean by influence and

by your leadership talents [turning liability into asset]. It must feel good to be that powerful [empathy].

E: Yes, sometimes, I guess. But usually I wind up getting into trouble because nobody understands, and I mean the, uh, stupid rules. I'm always in Mr. G's [principal's] office.

F: Sure must take a lot out of you constantly defending yourself. Boy, I guess talents can work against people at times. Is there any way you could use your leadership skills that wouldn't wind up giving you more trouble than pleasure? [perceptual alternatives].

E: (thinking) One way is as captain of the football team. There I could lead and not get into trouble.

F: Yes, I could see a smile on your face the other day when we talked about football. Football sure means a lot to you [empathy]. I'm looking forward to getting the inside scoop from you on next week's game [you are important and contribute in positive ways].

Another session:

E: The other day you said something about me going to college. Were you putting me on? I mean, me and college! Have you looked at my grades?

F: I've looked beyond your grades. I've looked at you. I've seen what you can do. College success requires intelligence, determination, responsibility, and confidence. You have the intelligence. Playing safety and halfback requires intelligence. Your IQ supports this. And determination—Eugene, when you make up your mind to get something, you get it.

E: But you said a couple of other things, I think, responsibility and something else.

F: Yes, responsibility and confidence. Responsibility is using your intelligence in a courageous way. It takes a gutsy person to say "I will take responsibility for everything about me—not blaming anyone else for my life." Irresponsibility is just thinking about the moment, not thinking ahead.

E: (laughs) You know what, Mr. F? The other day when I threw that cherry pie at Mrs. J, it was kind of funny, but I guess I wasn't thinking beyond the moment.

F: Yes, you probably thought, "She'll be impressed with this and perhaps will ask me if she should write a recommendation for college for me, huh? [humor]. (Both laugh.) You sure learn fast, Eugene [focus on strength].

E: (seeing time is up) Can we talk again soon?

When F felt that Eugene had internalized the perceptual alternatives of responsibility and confidence, they discussed the possibility of Eugene's going to college. Eugene had a great fear of being rejected as an applicant. The therapist encouraged Eugene to forget his past record and to say responsibly "What is my next step?" Eugene and the therapist continually enumerated his resources (perceptual alternatives), and Eugene was shown how his beliefs and talk ("It would be horrible to be rejected") affected his actions. More effective beliefs and talk were developed. When Eugene finally made a commitment to apply, the two "celebrated" the decision. Eugene concluded that even if he failed, at least he tried (effort focusing).

By early in his senior year, Eugene's grades had increased an average of 15 points, he served as football captain to a winning season, and presented only one major discipline problem. He applied to six colleges and was accepted by two. Five years after his high school graduation, Eugene wrote to F, telling him that he had completed his master's degree in counseling. Eugene wrote, "Without you, I would still be fighting the world and walking around feeling like the 'idiot.' When you helped me to realize what I could do rather than what I couldn't, my world changed."

SUMMARY

The central hypothesis of Encouragement Therapy is that regardless of which approach therapists use, in the end the major reason why clients change is because they themselves are motivated to change. Encouragement therapists seek to motivate client action by developing their responsibility ("It's up to me") and confidence ("I have strengths and assets and I can do it").

Responsibility and confidence are nourished by helping the client to look at self, others, and the world in more positive and productive ways. Encouragement Therapy is phenomenological in that a person's vision of things is believed to determine his or her actions. By enriching clients' vision through developing their perceptual alternatives, new emotions and actions are believed to follow. Although Encouragement Therapy is primarily cognitive, emotive and behavioral components are addressed throughout the four phases of encouragement.

This optimistic form of helping can be used with most clients to reorganize those assets that are already present. It is believed that Encouragement Therapy makes an excellent adjunct to any form of psychotherapy, especially at the "moment of movement" in the client's life.

Wherever successful therapy is done by a therapist, some form of encouragement is present.

REFERENCES

Adler, A. (1959). *Understanding human nature.* New York: Premier Books.

Ansbacher, H., & Ansbacher, R. (Eds.). (1956). *The individual psychology of Alfred Adler.* New York: Basic Books.

Dinkmeyer, D., & Dreikurs, R. (1963). *Encouraging children to learn.* Englewood Cliffs, NJ: Prentice-Hall.

Dinkmeyer, D., & Losoncy, L. (1997). *The Skills of Encouragement.* Boca Raton, FL: CRC Press.

Dreikurs, R. (1968). *Psychology in the classroom.* New York: Harper & Row.

Dreikurs, R., & Grey, L. (1968). *Logical consequences.* New York: Meredith.

Dreikurs, R., & Soltz, V. (1967). *Children: The challenge.* New York: Duell, Sloan and Pearle.

Ellis, A. (1962). *Reason and emotion in psychotherapy.* Seacaucus, NJ: Lyle Stuart.

Festinger, L. (1954). A theory of social comparison processes. *Human Relations, 7,* 117–140.

Glasser, W. (1965). *Reality therapy.* New York: Harper & Row.

Losoncy, L. (2000). *Turning people on: How to be an encouraging person.* Sanford, FL: InSync Publishing.

Losoncy, L., & Losoncy, D. (1998). *What is, is! How to accept what you choose not to change.* Boca Raton, FL: CRC Press.

May, R. (1977). *The meaning of anxiety.* New York: Norton.

Mozak, H., and Dreikurs, R. (1973). In R. Corsini (Ed.), *Adlerian psychotherapy.* Itasca, IL: F. E. Peacock, 1973.

O'Connell, W. (1975). *Action therapy and Adlerian therapy.* Chicago: Alfred Adler Institute.

O'Connell, W., & Bright, M. (1977). *Natural high primer.* Chicago: Alfred Adler Institute.

Paul, G. (1967). Strategy of outcome research in psychotherapy. *Journal of Consulting Psychology, 3l,* 108–118.

Rogers, C. (1961). *On becoming a person.* Boston: Houghton Mifflin.

Rogers, C. (1977). *On personal power.* New York: Delacorte.

Sartre, J. (1979). *Existentialism and human emotion.* New York: Philosophical Library.

Zastrow, C. (1979). *Self-talk therapy.* Englewood Cliffs, NJ: Prentice-Hall.

Chapter 19

ERICKSONIAN THERAPY

STEPHEN LANKTON

Milton Erickson was a handicapped person who suffered all kinds of disabilities, including dyslexia, tone deafness, and polio but who ended up as one of the most knowledgeable people in the field of psychology and psychiatry. Along the line he became interested in hypnosis, for which he is best known. Central to understanding his theory is the concept of the unconscious, which can be considered like an iceberg, the larger part of the individual, with consciousness the smaller part. Consequently in Ericksonian therapy the therapist attempts to communicate directly to the unconscious via hypnosis. Communications to the unconscious differ from communications to the conscious mind, stressing experiences rather than logic, with the therapist attempting to "go under" the person's limiting rationality.

Erickson did not limit himself to hypnosis but used a variety of techniques, and his followers also did not limit themselves to this procedure. For example, some research has shown that indirect suggestions are more successful than direct suggestions. Lankton suggests that the Ericksonian approach is somewhat like aikido in that one uses the energy of the client to essentially direct the individual in his search for the desired outcome. This unique system has already affected other psychotherapies.

DEFINITION

Ericksonian therapy is based on the innovative work of the late Dr. Milton H. Erickson. It is often characterized from two different perspectives, the most common of which involves defining it by its reliance on distinctive interventions such as hypnosis, indirect suggestion, therapeutic stories, double binds, homework assignments, paradoxical prescription, and so forth. These definitions may also indicate that Ericksonian therapy encompasses a spectrum of approaches including strategic therapy, brief therapy, and general psychotherapy, often with an emphasis on the use of hypnosis.

The other perspective on Ericksonian therapy emphasizes an approach that focuses on how clients dynamically use themselves, limit their resources, and create the problems they present for treatment. Therapists do not observe clients to discover a diagnosis and treat it by "doing something to" the client. Instead, therapists must approach therapy as a context in which they participate with clients to cocreate the meanings they reach. The interventions listed are, in this light, merely descriptions of the relationship with clients that help them come to use their experiential resources in the context in which they are needed.

HISTORY

The history of Ericksonian therapy, of course, begins with the life of Milton Erickson, M.D. (1901–1980). He was born in Wisconsin, lived in a small farmhouse, and attended a one-room schoolhouse. He had learning disabilities similar to dyslexia and was tone deaf, but that was only the beginning of the enormous physical challenges he would face. He contracted polio in 1919 and overheard doctors explain to his parents that their boy would be dead the next day. He was angry that a mother should be told such a thing based on opinion. That afternoon, he instructed family members to arrange the furniture in a particular way that allowed him to see out the west window, proclaiming, "I was damned if I would die without seeing one more sunset" (Rossi, Ryan, & Sharp, 1983, p. 10). He, of course, did not die and devoted his life to proving one could overcome imposed limiting expectations.

With great determination and effort, Erickson spent many introspective hours working to regain sensitivity in those muscles not completely destroyed by polio. Within a year he had control of his upper torso and sensation in his legs. He embarked, solo, on a 1200-mile canoe trip on the Mississippi River and was able to walk again on his return. He maintained that dealing with his various challenges made him more observant of others. For example, because he was tone deaf he learned to tell the quality of a pianist by the range of touch he or she employed. He also learned to attend to inflections in the voice and explained that left him less distracted by the content of what people say. Many patterns of behavior are reflected in the way a person says something rather than in what he says (Haley, 1967).

After the canoe trip, he entered the University of Wisconsin and studied premedicine. He became interested in psychology, psychopathology, and criminology and studied hypnosis with Clark Hull, obtaining a master's degree in psychology while completing his medical degree. He completed his psychiatric residency in Colorado and then joined the psychiatric staff at Worcester State Hospital in Massachusetts (1930–1933), eventually becoming chief psychiatrist. In 1933 he accepted a position at Eloise State Hospital and Infirmary in Michigan (1933–1945) and taught at Wayne State University.

Erickson did intense research on hypnotic phenomena such as color blindness, analgesia, time distortion, and age regression. During the 1930s, he was interested in Freud's notion of the unconscious and its influence on behavior. Early research focused on tracing a client's symptomatic presentation or neurosis to its origin in the past. Later in his professional development, however, Erickson shifted his focus from historical causes of symptoms to present functioning and interactions of clients. Eclecticism and pragmatism were always priorities.

In the mid-1940s, Erickson began to receive worldwide recognition for his work in hypnosis and was regarded as the world's leading practitioner of medical hypnosis. He wrote entries on hypnosis for Americana, Colliers (1952–1962), and Britannica (1945–1973) encyclopedias for as many as 20 years. His dedication to exploring the use of hypnosis in therapy was reflected in his publishing over 100 papers on this subject. He founded, in 1957, the American Society for Clinical Hypnosis and edited its journal for the next 10 years, but his influence extended beyond hypnosis. Margaret Mead became interested in his work while she was married to Gregory Bateson, and their friendship led to early collaboration that had far-reaching influence on the development of communication theory, Brief Therapy, and Family Therapy.

In 1952, Bateson's research project on communication elected to investigate Erickson's work since he, more than any other therapist known to the team, was concerned with pragmatics of how people change (Haley, 1985a). The team included John Weakland, Jay Haley, Don Jackson, William Fry, and later, Virginia Satir.

The lasting influence can be seen in such works as "Toward a Theory of Schizophrenia" (Jackson, 1968a) and subsequently, citations of Erickson by Bateson (1972), Haley (1963, 1967), Jackson (1968a, 1968b), and Satir (1964) as they developed models of Brief and Family Therapy. Under the later direction of Watzlawick, Weakland, and Richard Fisch, the Mental Research Institute (MRI) continued to attempt to develop communication models for techniques that originated in Erickson's work. These influences gave rise to systems models, brief therapy, strategic therapy, and family therapy.

CURRENT STATUS

Erickson's career spanned more than 50 years as he worked up to his death in March 1980. His developed ideas were embraced by earnest students who studied with him and collected his works, translated his actions into a set of heuristics, and continued educational, training, and supervision efforts for professionals worldwide.

The Milton H. Erickson Foundation, in Phoenix, Arizona, was founded in 1979 and coordinates institutes, education, and training. It was at the foundation's first international congress that the term Ericksonian Psychotherapy was first used, with Erickson's knowledge. Unfortunately, he died before this congress, but the invited faculty of over 123 professionals demonstrated a vast expertise in therapy following various aspects of Erickson's work.

Currently, over 70 institutes within dozens of countries teach or offer some form of Ericksonian Psychotherapy. However, there is no tight control over the actual practice or conduct often done under the rubric of Ericksonian Therapy. Some therapists seem to rely upon one or another of his techniques to the exclusion of others and, in many cases, it is likely that much of the underlying subtlety of Erickson's work is overlooked in striving for the dedication and hard work necessary to master the approach.

THEORY

Traditional therapy is based on the assumption of an objective reality that is independent of our efforts to observe it. The posture toward reality is separation from it and study by reduction. But while the simple act of reducing and labeling seems innocent enough, it does not credit the observer with the action of inventing the label that is applied. Furthermore, this description often pathologizes the individual and typically excludes his or her current life context.

The therapeutic stance of separateness and the pathology orientation results in an adversarial position that the language of therapy reflects with metaphors of resistance, conflict, defense, hidden motive, suppression, power, and attack. When placed in an adversarial position, either purposefully or inadvertently, labeled individuals will easily demonstrate more behaviors that will reinforce a therapist's conviction about the independent existence of an internal pathology. It was this very trend that Erickson wished to avoid throughout his career (Erickson, 1985).

There was clearly a progression from his early work with hypnosis when Erickson, like others in that time, used repetition, references to sleep, authoritative stance, and direct suggestion. Later in his life, however, he observed that indirection allowed him to show respect for clients by not directly challenging them to do what their conscious mind, for whatever reason, would not do. This was in contrast to earlier writing that referred to neurosis, resistance, conflict, and hypnoanalysis to reveal latent content in the unconscious. He considered anxiety due to the breakdown of defense mechanisms and the threat of previously suppressed material emerging. But over time, he departed from this vocabulary almost entirely and described anxiety as the result of a breakdown of relations between people and understood all problems to be the result of an inability to have desired resources in the context in which they were needed.

Erickson's approach was oriented to interactions that helped people change and aimed to be scrupulously unique with each client. Each question, silence, discussion, metaphor, or paradoxical directive was delivered with an ongoing sensitivity to the special needs of the listener. Interventions were seemingly reinvented for each individual and each goal. In this regard, the approach was extremely unconventional and was often misunderstood since it could not be explained according to a structural theory of personality. Erickson resisted even attempting to set forth an explicit theory of personality and warned that rigid adherance to theory often becomes a Procrustean bed that cuts the legs off clients in order to make them fit.

There were many stories, however, that described a theory of learning. For instance, a portion of one story concerned how his son explained events of a date to a malt shop and roller skating rink. The son's explanation of the superficial behavior was contrasted with Erickson's own interpretation about the same events. Erickson stated, "I knew what he'd really been doing. He'd been looking in her eyes, having mucous membrane stimulation, touching her, and having rhythmical physical activity."

This theory of human development assumes people are in a continuous cycle of learning experiences with ever increasing complexity. Success in learning simple sets of experiences provides a foundation for subsequent learning of greater complexity. Socialization experiences retrieve, encourage, and stabilize experiences. A person's awareness of this socialization experience is merely the tip of an iceberg, while the remainder is stored below the surface, as unconscious. Throughout life, we are learning as we are being socialized and simultaneously displaying and using previous learning. When the demands of our developmental tasks and current environment do not teach us how to perform, we rely upon previously learned patterns. These patterns of perception, cognition, emotion, behavior, and self-monitoring determine our success.

Fluctuations in family stability are most often precipitated by changes brought on when particular developmental stages require novel experiences or alterations in the usual types of transactions. For instance, the birth of a baby signals a change to the child-raising stage of development, and hundreds of new experiences, transactions, and behaviors must be learned: looking at the child and smiling, postponing gratification for the sake of the child's needs, learning to ask for help with the child, being able to experience joy in the child's growth, acquiring a vast array of caretaking skills, and so forth. If these experiences are readily available as resources due to previous learnings, the disorganization within the family system is relatively short and the transition to new organization easy. Conversely, to the extent that the resources are not available, the disorganization becomes more debilitating and resolutions more difficult. When problem-solving behaviors are greatly out of synchronization with contextual demands, people may seek therapy for various symptoms.

Central to the theory of learning is the unconscious and its relationship to consciousness. The unconscious is the complex set of associations outside awareness at any moment. These include a broad range of experiences and processes, some of which become conscious at times, though most do not ever become conscious. These unconscious patterns regulate, control, and guide moment-to-moment conduct. They are resources that can be used in therapy to cocreate different perceptions, experiences, and behaviors. In Ericksonian Therapy, the unconscious is considered a repository of resources and skills that can be employed for positive therapeutic change. Unconscious process and content need not be made conscious in order to be utilized.

Problems are the natural result of attempts to solve developmental demands in ways that do not fully work for the people involved. Intervention, then, should help clients actively participate in changing the way they live. As people find more effective ways of achieving goals and experiences they wish to have, previously learned patterns of behavior will drop away. In other words, clients will make the best choice possible for themselves at any given moment with the learnings they have.

Therapy is based on observable behavior and related to the present and future circumstances of the client. While people have memories, perceptions, and feelings regarding their past, preoccupation with the past to the exclusion of present and future will unnecessarily prolong and complicate the process of therapy. The hallmark of an Ericksonian approach is an emphasis on current interpersonal relationships and their influence on the development and resolution of problems. Individuals may have developed a symptomatic behavior in the distant past, but the Ericksonian view focuses on how the problem is maintained in the present. Efforts are concentrated on increasing new arrangements of learning that can be applied to solving problems in the client's present life.

METHODOLOGY

Several tenets that guide methodology in Ericksonian therapy can be crystallized from the preceding discussion of theory. These tenets affect the practice of therapy as they summarize the way in which problems and people are viewed.

1. Problems are thought to be the result of disordered interpersonal relations in that clients fail to use resources from earlier learning in the current context. Consequently, diagnosis is an activity that frames the presenting problem in terms of the developmental and interpersonal climate experienced by the individual and his or her family. Therapy is directed toward making a creative rearrangement in those relationships so that developmental growth is maximized.

2. The therapist is active and ultimately responsible for initiating therapeutic movement. This is done by introducing material into the therapy session, helping to punctuate experience and focus awareness, and by the use of extramural assignments. That is, therapy does not always wait until clients spontaneously bring up material but often sets the pace and challenges clients to grow and change.

3. Change comes from experience and not from insight. Mental mechanisms and personality characteristics need not be analyzed for the client. They can be utilized as processes for facilitating therapeutic goals. Indirect methods (metaphor, indirect suggestion, and ambiguous function assignment) are used to retrieve needed resources (attitudes, abilities, feelings, etc.) that can be directed to creating new adjustments to current life demands.

4. A major goal is getting clients active and moving in perceptions, cognition, emotions, and small and large behavior.

5. Utilization is employing clients' perceptions and resources for movement and change. It occurs in two areas. One is the here-and-now use of material presented from the client. If a client demonstrates relaxation, tension, talkativeness, silence, questioning, passivity, movement, stillness, fear, confidence, and so forth, it is to be accepted and used to further the therapeutic movement. So-called resistance is not seen or labeled as such, but rather is accepted and in some manner used to facilitate a context for change. The second area refers to using whatever talents, interests, and potential abilities a client brings as a vehicle to gain further experience and learning. Therapists make an effort to speak the clients' experiential language and join them at their model of the world.

6. Indirection refers to the use of controlled ambiguity. It encourages clients to make their own relevant meaning instead of being told what to do. The ambiguity in suggestions and stories gives rise to pleasant mental excitement and enhances communication. It is not limited to the hypnosis context.

7. Therapy is future oriented. Since the client has come to therapy due to an inability to meet developmental demands in his or her current life, therapy is focused on pinpointing and developing resources to meet these present demands. Recognizing the mechanisms by which a client can maintain needed resources in the current context is seen as much more important than analyzing how a shortcoming came to exist in the past.

These seven tenets guide the use of particular methods throughout Ericksonian Therapy, which begins as the assessment stage unfolds. For instance, imagine that a young man enters the office exuding inadequacy. An Ericksonian therapist recognizes that a logical set of behaviors and emotions is lacking in this client's behavior in the present context. But in speaking to the man in order to understand his presenting complaint, it is perfectly reasonable for the therapist to make comments that presuppose increased feelings of pride, confidence, and assertive behavior. Therapists observe how clients respond to such presupposition and minimal suggestions as part of the ongoing assessment that ascertains flexibility in experience and available resources. Therapy is not simply a two-part process consisting of an initial assessment followed by continued treatment; rather, it continues throughout communication and contact with clients.

Assessment does, however, include an intake interview that addresses four areas. First, the presenting problems as well as preliminary goals are determined. Next, family organization is assessed, including a conceptualization of the current stage of development (and related demands) as well as the likely demands of the next logical stage of development the family will be entering. An understanding is developed of the family's way of explaining typical time structuring, involvement with career and social networks, and each person's involvement with the symptom. Particular interest concerns how engaging in the symptom represents an adaptive response or "best choice" (Lankton & Lankton, 1983) to the interpersonal and developmental demands currently being encountered. Third, the initial assessment involves gathering background information about the problem itself: how each person responds to the problem, what is being accomplished by having the problem, what might be accomplished if the problem were not present, how the problem started, and previous treatment received for it. The fourth area determines cogent information about the family of origin of the client, even if it might initially seem unrelated to the specific presenting problem.

Goal setting usually includes the specific gains stated by the client as well as other subtle prerequisites, such as changes in perception, cognition, emotion, behavior, social role, family structure, and self-image that support the larger goal. Treatment is almost entirely centered on helping clients find and use experiential resources in the context in which they need them. Various interventions are employed to retrieve and reassociate experience, including those techniques identified with the Ericksonian approach, such as positive framing, utilization, paradoxical prescriptions, skill-building homework, indirect suggestion, therapeutic metaphors, ambiguous function assignments, dissociated visual rehearsal, reciprocal inhibition, and hypnosis. This does not preclude use of more common activities such as interpretation, confrontation, specifying, clarification, crystallization, and empathy.

Empathy, for Ericksonian therapists, means putting one foot in the client's world and leaving one in the therapist's own. Therapists need to literally speak the same vocabulary and speech patterns spoken by clients. This means therapists must be able to vary their behavior and perform a wide range of verbal and nonverbal styles. This means stretching oneself to mumble with almost inarticulate mumblers, matching the exasperated nonverbals provided by tentative clients, speaking rapidly, crudely, or eloquently depending on what is offered. Communication messages are packaged to be understood correctly by the receiver.

Positive framing is an attitude expressed in two ways. First, therapists attend to the ideas expressed by clients to scan for and monitor goals, attitudes, and desires that have been expressed in any form other than positive. Then, therapists sincerely restate those goals, attitudes, or desires in a positive and realistic manner acceptable to the client. Reframing such as this may apply to both the interpretation of a common daily event or a large portion of a client's life experience. Reframing is a transaction. It is not enough that a therapist has a terrific idea—

the idea must be communicated successfully to the client for reframing to occur.

Utilization is defined as recognizing and using the energy brought by clients to move their actions or thoughts in the direction of the therapeutic goal. In conventional therapy, certain behavior is considered to be resistant. However, in Ericksonian Therapy, all behavior is seen as problem-solving attempts. For instance, a person who continually disagrees with the therapist might realistically be seen as someone who has solved most of his problems by correcting others and thinking for himself. While this may not be appropriate social conduct and may even be detrimental to the treatment goals, it must nonetheless be recognized as a statement that he is trying to solve the problem in the way best known to him. The utilization technique is used correctly with such a person when the therapist asks him to "continue to try to solve the problem by discarding the things I say and doing a great deal of thinking for yourself." The potential adversary becomes a teammate when his behavior is framed as an attempt to solve the problem.

Paradoxical prescription is a request for clients to continue doing something they have been doing while making a minor alteration in some aspect of it. For example, spouses may be asked to refrain from having sexual relations but to keep a notebook and record in it, each day, compliments they would be reluctant to say to their spouse at this time. When this sort of intervention is used, clients are refusing to have sexual relations due to the therapist's demand and not due to their own anger toward one another. At the same time, an important behavior is being built to further marital intimacy. By writing in the notebook but not showing it to the spouse, each person is rehearsing skills needed to create positive communication in the marriage. Furthermore, there is mystery introduced in the marriage regarding the other spouse's positive comments. In effect, each spouse may begin to think, "I wonder what nice thing my partner is thinking about me." Thus, paradoxical intervention can skillfully help clients reach their goal of marriage fulfillment. It helps them find a way to give up the power plays and develop positive expectations without losing face and without winning or losing a game of "who's to blame?"

Skill-building homework assignments are intended to create a context outside the office in which clients can obtain bits and pieces of experience. Each assignment intends to evoke a small subset of experience such that, taken as a whole, the experiences approximate a complex socialization event. For example, an individual who is uncomfortable dating and has sought therapy for related issues might be given the following homework assignments without being told the reason. He may be asked to see the midnight showing of a popular movie. Another assignment might ask him to the go to a dessert restaurant and order two desserts and eat them. A third assignment might ask him to purchase new pants and a shirt. Still a fourth assignment might ask him to engage an attractive bank teller in a long conversation. In each of these four assignments, however, his attention would be diverted away from how they might be subsets of the dating goal. If the client were to think his success in dating depended on success in any of these assignments, his anxiety might be all that he learned while doing them. If, instead, he participates in skill-building assignments for reasons other than dating, his learned limitations will not prevent him from acquiring the experiences he needs.

Therapeutic suggestion refers to a large category of verbal and nonverbal communication. While all communication contains aspects of suggestion, few people realize how to consciously and effectively formulate those suggestions at the process level of communication. The goal of suggestion is to help the client search for and retrieve experiences. This refers to both experiences that are needed for ongoing understanding of therapy as well as experiences that pertain to the contracted treatment goals. The former category of experiences includes such things as listening with comfort, being specific, and taking risks. The latter category may include experiences that result from homework assignments, paradoxical interventions, visual rehearsal, and so forth. One of the intentions of Ericksonian Therapy is to use suggestions in such a way that clients do not feel obligated to respond to them. Clients respond to suggestions that are relevant to them. The more ambiguous a suggestion is, the greater the latitude and range of options available to the client. Indirect suggestions thus should not evoke resistance.

Therapeutic metaphors are stories with a specific structure. Unlike parables or fables, the goal is not usually to drive home some point, but rather to elicit experiences. This is accomplished in much the same way as viewers of a movie retrieve experiences. Watching the movie, a person will identify with particular characters and assign internal objects to stand for those characters in the movie. As those characters change relationships with one another, the internal objects used to represent them alter their relationship to one another as well. This results in certain predictable emotional experiences and attitudinal shifts. Clients listening to therapeutic metaphors can also be sensitized to certain behaviors. These changes provide a sort of window of opportunity for the client to reconsider available resources. They operate as an effective tool to evoke, retrieve, and associate relatively novel experiences into the context in which they are needed.

Ambiguous function assignments are a special category of homework designed to help a client suspend his rational limitations and understandings. While participating in this assignment, a client will attempt to understand the rather odd behavior that has been assigned. Attempts to understand will require that the client resurrect understandings and meanings that were evoked during the therapy session. In other words, this type of assignment helps the client search more deeply within him between therapy sessions. A typical ambiguous function assignment consists of specific behaviors pertaining to a specific object chosen by the therapist. These behaviors are assigned to be carried out at specific times in a specific location. However, the actual point or meaning behind these behaviors and this object are not explained. Instead, the client is asked to discern for himself what the meaning might be. Ideally, the therapist has absolutely no idea what sort of meaning might be derived. All the therapist needs to know is that the behavior is ethical, legal, doable, and not terribly unpleasant for the client.

Dissociated visual rehearsal refers to techniques that can be performed with or without the use of hypnosis but in each case have at least three features in common. The first of these features is that the client assumes a state of comfort and creativity. This state may be the result of previous empathy, suggestion, positive framing, or assignment. The second feature requires that the client disconnect current experiences from visual memories. Finally, the client needs to conduct an elaborate visual rehearsal of the past or anticipation of the future. In doing this, previous associations to the memories or anticipations are altered. The technique, when applied to mild or moderate traumatic memories, helps the client discover additional available positive resources in the context of the previously unpleasant memory. When applied to an anticipation, the technique helps clients prefigure their perceptions and add a longer anticipation of all the positive experiences they are feeling at the time of the therapy session. In one sense, this visual rehearsal is a self-generated metaphor that allows clients a context in which to associate desired resources to a situation in which they are needed. Future experiences of the same type are expected to become associated with the state of comfort and creativity that was established during the intervention. Even if some of the previous threatening experiences are evoked during future experiences of the same type, they will be "rechunked" or diluted since the client's participation in this activity has created an awareness for and experience of positive associations in the face of the trauma.

Reciprocal inhibition is the name given to the class of interventions that create change by interfering with the mind's ability to experience a previously unpleasant set of associations. The dissociated visual rehearsal discussed above is one example of reciprocal inhibition. Other means of facilitating reciprocal inhibition include working with a sequentially incongruent client in such a way as to evoke both major incongruities at the same time for the same event. Still other means involve urging a client to retrieve an avoided memory, pain, or symptom upon request in the office (out of context). For instance, a therapist might ask a client with "shooting pains" in his hands to "take a few moments and create them here in the office so I can better understand." If the client obliges, the pains are not happening to the client as a victim but rather are happening at the client's initiative. This is often the first step toward realizing responsibility for change and freeing oneself from the victim role.

Hypnosis is simply a modality for communication despite considerable misunderstanding to the contrary. It is a state of heightened internal awareness with a limited range of perceptual focus. During prolonged episodes of such internal absorption of attention, various phenomena are likely to be experienced. Trained subjects are better at producing these trance phenomena, but most people can experience a degree of each of them even in their first session. These experiences can be heightened and associated just as other experiential resources can. The experiences of dissociation, body distortion, amnesia, and time distortion, for instance, can be strategically applied to pain control. It is possible to focus and direct very subtle experiences in order to change perception and attitudes for problems as acute as pain. However, Ericksonian therapists often help a client use such focus to enhance a visual rehearsal, or to embellish desired experiences such as tenderness, confidence, joy, pride, or even sadness or anger. The use of hypnosis in therapy requires special training and often special licensing. This is not due to any inherent danger with hypnosis, but rather to the possible misuse of the tool by untrained therapists.

It is often believed that Erickson used hypnosis with all of his clients. Neither Erickson himself, nor the range of Ericksonian therapists who practice today, do this. Many Ericksonian therapists never use hypnosis and prefer to work primarily with homework assignments. Others prefer to work with only assignments and metaphor, while others prefer to rely on paradoxical interventions and suggestion. Erickson preferred that therapists employ a wide range of interventions and not be committed to any small subset of his techniques. Moreover, Erickson would urge therapists to invent new techniques for each client and not rely on any formula at all. He would insist only that the principles mentioned previously be followed within the theoretical frame he modeled.

The course of treatment often fluctuates greatly with each client. Some cases occur as single-session "cures," while most others are resolved within a few weeks or months. Rarely, a case continues for as much as a year or sometimes two. This situation is most often the result of the particular needs of the client and the existence of severely inhibiting childhood experiences.

APPLICATIONS

Contributions from Erickson's work have been reported in nearly all forms of therapy appropriate to outpatient populations. These include any imaginable concern for anxiety-related symptoms, sexual functions, pain control, habit control, childbirth, autism, phobias, asthma, Marital and Family Therapy. Some limited venues have reported work with inpatient populations, including patients showing psychotic symptoms and character disorders. A few treatment regimens have also reported the use of Ericksonian Therapy with substance abusers, counseling for gays, adolescents, and hospital venue work with cancer victims and grief patients. Many of these reports can be seen in the *Ericksonian Monographs*. These and other emerging and growing areas, including corporate consulting, can be found in the professional programs shared by invited faculty at the International Congresses of the Milton Erickson Foundation, Inc., in Phoenix, Arizona.

As popularity of Ericksonian Therapy has risen, so have criticisms due to a lack of published research. Despite the uniqueness of each intervention, specified protocols or intervention patterns do exist and are becoming more widely known. These may provide the basis for effectiveness studies. Some of the research finds limitations because the underlying clinical epistemology does not lend itself to procedures conforming to requirements of laboratory measurement. A few typical studies are cited below.

Alman and Carney (1980) reported that indirect suggestions were more successful in producing posthypnotic behavior than were direct suggestions. McConkey (1984) concluded that "indirection may not be the clinically important notion as much as the creation of a motivational context where the overall suggestion is acceptable such as making the ideas congruent with the other aims and hopes of a patient" (p. 312). Stone and Lundy (1985) investigated effectiveness in eliciting body movements following suggestions and reported indirect suggestions to be more effective than direct suggestions in eliciting the target behaviors.

Mosher and Matthews (1985), investigating a claim made by Lankton and Lankton (1983), found support for the structural effect of embedding metaphors on amnesia but also reported that indirect suggestion did not enhance the effect of amnesia. They indicated that as a result of stories told to six clients, five reported thinking about the meaning of the therapeutic stories during the intervening week and how they might act differently with regard to the presenting issue. Each of these five clients reported a positive change in the presenting problem. The sixth client reported almost total amnesia for each of the metaphor sessions.

Nugent (1989a) attempted to show a causal connection between Erickson's notion of "unconscious thinking without conscious awareness." In a series of seven independent case studies each client reported a clear, sustained positive change with respect to the presenting problem. While individual case study has certain methodological limitations, Nugent's (1989a) use of seven independent cases with a carefully followed treatment protocol makes his conclusion of causality more convincing. In a related study, Nugent (1989b) used a multiple baseline design to investigate the impact of an Ericksonian hypnotic intervention and found that target behaviors changed as a result of treatment intervention. Each of the Nugent studies has methodological weaknesses, as does the Matthews and Langdell (1989) study, but these still represent examples of current attempts to systematically investigate the clinical validity of Ericksonian interventions.

Despite these and other studies, it can be seen that in doing research it is easier to discuss Erickson's *techniques* than to discuss the subtle and perhaps more important contributions of his overall approach. With an overemphasis on technique, novice therapists have frequently been guilty of applying interventions without an adequate sense of how such techniques develop out of a natural interaction with clients. Effective application of Ericksonian techniques relies heavily on principles of utilization and cooperation in the clinical context.

CASE EXAMPLE

Frank, a 23-year-old single, white male, visited my office with a complaint of blood phobia. He had been a medical student but suspended his studies due to the development of his fear. He stood up in the waiting room as I approached him and when I reached to shake his hand I noticed that he held my hand limply and hesitantly. In my office he explained that he had a prolonged previous medical history. He related the following facts.

As a child of 14 he had developed lactose intolerance. He experienced an array of symptoms and saw many doctors before, at 16, he was diagnosed and his problem corrected. In the process of seeking many medical tests he decided that he might like to be a physician when he grew up. He never wavered from that dream again.

However, a most unpleasant incident occurred at age 16 when he was in a weakened state from vomiting and not sleeping well for days. On this occasion he recalls passing out briefly (he thinks due to low blood sugar) as he watched a vacuum needle draw a quantity of blood from his arm. At that point he developed a phobia. It was intense for a year, by the time he was 18 the phobia had been nearly forgotten. Even after undergraduate school his medical studies seemed to go well. In dissection labs, he had almost no memory of his past trauma.

Unfortunately, this comfort did not last. Eight months before seeing me, his reaction to a dissection lab was so frighteningly intense that he nearly passed out and had to run from the room. He even fainted in a movie when a surprising scene of blood appeared on one occasion. As a result of these events he sought therapy with another approach, Eye Movement Desensitization and Reprocessing (EMDR), to trauma resolution. After several treatments with that approach, his therapist declared that he was not making expected progress and recommended that Frank see me.

Inquiring about the constellation of symptoms, I discovered that he does not have any thoughts about death or irrational fears. He simply anticipates fainting if he sees blood. I was interested in what might have triggered the anxiety attacks associated with blood now, after he had been free of the disruption for several years. As I inquired about his life experiences I also asked about his life at 16 when the phobic reaction began. While I was interested in contrasting and comparing these periods, he believed they had nothing in common as far as the phobia of blood was concerned. It became clear, in fact, that he wished to find no other etiology at work.

However, as he answered my questions, it became most apparent that he had developed another unique set of experiences that might also have bearing on his present complaint. The onset of his first episode, his notable lack of aggression, even passivity, when he shook my hand, and his worried manner all gave rise to another line of inquiry. Eventually, Frank related that both of his parents were troublesome for him. His father had been quite passive as his mother was critical, aggressive, and controlling. It was her criticism that made him feel most hesitant, and he had developed a posture of being friendly and responsive to others rather than standing up to her or taking a dominant position of any kind. He avoided taking charge, expressing disagreement, competing, and so on.

In his recent life, the reemergence of his problem coincided with a week of efforts to begin dating a young woman that he met at school. He stated that this was no more than a coincidence and that the dissection lab had simply been scheduled to happen that week. It struck me as developmentally similar, at least in the use of experiential resources, to what one does as a 16-year-old: interest in girls, planning for independence, moving away from reliance upon a mother, becoming sexually active, and so on. All of these issues were not exclusively confined to his life at 16 and his life at 23. He had in fact headed off to college, moved away from home, and taken an apartment off campus prior to this. Such behavior had certainly involved breaking reliance on his parents and his mother and involved plans of moving toward independence. And yet something about this set of developmental demands was parallel and his behavioral and experiential responses employed the same phobic behavior as part of his problem-solving regimen.

During the discussion he confirmed the family dynamics and his hesitancy to become aggressive. A final additional concern for Frank was that his girlfriend had just broken up with him by means of a phone call. She did not wish to see him again or discuss the matter. He said she gave him no indication of the reason and he was only aware of her vague sense of distance lately. He reported being so upset by this that it "almost" took precedence over his concern about the blood phobia. Of course he needed to correct the phobia and return to medical school. We mapped out a rough treatment plan that would involve heightening his sense of confidence and assertiveness and using these experiences to inhibit and replace his conditioned response to seeing large volumes of blood. He scheduled two more sessions to follow his first visit.

Session 2 began with Frank reminding me that his problem was an example of phobic conditioning (and suggesting that it therefore had nothing to do with anxiety about his mother, his assertiveness, or any such emotional factors). I agreed that his awareness and understanding began at that time and quickly asked if I could help him get oriented to the session by relating one or two case stories that might be helpful to him as he unraveled this mystery and gained the resources he sought. He agreed and I explained to him that I would like to do something I had never done before. Usually, I ask clients to basically attend to me without distraction during such a story, as I want their reaction to help them form some creative experiences for approaching the solution to their problem afresh. However, in his case, as he was already distracted by a number of things, I asked him to purposely distract himself from me as I talked. Specifically, I asked him to doodle and sketch on my large notepad whatever ideas, images, foolishness, points, memories, or entertainment might come to his mind as I spoke. I reminded him that this was just a sort of creative warm-up for the crux of our agreed-on direction and that after 10 minutes or less, I would want to move on. He reiterated my instructions and emphasized that he really didn't draw well. I agreed that he understood my request and added that it would be fine to doodle or even jot down some words if he liked—although I favored his doing the novel act of drawing.

I handed him the pad and markers and began telling him of a case involving a man who sought therapy for hypertension and who insisted that his physical symptom had only a medical cause. I reminded Frank to ignore my speaking as much as he could and let it just be background noise, warming up his creativity by drawing what came to mind. The story continued for about eight minutes and detailed the therapy of the man with hypertension. In the story, the man's father had recently died of a

heart attack and the man actually carried a blood pressure monitor with him and measured his hypertension throughout the day in hope of confirming that he was not like his father in this way. He would run and perform relaxation exercises to reduce the readings on his monitor. However, whenever he would be before his students or with his wife, his blood pressure would rise again. He was unable to find that he was unlike his father in this way despite his efforts to improve himself.

As I spoke, Frank colored random doodles on the pad and split his attention between listening to the story and the art before him. He began drawing thick black lines between blotches of colors. Red was noticeably absent from the image.

In the story the protagonist came to discover that his almost obsessional concerns were an attempt to hide his emotional vulnerability. He subsequently used therapy to imagine returning to his father's deathbed, wept with sadness that he could not or did not express his own needs in the past, and expressed anger that he was provided such a model for how to be a man. Finally, he declared that he had needs he would no longer ignore and would essentially acknowledge them and act as his own father to see that they were met. In this act he firmly and aggressively asserted that he was not like his father and would learn more than his father could teach him—he would not remain limited just because his father could not teach him.

I had made the story as vivid and accurate as I could in the short time that it took to relate a very emotional session that had actually taken place with the protagonist. At that point Frank was not drawing but was sitting and staring off into space. He volunteered that he could identify with the man in the story in many ways. He asked if I thought something like that might be good for him as well.

In direct response to that interest, I asked him to do a two-part exercise for the remainder of the session. It consisted of the paradoxical directive to allow his phobia to continue for the next couple of weeks so his interest in learning from it could guide him better. He agreed, especially since working directly to destructure it had so far failed. I asked him to visually rehearse a scene with certain characteristics and tell me what he got out of it and what it meant. The fantasy involved recalling several moments when he demonstrated his strengths, confidence, pride, determination, and firmness. As his body and self-report reflected success in his amassing these feelings, I had him change the fantasy to become an image near the time of his traumatic past incident. I asked him to continue to stay confident but witness how he and his parents were getting along prior to the time of the trauma. In this waking-state concentration, Frank slowly shared what he remembered of his father's exasperation with Frank's eating and vomiting complaints, his parents' quarreling, and his mother's oppressive control of his life during the hours leading up to and including taking him to the hospital. He was asked to keep an image of his younger self in the fantasy and simultaneously be aware that he was a more confident older self, as it were, watching from my office sofa. I asked him not to conclude or change any of his reactions at this point, just to remember and learn anything that came to seem important.

As the session closed I asked Frank to do an assignment outside the office. I asked him to perform this activity three times before I saw him again; he could decide when those times would be. Since he was living at home, I wanted him to borrow his father's hammer and leave the house with it at sundown. I asked him to go to the pier or boardwalk on Pensacola Beach and use the hammer to pound down any and all nails that he saw protruding in any way above the wood. He was not to speak to anyone and could just act like this was his job if he needed to. In any case, he was to do this for at least an hour for three nights. If he pounded all the protruding nails in these two locations he could proceed to the wooden walkovers that bridged the sand dunes and connected the beach road to the shoreline. When he returned for the next session, I would want him to tell me what he thought the learning from such an assignment had been.

We began the third session with his rendition of the homework assignment. He said that while it was odd to say so, he had experienced it to be strangely freeing to be in public banging, making noise, hammering, and pounding. In fact, he did it four times instead of the assigned three. Frank said he had never done this sort of thing before, as he always felt or had been inhibited from anything like that. Asked what the learning of the assignment was, Frank concluded that maybe the point had been to show that he had more capabilities inside him than he expected. Still, he wasn't sure how this would cure his phobia.

Hearing that he had hammered for an extra night, I asked him to close his eyes and recall the freeing experience that he sought and found on that evening. Once again we used the time to dissociate from and visually rehearse the events of leading up to and including the phobia. Additionally, I asked that Frank also visually rehearse the newest onset of the phobia, eight months ago and, while he was at it, the moment leading up to meeting his girlfriend and beginning to date her. Finally, I asked him to visually rehearse the recent breakup with her.

Upon completing the dissociated review, Frank reported that he felt stronger about most all of these matters. He was still unsure of why his girlfriend had broken up with him, but thinking about did not seem as demoralizing as it had. Asked if he was ready to have the same

feeling about seeing quantities of blood or if he wanted to wait until he understood his former girlfriend, he replied that he was ready to get over the phobia. I asked him to set yet another appointment for the next week and used the remaining 10 minutes of session to elaborate about tools. I explained a number of characteristics about tools that my father had passed along to me. I put special emphasis on those tools that I had once thought were useless but which I later appreciated a great deal, such as the wood plane that I did not use as a child but which I had found irreplaceable for fixing closets and doors once I became a homeowner. I also elaborated on my appreciation for the pliers that used to belong to my mother and my favorite hammer that had been my father's, then mine, and which I passed along to my son. I explained what makes a hammer a "good" hammer.

Since he had found value in his father's hammer, I asked him to bring it in for the next session and let me examine it. I also asked him to write a short essay about the value of some of his father's tools so I could ostensibly evaluate his ability to express himself in writing. Finally, I asked that he approach his father, tell him in any way he could that he found the hammer to be valuable to him, and request that his father make a gift of it to him.

When he came back with his father's hammer, I examined it carefully and declared it a wonderful hammer. I asked if he had requested it as a gift yet, and he said he had not. I almost insisted that he do so, and in fact, do so immediately before therapy continued. Handing him the telephone, I urged him to call his father at work, tell him something had come up and he needed to know if he could have the hammer as his own and that he would explain later if necessary. At first he was embarrassed and reluctant. However, realizing that he had never really asked for anything so spontaneously, and remembering how excited he had become using it, and too, realizing the therapy session was about building such resources, he saw no harm in it. He called his father. His father was friendly and a little confused by the inquiry but had only minor hesitation and then agreed, saying that if the hammer meant that much to Frank he could certainly have it.

He said that while getting the hammer made sense at the time, having it now seemed a little silly. I asked him to be seated with it, close his eyes and revivify the memories of pounding with it during the previous week. He signaled me when he had the experience, and I asked that he imagine and come to believe as much as he could in fantasy, that he was still on the boardwalk on Pensacola Beach pounding nails. I counted backward from 20 to 1 and, in general terms, suggested that he could create an increasingly deeper self-induced trance hearing my voice and keeping the dual awareness of pounding the nails. After completing the deepening, suggestions were used to offer him the possibility of imagining that he was smashing vacuum needles filled with blood and other previously feared stimuli, including movie scenes, dissection lab carcasses, and objects in his memories of the original trauma. He reported being strong, not violent and angry, as he did this to all but the memories in the trauma. Toward these memories he reported being defiant and "sort of angry." He didn't want them to control him anymore.

I asked him to put the hammer down but keep the feelings and, in fantasy, to coach the younger Frank in the visual rehearsals. I suggested that he could pass along this feeling to Frank just as his father passed along the hammer to him. He could give the younger self the tools to express his desires that his mother stop controlling him. Finally, in due course, Frank was urged to switch to the visual fantasy with his former girlfriend and imagine doing the same in dialogue with her.

This was his last session with me. He left that session reporting that he would be curious about his reaction to blood now and would initially test it by renting a movie and call me with the outcome. That weekend Frank rented *Blade,* as it was reported to have a great deal of gratuitous violence and blood content. He said the scenes did not create a problem for him, that the movie was rather enjoyable, and I might enjoy watching it as well. He said it wasn't as bad as people made it out to be—he had seen a lot worse at the hospital. Three weeks passed from the last session and Frank moved back to the university in Alabama and restarted medical school with the new semester. After a couple of months he called to report he was a bit apprehensive at first but had not had any difficulty up to that time with duties at the hospital that used to frighten him. He jokingly said that he just had to keep "hammering on" to complete school. He said, however, that more interestingly he thinks the major gain from therapy turned out to be that he was more tolerant of himself and that he could make mistakes and have less anxiety.

SUMMARY

In summary, an Ericksonian approach to therapy is perhaps like the execution of a martial art known as aikido. Aikido is almost diametrically opposite karate and tae kwan do. In aikido practitioners are to do very little *to* an attacker but instead use the energy and behavior *of* the attacker to neutralize the attack.

Ironically, there are a number of skills the aikido practitioner must learn in order to do nothing to the attacker. Among these skills are understanding the dynamic energy brought by the other person and assessing where the other person is headed, and how the person is using himself to get there. Someone using aikido may, in a relaxed and rapid fashion, place himself in the path of the opponent—not so as to offer direct resistance, but so as

to deflect the vector of the attack and redirect the attacker's center. Doing so changes the outcome. Little, if anything, is added to the attacker that he didn't already have. In the end it appears that the person using aikido did nearly nothing.

In Ericksonian therapy, the therapist does not "do" anything to the client but instead accepts the energy given by the client. Assessing the direction and resources held by the client, the Ericksonian therapist may place ideas and tasks in his path—not to block or resist, but to alter the forward momentum. In the end the client changes himself with his resources and his momentum. The therapist does not want to take any credit for the gains made by the client. The therapist is only a catalyst for the outcome. Ericksonian therapy creates a context for change whether that is in the session, outside the session, or in concentrated internal absorption of self-hypnosis.

REFERENCES

Alman, B., & Carney, R. (1980). Consequences of direct and indirect suggestion on success of posthypnotic behaviour. *American Journal of Clinical Hypnosis, 23,* 112–118.

Bateson, Gregory. (1972). *Steps to an ecology of mind.* New York: Ballantine Books, division of Random House.

Erickson, M. (1985). *The seminars, workshops, and lectures of Milton H. Erickson: Vol. 2. Life reframing in hypnosis.* E. L. Rossi, M. O. Ryan, & F. A. Sharp (Eds.). New York: Irvington.

Fisch, R. (1990). The broader interpretation of Milton H. Erickson's Work. In S. Lankton (Ed.), *The Ericksonian Monographs: No. 7. The issue of broader implications of Ericksonian Therapy* (pp. 1–5). New York: Brunner/Mazel.

Haley, J. (1963). *Strategies of psychotherapy.* New York: Grune & Stratton.

Haley, J. (Ed.). (1967). *Advanced techniques of hypnosis and therapy: Selected papers of Milton H. Erickson, M.D.* New York: Grune & Stratton.

Haley, J. (1973). Uncommon therapy: The psychiatric techniques of Milton H. Erickson, M.D. New York: Norton.

Haley, J. (1985a). *Conversations with Milton H. Erickson, M.D.: Changing individuals.* New York: Norton.

Jackson, D. (Ed.). (1968a). *Communication, family, and marriage: 1.* Palo Alto: Science and Behavior Books, Inc.

Jackson, D. (Ed.). (1968b). *Therapy, communication, and change: 2.* Palo Alto: Science and Behavior Books, Inc.

Keeney, B. (1983). *The aesthetics of change.* New York: Guilford Press.

Lankton, S., & Lankton, C. (1983). *The answer within: A clinical framework of Ericksonian hypnotherapy.* New York: Brunner/Mazel.

Matthews, W. J., & Langdell, S. (1989). What do clients think about the metaphors they receive? *American Journal of Clinical Hypnosis, 31*(1) 242–251.

Maturana, H., & Varela, F. (1987). *The tree of knowledge.* Boston: New Science Library, Shambhala.

McConkey, K. (1984). The impact of indirect suggestion. *The International Journal of Clinical and Experimental Hypnosis, 32,* 307–314.

Mosher, D., & Matthews, W. (1985). Multiple embedded metaphor and structured amnesia. Paper presented at the American Psychological Association meeting, San Diego, CA.

Nugent, W. (1989a). Evidence concerning the causal effect of an Ericksonian hypnotic intervention. *Ericksonian Monographs, 5,* 35–55.

Nugent, W. (1989b). A multiple baseline investigation of an Ericksonian hypnotic approach. *Ericksonian Monographs, 5,* 69–85.

Rossi, E., Ryan, M., & Sharp, F. (Eds.). (1983). *Healing in hypnosis by Milton H. Erickson.* New York: Irvington.

Satir, V. (1964). *Conjoint family therapy.* Palo Alto: Science and Behavior Books, Inc.

Stone, J. A., and Lundy, R. M. (1985). Behavioural compliance with direct and indirect body movement suggestions. *Journal of Abnormal Psychology, 3,* 256–263.

Chapter 20

EXISTENTIAL-HUMANISTIC PSYCHOTHERAPY

JEFFREY G. SHARP and JAMES F. T. BUGENTAL

This method of psychotherapy evolved from the confluence of the rich traditions of existentialism and humanistic psychology. Existentialism developed with Kierkegaard and Nietzsche, and was popularized in the United States by Rollo May. Humanistic psychology originated in Post World War II American psychology. These two traditions address and emphasize human capacities such as choice, will, insight, creativity, intentionality and compassion within the unique context of each individual life. James Bugental has developed an approach to depth psychotherapy derived from existentialism's concern with an individual's immediate presence *and humanism's emphasis upon the integrity of each individual.*

The therapy process includes helping clients utilize a searching process as a means of addressing their deepest concerns. Close attention is paid to the client's immediate, ongoing experience during each session. A final aim is to help clients develop greater presence in their ongoing quest for meaning and purpose. This chapter calls for close reading since it involves a number of basic concepts that do not exist in other systems.

DEFINITION

The existential-humanistic view is an orientation to life-changing psychotherapy introduced in this country by Rollo May (May, Angel, & Ellenberger, 1958). Deriving from existential philosophy, it is characterized by a continual monitoring of the client's *subjectivity* as it is manifested through variations in the client's genuine *presence* to the therapeutic process.

This approach derives from the humanistic perspective the view that motivation is purposive and choiceful, and that the person or self cannot be reduced to the sum of its parts (DeCarvalho, 1991). It takes from the existential tradition an emphasis on confronting ultimate concerns with freedom, separateness, meaninglessness, and death (Bugental, 1978; Yalom, 1980).

A cornerstone of the therapeutic work is this focus on *presence.* That term refers to how genuinely, completely, and consciously a person is in a situation rather than standing apart from it as observer, commentator, critic, or judge (Bugental, 1987). The therapist draws attention to what interferes with the client's presence and recognizes these *resistances* as isomorphic with the life patterns that produce distress (Bugental, 1987).

The work is carried forward by helping the client engage in concern-guided *searching* (Bugental, 1978, 1987). Such searching is a latent potential of the human psyche, but the client needs help to make it actual and productive. That process calls for the client to focus on a life issue of genuine significance, and then to describe it fully while attending to concurrent associations and maintaining an expectancy of discovery. From this "set" the client may be able to explore significant life issues that have been disclosed.

Facilitating this process is a science and an art in which the therapist must use his or her subjectivity as well as cognitive and conceptual associations.

HISTORY

The existential-humanistic orientation to psychotherapy evolved out of two major streams of thought: European existential philosophy and psychiatry, and the American humanistic psychology movement. The rich, complex history of each of these related yet distinct intellectual traditions has been widely documented (DeCarvalho, 1991; Yalom, 1980). Here we call attention to a few key concepts and developments in each of these traditions, and look at recent efforts to integrate them.

Existential Psychotherapy

Existential psychotherapy evolved from the European existential philosophical tradition, which emphasized the importance of the experiencing subject. Kierkegaard and

Nietzsche, with their ground-breaking analyses of subjectivity and the emerging self, are widely viewed as the originators of the existential perspective. This perspective posits that truth depends upon the existing, experiencing person, in a given situation at a given moment. Existentialism developed, in part, in opposition to essentialism, the perspective that humans have a fixed or permanent nature. The European existential orientation also focused on human limitations and the tragic dimensions of life.

Rollo May is widely credited with introducing European existential psychotherapy into American psychology. His seminal book *Existence* (May et al., 1958) profoundly influenced many American psychologists who had begun to speak out in opposition to the narrow concepts of behaviorism and orthodox psychoanalysis that dominated Western psychology at that time. Bugental (1995b) has described the dramatic influence that May's writings, and presentations, had upon him (as well as upon others). He wrote that May's work

> exploded on me as a major emotional and professional experience: I had found someone who really knew about the unfamiliar territory into which my patients (not "clients" in those days) were taking me. Here was someone who could name, describe, and confirm the phenomena that my training had only vaguely known existed. With this perspective, and borrowing frequently from May's wisdom and experience I began to articulate what I'd been grappling with and to advance more satisfyingly in the endless work of trying to understand our human condition more deeply and more fully. From then on, I wrote out of my experience rather than solely in the cognitive style I had used before. (p. 103)

May went on to write several enormously influential books that continued to describe fundamental dimensions of human nature. He wrote scholarly studies that vividly and powerfully addressed issues at the very core of human nature. This included studies of normal and neurotic anxiety (*The Meaning of Anxiety,* 1977), creativity (*The Courage to Create,* 1975), the meaning of love and its relationship to will, wish, choice, and decision (*Love and Will,* 1969), and the nature of power (*Power and Innocence,* 1972).

Another writer who has been hugely influential in bringing existential thought into American awareness is Irvin Yalom. Yalom's *Existential Psychotherapy* (1980), the classic text on this topic, is a scholarly presentation of existential perspectives on clinical matters. In it he lucidly and forcefully addresses the importance of four dominant themes in human functioning and in the practice of psychotherapy: death, freedom, isolation, and meaninglessness. Yalom has continued to address existential themes through vivid case studies (*Love's Executioner and Other Tales of Psychotherapy,* 1989), a classic text on group therapy, *The Theory and Practice of Group Psychotherapy* (1995), and, in recent years, novels (*When Nietzsche Wept,* 1991; *Lying on the Couch,* 1996).

Many dominant voices in the existential tradition have argued that its contributions have significantly influenced other traditions (Bugental, 1987; May & Yalom, 1995; Schneider & May, 1995). Numerous authors continue to clarify and address existential themes inherent in contemporary clinical and research endeavors.

Humanistic Psychology

Humanistic psychology originated as a small movement in post–World War II American psychology, largely in reaction to the then-dominant fields of behaviorism and orthodox psychoanalysis. From its outset, humanistic psychology was interested in the experiencing subject and was opposed to the narrow, reductionistic conception of human nature that characterized the then-regnant orientations.

The movement, and tradition, was initially inspired by the vision, early works, and organizational efforts of Abraham Maslow. During the early 1950s, Maslow compiled a list of like-minded psychologists, and began circulating their names and respective writings. Initially this group was united more in what they protested than in an explicit, shared conception of human nature. Consequently, they initially described themselves as a "third force" in American psychology. Out of this initial group of psychologists eventually emerged an association (the American Association for Humanistic Psychology, which later became the Association for Humanistic Psychology), a journal (the *Journal of Humanistic Psychology*), an educational and research institute (The Humanistic Psychology Institute, now the Saybrook Graduate School and Research Institute), and a division of the American Psychological Association (Division 32, on Humanistic Psychology). Seminal leaders within this movement were the aforementioned Maslow, May, and Bugental, along with Gordon Allport and Carl Rogers (for a review, see DeCarvalho, 1991).

In 1963, about 75 individuals participated in the founding meeting of the American Association of Humanistic Psychologists. This spirited meeting addressed the isolation and frustration that these individuals experienced within academic psychology. An early effort to formally define humanistic psychology emerged from the association:

> Humanistic Psychology is primarily concerned with those human capacities and potentialities that have little or no systematic place, either in positivist or behaviorist theory or in classical psychoanalytic theory, e.g., love, creativity, self, growth, organism, basic need–gratification, self-actualization, naturalness, warmth, ego-transcendence, objectivity, autonomy, responsibility, meaning, fairplay,

transcendental experience, psychological health, and related concepts. (Bugental, 1964, p. 22)

Humanistic psychologists, from the outset, emphasized the experiencing and becoming aspects of human existence. The person at his or her best was viewed as proactive, choiceful, autonomous, adaptable, and mutable. Therefore one carries responsibility for the individuation and actualization of one's own existence. The process of becoming was not to be simply viewed as the byproduct of genetics, biology, unconscious conflicts, or external reinforcements. The rejection of being or of becoming was viewed as a dangerous psychological illness that plagued conformist American culture and was exacerbated by the doctrines of behaviorism and psychoanalysis.

The popularity and influence of humanistic psychology grew enormously during the 1960s and early 1970s. Membership in the Association of Humanistic Psychology (AHP) grew from 75 to 500 from 1963 to 1966. Graduate psychology departments with humanistic concentrations were founded. By the early 1970s the AHP had gained international status, with chapters in Europe, Asia, and Central and South America. International conferences were well attended, and humanistic growth centers were established in over a dozen countries (DeCarvalho, 1991).

During this era humanistic psychology went through dramatic phases of growth, popularity, chaos, trivialization, stagnation, and then reformulation and renewal. Yalom (1980) has colorfully described the early phases of this transformation:

> In the 1960's (and 1970's) the counterculture with its attendant social phenomena—such as the free speech movement, the flower children, the drug culture, the human potentialists, the sexual revolution—engulfed the humanistic psychological movement. Soon the association conventions developed aspects of a carnival. The big tent of humanistic psychology was, if nothing else, generous and soon included a bewildering number of schools barely able to converse with one another even in an existential Esperanto. Gestalt therapy, transpersonal therapy, encounter groups, holistic medicine, psychosynthesis, Sufi, and many, many others pranced into the arena. (pp. 19–20)

Yalom went on to criticize many dangerous elements in this movement, such as hedonism, anti-intellectualism, excessive emphasis on individual growth, and a naive optimism about the perfectability of man.

Greening (1984, October) chronicled an ongoing series of articles and debates within the humanistic community that emerged in reaction to concerns such as those expressed by Yalom. In 1984, 14 prominent humanistic scholars (Anderson et al., 1984), concerned about anti-intellectual tendencies within AHP, presented the following criticisms of the Association:

1. The deterioration of intellectual dialogue.
2. An ambivalence toward science.
3. A tendency to reduce concepts to jargon.
4. A confusion of optimism with hope.
5. A certain smugness about the superiority of group beliefs.

Such criticisms, conflicts, and ongoing debates have led to renewed efforts within the field of humanistic psychology to develop systematic and rigorous methods of studying human beings. These efforts are particularly evident in the *Journal of Humanistic Psychology,* Division 32 of APA, and humanistically oriented institutes such as the Saybrook Graduate School and Research Institute. Today scholars continue to address such critical and challenging questions as: What is human science? What research methods best serve psychologists? How can humanistic principles be applied to organizations? What is the relationship between humanistic psychotherapy and contemporary psychoanalytic theories, such as intersubjective theories? What role should phenomenology play in psychological research? What training methods most effectively imbue humanistic values?

Existential-Humanistic Psychotherapy

Both the existential and humanistic traditions emphasize the importance of subjectivity and the experiencing, evolving self. Existential-humanistic psychology embodies a confluence of complementary traditions. While each emphasizes the primacy of subjectivity and the importance of intentionality, existentialism does so in relation to limits, anxiety, and tragic aspects of life, while humanistic psychology does so in relation to possibilities, hope, and potential.

CURRENT STATUS

Although existential psychotherapy has had a pervasive impact on other schools of therapy, there have been few adequate training courses, or institutes, that fully address this kind of therapy. May and Yalom (1995) attribute this dilemma to existential psychotherapy's concern with broad generalizations about human beings rather than specific techniques.

In this context, two recent developments are quite noteworthy. The first is the creation, by Bugental and several colleagues, of an ongoing training program in Existential-Humanistic Psychotherapy. The second development, which largely emerged from the first, is the recent creation of the Existential-Humanistic Institute, a training, service, and support center (Schneider, 1997, Fall/1998, Winter).

The Art of the Psychotherapist

The Art of the Psychotherapist training program, derived from Bugental's (1987) book of the same title, is an ongoing, systematic series of trainings for mental health professionals. The arts program consists of five, five-day residential programs teaching an existential perspective, humanistic values, and the practical clinical skills to implement them. A concomitant outcome of these retreats has been the development of mutually supportive groups of professionals who have trained together for several years. Participants continue regularly to convene, from around the United States and Canada, in order to support each others' ongoing personal and professional development of one another.

This training program takes place in the context and atmosphere of a retreat. Participants commit five or six days to each of these trainings, which are separated by periods of at least six months of practice. In return, there is time not only for substantial submersion into one's own subjective experience during the trainings, but also for activities that complement the training, such as journaling, hiking, music, dance, yoga, meditation, poetry readings, or other expressive arts.

The initial phases of this program are structured primarily around a series of skill-building exercises. Through roleplays, taped interviews, observing others, journaling, and group process exercises, participants refine their clinical skills. Topics addressed include basic conversational arts, subject matter guidance, fostering greater depth, and becoming discerning of intrapsychic processes. The trainings are designed as vehicles to support participants in their own growth and development in relation to these dimensions, and to enable participants to better assist clients' isomorphic growth and development.

A central concern, throughout the trainings, is to create a context in which participants feel encouraged and safe to explore their own personal, subjective reactions to various aspects of clinical work and to examine what it means to be a psychotherapist in our contemporary world. Participants are encouraged to fully experience the fear, hope, frustration, dread, uncertainty, sadness and joy that accompany depth psychotherapy and life itself—and that are considered by some to be unprofessional, unacceptable, or at the very least, unsafe to discuss with colleagues.

Four distinct structured programs, each lasting five days and separated by at least six months, constitute the initial stages of this training process. Participants are taught specific skills and competencies. Each group of participants, however, takes on a character of its own, based on the participants' life histories, clinical experience, and contributions to the programs. After the four structured retreats, each group designs and implements its own agenda for further trainings.

A powerful aspect of these trainings is that individuals generally participate in this series of trainings with the same group of peers. Over a course of several years, perhaps a dozen individuals gather once or twice a year to refine their clinical skills, address their professional concerns, and support one another's growth and development. Considerable trust and cohesion develop within these groups, as demonstrated by the continuation of some peer groups for over 10 years.

These ongoing trainings provide a forum and context in which participants can explore and develop their professional interests with like-minded yet supportively critical colleagues. Thus individuals may present work in progress, such as drafts of professional papers, or use the retreats to experiment with experiential processes such as new therapeutic techniques or teaching methods. Pierson and Sharp (in press) have described the philosophy, content, atmosphere, and process of the arts program in far greater detail.

The Existential-Humanistic Institute

In February 1998, the Existential-Humanistic Institute was founded in San Francisco to create a "home" for like-minded therapists and scholars and to provide conferences and seminars on Existential-Humanistic Psychotherapy (Schneider, 1997, Fall/1998, Winter). The Institute was founded through the collaborative efforts of numerous graduates of the arts trainings, along with interested scholars from around the United States. The institute sponsors a variety of presentations and conferences, and publishes a newsletter, *The Existential Humanist*. This fledging organization provides a variety of ways for writers, scholars, and clinicians to share ideas and activities.

An initial project of this institute has been to provide training opportunities that enable participants to integrate existential-humanistic perspectives and practices into their clinical work. A systematic framework of courses, integrating philosophy and practice, is offered to graduate students and practicing therapists.

In an exciting and highly productive adaptation of this model, several founding members of the Existential-Humanistic Institute have conducted training programs with Russian psychotherapists over a period of several years. These trainings, held in the United States and in Russia, have led to extensive intercultural exchange (Boyd, 1997, Fall/1988, Winter). They have also led to the establishment of existential-humanistic institutes in Moscow and St. Petersburg.

THEORY

A principal point of distinction about the existential-humanistic perspective on psychotherapy resides in the underlying concept of the nature of psychological distress. Accordingly, the effort to alleviate that distress must be directed quite differently than is usual in the practice of many other perspectives.

While the sources of emotional-cognitive pain and malfunctioning are indeed legion, an important common denominator is often discovered in faulty ways in which a person conceives of his or her nature. Too often we have learned to regard ourselves as things, as objects, or, indeed, as elaborate machines. Our subjectivity, our inner life, is reduced to a by-product of interactions between environmental forces and internal physical-chemical processes.

As a consequence, psychological diagnosis often centers on behavioral indicators, objective tests, and detached study of personal histories. The more objective, quantifiable, and impersonal a treatment modality, the more likely it will be valued.

It is here proposed that we focus attention on what is *actual* in the living moment. This means on what is in fact going on in the client, not what the client may say or what the therapist may infer. This is an elusive concept. We are so accustomed to talking *about* ourselves, *about* our clients, *about* our observations. The preposition *about* is the key; what is about some topic is not that topic itself. To tell you about myself is to report on my image of my own being. But the map is not the territory. If you and I spend some hours together and then independently write an account of our time and of ourselves, it is not surprising that we will end up with contrasting statements. But which is the correct one?

The avenue to the living experience is, and can only be, the encounter with the living presence itself. That formulation is difficult to grasp. It is this contrast that requires that the therapist play a crucially important role—that of an engaged observer-reporter rather than detached detective or repairman.

The following fictional psychotherapeutic interview illustrates this perspective. The interaction is purposefully exaggerated in order to bring out the contrast to other therapeutic modes. It assumes a strong therapeutic alliance has been developing through prior sessions.

CLIENT: I am so miserable. I can't stop crying. You can see what a wreck I am. Just last week I was hopeful that my life would change, but it hasn't. It's the same miserable mess all over again.

THERAPIST: You sound very matter of fact as you tell me this.

CLIENT: Well, can't you tell what misery I'm in?

THERAPIST: It seems important that I recognize how disappointed you are.

CLIENT: (Aggrieved) Why, yes! Of course. That's why I come here.

THERAPIST: And now you are troubled that I seem not to appreciate how severe is your disappointment.

CLIENT: Well, yes! I don't know what you think you're doing, but your questions are certainly not helping me.

THERAPIST: Helping you what?

CLIENT: Get out of this funk, damn it! I'm sick of being depressed!

THERAPIST: You know, that's the first time you've said that you want to make changes in your life. Suddenly you sound involved in your life.

CLIENT: Yeah, well, I guess I kinda am.

THERAPIST: Now you sound resigned again.

CLIENT: I don't understand you, I don't know what you want from me!

THERAPIST: You seem more intent on figuring out what I want than on addressing your unhappiness and your struggles to bring about change.

The therapeutic intent in the above interaction is to bring forcefully to the client's attention his or her detachment, to call attention to the subjective experience of the client, and to explore the client's intentionality. Existential-Humanistic Psychotherapy pursues these goals by fostering *concern-guided searching* and examining the client's various forms of resistance to this process. We elaborate on these processes in the methodology section.

Our existential orientation leads us to focus on how an individual confronts the basic parameters, or givens, of existence. Various existentially oriented theorists have developed their own analyses of these fundamental conditions. For example, Yalom's classic text, *Existential Psychotherapy* (1980), examines psychological functioning in relation to confrontations with death, freedom, isolation, and meaninglessness.

Bugental (1987) identified five fundamental givens of existence and the inescapable circumstances, or confrontations, that accompany them. These givens are embodiedness, finitude, the ability to act or not act, choicefulness, and separate-but-relatedness. Our embodiedness, for example, forces us to recognize (or repress) that we are continually changing, that we and our world are continually in flux. Similarly,

> our being finite means that we will die, that we cannot do all things, that we cannot know all we need to, that contingency is always our partner in determining the outcomes of our efforts. Those efforts express our ability to take action, the fact that we are not hapless observers, that what we do makes a difference, and that we carry, therefore, responsibility. That responsibility is linked also with our choicefulness, with our being able to select from a repertoire of possibilities, and as a result with our continual need to relinquish. Finally, our paradoxical

circumstance of being at once related to but separate from all others leads to confronting our aloneness at times and at other times to accepting our being bonded to others whether we would or not, a condition given the name of "apartness." (Bugental, 1987, p. 240)

Schneider and May (1995) have provided another valuable framework for addressing the givens of existence. They highlight three themes that distinguish the historical perspective of existential psychotherapy:

1. Human experience is characterized by freedom (will, creativity, expressiveness) and by limitation (natural and social restraints, vulnerability, and death).
2. The dread of either freedom or limitation (usually due to past trauma) promotes extreme or dysfunctional counterreactions to that dread. These counterreactions often manifest themselves in either fanatical overreaching (if the dread centers on one's limits) or banal timidity (if the dread centers on one's freedom).
3. The confrontation with or integration of the polarities promotes a more vibrant, invigorating life design. This life design is exemplified by increased sensitivity, flexibility and choice. (Schneider & May, 1995, pp. 10, 11).

Existential-Humanistic Psychotherapy seeks to help clients confront and integrate these polarities.

METHODOLOGY

Existential-Humanistic Psychotherapy is both an art and a science (Bugental, 1987; Schneider & May, 1995; Yalom, 1980), built not only on studies of human development, interviewing, and psychotherapy, but also upon the evolving artistry of the therapist. As such, it cannot be formalized or reduced to simple formulas. Rather, guiding principles are to be followed.

This methodology section sketches the main principles that guide Existential-Humanistic Psychotherapy. Some of these principles are consistent with other forms of depth psychotherapy, while others are unique to our perspective. Each practitioner will, of course, select from these or others in keeping with his or her perception of the needs and resources of a particular client at a given time.

The principles that follow derive from the overriding conviction that the fundamental task of the psychotherapist is to help each client experience, attend to, and utilize his or her subjective world in relation to the existential givens of life.

An initial principle of this approach is to foster client *presence. Presence* refers to "how genuinely and completely a given individual is subjectively in a situation rather than standing apart from it as observer, commentator, critic, or judge" (Bugental, 1987, p. 26). *Presence* includes being attuned to what one is experiencing inwardly, or subjectively, as well as to the context or situation in which one is at the moment. A central therapeutic challenge is to help the client listen to what he or she is actually experiencing—which may or may not coincide with what he or she begins to talk about. A therapist may encourage a client to pause and reflect for a few moments on what feels of importance (e.g., "Rather than simply telling me further about what happened during the past week, listen closely to your immediate feelings and concerns, to what is emerging within you as you reflect on these events"). Similarly, a therapist may point out to a client that prematurely seeking solutions to problems impedes the client's ability to attend to the intensity and depth of what they are experiencing ("You seem to be trying to ignore your grief, as if it is not important to attend to it").

The two chief aspects of presence are *accessibility* and *expressiveness. Accessibility* refers to the extent to which one intends that what happens in a situation will matter or will have an effect upon oneself. This involves reducing the usual level of defenses against being influenced by another; thus it requires a measure of commitment. An often useful therapist intervention is to encourage the client to pause and take serious note of what he or she is experiencing, be it intense or low-key, confusing or illuminating, familiar or unusual.

Expressiveness has to do with the extent to which one intends to let oneself be truly known by the other(s) in a situation. This involves disclosing without disguise some of one's subjective experiencing, and it sometimes requires a willingness to put forth considerable effort. The therapist may facilitate this by reflecting back what is manifest, with such statements as: "You're finding it difficult to devote your main effort to self-discovery rather than telling me about yourself," or "You are so self-critical that you block your own inner discovery."

Presence, accessibility, and *expressiveness* are all ranges, not either/or processes. They shift and vary continually, in our daily lives as well as in therapeutic endeavors, depending on the material being addressed, the purpose and context of the interaction, and the persons involved. Our approach closely monitors, and at times feeds back, the client's different levels of presence during the clinical hour. A goal in this process is to heighten the client's in-the-moment awareness of, and ability to utilize, different levels of presence and engagement. Thus a therapist may say to a client, "You smile as you talk about your sadness," or "Your voice drops as you convey your anger." Such interventions call attention to the client's apparent resistance to experiencing fully his or her sadness or anger. Bugental (1978, 1987) has systematically described various levels of client presence and optimal therapeutic responses.

The therapeutic intent here is to enrich the client's inner experience by bringing in the intentional element that is evident to the therapist but may not be conscious to the client. Here, as in all of this work, the therapist's goal is to expand the client's awareness yet avoid making the client self-objectifying. This is a challenging task but an important one. When achieved it will greatly enrich the client's use of the therapeutic opportunity.

The immediate subjective experiencing of the client is a central focus of attention for Existential-Humanistic Psychotherapy. What distinguishes this approach's work is the use of *concern-guided searching,* a developed form of free association. It differs from traditional free associating in its emphasis on the element of concern.

Concern refers to the experience of allowing oneself to truly care about some life issue, to invest oneself in it, and to be ready to work to bring about desired change. *Concern* is defined as the subjective (cognitive-affective) recognition of what is of major importance to one's life. In Existential-Humanistic Psychotherapy, a client is encouraged to identify an important life issue, and to strive to remain as fully present, as attuned to subjective experiencing, as is possible while also exploring the concern. The client is also coached to maintain an expectancy of discovery.

The therapeutic challenge is to ascertain the client's level of presence, functioning, needs, and potential for growth. Based on these evaluations, the therapist calls attention to the client's efforts, moment to moment, to address his or her concerns.

This process involves attending to the various manifestations of *resistance* that inevitably arise when a client begins to face the possibility of significant life change. Bugental has defined *resistance* as

> the impulse to protect one's familiar identity and known world against perceived threat. In depth psychotherapy, resistance is those ways in which the client avoids being truly subjectively present—accessible and expressive—in the therapeutic work. The conscious or unconscious threat is that immersion will bring challenges to the client's being in the world. (1987, p. 175).

Consequently, resistance is not only a universal process, but an often necessary, healthy phenomenon. The therapeutic challenge is to gradually help the client ascertain ways in which his or her patterns of resistance may be sabotaging greater fulfillment.

An existential-humanistic therapeutic approach differs from many traditional forms of psychotherapy in the manner in which it addresses resistance. The emphasis is on continually helping the client see what manifests moment by moment (e.g., "Your voice drops as you say you are furious at your husband"). A fundamental treatment goal is to help the client persist with the searching process, and to become more conscious of resistances to

doing so, rather than relying on the therapist to hand out directives or explanations.

This generally entails addressing interview resistance, life-pattern resistance, and life-limiting resistance. Interview resistance refers to not allowing oneself to be subjectively present, and engaged, during the clinical hour. Life-pattern resistance refers to frequently repeated patterns in which the client is not present, or engaged, in his or her life. A key therapeutic task is to demonstrate to the client parallels between interview resistance and life-pattern resistance. That is, the therapist seeks to help the client see similarities between the client's way of being in the therapeutic relationship and his or her patterns of being outside of the office. Resistances in the therapeutic experience come to be seen as more than isolated, troublesome habits; rather, they are recognized as a segment of a larger, self-constricting pattern or life-limiting process intrinsic to the distresses in the client's life.

An existential-humanistic approach seeks to help clients perceive patterns of resistance within the larger framework of one's *self-and-world construct* (Bugental, 1987, p. 178). Our self-and-world construct system is broader than our resistive functions; it also includes the constructive, functional structures of one's life. That is, our self-and-world construct system includes our sense of our strengths and weaknesses, our needs, the dangers that threaten us, and the kinds of things or states of being we will seek or avoid.

In the process of depth psychotherapy, one's self-and-world construct system becomes challenged. Through deeper immersion into one's subjectivity, through greater self-awareness or consciousness, often one encounters conflicts between one's emerging experience of oneself or of the world and one's previous conception of oneself and of the world. This conflict may be relatively isolated and insignificant, such as pridefully conceiving of oneself as always honest and yet discovering half-truths one occasionally conveys in a work setting. Conversely, the conflict may be enormous and earth-shattering, such as during an existential crisis in which one discovers fundamental disjunctures between one's construct system and what is emerging as one's resistances are rolled back or diminished. Such crises are fraught with potency for life change—and with grave danger if poorly handled (Bugental, 1987).

This approach to psychotherapy seeks to help clients appreciate—through their experiences in the therapeutic interactions—that as humans we are, ultimately, processes, not things. We continually become who we are, we continually shape and rewrite our identity, through our doing, acting, reflecting, and relating. Existential-Humanistic Psychotherapy strives to help clients perceive and appreciate that a critical task of human life is to continually develop an evolving sense of personal identity.

APPLICATIONS

This therapeutic approach evolved out of depth psychotherapy with individuals and, not surprisingly, is most effective in that setting. That is, the goals of this approach include close examination, evaluation, and (generally) amendment of how one confronts the givens of existence. To address and achieve such goals requires substantial effort; client and therapist usually must be committed to an ongoing, consistent therapeutic process.

Bugental has written several books that detail such work through extensive case studies (1976), descriptions of the subjective processes of the therapist (1990), and analysis of fundamental elements of the therapeutic process (1978, 1987, 1999). The reader is encouraged to review these books for additional descriptions of the utilization of this approach in the context of depth psychotherapy.

Couples and Families

Many of the principles and methods of an existential-humanistic perspective are applicable to work with couples, families, and groups. Yalom (1995) has argued that the power of therapy groups is tied to the existential issues of assuming one's personal freedom and owning responsibility for one's participation, verbal and otherwise, ideally amid the lively subculture of a therapy group. He identified two essential therapeutic principles in working with groups: helping members to more fully be aware of their here-and-now experiencing, and illuminating group processes. These two principles can be applied effectively in work with couples and families.

A critical initial task in work with couples is to seek to create an atmosphere in which it is safe for each member to be authentically present. Often this is no small task. That is, a therapist must initially ensure that there are no threats to the physical well-being of each person. Abuse, destructive behavior, or violence must be interrupted and prohibited within the therapy office and proscribed elsewhere.

It is then necessary to explore the hopes, intentions, and psychological resources of each person: Have they come to therapy with the intention of blaming and attacking one another? Are they ready, willing, and interested in exploring their individual contributions to the strengths and weaknesses of their relationship? Do they have the desire and motivation to explore more fully their individual wishes, needs, disappointments, yearnings? Are they emotionally ready to empathically listen to their partner?

If sufficient safety has been established, and there is motivation for examining one's own contributions to relationship problems, many of the methods for work with individuals can be utilized in a slightly modified manner. Fostering presence, including accessibility and expressiveness, is often a powerful intervention in itself. Encouraging each member of a couple to reflect upon how they want to use the therapy session can interrupt a blaming/defending cycle of interactions. Many clients realize, on reflection, that continuing to attack one another is not likely to improve the quality of the relationship. If clients persist in attacks on one another, illuminating the process can be helpful. Often clients realize that they need new ways of dealing with their distress when directly confronted with the question "Does this sort of fighting help your relationship?"

Exploring the desire and willingness to be present—to acknowledge and take responsibility for one's unhappiness—frequently brings up numerous forms of resistance. Some of these resistances are due primarily to interpersonal concerns ("If I reveal vulnerability or neediness will I be attacked?"), while others emerge from concerns tied to one's evolving sense of self ("If I take responsibility for feeling unhappy and needy, how does that fit with my sense of myself as competent and in control?") Exploring these resistances—seeing their value and cost—can deepen each individual's sense of self and relatedness.

Similarly, existential-humanistic principles can be utilized in work with families. Again it is imperative initially to address issues of safety. This process may take a few minutes or a few months, depending on the nature and severity of the presented problems and the resources of the family members. Through creating a safe context in which individuals can be more present, more accessible, and more expressive, greater individuation and family cohesion can be fostered. The nature and depth of this work will of course be influenced by the goals, wishes and resources (internal and external) of the family members, as well as by their cultural values and mores.

Short-Term Applications

Bugental (1995a) has identified three principles that facilitate the application of an existential-humanistic approach to short-term therapy. The first of these is to emphasize the autonomy of the person who is the client; that is, to emphasize that the change agency is the client's own self-discovery rather than the insight, power, or manipulation of the therapist. The second principle is to demonstrate to the client the power of the natural searching process, and to help the client learn to continue to use this process outside of the therapy office. The third principle is to avoid building habits or expectancies that would be countertherapeutic if and when the client undertook further and deeper therapeutic work.

Short-term work requires a clearly defined and lim-

ited focus of effort. Treatment goals must be far less ambitious, and more overt structure must be imposed on
the therapeutic process. This structure generally consists
of a series of phases. The first phase, assessment, has
three components. Initially the therapist must evaluate
whether the presenting problem can be isolated to some
extent and made explicit or objective. The therapist then
must assess whether the client's urgency (pain, anxiety,
or distress) is such that he or she has sufficient ego
strength to sustain an apparently indirect approach. Finally, it is necessary to evaluate whether the client has
sufficient ego functioning to support intensive searching, and whether the client's observing ego can develop a
truly therapeutic alliance. Each of these conditions must
be met, if possible, before moving on to the next phase.
If a condition is not met—which is often the case—
longer term work will likely be required.

The second phase is to encourage the client to present
his or her concern in a succinct form. The therapist seeks
to shape the issue into as explicit or objective a form as
is valid, without distorting the concern by the therapist's
manipulations. A contract is then made to work toward
greater understanding and some resolution of the issue.

A third phase is to teach the searching process. This
generally includes teaching clients to get deeply centered
and to mobilize their concern.

In the fourth phase, as clients continue the searching
phase they invariably encounter resistances. They are
encouraged to take note of this process and to return to
the searching process. In stark contrast to longer term
work, there is no expectation of working through such
resistances. As a result, changes are likely to be more
shallow and less enduring. It is essential that the client
recognize this difference, for otherwise he or she may not
appreciate the limits of short-term work and may mistake them for limits of all therapy.

In the next phase, two crucial parameters of the work
must repeatedly be brought to the client's attention: First,
this is time-limited work; that limit needs to be recognized and not ignored. Second, this is work directed toward the identified concern. Other issues are likely to surface repeatedly, but they must not be allowed to derail the
focus on the initially defined concern. Attending to these
two parameters requires considerable therapeutic skill.
An overly literal or zealous rigidity about the focus can
lead to so superficial an exploration as to be therapeutically impotent. On the other hand, without considerable
structure this process could degenerate into such seeming
randomness—which might be beneficial in longer term
work—that there would be no therapeutic impact.

The final phase of this work involves termination.
Generally it is advisable to have identified a specific
number of sessions, and to adhere to that limitation.
Clients need to recognize the termination of their work
as arbitrary and as constrictive. They may gain from the
confrontation with their finitude that this ending
demonstrates.

During the termination of such therapy it is desirable
to help the client reflect on what has been accomplished
as well as what remains unaddressed. In addition, it is
generally quite valuable to urge the client to consider the
impact of incorporating the searching process into his or
her life outside the therapeutic experience.

We must emphasize that the preceding specifications
are for a very limited use of our approach. This is a compromise sometimes necessitated by circumstances (e.g.,
managed care programs), but in many instances such
short-term work is not desirable.

CASE EXAMPLE

Saul A., a portly, impeccably dressed Jewish man in his
late 50s, informed me at the outset of his first session, "I
have but one problem in life: My boss is a flaming ass-
hole. Outside of that, my life is wonderful. I'd like to deal
with this problem in the seven sessions paid for by my
employee assistance program, but I have no intention of
continuing in endless therapy sessions." I assured Saul
that I had no magic wand that could transform a ruthless
boss, but that I'd be happy to help him explore his concerns and options in light of his situation.

Saul went on to vilify his boss, in quite vivid language
and with great sarcasm, as an incompetent fool and an
unreasonable tyrant. Saul told elaborate anecdotes
about office shenanigans and gross violations of policy
orchestrated by his boss. He also described flagrant fa-
voritism that left Saul out of the power loop. His stories
about his frustration and rage were just that: stories,
seemingly designed to entertain me and to convince me
of his powerlessness in relation to his boss, but not as a
vehicle for exploring Saul's concerns and options.

A critical treatment goal early in Saul's therapy was to
confront him with his relationship to his concerns. He
seemed primarily invested in amusing me and convincing me that his situation was hopeless. I endeavored to
make this intent more explicit. After yet another witty
put-down of his boss, I commented, "You seem more interested in entertaining me than in exploring your concerns and options."

Saul was taken aback by my comment. He seemed
shocked that I had interrupted his storytelling. He then
informed me that while I was, no doubt, a well-
credentialed and well-meaning psychotherapist, I was
way off the mark in this case. It was clear to him that I
didn't comprehend the depths of malignancy and evil
within his boss. He provided me with new stories, each of
them underscoring his apparent helplessness.

"How fiercely, how adamantly, you insist that you are
powerless," I replied.

Again Saul appeared to be shocked, but this time he paused and reflected on what I had said and how he was using his time in my office. Repeatedly in our work together I pointed out how forcefully he insisted he was powerless.

I also continued to coach Saul to utilize the searching process: to pause, to reflect on his concerns, and simultaneously to focus inward on his emerging thoughts, images, concerns, and feelings. This was difficult for Saul. He was accustomed to relating to others through constantly attempting to entertain, which often included sarcastic or cynical humor. He was uncomfortable with the searching process, yet he reluctantly gave it a try.

Contrary to his opening comments during our first session, Saul was actually quite ready for ongoing, deeper psychotherapy. As he learned to look inward he began to see that some of his old, familiar ways of being contributed to his distress. He appreciated being encouraged to face his unhappiness and his self-sabotaging patterns of relating to his concerns. He agreed to continue in therapy and pay out of pocket after the seven sessions covered by his employee assistance program.

We then proceeded into a critical stage of Saul's therapy, in which I continued to push Saul to remain aware of how, during our sessions, he related to his concerns. We looked at how his wit often kept him from fully experiencing his unhappiness, and his sarcasm deflected and diffused the depths of his anger. Saul slowly began to see the value of owning and addressing the disappointment and anger that were beneath his wit and sarcasm.

Saul gradually realized that he held no hope of being fulfilled in his existing employment, and he began taking steps that would eventually lead to a valuable change of jobs.

As he made headway addressing his job dissatisfaction and career options, he began to open up about some "minor concerns" in other areas of his life. He acknowledged that he felt unhappy in his relationship with his girlfriend. At first this emerged via more angry, sarcastic stories, but this time the villain was his partner, Hilda. He described her as shallow and controlling, and he described a fundamental sense of disconnection from her. He never spoke of her with affection. Yet he raved about their great sex life and the advantages of dating a very wealthy woman.

I confronted Saul's need to again portray himself as a passive victim and his telling of stories in a manner that prevented exploration of his options. Initially Saul vigorously resisted acknowledging any options in his relationship with Hilda. He seemed terrified of owning freedom and responsibility within his relationship with her. He reverted to efforts to entertain me. He told me stories about their sexual escapades and about the advantages of Hilda's great wealth. Anything seemed better than acknowledging his current unhappiness and loneliness. Yet

Saul's stories were unconvincing. Despite his bravado, he seemed quite lonely.

My stance was threefold. First, I felt, and conveyed, empathy and compassion for Saul amid such an unsatisfying relationship. Second, I continually challenged his portrayal of himself as powerless. And third, I pointed out that endlessly joking or complaining about Hilda prevented him from addressing his pain, his fear, his wants, and his needs.

After months of such confrontations, Saul's dread of facing his fundamental aloneness gradually surfaced. Saul would visibly tense up, look away, and change the subject whenever the theme of loneliness surfaced. His experience of loneliness was exacerbated by concomitant feelings of humiliation, shame, and fear.

With my constant encouragement, Saul slowly, courageously addressed his memories and associations related to loneliness. We gradually began to better understand the intermingling of these feelings. As an eight-year-old he had been sent to England as part of the evacuation of Jewish children from Nazi Germany. At that tender age he had been torn away from his mother, father, extended family and culture, and sent off to live with total strangers.

Although Saul felt deep gratitude toward his foster family, he carried enormous bitterness about having been ostracized by the children in his new country. He was ruthlessly teased and ridiculed for being a Jew, for struggling with English, for being a German, and for being chubby and uncoordinated. This continued even after his mother joined him in England a year later. His father never escaped Germany and died in a concentration camp.

Saul knew I was moved—not entertained—by his emerging recollections. I was deeply saddened as I imagined his childhood and adolescence. I was stirred as I heard of his persistence and resilience in the face of such trauma and adversity. Saul's willingness to relinquish the role of entertainer reflected a significant positive change in our therapeutic alliance.

Saul spent months revisiting long-buried painful memories. We continually examined how such memories and related fears tied in with his current dread of being alone, and his struggles with intimacy in relationships. Gradually Saul was able to separate his lonely feelings from humiliation and shame, and he was more able to tolerate each of these.

At that point survivor guilt came powerfully into the foreground. Saul's guilt was amplified by his mother's admonition, before he was sent off to England, always to "do your utmost." She had to prepare her son for a cruel, harsh world and she sought to instill in him bravery, courage, and high standards. Unfortunately, her phrase (and her cold, distant temperament) came to mean to Saul that failure or weakness were unacceptable.

As Saul began to challenge his own perfectionism, he was more able to face existential anxiety: his anxiety about being alone, and about what to do with his life outside work. I encouraged Saul to explore and confront his anxiety; I wanted him to discern what this anxiety was telling him about his life.

Two dramatic changes transpired during the ensuing months. First, Saul became actively involved with an international organization of Holocaust survivors. As he faced his own painful memories, he found great meaning and satisfaction in helping others do the same. In order to deepen his sons' understanding of his past and their heritage, he took them to Auschwitz and to Israel.

Second, he faced the fact that he had no hope for saving his relationship with Hilda. Any love or affection that had been there was now gone. He realized how little they shared. No longer feeling the need to cling to her, he ended their relationship and spent more time with family and friends.

Saul later began dating again, and eventually met a woman with whom he developed a tender, playful, and affectionate relationship. When Saul ended his therapy he had been living with this new partner for several months. Although there were difficulties in the relationship, Saul had developed far more capacity to tolerate painful feelings and to address his desire and need for companionship. He had gained awareness of his tendency to use humor as a means of avoiding pain, anger, or anxiety. As he became more able to tolerate his own fundamental aloneness, he also developed greater desire and capacity for intimacy.

SUMMARY

Existential-Humanistic Psychotherapy has evolved from the rich, complementary traditions of humanism and existentialism. It emphasizes the importance of subjectivity and of the experiencing and becoming aspects of human existence. From the humanistic tradition there is an emphasis on possibilities, hope, and potential. From the existential tradition there is an emphasis on limits, anxiety, and the tragic aspects of life.

Existential-humanistic psychotherapists seek to foster and monitor client *presence*. Being authentically present includes being closely attuned to what one is experiencing inwardly, or subjectively, as well as to the context or situation in which one is at the moment. In our approach the therapist coaches the client to use *concern-guided searching* as a fundamental means of exploring and addressing life concerns. Examination of the client's *resistances* to this process is a central part of the therapeutic process. Resistances during the clinical encounter are examined in relation to self-constricting or life-limiting patterns elsewhere in the client's life. As a con-sequence, the client may challenge, and modify, his or her self-conception and way of being in the world.

Many contemporary movements in psychology reflect the larger culture we live in. Our society is increasingly driven by corporate values, an obsession with technology and the media, the objectification and manipulation of individuals, and the devaluing of subjectivity and autonomy. These cultural concerns manifest in psychology in the form of managed care and its emphasis on cost containment, brief therapy, and quantifiable behavioral change. Treatment plans, apparently processed by computers rather than by many clinicians, focus on trivial and often irrelevant behavioral indicators. Human concerns such as purpose, meaning, fulfillment, integrity, creativity, and passion are considered by many managed care executives to be too complex, amorphous, or ethereal to warrant attention.

Existential-Humanistic Psychotherapy chooses to reject this mold—and therein lies its strength and value. Clients, encouraged to honor their search for meaningful work and fulfilling relationships, feel understood and appreciated. Many choose to commit considerable time and effort to their therapy in order to address urgent, substantive concerns. Individuals, couples, and families convey considerable gratitude when their desires to create more fulfilling lives are met with compassionate support.

Similarly, many clinicians and scholars have been inspired by the ongoing interaction of humanistic and existential traditions. The continual development of training programs, scholarly institutes, APA divisions, journals, and newsletters devoted to the refinement and application of existential-humanistic principles, demonstrates the vitality and appeal of an existential-humanistic perspective.

REFERENCES

Anderson, W., Bridges, B., Bugental, J., Doyle, J., Farson, R., Greening, T., Haigh, G., Levy, J., Lyman, N., May, R., Michael, D., Ogilvy, J., O'Hara, M., & Polkinghorne, D. (1984, August). A challenge to all AHP members. *AHP Perspective.*

Boyd, K. (1997, Fall/1998, Winter). More Russians on my mind. *The Existential Humanist,* p. 9.

Bugental, J. F. T. (1964). The third force in psychology. *Journal of Humanistic Psychology, 4,* 19–25.

Bugental, J. F. T. (1976). *The search for existential identity: Patient-therapist dialogues in humanistic psychotherapy.* San Francisco: Jossey-Bass.

Bugental, J. F. T. (1978). *Psychotherapy and process: The fundamentals of an existential-humanistic approach.* Reading, MA: Addison-Wesley.

Bugental, J. F. T. (1987). *The art of the psychotherapist.* New York: Norton.

Bugental, J. F. T. (1990). *Intimate journeys: Stories from life-changing psychotherapy.* San Francisco: Jossey-Bass.

Bugental, J. F. T. (1995a). *Preliminary sketches for a short-term existential-humanistic therapy.* In K. Schneider & R. May (Eds.), *The psychology of existence: An integrative, clinical perspective* (pp. 261–264). New York: McGraw-Hill.

Bugental, J. F. T. (1995b). *Rollo May: Personal reflections and appreciation.* In K. Schneider & R. May (Eds.), *The psychology of existence: An integrative, clinical perspective* (pp. 102–105). New York: McGraw-Hill.

Bugental, J. F. T. (1999). *Psychotherapy isn't what you think: Bringing the psychotherapeutic engagement into the living moment.* Phoenix, AZ: Zeig, Tucker & Co.

DeCarvalho, R. (1991). *The founders of humanistic psychology.* New York: Praeger.

Greening, T. (1984, October). The *Journal of Humanistic Psychology* as a forum for controversy. *AHP Perspective.*

May, R. (1969). *Love and will.* New York: Norton.

May, R. (1972). *Power and innocence: A search for the sources of violence.* New York: Norton.

May, R. (1975). *The courage to create.* New York: Norton.

May, R. (1977). *The meaning of anxiety.* (Rev. ed.). New York: Norton.

May, R., Angel, E., & Ellenberger, H. (1958). *Existence: A new dimension in psychiatry and psychology.* New York: Basic Books.

May, R., & Yalom, I. (1995). Existential psychotherapy. In R. Corsini and D. Wedding (Eds.), *Current psychotherapies* (5th ed.) pp. 262–292. Itasca, IL: F. E. Peacock.

Pierson, J. F., & Sharp, J. (in press). Cultivating psychotherapist artistry: A model existential-humanistic training program. In K. J. Schneider, J. F. T. Bugental, & J. F. Pierson (Eds.), *The handbook of humanistic psychology: Leading edges in theory, research, and practice.* (Chapter 40). Thousand Oaks, CA: Sage.

Schneider, K. (1997, Fall/1998, Winter). An existential-humanistic institute is born. *The Existential Humanist,* p. 11.

Schneider, K., & May, R. (Eds.). (1995). *The psychology of existence: An integrative, clinical perspective.* New York: McGraw-Hill.

Yalom, I. (1980). *Existential psychotherapy.* New York: Basic Books.

Yalom, I. (1989). *Love's executioner and other tales of psychotherapy.* New York: Basic Books.

Yalom, I. (1991). *When Nietzsche wept.* New York: Basic Books.

Yalom, I. (1995). *The theory and practice of group psychotherapy* (4th ed.). New York: Basic Books.

Yalom, I. (1996). *Lying on the couch.* New York: Basic Books.

Chapter 21

EXPERIENTIAL PSYCHOTHERAPY

ALVIN R. MAHRER

In Mahrer's version of Experiential Therapy he states: "my therapy seems to have almost nothing in common with the nonexistent experiential family or with even a few of the 30–50 unrelated therapies in this mythical family." But in fact, it has. This system is at the same time old, based on his extensive readings, and new, based on his examination of the current literature and his personal experiences with it. Experiential Psychotherapy is an innovative attempt to change a person from what he or she is to what the person can be. It is organized in four steps and is based essentially on the writings and thinking of existential philosophers. Mahrer appears to have boldly gone past others in the field of experiential psychotherapy into what he himself says about his system: that it "outrageously depart[s] from and violate[s] what most professional practitioners are comfortable doing." Prepare for a completely new view of theory and practice. He says also: "This therapy has quite limited appeal to most practitioners. Perhaps the main reason is that both the actual therapy itself and the underlying way of thinking outrageously depart from and violate what most professional practitioners are comfortable doing and thinking."

Most surprising of all, Mahrer suggests that his system is incomplete, and he asks other therapists to improve on his work.

DEFINITION

Experiential Psychotherapy is defined as a person's going through an experiential session by, for, and with him- or herself. It is also defined as including a teacher who teaches-guides-shows a person how to go through an experiential session, and who joins with the person in going through the session.

Experiential Psychotherapy can also be defined by two goals to be achieved in each session. One goal is for the person to undergo a deep-seated qualitative change into becoming the kind of person this person is capable of becoming. Each session is a gateway into a whole new state, a radically transformational shift into being what this person can be. It is a powerful, quantum, qualitative shift. The related companion goal is for the qualitatively new person to be essentially free of the painful scene or situation, and the painful feeling in that scene or situation, that was front and center for the person in the beginning of the session.

A third way of defining Experiential Psychotherapy is in terms of its four steps that organize each session, steps designed to achieve the two important goals of each session. The purpose of the first step is to discover a much deeper quality, a deep-seated way of being, a deeper po-

tentiality for experiencing, inside the person in this session. The purpose of the second step is to enable the person to welcome, appreciate, accept, even love this newly discovered deeper potentiality for experiencing. The third step enables the person to undergo a radical, qualitative shift into being the deeper potentiality for experiencing in the context of earlier life scenes and situations. The final step provides an opportunity for the qualitatively whole new person to exist, to live and be, in scenes and situations from the imminent, forthcoming postsession new world.

HISTORY

The first picture that came to mind was being a little boy, hidden away in my grandmother's attic, secretly reading pornographic books by someone named Sigmund Freud. The next picture, much later, was being in my room at Ohio State University. Carl Rogers had just left for the University of Chicago, Julian Rotter was writing a seminal book on social learning theory, and George Kelly was pouring out the two volumes of his personal construct theory. The department was an exciting wellspring of bold new ways of thinking, and I, again hidden in my room, was enraptured by underground works on existential philosophy and philosophy of science: Bertalanffy, Binswanger, Bridgman, Buber, Buytendijk, Camus, Carnap, Derrida, Descartes, Dewey, Duhem, Einstein, Ellenberger, Feigl, Feyerabend, Gebsattel, Goethe, Hegel, Heidegger, Hume, Husserl, James, Jaspers, Kant, Kantor, Kierkegaard, Laing, Lakatos, Leibnitz, Locke, May, Merleau-Ponty, Minkowsky, Nietzsche, Ouspensky, Peirce, Polanyi, Popper, Quine, Reichenbach, Russell, Sartre, Scheler, Schlick, Schopenhauer, Spinoza, Straus, Tillich, von Uëxkull, Whitehead, Whorf.

The doctoral program gave me some precious gifts. It gave me a doctorate and the mantle of professional respectability. It introduced me to the world of existential philosophy and philosophy of science. And it let me be inspired by three exceedingly creative men who dared to face age-old questions, and to carve out their own distinctive answers.

A Long Search Yielded My Own Experiential Way of Making Sense of Myself and My World

I spent nearly 30 years trying to be clear about my own answers to many of these age-old questions in philosophy and psychology: How did I come to be the person I am? Why is it that I have these wonderful feelings and these awful feelings? What am I like deep down inside? What kind of person can I become? What accounts for the way we are together? How can we be better with one another? Why is my world the way it is for me? How does our world come about, and how can it change? So I wrote a book.

That book was published in 1978 and then reissued later (Mahrer, 1989a). Writing that book took 11 years. Those years allowed me to know my own way of making sense of myself and my world. When I was done, I knew how far I had departed from traditional schools of thought, from psychoanalytic theory, learning theory, biopsychological theory, cognitive theory, even theories with links to existential philosophers. Almost unintentionally, I had fashioned a distinctive experiential perspective on psychology.

A Longer Search Yielded My Own Experiential Psychotherapy

Beginning with my first job, my professional life had a fatal flaw. I worked in fine hospitals and universities. I did research and teaching and training. I published. I was engaged in some private practice. I did administrative work. I was involved in professional organizations and politics. I spent five years on a couch, talking to a nice old fellow. I did standard, nonintrusive psychotherapy. But there was a serious problem, a fatal flaw:

I still lived in a world of much the same kinds of painful scenes with the same kinds of painful feelings. I was still stuck being who and what I am. I had not taken a single step along a path toward becoming whomever and whatever I could become. I had not found a psychotherapy for myself or for the persons I worked with. This was the fatal flaw.

It took over 40 years to fashion, to put together, to develop, to ripen and mature a psychotherapy that could do what I vaguely dreamed a psychotherapy might be able to do.

I developed Experiential Psychotherapy over four decades of passionate, intense, detailed, exhaustive dissecting and learning from audiotapes of psychotherapists. Starting from the recordings that Carl Rogers had left behind when he went to the University of Chicago, I pleaded and begged for audiotapes of actual sessions from almost every practitioner I could nag. Many were well-known. Many were simply gifted artists, masters of their craft, virtuoso practitioners without fans, fanfare, publicity, or publications. For decades I dissected almost 500 sessions, discovering what psychotherapy could be and how to do it, trying out and learning from what I thought I was discovering. All the while, I felt a push to fashion some way of making sense of myself and human beings, and some way of making sense of what psychotherapy could be.

The search culminated in a way of making sense of and using dreams (Mahrer, 1989b), and a way of making sense of and doing psychotherapy (Mahrer, 1996a). Experiential Psychotherapy was my quest to find a way I could use by, for, and with myself, and for and with the persons I worked with.

Students and colleagues saw Experiential Psychotherapy as different, alien, intriguing, challenging, questionable, disturbing, compelling, weird, unique. Mainly through their eyes could I see how far I had departed from the main pack of psychotherapies. I believe they were right.

CURRENT STATUS

There Are Dozens of Unrelated "Experiential Psychotherapies"

I think I made a mistake in calling it Experiential Psychotherapy. One reason is that my therapy is so different from the pioneering 1950s experiential psychotherapy of Carl Whitaker, John Warkentin, Thomas Malone, and Richard Felder that a little simple respect would have been enough motive for my finding some other phrase. Another reason is that my therapy had almost nothing in common with Carl Rogers' approach, which changed its name from nondirective to client-centered to person-centered and then, with Eugene Gendlin, to experiential psychotherapy.

Calling my therapy experiential seemed almost deflatingly humorous when I found that there were about two dozen designated experiential psychotherapies, and an additional two dozen that used the word experiential in their title (Mahrer & Fairweather, 1993)!

What is even worse, a careful examination of these 30–50 experiential therapies seemed to reveal that they had essentially nothing in common. There were greater differences between these therapies than there were between these therapies as a group and all other therapies. Not only does there seem to be no such thing as an "experiential family," but my therapy seems to have almost nothing in common with the nonexistent experiential family or with even a few of the 30–50 unrelated therapies in this mythical family.

A few enterprising people try to co-opt and reorganize many so-called experiential therapies under their own grand megatherapy. Their war cry is that there indeed is a single experiential psychotherapy and it is ours! I believe such efforts fail to integrate the many experiential therapies into a single grand megaexperiential therapy, and instead produce yet another therapy, for example, a new client-centered–experiential-cognitive therapy. I do not try to reorganize all the many experiential therapies under the flag of my own psychotherapy. I believe it is far better to let all the unrelated experiential therapies flourish and develop in their own ways. Maybe it would have been better if I had done a better job of naming my own psychotherapy.

Its Appeal Is Quite Limited and Exceedingly Broad

This therapy has quite limited appeal to most practitioners. Perhaps the main reason is that both the actual therapy itself and the underlying way of thinking outrageously depart from and violate what most professional practitioners are comfortable doing and thinking.

On the other hand, this therapy's appeal is exceedingly broad because it speaks to any and every person, including the club of practitioners and their clients who might be interested in having a way of doing something by and for oneself, to discover and to become what you can become, and to be free of painful feelings in painful scenes.

I Do Research to Discover More and More About Psychotherapy, Not to Promote Experiential Psychotherapy

The main reason I do so much research is to discover the secrets of psychotherapy, to discover more and more about what psychotherapy can be and do, and how to help accomplish these wondrous things in actual in-session work. I do research to discover how psychotherapy, even my psychotherapy, can be better and better.

(For a summary of what I believe this research has discovered, please see Mahrer, 1996b).

I prefer this reason for doing research to research that seems aimed mainly at showing that one's favorite psychotherapy is indeed a good therapy, has a fine theoretical foundation, is of course an effective therapy, and is better than these lesser therapies. In other words, I decline doing research aimed at promoting, merchandising, selling my therapy, usually under the guise of scientific hypothesis testing.

I Prefer Helping This Therapy Get Better and Better, Rather Than Creating Priests and Disciples of an Institutionalized Experiential Psychotherapy

I hope that more and more people read my books that tell about this way of making sense of what people are like, and of what this psychotherapy can be (Mahrer, 1989a, 1989b, 1996a). I love teaching and training. I am pleased and proud that so many people share an interest in this way of thinking and in this psychotherapy.

My hope is that this experiential psychotherapy will keep getting better and better, keep growing and developing, keep extending further and further. Please help make it better. Apply it to your own work. Teach us what you have discovered. Help it to grow and develop.

I much prefer this picture to my trying to elevate this experiential psychotherapy into a hallowed institution with its bible and its rituals, its inner circle of Godlike figures, its gurus and disciples, leaders and followers, priests and dedicated congregations, its journals, postgraduate institutes and training centers, its conferences and societies, certifications and accreditations, its cadre of administrators. This picture does not fit me, and it does not fit whatever future growth and development may be in store for this way of thinking and of doing what I call Experiential Psychotherapy.

THEORY

The Experiential Conceptual System Is a Model That Is Useful, Rather Than a Theory That Is True

In the field of psychotherapy, almost without exception, most conceptualizations are theories that, first, are to approximate truth, to tell what the real world is really like. Theories are to tell the real structure of emotions, what accounts for dreams, how the brain works. Second, theories are to rest on fundamental propositions that are foundational truths. There are fundamental laws of human behavior. Psychological variables are reducible to more basic neurophysiological variables. Third, a theory is made up of pieces and parts that are real and true. There really are things like conceptual schemas, ego defenses, learned responses, pathological processes, and stages of biopsychological development.

In sharp contrast, the experiential conceptualization of human beings and of psychotherapy is a model, a convenient picture where the emphasis is on usefulness (Mahrer, 1989a, 1996a; Rorty, 1991; Speed, 1984). The premium test is usefulness, not approximation of truth. Second, models rest on a collection of basic notions and ideas that are understood as foundational beliefs, not truths; as helpful and useful beliefs, not eternal verities; as mere beliefs, not hallowed truths. Third, both the model as a whole and its component parts, its concepts and constructs, are conveniently useful fictions, hypothetical constructs, helpful representations, pictorialized metaphors, useful in helping to achieve the aims and purposes for which the model was conceived in the first place (Chalmers, 1982; Einstein, 1923; MacCorquodale & Meehl, 1948; Mahrer, 1989a, 1996a; Skinner, 1938; Whitehead, 1929).

In the Experiential Model, a Person Is Made Up of "Potentials for Experiencing" and Their Relationships"; That Is All

This model pictures a person as made up of potentials for experiencing. These are available kinds of experiencing that the particular person can have. The package of potentials in one person may be essentially unique to that person. For example, inside one person may be potentialities for experiencing tenderness, gentleness, softness; playfulness, silliness, whimsicalness; violence, explosiveness, destructiveness; strength, firmness, toughness; an experiencing of being mischievous, devilish, wicked; being dominant, controlling, in charge; being close to, one with, intimate; being risky, daring, adventurous; an experiencing of being docile, compliant, yielding.

That is all there is to the structure of a person. Nothing more. There are no egos or ids, no personality traits, no needs or drives, no unconscious impulses, no psychodynamics or psychic defenses, no cognitions or core schemas. Nothing.

Some potentials for experiencing are closer to the surface. They help account for the way the person acts, behaves, responds and reacts, makes sense of, builds, and constructs that person's world, how the person exists and operates in that world. These are called *operating potentials for experiencing.*

Other potentials for experiencing are much deeper, far from the surface. They are the underground foundation beneath the operating potentials. They are called *deeper potentials for experiencing.* Their nature and content generally vary from person to person. There are no universal deeper potentials for experiencing, no shared commonality. At the base, each of us may be quite different.

In addition to potentials for experiencing, there are relationships between and among these potentials. They may be friendly, accepting, welcoming, positive, integrative, or they may be unfriendly, rejecting, distancing, negative, disintegrative.

Potentials for experiencing and relationships between these potentials. That is all there is to this model of human beings. The picture is rather clean and simple, especially in contrast to all the concepts and constructs, pieces and bits, processes and dynamics, that are present in so many other theories, and are absent and unnecessary in this model.

One Builds One's Own Personal World to Enable One's Own Personal Experiencing

This model depicts a person as building, creating, organizing an external world to serve as appropriate and useful situational contexts to enable the experiencing it is important for this person to experience. And the external world is shaped and organized as externalizations of the person's own deeper potentials, again to enable the experiencing of what is important for this person to experience.

There are ways that a person builds and constructs his or her own personal external world. One is that the real external world presents itself to the person, and the person then receives it, uses it, gives it sense and meaning, in the person's own important way. Second, the external world is merely available, a rich warehouse or marketplace of stuff for the person to select from and use in the ways and for the purposes that are important for this person. Third, the person and the external world can work together, cooperate together, to create and build what is important for this person to create and build. Finally, the person can actively create and fashion the kind of external world it is important for the person to create and fashion. Whatever ways the person uses, the person is the one who builds, shapes, creates, constructs, gives meaning to, and uses the external world, and the person may use building blocks that are quite real or are utterly and fancifully unreal.

The Infant Is Created As the Personal External World of the Parents

Picture a period from about a year or so before conception to some years after birth. Picture that during this period the parental figures are at work building the infant into being an important part of the parental figures' own personal external worlds. Who and what the infant is, the system of relating potentials that is the infant, is determined by and includes the parental figures' own potentials for experiencing and their relationships. In effect, the infant-child is the external world that the parent creates, and the infant-child is the parent who creates that external world.

The bottom line is that a primitive, skeletal system of potentials for experiencing and their relationships is already present when the infant-child is being created. A partially developed whole infant-child is present from the very beginning. Furthermore, it is the parental figures who both are, and who construct, the system of potentials for experiencing and their relationships that is the infant-child.

This tiny capsule summary of a radical departure from traditional theories of where personality comes from in the first place is played out much more fully in a more appropriate volume (Mahrer, 1989a), and its implications for psychotherapy are explored in the volume on experiential psychotherapy (Mahrer, 1996a).

What Gets Ordinary Existence Going and Keeps It in Motion, and Where Is It to Go?

For virtually every person, existence throughout one's entire life consists of (1) providing for a safe, limited degree of experiencing of potentials for experiencing, but not too much, and (2) maintaining the present state of integrative-good or disintegrative-bad relationships between potentials for experiencing. By means of behaviors and the building of appropriate external worlds, the person enables a safe degree of mild-moderate experiencing to preserve and maintain the system of potentials for experiencing, and to preserve and maintain the state of relationships between potentials, whether relationships are integrative-good or disintegrative-bad.

In this model, there are no grand intrinsic forces, and no grand destinies, payoffs, elevated end-states. There is no notion of basic needs, drives, impulses, motivations, sources of energy or power. There is no notion of growth forces, actualization forces, built-in stages of human growth and development. There is no notion of intrinsic biological or social or psychological grand pushes or pulls, forces or powers. There is no notion of end-states of psychological maturity, uplifted states of psychological health, end-states or destinies of growth and development.

Movement Toward an Optimal State Requires Radical, Transformational Shifts into Becoming a Qualitatively New Person

According to the experiential perspective, a person will remain essentially the same person throughout life unless, and here is the wonderful opportunity and risk, the person is ready and willing and able to undergo a qualitative, radical, transformational shift. Then it is possible to become a qualitatively new person, a person who is closer to the optimal person that this person is capable of

becoming. Becoming an optimal person consists of two qualitative changes:

One is that deeper potentials for experiencing become operating potentials for experiencing. What is deeper inside becomes an integral part of who and what the qualitatively new person is. As you become a qualitatively new person, the risk, the almost certain risk, is that parts of the person you were, and parts of that person's own world, will drop out, fade away, no longer exist. This process of deeper potentials for experiencing becoming integral parts of the qualitatively new person is called *actualization of deeper potentials for experiencing.*

The related qualitative change is that relationships between potentials for experiencing become more welcoming, loving, accepting, integrated. This too is a radical transformation in the very person that you are, in your feelings, thoughts, actions, interactions, and in your own personal world. This process is called *integration of relationships among potentials for experiencing.*

The experiential model offers the possibility of becoming the optimal person you are capable of becoming. This is the precious and powerful gift of each experiential session. The opportunity is here. The risks are powerful. So are the opportunities.

METHODOLOGY

What Are the Goals of Each Experiential Session?

There are two goals that are to be achieved in each session. One goal is for this person to become a qualitatively new person, a whole new person both inside and outside, a transformed person who has achieved a radical shift in what this new person experiences, feels, thinks, in how this person is in the world, and in the world in which this new person exists. The goal is a qualitative shift toward becoming what this person is capable of becoming. The goal is to discover what lies deep inside this person, and to enable this deeper potential for experiencing to become an integral new part, an actualized and integrated new part, of the qualitatively new person. The goal is a qualitative, deep-seated change in who and what the person is, in what this new person experiences. This radical shift is one goal of an experiential session.

The other goal is that the qualitatively new person is essentially free of whatever painful scene-situation may have been front and center for the old person in the beginning of the session. The painful scene-situation is essentially gone, and gone also are the painful feelings in that scene-situation. The person may well have started the session with painful feelings in a painful scene-situation, but the painful feelings and the painful scene-situation are no longer a part of the new person and the new person's new world.

Magnificent and dramatic as these two goals are, they are what can be and are achieved in each experiential session. They may be achieved for a few minutes or forever, but these two goals define the session's success and effectiveness. They promise what each session is to achieve.

Each Session Follows the Same Steps, Whether There Is a Therapist and a Person or the Person Alone

Each session follows the same four steps, even the first session. There is no such thing as an intake interview, a diagnostic assessment or evaluation.

The session goes through the same four steps whether the person is having a session alone or whether the person is with an experiential therapist whose main job is to teach, guide, show the person how to proceed through the session. Picture an experiential session as the person alone or with the teacher-guide, which is what the experiential psychotherapist is.

In either case, picture the person's eyes closed throughout the session. If your picture includes a therapist-teacher-guide, picture the two as sitting very close together, both chairs facing the same direction, both with their eyes closed throughout the session.

Step 1. Discover the Deeper Potential for Experiencing

The aim of the first step is to access, to bring forth, to find, to discover, a deeper potential for experiencing.

The person is to be in a state of readiness for relatively strong feeling.   When you are ready to begin, put your body in a state of readiness for relatively strong feeling by doing things like heavy, exceedingly hard and deep breathing; make loud noises, whimpers, screams, sighs, hissings, moanings, shriekings, clackings, yellings, yelpings, shrill outbursts; move your arms and legs and torso with powerful energy and gusto. Do all this for perhaps a minute or so to get into a state of strong feeling. You are radically departing from your ordinary state of feeling, of control, and you have entered into an extraordinary state in which you are to remain throughout the entire session.

Find a scene of strong feeling.   Either the therapist or the person or both select some of the following questions, say them out loud, with feeling, over and over again until some scene of strong feeling comes to mind. Sometimes a scene of strong feeling is already front and center. Sometimes you have to use a number of these questions:

What is it that bothers me so much, tears me apart, makes me feel so awful, is almost always on my mind? When did I have this awful feeling?

In my life today, what kind of feeling do I have that is so awful, so painful, tears me apart, the terrible feeling? When did I have this awful feeling, some time when it was really bad? Anna, the client, begins crying.

> "I feel so terrible . . . Something about me that is cold, hurts people. My sister told me I . . . She's having trouble getting pregnant, and she got so mad at me. She said I don't ever really listen to her. She said she wished she had a real sister." (Anna cries harder.)

There are other ways of finding a scene of strong feeling:

When was it recently, when did I have maybe the worst feeling, the most horrible, a feeling I never ever want to have again? What was going on?

In my whole life, now and when I was little, when was it that I had one of the worst feelings, so powerful, so awful? What was happening?

In my whole life, now and years ago, when, even for a brief moment or longer, did I feel like I was losing my mind, crazy, something was really wrong with me? When did this happen?

In the last few days or so, when did I have a dream?

What kind of bad feeling have I had just about my whole life, from when I was just a kid, that same awful feeling, like it's just a part of me, the kind of person I am? When have I had that feeling?

Lately, what kind of nice change seems to be happening in me, in the way I seem to be, in the way I am with people, the way people seem to be with me, some nice change in the way I feel or act or just seem to be? When and where does this seem to happen?

Lately, recently, when did I have some wonderful feeling, really happy, excited, so wonderful, a great feeling? What was going on? When did this seem to happen?

When I go back in my life, my whole life, when was it that I had maybe the best feeling, wonderful, really happy, felt fantastic? When was this? What was happening?

Each time you get a scene, ask: "Earlier in my life, maybe even long ago when I was very little, when did I have that feeling even more powerfully, much more fully, deeply? When was it? What was happening?"

You will likely come up with several scenes of strong feeling. Choose which one you want to work with in this session. Which one seems most compelling, pulls you more?

> When Anna went back, she found a more powerful early time in her parents' home. Her mother is hurt, pulled in, crying, and her father is shaking, his voice quivering, as he accuses Anna of not caring about the family, of being cold and selfish, of slapping the family in the face with the things she does. Anna is numbly transfixed, her body filled with pounding pressure as his quiv-

ering voice booms: "We never want to see you again! Stay away! You are not our daughter!!"

Anna decides that here is the scene of strong feeling for her to work on in this session.

Fully live and be in the scene of strong feeling. You are to use the methods that enable you to enter into this scene, to live and be in this scene. It is exceedingly real. You are actually and wholly existing in this scene. You are filled with this same strong feeling.

Discover the peak moment of strong feeling in this scene of strong feelings. Freeze this scene of strong feeling. Keep it right here. As you are living and being in this frozen scene of strong feeling, actively search for precisely when the feeling is at its peak. This almost always means looking around, exploring, until you actually discover this precise instant.

It is truly a discovery. Anna discovers that the precise instant is when he is saying, "We never want to see you again!" His voice is very loud and, in the very instant, he averts his gaze from her. There is a numb look on his face.

This is the precise instant of peak feeling.

In the moment of peak feeling, the deeper potential for experiencing is discovered when there is a qualitative shift in experiencing. Freeze this discovered moment of peak feeling. As you are now living and being in this frozen, dilated moment, you and the deeper potential for experiencing are within breathing distance of one another. You actually touch, or are touched by, the deeper potential when there is a discernible, qualitative shift in experiencing. What you had been experiencing is now gone. The state qualitatively shifts. Here is a momentous change, yet it happens almost instantly, in a flash. If the feeling had been painful, it is gone. Suddenly there is a qualitatively new experiencing. This shift may happen subtly but dramatically.

There are several ways of living and being in this frozen moment of strong feeling to help you discover the deeper potential for experiencing:

Fill in the missing critical detail. Use this method first. As you are living and being in this frozen precise instant, fill in even more of the details.

Anna fills in the details of her agonizing feeling, what the awful heart pounding is like, the specific inner sense of pressure. She details everything she can about her mother, about Anna's own physical posture, the clarified racing thoughts in her head, that averted gaze of her father, about his physical posture, the specific words he is saying, how he says these words.

As you fill in more and more of the critical details, as you find and fill in the missing critical detail, what is actually happening in this precise moment can become vivid, can come to the foreground, can emerge out of the general scene.

When this happens, a shift can occur. A new experiencing happens.

However, when Anna fills in the critical details of her father saying those awful words, and looking away from her, no qualitative shift happens. Try another method:

Intensify the strong feeling. In the moment of strong feeling, raise the sheer level of feeling to a far higher level.

Anna's voice is drenched in powerful feeling as she belts out: "You never want to see me again! You hate me! My heart is pounding so hard it is going to burst! This pressure! My God! I feel like I'm going to die! OH! OH MY GOD! OH! OH! OH! THE PRESSURE! THE PRESSURE!" Suddenly there is a qualitative shift. Something new happens. She is almost hissing, and her voice takes on an icy, other worldly hardness. Here is the shift, as she says: "YOU CAN'T LOOK AT ME ... NOOOO ... AAAAHHHHHHHHHH, YYYEEESSSSSSS!!!"

Right here, Anna is touched by, or she touches, the deeper potential for experiencing.

But suppose that this method did not work. Use one of the remaining methods, especially one that seems to fit what is happening in the frozen moment of strong feeling:

Penetrate down into the awful feeling. Start with the feeling that is bad; painful, awful. Penetrate down further and further into the most horrible heart, the most catastrophic core, of the awful feeling. What is the most painful possibility, the worst consequence, the most terrifying implication of that awful feeling? It might be: "He hates me! He doesn't even want to look at me! I feel disgusting, hated!" Suppose it gets much worse. How bad could it get? How could this feeling be even more agonizing? As you penetrate deeper and deeper into the innermost pit of the awful feeling, a point will be reached when the qualitative shift occurs. This is when you are close enough to sense the breath of the deeper potential for experiencing.

Be the special other person-thing. In some of these frozen moments, your attention is compelled by, is magnetically drawn toward, is locked onto that special other person-thing. You are the object of, the passive recipient of, the far more active, central, powerful special other person-thing. Furthermore, you seem to know something of what is going on in the head of that special other person-thing. You know something of what it is thinking, knowing, intending. It is as if you are almost a little bit sensing, knowing, what it is like to be this special person-thing.

Go ahead and be the other person-thing. Put yourself inside the other person-thing. Live it. Take its place. Keep going until the qualitative shift occurs.

Replace the bad feelings with good feelings. In the moment of peak feeling, Anna is having awful feelings. Suppose that everything about the moment is preserved: the words the father says, the way he says these words, his averted gaze, the numb look on his face, Anna's posture and stance, Anna's mother in the background. Anna replaces her awful feelings with pumped-up joyful feelings:

"I love this! This is wonderful! Oh, how great this feels!"

Stay in the moment of peak feeling until a qualitative shift occurs, not the surface shift from bad to good feeling, but an inner qualitative shift to some new inner deeper experiencing. Anna exclaims,

"I feel great! This is wonderful! Yes! Oh this is just marvelous! . . . Keep trying, old man! Knock yourself out! I am staring at you, Pop! Hey, you are looking away! LOOK AT THAT! He can't even face me! YOU GOT THAT VACANT LOOK ON YOUR FACE. YOU CAN'T FACE ME. HA HA HA HA HA! YOU LITTLE WIMP!"

Anna is now touching or is touched by the deeper potential for experiencing.

Replace the bad feeling with exuberant good feelings, and wallow in the moment of peak feeling until the qualitative shift happens and there is a touch of, a glow of, a new inner deeper experiencing.

Step 1 is achieved when Anna is touching or is touched by, when she and the deeper potential for experiencing are in contact with one another; that is, when Anna has discovered the deeper potential for experiencing.

Step 2. Welcome, Accept, Cherish the Deeper Potential for Experiencing

What had been sealed off, kept deeper inside, is now right here. You are within breathing range. The purpose of the second step is to enable the person to move from a disintegrative relationship of fearing, hating, distancing, sealing off, holding down the deeper potential, to an integrative relationship of loving, welcoming, accepting, cherishing what had been deeper.

Anna has just hissed, "YOU CAN'T LOOK AT ME . . . NOOOOO . . . AAAAHHHHHH . . . YYY-EEESSSSSSS!!!" and the feeling is so good. But what is this deeper experiencing? One way of letting herself love and embrace the deeper potential for experiencing is (1) to name it, to describe what it is. Both Anna and the therapist try, and arrive at these words: "It is a sense of superiority . . . toughness, a one-on-one encounter . . . winning." The more she can name it, describe it, the more she is welcoming and cherishing it.

There are other ways of welcoming and cherishing the deeper potential. She (2) savors the wonderful bodily sensations accompanying its discovery, "When I said, 'You can't look at me', I felt strong, hard . . . my whole body felt so good." (3) She can check her feelings toward this deeper experiencing: "Yes, I love it . . . I never felt that, but I'd like to . . . I like being that." Anna laughs. There are other methods, yet they are all aimed at enabling her to move from a bad relationship to where she is genuinely loving, cherishing this deeper potential for experiencing.

The change is a magnificent one. There is a new felt sense of greater inner peacefulness, of being reunited with so much more that is you. And there are new felt bodily sensations that help make even more wonderful this second step of loving closeness with one's own deeper potential for experiencing.

Step 3. Undergo a Qualitative Shift into Being the Deeper Potential for Experiencing in the Context of Recent, Earlier, and Remote Life Scenes

The third step is achieved when the person wholly disengages from, no longer is, the ordinary person she has been, and enters wholly and completely into being the utterly new person who is the deeper potential for experiencing. It is a radical leap, a qualitative shift into being a whole new and utterly different person who literally is the living experiencing of sheer superiority, wholesome toughness, exuberant one-on-one encountering, wonderful winning. Here is a qualitatively new person in everything from the way she acts to the way she talks, from what she feels to the person who is present right here.

Find recent, earlier, and remote life scenes. Being this whole new person is helped by occurring in scenes and times from the past. She may use scenes from her recent life, or from further back, from many years ago, from later or earlier childhood, or from when she was a baby. She may even use scenes in the lives of her mother or father during the year or so before conception to some years after birth.

She gets herself ready by letting herself be in the general vicinity of recent times, or from earlier periods in her life, or when she was a child or a baby. She sets herself to see the first scene that comes to mind, whatever it happens to be, whether it is familiar or not, dramatic or not, whether it seems fitting and appropriate or not.

One way of finding these scenes is by describing the deeper potential for experiencing, even letting herself have a glow of this experiencing, until some scene appears: "I am little, five, eight, ten, and I feel superior, tough, winning, one-on-one encountering. . . ." In the first scene, she is about 10 years old. She locked herself in the bathroom and, with her angry mother just outside the door, she is glowering with reverberating self-pity because her mother accused her of stealing socks from the laundry of a neighbor in the next apartment.

Another way of finding these scenes is to use the general structure of the initial scene of strong feeling: "I am in my teen years. We live on Crandall Street. Someone is saying awful things at me, accusing me. . . ." Keep repeating these words until a scene appears.

We found four or six scenes by using these methods.

Undergo the qualitative shift into being the whole new person in these life scenes.   In each of these scenes, she is to hurl herself into being the qualitatively new person who is the live experiencing of sheer, undiluted superiority, toughness, winning, one-on-one encountering.

Picture her as this radically new person in the bathroom scene, and in each of the earlier life scenes. Picture her being this radically new person (1) fully and completely; (2) genuinely and authentically; (3) with powerful feeling, full of energy and saturation; (4) with wonderful, joyful, exciting, exhilarating feelings; and (5) all wrapped up in safety-providing craziness, zaniness, silliness, burlesque, and wholly free of all realistic constraints.

Step 4. Be the Qualitatively Whole New Person in Scenes from the Forthcoming New Postsession World

The final step is achieved when the qualitatively whole new person has an ample sample and taste, readiness and commitment, to live and be the whole new person in this new person's new world of today, tomorrow, and beyond. The person who leaves the session is qualitatively different from the old person who was there in the beginning of the session.

The qualitatively new person finds outrageously unrealistic imminent scenes and situations in which to playfully and fully wallow in being the qualitatively new person.   Look for imminent scenes and situations that are likely to happen soon, or might perhaps happen soon, or that Anna can make sure will happen soon. These imminent scenes become outrageously unrealistic when you picture them as the contexts in which you are to live and be as this qualitatively new person.

Elicit these scenes by asking this question: What imminent scenes (1) would optimally and ideally suit and be appropriate for the whole new person that you are; (2)

would come from the qualitatively new person's fantasies and daydreams; (3) would involve being the qualitatively new person in ordinary mundane daily living; for instance, while brushing your teeth, walking along the street, conversing with others; (4) would seem outrageously impossible and dangerously inappropriate; (5) are times when the qualitatively new person could-would-should be the qualitatively new person; (6) are times when the qualitatively new person would just love to be the qualitatively new person; or (7) are imminent reoccurrences of the initial scene of strong bad feeling, that is, when someone, perhaps her sister, criticizes her, berates her, hates her, accuses her of being cold, not listening, hurting people, being selfish?

By using these questions, Anna found a number of creatively useful scenes and situations within the context of the next few days or so. These scenes involved her sister and her father, situations at work in the hospital, spending an evening with a few friends at her place, ordinary little scenes with the butcher in the market and the fellow who was supposed to fix her refrigerator, and scenes with Jerry and his kids in her apartment.

Playfully and fully wallow in being the qualitatively new person in the wildly unrealistic scenes and situations.   Anna throws herself into being the qualitatively new person in each of these scenes, and does so (1) with absolutely full, saturated experiencing of pure superiority, toughness, winning, one-on-one encountering; (2) with sheer joy, ecstasy, exuberance, delirious hilarity and fun; and (3) in contexts of wildly unrealistic zaniness and playfulness. She is indeed the qualitatively new person in these imminent scenes and situations.

The qualitatively new person frames scenes that are realistically fitting and appropriate.   Now is the time to add reality constraints. When and where would the qualitatively new Anna be ready and eager to live and be this new way realistically, for real, in the real postsession world of the whole new Anna? It is reality time.

The new Anna selects two scenes. She is ready and willing to be this whole new person in having a real talk with her sister. She has never really talked with her sister. And, more excitingly, the new Anna sees a whole new world with men, new men, and even with the man she is with, Jerry, who is much older than she is, and who, with his two children, often stays at her place while she tries to be so graciously good to the three of them.

Rehearse and modify-refine being the qualitatively whole new person in these scenes until it is just right.   Try it out. The whole new Anna, including the new felt sense of superiority, toughness, winning, one-on-one encountering, rehearses what it is like to be with her sister. She checks her body. How does it feel? Are the bodily sensations wonderful, awful, dead and numb? Anna keeps rehearsing, modifying, refining what she does and how she does it until it feels just right, until the bodily sensations joyfully approve. Anna invites other parts of her to raise all sorts of serious objections. When there are no teeth-clenching objections, when overall bodily sensations are wonderful, when the final dress rehearsal is successful, Anna has experienced what it can be like to be this whole new person in undergoing this special talk with her sister.

Anna does the same thing in a forthcoming scene with Jerry and his children. They will be at her place tonight, again. How is the new Anna ready to be? Rehearsal and modification and refinement culminate in a newfound, solid, exciting rightness in facing their unspoken commitment, no longer suffocating this buried issue under her grudging graciousness. She is ready and eager to be this whole new Anna with Jerry and the children, perhaps tonight.

This whole new Anna sees what it can be like to be faced with an imminent reoccurrence of the initial painful scene of such painful feeling.

> "The little sister still isn't pregnant. She's mad at you! You don't really listen to her! You're bad! She wishes she had a real sister! Go ahead, Anna, cry! Feel rotten! She's right!" Anna is giggling. "Nice try, Kim. Come on. You can do better than that! Go ahead! Give it your best shot. . . . Then I have a few things to settle with you . . ."

The scene has lost its painful zing. Anna is a whole new Anna.

Commit yourself to being the qualitatively new person, with whole new ways of being and behaving, in the rehearsed scenes and situations. The session is over when Anna fully commits herself to being this whole new person in these whole new ways, in these whole new imminent scenes and situations with her sister, and with Jerry and his children. "Yes! I want to! I'm going to do it!" The person who leaves the office is a qualitatively new person, with the formerly deeper potential for experiencing as one integral part of who and what this new person is: pleasant, exciting, harmonious, well-fitting, experiencing a delightful sense of superiority, toughness, winning, one-on-one encountering.

After the session, actually be the qualitatively whole new person in the new ways, in the new scenes and situations of the new extratherapy world. The session is truly over when the new Anna does her homework. Becoming a whole new Anna in the session is an impressively prideful achievement. But actually being the whole new person in the new scenes and situations of the new extratherapy world is far more helpful in enabling the whole new Anna to come to life. So what happened?

CASE EXAMPLE

When Anna started her session, the foremost scene of strong feeling that was compelling her, bothering her, hurting her, was a recent scene in which her sister was so critical, hateful, accusatory, rejecting, and in which Anna felt so awful, so terribly hated, rejected, painfully hurt, put down, like there was something about Anna that was so awful, nasty, spiteful. The scene was ugly and painful, and so too were the feelings. Nor was this just one isolated scene. Her world seemed to contain similar scenes that took painful form and shape once or twice a week or so.

Within a few days after the session, Anna did her homework. During a family supper at her parents' home, including sister Kim, she found herself talking seriously with them, probably for the first time. With a quietly solid earnestness and self-confidence, she was saturated with a fulfilling sense of pleasant and easy toughness, superiority, winning, a willingness to engage in one-on-one encounters, as she declared new rules for the way things were to be with her and the family. And it worked! This new Anna seemed to be both reassuring, uplifting, freeing, and helpful, both for herself and for her parents and sister. Her Dad laughingly recounted stories about her as a tough little kid, and her sister had happy tears as she kept grinning at the new Anna, who was the superior yet cherished chairman of the board throughout the evening.

The natural new Anna felt so sound, so pleasantly well put together, as she engaged in a hard-fought argument with Jerry about her self-imposed one-sided commitment to him and his children, and she won, of course. It was as if the entire situation lost its painful edge, and she and Jerry could be together as much more real people.

And there were some spillover effects in other parts of her world. For example, she was so different in committee meetings with her boss at the hospital that the boss playfully asked if she could have whatever drug Anna had taken. Anna lightly wagged her finger at her boss. "Don't mess with me. I am always right!"

As Anna became more and more of this whole new person, what washed out of her world were painful scenes with her sister, with Jerry, and just about anyone else, of being hated, rejected, put down, together with the awful feelings that helped make such scenes so painful.

Anna had become a whole new person with a whole new part, namely, a wonderful, well-fitting, playful, and happy experiencing of new-felt toughness, winning, superiority, pleasant one-on-one encountering. The more she can be this whole new Anna, the more she can actually be and behave in the real world as this whole new person; and the more she can actually be and behave in the real world as this whole new person, the more she can truly be the qualitatively new Anna.

When she is this qualitatively new person, there is almost no further basis for a part of her working to hold down, seal off, hide and disprove what had been a deeper potential of ugly toughness, grotesque superiority, having to win, painful one-on-one encounters. There is almost no further basis for sporadic outbursts of being the twisted form of this potential for experiencing in tight, hurtful, painful ways. There is almost no further basis for her world containing outside agents, forces, people who are tough at her, win over her, gain superiority over her, one-on-one encounter her in ways that leave her hurt, torn apart, agonized, painful. The qualitatively new Anna is not only a magnificent new Anna, but is essentially free of those painful scenes, personal worlds, and bad feelings.

Anna and her therapist-teacher-guide did a good job of walking through the four in-session steps, and thereby achieving the two goals of an experiential session: (1) becoming the qualitatively whole new person that Anna is capable of becoming, and (2) essentially freeing herself of the compellingly painful scenes that were front and center for her in that session.

APPLICATIONS

This experiential system of thought is bursting with a whole range of applications in such fields as a new philosophy of science for the field of psychology, a way of thinking about the basic issues and questions in the field of psychotherapy, a discovery-oriented strategy for research, new applications and conceptualizations in education and training, new positions and answers to the basic issues and questions in the broad field of personality, and a new approach to social relations and change (Mahrer, 1989a, 1996a). It is so exciting to picture spelling out these new departures, these fascinating implications and applications. However, there is realistically room for a quick preview of two applications.

Virtually Any and Every Person Can Have Their Own Experiential Sessions—Sessions by, for, and With Oneself

Picture a person learning the skills of going through an experiential session by oneself. Picture a person as having his or her own experiential sessions every week or so, or whenever the person wishes, throughout the person's whole life, starting from later childhood or adolescence. If you can learn how to operate a computer, you probably can learn the skills of having an experiential session.

Picture a 13-year-old girl, or a young chef, or a cousin, or a buddy from work, each one having their own experiential sessions. Each one moves in the direction of becoming the kind of optimal person this person is able to become, a qualitatively whole new person, a person who is increasingly more and more integrated and actualized. Having sessions all by themselves, they become progressively free of the painful scenes and situations of their own personal words, and of the painful feelings in those scenes and situations. Just imagine half of the people that you know, and half of the people you do not know, learning how to have their own experiential sessions, and having their own sessions, all by themselves. Here is one side of the many-sided first application.

Picture a woman who is ready to be pregnant, or who is pregnant. Picture parents being with their babies. Suppose that the better the parents, the better are the babies. The more integrated and actualized are the parents, the more solid and well put together is the foundation for who and what the baby is. Not only are the parents attaining the important changes offered by experiential sessions, but the parents are thereby giving the baby a supreme gift of a precious foundational personality structure to start out with. Here is another side of this first application, all achieved without sight of professional practitioners and their clients or patients.

Picture a person having experiential sessions alone, and marvelous changes happening in this person's body. Just as there can be freedom from painful external scenes and situations, so too can there be a washing away of painful bodily feelings, states, conditions, growths, things called illnesses and diseases. The body need no longer serve as a painful, agonizing, malevolent, hurtful inner world. Furthermore, becoming more and more of what this person can become can include opening up the body to share in becoming more and more of what the body is optimally capable of becoming. Here is another facet of a person having one's own experiential sessions.

Picture psychotherapists doing all sorts of psychotherapies on clients-patients. Now picture psychotherapists having their own sessions by themselves, and clients-patients also having their own sessions by themselves. Now go one step further. Picture psychotherapists and clients-patients having their own personal sessions instead of their mutually fulfilling the roles of therapists and clients-patients with one another. What you have pictured is the virtual dissolution of the field of professional psychotherapy! If a person can achieve what can be achieved by having sessions by oneself, most of the field of professional psychotherapy gradually drains away. We can wave good-bye to most of the whole structure of professional psychotherapy. Much of what remains is the honest exchange of mutual pleasures when one person gets to talk about very personal matters to a special companion. If virtually any and every person can have their own sessions by, for, and with him- or herself, the field of psychotherapy ought to prepare itself for its own version of deep-seated radical changes that the field offers to some of its clients-patients.

These are some of the facets of just one application in which virtually any and every person can have their own experiential sessions—sessions by, for, and with oneself.

When People Undergo Their Own Personal Self-Change, the Consequence Is Qualitative Social Change

Picture a family, a larger group, a community, a nation, a society. Picture a fair proportion of these people engaging in their own personal experiential sessions. The power of the experiential way of making sense of collective people, of groups, of societies (Mahrer, 1989a) is that collective individual change is an awesomely powerful means of generating qualitative social change. When there are qualitative changes, truly deep-seated personal changes, in the persons who are parts of the larger group, a virtually automatic consequence is a truly deep-seated change in the group, in the society.

You may not be especially passionate about doing things to help change your group, your community, your society. You go about your daily life, read the newspaper, go to work, talk with the people you are close to and to those you are not especially close to. But something much bigger happens when you, and the other people like you, achieve more and more of what experiential sessions can achieve. The consequence is a social change that is as real, as impressive, as qualitative, as the personal changes achieved by each of you.

There are many people who work directly on making a difference in the family, the group, community, nation, society. These people make laws, build schools and dams, make war and peace, build cities and villages, provide services. They make changes in the group, whether the group is a small family or a large society. But something new happens when these people engage in experiential sessions, and accomplish what these sessions can help accomplish. A whole new world of cascading social changes opens up. Just as a person can become what that person can become, free of that session's central painful scene, so too can the group, the larger society, move toward becoming the optimal society its collective people can enable it to become, free of the collectively painful situations those people helped create in that family, neighborhood, group, community, nation, society. Do not stop doing what you do for your society. Just add a new ingredient: each person spends some regular time in personal experiential sessions to become more and more of the integrated and actualized person that person can become.

This second application involves members of a group or a society individually and quietly undergoing their own experiential sessions. If the group is small, the changes can occur right away. If the group is a vast society, the changes may slowly and gradually appear after many years, perhaps a hundred years or so. Yet a society can become what its collective people can become, by, for, and with themselves.

FINAL INVITATIONS

1. If you are a psychotherapist, if the ideas giving life to Experiential Psychotherapy fit well with your own, then the invitation is to grasp and do Experiential Psychotherapy. Help carry forward both the conceptual picture and the working practice.

2. If you are genuinely drawn toward what experiential sessions are designed to accomplish, learn how to carry out your own experiential sessions by, for, and with yourself. Or find and use some preferable other way of undergoing your own lifelong change toward becoming your own preferable version of the optimal person you can become.

REFERENCES

Chalmers, A. F. (1982). *What is this thing called science?* Queensland, Australia: University of Queensland Press.

Einstein, A. (1923). *Sidelights of relativity.* New York: Dutton.

MacCorquodale, K., & Meehl, P. E. (1948). On a distinction between hypothetical constructs and intervening variables. *Psychological Review, 55,* 95–107.

Mahrer, A. R. (1989a). *Experiencing: A humanistic theory of psychology and psychiatry.* Ottawa, Ontario, Canada: University of Ottawa Press.

Mahrer, A. R. (1989b). *Dream work: In psychotherapy and self-change.* New York: Norton.

Mahrer, A. R. (1996a). *The complete guide to experiential psychotherapy.* New York: Wiley.

Mahrer, A. R. (1996b). Discovery-oriented research on how to do psychotherapy. In W. Dryden (Ed.), *Research in counselling and psychotherapy: Practical applications* (pp. 233–258). London: Sage.

Mahrer, A. R., & Fairweather, D. R. (1993). What is "experiencing"? A critical review of meanings and applications in psychotherapy. *The Humanistic Psychologist, 21,* 2–25.

Rorty, R. (1991). *Philosophy and the mirror of nature.* Princeton, NJ: Princeton University Press.

Skinner, B. F. (1938). *The behavior of organisms.* New York: Appleton-Century-Crofts.

Speed, B. (1984). How really real is real? *Family Process, 23,* 511–517.

Whitehead, A. N. (1929). *Process and reality: An essay in cosmology.* Cambridge, MA: Cambridge University Press.

Chapter 22

EYE MOVEMENT DESENSITIZATION AND REPROCESSING (EMDR)

SANDRA PAULSEN INOBE

The first time I read about EMDR I thought it nonsense, but Gordon Bowers, who investigated it, assured me that it was a real phenomenon. Dr. Francine Shapiro, the developer of this system, has been busy explaining EMDR to many people, and it is probably the fastest growing system of therapy currently, although as yet its basic theory and method are not explained, at least to my satisfaction. There seem to be two levels of use of EMDR: pure use for immediate resolution and other psychotherapeutic methods, and EMDR for more deeply set problems.

Dr. Inobe in her explanation spends a good deal of time giving a good summary relative to research, although it has not yet been accepted by some people, with varying explanations including the placebo effect. While the methodology is well explained in seven phases, advertisements about this system warn against trying the system without appropriate training. Anyone reading about this system will realize such advice is sound.

DEFINITION

Eye Movement Desensitization and Reprocessing (EMDR) is a systematic clinical treatment for a range of dysfunctions that have resulted from traumatic or other experiences. EMDR integrates other therapeutic approaches, including cognitive and behavioral approaches, experiential, psychodynamic, and others, with a structured process that involves rhythmic stimulation of alternating sides of the body (usually involving lateral eye movements). The EMDR process leads to resolution of trauma and production of adaptive learning outcomes of the traumatic or other material. The EMDR-trained mental health professional employs a structured, but not rigid, systematic process to work from a carefully formulated treatment plan and targeted symptom through affective, cognitive, and behavioral material.

Although this treatment was originally formulated as a cognitive-behavioral treatment, EMDR practitioners of a cognitive-behavioral background typically acquire a deepened respect for psychodynamic theory as a result of participating in and observing the course of EMDR treatment. Typically, the use of the EMDR protocol to address a present-day problem, such as a phobia, causes psychodynamically oriented insights to spontaneously occur to the client during the EMDR processing, such

as awareness of early childhood origins of present-day problems. The clinical reality of the effect of unresolved early learning on present-day dysfunction is very clearly evident to EMDR practitioners, who observe the cause and effect of conflict or trauma and symptomatology. Unlike traditional psychodynamic treatment, EMDR treatment does not require the time-intensive reflective process. For single-trauma symptom pictures, a very few EMDR sessions—or sometimes a single session—will resolve the symptoms in most cases. For complex cases with multiple traumas or complex and extended dysfunctional learning histories, a long series of EMDR sessions that are well-integrated into an appropriate overall treatment plan will likely be needed.

Just as the cognitive-behaviorist becomes more psychodynamic with exposure to EMDR, so the psychodynamicist may become more cognitive-behavioral. Shapiro's carefully articulated therapy structure enables the rapid treatment effect to occur by processing affect to produce sometimes profound cognitive and behavioral shifts in a sometimes surprisingly short time span. Sometimes the patient experiences insights, as mentioned, and sometimes the processing produces shifts on a level not immediately evident to the patient's awareness, but evident by rapid and permanent shifts in behavior. In sum, many therapists will find their clinical worldviews tested and expanded by the experience of EMDR.

HISTORY

EMDR was developed by Francine Shapiro, PhD, in 1987. Shapiro observed a shift in her own experience of a personal event directly after engaging in spontaneous and rapid lateral eye movements while her attention was turned to the disturbing events. She hypothesized that eye movements were causally related to the affective shift she observed in herself. She tested this hypothesis informally with colleagues, then formally in her dissertation research with rape and combat trauma survivors. In her initial study of combat veterans and rape and molestation survivors, she found that most experienced rapid and permanent relief in their Posttraumatic Stress Disorder (PTSD) symptomatology (Shapiro, 1995).

Some have observed that Shapiro's contribution is half in her discovery of the effect of eye movements on affect, cognition, and adaptive functioning, and half in her conscientious development of a time-efficient protocol that should be followed to ensure the safe and effective use of the eye movements.

The 12 years since EMDR's inception have been remarkable for both the speed of its acceptance around the world by clinicians and by some in academia, as well as by marked out-of-hand dismissal of the method by others. At this point, the evidence in support of the veracity of the claims of a rapid and permanent cure for trauma-related symptoms has been borne out by a range of investigators, reviewed in the section on current status. A few critics have accused EMDR practitioners of following Shapiro as a cult; however, clinical experience finds that EMDR works whether or not the practitioner admires Shapiro or even believes that EMDR will work.

There are rare case reports of marked distress and negative outcomes associated with EMDR treatment. In the experience of the EMDR Institute (F. Shapiro, personal communication, 1995), and in the experience of this author and other senior practitioners of EMDR, those negative outcomes are rather uniformly cases in which EMDR was conducted on an undiagnosed case of a severe dissociative disorder, without the benefit of an appropriate protocol for EMDR with a dissociative disorder. Paulsen (1995) and Lazrove & Fine (1996) have provided such protocols.

In addition to being able to rapidly resolve the primary symptoms, such as nightmares and flashbacks, that cause trauma survivors to seek treatment, EMDR can produce both large and subtle shifts in adaptive functioning, when traumatic or other maladaptive learning has exerted influence on daily life. For example, feelings of helplessness, guilt, shame, hopelessness, and other states can emerge from maladaptive learning. Such learning can act as negative filters that create negative expectancies and maladaptive outcomes in situations that might be experienced very differently by others without those negative filters. Once EMDR has resolved the original maladaptive learning, those negative filters are replaced by more adaptive ones appropriate to the situation in the here and now, without negative influence of the early experience. This has been referred to as the progenerative transmutation of stored information (Shapiro, 1998; Shapiro & Forrest, 1997).

CURRENT STATUS

As of this writing, over 30,000 clinicians have been trained in EMDR worldwide. There is an international association (Eye Movement Desensitization and Reprocessing International Association) with membership from around the globe. Practitioners of EMDR have gone into natural disaster situations including the Loma Prieta earthquake, the Oklahoma City bombing, Bosnia, Hurricane Andrew, and many others, to treat traumatized individuals or to train local clinicians in the use of EMDR for trauma resolution.

Initially, all training in the EMDR procedure was conducted by the EMDR Institute. Currently, however, a number of trainers and graduate programs have been approved to incorporate EMDR training into their curricula. EMDR has been recognized by the American Psychological Association (APA) Division 12 Task Force on Psychological Interventions as a valid treatment for civilian posttraumatic stress disorder. The International Society for Traumatic Stress Studies (ISTSS) has evaluated EMDR as one of the PTSD interventions it examined, and assigned it a rating of A/B, or probably efficacious (Chemtob, Tolin, van der Kolk, & Pitman, 2000; Chambless et al., 1998). Indeed, there have been more controlled studies of EMDR for PTSD than for the entire field of PTSD outside EMDR (Shapiro, 1995).

A few of the most recent of the controlled studies of EMDR's effect include those of Carlson and colleagues (1998), who tested EMDR's effect on chronic PTSD in Vietnam combat veterans. Subjects evidenced substantial clinical improvement within 12 sessions, and some subjects became symptom free. Seventy-five percent no longer had PTSD after their 12 sessions of treatment. The comparison groups were a biofeedback relaxation group and a group receiving routine VA care. The outcome measures included a range of well-established devices, including the CAPS-1, the Mississippi Scale for PTSD, the IES, ISQ, PTSD Symptom Scale, Beck Depression Inventory, and the STAI.

Pitman and colleagues (1996) conducted a component analysis of 17 chronic outpatient veterans, with two treatment groups, one using eye movements, and a control group that combined forced eye fixation, hand taps, and hand waving. Both groups showed significant decreases in subjective distress. It is hypothesized that both groups were effectively EMDR groups because both groups used alternative forms of rhythmic stimulation.

Marcus, Marquis, and Sakai (1997) studied EMDR at Kaiser Permanente Hospital, evaluating its effect with 67 PTSD patients. They found EMDR superior to standard Kaiser care of individual therapy, group therapy, and medication. After EMDR treatment, 90 percent of patients no longer met criteria for PTSD. The study was based on independent evaluation using the SCL-90R, the Beck Depression Inventory, the Impact of Event Scale, the Modified PTSD Scale, the State-Trait Anxiety Inventory, and Subjective Units of Discomfort (SUD).

Rothbaum (1997) examined EMDR on a study of rape victims, finding that after three EMDR treatment sessions, 90 percent of participants no longer met full criteria for PTSD, as measured on the PTSD Symptom Scale, the Impact of Event Scale, the Beck Depression Inventory, and the Dissociative Experiences Scale.

Scheck, Schaeffer, and Gillette (1998) conducted a controlled study of 60 females between the ages of 16 and 25, with high-risk behavior and a history of trauma. The subjects were randomly assigned to either EMDR or active listening treatment groups. The EMDR group evidenced substantially greater improvement on the Beck Depression Inventory, the State-Trait Anxiety Inventory, the Penn Inventory for Post-Traumatic Stress Disorder, the Impact of Event Scale, and the Tennessee Self Concept Scale. After two EMDR sessions, the EMDR group's symptoms were reduced to within 1 standard deviation of the norm. A complete and current list of controlled studies of EMDR as well as of publications related to the use of EMDR can be obtained from the EMDR Institute in Pacific Grove, California, as well as on the EMDR website, http://www.emdr.org.

THEORY

Shapiro's theoretical formulation of EMDR has remained largely unchanged since the early 1990s. At that time, she articulated EMDR's effect within the framework of an information processing model of trauma and other maladaptive learning outcomes (Shapiro, 1995). In that formulation, Shapiro postulates that the human brain normally processes information spontaneously to a state of adaptive resolution unless that natural process is blocked. In the hypothesized normal process, negative emotions are released and resolved, and an adaptive resolution and learning occurs spontaneously. This natural and spontaneous healing process becomes blocked by overwhelming trauma as in PTSD genesis, or other mal-

adaptive learning outcomes, as in many clinical pictures that originate in childhood or adulthood experience. When blocked, the natural healing process cannot complete. Rather, the maladaptive outcome of PTSD or other symptom pictures occurs when the unprocessed material remains locked in the nervous system, in an unresolved state. Shapiro's accelerated information processing (AIP) model assumes a neurophysiological basis for both the resolved and unresolved states.

The AIP model has its roots in the language of information processing and associative networks pioneered by Lang (1977) and Bower (1981). According to AIP theory, the effect of EMDR occurs by unlocking the material that was frozen in the nervous system, desensitizing it to a neutral state, and reprocessing the meaning of the material to achieve an adaptive resolution. The latter component is so significant and notable an EMDR phase, that Shapiro and other EMDR practitioners find the behavioral formulation of desensitization alone is insufficient to explain the depth and extent of the meaning shift. Indeed, among the many inspirational experiences of the EMDR practitioner is that of not only observing desensitization of an anxiety response to trauma, but also witnessing the profound human drama of survivors finding positive meaning and personal growth in the ashes of horrific experiences.

AIP theory suggests that state-dependent trauma-related information is stored in a neurobiological stasis that, in PTSD cases, negates the possibility of additional learning or integration of the traumatic information. Under EMDR treatment, however, the traumatic material becomes catalyzed and released from its frozen state, and becomes organized into a dynamic state in which it is accessible to be processed, resolved, and integrated into the larger body of knowledge the individual holds. Additionally, new insights become available to the individual, and those insights seem invariably to be in the direction of adaptive resolution. As a result of EMDR, individuals do not shift beliefs to a less adaptive cognition or a state of greater maladaptiveness (Shapiro, 1998). Rather, the individual achieves a state of emotional neutrality and appropriate acceptance. When EMDR is used for nontraumatic maladaptive learning outcomes, the same result obtains. That is, the individual achieves a state of insight, repose, integration of related learning, and a more adaptive outcome.

The AIP model views many clinical syndromes as resulting from learning experiences that precipitated constellations of behavior, affect, and cognition. Those unresolved experiences remain in their static state, with their effects ranging from mild to severe impact on life functioning. Depression, phobias, panic disorders, dissociative disorders, personality disorders, and PTSD are all seen as expressing these unresolved experiences in a range of symptom pictures. Situational triggers in the present situation are seen as evoking the neural networks that contain the earlier unresolved and frozen maladaptive material. Related memories of events are linked associationally to like-kind memories or to more remote material that has become associated in the mind of the client. This view of the relational nature of associated memories is informed in the spontaneous way that EMDR sessions unfold. In the hypothesized neural network theoretical basis for frozen traumatic material, nodes of related information are accessed and resolved sequentially by the EMDR process. The organization of nodes is somewhat idiosyncratic to the individual's knowledge base, but follows predictable patterns related to such themes as helplessness, responsibility or guilt, and victimization. Processing resolves these maladaptive states to more adaptive and appropriate themes of freedom, appropriate responsibility, and choice.

Typically, an EMDR session begins with a current or past event as the object of focus. During the processing, however, the client likely spontaneously associates to other events with similar emotional themes or triggers. The recognition of the chain of associations often occurs spontaneously in the client, causing significant insight and shifts in affective arousal, cognitive meaning, and behavioral sequelae. The frequent observation of this spontaneous shift occurring in EMDR sessions gives rise to the theoretical notion that EMDR activates the brain's natural capability to process the information to an adaptive resolution, once the material is unlocked and the process is catalyzed.

One of the most interesting aspects of the model that the desired adaptive resolution often occurs spontaneously, once the procedure is properly conducted, with minimal additional intervention on the part of the clinician. Paradoxically, in other cases, the procedure requires maximal clinical acumen and experience to properly formulate the necessary EMDR targets within an appropriate diagnostic picture. Most EMDR practitioners find themselves significantly stretched by their experience with this therapy. As mentioned before, the cognitive behaviorist becomes more psychodynamic by seeing the primacy of affect in each EMDR cure. The psychodynamicist becomes more cognitive-behavioral by observing the speedy resolution of symptoms with a focused and structured treatment for which desensitization and cognitive restructuring is central.

METHODOLOGY

The practice of EMDR is defined with more articulation than most other psychotherapeutic practices are. In part, this is because the procedure is so powerful that it is imperative that the tool be appropriately harnessed and constrained. In part, this rigor is necessary in order

to produce successful results. Eye Movement Desensitization and Reprocessing represents a confluence of some of the best tactics of psychotherapy of the last decades.

The following steps are central to the EMDR process according to any EMDR training.

Phase 1: Client History

The method begins with a careful client history and treatment plan, as any treatment does. This history taking emphasizes ensuring that the client is ready for EMDR. It lays the groundwork for the selection of appropriate EMDR targets, as well as identifying any possible red flags that may contraindicate early EMDR intervention. Clients need to have a basic level of stability and social support in their lives before beginning EMDR, because EMDR processing can be emotionally intense temporarily. Without basic supports in place, the emotional processing could be destabilizing to the client. Acute physical health issues, safety, and living basics should be secure prior to beginning EMDR. Alcohol and drug abusers should have basic supports in place before beginning EMDR treatment. Any chemically based brain state, including medications, may effect EMDR processing. In some cases, individuals may need to repeat EMDR processing once they are clear of chemical substances. EMDR may alter the experience of recalling a traumatic event. The possibility of this occurring should be made known to any client in the middle of legal proceedings as well as to the client's attorney. Clinicians should be alert to the possible role of secondary gains in maintaining symptom pictures or interfering with resolution of those symptoms.

Treatment planning involves the careful assessment of the range of symptoms that the client reports, including behavioral, affective, and cognitive symptoms, their frequency, intensity, duration, and other characteristics. When traumatic events are reported, the circumstances and other past occurrences of the event are recorded along with other complaints that may or may not be related.

Phase 2: Preparation

Early in treatment, the therapist carefully prepares the client for EMDR, when early EMDR is indicated, by educating the client about what to expect, and enabling an informed consent. Establishing rapport early in treatment is important preparation. The clinician typically explains EMDR theory in plain language, offering metaphoric explanations for the process of EMDR. Commonly, the explanation is employed that the client may experience the processing as if he or she is on a train, and the "old stuff" of a traumatic memory will be going by, outside of the window, like scenery. The client is further prepared with instruction to just allow whatever comes up to come up, and is also empowered to stop the processing if necessary, though stopping is discouraged because it is like stopping the car in the midst of a tunnel; stopping lengthens the experienced period of darkness. The EMDR practitioner establishes with the client a comfortable speed and direction for the eye movements (or alternative bilateral rhythmic stimulation, such as hand-tapping or auditory stimuli) to occur. Because EMDR is so powerful and EMDR sessions can evoke intense affect, clients must have self-containment and relaxation skills before EMDR is used.

Phase 3: Assessment

An assessment phase is a necessary precondition to the EMDR treatment itself. In assessment, the clinician particularizes the component parts of the targeted memory and symptom cluster. Ideally, the affective, cognitive, bodily, and behavioral aspects of the symptoms are elaborated, though not all clients have ready access to all those features.

In this phase, the client selects the target or image that best represents the issue the client and clinician have agreed to work on. The client then identifies a self-statement that represents the negative cognition that the target/image evokes. A mirror-image positive cognition is identified collaboratively that best identifies the ideal self-statement to which the client aspires, in association with the target/image. This desired cognition is evaluated for how true the client experiences it viscerally to be on the Validity of Cognition (VOC) Scale, where 1 is completely false, and 7 is completely true. The neural network that is presumed to contain the blocked and unprocessed affective material is then evoked and opened up by holding the target image in awareness, coupled with the negative self-statement, and identifying both the emotions that arise and the body location of those emotions. The Subjective Units of Disturbance (SUD) Scale is used to derive a baseline measurement of intensity of distress prior to the initial eye movements. On this scale, 0 is completely neutral, no disturbance, and 10 is the most intense distress imaginable. In this state of affective arousal, the desensitization phase is ready to begin.

Phase 4: Desensitization

In the desensitization phase, the therapist evokes client eye movements (or other bilateral brain stimulation) by moving a hand, wand, or mechanical device (such as a flashing light or bilateral sounds through a headphone) for sets of approximately 24 saccades. Individuals, however, vary greatly on their preferred set length. Between sets of saccades, the therapist asks, "What are you getting?" or other neutral inquiries, to allow the client to express the current contents of his or her awareness. Although it also allows expression of the client's experience, the primary purpose of the talking between sets is for the clinician to observe whether the material being processed is shifting or appears to be stuck. The clinician's role is restrained and nearly silent as long as processing continues without being stuck, as is described in more detail following.

Typically, the client's attention systematically and spontaneously moves through series of experiences or affects, the organization and sequence of which is unique to the individual. These series of experiences are typically organized by type of experience, chronological sequence, type of affect, perpetrator, situational stimuli, body sensation, or almost any other theme.

The therapist typically stays "off the track so the train can progress" unless the processing gets stuck. The EMDR therapist is trained to use a systematic approach to getting the train back on the track using minimal intervention, such as shifting the direction of the saccades, or the speed. A more advanced intervention called cognitive interweave is used minimally when possible to enable the client to return to the most natural self-determined process. Samples of cognitive interweave to get processing unstuck include "Whose responsibility was it?" and "How would you feel if it had been your child it happened to instead of you?" Cognitive interweave is taught in the advanced EMDR training. Throughout the processing, the clinician is primarily tuned to whether the material is shifting in any sense. In fact, the client need not articulate much more than that things are changing for the therapist to have what is needed to continue, though typically clients want to tell much more. If the processing is stuck (also called "looping" or not changing), the therapist will require additional information to conduct appropriate cognitive interweave. As long as anything is changing, the therapist knows that the processing is continuing. Periodically, the therapist may request SUD levels to determine the status of the processing. For some clients, the contents of the processing are clear to the clinician and/or client because cognitive, bodily, and affective aspects of a traumatic memory are being recalled and reported. For other clients, the processing is mysterious, unclear, or limited to a very narrow range of experience such as bodily sensations only, without cognitive or affective components. It is not necessary for all components to be conscious or reported to the clinician for the processing to be effective. The measure of success is completion of the processing through a "clean" body scan, to be described below.

Phase 5: Installation

When the SUD level reaches 0 or 1, and the VOC reaches 6 or 7 (or the session is out of time though the desired

SUD and VOC levels may not have yet been achieved), it is time for the installation. In this phase, the therapist installs the predefined desired positive cognition, unless a new one has emerged out of the processing. The installation involves repeating the desired positive cognition while holding the target in awareness. Linking the desired cognition with the original target appears to markedly strengthen the associative bonding, and provide for maximal generalization of effect when combined with imagery of a successful future and self-mastery in a future situation similar to the target situation.

Phase 6: Body Scan

Typically, a body scan is conducted, which means that the client scans his or her body to see if any distress registers somatically while the target image is brought to mind. A body scan that evokes somatic discomfort means that additional processing is needed, either in the current session or a subsequent one.

Phase 7: Closure

As part of the proper closure of an EMDR session, the client is reminded that processing continues after the session, and to not be concerned if dream and waking states are slightly unusual or emotional following the session. The client is instructed to record such experiences on a log, or to take prearranged appropriate steps if significant distress occurs (such as notifying the therapist on an emergency basis). The log and subsequent SUD and VOC ratings will be instructive in the reevaluation phase that occurs in the next session, as to the direction any future EMDR sessions might take. Typically, new EMDR targets emerge between sessions, as the processing continues. Also typically, the prior EMDR targets remain permanently at the low levels of disturbance that were achieved at the end of a successful EMDR session.

The Role of Abreactions

It is not uncommon for EMDR processing to include the intense reexperiencing of emotions that occurred at the time of the traumatic event, but may not have been experienced or processed to resolution at the time of the trauma, due to the overwhelming nature of the experience. As a result, the emotional processing of the traumatic event may spill out of the client undergoing EMDR processing, as a necessary part of completing the traumatic experience. This abreactive process can be startling to a clinician not trained in the role of abreaction in emotional processing; however, EMDR clinicians learn to accept the occurrence of abreactions in EMDR. A critical component of a successful EMDR

session is for any abreaction that occurs to be allowed to complete in order to neutralize the emotional charge on the events being processed, and integrate the experience into the client's fund of knowledge. The client and clinician will have established a stop signal in the preparation phase of treatment, so that the client has control over whether to allow the processing to complete. It is by far preferable for the client to allow the processing to complete, emotional intensity and all, than to close down the processing in the middle of an abreaction.

A Range of Protocols

The EMDR protocols are slightly different depending on the type of dysfunction that is being targeted. For instance, the PTSD protocol necessitates targeting the original traumatic event, as well as any flashback imagery or nightmare or dream imagery, and any triggering stimuli that evoke traumatic reactions. In contrast, the simple phobia protocol involves targeting such elements as the first time the fear occurred, the most disturbing time the fear occurred, and the most recent time the fear occurred, as well as the physical sensations of fear and a positive future template for action. The clinical literature offered by EMDR practitioners offers a wide range of protocols for specific disorders well beyond the initial PTSD condition addressed in the controlled studies. These protocols are clinically derived from the literature and experience of the particular fields. For example, a careful protocol for the use of EMDR in substance abuse disorders has been offered by Shapiro, Vogelmann-Sine, and Sine (1994).

APPLICATIONS

In its short history, EMDR has been reported to be effective with a wide range of populations. Typically, for each application of EMDR, a modified EMDR protocol is required that integrates extant procedures for treating the condition with the EMDR procedure.

Trauma

The most commonly reported application of EMDR is with trauma survivors of all types, including combat veterans, rape and molestation survivors, police and emergency teams, crime victims, line-of-duty deaths, bereavement, assault, natural disaster, accident and injury victims, and burn victims. In these applications, the standard PTSD protocol is used to target trauma-related symptomatology and process them through to adaptive resolution (Shapiro, 1995). The standard protocol for a single traumatic event targets the memory of the actual event, any flashback or dream imagery associated with the event, and present stimuli that restimulate the PTSD response. The great preponderance of controlled studies and clinical case reports in the literature are studying the application of EMDR to this population of PTSD sufferers from a range of traumatic stimuli.

It is of considerable theoretical interest that for recent traumatic events, the standard PTSD protocol does not adequately process the symptomatology. Rather, a modified protocol is necessary, beginning with interviewing the narrative history of the recent traumatic event prior to the EMDR procedure. The EMDR targets the most disturbing aspect of the memory as usual, but proceeds to neutralize the particularized features of the event from the narrative history, repeatedly. The EMDR is repeated until the entire narrative can be processed through without arousal. Shapiro's interpretation of this effect for recent traumas is that the brain has not consolidated the traumatic material into a single addressable unit or neural network early in the post-traumatic time period, so the detail must be individually sought and desensitized (Shapiro, 1995). For this writer, the processing of recent traumas is comparable to groping to find snapshots that lie on the floor in a dark room—one has to keep returning and checking to see if all of the pieces have been found. In contrast, the relatively straightforward processing of an older traumatic memory is comparable to playing a videotape in a dark room. The room may be dark, but one can be confident that once started, the tape is likely to play to completion.

Other Anxiety Disorders

Early in its history, the standard EMDR protocol was modified to address other anxiety conditions (Shapiro, 1995). The protocol for simple phobias targets, typically, the first, worst, and most recent episodes of phobic avoidance, as well as associated current stimuli and physical sensations. Not uncommonly, the initial occurrence of phobia was a learning outcome in response to a traumatic event. Desensitizing the fear of fear component of phobic avoidance is part of the EMDR process.

For current anxiety, the protocol addresses the initial memory of the current anxiety or behavior, the most recent example of the anxiety-evoking situation, and future projection of the desired feeling and behavior in that situation. Typically, these anxieties too are revealed through EMDR to be related to traumatic origins in some sense.

Process phobias are those anxieties related to the execution of a series of behaviors, such as performance anxiety related to public speaking. For process phobias, the EMDR protocol is modified to address the key elements of that process. With the phobias, the end stage of EMDR typically includes an installment of positive imagery of being in the formerly phobically avoided situation in the future, in a state of being relaxed, calm, and free of fear.

Other Disorders

The protocol to address illness and somatic disorders with EMDR is conducted in conjunction with an action plan to address any real medical or other life needs (Shapiro, 1995). The protocol identifies the range of relevant memories, present situations, and fears associated with the medical condition, such as loss of personal function, social sequelae, and traumatic medical treatments or experiences. It also includes installing desired imagery for the future period of survival. Imagery is typically based on imagery for adaptive healthy body functioning and immune function, coupled with positive expectations for healthy outcomes and future. Treatment is coupled with assignments for self-care.

Addictions

Additional applications of EMDR exist for chemical dependency and pathological gambling. The standard EMDR treatment should not be conducted on a chemically dependent individual without the appropriate precautions and the specialized protocol (Shapiro, Vogelmann-Sine, & Sine, 1994). The protocol for chemical dependency involves targeting of situational triggers. EMDR is used to target not only urges, but to change beliefs (e.g., adaptation to victimization, or low self-worth), to increase tolerance for emotions, and to resolve traumatic learning, among other treatment directions.

Dissociative Disorders

EMDR theory focuses on unprocessed traumatic material, so it is not surprising that EMDR seems to uncover previously undiagnosed cases of dissociative disorder (Paulsen, 1995). For that reason, it is critical that all clients be screened for a dissociative disorder before EMDR is first used. Most of the case reports of maladaptive outcomes of EMDR sessions are subsequently identified to be undiagnosed dissociative clients for whom the standard EMDR procedure, rather than the protocol for dissociation, was incorrectly employed.

The dissociation protocol for EMDR is complex, and requires extensive knowledge of the field of dissociation. For the mild to moderate dissociative conditions, the protocol begins with informed consent of the complete self-system (Paulsen, 1995). For the severely dissociative, this may not be possible, and a fractionated abreaction approach is more appropriate, to prevent overwhelming the self-system (Lazrove & Fine, 1996).

Personality Disorders

In the treatment of personality disorders, EMDR has been used by integrating the EMDR procedure with established treatments ranging from psychoanalytic to cognitive-behavioral. It can be used to target long-standing maladaptive beliefs, or to address object relations by addressing early childhood memories with unresolved conflicts or distress associated (Manfield, 1998; Shapiro, Vogelmann-Sine, & Sine, 1994). Treatment of personality disorders with EMDR typically takes substantially longer than treating single traumatic events. Often the personality disorders can be understood as repetitive traumas of neglect or emotional abuse or impaired family relationships. As a result, the EMDR procedures take longer to untangle the defensive strategies and the results of the maladaptive learning experiences, but nevertheless have been reported to shorten treatment time considerably.

Performance Enhancement

Nonclinical applications of EMDR are available for enhancement of the performance of executives, athletes, and other performers (Foster & Lendl, 1995, 1996). In many cases, work and other performance issues can be understood as process phobias or other maladaptive learning outcomes from much earlier experiences. As such, they are addressable through EMDR. The performance enhancement protocol differs by focusing more on an adaptive functioning frame of reference, rather than a pathology frame of reference. The procedure treats negative cognitions as distractions from the focus of a high-performing outcome, and either desensitizes them or bridges over them, reducing the effect of the distractions.

CASE EXAMPLE

The EMDR literature is replete with examples of the use of the procedure on cases of trauma survivors. For this chapter, the author has chosen a case from the field of managerial performance enhancement. The following case illustrates the use of EMDR beyond the usual application to trauma, to produce shifts in current areas of performance attributable to early maladaptive learning outcomes. This innovative application of EMDR was pioneered in the mid-1990s (Foster & Lendl, 1996).

A 38-year-old Caucasian female middle manager in a technology organization was referred to the author by a senior executive at her workplace who knew that the author conducted executive coaching and performance enhancement. The presenting complaint was that the woman, Leah (not her real name), was limited in her career advancement because of her discomfort in the presence of male authority figures. A technologist, the woman had advanced to middle management under the supervision of only female direct superiors in her 15-year management career. She had been recently offered a promotion reporting to a senior male executive, and Leah experienced considerable trepidation about her ability to comfortably relate to this man. Leah knew that she couldn't expect her career to advance if she continued avoiding a direct reporting relationship with men, and accepted the referral to the author, specifically requesting an EMDR-focused brief treatment targeting this specific problem. Leah had both read and heard about EMDR from several sources, including television and magazine reports, as well as the reports of a friend. In the initial phone contact, the author and Leah agreed to four two-hour sessions with a specific focus on this work-related symptom. We further agreed that should that our work uncover a need for a more extensive clinical treatment, Leah would accept referral to a clinical provider for longer term treatment with a clinical focus.

The author sent to Leah, in advance of the first session, administrative and clinical history forms, and an information sheet and informed consent form for EMDR. Leah presented for her first visit having completed those presession forms. A personal history form invites self-report in a range of categories while carefully avoiding "sounding clinical," because the setting is not a clinical one but a coaching one. This distinction is largely one of packaging, as the material that emerges requires clinical expertise on the part of the EMDR provider.

Leah chose to be disclosing on the personal history form, and her history revealed no prior psychological treatment, medical problems, legal/criminal problems, substance abuse, or trauma history. Family history was significant for a stern and demanding father who, before his death three years prior, was simultaneously closely involved in his only daughter's life, and imperious and judgmental of her. Leah's mother had been affectionate but weak and avoided interfering in her husband's overinvolvement with Leah. Relationship history was significant for three long-term nonmarital relationships. The longest, currently ongoing, was with a gentle man with whom Leah had good communications and affection, and little conflict. The only relationship problems occurred when Leah responded intensely to perceived attempts to control her. Leah also brought with her to the initial visit a Myers-Briggs Type Indicator result from a business workshop, and was an ENTJ (Extravert, Intuitive, Thinking, Judgment) on that Jungian-style inventory.

The first 45 minutes of the initial visit was spent discussing Leah's history. Rapport was readily established, and Leah wanted to proceed directly in the first session with an EMDR procedure. We decided to embark on an initial EMDR procedure in the remainder of the initial visit. I felt this was appropriate because of the presence of a good rapport, her clear understanding of the procedure and what to expect, her motivation to work on a focused objective, the absence of red flags to contraindicate proceeding, and the presence of a good ability to self-soothe if necessary (she had learned self-relaxation from tapes). Note: In clinical practice, the author invariably conducted screening for dissociation prior to conducting EMDR, because problem EMDR outcomes almost invariably are the result of undiagnosed dissociation. In business coaching, it would make executives uneasy to be asked dissociative assessment questions about hearing voices, losing time, and other unusual symptoms. The author therefore does not formally screen for dissociation in coaching sessions when the executive has a personal history like Leah's, with a successful work history combined with a negative medical history, negative psychiatric and trauma history, and absence of such self-reported symptoms as headaches or memory difficulties. However, the author is fully prepared to recognize dissociation if it emerges in an EMDR session and use the appropriate dissociation protocol.

In preparing for the initial EMDR session, the standard EMDR protocol was established, with the modification that the predominant emphasis was on the desired work outcome as the targeted positive cognition. Leah's target positive outcome was of herself comfortably reporting to the male senior executive, disagreeing with him skillfully and professionally, and asserting herself appropriately. Her desired positive self-statement was, "I can do this, I'm good at this." Her negative imagery that interfered with this outcome, however, included self-consciously sitting in silence under her prospective boss's disapproving eye, while he quizzed her, or challenged her judgment, calculations, or reasoning. Negative self-statements included, "This probably isn't right"; "He's going to tell me I messed up, I can feel it"; and "I wish he'd just leave me alone." Leah's SUD level was 6 out of 10 possible, rated on anxiety, which Leah experienced in her stomach. The desired positive outcome prior to EMDR was evaluated as seeming viscerally true on the VOC scale at a level of 3 on a 7-point scale, where 7 is completely true.

In a clinical setting, the EMDR practitioner would have targeted Leah's relationship with her father, rather than the current work situation, in the first EMDR session. As a rule of thumb, when an early experience or relationship seems likely causally related to the current problem, it is targeted first as a feeder memory, that is, a memory that feeds the current problem from a reservoir of unresolved affect. Because the client came to treatment in a work performance enhancement setting, rather than a true clinical one, the focus is on the current

work situation. However, predictably, the early feeder memories emerge during the EMDR treatment anyway, and can be successfully resolved.

The EMDR session began with Leah turning her attention to the anxiety that arises in the imaginal exposure to sitting in her prospective boss's office, discussing a business issue on which they had different points of view. After each set of lateral eye movements, the author would ask Leah what she was noticing, and Leah readily reported cognitions, imagery, and emotions that emerged during the processing. Between the first several sets of eye movements, Leah reported such thoughts as, "He is frowning at me" and "His words are measured, but I can tell he is disappointed in me." Without prompting from the author, Leah then reported that her imagery had shifted to her father, and how he used to sit sternly while reading the paper. She recalled that he would require her to sit with him, read an article, and discuss it with him. She had little interest or knowledge of current events as a nine-year-old, and dreaded these discussions. Over the course of eight sets of eye movements, she reported how she would struggle to anticipate the "correct" answer, but her father would frown, and correct her. "I can't do it"; "I'm not smart enough." Leah recalled these thoughts without author inquiry beyond asking, "What are you getting?" between sets.

As the processing continued, the anxiety that began in her stomach shifted to a pressure in her chest. Between sets of eye movements, she reported feeling trapped by her father's scrutiny and criticism. She wished she could run out and play, but she had to stay and be interrogated and criticized. The pressure in Leah's chest then shifted to a "pang in her heart" and tears of hurt that he couldn't just love her as she was. She felt unloved because she needed so much improving. The tears continued through three or four sets of eye movements.

The physical sensations then shifted to a fullness or hurt in Leah's throat, and then a tension in the jaw. Between sets, she reported that she wanted to shout at her father, "Leave me alone!" As the sets of eye movements progressed, her mood shifted to wistfully sad, as her view of her father shifted, and she saw him as unable to relate authentically to anyone, except that he could feel intense feelings if they were negative, and if he was in a one-up position. With insight, she described him as fearful and constricted by his own father's fundamentalist religion and upbringing. She was startled by this perspective, as she had not thought of him that way before.

Because the two-hour session was almost over, the author then checked back in with the original target image of the prospective boss's office. Leah reported, "Well, I guess there's no mystery about where that problem started!" She wistfully reported that she wished she could have found the courage to relate to her father honestly and with affection before he died.

The EMDR session was prepared for closure by checking on the remaining levels of disturbance, which found Leah's SUD level at 2, and her VOC on the desired cognition at 6. Closure also included a brief relaxation to assure her comfort on leaving the office, and a reminder to log any feelings or thoughts that emerged following the session. The next session was scheduled for one week later, with an instruction to call in between in the unlikely event that she became acutely uncomfortable.

At the second visit, Leah excitedly reported that in the first several days following her initial session, she had an almost euphoric sense of a burden being "off her chest." After that feeling passed, she experienced memories of her father largely with affectionate and accepting overtones. Upon checking on the image of being in the prospective boss's office, her SUD was still a 2, including residual discomfort. Her belief in the statement "I can do this" was still 6, indicating some uncertainty. When the author inquired what stopped it from being completely true, Leah said that she did not know, but that she might feel guilty if she asserted herself. We agreed to target this in this second session. Before embarking on the EMDR, however, Leah apprised the author of developments in her work situation. She noticed decreased fear of the prospective boss, but was still unsure whether she felt comfortable reporting to him. Meanwhile, she knew she had only a short time to make up her mind or the opportunity would pass her by. She noticed that she had readily spoken up in disagreement in a meeting with a gruff male senior executive (not her prospective boss) who laid out an initiative he had planned. Leah thought that in the past she might have soft-pedaled her objection or remained silent. Her speaking up was well received because she felt she articulated her concerns skillfully, and others in the room agreed with her analysis. The gruff executive modified his plans in order to obtain more data. Leah was surprised by how smoothly and naturally this event transpired, although she did experience some anxiety about speaking up. We proceeded to the EMDR.

Leah selected her target as again being the prospective boss's office. Her desired cognition was, "I can do this with confidence," which was rated a VOC of 4. Her negative cognition was, "I better not say anything," accompanied by a vague feeling of guilt or distress located in her stomach, rated at a SUD level of 3 or 4.

We conducted a few sets of eye movements in which, at the author's suggestion, she ran through the imagined events of a discussion with her prospective boss in her mind, while her eyes were moving. Between sets she initially reported little change, except for a sadness "behind her eyes." Targeting that sensation, she abruptly reported

that her mother was in the kitchen while Leah was "interrogated" by her father. If Leah wasn't the one being interrogated, her mother would be. Leah recalled that her mother would be reduced to sobs by her husband's stern criticisms. Several sets of eye movements passed with Leah saying little in between sets, but many emotions showing on her face while the processing continued. Leah had felt it her responsibility to take the "torture treatments," as she called these sessions with her father, so that her mother would be spared. Between sets, Leah described anger and then sadness at the bitter silence between her parents, her mother's isolation and despair, and Leah's sense that her mother needed protection. Leah then shifted to surprise and then anger because this was backward, that her mother should have been protecting Leah, not the other way around. After several nearly silent sets punctuated by bodily sensations that were primarily located in the chest and throat, Leah spontaneously recalled with tears that her father had died in her mother's arms. Leah recognized that they had some measure of intimacy between them after all. When time was about to run out on the session, we shifted to installing with eye movements the desired cognition, "I can do this," although Leah wanted to change it now to, "I'm free to do this." We also ran through in Leah's mind the entire process of sitting in the prospective boss's office and standing up to him. Leah felt much more comfortable with her part of it. As she left the author's office, Leah turned and said, "I really don't like the jerk." We scheduled the next appointment for one week later.

Leah called during the week to say she needed to make the next session a one-hour visit and perhaps our last one. In our final session, we conducted no EMDR, and rather reviewed and discussed what had transpired and wrapped up our work.

Leah reported that she had decided she had no desire to work for the prospective boss because he was a dislikable person. Leah had, however, been offered a position with another firm, reporting to a senior male executive. She was excited about the new job and confident about her ability to do it and relate well to the new boss. Both of us were surprised and pleased with the turn of events. Leah said that she had always known that her relationship with her father was an issue, but that until EMDR she had not been able to resolve the discomfort she'd always felt about him. Leah's understanding was that her new feeling of empowerment caused her to redefine her initial work situation as one that she didn't want to stay in at all. The shifts in feelings toward greater empowerment and assertion remained relatively constant and seemed entirely natural to her. She agreed that she wouldn't hesitate to return if similar or new concerns emerged. She reported that she was speaking on the phone with her mother with a new understanding and acceptance. Leah felt she no longer had to protect anyone, except herself, in work situations.

On two months' telephone follow-up, Leah reported the new job was interesting and challenging but stressful because of workload. She had had a number of occasions where she was able to stand up to her new boss over issues, and it was, "no biggie."

This case illustrates several points beyond just showing a use of the procedure: (1) EMDR processing causes shifts in maladaptive learning outcomes that are affecting performance in current life, whether the person is aware or unaware of the early experience that feeds the current dysfunction; (2) EMDR treatment can be markedly brief and cost-effective; (3) EMDR has applicability beyond PTSD cases; (4) EMDR can produce significant turns in people's life events, not always in the way one might predict; and, finally, (5) EMDR's results spontaneously lead people in the direction of adaptive functioning. Although clinical cases can become infinitely more complicated, some clinical cases can resolve as rapidly as this case example.

SUMMARY

The impact of EMDR on the mental health field has been profoundly life changing, both for the professionals who use it and for the recipients of it. It challenges the beliefs of practitioners whose training and experience instilled the belief that change must be slow. When used for trauma survivors, it completely sets aside the notion that one can never get over a trauma such as rape or war. Certainly such experiences will bring permanent change, but EMDR practitioners see again and again that EMDR can help people make meaning out of senselessness, and healing and wholeness out of hurt and disarray (Shapiro & Forrest, 1997). Although the objective evidence is not yet amassed for nontrauma applications, the clinical case reports are legion for applications broader than trauma (e.g., Lovett, 1999; Manfield, 1998; Tinker & Wilson, 1999). Certainly, at this juncture there are sufficient controlled studies and a body of clinical case material to justify declaring EMDR the treatment of choice for trauma. At this point, an 84 to 90 percent remission rate is expected for PTSD within three EMDR sessions; however, treatment is not a race, and length of treatment will vary depending on the complexity of the case (F. Shapiro, personal communication, 1999). With EMDR in the clinical arsenal, one can begin to envision a world in which the psychological effects of war, disaster, violence, and other tragedies of the human experience can be subdued and reorganized into an adaptive, healthy, and meaningful survivorship. Beyond survivorship, with EMDR, our lives can be transformed into a thriving and adaptive wholeness.

REFERENCES

Bower, B. G. (1981). Mood and memory. *American Psychologist, 36,* 129–148.

Carlson, J. G., Chemtob, C. M., Rusnak, K., Hedlund, N. L., & Muraoka, M. Y. (1998). Eye movement desensitization and reprocessing for combat-related posttraumatic stress disorder. *Journal of Traumatic Stress, 11,* 3–24.

Chambless, D. L., Baker, M. J., Baucom, D. H., Beutler, L. E., Calhoun, K. S., Crits-Christoph, P., Daiuto, A., DeRubeis, R., Detwiler, J., Haaga, D. A. F., Bennett Johnson, S., McCurry, S., Mueser, K. T., Pope, K. S., Sanderson, W. C., Shoham, V., Stickle, T., Williams, D. A., & Woody, S. R. (1998). Update on empirically validated therapies, II. *The Clinical psychologist, 51,* 3–16.

Chemtob, C. M., Tolin, D. F., van der Kolk, B. A., & Pitman, R. K. (2000). Eye movement desensitization and reprocessing (EMDR). In E. B. Foa, T. Keane, and Friedman (Eds.), *ISTSS guidelines for PTSD.* New York: Guilford Press.

Foster, S., & Lendl, J. (1995). Eye movement desensitization and reprocessing: Initial applications for enhancing performance in athletes. *Journal of Applied Sport Psychology, 7* (Suppl.), 63.

Foster, S., & Lendl, J. (1996). Eye movement desensitization and reprocessing: Four case studies of a new tool for executive coaching and restoring employee performance after setbacks. *Consulting Psychology Journal, 48,* 155–161.

Lang, P. J. (1977). Imagery in therapy: An information processing analysis of fear. *Behavior Therapy, 8,* 862–886.

Lazrove, S., & Fine, C. G. (1996). The use of EMDR in patients with dissociative identity disorder. *Dissociation, 9,* 289–299.

Lovett, J. (1999). *Small wonders: Healing childhood trauma with EMDR.* Berkeley, CA: Free Press.

Manfield, P. (1998). *Extending EMDR: A casebook of innovative applications.* New York: Norton Professional Books.

Marcus, S., Marquis, P., & Sakai, C. (1997). Controlled study of treatment of PTSD using EMDR in an HMO setting. *Psychotherapy, 34,* 307–315.

Paulsen, S. (1995). Eye movement desensitization and reprocessing: Its cautious use in the dissociative disorders. *Dissociation, 8,* 32–44.

Pitman, R. K., Orr, S. P., Altman, B., Longpre, R. E., Poire, R. E., & Macklin, M. L. (1996). Emotional processing during eye-movement desensitization and reprocessing therapy of Vietnam veterans with chronic post-traumatic stress disorder. *Comprehensive Psychiatry, 37,* 419–429.

Rothbaum, B. O. (1997). A controlled study of eye movement desensitization and reprocessing for posttraumatic stress disordered sexual assault victims. *Bulletin of the Menninger Clinic, 61,* 317–334.

Scheck, M. M., Schaeffer, J. A., & Gillette, C. S. (1998). Brief psychological intervention with traumatized young women: The efficacy of eye movement desensitization and reprocessing. *Journal of Traumatic Stress, 11,* 25–44.

Shapiro, F. (1995). *Eye Movement Desensitization and Reprocessing: Basic principles, protocols and procedures.* New York: Guilford Press.

Shapiro, F. (1998). Eye movement desensitization and reprocessing (EMDR): Accelerated information processing and affect-driven constructions. *Crisis Interventions, 4*(2–3), 145–157.

Shapiro, F. (1999). Eye movement desensitization and reprocessing (EMDR) and the anxiety disorders: Clinical and research implications of an integrated psychotherapy treatment. *Journal of Anxiety Disorders, 13,* 35–67.

Shapiro, F., & Forrest, M. S. (1997). *EMDR: The breakthrough therapy for overcoming anxiety, stress, and trauma.* New York: Basic Books.

Shapiro, F., Vogelmann-Sine, S., & Sine, L. (1994). Eye movement desensitization and reprocessing: Treating trauma and substance abuse. *Journal of Psychoactive Drugs, 26,* 379–391.

Tinker, R., & Wilson, S. (1999). *Through the eyes of a child: EMDR with children.* New York: Norton.

Chapter 23

FEMINIST PSYCHOTHERAPY

BARBARA L. FORISHA

During the course of investigating the need for this book and important systems of psychotherapy, I kept being reminded of the importance of having a chapter on Feminist Psychotherapy. Although I had some doubts that there was any such thing as Feminist Psychotherapy as a system of theory and practice, and felt that the issue was really a political/ethical/professional one rather than a theoretical-procedural matter, I decided that it would be quite valuable to have in this book a point of view on this very sensitive issue.

In Barbara Forisha's chapter we obtain glimpses not only of the question of psychotherapy for a special group, that is, women, but also some of the major concepts that a small but relatively powerful group of individuals have about the state of the profession.

Since feminist therapy is essentially a political issue, I am positive that many will disagree with the conclusions, and may even, as I do, take umbrage at these views. Nevertheless, these views need to be heard—and at this point I regret that I have no means to permit counterarguments.

The essential message that Barbara Forisha expresses—of the need for a genuinely humanistic approach—is one that I am sure all therapists of goodwill will accept.

Feminist Psychotherapy is both a humanistic therapy and a force for social change. As a humanistic therapy, it promotes self-awareness, self-affirmation, and personal integration. However, feminists recognize that personal integration, particularly for women, is not encouraged by a sexist society that prescribes differing roles for women and men and that allots the marginal role to women. Thus, in facilitating personal integration in all individuals, feminists come into conflict with societal norms that are seen as creating dysfunctional behavior patterns for all individuals. Feminist Psychotherapy, therefore, turns inward to promote personal integration, but also turns outward to act as a force against the societal, sex-differentiated expectations that discourage personal integration in individuals within the society.

Feminists, therefore, are in accord with most other humanistic schools of thought that affirm the worth of the individual, postulate growth-oriented tendencies in the individual, and believe in the individual's ability to live the process of the complexities of life as a basis for trustworthy decision making. Feminists differ from adherents of other schools of therapy, however, in recognizing that no model of mental health encompasses a view of healthy womanhood and that it is incumbent upon therapists to facilitate the development of such a model in individual clients. Such a stance transforms the "personal into the political" and requires that feminist therapists stand against all social forces that attempt to pressure women into those unhealthy behavior patterns that are part of current societal norms.

HISTORY

Feminist Psychotherapy has developed out of a complex of historical conditions: the marginal status of women, which has made it relatively easy and convenient to label them as "deviant" in times of social stress; the emphasis on finding one's own personhood, which has been popularized by the humanistic movement; and the specific impact of the Women's Movement, which has crystallized the contradictions between societal marginality and the search for personal identity. Each of these is briefly reviewed in turn.

Women as Marginal Human Beings

Simone de Beauvoir, in her classic work *The Second Sex* (1953), developed the thesis that throughout history women have always been defined as the "Other," as opposed to men, who are the "One." In most societies, men have embodied (or been conceptualized as embodying) the socially valued traits of that culture. In our own society, such traits are assertion, independence, self-reliance, and other instrumental qualities. As a consequence, other devalued traits have been ascribed to women. Thus women have been conceptualized as embodying the desirable but not highly valued traits of nurturance and receptivity and also the undesirable traits of dependence, emotionality, and submissiveness. In general, women have been viewed, therefore, as demonstrating traits that are outside the mainstream of desirable social norms. As a consequence, women *are* somewhat deviant in times of stress when the One can scapegoat the Other.

Many writers and psychologists have lent support to the thesis that the marginality of women and the narrow definition of appropriate feminine behavior led to psychological distress. Virginia Woolf (1929/1957) suggests that any woman of talent would, historically, have been stifled by the lack of outlets for her gifts. She states that

> any woman born with a great gift in the sixteenth century would certainly have gone crazed, shot herself, or ended her days in some lonely cottage outside the village, half witch, half wizard, feared and mocked at. For it needs little skill in psychology to be sure that a highly gifted girl who had tried to use her gift for poetry would have been so thwarted and hindered by other people, so tortured and pulled asunder by her own contrary instincts, that she must have lost her health or sanity to a certainty. (p. 51)

The situation is only somewhat modified today. Osmund, Franks, and Burtle (1974) point out that women today may have more opportunities to use their gifts than previously but are still socially constrained from doing so. They state that medical science has improved the physical status of women so that they now have more leisure and better health, leading to a greater desire to exercise their abilities, yet societal norms have not changed sufficiently to allow them to do so. These changes are, therefore, "a source of stress and strain." Menaker (1974) echoes the same point of view, finding that social changes have increased expectations for women without necessarily increasing opportunities for action and that this creates a particular vulnerability in modern women who therefore seek psychotherapeutic help.

In part, the marginality of women explains the fact that women have accounted for greater numbers in the annals of madness. In the sixteenth and seventeenth centuries when mental illness was not yet defined, women were more often burned and drowned as witches than were men. With the redefinition of deviant behavior and the establishment of asylums in the eighteenth century, women were the more frequent inhabitants of these institutions (Osmund, Franks, & Burtle, 1974). In thera-

peutic settings of the twentieth century, studies show that women are more frequently mentally ill and/or in therapy than men (Gove, 1972) and that the larger group of women in therapy are white, educated, middle-class housewives and mothers (Fabrikant, 1974). Other research studies showed that women constituted two thirds of the therapeutic population and that women were twice as likely to be perceived as having psychiatric and emotional problems as were men (Locke & Gardner, 1969; Rosen, Locke, Goldberg, & Babigian, 1972).

Women have received more than their share of attention from psychotherapists, yet psychotherapy has historically been antithetical to the full development of women as human beings. Freud's early insistence that "anatomy is destiny" led him to the conclusion that women are merely defective men and that a woman's development is complete at 30 and she has nowhere else to go. Freud's work on hysteria was based primarily on clinical observation of his female clientele, and elaborated on the assumptions that women are remarkably passive and tractable, the mere objects of male desire. Osmund, Franks, and Burtle (1974) state that "The main female characteristic which emerged from the Freudian world appears to have been docility combined perhaps with envy that she was not a man" (p. 13).

Among other early therapists there were, however, glimmerings of a more sympathetic approach to women. Alfred Adler (1927), for one, recognized that many of woman's problems originated in the society in which she lived, which was designed to suit the male:

> All our institutions, our traditional attitudes, our laws, our morals, give evidence of the fact that they are determined and maintained by privileged males for the glory of male domination. (p. 123)

Yet in 1931 he could still write that women's problems basically stemmed from insufficient training for their secondary role in life (Janeway, 1975).

The first truly sympathetic approach to women was developed by Karen Horney. Just as did Adler, she realized the implication of living in a society designed for the One when one is only the Other. She wrote in 1926:

> Like all sciences and all valuations, the psychology of women has hitherto been considered only from the point of view of men. It is inevitable that the man's position of advantage should cause objective validity to be attributed to his subjective, effective relations to the woman, and . . . the psychology of women hitherto actually represents a deposit of the desires and disappointments of men. An additional and very important factor in the situation is that women have adapted themselves to the wishes of men and felt as if their adaptation were their true nature. That is, they see or saw themselves in the way that their men's wishes demanded of them; uncon-

sciously they yielded to the suggestion of the masculine thought. (pp. 56–57)

Women have allowed themselves to become the Other, for they have internalized views promulgated by a male world. Yet the options allowed by a traditionally sex-role-divided society make it difficult for women to do otherwise. Only recently has the psychotherapeutic emphasis encouraged women as well as men to disentangle themselves from internalized values and "find themselves." The conflict this produces for women, who have little societal support for so doing, has fed the fires of feminism.

Cultural Emphasis: Finding Oneself

The growth of humanistic psychology since World War II was spearheaded by the theoretical orientations of Abraham Maslow (1954/1970) and Carl Rogers (1961). In the late 1970s, the humanistic ethic of self-realization was popularized by many so that the importance of personal growth has become part of mass cultural expectations. Humanists write and speak of individuals "finding themselves" and detaching themselves from societal expectations. This orientation toward human beings emphasizes a present-centeredness, an individually based system of values, and an injunction to utilize one's potential. Within therapeutic relationships these principles are applied by establishing egalitarian relationships in which clients and therapists relate to each other as people, in which openness and transparency are encouraged, and in which the ultimate base for decision making rests with the client.

Humanistic psychologists have encouraged women as well as men to further their own growth in ways based on an "inner locus of evaluation" rather than on societal norms and thus have provided a theoretical framework for overturning existing societal sex-role stereotypes. However, the humanistic psychologists' focus is inward. There is little awareness of external, sociological forces that hinder full human development, nor is there much emphasis on the differential conditioning of the two sexes. Feminist psychotherapists thus build upon the humanistic theory by adding to the psychological process a sociological emphasis—and challenging the social norms that act against liberation from our conditioning.

Women, Self, and Society

Feminist psychotherapists have been particularly attuned to the difficulties women and men face in finding themselves in a society that denies to each a full repertoire of human action and feeling. In an oversimplified sense, men have been deprived of the experience of intimacy in the private sphere and women have been deprived of their power and the right to achievement in the public sphere. Neither women nor men have had full opportunity to maximize their capacities to work and to love, a definition of mental health since the time of Freud. The impetus provided by the Women's Movement, however, since the mid-1960s has led to the crystallization of a theoretical, therapeutic, and activist school that, to facilitate individual self-realization, is standing against the status quo and the historical heritage that argues that women should possess but half of human traits and the lesser half at that.

CURRENT STATUS

Feminist Psychotherapy has come of age since the rise of the Women's Movement in the mid-1960s. Many feminist therapists work primarily with problems arising out of the dysfunctional impact of sex-role norms on the personal and professional lives of women and men. Other therapists also have been sensitized to the problems of women and men and have adopted an orientation of "people's liberation," which is compatible with feminist theory.

A number of men as well as women claim to be feminist. This means that men as well as women are working for the liberation of both sexes from traditional patterns of behavior that do not suit the world in which we live. There is, however, considerable controversy over whether men really can be feminist therapists; many women feminists claim that patterns of sexism are so bred into our system that it is not possible for a male, raised in this society, to fully comprehend the problems of growing up female. In an ultimate sense this is no doubt true, and there are some women's issues that are perhaps beyond the understanding of anyone who is not female. Yet the collective failings in male understanding in many cases do no more disservice to specific clients than do the idiosyncratic failings of all therapists who, in some areas, fail to measure up to an unattainable ideal. The cause of human liberation is facilitated from many sources, and none provides the only or the surest source of guidance. Thus many acknowledge that feminist therapists may be male as well as female—and the clientele may also be drawn from both sexes. Yet the orientation remains predominantly female on both sides of the therapeutic relationship.

The general public as well as therapists have been sensitized to the particular difficulties of women in our society. Increasing numbers of individuals, primarily women, are now asking for and selecting therapists with a feminist orientation. This increased popularity of feminist thought must be viewed, however, against the backdrop of the patriarchal system that still dominates therapeutic circles. The larger number of therapists still act out, consciously or unconsciously, the mandates of a male-dominated society. Chesler's (1971, 1972) criticism of the therapeutic system is cogent. She states that the majority of psychologists and psychiatrists are middle-aged, middle-class, married males who see in therapy middle-age, middle-class married females, and who thus perpetuate the very problems from which women are suffering. The problems that women sustain living in relationship to males are then transferred to the therapeutic situation. A therapist, from his own orientation, may urge the woman to accommodate herself to the existing system, for his own comfort as well as for the male(s) with whom she lives. Chesler maintains, in fact, that men (including therapists) drive women crazy by urging them to maintain a submissive role in accord with the status quo. Some of Chesler's claims are supported by research studies that tell of the perplexity and lack of empathetic understanding male therapists demonstrate toward their women patients' complaints and dissatisfactions (see Rice & Rice, 1973).

If, as Karen Horney suggests, the view that men have of women is a record of their desires and disappointments when in the company of women, then men indeed do women an injustice and refuse to perceive them in fully human terms. Several studies document this view. The landmark study by the Brovermans and their colleagues (1970) shows that clinicians (both male and female) tend to see a healthy woman as contrary to all the norms of a healthy person. On the other hand, the healthy person is perceived as a healthy male. This is similar to the conclusions drawn by Neulinger (1968) in an earlier study; he concluded that men chose to see women as nurturant, sensuous playthings.

The result of this view in therapy is that women are urged to support their husbands, take care of their children, and please men. Since many of women's difficulties arise from the fact that they lose their own identity in the process of caring for others, the strong suggestion of further accommodation to others can only exacerbate women's malaise. Adjustment to the existing system has historically been detrimental to women, and traditional therapy has generally urged women only to "try harder" to accommodate this system rather than creating one more suited to their needs.

Feminist Psychotherapy thus stands against traditional views of women and society in urging women to find themselves. Feminists also recognize, however, that their stance, though popularly accepted, is still a minority point of view, and the development of new theoretical foundations requires that women work together to counteract the force of traditional institutionalized views of women. Hence in many ways Feminist Psychotherapy is a resocialization to a new system of being and requires the theoretical foundations, the individual examples, and the support networks that can support, strengthen, and expand a nonsexist view in a patriarchal society.

THEORY

In many ways Feminist Psychotherapy may be viewed as a form of resocialization to a new world—and in part to a world that does not yet exist. As such, Feminist Therapy requires detachment from previous cultural norms, many of which are internalized, and the conscious development of new patterns of behavior based on a new perception of women's needs and capabilities in a changing world. Such resocialization requires an understanding of the realistic options offered by society; an awareness of the learned patterns and internalized norms acquired in previous socialization; a knowledge of self, one's talents, abilities, limitations, and potential for growth; a new theoretical perception encompassing a view of the individual in society; and an interpersonal network that supports the individual's growth-oriented path. Each of these facets of the resocialization process of Feminist Psychotherapy is explored in the sections that follow.

Economic and Social Conditions

Contrary to popular mythology, woman's place is no longer in the home but in the workforce, where women are generally overqualified and underpaid (Forisha & Goldman, 1981). Many women must work, as their income is the sole or a necessary part of household survival: There are a large number of single-parent homes headed by women; the climbing divorce rate has left many women in a position where they must expect to work for the rest of their lives; in addition, more women are choosing to remain single or to be married and remain childless, and hence expect to be continuous members of the workforce.

The statistics on work and marriage are indicative of the changing status of woman in our society. Yet societal norms have changed but little. There is some general social support for women in the workforce when they *have* to be there, but there is still very little support for women leaving the nurturing functions traditionally ascribed to them. Thus women who choose to work, or who are overburdened by expectations of both working and caring for husband and/or children, find little support for the conflicts that they face. They are subject to feelings of guilt, inadequacy, and lowered self-esteem. The old model of traditional feminine behavior, for which all women have been socialized, no longer fits the world in which we live.

Feminine Socialization

Numerous writers have characterized the socialization of women as inculcating docility and responsiveness—traits counterproductive for women who must or who choose to earn their own way in the world. Weisstein (1971), for one, writes:

How are women characterized in our culture, and in psychology? They are inconsistent, emotionally unstable, lacking in a strong conscious or superego, weaker, "nurturant" rather than productive, "intuitive" rather than intelligent, and if they are at all "normal," suited to the home and family. In short, the list adds up to a typically minority group stereotype of inferiority; if they know their place, which is in the home, they are really quite lovable, happy, childlike, loving creatures. (p. 221)

Freeman (1976) concurs in pointing out that the traits manifested by girls in our society are those attributed to victimized groups by psychologists. Moreover, the victim's traits appear to develop in women as they grow up. They begin healthy and strong but later lose this advantage. As the impact of social expectations takes its toll, girls succumb to the expected attributes of inferiority. Freeman writes: "Girls start off better than boys and end up worse" (p. 139).

In the process of becoming feminine, then, girls become women who have lower self-esteem and less confidence in their ability to act in this world than they had in their early years. Steinman (1974) describes the result of this process:

> If for one reason or another, a woman is forced to suppress her need for self-expression, she will experience a loss of self-esteem, she will become less effectual in all spheres of her life. This is true for all women, but it is particularly severe for the educated woman who, in the process of her education, was given high aspirations for personal success in the world of business or the professions. (p. 76)

The resulting picture of the adult woman in our society, particularly the educated one, still emphasizes receptivity. The suppression of other areas of self-expression leads to lowered self-esteem. The extremes of this picture are those that, in many ways, resemble the typical clinical picture of hysteria and masochism.

Hysteria and Masochism.   Karen Horney (1926, 1935, 1950) was one of the first to comment on the similarity between the socially approved picture of femininity and the occurrence of masochism. She said these clinical pathologies were induced in whole societies by certain sociological factors—all of which occur in modern society. She wrote that masochism in women may appear in any culture-complex in which: expansiveness and sexuality have small outlet; the number of children is restricted; women are assessed as inferior; women are economically dependent on men; women are restricted to the spheres of life that are built chiefly on emotional bonds (family life, religious or charity work); and there is a surplus of marriageable women. In such a setting, as Douglas (1978) writes of nineteenth-century America, suffering may be eulogized because it is one of the few areas in which women can excel.

Similarly, hysteria is closely akin to the normal female personality (Wolowitz, 1972, p. 313). Cox (1976), drawing on the work of Belote (1976), explains this relationship by saying that women escalate to a hysterical pitch when they do not get emotional response from others (i.e., men). Trained to be emotional and responsive, women tend to expect this responsiveness in others. Yet men do not respond to women's needs because they do not think of it and because they do not know how, and other women do not do so either, because traditionally their attention has been focused on men. As Cox concludes, from a feminist point of view, taking into account the patriarchal context, women as a class may become "hysterical" because men as a class do not respond.

The socialization of women may be said, therefore, to lead not only to docility and responsiveness but often to hysteria and masochism. The fact that these behavior patterns are socially induced and yet regarded as pathological are part of the double-bind in which women's traditional socialization leaves them.

Awareness of Self

The process of women finding out who they are, in therapy, is necessarily interwoven with the social framework in which they live and the internalized view of women as nonassertive, other-oriented, and dependent. Increasing self-awareness thus requires that women differentiate their own needs from those that they have learned "ought to be" their needs, and learn to recognize their own worth and independence. The path to this self-awareness often leads through recognizing one's anger, learning to nurture oneself, and ultimately seeing oneself as an independent person.

Anger.   Women who have been trained to say yes have trouble saying no. Often the development of anger is necessary in order to break through this conditioning and ultimately seek an integration where one can say both yes and no. The development of the capacity to express anger is a necessary transition toward dismantling overly acquiescent behavior. As women come to disentangle their anger from their hurt, and to give expression to their anger as well as their pain, they may temporarily exaggerate their anger. Yet without this process of differentiation, the road to full humanness is barred. In a feminist poem, "For Witches," Susan Sutheim (1969) writes of this process:

today
i lost my temper.

temper, when one talks of metal
means strong,
perfect.

temper, for humans
means angry
irrational bad.

today i found my temper
i said,
you step on my head
for 27 years you step on my head
and though i have been trained
to excuse you for your inevitable
clumsiness

today i think
i prefer to head to your clumsiness

today i begin
to find
myself

tomorrow
perhaps
i will begin
to find you.

Self-Nurturance.   Discovering one's anger is often a necessary part of discovering one's self. Women have gone a long way down the other path of caring for others and disregarding themselves. A recent commentary by Ellen Goodman illustrates the tendency for women to "understand" others rather than to stand up for or defend themselves. In a newspaper column entitled "Understanding Woman," she says that such a woman is a good listener and helps others to put the pieces of their lives back together. However, she might be demonstrating too much of a good thing. Goodman (1979, August 21) writes of her "understanding woman":

> The last time I saw her I thought about the men in her life. I remember the husband who said he needed space. And she understood.
> I remember the guy who was, from time to time, unfaithful. And she understood.
> There was also a man who didn't want to get married and have children, after all, he had already been there. And now there is a man who has difficulty relating to her son because, after all, he has a boy the same age in another state. It is all very understandable. (p. 46)

Goodman compares such a woman to a marathon runner, a runner in a sympathy marathon, for which most women have been trained from childhood. Yet she points out that the "understanding woman" has understood too much and asked for too little and "has logged too many miles in other people's shoes."

Feminist therapists, then, are asking women to *ask* and to take care of themselves, to free themselves from always running in somebody else's place, and to give careful attention to their own course and the facilitation of their own record. For women, trained to excuse the other's inevitable clumsiness, this is often hard to do.

Independence.   Both anger and self-nurturance are steps on the way to differentiating oneself from others—in order to better relate to others when the transitional phase has passed. Learning to be angry and to take care of oneself are a part of seeing oneself as an independent person whose fortunes are not always dependent on the whims of others. Yet, traditionally, this has been the experience of women. Virginia Woolf (1929/1957), for example, writes that women have always served as reflections of men rather than independent human beings. She states: "Women have served all these centuries as looking-glasses possessing the magic and delicious power of reflecting the figure of man at twice its natural size." Yet the capacity to mirror another, when it becomes a way of life, precludes an active orientation based on one's own sense of self. Another novelist, in a popular work, has her main character, a nineteenth-century woman, elaborate on this tendency. After the loss of her husband, a young widow writes:

> But what will I be without him to tell me how beautiful and bright I am? Are other women as frightened as I am, wondering how much of what they are is merely a reflection of what others see in them? What am I when I am all alone? Am I strong and brave without children to assure me I am, out of their own need? Will I ever believe that I am beautiful and bright out of the sight of a man who loves me? I feel as if I have just been born—cut apart from the sustaining presence that made all my decisions for me and left helpless in the hands of strangers. (Hailey, 1978, p. 77)

The social sciences confirm the novelists' musings. Kaplan (1976) writes that women are socialized to be dependent and must learn to rely on self-evaluation rather than other-evaluation. The work of Bart (1971) illustrates this phenomena in a study of depression in middle-aged women. She finds that the more feminine her subjects were, the more depressed they were apt to become when the children left home. Bart says: "If one's satisfaction, one's sense of worth comes from other people rather than from one's own accomplishments, one is left with an empty shell in place of a self when such people depart."

The necessary struggle for independence is thus a struggle for self-differentiation. Women, embedded in their families and responsive to others in their circle, must come to see themselves as not only related but also separate, as not only responsive but also assertive, as not only together with others but also alone. For if women are to be fully human, they must be all of these, even accepting the loneliness often experienced in the initial steps of creating one's own path.

Theoretical World View

The worldview that supports the feminist orientation is generally based on humanistic theory and incorporates Rogers's (1961) view of fully functioning individuals, Maslow's (1954/1970) self-actualization, Fromm's (1941) spontaneous affirmation, and Horney's (1950) self-realization. This writer (1978a,b) has written of this view as process-oriented, based on a belief on living all of one's experience, allowing one's experience to shape one's sense of self, and seeking a harmonious integration of all parts of self.

Developmentally, this view encompasses a view of human growth as one of differentiation and integration in which new learnings cause new, differentiated behavior that eventually results in a higher integration of valued old and new learnings. Much of the desired integration can be termed androgynous in the sense developed by Bem (1974), and can be interpreted as bringing together characteristics associated with love (the expressive qualities) and those associated with power (the instrumental capacities) in an integration in which the person is both competent and caring, assertive and receptive, able to work and able to play.

The underpinnings of this theory developed by Maslow (1954/1970), Rogers (1961), Fromm (1941), and supported by the developmental work of Erikson (1950) were formulated primarily in regard to male development. The application of a model of process-oriented, androgynous living, when applied to women, is somewhat different and more problematic. The path to full human development, as outlined by the humanists, is not the same for women and for men.

For men, trained to be assertive, competent, and analytical, the path to full humanness requires the development and integration of the expressive qualities. Levinson (1978) tells us that in optimum development this occurs for many men during the midlife crisis. Maslow's (1954/1970) examples of self-actualizing individuals also illustrate that high levels of integration occur later in life. For women, however, trained to be receptive, nurturing, and global in thought, the path to full humanness requires the development and integration of the instrumental qualities. To seek a high level of androgynous development, women must, therefore, come to terms with power.

The difficulties that women have in doing so are illustrated in recent research. Analyses of development in educated and gifted women attest that women evolve at higher levels only with anxiety—and more anxiety than their male peers. In their longitudinal study of gifted individuals, Terman and Oden (1959) report that the gifted adult women have a higher incidence of nervous disorders than is found among women in the average population (which is already higher than that of men), whereas gifted adult men have a lower incidence of such disorders than the average male population. Helson (1967) also found that highly gifted women mathematicians were less emotionally secure than their male counterparts. In studies of college students, Marcia and Friedman (1970) and Orlofsky (1977) found that college women struggling toward the achievement of an independent identity were more anxious than a comparable group of men. Finally, Haan (1971) and her colleagues (Haan, Smith, & Block, 1968) found that female students of high ethical development were more anxious, moody, and discontented than a similar group of men.

Thus the androgynous, process-oriented model of health, developed from observations of men, is not so readily conceptualized in the case of women. Women who choose to move away from the dysfunctional feminine prescriptions in our society incur heightened anxiety and internal conflict when they seek a resolution that psychologists have argued is more fully human. As Maccoby (1963) states, the predicament of women is something of a "horror story," for if a woman is going to exceed normal, feminine expectations for her behavior, she "must be fleet of foot indeed to scale the hurdles society has erected for her and to remain a whole and a happy person while continuing to follow her intellectual bent." Thus women benefit by seeking external support for their nontraditional venture.

Resocialization and Support Systems

Women, with the encouragement of feminist psychotherapists, are turning to each other for such support and developing networks that support their new personal and professional choices. Barbara Bunker (1981) writes of the necessity of professional women devoting consciously directed energy into the creation of support systems. Mary Rowe (1981) writes of the creation of such a system within the academic professional world. Feminist collectives in large urban centers are also a wellspring for networking, for finding the necessary supportive framework for nontraditional choices. It is important to note, however, that the support women are seeking is not the traditional support they relied upon for survival in the traditional, other-oriented feminine model; nor is it the support traditionally offered by women to each other, which vanished when the man came home. Rather, women are seeking from each other the nurturance they have long denied themselves which is also a counterweight to the heavy impact of socialization. The new networks being created, in fact, do for the growing woman what society has traditionally done for the feminine woman—helped her stay in place. Yet the new worldview and its supportive networks offer greater promise for the process-oriented, androgynous view of full functioning than the old sex-role-differentiated model ever offered—to either women or men. Phyllis Chesler summarized this point of view:

> Women whose psychological identities are forged out of concern for their own survival and self-definition, and who withdraw from or avoid any interactions which do not support this formidable endeavor, need not "give up" their capacity for warmth, emotionality, and nurturance. They do not have to foresake the "wisdom of the heart" and become "men." They need only transfer the primary force of their "supportiveness" to themselves and to each other—and never to the point of self-sacrifice. Women need not stop being tender, compassionate, and concerned with the feelings of others. They must start being tender and compassionate with themselves and with other women. Women must begin to "save" themselves and their daughters before they "save" their husbands and their sons . . . and the whole world. (cited in Cox, 1976, p. 387)

METHODOLOGY

The basic model for therapeutic transactions in Feminist Therapy may incorporate gestalt, Rogerian, rational-emotive, or other humanistic techniques. Underlying the choice of technique, however, is basically a strong belief in the individual worth of the person.

What happens in Feminist Therapy? Lerman (1976) writes that the therapist assumes that the client is competent, that the client has personal power, and that "the personal is political," which means that the conflicts with which the client struggles have both internal and external referents. In general, the therapist stresses the forgotten side of the woman's socialization: issues concerned with power. Feminist Therapy thus is designed to fill in the gaps left in the woman's previous socialization.

Perlstein (1976) points out that the goals of Feminist Therapy are that a woman have access to herself and know her own feelings; that she be aware of and make decisions based on her relation to her own work; that she maintain and develop connections with others that bring meaning and support into her life (but that are not essential to her sense of self), and that she learn to relate to other human beings at the level at which we are all human. Once again, the process-oriented, androgynous view of personhood is emphasized: Women are to learn to relate both to their work and to others from a basic sense of self. In the process, they learn to combine both power and love.

The course of therapy proceeds through several stages, many of which are typical of other schools of therapy.

1. INCREASING SELF-AWARENESS
   a. *What is it that I want?* versus
   b. *What is it that I have learned to want?*

During this phase the client begins to discover her own needs and desires as separate from those needs and desires that she has been conditioned to recognize as hers. Because of the similarities in the conditioning of all women, generally she finds that she seeks some independent expression of self and that she has learned to confuse this with serving others.

2. ACCEPTANCE OF SELF-AWARENESS
   a. *Is it okay to want what I want?* versus
   b. *Is it only okay to want what you want?*

The realization of self-felt desires that conflict with the expectations of others is often experienced along with self-derogation ("I am bad because I do not want what you want") and guilt ("I ought to want what you want"). The acceptance of one's own needs as legitimate is often difficult for women who have learned that others' needs (men's and children's) are more important. The acceptance of one's own importance is thus a major step in the therapeutic process.

3. STRENGTHENING OF SELF-ACCEPTANCE
   a. *I am angry to have been so misled by you* versus
   b. *I have been rightly victimized by you.*

The path to acceptance of one's own legitimate needs and desires, for most women, leads through the recognition and expression of anger. Having realized the strength of her own self, a woman in therapy may still decide to retreat to the familiar position of "victim" and accede to the wishes of others with all the familiar costs. The healthier counterpoint to this is to express the anger that emerges as one realizes the negative effects of the feminine societal model. In the expression of appropriate anger, there is strength; in the channeling of anger, there is power.

4. DEVELOPING THE POWER TO ACT
   a. *Do I experiment with new alternatives and accept the risks inherent in such experimentation?* versus
   b. *Do I stay with the comfortable and familiar?*

The ability to act on one's own, to accept the consequences of one's actions, is difficult for many people but particularly for women, who have traditionally traded their independence for economic and social security. If one chooses to live only through others, as women have been trained to do, then one risks only through others; there is always an illusion of security in standing *behind* rather than *alone* (one never catches the first bullet!). Yet, if women are to come into their own as fully independent people, they must be able to stand alone and, reaping the rewards of independence, also risk the penalties.

5. RECOGNIZING SOCIETAL RESTRAINTS

At this point, women who have chosen to act on their world run into obstacles, external rather than internal, that may handicap the enactment of their desires. At such a point, a support group of other women often is necessary to sort out the external obstacles from the internal obstacles. A woman who works, for example, may not be promoted because of external sexism rather than personal competence, abilities, and attitudes. Collectively, these external difficulties may be recognized as such. Isolated, the woman may take them into herself and succumb to lowered self-esteem. The acknowledgment of common feminine experience guards against this personal inculpation.

6. ACCEPTING SOCIETAL RESTRAINTS

The increasing awareness of societal impositions is often met with anger, as is the process of realizing the internalized societal restraints. Beyond anger, however, lies acceptance of the world as it is and the motivation to act for change. This is concomitant with coming to accept oneself, which is the final stage of therapy.

7. ACCEPTANCE OF SELF, BOTH CAPABILITIES AND LIMITATIONS

At this point there is an increasing acceptance of self and others. As in most views of liberation, as stated by Alan Watts (1974), women will have moved beyond their conditioning and beyond hatred of their conditioning. They will have accepted themselves as they are, a composite of both what they have been and what they can be. Both powerful and loving, the fully integrated woman brings together both the reality of what she is and the vision of what she can be. She lives in the present with a view toward the future.

The course of therapy can be described as a process of differentiation—of self and others—and a new integration that brings together the best of the old and the new. The necessary steps in differentiation are somewhat similar for many women as they emphasize power-related issues: anger, self-nurturance, and independence. A similar process occurs in the therapy of men, yet the content generally differs as men learn to differentiate their feelings, to recognize their dependencies and vulnerabilities, and then to achieve an integration with other parts of themselves. For both sexes, the integration brings together power and love.

The process, of course, is never complete, and each new integration is the platform from which further dif-

ferentiation begins. Yet as in all development, successful transitions from one plateau to another develop the skills with which to move through the next transition.

APPLICATIONS

Clients of feminist psychotherapists are most often educated women, who are generally the first socioeconomic and sex status to experience the conflicts induced by social change (Forisha, 1978a). However, feminist psychotherapists also number men among their clients. Generally the clientele of a feminine psychotherapist, however, is composed of those who experience conflict between their own personal needs for self-realization and those of the society in which they live—and, as Virginia Woolf reminded us, it is often the gifted women who go crazy first. It is those with the best resources, both internal and external, who are the first to feel the stress involved by the creation of new options.[1]

In the lives of educated women—and most everybody else—there are often two primary issues. The first involves the woman's relation to her own work, the second her relation to others. Each of these will be examined in turn.

Women and Work

As Perlstein (1976) pointed out, one of the chief issues in Feminist Psychotherapy is the woman's relation to her work. In the kaleidoscope of human affairs, the woman's relation to *her* work is a new variable that affects the patterns established in all areas of her life—and in the lives of those with whom she lives. Formerly, men were related both to work and family, and women only to family. To add to these traditional relationships the relationship of women and work shifts all relationships mentioned above.

What does the introduction of this relationship mean? For many women who have been wives and mothers, it means that they are choosing not to be so any longer—or they fill these roles only part-time. For other women, it means choosing nontraditional relationships based on two-career patterns. For others, it means choosing to stay single. As one working woman said to her friend the other day, "I told him I loved him, but my work came first. I made that perfectly clear to him, but he didn't seem to understand why I couldn't go to New York over the weekend. So we split up . . . and now I'm seeing. . . ."

For women, who are perceived as basing their lives on

---

[1] Other feminist therapists reject this emphasis and turn their attention largely toward those women who are a subject of oppressive environmental circumstances. The emphasis on the educated woman expressed here is but one of many feminist orientations.

pleasing others, particularly men, this is a startling new occurrence. The woman above, like many others, is establishing new patterns of relationships in her life based on the premise that her work is important. The relationship of women to work (not just work when there are bills to be paid, or when the husband has departed, or when a child gets sick) has opened up for women a new range of possibilities with enormous ramifications.

Culturally, women are being offered new options—the chance to choose one's work and enjoy it. Yet in a changing society, and a predominantly sexist one, such options always lead to conflict, internal as well as external, and the costs of the new alternatives are often heavy. It is part of the educational process of therapy to point out the options available, the potential rewards, the potential costs, and affirm the fact that women *can* make a choice.

The second input of Feminist Therapy is to help women to sustain the choice once made. In relationship to work, this often involves providing confirmation for the "outsider" (female) on the "inside" (male) world, helping her to see her world and herself with clear eyes and to develop networks of other individuals who can pave the way or back her up when the "inside" ignores her, chastises her, or threatens to spew her out (Forisha & Goldman, 1981).

Women and Relationships

Women who relate closely to their work are powerful in the eyes of others in ways women have never been. Women have, of course, always been powerful, but the power was tolerable because they remained in the private sphere and did not intrude into the "real world." The image of the powerful mother figure in juxtaposition with women at work is, at root, terrifying to many men. The assumption of overt and external power by women has rocked the establishment boat and changed the nature of both work and professional relationships.

Therefore, the way in which women are relating to each other and to men is being shifted not only by women's relationship to work but by the increasing perception of power in women. The traditional arrangement in which men know they're powerful (and therefore okay) because they work in the "real world" and women know they are loved (and therefore okay) because they are protected from that world is outdated. Male and female sources of self-esteem have changed, and the stability of many relationships is threatened. Individuals are, therefore, in a process of experimentation with new forms of relating to others.

The result is increasing turbulence and uncertainty in relationships. In many cases the immediate rewards are greater, and perhaps the long-term ones (though not enough time has passed yet to really tell); but in many cases the immediate pain is also greater. However, the promise of what may be and the reality of what is may eventually come together in a higher integration of love and power in relationships as well as in one's work. Once again, however, women need each other and profit from the sharing of their collective experience as they try out new forms. The resocialization experience engendered by feminism and its therapeutic offshoots requires personal growth, theoretical understanding, and collective confirmation of the alternative courses of living.

CASE EXAMPLES

Each of the three cases below illustrates some of the difficulties with which women are grappling and some of the decisions they are living out. In all cases, these are women sensitive to the crosscurrents induced by social change, who are seeking to form a process-oriented identity in which they seek to find themselves, to find their work, and to find significant others in their lives. Juanita, though of Latin-American origin, illustrates the full panorama of changes through which women in the United States are passing, whereas Lynne and Aileen are still in transition at different developmental points in their lives. All three cases together illustrate the orientation of many women in feminist psychotherapy today.

Juanita is a very small, dark-haired woman of 30 who, when I first met her, was lost under a mass of long hair. Juanita's small voice, her slouched posture, and her lowered eyes contributed further to a picture of insignificance. Our initial work together revolved around her need to be "bigger" and not feel so at the mercy of others, particularly her husband and three small boys. During our early experience together Juanita became occasionally more bold, grew in intellectual understanding of her own capabilities, and occasionally spoke out for herself.

Six months later Juanita and her husband, John, requested a session in which they could work on their relationship. Juanita had recently entered a university and was no longer totally absorbed in her family's life. John had initially encouraged this move, but was now uncomfortable with Juanita's interest and enthusiasm in school. Juanita, on the other hand, felt that she was still regarded as a little girl by her husband and that she was rarely listened to in any serious way. During this session a cofacilitator and I monitored and clarified communication between Juanita and John. The session concluded with Juanita enthusiastically beaming at John and saying, "I think you've finally heard me," and John's pleased, but somewhat perplexed, acknowledgment of Juanita's newfound assertion.

A year later Juanita had finished her university education. John had divorced Juanita and was preparing to marry another woman, who was traditional in her outlook. During the next year Juanita struggled with the problems of singleness and single parenthood. Her new responsibilities challenged previously untouched resources in her, and she emerged from this time as a vivacious, lively person—with short, curly hair—who knew that she would handle the world. In that year she had not only handled divorce proceedings and school difficulties with her sons, and won a custody suit, but had also obtained a professional-level job working with people of Latin origin.

She returned to therapy shortly thereafter to continue her journey into self. During this time her increasing sense of self received additional confirmation, and Juanita finally came to terms with the fact that she was not "small" but as big as she wished to be. In a group session, this conflict came to the surface when Juanita remarked that a superior had praised her for a brilliant piece of work. At that point she ducked down and appeared small—discounting her capacity to do anything noticeable or brilliant. I asked Juanita then to stand up and deliver a speech based on the professional work she had done—and in fact to sell us her services as a consultant for bilingual peoples. She began reluctantly, but soon swung into the spirit of it and astonished all of us, including herself, with her straightforward self-assertion. She stood straighter, her face glowed, and when she concluded she leaped down and hugged everybody, exclaiming, "I really can do it!"

Juanita then spent the next few months exploring her relationships with men. A brief and explosive affair surfaced old feelings of dependency and her still present, though latent, desires for return to her former married state. In working through this episode, Juanita came to the conclusion, once again, that her happiness depended on herself and not others, and that this particular affair was a positive and groundbreaking experience for her. She learned that the value of an experience is not measured solely by duration but rather by the quality of the experience itself and what can be learned from it.

Juanita today is still unmarried, involved in an ongoing relationship with a man for whom she cares, and is excited and stimulated by her work. She has achieved, in many ways, the model of healthy womanhood proposed by Lerman (1976): She is aware of self, relates to her work and others, and experiences herself as part of the global connectedness of the universe. The same process is partially revealed in the cases of Lynne and Aileen.

Lynne has been married to a lawyer for over 20 years and is a young-looking, attractive, brilliant mother of teenage children. She dates her transformation from about two years ago when she began reading feminist literature and continuing her college career. She says within two years her husband watched "Gracie Allen at the breakfast table transformed into Gloria Steinem." At

the moment she is struggling with her desire to continue this relationship, which was satisfying as long as she continued to be her "old self," and her desire for further exploration of the options she sees opening out before her.

She tends to see these alternatives as mutually exclusive and feels caught on a pendulum. She rushed from her schoolwork and fantasies of romantic entanglements with like-minded intellectuals to a reenactment of her old role serving up carefully prepared four- and five-course dinners for the assembled family. She phrases her alternatives as extremes: either a room of her own (apartment) or continued cooking 24 hours a day. Recently, however, she has come to rephrase her alternatives in more moderate terms, recognizing that the process of change is slow and not always an all-or-nothing proposition. She is still caught by the swinging pendulum, but the swings have diminished now and a new direction is beginning to evolve that she will most likely act upon in time. Her major decisions are still in the future.

Aileen illustrates another aspect of a woman's search for self. A young and talented single woman, she has "fallen in love" with various men who often treat her badly. My work with Aileen has been to pull back toward herself the strings to her happiness that she has attached to others and to base her own sense of being more firmly in herself. In one session she talked about Jerry, who was "fantastic, intelligent, sensitive, and sexy" and who, nonetheless, periodically disappeared from her life without notice and turned up again at moments that suited his convenience. In the early part of the session, Aileen came to recognize the incongruence of her description of Jerry's character and her recounting of his behavior. Aileen, like many of us, was projecting her desired image of a man upon the nearest likeness of that image, yet the human being is always more complex than the projections.

In the second part of the session, Aileen made a list of all the qualities she felt in herself when she was with Jerry. The list included many of the qualities attributed to Jerry himself: sensitivity, intelligence, and sexiness. Yet Aileen claimed that she *was* these things because she was with Jerry and she lost them—and a desired part of herself—when he was gone. I asked Aileen to reclaim these qualities in herself by telling the group "I am . . . (sensitive, intelligent, sexy, etc.)." Aileen was at that time unable to do so. She claimed sensitivity, and hence the capacity to be hurt, but refused intelligence and sexiness. In succeeding sessions we worked through to the point where she finally could admit, in a straightforward fashion, that she was both sexy and intelligent, and hence could find in herself the resources that she had believed existed due to the benevolent attention of men.

Aileen, like Lynne and Juanita, is seeking herself. Like most women, she has learned to find happiness in others and is devastated when those others depart, partly because women have difficulty untangling what belongs to others and what belongs to themselves. The departure of significant others, then, is often experienced as taking part of the self, and devastation and depression are the result. The differentiation of self and another leads to a new integration in which the departure of another is the cause for further awareness and expansion of self rather than the diminishing of self. This is an important step for many women in therapy.

SUMMARY

Feminist Psychotherapy is directed both inward toward personal growth and outward toward recognition of the impact of social norms. Since many of these norms are seen as handicapping to women, Feminist Psychotherapy often takes a stand against the status quo and is thus a force for social change.

Women have always been deviant by virtue of their marginality. Their marginal status has not encouraged expression of their desire for independence or achievement. Further, the marginal status of women, who remain outsiders in the mainstream of society, has made them easy targets for projection of more severe deviance in times of social stress. The traditional response to women's discomfort with personal and social deviance has been for psychotherapists to urge women back into their marginal role and to remain content with things as they are. The role of Feminist Psychotherapy, since the 1960s, has been to urge women to assert their full individuality, and in doing so challenge the norms that define them as marginal.

The process of Feminist Psychotherapy is, therefore, one of resocialization. Women are urged to grow in the direction of process-oriented, androgynous behavior that presents greater scope for individual talent than do the traditional sex-role norms, and that is postulated as an appropriate model of mental health, displacing those based on masculine and feminine role characteristics. The process of therapy involves not only greater awareness of self but greater awareness of societal norms; not only change in self, but change in society. Because many of the afflictions of women have been suffered collectively, the process of change is also necessarily a collective one in which women are learning to work together both to support personal growth and social action.

Many of the concerns that are brought into Feminist Psychotherapy today revolve around issues that are traditionally associated with power (the ability to *do* things) as opposed to those traditionally associated with love (the capacity to *be* and to *care*). Because of the sex-differentiated socialization in our society, men more often than women have been groomed for the world of power; women have been sequestered in the world of love. Hence, in reclaiming part of their human heritage, women in therapy are coming to grips with power, affirming their own worth, recognizing their anger, and learning to care for themselves and each other. In this way, as in the case examples cited above, women are moving toward a fully functioning integration of love and power, which is pivotal in a model of human health.

REFERENCES

Adler, A. (1927). *Understanding human nature.* New York: Holt.

Bart, P. (1971). Depression in middle-aged women. In V. Gornick & B. Moran (Eds.), *Women in sexist society: Studies in power and powerlessness.* New York: Basic Books.

Belote, B. (1976). Masochistic syndrome, hysterical personalities and the illusion of a healthy woman. In S. Cox (Ed.), *Female Psychology: The emerging self.* Palo Alto, CA: Science Research Associates.

Bem, S. (1974). The measurement of psychological androgyny. *Journal of Consulting and Clinical Psychology, 2,* 153–162.

Broverman, I. K., Broverman, D. M., Clarkson, F. E., Rosenkrantz, P. S., & Vogel, S. R. (1970). Sex-role stereotypes and clinical judgements of mental health. *Journal of Consulting and Clinical Psychology, 34,* 1–7.

Bunker, B. (1981). Mobilizing resources: Creating a support system. In B. Forisha & B. Goldman (Eds.), *Outsiders on the inside: Women and organizations* (pp. 199–212). Englewood Cliffs, NJ: Prentice-Hall.

Chesler, P. (1971). Patient and patriarch: Women in the psychotherapeutic relationship. In V. Gornick & B. Moran (Eds.), *Women in sexist society: Studies in power and powerlessness.* New York: Basic Books.

Chesler, P. (1972). *Women and madness.* New York: Avon.

Cox, S. (1976). *Female psychology: The emerging self.* Palo Alto, CA: Science Research Associates.

de Beauvior, S. (1953). *The second sex.* New York: Knopf.

Douglas, A. (1978). *The feminization of American society.* New York: Avon.

Erikson, E. (1950). *Childhood and society.* New York: Norton.

Fabrikant, B. (1974). The psychotherapist and the female patient: Perceptions, misperceptions and change. In V. Franks & V. Burtle (Eds.), *Women in therapy.* New York: Brunner/Mazel.

Forisha, B. (1978a). *Sex roles and personal awareness.* Morristown, NJ: General Learning Press.

Forisha, B. (1978b). The role of love, power, and conflict: Socialization for creativity or alienation? Unpublished manuscript.

Forisha, B. & Goldman, B. (Eds.). (1981). *Outsiders on the inside: Women and organizations.* Englewood Cliffs, NJ: Prentice-Hall.

Freeman, J. (1976). The social construction of the second sex. In S. Cox (Ed.), *Female psychology: The emerging self.* Palo Alto, CA: Science Research Associates.

Fromm, E. (1941). *Escape from freedom.* New York: Holt.

Goodman, E. (1979, August 21). She runs sympathy marathon. *The Ann Arbor News,* p. 46.

Gove, W. (1972). The relationship between sex-roles, marital status, and mental illness. *Social Forces,* 51.

Haan, N. (1971). Moral redefinition in families as the critical aspect of the generation gap. *Youth and Society, 3,* 259–283.

Haan, N., Smith, M. B., & Block, J. (1968). The moral reasoning of young adults: Political-social behavior, family background, and personality correlates. *Journal of Personality and Social Psychology, 10,* 183–201.

Hailey, E. F. (1978). *A woman of independent means.* New York: Avon.

Helson, R. (1967). Sex differences in creative style. *Journal of Personality, 35,* 214–233.

Horney, K. (1926). The flight from womanhood. *International Journal of Psycho-Analysis, 7,* 324–339. Reprinted in K. Horney. (1967). *Feminine Psychology.* New York: Norton.

Horney, K. (1935). The problem of feminine masochism. *The Psychoanalytic Review, 22,* 241–257.

Horney, K. (1950). *Neurosis and human growth.* New York: Norton.

Janeway, E. (1975). *Between myth and morning: Women awakening.* New York: Delta.

Kaplan, A. G. (1976). Androgyny as a model of mental health for women: From therapy to therapy. In A. G. Kaplan & J. P. Bean, *Beyond sex-role stereotypes: Readings toward a psychology of androgyny.* Boston: Little, Brown.

Lerman, H. (1976). What happens in feminist therapy? In S. Cox (Ed.), *Female psychology: The emerging self.* Palo Alto, CA: Science Research Associates.

Levinson, D. (1978). *The season's of a man's life.* New York: Knopf.

Locke, B. Z., & Gardner, E. A. (1969). Psychiatric disorders among the patients of general practitioners and internists. *Public Health Report, 84,* 167–173.

Maccoby, E. (1963). Women's intellect. In S. M. Farber & R. H. L. Wilson (Eds.), *The potential of women.* New York: McGraw-Hill.

Marcia, J. E., & Friedman, M. L. (1970). Ego identity status in college women. *Journal of Personality, 38,* 249–263.

Maslow, A. T. (1970). *Motivation and personality.* New York: Harper & Row. (Original work published 1954)

Menaker, E. (1974). The therapy of women in the light of psychoanalytic theory and the emergence of a new view. In V. Franks & V. Burtle (Eds.), *Women in therapy.* New York: Brunner/Mazel.

Neulinger, J. (1968). Perceptions of the optimally integrated person: A redefinition of mental health. *Proceedings from the 76th Annual Convention of the American Psychological Association,* 554.

Orlofsky, J. (1977). Sex-role orientation, identity formation, and self-esteem in college men and women. *Sex-roles, 6,* 561–575.

Osmund, H., Franks, V., & Burtle, V. (1974). Changing views of women and therapeutic approaches: Some historical considerations. In V. Franks & V. Burtle (Eds.), *Women in therapy.* New York: Brunner/Mazel.

Perlstein, M. (1976). What is a healthy woman? In S. Cox (Ed.), *Female psychology: The emerging self.* Palo Alto, CA: Science Research Associates.

Rice, J. K., & Rice, D. G. (1973). Implications of the women's liberation movement for psychotherapy. *American Journal of Psychiatry, 130,* 191–196.

Rogers, C. (1961). *On becoming a person.* Boston: Houghton.

Rosen, B. S., Locke, B. Z., Goldberg, I. D., & Babigian, H. (1972). Identification of emotional disturbances in patients seen in general medical clinics. *Hospital and Community Psychiatry, 23,* 364–370.

Rowe, M. (1981). The minutiae of discrimination: The need for support. In B. Forisha & B. Goldman (Eds.), *Outsiders on the inside: Women and organizations* (pp. 151–170). Englewood Cliffs, NJ: Prentice-Hall.

Steinman, A. (1974). Cultural values, female role expectations and therapeutic goals; Research and interpretation. In V. Franks & V. Burtle (Eds.), *Women in therapy.* New York: Brunner/Mazel.

Sutheim, S. (1969). For witches. *Women: A Journal of Liberation.*

Terman, L. M., & Oden, M. H. (1959). *Genetic studies of genius, Vol. 5.* Stanford, CA: Stanford University Press.

Watts, A. (1974). *Psychotherapy east and west.* New York: Ballantine.

Weisstein, N. (1971). Psychology constructs the female. In V. Gornick & B. Moran (Eds.), *Woman in sexist society: Studies in power and powerlessness.* New York: Basic Books.

Woolf, V. (1957). *A room of one's own.* New York: Harcourt. (Original work published 1929)

Wolowitz, H. M. (1972). Hysterical character and feminine identity. In J. M. Bardwick (Ed.), *Readings on the psychology of women.* New York: Harper & Row.

Chapter 24

FIXED ROLE THERAPY

JACK R. ADAMS-WEBBER

My own love affair with therapeutic role playing is indicated by my having written three books and a number of articles on the subject. It is my belief that of all the methods of psychotherapy, none is either more logically correct or more therapeutically effective than psychodrama—which is, however, a very difficult process to do correctly. Consequently, I was most pleased to obtain Jack Adams-Webber's account of Kelly's Fixed Role Therapy, which uses psychodrama in an interesting and highly innovative manner. Goethe once said, "If you want a person to change, treat him now as though he were already how you want him to be." As I see it, this statement lies at the heart of Fixed Role Therapy. In the psychotherapy of the future, I am positive this approach will have a strong part.

Fixed Role Therapy is a form of brief psychotherapy developed by George A. Kelly from the basic principles of his psychology of personal constructs. Essentially, it is an experimental procedure for activating personality change in which the client plays the role of a hypothetical person for a period of several weeks. Kelly (1973) explained that this is not strictly a form of treatment, but rather an investigative project designed to elucidate specific problems in the client's life. The client is the "principal investigator," with the therapist more or less assuming the function of a "research supervisor." During the enactment period, therapist and client meet frequently, usually every other day, to plan specific experiments and to evaluate their outcomes. At the end of the enactment period, the client is invited to appraise the entire experience in whatever terms are most meaningful to him or her.

Other approaches to psychotherapy are derived from Kelly's ideas. Some of these are summarized by this writer (1979) and by Franz Epting (1984). Nonetheless, as Pervin (1975) points out, Fixed Role Therapy is that method of psychotherapy that is "particularly associated with personal construct theory, and it does exemplify some of the principles of the personal construct theory of change" (p. 300).

HISTORY

The first description of Fixed Role Therapy appeared in *The Psychology of Personal Constructs,* the two-volume work in which Kelly (1955) formulated the general principles of personal construct theory and summarized their applications in the practice of clinical psychology. This is still the best source of information available about the basic procedures. It also includes an illustrative case history.

Kelly (1955) specifically acknowledged the influence of J. L. Moreno upon the development of Fixed Role Therapy. As J. C. J. Bonarius (1970) notes, Moreno's (1934) psychodrama involves the client's reenacting particular episodes from her or his own biography, which can result in both catharsis and new insights into the effects of past experiences upon the client's current life. In Fixed Role Therapy, however, the client enacts the part of an altogether different person, which may afford an opportunity to place some alternative constructions upon one's potentials and life situation.

It is difficult to ascertain what, if any, impact Kelly's introduction of this new method of short-term therapy may have had in terms of actual clinical practice. He himself taught it to many trainees in clinical psychology at Ohio State University (including this writer) between 1950 and 1965, some of whom have taught it in turn to their own students (Bonarius, 1970). Bonarius (1967), a former student of Kelly's, published a brief account of Fixed Role Therapy in a Dutch journal. He followed this with a second paper in the *British Journal of Medical Psychology* (1970), in which he explicated the basic techniques more fully and discussed their underlying rationale in terms of personal construct theory. This paper also included a short case history. In the same year, T. O.

Karst (another of Kelly's former students) and L. D. Trexler (a former student of Albert Ellis's) published in the *Journal of Consulting and Clinical Psychology* the results of an experimental comparison between a modified form of Fixed Role Therapy and Ellis's (1958) Rational-Emotive Therapy in the treatment of public speaking anxiety. The outcome of their experiment is discussed in the applications section. Donald Bannister and Fay Fransella (1971) published another short description of Fixed Role Therapy in the following year.

A comprehensive review of the procedures and the theoretical rationale of this approach was completed by Kelly shortly before his death in 1967, and was eventually published in 1973. This work is an extremely useful source of basic information for anyone who wishes to become familiar with the details of Fixed Role Therapy.

Skene (1973), a British psychologist who, unlike Bonarius and Karst, had no direct contact with Kelly, reported a case history in the *British Journal of Medical Psychology* in which he described the successful treatment of an 18-year-old male homosexual by means of Fixed Role Therapy. This case is summarized as the case study. Since then no further case histories or experiments based on this technique have appeared in print. Analyses of the available literature have been provided by this author (1979) and by Epting (1984).

CURRENT STATUS

Kelly's (1955, 1973) own accounts of the theory and technique of Fixed Role Therapy are still the best sources of information about it. Apart from Kelly himself, Bonarius (1967, 1970) has made the greatest contribution to its development. Although, as noted in the preceding section, there have been relatively few relevant case histories (e.g., Skene, 1973) and experiments (e.g., Karst & Trexler, 1970) published so far, Fixed Role Therapy has been discussed widely in textbooks on personality as the method of psychotherapy most closely related to personal construct theory. Other psychotherapeutic techniques based on some of the same theoretical principles, and resembling it in several important respects, have been devised by Bannister and associates (Bannister, Adams-Webber, Penn, & Radley, 1975), Fransella (1972), and Landfield (1971). Their work has been summarized by this writer (1979) and by Epting (1984).

Fransella (1972), in particular, has developed a method for the treatment of stuttering in which the therapist assists the client in carrying out a series of experiments wherein the client enacts the role of a "fluent speaker." In these experiments, as in Kelly's original Fixed Role Therapy, the client is the principal investigator. Moreover, his or her speaking behavior is the main independent variable, rather than the dependent vari-

able as it is in many conventional methods of speech therapy. The purpose of Fransella's (1972) approach is to give the client an opportunity to learn what to anticipate from others in social situations when he or she enacts the part of a fluent speaker in contrast to that of stutterer. Her technique resembles somewhat the modified form of Fixed Role Therapy used successfully by Karst and Trexler (1970) in treating public speaking anxiety. She reported data from a sample of 20 stutterers whom she has treated with her method (Fransella, 1972).

THEORY

The rationale of Fixed Role Therapy derives directly from Kelly's (1955, 1969, 1970) personal construct theory (summarized by this writer, 1979). This theory is grounded on the "fundamental postulate" that "a person's processes are psychologically channelized by the ways in which he anticipates events" (Kelly, 1955). The basic unit of analysis is the *personal construct,* that is, a bipolar dimension of judgment such as *pleasant/unpleasant* used to organize information about the environment. Kelly assumed that each individual develops a hierarchically organized system of personal constructs, unique in terms of both its structure and content, to interpret and predict events. Thus, within the framework of personal construct theory, people must be understood in terms of the idiosyncratic constructions that they impose on their own experience.

Kelly (1973) pointed out that two specific features of this theory are central to the rationale of Fixed Role Therapy. The first of these is his underlying model of human nature; the client is seen as an incipient scientist with the capacity to represent and anticipate events, not merely respond to them. Within the context of this model, Kelly conceived of psychotherapy as essentially a program of experimentation in which the client assumes the role of principal investigator and should be fully aware of this fact. The chief responsibility of the psychotherapist from the standpoint of personal construct theory is to assist the client in formulating specific hypotheses, in carrying out relevant experiments to test these hypotheses, and in revising them in the light of the results. As Bannister and Fransella (1971) put it, "in construct theory psychotherapy the model for the relationship between the so-called therapist and the so-called client is somewhat that of research supervisor to research student." Indeed, in "The Autobiography of a Theory," Kelly (1969) described himself as having fulfilled pretty much the same functions as both therapist and thesis supervisor throughout his own career as a psychologist.

In short, the function of the therapist, according to Kelly, is to help the client to experiment actively with his or her own constructions of experience, not to represent "reality" to the client. Nonetheless, the therapist must contribute a great deal of what Landfield (1971) terms "methodological construction"; that is, the therapist must "assist the client in the ways of learning, focusing upon personal exploration and experimentation." Kelly (1973) characterized Fixed Role Therapy, in particular, as "an experimental procedure for activating personality change without resorting to applied psychology." That is, he regarded it not so much as a clinical technique but as a form of inquiry designed to elucidate important problems in the client's life. This is clearly consistent with his general assumption that the psychological processes that occur in psychotherapy should be fundamentally similar to those that take place in formal scientific research.

If we bear in mind that the behavior of the experimenter is ultimately the only "independent variable" in any kind of experiment, then Fixed Role Therapy implies a radical form of behaviorism in which the client's behavior is the independent variable, not the dependent variable as it is in conventional behavior therapy (cf. Skene, 1973). Thus, we can view the client in Fixed Role Therapy as a "scientist" carrying out an open-ended program of research in which he or she continues to pose new questions through his or her own behavior, and interprets the outcomes of these behavioral experiments in terms of his or her own personal constructs.

The second principle of personal construct theory fundamental to Fixed Role Therapy is Kelly's (1955) novel definition of the term *role* as a course of activity carried out in the light of one's own understanding of another person's point of view. This specific conception of role follows logically from Kelly's sociality corollary, which asserts that "to the extent that one person construes the construction processes of another, he may play a role in a social process involving the other." Thus, according to Kelly, an individual enacts a role only to the extent that his or her behavior is guided by inferences about another's interpretations of events. Kelly (1955) contended that the successful implementation of Fixed Role Therapy requires that both the therapist and client understand the meaning of *role* in precisely these terms.

Therefore, the role enacted by the client should portray explicitly a person who acts in the light of what he or she perceives to be the individual outlooks of particular other people in the client's life situation. Throughout the enactment, the client's attention, as well as that of the therapist, must be focused not only on the behavior of others, but also upon their personal points of view. In short, the client engages in "role relationships" with various important figures in his or her life, perhaps for the first time.

Kelly (1955) presents an excellent description of this kind of role enactment in his history of the case of "Ronald Barratt." There is no attempt on the part of the

therapist to directly interpret the client's problems. Instead, Fixed Role Therapy involves the client's undertaking unfamiliar modes of behavior, and progress depends primarily on his developing acute sensitivity to the responses of others, both inside and outside their skins.

METHODOLOGY

The first step in implementing Fixed Role Therapy is for the client—call her Joan—to write a brief character sketch of herself from the perspective of another person who knows her intimately. In eliciting this self-characterization, the therapist instructs her to write a sketch of herself just as if she were the principal character in a play. She is told to write it as it might be written by a friend who knows her very sympathetically, perhaps better than anyone could ever really know her. It should be written in the third person; for example, she might start out by saying "Joan Wilson is . . ." This specific format was adopted by Kelly (1955) in order to suggest to the client that she should represent her own personality as a coherent whole, rather than to simply catalogue all her faults and virtues.

The purpose of asking clients in Fixed Role Therapy to write self-characterization sketches at the outset is for the therapist to find out how they use their own personal constructs to elaborate their self-concepts and structure their behavior in a variety of different situations. The therapist studies the sketch until he or she arrives at a working understanding of the principal axes of references in terms of which the client identifies herself and what the client's own language means to her. It is also important for the therapist to learn how the client typically uses her experience to support her current conceptions of herself, and in what ways she sees herself as developing in the future.

After the therapist has analyzed the client's self-characterization, the *enactment sketch* is prepared. This is a sketch that could have been written by a hypothetical person—let us call her Nancy—whose role the client will be asked to play. Kelly (1973) insisted that this enactment sketch depict a role in the personal construct theory sense of the term (defined in the preceding section). That is, Nancy should be portrayed as a person who consistently acts in the light of what she perceives to be the outlooks of other people. In short, she concerns herself not only with their behavior and its consequences, but also with their interpretations of events, including her own actions.

In preparing this sketch, the therapist also tries to formulate at least one specific hypothesis to be tested during the enactment period. This hypothesis may either be stated explicitly in the sketch or merely implied. It can also be an alternative to a hypothesis that the client has proposed in her own self-characterization. For example, if the client has represented herself as a cautious person, the alternative *from her point of view* may be to play the role of someone who is assertive. Kelly recommends casting the enactment in terms of a novel dimension—one that never may have occurred to the client before, and that she may find quite difficult to fit into the current structure of her personal construct system. Nevertheless, she can explore the implications of this new dimension by playing the part depicted in the enactment sketch. That is, by using the new dimension to structure her own behavior, she can integrate it into her self-concept.

For example, Bonarius (1970) carried out Fixed Role Therapy with a client who construed himself as "free" in the sense that neither he himself nor other people could anticipate what he might do next. Since freedom, from his point of view, implied living on the impulse of the moment, everyone else had to be manipulated into going along with his own whims. The enactment sketch that Bonarius produced for this client portrayed a person whose deepest concern in life was "understanding people." The constructs *listening/persuasion, feeling/discussion,* and *forgiving/compulsive* were also included in the sketch to provide a specific context for elaborating the implications of being an understanding person. It was hoped that this client could experiment with the notion of his being understanding without reference to the basic issue of "being free" versus "being tied."

The purpose of the enactment is never to eradicate the client's "old" personality, that is, Joan, and to replace it with a "new" one, that is, Nancy. The therapist does not directly criticize or question the integrity of Joan as a personality. Joan is at all times treated with respect. The key to the whole undertaking is that Nancy, by virtue of her contrast to Joan, is clearly a hypothetical rather than a real person. Thus the enactment of the part of Nancy is explicitly a test of a hypothesis from the standpoint of both client and therapist.

The personality of Joan, which the client has come to know so well, is also, according to Kelly (1955), only a hypothesis. However, since the client cannot immediately envision any substantial alternatives to her being Joan, she cannot easily grasp the point that her current personality is a hypothetical construction that she herself has created. All of her everyday experiences represent the outcomes of behaving like Joan. Nancy, on the other hand, is so obviously a made-up personage that she can be treated as a hypothesis more readily by the client.

Once the enactment sketch is ready, the client is asked to pretend that Joan has gone away on holiday for a few weeks and Nancy has taken her place. The client is given a copy of the Nancy sketch and instructed to read it at least four times a day, especially at night when she goes to bed and again in the morning. She should also read it whenever she has difficulty playing the part. She is told

to act like Nancy, talk like her, eat the way she would, and, if possible, even have the dreams she might have. It is agreed that Joan will return after a specific period of time, say two weeks. In the meantime client and therapist do not have to be concerned about her.

Kelly stressed the importance of getting the enactment under way immediately. Rather than trying to persuade the client that she should act like Nancy, she is treated from the outset as if she actually were Nancy. The therapist expresses surprise or disbelief at any behavior that would be out of character for Nancy. Kelly noted that, although the client may be left completely speechless by this novel experience, her confrontation with a therapist who sees her as Nancy cannot be ignored. She must cope somehow with this situation, and the most obvious ways for her to act are the specific behaviors suggested in the sketch of Nancy.

A successful outcome does not depend on the ease with which the client assumes the prescribed role. On the contrary, Kelly indicated that the client who finds the experience disruptively novel, and whose first expressions in the new part are quite clumsy and inept, may be more deeply affected by the enactment than the skilled actress. This is because the former is likely to invest more of herself in the part.

The client and therapist meet regularly during the enactment period, usually every other day, to plan particular interactions with other persons and to evaluate the outcomes. In these "rehearsals," the therapist usually plays the parts of several figures in the client's life as "supporting roles." There also is a frequent exchange of parts between client and therapist. Kelly (1955) viewed this exchange of roles as an essential feature of each rehearsal for two reasons. First, without it, the client might perceive one part as dominant over the other. Second, playing the part of another person forces the client to attempt to reconstruct that person's point of view and thereby enter into a role relationship with him or her.

Throughout the entire course of the enactment, the therapist concentrates upon showing the client how specific hypotheses can be used as a basis for structuring interactions between herself and others, and in subsequently interpreting the results. The therapy sessions are planned to include, in succession, rehearsals for at least five different kinds of interpersonal situations, such as: (1) interaction with a supervisor, employer, or teacher, (2) with peers, (3) with a spouse, lover, or close friend of the opposite sex, (4) with parents or their surrogates, and (5) a philosophical or religious discussion.

The main advantage of beginning with a supervisor or teacher is that relations with such figures, even when they are strained, tend to be fairly simple. That is, they involve relatively few constructs and usually ones that can be readily verbalized. For instance, suppose that the client is a university student. The therapist might suggest that she start out with a brief interaction with one of her instructors. She could engage the instructor in a short discussion after class on some topic relevant to the course. It should be easy for her to concentrate on trying to understand the point of view of the instructor, and she can expect to receive immediate feedback on her own attempts to grasp his or her outlook.

In the rehearsal, prior to this interaction, the therapist can assist the client in formulating specific predictions about what the instructor will say and how it will be said. The client herself can assume the instructor's role during an exchange of parts, thereby concretely elaborating her anticipations of how the latter will respond at each stage of the interaction. In the next session the client can report the outcome of this particular experiment, and she and the therapist can go over it together, comparing what actually occurred with the client's original expectations. It will probably help to reconstruct the live interaction, again including an exchange of parts.

After this analysis of the first interaction has been completed, the next one can be planned. Once more the therapist assists the client in predicting what will happen and then in evaluating the outcome during the third session, and so on. It is hoped that, in this brief series of interactions, the client will learn gradually how to experiment more effectively in the context of interpersonal relationships. That is, she may discover how to elicit from others more definite answers to the questions that she poses through her own behavior.

Kelly (1955) indicated that the client is typically discouraged during the first week or so, and will probably come to a session complaining that she cannot play the part at all. She may be especially unable to think of how to initiate interactions with others in which she can assume the role of Nancy. Kelly warns that it is essential not to become embroiled in a debate with the client about whether she can play the part. Rather the therapist should emphasize that Nancy is only a hypothesis, and should encourage the client to experiment as thoughtfully as possible and observe what happens when a person behaves in a certain way. The therapist should also admit candidly that neither of them really knows what will happen or what sort of person the client will eventually become. This is something that should develop as therapy continues, and if it is successful, long afterward.

After a few weeks, the experimental enactment is terminated and Joan "comes back." She is asked to appraise the entire experience in whatever way makes the most sense to her. Kelly (1973) maintained that the therapist must see to it that the client herself assumes the responsibility for evaluating what has taken place and deciding what she subsequently will choose to undertake. He did suggest, however, that it is probably best for the client to abandon the fixed role of Nancy, no matter how valuable she may feel the enactment of that particular part turned

out to be (Kelly, 1955). Her next task is to create, by herself, a new Joan, a process that could take the rest of her life.

APPLICATIONS

Kelly (1973) did not find that Fixed Role Therapy was applicable to a majority of his own cases. Indeed, he estimated that he employed it with no more than one out of every 15 clients. On the other hand, he did not rule out clients in any specific diagnostic categories as candidates for this form of psychotherapy. He reported having used it successfully with schizophrenics, paranoids, depressives, neurotics, and even mental retardates.

Occasionally Kelly used Fixed Role Therapy when he had less than a month available to see a particular client. He sometimes employed it as a termination procedure following other kinds of psychotherapy. It can be used at the beginning of therapy to test the client's resistance to change. In addition, it can be employed as an adjunct to group therapy, with clients enacting fixed roles during group sessions. Kelly also viewed it as an alternative when other therapeutic approaches proved ineffective.

Kelly (1955) suggested that there is probably less danger of an inexperienced therapist's harming a client in Fixed Role Therapy than in many other types of psychological treatment. Since the entire sequence can be completed in as little as two weeks, there is not enough time for a strongly dependent transference to develop. It can provide extremely defensive clients an opportunity to experiment with therapy without exposing vulnerable areas. It is also, according to Kelly, useful for overcoming intellectualization. Moreover, by emphasizing here-and-now experience, it may help the client to avoid preoccupation with past problems and enhance contact with everyday events.

The most severe critic of Fixed Role Therapy to date has been Carl Rogers (1956). He claims that the client is kept from knowing the purpose of the "play-acting," and, therefore, it "could not be used by any client who had read about it or heard about it, since it is very important that the client regard the new role initially as simply an exercise, and not in any sense as a possible pattern for his personality" (p. 357). It is not clear why Rogers thinks that a client's previous knowledge of the specific objectives of Fixed Role Therapy as formulated by Kelly (1955) would prevent him or her from approaching the enactment as an experiment in every sense of the term. As Kelly pointed out, neither the therapist nor the client can know in advance what will be the outcome, a fact that is true of all scientific inquiry.

In a more positive vein, Bonarius (1970) argues that "only with FRT [Fixed Role Therapy] and behaviour therapy is a realistic falsification possible" (p. 219). Thus, if after two or three weeks this approach does not produce any positive changes, the client can be referred to an alternative method of treatment without much loss of time or money. Another major advantage noted by Bonarius is that the whole sequence can be planned fully in advance; that is, its duration, number of sessions, and so forth, are determined before it commences. Perhaps the most important feature of Fixed Role Therapy is that it is designed to help the client to cope with problems that may arise in the future and cannot be anticipated specifically by either client or therapist at the beginning of therapy. As Bonarius (1970) puts it, "FRT is fixated upon neither the past nor the present, but paradoxically provides the patient with a flexible approach to the future" (p. 218).

Only one relevant study regarding experimental evidence of the efficacy of this technique has been published thus far. Karst and Trexler (1970) demonstrated that a modified form of Fixed Role Therapy was more effective in the treatment of public speaking anxiety than was a version of Rational-Emotive Therapy (Ellis, 1958). Both methods of treatment proved more effective than did no treatment at all. A more extensive discussion of the results of this experiment is provided by this writer (1979). Further research along these specific lines is needed before we can begin to evaluate the relative efficiency of Fixed Role Therapy in comparison to other available forms of therapy.

CASE EXAMPLE

Skene (1973) employed Fixed Role Therapy in the treatment of a 19-year-old Englishman who had been admitted to a psychiatric hospital following his second appearance in court charged with homosexual acts with adolescent boys. He had been detained previously for nine months in a subnormality hospital after his first appearance in court for the same offense. Skene describes this client as an only child, whose mother both overprotected and overindulged him. The results of psychological testing revealed that he was of "borderline subnormal intelligence" (full-scale Wechsler Adult Intelligence Scale IQ of 77), as well as "conventional, defensive and highly submissive to authority." The latter interpretation is based on his responses to the Dynamic Personality Inventory (Grygier, 1961). Skene's direct clinical impression was that the client was both exhibitionistic and extroverted, "but at the same time felt inadequate sexually."

The client also completed a role construct repertory grid test (Kelly, 1955) prior to treatment, in which he rank-ordered eight photographs of strangers—four women and four men—successively on a sample of his own personal constructs that were elicited from him during a clinical interview. The purpose of this test was to evaluate his general attitudes toward sexual relations. The results, as interpreted by Skene, indicated that:

He had some confusion in his sexual roles. He did not differentiate homosexual from heterosexual feelings and he identified with neither. Homosexuality did not therefore exclude being attracted to the opposite sex. Nonetheless, he saw some differences in the two sexual roles; homosexuality implied being quite manly and happy-go-lucky, but getting one into trouble. Being manly was construed with anxiety. On the other hand, being heterosexual was construed with his being taken advantage of financially. He also put the concept of "money grubbing" at his own door, and this too was construed with anxiety. He felt that he experienced no guilt and would not like to change. He would like to have friends who were socially acceptable and liked by his mother. (p. 298)

Skene did not elicit a self-characterization sketch from this client, possibly because of his relatively low level of intellectual functioning. The necessary information concerning the client's self-concept and the system of personal constructs that he used to structure his impressions of his social environment was gleaned from the repertory grid test data just summarized.

In constructing the enactment sketch, there was no attempt to focus directly on the client's "problem behavior," that is, his sexual activities with adolescent boys. Skene specifically created the role of a hypothetical "John Jones," whom he depicted as a "bearded, jolly, very happy-go-lucky chap." John was portrayed further as both talkative and a good listener, who is usually casual in conversation and always agrees openly with others. He was described as also interested in current affairs, a good sportsman who organizes games with other patients, and as enjoying dancing.

The client was instructed to enact the role of John for six weeks. During this period he met with the therapist 12 times. He also kept a daily diary in which he recorded all of his experiences as John Jones. He did not, however, play the part of John while on weekend leave from the hospital with his parents. No medications were given to him during the enactment period.

Skene informs us that the client experienced very few problems with the part of John Jones. He participated actively in the functions of the hospital's social center, as well as those of several sports clubs. Also, he learned to dance. The client was able to become friends with several men of about his own age. Furthermore, he started to "go steady" with a woman of approximately his age outside the hospital. They went out together for several months, with her paying her own way and thus not "taking advantage financially." He claimed that he "demonstrated his affection towards her." Following the enactment, he confided to the therapist that she was married and separated from her husband.

At the end of six weeks, the client was advised that he could discontinue his enactment of the part of John

Jones. He was told also that he could adopt any role he found personally agreeable. Skene reports that the client "continued as happy-go-lucky, interested in sports and entertaining, but apart from this, abandoned the John Jones character." The client described his own experience in Fixed Role Therapy as "just like a play that went off well." Following further psychological testing, he was discharged from the hospital.

A second repertory grid test was administered to him six months later using the same photographs and personal constructs as those employed in the first grid test. Skene directly compared the grid data from before and after treatment in order to determine what significant changes might have taken place in the client's personal construct system during the enactment of the role of John Jones. He interpreted the results of this comparison in the following terms:

> In the grid . . . there is still the association between heterosexuality and homosexuality. In other words, his sexual orientation was still undefined, but the patient wished, and was able, to relate better to the opposite sex and felt less anxious in his current construing. The findings, therefore, indicated that his social anxiety had been alleviated to some extent and he felt more motivated for change. (p. 291)

Skene also reports the results of further testing with the Dynamic Personality Inventory, which revealed that the client had become more outgoing and sociable, more flexible, less conventional, and less submissive to authority. Moreover, Skene indicates that "he adopted sexual roles to a greater extent, although these were basically of a feminine identification (as seen from the Dynamic Personality Inventory)."

A five-month follow-up evaluation showed that the client had found a job, had a circle of male friends of his own age, and had joined a sports club. His girlfriend had become reconciled with her husband and had stopped dating him. He said that this had made him feel depressed; however, he was "contemplating courting another girl."

As part of this follow-up assessment, the client completed a third repertory grid test. This time a sample of his own personal associates were used as elements, and a set of personal constructs were elicited directly from the client (cf. Kelly, 1955). The results indicated, according to Skene's analysis, that "he currently construed himself as like people who were attracted to the opposite sex in the usual way."

At the time of this final evaluation, there had been no further reports of homosexual behavior. Skene concludes that "his adjustment might be considered of a more improved heterosexual nature." He also interprets the changes that were detected in the two grid tests following therapy as showing a general increase in social competence, together with less anxiety in relation to het-

erosexuality. Skene asserts that Fixed Role Therapy produced at least a partial resolution of the client's conflict and promoted the appearance of more heterosexual behavior. He does allow that similar changes might have resulted from Behavior Therapy; however, he feels that an advantage of Fixed Role Therapy over Behavior Therapy "would seem to lie in the fact that the patient himself feels that he is embarking on an adventure and feels that he is in control."

SUMMARY

Fixed Role Therapy is an experimental procedure for activating personality change in which the client enacts the part of a hypothetical character for a few weeks. Its rationale derives from the basic principles of personal construct theory as formulated by Kelly (1955, 1969, 1970) and summarized by this writer (1979). The two features of this theory that are most important from the standpoint of implementing Fixed Role Therapy are Kelly's model of "person-as-scientist" and his unique definition of the term *role*.

Kelly (1955, 1973) conceived of Fixed Role Therapy as essentially an investigative project in which the client serves as principal investigator and the therapist more or less fulfills the functions of a research supervisor. During the enactment, client and therapist meet frequently to plan particular experiments and to evaluate their outcomes. The purpose of these experiments is to elucidate specific issues in the client's own life. Following the enactment, it is the client who takes responsibility for appraising the entire experience.

The success of this venture depends on both therapist and client understanding the meaning of *role* in terms of personal construct theory, that is, as a course of activity carried out in the light of one's understanding of the points of view of one or more other persons. Throughout the enactment, the attention of the client, as well as that of the therapist, must be focused on the thoughts and feelings of significant figures in the client's life, and not only their behavior. This process can be facilitated by frequent exchanges of roles during rehearsal sessions in which the client must reconstruct the points of view of other persons in attempting to anticipate the outcomes of specific interactions with them. It is hoped that during the course of the enactment the client will gradually learn how to experiment more effectively in the context of interpersonal relationships, thereby eliciting more definite answers from others to the questions that he or she poses through his or her own behavior.

In creating the fixed role that the client is to play, the therapist tries to formulate at least one concrete hypothesis to be tested during the enactment. In rehearsal sessions, the therapist concentrates on helping the client discover how this hypothesis can be used as a basis for structuring his or her behavior during social interactions, and in interpreting the results afterward. The key to this undertaking is that the fixed role is so patently hypothetical rather than real; the enactment of this role is explicitly a test of a hypothesis from the standpoint of both client and therapist.

After a few weeks the experimental enactment is terminated, and the client is invited to evaluate the experience in whatever ways make the most sense to him or her. The therapist insists that the client assume the responsibility for appraising what has taken place and deciding what to undertake subsequently. Kelly thought that it would probably be best if the client were to abandon the fixed role and begin creating a new personality.

A major advantage of Fixed Role Therapy is that it can be planned fully in advance. Moreover, since it can be completed in a few weeks, if it does not lead to positive change, the client can be referred to an alternative form of treatment without much expense or loss of time. It can also be used as a termination procedure following other kinds of therapies, or when a therapist has less than a month available for seeing a particular client. Perhaps the most important feature of this approach is, as Bonarius (1970) points out, that it is designed to help the client to deal with problems that may arise in the future, and thus cannot be anticipated specifically by either client or therapist at the beginning of therapy.

There have been relatively few studies based on this approach published so far; however, the available evidence is fairly encouraging (see Adams-Webber, 1979; Epting, 1984). The best source of information about this technique is Kelly's (1955, 1973) own work. Apart from Kelly, Bonarius (1967, 1970) has made the greatest contribution to the development of Fixed Role Therapy, while Karst and Trexler (1970) have devised a successful modification of it for the treatment of public speaking anxiety. Clearly their efforts need to be augmented by further clinical and experimental research.

REFERENCES

Adams-Webber, J. (1979). *Personal construct theory: Concepts and applications.* New York: Wiley.

Bannister, D., Adams-Webber, J., Penn, W., & Radley, A. (1975). Reversing the process of thought disorder: A serial validation experiment. *British Journal of Social and Clinical Psychology, 14,* 169–180.

Bannister, D., & Fransella, F. (1971). *Inquiring man: The theory of personal constructs.* Baltimore: Penguin.

Bonarius, J. C. J. (1967). De fixed role therapy van George A. Kelly. *Nederlands Tijdschrift voor de Psychologie, 22,* 482–520.

Bonarius, J. C. J. (1970). Fixed role therapy: A double paradox. *British Journal of Medical Psychology, 43,* 213–219.

Ellis, A. (1958). Rational psychotherapy. *Journal of General Psychology, 59,* 35–49.

Epting, F. (1984). *Personal construct counseling and psychotherapy.* New York: Wiley.

Fransella, F. (1972). *Personal change and reconstruction.* London: Academic Press.

Grygier, T. G. (1961). *The dynamic personality inventory.* London: National Foundation for Educational Research.

Karst, T. O., & Trexler, L. D. (1970). Initial study using fixed role and rational-emotive therapy in treating public speaking anxiety. *Journal of Consulting and Clinical Psychology, 34,* 360–366.

Kelly, G. A. (1955). *The psychology of personal constructs* (Vols. 1–2). New York: Norton.

Kelly, G. A. (1969). The autobiography of a theory. In B. A. Maher (Ed.), *Clinical psychology and personality: The selected papers of George Kelly.* New York: Wiley.

Kelly, G. A. (1970). A brief introduction to personal construct theory. In D. Bannister (Ed.), *Perspectives in personal construct theory.* London: Academic Press.

Kelly, G. A. (1973). Fixed role therapy. In R. M. Jurjevich (Ed.), *Direct psychotherapy: 28 American originals.* Coral Gables, FL: University of Miami Press.

Landfield, A. W. (1971). *Personal construct systems in psychotherapy.* Chicago: Rand McNally.

Moreno, J. L. (1934). *Who shall survive?* New York: Nervous and Mental Disease Publishing Co.

Pervin, L. A. (1975). *Personality: Theory, assessment and research.* New York: Wiley.

Rogers, C. R. (1956). Intellectualized psychotherapy. *Contemporary Psychology, 1,* 357–358.

Skene, R. A. (1973). Construct shift in the treatment of a case of homosexuality. *British Journal of Medical Psychology, 46,* 287–292.

Woodward, C. A. (1998). Standardized patients: A fixed-role therapy experience in normal individuals. *Journal of Constructivist Psychology, 11,* 133–148.

Chapter 25

FOCUSING

JAMES R. IBERG

New concepts in psychotherapy arise periodically, as someone transcends usual thinking into a new dimension. The discovery or innovation may be valuable or it may be a kind of bubble that will burst upon fuller investigation. The basic work of Eugene Gendlin, the longtime editor of the journal Psychotherapy: Theory, Research and Practice, *a former colleague of Carl Rogers, and, incidentally, a fellow student of mine at the University of Chicago has been on the experiential aspects of psychotherapy. As in the case of Adrian van Kaam, who in this book writes on Transcendence Therapy, he is concerned with within-the-body aspects of psychotherapy and digs deeply into the cognitive aspects of the individual. In the process, it seemed necessary to develop a series of new terms, such as* felt *sense, focal completion, reconstitution, and* parturiency. *It appeared to me, as a student of Dr. Gendlin's thinking, that his conceptualizations were of extreme value—but extremely difficult to communicate. I very much wanted a chapter on Focusing, but was concerned that it should communicate well.*

In no other chapter was there more consideration of this issue, and no other chapter traveled back and forth more times between the author and me than did this one. Dr. James Iberg was very patient and cooperative in attempting to explain as clearly as possible within the space constraints some essentially new notions that may change psychotherapy in some fundamental ways of thinking and acting. I must warn the typical reader that despite everything, this next chapter will be tough reading—but I believe well worth the effort.

Focusing is a special kind of introspection that can resolve problems in which "the unconscious" is not serving the person well in some part of his or her living (see the theory section for a different metaphor for "the unconscious"). Clients and therapists each engage in their own Focusing. Focusing involves holding one's attention quietly, at a very low level of abstraction, to the *felt sense.* Felt sense is the *bodily* sense of the *whole problem.* In Focusing, one doesn't think about the problem or analyze it, but one senses it immediately. One senses *all* of it, in all its complexity, as the whole thing hits one bodily. At the more abstract levels of thinking used in Focusing, one forms verbal descriptions or images of the problem, but one keeps turning back to check their accuracy to the bodily sensed meaning. As one maintains this low level of abstraction, the meaning of the problem is processed so that what is sensed bodily changes. Ultimately, such change in what is sensed bodily restores the felt sense to a state in which it opens up and regains its optimal flowing quality. Once this *nascent state* is restored, insights

can be articulated verbally. More basically, however, the person's implicit meanings are then capable of changing and adapting in ways necessary to have fulfilling interactions with others. Self-understanding and a capability for cognitive organization are pleasant extra bonuses.

HISTORY

The concept of Focusing arose out of a confluence of existential philosophy and a long line of research in psychotherapy in the client-centered tradition. Carl Rogers's person-centered method (1951, 1957) minimized interventions by the therapist. Rather than attempting to diagnose or provide expert advice, the Rogerian therapist was trained to communicate understanding of the client's meanings as empathically as possible. This nondirective method represents a therapy in which the therapist's influence on the course of the interaction is minimized and the course of events most "natural" to the client is maximized. Rogers published his view of the process of therapy in *On Becoming a Person* (1961), in which he acknowledged the influence of his

I wish to thank Eugene Gendlin for his careful reading of the original manuscript and for his many helpful suggestions.

colleague Eugene Gendlin on his process conception of psychotherapy. Gendlin soon published his experiential philosophy (1962). He applied his theory to Rogers's data and from them abstracted the introspective procedures characteristic of successful therapeutic outcomes. *Focusing* is the term he selected for the type of introspective behavior conspicuously in evidence for successful clients and generally absent for unsuccessful clients. (See Leijssen, 1996/1997)

The answers to two questions discriminate Focusing from other kinds of inner exploration: (1) What of the person's thinking, emotions, and experiences is attended to; and (2) What kind of attention is given to that? Gendlin's answer to the first question is *experiencing,* which he describes as

> concrete experience. . . . the phenomenon I refer to is the *raw,* present ongoing *functioning* (in us) of what is usually called experience. . . . there always is the concretely present flow of feeling. . . . It is a concrete mass in the sense that it is "there" for us. It is not at all vague in its being there. It may be vague only in that we may not know what it is. (Gendlin, 1962, p. 11)

Examples that suggest the character of experiencing are available from Rogers's (1961) descriptions of the introspection of more successful clients. Successful clients "examine various aspects of . . . experience as they actually feel . . . as they are apprehended through . . . sensory and visceral equipment." They might be "talking about something when wham! [they are] hit by a feeling—not something named or labelled, but an experience of an unknown something which has to be cautiously explored before it can be named at all." For these clients "feelings 'bubble up through', they 'seep through.'" Sometimes experiencing seems at first foreign to the self. Rogers said, "there is surprise and fright, rarely pleasure, at the feelings which 'bubble through'" (Rogers, 1961, pp. 76, 129, 140).

Experiencing is something that is tangibly present to check thoughts and words against. Rogers found evidence of Gendlin's concept of experiencing as a direct referent. He saw clients making a "dawning realization that the referent of these vague cognitions lies within [them], in an organismic event against which [they] can check [their] symbolization and . . . cognitive formulation" (p. 140).

In more recent formulations, Gendlin (1979, 1981, 1996) emphasized that experiencing is distinct from body and emotions and the perception of external events. The *felt sense,* the direct referent to which the focuser attends, is the bodily sensed feel of the *whole* of the person's living of a specific concern. All considerations bearing on the concern (bodily symptoms, emotions, role expectations, habits, relevant past experiences, etc.)

can be sensed at once if the person takes a few moments to let form the felt sense of all that. As it forms, the felt sense is a peculiar bodily unease or discomfort. "It" does not seem particularly promising. It seems murky, or fuzzy, or vague. It is distinctly there, at times elusive, but with its own unique quality. This bodily experience, this peculiar "it," can be paid attention to.

In therapy once the felt sense forms, one opens oneself to it and invites it to say more about what is being felt. This begins to address the second question: *How does the focuser attend to the felt sense?* Gendlin (1981) says the focuser maintains an attitude of open questioning: "You ask a question, but then you deliberately refrain from trying to answer it through any conscious thinking process." A consistent emphasis in the focusing process is on freshly conceptualizing the personal meanings of experiencing, as opposed to using already existing concepts to categorize those meanings. Rogers (1961) believed his data supported this idea. He reported observing this type of attention in successful clients. He saw them "letting . . . material come into awareness, without any attempt to own it as part of the self, or to relate it to other material held in consciousness" (p. 78). These clients did not do anything to experiencing except to be receptive. Rogers describes them as formulating "self out of experience, instead of trying to impose a formulation of self upon . . . experience" (p. 80). A client's description conveys the kind of attention given to experiencing: "left to themselves the jumbled pieces fall quite naturally into their own places, and a living pattern emerges without any effort at all on your part. . . . the minute *you* tell it what it means, you are at war with yourself!" (p. 114). This represents a special kind of accepting attitude toward experiencing:

> One need *not* "accept" what comes in the sense of resigning oneself to it, or trying to think up some way of interpreting it as not so bad. . . . Rather, by letting whatever comes be for a little while, it will change, if it is felt as part of letting oneself feel all, the whole of what comes. Then all considerations which function implicitly and focally shape experiencing will play their role. (Gendlin, 1973, p. 343)

Cornell (1995, 1996) has also elaborated nuances of how the focuser can productively attend to the felt sense, calling this way of attending "inner relationship techniques."

Gendlin and colleagues developed an experiencing scale (Klein, Mathieu, Kiesler, & Gendlin, 1970) to assess the degree and quality of the focusing-type introspection characteristic of clients in therapy. The researchers initially expected that scores would increase over the course of therapy—that one effect of psychotherapy would be that clients would learn to introspect more effectively. Initial research provided a surprise in this regard, however. Scores on the experiencing scale did indeed predict successful and unsuccessful clients, but in neither group was there significant change on experiencing scores over the course of therapy (Gendlin, Beebe, Cassues, Klein, & Oberlander, 1968). Gendlin concluded that therapists and clients were seriously in need of a clearer understanding of Focusing. Focusing was the type of introspection that appeared to discriminate failure and success from the beginning of therapy. If this type of introspection is missing, years of therapy could be needlessly wasted. Gendlin has since endeavored to define clearly this specific therapy-success behavior and make it available to therapists, clients, and the general public (Gendlin, 1969, 1981, 1996). With a better grasp of Focusing, people should be better able to create productive therapeutic interactions.

CURRENT STATUS

The Focusing Institute, in New York, is organized to support the growth of focusing-related activities around the world The Institute publishes a journal, and lists many resources. Total membership in the year 2000 is about 900 people from 34 countries.

The Institute supports a web site (http://www.focusing.org) which makes much information easily available to people worldwide. It has material in Danish, Dutch, Finnish, French, German, Italian, Portuguese, Swedish, and Spanish. There is a large and growing group of people certified to teach focusing listed on the web site.

Some of E. T. Gendlin's most recent philosophical work is downloadable from the web site. In recent years, Gendlin has conducted annual workshops in New York called "Thinking at the Edge," which have been very well received and attended by people from around the world. At these workshops, Gendlin presents his method for thinking and theory-making which systematically utilizes the bodily felt sense. This method of making theory bridges the all-too-common gap between deeply meaningful personal experience and more abstract theory.

In the year 2001, the thirteenth annual Focusing International Conference will be held in Ireland. These conferences are occasions for focusers to share what they have been developing and learning, and to meet each other. In addition to the usual wealth of topical material to learn about at an international conference, these meetings have been remarkable for their consistent support of opportunities for all participants to personally focus several times during the meeting.

Considerable research has been done relating to focusing. Hendricks (2000) summarizes a good deal of this research. She says (in the section "Focusing and Psychotherapy Outcome"):

> Focusing-Oriented Therapy has been found to correlate with successful outcome for prison inmates (Wolfus & Bierman, 1996; Goldman et. al., 1996), psychotic patients (Gray, 1976; Hinterkopf & Brunswick, 1975, 1979, 1981; Egendorf, 1982), the elderly (Sherman, 1990) and in patients with health related issues (Katonah, 1999; Shiraiwa, 1998; Holstein & Flaxman, 1997). Focusing achieved desensitization as effectively as the use of behavior therapy (Weitzman, 1967) and Focusing was equivalent to RET in successful stress management (Weld, 1992). Focusing and Gestalt therapy were both found effective in resolving a specific therapy task and on outcome measures, compared to a control group, but Gestalt therapy was more effective than Focusing (Greenberg & Higgins, 1980). Focusing was included as part of the process experiential therapy treatment condition in several studies (Greenberg & Watson, 1998; Elliot et. al., 1990) which showed change effects comparable to behavioral studies with depressed patients.

Other bibliographical listings of related literature are also available on the site.

THEORY

The theory relating to Focusing involves several interrelated terms. In this section I define briefly key terms and then discuss them at more length. (See Gendlin, 2000)

Experiencing-Implicit Experiences. Both of these terms refer to all meaning functioning in an individual at a given moment. Experiencing includes much more meaning implicitly than is explicitly defined (for example, all relevant past experiences). Experiencing includes what has been called the "unconscious" to the extent that it is in any way functioning in the moment (Gendlin, 1962, 1964, 1973, 1979).

Felt Sense. This is the bodily feeling quality of the experiencing relevant to a particular situation or person, when it is felt as one whole from a perspective that accepts all parts and is not identified with any part of the experiencing. If one stops one's normal thinking and doing for a few moments, and asks oneself what is the bodily impact of *the whole meaning* of some particular situation or person in one's life, the felt sense will begin to form. When it forms, it is a subtle, unique, rather peculiar bodily stirring or tenseness that has one's whole complicated reaction in it. For example, if you stop reading this text and, for a minute or so, quietly pay attention to your bodily sense of all that is going on for you as you read, your felt sense of this moment will form. (Gendlin, 1969, 1973, 1979).[1]

Focal Completion.

Experiencing requires certain specific events, behavior, or objects from the person's environment to further the life process. Only certain events will fulfill, or complete, the meanings of experiencing. Hunger cannot be satiated by sexual activity. Interpersonal meanings often have very specific requirements for fulfillment: The other person's words must be just so, or the interaction remains blocked and unsatisfying. What is needed for completion is implied in experiencing: Hunger implies food. The felt sense of an interpersonal interaction implies what is needed from the other person (even though, at any given moment, one may not have identified what that is; Gendlin, 1973, 1979).

Carry Forward.

With focal completion, experiencing changes, moving forward to the next, different mesh of implicit meanings. This results in correspondingly different requirements for focal completion of the next moment's experiencing. To say this experientially, the felt sense that forms *after* carrying forward is different from the felt sense *before* carrying forward. The bodily experienced completion of the felt sense defines carrying forward. Without this bodily experience of completion, carrying forward has not occurred. Varying degrees of carrying forward short of full focal completion are possible by the right kind of verbal explication of experiencing (Gendlin, 1962, 1964, 1973, 1979).

Reconstitution.

In addition to the focal completion of meanings that already were functioning implicitly, carrying forward has another effect. Other implicit experiences that were formerly not functioning regain their functioning. A common example is what happens to all the "little things" one cannot do properly when upset (for example, social courtesies, and behavior expressive of one's higher values for interpersonal relating). When upset, the implicit meanings necessary to perform those things do not function. When carrying forward occurs that is focally completing for what *was* functioning implicitly, those implicit experiences that *were not* functioning implicitly—which are necessary for those little things—begin functioning again (Gendlin, 1964).

---

[1] If you do this, you will find that your felt sense includes, implicitly, not only your thoughts and reactions to what you read, but anything else you are reminded of, the other things that you would like to be doing with the time, your feelings about yourself as a reader of such material, and more. These and more contents spring from the felt sense of this moment. The contents are *not* the felt sense—the felt sense is immediately sensible—but are implicit in, and can be explicated from, the felt sense. It often helps the felt sense to form if the focuser refrains from verbal thinking at least until one bodily feeling-quality word is found for the whole of what is involved.

States of Experiencing

1. *Structure bound.* In this state, the implicit experiences necessary for fluid interaction with the environment do not function. The person "projects" the meanings that are functioning implicitly, but the absence of certain normal interactional capacities interferes with the person's ability to interact with the situation in ways that could lead to focal completion (Gendlin, 1964).

2. *Parturient.* Once the structure-bound person lets the felt sense form, focusing on that, he or she enters the parturient state. The meanings of experiencing are still effectively structure bound, but the person has assumed a different relation to them. An "opening up" of and to bodily feeling occurs here. In the parturient state, the focuser senses subtle intricacies of experiencing not perceived in the structure-bound state. Staying at this "edge" between known and unknown experiencing enables carrying forward, but reconstitution has not yet occurred (Iberg, 1979).

3. *Nascent.* When the meanings not functioning in the first two states regain their capacity to function in interaction with events, the person enters the nascent state. In Focusing this is a "shifting" of the felt sense. The person, as he or she enters the nascent state, feels the lifting of the problem; everything changes as the whole body of implicit meanings shifts and becomes a modifiable constellation of experiences. The person may say, "Ah, I see what is wrong here . . . yes, that's what it is. . . ." The change has occurred at that point, before much has been said about it. Once nascent, the felt sense will permit verbal expression that is deeply meaningful to the person or action that is "authentic" in that it is focally carrying forward (Iberg, 1979).

These terms provide the metaphor of *incomplete experiencing process* in place of the metaphor of the unconscious. This theoretical change eliminates certain problems that are unfortunate by-products of the unconscious metaphor. The latter suggests that personality change is a matter of uncovering certain contents of the mind in the therapy process, implying that those contents (for example, lost memories or id impulses) are hidden somewhere in the same form in which they eventually become articulated explicitly. This view goes hand in hand with the concept of resistance. While it is understood that the patient is not aware of what the analyst interprets as resistance, the patient and therapist are led (by the metaphor) to search for something not actually there at all. When unconscious contents are thought of as just like conscious ones, merely hidden, then it is these finished contents that the patient and the analyst look for within the patient. But this misses a crucial step in the process of identifying problematic implicit assumptions, interpretations, and memories.

The missing step is what the person finds when looking within, before the contents are knowable in a fully conscious, explicit form. What is found there is the *felt sense*. If the patient or client does not know to let the felt sense form, the contents of the unconscious may never be found, sine they do not first appear as fully formed. Therefore, therapy will be retarded.

Since the contents do not first appear fully formed, in what form do they come? At times, emergent contents will be inconsistent with one's self-concept and perhaps internally inconsistent with other contents of consciousness. The focuser may notice this and remark, "I have no reason to feel angry, but that's what the feeling is." Or: "She's the person I trust the most, how can I feel suspicious of her?" What is essential to effective Focusing is not an analysis of the relationship of emergent contents to existing contents, but a repeated return to the felt sense of which those contents are expressive (Gendlin, 1974).

The initial symbols that fit the felt sense may be primitive, in the sense that they are "childish" or immature when compared with the normal thought processes of the person. As Freud knew when he developed the technique of free association, the emergent material must be able to form *its own* symbolization (utilizing the wealth of extant symbols and experiences that anyone has, drawing analogies, making metaphors). If it must be forced into existing conceptual constraints, such as a therapist's conceptual categories or the client's existing concepts, the emergence will be delayed. Only after the emergence begins with its own just-right symbolization can the material change and become "adult" and consistent with the rest of the client's explicit conscious contents.

However, making unconscious contents conscious is *not* the primary goal. It is widely understood that much of what a person does and says is the product of unconscious processes. In focusing theory, we say that the bulk of what determines behavior from inside the person functions only implicitly without explicit contents to represent it. This situation is seen as unalterable: It is not possible to make explicitly conscious all of what functions implicitly (Gendlin, 1962). Therefore, the point of Focusing is not to "expand consciousness."

The reason for Focusing rests on the observation that there are different manners of functioning of the body of implicit experiences. Some manners of functioning are more optimal than others for living. At times there is a fluid flow of behavior, thought, and feeling in interaction with situations. The meanings and experiences functioning implicitly are capable of modification and subtle adaptation to permit fulfilling (focally completing) interaction with life's situations. The person's conscious and unconscious experiences serve well at such times. This optimal manner of functioning of implicit meanings is what is called the *nascent state* (Iberg, 1979), in which one need not make a special effort to focus because the meanings functioning implicitly are capable of receiving satisfactory focal completion in interaction with events.

For all of us at some times, and for some most of the time, the nascent state is not the state in which we find ourselves. When not nascent, one is in a state of varying degrees of *structure-boundedness* (Gendlin, 1964). When structure bound, implicit experiences do not function smoothly in interaction with situations. One cannot respond appropriately. One has whatever reaction one has, whatever feelings and emotions one has, but these cannot change and modify themselves in interaction with the situation. Hence, one "projects." That is, one acts the static structure that one has in one's reaction, rather than interactively responding to present events. Certain subtleties of implicit experiences are not functioning in this condition, so the person cannot effectively interact. In this state, the meanings implicit in experiencing fail to achieve focal completion in action and interaction. In effect, the person cannot get the situation to complete his or her implicit meanings in this state. When in this state Focusing is most appropriate. What is needed is the *reconstitution* of implicit meanings that permit satisfying completion in interaction with situations. Nonfunctioning implicit meanings must be brought back into functioning. The state of implicit meanings must be returned to nascent.

If the problem is that certain implicit meanings are missing, thereby preventing focally completing interactions, how can we restore their capacity to function? Allowing the felt sense to form permits reconstituting completion for meanings that are not completing in the external circumstances of one's life. Although it is not theoretically possible to complete what is not functioning, one can give further completion to what *is* functioning, by allowing the felt sense to form and repeatedly focusing one's attention there, waiting for a few words or an image that precisely describes the crux of what *is* functioning implicitly. This special intrapersonal relationship is *different* from just telling oneself what one is feeling. Implicit experiencing is not so readily available to our scrutiny. Even after the felt sense has formed, some additional time Focusing is usually required before state-changing words or images are found.

One must allow for the formation of the felt sense, which takes time. It is not there immediately when you turn your attention inward. Emotions may be there immediately, but the felt sense is not. It only forms after you begin sensing for it. It comes when you wait quietly to let your sense of the whole come to you. Even when it comes, it can be elusive. Often what first seemed to be the felt sense must be re-formed into a more complete whole when one discovers that one had been judging or reacting to the feelings originally thought to be the felt sense. The whole felt sense would then need the judging part included as part of the whole, sensed from a non-judging awareness. Once the felt sense forms, the implicit meanings that are functioning can be given further completion symbolically.

The first steps of the therapeutic process of Focusing often involve finding a word or phrase or image that is exactly right to capture the quality of the felt sense. Thus what first comes may only be a "handle" (Gendlin, 1981) for the felt sense, not revealing what it is all about, but definitely capturing the bodily felt sense. The felt sense remains mostly closed and vague, still, perhaps, "heavy," or "oddly tense" bodily. When the focuser attends to the bodily-felt quality of experiencing with an attitude that has been called "presense"[2], the *parturient state* (Iberg, 1979, 1990) is entered. The meanings remain mostly nonfunctional in this state, since they are not modifiable and ready to interact with situations or words. But they are not structure bound in the same way either, since the person is giving receptive attention to the implicit in this state. He or she is no longer projecting, but is, as it were, receiving the projection on his or her own screen, inviting it to make a really clear and accurate picture or statement of what is implicitly being experienced. Allowing the felt sense to form and accepting emergent material just as it comes is a different manner of experiencing, which already *is* the beginning of change (Gendlin, 1973).

The parturient state is a natural stage of Focusing. This point is often missed, even by experienced therapists, who may become impatient with time spent in the parturient state, as if it were up to one's own will how long it takes being parturient before nascence returns. Such impatience is itself a loss of presence: a divergence from the attitude of open questioning necessary for the further completion needed to return to the nascent state. We might say that an impatient focuser has slipped from parturient back to structure bound. If one becomes impatient while Focusing, that impatience is part of the whole and should be allowed in to reform the felt sense.

When the parturient state has been maintained just enough, the whole mesh of implicit meanings shifts in how it sits in the body (Gendlin, 1981). Carrying-forward words can then be found. A deep breath and bodily relaxation often occur at that time. Don (1977) found distinct electroencephalogram patterns in the seconds preceding such shifts. Certain meanings that were not functioning implicitly are reconstituted, regaining their capacity to interact with events. The person returns to the nascent state.[3] This writer (1979) found that the return to the nascent state while Focusing was followed by a more varied expression of self in the related situation. Once nascent, one "knows" what the trouble is. One has not yet found words, but one knows one can. The felt sense is then nascent, not only open to verbalizing but open also to actions that would carry it fully forward. If there were no time to tell oneself what it is, because action or interaction was needed instantly, one would move directly into satisfying, focally completing action.

The distinctions between structure bound, parturient, and nascent may seem odd, because these words all apply to what we have only implicitly. If one is structure bound and in a situation, one cannot respond appropriately. One has whatever reaction one has, whatever feelings and emotions one has, but these do not change and adapt to the situation. When such a troubled person stops acting and begins Focusing, allowing the felt sense to form in an atmosphere of presence, he or she goes from structure bound to parturient. While still parturient, the implicit is not such that carrying-forward words or actions come. But this state is one in which one can act more appropriately in situations (if need be) than while structure bound, since the parturient person is watching the felt sense, waiting for nascence to return, and therefore less likely to mistake external events for internal conflicts.

A second change that Focusing makes is from parturient to nascent. When nascent, implicit experiences return to the more optimal state of fluid functioning, capable of changing and recombining to permit satisfying and fulfilling interaction with events. The verbal and thoughtful insights that come once the felt sense is nascent are by-products, further results, of this basic change in how experiencing functions. Making formerly unconscious contents conscious is an additional capacity facilitated by the more fundamental change that Focusing makes in the state of experiencing. It is not that the quantity of conscious contents is expanded, but that in the nascent state of experiencing, consciousness is capable of forming new and carrying forward contents.

Focusing Therapy is never really finished. One can improve the ability to focus alone, and one can learn to arrange interactions that help one's Focusing. Therefore

---

[2] "Presence is what we call that state of non-judgmental awareness which can give company to any part of us . . . we reserve the word 'I' for Presence, as in 'I'm sensing something in me that . . .'" (Cornell and McGavin, 2000).

[3] If the focuser is unsure about whether the nascent state has been entered, this simple test may help. Can the focuser describe the problem purely in terms of which personal wants or values are being influenced, independent of the particular other persons who happen to be involved? If not, the focuser is not yet nascent, and more Focusing is advised.

one may no longer wish to have a therapist. Life being what it is, however, and people being what they are, it is unlikely that the need for Focusing ever stops. As situations and persons change, old patterns of behavior no longer fully complete one's changing body of implicit experiences. Focusing makes possible the discovery of new ways to be-in-the-world that more fully complete implicit meanings. Thus persons can benefit by making lifelong use of focusing skills.

METHODOLOGY

The Experiencing Scale (Klein, Mathieu, Kiesler & Gendlin, 1970; Klein, Mathieu-Coughlan, & Kiesler, 1986) is a long standing, widely used, and well-respected observer-rated instrument that is closely associated with focusing. It has been used to measure manner of experiencing in therapy, and to scale clients in relation to each other for their typical levels of experiencing. Level of experiencing has been repeatedly found to correlate with success in psychotherapy (Hendricks, 2000).

German researchers (Sachse & Newmann, 1983; Sachse, 1990) have been developing focusing rating scales and using them to study the relations between therapist focusing, therapist processing proposals, and client focusing.

Other researchers have begun to identify distinct types of obstacles to carrying forward, which call for differential therapeutic responses (Greenberg, Watson, & Lietaer, 1998, especially chapter 20; Greenberg, Rice, & Elliott, 1993).

The course of focusing from the structure-bound to the nascent state can be highly variable, depending on the person and the situation. Iberg (1996) described six variables involved in focusing experiences, the possible combinations of which make clear that there is a very large number of distinguishable courses of focusing (see Table 25.1).

Iberg (2000) has been gathering psychometric support for two post-session instruments to measure focusing activity, one client-rated, and one therapist-rated. Three sub scales on each instrument have good internal reliabilities and corroborate each other. These sub scales are called (1) Focusing Attitude, which measures the degree to which the client approached his or her experiencing from Presence (a witnessing position); (2) Opening of Feelings, which measures the degree to which the client-therapist interaction actualized the trust necessary for a bodily felt sense to form; and (3) Carrying Forward, measuring the extent to which there was a relieving shift in experiencing.

For addressing the practical methodological question of what the client and the focusing-oriented therapist actually do together, I offer table 25.2 (Also see Gendlin,

Table 25.1   Ways in Which Focusing Experiences Can Vary

I. Variables of relationship between focuser and external situation

   A. degree of complexity: low *vs.* high

   B. actuality of trust: bodily felt sense is faint or absent *vs.* distinct and tangible

II. Variables of focuser's inner psychic structure

   A. relationship between symbols and reality: incongruence *vs.* congruence

   B. position from which the focuser approaches feelings: ego-identified *vs.* witnessing

III. Variables of the focuser's existential stance

   A. attachment to existing forms *vs.* surrender to change

   B. attitude toward life and living things: self-centered/self-protective *vs.* self as one among equals

adapted from Iberg (1996)

1996). In the remainder of this section I discuss primarily the therapist's responsibilities, as I see them. In the case example section I will illustrate the specific client behaviors outlined in the first column.

One overall responsibility is essentially the same for both the client and therapist: to focus on their own felt sense. For the therapist, this is in the service of facilitating the client's Focusing. For the client, it is entirely to further personal growth.

The importance of the therapist's Focusing should be emphasized. The therapist can optimally perform only when nascent. Only then do all relevant implicit experiences enrich the therapist's understanding of what the client is expressing. Therefore, it is of the utmost importance that the therapist continually check with his or her own felt sense to keep it nascent as much as possible. (See Sachse, 1990 for some relevant research.) An example may clarify this.

I was listening to Mark about his difficulties in completing his proposal for his Ph.D. dissertation. Having recently completed my own doctoral work, I initially felt interested and eager to understand his struggles. About fifteen minutes into the session, I noticed feeling tense and worried about not being able to understand Mark as well as I wanted. At that point, I began limiting my responses to reflections of what I was being told, turning more of my attention to my felt sense, which first had the handle "intimidated." While parturient, I noticed that the feeling increased whenever Mark talked about his research, with which he was dissatisfied. I admired the scholarly thoroughness that I interpreted it to have. I compared my approach and felt intimidated by my judgment that his method was more scholarly. Had I not noticed that I needed to focus, my impulse would have been to insist that his method was excellent and that he should not change *that*. But that would have been the start of me

Table 25.2   Schematic of Responsibilities

For the Client	For the Therapist
Overall	*Overall*
1. Focus inwardly and let a fresh, bodily felt sense form for the whole of each specific problem on which you work.	1. Monitor your own felt sense of being with the client to maintain your own nascent state. If you get parturient, limit your behavior to what you can do that will not hamper the client's Focusing.
2. Monitor the therapeutic relationship so that it helps you focus.	2. Facilitate the client's Focusing.
Specifics	*Specifics*
1. Periodically stop talking and let the felt sense form. Say two or three things that describe the felt sense before going on with anecdotes, descriptions of events, thoughts, plans, and so forth.	1. Provide plentiful focusing opportunities.
	a. Communicate empathy.
	b. Stay quiet when the client is Focusing.
2. Try to maintain a balance so that:	c. Respond honestly and briefly to inquiries about what you are thinking. Immediately listen to the impact that has on the client (i.e., return to empathy).
a. You are not swamped and overwhelmed by feeling, but	2. Teach Focusing.
b. You have something to talk about that is somewhat unknown and vulnerable to discuss.	a. Provide Focusing exercises (Gendlin, 1969, 1981; Cornell, 1996).
3. Try to take therapist comments as aids to better get in touch with your felt sense. Use them to help you heighten and open your felt sense of what you want to be working on.	b. Point out bits of Focusing that you notice the client doing.
	c. Offer suggestions for getting the felt sense of the whole.
4. Specifically identify therapist behaviors that interfere with your Focusing or tend to close your felt sense or make it fade away. Ask the therapist to modify these behaviors.	3. Make invitations to focus.
	a. Make little invitations that point to the felt sense.
5. If you know of something the therapist can do, or does, that would help you focus, describe that to the therapist.	b. Make direct requests that the client stop talking and let the felt sense form.

arguing with him and asserting *my* authority over *his* experiencing. I would have failed to accept his dissatisfaction with his method. I refrained from that impulse and continued to listen to his perspective. Eventually, it evolved that he was relying too much on his ability to be a "workhorse" to forestall his fear that he would fall short on his incisiveness with the issues. By my staying out of his way, he was able to identify more clearly the cause of his dissatisfaction. He then took on his own challenge to get feedback on his incisiveness, rather than on his ability to work hard. Even though my parturiency had rendered my empathic responses relatively superficial, at least I had not interfered with Mark's Focusing. I was only able to enter Mark's world more fully after I became more nascent. My parturiency had to do with my own evaluation of myself as being less well read than I would like to be. I was confusing that evaluation with my performance as a psychotherapist. After some time Focusing, my bodily feeling of intimidation changed, and I relaxed. At that point, I recognized that evaluation as something meaningful in relation to an article I was working on, and that it applied to that distinctly different situation in my life—but not to doing therapy.

If the therapist becomes structure bound in some way with a client and fails to turn parturient, unfortunate confusion may result about who is feeling what. The likelihood that the therapist is perceived as an authority fig-

ure makes this an unfair situation for the client, so the therapist must exercise care to focus and turn parturient when necessary.

Often, a few moments Focusing will bring key words or a phrase to the therapist that catch the crux of the parturiency and return the felt sense to nascent, so that little attention to the client is lost. This should not be a time when the therapist ignores the client. Focusing is not a wordy inward working, since the felt sense can be attended to silently. Therapist Focusing is a being-receptive-to the therapist's full bodily experience of being with the client. If a parturiency is more disturbing and doesn't quickly return to nascence, the therapist may wish to indicate this to the client with some brief statement, such as "I'm feeling grumpy about something and I don't quite know what it is." This represents explicit acknowledgment that something in the therapist requires Focusing, and opens the way for clarifying how the client experiences the interaction. Such interactions often quickly clear up the therapist's parturiency. They may also provide instances of the therapist's Focusing that may be instructive to the client: The therapist can demonstrate how to feel into the unknown parts of experiencing, risking the vulnerability of what might emerge, and trusting his or her experiencing process and the relationship to carry things beyond the parturiency.

Occasionally, therapist parturiency persists, and further Focusing, perhaps in consultation with a colleague, is appropriate.

The nascent therapist benefits from taking a few moments to let experiencing enrich empathic responses. Experiencing is the implicit functioning of all meanings available to the therapist to understand the client, not just conceptual meanings. The therapist usually grasps what the client says immediately, but it takes a few moments of Focusing to let the whole felt meaning actually come home to the therapist. If this is done, empathic responses are meaning-rich rather than the outcome of a memory task. Therefore, the therapist generally withholds responses until experiencing gives a bodily sense of understanding the whole of what the client is experiencing.

Empathy is often all that is required to further the client's Focusing. Thus *communicating* empathy is extremely important. This therapist task must be accomplished to a high level and is a prerequisite to any other therapist task. If the client's bodily sense of being deeply understood is lost, the therapist must work to restore it by reflections or whatever means he or she has to communicate empathy (see Rogers, 1975; Rosenberg, 2000). The *client* is the judge of whether or not he or she is being understood. The therapist works to achieve an empathic understanding to the client's satisfaction. Anything the therapist does other than communicate empathic understanding runs the risk of leaving the client feeling misunderstood. Therefore, a therapist engaging in other activities (such as Specifics 2 or 3 in Table 25.2) must be attentive to signals that the client has lost the bodily sense of being understood. A return to straight client-centered listening is a good strategy when this occurs (Gendlin, 1974). At such times, the therapist should be wary of sending messages that have the following structure:

> You feel (paraphrase of what the client said), but I (therapist reactions, thoughts, feelings, wants).

Rosenberg's advice (personal communication, October 1979) to restore the client's sense of being understood is to "keep your big 'but' out of there."

When the client is quietly attending to the felt sense, the therapist should wait for the client to begin talking again. Focusing takes quiet time, which the therapist must avoid interrupting (Gendlin, 1996).

If the focuser expresses concern about what the therapist is thinking, the therapist should take a few seconds to focus and then say the essence of that which pertains to the interaction. The therapist should then immediately strive to understand what *that* means to the client (Gendlin, 1968). A productive outcome of such an exchange is that hearing the therapist's experiencing throws the whole of the client's feeling into relief *as a felt sense,* distinguishing it from external circumstances. This effect helps the client become more parturient and less structure bound, which can, with further Focusing, bring insight regarding how the client typically misperceives certain reactions of others. Achieving this effect depends on the therapist being nascent enough to communicate experiencing in a way that is not critical of the client as a person.

The nascent therapist may, if the client agrees, directly teach Focusing. The client may wish to attend a focusing training group or read about focusing (Gendlin, 1981; Cornell, 1996b).

Even with people who, when instructed in Focusing at first cannot do it, some specific parts of Focusing do occur. When they do, the therapist may point out to the person that they just happened, and what these events are. For example, a person might refer to feeling more than he or she can say. The therapist might say, "There, where you feel more than you can say, that is how the felt sense is *bodily.* In Focusing, you just sit quietly and pay attention there for a minute, to see what comes to you." The therapist may notice a felt sense has changed during Focusing. The therapist might say, "That way the whole feel of it changed, so that it really seems different to you now is something which often happens in focusing. When that happens, just stay with the new felt sense of it all."

Suggestions that help the focuser form the sense of the whole are frequently a matter of timing. The client may need to verbally lay out the various aspects of the problem before he or she can get the bodily sense of the whole. For example, one client had been discussing her reactions to the possible end of her primary relationship for 50 minutes. Then the following happened:

T: How are we doing?

C: There are so many things to consider, I could talk for hours.

T: I suggest that you check how all those things feel if you put them all in one big bag. What is the sense of all of that?

C: (10–15 second silence) Should I be graphic?

T: Sure.

C: I feel like throwing up.

T: Nauseous?

C: Tense, in here (pointing to her chest).

T: Just stay with that feeling—let's see what it tells you.

C: Fear is part of it, and confusion (10-second silence). Fear of being alone. Not just now, but for a long time.

T: It sounds like having a partner is something you really want, and the thought of not having one leaves you confused and scared of being alone for a long time.

C: Yeah (crying). But also I get down on myself for having the fear: I should be able to make it alone.

T: You would really value being able to make it alone?

C: Yes, but it *would* be lonely (30-second silence). You know, the feeling changed. I got in touch with my confidence that I *can* make it alone if I have to.

The nascent therapist may make little invitations to the client to focus throughout the session. Such invitations are woven into a context of empathy maintained by the therapist, so that each invitation is compatible with the client's flow of expression. The client may speculate about some possible meanings of certain reactions or feelings he or she has, perhaps culminating with "Maybe that's what it is." The therapist may then say, "But take a minute now, go down and check with your feel of it all. Is that it?" An invitation might be made if the person is talking about some experience but apparently not immediately feeling into it. The therapist could say, "Can you stop and sense right now how that is for you?"

There are many examples and a nuanced treatment of how therapists from any orientation can use focusing with their methods in Gendlin (especiallly see Gendlin, 1996).

APPLICATIONS

Focusing methods apply readily to any relationship in which the participants want continuing fulfillment of individual potentials and mutual harmony. Although the therapist and the client are distinct *roles,* an individual need not be limited to one role. We encourage people to learn both roles and to exchange them.

The range of applicability of Focusing can be seen by discussing clients at different levels of ego development (Loevinger & Wessler, 1970). Experienced therapists can likely identify two extreme groups of clients: (1) those who can readily communicate interpersonally and easily make distinctions between their own motives and the experiencing of others; and (2) those for whom there is consistent confusion between their feelings and wants and the behavior and intentions of others. Should we conclude that focusing cannot be learned by clients in the second group?

This would lead to a decision to work only with clients who need therapy the least. It would be tantamount to taking the current level of development as somehow permanent, and, in effect, giving up on attempting to foster growth and change. One of the central thrusts in the development of Focusing theory was just the opposite. Focusing instructions were developed precisely for persons who did not already know how to focus, to teach them this skill associated with successful therapy. Olsen (1975) found that nonfocusers' experiencing levels did improve with focusing training, although the increases were not fully maintained after the training stopped.

Leijssen (1996/1997) took a group of therapy clients with a history of failure in therapy and gave them focusing training. All improved in experiencing level during the training, and the average experiencing levels remained higher after the training than they had been before. However, two of the four clients had even lower levels than before the training, which in both cases had to do with their preferring the training therapy situation to the "regular" therapy sessions. Clients at lower levels of ego development may rely more heavily on the therapeutic relationship to help them focus than clients higher on ego development.

Hinterkopf and Brunswick (1979) reported measurable success in teaching elementary versions of both the client and the therapist roles (see Table 25.2) to "mental patients." Prouty (1976, 1977, 1994) has devised a "Pre-therapy" method for clients profoundly unable to make the "contact" necessary for usual psychotherapy. His adaptation of experiential methods to this population has expanded the relevance of the concepts and methods of Focusing to the most needy client populations.

But is Focusing difficult only for people who are low on level of ego development? In this writer's experience, this is not the case. People at higher levels of ego development also have difficulty focusing, but they have difficulties specific to their level of ego development. I (1979) found that two groups different on ego level (both relatively high) were roughly equal at achieving the nascent state while Focusing. About half the subjects in each group entered the nascent state. A problem specific to people at higher levels of ego development is that they have so much sophisticated conceptual machinery that they can easily spend all their introspective time analyzing the problem without Focusing. They intellectualize it extensively, but never stop to sense down into what is felt but not yet known about it all, which is where the desired change can begin. Elegant and comfortably familiar concepts can lure the mind away from the kind of quiet focusing attention to experiencing that so often brings rapid change and relief, once begun. Therefore the therapist, and focusing training, can provide an important service to clients at higher levels of ego development too.

The preceding ego-development discussion engenders a kind of thinking that is *fundamentally different from Focusing.* It takes the reader's attention away from his or her own felt sense and directs it to placing clients into diagnostic categories. While thinking in this way, you are concentrating neither on grasping the meanings of the client's felt sense nor on your own felt sense. Therefore, diagnostic activity interferes with the responsibilities of the focusing therapist (see Table 25.2).

Some writers make a distinction between diagnosing

the person of the client and diagnosing the state or processes the client engages in (e.g., Greenberg, Lietaer, and Watson, 1998; Greenberg, Rice, & Elliott, 1993; Iberg, 1979, 1990, 1996). This is an attempt to diagnose at a more subtle level of intrapsychic dynamics than the common nosological categories (e.g. American Psychiatric Association, 1994). It is crucial that the therapist not permit diagnostic thinking to overtake his or her mind during therapy to the point where the therapist role is sacrificed. Any diagnostic scheme that categorizes the person across time and situation is inherently at odds with the therapist's task of providing focusing opportunities. Such schemes are designed to reduce the client to a category (see also Rogers, 1975; 1951 on diagnosis). No category (even a process-diagnostic category) can ever capture the whole of the meanings that function in even the most trivial of a person's living activities. But attending to *the whole* in a focusing way can powerfully bring about change.

If the therapist communicates an investment in putting the client in a category measuring degrees of pathology, he or she may, in effect, gang up with the client's own self-deprecating images. Such images are often a big part of the client's difficulty in maintaining the proper attitude toward the felt sense, especially in major depression (Greenberg, Lietaer, and Watson, 1998). This difficulty, coupled with the attribution of expert authority commonly granted to the therapist, is an unfair double whammy that is almost certain to interfere with the client's Focusing. The message is this: *Do your diagnostic thinking at a different time from therapy, and strive to make sure you are not reducing the client to any category when doing therapy.*

The tendency to categorize persons is pervasive and compelling (Mischel, 1979). Suppose you wish to stop, but it keeps happening with a client. Then turn parturient! Let yourself stop talking to yourself about it for a few minutes. Pay attention to the whole situation for you with the particular client. Consider everything that is involved for you, and let yourself feel for the underlying bodily sense of all that. It might at first form as some feeling of "urgency," or some of your own despair, or some kind of enthusiasm. *You* have to let it form. I like to take myself through a focusing exercise in such instances (not while I'm with the client, but when alone or with a colleague) to make sure I stay with Focusing long enough. If you become nascent on one like this, you can expect the next interaction with that client to be richer and fuller.

Focusing can be advantageously integrated into any other therapeutic modality. When so used, it functions like a homing device for the client's growth path. Once the client learns what the felt sense is and how to focus on it, and the therapist can recognize Focusing, little time need be wasted on unproductive procedures. Whatever part of a procedure that does help the client carry experiencing forward can be capitalized upon.

Suppose the therapist is an analyst who offers an interpretation of the patient's motives. If the patient gets in touch with what the interpretation is about and focuses on the felt sense of that, whatever *is* true can come up. The part of the interpretation that misses accurately fitting the patient can be relinquished for another, better interpretation.

All clients, regardless of diagnostic category, and regardless of the orientation of their therapist, can benefit from focusing training and practice. Focusing teaches people how to let the felt sense form and to recognize the resulting bodily experience of change. This empowers them with the ability to evaluate specific therapeutic procedures according to whether the procedures foster that bodily change. Things that do not aid this bodily change can be eliminated, and things that do can be used more often.

In "good-enough" therapy, one should experience more bodily felt change than when one focuses alone. If the bodily experience of change rarely occurs with a particular therapist, even after the client has learned Focusing and the two people have tried to adjust the relationship, I believe the client should seek another therapist.

Focusing enables one to sense one's own as-yet-unclear bodily sense of what is right and wrong for one in life. To evaluate and improve or change one's therapy in accord with this inner source is an experience of relying on one's own organism for guidance. This is a direct learning of a capacity central to developmental growth.

The full realization of improvements made possible in the nascent state occurs outside the therapy hour. This further realization is enhanced if it is possible to go beyond giving therapy and medications. If people and situations can be made available to facilitate finding friends, employment opportunities, and appropriate community resources, therapeutic gains are more likely to be secured.

There are many applications of focusing outside of psychotherapy. It is used in creative activities like writing, art, and dance; in business decision-making, and in spirituality. See the Focusing Institute Web site (<www.focusing.org>) for references.

CASE EXAMPLE

This section illustrates specific client behaviors outlined in Table 25.2. The client is a 30-year-old single woman. A central issue for her involves how she handles feelings of vulnerability. In her words:

c: Somehow being vulnerable is one of the worst things that I can think of being.

T: Something about being vulnerable that's just—

C: Awful. It's like the worst thing you can do. There are probably lots of worse things you can do, but that's what seems the worst.

T: Being vulnerable is one of the worst things you can do?

C: Yeah. It shows a real lack or something.

T: It's indicative of a lack in you?

C: Yeah. (pause) Maybe that I'm not really worth anything, or—

T: (pause) Something total, real big. That your whole worth would be diminished?

C: Yeah. It's weird. Like it's probably not that bad a quality, and if you had some other synonym, like "sensitive," or "delicate," or (pause) I can't think of any other words.

T: There might be a way of looking at that feeling so that it wouldn't have that kind of impact, but mostly it does.

C: Yeah. Mostly it does. I feel really vulnerable. If people know that, they can take more advantage of you than they usually do.

This client is a delight to work with, in part because she gives me feedback regarding what I do. The following excerpt illustrates what I mean by Client Behavior Number 4 from Table 25.2: Specifically identify therapist behaviors that interfere with your Focusing or tend to close your felt sense or make it fade away. Ask the therapist to modify these behaviors. In this case the client is making reference to a previous session in which I had asked her to focus when she wasn't ready.

C: Well, that made me sort of mad, because I was trying to build up, and then by asking me what I was focusing on, I lost track.

T: That's where I pushed too hard, and you almost felt like giving up on it?

C: Yeah, but then, when you were finally aware of it, you said, "Well, let's start over again," or something like that. And that was really useful.

T: Then it was good. And that first thing, was that a place where I was a little too pushy?

C: Well, it was just that it was irrelevant. I was using it more as a buildup, rather than really wanting to get in touch.

T: I see. Now I understand a little better what you're saying about a buildup. That's something that I think maybe you do sometimes that I haven't quite recognized.

C: Yeah. I think I do it a lot. Even talking about my classes. A lot of times it's what I want to talk about, but sometimes it's sort of a way to come in and prepare my-self. Sort of an introduction. I mean, it's important, but it's maybe not the most important thing.

T: But it has another function of working up to what's more important.

C: It's not really like I'm testing you, because I know you're okay, but it's still sort of "How am I really feeling, today, and how are you really feeling today? What's going on between us," or "Let's use this as a way to find out."

T: Both about you, how you are, and about me. As well as the two of us together.

C: Yeah, yeah. It's the safe topic, or something.

This client also gives feedback illustrating Client Behavior Number 5: If you know of something the therapist can do, or does, that would help you focus, describe that to the therapist.

C: I've been thinking about what it is you do that seems to help me so much. A lot of it, I think, is not putting me into any particular category of "I won't do that," or "that's not the issue." I like it that you are able to take me as I come.

T: I don't have to have you too well defined.

C: Yeah. Or back off and say, "Therapists don't do this. And I am your therapist, so go away."

T: And *my* role isn't too rigidly defined.

C: Yeah. It's more open.

Another example of the same client behavior refers to the endings of our sessions.

C: It's time to go.

T: Yes, I'd like to stop. Let's just take a minute to see— is this an okay place to stop, or maybe do you want to do one more step of some kind to close it up, or get it so you can come back to it?

C: Yeah. It doesn't feel finished, but I don't think that one more minute would do it either, so it's probably not worth—but one thing I liked two sessions ago was your reluctance to end at a point where I was feeling vulnerable, and your just saying that now makes it a reasonable nonabrupt place to leave it.

T: In terms of the place that you're talking about, it makes a lot of difference if I indicate some reluctance to just drop it?

C: Yeah, rather than, "Okay, time is up."

T: Because you're feeling vulnerable.

C: So this feels much better, and that's enough.

Less often does this client spontaneously exhibit Client Behavior Number 1: Periodically stop talking and let the felt sense form. Say two or three things that describe the felt sense before going on with anecdotes, descriptions of events, thoughts, plans, and so forth. With my focusing invitations and suggestions, however, she eventually does it.

c: I seem to be more worried about, or more concerned about it, than other people. I don't know why.

t: But you've got it, you can feel it, right?

c: Yeah.

t: Well, just tell me about the feeling quality of it.

c: (long pause) It's just a real *need.*

t: Uh-huh. Can you just sit with that for a minute more? I think that might open up if you do.

c: Oh, I don't know. It probably has to do with my mother or something.

t: Hm. It reminds you of her?

c: Oh, I don't know. Dr. X's big thing was that I had to be a mother to my mother, to get her approval.

t: It doesn't sound like that was very helpful, though.

c: Well, I mean I think it's probably true. I mean I don't think that just localizing it changes it.

t: Right. It doesn't change it. I think you're analyzing it a little prematurely. I think it might be better to just stay with the feel of the need that reminded you of that stuff. Just keep it right over there where you can feel it.

c: Okay. (pause) Well, it's just, part of me is the teacher and part of me is the student, and in (pause) some ways they're probably equal parts, and in a sense to be rejected in the dependent role is like (pause) having my whole being rejected. And the sense that if I ever stop just being the teacher, then I'm no longer going to be accepted.

Risks are attendant to making any kind of suggestion as to what the client should do, such as the above focusing invitations. For example, the therapist may not recognize something the client was feeling at the time of the suggestion. For this reason, Client Behavior Number 2 is important: Try to maintain a balance so that: (a) you are not swamped and overwhelmed by feeling, but (b) you have something to talk about that is somewhat unknown and vulnerable to discuss. The following segment illustrates this kind of balancing.

c: It's sort of like nothing else in my life is any good either.

t: (pause) Uh-huh. The bad impact sort of bleeds into everything else, and colors your sense of yourself in all the different parts of your life.

c: Yeah. I mean nothing is going that (pause) well anyway.

t: There aren't other things that you're really feeling *good* about either.

c: Yeah.

t: Let's see. It might help to try Focusing on the bad feeling. But you might not want to do that. I know you have a mixed reaction to doing that sometimes. Part of you would like to put feelings like that in a closet, and part of you would like to go into them. So I want to check with you and see if you want to try Focusing on that or not.

c: I don't think I do at this point. (pause) I have a copy of another letter that I wrote. Would you look at it?

Sometimes the therapist's understanding of the client will not be especially accurate. Such times are when Client Behavior Number 3 is pertinent: Try to take therapist comments as aids to better get in touch with your felt sense. Use them to help you heighten and open your felt sense of what you want to be working on.

c: It makes me feel lousy. I mean it makes me feel defensive and upset, whereas a person who sees himself as accepted has all those groovy feelings à la Rogers. Not feeling accepted gives sort of the other—it does sort of make me want to lash out and feel defensive and hurt and makes it so much harder to communicate.

t: It kind of tightens everything up, and makes you want to strike back?

c: Yeah. I mean it's like I'm fighting against something.

t: Right. What's that? Can you stay with the sense of the fight for a bit? What's the quality of that?

c: Lack of appreciation. (long pause) And then I want a validation that I'm not getting.

t: (pause) A certain kind of validation of you as, uh, competent?

c: I think more than competent. Good.

t: Better than competent.

c: Yeah! (pause) I mean, I want a chance to rise, a chance to be in a situation where I can do more and better things.

When the therapist *is* closely understanding the client, Behavior Number 3 remains appropriate. The client can use good therapist responses to help focus attention inwardly to let the felt sense form. Tracking the changing felt sense is more important in Focusing than the logical sequence of thought. The end of the following segment illustrates this client doing this in an instance where her Focusing led to a more nascent state.

c: I haven't had a chance to be anything but bad. Part of me has been so eager to find me bad that I haven't really looked at me for a while.

t: You haven't taken a fresh look?

c: Yeah.

T: I wonder if you could do some of that now?

C: Intellectually, I'd like to do that.

T: Can you ask the feeling? What does the feeling say?

C: (pause) I think it wants to wait for a while.

T: It's got to be very careful about that?

C: Yeah. (pause) Also, I don't think it's had any real time to decide, you know, what it really feels, since it's been so busy fighting off the other. It's been in this stance of "keep away from me, keep away from me, I'm not so bad," without much beyond being really defensive.

T: Not much of a positive experience of itself. More it's had to keep fending off this other onslaught. No time to really feel into who it is.

C: And then that's scary too.

T: Even that is scary?

C: Yeah. If it really looks, it will find something out.

T: It's scary because it doesn't know what it will find out?

C: (long pause) It's feeling a little bit relieved (pause). Still tense, but—

T: Just a little bit of easing up.

C: Yeah. (sigh, and pause) It's good. (pause)

One goal of psychotherapy is change at the level of the whole personality. When successful, the person approaches all situations or subsets of life's situations in a manner systematically different from that prior to the therapy. This client reports change at this level.

> I'm more able to take risks and be more vulnerable with you. I feel more comfortable with you than with other people. I could cry with you. I can say more than I expected to be able to say. I can test things out with you, and my risks pay off, which has made me more able to take similar risks with others.

But change at the overall level probably only occurs if change is happening *throughout* therapy. This change involves (1) many specific therapy hours that result in nascent states, and (2) many corresponding differences in how the person interacts with situations outside the therapy hour. If neither of these kinds of change starts happening within three or four sessions, one should question whether the therapy is being productive.

When Focusing results in the nascent state, the person takes a different body home. Immediate change occurs in the manner of experiencing in relevant situations. For example, this woman received a letter from a former boyfriend whose marriage had broken up. The letter stirred many feelings, and she felt a need to speak to him. After Focusing, she was able to maintain a distinction when she called him. She could respond caringly without communicating a willingness to relate to him in ways he was suggesting that were no longer right for her.

A more dramatic example of this specific level of change followed a focusing session about her nail biting, which left her in a nascent state. This formerly persistent and disturbing behavior did not occur for the following two weeks. However, as is often the case, the nascent state didn't stay permanently the first time it came. The behavior reappeared along with the former state of experiencing. An overall objective in this area is the permanent elimination of the behavior. But one should expect to have to focus to nascent many times along the way to permanent overall change.

If the nascent state is achieved as the result of therapy sessions, we can be confident that overall change is in progress. On the other hand, if the client never or rarely experiences changing to nascent during the course of therapy, overall change is unlikely, and the client may be wise to try another therapist.

SUMMARY

Focusing-oriented psychotherapy's concepts and methods are deeply rooted in research on psychotherapy and in Gendlin's philosophy (Gendlin, 1962, 1996, 2000). The philosophy builds concepts, theory, and methods on a foundation that has interactive living processes as the basic starting point. This is quite different than starting, as do many other contemporary theories, with physical entities in a time and space comprised of uniform units.

Allowing actual lived experience with our methods to feed back to, and instigate change in our methods, is at the philosophical heart of this approach. Rather than placing clients into static categories of personality type, focusing theory defines activities pertinent to personality change.

Although the roles of the client and the therapist are distinct, those who assume the roles are on equal footing as persons. The therapist and the client are expected to become parturient, if not structure-bound, at times, each requiring Focusing to regain nascence and its fuller functioning.

The theory behind Focusing clarifies specifically how to determine whether productive change is occurring. Change is felt bodily; it is not just words. Such bodily change is not something that happens only within the person, separate from living in the world. When experiencing changes, the person in situations is different: He or she can more fully interact with situations immediately. There is no need to wait in confusion for many expensive sessions to find out if change is occurring; the experiential effects of Focusing should be experienced regularly from early in therapy.

Focusing theory is not a theory of persons; it is a theory of how symbols and persons interact during personality change. Thus, focusing methods apply to any theory of persons, lending a powerful perspective regarding the experiential impact of the theory on the persons whom the theory purports to describe.

REFERENCES

American Psychiatric Association (1994). *Diagnostic and Statistical Manual of Mental Disorders: DSM-IV* (4th Ed.) Washington, D.C.

Cornell, A. W. (1996a). Relationship = Distance + Connection: A comparison of Inner Relationship Techniques to Finding Distance Techniques in Focusing. *The Folio: A Journal for Focusing and Experiential Therapy, 15,* 1, 1–8.

Cornell, A. W. (1996b). *The power of focusing: A practical guide to emotional self-healing.* Oakland, CA: New Harbinger.

Cornell, A. & McGavin, B. (2000). The Argument about Action. Published on Focusing-disuss@focusing.org, August 21, 4:25 PM.

Don, N. S. (1977). The transformation of conscious experience and its EEG correlates. *Journal of Altered States of Consciousness, 3,* 147–168.

Elliott, R., Clark, C., Wexler, M., Kemeny, M., Brinkerhoff, V., & Mack, C. (1990). The impact of experiential therapy of depression: Initial results. In F. Lietaer, J. Rombauts, & R. Van Balen (eds.), Client-Centered and Experiential Psychotherapy in the nineties (pp. 549–577). Leuven: Leuven University Press.

Gendlin, E. T. (1962). *Experiencing and the creation of meaning.* New York: Free Press of Glencoe.

Gendlin, E. T. (1964). A theory of personality change. In P. Worchel & D. Byrne (Eds.), *Personality Change.* New York: Wiley.

Gendlin, E. T. (1968). The experiential response. In E. Hammer (Ed.), *Use of interpretation in treatment.* New York: Grune & Stratton.

Gendlin, E. T. (1969). Focusing. *Psychotherapy: Theory, Research, and Practice, 6,* 4–15.

Gendlin, E. T. (1973). Experiential Psychotherapy. In R. J. Corsini (Ed.), *Current Psychotherapies.* Itasca, IL: F. E. Peacock.

Gendlin, E. T. (1974). Client-centered and experiential psychotherapy. In D. A. Wexler & L. N. Rice (Eds.), *Innovations in client-centered therapy.* New York: Wiley.

Gendlin, E. T. (1979). Experiential Psychotherapy. In R. J. Corsini (Ed.), *Current Psychotherapies* (2nd ed.). Itasca, IL: F. E. Peacock.

Gendlin, E. T. (1981). *Focusing.* (2nd ed.) New York: Bantam.

Gendlin, E. T. (1996). *Focusing-oriented psychotherapy: A manual of the experiential methods.* New York: Guilford.

Gendlin, E. T. (2000). *A Process Model.* Available at http://www.focusing.org/philosophy.

Gendlin, E. T., Beebe, J., Cassues, J., Klein, M., & Oberlander, M. (1968). Focusing ability in psychotherapy, personality and creativity. *Research in Psychotherapy, 3,* 217–241.

Goldman, R., Bierman, R. & Wolfus, B. (1996). Relating without violence (RWV): A treatment program for incarcer-

ated male batterers. Poseter session presented at the Society for Psychotherapy Research International Meeting, June, Amelia Island, Florida.

Gray, J. P. (1976). The influence of experiential focusing on state anxiety and problem-solving ability. Unpublished doctoral dissertation, California School of Professional Psychology, Los Angeles.

Greenberg, L., & Higgins, H. (1980). The differential effects of two-chair dialogue and focusing on conflict resolution. Journal of Counseling Psychology, 27, 221–225.

Greenberg, L., Lietaer, G., & Watson, J. (1998). Experiential therapy: Identity and challenges. In L. Greenberg, J. Watson, & G. Lietaer (Eds.). *Handbook of experiential psychotherapy* (pp. 461–466). New York: Guilford.

Greenberg, L., Rice, L., Elliott, R. (1993). *Facilitating emotional change: The moment-by-moment process.* New York: Guilford.

Greenberg, L., & Watson, J. (1998). Experiential therapy of depression: Differential effects of client-centered relationship conditions and process experiential interventions. Psychotherapy Research, 8(2), 210–224.

Greenberg, L., Watson, J., & Lietaer, G. (1998). *Handbook of experiential psychotherapy.* New York: Guilford.

Hendricks, M. N. (2000). Research Basis of Focusing-Oriented/Experiential Psychology. Available at <http://www.focusing.org/research>.

Hinterkopf, E., & Brunswick, L. K. (1975, Spring). Teaching therapeutic skills to mental patients. Psychotherapy: Theory, Research and Practice, 12(1), 8–12.

Hinterkopf, E., & Brunswick, L. K. (1977). Teaching therapeutic skills to mental patients. *Evaluation, 4,* 63–64.

Hinterkopf, E., & Brunswick, L. (1979, Winter). Promoting interpersonal interaction among mental patients by teaching them therapeutic skills. Psychosocial Rehabilitation Journal, 3(1), 20–26.

Hinterkopf, E., & Brunswick, L. K. (1979). Promoting interpersonal interaction among mental patients by teaching them therapeutic skills. *Psychosocial Rehabilitation Journal, 3,* 20–26.

Hinterkopf, E., & Brunswick, L. K. (1981, Fall). Teaching mental patients to use client-centered and experiential therapeutic skills with each other. Psychotherapy: Theory, Research and Practice, 18(3), 394–402.

Holstein, B., & Flaxman, J. (1996, Fall/Spring). The Effect of Focusing on Weight Loss. The Folio: A Journal for Focusing and Experiential Therapy, 15(2), 29–46.

Iberg, J. R. (1979). *The effects of focusing on job interview behavior.* Unpublished doctoral dissertation, University of Chicago.

Iberg, J. R. (1990). Ms. C's focusing and cognitive functions. In G. Lietaer, J. Rombauts, & R. Van Balen (Eds.) *Client-centered and experiential psychotherapy in the nineties.* Leuven, Belgium: Leuven University Press.

Iberg, J. R. (1996). Finding the body's next step: Ingredients and hindrances. *The Folio: A Journal for Focusing and Experiential Therapy, 15,1,* 13–42.

Iberg, J. R. (2000). The *Focusing-oriented Session Report,* and the *Therapist's Report of Client Process:* The development of new measures of client experiencing. Manuscript under editorial review.

Klein, M. H., Mathieu, P. L., Kiesler, D. J. & Gendlin, E. T. (1970). *The experiencing scale: a research and training manual* (Vols. 1–2) Madison, WI: University of Wisconsin, Bureau of Audio-Visual Instruction.

Klein, M., Mathieu-Coughlan, P., Kiesler, D. (1986). The experiencing scales. In L. S. Greenberg and W. M Pinsof (Eds.) The Psychotherapeutic Process: A research handbook. New York: Guilford.

Leijssen, M. (1996/1997). Focusing processes in client-centered experiential psychotherapy: An overview of my research findings. *The Folio: A Journal for Focusing and Experiential Therapy, 15, 2,* 1–6.

Loevinger, J., & Wessler, R. (1970). *Measuring ego development* (Vols. 1–2). San Francisco: Jossey-Bass.

Mischel, W. (1979). On the interface of cognition and personality: Beyond the person-situation debate. *American Psychologist, 34,* 740–754.

Olsen, L. E. (1975). *The use of visual imagery and experiential focusing in psychotherapy.* Unpublished doctoral dissertation, University of Chicago.

Prouty, G. (1976). Pre-therapy—A method of treating pre-expressive psychotics and retarded patients. *Psychotherapy: Theory, Research, and Practice, 13,* 290–294.

Prouty, G. (1977). Protosymbolic method: a phenomenological treatment of schizophrenic hallucinations. *Journal of Mental Imagery, 1,* 339–342.

Prouty, G. (1994). *Theoretical evolutions in person-centered/ experiential therapy: Applications to schizophrenic and retarded psychoses.* Westport, CT: Praeger.

Prouty, G. (1994). *Theoretical evolutions in person-centered/experiential therapy.* West Port, CT: Praeger.

Rogers, C. R. (1951). *Client-centered therapy.* Boston: Houghton.

Rogers, C. R. (1957). The necessary and sufficient conditions of therapeutic personality change. *Journal of Consulting Psychology, 21,* 95–103.

Rogers, C. R. (1961). *On becoming a person.* Boston: Houghton.

Rogers, C. R. (1975). Empathic: An unappreciated way of being. *The Counseling Psychologist, 5,* 2–10.

Rogers, C. R., & Dymond, R. (1954). *Psychotherapy and personality change.* Chicago: University of Chicago Press.

Rosenberg, M. B. (2000). *Nonviolent communication: A language of compassion.* Encinitas, CA: Pudde Dancer Press.

Sachse, R. (1990). Concrete interventions are crucial: the influence of the therapist's processing proposals on the client's intrapersonal exploration in Client-centered Therapy. In G. Lietaer, J. Rombauts, & R. Van Balen (Eds.) *Client-centered experiential psychotherapy in the nineties.* Leuven, Belgium: Leuven University Press.

Sachse, R. & Neumann, W. (1983). ProzSModell zum focusing unter berucksichtigung spezifischer probleme. GwG-info: Informationsblatter der Gesselschaft fur wissenschaftliche Gesprachspsychotherapie, *53,* 51–73.

Weitzman, B. (1967). Behavior therapy and psychotherapy. Psychological Review, 74, 300–317.

Weld, S. E. (1992). Stress Management Outcome: Prediction of Differential Outcome by Personality Characteristics, Dissertation Abstracts International.

Wolfus, B. & Bierman, R. (1996). An evaluation of a group treatment program for incarcerated male batterers. *International Journal of Offender Therapy and Comparative Criminology, 40,* 318–333.

Chapter 26

HEALING THE DIVIDED SELF

MAGGIE PHILLIPS

This distinctively named system of therapy incorporates the basic ideas of John and Helen Watkins (who were in the previous edition of this book) and the procedures of Milton Erickson, whose work has a chapter in this book, and so represents an independent system based on two other systems. The specific subject of this therapy is the divided self, which includes the dissociative spectrum, with its many elements identified by Dr. Phillips throughout her chapter. Unusual is the specificity of her target group, though her model can be used with a broad array of clinical problems related to dissociation and ego-state conflicts.

This account spends considerable space discussing the origins and functions of dissociation, more than most people in the field probably know, and then goes on to the method of treatment, a four-stage model known as SARI for Safety and stabilization, Activation of inner resources, Renegotiation of dissociated traumatic events, and Integration of the therapy experience. All this calls for competence in direct and indirect hypnosis, even though, as the author suggests, other methods can be used. The processes are carefully explained, and any client whose diagnosis falls into this category should probably be treated by this method if at all possible.

Healing the Divided Self should be on every general therapist's list of available techniques for dealing with problems of self-division, including unnecessary fears, and symptoms which do not respond to other therapy methods.

The divided self is receiving growing attention in the world of psychotherapy. From this perspective, problems of self-division are viewed as the source of many presenting clinical symptoms. These can include anxiety and panic, depression, psychosomatic syndromes, eating disorders, posttraumatic stress, and the dissociative disorders.

One of the key concepts in understanding self-division is dissociation, which refers to divisions of consciousness in everyday experience. Dissociative issues are viewed as existing along a continuum, ranging from normal separations of consciousness that occur during absorbing activities such as driving or watching films, to the extreme pathology seen in the dissociative disorders. Although the study of dissociation was at the heart of early psychiatric and psychological investigation, emphasis on dissociative symptoms has been largely dissociated from consideration in formulating the parameters of clinical psychopathology (Spiegel, 1993).

With the reawakening of interest during the last few decades in dissociative difficulties believed to arise from exposure to various types of exogenous trauma, however, the *Diagnostic and Statistical Manual of Mental Disorders* of the American Psychiatric Association (*DSM-IV*, 1994) has acknowledged a wider spectrum of dissociative difficulties. This classification now includes Dissociative Amnesia, Dissociative Fugue, Depersonalization Disorder, Dissociative Identity Disorder (formerly Multiple Personality Disorder), and Dissociative Disorder Not Otherwise Specified, with important links to acute and posttraumatic stress, conversion, somatization, and somatiform disorders.

Healing the Divided Self is a method which incorporates clinical uses of hypnosis in the treatment of dissociative and posttraumatic symptoms that arise from dysfunctional divisions of consciousness. This model of therapy was developed by Maggie Phillips, PhD, and Claire Frederick, MD, and based on the work of John Watkins, PhD, and Helen Watkins, MA.

HISTORY

Until the nineteenth century, shamans, medicine men, and other healers attempted to help those afflicted by dissociative conditions by casting out demons. Exorcisms and the conditions they were used to treat were relegated to the church, with priests deemed the experts in this domain. The earliest secular work in this area is credited to Franz Anton Mesmer (1734–1815) and his theory of animal magnetism. Although his practices were largely discredited in his lifetime, many of his principles were kept alive by dedicated disciples, who continued to pursue the study and treatment of divided consciousness phenomena.

The basis for current research and treatment can be found in the systematic investigations of Pierre Janet (1859–1947). A philosopher turned physician, Janet made several noteworthy contributions to the study of divided self. He first coined the term *dissociation* (Janet, 1907) to describe the separation of thoughts, feelings, and perceptions associated with a particular traumatic event from the mainstream of consciousness. He then linked dissociation to traumatic antecedents, recognized the role of state-dependent memory, and acknowledged the contribution of altered states of consciousness to the disturbance of identity in dissociative pathology, which was then termed hysteria. Janet also pioneered abreactive and hypnotic techniques for the recall and reintegration of dissociated traumatic experiences since, from his point of view, cure occurred when the original trauma was discovered (Janet, 1907).

Others who contributed to this area of investigation included William James, Morton Prince, and Alfred Binet, who speculated that personality processes operated under the control of several subpersonalities. Although Freud was also interested in this area of exploration, he rejected the authenticity of child sexual abuse memories obtained through the use of hypnosis in his female patients because many of the accused perpetrators were among his colleagues (Ellenberger, 1970). This controversy continues to be echoed by the voices raised in the current false memory debate.

Freud's psychoanalytic theories and the advent of behaviorism temporarily pushed the study of dissociation into the background during the first half of the twentieth century. Treatment of soldiers suffering from battle fatigue during World Wars I and II, and later the Vietnam War, however, revived interest in hypnosis as a therapeutic tool. The subsequent explosion of the Women's Movement in the 1960s was the catalyst for a renewed concern for the well-being of children and led to social awareness of the prevalence of child abuse trauma.

Around this time, Milton Erickson (Erickson & Kubie, 1939), Ernest Hilgard (1977), and others conducted careful experiments involving hypnotic dissociation and personality division. These investigations led to further experimental evidence for the divided self. John and Helen Watkins (1979, 1997) built on these efforts, along with those of Paul Federn (1952), who was a colleague of Freud, to develop their model of Ego-State Therapy. Ego-State Therapy involves the hypnotic activation of ego states, or subpersonalities, within the core personal-

ity. The Watkins believe, along with Federn, that it is the conflicts which develop among and within these personality ego states which are responsible for creating dissociative, divided self difficulties.

Healing the Divided Self synthesizes the existing technology of clinical and Ericksonian hypnosis, including Ego-State Therapy, into a four-stage model that can be used to treat the full range of dissociative problems that are related to many common clinical syndromes. The codevelopers, Claire Frederick, M.D. and I, developed and tested our model in clinical and teaching practice, from 1988 to 1995. We published the results in our book, *Healing the Divided Self: Clinical and Ericksonian Hypnotherapy for Posttraumatic and Dissociative Conditions,* in 1995. In addition, many of our clinical cases that demonstrate the effectiveness of this model have been published in professional hypnosis journals from 1992 until the present time.

CURRENT STATUS

Clinical explorations with the Healing the Divided Self model are centered in the psychotherapy and supervision practices of the codevelopers. I direct the California Institute of Clinical Hypnosis, located in Oakland, California, which offers ongoing training and supervision for psychotherapists at the master's and doctoral levels. Dr. Frederick has consulted with many therapists using the Healing the Divided Self model in the Lake Tahoe, California/Reno, Nevada area and will now continue this work in Massachusetts. In addition, we have taught both separately and together numerous courses presenting Healing the Divided Self principles for the Northern California Society of Clinical Hypnosis, the American Society of Clinical Hypnosis, the European Society of Hypnosis, the International Society of Hypnosis, the Milton H. Erickson Congresses, and for many professional organizations within the United States and abroad.

Although we have not published empirical data, our results have been replicated and extended by students and colleagues who have emphasized various aspects of our model. Shirley McNeal, PhD, has written papers with Claire Frederick, M.D. (McNeal & Frederick, 1993, 1996), and one book, *Inner Strengths: Contemporary Psychotherapy and Hypnosis for Ego-Strengthening* (Frederick & McNeal, 1998), which emphasize the importance of ego-strengthening techniques with ego states when addressing divided self phenomena.

Other efforts have included investigations of methods to resolve unfinished developmental business that exists among and within divided ego states, such as self-soothing (McNeal & Frederick, 1994), development of positive transitional objects and experiences (McNeal & Frederick, 1997; Morton & Frederick, 1997a; Phillips &

Smith, 1996) and internal boundary formation and maintenance (McNeal & Frederick, 1995).

Another area of inquiry has been personality integration. The Healing the Divided Self model provides both for integration of therapy experiences and for reorganization of the personality system by reducing dissociation and increasing harmony and cooperation among ego states. Morton and Frederick (1997b) and Dickey, Nungary, and Frederick (1998) have explored ways of encouraging increased cooperation between conscious and unconscious processes as a way of healing self-division and facilitating an integrated wholeness.

Finally, several studies have extended the Healing the Divided Self model into work with populations other than individual therapy with adults. Toothman & Phillips (1998) have applied this model successfully in marital and couples therapy, while Grove (1995) and Hartman (1995) have reported using our model successfully with traumatized children.

THEORY

The understanding that human personality is naturally divided or segmented has been commonly held since the nineteenth century (Phillips & Frederick, 1995). Janet (1907) pioneered the use of the word *subconscious* to describe aspects of personality that held patterns of feeling and cognition and that could be activated only by hypnosis. Freud proposed a theory of tripartite personality development, consisting of the id, ego, and superego. This conceptualization was extended by several of his colleagues, including Carl Jung, who viewed personality as a multiplicity with different components that shifted between conscious and unconscious activity.

Paul Federn (1952) was the first of Freud's followers to suggest that the experience of self can vary depending upon which state a person is in at a given moment. His concept of ego state was adapted by both Eric Berne and John Watkins. Berne stayed close to Freud's model of personality to delineate three main ego states, parent, adult, and child, which formed the framework of his transactional analysis theory. Watkins, on the other hand, has viewed the personality as consisting of innumerable ego states that do not fit neatly into Berne's three categories.

Ego States

Ego states are defined as an organized system of behaviors and experiences bound together by some common principle. They may be large and include, for example, all the knowledge, experience, and behavior contained in an adult's work identity. Conversely, they may be limited and include specific behaviors and experiences that oc-

curred as part of a memory from the first month of second grade. Ego states may be related to current experience or include memories, feelings, behaviors, and cognitions that are connected with a past event. They may be relatively isolated from each other or they may overlap, sharing common experiences, yet differing significantly in terms of strategies they use to accomplish a common goal. Ego states that are dissonant, or have different purposes and goals, may often develop conflicts that can create symptoms.

According to the Watkins, ego states can be formed in three ways (Watkins & Watkins, 1979, 1997). The first is normal differentiation. Here, the child develops ego states in order to develop patterns of adaptation to deal with different external stimuli, including people and situations. Through the formation of different ego states, the child learns to discriminate and develop appropriate responses for playing on the playground versus completing schoolwork or sitting quietly in church. A second way these states are formed is through introjection of parental or other significant authority figures as well as significant early life events. Third, when confronted with overwhelming trauma, the child may dissociate and form one or more ego states to contain and/or to cope with the traumatic situation.

Ego states exist on a continuum of dissociation, from the least to the most differentiated. Normal situations include those where the personality is rich with an integrated complexity of ego states that are in communication and work together cooperatively (Phillips & Frederick, 1995). Boundaries between these ego states are flexible and permeable, allowing for a dynamic flow of information in and out. For example, an individual may have a child ego state who loves to eat ice cream when the adult states in the personality are overworking. This behavior may be accepted and cooperated with by the other ego states, who keep weight in balance by increasing exercise and choosing healthy foods at mealtime.

In the middle of the spectrum are situations where ego states are in active conflict, resulting in common clinical problems such as depression, anxiety, Posttraumatic Stress Disorder (PTSD), eating disorders, and panic attacks. There is a higher degree of dissociation here, and boundaries between ego states are less flexible, with at least some ego states separated from the mainstream of consciousness. The source of ego-state problems is usually outside of consciousness and occurs when one or more parts are not in harmony with the others, act on their own, and produce symptoms. If the preceding example were extended, there might be a conflict between an older adult ego state who derives primary satisfaction from overworking and a younger adult state who receives satisfaction from maintaining a trim, fit body through intensive exercise. Both of these may be in conflict with the child state who overeats ice cream and an adolescent state who withdraws during times of stress and engages in a binge-purge cycle.

At the extreme end of the continuum, ego states are separated by a high degree of dissociation, commonly resulting from trauma. Their boundaries are thick so that ego states are walled off from each other, disconnected, and not in communication. Dissociative Identity Disorder, previously termed Multiple Personality Disorder, occurs when ego states, or alters (i.e., alternative personalities), take executive control spontaneously while the rest of the personality experiences some degree of amnesia.

To extend the preceding example toward the dissociative end of the continuum, an individual who has experienced extensive sexual abuse in childhood might have an internal system with numerous dissociated states engaged in conflict similar to the situations described but with important differences. An adult ego state might overwork not only to derive satisfaction but also to avoid times of introspection that might lead to flashbacks of the abuse. The younger adult state might engage in addictive patterns of exercise, using steroids to produce more bulk and physical protection from unwanted sexual activity that might reactivate sexual trauma. Other adult states, who serve as alcoholic parent introjects, might take over personality functioning to engage in abuses of alcohol and drugs that result in periodic losses of time and fugue experiences of "coming to" in a town miles away from home with no memory of traveling there. The child and adolescent ego states might also take over the executive functioning of the personality at times of acute stress, leading to dissociative episodes of overeating, binging, and purging that can result in a life-threatening anorexic-bulemic disorder. If there is little or no co-consciousness between the ego states engaged in these behaviors, then many of these self-destructive episodes will take place outside conscious awareness, triggering anxieties that might evolve into panic attacks, along with periods of despair that could elicit cycles of suicidal feelings and behavior.

With prevalent losses of time and executive functioning, Dissociative Identity Disorder becomes a diagnostic reality, especially if the ego states are complex and relatively complete in their organization. If treating professionals are not aware of divided self phenomena, the focus of treatment might be restricted to discrete symptoms, such as eating disorder, alcoholism, depression, or panic attacks. Without an understanding of dissociative fragmentation and the ego-state conflicts that drive these symptoms, however, treatment may fail or stop short of the depth of discovery necessary for full resolution of divided self problems.

Regardless of the nature of its formation, or its place on the dissociative continuum, however, every ego state is considered adaptive. That is, its purpose is one of attempting to help the personality in some way. Even when ego states are related to destructive behaviors or symptoms, their intentions are considered to be positive. Because of the dissociation related to trauma that often exists within the personality, ego states with significant separation from the main personality can be thought of as "frozen in time," continuing to think, feel, and respond as they did at the time of traumatic dissociation. Because of this separation, they have not been able to participate with the rest of the ego states in experiences that would have likely contributed to their growth, maturation, and healing (Phillips & Frederick, 1995).

Related Theoretical Models of Self-Division

State-dependent learning refers to the connection between the learning experience and the psychophysiological state of the central nervous system at the time that the learning is taking place. Ernest Hilgard (1977) has postulated that divided consciousness is related to the state-dependent learning paradigm. Hilgard's experiments with hypnosis involving perceptions of sound and pain indicated that psychological functioning results from the interaction of many subordinate systems. His theory, termed neodissociation, makes a distinction between dissociation and repression, suggesting an inner vertical splitting between the dissociated event and the aspect of self that knows and remembers. He determined from his investigations that covert observing aspects of the mind could register experiences even when the hypnotized individual denied knowledge. Hilgard called these self aspects "hidden observers" (Hilgard, 1977).

The Watkins (Watkins & Watkins, 1979) also studied the hidden observer phenomenon, replicating Hilgard's results and interviewing these covert self aspects, whom they later called ego states. Through their investigations with college students, the Watkins (Watkins & Watkins, 1997) found that activation of hidden observers and subsequent inquiry seemed to yield organized ego states. They have concluded that ego states and hidden observers are in the same category of personality phenomena.

The SARI Model

In our study of the divided self, Claire Frederick and I (Phillips & Frederick, 1995) have recognized the centrality of ego state phenomena in explaining personality fragmentation and suggesting guiding principles for treatment.

We have gone beyond the ego state model, however, to propose a four-stage model of therapy we call SARI that includes approaches other than hypnoanalytic Ego-State Therapy to address clinical problems resulting from self-division. SARI is an acronym for the following stages and tasks of therapy: (1) Safety and Stabilization; (2) Activation of inner resources and conflicts of the divided self; (3) Resolution of symptoms and inner conflicts and Renegotiation of past dissociated trauma experiences; and (4) Integration of therapy experiences and personality functioning and development of new Identity. The SARI model parallels the basic sequence of recovery from trauma identified by numerous experts in the trauma/dissociation field.

During the first stage of treatment, the emphasis is on the uses of direct and indirect suggestion to facilitate mastery and ego strengthening. From the SARI perspective, no other therapy work should be attempted until a reasonable degree of safety and stabilization has been achieved within the therapy situation and in the client's everyday functioning. This beginning stage must address the client's safety needs in a variety of areas, including health issues, emotional and interpersonal difficulties, alcohol and drug use, management of posttraumatic symptoms, and work environment.

Many individuals with divided self difficulties, especially those at the extreme dissociative end of the spectrum, present in acute crisis states and must be evaluated for suicidal risk and referred for medication to reduce depression, anxiety, hyperarousal, and other PTSD symptoms. Self-destructive behaviors must be addressed, including self-mutilation, impulsive risk-taking, and involvement in exploitative or abusive relationships. Adjunctive services, including hospitalization, can be considered.

Once Stage 1 tasks have been actualized to the satisfaction of both therapist and client, the next step is activating the origins of divided self symptoms while activating the inner resources needed to correct and heal the divisions. Sometimes the client is aware of the past experiences that contribute to inner conflicts. In other situations, traumatic events have been walled off from consciousness by the dissociative barriers of state-dependent memory and may require deeper exploration (Phillips & Frederick, 1995). The therapist's role is to help the client elicit enough internal information about the sources of presenting symptoms, but not so much that the individual is overwhelmed and debilitated. Destabilization is often a risk during this stage of work, and can be resolved by further focus on Stage 1 tasks.

The third stage, which is often interwoven with the previous phase, involves reconnecting dissociated experiences and parts of the self to resolve symptoms. From an ego-stage perspective, this means that the client is helped to connect with split-off personality states. Relevant ego states are reconnected with each other, conflicts between them examined and resolved, and corrective experiences provided to promote growth and maturation.

As the client is helped to reconnect with dissociated affects of rage, grief, helplessness, confusion, and terror,

restabilization through a return to Stage 1 tasks may again be necessary. If past traumatic events are found to contribute to the symptoms of self-division, they must be confronted in safe, productive ways. Experts in the field of posttraumatic stress and dissociative disorders concur that reliving of traumatic experiences is insufficient for healing (Kluft, 1993; van der Hart & Brown, 1992). Instead, hypnosis and other techniques are used to facilitate a sense of mastery and personal control over the past, integrated self-awareness and functioning, and reframing of past traumatic experiences to provide new internal meanings. Traumatic events must also be renegotiated by identifying traumatic responses in the body and somatosensory systems and restructuring these into flexible somatic resources.

In the final phase, the client is helped to fully integrate growthful experiences of therapy and begins to sustain a more positive and realistic future orientation. More complete co-consciousness is achieved within the inner family of self as the client becomes aware of the strengths and vulnerabilities of significant ego states. As more cohesive self-identity evolves, individuals whose decision making may have long been governed by a divided self may now reclaim aspirations that were shattered by inner conflicts or discover deep longings for the first time. Forward movement toward life goals is supported by inner cooperation and harmony.

The SARI model is an integrative model of therapy because it draws from Ericksonian principles and indirect methods of hypnotic suggestion as well as more direct, formal trance techniques that originate from classical hypnoanalytic, medical, and clinical hypnosis traditions, as well as other therapy approaches. This model provides more comprehensive treatment that can heal the complexities of the divided self.

METHODOLOGY

Healing the Divided Self methodology is organized around the SARI model. Direct and indirect techniques that include hypnosis are offered at each stage of treatment to facilitate achievement of specific goals.

Stage 1

During the safety and stability phase, the focus is on ego strengthening and mastery of presenting symptomotology. Strategies range from Ericksonian indirect techniques, such as metaphor, seeding, reframing, and utilization, to formal hypnotic techniques such as ideomotor signaling, age progression, and age regression to positive experiences in the past. Cognitive behavioral methods, imagery, and other approaches are also useful.

Assessment Phase

During the assessment interview process, the therapist is advised to determine whether the client's presenting problems reflect self-division. Some of the indicators (Phillips & Frederick, 1995) can include:

1. Amnesia for significant portions of childhood;

2. Recollections or information from others about incidence of childhood trauma;

3. A history of significant changes in behavior during childhood;

4. The presence of symptoms that are ego-dystonic;

5. A clinical picture that has proven refractory to a variety of previous therapy approaches;

6. Use of the "language of parts" to describe difficulties (e.g., "Part of me wants to do this, while another part of me wants to do that" or "Some part of me seems to stop me from making this change");

7. References to dissociative experiences, such as a loss of time, significant change in mood, affect, or personality out of proportion to external circumstances; transient sensory experiences such as pain, trembling, parasthesias, itching, inexplicable sensations of heaviness or lightness;

8. Intrusive behaviors, such as muscular jerking, trembling, catalepsy, tics, spasms, and changes in voice and mannerisms while speaking.

The most critical factor in diagnosing clinical problems involving self-division is an "awareness of the *possibility* that dissociation *could be* involved as a causative agent" (Phillips & Frederick, 1995, p. 17). Frequently, dissociative conditions are confused with other clinical problems, such as bipolar disorders, depression, anxiety, personality disorders, and even psychotic symptoms. If the therapist believes that there is a likelihood of the diagnosis of a dissociative disorder, use of assessment instruments designed for this purpose, further training in the diagnosis and treatment of dissociative disorders, and/or consultation with a clinician who has extensive experience in this area is appropriate.

When self-division is believed to be at issue, treatment based on the use of hypnosis and hypnotic principles is viewed by many experts to be the treatment of choice. Yet formal hypnosis must be used with caution with clients who are actively suicidal, exhibit psychotic symptoms currently or in their history, are impaired by alcohol or drug use, who have loose boundaries or impulse control, or who demonstrate significant emotional lability or dependency. An additional contraindication for the use of hypnosis exists when the client is currently involved in, or plans to be involved in, legal proceedings. Prospective hypnotic subjects must be informed that, in many states, uses of hypnosis may disallow testimony. Discussion of relevant issues and obtaining written informed consent is recommended.

Clients who may have trauma in their backgrounds or a significant degree of dissociation in their current personality organization pose additional risks. The use of formal hypnosis before the client has achieved adequate internal and external safety and is stabilized in the therapy situation may result in retraumatization if hypnosis elicits powerful material that is overwhelming to the client or stimulates anxiety or confusion. For this reason, it is important to assess clients carefully for the appropriate use of formal hypnotic states in therapy. One way of obtaining informal hypnotic assessment is to ask interview questions that elicit an inner focus. For example, in interviewing a client who believes his symptoms of depression and inability to concentrate are related to sexual abuse by his grandmother, the therapist might suggest, "Just go back in your mind to a recent time when you felt unable to concentrate or felt depressed. That's right. Just explore that experience for a moment. What else comes to mind now about this? Does this remind you of similar experiences in the past? If so, what?" If the client is uncomfortable with this type of approach, begins to move into a more regressed state, or seems to lose contact with the immediate therapy situation, the therapist is advised that this individual may have loose internal boundaries for containment so that formal hypnosis will need to be used cautiously and only after careful preparation.

If hypnosis seems appropriate, the therapist needs to examine the client's beliefs, fears, misconceptions, and questions about hypnosis and discuss mutual expectations about hypnosis sessions (Phillips & Frederick, 1995). Initial sessions with formal hypnosis should be viewed as explorations in order to obtain further assessment information and to find out what the client already knows about how to respond to hypnotic suggestion. It is important to present several initial tasks (Phillips & Frederick, 1995) that have a positive focus and can begin the process of ego-strengthening. These include:

1. Focus on the breath and the initiation of diaphragmatic breathing

2. Progressive muscular relaxation involving various parts of the body

3. Comfortable eye closure

4. Developing a comfortable internal focus

5. Deepening a light trance state in a comfortable way

6. Comfortable responses to suggestions of imagery and other sensory suggestions

7. Ability to start and stop initial experiences at will

8. Reorientation to external surroundings at the end of a formal induction

The main guideline during this time of exploration with formal hypnosis is mastery. That is, it is essential that a client experience mastery of each of these tasks and self-control of mind/body processes. This will prove ego-strengthening and will also serve the overall purposes of safety and stability for this stage of work.

Uses of Direct and Indirect Hypnosis

Once initial assessment is complete, the therapist who follows the Healing the Divided Self SARI protocol begins to use a variety of direct and indirect hypnotic approaches to help the client achieve the goals of safety and stability through experiences of mastery and ego-strengthening.

Indirect Ericksonian techniques are often used in situations where the cautions indicated about the use of formal, direct trance states must be considered. Indirect methods can help to introduce clients more gradually to hypnotic principles and prepare them for more formal techniques. Metaphor and storytelling can be introduced in a nonthreatening way that facilitates rapport, deepens internal communication, and allows the client to respond comfortably at his or her own pace. During this first stage of therapy, metaphors can also be used to "seed" an idea that may be threatening or challenging, followed by an associational "bridge" that is more closely related to the client's problem and offers a strategy for resolution, and then reinforced with more direct communications (Hammond, 1990).

For example, metaphors can seed the experience of internal safety, which often seems difficult for many dissociated or highly fragmented clients to achieve, by telling a story that develops the image of a tree with deep, strong roots. No matter how hard the winds shake its branches or storms threaten its stability, the roots hold the tree securely through seasons that are full of adversity as well as those that are relatively calm. After elaborating the image with further detail and perhaps use of a story line, an associational bridge can suggest that even though the client does not currently feel a sense of inner security, his/her creative inner mind can act as the roots of the tree, providing invisible, deep possibilities for support through times of imbalance and turmoil. If the client responds to these kinds of metaphorical suggestions, the therapist can follow with more direct suggestions about ways of evoking inner safety.

Another important Ericksonian technique used with clients who present divided self difficulties is the principle of utilization. Milton Erickson defined utilization as the acceptance of all the symptoms, behaviors, attitudes, and emotional reactions of the client, no matter how negative or destructive they might appear, as potential assets and resources in the treatment process (Erickson, 1959). In contrast to more classical hypnosis, which traditionally required the hypnotic subject to cooperate with the therapist's suggestions or be considered resistant, utilization approaches require the therapist to cooperate fully with the client's presenting style. Because utilization approaches do not require clients to abandon beliefs or feelings about themselves that are often negative, they can help to strengthen the therapy alliance and begin to create feelings of security and self-acceptance.

For example, many clients present in therapy with debilitating somatosensory flashbacks of childhood sexual abuse or adult rape that make it difficult for them to have positive intimacy experiences. Other therapeutic approaches might begin by working to eliminate or modify the flashbacks, or to analyze their origins. The Healing the Divided Self SARI model, however, holds that it is best to help the client utilize these symptoms in order to help achieve safety and stabilized functioning during the early phases of treatment rather than attempting to alter them. The therapist might suggest that the client begin to notice how the onset of flashbacks might allow him/her to slow down the pace of intimacy to allow for a gradual development of safety, provide an opportunity for deepening communication with the partner, and help to focus on inner needs rather than the needs and wishes of the partner. Utilization of the flashbacks in this way can help the client achieve a sense of mastery and provide for important self-learning.

Formal uses of hypnosis include suggestions that stimulate ego-strengthening, expanding both observing and experiencing ego capacities. Suggestions might include a hypnotic review of past experiences of accomplishment and mastery to increase self-confidence and esteem, the use of imagery for containment of negative affects such as safe place imagery, and age regression to find positive nurturing figures from the past outside the family of origin, such as neighbors, surrogate parents, and positive adult role models.

Projective/evocative techniques can also be used, such as the activation of *inner strength,* a powerful inner resource that is connected to the survival instinct (Frederick & McNeal, 1998; McNeal & Frederick, 1993). If Ego-State Therapy is to be used, the emphasis during Stage 1 should be on finding positive ego states that can help to strengthen the client and provide assistance in achieving mastery of presenting symptoms.

Finally, the use of age progression, or positive orientation to the future, is also introduced to the client. Many clients who experience problems resulting from self-division that are linked to past trauma have extremely negative views of the future, or cannot think about the future at all. It is extremely important to seed the idea that a positive future can be developed. The client's negative views of the future can function as prognostic indicators that extensive strengthening may be needed, or that adjustments may be needed in the therapy alliance or the treatment framework (Phillips & Frederick, 1992). The client's production and use of positive age progressions is viewed as an indicator of more adequate ego strength.

Stage 2

Once a reasonable degree of safety and stabilization is evident in the therapy situation as well as in everyday functioning, the next stage of work can begin. The "A" stage of the SARI model involves the dual tasks of accessing the origins of self-division difficulties while activating inner resources that can reduce dissociation and provide reconnection. In this phase of work, hypnosis is used primarily for the uncovering of dissociated traumatic past experiences as well as creative, healing ones.

It is important to begin this stage with the client's conscious understandings of how past experiences are related to current difficulties and expand on these through journaling, dream explorations, art, and other expressive work. This validates the client's own knowledge base and gives the therapist a number of entry points for inner examination.

Uncovering

The purpose of inner investigations during this stage of treatment is to help the client find his/her own inner subjective truth rather than to prove details of objective truth. Failure to be clear about expectations on the part of both therapist and client can result in false memory problems. Regardless of the methods used, care must be taken to balance uncovering of past events with attention to current functioning and future possibilities.

Here, indirect hypnotic approaches, such as Dolan's (1991) safe remembering technique, can be valuable in keeping the client connected to the present context of therapeutic safety while exploring traumatic experiences in the past. Clients can choose a symbol of autonomy and personal freedom in their present lives, such as car keys, and hold them as tangible or imaginal anchors, linking to feelings of security and protection. Once these anchors are used consistently to elicit desired feeling states through the use of specific word cues, the client can be guided into an eyes-open trance state to review painful events of the past believed related to current difficulties. These light trance states can be deepened through suggestions, provided that the client remains in a state of relative comfort. If destabilization or undue anxiety occurs, the client can be reminded to focus on the identified anchor to safety back in the present time.

More direct hypnotic approaches are also useful with individuals whose divided self difficulties appear to originate from less conscious sources. Many types of age regression techniques can be used, such as ideomotor and ideosensory signaling, imagery that allows the viewing of a videotape of the client's life during a particular time period, or the affect or somatic bridge, which involves bridging from a current symptomatic feeling or body sensation back to the source of this reaction. Before initiating these techniques during a formal trance state, however, it is helpful to reintroduce ego-strengthening experiences instituted during Stage 1, such as the recall of safe place imagery or activation of inner resources, such as confidence and strength. Regardless of the method used, the therapist is also advised to begin with an experience of regression back to a positive experience. Not only is this further strengthening to the client, but it also provides a connection to important positive experiences that the client may have dissociated from awareness along with traumatic ones.

Until the early 1990s, the focus for traumatic uncovering work was on achieving abreaction or discharge of painful affects believed to be somewhat curative. More recent emphasis in the trauma and dissociation literature has shifted to mastery of traumatic material, reeducation, restructuring, and correction, continuity of experience, and ego-integration (van der Hart & Brown, 1992). For this reason, Healing the Divided Self protocols suggest that corrective experiences are provided for past traumatic events as they are retrieved.

For example, if the therapist is using ideomotor signals, the client can be asked to identify and add resources that are available at the present time that were not available at the time of the traumatic event. These resources may involve adult understandings, the presence of the client's adult strength in a scene where she or he was a vulnerable child, the inclusion of other adult or spiritual allies, and even the mechanism of dissociation itself, such as the perceptual possibilities of viewing the scene from far away, from a protected safe place, or through the lens of a special effects camera.

Direct or indirect regression should be followed by orientation back to the present, helping the client to apply information that has been retrieved from the past to current situations, and then progressing on into the future, to provide further integration of dissociated past material and continued seeding of positive future perspectives.

Ego-State Therapy

Any hypnotic technique that can be used with an individual client can be used with an individual ego state. If ego-state therapy is being used to address divided self difficulties, the therapist can uncover the source of client difficulties through ego state exploration. This means that ego states can be activated using formal hypnosis or through more indirect means, such as Helen Watkins's chair technique (Watkins & Watkins, 1997), or the use of sand tray figures or other visual representations (Toothman & Phillips, 1998).

The therapist can initiate communication with ego states either verbally or nonverbally through ideomotor/ideosensory signalling, depending on what is comfortable and possible at this stage. A positive therapeutic alliance is formed and inquiry conducted in terms of information the ego state can provide about inner conflicts that contribute to symptoms.

I worked with a client (Phillips, 1993) who complained that previous therapy had failed to get to the "root" of her problems. She was suffering from hypnagogic sleep disturbance, affective numbing, depression, panic and anxiety attacks, and difficulties with concentration. Symptoms of intermittent leg pain were used to provide a somatic bridge back to a dissociated experience of sexual abuse by her father. A child ego state was activated who provided extensive information about the nature of this trauma as well as important information about inner conflicts with two adolescent ego states, which contributed to her symptoms and prevented her from resolving related life issues. Without identifying and working with this ego state, it is likely that our work might have continued the trend of not getting to the base of her clinical difficulties.

Stage 3

The third stage of the SARI model involves the reassociation of dissociated experiences and parts of the self and the resolution of posttraumatic and dissociative symptoms. The first task within this phase of work is helping the client in a conscious waking state to reconnect with dissociated material elicited during hypnosis and to organize it into a cohesive form. Therapist and client must explore, further process, and work through related feelings, associations, and somatosensory responses that may surface. Cognitive restructuring is also important during this stage because basic beliefs related to safety and trust may have been shattered or disrupted. It is essential that this task be given equal emphasis to uncovering work. If adequate attention is not given to this reworking, full resolution may not be possible.

Developmental Repair

During the reprocessing of past dissociated experiences, unresolved developmental issues are likely to emerge. Often such issues, such as self-soothing, affect regulation, boundary formation and stabilization, and object permanence and constancy, if left unaddressed, can continue to fuel self-division.

Hypnosis is useful in facilitating the inner completion of maturational steps. For example, Milton Erickson's famous case of the February Man (Erickson & Rossi, 1989) illustrates an indirect metaphorical method of renurturing. Working with a young woman who was conflicted about getting pregnant for fear that her lack of a mother during formative years might compromise her own ability to provide good mothering, Erickson led her through a series of renurturing experiences in a deep trance state. Posing as a good friend of her father who visited every February, Erickson was able to provide many corrective experiences that occurred on multiple levels. Other more direct types of hypnotic renurturing approaches involve using the adult self to provide missing reparenting experiences for the child self, or making use of ideal nurturing figures.

Ego-State Therapy can be particularly useful in addressing developmental deficits. More mature ego states can be asked to help younger ones deal with specific issues. For example, one young ego state who has difficulty with transitions related to separations might be helped by an older adolescent state to engage in appropriate positive activities that could generate feelings that can be used for successful self-soothing. When clients have inner systems where there are no ego states available for nurturing, hypnosis can be used to internalize appropriate models from present or past experience.

Again, as with any other stage, clients may destabilize as a result of internal work during therapy sessions or due to triggers in the external environment. Under these circumstances, the therapist must be prepared to revisit Stage 1 tasks of rebuilding or deepening a sense of safety and stability before continuing with the working through of painful material and the repair of related developmental problems.

Stage 4

In the final stage of work, the "I" stage, the client is helped to integrate the work of previous stages as well as to achieve more integrated personality functioning, which can lead to expanded identity. Because most clients are feeling significantly better at this stage, many want to terminate prematurely. It is important that the therapist help them understand the rich possibilities that may unfold during this phase of completion.

Integration of therapy experiences can often be accomplished through homework directives designed to help clients use the tools they have developed, through analysis of integrative dreams that frequently occur, and through explorations of trance material that emphasize gains and learnings the client has made over time.

At this stage, frequent use of more structured hypnotic age progressions can help the client make ongoing contact with unconscious resources for future development. Related techniques useful here are strategies asking clients to write themselves letters from the future or the use of rituals to prepare for a change in identity.

Ego-state therapy provides a particularly helpful model for personality integration. As ego states discover increasing communication and cooperation through the work in the previous stages of therapy, dissociative barriers defuse or collapse so that inner boundaries are more flexible as clients move through predictable stages of integration (Phillips & Frederick, 1995). Ego states share information freely, have empathy for diverse needs and interests, and work together for the common good of the whole personality. When co-consciousness has become a continuing process, some ego states spontaneously merge with each other while others adopt functions that are more responsive to changing needs and demands.

More integrated personality functioning leads to the development of a generative self, which is related to the seventh step of Erik Erikson's developmental ladder (Erikson, 1980) and involves resolving his stage of generativity versus stagnation. Hypnosis is one of the most effective tools for enhancing the development of self-identity that is not only unique but can generate whatever is needed for continued integration and growth. The issue of spirituality can now be explored, since many of the inner barriers that tend to block spiritual growth have been removed or reduced. Here, the therapist can help the client construct contemporary views of spirituality that are not based on projections or fears from the past.

APPLICATIONS

Healing the Divided Self's SARI model and its incorporated approaches have been used with a wide range of clinical problems ranging from simple presenting symptoms such as airplane or bridge phobias and behavioral habit issues to more complex symptoms of major depression, eating disorders, addictions, psychophysiological symptoms, generalized anxiety, and personality disorders. SARI is also highly effective with Posttraumatic Stress Disorder and the dissociative disorders including Dissociative Identity Disorder (MPD). SARI is an integrative model, because it integrates powerful aspects of Ericksonian and indirect approaches to hypnosis with classical hypnoanalysis; formal, structured strategies; and Ego-State Therapy.

Research has found very few situations where SARI is contraindicated, simply because it is such a flexible protocol. When formal hypnosis is inadvisable, as indicated in the assessment phase of Stage 1, more indirect techniques can be used to maintain greater stability as well as preparing for the use of more formal techniques,

if appropriate, later on. Many techniques can also be incorporated easily from other therapeutic orientations, such as Cognitive-Behavioral Therapy, family systems, Eye Movement Desensitization and Reprocessing (EMDR), and psychodynamic therapies.

One common question that arises involves the use of Ego-State Therapy. The appropriate use of this method is invaluable in identifying and treating the source of complex problems related to self-division. Almost all of the time, clients report an immediate sense of greater wholeness and a reduction in inner fragmentation. Occasionally, however, some clients seem to experience an increase in fragmentation. When this is the case, there is usually an underlying developmental or transference issue that must be addressed before Ego-State Therapy can continue effectively (Phillips, 1997). Under these circumstances, it is important to stop the use of Ego-State Therapy involving formal hypnosis until the client can be restabilized and the obstacles identified and worked through. Other clients who greatly fear exploring inner fragmentation or who resist the loss of control may not respond well to this approach, although indirect ego-state techniques may be helpful.

Because Ego-State Therapy can rapidly activate complex intrapsychic processes, it is recommended that this method be used by therapists already experienced in other therapy procedures, including psychodynamic approaches and work with unconscious processes. Receiving specialized training in Ego-State Therapy and in direct and indirect hypnotic methods and their uses is also important for any therapist who wishes to apply the SARI model to clinical practice.

CASE EXAMPLE

Sylvia, a children's book editor in her mid-40s, was referred by a colleague for hypnosis with daily tension headaches, which appeared to be of the muscle contraction type (Phillips, 1998; 2000). She described the headache pain as a narrow band tightening along her forehead behind and above her eyes. Variations included sharp, intermittent shooting pain in her temple area.

She had temporarily been helped by biofeedback some years before, and had had marginal success with techniques obtained from participation at two local pain clinics. Her current condition was relieved only by prescribed medications, which she rotated on a daily basis, and included Cafergot, Fiorinol, and Emetrex. Sylvia sought hypnotic treatment to reduce her headaches so that she could discontinue medication, to which she felt addicted, and to help her manage the pressure of book deadlines, which seemed to trigger the headaches.

Relevant history included the fact that a significant trauma occurred at the age of seven when Sylvia had a severe concussion as a result of being struck by a truck suddenly backing into her as she was riding her bicycle. She recalled being unconscious for longer than 24 hours and convalesced at home for several months. When she returned to school, Sylvia remembered being far behind her class. Her teacher was unsympathetic with her anxiety and frustration, as were her parents, who threatened to send her to a psychiatrist if she didn't "straighten up." Sylvia remarked that after this experience, her self-confidence was shattered and that she had continued to have confidence issues throughout her school years.

After explaining the SARI model and its uses of hypnosis to achieve safety and stability during the first stage of work, I conducted an informal assessment of her responsiveness (Phillips & Frederick, 1995). We began working with basic hypnotic inductions to activate feelings of safety, calm, and relaxation. During initial hypnotic experiences, Sylvia reported extreme sensitivity to street noises, light, and body position. We corrected distractions caused by the latter two factors, but she continued to complain of noise distractions, despite various kinds of suggestions designed to increase a positive mental focus. Because Sylvia seemed to become increasingly anxious and frustrated by her difficulties concentrating, I decided to use a structured approach that might help her develop a sense of mastery that could later be generalized to the management of her headache symptoms.

We established ideomotor signals and used them to achieve gradual elimination of noise sensitivity by having Sylvia calibrate her sensitivity on a 1–10 subjective scale and then directing her fingers to signal as her unconscious mind was willing to reduce her sensitivity one level at a time all the way down to zero. After three sessions using this approach, Sylvia's sensitivity to noise completely disappeared; no recurrence was reported throughout the subsequent duration of treatment.

Attempts to apply this approach to her headache pain, however, brought mixed results. Although she could use ideomotor signals to reduce pain successfully in the office, she was not able to sustain these results with self-hypnosis practice on her own. Sylvia became noticeably anxious and expressed strong doubts that she would be able to find a solution that would work consistently for her headaches. Reminding her about our success with the noise sensitivity helped to provide reassurance and an anchor to experiences of successful mastery.

I suggested that we prepare for Stage 2 work, which would involve conducting a more thorough investigation of underlying psychological factors, including the possible relationship of the early head trauma to her current headache condition. Since Sylvia reported that her headaches were accompanied by "internal chatter" that was distracting to her, and described difficulties in meeting editorial deadlines as if she was being pulled in different directions by different parts of herself, I decided to present Ego-Stage Therapy as a method that might help us discover more about the source of the headaches and help to resolve related inner conflicts.

After several more sessions of hypnotic ego-strengthening with the whole personality, we began use of the inner strength technique (McNeal & Frederick, 1993) to introduce her to a resource state that could help with headache pain. Sylvia soon acknowledged that she felt more confident and that she was using pain medication only four to five times a week rather than daily. We then decided to attempt ideomotor activation of an ego state who might be associated with current headache pain.

We first identified the image of a seven-year-old ego state who was lying on the sofa in the living room waiting for her parents to come home from work in a distressed state of fear and loneliness. Further exploration revealed that this ego state was recovering from a head injury that occurred a few months earlier when she was riding her brother's bicycle, which was too big for her and hard to control. A large truck backed into her as she crossed a driveway and she hit the concrete on her head. The seven-year-old ego state told us that she was just lying still and waiting because the doctor told her not to move around, that it was too dangerous.

With additional questioning, we determined that this state of inertia was triggered currently in Sylvia's work-life when a deadline was approaching. To the seven-year-old state, it felt that she was being hit out of nowhere by something much bigger than she was and that the only way to survive was to lie very still. When she was given information that she was now safely past the time of danger and could move about freely, the seven-year-old state tested out this new reality by first going up and down the stairs and then going outside to play in fantasy for increasingly longer periods of comfort and enjoyment.

After several sessions designed to integrate these changes, Sylvia reported a further decrease in headaches. Several weeks later, however, increased stress related to several deadlines seemed to trigger a different type of headache, which she described as a "plate" of pain running through her left eye into her right temple. Ideomotor exploration revealed that the seven-year-old ego state was back at school and feeling paralyzed. This state told us that she was giving adult Sylvia the headaches because if she kept trying to write, she would be found out as incompetent. With more questioning, the ego state revealed that this was her mechanism for dealing with her own fears of incompetency as she fell further and further behind her classmates.

Following the protocol for Stage 3, we decided to provide several important corrective experiences for this ego state. First, we connected her with an adult ego state who was able to provide emotional support and help with schoolwork, especially tasks that involved writing. An important turning point occurred when "adult Sylvia" entered the writing class, sat next to the child state, and encouraged her to approach the lessons one step at a time. Inner strength was also used to teach her that inner confidence and mastery feelings could become more powerful than the fear and inadequacy that had plagued her throughout her school years.

Other ego states were also identified as contributing to various types of recurring headaches. These included a subpersonality named Fear, who appeared to be triggered by unpredictability and linked back to head trauma survival issues; Anger, an introject of Sylvia's father's voice, who doubted her competency and warned that she would be exposed as a phony; and Anxiety, who was connected with another recurring childhood trauma experience that occurred when Sylvia's brother terrified her by putting his hand over her nose and mouth and holding her head under water during family vacations at a nearby lake.

Appropriate corrective experiences were provided for these states, and each of them was given a more helpful way to channel ego energy. For example, Anger was employed to help Sylvia set limits with an administrator of a company that was one of her main clients for writing assignments; Anxiety was used to warn Sylvia that she was feeling overwhelmed by pressures and needed to take time out to engage in self-hypnosis or physical exercise; Fear became an advocate for constancy in adhering to regular times for writing each morning without distractions.

Over a six-month period, Sylvia reported a gradual decrease in headaches. We developed a medication plan that continued to promote self-constancy and trust. If her headache discomfort remained at a four or lower on her subjective pain scale, Sylvia took two Bufferin and ½ an Excedrin every four hours as needed for management. If her headache increased to between four and six on her scale, she took a Fioricet. We agreed that there should be no circumstances now where she needed to take a shot of Emetrex. Sylvia's confidence increased as she was able to keep this plan consistently. She began to have more weeks that were headache free. Recurrence of symptoms was viewed as an opportunity to achieve further resolution of inner dynamics related to early trauma and internalized dysfunction parental messages. The use of self-hypnosis, which was difficult for her earlier in our work because of inner fragmentation and conflict, became effective in managing occasional headache discomfort and in maintaining a positive focus on writing tasks.

As Sylvia began to approach the fourth stage of integration, she decided to leave her job with the publisher and begin a freelance editing business. Although a sign of her increased strength, this change triggered old inner insecurities and the headaches resumed. I reminded Sylvia that we would need to revisit the tasks of safety and provide further strengthening to stabilize her in her new situation. As she began to emerge from a downward spiral of anxiety, we activated an ego state named True Self, who provided balanced perspectives and was able to engineer plans for more productive and comfortable daily functioning. Over time, Sylvia was able to reduce her pain medication again. She formed associational imaginal anchors to times of confidence and mastery, such as recent speeches she had given on behalf of a struggling nonprofit organization. These images, plus the results of several EMDR reprocessing sessions, reminded her of times during therapy when her ego states had learned to work together as a cooperative team. She then linked these good feelings to future views of the states helping her in freelance writing just as they had with her editing job and speechwriting.

Six months after terminating therapy, Sylvia is continuing to integrate these changes into her new career and into other areas of expanded identity. The headaches rarely occur. When they do, she is able to use them as further opportunities for self-examination and growth. She is also becoming a more spiritual person, finding time to meditate and using more images of her peak experiences in nature to provide deeper healing and integrative experiences.

SUMMARY

The problems of self-division pose formidable challenges to the clinician. Often, they prove unresponsive to traditional methods of therapy and can lead to entrenched dysfunctional patterns of behavior, cognition, affect, and sensory experience.

The SARI model presented here is a comprehensive, carefully paced method of healing the divided self. An organizing principle is the use of sequential stages and corresponding methods which, from the beginning of therapy, emphasize the importance of strengthening. As clients are helped to gain a positive sense of inner control and mastery, they begin to initiate positive changes on their own. Focusing more on strengths than pathology and on generative solutions more than causality is integral to the operation of this model.

When working with problems of self-division, it is essential to address internal fragmentation. Since every client is a whole that is composed of many units or states of identity, the issue of whether to address interventions to the whole personality or to component parts can be answered only by discovering which approach is most beneficial to the client and most likely to facilitate a cohesive self. Fortunately, if direct ego-state methods are not effective, indirect ego-state approaches can provide avenues into the inner self that widen the therapeutic window of possibilities for many clients who otherwise might not be able to make use of treatment. Underlying developmental issues that maintain self-division can also be addressed in this manner.

In this age of increasing violence, abuses of power, and boundary confusion that continue to contribute to self-fragmentation, Healing the Divided Self stands as a model that can provide transformational resolution. As new technologies emerge and are proven in their effectiveness, they can easily be integrated into this flexible protocol designed to promote multilevel change that leads ultimately to wholeness.

REFERENCES

American Psychiatric Association. (1994). *Diagnostic and statistical manual of mental disorders* (4th ed.). Washington, DC: Author.

Dickey, T., Nungary, V., & Frederick, C. (1998). You must be present to win: Attentional training for the management of serious ego-state problems. Paper presented at the annual meeting of the American Society of Clinical Hypnosis, Fort Worth, TX.

Dolan, Y. (1991). *Resolving sexual abuse.* New York: Norton.

Ellenberger, H. (1970). *The discovery of the unconscious.* New York: Basic Books.

Erickson, M. (1959). Further clinical techniques of hypnosis: Utilization techniques. *Journal of the American Society of Clinical Hypnosis, 2,* 3–21.

Erickson, M., & Kubie, L. (1939). The permanent relief of an obsessional phobia by means of communications with an unsuspected dual personality. *Psychoanalytic Quarterly, 8,* 471–509.

Erickson, M., & Rossi, E. (1989). *The February man: Evolving consciousness and identity in hypnotherapy.* New York: Brunner/Mazel.

Erikson, E. (1980). *Identity and the life cycle.* New York: Norton.

Federn, P. (1952). *Ego psychology and the psychoses.* New York: Basic Books.

Frederick, C., & McNeal, S. (1998). *Inner strengths: Contemporary psychotherapy and hypnosis for ego-strengthening.* Mahwah, NJ: Lawrence Erlbaum.

Grove, M. (1995). Ego-state therapy with small children. In G. Burrows & R. Stanley (Eds.), *Contemporary international hypnosis* (pp. 141–148). Chichester, West Sussex, England: Wiley.

Hammond, D.C. (1990). *Handbook of hypnotic suggestions and metaphors.* New York: Norton.

Hartman, W. (1995). Ego-state therapy with sexually traumatized children. In G. Burrows & R. Stanley (Eds.), *Contemporary international hypnosis* (pp. 149–158). West Sussex, England: Wiley.

Hilgard, E. (1977). *Divided consciousness: Multiple controls in human thought and action.* New York: Wiley.

Janet, P. (1907). *The major symptoms of hysteria.* New York: Macmillan.

Kluft, R. P. (1993). The initial stages of psychotherapy in the treatment of multiple personality disorder patients. *Dissociation, 6(2/3),* 145–161.

McNeal, S., & Frederick, C. (1993). Inner strength and other techniques for ego-strengthening. *American Journal of Clinical Hypnosis, 35,* 170–178.

McNeal, S., & Frederick, C. (1994). Internal self-soothing: Other implications of ego-strengthening with ego states. Paper presented at the annual meeting of the American Society of Clinical Hypnosis, Philadelphia, PA.

McNeal, S., & Frederick, C. (1995). Good fences make good neighbors: Boundary formation in ego states as precursors to integration. Paper presented at the annual meeting of the American Society of Clinical Hypnosis, San Diego, CA.

McNeal, S., & Frederick, C. (1996). Inner love: Projective/evocative ego-strengthening of ego states with inner resources of unconditional love. Paper presented at the annual meeting of the American Society of Clinical Hypnosis, Orlando, FL.

McNeal, S., & Frederick, C. (1997). New vintages in old vessels: Activating and utilizing transitional phenomena with ego states. Paper presented at the 14th International Congress of Hypnosis, San Diego, CA.

Morton, P., & Frederick, C. (1997a). Intrapsychic transitional space: A resource for integration in hypnotherapy. *Hypnos, 24,* 32–41.

Morton, P., & Frederick, C. (1997b). Re-alerting in the middle of a tightrope: Promoting conscious/unconscious complementarity during the integration process in ego state therapy. Paper presented at the 14th International Congress of Hypnosis, San Diego, CA.

Phillips, M. (1993). The use of ego-state therapy in the treatment of post-traumatic stress disorder. *American Journal of Clinical Hypnosis, 35(4),* 241–249.

Phillips, M. (1996). The importance of role integrity for therapists working with traumatic memory issues. Paper presented at the 13th international fall conference of the International Society for the Study of Dissociation, San Francisco, CA.

Phillips, M. (1997). Spinning straw into gold: Utilization of transferential resources to strengthen the hypnotic relationship. *American Journal of Clinical Hypnosis, 40(2),* 118–129.

Phillips, M. (1998). Hypnoanalytic interventions with atypical headache and seizure disorder patients. Paper presented at the annual meeting of the American Society of Clinical Hypnosis, Fort Worth, TX.

Phillips, M. (2000). *Finding the energy to heal: How EMDR, hypnosis, TFT, imagery, and body-focused therapy can help restore mind-body health.* New York: Norton.

Phillips, M., & Frederick, C. (1992). The use of hypnotic age progressions as prognostic, ego-strengthening, and integrating techniques. *American Journal of Clinical Hypnosis, 35,* 90–108.

Phillips, M., & Frederick, C. (1995). *Healing the divided self: Clinical and Ericksonian hypnotherapy for post-traumatic and dissociative conditions.* New York: Norton.

Phillips, M., & Smith, A. (1996). Transitional states of consciousness and the hypnotherapeutic relationship. Paper presented at the annual meeting of the American Society of Clinical Hypnosis, Orlando, FL.

Spiegel, D. (1993). Dissociation and trauma. In D. Spiegel (Ed.), *Dissociative disorders: A clinical review* (pp. 117–131). Lutherville, MD: Sidran.

Toothman, D., & Phillips, M. (1998). Coming together: Working with couples from an ego-state therapy perspective. *American Journal of Clinical Hypnosis, 42*(2), 174–189.

van der Hart, O., & Brown, P. (1992). Abreaction re-evaluated. *Dissociation, 5*(3), 127–140.

Watkins, H. (1993). Ego-state therapy: An overview. *American Journal of Clinical Hypnosis, 35,* 232–240.

Watkins, J., & Watkins, H. (1979). The theory and practice of ego-state therapy. In H. Grayson (Ed.), *Short-term approaches to psychotherapy* (pp. 176–220). New York: Wiley.

Watkins, J., & Watkins, H. (1997). *Ego states: Theory and practice.* New York: Norton.

Chapter 27

HOLISTIC EDUCATION

WILL SCHUTZ

In my experience, psychotherapists as a group differ from most other people in that they are relatively free. They have, for the most part, achieved the aim of being themselves. And those in this field who have the personal qualities needed to establish new systems of psychotherapy, a pure inner vision of what life should be, tend to test the limits of this freedom and generate a world of their own. Then they attempt to give this message to the world as their most precious gift.

I know a number of the chapter authors in this book, and what I have just said is generally true of them: They are in their own private worlds, more or less. And at the head of the list in terms of this vision is Will Schutz, who, as the reader will soon discover, differs from almost everyone else in practically every dimension in his generation of a new world of logic and beauty as seen by his Holistic Education. It was my pleasure to dedicate a book I coedited, Great Cases in Psychotherapy, *to him.*

Schutz is in the multimodal mode, and he attempts, to develop the total individual in all possible views. Schutz emphasizes personal responsibility and the importance of choices as much as anyone does. He is an optimist, believing in the strength and goodness of people, that we have the power and capacity for the good and joyful life. The reader is in for a powerful experience in meeting Will Schutz, a truly seminal thinker who pushes back all frontiers.

Holistic Education is a process occurring between two or more people in which one person, the educator = therapist/teacher/parent/administrator/physician, creates conditions within which the other person or persons, the learner = client/student/child/employee/patient, may choose to learn. The educator's skill is expressed through selection of which conditions to create. The educator is useful to the degree to which the learner chooses to learn. The educator does not educate, does not teach, does not heal anyone. He or she merely creates conditions by talking, by doing, and by being; that is all. Whether learning takes place is determined by the learner.

Holistic refers to the assumption that growth is a property of all aspects of a person—physical, social, emotional, intellectual, aesthetic, and spiritual.

For maximum growth of the individual holism asserts that each of these aspects or properties of the individual must be developed to its fullest, and that all relations among the properties be harmonized. When this is accomplished, the person is an integrated whole, literally, a person of *integrity.*

HISTORY

Holistic Education developed from the encounter group movement, which, in turn was influenced by Group psychotherapy T-groups, group dynamics, psychodrama, gestalt therapy, body methods, and theater games (Schutz, 1973). The encounter format allows new methods and new concepts to be incorporated into the small-group format, thus providing a unique arena for working directly on individual and interpersonal issues simultaneously.

The most recent developments to be assimilated into the encounter format are new body methods, mental imagery techniques, and the concepts of choice and limitlessness. These approaches have helped the encounter group to evolve into Holistic Education (Schutz, 1979).

As holistic education theory developed, it became clear that the therapeutic technique derived from it must (1) work on all aspects of the person, (2) focus on truth, and (3) emphasize individual responsibility. Individual responsibility is the key concept that led to the extension of the therapeutic method and to the realization that therapy is simply one form of education.

In the holistic education process the person is dealt with at all levels—physical, aesthetic (sensational), intellectual, spiritual, social, and emotional. Activities are designed to exercise and explore these aspects and their integration. The way Holistic Education works is best demonstrated by the first major application of the technique, the graduate program in Holistic Studies at Antioch University West in San Francisco.

CURRENT STATUS

In January 1979, the first application of Holistic Education was inaugurated at Antioch University West in San Francisco (Schutz, 1979, May). A group of 40 students began a 12-week program in Holistic Education. Their schedule reflects the holistic theory:

1. 9:00–10:00   Running (physical activity)
2. 10:00–11:00   Feldenkrais Exercise (aesthetic activity)
3. 11:00–12:00   Meditation (spiritual activity)
4. 12:00–1:30   Lunch
5. 1:30–3:30   Lecture (intellectual activity)
6. 3:30–5:30   Encounter Group (social, emotional activity)

Each activity and the interactions among the activities were approached from the standpoint of personal awareness. Here are some examples of the interactions that occurred in the program.

Running.   Most people found that running sharpened their awareness and freed them for other activities. In the second week of a subsequent academic quarter, students fasted (water only) for five to nine days while participating in the program. This, too, helped them to be in touch with their bodies and to grow more confident that their bodies were accurate indicators of self-harmony.

Feldenkrais Exercises.   In these exercises, many people learned how their body movements reflected their total beings. Some people could not do the movements gracefully because they held on to the floor for support too long. They were people who needed security. Others did the movements properly and then could not stop. They were people who went a little too far in their life activities.

Meditation.   This practice helped many people to shut down their verbalizing and to "hear" other activities of their organism. The defensive use of intellect and the subsequent blocking of being in tune with the self through talking and other activities thus became evi-

dent. Learning to stay in touch with one's inner self illuminated the difference between public behavior and private feelings, between the behaviors people do for effect and the behaviors people really feel.

Lunch.   The lunch hour was an important part of the program. It gave time for assimilation, both of food and of the emotional and intellectual experiences that had occurred earlier in the day. It also provided time for people to be together in smaller, self-selected groups to process their personal material.

Lecture.   The effect of emotions on intellect was clarified by the insights, developed during the encounter group (next stage), into the ways in which people listened to the lectures. Those who were anxious about looking bad or believed they had bad memories or felt they could not assimilate scientific material or did not want to hear from an expert an idea that contradicted their own ideas, learned about their blocks to learning.

Encounter Group.   This group was the central experience. It provided a "home room" for the myriad experiences the students were having. It was the place where each student explored his or her own being and where each had an opportunity to reflect on and to integrate all activities.

The total program led to a greatly increased experience of the total oneness, the integrity of the organism, to the realization of how truly unified we are and of how essential it is that we view ourselves as a whole if we are to have any opportunity to understand ourselves fully.

THEORY

Assumptions

Holism.   For maximum growth of an individual, all aspects—physical, intellectual, emotional, aesthetic, social, and spiritual—must be developed to their fullest, and all relationships among these aspects must be harmonized into an integrated whole person.

Limitlessness.   Each person is seen as limitless. The only limits people have are limits of belief. If they believe that they are unlimited, then they may spend their energy learning how to reach their own potential (if they choose to do so).

Problems.   Psychological problems result from lies and from incomplete experiences. Holistic Education is aimed at creating conditions within which learners will complete incomplete experiences, become aware of the lies they have told themselves, and choose to know their truth. A common lie is that other people are to blame for the events of one's life.

Process

Education.   Therapy is accomplished through the same educational process as teaching, parenting, healing, curing, and managing. In all these cases, the educator creates conditions—psychological, economic, physical, and political. The learner chooses to respond to those conditions in a certain way—to perceive them, to ignore them, to fight them, to escape them, to subvert them, and so forth. Growth occurs when the learner uses these conditions to grow.

Change.   A therapist does not heal or cure a client. Therapists simply create an environment through talk, nonverbal communication, atmosphere, and their own being. The client decides how to perceive the situation and how to make use of it to change. Clients may perceive therapists as domineering, helpful, evaluative, primitive, perverted, supportive, threatening, et cetera. Clients may choose to hear words accurately, understand them, and use them productively, or may choose to distort them, not understand them, and use them destructively.

Skill.   Therapists' skill lies in their ability to create conditions that clients choose to use productively. Therapists are "responsible" for creating these conditions. Clients are "responsible" for what they do with these conditions.

Principles

Responsibility.   The holistic educator makes clear to clients, from the start of the relationship, the division of responsibility—namely, that clients are responsible for whatever happens to them in the therapy; that they have chosen the therapist freely; that they may leave whenever they wish; that they may follow or not the suggestions of the therapist; that they may arrive late, leave early, go crazy, become ill, get injured, profit enormously, be bored, or whatever they wish. Holistic educators are responsible for whatever they themselves do and whatever they are. They may make agreements with the learner, lay down conditions, terminate the relationship, or do whatever they wish. The holistic educator makes this clear from the outset and throughout the relationship acts in a manner consistent with this concept.

Truth.   The holistic educator is committed to truth, that is, self-awareness and honesty, and agrees to be totally honest throughout the relationship and committed

to maximizing self-awareness. The holistic educator asks the learner to commit to honesty to the utmost degree. This is the fundamental basis of the "contract" in Holistic Education.

Technique

Initiative.   The holistic educator takes little initiative in the conduct of a therapy session, especially in the early meetings. After the opening statement regarding responsibility, participation is invited by saying that if anyone in the group wants anything to happen, it is up to him or her to make it happen. The holistic educator then actualizes that statement by waiting for group members to initiate. The beginning activities of the holistic educator are aimed at helping to expose "games," bringing defenses to awareness, and focusing on the learners' willingness and ability to tell the truth and to be aware. After a learner has initiated, the holistic educator typically takes a more active role.

Methods.   In Holistic Education, all modalities are worked on and any techniques may be used, as appropriate. The body, intellect, feelings, sensations, and spiritual elements are viewed simultaneously and dealt with as an integrated whole. Techniques such as Rolfing, imagery, Feldenkrais, acupuncture, bioenergetics, psychodrama, running, free association, aikido, tai chi, meditation, or any other methods are available depending on which seem most beneficial at the time.

Training.   Each person may profit from different experiences at different points in his or her evolution; therefore, the most successful holistic educator has learned a large repertoire of techniques and has accumulated the experience to know the proper time to use each method.

METHODOLOGY

In Holistic Education all methods are potentially valuable. The question is not "Which methods are best?" but rather "Which methods work best for which people at which point in their evolution?"

From this perspective, virtually all therapies are of value to some people. Rather than attempting to show that other methods are not of value—a risky enterprise considering the sorry state of research on the evaluation of traditional therapy—it is more useful to explore the circumstances under which each technique is valuable.

The methods used in the Antioch experiment with Holistic Education are, of course, not the only ones available. The following are a few methods that are appropriate.

Physical Activity. Running, cycling, swimming, handball, racquetball, tennis, skiing, or walking might be included in the program. These activities should all be done with awareness and with a focus on sport as metaphor for the way a person is in life.

Aesthetic (Sensational) Activity. These methods might include Feldenkrais, Rolfing, Alexander, hatha yoga, Trager Mentastics, tai chi, and aikido. These methods also must be done with awareness and with an emphasis on total body harmony and integration.

Spiritual Exercise. Meditation, prayer, chanting, and Arica spiritual exercises can be included. Any of the various types of these exercises is acceptable; for example, of the many types of meditation—sitting, walking, chaotic, kundalini, or transcendental—any may be employed.

Intellectual Activity. Lectures, discussions, reading, and academic coursework are used. Any intellectual activity of personal relevance experienced with an awareness of the emotional blocks to learning is beneficial.

Social Activity. Encounter, psychodrama, Synanon, and so on, can be employed. Several other useful social activities, such as Dale Carnegie training, Toastmasters, Alcoholics Anonymous, and Recovery, are generally more immediate and are usefully continued into deeper realms. They are often useful as an introduction to social relationships based on truth.

Emotional Exercise. Methods including encounter, gestalt, psychodrama, est, bioenergetics, imagery, Fischer-Hoffman, rebirthing, and psychoanalysis might be employed.

This is obviously not an exhaustive list. A recent compendium (Matson, 1977) cites and describes dozens of available methods.

APPLICATIONS

The tenets of Holistic Education form a social philosophy that directs action in fields beyond psychotherapy. This philosophy is directly applicable to politics, sports, birthing, law, medicine, education, and many other areas of living. This is true because Holistic Education is based on principles of interaction between people. With appropriate adaptation, the principles apply wherever people interact.

Principles of Application

The following is the translation of the tenets of Holistic Education, especially limitlessness, truth, choice, and holism, into a basis for application to society.

Self-Determination. The aim of any social institution is the creation of social conditions within which individuals find it easiest to determine their own lives. These conditions include removing blocks to and encouraging development of self-determination.

Freedom. Permit any action done by an individual that does not impinge on another individual.

Agreement. Allow any action between two or more people, performed with awareness by both, that does not impinge upon others.

Truth. By eliminating dishonesty, create conditions that make awareness easier.

Simplicity. Provide profoundly simple solutions to problems that individuals choose to have dealt with by institutions (e.g., traffic, welfare).

Choice. Create conditions within which individuals choose to find it easier to realize that they choose their own lives.

Options. Create conditions within which people choose to find it easy to be aware of options.

Self-Responsibility. Reward self-responsibility.

Awareness. Reward awareness.

Transition. Provide for a minimum delay in changing social practices to allow the unaware person to become aware and to make a conscious choice.

Obviously, these principles are to be progressively clarified, defined, and measured much more extensively during the course of Holistic Education (see Schutz, 1979 for a start), but even in outline form they provide an adequate basis for many social applications.

The following are some applications of these principles to social phenomena.

Medicine

In the holistic education approach to medicine, the patient is acknowledged as the sole source of his or her own healing and as the one who has chosen to be ill. (Choosing to be ill is neither an accusation nor an assignment of blame. It is simply a statement of what happened.) Doctors are regarded as teachers who create conditions under which patients choose to heal themselves.

Holistic Education assumes that all illnesses result from out-of-awareness conflicts and are an expression of the total organism, not the expression of just a part.

Usual explanations of illness are incomplete, such as "he picked up a bug," "he sat in a draft," "it's something she ate." The patient is seen as the active agent in acquiring the illness or, at least, in choosing not to prevent it.

One of the most dramatic examples of choosing one's illness occurred in the case of Karen Quinlan, the young woman who remained curled up in a comatose, vegetative state for years after being taken off life-support equipment following a highly publicized court battle between doctors and her parents.

Her mother reported the "irony" of a poem she found that Karen had written just prior to her illness.

> The constant struggle with submission is tiring.
> The so-called strength I've gained is just another heavy load.
> I wish to curl myself into a fetal rose and rest in the eternal womb a while.

Preferred treatment methods in Holistic Education are those that enhance the organism's own capacities for healing (Glasser, 1976). These methods include fasting (so that the body can detoxify itself), exposure to fresh air and sunshine, feldenkrais exercises, imagery, and a deep understanding of the process of choosing an illness and the self-rewards that accrue from making that choice.

Standard medical practice is recognized as valuable in many instances. Medical research is often useful in discovering the mechanisms, though not the causes, through which illness occurs. Physical diagnosis is helpful for promoting self-awareness. Emergency treatments are still essential, since most people have not mastered the ability to become aware of or to control their own body functions; however, more people are becoming aware of these body functions, and Holistic Education holds that their control is well within human capacities.

Law

The law is frequently supportive of the lack of self-responsibility:

—Dan White escaped serious punishment for killing two men, including the mayor of San Francisco, partly because of the "Twinkies defense"—he ate a great deal of sugar and sugar leads to violence.
—A man ignites his bed falling asleep with a lit cigarette and sues the tobacco company.
—Bartenders are often held responsible when their customers later get into accidents through drunken driving.

These are instances of almost total disregard of the principle of self-responsibility. They illustrate the notion that the law is often so supportive of our being our brothers' keeper that it neglects to require that we be our own keeper.

The holistic education approach to this issue is exemplified by an experiment in two large cities made by a law agency (Graecen, 1972). In this test first felonies, such as burglaries, were punished through direct interaction between burglar and victim in the presence of a facilitator. This trio was charged by the court to discuss the crime and to agree on a proper punishment. If they agreed, the court would accept it.

The results were astonishing. Agreement was reached in 96 percent of the cases. Court costs were reduced 80 percent. And the solutions reached were extremely imaginative. One man, for example, who stole a TV set from an aged woman agreed to mow her lawn and to drive her to the hospital every week for a year, certainly a much more useful solution than incarceration for some period.

Licensing

Holistic education principles indicate that the current approach to licensing psychologists is on the wrong track. It is now widely acknowledged that licensing psychologists does not protect the public; nor does it guarantee excellence (Hogan, 1979). Licensing procedures are often politicized to maintain the status quo.

The government is not in a good position to decide on technical competence. It *is* in a good position to make certain that people tell the truth. The holistic education approach to licensing would expect truth from therapists and self-responsibility from clients. This may be accomplished through requiring therapists to post publicly, and to make available to prospective clients, full disclosure of all their qualifications—education, experience, and so forth. It is then the responsibility of the client to select a therapist. The government's role is to assure that the therapists' statements are true and to punish lying.

Health Insurance

The liberal strides toward a national health insurance that would cover everyone in case of illness are well-meaning but not consistent with holistic education principles. Health insurance rewards the sick at the expense of the fit. If we both pay into the plan and I am sickly and you are healthy, then you pay for me.

A holistic education health plan would reward those who take responsibility for their own health and would encourage everyone to take care of his or her own health (Schutz, 1979, August 1). This may be accomplished through government-sponsored fitness centers where everyone is tested and given a regimen to follow—exercise, diet, stress reduction—to keep healthy. In a year, everyone would be retested and given a number indicating the percentage of their optimal health they have achieved, based on their original condition.

People as healthy as they could be, probably people who followed the regimen, would be given a score of 100. Those who totally neglect themselves would be given a minimum score of 25. *The number received is equal to the percentage of sickness care covered by the insurance.* If you take good care of yourself, your sickness care is fully paid for. If you do not take good care of yourself, you pay a high percentage of your sickness care if you become ill.

This plan involves no coercion, no special favors. It simply rewards treating your body responsibly. Instead of rewarding the ill, as do the present plans, it rewards those who keep themselves healthy.

Suggestions like these follow directly from the holistic education principles. They apply to child rearing, birthing, politics, business, sports, and many other realms. Wherever there are people interacting, the holistic education principles are applicable. The principles of everyday living are consistent with the therapeutic technique.

CASE EXAMPLE

Cora was a binge drinker. She was 28 years old, married, had an eight-year-old child, and had been binge drinking regularly for seven years. She never touched alcohol between binges, but, at first every six months, then every three months she would go on a bender, drinking beer, wine, vodka, NyQuil, vanilla extract, or whatever was available. Cora would drink herself totally out of commission for about five days, sleeping the whole time except for sallies forth to reinforce her drunken state.

When sober she was totally opposite the liquor-soaked, straggly haired, rubber-legged, blankly staring Cora of the binges. She was very attractive, extremely efficient, charming, talented, and extraordinarily reliable. The contrast between the two Coras strained credulity.

She had become the despair of her family. They handled her binges by putting her in the detoxification tank until she dried out, then taking her home and saying little about it.

Cora began working on her drinking problem by going to gestalt and transactional analysis groups, going through psychoanalysis, and by attending an occasional Alcoholics Anonymous (AA) meeting. Through these approaches she acquired insight into the many reasons for her condition:

1. The premature responsibility entailed in having a child at 19.
2. The demands of her very responsible job.
3. Her strained relationship with her mother, who had not spoken to her for five years even though she lived nearby.
4. Her unhappy marriage, which was a model of non-communication.
5. The stress and guilt of her extramarital affairs.
6. The rejection by a lover on whom she had become very dependent, but who would not leave his wife to be with Cora.
7. The abandonment by her father when she was one and her subsequent fear of abandonment by all men.
8. Her body, which could not assimilate alcohol properly.

With each insight, Cora saw her situation more clearly. Slowly she was uncovering the basis for her trouble. The solutions offered by the various therapists all made sense: make up with your mother, quit your job, leave your lover, get a divorce, stop drinking. Most of these options were feasible since she was financially comfortable.

She came to see me after considering these solutions and because she was being fired from her job for the second time—for drinking. Clearly, something was not working.

After interacting with her for a while, it became clear that Cora had great insight into her situation and had worked through many of her background circumstances emotionally as well as intellectually. She understood that her last binge had been partly to escape the pressure of her job. She was learning how to take better care of herself.

All of her insights pinpointed the circumstances responsible for her situation: her lover, her husband, her unprepared motherhood, her high-pressure job, her cold mother, her abandoning father, her physiology. The solutions she had entertained, such as quitting her job or getting a divorce, were attempts to alter her environment.

The missing part was Cora taking responsibility for what was happening to her. As we progressed, what became clear to her was:

1. She did not drink because of the pressures of the job. Many nondrinkers have demanding jobs.
2. She did not drink because of her bad marriage. There are many nondrinkers in bad marriages.
3. She did not drink because of her lover's rejection. Many nondrinkers have been rejected.
4. She did not drink because her father left home or because her mother would not talk to her.
5. She did not get drunk because of her physiology.

Cora drank because Cora chose to drink.

As soon as she began to accept this idea, which she did very quickly, Cora's whole approach changed. She realized that changing external circumstances, such as quitting a job or leaving a marriage, becomes, at best, temporary relief until a new threatening circumstance arises. She saw that blaming others, such as mother, father, husband, job, must be abandoned. Cora recognized that they did not drive her to drink. They just did whatever they did. *She* chose to drink.

Her attitude toward her alcoholism also changed. No longer did she accept the AA description of herself as an alcoholic, no matter how long she remained dry. Even the solution of abstaining from drinking seemed inadequate. That meant Cora would forever have to expend energy to not take a drink, in the belief that, since she was an alcoholic, one drink would lead her to resume her "addiction."

Cora internalized the idea that she was totally responsible for her condition. She accepted that she had colluded with her parents to elicit the behavior she received from them, that she had chosen her husband, that she had elected to get pregnant at the age of 19, that she had chosen a lover whom she knew would not leave his wife, that she had chosen a hectic job and had decided to interpret her duties as overwhelming. After doing all of that, she had decided to perceive her circumstances as beyond her ability to handle and to drink herself into periodic stupors to get herself out of the situation.

Once she accepted responsibility for her situation, she realized the vital correlate: Cora could *choose* to change.

While she believed she was a victim, she had no power. She could only try to alter or escape from her circumstances. Once she accepted responsibility, she was in a position to change herself into a nonbinger. She had the power.

The path that we set out upon was for Cora to take charge of her life. The key to this path is the willingness to be completely truthful. Without truth, growth stutters and often founders. As a first step, Cora had lunch with her lover and expressed to him all the feelings that she had withheld and found out all the things she wanted to know from him. She left the lunch with many warm feelings toward him and knowing that she could let go of him.

Next, through one of those synchronicities the universe often provides, Cora's father came to visit for the first time in 12 years. Cora told him exactly how she felt about him now and how she had felt for all of their years together. He responded, as most people do to the deep truth, by being truthful in return. Their visit ended on a warm, loving note with the expectation of a growing, continuing relationship.

After holding back for seven years, Cora finally told her husband exactly what she was feeling and decided to get a divorce. After some early difficulty, their relationship developed into one of friendship and cooperation around the child.

She also talked honestly to her son, who subsequently has made the adjustment with great ease.

Her relation with her mother remained difficult, and Cora and I felt that there was some unfinished business in that area. We decided that intensive work on clearing out her relations with the parents would be an important step. Cora entered the Quadrinity Process, an intensive 12-week experience that is often effective for people who are ready to deal with their unresolved parental issues. She did extremely well in that program.

It has been quite a while now since Cora's last binge. She feels that her binge drinking is over, not just because of the time she has spent without a binge, but because situations have arisen that were even more pressured than those that formerly led to the benders, and she does not even consider the possibility of a drink. Apparently the desire for alcohol has been replaced by the feeling that she can deal with the situation without outside help.

This is what Cora has to say now:

I feel totally different about my binge drinking now than ever before. I am beginning to see who I really am and that I do not need to be stuck in a role of "alcoholic," nor do I need to experience physical withdrawal symptoms. I had totally accepted the AA philosophy that if I took one drink, I was doomed I felt that something beyond me controlled my life.

I am now clear that *I control my life* and all I need to do is to fearlessly and truthfully pursue what is ME. Through imagery during a severe alcohol withdrawal, I became aware of knowing what my body was doing in order to eliminate the alcohol and that I was not going to die. I saw that I could assist my body to speed up detoxification by working with it rather than fighting against it.

What amazes me most is the knowledge/gut feeling that binge drinking is not a part of ME anymore. I choose not to be a binge drinker not by abstaining, but by knowing that is not who I am. I have changed not because of external threats—job firing, divorce, abandonment—but because I was a fool who saw what a fool I was and who chose to change because I was not that person. I do not fear alcohol anymore! I am regaining daily a greater sense of self-power and testing out my beliefs in my limitless abilities. I feel soft and vulnerable and porous to the universe—my armor is dropping off, and I am truly being reborn in the sense of knowing that I am in charge of myself.

As Cora said, she does not regard herself as an alcoholic. She is someone who *used to* go on benders. When she felt sufficiently sure, and not before, she took a drink in my presence. She remained totally aware of her thoughts, feelings, and total experience while drinking. Next she took a drink alone, also with awareness. She now feels she can drink, if she wishes to, without getting drunk. She does not have to avoid drinking, nor does she have to drink. She is the master of her drinking.

The turning point of the "therapy" was Cora's acceptance of total responsibility for her problem. Once that occurred, her abilities and power were mobilized and she went directly toward mastery. The principles of truth and awareness were followed, and a variety of techniques—encounter, gestalt, imagery, Quadrinity—were used as they became appropriate. Cora was regarded as a whole person and her problem understood as a function of her whole being, not just her physiology, her history, or her present job. The Holistic Education assumption about Cora is that her drinking is a choice she is making to deal with her total life situation, and that she is fully capable of making the choice to stop drinking.

SUMMARY

Holistic Education is the name of this method rather than Holistic Therapy, because "therapy" is a misleading word in that it implies that someone cures someone else. The therapeutic relationship is regarded as one type of education, just as is parenting, administrating, and doctoring. The basic relationship is educator-learner in the sense that educators do nothing but create conditions, and learners decide how they respond to these conditions.

"Holistic" refers to the assumption that the person is a whole organism—physical, spiritual, emotional, intellectual, aesthetic, and social. This is not just a cliché, but it is an integral, guiding part of the process.

The main principles of Holistic Education are: (1) *limitlessness:* All people are limitless; (2) *truth:* The truth, which includes awareness (self-truth) and honesty (truth to others) is essential for the change to happen. The truth really does make one free; (3) *responsibility:* Everyone chooses everything in his or her life and always has.

All therapeutic techniques are usable within Holistic Education. The educator has a large repertoire and, through experience, uses whichever methods are most appropriate.

The principles of Holistic Education are equally applicable to all phases of human interaction: that is, they form a social philosophy. This philosophy generates social policy in medicine, law, politics, business, sports, birthing, parenting, and daily life.

The theoretical background and applications of Holistic Education are presented at greater length in *Profound Simplicity* (Schutz, 1979).

REFERENCES

Feldenkrais, M. (1973). *Awareness through movement.* New York: Harper & Row.

Glasser, R. (1976). *The body is the hero.* New York: Random House.

Graecen, J. (1972). "Arbitration, a tool for criminal cases? A proposal for bringing the wisdom of civil settlements into our criminal justice system." Washington, DC: National Institute of Law Enforcement and Criminal Justice.

Hoffman, B. (1979). *No one is to blame.* Palo Alto, CA: Science and Behavior Books.

Hogan, D. (1979). *The Regulation of Psychotherapists* (Vols. 1–4). Cambridge, MA: Ballinger.

Huang, A. (1977). *Embrace tiger return to mountain.* Moab, UT: Red People Press.

Matson, K. (1977). *The Psychology Today omnibook of personal development.* New York: Morrow.

Schutz, W. (1973). *Elements of encounter.* Big Sur, CA: Joy Press.

Schutz, W. (1979). *Profound simplicity.* New York: Bantam.

Schutz, W. (1979, May). Antioch University's experiment with holistic education. *Association for Humanistic Psychology Newsletter.*

Schutz, W. (1979, August 1). A health-care plan that rewards the fit. *San Francisco Chronicle.*

Chapter 28

IMMEDIATE THERAPY

RAYMOND J. CORSINI

I feel somewhat uncomfortable introducing my own chapter, but I suppose that if I am bold enough to include it, even though no one to my knowledge is using this system, I should be bold enough to say something about it.

In my many years of practicing counseling and psychotherapy, I have had hundreds of bright ideas and thousands of various new insights, most of which soon dissipated. I have read probably a thousand articles and books on psychotherapy—and they all impressed me, but in my practice I more or less operate today as I did 25 years ago. I imagine that this is what happens to most of us. As time goes on, we get more set in our ways, and we tend to find comfort in our own procedures. And this is what has happened to me regarding Immediate Therapy: I no longer use it, yet I believe that it is useful in institutional treatment, especially in prisons, where I employed it, as I recall, so successfully. But that is what this book is all about: to show new methods for various individuals and various institutions and settings.

What has kept me going through the years in this terrible profession has been the relatively few instances in which I knew that what I had done really made a difference. I feel certain there must be at least two dozen people "out there" formerly in durance vile who are now "normal" as a direct result of Immediate Therapy. And so I suggest that those who work in corrections learn about Immediate Therapy.

Immediate therapy is based primarily on Heider's (1958) theory of interpersonal relations and Festinger's (1957) theory of cognitive dissonance as well as Zeigarnik's theory of incomplete gestalts. Essentially, Immediate Therapy holds that people can make rapid, lasting, ameliorative personality changes under proper conditions. While preparation before Immediate Therapy may take considerable time, nevertheless the therapy itself is of the instant type, occurring with extreme emotionalism on the part of the client. The method of treatment is ordinarily done in a group and the actual procedure is either psychodrama or the behind-the-back technique.

HISTORY

Throughout history are examples of individuals having made rapid and lasting changes of their personalities (Corsini, 1945). This phenomenon, known as *conversion,* is defined by English and English (1958) as "Radical and relatively rapid change of belief or attitude, especially of religious attitude, with or without corresponding change in character or conduct." The classic example is that of Saul of Tarsus who, en route to persecute the Christians, fell from his horse and heard a voice asking him why he was persecuting his people, and as a result had an immediate and lasting change of heart. He changed his name to Paul and became a Christian. In theatricals dramatists often make a central point of a character having a particular attitude that he or she holds on to with great tenacity. The audience, however, knows something that the protagonist does not know. Someone in the drama has this information, but either cannot get it to the protagonist or the protagonist will not permit that person to give him the information. However, when the protagonist learns that information—such as that the condemned person is his own son, or that the vilified individual is actually an ally—then there occurs an immediate change of attitude.

A good many of the "miraculous" cures by the laying on of hands on hysterics are probably nothing more than what I call Immediate Therapy. A person held in high repute by the client informs that person that he or she is now cured of the disability, whereupon that individual announces that this is indeed so. The best-known examples of this in the early history of psychotherapy were the antagonists Johann Joseph Gassner, the exorcist, and Franz Anton Mesmer, the hypnotist, who in the eighteenth century demonstrated all kinds of miraculous immediate cures. Over the centuries many other people have performed such "miracles," and even today a variety of ministers do spiritual healings.

Perhaps the best known people who performed such rapid psychological cures in our time were J. L. Moreno, who on the psychodrama stage would treat and "cure" patients in a single session, and Frederick C. (Fritz) Perls, who used the "hot seat" technique.

The history of Immediate Therapy dates back to two incidents, both of which occurred in prisons. The first took place about 1945 at Auburn Prison in New York and the second, nine years later, in San Quentin in California. Only after the second one (cited in the case example) did I understand what I had witnessed.

The first case went as follows: An inmate at Auburn Prison requested an interview with me, the prison psychologist. My duties were mostly psychometric in nature. The man who came to see me was about 30 years of age. His statement went approximately as follows:

> I used to be skeptical of bug doctors [psychologists and psychiatrists] but now I know I was wrong. Because of you, my whole life has changed. After seeing you I gave up the criminal crowd I had been associating with. I gave up the easy job I had and changed to one in the machine shop. I finished my high school education and passed the Regents' tests, and I am also taking college-level correspondence courses. I have taken a correspondence course in drafting and will work as a draftsman when I get released next week. I have returned to my religion, and I have reunited myself with my family. All on account of you. My parents bless you and pray for you for what you did for me.

I was astounded to hear this paean of praise for me, especially since I was fairly certain I had never met the man before. "Do you have the right person?" I asked. "I don't remember you at all."

"It's you, all right," he replied. "I'll never forget the words you said which so changed my life."

"What were they?" I asked, having thoughts of becoming one of the giants of psychotherapy.

"About a year ago when you tested me you told me I had a high IQ," he replied.

Shocked by the triviality of the reply, I learned upon further questioning that this remark really had had the effect of changing this man's whole life. I did not understand the meaning of this incident and on several occasions I told others this story with the intention of showing the irrationality of some people. Other clients exhibited such rapid changes after hypnosis, but not until the incident recounted in the case example following did I begin to understand what Immediate Therapy was all about.

CURRENT STATUS

In medicine powerful therapeutics are inherently dangerous and can lead to death. Radical operations, miracle drugs, and the like tend to have serious side effects. No one, except highly qualified people, would dare practice coronary bypass operations or administer powerful drugs. It is my opinion that Immediate Therapy should be restricted only to individuals with proper training in (1) personality theory, (2) psychotherapeutic techniques, and (3) this specific methodology. Due to personal limitations—that is to say, inability to find a proper teaching forum, plus my own personal conservatism in training others—no attempts have been made to propagate this theory or method. On the other hand, in the best interests of science, the findings and the underpinnings as well as the methodology of Immediate Therapy should be known to others in the field of psychotherapy for their consideration and possible utilization.

Essentially, at the present time, I believe I am the only practitioner of Immediate Therapy, and even I use it only rarely and sparingly. However, this technique and the theory itself have been employed by several others, but generally without full understanding. The behind-the-back technique, for example, is being employed by some people who include it in their repertoires in various so-called "encounter" groups.

THEORY

Essentially the theory of Immediate Therapy goes something like this: The human mind, like the human body, has a built-in tendency to perfection, and will cure itself under proper circumstances. This so-called growth tendency or self-actualization tendency is implied or made explicit in the writing of many personality theorists, Abraham Maslow (1970) and Kurt Goldstein (1940) most prominently. What this means is that the mind seeks to be free and perfect and well, and that it is the job of the therapist to help nature. The statement made by Ambroise Pare, "I treated him, God cured him," holds. We treat patients, but they cure themselves.

The essence of the theory of Immediate Therapy is that every individual has the potential for improvement or cure or change in him or her, and it is the function of the therapist to help release this potential. Carl Rogers (1951) made the central point of his theory the capacity of people to cure themselves. And essentially this is what all therapists do: establish conditions under which the patient can cure himself or herself.

What is psychoanalysis? A formal method for self-reflection. *What is client-centered therapy?* A means for a person to analyze himself. *What is psychodrama?* A method for allowing oneself to cure oneself. "I treat, God cures" is what all therapists can say.

Physicians know that the body heals slowly, and so they are trained and are biased in the direction of slow, gradual cures. This bias has been translated into their psychological treatment methods and into their theories, with the notion that personality changes slowly and that psychotherapists should operate slowly and carefully. This bias has been accepted by nonphysicians generally and has become a kind of self-fulfilling prophecy. It is well-known that therapists can affect patients in curious ways. Patients of Freudians have Freudian dreams, Jungian patients have Jungian dreams, and Adlerian patients have Adlerian dreams. If a therapist makes the assumption that therapy must last at least a year, then the patient will pick up this concept and will cooperate, albeit unknowingly, with the therapist to make the therapy last that long.

This concept also translates into learning theories, which fall into two groups. One is that personality learning is of the gradual, incremental type, just as in learning how to ski or speak a foreign language. The second kind of learning is of the saltatory (from *saltatorius,* which is Latin for "leap") type, and is sudden and immediate, as for example when one learns the point of a joke. Most therapists see psychotherapy as learning of the first type, incremental, and so they operate in this manner—as though this were the right, the correct, and the only way. Other therapists, such as Moreno, Perls, and Albert Ellis, start off with a bang with practically instant diagnosis and correction, having no use for long, drawn-out therapeutic processes.

Naturally, psychotherapists who have been imbued with ideas that stem from an analogy to physiotherapy, or from the incremental theory of learning and unlearning, will consider those who use Immediate Therapy to be doing superficial therapy, since deep therapy must be long-lasting. Nonsense!

Good therapy need not be interminable. Quick therapy is better than drawn-out therapy. The elegant way to do therapy is to do it quickly, simply, cheaply. Consider the concept of resistance, the single major enemy of all therapists. As was realized by Sigmund Freud, and reaffirmed by all therapists since, practically every patient who comes for therapy shows resistance, and the cleverer the patient, the more the resistance. Therapy essentially becomes a power contest in which the therapist says, "Get cured" and the patient says, "No!"

The main intent of Immediate Therapy is to avoid this power contest and to achieve therapy through single-minded cunning, guile, stealth, and forceful action. These pejorative terms are deliberately selected, since the therapist must "betray" his patient by hurting him deeply, suddenly, unexpectedly—for his own good.

The following analogies help explicate the theory behind Immediate Therapy.

The Balloon Analogy. Let us imagine the total personality, the psyche, as a helium-filled balloon that wants to soar to its proper destined height of appropriate adjustment. The balloon, however, is weighted down by a heavy rope. Were the rope to be released, the balloon would go up to 1,000 feet; but the balloon is now only 25 feet from the ground. The rope is 25 feet in length and so the bottom of the rope just touches the ground. Working in conventional ways, to release the balloon we pull the rope down a bit at a time, and this takes a long time. Were we able to get on a ladder, we could cut the top of the rope in one clip. This is what Immediate Therapy is all about: to cut that rope immediately at the very top, so that the balloon immediately soars to its proper level.

The Logjam Analogy. A second analogy has to do with a logjam. Imagine a thousand logs have been cut down in a forest and are being floated down the river. Imagine that a single log manages to get caught between some rocks and that this single log now generates a logjam. When the lumberjacks discover the problem, they approach it from the back, as it were, going to the very last log, carrying it past the other logs and over the crucial log; then getting another log, and so on. Eventually, they finally get to the key log and remove it from its jammed position. In contrast, in Immediate Therapy, we find the key log and we blow it out of place; then all the logs come down the stream.

The Splinter Analogy. One further analogy is needed to complete the theory: Imagine that a person has a splinter in his hand, and that another person is to take the splinter out. Let us assume that the one who is to serve as the "surgeon" is blind and does not know where the splinter is. The blind surgeon now begins to probe but can only tell where the splinter is in terms of the pain he causes the patient. The patient "knows" where the splinter is, but the surgeon can only know when the patient cries out. Immediate Therapy's view is that the patient is his own therapist and knows where the treatment is needed, but he enters into a power contest with the therapist because he fears the hurt necessary for therapy.

Immediate Therapy can be explained in this way: Over time a person comes to have a rather set series of concepts and ideas about self and others. Alfred Adler (1960) referred to this personal set of concepts as private logic and private intelligence. The combination of these ideas, of which some are incorrect, leads to maladjustment. In Immediate Therapy matters are arranged so that there will be a confrontation between the person's concepts and reality. The resulting contrast leads to a situation of "cognitive dissonance" (Festinger, 1957) that upsets the person's pattern, or gestalt, of thinking; leads to confusion and disruption, which is shown by dissonant feelings and external evidence of tension; and then moves inevitably to a new restructuring of thinking due to tension resulting from the disturbed gestalt, as explained by Zeigarnik (1927) and called "unfinished business" by Holt (1959).

METHODOLOGY

The first step in the methodology of Immediate Therapy calls for the patient to be "prepared" or "set up" to receive the treatment. A sensitive and competent therapist generally knows when and where to operate. The next step is to have a one-time confrontation, so orchestrated as to achieve maximum results in minimum time. This confrontation must be of such intensity as to transcend the individual, to send him or her into an emotional state so that he or she will lose control. The third step, crucial for Immediate Therapy, is to stop everything immediately when the individual gets to an unbearable moment, and to cast that individual out of the group to work out the problem on his or her own.

The three steps of Immediate Therapy are warmup → confrontation → expulsion.

Warm-up. This step calls for gaining the client's confidence, leading him to the point where he will want to participate in the therapeutic procedure. Since Immediate Therapy almost always occurs in group therapy, the most obvious way to achieve this confidence is for the patient to see others benefiting from this treatment. So if client D sees A, then B, then C, participating and getting benefit, this observation will tend to give him confidence that when his turn comes, he too will benefit. It also calls for the therapist to be determined, patient, wise, and courageous, since Immediate Therapy is extremely exhausting and fatiguing emotionally. The length of time for the warm-up varies. In the case cited earlier, the client who heard the words "You have a high IQ" was already "warmed up" (ready to change); otherwise the words would have had no meaning for him.

Confrontation. This is the moment of therapy in which the therapist orchestrates the treatment in such a manner as to achieve the desired results of "blowing up the logjam"—getting to the heart of the matter.

Expulsion. The last step is simple: During the moment of most extreme excitement, when the patient has been driven to the edge of anguish, screaming in agony, the group expels—immediately and in silence—the patient, who now must reassemble himself.

One technique frequently used in Immediate Therapy is psychodrama. I shall not attempt to describe this process, since there are several books on the subject (see Corsini, 1965; Moreno, 1946; etc.). The procedure sometimes used is the behind-the-back technique (Corsini, 1953, 1968, 1973), which I now describe.

1. Group meets in a circle and members agree to volunteer in a predetermined sequence. Should B not take his turn, then C must take his place.

2. The client has this assignment: "Tell everything about yourself." Each client will usually be given one-half hour to do this.

3. Everyone plans what to say when his turn comes, which may be from one week to several weeks ahead.

4. At the treatment session, the person who was the subject the week before tells the group what the session meant to him or her.

5. Then the current subject speaks for a half hour (or whatever time is established), telling the others *everything* about him- or herself.

6. When the statement is finished, the protagonist "leaves" the room symbolically, by going to the outside of the group and facing outward. The rest of the group discusses him "behind his back," while he listens but does not look.

7. Meantime the director keeps notes of what was said by the group. When the client comes back into the group, the director reads from the notes and informs the client of what was said. (The fiction is that the patient was actually out of the room.) The purpose of this is to repeat the highlights.

8. The protagonist is asked to comment or defend him- or herself. He or she sits in the center of the circle.

9. Now the therapist and the group members ask questions, make comments, and proceed deliberately to upset the client, with the client defending him- or herself.

10. If the technique is to succeed, the client, goaded by the questions and comments, will get upset, and this degree of upset is carefully noted by the therapist. If the client gets terribly upset, the group must fall silent at a quick clap of the therapist's hands and the client is "pointed out of the room" by the therapist. Not until he or she leaves does the group continue with further business.

11. When the client returns at the next session, he or she is asked to recapitulate what happened to him or her after being sent out of the group. Whenever the therapy is successful, statements such as the

following are heard: "I left the group in a daze"; "I was terribly upset"; "I don't know how I got home"; "I walked the streets for hours"; "I couldn't sleep"; "I didn't have any appetite"; "My head went round and round for hours."

Follow-Up. After the client comes back next session and gives his or her report, the general question is: "Did you learn anything?" Generally, the client begins with such statements as, "I really never believed . . ." or "I suddenly realized . . ." and then typically has some explanation of the origins of his or her behavior pathology. The therapy is completed! After listening, the next client presents him- or herself and the group goes through the same process again.

Perhaps the most important part of the methodology is the respect paid to all members of the group by the therapist, who takes them on as full partners and who also operates as a full partner in the enterprise. The therapist is merciless in his analysis, and must speak fully from his heart, thereby encouraging all others to be equally honest and forceful.

APPLICATIONS

Immediate Therapy is especially designed for those individuals who are resistant to therapy, who are smart and highly likely to use ingenious methods to avoid the benefits of therapy. While it can work well with those who are innocent and willing to go along, Immediate Therapy is especially useful with those complex, complicated characters who ordinarily will make their therapy interminable and who delight in defeating the therapist. Therapists and patients are in a power struggle; the patient who wants therapy, who pays for it, who takes time out to pursue it, nevertheless is bound generally to do whatever he or she can to defeat the therapist—and not change. Resistance is the means used to win the game. The cleverer the person, the cleverer the form of resistance. Immediate Therapy is directed to destroy resistance.

The following summaries of some individual cases will serve to explicate the kinds of problems that can be solved through Immediate Therapy.

1. A black prisoner, in solitary confinement for refusing an assignment, stated that he would rather serve the rest of his life in solitary than take on a mopping job, which he considered beneath him and which he felt was intended to make him feel violated. As a result of a behind-the-back treatment, he changed his mind and admitted that he was prejudiced against whites and that he provoked them into mistreating him so that he could get even with them.

2. A man learned that he had abused a child sexually in front of witnesses in order to go to prison to atone for his desire for his father's death (Corsini, 1951b).

3. A man stated he wished to kill his brother, who he felt had mistreated him; however, as a result of psychodrama, he realized that he loved his brother and did not want to harm him any more.

4. A man who had committed a number of senseless crimes involving bad checks discovered, following a behind-the-back session, that his secret hatred of his father was the cause of his actions; he desired that his father be disgraced.

5. An alcoholic woman with anorexia nervosa, who weighed less than 70 pounds, was "killed" in role playing and had a talk with "God." During the talk she was led to understand that her great "sin" of marrying a Catholic priest would be forgiven.

6. A completely reckless psychopathic youth was "killed" in a psychodrama demonstration and "buried" amid weeping "relatives." He changed his personality immediately, to the surprise of all who knew him.

Every one of these individuals was essentially a hard-core person, resistant to psychotherapy, and was "blasted" into a confrontation-type encounter. They were all put into a situation as described by Zeigarnik (1965) in which their tight gestalt of concepts was shattered by the logic of the situation and of the opinions of the group members. This generated unbearable tension, which could only be resolved by a complete personality restructuring, that is to say, by new conceptions of their fundamental views of self and others.

The behind-the-back technique has been employed with hospitalized paranoids, with criminals, with ordinary neurotics, with fighting husbands and wives. If employed properly—that is, if the therapist is able to generate the unbearable tension that is the essence of Immediate Therapy—then rapid changes occur. Essentially, the ideal client for this kind of therapy should be strong, opinionated, and certain of self. This system's intent is to take such people and shake them up so that they now have to deal with the cognitive dissonance between their original opinions and beliefs and strong evidence of the incorrectness of their position.

To give an analogy: Suppose that one believes (and some still do) that the Earth is flat, not round. Suppose that all contrary evidence is discounted as propaganda. Now, suppose that person goes up in a spaceship. The earth gradually recedes until it can be seen that it really is round. We now have a conflict within the person, between the old beliefs and the new vision. This is exactly the situation in Immediate Therapy. Evidence is put in front of the client that contradicts past concepts. The resulting internal upheaval is due to the incompatability of the two notions: When therapy occurs, truth wins out.

CASE EXAMPLE

Frank was an inmate at San Quentin, serving a sentence for a series of crimes of the same type. He would meet a woman, woo her, marry her, then steal her money, car, and so forth, and run away, and then search for another victim. A heavyset person with a sneering expression, Frank was nominated to attend this writer's therapy group by another inmate. I had a short talk with Frank about the group, which featured psychodrama (see Corsini, 1957, pp. 198–217), and accepted him, though I was not impressed with him or his attitude. I explained that he should attend at least three group sessions before deciding whether to remain. He accepted these terms.

In the group, he was more or less a spectator. Psychodrama was the main instrument of treatment, but he did not volunteer to participate as a subject. According to our pattern, every eighth session was a breather, a relaxer, run nondirectively, and at one of these sessions the discussion got onto Frank and his nonparticipation. Other group members questioned Frank's motive for joining the group and his lack of involvement. He then agreed to participate at the next regular session. However, the next week when I gave him the floor, he stated that he had nothing to say and had no intent to role play.

This was an impasse. I then suggested that he tell the group "everything about yourself" and that we would listen to him for 15 minutes in silence. He agreed to this, and a summary of his statements went as follows:

> My father was Jewish and my mother was Italian. My mother told me never to trust anyone, because people will take advantage of you. My father used to tell me the story of the Jewish man who wanted to teach his son about business. He got the son to climb on a table and then on a chair and asked the son to jump and that he would catch him. When the son jumped, the father moved aside and the child fell. The father then told his son that he had shown him the secret of success in business: "Never trust anyone."
>
> Well, throughout my life I have been screwed by others. Once on a train ride, there was a mother with a child. The child was crying. It was hungry. The mother told me she had no money to buy it food. The kid kept crying and bothered me. So I offered to buy the kid a container of milk, and gave the mother fifty cents. Then she came over and sat by me. We talked and she told me her troubles. Then I fell asleep. When I woke up she and the kid were gone and so was my wallet. See, I was a nice guy, bought the kid milk, befriended the mother and what happened? She stole my money.

> That's how life has been. Everyone is out to get you. You got to look out for yourself. . . .

Frank went on and on with his account. Some background information and details of my previous interactions with him will help clarify my attitude toward him at the time he was telling his story.

In the first week of membership in the group he had asked me to violate one of the rules of the prison. He asked me to "kite" (mail out) a letter to his "wife." Ordinarily, I did not care to know what a person's crime was; curious, I checked his records and discovered that this "wife" was one of several women he had married bigamously and who had filed charges against him in another state. In the files was a piteous letter from her, intercepted by the censor, asking him why he had stolen her money and ruined her life.

One time while I was walking in the prison yard, he called me over. When I came over, he waved several of his buddies toward us. Surrounded by them, he faced me, pulled out from under his jacket a two-pound brick of cheese, stolen from the kitchen where he worked, and told the others, "See, he's my therapist. He can't tell them that I did this." Angry with this mistreatment of me, I broke through the circle and went on to my office.

Frank eventually finished his story, and there was silence. I then asked Frank to go outside the circle, to sit with his back to me, and to listen to what we would say. I asked the other members to come closer to each other so that we formed a tight circle.

"Now, men," I said, "we have all heard Frank. Now, what I want to ask you is this: will each of you give your opinion of Frank, your overall impression—in the group and in the institution. Jim, will you start?"

Jim replied: "I have nothing to say."

"Pete?"

"Sorry, I have nothing to say either."

"Danny?"

"Me neither. . . ."

I looked around the group. They were all tight-mouthed, their features firmly set. I could tell none would speak up unless I was able to convince them.

"Let me tell you something, every one of you. We are not fooling around. I can see you fellows don't like Frank. I don't like him either. But he is a member of our group. He has attended seven or eight sessions. He has not participated much. I don't like his attitude here, but it is our duty to try to help him. And the way you can help him, me, yourself, the other members of the group, and even society, is to tell the truth, exactly how you feel about Frank. What do you say, Jim?"

Jim looked me in the eye, took a deep breath, and began. "He is a shit. A bastard like him doesn't deserve to live. . . ."

When he finished, Pete began. "I feel ashamed that I

belong to the human race if a scum like Frank is one too. Why, that son of a bitch hesitates about buying a hungry baby some milk. . . ." and on he went.

"Danny?"

"I wanted to quit this group when Frank came in. People say that no one is all bad. They never met Frank. I know him well. He is the laziest, crookedest, meanest bastard in the world. It's guys like him that make it hard for others. . . ."

When it came my turn, I said nothing about his crimes, the letter from one of his "wives," his asking me to kite the letter, or the incident in the yard but I said something like this:

"I dislike the man. I think he is cunning, sneaky, vicious. But I don't know enough about him to understand what made him the way he is. I am sorry he is in the group, but he is in, and I am happy we are having this discussion."

We continued until we had all finished, and then I called Frank and asked him to comment on the comments. He entered the group, remained standing, and his remarks went something as follows:

"I heard what you bastards said. As far as I am concerned you are a bunch of ——suckers, all of you. You are all full of shit. This is what I think of you. . . ." He then cleared his throat, spit on the floor, turned around and left the room.

I thought that was the end of Frank. I was happy to see him go, and so were the others. He was just no good; no damned good. . . .

About three months later I got a note from Frank asking me for an interview. I threw it into the wastebasket. I just didn't want anything to do with him. However, as I pondered the situation, I had a kind of personal confrontation. Here I was, a prison psychologist, supposed to be "rehabilitating" persons and refusing a man an interview. Ashamed of myself, I made arrangements for Frank to see me the next day, not knowing what to expect.

When he arrived, my attitude was cold and hard. "What can I do for you?"

"Why did you kick me out of your group?"

"I didn't kick you out. You got up, told us what you thought of us, spit on the floor, and that's the last I saw of you."

"Why did you and the rest say all those terrible things about me?"

"We only said what we believed."

"Well, they are all untrue. I am a nice guy."

"Is that what you really think?" The concept of Frank being a nice guy was so monstrous that I was shaken by the very idea.

"Sure, everyone is against me. I don't deserve what they said."

"Why do you think they said it?"

"Did you put them up to it?"

"Do you believe that?"

"No."

"Well, what do you want?"

"Christ, I haven't been able to sleep well since that day. I can't get over what they said. All of them. What they think of me."

"I am sure everyone said just what they thought about you."

"Well, then I need help to change. I came here to ask you to let me back in the group."

"No way. You left. You are out. That's final."

"Then, see me personally. Give me individual treatment. I need help."

"No way. Frank, I want to tell you I can't work with you because I don't like you. You know what you did, tried to get me to kite a letter. Remember that incident in the yard with the cheese? Besides which, I want to tell you that I have contempt for you because of your record. I have more respect for murderers than a man who did what you did. So I would be the last one for you to have therapy with."

"You are supposed to rehabilitate me. What the hell is all this about rehabilitation?"

"Look, there are others in the psych department: psychiatrists, psychologists, social workers. Ask one of them."

"I want you."

"And I don't want you."

We looked at each other in silence. Finally a thought came to me. Some time before, the male nurse in the prison psychiatric hospital unit in which I worked reported that he could not find attendants for the geriatric ward, and asked us to search for possible attendants. No one would want to work with these old, senile convicts. For the most part they were just waiting to die. Working in the B ward was the least desirable job in the institution. "Frank, I'll make a deal with you."

"What's that?"

"They need attendants in the old men's ward in the hospital. You volunteer for a job there, you stick with it six months, and you never talk to me. If you keep the job six months, then I'll see you for therapy."

To my surprise, he agreed.

The next day the chief nurse came to see me. "How did you do it, Corsini?" he asked. "This fellow Frank volunteered to work in B ward."

"Bill, do me a favor. Keep an eye on Frank and let me know from time to time how he is doing."

Periodically, Bill would inform me of Frank. The first week, Frank kept vomiting, showing great distaste for having to clean these old men who urinated and defecated in their beds. He had trouble feeding them or dealing with them. "If he finishes the first week," Bill told me, "I'll be surprised."

But Frank stuck it out, and Bill's reports were enthusiastic as time went on. "He's very devoted." "He turns the men over very carefully." "He is there when they want him." "He is very gentle with them." "He's my best man." "I saw him crying as one of them died." "He's reading nursing books." "The other attendants look up to him." "The old men brighten up when he shows up." "He's really devoted." "He stayed all night with a dying man, holding his hand."

I wondered about this magical transformation. When I would pass Frank in the hallways, he would pay no attention to me. He was losing weight, and from an estimated 200 pounds, he now probably weighed about 150. His appearance and his expression were different. I noted that the other inmates respected him. One or two of the men of my therapy group referred to the change they had noted in him.

Six months to the day after that interview, Frank showed up, waiting in a chair outside my room. I motioned him in.

"Well, I am ready for my therapy."

I shook his hand. "Frank, you have had it. You don't need any more therapy."

"I think you're right."

"What happened? What made the change?"

"It was that behind-the-back session. It bugged me. I couldn't believe that everyone in the group really hated me like they said they did. The difference between what I thought of myself and what they—and you—thought was too much. When I left the group I was very angry with all of you. I figured you all plotted against me. But then I figured that couldn't be. Then I had to face the fact that you all really believed what you said; each of you had independently come to the conclusion I was no good. This contradicted what my mother and father told me. It contradicted what I thought of myself. And then I began to think that maybe you guys were right, that maybe I was a bastard. Now, that really took a lot of time to believe. I was terribly upset for a whole week, and finally I came to the conclusion, hell, look what I did to those women. They really didn't deserve it. So I agreed with you all. So I decided that I'd change. But it still bothered me that you and the other guys had that bad opinion of me. I hated you and I didn't want to have anything to do with any of you. I stuck by myself, but that bothered me. I wanted you to like me. That's why finally I came to see you. And when you refused to see me I could understand why. And when you offered to see me in therapy if I would become an attendant I jumped at the chance to prove to you that I was okay. Boy—that was some shithouse you sent me to. I thought I'd puke my brains out the first week. God—I was always afraid of death. Those old, dying men. But I stuck it out, and now I love my work. I'm going to become a nurse. I'm studying books. I've found my vocation. I really want to thank you."

"Anything you want from me?"

"Nothing."

"How about a letter or something telling about your rehabilitation? Maybe the other state will go easy on you." (I still had my reservations about Frank.)

"Nothing. I'll take my medicine. I'm going to the parole board here and then I have to face the jury in the other state. No, I'll take life as it comes."

Frank was in the institution for another three to four months, during which time we met informally several times. There was no doubt in my mind that he had experienced a 180-degree change. This change was confirmed by all other prisoners who had dealings with him; Frank had changed—for the better.

SUMMARY

Immediate Therapy is not a system of psychotherapy in the same sense as, for example, psychoanalysis or reality therapy, which have a more or less complete system of conceptualizations about personality growth and development. It is instead a psychotherapeutic system that could well be fitted into other personality theories. I myself am a follower of Alfred Adler's individual psychology theory, and at various times I use a variety of techniques, such as nondirective interviewing, free association, group therapy, family counseling, and so forth. One of these techniques is Immediate Therapy—an attempt to break through a person's defenses by a swift, powerful, coordinated attack.

In my opinion, some forms of therapy are based on the fallacious notion, rooted in physical medicine, that psychotherapy, to be effective, has to be "deep" and long-lasting. This is just not so. Good, significant, meaningful therapy can be short. Long-lasting, permanent changes can occur quickly. Traditional methods of operation can be counterproductive. The work of Moreno, Perls, Ellis, as well as many others, including those who use hypnosis and a variety of encounter techniques, indicate that Immediate Therapy is a valid means of treatment.

REFERENCES

Adler, A. (1960). *What life should mean to you.* New York: Capricorn Books. (Original work published 1931)

Corsini, R. J. (1945). Criminal conversion. *Journal of Criminal Psychopathology, 7,* 139–146.

Corsini, R. J. (1951a). The method of psychodrama in prison. *Group Psychotherapy, 3,* 321–326.

Corsini, R. J. (1951b). Psychodramatic treatment of a pedophile. *Group Psychotherapy, 4,* 166–171.

Corsini, R. J. (1952). Immediate therapy. *Group Psychotherapy, 4,* 322–330.

Corsini, R. J. (1953). The behind-the-back technique in group therapy. *Group Psychotherapy, 6,* 102–209.

Corsini, R. J. (1954a). Criminal and correctional psychology. In F. L. Marcuse (Ed.), *Areas of psychology.* New York: Harper.

Corsini, R. J. (1954b). Group psychotherapy with a hostile group. *Group Psychotherapy, 9,* 184–185.

Corsini, R. J. (1957). *Methods of group psychotherapy.* New York: McGraw-Hill.

Corsini, R. J. (1964). Group psychotherapy in correctional rehabilitation. *British Journal of Delinquency, 15,* 272–278.

Corsini, R. J. (1965). *Roleplaying in psychotherapy.* Chicago: Aldine.

Corsini, R. J. (1968). Immediate therapy in groups. In G. M. Gazda, *Innovations to group psychotherapy.* Evanston, IL: Charles C. Thomas.

Corsini, R. J. (1973). The behind-the-back encounter. In L. Wolberg & E. K. Schwartz (Eds.), *Group psychotherapy, 1973.* New York: Intercontinental Medical Books.

Ellis, A. (1962). *Reason and emotion in psychotherapy.* New York: Lyle Stuart.

English, H. B., & English, A. C. (1958). *A comprehensive dictionary of psychological and psychoanalytic terms.* New York: Longman, Green.

Festinger, L. A. (1957). *A theory of cognitive dissonance.* Evanston, IL: Row, Peterson.

Goldstein, K. (1940). *Human nature in the light of psychopathology.* Cambridge, MA: Harvard University Press.

Greenwald, H. (1975). *Direct decision therapy.* San Diego: EDITS/Educational and Industrial Testing Service.

Heider, F. (1958). *The psychology of interpersonal relations.* New York: Wiley.

Holt, R. R. (1959). Discussion of "Further observations of the Potzl phenomenon: A study of day residues" by Charles Fisher. *Psychoanalytic Quarterly, 28,* 442.

Maslow, A. H. (1970). *Motivation and personality.* (2nd ed.). New York: Harper & Row.

Moreno, J. L. (1946). *Psychodrama* (Vol. 1). New York: Beacon House.

Perls, F. (1969). *Ego, hunger, and aggression.* New York: Random House.

Rogers, C. R. (1951). *Client-centered therapy.* Boston: Houghton Mifflin.

Schutz, W. (1971). *Joy.* New York: Grove.

Zeigarnik, B. V. (1927). Über das Behalten von erledigten und unerledigten Handlungen. *Psychologische Forschung, 9,* 1–85.

Zeigarnik, B. V. (1965). The task of psychopathology. In *Problems of experimental psychopathology.* Moscow: Gosudarstvennyi Nauchno-Issledovatel's Kii Institut Psikhiatrii.

Chapter 29

IMPASSE/PRIORITY THERAPY

NIRA KFIR

I was present in 1971 at a workshop given in Jerusalem on Adlerian Therapy when Nira Kfir introduced her highly original ideas about priorities and impasses. Interestingly enough, Kfir's views have generally been incorporated into Alfred Adler's system of individual psychology, which is a great compliment since very little that is new has been accepted as part of the theory since its founder's death in 1937. Kfir has therefore made a substantial contribution to personality theory.

And now she has further developed her concepts into a total therapeutic approach, innovative and unusual in many ways, not the least being the length of the therapy—it generally lasts for two years. The reader is in for a real treat and an absolutely unique conception of what psychotherapy is all about.

Impasse/Priority Therapy (IPT) is a four-part therapeutic structure developed with the primary goal of leading individuals from a minus to a plus position. A minus position is defined as one in which an individual has a distorted view of the human social environment, perceives others as threatening, and, consequently, is paralyzed in moving in life. Situations of the minus type are those in which the human encounter is seen as a threat—a hindering force.

In line with Alfred Adler's holistic personality model, every person is seen as a creative, self-determining, "becoming" being who moves toward fictional goals within a phenomenal social field. The minus situation is normally an impetus to growth and the feeling of significance, but it can lead to impasses and a reduction of behavioral repertoires—even to "illnesses"—owing to a distorted social learning process developed in early childhood.

IPT involves a repetition of the child's socialization process as well as training in social interest, advancing clients to a higher state of being, in which they are open-ended, active, and always oriented to other people.

IPT is designed as four-stage process, including: (1) meeting individually with a therapist for diagnosis and a treatment plan, (2) participating in an intensive marathon, (3) being in an extended workshop program, and (4) studying human relations.

HISTORY

An unattributed saying is that when a person says "I think," he is probably lying, or at least uttering a half-truth, because our thoughts are an accumulation of previous thoughts, our reaction to them, and our associations connected with the actions of other people. The finished thought that accompanies the "I think" encompasses all these previous thoughts. That is why the concept of priorities and Impasse/Priority Therapy—which is, as far as I can determine, my own creation—evolved through a process of filtering and absorbing the ideas of other people, beginning in childhood with what was learned in the family. I also incorporated the ideas of Hillel, Alfred Adler, Rudolf Dreikurs, Jean-Paul Sartre, Viktor Frankl, and many others. Hillel's basic thought, "Love thy neighbor as thyself," is the essence of the Torah he proclaimed. This idea, similar to Adler's concept of "social interest," places supreme value on social relationships. I regard the purpose of the therapeutic process as mainly one of helping individuals find their place among other human beings, helping them to enlarge their social interest and to develop a personal significance in connection with others.

In my training with Rudolf Dreikurs I learned and accepted Alfred Adler's individual psychology as a socio-teleological system that emphasizes looking at the individual holistically within the present social field. What is important is not so much what happened in the past but rather where one is now heading. The individual's lifestyle, the apperceptive ways one looks at oneself and the external world, and how one moves behaviorally through life toward an idealized goal of superiority (the "plus") is believed to be formed by the age of four to six years.

After working for several years with the basic Adlerian tool of the lifestyle, I found that uncovering it does not show the therapist or the client the individual's mode of behaviors but only one's perception of the self, one's outlook on life and the way in which other people are perceived. This realization led to my formulation of the concepts of *impasse* and *priorities,* both of which are regarded as being created by each individual in the preconceptual stage of development; that is, they are created both prior to and coincident with the establishment of the lifestyle. The concepts of impasse and priorities appear to indicate the different conditions under which an individual feels a sense of belonging and, consequently, feels significant. The idiosyncratic condition(s) under which each person sets to find the sense of belonging leads to the establishment of a preferred mode of behaving—of moving on the social map. Four basic categories of impasse/priority have been postulated and are elaborated on in the theory section.

The development of the IP theory also coincided with certain professional developments in Israel. Following the Yom Kippur War (1973), therapists came to realize that people suffering from shell shock are best treated in a group rather than in the traditional one-to-one setting. The traumatic events that trigger shell shock symptoms are social ones. When a soldier is traumatized by seeing his closest friend killed, he tends to feel unbearably guilty because he alone was spared. Since the trauma is a socially connected event, then theoretically the therapy, a remedial experience that reprocesses the traumatic event, should likewise be done in a social, that is, group, setting.

The impasse as described in IP theory also results from a social shock arising from relationships with others. Consequently, in IPT are incorporated social therapeutic techniques, specifically an intensive marathon and workshops that involve working closely with other people, thus providing a remedial experience where the patient can *relearn* and *unlearn* inappropriate interpersonal relationships. The workshops and the intensive marathon are designed to be "guided self work" that instills the concept of "the other(s)" into the life of the patient.

IP theory has enabled clinical staff to develop techniques for diagnosing, confronting, and treating in an efficient and reliable manner.

CURRENT STATUS

The concept of priorities was first enunciated in 1971 at the International Adlerian Summer School session held in Israel. It aroused much interest and was subsequently introduced at meetings in the United States and in Europe by myself and colleagues from other countries. A theoretical paper on the concept was first published in 1974 (Kfir & Corsini, 1974). Jacqueline Brown adopted the priorities concept and independently developed it into an action-oriented diagnostic process (Brown, 1976). John M. Sutton (1976) tested the validity of the priorities concept with 385 college students with encouraging results. Donald E. Ward (1979) wrote an analytical review of the concept in which he said:

> Priorities constitute a cognitive framework which can help the client feel a strong sense of mastery and ability to handle him or herself. . . . the personality priority assessment strategy allows a person to retain the "who" of what he or she is [i.e., the priority] but encourages [its] use in more useful, social-interest directed ways. (pp. 14–15)

Impasse/Priority Therapy is actively practiced in Israel, principally at the Alfred Adler Institute of Tel Aviv. Since 1978 many therapeutic and educational institutions in Israel have referred people to the workshops at the institute. Today a skilled team of leaders carry on the work. The IPT intensive marathon was introduced for the first time outside Israel during the summer of 1979 in Washington, D.C. There the purpose was essentially didactic, to show professionals the kind of work we are doing.

As yet a systematic inquiry has not been done to measure the effectiveness of the therapeutic method of IPT, and this chapter is one of the first attempts at describing the system. The psychologists and social workers now using this approach periodically assess their experience and refine the workshop and marathon techniques. The general impression is that IPT is a promising innovation in psychotherapy, which we at the institute believe could be effectively used throughout the world.

THEORY

It might seem pretentious to propose yet another concept aimed at changing people's behavior, not only because of the French proverb *Plus ça change, plus c'est la même chose,* but because, in a world of accelerating change, the attempt to define the concept *change* becomes ever more elusive. Change in our present era might actually act to preserve existing values in a changing world. Yet people feel compelled to find a better way of living, whether for immediate benefit or in order to find a meaning and purpose in their lives.

This model of psychotherapy holds as a basic underlying concept that people are in constant motion; that change is inevitable; that, as Heraclitus said, it is not possible to step into the same river twice. Motion in life is always directed toward an ideal, a goal. Changes in our relationships are likewise directed toward attainment of those goals in terms of our idealized conceptions of self, of others, and of the final result.

A therapist who operates on the premises of Adlerian theory assumes the position of leader in the therapeutic process. The therapist's role aims at enlarging the individual's social interest, helping him or her to overcome feelings of inferiority, helping the individual modify his or her goals, as well as training the client toward greater contribution within interpersonal relationships. The therapeutic process is thus essentially an educative one that results in a tangible movement forward for the individual.

Psychotherapy as directed movement involves a reprocessing of the childhood pattern of development, and especially its social aspect. Socialization is a process, beginning in childhood, of finding one's place in society, of feeling a sense of belonging and of contributing, which occurs simultaneously with the individual's constant forward movement in life. The flow of life thus involves a developing sequence of circles of belonging with widening possibilities of contribution and new goals.

Circles of Belonging

Every new human being becomes the center of a new world, the center of a human circle. The infant forms a first human relationship with the person who takes care of him or her, generally the mother. However, the infant's efforts and creativity in the development of this relationship must be stressed. He or she is definitely not simply a receptive object of the mother's ministrations, but is an active participant in the transaction. Since he is a creative being, the child's development is directed from the interior to the exterior, to the world of other objects. Generally, psychologists have ascribed variable personality development to the environment of the child. They focus on the attitudes of others toward the child, the projection of their personal needs in the relationship with the child, and their responses to the child's existence and behavior. In contrast, and taking the existential viewpoint, IP therapists regard the life movement of all people, including the newborn, as directed from the inside to the outside, as a reaching out from a relatively secure and comfortable existence to an unknown condition. This risk taking in reaching to the external world is the heart of the development process, the motivation for advancement.

The relationship with the mother is the first ring in the development of the child's circle of belonging. The child's social development proceeds through a sequence of widening concentric circles, which can be pictured as a radius projected outward from the nuclear center to encompass the enlarging circles of belonging that develop in life. As illustrated in Figure 29.1, the first circle

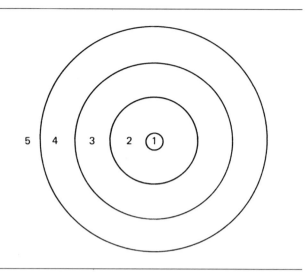

Figure 29.1   Circles of belonging: How they might be for a particular person. (1) Mother. (2) Family. (3) Social group. (4) Professional group. (5) Political party.

is likely to be the mother. The second circle includes other members of the nuclear family; subsequent circles represent the widening social experiences of the individual, which are unique to each child. When such a diagram is created for an individual, not every social framework is included; only those where the individual feels belonging by contributing to and receiving meaningful feedback. Social frameworks that are not a meaningful part of the individual's existence are not included.

Contribution

Contribution, a concept related to social interest, is central to IPT. During the socialization process, the individual acquires skills, such as being able to speak up and address people, to find assistance, to inspire affection and appreciation, to relate the body to various configurations of space, to listen and use feedback, and so on. These skills become part of the individual's behavior repertoire, but for some people these skills are underdeveloped or missing. IP therapists attempt to give individuals new social skills and associated attitudes so that they can contribute more meaningfully and thereby enlarge their feeling of significance. Where there is a severe limitation in the development of the social repetoire, there we find impasses.

Impasses

The impasse concept developed from a determined search for the precursors of the lifestyle. IP therapists came to understand that the child's self-determination process and adoption of a lifestyle pattern was not only a process of selective choice but also a process of wary elimination. Every positive decision is also a decision to avoid and negate alternatives. When a person decides to go to the movies, he also decides not to stay home or to read or to be with friends. In other words, any decision reflects a process of elimination. In childhood the process of elimination is not a random matter but often arises from a negative or traumatic social experience.

Human life involves a process of searching how to be significant. This process begins at birth—with mere survival—since survival is a condition of life. To survive, the child first learns what must be avoided—which is a negative learning. Negative learning can be divided into two forms: (1) *physical negative learning*—the avoidance of fire, water, falling, and so on; and (2) *social negative learning*—the avoidance of ridicule, stress, mistakes, self-depreciation, and so forth. This learning becomes rigidly fixed in the early years of life and serves as a reminder of what is dangerous, both physically and psychologically. This learning is based upon the child's biased perception of self and the world. This may explain why a child disregards many influences of the social environment once the lifestyle is formed, especially if those influences do not fit his or her apperceptive schema. If social experiences remain equally influential throughout life, then one's lifestyle would change with varying influences. However, once the lifestyle is formed, the basic personality appears to remain fixed; despite a myriad of later social influences, it does not change to any significant degree. Negative learning probably precedes positive learning in the creation of the personality, and leads to the development of physical and social avoidance strategies. Just as the child learns to avoid fire or being burned, falling, and so forth, he or she develops a similar avoidance strategy toward social situations where he or she feels nonsignificant. The child's behavior then becomes focused on conduct and actions that assure a feeling of significance.

An impasse is viewed as a nexus or a complex of feared social behavior that the person always avoids. The term *always* is used deliberately because I am convinced that a persona always operates in terms of impasses, avoiding them like a burned cat avoids a flame.

The traumatic experience that produced the impasse was always a social one and so leads to an avoidance strategy in the social living of the individual. *Impasse* implies the end of the road, a roadblock, from which one cannot advance further. And, as a driver avoids roads marked "dead end," so in life also a person stops moving in a certain direction when he or she psychologically reads "dead end."

Some other psychological theories include a concept of impasse or deadlock. Psychoanalysis traces deadlocks to the unconscious formation of intrapsychic conflicts. In Primal Therapy, the impasse is traced to shock experiences that took place in infancy or early childhood, and its therapy is directed to releasing the person from this shock through abreaction techniques. Gestalt Therapy deals with present deadlocks in a concrete and holistic manner; here the individual works on the deadlock himself, but it is carried out in a group setting. Forms of therapy such as Encounter, Rebirthing, and Creative Aggression all deal with breaking down of deadlocks by means of support, release of aggression, or relearning. What distinguishes the IP approach to deadlock or impasse is its strong emphasis on the social setting and relations that initiate the impasse and are involved in its resolution.

Even though the original traumatic events may have been diverse and may have occurred at different times during the child's early development, they tend to fall into four generalized categories, which are called the four basic impasses. They are: (1) appearing *ridiculous;* (2) being *insignificant;* (3) being *rejected;* and (4) avoiding *stress.*

Ridicule.   A person who has this impasse is afraid of being in a situation in which he or she is not in control, where he or she might behave in a socially unsuccessful manner, or might seem not to understand the rules of the environment. A person blocked by ridicule sees others as scornful and hostile.

Meaninglessness.   A person with this block is afraid of being insignificant, having no influence on the environment, having no value, no possibility of proving himself, being unimportant.

Rejection.   Persons with this impasse fear rejection— being unwanted, unappreciated, disregarded, overlooked, unloved. Therefore, they believe themselves incapable of living alone and think that others provide justification for their existence.

Stress.   People with this impasse fear for their very existence. They feel a lack of energy, lack of breath, when confronting an anticipated stress. To them, others seem to be constantly confronting them, which heightens their feeling of threat to their existence. Even routine tasks are viewed as stressful—and something to be avoided.

These impasse situations appear as existential dangers, as though one were entering a dark tunnel with no exits. Dread of confronting these impasses is inflated beyond proportion. Through repetitive experiences, first within the family and then later in larger and larger circles (see Figure 29.1), we begin to form a strategy of living, dominated by our desire to avoid those situations that could bring forth the impasses we dread. As a consequence, one's choices in life are restricted and one is operating minimally, always in fear of the impasses. The paralyzing fear and limited choices therefore restrict possibilities for living fully, for contributing and finding meaning and happiness in life.

Priorities—The Existential Precondition

Avoidance strategy, the movement away from expected social danger, is the first stage in the development of the lifestyle. The young child either overcomes the basic fear that the social trauma/impasse generates or the fear becomes intensified, leading to an avoidance strategy. At this point one of the most important decisions in life is made: whether movement in life will be mainly toward goals or away from dangers.

Both are movement strategies, since all life is movement. But there is a difference between when we move toward something or away from something. When we move toward something, there is a sense of positive direction; when we avoid, out of fear, there is no direction, only chaotic flight. Priorities arise out of our creative power to organize chaos. Priorities clear a pathway for organizing human relations. As the choice of the priority arises from the impasse, the best way to discover each priority is to trace it back to the impasse. Priorities are there not because they are preferred behavior, but because they are seen as the *only* way to significant social survival.

Four priority dynamic patterns have been identified. They are:

The Controller. Being a controller is a guarantee against being ridiculed. This means that the person must not be laughed at, must not appear ridiculous, and must be in complete control of the current situation so that he or she will not suffer any embarrassment. Such people are socially sensitive and are greatly concerned with proprieties.

The Pleaser. Pleasers must avoid rejection. To do so, they seek constant acceptance and approval. They will do anything to achieve approbation since they dread being disliked or found unimportant. The pleaser is agreeable only as long as approval is given.

The Morally Superior. Such persons avoid anonymity. They obtain significance and influence on people by high achievement, leadership, martyrdom, or in any fashion that makes them feel that they are "superior" persons.

The Avoider. Avoiders are reactors; they use delay and specialize in unfinished business, unresolved problems, and unmade decisions—avoiding anything that implies *stress.* In avoiders, unlike in the other dynamic patterns of behavior, the chaotic flight generated by the social im-

passe was never organized in a behavioral or temporal sense. Avoiders see their lives as always in a temporary state.

Each priority gives us different ways of being significant. In each priority one can be more active or passive, more cooperative and contributing, more useful or useless—there is a whole range of possible expressions. For example, one might ask, "How does an avoider gain significance?" The logic behind this behavior might be: "I am significant when I am secure, and I am secure only when I am left alone." This is a passive way of life as an onlooker. Noninvolvement, watching others, becomes a way of being on top of the situation. With moral superiority, significance can be achieved by contribution, but one can also feel superior in a negative way by being a victim.

To become fully aware of ourselves, we have to learn: (1) what our priority and condition for feeling significant is; (2) what our avoidance strategy is based on—in other words, what the impasse was; and (3) how we can find alternative ways to gain significance using a larger repertoire.

Structured Stages of Therapy

Psychotherapy is not generally studied in universities; rather it is usually learned during unstructured transactions between supervisors and trainees. Psychotherapy is undoubtedly a creative art. Yet unlike Leonardo da Vinci's apprentices, who spent some of their best years in study, we allow novices only a brief glimpse into the holy of holies—the therapy room—because most of us have difficulties describing what actually takes place there. In constructing a therapeutic setting, I have tried to turn a mysterious process into a teachable one that is not over-affected by the charismatic personality of the therapist.

In Impasse/Priority Therapy, the emphasis is placed on work caried out by the client under the guidance of the therapist. This involves a reprocessing of the patient's socialization, with the goal being to encourage movement forward in conjunction with an activation of social interest. The different stages of therapy designed to reach this goal are part of the resocialization process.

The first stage is a *diagnosis* and *structuring;* a one-to-one relationship between client and therapist that mirrors the first circle of belonging. The second stage, the *marathon,* is similar to the social setting of the family. The third stage, the *workshop,* represents the larger social sphere (school, work, community). The fourth stage, *study,* represents independent functioning in the social world. This four-part therapeutic structure is designed to guide the individual from awareness to breaking through the impasse, a process that takes place during the first two stages. Thereafter, the workshop stage encourages the acquisition and practice of broader social skills, which are further developed in the fourth stage. One can view these four stages as a process of learning, unlearning, relearning, and reinforcing goals.

METHODOLOGY

In some places psychotherapy has acquired a negative stereotype. In Israel the client's encounter with therapists prior to the intake interview generally involves a series of bureaucratic procedures—coming to an office, registering, paying in advance, and then waiting up to six weeks for the first interview to take place. No wonder the client has a low level of expectation at this point and is totally unaware that he or she is about to enter an unforeseeable experience.

The creativity of the therapist in IPT is of crucial importance, especially during the intake interview and in the first stages of the therapeutic relations. In this field there is no greater danger than routine. The therapist needs to be original, thinking constantly in terms of new ideas and forms; he or she must always be sure of being understood. Regarding creativity, solo private practice is not a satisfactory therapeutic approach because it lacks the feedback and contributing ideas of a team. The one-to-one pattern similar to parent/child, teacher/pupil, sinner/confessor common to private practice work is too limiting for IPT.

The Intake Interview and Individual Therapy

The intake interview is conducted by a senior therapist in conjunction with another member of the staff. The interview is a diagnostic one in which we discuss problems, bring them into focus, and arrive at a common goal. The goal is a guideline by which to assess the client's advance in therapy. A typical question explored is: "If you could change your life by pressing a button, what would it be like?" This question is particularly useful when people come in with a generalized problem or condition. In such cases, we tell the client to come back with a more concrete idea of what is wanted. For example, the general complaint of "depression" is insufficient as a reference point for therapy. We have to focus and find a common desired goal from which to proceed.

We approach the intake interview in an antibureaucratic way. We do not focus on the collection of many personal details or facts, but rather concentrate on the therapeutic contract and the setting of goals. Here creativity and flexibility are essential. To illustrate: N., a man of 38, came to the first interview well supplied with information about himself. A student in a rabbinical academy, he was well read in psychological literature and identified himself as a schizophrenic. He felt therapy offered no chance for him, but because he had found Adler's theory plausible he was willing to give it a try. His manner was both arrogant and engaging. He was clearly testing us; and, indeed, he succeeded—so much so that it was very tempting for the therapist to roll up sleeves and plunge into an intellectual power conflict, which sometimes is taken for therapy. It was clear that there was no common goal. Paradoxically, we asked N. to prepare a paper on schizophrenia, comparing at least three theories, and for him to try to establish which theory was most applicable to him. We promised that after examining his work, we would present it to the staff. In this way we hoped to gain his commitment and cooperation. And it worked.

Individual Therapy.   The first stage of the IPT process generally involves 15 to 20 individual sessions that continue at the same time as participation in the marathon or workshop stages. During this stage the client learns about his or her lifestyle, early deadlocks or impasses, existential preconditions or priorities, and the way he or she moves on the social map. This is the only stage that deals with interpretation and self-awareness through exploratory exercises and homework. Members of the client's family—the family of origin or one the client has built; in the absence of either, a close personal friend—are invited to participate. The purpose of including significant others is to get a three-dimensional insight into the client's position in the family constellation, and, at the same time, to check the credibility of the client's self-image with others. From this point the client moves on to the next stage.

The Marathon.   The marathon is structured as an intensive group experience that runs for five consecutive days, eight hours each day. About 20 participants have an opportunity to work on the various concepts introduced each day. These personal observations are discussed and actively experienced in the group setting. A variety of learning techniques are utilized that expose the participants to the concepts in an intensive way through lectures, guidance, short therapy, and help from the group. The marathon is designed to be a self-growth process, in which clients are aided by the help from and support of other group members.

The marathon is designed to provide the time, concentration, and guidance for the individual participants to move from *awareness,* a passive state, to *connections*—energized, gestaltic moments. In the marathon, awareness becomes integrated into a holistic, encompassing focus for action.

To distinguish *connection* (bonding) from *awareness* (insight), it is useful to use the example of orgasm. The literature on sexual techniques explains well what takes place within ourselves during sexual intercourse, and also guides us, via positions and operations, to learn how we can attain the longed-for result. However, even if we follow instructions to the letter, an orgasm is not guaranteed, because the orgasm is an authentic occurrence involving all our mental and physical being. An orgasm takes place in the brain and can even occur without physical stimulation. Paradoxically, orgasm appears to occur at a peak point of self-control and concentration and at the same time calls for loss of control and abandonment. In this paradoxical condition the authentic orgasm is experienced.

Similar to the orgasm, connection occurs on a different level from awareness. A combination of physical and mental states is necessary for a connection to take place. Like the orgasm, the moment of connection is brief, fleeting, and cannot be sustained. Another similarity between the two phenomena is the difficulty of describing either experience in words. By their nature, they are personal phenomena whose meaning exists solely for the self. And, notwithstanding all the help of others, the individual experiences them alone.

Individual therapy supplies the patient with good insights, and he learns much about himself by clarifying experiences that had previously been unclear. However, movement forward (energized action) cannot take place without "orgasmic" connections.

Connections may occur in therapy only if the following conditions exist: (1) an intensive social setting; (2) a specific system of stimuli combining mental and physical activities that lead to intense concentration and release; and (3) hard work. At the moment of connection one feels energy flowing out from one's center to the world. It is a metamorphic experience.

The concentrated group work of the five marathon days forms the link in a chain that enables the individual to make connections. Following the first stage of individual therapy, where the main objectives are to form a therapeutic contract and to provide insight, awareness, and clarification of goals, the marathon fosters a breakthrough of impasses, thus opening up new possibilities for growth.

The techniques used in the marathon are varied and specifically designed to aid the participants in reexperiencing the basic social impasses, to "survive" them, and to discover new strengths and energy. Screaming, fantasizing, relaxation versus physical exertion, breaking into a closed circle, physical closeness, singing, dancing, and so forth, are characteristic activities. Other activities include elaboration of the lifestyle and the priorities, or existential preconditions, both through personal writing and group experiences. All of these activities serve mainly as catalysts for making connections.

In the marathon, as in the sexual act, there are those who "come quickly"; that is, for some the climactic connection happens on the second or third day. However,

unlike the sexual act, those who come quickly remain with the group and supply others with the new energy discovered within them. Others "come" slowly, or on the last day, and sometimes only later, at home, does the longed-for connection take place.

Workshop. The workshop stage of therapy takes place over the course of a year. Usually the client starts to participate in a workshop shortly after completing the marathon.

The workshop approach evolved as a fruitful alternative to classical group therapy. The institute staff in Israel has worked with group methods since its inception in 1963, and has found there are definite limitations to group therapy as generally practiced. These limitations include: (1) the burned-out therapist phenomenon; (2) the problems posed by passive members and the efforts spent trying to activate them; (3) the difficulty of determining when to end a group; (4) the dependency and pressure on the therapist as the leader, teacher, and authority figure; (5) the inadequacy of verbal communication (typical of classical groups) to meet the needs of certain participants; and (6) the fact that classical group methods, while adequate for providing feedback to individuals, are not a good tool for helping them move forward within and without the group. As a consequence, the staff at the Alfred Adler Institute of Tel Aviv developed a new group work model, the workshops, that stimulate clients to activate and actualize their advancement better.

Six kinds of workshops were developed to fit the needs of the client population. There are workshops for (1) married couples, (2) young adults, age 20 to 30, (3) midlife adults, age 30 to 50, (4) elderly people, age 50 to 70, (5) teenagers, age 15 to 18, and (6) families. Each workshop involves between 20 and 30 participants and includes both men and women. A team of two staff members conducts each workshop, which runs for between eight and nine months with a total of 40 weekly sessions.

Every other week all workshop members attend a five-hour session. On alternate weeks, from the second meeting on, workshop members are divided into "home groups" of six to eight people. Thus, all participants meet together for 20 sessions; for the other 20 sessions they meet in small groups in private homes on a rotating basis and work in leaderless fashion discussing topics brought up in the large workshop meetings.

The workshop approach is designed to enable people to learn in their own way. There are basically three ways in which people learn: (1) rational or cognitive, (2) experiential-emotional, and (3) passive observer. Every large assembly workshop is designed to foster all three forms of learning. A topic that needs thinking, interpretation, teleological reasoning, and so forth, is presented, and part of the evening is designed for experiencing through active, physical movement—body image work, fantasizing, creative drama, art therapy, and so on. Last, part of each large session is set aside for demonstrations where participants can learn by observing other people who are the focus of attention. Such demonstrations are likely to include an exposition of a lifestyle, work with early recollections or family constellation, or focusing on a married couple or family. Thus, in the course of the five-hour session, all participants can find a meaningful way to learn.

Skill building and the social framework is another important aspect of the workshop's therapeutic endeavor. Over the course of the year, the participants become mutually responsible and help each other in meeting certain life challenges. They provide the support and encouragement for the individual to carry out a change in his or her life patterns.

The home groups contribute much in this respect. The rotational scheme of meeting in homes means that everyone, without exception, must serve as a host to the others and provide a basic refreshment (simple coffee and biscuits with minimal time involvement). This process enhances the development of social skills for young people and those who feel socially inadequate. It emphasizes the social equality of all members, and provides an opportunity for them to observe the host member in a home setting. Through feedback and support, the group exerts a strong influence on the others. Through sharing and mutual help, the individuals experience the rewarding sense of contribution and the concrete meaning of social interest.

The feeling of belonging generated encourages group members to meet the challenges in other aspects of their lives. The groups provide an antidote to the alienation and loneliness of contemporary society by creating a feeling of family in the best sense, beyond the petty competition and rivalry that infects so many real families. In sum, the home groups have become a remarkable meeting point from which all sorts of things emerge for the participants despite their wide-ranging backgrounds and interests. The home groups are the most influential part of the program, but most participants feel this could take place only as an outgrowth of the larger workshop framework.

Advanced Study and Community Work. By the time the clients have completed the three stages of individual therapy, the marathon, and the workshop, they are ready for advanced study. In the prior stages they were focused mostly on themselves. Now they need a larger conceptual framework in which to relate and practice what they have learned on the world at large. At this level, it is strongly recommended that clients—who are now referred to as *students*—enroll in courses in social studies

and human relations provided by the Adler Institute and other institutions. Such courses open the way for them to become involved in community work and thus actively contribute to others. Some students have volunteered to answer telephones for "hotline" mental first aid programs, while others have worked with underachieving children in volunteer programs, and so forth.

APPLICATIONS

It is necessary to see Impasse/Priority Therapy in its larger context as a functional unit of the Adler Institute, which is primarily oriented toward improving human relations for the individual, the family, social organizations, and the community at large. This ties in to the concept of the circles of belonging described earlier, and to the basic Adlerian belief that individual growth is a movement toward increased contribution or social interest. The institute is designed to foster the realization of these goals whether through IPT for individuals and small groups or various other educational programs and community services.

CASE EXAMPLE

M was 26 when she entered therapy. She was on probation and referred for therapy by her parents under pressure from the court. Her transgression: She had been caught in an apartment where police uncovered a brothel, drug dealing, and orgies. A firstborn daughter, M had a sister three years younger. Her parents had survived the Holocaust and met and married on a refugee ship that brought them to Israel in 1948.

My first impression upon meeting M was that she was an attractive and provocative person who possessed an uncommon intuitive sensitivity to people, odors, feelings, and nature. She was imaginative, audacious, and daring with a rich, internal world. Her vocabulary, however, was poor and strongly infused with street slang. She had a considerable capacity for creating contact with almost anybody.

Intake Interview

M appeared at the therapist's office at the appointed day and hour. She came into the office barefoot, having walked miles on the blazing roads from her house. The soles of her feet looked like those of the Bedouins who are accustomed all their life to walk barefoot on the sands and rocks of the desert. She was wearing a bright, transparent, light cotton dress with nothing underneath, and her large breasts were almost uncovered. An enormous mass of blond hair curled almost down to her hips.

She had no purse or any other article of dress. Our opening dialogue went as follows:

M: You gonna be my therapist?

T: No.

M: Why, don't you deal with whores?

T: No.

M: Junkies?

T: No.

M: Tough asthmatic cases?

T: No.

M: So who do you deal with in this office anyway?

T: With children who don't like to do their homework. (Laughter)

M: Last night I made it with five men. Don't that blow your mind?

T: No.

M: For a therapist, your vocabulary is quite poor. (Laughter; both are still standing. Long silence, watching each other)

M: I didn't make it with them—they raped me. They were five marketstand owners, regular clients of mine. They all came up together, but when I wanted to split, they raped me. In the end, they left some dough anyway. (Her expression was unemotional with a penetrating gaze that didn't fit the silly smile on her face.) Wanna hear the details? (Provocatively.)

T: I don't think so.

M: Maybe we'll sit down already?

T: Sure.

M: When we are standing, we look like two suspects waiting in the corridor of the Hall of Justice. You ever been there?

T: Yes, but I didn't wait. I was in the judge's chamber.

M: How long will my therapy take?

T: I haven't decided to accept you yet.

M: If you're thinking of putting me through tests, forget it—I always fail. In all tests I've taken in my life, I have failed.

T: In what didn't you fail? (Both sitting down)

M: You tell me.

T: In impressing people. (Laughter)

Summarized History from the Probation Report

M was born in 1948 and suffered from severe asthma during her childhood. At school she was considered almost retarded and did not form any contacts with teachers or students. As the eldest daughter whose parents had survived the Holocaust, she had been overprotected to the point of suffocation, while at the same time she was severely punished by her mother for her disobedience, low achievement, escapes, wandering the streets, and so forth. She had always been close to her father, but as the weak person in the family, he felt obliged to be loyal to his wife, and thus "betrayed" M in her most difficult moments. There was no meaningful relationship with her sister.

M's beauty, height, and wit were impressive, and she irritated others because of her indifference toward the world and achievement. At the age of 14, she was sent to a kibbutz from which she absconded after a year and returned home. Following months of idleness, she met Y by chance, and he induced her to work the streets as a prostitute. At 16 she left home and has had very little contact with her parents since. After a brief period working as a model, she left Israel for Germany and worked as a hooker in Hamburg for three years. There she was abused by Y, whom she loved. She was arrested and spent two weeks in the Hamburg city jail, which she passed in continuous fantasizing. She imagined being in Auschwitz where her mother had been incarcerated. Her release from jail, expulsion from Germany, and return to Israel are remembered as if seen through a screen. When she returned to Israel three years ago, she resumed working as a call girl. Y disappeared from her life; he went to work at sea, smuggling. She, meanwhile, made a lot of money, got involved with drugs, and her asthmatic condition worsened.

Stages of Therapy

Individual therapy with M, the first stage, extended for six months. In spite of her using a variety of symptoms, her repertoire of skills for life were very limited. During this stage, we elaborated upon her impasses and priorities. Her social repertoire had become so small because all alternatives had been eliminated or become impossible for her. It was impossible for her to deal with people because any slight feeling of rejection was alarming to her. She also had to be on top of every situation, in complete control. That limited her mostly to one-to-one relations and, further, to relate only to others whom she could dominate. Such persons were typically social misfits, drug addicts, or frustrated artists and others who depended on her economically and for ego support.

That helped to explain her sense of persecution. She felt persecuted by herself, by her crazy fears, and by her own power of destruction. She also suffered from the impasse of avoidance of stress, because she had not had any successful experiences in coping with life tasks. Thus she couldn't dare to take a job or even to do something about her asthma. Apart from our meetings, she was always late for anything she did, wore no watch, and had no daily schedule. The idea of planning was not in her repertoire, because planning itself was stressful. But the strongest impasse for M was not to be insignificant, and her number one priority became striving for moral superiority. Even her imbecilic behavior enabled her to gain significance because of its shocking effect on others. The biggest issue for her was overambition within, which was combined with the desire to be perfect in all the priorities, which in turn only reinforced and strengthened the impasses.

As part of M's individual therapy stage, different members and then her entire family participated in order to start a new, accepting relationship that gave her a feeling of belonging in the first circle of belonging. Then she was ready to move beyond one-to-one relationships and from awareness to connections.

Her main benefit from participating in the marathon was that she engaged in intensive group work in which she worked only for herself, neither attempting to excel or be different in any way. She thus discovered a sense of belonging by merely participating as all the others did. All her bizarre behavior, which usually brought her attention, was permitted but ignored. She came as close as possible to her impasse, and there made the most important connection of all. She discovered that she was always significant to herself, that she provided her own significance and no longer needed to depend on others to be significant.

During the workshop stage, M moved from attention-getting to leadership, undertaking responsibility in the process. Through other people she learned about life tasks and how they are met by others. She also learned firsthand the roles of both the helper and the helped. She developed skills such as expressing herself in a group setting, listening, being passive, and not quitting when she felt like it. She also learned for the first time in her life the "we" feeling in a setting that permitted her to stay "I." During this period she was encouraged by the group members to start a business, which she later did. For her, the most important experience of the workshop was just being with people and feeling at ease with them. Although prostitution was never a major issue between us, symbolically she stopped this work as she prepared to host the home group for the first time.

Fourth Stage

By the end of the workshop, one and a half years had passed since M started therapy. She was ready to move and to learn. She was hungry to be significant in the real world, and thus she enrolled in the Open University to study Judaism and Jewish history (symbolizing her desire for belonging and roots). At the same time, she began her own fashion boutique. To the time of this writing some two years later, she sees her therapist occasionally. She now owns three boutiques, does her own designing, employs 15 people, including two former

workshop members, and, after a long period of exclusively platonic social relations, is preparing, at age 30, for a mature love relationship. As busy and as self-actualizing a person as she has become, she revealed not long ago that the only thing she truly wants is to change her childhood memories.

SUMMARY

In Impasse/Priority Therapy, movement forward, from a minus to a plus situation, is regarded as an integral part of therapy. Meaningful interpersonal movement is considered the criterion for mental health. Disturbances in the flow of life are seen as stemming from early deadlocks, or impasses, due to failures in social learning. The impasses we acquire early in the socialization process are always one or more of the following:

1. I cannot move while I am ridiculous.
2. I cannot move while threatened with being insignificant.
3. I cannot move while I am in danger of being rejected.
4. I cannot move while under pressure.

After the formation of one or more of these impasses, the life style crystallizes, incorporating the individual's idiosyncratic view of the self, the world, and his or her position in the world. Because the lifestyle emerges after the impasses have been created, it is derivative of the prior deduction and the elimination of alternatives. Through the lifestyle, for instance, especially as it is mirrored in childhood recollections, we can determine the strategic priorities the individual has chosen because we can see which directions of movement are considered "impossible." In the lifestyle we can discern four personality priorities: (1) *control,* (2) *moral superiority,* (3) *pleasing,* and (4) *avoidance.* These are not preferred behaviors, they are "musts." Only permanent control of the situation precludes the danger of seeming ridiculous; only superiority guarantees against being insignificant; only pleasing averts rejection; and only avoidance prevents pressure and stress.

The diagnostic process in IPT clarifies the individual's movement on the map of life that is always populated by other people. How does the individual move among them? What is the direction of the movement? What is seen as an obstacle? By what direction is this obstacle evaded? Therapy, then, deals with these issues in a connected approach through: (1) priorities evaluation (individual consultation and family therapy); (2) experiencing deadlocks or impasses (the marathon); (3) enlarging the social repertoire (the workshop); and (4) activating social interest (studies, community work).

The impasse/priorities therapeutic program has four parts, some of which may overlap with others: (1) individual sessions for diagnosis and planning of the program; (2) an intensive marathon that runs for eight hours a day for five consecutive days; (3) a workshop that meets weekly, for eight to nine months, consisting of one group session of about 20 people or one home session of about six to eight people; and finally, an open-ended self-development program intended to help people to help others.

IP philosophy is consonant with Alfred Adler's idealism in stressing social interest and with the ideas of Hillel, who said, "If I am not for myself, who will be? But if I am only for myself, what am I?"

To contribute, to learn, to move forward, to feel the need to move others along with us—IP therapists are doing just what the moon is doing, illuminating the world.

REFERENCES

Adler, A. (1956). *The individual psychology of Alfred Adler* (H. L. Ansbacher & R. Ansbacher, Eds.). New York: Basic Books.

Adler, A. (1964). *Superiority and social interest* (H. L. Ansbacher & R. Ansbacher, Eds.). Evanston, IL: Northwestern University Press.

Adler, A. (1972). *Study of organ inferiority and its psychical compensation.* New York: Johnson Reprint Corp. (Original work published 1917)

Brown, J. F. (1976). *Practical applications of the personality priorities* (2nd ed.). Clinton, MD: B & F Associates.

Buber, M. (1958). *I and thou.* New York: Scribners.

Dreikurs, R. (1960). *Group psychotherapy and group approaches: Collected papers.* Chicago: Alfred Adler Institute.

Dreikurs, R. (1967). *Psychodynamics, psychotherapy and counseling: Collected papers.* Chicago: Alfred Adler Institute.

Dreikurs, R. (1973). Private logic. In H. H. Mosak (Ed.), *Alfred Adler: His influence on psychology today.* Park Ridge, NJ: Noyes Press.

Frankl, V. (1965). *Doctor and the soul.* New York: Knopf.

Frankl, V. (1968). *Psychotherapy and existentialism.* New York: Simon & Schuster.

Janov, A. (1970). *The primal scream.* New York: Dell.

Kfir, N. (1971). Priorities—A different approach to life style and neurosis. Paper presented at ICASSI, Tel Aviv, Israel.

Kfir, N., & Corsini, R. J. (1974). Dispositional sets: A contribution to typology. *Journal of Individual Psychology, 30*(2), 163–178.

Perls, F. (1969). *Gestalt therapy verbatim.* (J. O. Stevens, Ed.) Toronto: Bantam Books.

Perls, F. S., Hefferline, R., & Goodman, P. (1951). *Gestalt therapy: Excitement and growth in the human personality.* New York: Delta.

Pew, W. L. (1976, August 1). The number one priority. *International Association of Individual Psychology Monograph* (Munich, Germany).

Sartre, J.-P. (1956). *Being and nothingness.* New York: Philosophical Library.

Sutton, J. M. (1976). *A validity study of Kfir's priorities: A theory of maladaptive behavior and psychotherapy.* Unpublished doctoral thesis, University of Maine at Orono.

Ward, D. E. (1979). Implications of personality priority assessment for the counseling process. *Individual Psychologist, 16*(2), 12–16.

Chapter 30

INTEGRATION THERAPY

SAYID MUHAMMAD MUHSIN JALALI-TEHRANI

This unique system of therapy, intended to achieve the same goals of growth therapies, is written by an Iranian, a follower of Islamic values, and was developed first in a university setting (Ferdowsi in Mashhad) and then in a prison setting. Dr. Jalali-Tehrani first got in touch with me because he had read some of my prison writings. It turned out that he had developed a unique psychotherapy system that helped inmates to turn their lives around, and which I believe has value not only in prisons throughout the world but also for people everywhere, regardless of their religion or belief system.

Readers will have an extra benefit from examining this system since it will explain to some extent Muslim philosophy and theory as well as purely psychotherapy theory and practice. It falls chiefly into the area of existential-humanistic psychology, of which there are several examples in this book. Dr. Jalali-Tehrani makes the cogent point that universities are not as congenial to innovation as are prisons. To that, I say, amen. The concept of integration involves having a unifying life theme that serves to give the person direction. This theme can be based on a genuine religious or spiritual orientation, a theme also mentioned by Viktor Frankl and O. Hobart Mowrer.

The methodology covers six points, described as a treatment of the whole individual, and is put into action by a team, usually consisting of the clinical director, therapist, social worker, educational specialist, medical specialist, and peer counselor. This compares with Dr. Kefir's method in Israel and Dr. Gazda's approach in the United States, present in this book.

DEFINITION

Integration Therapy, as a method of promoting human growth and development, has a common history with all growth psychologies. Other disciplines, such as religion and philosophy, the arts and humanities, which have focused on the nature of the human being, the role of values in human life, what blocks human growth and what facilitates it, share this history as well. Thus, the roots of integration therapy can be said to extend to the human being's earliest search for self understanding, at finding and developing a way of life that leads to the highest fulfillment and development.

HISTORY

In its current form, Integration Therapy has a 25-year history. Integration Therapy can be said to be a natural combination of the Islamic understanding of the nature of the human being and the theory and practice of humanistic psychology. This represents the first time that Islamic theory has taken shape as an explicit, mod-

ern psychological theory and method of psychotherapy. Although Integration Therapy grows from Islamic emphasis on integration as a governing principle in the universe, it shares a rich background with other techniques, especially in the humanistic, gestalt, existential-phenomenological, person-centered, and cognitive approaches.

Coming from a family background of Islamic scholars as well as a lived experience of Islam, the author began psychology studies in Iran in the early 1970s. This coincided with a remarkable revival of Islamic thought that was occurring in many places in the world. Outstanding contemporary scholars, such as the late Allamah Sayid Muhammad-Husain Tabatabai and the late Sayid Muhammad-Husain Husaini-Tehrani, were shedding new light on centuries-old wisdom found in the works of philosophers such as Sadr-al-din Muhammad Shirazi, also known as Mulla Sadra.

These writings served to revive Islamic thought and showed Islam as more than a series of religious practices. Islam was found vital to present-day concerns, a way of living in integration and harmony with all of creation, a vibrant path to human growth and development. Central to this was the Islamic viewpoint on the positive nature and potential of the human being, identifying obstacles to development, and outlining goals and values.

Poetry provided an experiential arena for this revival. An inclusive list of the precursors of integration therapy must include the poets Jalal-al-din Muhammad Balkhi, also known as Maulavi, or Rumi, and Shams-al-din Muhammad Shirazi, known widely as Hafiz. These poets, each in his own inimitable style, exhibited remarkable insights into the human personality, assigning a central place to spiritual longing and the human being's struggle to reconcile the self with virtue. Their poetry, in ways transcending form and content, often provokes experiences which transform the lives of their readers.

This renewed interest in religion and spirituality seemed to speak in a timely manner to the human being's quest to find harmony between a deep inner truth and what many sensed as a call to the spiritual. It helped to strike the balance between the material and the spiritual, to understand the relation between the human and the divine. Enthusiasm for these ideas spread throughout the culture, in a movement that crossed class and generational lines. Islam, as newly understood, became a source of meaning for many lives.

The author pursued a master's degree in psychology at United States International University in San Diego, California, which at the time was a noted center for humanistic studies. Visiting lecturers such as Viktor Frankl, Carl Rogers, Albert Ellis, and J. F. T. Bugental were complemented by full-time faculty such as Harold Greenwald. It was intriguing to find that humanistic theory and philosophy echoed several key principles of Islamic thought. Many humanistic models for psychotherapy, as well as their underlying theories, were in harmony with Islamic thought, as though both were flowing from some common stream of knowledge. Excitement began to grow about building a theory that would articulate the similar core concepts in these two systems. Being able to build bridges of understanding between these two disciplines, between Islam and psychology, seemed increasingly possible.

Further input to the humanistic underpinning of integration therapy came during master's study in the Institute for Islamic Studies at McGill University. Interestingly enough, the greatest contribution to integration therapy came not from the Islamic Studies department, where the emphasis was mostly on interpretations of Islamic theory and history, but through elective courses taken in the departments of philosophy and pastoral studies.

Greek philosophy addressed such classic issues as what is the good, final causes, the good society, and in general served to sharpen critical and logical skills. The pastoral studies department offered works by Gordon Allport, Abraham Maslow, and Gabriel Marcel. These

were to prove critical building blocks. Allport's ideas of values, and the importance of religious values as integrating forces in the human personality, Maslow's quest for "the good person in the good society," of being-growth versus deficiency growth, all struck familiar chords and took their place in this developing theory. Marcel's respect for the human being and emphasis on values, as well as his inclusion of an attitude toward the divine as an essential part of full human experience, were inspiring and encouraging.

Integration therapy grew further during doctoral studies at the Humanistic Psychology Institute, now known as Saybrook Institute. There, with Stanley Krippner as sponsor and chief advisor, the author was free to fully develop his understanding of ideas that were growing and converging so powerfully. A doctoral thesis on religion as a factor in integration, a factor in mental health, was chaired by Stanley Krippner and confirmed by committee member the late Rollo May.

In this work, integration was identified as an essential factor in mental health; further, integration was shown to be achieved through focusing on goals and values. The results of research showed religious values to have more integrating potential than other values, providing that the religion is genuinely adopted.

Integration therapy was first practiced on the author's return to Iran, where he accepted a teaching position at Ferdowsi University in Mashhad. As head of the psychology department, director of the university's mental health and counseling center and founder of Iran's first graduate program in clinical psychology, the author taught, demonstrated, and practiced Integration Therapy. Scores of graduate and hundreds of undergraduate students were trained in this technique. In a culture where psychotherapy was nearly unknown, the waiting list for this unique experience grew in the mental health center, which served the public as well as the university community.

Unfortunately, as is the case in many places throughout the world, the structure of a university is not always congenial to innovation and creativity. Humanistic theories and practices, in particular, require a free and open atmosphere, which may be one reason that they are encountered somewhat infrequently. Ironic as it may seem, such freedom was found in the Iranian prison system, in Mashhad, the capital of the province of Khorasan, in northeastern Iran.

It was not until the author left university responsibilities to accept a position as program coordinator at the Mashhad Bureau of Security and Corrections, in 1994, that Integration Therapy became known worldwide. A successful prisoner rehabilitation program was developed there, based on Integration Therapy. Careful accountability studies using extensive pre- and posttesting showed remarkable changes in inmates and staff alike following a few months' experience in the Integration Therapy milieu. Reports at international conferences and publications in international journals led to transcultural awareness of this new method of promoting human growth and overcoming blocks and obstacles to development.

It would be unfair and inaccurate to report that the history of Integration Therapy came solely from merging two theories, no matter how fine these theories may be. A very important part of its history lied in the application of integration therapy in practice. The lives of clients, the change, frustration, and challenges, which they so generously and bravely shared in the therapeutic experience, were essential ingredients in the development of this therapeutic approach.

Integration therapy continues to grow and develop through insights gained through study, practice and input from colleagues. In some way, this chapter is a still snapshot of a moment in time of this therapy, rather than a complete description of this innovative psychotherapy.

CURRENT STATUS

The principles of integration therapy have been effective in the training and practice of a generation of psychology graduate students throughout Iran, who are currently practicing counseling and therapy both within and outside the country. Individuals interested in ongoing training and practice of integration therapy have formed the Islamic Association for Humanistic Psychology, Iran, part of the larger community of the Association for Humanistic Psychology (AHP). AHP has shown its interest in this approach by printing articles describing its use in several of its publications.

The practice of integration therapy is carried out at the present time in its most intensive form in the Bureau of Prisons and Corrections in Iran. The Islamic Association for Humanistic Psychology in Iran, is also involved in teaching and practicing Integration Therapy. Integration therapy is also applicable to conflict resolution and there is currently a worldwide network of conflict resolution workers who are aware and informed of the techniques and methods of integration therapy.

Further, the author has founded, along with other colleagues in the region, the Middle Eastern Psychologists Network (MEPN), a clearinghouse and center for increasing levels of expertise in the study and practice of psychology thoughout the Middle East. Integration therapy is one of the techniques offered through the MEPN and is offered at its seminars and workshops. Its principles have been presented in teacher and counselor training programs and are currently being applied in community mental health, and substance abuse programs.

THEORY

Integration, Values, and Religion

Integration is essential to the healthy personality. From the inception of modern personality psychology, integration and its related concepts have been found in the very definition of personality (Allport, 1951; Angyal, 1956; Bonner, 1961; Lecky, 1961; Levy 1970; Ryckman, 1989). Integration is facilitated by having a unifying life theme, an overriding goal that gives meaning to all lesser goals, and values give direction to this goal (Csikszentmihalyi, 1990).

Among different life themes are the aesthetic, political, theoretical, social, economic, and religious (Allport, 1968). The religious or spiritual life theme is unique in its ability to give an overall view and impart a comprehensive meaning to all aspects of the individual's life (Radhakrishnan, 1956; Tillich, 1957), a quality known as transcendence.

A religious or spiritual life theme is imbued with certain values, which are enacted as virtues. Through embodying these virtues, one becomes nearer to the goal, to approaching the Essence of these virtues, known in some religions as God, and in the religion of Islam as Allah. This goal, this Essence, acts as an organizing, integrating force on the individual, and is responded to with love and its expression, worship.

Many persons turn to religion to provide a method for this expression, to suggest forms of practice and worship. A religion can provide a structure or way of life. It would be preposterous to claim that adopting a religious attitude automatically confers integration or that all persons who consider themselves religious enjoy mental health, or conversely, that mental health is exclusive to persons who practice a religion. To understand this more clearly, we can turn to Allport's (1967) introduction of the concept of intrinsic or genuine religious orientation to refer to a comprehensive motivational commitment, an end rather than a means. Integration Therapy submits that only the intrinsic religious or spiritual orientation, one based on love and acceptance rather than conformity or opportunism, can yield integration.

The route to integration is opened any time a person responds to the call, the attraction from the Essence. The stronger the response, the stronger the integrating effect. An individual may turn to religion to provide guidance, some pattern for expressing this love in everyday life, otherwise known as worship. At its best, worship is a comprehensive lifestyle involving ethics, values, virtuous behaviors, and perhaps rites and rituals which express the indivual's inner yearnings and sentiments. Such a genuine, intrinsic, religious or spiritual orientation can have extensive effects.

Worship that is only an exterior form, empty of meaning and commitment, is never integrating. Such religious or spiritual orientation, which is not authentically adopted, which serves other purposes such as security, status, social benefits and the like, is what Allport termed an inauthentic religious orientation and deserves the criticism that it breeds hypocrisy, prejudice, (Myers, 1994), alienation, and neurosis (Freud, 1964).

To summarize, the important element in integration, is experiencing the attraction from the Essence, and responding to it genuinely, in whatever form. Persons of all religions and spiritual bents, Islam included, recognize the universality of this worship and commitment, and recognize all such worshippers as fellow travelers along the same path, a path of unity and integration.

Islam and Integration

In the religion of Islam, the process of integration is given special attention. The religion of Islam is based on integration and unity, as God the creator is seen as one indivisible Essence (Tabatabai, 1980). Creation is also seen as one unified system, with each element having an internal integration as well as an important role in the harmony of the created realm itself. The human personality is no exception to this rule.

> By the self and One who ordered and arranged it
> Then inspired it as to its dissolution and its goodliness,
>   to understand what is right and wrong for it;
> Surely whoever maintains its integrity and is pure in
>   heart will prosper and thrive
> And who corrupts it will fail.
> —*Glorious Quran* XCI, 7–10.

These verses are perhaps the most succinct expression of Islamic psychology. The human being has a soul, or self. This contains elements or systems that originally, in a natural and healthy state, exist in balance and proportion to each other, are ordered and arranged. This self is divinely inspired to know what is best for itself, to keep this proportion and balance. It also knows, by inspiration, what is harmful and destructive to it. Human success is defined by the maintenance of this balance and order.

Further, it can be explained that the way to maintain this balance comes by inspiration to an agent in the self, which can be called the seat of wisdom. Divine inspiration, and its outward manifestation, revelation, sent to the prophets through time, is naturally drawn to this center. The response is love and attraction, which is expressed in virtuous behaviors. The more virtuous behaviors are implemented, the closer one becomes to the source. The individual becomes more in tune with the integrative principle, and this resonates throughout the individual's life.

Conversely, a failure to respond, or to employ virtues, will create a distance. Reception is blocked, the path of virtue becomes unclear and unapproachable. This leads to further distance as inspiration is progressively lost and revelation loses its meaning for the person. Unless the individual purifies himself, that is, unless he removes these blocks, disintegration and disharmony will eventually take the place of integration and balance.

It is the purpose of this chapter to show how this metaphysical, spiritual, religious explanation of the human personality, of mental health and illness, fits into a modern innovative psychotherapy schema, integration therapy. The aim of integration therapy is to strengthen the seat of wisdom, to reawaken the attraction and love for the source, thus effecting integration. Removing blocks to this attraction, refreshing awareness and commitment to virtuous behaviors, are integral parts of the treatment plan.

METHODOLOGY

The method of integration therapy can be understood by considering six main components. These include (1) the therapeutic team, (2) the intake interview, (3) orientation, (4) the therapeutic relationship, (5) dealing with content, and (6) maintenance.

The Therapeutic Team

Integration therapy treats the whole individual, and gives importance to all aspects of human functioning and concern. A therapeutic team is usually employed at each clinical site to ensure a full range of treatment. The team is typically composed of a clinical director, therapist, social worker, educational specialist, medical specialist, and peer counselor. These individuals may be full or part-time, paid staff or volunteer.

The clinical director supervises cases, chairs intake meetings, influences treatment decisions and plans, and helps assign responsibilities. Therapists give input to intake and treatment decisions and hold individual, group, and family therapy as required. They may also conduct orientation classes, or perform specialized therapies such as cognitive therapy, problem-solving skills workshops, or behavior modification programs. Therapists coordinate cases assigned to them and serve as supervisors for the peer counselors.

Social workers, familiar with local governmental and private sector support agencies, social services, and employment opportunities, help the client gain access to resources in meeting basic needs. An educational specialist may assist in furthering the educational level of the patient or in overcoming educational deficits. A medical specialist is available for regular assessment and referral when necessary for medical or rehabilitative service.

Peer counselors are individuals who have reached the later stages of therapy and are willing and skilled to serve on the team. They may be involved in the intake process, keep records, or perform secretarial functions. If qualified, the peer counselor may also serve as a social worker educational specialist. Peer counselors are coleaders in group therapy, educational social workers, or educational specialists. The use of peer counselors not only reinforces their own progress, but provides a source of hope and example for others entering therapy. Peer counselors have been found especially helpful in institutional settings such as schools and prisons.

The Intake Process

Clients usually have first contact with integration therapy through an intake worker who gathers certain demographic information, such as age, marital status, education and the like about the client. Any history of difficulties, as well as the presenting problem, are ascertained, and are counterbalanced with a report of the client's understanding of his own strengths and positive points. This information is used not only in reaching a treatment decision but for ongoing research in program development and evaluation. Psychological testing, either projective or self-reports, may be used to this end as well.

Each case that passes through the intake process is presented at a general staffing meeting in order to arrive at a treatment decision. A representative of each section of the team must be present at the meeting and all members of the team are invited to attend. The treatment decision refers to whether the client is invited to participate in therapy; what types of therapy will be employed (individual, group, family); what social support services or medical care is indicated.

The decision to enter treatment is arrived at through mutual agreement between the therapeutic team and the client. In order for the client to be able to make an informed choice about treatment, there is an orientation to Integration Therapy.

Orientation

Each client is given a general orientation to the therapeutic outlook and process of integration therapy before entering into an active phase of treatment. Every therapy has some underlying presuppositions about the nature of the human being, what constitutes mental health and illness, what process needs to be followed to restore mental health, and what the client's role will be in this process. Integration therapy sees therapy as a commitment, and thus considers it necessary, both from an ethical and a process perspective, that the client have a basic understanding of the clinical and philosophical presuppositions of the therapy before making a commitment. Orientation helps the client make this informed choice about therapy. Orientation may take the form of a brief handout, one or two discussions, viewing a brief video presentation, or attending a series of classes or question-and-answer sessions. The particular form is determined by the resources of the clinical site and the needs of the client.

Individual clients who are familiar with the general goals of therapy can often be oriented through reading materials or short explanations. More extensive methods may be used in institutional settings or in groups with lower socioeconomic backgrounds and less general awareness about psychotherapy. Orientation classes and workshops that involve question-and-answer sessions are often particularly effective in settings such as schools or prisons in which there are many "referred" cases. This allows the population to become familiar with the principles of therapy, as well as to distinguish the therapeutic team from the referral source. Such meetings often pique interest in therapy, inspire hope for change, and stimulate motivation for self-referral.

The client is given the following information, in condensed or expanded form, in the orientation period. The client is informed that the therapeutic team views the human being as basically healthy and positive, that the individual is capable of knowing and acting in his or her own best interests, able to contribute to or detract from his or her own growth and happiness. The client is also informed that should the individual choose to grow through entering therapy, the therapeutic team will be available to support such growth. This will be done by helping to eliminate barriers to growth and by facilitating the development of certain attitudes and behaviors that lead to success and health.

Further, the client's role in therapy may be explained. There are certain necessary elements to therapy that only the client can supply. Briefly, these include a hope for change, a commitment and resolution to hard work, and a decision to withstand peer and social pressure toward one's changes. The client is also told that he or she will need to make a commitment to maintain progress, to take a daily accounting, as well as to face the entire project with patience. The client is informed that psychological strength, like physical strength, is built gradually and progressively (Husaini-Tehrani, 1967).

Following the orientation period, the client is informed of the outcome of the staffing meeting and is asked to make a decision about treatment. If the client is willing to make a commitment to enter therapy, the intake worker helps arrange and explain the time, places, fees, and other scheduling details.

The Therapeutic Relationship

Great emphasis is given in integration therapy to the therapeutic relationship since this is recognized as the primary vehicle for change. The therapeutic relationship includes two aspects, the therapeutic attitude and the therapeutic approach.

The Therapeutic Attitude

The humanistic and Islamic views of the human being as innately good, capable of error, and charged with the responsibility of working toward perfection and development are reflected in the therapeutic attitude. The therapeutic attitude of integration therapy is one of belief, respect, and acceptance.

The effective integration therapist holds the belief that the human being has a positive nature, is motivated toward perfection, and may choose to work toward this motivation, or abandon this responsibility. This therapist further believes that the power and motivation for change, while enacted from the self, ultimately issues from a source. For the Muslim, this source is known as Allah, for others as God, for still others Spirit, Truth, or some other transcendent force.

The therapist has respect for the client and thus recognizes that therapy is a way of performing the work innately sensed by and incumbent upon every individual, striving toward growth and perfection. The symptoms of what is known as mental illness are seen as a sign that the individual is undergoing a deep and painful struggle. The pain and crises that bring a person to therapy may be seen as assets, because they prod the individual to seek help and to attend more carefully to the growth process.

The therapist is him- or herself involved in the growth process, has faced many challenges, has known failures, and has experienced success. Since the source of change transcends the self, the therapist has no basis for pride or for feelings of superiority in relation to the client.

The therapist accepts the client as a fellow traveler along the road of development. The therapist does not see him- or herself as the ultimate in mental health, but as someone who is committed to striving to follow a path that leads to growth and development. This is a lifelong commitment, thus the therapist is a traveler also, a fellow pilgrim, as it were. The therapist welcomes the chance to accompany the client on this journey and feels empathy for the struggle and difficulties that the client is facing, no matter how different in form and detail from the therapist's own personal struggle.

The Therapeutic Approach

It is not enough for the therapist to have these attitudes. The therapist must express them to the client through the therapeutic approach. Therapeutic presence, empathy, and personal involvement comprise the therapeutic approach.

Therapeutic presence means expressing to the client that during the therapy session, the life, struggles, and presence of the client are of primary importance to the therapist. To be present, the therapist puts aside whatever may block attention to the client. Such blocks may be the therapist's personal problems and concerns, psychological theories and diagnoses about the client, or even some image he may have of the client based on personal background or on previous therapy sessions. Each session takes place in the here and the now. The therapist must be present in order to enjoy the presence of the client.

Empathy is expressed through the reflection of feelings and content of the session. Empathy means trying to understand, but never judge, what the client is experiencing, and offering this understanding in the way of feedback. The client then affirms or modifies the therapist's understanding.

By basing all interactions on empathy, the therapist follows the client's lead in the session, sharing the experience that the client undergoes, trying as much as possible to understand it from the client's point of view. The therapist may also ask for clarification, but does not use the therapeutic session to probe for information, to express his own opinions, or to direct the sessions. Direct help and assistance are left to the support team and take place outside the therapy session.

This approach conveys the message that the client is the only one with direct access to the personal seat of wisdom. It is the client who must reveal this world to the therapist, and not the other way around. Further, although the inner seat of wisdom may be in some ways a shared phenomenon for all human beings, the blocks to this are unique. They are related to variables such as past experience, temperament, genetic endowment, cognitive structures, education, cultural background, and the like. The way to the inner seat of wisdom is by following the client, with empathy, along his or her own personal path to that center, observing and helping the client remove the blocks that the client finds along the way. It has been the experience in integration therapy that the most common mistake a therapist can make, the one mistake that will surely lead the therapy away from productiveness, to finding that inner self of the person, is to try and analyze, direct, rush, or otherwise interfere with the client's inner journey. Instead, the therapist relies on empathy, a continuous attempt to understand, and to reflect that understanding, to be able to accompany the client on what is necessarily a very personal path to development.

Finally, the therapist is *personally involved* with the client. In words and in actions the therapist conveys a personal belief in the client's ability to change. Glimpses of the therapist's personal struggles, including failures and successes, may be injected into the therapeutic process at appropriate times, allowing the client to have a more personal picture of the therapist. The therapist is also committed to working toward change with the client, and through patience and belief expresses care and concern for the client. Through the therapeutic attitude, the client finds a new belief, hope, and acceptance for him- or herself as someone who will be able to follow a life based on virtue and integrity, to be able to live up to his or her own true, inner values.

The therapist's approach can reveal a role model for many of the values that the client will come to incorporate. Values and virtues must radiate from inside the individual, not be preached from the outside. Virtuous behaviors that the client witnesses in the therapist act as attractive forces, drawing out the client's own virtues. This approach implies not that the therapist is some sort of saintly person, but rather is one clearly committed in actions to maintaining a certain standard of behavior. The therapist is in touch with the personal seat of wisdom, and will be able to communicate, from that base, to the client's inner wisdom. The therapist will embody characteristics such as integrity, faith, respect, care, moderation, patience, honesty, and acceptance (Bahr Al-Ulum, 1967).

Dealing with Content

The work of therapy, dealing with the content of the sessions, involves three elements: (1) problem solving, (2) uncovering the seat of wisdom and activating the virtues, and (3) integrating meaning. All of these phases tend to occur simultaneously, although their proportions change in the course of therapy. Beginning sessions are more heavily weighted toward problem solving, followed by an awakening of the seat of wisdom and activating of inner guidance and virtues. In the later stages, integration of meaning is of prime importance to the client.

Problem Solving

The client who presents for therapy is someone who is under pressure. This pressure is experienced as distress and is brought to the attention of the therapist as the presenting problem. This problem becomes the focus of the therapeutic relationship.

The therapist's first function is to empathize with the patient, and strive to find a solution that will eliminate this pressure. Empathizing here means not only recognizing emotions but recognizing that the presenting problem is causing the client real pain and needs to be solved. For example, should a client report having been unable to find work, sleeping excessively, and feeling like a failure for being unable to support the family, the therapist's empathy does not end with saying, "You seem to feel worthless because you are unable to find a job."

In the therapy session, the therapist may concentrate on the emotions, and possibly on the self-defeating thoughts and behaviors that aggravate this problem. The therapist will also arrange for other ways of solving this problem outside the therapy session. The therapist may refer the client to an employment specialist to review job-finding skills and access job opportunities. A social worker may also be called on to assess the level of family distress and help the family connect to a support network until the client proceeds sufficiently in therapy to be able to support the family. Thus, simultaneous with ongoing therapy, the client may be involved in remedial education, problem-solving skills seminars, group lessons in rational thinking, physical rehabilitation, and receipt of social services, as the situation requires. Reading assignments or homework may complement these processes.

The therapist follows the client's lead, as successive presenting problems are entered into the therapeutic relationship. These concerns are handled with empathy and respect. The client, however, tends to require less support and feels less distress about these problems as the therapy continues.

Awakening the Seat of Wisdom and Activating Virtues

As the client solves the most urgent problem, pressure is relieved. Blocks to the seat of wisdom, caused by panic, fear, tension, guilt, and other such emotions, gradually are released. The client gains access to inner guidance, thus being able to follow his or her own wisdom in dealing with situations. Through becoming more able to solve problems, the client comes more to believe in this wisdom and thus becomes more likely to trust this inner guidance. So not only does dealing with the presenting problem help relieve immediate pressure, it also activates, in general, the seat of wisdom.

As the preoccupation with a problem lessens, the client is able to be aware of issues outside the self, and so is more able to see the therapist. Through patience and support for the client, the therapist wins the client's appreciation and respect as the client begins to be attracted to the qualities and virtues that he or she finds in the therapist. This, in turn, attracts and activates these virtues within the self.

As the client faces life through this awakened seat of wisdom and virtues, he or she often finds great relief and satisfaction. That is, the client is not simply learning skills or changing behaviors. Rather, perhaps for the first time, the client is able to act in a way that is sensed as being in harmony with his or her inner nature, a way that is deeply satisfying. This approach is self-reinforcing, effecting deeper and deeper involvement with virtue, increasingly opening the seat of wisdom. Virtuous states eventually lead to virtuous traits.

Integrating Meaning

Facing life's situations with virtuous behaviors, acting from the inner seat of wisdom, in turn invokes new meanings. The individual who has been successful in learning to solve practical problems and who begins to trust the inner seat of wisdom, and has activated internal virtues, is well on the way to developing a coherent life theme. This is a values system, with a goal, which integrates and gives meaning to all an individual's behaviors. It involves a moral code, a method or way of life, which is totally harmonious to the goal. That is, there is no conflict between goal, and means. There is no sacrifice of what the individual considers to be virtuous or appropriate behaviors for the sake of expedience in reaching a goal, nor is the person satisfied with discreet individual actions while losing site of a long-term goal. The goal, the essence of virtue, is harmonious with the method, virtuous behaviors. All of life's events are viewed in the context of this life theme, deriving their meaning from their place in this overall background. Consequent to this change in perspective from a fragmented to a whole perceptive, from mundane to transcendent, the individual is usually less disturbed by life's events.

In this new life theme, events and difficulties are often no longer seen as disasters and distress, but are often seen as challenges, opportunities for growth, and lessons to be learned. Each difficulty is valued for its ability to uncover yet another block, to be removed on the way to fully opening the inner seat of wisdom. Life's challenges and difficulties lose their pressure and sense of urgency. The client is more patient while seeking to absorb the meaning that each challenge holds. Consequently, the client calls for less use of support systems. During this stage, as in other stages, the therapist and client are involved in the therapeutic relationship, and face each session within this context. Their relationship, however, may be less active, but deeper, because of shared experience in growth and life themes.

Throughout the therapeutic process, the type of approach, the exact degree of problem solving in relation to meaning application, is related to the level of the individual's growth. That is, integration therapy never withdraws support from the person until the client has developed practical skills to deal with his or her problems. That is, the client is never ordered or urged to make a transition between stages but is allowed to progress at his or her own rate. The client always is supported in solving his own problems according to his or her own level of development. Typically, in the beginning stages of therapy, the client requires more practical problem-solving sup-

port, and becomes more involved in meaning and integration in later stages. Breakthroughs to meaning, however, do occasionally occur in the beginning stages, and significant crises can demand practical support even in the later stages of therapy.

Maintenance

After entering the meaning stage, the main work of the individual remains to keep abreast of daily living, to give a continuous meaning to life, to work toward integration. Growth on a path of meaning does not ever promise a life without difficulties. In fact, often challenges seem to take on mounting proportions as the individual progresses, according to that person's ability to deal with them. But as the individual grows, situations that once would have been devastating are dealt with through patience, faith, and wisdom.

At this stage, individuals are often drawn to seek out deeper, transcendent sources of meaning and may find new commitment to their own religious traditions, or seek some tradition in which to ground their journey. Again, although integration therapy sees great wisdom in the teachings of Islam, and may make them available to the client upon request, these are never thrust upon him. Resources for religious and spiritual inquiry and study in the form of books, tapes, counselors, and most importantly, meditative and introspective opportunities are provided for individuals who request them.

Continuous support in integration may be lifelong, with the individual being free to drop in to therapy at any time. Clients often keep in touch with the clinical site, accessing books, acting as peer counselors, or participating in growth sessions, attending classes, or group therapy.

APPLICATIONS

Integration therapy can be applied in many clinical, institutional, and private settings (Jalali-Tehrani, 1996a). The full range of services offered by integration therapy makes it particularly appropriate for use in community mental health centers where a wide range of services and service providers are usually on staff. It has also been used successfully in university mental health centers.

Integration therapy has had widespread use and success as an effective program against substance abuse. It has also been proven to bring about vast widespread changes in institutional populations such as prisons (Jalali-Tehrani, 1996b) and schools, where populations are traditionally known to be resistant to change and treatment.

Integration therapy has been used successfully with a

wide range of socioeconomic groups and diverse cultural backgrounds. This is accomplished through adjusting the extent of pretherapy orientation as necessary to accommodate individuals who may not be aware of the purposes or process of therapy. Its success is also due in part to its appeal to the religious or spiritual sense in individuals, which is not limited to a particular class. The support system also allows it to serve the needs of a range of individuals who might not otherwise be able to seek or remain in therapy.

Integration therapy has been applied in individual, group, family, and marathon therapy settings. These modalities may be used separately, or in any combination, depending on the need of the client. Research has shown it to be successful with patients diagnosed according to testing as psychotic, psychopathic, depressive, anxious, and obsessive-compulsive. Individuals who showed no pathology also reported increases in meaning and purpose in life through participating in integration therapy (Jalali-Tehrani, 1997).

CASE EXAMPLE

The following is an example of a group therapy session. This group therapy takes place in a prison where integration therapy is the primary mode of treatment for a large group of members who have chosen to take part in it. The members of this group are individuals who are serving sentences that are non-commutable to date. Because of the progress they have made in this program, documented by pre- and posttreatment standardized psychological testing using Cattell's Clinical Analysis Questionnaire (CAQ) (Krug, 1980), as well as prison records, they are permitted to serve their time in different types of halfway houses devised under this program.

This case example focuses on three group members who represent different levels of development in Integration Therapy. One of the clients, Mr. A, is married, has four children, and is serving time for armed robbery. A repeat offender, he works outside the prison in the days, visits his family in the afternoon, and sleeps in the prison at night. Another client in this group, Mr. B, formerly had a plumbing business and was arrested for fraud, forgery, and check kiting. He is also married and has three children. He lives in prison facilities recently built by the prisoners themselves, outside the main prison grounds. He visits his family regularly, but lives in the new compound.

The third client highlighted in this vignette is Mr. C. Mr. C is serving time for a drug-related offense in a special prison unit where milieu therapy is employed. He also participates in biweekly large-group therapy. He left his wife and two daughters, virtually abandoning them, a few years before his arrest.

MR. C: I really need to talk about what happened last week on my leave. I feel so devastated, I don't know how I can face this.

GROUP MEMBER: I, for one, am ready to listen.

ANOTHER GROUP MEMBER: Me too, Mr. C. I remember you said last time that you were going to try and see your wife, try and see your girls.

(A long silence occurs, as members allow Mr. C time to reach the point where he can begin to share his experience. Finally, Mr. C begins, speaking in a measured way. His face is flushed, and his voice is choked. He keeps his head down, repeatedly shaking it back and forth, looking up only occasionally.)

MR. C: I went to my wife's school, where she teaches. I asked for her address. At first, they wouldn't give it to me, but I told them I was from the teacher's welfare bureau. I guess I can still fool some people. (Pauses and grimaces.)

ANOTHER MEMBER: You don't seem to feel too good about having to lie to get done what you wanted to do.

MR. C: I hated to tell that lie, I felt like I was burning up inside when I told that man a lie right to his face. But when he handed over that address, I felt relieved, and actually kind of glad that I knew what to say to get the job done. (He smiles here, then his face twists in pain as he continues.)

So, I went to her house, rang the bell and she opened the door. After 15 years, there she was. But her face was broken, so broken. (Here he bursts into tears rolling his head back and forth.) And I could see so many white hairs. I ruined her life. I ruined her life. (He cries again and it takes time for him to control himself.) She said to me, "So it's you, what business do you have here, what could you possibly want from me?" I could hear noises in the background, someone moving around. I told her "I came to see my daughters." She said, "You don't have any children here. These children have no father. If they had one, he would have shown up by now." I felt so ashamed. I just didn't expect her to answer like that. She has the right . . . but I just didn't expect it. (Here, the client withdraws into sobs.)

THERAPIST: You felt that if you were sorry about what you did, and willing to make amends, then all would be well. Her reaction surprised you.

MR. C: Yeah. I just felt so worthless, like such a bum for having let her and the kids alone for all these years.

Therapist: You just feel no good.

(A long silence follows.)

MR. B: I have problems with my family too. As long as I was in prison, and didn't have the chance to see them except when they came to visit, they didn't ask too much of me. Now that I am on the outside more, and come and go more, they want more out of me. Every time I go home, my wife just sits at the table and tells me of our problems. She talks about all the hard times they had while I have been on the inside, the sacrifices, and all the things they had to do without . . . Now she tells me my son is going to get an award at school, and he doesn't have a decent shirt to wear. My daughter's school uniform is torn, just plain worn out. There is no meat in the house, and no money for fruit either. What can I do? I always was able to handle these problems before. I knew how to wheel and deal, even if it meant doing something that might get me in trouble. Now, I don't want to do anything illegal, but . . . I mean, what else can I do? Doc, you got to help me, you got to help me find some way to make more money. I'm a good plumber, but I don't have the money to get together any tools. (And he mentions some basic tools he would need.) If I had these at least I could get something going. I got to have this help. What good is all this talk, when I go on the outside and feel useless?

ANOTHER MEMBER: You really feel useless and worthless because you can't take care of your family, you can't meet their demands.

MR. B: Yeah, I mean a man's value, being a man, means that when you walk in that house, and the kids and the wife look at you, you have something in your hand to show them. I mean, they don't say anything, but when I come in empty-handed, I see the disappointed look on their faces and they just turn off and go to their rooms. It rips me up inside. You just gotta do something, Doc.

MR. A: I have the same problem, in a way. We can't afford a lot of things, like we can't buy chicken, or even rice [a staple food in his culture]. But, to me, I mean, this doesn't make me feel worthless. 'Cause I know that if I do something, anything, outside the law, or even something that just doesn't sit right with me, then that would really make me feel useless. It would make me feel as if all of these years, all of this hard work in these sessions were wasted. I would really feel worthless then. I would feel that I betrayed myself and all the people who care about me. My family has gotten used to it. I know what they need, and they know I care. But they have gotten used to me like this, and they may even prefer me like this. I don't know. But I know I just can't go back to being any other way.

In the examples of Mr. A, Mr. B, and Mr. C, we see the three phases of progress—facing the presenting problem, uncovering the seat of wisdom and developing virtues, and integrating meaning. Mr. C has a very painful presenting problem he has shared with the group. He is trying to employ some virtues, to make up for what he considers to be his mistakes, but things are not going to be easy for him. He is still in conflict, ready to lie sometimes if it means getting what he wants done.

Mr. B is agitated, but not as much as Mr. C. He is frustrated as he finds that the virtues that he would like to apply, such as honesty and straight dealing, are in conflict with the demands of his family. Further, he has not adopted a religious or spiritual life theme that can give integrative meaning to his life. He still gains meaning from social values, being a good husband and father.

This is, of course, laudable, but is causing him conflict between an attraction to illegal behavior, which he sees as a way to keep up his image as a man, as a good husband and father, and a desire to keep crime free. Thus this life theme, being a man according to his definition of manhood, is unable to provide him with harmony and integration. He is still in a transitional phase. His inner seat of wisdom is awake to some virtues, but he has not adopted a system that can give him integrative meaning and help eliminate conflicts.

Mr. A, however, finds meaning in virtue itself. He has an inner commitment to a religious and ethical life theme. Stepping outside this commitment would cause a meaning crisis and feelings of worthlessness. The method of being virtuous has become a goal, it has become central to his life. He has been able to withstand peer and social pressures, allowing others to adjust to his new characteristics, rather than forcing himself to change to meet others' expectations.

Because Mr. C is currently in a deep emotional crisis, he may be seen in individual therapy, to complement his regular twice-weekly group sessions. His needs for support will be explored. He and the social service team will decide whether visits from a social worker or other personnel to the family home would be beneficial. The option of pursuing legal means to obtain visitation rights to his daughters would also be explored.

Because Mr. B has not yet reached the point where his ethical commitment can overcome his presenting problems and conflicts, he will also be given some help. He will be referred to the occupational worker to see if there are any community openings for plumbers that might not require his having a full outfit of plumbing equipment. Alternatively, sources might be explored for a loan for at least a basic set of tools to start him off. Mr. B was moved by Mr. A's feedback. On the way out the door after the session, he gravitated toward Mr. A, who put his arm around him as they walked out the door. Although Mr. B does not share Mr. A's awareness, he does recognize that he and Mr. A are in similar situations and that Mr. A's commitment to values allows him to be free of conflict and stress in this regard. Mr. B will continue in group treatment.

Mr. A will also continue in treatment, and may eventually become a peer counselor. Although his situation, financially, is as difficult as Mr. B's, he will not be offered support services, because he does not feel the need for them. His growth will be facilitated by allowing him to continue to stretch, to seek his own values and to employ his virtues to deal with difficult situations. Should his situation, however, become such that he asks for some help, support services would be enlisted for him.

SUMMARY

Integration therapy has as its goal the uncovering of a life theme, an overall sense of meaning and purpose, a central motivation. A genuinely adopted religious life theme is uniquely integrative, because it comprehends and transcends all aspects of life. Integration therapy accepts the tenet of humanistic psychology that the human being has a positive core, and the Islamic tenet that this core is the seat of wisdom. Therapy aims at uncovering this seat of wisdom. A wide range of support services and treatment modalities are offered to be able to reach and put aside each individual's personal blocks to wisdom. Once uncovered, the seat of wisdom guides the individual in virtuous behavior, in attraction to the source of all virtue.

The main vehicle for change is the therapeutic relationship. Key to this relationship is the therapeutic attitude of belief, respect, and acceptance. The therapist approaches the client through therapeutic presence, empathy, and personal involvement.

The beginning phases of integration therapy are characterized by working on the presenting problem. In addition to using classic techniques of empathy, more extensive attention to the presenting problem is given through use of the support team. When the pressure of the presenting problems begin to become eased, the individual becomes in touch with his seat of wisdom.

Taking the nature of the therapeutic relationship and the characteristics of the therapists, which he observes as a model, and acting on inner motivation, the client begins to employ virtues in meeting the demands of his life. The client finds these virtues deeply satisfying and seeks ways to employ them more extensively. Therapy supports these efforts and the individual finds these virtues and the measuring system that they grow into to be the prime source of integration in life.

This meaning framework is one in which virtue is uncovered and applied throughout life. Therapy, therefore, is ongoing. The client who develops a meaning system may become less active but more deeply involved in therapy. Maintenance therapy allows for drop-in therapy and participation in groups or seminars. Many clients go on to serve as peer counselors.

REFERENCES

Glorious Quran (1996 Ed.). Tehran, Iran: Usveh Publishers.

Allport, G. W. (1951). *The individual and his religion.* New York: Macmillan.

Allport, G. W. (1967). Personal religious orientation and prejudice. *Journal of Personality and Social Psychology, 5,* 432–443.

Allport, G. W. (1968). *The person in psychology.* Boston: Beacon Press.

Angyal, A. (1956). A theoretical model for personality studies. In C. E. Moustakas (Ed.), *The self* (pp. 44–58). New York: Harper & Row.

Bahr Al-Ulum, S. M. (1967). *Sayr va suluk* [Observing the journey]. Mashhad, Iran: Tabatabai Publishers.

Bonner, H. (1961). *Psychology of personality.* New York: The Rand Press.

Csikszentmihalyi, M. (1990). *Flow: The psychology of optimal experience.* New York: Harper & Row.

Freud, S. (1964). *The future of an illusion.* Garden City, NY: Doubleday.

Husaini-Tehrani, S. M. H. (1967). *Lub Al lubab* [The heart of the matter]. Mashhad, Iran: Allameh Tabatabai Publishers.

Jalali-Tehrani, S. M. M. (1985). *Religious commitment as a factor in personality integration.* Unpublished doctoral disseration, Saybrook Institute, San Francisco.

Jalali-Tehrani, S. M. M. (1996a). Islamic theory and humanistic psychology. *The Humanistic Psychologist, 3*(24), 341–349.

Jalali-Tehrani, S. M. M. (1996b). An application of Cognitive Therapy in Iran. *Journal of Cognitive Therapy, 3*(10), 219–225.

Jalali-Tehrani, S. M. M. (1997). A prison reform project in Iran. *Journal of Humanistic Psychology, 37*(1), 92–109.

Krug, S. E. (1980). *Clinical Analysis Questionnaire Manual.* Champaign, IL: Institute of Personality and Ability Testing.

Kulayni, M. (1978). *Usul al-Kafi* ([Sufficient principles]): *Vol. 1., Book 1. The book of wisdom and ignorance* (S. M. H. Rizvi, Trans.). Tehran, Iran: World Organization for Islamic Services.

Lecky, P. (1961). *Self-consistency.* USA: Shoestring Press.

Levy, L. H. (1970). *Conceptions of personality.* New York: Random House.

Myers, D. G. *Social psychology* (4th ed.). New York: McGraw Hill.

Radhakrishnan, S. (1956). Human personality. In C. E. Moustakas (Ed.), *The self* (pp. 101–123). New York: Harper & Row.

Ryckman, R. M. (1989). *Theories of personality.* Pacific Grove, CA: Brooks/Cole.

Tabatabai, S. M. H. (1980). *A Shi'ite anthology.* Albany, NY: State University of New York.

Tillich, P. (1957). *Dynamics of faith.* New York: Harper & Row.

Chapter 31

INTEGRITY GROUPS

ANTHONY J. VATTANO

The creators of the therapies described in this book are a group of remarkable people—highly inventive, strongly motivated to change the world, having the capacity to see clearly where others cannot see at all—they are people who have the ability to restructure reality. But possibly none is more of an intellectual rebel than O. Hobart Mowrer, who has attempted a kind of Copernican revolution in the field. His primary view is that neurosis is the result of secret violations of commitments and contracts, what some people call "sin."

I know Hobart, as he is generally called, quite well, although I have met him only a few times. A man totally devoid of artifice, he is similar to Albert Ellis and Carl Rogers, two of my favorite humans in our profession. Mowrer, who has made important contributions to learning and personality theory, has attempted to generate a Utopia, and he should be considered, I believe, a religious leader.

Anthony Vattano's account of Integrity Groups should be read carefully since it is essentially a complex moral tract. The time has come for us all to realize again that morality has a central importance in human affairs.

Integrity Groups (IG)[1] are mutual-aid or self-help groups that assist people in dealing with problems of alienation and identity. They provide a uniquely structured opportunity for individuals to examine and disclose their thoughts, feelings, and actions with a group of concerned others. The focus for exploration and discussion is on the group members' practice of honesty, responsibility, and involvement, since it is hypothesized that these are significant factors in achieving and maintaining one's personal integrity and sense of community with others.

These groups were developed by O. Hobart Mowrer in the 1950s following his reconceptualization of the causes and treatment of "neuroses." The hypotheses of Sigmund Freud and Joseph Wolpe that related these disorders respectively to an overstrict conscience or false fears were replaced by an alternative view. The central concept of IG is that people become alienated from themselves and others when they have not been honest, responsible, and involved with the significant people in their lives. Integrity Groups provide a community-based support system for helping individuals examine and

modify their behavior in other social contexts. The IG procedures that guide this support system enable people to change their actions, thoughts, and feelings in such a manner as to enhance their sense of identity (Mowrer & Vattano, 1976).

The objectives of IG are accomplished by means of a group social learning approach that has the following features: a distinctive group structure; group intake, with modeling procedures demonstrated by experienced members; specific goals that focus on each member's responsibility for personal behavior change; contractual agreement to embrace the core values of honesty, responsibility, and involvement; a commitment to move beyond self-disclosure by translating words into deeds; leadership shared by the participants; and group support and reinforcement for individual behavior change. The combination of self-responsibility and mutual support is expressed in the IG motto: "You alone can do it, but you can't do it alone" (Mowrer, 1971).

HISTORY

Precursors

The origins of Integrity Groups are found in the self-help or mutual-aid groups that have been part of human ex-

---

[1] In 1969 Mowrer changed the name of his approach from *Integrity Therapy* to *Integrity Groups.* This was done to reflect the fact that the groups emphasize mutual-aid or self-help endeavors rather than professionally directed therapeutic activities.

332

perience since the beginnings of tribal and social life. In these groups the healing power of discussing one's misbehavior with friends and relatives was known throughout the ages, and to people in all parts of the world (McNiell, 1951; Mowrer, 1976; Mowrer, Vattano, Baxley, & Mowrer, 1975). Both the Old and New Testaments contain accounts of individuals experiencing troubled emotions after engaging in deviant behavior. Prior to the development of the institutional church, early Christianity was essentially a small-group movement. The members engaged in a close form of fellowship, with mutual openness, the making of amends, and concern for one another. There was an emphasis on public admission of wrongdoing, restitution, and the rehabilitation brought about by these practices. The growth of this movement was in no small way due to the psychological peace of mind and feeling of support that these groups engendered in their members.

More recently, outside the church, Alcoholics Anonymous (AA) pioneered the use of openness, personal responsibility, and fellowship to assist people with their drinking problems. AA has demonstrated how structured procedures, a defined value system, and group support can foster individual behavior change. Much of AA's success is due to the belief that one can help him- or herself by assisting others who share the same problem. AA has served as a model for Integrity Groups and for many of the other clinical self-help groups that are being developed.

Beginnings

To understand how Integrity Groups evolved, it is necessary to consider some important events in Mowrer's personal and professional life. Mowrer's special understanding of the aforementioned historical developments and their implications for present-day mental health came about through his own intimate experiences with psychopathology. He was born on a modestly prosperous farm near Unionville, Missouri, in 1907. His early years in the country and later in town were characterized by a love of nature and a penchant for learning that limited his social interaction and his involvement in household chores. He experienced a good measure of affection and support from his parents, his brother and sister, and the many relatives living nearby. This idyllic childhood was shattered when he was 13 by the unexpected death of his father. That event was closely followed by the loss of his family home, separation from his mother and siblings, and the stress of beginning high school while rooming in a run-down boarding house.

Mowrer's high school career was marred by periodic episodes of anxiety and a variety of depressive symptoms, including feelings of depersonalization. Mental health resources were in short supply at that time and

place. The young student was seen by several practitioners, who attempted to treat him by means of diet, bed rest, chiropractic treatments, and a tonsillectomy (Mowrer, 1966a). He also joined the church and attempted to obtain help through prayer.

When neither medicine nor theology cured him of his recurrent anxiety and depression, Mowrer resolved to enter college and study psychology in the hope of finding a solution. This pursuit embarked him on a journey that resulted in his signal contributions to psychology and the development of Integrity Groups. Along the way he was to be hospitalized for depression in 1953 and 1971.

After graduating from the University of Missouri, Mowrer entered Johns Hopkins University in 1929 for graduate work in psychology. He also started psychoanalysis in the continued effort to find relief from his emotional difficulties. Following graduation, his reputation as a researcher on learning and personality enabled him to obtain teaching and research positions at Northwestern University, Princeton, Yale's Institute of Human Relations, and Harvard's Graduate School of Education.

Despite his academic success, Mowrer continued to experience periods of anxiety and depression. His work with three different psychoanalysts did not prove helpful. Eventually, his long-time association with Freudian theory and therapy convinced him that Freud's views of neurosis were in error. This impression was further strengthened when Mowrer attended several of Harry Stack Sullivan's seminars at the Washington School of Psychiatry. There he heard Sullivan describe neurosis as a manifestation of *interpersonal disturbances* and the fear of having one's personal pretenses revealed to oneself and to others.

In 1948 Mowrer was appointed a research professor of psychology at the University of Illinois. From the middle 1940s to the early 1960s, he pursued his systematic work on an alternative to Freud's view of neurosis. In this connection, Mowrer studied the practices of the early church. He also worked with some of the leading religious and moral scholars in the United States and abroad (Mowrer, 1967).

In 1961 the Eli Lilly Foundation established a fellowship program at the University of Illinois under Mowrer's direction. This program supported his collaboration with Protestant, Jewish, and Catholic educators to explore the mental health contributions of psychology and religion. Some of Mowrer's fellow psychologists across the country took a dim view of one of their most prestigious researchers fraternizing with members of the clergy. They also did not appreciate his work, which resulted in such articles as "'Sin,' the Lesser of Two Evils" (Mowrer, 1960). Several even erroneously believed he had been converted to Catholicism. It is interesting to note that while Mowrer's use of theistic terms, such as *confession* and *sin,* stirred up controversy, his later employment of their secular counterparts, "self-disclosure" and "breaking commitments and contracts," became quite acceptable to most mental health professionals.

Mowrer's exploration of the church's potential contributions to the current problems of mental health led to disappointment. He discovered that many of the healing practices of the early church, such as openness and fellowship in small groups, had been abandoned. Furthermore, a large number of the clergy had embraced Freudian psychology. Thus, after exploring psychiatry and religion, Mowrer (1961) concluded that neither discipline was dealing effectively with the problems of emotional disturbance. Nevertheless, he maintained his interest in the nontheistic practices of *religion* in the literal sense of that word, that is, *reconnection.* The practices center on the healing power of self-disclosure to others, individual responsibility for behavior change, and the support found in the small-fellowship group. Mowrer noted that these elements were also presently found in Alcoholics Anonymous, and AA had proven successful with problem drinkers, whereas professional approaches had not. Along with others, he began to wonder if AA's procedures could be employed to help other types of troubled people.

While Mowrer was exploring new ways to conceptualize emotional problems and their treatment, students and others sought his help. As he worked with these people, Mowrer focused on the details of their interpersonal relations. He discovered that many individuals were concerned about instances of dishonesty and failure to remain open in their transactions with others. However, apprehension and guilt made it difficult for them to discuss their deceptive practices. In an effort to help his clients trust him and give up their evasion and denial, Mowrer hit upon the idea of modeling. He would in effect "go first" and relate examples of guilt-producing behavior from his own life. The persons who consulted him responded favorably to this procedure and to his suggestion that they move beyond discussing their deviant behavior with him. They agreed to disclose the same material to the people who had been hurt by their deception and also resolved to make restitution. Some clients were surprised at Mowrer's "homework assignments," since they expected that "treatment" would occur in the office. Occasionally, secretive, guilt-ridden persons would resist Mowrer's best efforts to help them disclose their misdeeds to their significant others. However, he found that such people were willing to have a joint session with another individual in Mowrer's caseload. In these sessions, clients freely discussed their guilt-producing behavior. From this beginning, Mowrer moved to the establishment of groups—Integrity Groups—composed of eight to ten persons. He also increased the time for each session to three hours and cen-

tered the group's focus on the three cardinal principles of honesty, responsibility, and mutual involvement (Mowrer & Vattano, 1976, pp. 421–424).

CURRENT STATUS

Integrity Groups began and continue as lay mutual-help organizations (Gartner & Riessman, 1977; Lieberman & Borman, 1979). They are part of the general small-groups movement and are a useful community mental health resource. The first "IG Community" of several groups was established by Mowrer in the cities of Urbana-Champaign, Illinois, in the middle 1960s. At first Mowrer and his wife, Dr. Willie Mae Mowrer, a former classmate at Johns Hopkins, operated these groups in their house. Later, the current practice evolved of meeting in members' homes on a rotating basis or in the meeting rooms of churches or other community buildings. Mowrer also organized Integrity Groups at the Galesburg State Research Hospital with the assistance of the clergymen who attended the Lilly Foundation program. These clergymen later returned to their home communities across the nation and began a number of Integrity Groups. The largest IG community has been developed by Dr. John Drakeford (1967) at the Southwestern Baptist Theological Seminary in Fort Worth, Texas.

In 1969 the Mowrers started teaching a seminar and practicum in IG for graduate students in psychology, social work, child development, and education at the University of Illinois. Since the course began, many students have learned how to facilitate Integrity Groups. Following graduation, they have settled in different parts of the country and abroad. Many have taken jobs in community mental health or in academic settings where they continue to group and train others in the IG process (Bixenstine, 1970; Madison, 1972).

A number of publications[2] are available that describe the theory underlying Integrity Groups and its operations. Some of these publications have been translated into other languages.

Mowrer's views on psychopathology are summarized and IG theory and practice are described in a "manual" titled *Integrity Groups: The Loss and Recovery of Community* (Mowrer et al., 1975). This text describes the history and operation of Integrity Groups in considerable detail. It provides students and others with the information they need to organize and operate these groups.

As with most self-help or mutual-aid groups, there is not a great deal of systematic research available on IG. However, graduate students and psychologists have in-

[2] See Mowrer, 1961, 1964, 1966a, 1966b, 1968, 1972, 1973, 1979; Mowrer & Vattano, 1976; Johnson, Dokecki, & Mowrer, 1972

vestigated Mowrer's approach to dysfunctional behavior and have generally corroborated his views (Jessop, 1971; Kaye, 1973; Peterson, 1967; Rolls, 1968; Vogel, 1976). Mowrer (1968) has summarized the research evidence for his work on the nature of psychopathology.

THEORY

Many individuals have had experience with one or more natural groups where they could talk about their daily problems in living and receive counsel and support. In so doing, they became socialized and personally involved with others. If all went well, they also learned the important characteristics of honesty, responsibility, and trust. Such experiences facilitated the harmonious development of thoughts, feelings, and behavior. The mutual sharing that occurred in these interactions gave people the knowledge and skill needed to deal with life's problems.

These natural groups furnished their members with valuable interpersonal experiences. They also provided them with an important social support system for coping with the joys and sorrows of everyday existence. However, not everyone is fortunate enough to have had such experiences or to have support systems available when they are needed. This has been particularly true since the industrial revolution began to produce drastic changes in the culture and institutions of society. Technological advances in the United States and elsewhere have increased the material standard of living for many people at the expense of the support systems that traditionally helped individuals develop a sense of personal integrity and identity. Many of our basic institutions have been affected by these developments, especially the family, the community, the neighborhood school, and organized religion (Mowrer, 1972). In addition, the mobility and transient human relationships characteristic of modern-day society provide little opportunity for the development of trust, intimacy, and involvement with significant others (Keyes, 1973; Sarason, 1974). These societal changes have been associated with a media-fed emphasis on the pursuit of happiness and personal fulfillment through material possessions. It becomes increasingly apparent that the present culture of rising expectations is incompatible with our diminishing economic and natural resources. This situation has caused some observers to refer to our era as the "age of anxiety."

Many of us have encountered individuals who are struggling with the consequences of these developments, particularly the discrepancy between desires and reality. In attempting to meet their needs, people often blame others and engage in behavior that violates their personal values and their interpersonal commitments or contracts. Such behavior has a negative effect on a person's thoughts, feelings, and actions. He or she may experience a variety of symptoms, such as anxiety, guilt, and alienation. These symptoms lead to a breakdown in personal integrity and result in the condition Mowrer and others call an identity crisis.

Following Freud, the traditional view of psychopathology is that the crux of neurosis is an emotional problem caused by people's reactions to the unrealistically stringent moral standards imposed by the significant others in their lives (parents, teachers, associates, etc.). Some people have been taught the rules and standards of society so well that they are, in effect, "oversocialized." From this perspective, it is the behavior of others that is responsible for their "inappropriate" emotions. These emotions in turn lead to symptoms of neurotic behavior, such as anxiety, guilt, and alienation. The therapeutic task in this model is to alleviate the symptoms by assisting the individual in undoing the effects of the presumed oversocialization. This is accomplished through helping him or her "understand" that it is wrong to feel responsible for emotions. (See Figure 31.1)

Mowrer's alternative view is that the essence of psychopathology is primarily behavioral rather than emotional. The major difficulty lies in the individual's violation of the norms of his or her own reference group. This includes breaking commitments and contracts with the significant people in his or her life. The problem is one of being "undersocialized" in one's behavior with others. The practice of deception with oneself and others results in *appropriate* emotional discomfort and symptoms of anxiety, guilt, and alienation. These symptoms produce an erosion in personal integrity and a crisis in identity. Since the disorder, or "osis," is in the individual's interpersonal relationships rather than neurons, the term "sociosis" comes closer to describing this condition than the more common term *neurosis* (see Figure 31.1).

Mowrer recognizes that our behavior is influenced by the actions of others as well as by the social events in our environment. However, he holds that we are not totally controlled by such forces. We can learn to keep our commitments and contracts by engaging in self-management and can thereby influence people and the environment through our own actions. The most direct way to do this is not through supportive "therapy" or the achievement of insight, but by participating in open and honest transactions with a group of similarly engaged people who will assist us in changing our behavior. The beneficial effects to the individual of such transparent interactions have been documented by Sidney Jourard (1971).

After practicing honest, responsible, and involved behavior with the support of the group, individuals transfer this activity to other people in the natural environment. These people ordinarily respond to such positive

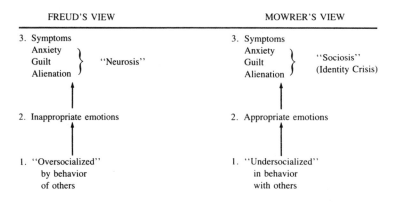

Figure 31.1. Schematic representation of Freud and Mowrer's views of psychopathology. From "Abnormal Reactions or Actions? An Autobiographical Answer" by O. H. Mowrer, 1966, in *Introduction to Psychology: A Self-Selection Textbook*, ed. J. A. Vernon. Dubuque, IA: William C. Brown.

actions in a favorable manner, thus reinforcing their continued occurrence. If difficulties in such transfer arise, the group serves as a backup social support system providing feedback, clarification of problems, and a place to test out alternative responses. Taking affirmative action to change one's behavior alleviates guilt, anxiety, and alienation. This leads to positive changes in thoughts, feelings, and actions. As these are brought into harmony, the crisis in identity diminishes. The individual is then ready to experience a renewed sense of personal integrity in community with others.

METHODOLOGY

There are two types of Integrity Groups: those that operate in the community (nonacademic) and those that operate in academic groups. The community groups are primarily composed of people from all segments of the population who participate because of a variety of painful experiences in their interpersonal life. Academic groups consist of students in the different mental health professions who wish to study the operation of Integrity Groups as part of their education. However, over the years it has been noted that the concerns and interests of the two groups overlap to a considerable extent. Along with their treatment, community group members also receive training in IG theory and practice; and all learn how to establish and facilitate the operation of new groups. While students are primarily interested in learning the principles and operations of IG, they also learn to practice honesty, responsibility, and involvement in their practicum group. In so doing, they open up important areas of their life for examination. Most report that their IG experience provides them with treatment as well as training.

The community (nonacademic) and academic groups

employ the same practices and procedures in their operations. However, community group members are admitted through an intake procedure. Potential members submit a letter of application and participate in an intake interview. The interview is with a committee of current IG members, who inform the applicant about the IG process and requirements, discuss how they are currently working in their group, and explore the applicant's interest and potential for benefiting from such an experience. The practicum groups associated with the student seminars of necessity employ academic procedures for admitting members.

The most current and detailed description of IG methodology is contained in the "manual" *Integrity Groups: The Loss and Recovery of Community* (Mowrer et al., 1975). The following material is taken from this manual with minor changes.

New IG members are expected to commit themselves to the principles of honesty, responsibility, and involvement. However, it is only as individuals disclose painful information about themselves and give others feedback about how they are "coming across" that these principles become meaningful. In the process, group members engage in self-disclosure, confrontation, and emotional support. They examine their behavior in relation to the three principles by asking: (1) How truthful am I with myself and others? (2) To what extent do I carry out my accepted responsibilities (commitments)? (3) How much love and concern do I express for my significant others?

Behavioral Guidelines

In exploring these questions, group members follow a series of 10 behavioral guidelines that have evolved over the years. In the interest of space, these guidelines will merely be listed here. The reader is referred elsewhere for specific details (Mowrer & Vattano, 1976; Mowrer et al., 1975). The "won'ts" in the guidelines relate to behavior both in and outside the Integrity Groups. The first word "I" is understood.

1. Won't interrupt, but will listen to others.
2. Won't blame, or complain about other people.
3. Won't "act-off" negative feelings, but will talk about them.
4. Won't subgroup, but will participate in the group as a whole.
5. Won't "yes . . . but!" I will simply say, "I did it, and I will not do it again."
6. Won't "talk back or argue." When corrected, I will say "Thank you."
7. Won't mind-read or expect others to do so.
8. Won't cheat. I will keep or renegotiate agreements.
9. Won't double-talk or lie, but I will "say it like it is."
10. Won't tit-for-tat when challenged by another.

Ground Rules

In addition to the 10 guidelines, the following ground rules govern the operation of Integrity Groups. (Details may be found in the sources listed for the behavioral guidelines.)

1. IG meetings last for three or three and one-half hours.
2. Groups meet once each week, but extra or extended-time meetings may be called if necessary.
3. Members will be responsible to inform the group if they are unable to attend a meeting.
4. If a person is late to a meeting, he or she should give an explanation.
5. Meetings are chaired on a weekly rotating basis. The chairperson may be flexible, but ordinarily will begin with a "go-round," asking each member "where he or she is" and whether he or she wants time to talk.
6. Members are free to use any language or sounds they wish (yelling, crying, etc.) during a meeting.
7. A member may be expelled from a group for any act of physical violence.
8. If necessary, a member may ask to attend another person's group for the purpose of challenging or giving feedback to that person.
9. A person who "walks out" during a "run" (i.e., during active interchange about his or her prob-

lem or feeling) automatically "resigns" from the group. He or she must apply for readmission.
10. A person may quit, or "split," from a group. However, it is recommended that the intention to leave be discussed with the group.
11. It is desirable to end IG sessions with general feedback. This consists of going round, with each person giving an overall reaction to the session and to the behavior of others and him- or herself.

Despite what may seem like a considerable amount of structure, the guidelines and ground rules permit a large measure of individual choice, freedom, and flexibility in the operation of Integrity Groups. Experience has demonstrated their usefulness in facilitating effective group interaction.

How Integrity Groups Change Individual Behavior

Integrity Groups contain all of the "curative factors" that were first described by Corsini and Rosenberg (1955) and later elaborated by Yalom (1975) to account for the changes that occur in professionally directed group psychotherapy. These factors are: (1) instillation of hope; (2) universality; (3) imparting of information; (4) altruism; (5) the corrective recapitulation of the primary family group; (6) development of socializing techniques; (7) imitative behavior; (8) interpersonal learning; (9) group cohesiveness; (10) catharsis; and (11) existential factors.

However, the mutual-aid or self-help orientation of IG, with its particular constellation of structure, goals, and leadership, modifies the operation of these factors. They are also affected by the specific behavioral components in IG. These are apparent in the specification of discrete aspects of behavior, the use of commitments, and reinforcement for behavior change.

As group members practice introspection, self-disclosure, and feedback, they become aware of specific aspects of their behavior that are personally and interpersonally dysfunctional. This awareness permits them to decide whether they want to engage in the difficult process of modifying their behavior. When an individual indicates the areas he or she wants to work on, the group helps him or her pinpoint specific experiences in or outside the group where new ways of behaving can be tested. After group members have carefully considered the behavior changes they wish to make, they are expected to give a verbal or written commitment of their specific intention to carry out some action. These pledges are taken very seriously in IG. Once a commitment is made, there is a strong expectation that it will be honored. Commitments that are kept are always reinforced by verbal praise and support. Group members may also provide a physical embrace for a job well done. Broken commitments call for careful examination. If the results indicate irresponsible behavior, confrontation and group reprimand may follow.

IG members have been able to initiate and sustain difficult behavior change through the use of commitments. The external support and reinforcement from the group has been instrumental in developing internal "self-control." As people modify their behavior in the natural environment outside the group, they receive additional reinforcement from their significant others. Alienation is diminished, and a sense of community is enhanced.

APPLICATIONS

The major concern of Integrity Groups is to help people combat alienation through recovery of personal integrity and identity. The theoretical views related to alienation have already been discussed. However, there are a number of biopsychosocial events that may be associated with this condition. These include intrapersonal, interpersonal, and environmental concerns.

Integrity Groups were specifically designed to help troubled individuals cope with anxiety, guilt, and alienation in their struggle for a sense of identity. These symptoms are experienced by a considerable number of people irrespective of age, race, sex, and social class. Integrity Groups have been employed to help students, adults, and the elderly change their thoughts, feelings, and actions. The level of psychosocial integration in IG members has ranged from mild anxiety to frank psychotic symptoms. While the latter are best helped by means of other strategies, such as medication, IG has served as an important social support system for the acute or chronic mentally ill who are attempting to reestablish themselves in the community. Integrity Groups have been less successful with the severe character problems of the so-called sociopath or antisocial personality. However, they have been of assistance to persons suffering from other kinds of character disorders, depression, and reactions to physical illness. This is particularly true in those cases where self-disclosure, confrontation, feedback, social reinforcement, and support are indicated.

Interpersonal problems that have been helped by IG are: marital and sexual conflict, parent-child relations, difficulties with coworkers, and troublesome social relations. There is a standing rule in IG that any significant other with whom one needs to work out interpersonal difficulties may join the group at any time, if this will not unduly affect group size. Ongoing groups have been composed entirely of marital couples. However, in marital conflict it may not always be indicated for a couple to be in the same group continuously or in a group composed solely of other couples. In the student groups, additional concerns have centered on academic responsibilities, emancipation from parents, men-women relations, and conflicts between roommates.

While the major thrust of Integrity Groups is directed toward individual behavior change, these groups also help their members by intervening in the social environment. This is done, for example, by encouraging a member to invite a significant person from his or her environment into the group where both people can work out their transactions in the here and now. At times individual group members will accompany a troubled member outside the group and help him or her interact more effectively with a person or agency in the natural environment.

In the history section it was explained how Integrity Groups developed partly in response to significant changes in our social environment. Many of the societal changes have proven to be a mixed blessing for those who have achieved greater economic security at the expense of emotional insecurity. Through the experiences and struggles of individual group members, we come to learn the aversive nature of our "natural" environment and identify targets for social change. For example, before she could get in touch with her own feelings and true identity, a former airline stewardess in one of our groups had to unlearn all of the artificial behaviors (including inappropriate smiling) that her employers had reinforced her for manifesting. Another example of a dysfunctional environment was seen in an Integrity Group composed of medical students. The group was the only place where the future doctors could relate to each other without intense competition, evasion, and defensive behavior. The caring and sharing that developed in this group provided these students a major source of support in dealing with the stress of medical school. These experiences raise questions about environmental arrangements that distort identity and prevent the development of a sense of community with one's peers.

It is difficult for an Integrity Group to act as an advocate for its members with institutions such as airline companies or medical schools. However, Integrity Groups belong to a larger constituency of mutual-aid or self-help groups whose impact on the social environment is being increasingly felt in this country and abroad. Perhaps in the not too distant future Integrity Groups will be as active in bringing about change in the environmental dimension as they are in the other areas discussed here.

CASE EXAMPLE

Joe and Jean were a married couple, both 24 years old. They had referred themselves to the community Integrity Group and indicated that they needed help in achieving better "communication" in their marriage. They were an attractive couple. Joe was an accountant for a large firm and gave the impression of being an ambitious, hard-working man. Jean was two months pregnant with their first child. She had recently quit her job as a secretary in a local bank.

During the first group session, both people discussed their relationship in somewhat neutral terms. Some members commented that Jean appeared particularly tense. In the second session, Jean came in red-eyed and tearful. During the go-round at the beginning of the session, she said she and Joe needed time to run something important. The chairman suggested that they bring up their concern first. Jean began crying, and Joe looked pale and upset. Jean said that she had recently discovered that Joe was having an affair. She felt completely devastated by his cheating, particularly since she was pregnant. She was angry and depressed and said she was frantically checking up on all of Joe's actions.

Group members asked Joe for his comments. He reluctantly admitted that he had become friendly with one of his coworkers and that he had slept with her on one occasion. He tried to hide the affair from Jean because she had always been jealous of him, even though she had slept with another man when they were engaged. Joe had promised Jean that he would not have further outside sexual affairs, but he wanted to "grow emotionally" by having close friendships with other women. He resented Jean's mounting suspicions and her constant checking up on him. Jean sobbed that her suspicions were well founded. She could not trust him. She felt vulnerable because of her pregnancy. Thus the couple had reached a standoff in their involvement with one another. Communication had broken down in their relationship outside the group. Joe and Jean received confrontation and support from different members of the group. Even though they felt uncomfortable with one another, it was suggested that they face each other and hold hands while they discussed their painful feelings.

After considerable exploration and expression of emotion, Joe said that he had acted irresponsibly by cheating on his wife. Jean was informed that she was being irresponsible in not being willing to trust him when he had given her his word to be faithful. Before the session ended, group members encouraged the couple to make a joint commitment. Joe would agree not to have sexual relations with anyone else, and Jean would stop mistrusting him and checking up on his whereabouts. Both people felt uncertain of the other's ability to uphold the commitment, but they agreed to go along with the suggestion of the group members. It was understood that both people would feel free to ask for a "special" group session, or phone one of the group if they needed help before the regular weekly meetings.

During the subsequent sessions, Joe and Jean had periods of pain and doubt about each other, but they worked on their commitments with the continued monitoring and support of the group. With further exploration of their feelings and behavior, it became apparent that the prospect of impending parenthood had reawakened old conflicts over Joe's need for independence and Jean's control of his behavior. During their runs over a period of several weeks, they were able to communicate their concerns to each other directly with the interested exploration and support of the group.

By the end of three months, Jean and Joe were still keeping their commitments. They had learned to talk over their feelings both in and outside of the group. As Jean began to trust Joe and communicate with him in a more meaningful way, he had less need to seek companionship outside the marriage. One year after the couple left the group, they visited one of the group resource people. They were both enjoying their role as parents of a baby girl. Joe had been promoted, and Jean was looking forward to returning to work when the baby grew older. Both people commented that their IG experience had helped them to be more honest and involved with each other and this had helped to strengthen their marriage.

SUMMARY

Technological progress has produced a society characterized by a general absence of community. The report of the President's Commission on Mental Health (1978) revealed that as much as 25 percent of the population may suffer from depression, anxiety, and other types of emotional disorder. Many individuals today are alienated, isolated, lonely, and in need of help. There has recently been a reemergence of mutual-aid or self-help groups that assist people in coping with a wide array of human concerns.

Integrity Groups are part of this movement. They are designed to aid those who are troubled by alienation and the lack of identity. Integrity Groups help individuals move into community with others by encouraging the practice of honesty, responsibility, and involvement. These groups are highly democratic, and they do not charge a fee. While providing help, they also furnish their members with training that equips them to organize additional groups in the community. The social learning approach employed in IG has a strong behavioral emphasis. However, these groups are equally concerned with the thoughts and feelings of their members. The distinctive aspects of IG are its unique group structure, shared leadership, and specific goals.

Integrity Groups provide an ideal support system for delivering community mental health services. The cost is minimal since there are no salaries to pay or buildings to rent. Two or more experienced "resource people" can start a group with seven or eight other individuals who will in turn "seed" additional groups. This "pyramid training" model (Jones, Fremouw, & Carples, 1977) provides an effective way of supplementing other kinds of community mental health services over a wide geographic area.

Some individuals believe that professional involvement is incompatible with the aims of self-help groups. Therefore, it is significant that Integrity Groups were developed by Mowrer, who is a professional psychologist. The IG experience has shown that professionals and community people have much to learn from each other. It has also demonstrated that professionals can make important contributions to a self-help group without co-opting or controlling its members. Professionals may operate as organizers or facilitators of new groups, particularly in the beginning stages. They also are in the best position to do needed research on the problems the group is dealing with and the effectiveness of the group's methods and procedures. Professionals can also conceptualize the self-help group's experiences and provide the feedback and theory building necessary for further development (Vattano, 1972).

A final word about Mowrer's search for the causes and treatment of emotional difficulties. Despite two hospitalizations for depression, his personal and professional life has been rewarding and productive. Mowrer has concluded that his depressions were most likely the result of several circumstances. Most important were the deception and alienation of his early years and the combination of constitutional predisposition, nutritional factors, and personal loss. As for the present, Mowrer continues to teach, write, and enjoy life. These activities are associated with his ongoing practice of honesty, responsibility, and involvement with others. Mowrer's search ended with his discovery that "You alone can do it, but you can't do it alone."

REFERENCES

Bixenstine, V. E. (1970). *Community house and its groups: A new approach to community mental health.* Mimeographed. Kent, Ohio: Department of Psychology, Kent State University.

Corsini, R., & Rosenberg, B. (1955). Mechanisms of group psychotherapy: Processes and dynamics. *Journal of Abnormal Social Psychology, 51,* 405–411.

Drakeford, J. (1967). *Integrity therapy.* Nashville, TN: Broadman Press.

Gartner, A., & Riessman, F. (1977). *Self-help in the human services.* San Francisco: Jossey-Bass.

Jessop, N. (1971). *A semantic differential analysis of integrity groups.* Unpublished doctoral dissertation, University of Illinois.

Johnson, R. C., Dokecki, P., & Mowrer, O. H. (Eds.). (1972). *Conscience, contract and social reality.* New York: Holt, Rinehart, Winston.

Jones, F., Fremouw, W., & Carples, S. (1977). Pyramid training of elementary school teachers to use a classroom management "skill package." *Journal of Applied Behavior Analysis, 10,* 239–253.

Jourard, S. (1971). *The transparent self: Self-disclosure and well-being.* New York: Van Nostrand.

Kaye, B. (1973). *An inventory for evaluating Integrity Groups.* Mimeographed. Champaign-Urbana, IL: University of Illinois.

Keyes, R. (1973). *We, the lonely people: Searching for community.* New York: Harper & Row.

Lieberman, M., & Borman, L. (1979). *Self-help groups for coping with crises: Origins, membership, processes, and impact.* San Francisco: Jossey-Bass.

Madison, P. (1972). Have grouped, will travel. *Psychotherapy: Theory, Research and Practice, 9,* 324–327.

McNiell, J. (1951). *A history of the cure of souls.* New York: Harper & Row.

Mowrer, O. H. (1960). "Sin," the lesser of two evils. *Contemporary Psychology, 15,* 301–304.

Mowrer, O. H. (1961). *The crisis in psychiatry and religion.* Princeton, NJ: Van Nostrand.

Mowrer, O. H. (1964). *The new group therapy.* Princeton, NJ: Van Nostrand Reinhold.

Mowrer, O. H. (1966a). Abnormal reactions or actions? An autobiographical answer. In J. A. Vernon (Ed.), *Introduction to psychology: A self-selection textbook.* Dubuque, IA: William C. Brown.

Mowrer, O. H. (1966b). Integrity therapy: A self-help approach. *Psychotherapy: Theory, Research and Practice, 3,* 114–119.

Mowrer, O. H. (Ed.). (1967). *Morality and mental health—A book of readings.* Chicago: Rand McNally.

Mowrer, O. H. (1968). New evidence concerning the nature of psychopathology. In M. Feldman (Ed.), *Studies in psychotherapy and behavior change.* Buffalo, NY: University of Buffalo Press.

Mowrer, O. H. (1971). Peer groups and medication: The best "therapy" for professionals and laymen alike. *Psychotherapy: Theory, Research and Practice, 8,* 44–54.

Mowrer, O. H. (1972). Integrity groups: Principles and procedures. *The Counseling Psychologist, 3,* 7–32.

Mowrer, O. H. (1973). Autobiography. In G. Lindzey (Ed.), *The history of psychology in autobiography* (Vol. 6). Englewood Cliffs, NJ: Prentice-Hall.

Mowrer, O. H. (1976). Therapeutic groups and communities in retrospect and prospect. *Proceedings of the First World Conference on Therapeutic Communities* Montreal, Quebec, Canada: Portage Press.

Mowrer, O. H. (1979). Is much psychotherapy still misdirected or misapplied? *Canadian Counsellor, 13,* 120–126.

Mowrer, O. H., & Vattano, A. J. (1976). Integrity groups: A context for growth in honesty, responsibility, and involvement. *Journal of Applied Behavioral Science, 12,* 419–431.

Mowrer, O. H., Vattano, A. J., Baxley, G., & Mowrer, M. (1975). *Integrity groups: The loss and recovery of community.* Urbana, IL: Integrity Groups.

Peterson, D. (1967). The insecure child: Oversocialized or under-socialized? In O. H. Mowrer (Ed.), *Morality and mental health.* Chicago: Rand McNally.

President's Commission on Mental Health. (1978). *Report to the President from the President's Commission on Mental Health* (Vol. 1). Washington, DC: U.S. Government Printing Office.

Rolls, L. J. (1968). *The interrelation between guilt and anxiety in the Freudian and Mowrerian hypotheses.* Unpublished doctoral dissertation, University of Ottawa.

Sarason, S. (1974). *The psychological sense of community: Prospects for a community psychology.* San Francisco: Jossey-Bass.

Vattano, A. J. (1972). Power to the people: Self-help groups. *Social Work, 17,* 7–15.

Vogel, P. (1976). *The development of a social integration measure (SIM) for the study of small-group process.* Unpublished doctoral dissertation, University of Illinois.

Yalom, L. (1975). *The theory and practice of Group Psychotherapy* (Rev. ed.). New York: Basic Books.

Chapter 32

INTERPERSONAL PROCESS RECALL

NORMAN I. KAGAN AND RICHARD MCQUELLON

In a famous couplet Robert Burns wrote:

O wad some Pow'r the giftie gie us
To see oursels as others see us!

Generally, in the psychotherapeutic setting electronic recording devices have two major purposes: either re-production of the therapy situation for training purposes or reproduction to see ourselves as others see us. In some police departments audiovisual recordings are made of drunks so that when sober they can see how they looked, acted, and spoke when they were intoxicated.

Norman Kagan and Richard McQuellon discuss the use of audiovisual devices in ways that are unusual both in terms of purpose (greater insight through introspection) and process (having a neutral inquirer deal-ing with the repeat process). Another important aspect of this chapter is the story of how the therapy devel-oped, which is the same as for a scientific experiment. This method is contrary to almost all of the other sys-tems in this book, which are generally brilliant insights that developed from creative thinking and were then tested in the field.

In my judgment IPR represents a powerful technique with great promise, and it may be the technical solu-tion to what I consider a major problem of psychotherapy—the economic aspect, or how to provide the most therapy for the least money.

Interpersonal Process Recall (IPR) consists of specific techniques for examining interpersonal behavior. The heart of the method is the recalling of thoughts, feelings, intentions, and images that occur during an interaction through immediate videotape playback of the partici-pants and by open-ended questioning by a third party called an inquirer. An inquirer helps subjects examine re-actions that occurred during the videotaped session by means of noninterpretive in-depth probing, from a rela-tively neutral frame of reference.

HISTORY

Precursors

The key elements in the Interpersonal Process Recall method—that is, the use of immediate videotape play-back and a trained inquirer—have philosophical as well as technological precursors. The inquirer role and func-tion has its roots in the Socratic method, in which ques-

tions were posed as a way of stimulating learning. In IPR the learning occurs in the context of the client-counselor relationship relived through videotape playback. The crucial difference between the Socratic method and the inquirer role is that the inquirer does *not* have a prede-termined goal or answer in mind. The inquirer's primary function is to pose questions and facilitate client self-exploration about the videotaped session.

Efforts at self-exploration and understanding have been with us in one form or another for centuries, long before Socrates uttered his famous dictum, "know thy-self." The scientific study of mental processes began in the laboratories of the early psychological experimental-ists who attempted to understand the human mind through introspection, which was seen as a skill requir-ing training and practice. People were trained to report what was going on in their minds. Wilhelm Wundt and other introspectionists observed that many things were forgotten when subjects were asked to recall specific events. The advent of audio and video recording permits psychologists to once again use a form of introspection as a refined experimental procedure. IPR employs videotape and an inquirer as aids to recalling specific reactions during an interaction. These techniques stimulate considerably more introspective analysis than can be achieved by memory alone.

Bernard Covner (1942, 1944) reported the use of self-confrontation techniques in counseling practice and research, and Carl Rogers (1942) used audio recordings in research and teaching, but Herbert Freed (1948) appears to have been the first therapist to report the use of audio recordings as a central component of the therapy process as a means to initiate self-confrontation, which he claimed was particularly helpful with children and in the treatment of character disorders. Today it would be difficult to find a therapist who has not used some form of recording technology either in training or in treatment.

Closed-circuit television was used as early as 1953 in a mental hospital so that ongoing group psychotherapy sessions could be viewed by other patients (Tucker, Lewis, Martin, & Over, 1957). It was reported that patients improved with this brief exposure. Moore, Chernell, and West (1965), who conducted the first controlled experiment with video procedures, reported improvement in psychotic patients. Others have also reported positive effects from using television in therapy (Walz & Johnston, 1963). Recent developments include more systematic, structured applications of the new video recording technology. A number of such applications are described by Berger (1978). The IPR method is one such approach.

A technique similar to IPR was used by Bloom (1954), who used audiotape recordings to stimulate recall of students in classroom interactions. Tapes were replayed to students and stopped at what appeared to the investigator to be significant points. The subject was asked to recall what thoughts were occurring at that time. Students reported their experiences and thoughts in remarkable detail. In studying self-confrontation, Gerhard Nielson (1964) used films to stimulate recall and found that subjects could engage in self-confrontation, but also could recall many of the feelings they had at specific points even though there was a time delay because the film had to be developed.

Beginnings

The Interpersonal Process Recall method was developed by Kagan and associates (Kagan & Krathwohl, 1967; Kagan, Krathwohl, & Miller, 1963; Kagan & Schauble, 1969) following Kagan's observation in 1961 that viewing a videotape playback with the help of a probing, nonevaluative inquirer who allowed the viewer full responsibility for determining when the tape would be stopped provided a powerful stimulus for self-examination and change. This serendipitous discovery occurred when distinguished psychologists were invited to lecture at Michigan State University. Their lectures were videotaped and subsequently viewed by them, curious about themselves as well as the new video recording technology. The psychologists often stopped the tape to react to their own images. They were politely questioned by Kagan (assistant professors question distinguished psychologists politely); the visitors were intrigued by the process, could recall covert processes in remarkable detail, and noted that they were learning important facts about themselves. This led to a series of research projects using the recall of interpersonal processes via videotape playback as an aid to introspection.

Initially, the focus was on training of counselors by applying the IPR technique to supervisory sessions. Numerous applications of IPR proved it a useful method by which mental health workers, teachers, physicians, and a myriad of other professional and paraprofessional caregivers could improve their ability to interview, communicate with, or help other people. A logical next step was to investigate its potential for accelerating client growth in therapy, since in many graduate school training programs the supervisor-supervisee relationship is analogous to the counselor-counselee relationship (Doehrman, 1976; Mueller & Kell, 1972). It may have been logical to proceed in this direction, but it certainly was not without difficulty.

A research group[1] began by developing specific outcome measures. They operationalized specific criteria of client growth—the so-called *Characteristics of Client Growth Scales*—and proceeded to conduct a series of studies. From this early research there were indications that the application of a structured approach to the examination of the videotape accelerated movement in therapy (Kagan, Krathwohl, & Miller, 1963; Resnikoff, Kagan, & Schauble, 1970). Initially, intensive case studies were conducted and then followed by research with a larger sample of counselors and clients (Kagan & Krathwohl, 1967).

These initial observations led to further research comparing traditional counseling with traditional counseling plus IPR techniques. While the results of this research are not conclusive, some studies have found significant evidence that IPR accelerates client improvement under certain conditions.

CURRENT STATUS

The IPR method is currently being applied in a variety of settings. When applied in a training setting, the coun-

[1] During the first four years David R. Krathwohl and William Farquhar were coresearchers with Kagan.

selor/trainee is in some sense viewed as a client. The focus is not on problem resolution of psychopathology but rather on interpersonal behavior and its consequences. The model focuses on counselor as client in the sense that self-exploration of interpersonal behavior and understanding underlying processes are the goal of both training and treatment.

Reliable replication of the IPR model by others has been a primary concern to us. The inquirer role, so basic to the client recall process, is very difficult to communicate in writing. This concern has led us to experiment with "packaging" the entire model to simplify the instructor's task and to make the IPR model reliably replicable without the need for outside consultants. The first attempt was a black-and-white film and videotape series containing illustrations, instructions, demonstrations, and didactic presentations aimed primarily at mental health workers. The package was used by more than 40 universities, schools, and social agencies, most of which reported satisfactory experiences. A controlled evaluation at New York University (Boltuch, 1975) indicated that counseling students taught by instructors using the package made significantly greater gains than a control group receiving an equivalent amount of other curriculum offerings. The film series, known as *Influencing Human Interaction,* was revised and expanded so that it now consists of color films or color videotapes (Kagan, 1975a) and contains illustrations from medicine, teaching, and family therapy as well as counseling. The new series also contains scenes designed to stimulate discussions on sexism and racism. An instructor's manual and student handouts were also prepared. The new program, like the original one, can be implemented with a minimum of instructor preparation and is currently in use in medical, pharmacy, and law schools, hospitals, secondary schools, agencies, and prison personnel programs in the United States, Canada, England, Australia, Sweden, Denmark, Norway, Germany, Puerto Rico, Israel, and elsewhere. At Michigan State University it is an integral part of several graduate programs, including medical education.

The revised IPR model consists of a number of modules that have specific applicability to the settings mentioned earlier. The model includes seven basic units. The first, titled *Elements of Effective Communication,* presents four verbal response modes—exploratory, listening, affective, and honest labeling responses. The second unit, *Affect Simulation,* makes use of stimulus films or videotapes consisting of brief vignettes depicting people communicating "difficult-to-deal-with" messages directly to the viewer. The vignettes might be thought of as depicting "the worst possible things" that might underlie fear or excess cautiousness in the neophyte. The vignettes are usually perceived as stressful for the viewer. They are designed to stimulate thoughts, feelings, and reactions, and to help the viewer increase sensitivity to his or her own reactions and overcome fears of involvement with clients. The third component in the IPR model, *Interviewer Recall,* introduces the inquirer role and the recall process. First the trainee conducts an interview. The client (a fellow trainee or paid actor who simulates a genuine concern) then leaves the room and the recall session follows immediately. The trainee is encouraged to report reactions to the interview while reviewing the videotape. The trainee is given control of the recorder and is asked to stop the playback whenever any thoughts or feelings are recalled. The purpose of this unit is to help trainees learn to study themselves in action by making explicit important information they perceived but did not act on. The fourth unit is titled *In-Depth Study of the Inquirer Role.* The inquirer's function is to conduct the recall session. This is the heart of the IPR process, because the ability and willingness of a person to recall interpersonal process events depends largely on a skilled inquirer. The role is clearly defined and teachable. The fifth unit, like the third, focuses on the recall process again, but in this instance on the *Client's Recall.* This experience is designed to help the counselor learn about client dynamics directly from the client. The client's recall is the basis for learning about client needs and wants. The sixth unit brings the trainee and client together for a *Mutual Recall Session* where either participant stops the video playback to comment about reactions during the previous interview. The inquirer encourages each to talk about unexpressed thoughts, feelings, and intentions in each other's presence. The purpose of mutual recall is to help trainees learn to be able to turn the implicit process of an interaction into explicit content, to talk about the here-and-now in interaction whenever such dialogue might be of use. The final IPR unit provides a *Theory Discussion* and is designed to give the trainee a cognitive framework to make some "sense" of the largely experiential program.

Although the IPR model was originally intended as a training device, its use has not been confined to this area. One of the more exciting areas for development lies in its potential for accelerating client growth in therapy. Research on applications in this area has produced conflicting but promising results (Tomory, 1979).

THEORY

Constructs from a variety of theorists, both analytic (Horney, 1950; Sullivan, 1953) and behavioral (Lazarus, 1971), can be used to explain why Interpersonal Process Recall is effective in fostering growth and behavior change.

Basic Assumptions and Interpersonal Manifestations

Two basic dynamics have been observed or inferred from the application of the IPR method. First, people need each other, not only for physical survival but for an optimum level of interpersonal stimulation. People are potentially the most complete source of joy for each other—more interesting, stimulating, and satisfying than any other single source of satisfaction in the environment. The second basic dynamic is that people learn to fear each other. Just as relationships can provide a potent source of satisfaction, so they can also be a source of intense pain.

The fears we have of each other cluster into one of the following four categories:

1. *You will hurt me:* If we develop an intimate relationship, you will do something that will cause me pain.
2. *I will hurt you:* In like manner I could hurt you.
3. *You will engulf me:* If we relate intimately, you will somehow overwhelm me, negate who I am. My sense of self will be engulfed in who you are.
4. *I will engulf you:* In a similar manner I could engulf you.

These fears develop early in life and are the product of being a "small person in a big person's world." Vague feelings of fear and helplessness are the natural result of lengthy childhood dependence, and such feelings may persist throughout life. IPR therapists think this is the reason why so many of the intense feelings described by clients in recall sessions appear infantile—living vestiges of early fears. Such feelings are usually unlabeled, unstated, and thus inaccessible to the logic of language.

These basically opposed states, the need for people and the fear of people, evince themselves in many interpersonal behaviors. Each attitude is reflected in interpersonal behavior designed to avoid the feared consequences of intimate human interaction. One manifestation can be seen in the approach–avoidance behavior that seems to characterize most human interactions. People appear to both approach and retreat from direct, simple intimacy with others in a cyclical fashion—intimacy followed by relative isolation, followed by new bids for intimacy. This process appears to establish a specific range of "safe" interpersonal distance unique for each individual. An established psychological distance allows for some level of intimacy along with a feeling of safety from the potential risks that accompany close relationships. The attempt at establishing a safe interpersonal contact range may be seen as an effort to find a balance between the pain of boredom and sensory deprivation when contact is too distant and the experience of anxiety

when it is too close. The stronger the fear, the more likely the person will be to avoid intimate relationships. Conversely, if people are not frightened of each other, they will be more able to achieve sustained, intimate contact. This genuine intimate contact with another also then allows for periods of aloneness without panic. Maslow (1968) suggested that more fully functioning people are capable of gratifying periods of being alone possibly because of their ability for deep levels of intimate relating. It is as if knowing that the potential for intimacy is available frees one to experience aloneness without fear.

As people interact they sense each other on many levels, but they label or acknowledge only a very limited range of what they send or perceive. This is a part of all human interactions and serves to reduce the level of genuine intimacy.

The fears people have of each other usually become translated into an interpersonal mythology and expectations—a "slogan" that enables one to avoid frightening interpersonal nightmares, such as "People have always perceived me in certain ways and ultimately react to me accordingly, and they always will." These anticipated reactions by others then foster a self-fulfilling prophecy in which people make their nightmares happen.

Interpersonal closeness or distance is a subjective event not easily observed. Such events have behavioral consequences that can be organized in a two-stage model. The first stage consists of typical response modes in the immediacy of interaction, the way a person acts in daily encounters. The second stage is characterized by a long-term interpersonal posture. The recurrent use of specific interpersonal behavior (Stage 1) leads to the development of a pattern of interaction (Stage 2). Some of these observations closely parallel those of Karen Horney (1950).

The basic interpersonal response modes in Stage 1 are characterized by three behaviors—attacking, withdrawing, and conforming. As one perceives other people impinging, one can attack or strike out. On the most extreme end of the aggression continuum the word attack is appropriate, for the behavior that occurs is a vicious, angry striking out. On the other end of the aggression continuum, one might think of simple assertiveness. This continuum is referred to as *attack*. Some people operate almost exclusively on an attacking response mode.

A second basic social response mode is withdrawal. On the most extreme end there is complete "withdrawal" and on the other end the ability to back out graciously. Some people rely almost exclusively on a withdrawal modality.

The third basic mode is conformance. At one extreme end is the pure conformist, the chameleon. A less negative extreme position would be the ability to be agreeable.

Some people who attack achieve a lifestyle not of engagement and stimulating direct involvement, but rather of withdrawal. The person may attack not to engage people, but as a way of ultimately withdrawing. The attacking posture may achieve a long-term posture of withdrawal.

Another pattern is attack with conformity as a long-term achieved status. People strike out so that they can maintain an unchallenged loyalty to a set of beliefs or a family. Such basic conformists as the television character Archie Bunker fit that description. An attacking interpersonal style then may be developed to conform or to withdraw from involvement.

Withdrawal can also be a way of achieving a long-term attack or hostile posture. The classic passive-aggressive personality type develops a long-term posture of attack through passive withdrawal.

Withdrawal can also be a way to conform, to maintain a belief system, a loyalty, a set of interpersonal relations unchallenged. Here we find people who will go limp interpersonally, withdrawing to protect themselves from change. It is very hard to have an impact on such people.

Conforming can serve a long-term posture of attack. This can be seen in the pseudoconformist who strikes out when backs are turned. The hostile social manipulator is of this type.

Finally, a conforming reaction can be a vehicle for ultimate withdrawal and avoidance of human interaction. One can conform to maintain distance and safety, but often boredom and loneliness result.

More fully functioning people appear to be those who have a wide repertoire of behavioral patterns—who can be assertive but are not driven to be, who can back down as well as conform.

IPR Applied in Psychotherapy

The potential effectiveness of IPR with clients in treatment can be understood from a relationship theory of counseling in which the client-counselor relationship is the critical variable in client growth. This perspective, first described by Carl Rogers (1957) and later by Patterson (1974), views the client as a positive force in the resolution of his or her conflicts. The client is capable of achieving insight leading to more appropriate behavior. The client has learned an interactional style, a way of coping and behaving, that will be demonstrated in the counseling session. The maladaptive interpersonal behavior that brings the client to treatment will be manifested with the counselor, usually in the intra- and interpersonal behaviors and perceptions previously described. It becomes the task of the counselor to help the client explore this interactional behavior.

A client's response to anxiety in the counseling situation is assumed to trigger the same defenses and interpersonal patterns characteristic of client interactions outside the counseling session. Kell and Mueller (1966) and Kell and Burow (1970) have described a theory of counseling based on this idea. They suggest that while the client wants to change, there are no alternatives to the maladaptive coping behaviors that have become so familiar. These behaviors are mobilized in the counseling situation because the prospect of change is threatening and anxiety-provoking. Since anxiety can hinder the client's efforts at change, it is crucial that the counselor reduce nonproductive anxiety and create a therapeutic atmosphere.

If one considers the counseling session as an emotional experience characterized by frequent high levels of anxiety, then the value of IPR for accelerating the counseling process becomes evident. Anxiety interferes with the perceptions of client and counselor and often acts as a hindrance to therapy. The "acknowledged" content usually does not include the most pressing client issues because of high levels of anxiety. The IPR method serves to create an environment characterized by reduced anxiety levels. This is achieved by viewing interactional behavior immediately after it has occurred so that the accompanying thoughts and feelings can be recalled in depth. Videotaped interaction is less threatening than actual interchange since both participants know they survived the encounter, a fact not known in an ongoing interaction. A second source of safety is the nonjudgmental inquirer.

The basic IPR process has two central therapeutic features: (1) videotape technology, which provides an immediate re-creation of the previously experienced interaction, and (2) the use of stimulated recall methodology to facilitate the client's ability to introspect, a necessary skill if therapy is to proceed successfully. The recall process and inquirer role in the IPR model provide structure and a rich theoretical foundation for accelerating client growth in therapy.

The Recall Process. The IPR format consists of the client and inquirer viewing the videotape replay of a portion of the counseling session without the counselor present. The client stops the playback at any point where thoughts or feelings were stimulated but not discussed fully. In such sessions clients usually begin to recognize ways in which their relationship with the counselor parallels their relationships with significant others. In *mutual recall* both client and counselor tell each other and the inquirer of their covert processes in the recorded session, and behavioral rehearsal of immediate intimate exchange can also occur, with client and counselor given practice at talking about their relationship. Both then become more like participant-observers of their own interaction—stepping back from the immediacy of their interaction and replaying the "videotape in their head."

In this manner they learn to discuss what happened in the session. This also happens in real life with a significant other when a recall session is held between the client and a friend, spouse, or some significant other with the counselor functioning as inquirer. In each format the inquirer is to pose questions in a gentle, probing fashion.

Therapy is an emergent process, developing as the client becomes increasingly aware of interpersonal processes through recall. Engaging in the recall process enables clients to label (in spoken language) their perceptions and expectations. This often invokes the logic of language onto emotional experiences that ordinarily are unreported and unrecognized. This amounts to finding words for what had been prelanguage feelings, learning about oneself in language. The labeling process may literally be informing one part of the brain about the content of another (Sagan, 1977).

Tomory (1979) has suggested further reasons to justify client recall in psychotherapy. First, the videotape recall provides the client with a neutral source of feedback. The client is not being told *about* his or her behavior. The client views it in relation to the counselor. The videotape is objective and valid in providing feedback. Second, with the help of the inquirer, the client is free to explore in depth the covert processes underlying the interactional behavior. Since the feedback is neutral, clients are free to accept or reject it without challenge. Given accurate feedback and nonthreatening environment, clients are less likely to deny or rationalize and can take responsibility for their behavior. The playback allows clients to examine the client-counselor relationship from a relatively safe vantage point (the immediate outcome of the interactional sequence is known since it has already occurred). Lowered levels of client anxiety provide favorable conditions for emotional, cognitive, and behavioral relearning. Third, clients may learn that they invest a lot of energy in the client-counselor relationship even when discussing third-party concerns that lie outside the dyadic counselor relationship. The client can literally "see" how he or she relates to his or her presenting problem. Fourth, in client recall, the client can explore interpersonal patterns without relating directly with the therapist.

The Inquiry.   The effectiveness of the recall process largely depends on the inquirer. The inquirer's function is to facilitate stimulated recall and self-analysis. The inquirer helps clients direct their energy into self-analysis as the videotape is reviewed. (It is not unusual for clients and counselors to incorporate inquirer questions into their repertoire and then to function as their own inquirers.) Clients are discouraged from talking with the inquirer at length about external relationships or material not discussed on the videotape. The focus during the inquiry is on examining the recorded interactional behavior and avoiding a therapeutic relationship with the inquirer. The task is to "debrief" the videotape, with the client serving as authority on the meaning of the interaction and the inquirer as expert in asking questions. It is assumed that as clients reflect on their behavior and the concomitant, covert thought processes, they will begin to discover the antecedents and consequences of specific interpersonal behaviors.

A social-psychological perspective provides an alternate explanation for the effectiveness of the inquiry. A powerful influence in facilitating the therapy is the manner in which the inquirer handles the recall session and, by implication, defines a theory of human interaction for the client. From this perspective, the defining of the situation, as described by McHugh (1968), is the key to the power of the inquirer role. In any social encounter the people involved have the task of organizing meaning in social interaction, thus producing a highly unique definition of the situation. This definition stems from the question Goffman (1974) suggests all people pose when engaged in face-to-face encounter: "What is it that's going on here?" The inquirer defines the therapy session as a situation in which the client will discover and express heretofore hidden aspects of interpersonal behavior. The inquirer helps the client find an answer to "What is it that's going on here?" This is done in several ways. First, a series of specific instructions is presented to the client, suggesting that there is a universal human phenomenon in which many possible interactional responses are censored for a variety of adaptive purposes, but this censoring may be maladaptive. An expectation is thus set for discovering "censored" items. The client is expected to see and explore things glossed over in the session. Second, the posing of probing questions by a nonjudgmental inquirer helps the client self-explore in a nonthreatening relationship. The inquirer is neutral but curious about the meaning of the client's behavior. The questions the inquirer asks stimulate the client to ask "What were my implicit thoughts, feelings, beliefs, attitudes that occurred with my counselor?" The inquirer defines the recall session to create the expectation of exciting self-discovery.

These discoveries, along with curiosity about self, are integrated into the therapeutic relationship where the counselor facilitates client change by addressing interactional themes characteristic of the client. The parallel process of client-counselor and client-other interaction can then be elucidated.

METHODOLOGY

The first step in employing Interpersonal Process Recall is to assure adequate videotape facilities. The equipment is located in one room where both the counseling and recall session are held.

Before the taping process begins, the rationale for IPR and the use of video equipment is explained. The client is free to voice any reservation about the procedure and, as in any form of counseling, choose not to engage in the procedure. If the process is accepted, the client and counselor tape a session, which can be as brief as 10 minutes or the traditional 50 minutes. If the IPR format is to be client recall, the counselor leaves the room after the taping and the inquirer takes his or her place.

The inquirer then instructs the client on the purpose of the recall process. The following assumptions taken from Kagan and Krathwohl (1967) are made explicit to the client before recall is begun:

1. We know that the mind works faster than the voice.
2. As we talk with people, we think of things which are quite different from the things we are talking about. Everyone does this and there is no reason to feel embarrassed or to hesitate to "own up to it" when it does occur.
3. We know that as we talk to people, there are times when we like what they say and there are times when we are annoyed with what they say. There are times when we think they really understand us and there are times when we feel they have missed the point of what we are saying or really don't understand what we were feeling, or how strongly we were feeling something.
4. There are also times when we are concerned about what the other person is thinking about us. Sometimes we want the other person to think about us in ways which he may not be.
5. If we ask you at this moment just when you felt the counselor understood or didn't understand your feelings, or when you felt you were making a certain kind of impression on him, or when you were trying to say something and it came out quite differently from the way you wanted it to, it would probably be very difficult for you to remember. With this T.V. playback immediately after your interview, you will find it possible to recall these thoughts and feelings in detail. Stop and start the playback by means of the switch as often as you remember your thoughts and feelings. The recorder is on remote control so that you are not troubling anyone no matter how often you stop and start the playback. As you remember thoughts and feelings, stop the tape and tell me what they were. (p. 13)

Clients differ widely in their ability to engage in this process, requiring more or less encouragement by the inquirer. The inquirer avoids counseling or interpreting. Recall sessions last approximately 40 minutes and, de-pending on the client, only 10 to 15 minutes of the interview may be covered. Exploratory, brief, open-ended questions about thoughts and feelings are posed.

A number of general areas often prove fruitful for inquiry. When the client stops the tape to make observations about a theme, the experienced inquirer pursues that theme and then introduces other areas. For example, questions that stimulate affective themes include: Were you aware of any feelings? What did you decide to do with that feeling? How did you decide not to express that feeling? To encourage cognitive examination an inquirer might ask: What were you thinking at that time? What was going through your mind when you said that? What thoughts were you having about the other person? Did you want to say anything else at that time? Further exploration can be encouraged in the area of physiological and other nonverbal behaviors—body sensations, images, and expectations—by asking questions such as: Do you recall how your body was feeling at that time? Were you having any fantasies or images at that moment? What did you want your counselor to tell you? Were you expecting anything from your counselor at that point? Also, questions might lead into other associations or help to check out unstated agendas: Did your counselor remind you of anyone else in your life? (If the answer is yes, then ask: What effect did that have on you?) What reaction did you have toward your counselor's statements? What would you have liked to have said at that point? Was there anything you felt like doing at that time?

One area to explore is the client's perception of the counselor's view of him or her, which strongly influences the interaction during the session. Inquirer probes include: What do you think your counselor was feeling about you? What message do you think he was trying to communicate to you? How were you being seen at that point? How did you want to be seen? How did you not want to be seen? How do you think he felt about discussing this problem?

Clients vary in their ability and/or willingness to explore particular areas. For example, if the counselor is observing the recall process, the client may be somewhat less willing to reveal perception of the counselor.

Inquirer leads (Kagan & Burke, 1976) can be used in a variety of areas in order to encourage active client involvement during the inquiry. This involvement centers around (1) the origin and development of the client's thoughts and feelings as experienced during the interview; (2) the way the client sees him- or herself in terms of likes, dislikes, fears, fantasies, and so forth, about self; (3) the way the client would like to be seen by the counselor; and (4) the way the client believes the counselor actually does perceive him or her. We have found that inquirer questions can facilitate self-exploration and increased awareness and involvement if they encourage a self-questioning rather than a self-explanatory attitude. We do not want clients to attempt to explain *why* they behave the way they do; rather we want the client to fully explore the *what* and *how* of his or her interpersonal behavior. Consequently, "why" questions are avoided in the recall session. This is not to suggest that client motivation and historical antecedents are not important, but rather that the recall session is designed to focus more on the "what" of behavior. The therapeutic relationship is the place for the client to further explore the reasons of idiosyncratic behavior.

APPLICATIONS

Interpersonal Process Recall has been researched extensively as a training device and to a lesser extent as a method for psychotherapy. In both applications the emphasis is on self-study through observation and discussion of interpersonal behavior and exploration of concomitant covert processes. It is postulated that knowledge about one's own interpersonal behavior is invaluable in learning to be an effective therapist. Relationship conflicts emerge between client and counselor that parallel (Doehrman, 1976) those that develop between counselor and supervisor (Mueller & Kell, 1972). The relationship dynamics in the client-counselor relationship reflect, to some degree, the presenting problem for which the client is seeking therapy. Thus a counselor in training is viewed much as a client is viewed, although there is an obvious difference—the counselor uses self-study to become an effective therapist, whereas the client usually seeks resolution of personal problems. The reasons that counselors and clients use IPR are different but the processes are similar. In many ways the dynamics of supervision are analogous to those seen in psychotherapy (Chiles & McQuellon, 1978). The research based on IPR in counselor training and other areas is available elsewhere (Kagan, 1975b).

IPR as a method for accelerating client progress in counseling and psychotherapy has been reported in several controlled experimental research studies (Hartson & Kunce, 1973; Hurley, 1967; Schauble, 1970; Tomory, 1979; VanNoord, 1973) and in case studies (Kagan & Krathwohl, 1967; Kagan, Krathwohl, & Miller, 1963; Resnikoff, Kagan, & Schauble, 1970).

Hurley (1967) conducted one of the first studies using IPR recall in small counseling groups. A single recall session was introduced during the fifth session of a 10-session group. The IPR intervention did not result in a statistically significant advantage on measures of self-disclosure when compared with two control groups, but it did alter the style of group interactions in a positive direction as reported by group leaders and supported by analysis of pre- and postsession tape recordings. It was

concluded that more IPR treatments might have increased self-disclosing behavior, the main criterion measure used.

Affect simulation through filmed stimulus vignettes was incorporated into the IPR model to facilitate the client's discussion of reactions to highly emotional interpersonal situations, to discover individual client stereotypes in interpersonal behavior, and to uncover conflict areas (Danish & Kagan, 1969; Kagan & Schauble, 1969). The vignettes depicted mild to intense degrees of affect in the areas of hostility, fear of hostility, affection, and fear of affection. These brief filmed vignettes were used in a variety of formats. In one format vignettes were shown to clients while they were being videotaped. This was followed by a recall session. The vignettes were also used without videotape and recall. It was found that the vignettes were particularly helpful in the initial stages of counseling. This finding influenced later researchers to apply IPR methodology with clients in a developmental manner from least to most threatening experiences.

Schauble (1970) compared traditional counseling with IPR techniques using two advanced doctoral candidate intern therapists and 12 female counseling center clients. Both treatments consisted of six sessions. The IPR treatment group followed a structured sequence proceeding from least to most threatening experiences. This approach stemmed from an earlier pilot study suggesting a series of developmental tasks facing the client during the counseling or therapy process. The theory underlying this developmental approach was: (1) Clients first needed to learn how to talk about feelings and explore them in a safe environment (videotape recall or stimulus films). Under these conditions, that is, without debilitating anxiety, emotionally stressful interpersonal situations could be examined for maximum learning. (2) Clients needed to begin to identify the behavior patterns and feelings experienced during the counseling session but had to do this in the relative safety of an objective third person—the inquirer (client recall). (3) Finally, clients needed to learn to be able to discuss their behavior and feelings as they occur, that is, to deal with the "here-and-now" of the counseling relationship (mutual recall). Significant between-group differences favoring the IPR group emerged on most of the five dependent variables employed as pre- and postmeasures. Client feelings about coming to the session and client feelings about progress made in the session as measured by *The Therapy Session Report* (Orlinsky & Howard, 1966) favored the IPR treatment group.

VanNoord (1973) conducted a similar investigation using a highly structured sequencing of the IPR model, employing 12 therapists, each seeing only one client (half were in the IPR treatment group and half in the control group) and adopting a posttest only design. He made several other modifications, most notably adopting different criterion measures. The sequencing of the IPR model proceeded in the following manner: (1) Session 1—*traditional;* (2) Session 2—*stimulus films;* (3) Session 3—*video recall of stimulus films;* (4) Sessions 4 and 5—*client recall with counselor observation through a one-way mirror;* (5) Session 6—*mutual recall.* No significant differences were observed between groups on the objective measures, although subjective comments by clients suggested that IPR techniques were beneficial in self-exploration and in exploration of the client-counselor relationship.

Tomory (1979) attempted to build on the Schauble and VanNoord researches in evaluating the potential of IPR in accelerating client growth. He noted that both Schauble and VanNoord reported a frequent therapist criticism of the rigid structure in the IPR treatment groups. The therapists did not view this as helpful because it did not allow for individual client differences in terms of growth rate and needs. Tomory introduced flexibility into the research design by allowing therapists to apply five IPR techniques (stimulus films, video recall of stimulus films, client recall, mutual recall, and significant other recall) whenever they deemed it appropriate. He increased the number of subjects to 50 and allowed for variability in the number of treatment sessions. Unfortunately, the therapists received only five hours of training in the IPR methods. The therapists in the IPR treatment group were required then to use the techniques in (1) 50 percent of the first 10 sessions and (2) at least every other session or in two consecutive sessions followed by two traditional sessions. Like VanNoord, Tomory found no significant differences between the traditional counseling group and the traditional counseling in addition to IPR treatment on the objective measures used, but clients' statements on the use of the videotape feedback were overwhelmingly positive. Therapists without exception stated that IPR videotape and stimulus film intervention techniques were helpful with their clients.

In a study assessing the effectiveness of IPR in accelerating group psychotherapy, Hartson and Kunce (1973) used a combination of stimulus films, dyadic recall, and group recall techniques. In six sessions IPR treatment clients demonstrated significantly higher changes in self-disclosure and readiness for group behavior and participated in more therapeutic interchanges than clients in traditional *T*-groups. The *T*-group clients did, however, show significantly higher satisfaction scores. A differential treatment effect was reported with the two sample groups observed: IPR self-confrontation methods were helpful to low self-esteem, socially inactive (counseling center) subjects on whom the direct confrontation methods of the *T*-group had an adverse effect. No treatment differences were observed between high self-esteem, socially active (YMCA) subjects. The authors suggested that further research should focus on the appropriate-

ness of specific IPR techniques according to client needs and personalities.

Additional applications of the IPR model in controlled experimental studies have investigated the effects of varying the frequency of videotape feedback during short-term counseling (Grana, 1977) and have examined the ability of clients to accurately recall feelings of comfort and discomfort while watching a videotape of a previous session (Katz & Resnikoff, 1977). Kingdon (1975) explored the cost/benefit of IPR application in terms of the inhibitory effect of using videotape on client self-exploration (cost) and client satisfaction, increased counselor empathy ratings, and increased supervisor ratings. Rather than inhibiting self-exploration, she found that IPR served to positively influence depth of client exploration.

Intensive case studies have been reported with a 30-year-old female who suffered from periods of depression and a rigid, nonsexual relationship with her husband (Kagan, Krathwohl, & Miller, 1963); a 21-year-old male who had problems with dependency, social inadequacy, and sexual uncertainty (Woody, Kagan, Krathwohl, & Farquhar, 1965); and with more severely disturbed clients (Resnikoff, Kagan, & Schauble, 1970). In these studies and others, IPR methods have been used in a variety of ways, with variations in the structure and technique applied.

Other applications could be developed. The entire IPR training course could be given to groups of clients as an adjunct to therapy not only to facilitate their work in therapy but also to improve their communication skills. The IPR model could be used directly to influence clients' relationships with significant others by videotaping couples or families and having the therapist then serve as the inquirer (Kagan, 1975a). In the IPR counselor training program the counselor and inquirer review a tape without the client during the first recall experience. The focus is on therapist recall. The therapist is encouraged to label impressions and strategies as well as aspirations, frustrations, satisfactions, and anxieties evoked by the interaction with the client. In accelerated therapy applications, this possibly critical aspect is usually omitted by therapists, who "prescribe" only client recalls. Perhaps therapist recall alone should be included as part of the use of the process in psychotherapy.

CASE EXAMPLE[2]

Background

The client (referred to as George) was a very bright and well read 18-year-old college-bound high school senior.

---

[2] Originally reported by A. Resnikoff, N. Kagan, and P. G. Schauble, 1970, "Acceleration of psychotherapy through stimulated videotape recall," *American Journal of Psychotherapy, 24*(1), pp. 102–111.

His immediate family consisted of his mother and two younger sisters, one an illegitimate child. When George was only two years old his father had died of natural causes. His mother had remarried and divorced twice; she was hospitalized with emotional problems following her second and third marriages and used alcohol excessively. She had wanted a girl and clearly communicated a rejecting attitude toward George. George lived with a number of relatives who often beat him and considered him a burden until the age of 14, when he entered an agency. When he began therapy he was still residing in the agency setting.

Problem

George was diagnosed as suffering from mild to acute psychotic reactions. He had trouble with authority figures, a fear of people generally, and his behavior with women was highly sexualized and acting-out. At the age of 14 he had begun drinking heavily and eventually became an alcoholic. Shortly before he entered therapy, he made his second suicide attempt.

Treatment

The client was seen twice a week for hour-long interviews by a clinical psychologist who planned an intensive 20-week insight-oriented treatment regimen. The initial two sessions were filled with many painful childhood and adolescent memories in addition to repeated questions regarding his sanity, capacity to love, and his worthiness to receive love. The third interview was focused on the first of a series of dreams reported by George. These proved to be helpful in sorting out his mixed feelings toward his mother and discovering that his angry thoughts and feelings were not, of themselves, destructive. The themes uncovered in the four interviews were examined more fully in Sessions 5 through 8. George began to see the origin of his generalized fear of people in his earlier mistreatment at the hands of his relatives. Sessions 9 through 11 consisted of client attempts to connect his intense feelings with his recognition of anger and, at length, love. He became increasingly aware of his confusion concerning sexual intercourse and also of ambivalent feelings toward his therapist. When George's affect became noticeably depressed in the 11th interview, it was decided to employ an IPR intervention in order to more clearly understand the dynamics underlying the depression.

Twelfth Interview—IPR Session. To keep the entire session one hour in length the therapist conducted a 20-minute interview followed by a 40-minute recall session. George was not aware of the method when the session began, but was informed of the procedure in general and introduced to the inquirer following the 20-minute interview. During the recall only nine minutes of video material stimulated all of the 40 minutes of client recall.

The client seemed mildly depressed during the interview session with the therapist. He told of a visit by his mother, who had given him a cigarette case and made reference to his sister. He also noted that his plans for summer vacation were unclear.

During the recall session the client communicated freely with the inquirer. There was a marked difference in George's participation during the recall when compared with the 20-minute therapeutic session. He spoke with added clarity and rapidity of speech and he stopped the videotape playback often—a characteristic of productive recall sessions. George was both surprised and pleased at what he was learning about himself. It became clear during the recall that his imagery had been very rich but not entirely revealed to the therapist and that he had worked through much of the material covered in earlier interviews without reporting such gains to his therapist. Also, George's commitment to his therapist and their relationship was much stronger than he had been willing and/or able to admit and stronger than the therapist had realized.

One of the client's intense reactions to the recall session was anger at the point in the tape where he spoke about his grandfather's not caring for his father following a brain tumor operation. This theme had been addressed during the interview with the therapist, but little affect had been demonstrated. The intensity of anger associated with this recollection was much more clearly demonstrated during the recall session. Several other associations were prompted, including thoughts and feelings about his mother and sisters.

An apparently important discovery was made when George described that he had avoided revealing his "real" thoughts to his therapist. The recall session seemed to help George expand on his feelings toward his family and begin to understand the nature of his irrational feelings toward people and his ambivalent feeling toward women. Subsequent therapy sessions were rich in associations and more spontaneous. This change resulted from the therapist's new approach to inducing associations.

The recall data (the therapist had reviewed the recall session with the inquirer) helped the therapist to better understand George's ideational systems and to modify his approach to include, for instance, asking that George focus on the images he "saw" when discussing problem areas. This single statement stimulated a flow of material relevant to his dynamics and concerns. George's avoidance behavior, that is, discussion of authors and their works, began to disappear in favor of the issues that presented difficulties for him.

This single exposure to an IPR session served to help

George move through a therapeutic impasse by opening up areas that had not been addressed in the therapy session. George demonstrated different behavior in therapy following the IPR treatment, perhaps as a result of that session. He began to own up to his own discomfort, make a commitment to change, differentiate his thoughts, feelings, and visual imagery, and finally behave differently.

SUMMARY

Interpersonal Process Recall is a method of influencing and improving human interaction using stimulated recall and learning-by-discovery. When applied in training or in counseling/psychotherapy, audio/videotape is used for stimulated recall so that the original experience of the client-counselor interaction may be viewed and relived. The core of the IPR process lies in the immediate replay of the counseling session and the skills of an "inquirer" in helping participants relate their recalled thoughts and feelings. Filmed vignettes are also used to help clients identify their worst "interpersonal nightmares."

The method relies on both analytic and behavioral constructs and does not evolve from any specific personality theory. The basic assumptions of IPR center around the conflict of (1) a universal need for interpersonal stimulation and (2) the learned fear of intimate relationships. These opposing needs motivate interpersonal behaviors that can be categorized into a typology of attacking, withdrawing, and conforming behavior. These interpersonal behaviors may function to create certain long-term consequences or interpersonal "postures." Six basic typologies are postulated, including: (1) *attack to withdraw;* (2) *attack to conform;* (3) *withdraw to attack;* (4) *withdraw to conform;* (5) *conform to attack;* and finally (6) *conform to withdraw.*

Behavior in the counseling situation is assumed to reflect the interpersonal patterns characteristic of client interactions in other settings. Thus the study of client-counselor interaction becomes a major focus of counseling to help the client learn about interpersonal behavior elsewhere.

The inquirer role consists of helping the client engage in the recall process and become an active participant in self-analysis and learning. Through the recall process clients come to know their interactional processes with the counselor and to try out new behaviors within the client-counselor relationship. The inquirer role functions to increase client awareness of such vaguely perceived ideas about interpersonal behavior by encouraging the client to verbalize his or her perceptions. Through the recall process clients come to know their fears of others and their "less adaptive" behaviors. If observation and analysis of one's own interpersonal behavior, mental processes, and emotional states is a necessary condition for behavior change, then the value of IPR in counseling and psychotherapy becomes evident.

REFERENCES

Berger, M. A. (1978). *Videotape techniques in psychiatric training and treatment* (Rev. ed.). New York: Brunner/Mazel.

Bloom, B. S. (1954). The thought processes of students in discussion. In S. French (Ed.), *Accent on teaching.* New York: Harper.

Boltuch, B. S. (1975). *The effects of a pre-practicum skill training program. Influencing Human Interaction, on developing counselor effectiveness in a master's level practicum.* Unpublished doctoral dissertation, New York University.

Chiles, R., & McQuellon, R. (1978). A growth model of supervision: Training the beginning psychotherapist in the community mental health center. *North Carolina Journal of Mental Health, 8*(9), 35–40.

Covner, B. J. (1942). The use of phonographic recordings in counseling practice and research. *Journal of Counseling Psychology, 6,* 105–113.

Covner, B. J. (1944). Written reports of interviews. *Journal of Applied Psychology, 28,* 89–98.

Danish, S. J., & Kagan, N. (1969). Emotional simulation in counseling and psychotherapy. *Psychotherapy: Theory, Research and Practice, 6*(4), 261–263.

Doehrman, M. (1976). Parallel processes in supervisor and psychotherapy. *Bulletin of the Menninger Clinic, 40*(1), 3–104.

Freed, H. (1948). On various uses of the recorded interview in psychotherapy. *Psychiatric Quarterly, 22,* 685–695.

Goffman, E. (1974). *Frame analysis: An essay on the organization of experience.* Cambridge, MA: Harvard University Press.

Grana, R. K. (1977). *Videotape feedback: Frequency of usage and its value as a counseling technique.* Unpublished doctoral dissertation, University of Akron.

Hartson, D. J., & Kunce, J. T. (1973). Videotape replay and recall in group work. *Journal of Counseling Psychology, 20,* 437–441.

Horney, K. (1950). *Neurosis and human growth.* New York: Norton.

Hurley, S. (1967). *Self disclosure in counseling groups as influenced by structural confrontation and interpersonal process recall.* Unpublished doctoral dissertation, Michigan State University.

Kagan, N. (1975a). Influencing human interaction [filmed training series]. Mason, MI: Mason Media.

Kagan, N. (1975b). Influencing human interaction: Eleven years with IPR. *The Canadian Counselor, 9,* 74–97.

Kagan, N., & Burke, J. B. (1976). *Influencing human interaction using interpersonal process recall (IPR): A student manual.* East Lansing, MI: Michigan State University Press.

Kagan, N., & Krathwohl, D. R. (1967). *Studies in human interaction: Interpersonal process recall stimulated by videotape*

(Research Report 20). East Lansing, MI: Educational Publication Services.

Kagan, N., Krathwohl, D., & Miller, R. (1963). Stimulated recall in therapy using videotape. *Journal of Counseling Psychology, 10,* 237–243.

Kagan, N., & Schauble, P. G. (1969). Affect simulation in interpersonal process recall. *Journal of Counseling Psychology, 16,* 309–313.

Katz, D., & Resnikoff, A. (1977). Televised self-confrontation and recalled affect: A new look at videotape recall. *Journal of Counseling Psychology, 24,* 150–152.

Kell, B. L., & Burow, J. M. (1970). *Developmental counseling and therapy.* Boston: Houghton.

Kell, B. L., & Mueller, W. J. (1966). *Impact and change: A study of counseling relationships.* New York: Appleton.

Kingdon, M. A. (1975). A cost/benefit analysis of the interpersonal process recall technique. *Journal of Counseling Psychology, 22,* 353–357.

Lazarus, A. A. (1971). *Behavior therapy and beyond.* New York: McGraw-Hill.

Maslow, A. H. (1968). *Toward a psychology of being* (2nd ed.). New York: Van Nostrand.

McHugh, P. (1968). *Defining the situation: The organization of meaning in social interaction.* Indianapolis, IN: Bobbs-Merrill.

Moore, F. J., Chernell, E., & West, J. M. (1965). Television as a therapeutic tool. *Archives of General Psychiatry, 12,* 217–220.

Mueller, W. J., & Kell, B. L. (1972). *Coping with conflict: Supervising counselors and psychotherapists.* Englewood Cliffs, NJ: Prentice-Hall.

Nielson, G. (1964). *Studies in self-confrontation.* Copenhagen, Denmark: Munksgaard.

Orlinsky, D. E., & Howard, K. I. (1966). The therapy session report. Chicago: Psychotherapy Session Project.

Patterson, C. H. (1974). *Relationship counseling and psychotherapy.* New York: Harper & Row.

Resnikoff, A., Kagan, N., & Schauble. P. G. (1970). Acceleration of psychotherapy through stimulated videotape recall. *American Journal of Psychotherapy, 24*(1), 102–111.

Rogers, C. R. (1942). The use of electrically-recorded interviews in improving psychotherapeutic techniques. *American Journal of Orthopsychiatry, 12,* 429–434.

Rogers, C. R. (1957). The necessary and sufficient conditions of therapeutic personality change. *Journal of Consulting Psychology, 21,* 95–103.

Sagan, C. (1977). *The dragons of Eden: Speculations on the evolution of human intelligence.* New York: Random House.

Schauble, P. G. (1970). *The acceleration of client progress in counseling and psychotherapy through interpersonal process recall (IPR).* Unpublished doctoral dissertation, Michigan State University.

Sullivan, H. S. (1953). *Interpersonal theory of psychiatry.* New York: Norton.

Tomory, R. E. (1979). *The acceleration and continuation of client growth in counseling and psychotherapy: A comparison of interpersonal process recall (IPR) with traditional counseling methods.* Unpublished doctoral dissertation, Michigan State University.

Tucker, H., Lewis, R. B., Martin, G. L., & Over, C. H. (1957). Television therapy: Effectiveness of closed circuit TV for therapy and treatment of the mentally ill. *Archives of Neurology and Psychiatry, 77,* 57–69.

VanNoord, R. (1973). *Stimulated recall with videotape and simulation in counseling and psychotherapy: A comparison of effects of two methodologies with undergraduate student clients.* Unpublished doctoral dissertation, Michigan State University.

Walz, G. R., & Johnston, J. A. (1963). Counselors look at themselves on videotape. *Journal of Counseling Psychology, 10*(3), 232–236.

Woody, R. W., Kagan, N., Krathwohl, D. R., & Farquhar, W. W. (1965). Stimulated recall in psychotherapy using hypnosis and videotape. *American Journal of Clinical Hypnosis, 7,* 234–241.

Chapter 33

LIFE SKILLS TRAINING

GEORGE M. GAZDA

This system, termed Multiple Impact Training in the first edition of this Handbook, takes the position that many people cannot function as well as they could because they are likely to have correctable deficits of skills in various areas of their lives. The presence of such deficits can have mental health consequences. The process of training (or therapy if you wish) is to evaluate any person, generate a graph of some sort, and apply corrective measures. The system has impressive antecedents that fit neatly together, and the more recent additions are Loevinger's ego stages of development and Dupont's emotional stages.

Once the life skills are evaluated, group therapy, relaxation therapy, physical therapy, assertiveness training, occupational therapy, corrective therapy, problem solving, and interpersonal communications skill training are provided by capable professionals until a satisfactory level of achievement has been attained.

Life Skills Training (LST[1]) formerly Multiple Impact Training (MIT), is therapy but not in the traditional sense, because it is based on an educational rather than a medical model. Persons who seek therapy rarely suffer from a single life-skill deficit; however, some life-skill deficits are more important than others for effective functioning. For example, poor interpersonal relationships may be more crucial to a person's effective functioning in life than poor decision-making abilities. In working with clients in a variety of locations, I have noted that practically everyone is in need of counteracting some life skill deficit.

LST therapists/trainers recognize that a variety of skills are needed to succeed in life. These skills are defined within the psychosocial, physical-sexual, vocational, cognitive, moral, ego, and emotional areas of human development. Many so-called "mental problems" will be alleviated or resolved if people learn such skills. LST is concerned with training/teaching such skills as an essential part of any comprehensive psychotherapy/counseling process.

HISTORY

Life Skills Training was first called Multiple Impact Training in 1978; however, the concept was first pre-

sented in *Group Counseling: A Developmental Approach* (Gazda, 1971). Only two major human developmental areas were included in this publication: the *psychosocial stages* of development of Havighurst (1953, 1972) and Erik Erikson (1963) and the *vocational stages* of Super (Super, 1963; Super et al., 1957). In the second edition of this publication (Gazda, 1978), the *physical-sexual stages* of Gesell (Gesell, Ilg, & Ames, 1956; Gesell et al., 1946), the *cognitive stages* of Jean Piaget (Flavell, 1963; Wadsworth, 1971), and the *moral stages* of Kohlberg (Kohlberg, 1973; Kohlberg & Turiel, 1971) were included. Since then two more areas were included: the *ego stages* of development of Loevinger (1976) and the *emotional stages* of Dupont (1978).

The basic human development areas are considered major intervention domains for individual and group counselors. Figure 33.1 illustrates how the impact is conceptualized currently.

There is a similarity between the Multimodal Behavior Therapy (MBT) of Lazarus (1975) and the Life Skills Training model. Lazarus defined Multimodal Behavior Therapy as "a systematic problem-solving process that examines and, if necessary, endeavors to remedy maladaptive responses across six separate but inter-related modalities—behavior, affect, sensation, imagery, cognition, and interpersonal relationships" (p. 150). There are however, several basic differences between Life Skills Training and Multimodal Behavior Therapy. The central difference concerns the conceptualization of the human dimensions subject to deterioration or ineffective func-

---

[1] For a more detailed presentation, see Chapters 8–12 in G. M. Gazda, W. C. Childers, & D. K. Brooks, Jr., *Foundations of Counseling and Human Services* (1987), New York: McGraw-Hill.

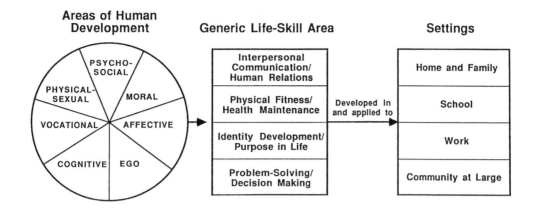

Figure 33.1   A model for the development and application of generic life skills.

tioning and consequently needing improvement. In certain areas, however, the two systems overlap. For example, Lazarus's *interpersonal relationships* are similar to the life skill of *interpersonal communications.*

Another major difference is Lazarus's emphasis on locating deficits versus the LST emphasis on locating areas of strength as well as areas of weakness. However, insofar as Multimodal Behavior Therapy emphasizes an education approach to solving problems versus the medical "treatment" model, the LST and MBT models are quite similar.

LST and MBT are alike in their assumption that individuals experiencing psychological/emotional problems suffer from multiple deficits that require multiple intervention strategies. Lazarus (1975) states his position on this issue as follows: *"The multimodal behavior therapy approach stresses the fact that patients are usually troubled by a multitude of specific problems that should be dealt with by a similar multitude of specific treatments"* (p. 165).

Insofar as Ellis's (1975) Rational-Emotive Behavior Therapy uses an educational rather than a medical or psychodynamic model, it too has components that are similar to LST. Ellis contends that REBT therapists use group processes as the method of choice, and in that regard REBT is similar to LST.

CURRENT STATUS

The life-skills training model has been under constant development since it was described in *Group Counseling: A Developmental Approach* (Gazda, 1971). The setting in which this model has been developed most completely (though is still not complete) is the psychiatric division of the Veterans Administration Medical Center in Augusta, Georgia. The writer of *Group Counseling* served as a consultant to this center from 1972 until 1994. A psy-

chiatric hospital such as a Veterans Administration hospital provides an ideal setting for LST. Any other setting in which there are numerous professionals in the "helping" professions with a great variety of interests and skills would be equally suitable.

Because so many different life-skills areas are involved, "helping" professionals involved in LST have the opportunity to choose one or more areas in which to specialize and therefore do not have to be everything to everybody. The system thus permits maximum skill development in the life skills areas of interest to the staff members. For example, certain staff members are interested in marriage and family counseling and teaching parenting skills. They can develop a model for teaching "family relationship" skills for those patients who need to develop such skills. Because chaplains are already doing spiritual counseling, they are usually interested in developing a model dealing with purpose or meaning in life (identification of personal values).

Because of the several life skills deficits generally found in their patients, psychiatric staff must develop many areas of expertise. However, because of the interdisciplinary nature of the staff, there is usually much expertise available for utilization in the typical clinic or mental health center. With proper encouragement and management, a built-in team approach to the delivery of psychiatric care is possible through LST. One of the positive side effects is the staff's increased feeling of self-worth, their greater cooperation, and their higher morale as a result of working together in a common project, each utilizing his or her best skills.

THEORY

Life Skills Training had its origin in a developmental conceptualization of human growth and development

(Gazda, 1971, 1978). The assumptions that underlie LST are essentially the same as those of developmental psychology/education (Gazda, 1977). Several primary assumptions are at the heart of LST:

1. There are at least seven well-defined areas of human development: psychosocial, physical-sexual, vocational, cognitive, ego, moral, and affective (see Figure 33.1).

2. From the seven well-defined areas of human development, coping behaviors (life skills) can be determined that are appropriate to age or stage.

3. There are identifiable stages in each of the seven areas of human development through which individuals must progress if they are to achieve mastery of later, more advanced stages.

4. Accomplishment of developmental tasks is dependent upon mastery of life skills, or coping behaviors appropriate to stage and task.

5. In general there are certain age ranges when certain coping skills (life skills) are optimally learned.

6. Individuals achieve optimal functioning when they attain operational mastery of fundamental life skills.

7. Neuroses and functional psychoses frequently result from failure to develop one's life skills.

8. Instruction or training in life skills, introduced when a person is developmentally ready to learn given concepts and skills, serves the role of preventive mental health.

9. Instruction or training in life skills, introduced when a person is suffering from emotional or mental disturbance of a functional nature, serves the role of remediation in mental health.

10. The greater the degree of functional disturbance, the greater the likelihood that the individual will be suffering from multiple life skills deficits.

The theory underpinning LST is based primarily on education or reeducation rather than medical treatment. Teaching and training in life skills is based on the assumption that they can be taught in much the same fashion as the 3 R's are taught in schools. Different life skill areas will require different educational models for most effective and efficient learning. For example, developing physical fitness and health maintenance skills includes more direct physical action or practice than discovering one's purpose or values in life.

The assumption is made that one's self-concept, emotional status, and behavior are modified through learning and perfecting basic life skills. The more mastery one has over his or her life skills, the more capable he or she will be in meeting and solving life's daily problems. The more often one is able to meet and solve daily problems, the better will be his or her self-concept, emotional state, and behavior. Persons who gain mastery in basic life skill areas will be able to use these skills in creative ways to solve complex problems. They will gain security and happiness because they have achieved at least some control over their environment through their increased capacity to cope.

METHODOLOGY

Life Skills Training is based on the assumption that most clients or patients seeking help for psychological or emotional problems have deficits in multiple life skills areas. Determining these deficit life skill areas can be done through individual, group, or combinations of individual and group approaches.

The model of LST methodology to be outlined herein was developed at a Veterans Administration hospital. The process begins with a referral by the client's primary therapist to an "interdisciplinary screening group." This group may be led by any staff member or members from any of several departments of the hospital. At any one time it may be led by a psychologist and a nurse, or a nurse and a social worker, or a chaplain and a nurse, and so forth. Although usually there are at least two professionals leading these groups, this is not a requirement.

These interdisciplinary screening groups function in a manner similar to the traditional open-ended interview therapy groups. They meet two or three times a week and the leaders attempt to diagnose the patient's life skill deficits within three sessions. In addition to these interviews, the staff, of course, uses other available opportunities and data such as individual patient interview, examination of the patient's social and medical history, ward observation by staff, interviews with the patient's family, and the like.

Life skill training groups are then made available for the areas in which the majority of patients have skill deficits. In the Augusta Veterans Administration Medical Center, the most frequent areas of life skill deficits are interpersonal communications, physical fitness, meaning or purpose in life, decision making and problem solving, use of community resources, vocational choice, and parenting and family/marital relationships. A patient is encouraged to choose as may of these life skills groups as he or she wishes to attend, but when the patient has more deficits than he or she has time for group attendance, the patient ranks the groups according to preference and then attends the two or three of highest priority. When it appears that a patient will be in the hospital for several months, he or she is encouraged to attend certain groups as prerequisite to others to follow. For example, the "purpose-in-life" group is a good prerequisite for the vocational choice group because once the patient achieves some purpose in life, he or she is more highly motivated to explore a vocation.

An open-ended traditional therapy group is always available for those patients who need the opportunity to continue exploration of self along with life skill training groups. This group also helps patients integrate the skills from their training groups as well as isolate new areas of strengths and deficits. In this particular setting the patient's primary therapist is responsible for monitoring the patient's progress and for recommending the patient's release. Ward-team staffing of patients, along with a written progress chart, provide the interdisciplinary treatment group with opportunities to exchange information about the patient's progress and to make recommendations regarding life skill group placements.

It should be obvious by now that LST is basically a multigroup treatment/training model. Since LST is most effectively and efficiently done in a small group of eight to ten members, group instructional methods are most commonly employed. However, all LST groups are designed to include a combination of didactic and experiential (action) methods. All groups heavily emphasize the practice of the life skills in the small group setting.

APPLICATIONS

Life Skills Training was developed in a Veterans Administration psychiatric hospital and even difficult psychiatric patients have been found to be suitable clientele. Obviously, patients who are acutely psychotic and unable to attend meetings and to communicate would be excluded from LST. These might include the hebrephrenic, paranoid, and catatonic schizophrenic types and manic-depressives in the manic stage. Any patient who could not control him- or herself or was otherwise disruptive would be excluded from the group training. However, some of these patients could still be assisted by LST through individual training or instruction.

Because LST is essentially an all-inclusive treatment model, virtually all individuals suffering from any of the life skills deficits would be suitable clientele. Let us, for example, consider the application of LST to persons suffering from substance abuse, specifically alcoholism. It is likely that the person classified as an alcoholic is lacking in some of the basic life skills. It is apparent that virtually all alcoholics have deficits in the area of physical fitness and need a physical fitness/health maintenance program. Many alcoholics are without a purpose in life and can benefit from a group that focuses on this issue. Still another area of deficit for the alcoholic is interpersonal communications. Most substance abusers can benefit from direct training in interpersonal communication, including assertiveness training. Some very anxious alcoholics can benefit from relaxation therapy. Others with marital problems need family relationship training (marital therapy).

Life Skills Training is especially suitable in institutional settings in which there are a variety of trained professionals with differing interests and life skill training expertise. For example, a university counseling or mental health center would usually have psychologists, psychiatrists, social workers, and nurses on staff. Some of the personnel might be counseling psychologists who could help students with life skill deficits in career choice or vocational development. Some of the staff might be experts in interpersonal communication training. Still others will need to be able to teach purpose-in-life groups. There will be students with health maintenance deficits who will need instruction in nutrition, diet, and so forth. In other words, college and university students represent a broad spectrum of the population with life skill deficits in all areas and in varying degrees.

Community mental health clinics are similar to college and university mental health centers, but generally their clientele are more seriously lacking in life skills. The professional staffs of community mental health clinics are generally interdisciplinary in training and therefore have the potential to develop expertise in all the life skills areas. Insofar as the staff generally functions from a medical model, reorientation in philosophy may be necessary. That is, the concept of "mental illness" will need to be changed to "life skills deficits," for which teaching and training are the preferred treatments.

LST, with its emphasis on "training" rather than "therapy," is also an ideal model for use in elementary and secondary schools because it is an educational preventive model. Prevention of psychological and emotional problems can best be achieved through a comprehensive life skills curriculum in the schools. Operating from the LST model, counselors, school psychologists, school social workers, school nurses, special education personnel, and so forth would all be involved in teaching life skills. All students would be taught effective life skills models for interpersonal communication, decision making and problem solving, physical fitness/health maintenance, emotional awareness, conflict resolution, group skills, family relationship skills, self-evaluation skills, principles of applied learning, organizational/institutional functioning, and so on. The life skills hold a striking resemblance to the seven cardinal principles of secondary education: health, command of fundamental process, worthy home membership, a vocation, good citizenship, worthy use of leisure time, and ethical character. Shane (1977) contends that the seven cardinal principles "have retained their usefulness and their importance even after the passage of nearly 60 years." The National Assessment of Education Progress (1975), a division of the Commission on Education of the States,

Table 33.1 Mr. Banks's Treatment Program

	Group Therapy	Relaxation Therapy	Physical Fitness/Health Maintenance	Assertiveness Training	Occupational Therapy	Corrective Therapy	Problem Solving	Interpersonal Communications Skill Training
Psychosocial	X			X				X
Vocational					X			
Physical-sexual		X	X			X		
Moral								
Cognitive							X	
Ego								X
Affective		X						

cited seven areas that were recommended by a planning committee as *basic skills*. The seven skills areas were consumer, health maintenance, interpersonal, citizenship, family relationship, community resource utilization, and career and occupational development.

Because LST is an educational model and because it is most effectively and efficiently applied in the small group setting, it is especially appropriate for use in institutional settings in which there exist a variety of trained professionals with a variety of interests and expertise. It would be least suitable for private practitioners unless they were a part of a larger practice with referral possibilities to other professionals who specialize in three or four areas of life skills training. For those private practitioners who would be willing to work as part of a large team, LST can be a valuable therapeutic modality.

CASE EXAMPLE[2]

This is the first psychiatric admission (5/11/89) for a 51-year-old white male diagnosed as a passive-aggressive personality with depression. Mr. Banks has hypertension and arthritis, and is obese. On admission this patient was red-faced, unkempt, weighed 310 pounds, and had a blood pressure (B/P) of 168/110. He was very shy, unable to make eye contact, and spoke in a low monotone. Mr. Banks stated that he lost his temper easily, had been explosive at times, had crying spells, felt tired all the time, and had been socially withdrawing for the past six months. The patient also related that his wife failed to have sexual relations with him because he was fat, sloppy, and fearful that she would get pregnant. Although Mr. Banks worked, he had no social outlets.

Mr. Banks's treatment plan included a mild anti-

depressant, 1,200 calorie diet, antihypertensive drug, and group therapy. He had Interpersonal Communications Skill Training, Assertiveness Training, Reality-Oriented Problem Solving, Relaxation Therapy, Diet Therapy (Physical Fitness/Health Maintenance), Occupational Therapy, and Corrective Therapy (see Table 33.1).

On discharge on July 31, 1989, Mr. Banks weighed 291 pounds, had a lowered B/P of 128/80, had a vasectomy, had initiated marital counseling, and was active and neat in appearance. During his hospitalization the patient was able to learn how to initiate conversation with others and was able to assert himself as chairman of ward government. He signed a nursing referral to be followed up in his community, and he plans to attend the local mental hygiene clinic. Mr. Banks will return to his carpenter's job (see Table 33.2 for Mr. Banks's progress report).

SUMMARY

Several features make Life Skills Training a unique model. First, LST is a potent form of treatment-training because the recipient is learning simultaneously new skills in several areas of functioning. Second, LST is an educational model that teaches life skills and therefore should endure or result in fewer relapses for the recipient. Third, because LST is an educational model, there is much less stigma attached to it. Fourth, participants are *actively* involved in learning or perfecting life skills and therefore are likely to feel more ownership of the process. Fifth, LST is appropriate both in prevention and remediation of mental health problems. The basic assumption of LST is that the so-called functional neuroses and psychoses are the result of deficits in life skills, that life skills can be learned, and that the most effective and efficient way for life skills to be learned is to teach them directly.

The paradox of LST is that its real strength lies in its

---

[2] The case used here is fictitious to protect identity of the patient. Mildred Powell, R.N., of the Augusta Veterans Medical Center, developed this case.

Table 33.2   Patient Progress Report[a]

Client: Ed Banks				Counselor: John Herman	
Dates:	5/11[b]	5/25	6/9	7/23	7/31
Area of Development					
Psychosocial	D	D	C	B	B
Vocational	C	C	B	A	A
Physical-sexual	C	C	B	A	A
Cognitive	C	C	B	B	B
Moral	B	B	B	B	B
Ego	D	D	C	B	B
Affective	D	C	B	B	B

[a]Typical rating scale, based on Life Skills Training. Numbers refer to dates of evaluation: 5/11 represents initial evaluation of the client; 5/25 represents first evaluation, and so on. (Time periods may vary, but we recommend twice-a-month evaluations).

[b]D—gross deficit; C—deficit; B—average: A—good.

conceptualization as an educational model. Because the majority of "helping professionals" in the mental health domain still accept the medical treatment model, LST can be expected to meet with much resistance.

REFERENCES

Dupont, H. (1978). Meeting the emotional-social needs of students in a mainstreamed environment. *Counseling and Human Development, 10,* 1–12.

Ellis, A. (1975). Rational-emotive group therapy. In G. M. Gazda (Ed.), *Basic approaches to group psychotherapy and group counseling.* Springfield, IL: Charles C. Thomas.

Erikson, E. H. (1963). *Childhood and society* (2nd ed.). New York: Norton.

Flavell, J. H. (1963). *The development psychology of Jean Piaget.* Princeton, NJ: Van Nostrand.

Gazda, G. M. (1971). *Group counseling: A developmental approach.* Boston: Allyn & Bacon.

Gazda, G. M. (1977). Developmental education: A conceptual framework for a comprehensive counselling and guidance program. *Canadian Counsellor, 12,* 36–40.

Gazda, G. M. (1978). *Group counseling: A developmental approach* (2nd ed.). Boston: Allyn & Bacon.

Gesell, A., Ilg, F. L., & Ames, L. B. (1956). *Youth: The years from ten to sixteen.* New York: Harper.

Gesell, A., Ilg, F. L., Ames, L. B., & Bulliss, G. E. (1946). *The child from five to ten.* New York: Harper.

Havighurst, R. J. (1953). *Developmental tasks and education* (2nd ed.). New York: McKay.

Havighurst, R. J. (1972). *Developmental tasks and education* (3rd ed.). New York: David McKay.

Kohlberg, L. (1973). Continuities and discontinuities in childhood and adult moral development revisited. In P. B. Baltes and K. W. Schaie (Eds.), *Lifespan developmental psychology: Personality and socialization.* New York: Academic Press.

Kohlberg, L., & Turiel, P. (1971). Moral development and moral education. In G. Lesser (Ed.), *Psychology and educational practice.* Chicago: Scott Foresman.

Lazarus, A. A. (1975). Multimodal behavior therapy in groups. In G. M. Gazda (Ed.), *Basic approaches to group psychotherapy and group counseling.* Springfield, IL: Charles C. Thomas.

Loevinger, J. (1976). *Ego development.* San Francisco: Jossey-Bass.

National Assessment of Educational Progress. (1975, August). *Draft of basic skills objectives.* Denver, CO: National Assessment of Education Progress (division of the Commission on the Education of the States).

Shane, H. G. (1977). *Curriculum change toward the 21st century.* Washington, DC: National Education Association.

Super, D. E., (1963). Vocational development in adolescence and early adulthood: Tasks and behaviors. In D. E. Super (Ed.), *Career development: Self-concept theory.* New York: College Entrance Examination Board.

Super, D. E., Crites, J., Hummel, R., Moser, H., Overstreet, C. B., and Warnath, C. (1957). *Vocational development: A framework for research.* Monograph No. 1, New York: Teachers College Press.

Wadsword, B. J. (1971). *Piaget's theory of cognitive development.* New York: McKay.

Chapter 34

MAINSTREAMING

WERNER M. MENDEL and SOPHIE GOREN

I am grateful to my friend Dr. Arnold D. Schwartz for directing me to Werner Mendel and to Mainstreaming, the subject of this chapter. We all are well aware of the social movement away from the huge state institutions for the mentally ill, who are now being returned to society.

But such people need special assistance; they often face negative attitudes from the community; they often just do not have the practical skills for getting along in the community. And they do not know how to deal with these negative attitudes or with the necessary obligations of social living. How can such people be helped to make adjustment to society and to themselves? How can we counteract the harm that has been done to them by their families and the institutions they have been in?

The solution offered here is sensible, bold, imaginative, and practical, and represents a new social way of looking at and dealing with a new class of humans, those formerly and presently incapacitated people who are put back into society. Mainstreaming is a most important humanistic project, and one that I suspect will gain momentum in the years to come.

Mainstreaming is a unique concept and quite different in its character and approach from almost all other systems in this book. It has close ties with Direct Psychoanalysis and Life Skills Training, which should be read in conjunction with this chapter.

Mainstreaming is the technique of using the normal support resources available to all citizens, outside of the mental health network, as a means of helping the chronically and severely mentally ill patient to live and function in the community. Ordinary people in a normal environment and everyday life activity in the real world are the matrix for this treatment program. Mainstreaming provides special services to help the patient to learn to use usual community resources as a means of support. Embedded in the community, such chronic patients show relief of symptoms and a minimizing of discomfort, distress, and dysfunction.

HISTORY

At the close of the 1970s, the chronically ill psychiatric patient remains a major treatment problem. Over the past 30 years there have been changes in treatment approaches for such patients (Mendel, 1968). These changes have moved the patient out of the hospital and provided medication for suppression of target symptoms. Various attempts at community support have been developed, but all rely heavily on supporting services provided by a mental health network (Erickson, 1975). These support services are delivered as partial hospitalization, day treatment, outpatient clinics, rehabilitation workshops, and community mental health centers. All of these services require special funding, highly skilled and expensive mental health personnel, massive financial support by various branches of government, and a huge overhead of coordinating and regulating agencies representing the federal, state, county, and local government. This community mental health approach, if properly staffed, funded, and carried out, seems to be beyond the financial means of society and has recently been limited by the spreading taxpayer revolt. To discharge chronically ill resourceless patients into the community has not worked. The response of the community generally has been characterized by hostility and rejection, and the patient has suffered and lived in circumstances that are unacceptable both to him and to society. Returning the patient to the hospital is no longer an acceptable alternative for all the reasons that the state hospitals have been dismantled.

Out of this perspective the technique of Mainstreaming was developed. Over the past 25 years the writers have worked with the chronically impaired, severely disorganized, psychiatrically ill patients (Mendel, 1975). In the attempts to provide a supporting network through mental health services, it has been noticed that patients often used informal support in the community that had not been taken into account by the therapists. A neighbor, a church group, a grocery clerk, a bus driver, a telephone operator, a school crossing guard, even an automatic telephone service giving a prayer for a day or the time of day provided important means of support.

These ordinary community services are often not used by patients because the severely impaired psychiatric person ordinarily lacks the skills to use them. With some special assistance and training, the patients can learn to get support from such common resources in the community, which are also used by ordinary citizens. The development of such skills is the purpose of the mainstreaming technique.

CURRENT STATUS

The Mainstreaming program started in 1968, specifically for the treatment of patients with schizophrenia. (Schizophrenia is used as the model illness for the chronic, severely ill psychiatric patient [Mendel & Allen, 1977]). However, the technique and program is useful for all people who have chronically impairing psychiatric difficulties that cannot be resolved by definitive treatment. Many severely and chronically ill patients have thus far participated. Even though all these patients spent most of their time in hospitals prior to Mainstreaming, during the program the longest hospital stay was for 10 days and hospitalization was prescribed in only 4 out of 50 cases at any time. Hospitalization was rarely indicated because the major function of the hospital could be better carried out and less expensively provided, and fewer side effects were created, when resources in the community were mobilized for the patient. The mainstreaming program provides the catalytic agent essential for the chronic patient to be able to use ordinary community resources. The decreased need for hospitalization is of benefit to patients; it avoids the complications of excessive dependency gratification, prevents reifying the patient's failure in life, and averts further removal from contact with the real world.

Over the past twenty years the Mainstreaming technique has been refined and formalized. However, the lack of funding for mainstreaming services is a serious problem. Since such services do not fall into the usual model of psychotherapy—counseling, psychiatric treatment, or hospitalization—insurance companies, health plans, and government agencies do not provide payment through customary reimbursement channels. This shortsighted policy has continued, even though Mainstreaming can be demonstrated to be more cost effective in reaching specific treatment goals than either prolonged hospitalization or the usual revolving-door arrangement between the hospital and community mental health systems. Mainstreaming moves the patient toward partial independence and away from professional care; in effect the program refers the patient to "life." Goal-attainment scaling and critical-incident cost accounting can be used to demonstrate that Mainstreaming is less expensive than other approaches to supportive care. However, all funds for Mainstreaming come either from the patient and his family (private resources) or from specially funded programs supported by various government agencies as demonstration projects.

THEORY

The theory of Mainstreaming rests on three observations:

First, it is recognized that the normal population uses both formal and informal resources in the community as a means of support. These resources are generally free and are in no way identified with the mental health network. Were they to have the skills to use them, these same resources are available to the chronically mentally ill members of society. Most chronically ill psychiatric patients do not have these skills; they require training and assistance to develop the necessary skills to use these resources.

The use of support resources in the community that are not related to the mental health system has many advantages. Because these resources do not involve professional services, they are much less expensive. Because they do not group patients together, each patient can be surrounded by a normal group of people. This helps the patient avoid some of the stigma of being mentally ill that follow him throughout life as long as he is associated with the mental health establishment.

These support resources include groups with cultural, political, religious, community action, and educational interests. A wide spectrum of these groups is available, providing a great possibility of connection for the patient. The patient's ability to use that support resource and to function within the group does not depend on his identifying himself as mentally ill or as a patient, but rather depends on his social and interpersonal skills, skills he can learn from the team members who function as social preceptors in the mainstreaming program.

Second, it has been noted that severely chronically ill psychiatric patients change their behavior, thinking, and feeling by modeling themselves after other people in their immediate environment who are available as concrete examples of how to be in the world (Bellack, 1976). If these patients spend their time in the mental health network, be it in the hospital or in the community mental health system, they are in contact with other patients and therefore identify with "sick" models.

In providing supportive care within the mental health network to chronically ill schizophrenic patients, we have been concerned with the problems created by grouping severely ill patients with each other. Such grouping insures that each patient has major interpersonal contacts with other severely ill and disturbed psychiatric patients in a "sick"-oriented environment. Even when the patient gets a great deal of attention—by seeing a therapist daily or by participating in group or milieu programs—this represents only a small portion of his 168-hour week. The major part of the week is spent with other psychiatric patients. Mental hospitals and community mental health systems, therefore, tend to teach patients how to be sick rather than how to be well.

By participating in Mainstreaming, psychotic patients improve clinically, not only as a result of medication and psychotherapy, but also because they learn how to be normal and to become "as if" persons. They do this by learning from others how to feel, think, and behave. They model themselves after the people around them. One crucial function of treatment is providing the severely ill patient a "healthy" role model. We must show how normal people respond to anxiety in ways other than going crazy. We must demonstrate behaviorally that normal people respond to anger in socially acceptable ways. We can teach our patients how to respond to fear and loneliness in ways other than cutting wrists or overdosing on medication (Serban, 1975).

Mainstreaming pays a great deal of attention to the role models provided during the entire 168 hours per week that the patient spends in the world. The severely ill psychiatric patient has the usual life problems of normal people. The difference is that he or she has a severely impaired ability to respond to life's usual crises. Social remission is achieved when the patient has learned to manage anxiety, to develop interpersonal skills, and to live as an "as if" person. The major task of the mainstreaming program is to teach more adaptive ways to deal with life's problems by providing health role models.

Third, it has been recognized that the medical model of intervention, which in its ideal form includes diagnosis, treatment, cure, and the abolition of the defect, is not applicable in the care of the chronic psychiatrically ill person. The rehabilitation model, which accepts a stable defect caused by illness but then focuses on minimizing the disability caused by the defect, seems more appropriate for the chronic psychiatric patient. This model of intervention develops techniques that allow for limited goals while maximizing the patient's function and satisfaction in life.

There is great advantage in the rehabilitation model for this patient population. They, for the most part, have defects that we cannot correct with our present knowledge of biological, psychological, and social processes and interventions. Working with limited goals is difficult for the patient, the community, and the treatment staff. The rehabilitation model provides the potential for success both to the patient and to the treatment staff. Within this model a much wider spectrum of goals is available, because for each individual patient there are infinite gradations of improved function in a multitude of areas. The experience of success is absolutely essential. These patients do not tolerate failure well because most of them have failed much of their lives.

In the medical model treatment staff burns out quickly in dealing with chronic patients. They are constantly faced with their impotence, helplessness, and uselessness in treating these patients. However, in the rehabilitation model the staff can adopt more realistic goals for specific patients. They can measure and experience improvement in function and satisfaction in the patient's life.

METHODOLOGY

When a patient is first referred to the Mainstreaming program, the diagnosis is confirmed. Psychiatric evaluation includes a detailed history, psychometrics, and a present state examination. After the diagnosis of schizophrenia is confirmed, the chronicity of the illness demonstrated, and the stability of the defect clearly established, the treatment history is then reviewed in detail. Usually the people referred to the program have been ill at least 10 years, have been treated with a wide variety of approaches including the use of medication, electroconvulsive treatments, extensive hospitalization, and extensive individual and group psychotherapeutic interventions. Usually the patients have also had major dietary treatment and special fad approaches. As a group they would be described as poor prognosis and process schizophrenic patients.

Once the patient is accepted for treatment in the Mainstreaming program, he or she must consent to live in the community and to participate with a mainstreaming team. Acquiring this consent usually poses no difficulty, because the program is certainly more desirable than the usual hospital situation and is the least restrictive environment offered to the patient.

The patient is assigned to a team consisting of a team leader, who is usually a graduate certified rehabilitation counselor or a social worker, and three or four team members called rehabilitation technicians who serve as social preceptors. These team members are generally graduate students at various local colleges engaged in studies of the helping professions. Team members are chosen to represent the dominant culture to which the patient must adjust. The ideal member would be one who resembles the patient in family background, level of vocational expectations, and social class values. He or she should have achieved some degree of self-sufficiency and have demonstrated the ability to support him- or herself emotionally, intellectually, and economically. The team member should be similar to the person the patient was becoming when he became ill. It is not possible to have as team members only persons who exhibit all of these ideal characteristics. However, three or four team members together can represent these qualities.

Two general approaches to helping people are taught in the graduate programs from which interested and talented students are chosen. The training offered in graduate programs in psychology and social work emphasizes self-awareness and self-understanding so that the person being helped can understand his motives for his behavior and can choose to change his behavior to better meet his needs. Team members trained in this manner seem to be more effective for neurotic patients than for the chronic mentally ill. The second approach—taught in the disciplines of nursing; rehabilitation; and occupational, recreational, and activity therapy—emphasizes the evaluation and modification of maladaptive behavior to conform better with current social standards. The student who has had training in these programs is well able to evaluate behavior and finds it easy to work with chronic psychiatric patients. The patients respond better to an activity-oriented here-and-now approach. Therefore, most team members are drawn from these programs.

Graduate students are generally excellent team members because the program offers them valuable professional experience; however, other individuals without such training have also become successful team members as long as they meet the basic requirement of wanting to help people and are willing to do so in direct, practical ways.

The size of the team depends on how many services the patient needs. If the patient is just leaving the hospital and is very frightened by the thought of living alone in the community, he may require a great deal of service for the first few days while becoming embedded in the community resources. However, soon the typical patient will require only a few hours' help every day in finding a job and attaching himself to various community resources.

Members of both sexes are included in each team, except in occasional cases where the patient might feel threatened by the opposite sex. The inclusion of both sexes on the team gives the patient the opportunity to identify with members of his own sex and to practice social skills with both.

The primary function of the mainstreaming team is to provide immediate and helpful feedback and emotional support to the patient and to act as role models and so-

cial preceptors. Team members teach the patient by modeling and direct instruction on how to behave in the community and how to attach to the social support systems available. The chronic mentally ill patient has great difficulty with interpersonal relationships and therefore frequently is quite socially isolated. He has often spent years in hospitals, board and care homes, and day-care programs. His social skills are clumsy and his social behavior tends to be regressed and idiosyncratic. The team provides a customized social circle where undesirable behaviors can be selectively ignored or pointed out as maladaptive and more mature behavior can be explained, modeled, and reinforced. The team gives realistic, immediate feedback whenever possible so that the patient can gain an understanding of society's reaction to him. Team members react to the patient's attitudes, values, and behavior much as the ordinary person in the community would. Bizarre, idiosyncratic behavior is experienced by the team members as sharply different from the norm and is pointed out by them to the patient as unacceptable or uncomfortable to others. This feedback, however, must always be given to the patient with sensitivity and kindness so that he or she can modify maladaptive behavior to more acceptable conduct without further impairment of the already severely damaged self-esteem. Some patients who are unaware of the effect of their behavior on others often experience rejection without ever knowing why. When a team member can point out such behavior as seeming rudeness and the effect it causes in the other person, such as withdrawal or the wish to retaliate, then the patient can learn to modify his or her behavior. From the beginning in the mainstreaming program team members offer support, encouragement, and positive reinforcement to the patient. After a time, the patient begins to trust that he will be supported. He may choose his team members as a special circle of confidants.

The team provides role models for the development of the patient's coping skills and problem-solving abilities. As the patient engages in the various activities, a team member demonstrates appropriateness in manner, proper interchange with persons in the community, and useful coping devices to manage the common problems in living. Team members of the same sex provide an opportunity for the patient to strengthen his sexual identity by adopting an appropriate role.

All of the patients in the program live by themselves, in an apartment in the community. At the beginning of the program the patient may still be living with his or her family, but one goal is to have the patient move toward independent living as quickly as possible. For many patients this requires a great deal of training in the ordinary, everyday skills of caring for self, meal planning and preparation, grooming, managing money, and shopping.

Countertransference problems for team members are many, because providing support to the chronic patient is a difficult task (Mendel, 1979). The mainstreaming program takes several years to complete. Because progress is slow, team members have a tendency to either burn out or to become overinvolved with the patients. These patients exhibit behavior that has developed over many years of illness, has been learned from other psychiatric patients in hospitals, or is the result of their family's accommodation to idiosyncratic and bizarre behavior patterns. Maladaptive behavior that has not been modified by the usual social contacts is overlearned, and it requires patience, consistency, and firmness on the part of team members to change it. The work can be stressful, exhausting, discouraging, frustrating, and irritating. Frightened, severely impaired patients require dependable, sustained supporting relationships. This is demanding and difficult for the team members. There is a tendency to slide from the therapeutic rehabilitative position to one of parentlike scolding, correcting, and nagging, which is antitherapeutic. The team member must not react to frustrations and irritations in a spontaneous and thoughtless way, but must always run the response through a therapeutic filter, asking whether his or her response or confrontation is helpful in accomplishing the therapeutic goal with this patient at this time. Yet team members must be allowed the opportunity to share their negative feelings in some way to guard their own well-being and effectiveness as helpers. All of this is accomplished by providing ongoing training and support to the team members. The team leader's role is to provide such support and to organize the in-service training. The primary therapist in charge of the case and who meets with the patient, team, and team leader usually once every two weeks must deal with these countertransference problems by giving support, instruction, and by setting appropriate goals. At these biweekly meetings both short- and long-term goals are set and goal attainment is evaluated. In setting goals the therapist must keep in mind the need of the patient for success, as well as the needs of the team members for structure, support, and encouragement. Goals must be set in such a way that they are not beyond the emotional means of the patient, yet they must not be so low that they tend to hold the patient back. One of the great difficulties for the therapist is determining the fine line between expecting too much or too little. The therapist should not forget that patients change constantly and that any particular patient is not the same as he was two weeks previously. The problem of both underestimating and overestimating a patient's abilities is a constant issue even for the experienced therapist.

The ultimate goal for each patient is maximizing pleasure and function within his limitations and minimizing pain and dysfunction. The expected outcomes include independent living, involvement in the social network, and competitive employment in an appropriate and satisfying job. The task of goal planning is to evaluate the patient in relation to these long-term goals and to set intermediate (two-week) goals in the time frame in which they can be accomplished.

An early task is that of acquainting the team members with the patient and of engaging the patient in the activity of finding an apartment. This is usually accomplished in the first 15 days. Subsequently, the team will help the patient to get acquainted with necessary services, such as grocery stores, banks, and libraries, in his or her immediate community. During the early phase of the program, the emphasis is on building a working relationship between the patient and the team in the context of activities that may include marketing, taking walks, riding a bicycle, touring a museum, or opening and managing a bank account. Patients are often fearful and reluctant to participate in activities that involve a change from their customary patient role. The team members' attitude should be one of encouragement and firmness, with specific instruction if necessary.

Team meetings are used to guide the direction and timing of the effort and to decide whether the patient is to be urged gently forward to new involvements and activities or to be allowed to slip back to a more familiar ground. The patient must be constantly evaluated for the ability to tolerate increased anxiety and for potential for disorganization. The team must be sensitive to the patient's tolerance of stress and must learn to recognize the patient's level of discomfort. When members of the family are available and supportive, they are invited to participate in the program as much as possible and as appropriate for the age and status of the patient. If family members do participate, they frequently require support and instruction to help them modify prior unsatisfactory relationship patterns.

As mentioned, one important function of team members is to help the patient become embedded in the community. Team members make contact with potential employers, recreational and educational resources, and special interest groups. Since prior discussion with members of these groups on behalf of the mainstreaming patient may produce an undesirable prejudicial set, this is a most delicate task. Frequently team members will need to accompany the patient as he first participates in some of these activities. In some instances their presence may appear quite appropriate, as when a patient goes with a friend to a club or class activity. However, in work and other situations, the presence of what appears to be a chaperon will be questioned, and some explanation may be necessary. Individual team members need a great deal of creativity, which comes from experience, in dealing with this particular problem.

APPLICATIONS

Mainstreaming is particularly suitable as a technique of supportive care for schizophrenic patients who live in the community. Schizophrenia is a psychobiological illness characterized by a cluster of three simultaneously occurring basic defects. These are (1) ineffective and expensive anxiety management, (2) clumsy and disastrous interpersonal misadventures, and (3) failing historicity. All psychotic symptoms can be understood either as consequences or attempted restitution secondary to these three basic defects. The illness usually begins in late adolescence, is characterized by periods of exacerbation and remission, and is chronic in nature (Mendel, 1976).

Supportive care minimizes the disruption and disorganization caused by intermittent exacerbations and minimizes the symptoms caused by the three nuclear defects. By providing ongoing support, the schizophrenic patient can minimize dysfunction and maximize the difference between his defect and disability.

Mainstreaming is also of value in treating other chronic conditions that require ongoing support. As a technique of supportive care, Mainstreaming is suitable for any patient who lives in the community and suffers from an incurable illness that requires lifelong care. Mainstreaming aims to convert the chronic psychiatric patient who relies on services provided by the mental health network to a person who lives in the community and uses the ordinary support services available to all citizens. A good outcome is to have the person function as an interesting and lovable eccentric without having to make a career of patienthood.

Mainstreaming is not a suitable system of treatment for patients who require definitive care for conditions that can be cured, resolved, or are self-limited. These patients mainstream themselves once the illness is terminated. They do not require long-term supportive care.

CASE EXAMPLE

Susan is a 31-year-old single Caucasian female, the youngest of two children. Her sister, who is two years her senior, is a successful attorney, living 4,000 miles away. Her father was a well-known attorney, hardworking and successful, who died about 10 years ago of a sudden heart attack. Her mother, now 64, has devoted the past 11 years of her life entirely to the care of Susan.

In 1965 Susan was graduated from high school at age 17. She had an excellent academic record and was accepted at three major universities. She entered a university but during the first semester took LSD and experienced severe side effects. She withdrew from school after two months.

In January 1966 Susan entered another university. During her second semester she was recommended for a scholarship by her art professor. When she did not receive the scholarship, she considered herself a failure. She compared herself unfavorably to her sister, who has always been successful. The patient's disorganization increased and her dormitory friends referred her to a psychiatrist. Susan's parents met with the psychiatrist, who told them that the patient was "hanging on by a thread." Subsequently Susan and her parents met regularly with a psychologist.

Susan dropped out of the university before completing the semester. She moved to a small apartment in a poor area of town. She took a job as a file clerk in an automobile insurance company (her father knew the president of the company and obtained the job for her). She walked off the job a short time later and has not worked since.

She became hostile, wandered away from home many hours each day, and smoked marijuana with other young people. On the evening of Susan's twentieth birthday, after a luncheon party in the family home attended by a number of her dormitory friends, she overdosed with sleeping pills. She was hospitalized in the psychiatric ward of a local hospital. Four months later her father suddenly died of a heart attack. While on a pass home from the hospital, Susan searched out some pills and took them back to the hospital and overdosed there. She remained in the hospital for one and one-half years. Then her mother decided that more had to be done for her daughter, and they visited five psychiatric hospitals in the East. She then arranged for two independent psychiatric evaluations of her daughter. Both evaluations concluded that the patient needed further hospitalization.

Susan was then transferred to a large private hospital in the East where she remained for one and one-half years without change. In fact she learned even more bizarre behaviors, identifying with other patients on the ward and learning how to be crazy. In addition, those patients who had been on pass brought in drugs, and she learned how to get high by drinking coffee loaded with nutmeg.

As the hospital stay was not improving Susan's condition, her mother was told by a treating psychiatrist to place her in a long-term state hospital. Susan and her mother returned to California, where another psychiatrist was consulted. He suggested that Susan should go to a foster home, since he felt it might be traumatic for the patient to go home. The mother agreed to this plan, believing Susan might do better with foster parents. In addition, she hired a woman who had been acting as a therapeutic companion to patients to be with Susan.

While in the foster home, Susan was given responsibility for taking her own medications; she swallowed the entire prescription, 100 tablets, and was found unconscious, her face covered with vomitus. She developed aspiration pneumonia and was placed in the intensive care unit of a local hospital. On her medical recovery Susan moved back to her mother's home.

The mother, who had taken workshops at the Los Angeles Institute of Reality Therapy, engaged one of the staff psychiatrists to treat her daughter. Another year went by without change. During this year a psychiatric social worker was also engaged to assist with the treatment of Susan, but there was no improvement.

A new psychiatrist, the medical director of the local day hospital, was consulted. After a year of treatment, Susan entered the day hospital program. Even though the structure of the program was excellent, she was not able to function in the facility due to her fears and paranoia, which had become her way of life.

After two years in day care, Susan moved to a board-and-care home. During a year's stay there, no improvement was noted. Susan was placed in another foster home recommended by the previous social worker. A new psychiatrist was engaged. Family meetings were held including the foster parents and the patient. The foster parents and the two young children in the home were a fine family, but the foster mother was home very little and Susan was left alone most of the day. After a nine-month stay, no improvement was noted. The patient was not willing to stay any longer—she threatened suicide several times, and she was allowed to return to her mother's home again.

Another psychiatrist, the medical director of a private psychiatric hospital, was consulted. He made a house call, saw the patient, and had her involuntarily hospitalized. There she was given lithium, without therapeutic response. All medications were discontinued at once and the patient suffered severe withdrawal. She stayed in bed, cried much of the time, and begged to go home. After three months the psychiatrist said that Susan might as well go home.

Susan became very agitated and violent at home and was again hospitalized. This time she was placed in the local county hospital and treated with propranolol for a six-week period. Upon leaving the hospital, she returned to live with her mother but also began Mainstreaming. A team was developed consisting of four female team members who visited with her every day for three or four hours and took her to various activities, including cooking and sewing classes at the local high school, bicycle riding, and visits to the museums. At the biweekly team meetings the mother, therapist, team leader, and team members met. The patient attended two team meetings, but she could not stand the discomfort of being discussed and chose not to attend future meetings. Every two weeks the patient was evaluated and new goals were set.

In the course of the last seven months the patient has moved out of her parental home into an apartment to live independently. Unfortunately, soon after she moved out the first time, her apartment building was sold to be converted to an office building. At that time the patient developed considerable exacerbation of her symptoms, became frightened, developed fantasies of being raped and followed, and decided that she had to return home. After an uncomfortable two months of living at home, she moved into another apartment. This time she became embedded in the community in which she lived. She learned to cook her own meals, clean her own apartment, and live her own life. She continued with some classes and activities and now works as a volunteer clerk in a senior citizen center three days per week. Each time she goes to work, one of her team members goes with her and helps her in the work. She has changed her image from being a patient to being a working young woman. She has a work wardrobe and work ethic. It is planned that within the next few months she will move on to competitive employment in the facility in which she now volunteers. She manages her own money ($7 per day allowance), which is given to her three days at a time. She frequently spends this money foolishly and then finds that she has nothing to eat in the house for a couple of days. However, her freezer is well stocked with supplies provided by her mother. Her visits home are now limited to one afternoon and evening every two weeks, including a dinner at home with her mother. She has telephone contact with her mother once every two days and the relationship has generally improved. She no longer feels like a little girl under the control of her mother, and her mother no longer feels so responsible for the behavior of her daughter. Approximately six months ago an attempt was made to introduce a male member into the team. The patient found this impossible to tolerate. She became increasingly anxious, showed marked exacerbation of symptoms, and it was necessary to back off from that plan. At this time she is again talking about wanting a male member on the team, although she wonders how she will handle that relationship without making it either sexual or inappropriate.

At this point, approximately 11 years after the beginning of her illness and at age 31, the patient has had the best and longest period of good adjustment. She lives independently, appears generally appropriate, takes small doses of antipsychotic medication, and works at a volunteer job in the community. She spends her time with healthy companions—the team members who make up her social circle. The major emphasis of the team members is to shape her behavior and her appearance so that she has now learned to appear, behave, and think in a much more healthy way. The therapeutic thrust is to constantly say to her in our behavior and verbalization "Let us show you what to do about your fear and your loneliness and your anger other than going crazy or cutting your wrists or being inappropriate." The patient also sees the therapist once a week for both the management of her medication and for psychotherapeutic reinforcement of the supporting position and the normalizing attitude.

SUMMARY

Mainstreaming is a technique of supportive care for chronically and severely ill psychiatric patients carried out in the community. It is an alternative to both hospitalization and the usual community mental health system. This approach allows for severely impaired patients who live with schizophrenia or other chronic psychiatric illness who otherwise could not be maintained out of the hospital to function in the community. Mainstreaming allows the patient to use the usual and normal support systems available to the average citizen in the community that are outside of the mental health network. The interventions are structured within the rehabilitation model. The Mainstreaming technique makes it possible for severely ill psychiatric patients to use healthy people as role models and social preceptors. Even at the beginning of treatment Mainstreaming is less expensive than the usual mental health services in the community. The final goal for each patient is to obtain as much support as necessary from the usual community resources that are free of charge. Mainstreaming takes individuals who are unable to live in the community because they are sick and disorganized, and helps them to develop techniques to enter the "normal" world. Patients who have been mainstreamed can often live independently, support themselves, and take a more useful position in society than patienthood would offer.

REFERENCES

Bellack, A. S. (1976). Generalization effects of social skills training in chronic schizophrenics: An experimental analysis. *Behavior Research & Therapy, 14,* 391–398.

Erickson, R. C. (1975). Outcome studies in mental hospitals: A review. *Psychological Bulletin, 82,* 519–540.

Mendel, W. M. (1968). On the abolition of the psychiatric hospital. In L. M. Roberts, N. S. Greenfield, & M. H. Miller (Eds.), *Comprehensive mental health.* Madison, WI: University of Wisconsin Press.

Mendel, W. M. (1975). *Supportive care: Theory and technique.* Los Angeles, CA.: Mara Books.

Mendel, W. M. (1976). *Schizophrenia: The experience and its treatment.* San Francisco, CA: Jossey-Bass.

Mendel, W. M. (1979). Staff burn-out: Diagnosis, treatment, and prevention. *New Directions for Mental Health Services, 2,* 75–83.

Mendel, W. M., & Allen, R. E. (1977). Treating the chronic patient. In J. H. Masserman (Ed.), *Current psychiatric therapies,* vol. 17. New York: Grune & Stratton.

Mendel, W. M., & Allen, C. (1978). Rehabilitation model in psychiatry. In *Conference Proceedings, Adult psychiatric day treatment: 2d multi-disciplinary national forum.* Minneapolis, MN: University of Minnesota Press.

Serban, G. (1975). Stress in schizophrenics and normals. *British Journal of Psychiatry, 126,* 397–407.

Chapter 35

MEDITATION

ROGER N. WALSH

It would be a kind of cosmic joke if the key to understanding the self and curing maladjustment were to be under our noses, and to have been there for some 3,000 years. This is the implication of the next chapter by Roger Walsh.

Meditation, an import from Asia, has become quite fashionable and popular in a variety of guises; and in this book, a number of the systems, including Autogenic Training, some of the Body Therapies, Comprehensive Relaxation, and Covert Conditioning, just to name a few, contain elements compatible with classical meditation. Even though people brought up in Western philosophical traditions, where an outward, interactional approach rather than an inward, autochthonous approach is emphasized, seem strongly resistant to Meditation, there seems to be not only growing interest in Meditation, but also some laboratory evidence that the process can produce measurable physiological changes.

I found this chapter quite exciting. In discussing his own experience Dr. Walsh makes the challenge of Meditation real, and in this chapter the reader will be given an opportunity to experience Meditation for himself or herself. Would it not be amazing if eventually Meditation becomes the ideal therapeutic system: cheap, simple, and effective? We looked so long and so hard, and people have been doing it for three millennia. It could be. . . .

It is the mind that maketh good or ill
That maketh wretch or happy, rich or poor.
　　　　　　　　　　　—*Edmund Spenser*

The term "Meditation" refers to a family of practices that train attention in order to heighten awareness and bring mental processes under voluntary control. Their ultimate aim is the development of the deepest insight into the nature of mental processes, consciousness, identity, and reality, and the development of optimal states of psychological well-being and consciousness.

HISTORY

Specific meditation practices have evolved across the centuries, reflecting the insights, proclivities, and cultures of its practitioners. For example, the basic practices taught by the Buddha some 2,500 years ago have been largely maintained in their original forms in Southeast Asia, elaborated into a complex family of practices emphasizing visual imagery in Tibet, and merged with Taoism and other disciplines to form Zen in Japan.

Recent decades have seen an explosion of interest in

Meditation in the West. Until then there was only scattered episodic interest punctuating general skepticism and disbelief. Several factors seem to have facilitated this shift. These include the human potential movement, the diminution of the materialistic dream, and a search within for the satisfaction that was not found outside, a growing interest in nonwestern cultures and philosophies, and research into the nature of altered states of consciousness (Wilber, 1996).

From the research on altered states came the recent and startling recognition that portions of some of the world's great religions can be viewed as state-specific technologies for the induction of higher states of consciousness. At the esoteric core of these disciplines, as opposed to the articles of dogma to which the masses adhere, lie precisely delineated practices aimed at training awareness and mental processes. One of the most widespread and central of these practices is Meditation, which is often regarded as a cornerstone of advanced work in these disciplines.

These recognitions led to the awareness that self-actualization was not the summit of psychological well-being. Rather it began to be recognized that there lay realms and states of consciousness beyond those encompassed by traditional Western psychological models and that some of these states held radically different and larger potentials than those we had formerly acknowledged (Wilber, 2000).

CURRENT STATUS

Meditation is probably the most widespread and popular of the "innovative therapies," having been learned by several million people in the United States and some 100 million worldwide at a conservative guess. Its status in the East remains much as it has for centuries; namely, it is a widely practiced discipline that is regarded as a central practice for any people wishing to explore or develop themselves to the highest psychological or religious levels.

In the West a relatively small percentage of people also practice it with this perspective. However, a much larger population uses it for its short-term benefits, such as relaxation, stress management, self-confidence, and a generally heightened sense of psychological well-being.

Behavioral scientists and mental health practitioners have also become interested, seeing Meditation as a tool with potential both for facilitating the therapist's effectiveness and as a self-regulation strategy useful for a variety of clinical disorders. A sizable body of research provides evidence of its clinical effectiveness and lends support to some of the claims made by practitioners across the centuries. For reviews see Murphy and Donovan (1997), Shapiro and Walsh (1984), Walsh and Vaughan (1993), and West (1987).

For those who wish to learn to meditate there are several helpful books. Those beginners may find helpful include Goldstein (1983) Ram Dass (1990), and Walsh (1999). However, books by themselves are rarely sufficient, and it is extremely helpful to have the support and guidance of a teacher and fellow meditators. Meditation teachers and centers can often be found by a perusal of the phone book, particularly for the more popular varieties such as Transcendental Meditation or Zen. A useful reference book listing centers and teachers is contained in the appendix of the book by Ram Dass (1990).

THEORY

Meditation stems from and leads to a view of human nature, mind, psychology, and consciousness that differs markedly in some ways from our traditional Western psychological perspectives. In this section we will first examine the nature of the meditation model, then compare the traditional Western view with it, and finally examine the mechanisms that may be involved in producing the effects of Meditation.

The Meditation Model of Consciousness

Our traditional psychological and psychiatric models posit a limited number of states of consciousness, and our usual waking state is assumed to be optimal. Some other states may be functionally useful—for example, sleep and dreaming—but most are viewed as degenerate and dysfunctional in one way or another—consider delirium, psychosis, or intoxication. No consideration is given to the possibility that states may exist that are even more functional than our usual waking one.

On the other hand, most meditation theories view the waking state as suboptimal. The mind is seen as largely outside voluntary control and continuously creating a largely unrecognized stream of thoughts, emotions, images, fantasies, and associations. These are held to distort our awareness, perceptual processes, and sense of identity to an unrecognized degree. This distortion is described in various traditions as *"maya," "samsara,"* or "illusion" (Goldstein, 1983). The term "illusion" has often been mistaken to mean that the world does not exist. However, it actually refers to the concept that our perceptions are distorted to an unrecognized degree and hence are rendered illusory. From this perspective we might argue that many human problems originate from the unrecognized inability to differentiate mind-produced distortions from objective sensory data. For example, how rarely do we directly recognize and experience that we are the active creators of our perception and that the unpleasantness, beauty, ugliness, and so on, that we think we see in the world are actually creations of our own mind? According to Ram Dass (1990), "We are all prisoners of our own mind. This recognition is the first step on the journey to awakening."

Fortunately, these claims about the nature of our usual state of consciousness, or lack of awareness, the unrecognized involuntary nature of much of our mental processes, and the distortions to which they are subject are readily open to personal testing. Anyone willing to undertake a period of intensive training in observation of his or her own mental processes—such as an insight meditation retreat of one or two weeks' duration—will become painfully aware of this fact. Indeed, one of the major dictums of all the meditative traditions is that these phenomena should be experienced and known directly by the individual rather than by what others say about them. Many a behavioral scientist and therapist who has heard of these things has been grudgingly shocked into acknowledging their potency only after personally experiencing them (Walsh, 1977, 1978; Ram Dass, 1990).

Trained meditative observation reveals that our usual consciousness is filled with a continual flux of subliminal thoughts, internal dialogue, and fantasies (Goldstein, 1983). In becoming lost in and identified with this mental content, awareness is reduced and distorted, resulting in an unappreciated trance state. Thus from the meditative perspective our usual state of consciousness is seen as a state of hypnosis. As in any hypnotic state, there need not be a recognition of the trance or its attendant constriction of awareness, or a memory of the sense of identity prior to hypnosis. Those thoughts with which we have identified create our state of consciousness, identity, and reality (Walsh, 1999). In the words of the Buddha, "We are what we think. / All that we are arises with our thoughts. / With our thoughts we make the world" (Byrom, 1976).

From this perspective the ego appears to represent the constellation of thoughts with which we usually identify. Indeed, deep meditative observation reveals that what we take to be our continuous abiding ego, or "self," turns out to be a rapid flux of individual thoughts and images that, because of our usual limitations of awareness, is perceived as solid and continuous (Goldstein, 1983). This is analogous to the experience of continuity and motion that our perception of the individual frames of a movie provides: the so-called "flicker-fusion" phenomenon.

Because they view the usual state as suboptimal, the meditative traditions obviously hold that more optimal states exist. Indeed they suggest that a large spectrum of altered states of consciousness exist, that some are potentially useful, and that a few are true "higher" states. The term "higher" indicates that a state possesses all the capacities and potentials of the usual states plus some additional ones (Tart, 1975). These higher states are seen as realizable through mental training, with Meditation being one particular type of such training.

At the summit of mental development lie those states of consciousness that are the goal of advanced Meditation, known variously as enlightenment or liberation (Walsh & Shapiro, 1984; Wilber, 1996, 2000). These are states in which awareness is said to no longer identify exclusively with anything. Without exclusive identification the me/not me dichotomy is transcended and the individual thus perceives himself or herself as both no thing and every thing. That is, such people experience themselves as both pure awareness (no thing) and the entire universe (every thing). Defenses drop away, because when experiencing oneself as no thing there is nothing to defend; when experiencing oneself as every thing there is nothing to defend against. This experience of unconditioned or pure awareness is apparently very blissful. It is described in the Hindu tradition as comprised of "sat-chit-ananda": awareness, being, and bliss (Feuerstein, 1996).

To those with no experience of these states, such descriptions sound paradoxical if not bizarre. However, there is a remarkable similarity in such descriptions across cultures and centuries by those who have taken these practices to their limits. So consistent are descriptions of these states of consciousness and the worldview that originates from them that they have comprised the basis of what has been called "the perennial philosophy," a description of consciousness and reality that can be found at the core of all the great meditative and yogic traditions (Wilber, 1996).

Comparing the Meditative and Western Psychological Models

When the traditional Western psychological and the meditative models are compared, a "paradigm clash" necessarily ensues (Walsh, 1980). What happens when the claims of the consciousness disciplines are examined from within the Western framework?

First, all claims for the existence of true higher states will be automatically dismissed, because the usual state is believed to be optimal and there is thus no place in the Western model for anything better. Not only will they be dismissed, but because many of the experiences accompanying these states are unknown in the Western model, they are likely to be viewed as pathological. Thus, for example, the experiences known as *satori* or *kensho*, intense but short-lived enlightenment experiences, include a sense of unity or oneness with the rest of the universe. However, because our traditional Western model recognizes such experiences only when they occur in extreme psychosis, they are likely to be pathologized. This is an example of the "pre/trans fallacy," in which prepersonal regression and transpersonal regression are infused (Wilber, 1996). Without an awareness of paradigmatic assumptions, it becomes easy to dismiss such phenomena as nonsensical or even pathological, a mistake that has been made even by some of the most outstanding Western mental health professionals. Thus, for example, Freud (1962) dismissed oceanic experience as infantile helplessness. Alexander (1931) interpreted Meditation as self-induced catatonia, while the Group for the Advancement of Psychiatry (1976) viewed mystics as borderline psychotics (Deikman, 1977).

When we reverse viewpoints and examine the Western model from the perspective of the meditative model, even more startling conclusions arise. The meditative model is inherently broader than the traditional Western perspective, because the former encompasses a wider range of states of consciousness, including all those recognized by the latter. Indeed the Western model can be viewed as a specific subset of the meditative one.

Thus the Western model has a position vis-à-vis an Einsteinian model in physics. The Newtonian model applies appropriately to objects moving at relatively low velocities but no longer fits when applied to high-velocity objects. The Einsteinian model, on the other hand, encompasses both low and high speeds; from this broader perspective the Newtonian model, and its inherent limitations, are perfectly logical and understandable (employing Einsteinian and not Newtonian logic, of course). However, the reverse does not hold, for Einsteinian logic and phenomena are not comprehensible from within a Newtonian framework. To try to examine the larger model from the perspective of the smaller is inappropriate and necessarily productive of false conclusions, because what lies outside the range of the smaller model must necessarily be misinterpreted by it (Walsh, 1980).

Viewing our usual state of consciousness from this expanded model results in some extraordinary implications. Our traditional model defines psychosis as a state of consciousness in which reality is misperceived or distorted without recognition of that misperception. From one perspective of the meditative model our usual state fits this definition because it is suboptimal, provides a distorted perception of reality, and fails to recognize that distortion. From this perspective, our usual state is seen as a hypnotically constricted trance. Like individuals who live their lives in a smog-filled city and only recognize the extent of the pollution and limited visibility when they climb into the surrounding mountains, most of us live our lives unaware of our restricted awareness.

In developmental terms, the Meditative perspective sees our "normal" psychological condition as a form of collective developmental arrest. Development has proceeded from prepersonal to personal (from preconventional to conventional), but has there ground to a halt rather than continuing into the transpersonal (postconventional) stages that are potentially available to us and that can be realized through practices such as Meditation (Wilber, 2000).

Possible Mechanisms Involved in the Production of Meditation Effects

In all likelihood a large number of mechanisms are involved in producing the effects of Meditation. In this section we will first examine possible mechanisms proposed by Western psychology and then discuss a nonwestern model from Buddhist psychology.

From one perspective Meditation can be viewed as a progressive heightening of awareness of, and disidentification from, mental content. In practices such as Insight Meditation, the student is trained to observe and identify all mental content and processes rapidly and precisely (Goldstein, 1983). This is a slow process in which a gradual refinement of perception peels awareness from successively more subtle layers of identification. Thoughts with which one formerly identified become recognized as just thoughts.

For example, if the thought "I'm scared" arises and is seen to be just a thought, then it exerts little influence. However, if the individual identifies with that thought, the experiential reality is that he or she is scared. This identification sets in motion a self-fulfilling, self-

prophetic process in which experience and psychological processes appear to validate the reality of that which was identified with. This thought "I'm scared" is now not something that can be seen; rather, it is that from which everything else is seen and interpreted. Awareness, which could be transcendent and positionless, has now been constricted to viewing the world from a single self-validating perspective.

"There is nothing more difficult that to become critically aware of the presuppositions of one's own thought. . . . Every thought can be scrutinized directly except the thought by which we scrutinize" (Schumacher, 1977). However, with the heightened awareness a trained mind can bring to bear, the individual thought may now be recognized again. In recognizing it as only a thought, the individual goes from thinking that he or she is a scared person to the experience of being aware of the thought. This may be seen as *dehypnosis* (Walsh, 1999).

A number of other mechanisms are clearly also involved. Suggested psychological mechanisms include relaxation, global desensitization to formerly stressful stimuli, habituation, expectation, deautomatization, counterconditioning, and a variety of cognitive mediating factors. At the psychological level, suggested mechanisms include reduced metabolism and arousal, hemispheric lateralization (a shift in the relative activity of the two cerebral hemispheres), brain-wave resonance and coherence, and a shift in the balance between the activating and quieting components of the autonomic nervous system (Shapiro & Walsh, 1984; Walsh & Vaughan, 1993).

Another way in which meditative mechanisms can be viewed is in terms of Charles Tart's systems model of consciousness. Tart views consciousness as a complex, dynamic system constructed from various components such as thought, emotion, attention, identity, arousal, and so forth (Walsh & Vaughan, 1993). Different types of Meditation can be viewed as cultivating specific components. While Insight Meditation specifically trains attention, other types work with, for example, emotion or the sense of identity. Some practices use specific strategies that we would now recognize as counterconditioning and classical conditioning to cultivate love. When this or any other component of consciousness is cultivated to a sufficient degree, it may result in significant shifts in the state of consciousness.

A Buddhist Model of Mind

Several nonwestern psychologies also contain models that attempt to explain how meditative effects are produced. One Buddhist psychological model based on "mental factors" is particularly useful in making comparisons with Western psychotherapeutic practices.

Mental factors are qualities of mind said to determine the relationship between consciousness and the object of consciousness (the sensory stimulus of which consciousness is aware). Thus, for example, the mental factor of aversion describes a state in which consciousness tend to withdraw from or avoid a particular stimulus. Buddhist psychology describes some 50-odd mental factors; of these, the seven so-called "factors of enlightenment" will be examined here. These are seven qualities that are deliberately cultivated by Buddhist meditators, because it is held that when they are cultivated and balanced one with another they result in an optimal relationship of awareness to each moment of experience (Goldstein, 1983; Walsh & Vaughan, 1993).

The first of these qualities is *mindfulness,* which is the quality of being aware of the nature of the object of consciousness. Thus, for example, a fantasy is recognized as such, rather that the individual becoming lost in it without recognizing that it is merely a fantasy.

The remaining six mental factors are divided into two groups of three that should be balanced for optimum psychological well-being. The first group are energizing or arousing factors of *energy, investigation,* and *rapture.* These are balanced by the three calming factors of *concentration, tranquility,* and *equanimity.*

The energy factor refers to the arousal level, which should be balanced between the extremes of agitation and torpor. Investigation refers to the active exploration of the moment-to-moment experience and state of mind, while rapture refers to a positive state of joy and intense interest in the moment-to-moment experience. The calming factors involve concentration, which is the ability to maintain attention on a specific object; tranquility, which is calm and freedom from anxiety and agitation; and equanimity, the capacity to experience sensations without disturbing the mental state.

Western therapists of all persuasions have tended to emphasize the active factors of energy and investigation in psychological exploration. What has not been appreciated is that perceptual and intuitive sensitivity and insight are limited without a complementary development of concentration, tranquility, and equanimity (Walsh & Vaughan, 1993). On the other hand, Eastern traditions have sometimes overemphasized these factors so that the individuals may develop intense concentration and calm without a balanced complementary cultivation of investigation and energetic observation. Such practices lead to euphoric experiences but relatively little deep wisdom or permanent liberation from mental conditioning. Rather, optimal effects are held to occur when all seven factors are cultivated in a balanced, mutually facilitating manner.

METHODOLOGY

While the general principles and methods of practice are the same, the intensity and degree of commitment required for a person wishing to use Meditation for intensive exploration and growth is far greater than that of the person who wishes to employ it as a self-regulation strategy for a limited psychological or somatic benefit. The major part of this section will deal with intense practice because this also encompasses the lesser demands of using Meditation as a clinical self-regulation strategy.

For an individual committed to deep and thoroughgoing self-transformation, Meditation is best viewed as but one component of a shift in attitudes, thought, speech, and behavior aimed at the transformation of mind, awareness, identity, lifestyle, and relationship to the world. Any meditator soon recognizes that while behavior originates from the mind, all behavior also leaves its imprint on the mind, and conditions and imprints the state in which it was performed. Training in Meditation is therefore usually accompanied by preliminary and concomitant shifts in lifestyle designed to enhance positive mental states and reduce negative ones.

Thus, for example, the meditator is advised to be strictly ethical in all behavior. Buddhist psychology recommends at a minimum refraining from lying, stealing, sexual misconduct, killing, and the consumption of mind-clouding intoxicants. Traditionally this is said to lead to what is called "purification" in which unskillful, lower motives and behavior are gradually winnowed away. This can be seen in part as movement up Maslow's hierarchy of needs.

This ethicality is not to be confused with externally imposed or sanctioned moralism that adopts a judgmental right/wrong, good/bad perspective on behavior. Rather, no meditator can long remain unaware that unethical behavior is motivated by emotions and states such as greed, anger, and aversion, that unethical behavior reinforces these states, and that they in turn disrupt the mind, leaving it agitated, guilty, and trapped still more deeply in painful conditioning.

Other useful practices include the cultivation of generosity and service to others as ways of reducing egotistical self-centeredness and desire. The meditator may wish to be selective in friendships, because people without such motives may not provide a supportive environment for these initially difficult practices (Walsh, 1999).

Practitioners may also be drawn to a life of what has been termed "voluntary simplicity" (Elgin, 1993). With deepening practice meditators recognize the disrupting effects of greed and attachment. At the same time, they find themselves better able to generate a sense of well-being and the positive emotions for which they were formerly dependent upon external possessions and stimuli. They may thus experience less need to own the latest and biggest car, boat, or color television. Rather, greater pleasure is found in a deepening sensitivity to the moment-to-moment flow of experience and each moment, no mater what one is doing, becomes a source of rich and multifaceted stimulation (Feuerstein, 1996; Goldstein, 1983).

For most people Meditation is a slow, cumulative process; people should be prepared to commit themselves to daily practice for a minimum of about a month. Practice may be begun with either short daily sessions of 20 minutes or half an hour once or twice a day, or for individuals who wish to jump in, with a retreat in which one engages in more or less continuous meditation for a period of days or weeks. The latter is more difficult in that initial intensive practice can often be quite arduous, but it is also more rewarding; even several days of intensive, continuous practice will be sufficient to produce a range of experiences and insight beyond the ken of normal daily life. While it is possible to make some progress unaided, any deep practice is greatly facilitated by a good teacher or guide with considerable personal experience of the discipline.

Meditation practices can be subdivided into two main categories: concentration and awareness practices. Concentration meditations aim especially at developing the ability of the mind to focus attention imperturbably on a specific object such as the breath, an emotion, or a mental factor. Awareness meditations, on the other hand, aim at examining the nature of mind, consciousness, and the ongoing flux of moment-to-moment experience. Meditations on the breath or on a repetitive internally generated sound can be seen as concentration practices; Zen or Insight Meditations, which aim to open the individual to an awareness of whatever passes through the field of awareness, can be seen as awareness trainings (Goldstein, 1983).

In Concentration Meditation, the individual attempts to fix attention on a specific stimulus, such as the breath. However, attention remains fixed for a remarkably short period and the individual soon finds himself or herself lost in fantasy, inner dialogue, or unconscious reverie of some type. As soon as this is realized, attention is brought back to the breath and maintained there until lost again. This rapidly results in a startling and disconcerting recognition: awareness and control of attentional processes are far less than we usually recognize. Most beginning meditators are astonished to recognize just how much of their lives and mental processes are on unconscious automatic pilot. From a meditative perspective we all suffer from attention deficit disorder.

Because the power and extent of this automaticity is so difficult to convey to someone without personal experience of it, it is worthwhile for any nonmeditator to try the following exercise.

Set an alarm for a minimum of 10 minutes. Then take a comfortable seat, close your eyes, and turn your attention to the sensations of breathing in your abdomen. Try to stay with the sensations continuously as the abdominal wall rises and falls, and focus your attention as carefully, precisely, and microscopically on the sensations that arise and pass away each instant. Do not let your attention wander for a moment. If thoughts and feelings arise, just let them be there, and continue to focus your awareness on the sensations of the breath.

While you continue to pay close attention to the sensations, start counting the breaths from 10 down to one and after you reach one go back to 10 again. However, if you lose count or if the mind wanders from the sensations of the breath, even for an instant, go back to 10 again. If you get lost in fantasy or distracted by internal or external stimuli, just recognize what has happened and gently bring the mind back to the breath and start counting again. Continue this process until the alarm clock tells you to stop; then estimate how much of the time you were actually fully aware of the experience of breathing.

Most people find that only a very small percentage of their time was spent fully aware of the sensations of the breath. With continued practice you would find that this awareness was even less than you initially thought because much of the time spent lost in fantasy is not initially recognized. However, this brief exercise should be sufficient to give a beginner an idea of the problem.

With prolonged practice, concentration gradually improves and meditators are able to maintain their focuses for progressively longer periods. As they do so, a number of concomitant experiences occur such as calm, equanimity, a sense of lightness and well-being, and ultimately a range of altered states (Kornfield, 1979).

Although the practice of concentration can be useful and pleasurable, some traditions view it more as a facilitator of Awareness Meditation than as an end in itself. Insight or awareness practices also aim at directing attention but allow it to shift to focus electively on whatever is predominant within the field of awareness. Thus, the individual practicing Insight Meditation might begin by focusing attention on the breath. Then, as other stimuli such as thoughts, sensations, or emotions become predominant, attention is allowed to focus on and examine each of them in succession.

In doing this the first level of insights that develop are what might be called psychodynamic. That is, the individual recognizes patterns of thought and behavior such as might be recognized in traditional psychotherapy. However, as the practice deepens, the significantly enhanced capacities of concentration, calm, and equanimity allow deep insights into the nature of psychological processes. This level of insight brings an illumination of the how the mind is constructed. One begins to see, for example, the way a single thought may arise into awareness and modify perception. The arising of desire may be seen to modify perception and result in the production of a state and motivational system aimed at not only obtaining, but clutching to and resisting detachment from, the object of the desire. Simultaneously, associations and fears concerning the possible loss of the object may be observed. One begins to gain insight into the fundamental nature of processes such as motivation, perception, and ego. Everything in the mind is seen to be in constant change, and the illusion that there abides deep within the psyche a permanent unchanging ego or self is seen to be an illusory construction of perceptual insensitivity. With this recognition there occurs a letting go of egocentric motivation and an enhanced identification with others and the universe at large (Goldstein, 1983; Feuerstein, 1996).

The range of experiences is extraordinarily large and intense, far beyond anything experienced in daily life, and suggests that almost any experience may occur in Meditation as a result of greater openness and sensitivity (Kornfield, 1979). Indeed, more experienced meditators state that what tends to emerge as one continues to have more and deeper experiences is an underlying calm and nonreactive equanimity so that this greater range of experiences can be observed an allowed without disturbance, defensiveness, or interference. More and more the individual identifies himself or herself with the calm observer or witness of these experiences rather than the experiences per se (Goldstein, 1983; Kornfield, 1995).

Many meditators, including behavioral scientists, have reported that as they continued to meditate there was a deepening of their intellectual understanding of the statements of more advanced practitioners. It therefore appears that intellectual understanding in this area demands an experiential basis and that what was incomprehensible at one stage may subsequently become more understandable once the individual has experienced more of the meditative process.

Occasionally some of the experiences that occur may be disturbing—for example, anxiety, tension, anger, perceptual changes in sense of self and reality (Kornfield, 1979; Walsh & Vaughan, 1993; Wilber et al., 1986). These may sometimes be quite intense but generally are short-lived and remit spontaneously. In many cases they seem to represent a greater sensitivity to, and emergence of, previously repressed psychological memories and conflict. Thus the initial discomfort of experiencing them may be a necessary price for processing and discharging them.

APPLICATIONS

The applications of Meditation can perhaps be best considered in terms of the levels and degrees of psychological intervention that are available. One useful division views such interventions in terms of three levels: therapeutic, existential, and transpersonal (Wilber, 1977). The therapeutic level is essentially aimed at reducing

overt pathology, while the existential aims at confronting the givens of existence such as responsibility, finitude, death, and so forth. The transpersonal level is aimed at liberation or enlightenment and, as such, has been little recognized in traditional Western models.

At the therapeutic level a considerable body of research data is available to suggest that Meditation may have a wide range of application from both psychological and somatic, particularly psychosomatic, disorders. The general picture that is emerging suggests that Meditation may enhance psychological well-being and perceptual sensitivity (for reviews see Alexander & Langer, 1991; Murphy & Donovan, 1997; Shapiro & Walsh, 1984; Walsh & Vaughan, 1993).

Many studies have reported that Meditation reduces anxiety, either for nonspecific anxiety and anxiety neurosis or for specific phobias, such as of enclosed spaces, examinations, being alone, or of heart attack. Clinical research indicates that drug and alcohol use may be reduced, and prisoners show reduced aggression and recidivism.

There have also been many reports of psychosomatic benefits. In the cardiovascular system, Meditation can reduce high blood pressure and cholesterol levels, enhance rehabilitation after myocardial infarction, and has proved a valuable component of Dean Ornish's (1990) successful program to reverse coronary artery disease through lifestyle changes. Other responsive diseases that may be ameliorated by Meditation include premenstrual syndrome, migraine, psoriasis, Crohn's disease, fibromyalgia, and chronic pain (Murphy & Donovan, 1997). Even mortality rates in the elderly have been found to drop (Alexander et al., 1989).

Positive effects have also been noted in healthy nonclinical populations. A number of studies have suggested that meditators change more than controls in the direction of enhanced confidence, self-esteem, sense of self-control, empathy, and self-actualization (Alexander & Langer, 1991; Murphy & Donovan, 1997).

In summary, experimental evidence clearly indicates that Meditation may have considerable therapeutic potential. However, many points remain unclear. For example, many studies have been flawed by such methodological problems as the lack of adequate control groups, uncertain expectation and placebo effects, and dubious measurement procedures. Furthermore, some studies have suggested that Meditation may not necessarily be more effective for clinical disorders than are other self-regulation strategies such as relaxation training and self-hypnosis. On the other hand, in several studies subjects have reported meditation experiences to be more meaningful, pleasurable, and relaxing than those of other strategies, even where objective measures did not separate them. Patients who are most likely to benefit from Meditation are probably those who are not severely disturbed and who perceive themselves as possessing an internal locus of control (Murphy & Donovan, 1997).

Experimental measures also indicate greater perceptual sensitivity. Sensory thresholds, the lowest levels at which a stimulus can be detected, are lowered, while the capacity for empathy and field independence increase. Thus both phenomenological and objective studies agree with classical literature that Meditation enhances perceptual sensitivity.

Meditation may also be useful for therapists. A number of subjective reports and experimental papers suggest that Meditation may enhance empathic sensitivity and accuracy (Shapiro & Walsh, 1984). The deep insights into the workings of one's own mind that Meditation provides also seem to allow for insight into, and compassion toward, the painful mental patterns that clients bring to therapy. As in many traditional Western psychotherapies, the meditator's own self-insight and wisdom are limiting factors for successful help to others. Therefore, the meditator is urged to continually deepen his or her own practice as the most effective way of benefiting others.

Finally Meditation is available as a tool for those who wish to plumb the depths of their own beings. Here it can be used to explore the nature of mind, identity, and consciousness, to grapple with the deepest questions of existence that any human being can confront, and to seek to ultimately transcend them all in a radical transformation of consciousness and the seeker (Walsh, 1999).

For such a person Meditation provides an invaluable tool that can be used from the beginning to the end of the quest. Such a path is not for the fainthearted, because the individual must be willing to confront any experience that the mind can create, and that range is vast indeed.

Although the deepest insights may occur at any moment, such a practice is usually to be reckoned in years rather than hours or even months. As Ramana Maharshi, one of the most respected Hindu teachers in the last century, noted, "Mind control is not your birthright. Those who have succeeded owe their liberation to perseverance" (Kornfield, 1995). This recognition prompted Medard Boss (1963), one of the earliest Western psychiatrists to examine meditative practices firsthand, to comment that compared with the intensity of yogic self-exploration "even the best western training analysis is not much more than an introductory course."

Coming to full voluntary control of one's own mind has been called the art of arts and science of sciences. While this has a hyperbolic ring to it, few people who have tried it would probably disagree.

Of course one does not have to commit oneself totally to this path. All of us can explore it as little or as much as we wish and can expect proportionate benefits. Nowhere is the old maxim about getting out of something what you put into it truer than in Meditation. Although initially often quite difficult, the practice is both self-reinforcing and self-fulfilling, and the progressive experiences of deepening calm, equanimity, understanding, and compassion may draw one gently and pleasurably into deeper and deeper exploration.

> The thought manifests as the word, the word manifests
> as the deed.
> The deed develops into habit, and the habit hardens
> into character.
> So watch the thought and its ways with care.
> And let it spring from love born out of respect for all
> beings.
> For all beings are One.
>
> Anonymous

CASE EXAMPLE

As an example of a successful outcome, I am presenting a condensation of papers describing my own meditative experiences (Walsh, 1977, 1978). Some readers may suspect that I am biased in presenting this particular case and describing it as successful. They are, of course, correct.

However, for obvious reasons I have better insight into these experiences than I do those of other people. In addition, the practice was undertaken out of curiosity and for personal growth rather than to deal with any specific clinical problem and was pursued more intensively and further than most westerners do. Such a report by a fellow mental health professional may be of personal interest to readers of this volume who are considering the possibility of trying Meditation for themselves. For those readers who wish to see a detailed case study of Meditation employed for a specific clinical disorder, an excellent account by Dean Shapiro is available in Wedding and Corsini (2000).

Because parts of this account describe experiences that occurred during very intensive continuous Meditation in retreats, many of the experiences are far more intense and difficult than those usually encountered by people practicing for brief daily periods.

This is an account of my subjective experiences of some two years of Vipassana, or Insight Meditation. During the first year this practice took an average of one hour per day; during the second this was increased to about two hours, as well as some six weeks of intensive meditation retreats, usually of two weeks' duration. During these retreats about 18 to 20 hours per day were spent in continuous walking and sitting Meditation performed in silence and without eye contact, reading, or writing. While this amount of practice may be vastly less than that of more experienced practitioners, it certainly proved sufficient to elicit a range of experiences beyond the ken of day-to-day nonmeditative living.

I began Meditation with one half-hour session each day. During the first three to six months, there were few times during which I could honestly say with complete certainty that I was definitely experiencing benefits from it. Except for the painfully obvious stiff back and sore knees, the psychological effects other than occasional relaxation were so subtle and ephemeral that I could never be sure that they were more than a figment of my wishes and expectations. The nature of Meditation seems to be, especially at first, a slow but cumulative process, a fact that may be useful for beginners to know.

However, with continued perseverance, subtle effects just at the limit of my perceptual threshold did begin to become apparent. I had expected the eruption into awareness of powerful, concrete experiences that, while perhaps not flashes of lightning and pealing of bells, would at least be of sufficient intensity to make it very clear that I had "gotten it", whatever "it" was. What "it" actually turned out to be was not the appearance of formerly nonexistent mental phenomena but rather a gradual, incremental increase in perceptual sensitivity to the formerly subliminal portions of my own inner stream of consciousness.

"When one sits down with eyes closed to silence the mind, one is at first submerged by a torrent of thoughts—they crop up everywhere like frightened, nay, aggressive rats" (Satprem, 1968, p. 33). The more sensitive I became, the more I was forced to recognize that what I had formerly believed to be my rational mind, preoccupied with logical planning, problem solving, and so forth, actually comprised a frantic torrent of forceful, demanding, loud, and often unrelated thoughts and fantasies that filled an unbelievable proportion of consciousness even during purposive behavior. The incredible proportion of consciousness that this fantasy world occupied, my powerlessness to remove it for more than a few seconds, and my former state of mindlessness or ignorance of its existence staggered me. Interestingly this "mindlessness" seemed much more intense and difficult to dealt with than in psychotherapy (Walsh, 1976), where the depth and sensitivity of inner awareness seemed less, and where the therapist provided a perceptual focus and was available to pull me back if I started to get lost in fantasy.

The subtlety, complexity, infinite range and number, and entrapping power of the fantasies that the mind creates seem impossible to comprehend, to differentiate from reality while in them, and even more so to describe to one who has not experienced them. Layer upon layer of imagery and quasilogic open up at any point to which attention is directed. Indeed it gradually becomes apparent that it is impossible to question and reason one's way out of this all-encompassing fantasy because the very process of questioning, thinking, and seeking only creates further fantasy.

The power and pervasiveness of these inner dialogues and fantasies left me amazed that we could be so unaware of them during our normal waking life; they reminded me of the Eastern concept of *maya,* all-consuming illusion.

The First Meditation Retreat

The first meditation retreat, begun about one year after commencing sitting, was a difficult two-week affair. A marked hypersensitivity to all stimuli, both internal and external, rapidly developed, resulting in intense arousal, agitation, discomfort, and multiple chronic muscle contractions, especially around the shoulders.

One of my most amazing rediscoveries during this first retreat was the incredible proportion of time, well over 90 percent, which I spent lost in fantasy. Most of these fantasies were of the ego self-aggrandizing type, so that when eventually I realized I was in them, it proved quite a struggle to decide to give them up and return to the breath, but with practice this decision became slightly easier, faster, and more automatic. This by no means happened quickly; in fact, in the first four or five days the proportion of time spent in fantasy actually increased as the Meditation deepened. During this period, each time I sat and closed my eyes I would be immediately swept away by vivid hallucinations, losing all contact with where I was or what I was doing until, after an unknown period of time, a thought would creep in such as, "Am I really swimming, lying on the beach?" and so forth. Then I would either get lost back into the fantasy or another thought would come: "Wait a moment, I thought I was meditating." If the latter, then I would be left with the difficult problem of trying to ground myself; that is, to differentiate between stimulus-produced percepts ("reality") and entirely endogenous ones ("hallucinations"). The only way this seemed possible was to try finding the breath, and so I would begin frantically searching around in this hypnagogic universe for the sensations of the breath. Such was the power of the hallucinations that sometimes I would be literally unable to find it and would fall back into the fantasy. If successful, I would recognize it and be reassured that I was in fact meditating. Then in the next moment I would be lost again in yet another fantasy. The clarity, power, persuasiveness, and continuity of these hallucinations is difficult to express adequately. However, the effect of living through three days during which time to close my eyes meant to lose contact almost immediately with ordinary reality was extraordinarily draining, to say the least. Interestingly enough, while this experience was uncomfortable and quite beyond my control, it was not particularly frightening; if anything, the opposite. For many years I had feared losing control if I let down defenses and voyaged too far along the road of self-investigation and discovery. This appears to be a common fear and seems to serve a major defensive function. Having experienced this once-feared outcome, it now no longer seems so terrifying. Of course, the paradox is that what we usually call control is often exactly the opposite, a lack of ability to let go of defenses.

While a good 90 percent or more of this first retreat was taken up with mindless fantasy and agitation, there did occur during the second week occasional short-lived periods of intense peace and tranquility. These were so satisfying that, while I would not be willing to sign up for a lifetime in a monastery, I could begin to comprehend the possibility of truth in the Buddhist saying that "peace is the highest form of happiness."

Affective lability was also extreme. There were sudden, apparently unprecipitated, wide mood swings to completely polar emotions. Shorn of all my props and distractions, it became clear that I had little more than the faintest inkling of self-control over either thoughts or feelings and that my mind has a mind of its own.

This recognition is commonly described as one of the earliest, strongest, and most surprising insights that confronts people who begin intensive meditation practice; they are always amazed that they had not recognized it previously (Goldstein, 1983).

Attachments and Needs

It soon became apparent that the type of material that forcibly erupted into awareness and disrupted concentration was most often material—ideas, fantasies, thoughts, and so on—to which I was attached (addicted) and around which there was considerable affective charge. There was a definite sense that attachments reduced the flexibility and power of the mind, because whenever I was preoccupied with a stimulus to which I was attached, I had difficulty in withdrawing my attention from it to observe other stimuli that passed through awareness.

Paradoxically, it seems that a need or attachment to be rid of a certain experience or state may lead to its perpetuation. The clearest example of this has been with anxiety. I suddenly began to experience mild anxiety attacks of unknown origin that, curiously enough, seemed to occur most often when I was feeling really good and in the presence of a particular person whom I loved. At such times I would try all my various psychological gymnastics to eradicate the anxiety because I did not want to feel anxious.

However, these episodes continued for some five months in spite of, or as it actually turned out, because of my resistance to them. During this time my meditation practice deepened, and what I discovered was that I had considerable fear of fear; my mind therefore surveyed in a radarlike fashion all endogenous and exogenous stimuli for their fear-evoking potential and all reactions for any fear component. There was a continuous

mental scanning process preset in an exquisitely sensitive fashion for the detection of anything resembling fear. Consequently there were a considerable number of false positives; that is, nonfearful stimuli and reactions that were interpreted as being fearful or potentially fear-provoking. Because the reactions to the false positives themselves comprised fear and fear components, there was of course an immediate chain reaction set up with one fear response acting as the stimulus for the next. It thus became very clear that my fear of, and resistance to, fear was exactly what was perpetuating it.

This insight and the further application of mental awareness to the process certainly reduced but did not eradicate these episodes entirely. Paradoxically, they still tended to recur when I felt very calm and peaceful. It was not until the middle of the next meditation retreat that the reasons for this became clear. After the first few days of pain and agitation, I began to feel more and more peaceful. There came a sitting in which I could feel my Meditation deepen perceptibly and the restless mental scanning slow more and more. Then, as the process continued to deepen and slow, I was literally jolted by a flash of agitation and anxiety accompanying this thought: "But what do I do now if there's no more anxiety to look for?" It was apparent that if I continued to quieten, there would be neither anxiety to scan for nor a scanning process itself, and my need to get rid of anxiety demanded that I have a continuous scanning mechanism, and the presence of the mechanism in turn created the presence of the anxiety. My "but what do I do now?" fear had very effectively removed the possibility of the dissipation of both, and its occurrence at a time when I was feeling most peaceful, relaxed, and safe of course explained why I had been subject to these anxiety episodes at the apparently paradoxical times when I felt best. It appears that, within the mind, if you need to be rid of certain experiences, then not only are you likely to have a number of false positives but you may also need to have the experiences around continuously so that you can keep getting rid of them. Thus within the province of the mind, what you resist is what you get.

Perception

With continued practice the speed, power, loudness, and continuity of thoughts and fantasies began to slowly diminish, leaving subtle sensations of greater peace and quiet. After a period of about four or five months there occurred episodes in which I would open my eyes at the end of Meditation and look at the outside world without the presence of concomitant internal dialogue. This state would be rapidly terminated by a rising sense of anxiety and anomie accompanied by the thought, "I don't know what anything means." Thus I could be looking at something completely familiar, such as a tree, a building, or the sky, and yet without an accompanying internal dialogue to label and categorize it, it seemed strange and devoid of meaning.

It seems that what made something familiar and hence secure was not simply its recognition, but the actual cognitive process of categorizing and labeling it. Once this was done, then more attention and reactivity was focused on the label and labeling process rather than on the stimulus itself. Thus the initial fantasy and thought-free periods may feel both strange and distinctly unpleasant; we are at first punished by their unfamiliarity. We have created an unseen prison for ourselves whose bars are composed of fantasies and thoughts of which we remain largely unaware unless we undertake intensive perceptual training. Moreover, if they are removed we may be frightened by the unfamiliarity of the experience and rapidly reinstate them.

Presumably this labeling process must modify our perception in many ways, including reducing our ability to experience each stimulus fully, richly, and newly, by reducing its multidimensional nature into a lesser dimensional cognitive labeling framework. This framework must necessarily derive from the past, be less tolerant of ambiguity, less here now, and perpetuative of a sense of sameness and continuity to the world. This process may represent the phenomenological and cognitive meditational basis of Deikman's (1966) concept of "automatization."

Interestingly, the extent of reaction to the stimulus itself as opposed to the label seems to be a direct function of the degree of mindfulness or meditative awareness. If I am mindful, then I tend to be focused on the primary sensations themselves, to label less, and to react to these labels less. For example, there was a period of about six weeks during which I felt mildly depressed. I was not incapacitated but was uncomfortable, dysphoric, and confused about what was happening to me throughout most of the waking day. However, during daily Meditation this experience and its affective quality changed markedly. The experience then felt somewhat like being on sensory overload, with many vague ill-defined somatic sensations and a large number of rapidly appearing and disappearing unclear visual images. However, to my surprise, nowhere could I find stimuli that were actually painful. Rather there was just a large input of vague stimuli of uncertain significance and meaning. I would therefore emerge from each sitting with the recognition that I was actually not experiencing any pain and was feeling considerably better. This is analogous to Tarthang Tulku's (1974) statement that "The more you go into the disturbance—when you really get there—the emotional characteristics no longer exist."

However, within a very short time I would lapse once more into my habitual nonmindful state. When I next became mindful once again I would find that I had been automatically labeling the stimulus complex as depression and then reacting to this label with thoughts and feelings such as "I'm depressed; I feel awful; what have I done to deserve this?" A couple of moments of relaxed mindfulness would be sufficient to switch the focus back to the primary sensations and the recognition once again that I was actually not experiencing discomfort. This process repeated itself endlessly during each day. The effect of mindfulness on phenomenology and reactivity should lend itself to experimental investigation. It is also an interesting example of one difference in the therapeutic processes of Meditation and traditional Western therapies. While the latter attempt to change the content of experience, Meditation is also interested in changing the perceptual-cognitive processes by which the mind produces such experiences.

Perceptual Sensitivity

One of the most fundamental changes has been an increase in perceptual sensitivity, which seems to include both absolute and discrimination thresholds. Examples of this include both a more subtle awareness of previously known precepts and a novel identification of previously unrecognized phenomena.

Sensitivity and clarity frequently seem enhanced following a meditation sitting or retreat. Thus, for example, at these times it seems that I can discriminate visual forms and outlines more clearly. It also feels as though empathy is significantly increased and that I am more aware of other people's subtle behaviors, vocal intonations, and so forth, as well as my own affective responses to them. The experience feels like having a faint but discernible veil removed from my eyes, a veil comprised of hundreds of subtle thoughts and feelings. Each one of these thoughts and feelings seems to act as a competing stimulus, or "noise," that thus reduces sensitivity to any one object. Thus, after Meditation any specific stimulus appears stronger and clearer, presumably because the signal/noise ratio is increased. These observations provide a phenomenological basis and possible perceptual mechanism to explain the finding that meditators in general tend to exhibit heightened perceptual sensitivity and empathy (Murphy & Donovan, 1997).

One unexpected demonstration of greater sensitivity has been the occurrence of the synesthetic perception of thoughts. Synesthesia, or cross-modality perception, is the phenomenon in which stimulation of one sensory modality is perceived in other modalities, as, for example, when sound is seen and felt as well as heard (Marks, 1975). Following the enhanced perceptual sensitivity that occurred during my prior psychotherapy, I began to experience this phenomenon not infrequently, suggesting that it may well occur within all of us though usually below our thresholds (Walsh, 1976). Now during moments of greater meditative sensitivity I have begun to experience this cross-modality perception with purely mental stimuli—with thoughts, for example. Thus, I may initially experience a thought as a feeling and subsequently become aware of a visual image before finally recognizing the more familiar cognitive information components.

Another novel type of perception seems to have occurred with continued practice: I have gradually found myself able to recognize increasingly subtle mental phenomena when I am not meditating but rather am involved in my daily activity. This has resulted in an increased recognition of affects, motivations, and subtle defensive maneuvers and manipulations. Indeed these latter recognitions now seem to constitute the sensitivity—limiting factor, because the discomfort that attends their more frequent perception is often sufficient to result in a defensive contraction of awareness.

Trust

These experiences have led to a greater understanding of and willingness to surrender to the meditative process. In the West, surrender has connotations of succumbing or being overwhelmed, but with increasing experience I have begun to surrender to the process in the sense of trusting, following, and allowing it to unfold without attempting to change, coerce, or manipulate it, and without necessarily requiring prior understanding of what I may be about to go through or predicting the outcome. Thus, for example, one of my major fears has been the threat of losing certain psychological and intellectual abilities—for example, of losing intellectual skills, scientific capacities, and control. This seems reminiscent of the idea that one of the major barriers to moving on to the next level is the fear of losing what we have.

Although I must emphasize that this trust is far from complete for me, I have come a long way. The experiences that have contributed to this trust are as follows. First of all, to the best of my knowledge the feared catastrophes have not eventuated. My intellectual and scientific skills seem to have remained intact. In addition, Meditation seems to have provided a range of experiences, insights, and developments formerly totally unknown to me. Thus, to expect, demand, and limit learning to extensions of that which is already known can prove a major limitation. As Bugental (1965) indicated, psychological growth is a voyage into the unknown.

Furthermore, it now seems clear that allowing experiences to be as they are and experience them without forcibly trying to change them is effective. This is especially true when it is recognized that any experience can be used for growth even to the point of perceiving the experience as necessary and perfect for the process.

Indeed, recognizing the perfection and functionality of each experience appears to be a highly productive perspective for several reasons. First, it reduces the deleteri-

ous agitation, resistance, and eruption of defenses and manipulations that occur secondary to judgment and negative perspectives. Second, contrary to my previous beliefs, acceptance and a nonjudgmental attitude toward an experience or situation do not necessarily remove either the motivation or capacity to deal with it in an effective manner. (My prior beliefs were that I needed my judgments, aversions, and negative reactions in order to power my motivation to modify the situations and stimuli eliciting them.) It should be noted here that the experience of perfection is just that, an experience. This may say more about the psychological state of the individual perceiving it than about the stimulus per se and may not necessarily in any way vitiate the perceiver's perception of the need to modify it.

Finally, there has been the recognition that the great meditation teachers really knew what they were talking about. Time and time again I have read descriptions, explanations, and predictions about Meditation, the normal psychological state, the states that arise with more and more Meditation, latent capacities, and so forth, and have scoffed and argued against them, feeling that they were just so removed from my experiences and beliefs that they could not possibly be true. However, I have now had a variety of experiences that I formerly would have believed to be impossible and have gained the experiential background with which to understand more of what is being taught. I now have to acknowledge that these people know vastly more than I do and that it is certainly worth my while to pay careful attention to their suggestions. Thus experiential knowledge may be a major limiting factor for intellectual understanding of psychological processes and consciousness; even highly intellectually sophisticated nonpractitioners may not fully understand such phenomena. This is a specific example of Immanuel Kant's idea that concepts without relevant experience are "empty."

SUMMARY

Meditation is a 3,000-year-old "innovative psychotherapy," which across centuries and cultures has been held to be capable of leading to the summa of human psychological development. Its recent discovery by the West has meant that millions of Westerners have joined tens of millions of nonwesterners in this practice. However, in the West its most popular application has been for relaxation and stress management rather than for the deeper psychological insights, higher developmental stages, and altered states of consciousness for which it is most frequently used in the East.

Empirical research has clearly demonstrated significant psychological, physiological, and chemical effects of Meditation. It has also been clearly demonstrated to be an effective treatment for a variety of psychological and psychosomatic disorders, although it remains less clear whether it is more effective for these purposes than are other self-regulation strategies, such as relaxation training and self-hypnosis. However, in general the effects that Meditation was originally designed to induce, such as subtle shifts in perception and consciousness, remain less tested by Western empirical approaches.

This is regrettable in that Meditation challenges some of the most fundamental assumptions of Western behavioral sciences. For example, its claim that our usual state of consciousness is suboptimal and that our usual perception is clouded and distorted to an unrecognized degree runs counter to our basic assumptions that our usual state is best. Similarly, Meditation suggests the existence of higher states of consciousness and higher developmental stages, and claims that these are realizable through training. In the West, because we regard the usual state and stage as best, there is no space for anything better. These claims are so fundamentally divergent from our usual assumptions that until recently they were dismissed as nonsensical. However, it is clear that we can no longer afford to dismiss such statements so casually. A growing network of concepts and data points to their validity and has already begun to shift our own assumptive framework (Wilber, 2000).

Meditation may offer several advantages. First of all, it is certainly cheap. The practitioner is independent of location and instruments and can practice as much or as little as desired. As a self-therapy or self-regulation strategy there is very little difficulty with dependency. In fact, there may be relatively little need for professional time and energy once the basic practice has been established. It has a wide range of application, being useful for clinical difficulties as well as for psychological growth at all levels. Casualties are rare, and both clients and therapists may find it beneficial. It can be used as a useful adjunct to more traditional therapies and, last but not least, it is often very enjoyable.

These are unusual claims: an inexpensive, widely applicable, relatively harmless, enjoyable self-regulation strategy, useful for both clinical difficulties and the heights of psychological well-being. Are these claims valid? All meditation traditions would agree that the ultimate test it to try it for oneself. Their traditional advice is, "To see if this be true, look within your own mind."

REFERENCES

Alexander, F. (1931). Buddhistic training as an artificial catatonia (the biological meaning of psychic occurrences). *Psychoanalytic Review, 18,* 129–145.

Boss, M. (1963). *A psychiatrist discovers India.* New York: Basic.

Bugental, J. F. T. (1965). *The search for authenticity: An existential analytical approach to psychotherapy.* New York: Holt.

Byrom, T. *The dhammapada: The sayings of the Buddha.* New York: Vintage.

Deikman, A. (1966). Deautomatization and the mystic experience. *Psychiatry, 29,* 324–328.

Deikman, A. (1977). Comments on the GAP report on mysticism. *Journal of Nervous and Mental Disease, 165,* 213–217.

Elgin, D. (1993). *Voluntary simplicity* (2nd ed.). New York: William Morris.

Freud, S. (1962). *Civilization and its discontents.* New York: Norton.

Goldstein, J. (1983). *The experience of insight.* Boston: Shambhala.

Group for the Advancement of Psychiatry. (1976). *Mysticism: Spiritual quest or psychic disorder?* New York: Author.

Kornfield, J. (1979). Intensive insight meditation: A phenomenological study. *Journal of Transpersonal Psychology, 11,* 41–58.

Marks, L. E. (1975). On colored-hearing synesthesia: Cross modal translations of sensory dimensions. *Psychological Bulletin, 82,* 303–331.

Ram Dass. (1990). *Journey of awakening: A meditator's guidebook.* New York: Doubleday.

Satprem. (1968). *Sri aurobindo, or the adventure of consciousness.* New York: Harper and Row.

Schumacher, E. F. (1977). *A guide for the perplexed.* New York: Harper and Row.

Shapiro, D. (1980). *Meditation: Self regulation strategy and altered states of consciousness.* New York: Aldine.

Shapiro, D., and Walsh, R. (Eds.). (1986). *Meditation: Classic and contemporary perspectives.* New York: Aldine.

Tart, C. (1975). *States of consciousness.* New York: Dutton.

Tarthang Tulku. (1974). On thoughts. *Crystal Mirror, 3,* 7–20.

Walsh, R. N. (1976). Reflections on psychotherapy. *Journal of Transpersonal Psychology, 8,* 100–111.

Walsh, R. (1977). Initial meditative experiences: I. *Journal of Transpersonal Psychology, 9,* 151–192.

Walsh, R. (1978). Initial meditative experiences: II. *Journal of Transpersonal Psychology, 10,* 2–28.

Walsh, R. (1980). The consciousness disciplines and the behavioral sciences. *Journal of American Psychiatry, 137,* 663–673.

Walsh, R., and Shapiro, D. (Eds.). (1983). *Beyond health and normality: Explorations of extreme psychological well-being.* New York: Van Nostrand.

Wilber, K. (1977). *The spectrum of consciousness.* Wheaton, IL: Theosophical.

Chapter 36

METAPHOR THERAPY

RICHARD KOPP

This mode of therapy is an example of a system by an Adlerian, as are Encouragement Therapy, Immediate Therapy, Natural High Therapy, Impasse-Priority Therapy, and Primary Relationship Therapy. Alfred Adler's personality theory of Individual Psychology differs from both Freudian and Jungian systems in being open to every system and there are no limits, as can be seen by examining these other systems.

Richard Kopp has found that the device of focusing on metaphors presents a royal road to understanding of clients, much as Sigmund Freud used dreams. The system has a clearly defined pattern of steps, beginning with taking notice of metaphors and going on through changing the metaphor representing a client's current subjective experience. This procedure gives eclectic psychotherapists an additional tool to in their repertoire of therapeutic devices, one that may be particularly useful for some difficult cases.

DEFINITION

Metaphor Therapy describes a theory and method that identifies metaphor as a powerful source of insight and change in psychotherapy. Metaphor Therapy distinguishes between two broad categories of interventions, *client*-generated and *therapist*-generated metaphors, and introduces two new client-generated interventions: exploring and transforming a client's metaphoric language, and exploring and transforming a client's early memory metaphors. The power of these brief, structured interventions lies in their ability to help clients use their imaginations for creative problem solving of current conflicts and problems.

As a theoretical system, Metaphor Therapy proposes three frameworks for integrating cognitive, family systems, and psychodynamic therapies. First, a three-dimensional model of cognitive-affective processing views metaphor as a unique mode of mentation that integrates two other distinct cognitive modalities: propositional/syllogistic cognition and imaginal/sensory-affective processing. Second, it is proposed that individuals, families, social groups, cultures, and humanity as a whole structure reality metaphorically. The structure of individual reality is comprised of metaphoric representations of self, others, and situations, and relations among these: self-other, self-situation, and self-self. The metaphoric structure of family reality is found in the structure of family systems and subsystems, and in family communication and behavioral interaction patterns. The metaphoric structure of sociocultural and transcultural reality is revealed in language and myths, respectively. Third, metaphor is viewed as a common factor for promoting insight and change in many forms of individual and family therapy.

HISTORY

The word metaphor is derived from the Greek *meta,* meaning "above or over," and *pherein,* meaning "to carry or bear from one place to another." Thus, metaphor carries meaning from one domain to another. When Romeo declares, "Juliet is the sun," for example, the sun's qualities convey the meaning that is "carried over" to Juliet. Linguists refer to Juliet as the *topic* in this metaphor, and the sun as the *vehicle*—a fitting term (metaphor)—for that aspect of metaphor that "carries or bears" meaning from one thing or domain to another (Winner, 1988).

Aristotle held that to "metaphorize" well is a sign of genius in the poet and that "the greatest thing by far is to be the master of metaphor" (quoted in Ricoeur, 1984, p. 23). In Aristotle's view, metaphor involves giving a thing a name that belongs to something else. Ricoeur (1979) points out that, according to Aristotle, making good metaphors requires the capacity to contemplate similarities. Moreover, good metaphors are vivid because they can "set before the eyes" the sense that they display. It is through this "picturing function" that metaphoric meaning is conveyed (Ricoeur, 1979). In contrast, philosophers following a positivist tradition that emphasizes objectivity, fact, and logic have maintained that metaphors are frivolous and inessential. From this perspective, metaphors do not contain or transmit knowledge, have no direct connection with facts, and convey no genuine meaning (Cohen, 1979).

Because metaphors are untrue as literal statements (e.g., Juliet is not actually the sun), we can see why metaphor would be viewed as frivolous and inessential by those for whom reality and truth are restricted to the domain of literal meaning and logical thought. In the "either-or" domain of linear logic, sameness and difference are incompatible.

The positivist perspective has been challenged by recent developments in a variety of disciplines, including linguistics, philosophy, and cognitive psychology. Winner (1988) suggests that it wasn't until the 1970s that psycholinguists and cognitive psychologists became interested in metaphors because of their realization that metaphor was not a unique, atypical form of language found primarily in poetry. "Instead, metaphor was recognized as a pervasive aspect of ordinary language and as the primary vehicle for language change" (Winner, 1988, p. 16). Metaphors came to be appreciated as the root of the creativity and openness of language and thus as an essential aspect of cognition (Winner, 1988).

In her landmark book, *Philosophy in a New Key* (1942/1979), Langer presents a persuasive argument for the central role of metaphor in the evolution of language and symbolic thought in humans. Drawing on the work of Wegener, published in 1885, Langer suggests that metaphor is the principle through which literal language develops and that our literal language is the repository of "faded metaphors" (p. 140). Metaphor Therapy advances this view a step further; in other words, just as metaphor is the source of novelty and change in language, exploring and transforming a person's metaphoric imagery can be a source of novelty and change in psychotherapy.

I first became interested in metaphor as a source of data for identifying the Adlerian concept of lifestyle (Adler, 1956; Shulman & Mosak, 1988). For example, a client who repeatedly uses the metaphor, "I'm sinking in quicksand" might be seen as holding certain lifestyle beliefs such as "I am helpless; life is overwhelming, therefore I can't save myself." A key step in the development of Metaphor Therapy occurred as a result of my reading *Metaphors We Live By* by Lakoff and Johnson (1980).[1] These authors argue that we construct our social reality metaphorically. It occurred to me that their hypothesis may hold true for psychological reality as well. If so, then an individual's metaphoric language could be a direct expression and indicator of their metaphoric structure of personal reality.

This insight lead to a figure-ground shift in how I viewed metaphor—instead of regarding metaphor as a means for interpreting one's lifestyle beliefs and assumptions, metaphor could be seen as a direct expression of one's subjective experience. This awareness, in turn, leads to a broader hypothesis; the interpretation of a client's metaphors from any theoretical perspective can create distance from the client's spontaneous expression of his or her subjective experience and unconsciously rooted structure of reality. When this occurs, theoretically grounded interpretation serves to substitute the theorist's theoretical metaphors for the client's personal and spontaneously generated metaphors.

These theoretical developments raised an interesting question: Could interventions that use clients' creative imaginations to explore and change their metaphors in the domain of imagery, stimulate a change in the experiential meaning of the "topic" of the metaphor, or lead to change in the original situation? These issues are discussed below.

CURRENT STATUS

My book, *Metaphor Therapy: Using Client-Generated Metaphors in Psychotherapy* was published in 1995. I began developing the material for the book over the previous 12 years. Teaching courses in metaphoric approaches to psychotherapy at the California School of Professional Psychology (CSPP) at Los Angeles offered an opportunity to develop and refine the concepts and interventions with a wide range of clients in a variety of settings which serve as field placements for our students.

Since the publication of *Metaphor Therapy,* interest in this approach has grown steadily. Seminars in this approach have been offered at mental health facilities throughout Los Angeles, and professional presentations and workshops have been made at conferences, universities, graduate institutes, and mental health agencies in the United States and Canada. An eight-week multimedia distance learning course in Metaphor Therapy was developed in 1995 and is offered through CSPP Continuing Education. Students include counselors and therapists from China, Canada, and England. Metaphor Therapy is also offered as part of the curriculum of ICASSI (the International Committee on Adlerian Summer Schools and Institutes). This two-week 15-hour course has been taught in Austria, England, Canada, Holland, Ireland, and the United States. Workshops in "The Creative Imagination in Psychotherapy" that integrate Metaphor Therapy, psychodrama, and dream interpretation have been conducted in the United

---

[1] I would like to thank Lynn Thomas for suggesting this book to me.

States (in 1992[2], 1993, 1995, 1999) and Canada (in 1993). An Italian translation of *Metaphor Therapy* (*Le Metaphore—Nel Colloquio Clinico: L'uso delle Immagini Mentali del Cliente*) was published by the Milton Erickson Foundation of Italy in 1998.

THEORY

Viewing current approaches to individual and family therapies through the eyes of Metaphor Therapy highlights their shared metaphoric properties. There are four ways that Metaphor Therapy integrates various approaches to psychotherapy.

Metaphor: A Common Factor in Psychotherapy

Metaphor Therapy identifies metaphor as a specific class of therapeutic interventions that emphasizes metaphoric communication between client and therapist. Two broad categories are identified: client-generated metaphors and therapist-generated metaphors.

Two types of client-generated metaphoric interventions are introduced in the book, *Metaphor Therapy: Using Client-Generated Metaphors in Psychotherapy:* exploring and transforming a client's metaphoric language, and exploring and transforming a client's early memory metaphors. Interventions that use therapist-generated metaphors are found in psychodynamic, Ericksonian, and family systems approaches (especially Structural and Strategic family therapy). These include using metaphors to interpret psychodynamics and symptoms, and using metaphors to communicate and to suggest changes in family structure (Minuchin & Fishman, 1981), metaphoric enactments, and metaphoric stories and anecdotes (Lankton & Lankton, 1983). Madanes (1981) also identifies five levels in which a family member's symptom, such as physical neck pain, may be considered metaphoric for other family members' internal states and for various interactive patterns between and among family members. This is the first way in which Metaphor Therapy makes a contribution to psychotherapy integration: by showing that metaphoric interventions are a common factor in a variety of approaches to individual and family therapy.

A Three-Dimensional Theory of Cognition

Metaphor Therapy discusses three types of cognition. The first is logical/propositional cognition, also referred to in the cognitive science literature as syllogistic cognition (Kosslyn, 1980; Kosslyn & Koenig, 1992), which

---

[2] Available on videotape from the North American Society for Adlerian Psychology, Chicago, Illinois.

proceeds logically from premise to conclusion. Socrates' syllogism illustrates this form:

Major Premise: Men die.
Special Case: Socrates is a man.
Conclusion: Socrates will die.

The primary entities that cognitive therapy seeks to identify and change, such as core or irrational beliefs, schemas, and automatic thoughts, are represented using propositional cognition. For example, Beck, Rush, Shaw, and Emery (1979) suggest that dysfunctional cognitions function as rules that are often stated in if-then statements the person uses to make sense of the world.

Major Premise: "If I don't have love then I am worthless."
Special Case: "Raymond doesn't love me."
Conclusion: "I am worthless." (p. 100)

The second type of cognition is imaginal cognition. Research in cognitive science suggests that imagery is a form of cognition in its own right, existing independently of propositional cognition with its own set of rules, principles, and characteristics (see Kosslyn, 1980; Kosslyn & Koenig, 1992, for a summary of this research). Propositional cognition describes relationships using words, whereas imaginal cognition directly depicts relationships using images. Thus, the statement *the ball is on the box* describes the relationship between the ball and the box, while a mental image of a ball on a box directly depicts the relationship between the ball and the box (Kosslyn, 1980).

The third cognitive modality is metaphoric cognition, which draws on and integrates both propositional cognition and imaginal cognition. Metaphoric cognition is expressed in language through verbal metaphors—word-pictures in which an image is employed as a word to convey meaning (Kopp, 1995).

Langer (1942/1979) observes that when a precise word is lacking, we resort to the power of logical analogy by using a word that is a symbol for the thing that we mean. Langer's use of the term logical analogy highlights the quality of metaphor that integrates the logic of words and the "analogic" of imagery. Similarly, Lakoff and Johnson (1980) suggest that metaphor employs imaginative rationality which unites reason and imagination. Clearly, the concepts of logical analogy and imaginative rationality are consistent with the hypothesis that metaphoric cognition integrates imaginal and logical/propositional cognition (Kopp, 1995).

Freud notes that thinking in pictures (i.e., imaginal cognition) is closer to unconscious processes than thinking in words (Freud, 1923/1960). In contrast, we have noted that cognitive therapy emphasizes propositional cognition in formulating a client's automatic thoughts, beliefs, and schemas. By proposing a three-dimensional model of cognition that integrates propositional cognition and imaginal cognition, Metaphor Therapy offers a framework within which aspects of psychodynamic and cognitive approaches to psychotherapy may be integrated.

The Metaphoric Structure of Reality

The theory of Metaphor Therapy rests on the proposition that individuals, families, social groups, cultures, and humanity as a whole structure reality metaphorically. At an individual level, the metaphoric structure of reality is comprised of six substructures representing self, others, and life and the relations among these elements (i.e., self-in-relation-to-self, self-in-relation-to-others, and self-in-relation-to-life). Various approaches to individual psychotherapy (e.g., psychoanalytic/psychodynamic, Adlerian, Jungian, and Ericksonian hypnotherapy) are conceptualized as ways to understand and change the metaphoric structure of individual reality (Kopp, 1995).

At the family level, the metaphoric structure of reality involves the metaphoric structure of the family system and subsystems, and the metaphoric structure of family communication and behavioral interaction patterns. Structural and strategic approaches to family therapy make the important contributions to this level of understanding and changing the family's metaphoric structure of reality (Kopp, 1995).

At the sociocultural level, our language reflects the metaphoric structure of reality. For example, metaphors such as "He shot down my argument" or "I attacked the weak points in his argument" suggest that we speak and think of arguments as war in our society (Lakoff & Johnson, 1980). The metaphoric structure of sociocultural reality has implications for integrating social and cultural factors within a metatheory of psychotherapy (Kopp, 1995).

At the transcultural level, the metaphoric structure of transcultural reality resides in myths. Campbell (1986) notes that myth and archetype are universal metaphoric images. "Every myth . . . is *psychologically* symbolic. Its narratives and images are to be read, therefore, not literally, but as metaphors" (emphasis in original; p. 55). Taken together, Jung's concept of archetype, understood as a "universal metaphor," and Campbell's insight that myths in human culture reveal universal metaphoric images, suggest that myth and archetype point to a universal dimension of human experience—the metaphoric structure of transcultural reality (Kopp, 1995).

In summary, this multilevel theory of the metaphoric structure of reality offers a metatheoretical framework for integrating individual and family therapy. This is the third contribution that Metaphor Therapy makes to psychotherapy integration.

Metaphor in Mind and Brain: Toward a Neuropsychology of Metaphoric Language and Cognition

The theory of Metaphor Therapy also proposes hypotheses regarding the brain mechanisms that mediate linguistic and cognitive-affective metaphoric structures and processes. Hypotheses are also suggested that explore the neuropsychological processes involved in therapeutic changes produced by the client-generated metaphoric methods. Thus, Metaphor Therapy proposes an interdisciplinary model of how linguistic, cognitive, sensory-affective, and neuropsychological processes interact in the therapeutic change process. This the fourth way that Metaphor Therapy proposes an integrative model of psychotherapy.

Metaphor, Creativity, and Therapeutic Change

Clients often use metaphors to express their experience of themselves, others, and situations, such as "I feel like I'm the invisible man,"[3] "She treats me like a maid," "I'm up against a wall," "I can't handle this," and "I feel like I'm drowning." A Vietnam veteran complained that he was under "constant pressure," stating, "I feel like a tea kettle that can't let the steam out" (Kopp, 1995, p. 102). A woman who was angry with her estranged husband for repeatedly coming over to the house without calling in advance in spite of her persistent requests exclaimed, "He barges into the house like a locomotive" (Kopp, 1995, p. xiv).

Research on imaginal cognition, as well as reflections of creative physicists such as Einstein, Poincare, Bohr, and Heisenberg, suggest that imaginal cognition is essential to the creation of new ways of looking at things (Miller, 1986). These scientists emphasized the central role of mental imagery in contrast to purely syllogistic or verbal modes of thinking in their creative scientific work.

The metaphor-maker draws out of his or her imagination an image that resembles a pattern of meaning present in a specific situation to which the metaphor refers ("I'm just spinning my wheels at this job"). Metaphor Therapy posits that, because imaginal cognition plays a central role in metaphoric language and metaphoric cognition, metaphoric interventions that guide clients to explore, elaborate, and ultimately transform the imagery dimension of their metaphor can facilitate the therapeu-

---

[3] This phrase is technically a simile because the word "like" is employed; the true metaphoric form would be "I am the invisible man." Although simile and metaphor differ as linguistic forms, they are equivalent psychological forms (Kopp, 1995).

tic goal of creating new patterns, perspectives, meaning, and understanding (Kopp, 1995).

METHODOLOGY

Metaphor Therapy identifies two brief, structured interventions for working with client-generated metaphors. In the first method, the therapist chooses a metaphor that has been generated by a client and guides the client in exploring his or her metaphoric imagery. Thus, the therapist's first task is to develop the ability to listen for and identify metaphors. This skill requires practice because our natural tendency is to attend to the topic of the metaphor (i.e., the situation, person, or relationship to which the metaphor refers) rather than to the vehicle (imagery) used to convey meaning about the topic. Therapists can facilitate this process by keeping a metaphor log in which they record metaphors that others use, and a second metaphor log for recording metaphors that they use in their own spoken communication. For most people, noticing metaphors used by others is easier than attending to one's own metaphoric speech. Also, experience has shown that it is necessary to write down the metaphors as they occur because most people find it extremely difficult, if not impossible, to remember metaphors used even several minutes earlier. It appears that, like dreams, metaphoric imagery tends to fade from memory in the face of our dominant linear verbal logical mode of communication and cognition.

It has been interesting to observe that therapists tend to move through a sequence of stages in the process of acquiring the ability to listen to metaphoric speech. In the first stage the therapist primarily attends to the content of the client's communication and misses most of the metaphors present in the client's speech. For example, a therapist at this stage would not pick up on the metaphor used in the previous sentence ("misses") or in the present sentence ("not pick up on"). In the second phase, the therapist begins to hear and identify metaphors. The therapist knows that he or she has progressed to the third phase when metaphors seem to appear "all over the place"; so much so, in fact, that many therapists report have difficulty attending to the content of what their clients are talking about. This conflict between attending to metaphoric language and the content (topic) of communication highlights the dual-channel nature of metaphoric communication and linear verbal communication. The former relies on imagery and analogy, while the latter emphasizes words and logic. With practice, this stage yields to the final stage, in which the therapist can note and quickly jot down key metaphors in the client's speech while continuing to attend and respond to the consent of the client's communication.

Once the therapist has learned to identify their clients' linguistic metaphors, the therapist must decide which metaphor to explore. The therapist's clinical experience and judgment is essential in this regard, since metaphors that are most helpful tend to be those which point to key issues in the therapy and core dynamics in the client. When more than one metaphor seems potentially fruitful for exploration, the client can be asked which they feel might be potentially helpful to explore.

Experience has shown that metaphors which include a representation of self in the metaphor (e.g., "I feel like a tea kettle that can't let the steam out," "I feel like I'm walking on eggshells with him," or "I feel like I'm sinking in quicksand") tend to be more helpful than metaphors that refer only to situations or others. One way of dealing with this situation is to begin with a metaphor for another or for a situation and then ask the client to create a metaphoric image in which the client represents himself or herself in relation to the other or the situation. For example, the client who referred to her husband, saying "He barges into the house like a locomotive" was asked by her therapist, "If your husband is a locomotive, how do you picture yourself?" After some thought, she said, "I guess I'm the tunnel."

Once the metaphor has been selected, the intervention continues with the therapist asking, "When you say [the metaphor], what image comes to mind?" This question invites the client to shift his or her attention from the external situation to the image used by the client to convey the client's subjective experience of the situation. Using prompts such as "What else do you see?," "Is anything else going on in the image?," and "What was happening just before this image?," the therapist encourages the client to elaborate the metaphoric image and to explore the feelings and experience associated with the imagery. Note that these questions are relatively nondirective, and the therapist is cautioned to avoid directive inquiry that intrudes on the content of the client's imagery. For example, a client told her therapist that she felt like she was sinking in quicksand. Instead of asking the client to describe what image came to mind as she pictured herself sinking in quicksand, the therapist asked, "How deep is the quicksand?" By asking a question about the depth of the quicksand, the therapist introduced his or her own concerns and interests and directed the client's attention to respond to this dimension. In so doing, the therapist interrupted the client's inner exploration and elaboration of the metaphor.

A key moment in this intervention typically occurs when the therapist invites the client to change the image, asking, "If you could change the image in any way, how would you change it?" In the last phase of the intervention, clients are invited to explore the connections between their metaphoric imagery and the original situation. They are then asked, "Does the way in which you changed your image suggest any ways in which you might better deal with your problem?"

It should be emphasized that the effective use of this intervention hinges on the therapist's skill in keeping clients focused on the client's imagery in contrast to the actual situation, or to the therapist's imagery that emerges in response to the client's description of his or her imagery. It is the client's work—the therapist guides the process, the client creates the content.[4]

The second intervention uses a structured interview protocol to elicit an early childhood memory that will be a metaphor for a problem situation the client is experiencing. The client is asked to focus on where they are "most stuck" with the problem they are discussing, and then to think of a recent time this problem occurred. The client recalls the incident as vividly as possible, using as many aspects of sensory memory as they can. The client is given time to silently form a vivid image of the incident "so that you begin to get the feelings in your body now that you had at the time of the incident." When the client reports that they are feeling the feelings in their body, the therapist asks, "What is the first early childhood memory that comes to mind right now . . . the first image from childhood that pops into your mind right now?" The early recollection—a one-time, specific incident from childhood—is elicited and recorded by the therapist (Adler, 1956; Mosak, 1958). Once the memory is collected, the therapist invites the client to change the memory, asking, "If you could change the memory in any way, how would you change it?" The changed memory is described in detail by the client and recorded by the therapist.

In the last phase of the intervention, the therapist reads the original memory back to the client and asks the client what parallels or connections the client sees between the original early memory and their current problem. The therapist then reads back the changed memory, asking the client to listen to the changed memory to see if it suggests to the client any ideas the client may use in the current situation.

We have observed that the changed memory can provide a guide for new approaches to the problem situation when the client has changed themselves (what they said or did or how they reacted) in the memory. Clients who change the situation or who focus on changing the way others behave in the memory tend to find these changes not very helpful because they cannot change the current situation or the response of others in the current life. This awareness can be extremely helpful, however, because clients can realize that their inability to solve or improve their current situation is due to the fact that they are relying on a change that they cannot create.

---

[4] This distinction is credited to Achi Yotam, an Israeli Adlerian therapist.

APPLICATIONS

Psychotherapy

One or both interventions described above have been used in brief and long-term psychotherapy with a wide variety of patients and in a wide variety of settings. Because they can be completed within a single session, they can be used effectively in brief psychotherapy (Kopp, 1989) and thus are especially well-suited for clients covered by managed care insurance or who are members of health maintenance organizations.

Early memory metaphors have been used to uncover unconscious countertransference issues that contribute to resistance and impasse in psychotherapy (Kopp & Robles, 1989; Maybell, Christensen, Kopp, & Powers, 1992). The use of early memory metaphors in psychotherapy has been compared to the role that early recollections play in Adlerian therapy (Kopp, 1998).

Kopp and Craw (1998) explored the implications of Metaphor Therapy for the theory and practice of cognitive therapy. It was proposed that client-generated linguistic metaphors represent deep, tacit metaphoric knowledge that can be directly accessed, explored, and ultimately transformed by the client, creating the potential for new insights into the nature of the client's problems and new possibilities for constructive problem solving. These authors conclude that Metaphor Therapy offers a theory of cognition and meaning that incorporates metaphoric, imaginal, and analogic processes along with verbal/logical cognitive forms found in traditional cognitive approaches. Within this broader theoretical framework, metaphor can play an important role in cognitive therapy.

Diversity

Developing therapeutic approaches that are responsive to issues of human diversity such as ethnicity, sexual orientation, and gender has gained increasing importance. Sue and Zane (1987) point out that therapists' knowledge of the general characteristics typical of various large cultural and ethnic groups may or may not impact the outcome of psychotherapy. These variables are "distal" to therapeutic outcomes because knowledge about these factors must be transformed into concrete therapist behaviors (therapeutic strategies and procedures). The meanings of ethnicity are more important than ethnicity itself because they are more likely to influence therapy outcomes (Sue, 1988). Thus, the client's problems must be understood by the therapist in a manner that is congruent with the client's belief system (Sue & Zane, 1987). The client-generated metaphors described earlier aid both therapist and client to expand and deepen their understanding of the client's belief system.

Dwairy (1997) notes that psychologists who work with nonwestern clients who adopt traditional nonwestern cultural beliefs are faced with a decision. They can emphasize their scientific, objective-psychological language, or they can develop intervention techniques that fit the client's metaphoric-physical language (which is characteristic of nonwestern cultures that have a non-dualistic, holistic view of reality) without differentiating between mind and body. Dwairy (1997) identifies Metaphor Therapy as a way of avoiding psychologically based interpretation and instead facilitating the clients' inner searches through their own metaphoric imagery. He concludes that this type of metaphoric work influences the mind-body system and helps clients from nonwestern cultures to find solutions within their own sociocultural beliefs.

Organizations

Metaphor Therapy has been applied in organizations and to workplace coaching (Kopp, 1999). Metaphor bridges the gap between internal, subjective, psychological dynamics and external, objective, organizational dynamics. Thus, helping executives, managers, and others explore and transform their metaphoric representations of organizational problems helps them to create new actions they can take to implement organizational solutions that are consistent with their own beliefs and values.

CASE EXAMPLE

Exploring and Transforming Spoken Metaphors[5]

TJ, a 29-year-old female, sought individual therapy to help her deal with symptoms of depression.[6] She reported feeling sad and anxious, having difficulty sleeping, feeling lonely, and having difficulty engaging in and maintaining social and romantic relationships.

Step 1: Notice Metaphors

TJ discussed her feeling of depression in an early therapy session, stating that she was doing a lot of schoolwork but feeling like she wasn't doing enough. TJ said that "I feel like I'm barely treading water." The therapist chose to explore this metaphor because it was a vivid representation of TJ's experience and because TJ used it several times to describe her experience and feelings in different situations. The repeated use of a metaphor such as "I feel

---

[5] This case example and discussion (pp. 742–748) is adapted from Kopp (1999). Used with permission.

[6] The author would like to thank Lisa Staab, who was the therapist for this case.

like I'm barely treading water" suggests that it is likely to reflect a personality pattern. Thus, TJ's feeling that she is barely treading water with regard to her schoolwork represents one instance of a broader lifestyle theme.

Step 2: Describing the Metaphoric Image

THERAPIST (T): When you say that you are barely treading water, what image comes to mind?

CLIENT (TJ): Well (pause), it's like I'm out in the middle of the ocean, treading water.

Step 3: Exploring the Metaphor as a Sensory Image

T: While you're out there in the middle of the ocean, treading water, what else do you see?

TJ: Well, there's a lot of water all around me, and I'm trying to swim in it but I feel like I'm barely moving. The water is cold and I think it's pretty deep.

T: What else in going on in the image?

TJ: Well, there's just a lot of water, it's a really big ocean. And there's an island, but it's pretty far away.

T: What led up to this? If this were a scene in a movie, what would the scene before it look like?

TJ: I was on a boat. A really big boat, a brown one.

T: What was happening on the boat?

TJ: My family was there. I'm not sure what they were doing, but I wanted to get off; I didn't want to be on the boat any more. So I jumped overboard. Then the boat left. I'm not sure if the rest of the family even noticed that I was gone . . . that I wasn't on the boat anymore.

Step 4: Describing Feelings Associated with the Metaphor.

T: So you are in the ocean treading water. What are you feeling?

TJ: I'm scared to be trying to stay afloat because the ocean is so big and so deep, but I am happy that I am not on the boat anymore.

Step 5: Transforming the Metaphoric Image

T: If you could change your image in any way, how would you change it?

TJ: Well . . . I wouldn't be staying still in the water, treading water, I guess I would be on the island.

T: How would you get there?

TJ: I would swim.

T: What would your image look like then?

TJ: I would be lying on the sand on the island, and it would be warm and sunny . . . and I would be drying off and getting warm. I wouldn't be so tired anymore.

Step 6: Making Connections between the Metaphor and the Original Problem Situation

T: What connections do you see between your image of treading water and your original problem regarding your school situation?

TJ: (Smiles and laughs; pauses) Well, I can definitely see some connections. Sometimes I feel like I'm working hard but going nowhere in school, just like I was working hard but going nowhere treading water.

T: What about your "before" image of being on the boat and jumping into the water? Do you see any parallels there?

TJ: Well, yeah, 'cause I was with my family. I wanted to get out of that house so badly, just like I wanted to jump off the boat. I didn't feel like they really wanted me there.

T: And about them not noticing you jumping. . . .

TJ: Well, I felt like they never noticed me while I was there, they never paid attention to me. So why should they notice me when I'm gone? They still hardly ever talk to me, except for one of my brothers who I talk to on the phone sometimes.

Step 7: Relating the Changed Metaphoric Image to the Current Situation

T: And what about your changed image? How might the way you changed the image apply to your problems with your schoolwork?

TJ: Well, I guess the biggest thing is that I have to try to stop wasting my energy on being afraid and on beating myself up, and work on moving toward, or "swimming" toward my goal, which is a four-year college. I guess I'm just so afraid that my grades won't be good enough for me to get in.

T: Could it be that treading water is a way of protecting yourself because it keeps you from getting closer to confronting your fear that you will be rejected from a four-year college?

TJ: Yeah.

T: How might you help yourself move toward the island?

TJ: I've just got to stop being so frightened, and look at my goals rather than trying to avoid thinking about them.

T: From what you have told me, it sounds like you have a really good chance of getting into a lot of the schools that you are applying to.

TJ: Yeah, thanks. As long as I don't stop swimming.

Results of the Intervention

TJ seemed to develop insight in the connections she made between her image and the original situation, and

was able to use her changed metaphor to help her focus on her goal of attending a four-year college. TJ was less self-critical in subsequent therapy sessions and reported being more productive in her academic work. She also began taking tours of universities to which she had been thinking of applying, and met with a member of the admissions committee at a major university to find out more about their admissions process.

TJ became more willing to explore the childhood origins of her fears and self-critical thoughts. The therapist reported that the biggest change was her discussion of her childhood experiences and family dynamics, which she had avoided in earlier sessions. For example, she began to explore her feelings about being alternately criticized and ignored by her parents, and looked at how that may have influenced her lifestyle regarding meeting the tasks of work, love, and friendship.

Discussion

The metaphor, "I'm barely treading water," is a *self-situation* metaphor, because the "self" is represented in the metaphor as the one who is treading water, the situation (schoolwork) is represented in the metaphor by the water, and the feeling of working on her schoolwork without making progress is symbolized by the activity of barely treading water. The metaphor expresses TJ's subjective experience, meaning and movement of self in relation to her school workload. Vaihinger noted that "All cognition is the apperception of one thing through another. In understanding we are always dealing with analogy" (Adler, 1956, p. 79). Vaihinger's "as if" philosophy is expressed in metaphoric language and metaphoric thinking. For example, TJ creates the metaphoric image of "I'm barely treading water" to symbolize and communicate the apperceptive meaning of her school workload. Note that the comparison is not literal—TJ is not actually treading water. Rather, the metaphor communicates that it is *as if* TJ is barely treading water. This metaphor also conveys TJ's movement with respect to her school workload; in other words, exerting energy but not making any progress and barely being able to keep her head above water.

As TJ expands and develops her metaphor in Step 3 she draws on her creative imagination to create a story—a kind of waking dream—that starts with and elaborates her metaphor of "I'm barely treading water." Step 3 also invites the client to create a history to the current metaphoric imagery. TJ introduces the image of a "really big boat" and places her family on it. By creating this history of what preceded her treading water, TJ links the metaphor of barely treading water to an earlier decision of jumping overboard to escape her family. This reframes the meaning of being in the ocean and symbolizes the fact that her current experience in college is related to her decision to be independent from her family. This eventually leads to a new conscious perspective, expressed in Step 4; although TJ is still "scared to be trying to stay afloat because the ocean is so big and deep," she now is aware that "I am happy that I am not on the boat anymore."

Step 5 invites the client to change the metaphoric image, thereby introducing the opportunity to create new possibilities for movement and problem solving in the domain of metaphoric imagery. TJ says that she would no longer be treading water, and then adds, "I guess I would be on the island." The therapist wisely asks, "How would you get there?," encouraging TJ to create a visual image of how she might get from her current (metaphorically represented) situation of treading water to being on the island. This is a way that clients are helped to create a solution to their problem in the domain of metaphoric imagery using their creative imagination. Later in the interview protocol (Step 7), TJ will be invited to use the metaphoric solution as a guide to exploring what she might do in the actual situation which was represented by the original metaphor.

Step 6 invites clients to gain deeper insight into the problem situation by drawing parallels between their imaginative exploration and elaboration of their metaphor on the one hand and their current situation on the other. We can see how TJ's images of being on the boat with her family and then deciding to jump off the boat become a metaphor for her actual experience with her family. Note that the images become metaphors as TJ creates connections between the images and her current life situation. For example, the image of jumping off the boat is not a metaphor in and of itself. However, the image becomes a metaphor when TJ creates a resemblance between this image and her decision to get out of the house. Thus, clients create metaphoric meanings with each connection they create between the imagery they have generated and how that imagery represents the actual situation in their life.

In Step 7, TJ creates the image of swimming as an alternative movement to treading water. She also appears to have developed insights regarding the relationship between treading water and her self-criticism, and that swimming represents movement toward her goal of attending a four-year college.

Exploring and Transforming Early Memory Metaphors[7]

John, a 33-year-old White male, has been married for almost two years. In recent weeks, John has begun to snore

[7] Adapted from Kopp (1995), pp. 46–50. The author would like to thank Daniel Goldberg, PhD, who was the therapist in this case example.

so loudly that it seriously disturbed his wife's sleep. After a brief discussion of the problem, the therapist begins the intervention with the question:

T: Where in all of this are you most stuck?

J: It scares me that my snoring could stop us from sleeping together. It's really upsetting to think that I'm driving away the person I love most. And there's nothing I can do about it. I mean, snoring is involuntary.

T: Can you remember a recent time when you felt this way?

J: Yes . . . a few nights ago when my wife spent part of the night on the living room couch because of my snoring.

T: I'd like you to form an image in your mind of that situation . . . the part of it that stands out most for you. [Pause] Picture it as vividly as you can . . . where you were . . . what was happening . . . what was being said. [Pause] Picture that scene as vividly as you can, so that you begin to feel the feelings that you felt in that situation in your body now: [Pause. T watches as J silently recalls his recent example of the problem.] Are you feeling the feelings in your body now?

J: Yes.

T: What's the first early childhood memory that comes to mind right now . . . the first image from childhood that pops into your mind right now?

J: I remember when I was five, Fred [John's older brother] and I were staying with my aunt and uncle. My parents were on a vacation, and my aunt and uncle were taking care of us. Anyway, while I was there I really got sick. In fact, I came down with pneumonia. I remember having to get sponge baths to get my temperature down, and I had a hacking cough. I would cough all night and Fred would get really angry at me. The two of us were sharing a room. He'd keep on yelling at me to be quiet. He didn't believe that I couldn't stop myself from coughing. At one point, he tells me if I cough one more time, he's gonna go sleep somewhere else and leave me by myself. So, I try to stop myself from coughing, but of course, within seconds I cough, and Fred jumps out of bed and grabs his blanket and his pillow and starts to leave. So I start crying and beg him not to go. I mean you know, I was feeling really sick and homesick too, and I didn't want to be left alone. But he just left, and I was all alone. [Pause] I guess that's about it.

T: Okay. As you think about what you just told me, what stands out most for you? If you were to take a snapshot of the most vivid moment in the memory, what image stands out most?

J: Just me sitting up in bed, crying and coughing while Fred is storming out of the room.

T: How did you feel at that moment?

J: Alone and hurt.

T: Why did you feel that way?

J: Because Fred was leaving, and he was angry with me.

T: If you could change the memory in any way so that it would be ideal—the way you would have liked it to turn out—how would you change it?

J: All right, let's see. Well, first of all, my brother wouldn't have yelled at me. Maybe he would have said in a nice way that my coughing was keeping him awake—that he knew I couldn't help it, but that it was still bothering him. Maybe we would have talked for a little while and he would have been really understanding and sympathetic. I know. Maybe he would have gone and woken up my aunt and asked her to give me some cough medicine. [Laughing] And maybe she would have given him some earplugs. That would have been good.

T: What stands out most vividly in the changed memory?

J: Me in bed, coughing but also smiling. And my brother would be getting into bed with earplugs in his ears. And we'd both be laughing about the earplugs.

T: And how would you be feeling?

J: I'd be feeling good. I mean, I'd still be sick, but I'd be feeling happy inside . . . and safe.

T: And what is it that would be making you feel that way?

J: That my brother cared about me and that he was there to look out for me.

T: Now I'm going to read the memory, and I'd like you to tell me any connections you see between the memory and your current situation with your wife.

J: Okay.

T: [Reads the memory.] What connections do you see between the memory and you current situation?

J: I guess the snoring is pretty much the same thing that the coughing was. Well, I mean, they're different, but the effect is the same. Both are something I can't help and something that leads to me being alone. My wife left the room the other night, just like my brother did. I mean, she didn't act mad or anything, but I still felt hurt. I don't know, it was like I was being abandoned.

T: And that does hurt.

J: Yeah. [Pause] You know, I wonder if that's why this whole thing bothers me so much. I mean, I haven't thought about that coughing thing for a long time. But at the time, it was a big deal. It really upset me. And now this situation is so similar. It's kind of funny [laughs].

T: What feels funny to you?

J: I don't know, I guess it's just the whole snoring thing seemed to be such a big deal. I mean, when I woke up and realized that Joan [his wife] wasn't in bed with me

and then I found her on the couch in the living room, I got really upset. She even said that I was making too big a deal about the whole thing. But it scared me.

T: It made you feel . . . unsafe.

J: Yeah.

T: Now I'd like to read back your changed memory, and see if your changed memory suggests any things that might be helpful to you in dealing with your current situation.

J: Okay.

T: [Reads the changed memory.] Does this give you any ideas in terms of your current situation?

J: Well . . . [Laughs] Yeah! My wife could get earplugs. I mean, it sounds funny, but it could work. We didn't think of it . . . Well, to be honest, we didn't really talk about it at all. I was too upset. I guess that's the main thing—we have to sit down and discuss the problem like two adults—two adults who love each other.

T: In your revised memory your brother went to ask your aunt for help.

J: Yeah, well, I don't know. I really don't want to ask . . . Well, actually, about a month ago I was at the doctor, sitting in the waiting room, and I saw this pamphlet about snoring. [Laughs] This is gonna sound really dumb, but I didn't pick it up because I thought someone would see me and think that I have a problem with snoring. Well, anyway, I guess that might be worth looking into.

SUMMARY

Therapist-generated metaphoric interventions have been used for quite some time in psychodynamic, Ericksonian, and family systems approaches to psychotherapy. Metaphor Therapy introduces two new methods for using client-generated metaphors in psychotherapy. By helping clients identify, explore, ultimately transform their metaphors, therapist are better able to understand the subjective experience and cognitive belief system that is reflected in their clients' metaphoric speech and early memory metaphors. Using structured interview protocols, these interventions also empower clients to create self-generated insight and new directions for constructive problem solving. Because both of these methods are brief, they are especially well-suited for short-term psychotherapy.

As a theory, Metaphor Therapy proposes four ways that various approaches to psychotherapy may be integrated. First, by taking a transtheoretical approach to the role of metaphor in psychotherapy, Metaphor Therapy demonstrates that metaphoric interventions are a common factor in a variety of schools of individual and family therapy. Second, Metaphor Therapy proposes a three-dimensional model of cognition that views metaphoric cognition as a distinct cognitive modality that integrates propositional (logical) cognition and imaginal cognition. This framework offers the possibility of integrating psychoanalytic therapy approaches that draw heavily on imaginal processes with cognitive therapies that emphasize automatic thoughts, cognitive beliefs, and cognitive schemas using propositional forms of cognition. Third, Metaphor Therapy proposes a multilevel theory of the metaphoric structure of reality, suggesting that, as humans, we structure our individual, family, social/cultural, and mythological transcultural reality metaphorically. This multilevel theory has the potential to integrate individual, family, and sociocultural elements of psychotherapy. Finally, Metaphor Therapy offers a range of interdisciplinary hypotheses regarding how linguistic, cognitive, sensory-affective, and neuropsychological processes may interact to produce therapeutic change.

REFERENCES

Adler, A. (1956). *The Individual Psychology of Alfred Adler: A systematic presentation in selections from his writings.* New York: Basic.

Beck, A., Rush, A., Shaw, B., & Emery, G. (1979). *Cognitive therapy of depression.* New York: Guilford.

Campbell, J. (1986). *The inner reaches of outer space: Metaphor as myth and as religion.* New York: Harper & Row.

Cohen, T. (1979). Metaphor and the cultivation of intimacy. In S. Sacks (Ed.), *On metaphor* (pp. 1–10). Chicago: University of Chicago Press.

Dwairy, M. (1997). A biopsychosocial model of metaphor therapy with holistic cultures. *Clinical Psychology Review, 17*(7), 719–732.

Freud, S. (1923/1960). *The ego and the id.* New York: W. W. Norton.

Kopp, R. (1989). Holistic-metaphorical therapy and Adlerian brief therapy. *Individual Psychology: The Journal of Adlerian Theory, Research, and Practice, 45*(1 & 2), 57–61.

Kopp, R. (1995). *Metaphor therapy: Using client-generated metaphors in psychotherapy.* New York: Brunner/Mazel.

Kopp, R. (1998). Early recollections in Adlerian and metaphor therapy. *Journal of Individual Psychology, 54*(4), 480–486.

Kopp, R. (1999, March). *Metaphoric methods of corporate coaching.* Course presented at the Adler School of Professional Psychology, Toronto, Ontario, Canada.

Kopp, R. (1999). Clinical strategies column: Metaphoric expressions of lifestyle: Exploring and transforming client-generated metaphors. *Journal of Individual Psychology, 55*(4), 466–473.

Kopp, R., & Craw, M. (1998). Metaphoric language, metaphoric cognition, and cognitive therapy. *Psychotherapy, 35*(3), 306–311.

Kopp, R., & Robles, L. (1989). Single session supervision and Adlerian psychotherapy. *Individual Psychology: The Journal of Adlerian Theory, Research, and Practice, 45*(1), 212–219.

Kosslyn, S. (1980). *Image and mind.* Cambridge: Harvard University Press.

Kosslyn, S., & Koenig, O. (1992). *Wet mind: The new cognitive neuroscience.* New York: Free Press.

Lakoff, G., & Johnson, M. (1980). *Metaphors we live by.* Chicago: University of Chicago Press.

Langer, S. (1942/1979). *Philosophy in a new key: A study in the symbolism of reason, rite, and art.* Cambridge: Harvard University Press.

Lankton, S., & Lankton, C. (1983). *The answer within: A clinical framework of Ericksonian hypnotherapy.* New York: Brunner/Mazel.

Madanes, C. (1981). *Strategic family therapy.* San Francisco: Jossey-Bass.

Maybell, S., Christensen, O., Kopp, R., & Powers, R. (1992, June). *Adlerian case supervision.* Paper presented at the 40th Annual Convention of the North American Society of Adlerian Psychology, Chicago, IL.

Miller, A. I. (1986). *Imagery in scientific thought: Creating 20th-century physics.* Cambridge: The MIT Press.

Minuchin, S., & Fishman, H. C. (1981). *Family therapy techniques.* Cambridge: Harvard University Press.

Mosak, H. (1958). Early recollections as a projective technique. *Journal of Projective Techniques, 22*(3), 302–311.

Ricoeur, P. (1979). The metaphorical process. In S. Sacks (Ed.), *On metaphor* (pp. 151–157). Chicago: University of Chicago Press.

Ricoeur, P. (1984). *The rule of metaphor: Multi-disciplinary studies of the creation of meaning in language.* Toronto, Ontario: University of Toronto Press.

Shulman, B., and Mosak, H. (1988). *Manual for lifestyle assessment.* Muncie, IN: Accelerated Development.

Sue, S. (1988). Psychotherapeutic services for ethnic minorities: Two decades of research findings. *American Psychologist, 43*(4), 301–308.

Sue, S., & Zane, N. (1987). The role of culture and cultural techniques in psychotherapy. *American Psychologist, 42*(1), 37–45.

Winner, E. (1988). *The point of words: Children's understanding of metaphor and irony.* Cambridge: Harvard University Press.

Chapter 37 ———————————————————

MORITA PSYCHOTHERAPY

DAVID K. REYNOLDS[1]

I was quite fortunate in being able to persuade David K. Reynolds to write this chapter on Morita Therapy as well as the one on Naikan. I was very eager to get some Asian systems in this book, and through the efforts of my friend Dr. Paul B. Pedersen I eventually was able to persuade Dr. Reynolds to contribute the two chapters.

Morita is quite similar to an almost completely forgotten rest treatment approach to the treatment of neurotic conditions, originally developed by Dr. S. Wier Mitchell, a psychiatrist who died in 1914. From one point of view both systems involve regression to infancy. From another point of view Morita is a stern injunction that people should do their duty and accept their feelings.

In this chapter, the perceptive reader will learn that many apparently complicated systems essentially are based on simple injunctions about life, such as "Do your duty" or "Suffer without complaining." Here is a simple, novel, and workable system applicable to any society.

Morita Psychotherapy is a Buddhist-based treatment for neurosis developed in Japan by Shoma Morita, a psychiatrist, around the turn of this century. Through verbal instruction and guided activity the therapy aims at teaching the patient to accept his or her symptoms as part of everyday reality. The patient learns to live a constructive life in spite of feelings of shyness, anxiety, tension, and fears.

HISTORY

The first paper on Morita Therapy appeared in 1917. It outlined a treatment method developed during the previous 15 years by a Japanese psychiatrist named Shoma Morita. A graduate of Tokyo University and chairman of the department of psychiatry and neurology at Jikei University School of Medicine, Morita was influenced by both Eastern and Western treatment modalities. His method grew out of his personal experience as a self-cured neurotic, his practical experience treating Japanese patients, and his familiarity with contemporary Western modes of treatment.

As a young man Morita suffered from a variety of neurotic complaints, including inability to concentrate, death anxiety, palpitations, and gastrointestinal complaints. The more he struggled with himself in an at-

tempt to overcome these problems, the deeper he found himself enmeshed in them. Only after "giving up" on the struggle and focusing on the tasks at hand did his symptoms recede. Morita began applying the same approach to his patients, generally treating them in his home so that they could see the working out of his thought in everyday life.

Specific techniques were borrowed from S. Wier Mitchell's system of absolute bed rest and Paul Dubois's method of regulated living, but these external forms were put to different uses. For example, Wier Mitchell saw neurosis as a physiological exhaustion of the nervous system that required long-term bed rest for recuperation. Morita used the bed-rest method, but he, like Freud, perceived the essentially psychological nature of neurosis and so employed bed rest in order to affect the mental state of his patients.

Following Morita's death in 1938, students and former patients carried on the treatment method within an inpatient setting. After World War II outpatient treatment became increasingly popular among Morita therapists, although Moritist hospitals have not yet disappeared from the scene. In the late 1960s a nationwide Moritist mental health organization emerged with chapters in all the major cities of Japan. Called Seikatsu no Hakkenkai (literally "The Discovery of Life Organization"), this movement is now the most powerful force for uniting practitioners, developing theory, and training new therapists.

---

[1] Case material by Radmila Moacamin.

Historically, Morita Therapy has moved from a narrow inpatient focus to encompass outpatient therapy, group therapy, public education, and recently, therapy by correspondence and cassette tapes. Similarly, the power base has moved from Jikei University to several Japanese universities (Kyushu, Okayama, and Hamamatsu) and finally, out of the university system altogether into the public organization mentioned above. Correspondingly, the initial core of psychiatrists (e.g., Nomura, Noda, Kora, and Suzuki) has been augmented by communications professionals, psychologists, physicians in other specialties, and laypersons who have had personal experience with Morita's methods (Morita & Mizutani, 1956).

Similar trends may be seen in the broadened definitions of which sorts of patients may be appropriately treated by this therapy (see "Applications" section). Furthermore, widening theoretical perspectives have gradually permitted other therapies (such as hypnosis, Behavior Therapy, and autogenic training) to be used in conjunction with this method (Yokoyama, 1968; Ohara & Reynolds, 1968).

In sum, Morita Therapy has been able to maintain a core theory and practice while adapting to the extreme sociocultural changes in Japan over the past 80 years. It was introduced in the United States in the late 1940s. Classical Freudians did not accept it because it refused to deal directly with the unconscious (Jacobsen & Berenberg, 1952), but it received a more sympathetic reception among neo-Freudians such as Horney (Kondo, 1953). Formal training of American psychiatrists, psychologists, and social workers in Morita Therapy began in the early 1970s at the University of Southern California School of Medicine (Reynolds, 1976). Although English-language articles on the subject have existed for 30 years, the first book in English on Morita Psychotherapy appeared in 1976 (Reynolds, 1976).

CURRENT STATUS

Morita Therapy is currently being practiced on an inpatient basis in many hospitals and clinics in Japan. In addition, therapists at these facilities treat outpatients with the method, as do physicians at several university outpatient clinics (among them Jikei University, Hamamatsu University, and Okayama University). The national Seikatsu no Hakkenkai organization has a large membership. The central office of Hakkenkai is in Tokyo. Local chapters meet monthly throughout Japan with supplemental retreats and training courses offered widely.

There is a vast literature on the subject in Japanese. A number of scholarly and popular books dealing with Morita Therapy appear each year. The Hakkenkai organization publishes a monthly magazine, and several Moritist hospitals also put out magazines for patients and former patients.

The impact of Morita's ideas on psychotherapy in Japan cannot be accurately assessed by the number of psychotherapists who call themselves Morita therapists. Just as Freud's ideas have permeated the psychotherapeutic establishment in the West, providing a reference point for agreement or dissent, so Morita's ideas have provided a benchmark for practice in Japan even though the number of trained Morita therapists probably is less than 100.

In the United States nearly 100 psychiatrists, clinical psychologists, and social workers have received some formal training in Morita Therapy. Only a handful of practitioners have had direct supervision, however. Until 1979 training was centered at the University of Southern California School of Medicine. There are Morita therapists practicing on an outpatient basis in the Los Angeles, San Francisco, and Houston areas.

THEORY

The flow of awareness and attention is the basis of understanding neurosis and psychotherapy, because that flow is all that any of us knows. The stream of consciousness normally flows from topic to topic in concert with the requirements of the situations in which we find ourselves. Each moment brings ongoing or fresh "tasks" that require our attention and appropriate response. These "tasks" may be weeding a garden, following a conversation, daydreaming, writing an article, planning a vacation, answering a telephone, and the like. The awareness of a mature individual recognizes these tasks and loses itself in them. The healthy person finds himself immersed in constructive activity (including the constructive behaviors of napping, recreation, and so forth).

The flow of awareness in the neurotic person is blocked and turned inward, away from the circumstances in which he finds himself. The neurotic person is characteristically *self*-centered in the sense that he is attending to internal events—shyness, fear, sadness, feelings of abandonment or inferiority—rather than to the environment. He may be living in a world of unreality, not the unreality of the psychotic world, but the unreality of "I wish," "if only she had," "I shouldn't have," "what if," and so forth (Reynolds, 1980). Again, attention has drifted from what *is* to what could happen or what did not happen. The beginning of realistic change comes with acceptance of what is. Acceptance of reality is not passive, it is the only first step for active intervention in the world. The neurotic person, however, faces not reality but perfectionistic ideals, abstract possibilities, and his own feeling states.

Thus far, the argument has been written as if there

were neurotic and healthy *persons*. To be more precise, there are neurotic and healthy periods of time for all of us. We all experience moments of blocking and freezing of our thoughts. We all have periods of dysfunctional self-consciousness. The internal struggle to make oneself want to get out of bed on a cold morning or the effort involved in trying to create inspiration as one sits before the typewriter are examples of neurotic moments. The discomfort as conversation dwindles over dinner with a new acquaintance or the spiral into passive misery as one sits at home alone trying to decide what to do that evening are further examples of the turning inward of attention away from awareness of and commitment to the requirements of the situation. In essence, the neurotic person has more neurotic moments and blocks over a wider variety of situations than the healthy person, but qualitatively his experience is not unlike that of the normal person.

The normal person feels a range of emotions, as does his neurotic counterpart, but he does not allow the emotions to interfere with his doing what he perceives needs to be done in most situations. Moritists make a clear distinction between feelings, moods, and thoughts on the one hand, and behaviors on the other. Feelings are not controllable directly by one's will. They arise from nothingness, as do thoughts, and they pass away in time unless they are restimulated behaviorally. Put more concretely, there are times when we believe we can pinpoint the source of a feeling or mood, but it is likely that similar circumstances may have provoked a different emotion in the past, and often we cannot find an apparent origin for a mood. So Moritists take feelings as "givens" in a way no Freudian would find acceptable. Similarly, thoughts seem to bubble to the surface of our minds and pass away to be replaced by other thoughts. One begins an utterance without knowing precisely how the sentence is to end, yet word follows word, appearing from chaos. If we have no direct control over such internal events, we have no responsibility for them (i.e., all feelings are acceptable), and our best strategy for dealing with terror, panic, depression, joy, lack of confidence, timidity, and the like is to accept them as part of the reality of the moment in which they appear. Thus, the Moritist gives "permission" to the patient to feel as he feels. What else can he do? There is no need to struggle with this side of the self.

In contrast, behavior is controllable at all times despite what one is feeling. This position holds that one is morally, socially, and personally responsible for what one does, regardless of whatever feelings are present. Neither Americans nor Japanese customarily make clear conceptual distinctions between feelings and behaviors. Often when distinctions are made, feelings are cited as excuses for acts that are harmful to the self or to others. Such statements have no meaning within the Moritist system. When one has the experiential sense (not a mere intellectual understanding) based on practice of the principle that behavior is controllable despite one's emotional state (read: despite the presence of symptoms) a new condition of freedom occurs. One is free to feel the depths of anger at an impolite bus driver, love for a charming student, fright at a horror film, because one knows that one's behavior is under control and will not produce some act that will cause embarrassment or other trouble. A basic trust in one's ability to behave appropriately in each moment grows out of a history of behaving appropriately, not before.

This trust exemplifies the principle that links feelings and behavior in Moritist theory. The principle is that behavior indirectly influences feeling. By behaving in a loving, caring way toward some person or animal or plant, feelings of love and concern begin to emerge. Confidence in behavior control comes after repeated experiences of controlling behavior, not before. The client works out his or her own cure in Morita Therapy.

In a sense, one can say that when the patient is not attending to depressed or anxious feelings, he is not depressed or anxious. Most of life is not experienced as happy or sad or pleasant or lonely. We spend most of our existence attending to the moment's task without any awareness of our feeling states at all. Such a condition is normal.

It is important to emphasize that Morita therapists do not propose that patients should attempt to ignore or deny their feelings. Emotions are to be recognized and accepted as they are when they appear in awareness. Then the patient is to go about doing what needs to be done regardless of the feelings. He is to build his life on behavior that is directly controllable by his will.

There is a third principle to be added to acceptance of feelings and control of behavior; it is recognition of purpose. This principle is the formal expression of the attention to what needs to be done in any given situation. Feelings may provide information about what needs to be done, and recognition of the situational requirements guides one's behavior. The three principles are linked in this way but remain conceptually separate.

Finally, Moritist theory offers some broad explanation for why some people become neurotic. This explanation applies particularly to one type of neurosis common in Japan called *shinkeishitsu* (see "Applications" section) but may have broader application, as well. Briefly put, the neurotic person is considered to have a surplus of the need to actualize the self, to succeed in life. This excess may have roots in genetic disposition and in childrearing practices. In any case, the neurotic person perceives that what he wishes to do and be is in conflict with his actual limitations (much as Horney's neurotic struggles between his ideal self and real self). He becomes obsessed with the limitations of the self rather than the potentials of the situation.

Just as Freud used hysteria as a model for the development of his theory of neurosis, so Morita used obsession as the model for his theory. All neurosis is a kind of obsession with the self. Moritist theory holds that when this strong need to achieve and excel is properly channeled so that attention is directed away from the self to the accomplishment of each moment's tasks, the neurotic person has the potential of becoming not merely a normal human being but a superior one.

METHODOLOGY

Morita therapists are explicitly directive. They are teachers, experienced guides who, for the most part, have surmounted their own self-imposed limitations through this method (Reynolds & Yamamoto, 1973). Although the therapist offers authoritative advice, he does express genuine interest in the patient. Avoiding a cold, authoritarian approach, he seeks to establish rapport knowing that a positive relationship will facilitate the therapy process. Nevertheless, the therapist cannot directly control his own feelings of likes or dislikes for certain patients. Much less can he control the patient's feelings for him. So he goes on with instruction in the Moritist lifeway whatever the relationship. The therapist, like the patient, must know his behavioral purpose and cling to it.

Inpatient treatment by Morita Therapy is not practiced in the United States, and it appears to be on the decline in Japan. It is time-consuming (lasting several months or longer in recent times), relatively expensive, and necessary only for severely disturbed neurotics who cannot work or study under normal circumstances.

A detailed description of inpatient treatment may be found in *Morita Psychotherapy* (Reynolds, 1976). Briefly, its chief characteristics include absolute isolated bed rest and guided work therapy. Absolute isolated bed rest involves a week of bed rest with no reading, writing, television, or other diversions. Only three meals a day and the carrying out of necessary bodily functions are permitted. The patient must lie alone with his own thoughts and feelings. There is no escape from the task of coming to terms with the self. He must accept himself with all his limitations. He observes the capriciousness and the natural decline of his own feelings. He realizes that isolation and extended inactivity are unnatural and unpleasant. At the end of a week he is quite bored and eager to involve himself in work, that is, in the losing of himself in various tasks. Other inpatient treatment techniques are similar to those used in the outpatient setting (Kora, 1965).

Outpatient treatment as practiced in Japan and the United States has a broader appeal and is more economical for patient and for practitioner. Treatment begins with the therapist listening to the patient's account of the troubling symptoms. It proceeds in an instructional mode with the therapist explaining the principles of the natural decline of feelings unless they are restimulated, the controllability of behavior despite one's emotional state, and so forth. Examples, demonstrations, and illustrations are taken from everyday life to insure that the patient understands intellectually what he is to do.

The patient may then be required to keep a diary. The diary format may vary somewhat, but the one in common use in the United States involves dividing a sheet of paper in half lengthwise and writing on one side of the page what was done at a particular time. Opposite that entry the patient writes what he felt and thought at that time. At least a page a day is written. The diary is brought to the weekly therapy sessions for the therapist's inspection and comment. Through diary guidance the patient gains the ability to analyze his daily life into the categories of controllable and uncontrollable aspects. Furthermore, he begins to see that much of what we do is done because there is something that must be done, not because the activity and our feelings or desires to do the activity necessarily correspond. The patient perceives the fluctuation of his unstable feeling states and the possibility of steady behavior in spite of that fluctuation. The diary becomes a permanent record of what he was able to do in spite of his fears or tension or other misery.

In similar fashion the patient may be asked to describe in detail the events of the recent past. Neurotic persons tend to describe their world in global generalities and broad abstractions—"All this week I felt terrible," "No one cares about me at all," "Yesterday I didn't do anything." The therapist forces the patient to examine minute details of the morning of the therapy session, for example. Questions might include: What side of bed did you get up on? Did you put on slippers? Which hand did you use to throw off the covers? In what order did you wash your body in the shower? and so forth. Knowing that he will be quizzed by the therapist, the patient begins to observe his everyday behavior and surroundings. He is being brought out of focus on himself into "reality." He may realize that while he showered and brushed his teeth he was not noticing whether he felt good or bad. He may begin to recognize the waves of feeling, the variation in what seemed an overwhelming constancy before.

Readings may be assigned or specific tasks. In lieu of a fee I may ask some of my patients to bring me something they have made while feeling depressed or tense or lonely. Thus they get the experience of constructive activity and fulfillment of a social debt while feeling bad.

The principles of Morita Therapy, as stated above, are neither complex nor many in number. Therapy sessions focus on the application of these understandings and suggestions for living to the patient's daily life. The applications, of course, are numberless. But after a few months of therapy (and even sooner for some) the patient has a pretty good idea of what the therapist will say in a given situation. In other words, the patient perceives what needs to be done in given life situations. Only the patient can do what is necessary. The result of the repetitions in therapy is that there is a gradual decline in the need to meet. Interest can be sustained somewhat longer by role reversals in which the therapist asks the patient what he would suggest to a patient who came in with this or that complaint.

When the patient responds to each life situation with the cognitive process "What needs to be done now?" "Hmmm, now I'm feeling anxious (sad, excited, pleased, terrified). That's interesting. What needs to be done now?" and then goes about doing what needs to be done, he is no longer in need of further work on Morita Therapy. Long before this ideal state is reached a natural termination of therapy will occur. The patient will have realized that there is nothing further to learn from the teacher/therapist. The patient's own effort in applying the principles will result in further progress.

APPLICATIONS

The Japanese patients for whom Morita Therapy was devised were said to be suffering from *shinkeishitsu* neuroses. *Shinkeishitsu* neuroses are characterized by a strong desire to get rid of symptoms and by perfectionism, idealism, and extreme self-centeredness (Kora & Ohara, 1973). These neurotics are usually brighter than normal with better than average school histories. Initial difficulties in living generally occur during the junior or senior high school and usually worsen until treatment despite the patient's strong efforts to control the symptoms. *Shinkeishitsu* neuroses are of three subtypes: obsessions and phobias, anxiety neuroses, and neurasthenia. The most common symptom complex treated in Moritist hospitals and clinics involves a sort of social phobia called *taijin kyofusho*. This social phobia begins in adolescence and takes the form of sensitivity to what others are thinking about oneself, concern with where to look when conversing, worries about blushing, trembling, and general discomfort around social superiors and persons of the opposite sex. This extreme shyness may make difficult such activities as riding in buses or trains, shopping, attending classes, going to work, and dating. Such patients in Japan and in the United States respond most satisfactorily to Morita's style of treatment.

Perhaps two-thirds of the patients treated in Moritist clinics and hospitals are in their teens and twenties. The remaining one-third are mostly middle-aged. The clients suffer from a variety of neurotic complaints not unlike those found in most clinics in the United States.

Psychotics and depressives are treated with medication and Morita Therapy. Customarily, sociopaths, children, addicts, and mentally retarded persons are not treated by this method. The clients, however, need not be highly verbal, and neither a high level of formal education nor cultural sophistication in the client is necessary.

In the United States a variety of neurotics and mild schizophrenics have been effectively treated, the latter with concomitant psychopharmacological intervention. At the University of California at Los Angeles, Andrew Kumasaka, a psychiatry resident, and Millie Warwick, a nurse, have begun to apply Morita's ideas to treatment of the long-term physically ill patient and patients in chronic pain. Dr. Karem Monsour and his staff of the Student Counseling Services at the Claremont Colleges have focused on adolescent study problems. Radmila Moacanin, a psychiatric social worker at the Los Angeles County General Hospital-U.S.C. Adult Psychiatric Outpatient Clinic, has used Morita Therapy as a primary and adjunct treatment form in her practice.

It might be noted that commitment to a Buddhist belief system is not required of the patient. Suitably translated, "accepting reality as it is" can be taken to mean "accepting God's will as it is." A doctoral dissertation by Brian Ogawa (1979) at the San Francisco Theological Seminary examines the implications of Moritist thought for pastoral counseling and Christian clients.

The highly motivated client is likely to do well in most therapies; Morita Therapy is no exception. Particularly because the burden of living out the instructions lies with the patient, those with high secondary gain from their symptoms are unlikely to continue with a therapist who uses a Moritist approach.

CASE EXAMPLE

A question has been raised by Jacobsen and Berenberg (1952), Levy (1965), Kumasaka (1965), and others concerning the effectiveness of Morita Therapy outside the Japanese cultural milieu. The issue can perhaps best be considered a testable hypothesis. Rather than reject Moritist methods on a priori grounds, we have begun treating Western patients and evaluating results. This section describes the therapy course of the first patient treated by Morita Therapy at the University of Southern California Adult Psychiatric Outpatient Clinic. Radmila Moacanin, MA, MSS, was the therapist, with consultation by the author. More detailed case-history material appeared in Japanese in Reynolds and Moacanin (1977).

Certainly, a single successfully treated case does not demonstrate the effectiveness of a therapy. This case is presented to provide an illustration of one way of adapting an Eastern therapy to the treatment of a Western patient. It is organized in Moritist style, with progress notes along with commentary—a blend of concrete example and interpretation—just as everyday reality is encountered in a blend of what is and what we attend to. The commentary is in brackets.

Presenting Complaints

Mr. W was a 31-year-old Caucasian, Catholic, married man, father of a three-year-old son. He was a college graduate and was employed as a clerk in a government office. He had been seen in the psychiatric outpatient clinic by several different therapists both individually, and in groups for seven years. He terminated treatment about a year previously, but returned at this time seeking further treatment for anxiety and depression subsequent to eviction from the apartment where his family lived and his wife's threat to leave him. Other complaints included dissatisfaction with his job (which he perceived to be insignificant, routine, and much below his abilities), lack of friends, and financial problems. Mr. W felt overwhelmed by these life circumstances.

October 28

Since the initial interview on October 21, the housing problem has been resolved. Mr. W found another apartment. [Actively seeking an apartment, in spite of his overwhelming feelings of despair, has paid off for him.]

His wife has returned to him. Now his main desires are for further education and training. He is convinced that he will "fall apart" if he continues in his present job.

November 4

Mr. W quit his job and is now exploring the possibility of enrolling in a training program. In the meantime his wife has started working and has agreed to support the family until he gets on his feet. We discussed goals in therapy and the need to focus on his behavior rather than wander in many different directions allowing his feelings to control and overwhelm him. [A key feature of Morita Therapy is acceptance of one's feelings as they are—not denying, suppressing, trying to ignore them—yet acting with consistency, responsibility, and productivity regardless of the feelings.] Morita Therapy was explained to him briefly.

November 10

Mr. W went to the Department of Vocational Rehabilitation and discussed with a counselor the possibility of enrolling in a training program. He is already more focused on the goal he wishes to pursue and realizes that one of the major problems all his life has been "I am general about everything and unwilling to commit myself to anything." He now accepts the need for some discipline in his daily activities. [The neurotic person tends to "overthink and underact." He plans, speculates, evaluates, wishes life were otherwise, daydreams, and focuses on inner conflicts and processes to the degree that he fails to behave appropriately in the situation in which he finds himself this very moment.] Further explanations about Morita Therapy and its methods were given to him, and he was asked to keep a daily diary. On one-half of each page of the diary he was directed to write what he felt and thought; on the other half of the page, what he did, what he accomplished. [This clear dichotomy between feelings, moods, fantasies, and thoughts on the one hand and behavior on the other hand is fundamental to Morita Therapy.] Patient stated that the assignment made sense to him.

November 17

Mr. W brought his diary and reported it has been helpful to him. He accomplishes more work now. At this time he works as a night watchman. He is alone and afraid on the job. It entails some realistic risks to his life, but nevertheless he goes to work. He wants to build a better work record than the one he has had in the past. He is also exploring further possibilities with the Department of Vocational Rehabilitation.

Mr. W's new job is not significantly different from his last one in terms of the interests and stimulation that it offers him. The difference is that he is more accepting of it now.

November 25

Patient reads entries from his diary and states he understands Morita Therapy better. He intuitively feels this is a logical and simple way of working with his life, but also a very difficult one. [Gains in therapy follow from the patient's effort. The goal is a sort of character development. The successes are his, earned through his moment-by-moment struggles.] The diary organizes his thinking, and after completing the necessary daily chores he feels a burden off his shoulders. [How much of our energy is wasted rescheduling, avoiding, putting off chores that could be done now and then forgotten.] He already feels better, although he does not know why.

[It is not important to have elaborate intellectual/theoretical understanding about why these principles are effective. To put them into practice brings experiential understanding. Again, we cut through the neurotic's tendencies for mental wheelspinning with direct, straightforward action.] At this point, as after similar statements, the patient is reminded that feeling better is not the goal of therapy, but rather the aim is a vigilant adherence to his immediate tasks. [The beginning patient may be attracted to this therapy when he discovers that his misery goes unnoticed as he involves himself (loses himself) in his activity. He also learns that negative feelings diminish over time unless they are restimulated. But so do positive feelings. Life need not be constructed on the unpredictable fluctuating base of emotions. Successful behavior patterns are likely to bring overall satisfaction, but satisfaction or not, each moment requires our full attention and appropriate behavior.]

Several times this past week Mr. W did not want to go to work, but he did go anyway. On his days off he had an urge to go to a bar in the evening, but instead he stayed home knowing that he needed the rest in order to be able to go to work the following evening.

December 1

Mr. W has been accepted into a vocational school. During this session he comes to the recognition that the only time he is "happy" is when he is not worried about his past or his future. He is instructed to focus on the present moment without lingering in the past or daydreaming about the future. [Of course, some evaluation of past actions and some future planning are necessary tasks of life. It is the excessive rumination that debilitates and paralyzes the neurotic person.]

December 10

Patient has been anxious and depressed this past week after he met with a friend and the two reminisced about old times in their native home. [Feelings, moods will fluctuate. When he is anxious, he is anxious. That is reality. But when he knows by experience that his behavior is under control regardless of his anxiety, he is free to feel that anxiety fully, even to treasure it.] Patient's attention was redirected to his present life situation. He expressed satisfaction with the prospect of starting school the following week and with the progress he has already made in therapy. He has started working on a second job part time.

January 5

Mr. W likes his school, wants to complete it, and then give something of himself to others. [Note the emerging social consciousness. Neurotic persons tend to be self-centered. Most Western therapies focus even further attention on the self. This spontaneous budding of selflessness in Mr. W is a consequence of the new outer-direction of his awareness.] He perceives as "illusion" his constant desire for something other than what he already has, such as another woman, a close male friend, and another country. He believes his marriage is working out at this time.

January 13

Mr. W has been depressed this past week, but kept on with his tasks, went to school regularly, and drove his wife to and from work. At times he feels he is not advancing, but nevertheless he keeps up.

Today Mr. W wants to know more about Morita Therapy, particularly how it is like and unlike Behavior Therapy. He recognizes deep urges in himself for a fuller life, which he realizes were there even before therapy. [This desire to live fully, the drive for self-actualization (called *sei no yokubo* by Morita therapists) provides the momentum for cure but also for neurosis. In the past, this energy source has been misdirected; during therapy it is refocused on productive living.]

In response to his observation that Morita Therapy somewhat resembles Behavior Modification Therapy, it was stressed that our goal is not to mold him to produce any particular behavior but to make him a freer individual. At the same time the therapist pointed out the necessity of learning and adhering to discipline—which he himself has identified as lacking in his life so far—in order to reach and maintain that freedom. [The environment holds "responsibility" for what we do, according to Behavior Therapy. And changing the reinforcers of the environment produces cure (i.e., symptom reduction) as well. Morita's method holds the patient responsible for his or her behavior. And the goal is not the symptom reduction but symptom transcendence through acceptance of feelings and self-control of behavior.]

Through his diary Mr. W has learned that his main conflict revolves around his sexual identity. [Patients often try to simplify their problems into a single complaint. "If only I had been born to other parents." Or, in this case, "if only I were more masculine. . . ."] He feels incapable of resolving that problem, yet he has been attentive to his wife and has not failed to satisfy her needs. The therapist pointed out that despite some conflicting emotions, Mr. W has been attending to his duties as husband. The patient also reports that although he often feels "bad" while in school, he pursues his classes. He sees a similarity between the required discipline in school and in therapy.

February 10

The past week Mr. W felt good, happy, very happy, depressed, anxious, fatigued, and so forth, but pursued his work and concentrated on his daily tasks. Occasionally he suffers mild anxiety attacks in class, but keeps on with the work. He asked what he should do in such instances. He is urged to continue the work he is engaged in at that moment. He again discusses the need to make some judgment at times when faced with two or more simultaneous conflicting demands for action. He is now more confident about making his own decisions at such times, implementing his decisions, and assuming responsibility for them.

February 24

We continue to work on the recognition that despite fluctuation of his feelings—within one single day and from moment to moment—he can maintain constancy in his actions. Mr. W can see this very well as he goes over his daily diary. He further recognizes that often when he does not feel good but keeps on with his tasks, the feeling changes. He has been able to take the pressures at school although many of his fellow students quit. [He is building a history of perseverance and success. Confidence follows accomplishment more often than it precedes it.]

Mr. W is eager to spend more time with his son and participate more actively in the child's upbringing. He decides to make it his task to do so. After each session the patient reviews what we have discussed.

March 2

Mr. W is having trouble concentrating on his reading assignments. When intruding thoughts of possible failure appear, he is to keep on scanning the page, keep on repeating the definitions to be learned so as not to divert his attention to useless worries over his future. [Intrusive or wandering thoughts are problems for all of us. To try to get rid of them is to focus even more attention on them. They are to be accepted while we continue to go about what we are doing. Eventually, a word of phrase from the text will "catch" his attention and he will be "lost" again in his studying.]

March 9

Mr. W's grades at school have gone up, and he has been able to study well. Once again he realizes that "this therapy works."

March 16

Mr. W did well on his examinations. He reports that when he does what needs to be done and pursues the required actions, his feelings spontaneously change so that he becomes less lonely and depressed. Loneliness never fades away completely, but he now accepts the fact that he may never be able to conquer it. He discovered that when focusing his thinking on one task at a time, he is more likely to be successful. For example, when he studies anatomy, he now thinks of anatomy only, and not how he is going to pay his rent. Then when he passes his examination he feels relieved and may even no longer worry about the rent. Furthermore, he has learned to handle previously distasteful tasks. For instance, although cleaning up an incontinent patient used to make him vomit, he now performs his job without being bothered by it. He believes that if he had not learned to focus on and accept whatever the demands of the tasks, he would not have been able to continue his studies.

April 6

Today Mr. W says he is "in good shape." He finds himself more efficient the more he is bombarded with problems. He has learned to "get into the rhythm of things" and accomplish one task after another. His wife may be pregnant, and he is accepting this possibility without worrying unnecessarily about their meager financial resources.

May 17

Mr. W and his wife will leave for Europe in two days. He considers this trip to be a vacation, but, moreover, an educational experience. Reviewing his gains in therapy, he states that even though he did not complete his vocational school at this time, he learned a more important lesson in life. He learned "to take every day as a new birth." He has surmounted his difficulties and revulsion about certain nursing chores, and he is now able to do anything that is required of him.

We reviewed his progress in other problem areas that he presented at the onset of therapy. The relationship with his wife has significantly improved. He now has a skill in a field that gives him genuine satisfaction, a field in which he can always obtain employment. Consequently, he no longer has financial worries. He no longer has the feeling of lacking control over his life. Mr. W now realizes that he does not need to stop and be overwhelmed by an event, but, as he proceeds, the event assumes smaller proportions and often resolves itself. He gave as an example a recent incident in which he got a $25 traffic ticket on his way to work. His first impulse was not to go to work, for in one day he would not make enough money to pay the ticket. Nevertheless, he did go to work, and as he kept working his preoccupation with the ticket lessened and the problem diminished. Mr. W also remarked that until recently he had many "dualities" in himself that kept him from going ahead. He feels that now he has resolved those dualities.

Summary of Case History

The patient maintained a daily diary. He read his diary entries aloud at each therapy session. His diary was a key instrument of therapeutic work between sessions and became the focus of our discussion during each session. Occasionally Mr. W would dwell on the past or would question the Moritist method, finding it confining, restricting, demanding of excessive discipline, and apparently irrelevant to the more creative aspects of life. His anxieties, worries, and questions were acknowledged with empathy, but his attention was firmly redirected to his current tasks. There was neither avoidance of feelings nor focus on them, no psychodynamic analyzing or interpreting as they arose in the therapy sessions or in his diary. By directing his energies to specific tasks, the waste and diversion of energy on fruitless emotional and mental activities was minimized. Without undue worry about future problems, regrets over past failures, or avoidance of present tasks, the patient became able to use his energies to more fully involve himself in life. A meaningful occupation, satisfying relationships with his wife, son, and mother, and a broadened social awareness have resulted.

Mr. W was repeatedly reminded by the therapist and by his daily living of the fluctuations in feelings from day to day and moment to moment (as were clearly reflected in his diary) despite a constancy and regularity in his actions. The inevitable ups and downs of his emotions, from depression and acute anxiety to peacefulness to exhilaration to feelings of harmony, did not necessarily deter him from his pursuit of daily tasks. He was thus gradually but steadily building up positive and constructive behavior patterns. Deep urges from an unknown source within himself directed him toward a meaningful life for himself, and a usefulness to society. (We must recognize the possibility that we have no real grasp of the source of our impulses and feelings, accept them, and get on with using them. In this manner we transcend them.) By focusing on specific daily activities his personality could unfold spontaneously, unhindered by useless habits and obsessive destructive thought patterns.

The diary fostered a sort of meditative process by which Mr. W developed an increased capacity for observation of his feelings and thoughts from moment to moment in a neutral way.

The patient's trust in the therapist was a critical element in his willingness to undergo Morita Therapy and give it an experiential try in his daily life. Yet once the unique insights and strategies for dealing with feelings and behavior are mastered by a patient, they can be maintained and strengthened after therapy has been formally terminated.

SUMMARY

Through application of three principles—*recognize purpose, accept feelings,* and *control behavior*—the client in Morita Therapy seeks to build his or her character rather than merely reduce symptoms. In fact, from the Moritist perspective, symptoms such as anxiety and lack of confidence are not considered accretions to be removed as a surgeon would excise a tumor. Rather such feelings and attitudes are part of the reality that exists for a patient; they are elements in the flow of his awareness. They are neither good nor bad, they simply are.

In practice, symptom complaints *are* reduced (Suzuki & Suzuki, 1977), but that is merely a side effect. What is important is the growing ability of the patient to live responsibly and constructively whether symptoms are present or not. The normal person has anxiety too. However, the normal person is not "trapped" by his anxiety; he is not boxed into a corner of excessive self-focus and passive dependency by his feelings.

The therapist cannot make a patient feel better. He cannot control his own feelings, much less those of his client. The Morita therapist only offers what he has experienced himself. When success comes to the patient, it is the result of the patient's putting what he has learned into practice. That effort is the solid behavioral basis for a lasting sense of self-worth.

REFERENCES

Jacobsen, A., & Berenberg, A. N. (1952). Japanese psychiatry and psychotherapy. *American Journal of Psychiatry, 109,* 321–329.

Kondo, A. (1953). Morita Therapy: A Japanese therapy for neurosis. *American Journal of Psychoanalysis, 13,* 31–37.

Kora, T. (1965). Morita therapy. *International Journal of Psychiatry, 1*(4), 611–640.

Kora, T., & Ohara, K. (1973). Morita therapy. *Psychology Today, 6*(10), 63–68.

Kumasaka, Y. (1965). Discussion. *International Journal of Psychiatry, 1*(4), 641–642.

Levy, J. (1965). Discussion. *International Journal of Psychiatry, 1*(4), 642–643.

Morita, S., & Mizutani, K. (1956). *Sei no Yokubo (The Desire to Live Fully).* Tokyo: Hakuyōsha.

Ogawa, B. K. (1979). *Morita psychotherapy and Christianity.* Ph.D. dissertation. San Francisco Theological Seminary.

Ohara, K., & Reynolds, D. K. (1968). Changing methods in Morita psychotherapy. *International Journal of Social Psychiatry, 14*(4), 305–310.

Reynolds, D. K. (1976). *Morita psychotherapy.* Berkeley, Calif.: University of California Press.

Reynolds, D. K. (1980). *The quiet therapies.* Honolulu: University Press of Hawaii.

Reynolds, D. K., & Moacanin, R. (1977). Eastern therapy: Western patient. *Japanese Journal of Psychotherapy Research, 3*(2), 65–74. (In Japanese)

Reynolds, D. K., & Yamamoto, J. (1973). Morita psychotherapy in Japan. *Current Psychiatric Therapies, 13,* 219–227.

Suzuki, T. (1967). Morita rhyōhō no tachiba kara (From the standpoint of Morita therapy). *Seishin Igaku, 9*(7), 11–19.

Suzuki, T., & Suzuki, R. (1977). A follow-up of neurotics treated by Morita therapy. VI World Congress of Psychiatry, Honolulu.

Yokoyama, K. (1968). Morita therapy and seiza. *Psychologia, 11*(3–4), 179–184.

Chapter 38

MULTIPLE FAMILY THERAPY

JOHN W. RAASOCH

Many years ago I searched for the origins of group psychotherapy and found that about a dozen people had discovered or developed it in about the same decade, all quite independently of each other. The same is true of Multiple Family Therapy, which in this next chapter is credited to H. Peter Laqueur. I was trained in it by Dr. Rudolf Dreikurs in about 1950, and he in turn had been trained by Alfred Adler about 1920. When I first moved to Hawaii I discovered that a form of this kind of Multiple Family Therapy, with the additional innovation that there were also multiple therapists, was being done by Dr. Daniel Fullmer. I suppose that it is either a case of great minds going in the same directions or perhaps, even more likely, that procedures such as Multiple Family Therapy, as well as group psychotherapy, are a function of the cultural Zeitgeist—an idea whose time has come.

This chapter by John Raasoch gives a clear indication of a most useful and practical method of family counseling and psychotherapy. It seems to be a more complex version of what occurs in primitive cultures when the extended family group meets in council for the purposes of settling disputes, making decisions, and the like. In my judgment MFT is an important technique, with many economic and social values, and bears further investigation and replication.

Multiple Family Therapy (MFT) is a combination of individual family therapy and group therapy. In MFT three to five families are seen simultaneously.

There are two basic models of MFT. The first model entails doing family therapy for one family while the other families observe. One family is on the "hot seat" each week. The second model involves maximizing group interaction and group process. Here each family's concerns are addressed at each session. The second model will be described here.

HISTORY

H. Peter Laqueur is usually cited as the pioneer of Multiple Family Therapy because of his work at Creedmore State Hospital in New York. His first publication regarding MFT appeared in the *Journal of Neuropsychiatry* (1962). However, Detre, Kessler, and Sayers (1961) as well as Hes and Handler (1961) described meetings of patients and families occurring earlier.

Laqueur fondly recalled those early Sunday afternoons at Creedmore in an auditorium with 50 patients and families together for both an educative program and patient government. After achieving many successes

even from that chaotic interaction, he followed the suggestion of a family therapist friend and began seeing 10 groups of five families each. When Laqueur realized that these groups fared better and had decreased readmission rates, MFT as a legitimate therapy was born.

MFT was later refined as a therapy when the Laqueurs moved permanently to their summer home in Vermont. Even rugged, private, backwoods Vermonters would brave two hours of traveling through ice and snow to attend these highly valued MFT groups. Initiating group therapy, especially in Vermont, was difficult. Asking three to five families to "go public" for MFT was an almost insurmountable task. When the MFT group was finally formed, it was a tedious process to build trust and encourage sharing of meaningful information. Techniques and exercises to accelerate this process have been published elsewhere (Laqueur, 1976). These exercises include all the mothers coming to the center of the room to discuss with each other what kind of spouses and parents they are. The fathers then follow the same procedure. Other subgroups identified by the therapist, such as "good kids" and "bad kids," also meet separately to identify their similarities. This process facilitates early cohesiveness and identification with subgroups.

The method of training therapists has also been modified over the years. The early process of training MFT therapists required at least five steps, each usually lasting for about six months. The progression of training steps was from silent observer, to operator of the video camera, to active observer, to cotherapist, to therapist. Innovative techniques to accelerate this learning process, such as simulating MFT in workshops for professionals, have been developed (Raasoch & Laqueur, 1979).

CURRENT STATUS

Multiple Family Therapy has grown by leaps and bounds and is currently in practice throughout the world. MFT-type meetings with families now occur in schools, prisons, and nursing homes as well as in traditional psychiatric hospitals and outpatient clinics. The MFT method is applicable to mental health centers with long waiting lists and is useful to the many different specialty populations that a mental health center serves.

It is interesting to compare and contrast MFT with different models of family education. Most traditional models of family education teach parents about parent-child communication in a structured, intellectual manner without children present. In MFT, parents learn informally along with their children by modeling and example. Out of the knowledge gained from MFT, it has been recommended that children be present when courses are taught to parents on how to communicate more openly with their children (Raasoch & McCollester, 1977).

An excellent review of the literature of MFT was done by A. H. Strelnick (1977).

THEORY

Multiple Family Therapy theory borrows from systems, family, and group theory. MFT takes exception to the often cited eight to ten client maximum thought to be desirable for functional group therapy (Yalom, 1970). Even though MFT has been referred to as crowd control or a three-ring circus, it can be organized. Meeting with 20 individuals from four families is not the same as meeting with 20 unrelated individuals. In MFT the therapist can divide a large group into subsets. The therapist is then essentially dealing with four or five entities at a single moment. The situation then becomes almost analagous to doing group therapy with four to five clients. These subgroups, however, are constantly changing. For the first 10 minutes of a session one may be dealing with the Browns, the Smiths, and the Joneses, and then switch to the mothers, fathers, problematic kids, and "good kids." By the end of the session there may be groups of angry screamers, quiet stompers, and passive observers. With such a large group the therapist needs to encourage identifica-

tion with subgroups among clients by pointing out similarities among members. Frequently the therapist needs to physically maneuver clients into various groupings.

Objectivity is another major asset of MFT. Family members can be much more objective in viewing another family's dynamics than their own. It is common for Mr. Brown to comment on Mr. Smith's interaction with his family and then reflect on his own family; for example, "George, you're really lecturing Johnny. Hmmm. . . . Maybe I do the same to my son."

Support among clients is probably the greatest benefit of MFT. A great deal of support can occur between families in a well-functioning MFT group. A family's crisis does not have to become a crisis for the therapist when the other families empathize and help solve the problem. If the therapist has modeled helpful behavior in past sessions without rescuing, he frequently needs to only direct traffic while the other families do the "therapy."

Modeling is another benefit provided by MFT, especially with cotherapy teams. The ideal is to have a harmonious male-female cotherapy dyad that models openness and sharing of decision making. MFT can be an open modality for sharing therapeutic techniques with the entire group. When MFT groups are used for training professionals, a supervisor may confront a learning therapist in the midst of an MFT session and ask him to justify to everyone what he is trying to accomplish. Maximizing openness of techniques in front of clients facilitates the process of their becoming cotherapists.

Cotherapy by clients is another achievable goal. Many families with "seniority" in the group have returned for several sessions after their logical termination to help engage new families in an MFT group. Long before logical termination, certain families or members are far advanced in specific areas and can be referred to as models—there may be bedtime-setting experts, relating-to-adolescents experts, or the experts at bringing up parents.

In various stages of MFT, competition can be encouraged. Competition is a positive factor when clients and families compete to see who gets better faster. Competition to become a good example or a cotherapist is also desirable.

In this day of fragmented families, it is striking how well MFT is suited to deal with absent members. The anger toward an alcoholic father who has practically deserted the family can be worked through with another father in the group. In individual family therapy these resentments may come out much slower and take longer to work through.

METHODOLOGY

Beginning any group takes a lot of a therapist's energy, and Multiple Family Therapy is no exception. To begin

MFT requires a directive salesman who is totally sold on the value of his service. The enthusiastic salesman also needs endurance, because many families who are screened may reject the idea of MFT as totally absurd before three to five families willing to participate are found. Dropout rates are at least as high as for other group therapy modalities (Yalom, 1970).

Not being directive enough in the early sessions is an easy trap to fall into. Lack of direction leads to individuals and families feeling neglected in such a large group. It also allows aggressive or crisis-prone clients to dominate.

Families feel very uncomfortable being "exposed" to other families, and the therapist has to demonstrate his abilities and the benefits of MFT very early in the sessions. In spite of these efforts, it is not uncommon for it to take a year or two for members of an MFT group to engage themselves in the therapeutic process and for the group to become well established.

The ideal process of an MFT session includes six stages. The first stage is to *gauge the affect;* that is, obtain the feeling tone of each member of the group, including general information of most recent events in the family.

The next stage is to *develop a common theme.* It is important to find and label a theme common to all or most of the families. When a more specific discussion involves a particular family, the other families can then relate their own problems to the discussion. If three families each presented with a crisis—such as a suicidal mother, a son arrested for drug charges, a grandmother moving out of the family home—the common theme could be defined as a power struggle. Given the many diversities of content that can be presented, it is most important to reduce issues to the most basic, feeling levels.

The third stage is to *find a relevant exercise.* The goal is to utilize a nonverbal exercise to break through much of the verbal preoccupation with minute details and deal instead with the gut-level responses. To deal with the power struggles cited above, a sculptured "back-to-back" exercise can be utilized effectively. The two clients involved are asked to stand in the center of the room with their backs together, arms folded across their chests. They are instructed to solve their problems *without* words: "Show us action, not talk." If one of them chooses to walk away from the conflict, the therapist states that that is one alternative. The therapist then yanks the client back into the center of the room and instructs him to find another alternative. Sculpturing is a visual representation of family dynamics first developed by Duhl, Duhl, and Kantor (1973).

Stage four is a decision to *intensify or diffuse the process.* Because there are so many ages in families, it is important to maintain a level of intensity that keeps everyone's interest. Nonverbal techniques, such as family sculpturing, can hold children's interests, while they intensify the tone for adults and force them to function on a more primary process level. Depending on the timing, the therapist can either intensify or diffuse the session by having group and family members talk about themselves as colors or animals. A father's intense anger can be diffused by comparing him to a grizzly bear with subsequent discussion of the bear's positive attributes.

Stage five, *winding down,* and stage six, *leaving with positive feelings,* frequently run together. If, somehow, someone in each family does not leave with a positive feeling, the MFT group likely will not survive. With entire families coming each week, it is difficult to keep everyone engaged. Many conflicts in schedules arise and frequently someone ends up pleading not to come back. It is valuable to give the clients a chance to catch their breath and leave on a friendly social note with the others. Summing up, providing some resolution, and assigning homework tasks are helpful.

The essential ingredient in the above stages is the directiveness of the therapist. MFT is unique because of the large numbers of clients dealt with at one time, which necessitates that the therapist adopt the role of a ringmaster. The therapist may gradually evolve a laissez-faire stance as the group becomes cohesive, but initially an enthusiastic optimist must take charge. An earlier reference was made to the therapist *yanking* a client back to the center of the room. This is not an overstatement when it comes to nonverbal exercises. If the exercise is to have any chance of success, it must be spontaneous. The therapist cannot take no for an answer; he has to feel confident that the client will stand up. This is analogous to admitting ambivalent schizophrenics to the hospital. Young psychiatric residents may spend hours in the emergency room trying to talk future inpatients out of their ambivalence. However, the resident soon learns to elicit family support. He also learns that gentle, firm, constant pressure on the patient's back will succeed in getting the patient to the elevator.

Another analogy is that of an aggressive coach pacing the sidelines and yanking players off the bench to enter the game. The time of inserting someone into the action is crucial and, like the coach, the MFT therapist must know his players' strengths and vulnerabilities very well.

APPLICATIONS

Multiple Family Therapy works for almost every diagnostic category and level of psychopathology. The benefits of MFT include simultaneous training of many professionals and reduced boredom of therapists. It can also be justified on economic considerations. Even more so than in traditional Group Therapy, the professional can see large numbers of clients with a minimal expenditure of time. MFT can even be justified for clinical needs. Chronic schizophrenics and their families can be boring after a few years and, if seeing groups of these families stimulates the interest of a therapist, certainly the quality of clinical treatment will improve.

In discussing applications of MFT the needs of two groups of people should be considered—the professionals and the clients. The professional category includes third-party payers to whom the economic benefits of MFT are obvious.

Training therapists is quite applicable to MFT. Many observers can watch and participate in meaningful ways, such as behind a video camera. It also presents an opportunity for a trainee to observe several families' dynamics in one session. Much more time would have to be spent in order to see those same families individually. Medical students especially find MFT useful in providing maximum exposure to families in a limited time period.

Clinical indications for MFT are not as obvious. Two questions arise: What can a client do for the group? and What can the group do for a client? The group needs diversity—socioeconomic diversity, for example. If five corporate lawyers and their families meet together they inevitably discuss corporate law. Families of a college professor, a welfare mother, and an old New England farmer will comprise a far superior group, since the fact that they have so little in common forces them to deal with the common denominator of basic family conflicts. In a specific MFT group it may be preferable to have families whose children's ages are similar; for example, families with adolescents or families with preschoolers. Laqueur, however, preferred to have the most diverse ages possible.

Most family problems are included when considering indications for clients to benefit from MFT. Because of the enormous group support, MFT is especially helpful for adolescents separating from their families. This is clearly effective when an older adolescent has resolved this conflict and can serve as a role model.

MFT groups can also help parents recognize when they are scapegoating their children for marital conflicts. Single parents can receive the support they so desperately need to make it on their own, which helps prevent them from immediately turning to the first available spouse. MFT has also risen to the occasion to help an "untreatable" individual or family so labeled by the referral source. Seeing an individual in the context of his family and, particularly, in a group of families facilitates work.

Before a family can benefit from MFT, it must be convinced to "go public," which is no small task. Because of this difficulty, sometimes the only criteria left for a family to pass the screening process is its willingness to be exposed in front of other families.

A relative contraindication for inclusion in the group would be the acutely psychotic individual, as Guttman (1973) mentioned. However, the present MFT group composition would be an important factor to consider since a supportive, well-functioning group could probably handle this individual with a very nonthreatening, slow-pace approach.

Other categories that signal the need for caution because of possible detrimental effects to the client include the extremely sub-assertive individual and the passive schizophrenic. As published previously (Raasoch & Laqueur, 1979) these clients may be double bound by feeling abandoned yet unable to mention it.

CASE EXAMPLE

The following example represents a composite of several. MFT groups; specifics have been changed to protect confidentiality. The MFT group consists of the following families.

The Red-Blue Family (Blended Family)

Mr. Red: Father, lawyer, age 47, previously married, nearly constantly angry.

Red Jr.:   Son, age 17, product of father's first marriage, in conflict with father because he does not want to be a lawyer.

Mrs. Blue: Mother, salesclerk, age 38, previously married, usually depressed.

Bluette: Daughter of Mrs. Blue's first marriage, age 17, usually bubbly.

(Two other daughters of Mrs. Blue, ages 23 and 21, live out of the home and are non-descript. They attended sessions 3 and 4 respectively.)

The White Family (Single Parent)

Mrs. White: Mother, schoolteacher, divorced, age 37, usually righteous.

Black: Son, age 19, always in trouble.

Gray: Daughter, age 16, not as much trouble.

The Green Family (Single Parent)

Mrs. Green: Welfare mother, age 30, eighth-grade education, constantly worried about money.

Greener: Son, age 12, always "better" than Greens.

Greens: Daughter, age 11, vegetarian.

Greenie: Infant daughter, age 9 months.

The Burgundy Family

Mr. Burgundy: Father, machinist, age 56, alcoholic.
Mrs. Burgundy: Mother, age 55, a happy homemaker.
Burgy: Daughter, age 23, unmarried, tomboy, still living at home.
Burnt-Out: Daughter, age 17, schizophrenic.
Bundy: Daughter, age 7, always fighting with siblings and peers.

Summary of First Four MFT Sessions

Session 1.   The Red-Blue, White, and Burgundy families, along with a fourth family X, were introduced to each other. Mothers, fathers, "good kids," and "bad kids" all came to the center of the room sequentially and were encouraged to identify with each other. Parents became polarized with the group of "bad kids" when the therapist redefined "bad kids" as having more fun. When the Burgundy family was sculptured, this polarization was slightly diffused. (See Figure 38.1*a*.)

Session 2.   Only the Red-Blue, White, and Burgundy families returned, while family X was absent. The group was very slow starting but by the end of the session some early cohesiveness was beginning to build. (See Figure 38.1*b*.)

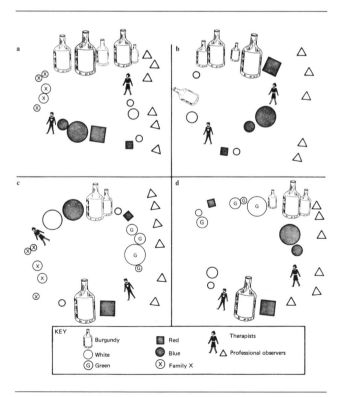

Figure 38.1   Sessions 1 to 4.

Session 3.   The Green family was added to the Red-Blue, White, and Burgundy families, and family X returned. Family X was very negative about MFT, which made it difficult to convince the Greens that this was a workable treatment modality. Family X never returned. (See Figure 38.1*c*.)

Session 4.   The Green family returned with the Red-Blues, Whites, and Burgundys. The four families began functioning as a group. After the Green family was sculptured, they were well integrated into the group. (See Figure 38.1*d*.)

In figure 38.1*d,* showing sessions 1 to 4, the shift from families sitting together to dispersing throughout the group can be noted. This shift of seating attests to the alliances that are formed between mutually supportive clients. When a new family (the Greens) is added in session 3, they cling together for security. By session 4, however, they are already beginning to disperse throughout the group. By session 4 alliances are established between fathers, mothers, and "bad kids."

Session 10—All Four Families Present

Mr. Burgundy announced his third consecutive week of sobriety and was very active throughout the session, emerging as the first client cotherapist.

Red Jr. presented a huge fight with his father, which resulted in his decision to go and live with his biological mother. He also accused his stepmother, Mrs. Blue, of having an affair. At that point Greens broke into tears over not having seen her divorced father for three years and even Black was able to relate what a hassle a divorce was for a son. At this point, one of the therapists crossed the room to Greens, asked Mrs. Blue to watch Greenie, and encouraged Greens to physically join Red Jr. and Black (See Figure 38.2.)

Mr. Burgundy pointed out how Mr. Red and Mrs. Blue must not allow Red Jr. to continually threaten to return to his mother and play on their guilt. Red Jr. admitted that he really did not want to return to his mother because she was an alcoholic like Mr. Burgundy. He then described in detail how totally obnoxious a drunk parent can be. Talking about divorce and separation led Black to a very emotional resolution that his parents would never reunite.

The session ended on a light note when Greenie, the nine-month-old, poured soda into Mrs. Blue's pocketbook.

Session 20—Red-Blue, Green, and Burgundy Families Present

This session began with a long intellectual discussion between Mr. Red and Mr. Burgundy. Mr. Burgundy's plant

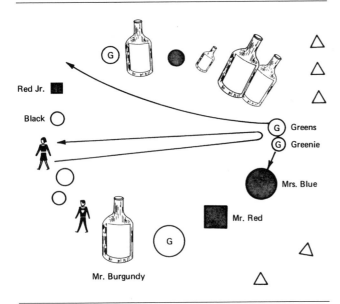

Figure 38.2　Session 10.

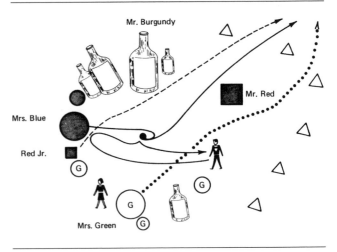

Figure 38.3　Session 20.

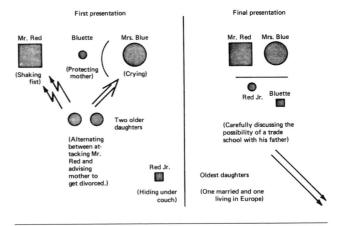

Figure 38.4　Session 40.

was about to unionize and Mr. Red was expounding on all the legal ramifications of unions. On a hunch, one of the therapists sat Mrs. Blue on the floor in the center of the room, positioning her head down. Within seconds she began to cry intensely, whereupon Mr. Red began swearing at Mr. Burgundy. Then Mrs. Blue rose to her feet, threw her glasses across the room, and stormed out the door, slamming it behind her. Red Jr. ran out after his stepmother. When the two did not return to the group, Mrs. Green left the room and eventually convinced Mrs. Blue to return. In the ensuing discussion a pattern was identified between Mr. Red and Mrs. Blue. Every time Mrs. Blue got depressed Mr. Red became extremely angry and Red Jr. always ended up in the middle.

During the discussion that followed, Mrs. Burgundy was able to confront Mrs. Green with the observation that her interaction with her 12-year-old, Greener, was very similar to Mr. Red's interaction with Red Jr. The therapists were able to use Mrs. Burgundy's style of very openly relating to adolescents as an example of listening to and truly respecting them. (See Figure 38.3.)

Session 40—All Four Families Present

This session had been previously set as the termination date for the Red-Blue family. The Red-Blue family was sculptured—first, the way they had presented almost a year earlier and then their present status. (See Figure 38.4.)

The progress and shifts of this family were very dramatic and obvious to everyone. The Red and the Blue families were finally integrated and a new family—Purple—emerged. The Greens were also discussing ter-

mination, and a tentative termination data was set two months away. The families were updated about the screening process for new families for the group.

Throughout most of the session the younger children—Greener, Greens, and Bundy—had been drawing and seemed fairly distant from the group process. Near the end, when asked if they wanted to give their drawings to anyone, they unanimously chose Burnt-Out as the recipient. Burnt-Out had been almost catatonic recently and was clearly moved when she was awarded the drawings. She then volunteered that it was her birthday. It was interesting to note that all of the drawings were of cats and that Burnt-Out's T-shirt had a picture of a tiger on it.

SUMMARY

MFT utilizes the best of both worlds, combining the excitement and advantages of group and family therapy.

This modality represents much more than merely a large group of 20 individuals. Each member is already a member of a family in the group, and the cotherapists continually look for innovative ways to help the clients see themselves as part of other subgroups. Through these subgroups and the natural caring that is fostered in this process, a tremendous amount of support emerges for troubled individuals.

Objectivity is another advantage of having several families present. Seeing one family alone, a single professional can easily get caught up in that family's psychopathology. In MFT more than one professional is usually present and the rest of the group provides valuable input. In fact, other family members are encouraged to become "cotherapists."

The rich supply of family dynamics and psychopathology makes MFT a very efficient modality for training professionals. Innovative ways to learn MFT process are also available such as workshops for professionals that simulate MFT groups (Raasoch & Laqueur, 1979).

Whether in a workshop or an actual MFT group, a very directive salesman-type therapist is needed. The MFT therapist must be confident and comfortable with moving people physically about. This person is frequently "on stage" and is a continual model for the group. The "performance" part—utilizing nonverbal exercises with spacial imagery—is needed to maintain interest.

REFERENCES

Detre, T., Kessler, D., & Sayers, J. (1961). A socio-adaptive approach to treatment of acutely disturbed psychiatric inpatients. *Proceedings of the Third World Congress in Psychiatry, 1,* 501–506.

Duhl, F., Duhl, B., & Kantor, D. (1973). Learning, space and action in family therapy: A primer of sculpture. In D. Block (Ed.), *Techniques of family psychotherapy.* New York: Grune & Stratton.

Guttman, H. A. (1973). A contraindication for family therapy. *Archives of General Psychiatry, 29,* 352–355.

Hes, J., & Handler, S. (1961). Multidimensional group psychotherapy. *Archives of General Psychiatry, 5,* 92–97.

Laqueur, H. P. (1976). Multiple family therapy. In P. J. Guerin, Jr. (Ed.), *Family therapy theory and practice.* New York: Gardner.

Raasoch, J., & Laqueur, H. P. (1979). Learning multiple family therapy through simulated workshops. *Family Process, 18,* 95–98.

Raasoch, J., & McCollester, G. (1977). Multiple family therapy or education. Workshop presented for The American Association of Psychiatric Services for Children, Washington, D.C.

Strelnick, A. H. (1977). Multiple family group therapy: A review of the literature. *Family Process, 16,* 307–35.

Yalom, I. D. (1970). *The theory and practice of group psychotherapy.* New York: Basic.

Chapter 39

NAIKAN PSYCHOTHERAPY

DAVID K. REYNOLDS

Naikan Therapy reminds me very much of the Catholic Church's viewpoint about sin, as it was explained to me some 50 years ago when I went to a parochial school. It is a moralistic, philosophical point of view, and this position is very similar to O. Hobart Mowrer's theory, which is summarized in the chapter on Integrity Groups by Anthony Vattano. In traditional Catholic practice, before one goes to sleep one is supposed to go over the day's events, meditate on what one did that was right and what was wrong, to feel truly sorry for one's mistakes and grateful for what one has received, to pray for guidance and understanding and the strength to live the good life—and to consider making reparations for any wrong one has done. Generally, this is known in Catholic thinking as examination of the conscience.

As I read it, this essentially is the message of Naikan Therapy. Note that in this Asian process the therapist plays a genuinely nondirective role. The therapy is a true self-therapy of the kind that Sigmund Freud did, that Karen Horney wrote about, and that Theodore Reik said was the best of all modes of psychotherapy. This chapter has many important implications for the future of psychotherapy and should not be considered an alien system; rather, it calls for very close examination. David Reynolds presents a most persuasive point of view relative to an innovative approach to psychotherapy.

Naikan Psychotherapy is a meditative treatment form developed in Japan from Jodo Shinshu Buddhism by Isshin Yashimoto, a lay priest and former businessman. Through guided self-reflection on his past, the Naikan client comes to realize how much others have done for him, how little he has returned to them, and how much trouble and worry he has caused the significant others in his life. The therapy explicitly aims at producing an existential guilt and, simultaneously, a sense of having been loved and cared for in spite of one's own inadequacies. These preparatory realizations produce a desire for self-sacrifice in the service of others in order to begin to right the social balance. In the process, excessive self-concern diminishes and symptom focus is relieved.

HISTORY

Naikan Therapy grew out of *mishirabe,* the religious practice of a subsect of Jodo Shinshu Buddhist priests. In order to achieve enlightenment these priests would enter caves or other isolated settings to meditate for long periods of time on the expression of the Buddha's love in their lives. Going without food, water, and sleep, they sought to abandon the comforts of life in the effort to

gain spiritual insight. After some initial failures, Isshin Yoshimoto gained *satori* ("enlightenment") by this means. He decided to adapt the *mishirabe* practice for the lay person as a character-development technique. Yoshimoto added structure to the meditative process by developing the three themes of (1) what was received from others, (2) what was returned to them, and (3) what troubles were caused them. He removed the ascetic elements of fasting and sleeplessness. Finally, he simplified the isolation restriction and devised a process of frequent checks on the progress of the client's self-reflection.

In the early 1950s, having become wealthy in the synthetic fabric business, Yoshimoto turned over to others the running of his commercial enterprise and devoted himself entirely to Naikan Therapy. Naikan's first successes came within the Japanese prison system. Naikan was used in the rehabilitation program for sociopaths and addicts in juvenile reform centers and prisons for adult offenders (Kitsuse, 1965). Recidivism rates for prisoners who had done Naikan were significantly lower than for those who did not, and the treatment flourished for a while before political pressures severely restricted its use in the country's penal institutions.

Meanwhile the number of private clients treated at

the Nara Naikan Center were increasing to upward of 30 per week. These clients came for treatment because of family problems, difficulties at work, unhappy love relationships, psychophysiological complaints, and a wide variety of neurotic symptoms. Others wanted to strengthen their character or find a practical method for developing their spiritual self.

In the mid 1970s other Naikan centers opened, and by 1979 more than 15 private Naikan settings were in operation. Some catered to devout believers in Shinshu Buddhism or other religions; some were psychiatric facilities with strong programs of rehabilitation for alcoholics; others used Naikan with hypnosis (Ishida, 1969), autogenic training, and other meditative techniques.

Since the 1960s two other areas in which Naikan has operated are the business world and the school system. One facility in Tokyo provides special services for businessmen. Many companies in Japan send their employees, particularly new ones, to special programs for character training (Rohlen, 1976). Some companies (including hospitals) utilize Naikan as part of these *seishin kyoiku* training programs, paying their employees' fees and travel expenses. In schools individual teachers have encouraged Naikan practice both in the classroom and on sports teams. However, Naikan's resemblance to religious practice and the lack of apparent immediate relevance to success in college entrance examinations prevents this method from gaining wide popularity in the public educational institutions of Japan.

Very few westerners have undergone a week of intensive Naikan in Japan, although perhaps 10 researchers and clinicians have visited the Nara Center for brief periods of observation. Even fewer neurotics have been treated by Naikan in the West. The therapy remains essentially untried in the United States. However, recent innovations in technique make Naikan a more likely candidate for serious trial in the West.

The literature on Naikan in Japanese is not as extensive as that of Morita Psychotherapy. Much case history material exists, however, and verbatim audio tapes and transcriptions of Naikan interviews are readily available. Within the past few years a concerted effort has been made to broaden the scope of Naikan and to make it more respectable in academic psychology and medical circles (Murase & Johnson, 1973). Careful scientific study has begun and a national organization of therapists, researchers, and former clients was founded in 1978. Annual meetings attracted some 150 members from Hokkaido in the north of Japan to Kagoshima in the south. The heart of Naikan influence remains in the history-rich Kansai area of central Japan.

Few works dealing with Naikan have appeared in English (see references). The first book-length manuscript on the subject in English was submitted for publication

(Reynolds, 1981), and translations into English of Japanese volumes are also available.

CURRENT STATUS

Some 2,000 clients undergo intensive Naikan Therapy each year. Some of them continue to do daily Naikan at home, but a sizable number return to do intensive Naikan a second or third time.

Recently Naikan has been used with increasing frequency in the Japanese prison system, and particularly in juvenile rehabilitation centers, because of its strong impact within a short period of time. The trend in Japan, as in the United States, is toward shorter sentencing for most criminal offenses. Reports of cure and improvement rates of 60 percent over a two-year follow-up period have drawn much interest toward this method as a treatment form for alcoholism. Several psychiatric hospitals regularly use it in conjunction with broader rehabilitation programs.

The heart of Naikan in Japan remains at the Naikan Kenshu Jo, the Naikan Training Center in Nara, Japan. Though a national organization exists with a business office in Tokyo and members throughout Japan, the organization functions primarily to coordinate the annual meeting, encourage research, and distribute *Naikan* magazine.

Physicians, psychologists, priests, educators, nurses, and lay people practice Naikan. Training to become a Naikan therapist involves undergoing a week of intensive Naikan at one of the Japanese centers, preferably the one in Nara. During this week the potential therapist is given the opportunity to accompany the attending therapist on his rounds of the Naikansha clients and then to make the rounds on his own.

THEORY

Naikan holds that from early childhood we learn to use other people to our own ends. In myriad ways each day we take from others without adequately appreciating or reciprocating their contributions to our lives (Murase, 1974). We ignore or rationalize this selfishness because we fear the guilt and self-blame that comes as a natural consequence of taking a straight look at ourselves. Maintaining a positive self-image through this process of distortion requires energy and a sort of twisted perspective on living. The Naikan technique is designed to force the client to take a cold, hard look at himself for perhaps the first time in his life. He is instructed to prosecute himself as an attorney would in court (Takeuchi, 1965). The result of this seemingly harsh tactic, however, is rather surprising. Along with the tears of sorrow and repentance come a recognition that we have been loved and cared for by others in spite of our taking them for granted, hurting them, using them. An existential relief follows from squarely facing one's self at one's worst. The myth of individualism and the self-made person is exploded (Reynolds, 1977). The natural consequence of this cathartic realization is intense gratitude and the desire to try to begin righting one's social balance by offering oneself in the service of others.

The initial model for the giving significant other is the human mother. Whatever faults our mother (or mother surrogate) may have had, it was her effort that brought about our birth and kept us alive during the helpless dependent years when we were unable or uninterested in returning her services in equal measure. One begins Naikan reflection on the topic of one's mother.

To the Western theoretician this approach may seem rigid and antitherapeutic at first glance. We all know persons whose mothers seem at least to share large responsibility for psychologically deforming their offspring. It would appear almost obscene to suggest an attitude of gratitude and guilt toward such mothers. Yet on another level, the Naikan therapist is not seeking to change or evaluate critically *the mother* at all. Whatever evil she inflicted on the client, a careful reflection on the past will turn up positive, nurturant behavior as well. If not, the client would probably not be alive. At any rate, the focus is not on the mother herself but on what the client did (or did not) do for her and to her. Whatever may have been her faults in the relationship, it is certain that the client was less than a perfect child. It is the *client* who is to grow by reexamining his harsh evaluations of others and appreciating and serving them. The client is not told that he must find his mother to have been an ideal person. Rather he is to seriously consider those things she did for him, those things he returned to her, and the troubles he caused her. In most cases, the result of such a review of the past is a new recognition of the detailed ways in which, as the Japanese put it, "one was caused to be lived."

Viewing the therapeutic process from a broader perspective, it is clear that our current behaviors are influenced by what occurred in our past. It is also obvious that the past cannot be changed. It is frozen, unalterable. However, if we can come to restructure our perception of the past, its influence upon us may be altered. Restructuring our view of the past is precisely what Naikan is about.

Perhaps the theoretical perspective in the West that most closely fits that of Naikan is O. H. Mowrer's. Simply put, Mowrer (1964) argues that the sources of neurotic symptoms are our misdeeds and our attempts to conceal those misdeeds from significant others in our lives. He places the locus of responsibility for neurosis not on the environment, not on childbearing, not on some abstract "society," but on the neurotic individual himself. I am reminded of the problems I had in Japan during my first period of fieldwork there. My ability with the Japanese language was very poor at that time. Yet I attempted to conceal my inadequate language preparation by nodding and acting as if I understood even when there were gaps in my vocabulary, when I wasn't following the conversation. As a result of this effort to hide my limitations, it was necessary to keep conversations brief and to remember whom to avoid. Long conversations or repeated conversations with a person increased the likelihood of discovery of my secret, my lie. Social relationships became unsatisfying, even burdensome. When I was finally able to admit my inadequacy to others, to ask for repetitions and slower rates of speech, the unnecessary tensions that had been added to these interactions disappeared.

Mowrer indicates that the appropriate therapy for the neurotic who is attempting to conceal his weakness and "badness" from others is to confess his deviousness to them and to attempt to make restitution for his wrongs. Effectiveness aside, that is surely a difficult solution to the problem. It is easier to sit quietly in the therapist's office in an attempt to convince oneself that what one is doing is all right as it is. Yet Mowrer's solution is character building, in a way, and character development is precisely the tack that Japanese therapists in general and Naikan in particular take in treating neurosis.

As we shall see, the client confesses his social omissions and misdeeds to the therapist, then to a group of his peers, then to the significant others in his daily life outside the therapy setting. Finally, he attempts to repay those in his social world out of the feelings of gratitude and obligation that have welled up from within.

METHODOLOGY

The practice of Naikan is simple and readily described. In essence, it requires the *Naikansha* (client) to reflect on his past and report those reflections to his therapist, or *sensei*. The settings and styles vary somewhat, but the process is likely to go somewhat as follows.

The Naikan client may have read in the newspaper about Naikan; he may know someone who has done Naikan; or he may have been sent by his school principal, boss, or doctor. On arrival at the Naikan Center, he talks briefly with the therapist about his reasons for coming, then he listens to a short orientation tape. Within 30 minutes after his arrival he is doing Naikan seated behind a folding screen in the corner of a room (or facing the wall). He sits in any position that is comfortable on the pillows provided for him. He is not to lie down for fear of drifting off to sleep.

His initial assignment is to reflect upon how he behaved and felt toward his mother through the first years of grammar school. He is to consider what she did for him (20 percent of his meditation time), what he returned to her (20 percent), and what troubles and worries he caused her (60 percent). The aim is to recall in vivid detail specific events and acts during that period. Within an hour or two the therapist comes, bows before the screen, opens it, bows again, and asks the *Naikansha* what he has been reflecting on. The client then "confesses" within the structured format of what was given, what was returned, and troubles caused. He is then told to continue recalling his past self in relation to his mother up through the sixth grade. If he has no questions, the interview is ended with bows and he is left to continue with his memories.

During each interview the therapist simply listens humbly and gratefully to the outpouring from the client. The therapist then assigns the next topic, answers questions, and perhaps offers a word of encouragement, such as "Reflect deeply, please."

Usually assignments proceed in three-year steps up to the present (five- or ten-year steps may be used for elderly clients). Then the topic for reflection may change to the father. Again, the time periods begin with early school years and work up to the present. The pattern is repeated for mother, father, siblings, aunts, uncles, teachers, bosses, schoolmates, workmates, husband, wife, children, and other significant persons in the *Naikansha*'s life. Special topics such as lying, stealing, breaking school rules, gambling, and drinking may also be assigned. Time frames may be adjusted to fit the topic or to focus in on yearly or even monthly steps in the recent past.

The interviews may be taperecorded. With permission from the clients, the best tapes are reproduced and sold to clients with similar problems. Several times during the day, sample tapes are broadcast over a loudspeaker system. They provide models of proper Naikan and an education in the Naikan way of thinking.

The first few days are the most difficult ones. Inability to remember, muscle cramps, and boredom are common. But once the client gets into deep Naikan, the therapist, rather than assigning the subsequent topic, may ask the client who he wants to reflect on during the next time period. The Naikan reflection lasts from 5 AM until 9 PM for a week. In most settings clients arrive Sunday afternoon and leave the following Sunday morning.

At the Naikan Center the day is broken up by three meals, a bath, toilet functions, and a brief cleanup period each morning. The client eats his meals behind his screen. He is assigned a 10-minute bath period. He is told not to do Naikan while bathing but to bathe while doing Naikan. The same advice applies to eating and even urinating. Outside of the interview exchange, he is to remain silent.

Twice during the week, once on Monday and once on the final Sunday, group meetings are announced. The *Naikansha* assemble to hear the therapist's lecture and to ask questions. On the last day those who wish to are encouraged to talk about their experience before the whole group. This meeting is recorded, and the tape is duplicated for those who wish to purchase it.

Some clients maintain contact with their therapists through correspondence after discharge. Recently the national magazine and ex-client groups provide the opportunity for periodic reinvolvement with the people and ideas of Naikan. Discharged clients are encouraged to do Naikan reflection for at least one half hour twice daily. In the morning they are to reflect in sequence as they did during intensive Naikan. In the evenings they are to reflect on the events of that day—what they received, returned, and what troubles they caused others. Follow-up studies indicate that only a few continue with *nichijo*, or everyday Naikan. Fewer still report their reflections to a therapist by postcard.

APPLICATIONS

Naikan has been applied to a broad spectrum of clients. Psychosomatic problems, interpersonal difficulties, neuroses, addictions (including alcoholism), and criminal behavior problems have responded well to this treatment. Normal persons seeking character development or spiritual insight have also found Naikan useful.

Psychoses, senility and other organic brain syndromes, physical disorders, and many neurological conditions are not appropriate for Naikan treatment. Some practitioners, however, claim individual cures for clients previously diagnosed as suffering from schizophrenia, senile dementia, depression, and Parkinson's disease.

In practice, the number of dropouts during a week of Naikan varies from almost none to one-third, depending on the setting. Some settings have large percentages of clients who have been sent by school or legal authorities or by their employers or families. Such clients are not motivated to exert themselves in effortful Naikan, though some, in fact, do complete the week successfully. As yet there are no good predictive scales for determining who would benefit from Naikan.

Subjective ratings of Naikan depth maintained over a number of years at Nara indicate that the best clients tend to be middle-aged persons of both sexes.

Elderly persons present special difficulties in terms of memory deficits. On the other hand, adolescents may have motivational deficits. The youngest *Naikansha* was six years old at the time, but twelve or thirteen years seems to be an appropriate lower age limit.

Recent innovations have expanded the applicability of Naikan somewhat. A week of intensive Naikan is impracticable for some who might benefit from this form of self-reflection. A Naikan diary maintained at home covering recollections for an hour or more each day and brought to the therapist's office for weekly comment is one new possibility. Another involves the use of correspondence or audio tapes covering Naikan meditation at home. Since Naikan as practiced today is already an adaptation of another process (*mishirabe*), there is no substantial opposition to other innovative techniques provided that the fundamental self-reflection on the three themes is followed by some sort of confession to a caring other.

Naikan has been used in conjunction with hypnotherapy, autogenic training, various other forms of meditation, and psychoanalysis. It has been used to educate and motivate prisoners and alcoholics in programs of rehabilitation.

CASE EXAMPLE

This client, Mrs. O, is a middle-aged woman, a housewife and innkeeper. Her husband is the owner of a *ryokan* (a Japanese inn) and head of a construction company. Her complaints were as follows:

> Every day my head was heavy; I couldn't do my work well. I kept going over and over things in my mind. I couldn't express myself well to others. I walked around with a depressed-looking face and caused a lot of trouble for my family. Someone told me to go to Nara for Naikan, that there was someone in Nara who could help depressed people. I didn't really know anything about Naikan, hadn't heard anything about it, hadn't read a word about it, but why not try it? I thought.

The depression had begun about five years earlier, occurring a few times a year for a week or two each time, but it became a severe problem about six months prior to Mrs. O's admission to the Nara Naikan Center. More specifically, the symptoms involved a sudden dislike of work, a dissatisfaction with life. She would simply go to bed and stay there, getting up only when she felt like it. Her husband was an easygoing fellow; he never scolded her for her actions, though he couldn't have been pleased with this sort of behavior. She had no particular pains, but she felt tired and unwilling to do housework.

Mrs. O's Naikan reflection began with the assignment of considering herself in relation to her husband on a month-by-month basis from six months earlier. We pick up the transcription of her Naikan interviews about midway through the week. Yoshimoto Sensei is the interviewer.

Y: What did you reflect upon for the month of August?

O: My husband calls the family together each year in August for a family trip. All the children and grandchil-dren come. We all go somewhere together. There's nothing so wonderful as that, but I always put on a grumbling face. "Well, since everyone is here I suppose I'll go too," I'd say and go along with them.

Y: What did you receive from your husband, what did you return to him, and what troubles did you cause him?

O: That he took me along on the trip was something I received from him.

Y: And what did you return to him?

O: Well, the family asked me to make riceballs for everyone, and though I didn't feel like it, there was no way out of doing it. But I made them too salty.

Y: What trouble did you cause him?

O: Even though it was a pleasant trip, an enviable trip, I never showed any happiness, never spoke a word of gratitude. The crowd of grandchildren never called for me, and I never minded at all. I don't like children, I told them. They all liked Grandpa. When my daughter asked them who they liked best, they all said they loved Grandpa. When they said they didn't like me, my daughter asked them if it was nice to talk like that with me standing right there. Well, they said, she's just average. Whenever I went shopping I never got anything for the grandchildren. Now I've been reflecting on why I never bought anything for them.

Y: How have the first few days of Naikan been for you?

O: The first few days I really didn't know the meaning of Naikan. What shall I say? The first few days I simply sat and wasted time. At night I couldn't sleep. Then on the fifth evening I got to thinking. What are you doing here? I've been hearing the tapes of other *Naikansha*. By the third or fourth day they all seemed to be able to do Naikan, giving proper replies to the *sensei*. What's the matter with me? I wondered. I must be some sort of idiot. I was terribly sad. What should I do? Even during the war years we had plenty of rice, traded rice for medicine. We didn't lack anything. Maybe if I gave something up. Tomorrow I'll do without breakfast, I thought. So even though Mrs. Yoshimoto's meals are outstanding, I did without breakfast. Also instead of shifting my sitting position and standing once in a while, I sat all morning in formal position with my legs tucked under me. I think that's when I began to do Naikan.

Y: You went without lunch and dinner yesterday also, didn't you? Didn't you feel hungry?

O: Not a bit. Before, even when I ate a lot, my stomach rumbled, but not now. And I'm not in the slightest bit bored. Whether I have two or three days left I want to use them wholeheartedly, without eating.

Y: Fasting isn't an essential part of Naikan, but it is true that when one is really involved in self-reflection and forgets to eat, one's appetite doesn't seem to give much trouble.

O: That's certainly true. I'm not a bit hungry.

Y: Now please continue reflecting on your husband. Time is getting short, so bear down.

O: I shall. Thank you.

* * *

Y: What have you been reflecting upon this time?

O: I've been reflecting upon myself in relation to my husband in the month of September, what I received from him, returned to him, and the trouble I caused him. (Her voice has become soft and seems to come from far away.) At that time my blood pressure rose. I went to bed and I began to have stomach trouble. My husband assisted me in getting to the bathroom. He held me up and did other kind things for me. He even cleaned me off. As I did Naikan I realized what a special thing he did for me.

Y: Now you feel gratitude. What about at that time?

O: Then I didn't think a thing about it, only that it was part of being a husband. My children told me how fortunate I was to have a husband like that. He is a good provider, manly, and kind. They told me I should be thankful to have one like him.

Y: When they said that what did you think?

O: I just thought that this was natural, he was merely the way he should be. He was my husband; after all, when I'm sick he should take care of me.

Y: How do you feel about him now?

O: I realize how selfish I've been. I feel sorry and apologetic. (She cries.)

Y: What did you return to him in September?

O: Nothing in particular.

Y: What trouble did you cause him?

O: I always slept when I felt like it and got up when it suited me. I didn't do anything for him that a wife should do.

Y: If you were your husband in such circumstances, what would you have done?

O: I'd become sad.

Y: If you saw your daughter-in-law doing as you've been doing, what would you do?

O: I'd warn her. You can't do such things. Behave more properly.

Y: How did your husband react?

O: He always stayed the same. Perhaps he had given up on me. He laughed around the house, as usual. And he continued to treat me with kindness.

* * *

Y: What have you been reflecting on during this period?

O: December, what I received from, returned to, and the troubles I caused my husband. December is a very busy time for us at work. My husband's head is filled with thoughts about bills and the like. The year-end bonuses for employees at the inn were all prepared by him. I'm really grateful for that. As for what I returned to him, on December first I had responsibility for preparing the meal for a big celebration. About the trouble I caused him, on the day of the celebration I did what I had to do, but I grumbled and only appeared before the guests when I absolutely had to. As I think back over the day, I only said unpleasant things and presented a troubled face to the guests. Later that month when my daughter came home suddenly I treated her as if I didn't know her. That's the only time I've ever seen my husband cry. Whatever she said I felt nothing. She even told me that I wasn't much of a mother. To think that my husband had to raise the children practically alone. (She cries.)

Y: Next time, will you reflect on January?

O: Yes, thank you.

Y: Please reflect deeply. Do you have any questions?

O: I had a question but I seem to have forgotten it.

Y: Such a question isn't worth worrying about; please continue with your Naikan.

O: Thank you.

* * *

Y: You haven't been eating. How do you feel?

O: Not a bit hungry.

Y: How many meals have you skipped now?

O: Five.

Y: Have you done such a thing before?

O: Never.

Y: At home do you eat a lot?

O: When I'm sick I don't have much of an appetite, but otherwise I eat a lot, always three meals a day. People tell me I'll get fat.

Y: What is the greatest number of meals you have skipped before?

O: One meal, when I was depressed.

Y: Now if you were to return home and someone asked you about your depression, what would you reply?

O: I am completely cured. (Her voice is bright with enthusiasm.) Naikan is marvelous! I plan to tell everyone and encourage them to try Naikan too.

Y: Do you have any questions?

O: Three years ago I saw a couple that really impressed me. The husband's face was bright and the wife seemed to be taking good care of him. She respected him and showed him so. I want to be like that, I thought. But I couldn't put that hope into effect, unfortunately.

Y: Did you want to ask me something about that?

O: Oh yes, when I thought of that event three years ago I thought also of your face. Your wife shows you the same supporting respect I saw back then. Comparing myself with them, I realized how lax I've been.

Y: Well, tomorrow you leave here, don't you? Use every second as if your life depended upon it.

O: Yes, thank you.

About two weeks after she returned home, Mrs. O telephoned the center. She was doing exceptionally well, working hard. Her husband was pleased with the change, and her friends were talking of coming for Naikan too. She said that she was not continuing to sit in formal Naikan, but each day she thought about the three themes as she worked. Her work had become interesting again. Her children remarked on the complete change in their mother. "I really understand how bad I've been," she said. She expressed her gratitude again and again, and promised to call Mr. Yoshimoto periodically to report on her progress. At that time she also made a reservation to return for another week of Naikan in the early summer, accompanied by her daughter.

SUMMARY

A week of intensive Naikan is, for many clients, an impactful life-altering experience. A new perspective on life is obtained. One feels guilty but grateful, one feels unworthy but loved in spite of the unworthiness. Ordinary feelings of guilt and inferiority are trivial in comparison with the existential blows to one's self-image received in Naikan. So a new benchmark is created, a new standard for self-assessment is formed. Evaluation of one's day shifts from "Why did this have to happen and did I get my share?" (with the implication that *I* deserve better) to "How grateful I am for whatever happened today, and what did I do for those around me?" On one level it is certainly unreasonable to be grateful for unnecessary delays, missed telephone calls, or an engine breakdown. But on another level gratitude is not unreasonable at all. Moreover, after learning Naikan clients exhibit a shift from the mode of passive recipient of "the slings and arrows of outrageous fortune" to the actor in others' behalf, a shift from self-centeredness to other-centeredness. That shift, for some, is the marker for the change from childishness to maturity. Furthermore, it may signal a movement from misery to joy.

REFERENCES

Ishida, R. (1969). Naikan analysis. *Psychologia, 12,* 81–92.

Kitsuse, J. I. (1965). Moral treatment and reformation of inmates in Japanese prisons. *Psychologia, 8,* 9–23.

Mowrer, O. H. (1964). *The new group therapy.* Princeton. N.J.: Van Nostrand.

Murase, T. (1974). Naikan therapy. In Lebra, T. and Lebra, W. (Eds.), *Japanese culture and behavior.* Honolulu: University Press of Hawaii.

Murase, T., & Johnson, F. (1973). Naikan, Morita and western psychotherapy: A comparison. Paper presented at the American Psychiatric Association Meetings, Honolulu.

Reynolds, D. K. (1977). Naikan therapy—an experiential view. *International Journal of Social Psychiatry, 23*(4), 252–264.

Reynolds, D. K. (1980). *The quiet therapies.* Honolulu: University Press of Hawaii.

Reynolds, D. K. *Naikan therapy: Meditation for self development in Japan.* Submitted for publication.

Rohlen, T. (1976). *For Harmony and Strength.* Berkeley: University of California Press.

Takeuchi, K. (1965). On "Naikan." *Psychologia, 8,* 2–8.

Chapter 40

NARRATIVE THERAPY

JEFFREY L. ZIMMERMAN and VICTORIA C. DICKERSON

This may be a difficult but important chapter to understand. The main reason, I believe, is that although both authors write well, they use words that are not familiar to the psychotherapy field. Their language draws from philosophy, linguistics, literary criticism and contemporary social thought. For example, deconstruction *a word devised by Derrida which in my dictionary, means "The undoing or the exposition of assumptions or of internal contradictions of any system of thought, such as a theory" and the definition goes on. The authors are interested in deconstructing therapeutic approaches, exposing the assumptions behind them (including their own) and taking them out of the status of truth.*

As I understand the system, I view it as referring to a problem that the therapist and client create together, that the client gets to recognize as bad narrative therapy would help as the therapist helps the client notice experiences that are outside or unaffected by the problem. This is done through the medium of language. To give an example, someone who worked for me called me and announced in a happy manner that she was dying. She reported how she enjoyed being able to see the trees and the sea, how good everyone was to her, and how wonderful life was. While she did not prefer to die, she was able to live her life without the dying totally influencing the rest of her life.

It might be useful to read the authors' case example first, then their methodology, leaving the theory for last. As their approach dictates, you will then have some experience to understand their perspective.

Narrative therapy is characterized by the use of a narrative metaphor to conceptualize problems, persons, and change. This approach locates problems in the dominant stories that influence people's lives. Stories are created by the meaning people give their experiences. They are not located in or produced by personality, but, instead, they have been shaped by cultural meaning systems, and thus viewed as separate from persons. Not only are problems viewed as existing in external stories, but who a person is, is also viewed as having been created by these stories. Stories influence how persons interpret their experience and how they decide what is significant. The effects of these stories likewise affect other persons, so that they respond in ways that inadvertently support the other's dominant story. The narrative therapist facilitates change by creating a context in which clients can separate from stories that have undesired effects, and by helping them attend and give meaning to other life experiences, currently unstoried, considered as entry points to more preferred narratives.

A critical aspect is an understanding of stories as profoundly cultural in origin. Narrative therapists help clients notice the influence of the cultural constructions of gender, race, class, sexuality, and age, and see the relationship of these constructions to their own experience of problem stories. Clients might then identify cultural constructions, likewise shaping of their identities, that better fit their preferences.

Narrative therapists see all therapies, including their own, as stories or constructions created in particular social contexts. They raise the question of effects, seeing clients as the ultimate judge of the usefulness of any work.

HISTORY

The origins of narrative therapy as it currently exists rest with Michael White, of Adelaide, South Australia, although certainly others (notably David Epston of Auckland, New Zealand) are critical to its development. I (JLZ) met Michael White in 1986 when Karl Tomm brought him to North America for the first time. Then, Michael (1986) was situating his innovative work in Batesonian theory, reinterpreting and emphasizing aspects of Bateson's work differently than family systems therapists had done previously. Gregory Bateson (1972, 1979) was part of a group that developed some of the fundamental ideas in family therapy, including the basic cybernetic model (i.e., viewing the family as a homeostatic system with circular causality). The family therapy field was also evolving in the mid-1980s, again influenced by Bateson's thinking, but emphasizing a "second-order" cybernetic model (See Zimmerman & Dickerson, 1994b, for a description of this evolution). This emphasis acknowledged the role of the observer (e.g., the therapist) in creating views that dictate the way things become known. In other words, what therapists said represented their own view about what was happening more than some "objective" truth about the family.

In a related area, constructivism was becoming popular among family therapists (Watzlawick, 1984). Newer therapeutic approaches began to account for the idea that individuals create their own reality rather than traverse along planes of objective truth. These developments paralleled overall changes in the arts, sciences, and humanities, which had moved from the "modern era" with its emphases on objectivity and specification, to the "postmodern era" (Kvale, 1993; Lax, 1992; Lowe, 1991), reflecting multiple points of view and multiple possibilities for the way things might work.

Given this cultural backdrop it makes sense that Michael White changed the procedure from the therapist wondering what was "true" to the therapist asking clients about the "real effects" of what they were experiencing. In addition, Michael began a process of decentering the therapist by considering the client to be the person with the knowledge and experience to answer questions about the problem. Michael privileged his client's knowledge and problem-solving possibilities over his own. This belief in people was not an intervention; it was real. Those of us who were learning from Michael experienced the real effects of this "belief" in our own knowledge and abilities.

Another shift was away from causal thinking, which was dominant in the field, to a theory of restraints (Bateson, 1972, 1979). Michael talked about the problem as a restraint—had effects that encouraged certain responses and discouraged others, but did not quite cause something to happen. This thinking fit nicely with a practice he developed called "externalizing the problem," in which the therapist talks about the problem as separate and asks the client to describe and evaluate its effects. Clients (and therapists) have found it useful to notice a problem's effects, develop for themselves what they think about it, and then feel agency in being able to turn down the problem's "invitation" to react in certain ways (an advantage of not thinking from a causal perspective).

The French poststructuralist Michel Foucault (1979, 1980, 1984a, 1984b) was another strong influence on Michael White's thinking. Foucault was interested in how dominant discourses shape people's lives. For example, systems of scientific classification (for example, the DSM) achieve truth status, rather than being seen as just the point of view of the privileged some (see also Gaines, 1992) and therefore not necessarily consistent with many people's experiences. When these systems of classification do achieve truth status, they can have a profound effect on people's identities as people begin to believe that the truth about themselves is the one produced by scientific points of view. They begin to know themselves and be known through these systems of knowledge as opposed to their own personal experience or local (i.e., relevant small community) systems of knowledge. Foucault wrote about how persons get objectified in this culture, becoming the thing these systems specify (e.g., a schizophrenic). Furthermore, through a process called subjectification, Foucault noted how we learn to do the same to ourselves—to "torture" ourselves to fit the mold the dominant culture says is correct. Those whose work, life, and self fit the dominant specifications achieved a position of power and privilege relative to others. Michael's externalization of the problem was a way to reverse this political process—by objectifying the problem, not the person.

Other writers (e.g., Gergen, 1985, 1991), identified as social constructionists, were also examining how the sociopolitical context of ideas shapes people's lives and identities. From this point of view, the use of language and the effects of current cultural practices shape and create individual meaning in the culture. In contrast to many constructivists, who might consider all meaning to be relative to any individual, social constructionists look at the effects of various viewpoints, situate them culturally, and are often willing to take a personal stand about these effects. This emphasis on the sociopolitical context appealed to those who had some background in standing up against oppression and against the marginalization of people whose beliefs and practices did not fit the status quo. This included certain pathologizing practices in the mental health field, which had the effect of making people feel "less than." Clients say they often experience the relief that comes when they are freed from evaluation by dominant discourse.

In the late 1980s, at the suggestion of Michael's close colleague, David Epston, and Michael's partner, Cheryl White, Michael situated the work in a narrative metaphor (Bruner, 1986, 1990). This metaphor was becoming popular in various areas of intellectual and social thought. It allowed a greater flexibility in the work by introducing time as an integral variable, an advantage over the original Batesonian cybernetic/information metaphor. Bruner's work fit well into the developing philosophical base, as he noted that people tend to create stories to explain their own or others' deviance from the status quo. Bruner's ideas, as well as the work of My-erhoff (1982), helped contribute to Michael's thinking about how to ask questions in the therapy room in a way that supports a "reauthoring" process. The therapist's expertise evolved from knowing what was best or how things should be, to how to create a context, through language and questions, that would allow clients to leave problems behind and embark in directions they thought would have preferred effects. The use of ritual and ritual processes, including a "rite of passage" metaphor (Turner, 1969; van Gennep, 1960), represent contributions to the work that Michael took from anthropology and sociology.

It is critical to reiterate that the backbone of narrative therapy is an emphasis on challenging dominant structures of power and how they affect people. This began with the early influences of the feminist challenge to gender relations (and models of therapy) and continued with Foucault's ideas. Currently the work of the Just Therapy Team (Kiwi Tamasese, Flora Tuhaka, and Charles Waldegrave) of New Zealand (Tamasese & Waldegrave, 1993; Waldegrave, 1990) adds to this challenge by providing a model for social justice and accountability.

CURRENT STATUS

Since 1988, when Michael White began to situate his work in a narrative metaphor, narrative therapy has interested more and more practitioners, particularly those with family therapy backgrounds. Despite not being a systems therapy (as are most family therapy models), narrative therapy is one of the growing trends of post-structuralist models gaining popularity in the family therapy field. In 1996, narrative ideas and practices were the main thrust of both a preconference and a conference plenary at the Annual Meeting of the American Family Therapy Academy, the most prestigious group of family therapy teachers, researchers, and clinicians. There were strong reactions to the plenary presentation, which were compared to similar reactions to a meeting some years prior that had represented the feminist challenge to family therapy. It might have seemed that a revolution was occurring. However, although narrative therapy includes passionate groups of devotees, their limited influence reflects the lack of promotion given to narrative ideas by mainstream groups (i.e., psychiatry and psychology journals and conferences).

Even so, the mid-1990s saw a rise in interest in the narrative metaphor. Nationally (United States), *Newsweek* magazine (Cowley & Springen, 1995) ran a short article on narrative work. The *Family Therapy Networker* (O'Hanlon, 1994), the most widely read family therapy publication, presented narrative therapy as possibly "the

third wave." There have been frequent articles in all of the family therapy journals, including a special edition on narrative therapy in the *Journal of Systemic Therapy* (Zimmerman & Dickerson, 1996a). Dulwich Centre Publications, run by Cheryl White in Adelaide, South Australia, publishes the *Dulwich Centre Newsletter,* which has been providing articles on narrative ideas since 1985. In 1997, *Gecko* was added as a journal focusing on narrative practices. Dulwich Centre Publications has also published several books highlighting different aspects of narrative work. Michael White and David Epston's seminal book, *Narrative Means to Therapeutic Ends* (1990), was originally published in Australia as *Literate Means to Therapeutic Ends* (1989). Other books followed, including those by Zimmerman and Dickerson (1996b); Freedman and Combs (1996); Freeman, Epston, and Lobovitz (1997); and edited books by Monk, Winslade, Crocket, and Epston (1997); Smith and Nylund (1997); and Madigan and Law (1998). Numerous chapters appear in edited books covering constructivist and social constructionist models.

In 1993, the first annual Conference on Narrative Ideas and Therapeutic Practices occurred in Vancouver, BC. Biannual Therapeutic Conversation Conferences, which include narrative work, started in 1991. Narrative presentations have taken place at the American Association of Marriage and Family Therapy Conferences, including a narrative track in 1997. The First International Narrative Therapy and Community Work Conference was held in Adelaide, Australia, in February, 1999. Narrative work is noticeably present in Australia and New Zealand, California, Vancouver, BC, Chicago, and Boston. Tulsa, Oklahoma, where Michael White first visited the US, has many narrative practitioners. Pockets of narrative groups are springing up all over the world (e.g., South Africa, Zimbabwe, Israel, and Denmark to name a few). Although there is no formal listing of narrative therapists, continued sharing of ideas at conference venues has allowed for informal networking, and it is likely narrative therapy is practiced in most large US cities.

THEORY

As stated previously, narrative therapy is based on radically different notions of what a problem is, how to conceptualize persons, and what creates change.

The Problem

In many forms of therapy, therapists conceptualize problems to mean something more than how their clients present them. For example, some therapies understand problems as evidence of structural differences or deficits (structuralism), either of the person or the family. Other therapies see problems as symptoms that serve a function (functionalism). In both of these cases the problem is located in the person or in the relationships. A narrative therapist understands the problem to be the one the client's experiences and thinks about the cultural meaning systems that influence that experience. For example, tension is tension and not representative of something else. What the problem is may change as the client's meanings of his or her experience are explored, but the client's opinion about the problem is privileged. In addition, narrative therapy sees these meanings as produced externally to the person. What does this mean, and how does this relate to how we clinicians make sense of what we hear?

From our perspective we believe that language and dominant discourses in the culture shape the way people make meaning of their experience. A discourse is a set of ideas that create meaning in a particular domain. We are all influenced by some discourse all of the time. Discourses have the effect of putting some in the majority while leaving others marginalized (if they don't fit the dominant specifications). In this way, they organize relations of power. Thinking in terms of how dominant cultural discourses shape meaning, one can understand the problem as residing in these discourses and the meaning they create. If so the problem is seen as separate/external to the person. As we listen to clients, we can imagine what discourses are shaping meaning for them. We ask about discourses when they seem close to our clients' experience and wonder about their effects on our clients' lives and what they think of these effects (although we are careful to leave the problem constructed in the language and domain of our clients' experience).

What are some dominant discourses that we find useful to bring forth? We are very interested in the effects of patriarchy and gender specifications (separate ones for men and women), classism, racism, heterosexual dominance, adultism, developmentalism, capitalism, moralism, individualism, and others. Examples of how some of these discourses affect/shape problems will be given in a later section. All of these discourses could have both positive and negative effects, given an individual's preferences. Narrative work is political in that it focuses on what ways people cooperate with the specifications of certain discourses, what ways they do not, and what are the effects of cooperating or not. We want our clients to reflect on how these choices fit their own preferences for how they want to live their lives and what kind of persons they would like to be. In this way, we are inviting clients to see themselves as separate from these discourses, so that discourses no longer speak the truth about who the client has to be. Often, we understand problems as an effect for persons of their not being a way these discourses prescribe, particularly for those persons who don't believe in prescribed ways but feel they have no choice. Or, one could follow these prescriptions but not really want to be the way the discourses direct one to be. For example, "self-doubt" may influence persons of a so-called "lower" class who believe they have failed because they have not achieved a certain economic status. They may notice and value their rich relationships but not give this much weight in evaluating themselves. Given the discourses of capitalism and classism, economic status is privileged and valued over relationship. People blame themselves for not achieving more, instead of seeing clearly the economic inequities in the culture and how these inequities make it difficult to "move up." They may also not prefer to engage in competitive tactics but feel inadequate when they don't.

How and why are these personal stories (e.g., self-doubt) created and why are they so individually-oriented? Often, stories are created to explain deviance from normative social functioning (Bruner, 1990). These stories support or justify a person's behavior, explaining why they are not doing something they "should" or why they have to be doing what they are doing. Events from the past (small stories or pieces of experience) are strung together in a causative plot to account for why what is occurring in the present was inevitable. The story in the present (e.g., "self-doubt") is supporting stories from the past as well as events in the present. When these stories get created they get the person to notice only the events that fit the storyline and to make interpretations of events that support that particular story. This is just as true for stories with good effects (e.g., self-acceptance) as for those with bad ones. When a problem dominates a story, we say it is problem-saturated (White, 1989) or that someone has a problem-dominated identity. Given how the discourses of individualism and essentialism have shaped our notion of persons, people experience the story as who they truly are and assume the problem resides in them. How do the assumptions in narrative work about persons challenge this way of thinking and the effects it has on people's identity?

Person

Psychology was created, as a discipline, to detect and account for those persons who wouldn't fit into major social institutions (Gaines, 1992). Individualism and essentialism (the idea that there is one, basic core self) set the backdrop for psychology and psychological practices from the beginning. In narrative work we are not thinking of persons as self-contained or relatively fixed. Instead, we believe that stories, which are culturally produced and maintained, have the effect of creating versions of the person. From a narrative perspective, we would say these stories are constitutive of the self. Whatever story is affecting us, it creates a version of the self that is consistent with that story. In this sense, all of us are multiversioned or multistoried, as we have the potential to respond in any way that might be encouraged based on which story is influencing us. For example, under the influence of patriarchy a man might be inclined to dominance and over entitlement. However, the same person, under the influence of compassion (as a way of being) might respond quite differently. The implication here is that problems do not reflect any deficits or a lack of capacity. Narrative therapists can invite people to decide on preferred versions of themselves and then help them notice experiences in their lives that fit that version. People can begin to let that version be the story of influence in their lives. This has the effect of their responding in ways that previously may have seemed to them and to others that they "couldn't."

Narrative therapists are concerned about the effects of the traditional psychotherapy view of the self that questions one's capabilities or motives and views them separate from the social context in which they occur. From our point of view, the effect of dominant discourses and participation in dominant social institutions is both to shape and value certain versions of the self. Because traditional approaches to therapy are often pathologizing, those versions that don't fit the mold are misrepresented as something "less than" or bad. Given that these versions of the self have been created by a viewing of the self through powerful institutions (e.g., media, schools, therapy), they achieve truth status and become constitutive of a person's identity. In other words, these versions gain more influence and have profound effects on the person's behaviors and conclusions about themselves and others. As people engage in these thin conclusions (White, 1997), the possible rich descriptions, which would incorporate other experiences in their lives and connect to more preferred versions of the self, fall into the shadows.

Change

Given these ideas about problems and persons from the perspective of a narrative metaphor, how does change occur? Since the therapist does not consider him- or herself to be the expert in how others should live their lives, clients must first articulate a picture of how they want to be, and how this is different from the ways the problem is currently encouraging. We are ever on the lookout for hopes, dreams, attitudes, and behaviors that are already present within the client's experience. These experiences have occurred throughout the client's life, but have gone unstoried, or without meaning being attributed to those experiences. The task of the therapist, then, is to create a context in which the client can notice those experiences and create meaning around them. This can be quite difficult as problems supported by dominant cultural

meaning systems can blind clients to the significance of those other experiences in their lives.

The therapeutic conversation from a narrative perspective is very different from other approaches. First, all the versions of the therapist's self are available to share with the client when appropriate. In this way, the work is more like two persons standing together without some of the usual hierarchy. Second, the therapist supports, usually through externalization, a process whereby clients can experience some separation from the problem and its effects. Once this occurs, space is available for them to notice other occurrences (events, actions, habits, or ideas and beliefs) in their lives that would, perhaps, be more preferred by them. Third, the therapist and client coconstruct meaning around these events. This meaning is not something that the therapist thinks would be better for the client, but is instead situated within the client's store of experience. Constructing an alternate story, a preferred one, and stringing together those events that hold that story is the core of narrative work.

METHODOLOGY

As suggested in the previous section, the beginning part of narrative work involves a separation—from problems, problem identities, and from conventional ways of knowing the self. It also involves a separation from dominant understandings about relating to professionals (e.g., therapists) and beliefs in their greater expertise regarding knowing oneself (e.g., clients). As narrative therapists, we set the process of separation in motion by asking the person or family to share something about their lives separate from the problem, and then by offering to answer some of the same types of questions the client or family might have in return. This practice sets a direction for the work and for the relationship we want to have with our clients.

Two sets of ideas orient us in the beginning sessions. One is the *statement of position map* (White, 1998), and the other is the practice of *following*. The statement of position map helps us to organize the conversation toward the goal of separating the person from the problem. We start by asking clients to tell us about what problem is affecting their lives. We are interested in hearing their experiences and having them help us try to get the meaning they are giving these experiences. For example, if they tell us about some things they have trouble doing and say that this is because they are afraid, then "fear" becomes the problem. If a child, brought in for lack of performance at school, complains that he or she does not feel like doing the work, then the "don't want to's" can become the problem. The first step in the map, then, is to get at the client's version of the problem. We respond to this by talking about the problem as if it were a thing, a practice we call *externalizing the problem.*

Step two in the map involves looking at the effects of the problem. We are interested in behavioral effects, on how the problem encourages conclusions about the self and others, how it stops people from doing some things they want to do, how it demands that they do some things they would prefer not to do; generally, how the problem influences the clients' lives and relationships. In asking about effects, and effects of effects, we are hoping to get some separation of the person from the problem as well as to help them notice the ways the problem is creating havoc in their lives. One common strategy that problems employ is to isolate people from the world or from each other. When people notice this, they often become alarmed and maybe even angry at the problem.

Steps three and four of the map involve asking people to evaluate what they think of the problem and to justify that evaluation by explaining why their conclusion makes sense to them. In our experience most people quickly begin to evaluate the problem as bad, realizing its impact on their lives in ways they previously did not appreciate. With separation from the problem and with increased awareness of its effects, people begin to argue against its future intrusion into their lives. We believe this is an advantage of the externalizing process. If the problem is separate and it is bad, then people take more responsibility in beginning to stand up to it (as opposed to when they think they are the problem and feel blamed). Their interest in standing up to the problem is justified by them when questioned about why the problem or its effects don't fit for them. Their values, goals, intentions, and commitments are in direct opposition to the direction the problem has in mind for them.

Sometimes, when questioning about effects, one of the effects becomes a more useful candidate for what the problem might be (as determined by the client). For example, if one of the effects of "fear" is "self-doubt," then this problem might capture more of the client's experience and be named as the problem. "Fear" can then be considered an effect of "self-doubt." We tell our students to remember we are not searching for truth or causality, just the ways of making sense of people's experience that are most helpful. This evolution of what the problem is (how it is named) can occur in the first half hour or in a later session. The direction of the session and our questions, always follow the experience of the client.

We don't want this to sound easy or facile. Some problems, like anorexia, are quite big with huge negative effects. Anorexia, with its wide-reaching cultural support, can make people think it is their friend while it is killing them. These kinds of problems require more time and effort to make the problem noticeable. We find it useful to situate such problems in the culture by asking questions like, "Why is anorexia more likely to pick on

women than on men." In general, we look for opportunities to ask questions that situate the problem in dominant cultural meanings, a process we refer to as *deconstruction* (i.e., bringing forth the context of ideas that help produce meaning). For example, a man I (JLZ) saw came in for anxiety, which through questioning, evolved into a "real man" problem. This situated the problem in dominant cultural specifications for men. Deconstructing questions further alienate the person from the problem, implicitly question the truthfulness of the problem, and help the person see that the roots of the problem are separate from who they are as a person and from their relationships. It allows for the conversation described in the theory section about how a person's preferences may or may not fit with the specifications prescribed by the culture. It can also be useful to ask questions about people's shame and embarrassment about their problems, situating these feelings in dominant and traditional ideas about problems and therapy.

Although the process of externalizing is one of the major ways by which narrative therapy has come to be known, we believe it does not constitute the major thrust of the work. Certainly, the process of helping people separate from the problems that constitute them is a sine qua non for the rest of the work, for reauthoring cannot occur as long as one's life and person are taken over by a problem-saturated story. However, once separation has occurred, reauthoring becomes the stuff of narrative work. To engage clients in the "thickening" of a preferred story, the therapist collaborates with the client in the coconstruction of an alternative narrative. The practices that encourage a reauthoring process include: telling and retelling, creating reflexivity, re-membering, outsider witness groups, definitional ceremonies, and taking back, among others.

What gives a problem story life is the telling and retelling of that story over time with the concomitant searching of past events that corroborate the story. To help persons "reconstitute" themselves along preferred lines, the same process of telling and retelling must occur. Entry points to an alternative story are often noticed as the therapist engages with the client in a conversation about the problem story and its effects; these entry points are events or incidents that are "outside" the problem story that would not be predicted by a telling of it. Narrative therapists refer to these events as "unique outcomes" (White, 1988; Goffman, 1961, 1974). When these events are noticed, and the client acknowledges their importance, the therapist tries to develop these unique outcomes by inviting the client to respond to "landscape of action" and "landscape of identity" (also called consciousness) questions. Landscape of action questions refer to the plot, the events over time that support a preferred story, and the when, where, who, and what questions; landscape of identity questions include the how and why, the person's intentions, purposes, preferences, philosophies, values, desires, and goals. So, for example, if "fear" is the problem, then a client might indicate an event when he or she approached a situation with courage (a unique outcome). The therapist might ask questions such as, "When did this event occur? Who was there? What happened just before the event? How did the client notice the courage? Had the client acted with this courage on previous occasions?" These are action questions. Identity questions might be, "What was the client thinking? How did courage fit his or her preferences? Or goals? Or values? Who else might have noticed it, and what did this tell that person about the client?" In other words, the therapist engages the client in a process of telling another story about themselves in relation to the problem. This is a heroic story of persons standing up to problems that are primarily not of their making and putting them out of their lives (as opposed to a pathological story of the person or family).

The telling and retelling continue through subsequent sessions, with the focus of the work on experiences that are a performance of the preferred story in the client's life. The therapist also begins to ask questions, such as "Who do you think is noticing these developments?," wondering who might be witnessing the performance. Through more questions, the practice of re-membering, or the creation of a "membered" community, is extended to include persons from one's past who might have witnessed the precursors to the developing preferred story. A question like "Who would be least surprised at the steps you've taken?" can be very evocative when there is enough connection to the new story. Indeed, many "new" memories start popping out once there is a context for them (i.e., the alternative story). Individuals get reconnected to versions of themselves that have been in the shadow of the problem. In addition we might even suggest that the client actually invite others to a session to share experiences of the person that support the developing story or to become members of a community of concern and support for the client.

A similar witnessing can occur in the responses of what are called *reflecting teams* or *outsider witness groups*. Reflecting teams are made up of professionals (or sometimes friends of the client) who watch the session. The team in turn is watched by the client and therapist as the members ask further questions to make the preferred story more noticeable. These are reauthoring questions of the type mentioned above, with the difference being that the client is in a "reflexive" position while listening to the questions being raised. That is, he or she can overhear (or eavesdrop) on the conversation without having to respond (Janowsky, Dickerson, & Zimmerman, 1995; White, 1995b). The team members say how their questions are related to their own lives and experience, allowing the client to compare his or her own experience to theirs and decide the relevance of the question or comment. Letters are also often used to summarize sessions and to raise further questions. In addition, ceremonies, including certificate giving or gathering people together for parties to mark new identities, are also used to make the preferred story more visible and more salient.

Finally, there are additional narrative practices that help mark a shift in story. These include "taking it back" practices as well as inviting the client to be a consultant to others. "Taking it back" refers to a process whereby the therapist (or reflecting team) share with the client the ways they have been transformed by the client's experience. For example, a client recently commented to me (VCD) that she (a teacher) could "call in sick" but couldn't "call in dead," continuing with the idea that it had become foremost in her mind to pay attention to her own health. I asked if I could share that comment with others and, in a subsequent session, let her know the profound influence the comment had on my personal health decisions. In gaining a client's permission to share his or her knowledge and learning, others who have similar difficulties can also learn. The process of sharing knowledge, and taking it back to the client, continues a telling and retelling. This is similar to asking the client to act as a consultant. In other words, would he or she be willing to call another client, write a note, even come into a session, or let the therapist act as a conduit of information? Clients have been known to form groups (such as the Anti-Anorexia, Anti-Bulimia League of Vancouver, BC, Canada), to establish short- and long-term relationships, and to even write short articles for an Internet web site. See www.voices.com, created by Marie-Nathalie Beaudoin as described in *Gecko* (Dickerson, 1998).

Throughout the work, narrative therapists employ accountability practices. These include having the client interview therapists about their questions and practices or letting them know what fits or does not. We might also consult with members of the clients' group if they are not the same as that of the therapist (e.g., male therapists with women for women clients, white therapists with persons of color, heterosexual therapists with persons who identify as lesbian or gay, and so on). We continue to look for ways to be accountable where issues of power and hierarchy exist.

APPLICATIONS

Narrative therapy has been used to address a wide range of problems with persons of many different ages. In the following section, we will provide a brief survey of problems along with examples of how we address dominant cultural discourses, either implicitly or explicitly, in this work.

Adults

Narrative work has been useful with the typical problems that affect adults, such as anxiety and depression, as well as even more difficult problems, such as anorexia and chronic pain. If these problems have been around a short time, the work can go very quickly. However, problems that have been around a long time often speak to people of their identity (Zimmerman & Dickerson, 1996b). Such problems affect persons differently, depending on gender, race, and class, or the intersection of these. For young middle-class women in their 20s (usually white, but also some Asian women in North America), anxiety and depression often can be understood as effects of tremendous societal pressure to "do it all" (i.e., get married, have a family, have a career, make money, and be happy, as well as make others happy). For example, I (VCD) have worked extensively with such young women, and have been astounded at their experience of pressure to perform. Two young women in particular, one 22 and the other 27, one white, the other Asian, both extremely bright and talented, have suffered greatly at the hands of depression and anxiety, so much so that it has eroded their future. In one case, an experience of chronic fatigue has made it close to impossible for the young woman to create the kind of career and relationship possibilities she desires. My work with her has helped her separate from the anxiety and move slowly but surely forward. The other young woman, struggling since high school to find her way, is now completing general education requirements so that she can go to a four-year college. She is also finding new ways to relate to her family, who have remained her strongest support system.

These problems may become influential in a context where women are not experiencing the kinds of connections they've been taught to value or are experiencing situations of oppression (e.g., male domination in a relationship). For men, these problems might evolve in a context where their adequacy is in question. An example, mentioned previously, is where anxiety was later talked about as being an effect of not living up to dominant specifications for men (i.e., the "real man" problem).

Pain (similar to anxiety) has very specific behavioral effects. A careful examination of these, juxtaposed with noticing any departures from the problem, can support a dramatic shift in direction away from the problem and the lifestyle it creates. One woman was seen by me (JLZ) in the hospital, her life 98% taken over by pain. What did it mean that she was able to get out of bed, or do her crossword puzzle? Soon she had recaptured much of her life.

Anorexia and bulimia are problems frequently addressed by narrative therapists (Epston, 1994; Madigan, 1994; Zimmerman & Dickerson, 1994a). We are particularly interested in this problem because of the extraordinarily powerful way the culture supports it. Women are literally surrounded by encouragement toward it through the movies and television, advertisements, magazines, and so on. David Epston, who pioneered the first Anti-Anorexia League in New Zealand (an effort to create an alternative body of knowledge for women) suggests that all women are affected to some extent by pro-anorexic/bulimic thinking. A therapy that situates problems primarily in a cultural context seems useful here. In addition, we believe that the traditional practices of psychiatry replicate the experience of anorexia for women (Gremillion, 1992, 1996) by making the psychiatrist, therapist, or nurse (on an inpatient unit) the authority. In contrast, narrative work explicitly sets up a context where people access their own authority.

In many ways, the narrative work being done with those who are labeled schizophrenic is also about reversing the usual hierarchy of authority (White, 1987). If we understand persons labeled in such a way as those who don't have the strengths privileged by the dominant culture (e.g., self-containment, coherence, self-maximizing), then we can be alert to the insidious process of their identities being marginalized. The profound sense of failure they might experience can be understood as an effect of not being certain ways the culture privileges, and their believing it has to do with their adequacy and not the culture. One of the ways that has been created to counter this was the formation of an Australian group who called themselves "Power to Our Journeys" (White, 1997). This group has shared with professionals their experience of what they found helpful. The common narrative practice of assuming the client has the expertise and relevant knowledge fits here, as it allowed this group to return to their proper place of authority in their own lives.

Couples

With couples, we always pay attention to the effects of gender-training, particularly in heterosexual relationships, although gendered implications influence partners in same-sex relationships also. We notice the effects of patriarchy on men and women alike, how they respond to each other and to problems when they occur. For example, men are often trained to believe in the "rightness" of their ideas, and sometimes feel insecure if they believe their competency is being threatened. In a similar vein, women are usually taught to accommodate, to be overly responsible, to put others first, sometimes sacrificing their own wants and needs. See our problem example in this chapter for a further description of this work. Also, see Neal, Zimmerman, & Dickerson, 1999, for other examples of work with couples.

Adolescents

With adolescents, we notice that often parents complain about their kids by saying they are rebellious or defiant, and then follow up with the idea that "teenagers are just like that" or "they probably just need to separate." Historically, traditional psychological theory shapes this thinking. For example, Anna Freud (1936) points to adolescence as a time of "storm and stress." Erikson's (1968) eight-stage developmental theory situates adolescence as "pivotal," since it is the stage that has to do with "separation-individuation." These ideas have found their way into the conventional wisdom and have achieved truth status. Noticing these accepted ideas, we began to challenge separation as a necessity, and thought about "continuing connection" as a possibility (Dickerson, Zimmerman, & Berndt, 1994). In our current work with teenagers and their families, instead of believing the problem to be "difficulty in separating," we wonder if the problem is (the demand for) separation itself, supposing it might be making it difficult for parents and their adolescent children to work together. We have found that parents are relieved when they hear these ideas and teenagers end up feeling safer, more secure, and less anxious about the future. In one family, for example, the parents commented, "This is a new paradigm, the idea of staying close with our son and working with him to solve our difficulties. We want to try looking at it this different way."

Children

Narrative work with younger children is extremely effective and a great deal of fun. Interviewing them about their strategies for managing problems or banding together with them in imaginative ways against the problem makes us really appreciate kids' particular knowledges and abilities. We believe these knowledges have been marginalized by adults as merely fun or fantasy as opposed to useful and important. Furthermore, we believe the assumption that children's problems can only or best be addressed indirectly through play is an example of adultist thinking that affects children in this culture. This "adultism" is reflected in certain maxims about children, like "children are to be seen and not heard," "spare the rod, spoil the child," and "father knows best." These words illustrate the dictum that adults are considered more "right" and that children have no "rights." Narrative work with children would challenge this assumption by privileging what the child knows about him or herself, by speaking their language, and by working together with the child to help them author their lives in ways that work better for them. Michael White's (1984) work with children around "sneaky poo" (encopresis) is well-known, and David Epston (1993; Epston & White,

1992) has archives of children's knowledges about handling various problems (e.g., asthma, obsessive-compulsive disorder). Recently, a six-year-old made a tape for me (JLZ) on how to handle "scary feelings" when leaving his parents at school or in social situations. Also, I have been working with a young boy to develop a way to manage "forgetfulness," by having remembering sessions where he notes his victories over forgetfulness and what strategies he employs.

Supervision and Our Lives

Finally, two other areas deserve brief mention. First, as supervisors, our approach is isomorphic to the therapy we do. When meeting with students we notice the developments in their work that fit what they want to learn. We may also interview them if a problem overtakes them, like it has their client, and blinds them to some possibilities toward which they might ordinarily gravitate.

Second, as persons, this work has transformed our lives. I (JLZ) feel this is the only approach I can use with myself. It continues to help me be more the person I prefer. For me (VCD), narrative ideas have helped me think in terms of multiple possibilities and multiple versions of myself and thus allowed me to make sense of my life experience in a way that no other set of ideas has.

PROBLEM EXAMPLE

When Donna called, she said she wanted help for herself. She was experiencing a great deal of sadness, some of which was work-related, but she suspected mostly because she and her husband, Robert, had just learned they could not have children. As I usually do with couples, I asked how this sadness (and the news about not having children) was also affecting her partner. She said he was really frustrated, mostly about what to do to help her, and wanting her to "just get over it." She also said he didn't think much of therapists. Preferring to start with both of them, I asked if she thought he might also come to the session.

When the couple arrived, I spent a bit of time finding out a little about each of them. I then asked Donna to tell me about the "sadness" she had mentioned on the phone. She gave a poignant description of her experience, the sadness that was the effect of learning she and Robert could not have children, how she felt the sadness had taken away her future and removed not only the possibility of having a child but all possibilities. It is not unusual, in a first session, to spend a great deal of time mapping the field of influence of the problem, asking how it affects the person, their lives, their relationships. In this process, Donna talked about what it meant to her to have a child. When she learned they could not have children, it felt to her like her life had ended and had no purpose or meaning. The sadness had taken away her future. In terms of the relationship, she said the sadness had created a huge distance between her and Robert.

In this process of questioning Donna, I was trying to understand what she thought the problem was (her experience) and how it made sense to her (the meaning she attributed to her experience). I was also thinking about how the gendered discourse regarding being a mother and having children was affecting her by making her think her life was meaningless if she could not have children. Without having to refer directly to this discourse, I could question her about "sadness" in an externalizing way, so she could experience some separation from it.

I was also questioning Donna separately from Robert, which left him in a "reflexive" position. The reflexive position allows people to think about what they are hearing without having to respond or react. Thus, Robert could listen to, or overhear, the conversation, and perhaps understand things differently than he would in an ordinary conversation. We tend to work this way with couples and families, believing that our way of talking about problems creates a different experience for our clients, and if they have enough separation from the problem, they can reconnect with preferred ways of being. In this case, talking with Donna and Robert separately had a good outcome.

When I turned to talk with Robert, he agreed there was a great deal of distance between them. His experience was one of increasing frustration. He knew Donna was sad, but he had no idea what to do, believing that there was something he "should" do. The frustration made him impatient, irritable, withdrawn, and thus contributed to distance in the relationship. For him, having a child simply meant "the next phase" in a marriage. Not being able to have a child didn't have the same impact on him as it did on Donna—he would just do "something else." He said he could see how he got into trying to "fix" things like men do, saying "You know, the Mars/Venus thing."

At the end of that first session, I did what I often do when it seems that people have gotten clear on what the problem is and how much it is affecting them. I ask them to pay close attention to the problem in their lives, to "spy" on it, so to speak. I asked Donna to attend to sadness and all the ways that it was interfering in her life, her future, and her relationships, and Robert to watch out for frustration and how it was influencing him to pay attention to some things, like fixing, and not others, like Donna's experience.

When they returned two weeks later, Donna started by saying that things were "much better;" specifically, she and Robert were closer, doing things together, were

even romantic, and she didn't feel so sad. I asked what had happened to her relationship with sadness. She said she realized there were other things she wanted to do in her life, and though she wasn't sure exactly what these things were, she was open to it. In fact, she said there were "tons of possibilities"—quite a different story from two weeks earlier. It seemed that she had reclaimed her future. Although this might seem like a facile shift, too quick, too easy, I understood this shift as an effect of Donna experiencing separation from the problem. I also saw it as a beginning, a step toward a preferred direction (based on what Donna had told me). I think of the next phase of the work as "thickening" the preferred story and gathering support for it. To start this reauthoring process I asked what she would call the step she had taken; she responded, "Courage."

Robert then reminded me that he was supposed to pay attention to frustration. He told a story of how he tended to notice the flaws in life, even if they were only 10%, how his inability to fix things contributed to an experience of frustration. He said he would rather focus on the 90%, and that he could often do so in his own life, but that it was harder when it was something upsetting to Donna. Then, with tears in his eyes, he said he "got how much this meant to her" (having a baby) and realized how much he wanted her to be happy. I understood his comment as an effect of the work we had done in the first session, my questioning them each separately, and Robert hearing Donna almost as if it were the first time. As I was listening to this conversation, I heard him use the word "compassion," so I wondered whether he thought of himself as a "compassionate" person, knowing that male gender-training does not usually privilege that way of describing oneself. Robert responded by saying compassionate wasn't the way he thought of himself, nor was he sure he would want to be described that way, but it clearly fit for him in that moment. He could also see how much it meant to Donna to see him as a "compassionate" man. We ended the second session by focusing on Donna as a woman of "courage" and Robert as a man of "compassion," wondering what that might mean for the future of their relationship (both to themselves and to each other).

I saw them two more times, continuing to focus on the "courage" and "compassion" descriptions rather than the problem descriptions of "sadness" and "frustration." The conversation extended beyond the original issue, not being able to have children, to a longer-standing relationship issue between them, which was about having conversations that felt acknowledging to both parties. (Donna experienced "sadness" when she thought Robert wasn't listening to her, and he got taken over by "frustration" and "fixing" rather than paying attention to what she was saying. When he accessed "compassion" and could listen to her, and she stayed in a position of "courage," hanging in there so her point of view could be heard, their conversations went much better.)

From a narrative perspective, we think of this work with Donna and Robert as a process of deconstructing gendered ways of being and opening possibilities for alternative identities. These alternative identities are not as constricted as prescribed gender identities tend to be. In this way, narrative work extends the margins and opens up other possibilities in people's lives.

SUMMARY

Narrative therapy represents a set of ideas and practices in what we predict will be a growing trend of poststructuralist therapies, which do not rely on objective descriptions of how individuals or relationships are organized. Instead, the therapist is able to create a context for change through the use of language that allows persons to leave problems behind and move to ways of being they define as more preferred. In this process, client experience is not reinterpreted into diagnostic categories predetermined by the therapist's model or view of the world. Given that most models involve categories that represent deviances from the norm, the inevitable pathologizing of person's lives and relationships is avoided in this approach.

Narrative therapy is also an efficient way to address problems, as the solutions are considered to be already present in the person's experience. There are no hypothetical deficits to remediate or lack of capabilities to address. Often the work can go quickly. Sometimes, when the problem has been around a long time and involves a problem identity, this way of working provides clear and direct practices to help the person leave that identity behind.

Narrative therapy is inherently political; its practitioners often see themselves as activists trying to organize processes that stand against the oppression and marginalization of those individuals who, for whatever reason (gender, race, class, sexuality, age, or personal preference of any kind), have less space to be the kind of person they choose. They are aware of issues of power and try to address them as they occur both in the therapeutic process and in the world.

Finally, narrative work allows for a less restricted and constrained connection between therapist and client, leading to encounters that are emotionally rich and inherently human. Therapists connect with clients in a context that is respectful of the other's preferences, attitudes, and experience, and they expect to be open to the process in a way where they "take back" something from their clients into their own lives. In this way, the process can be, as Michael White (1997) points out, a "joyous" one for all.

REFERENCES

Bateson, G. (1972). *Steps to an ecology of mind.* New York: Ballantine.

Bateson, G. (1979). *Mind and nature: A necessary unity.* New York: Dutton.

Bruner, J. (1986). *Actual minds, possible worlds.* Cambridge, MA: Harvard University Press.

Bruner, J. (1990). *Acts of meaning.* Cambridge, MA: Harvard University Press.

Cowley, G., & Springen, K. (1995, April 17). Rewriting life stories. *Newsweek,* 70–74.

Dickerson, V. C., Zimmerman, J. L., & Berndt, L. (1994). Challenging developmental "truths": Separating from separation. *Dulwich Centre Newsletter, 4,* 2–12.

Dickerson, V. (1998). Silencing critical voices: An interview with Marie-Nathalie Beaudoin. *Gecko, 2,* 29–45.

Epston, D. (1993, March 9–10). Narrative therapy with children. A workshop in the Narrative Therapy Series for Bay Area Family Therapy Training Associates, Cupertino, CA.

Epston, D. (1994, February 10–11). The anti-anorexia league: Resistance and counter-practices. A workshop in the Narrative Therapy Series for Bay Area Family Therapy Training Associates, Cupertino, CA.

Epston, D., & White, M. (1992). *Experience, contradiction, narrative, and imagination: Selected papers of David Epston & Michael White, 1989–1991.* Adelaide, South Australia: Dulwich Centre Publications.

Erikson, E. (1968). *Identity, youth, and crisis.* New York: Norton.

Freeman, J. C., Epston, D., & Lobovitz, D. H. (1997). *Playful approaches to serious problems: Narrative therapy with children and their families.* New York: Norton.

Freedman, J., & Combs, G. (1996). *Narrative therapy: The social construction of preferred realities.* New York: Norton.

Freud, A. (1936). *The ego and the mechanisms of defense.* New York: International Universities Press.

Foucault, M. (1979). *Discipline and punish: The birth of the prison.* Hammondsworth, England: Penguin.

Foucault, M. (1980). *Power knowledge: Selected interviews and other writings.* New York: Pantheon.

Foucault, M. (1984a). *The history of sexuality.* Hammondsworth, England: Penguin.

Foucault, M. (1984b). The subject and power. In H. Dreyfus & P. Rabinow (Eds.), *Michel Foucault: Beyond.* Chicago: University of Chicago Press.

Gaines, A. (1992). From DSM-I to III-R; Voices of self, mastery and the other: A cultural constructivist reading of U.S. psychiatric classification. *Social Science and Medicine, 35*(1), 3–24.

Gergen, K. (1985). The social constructionist movement in modern psychology. *American Psychologist, 40,* 266–275.

Gergen, K. (1991). *The saturated self: Dilemmas of identity in contemporary life.* New York: Basic.

Goffman, E. (1961). Asylums: Essays in the social situation of mental patients and other inmates. New York: Doubleday.

Goffman, E. (1974). *Frame analysis.* New York: Harper.

Gremillion, H. (1992). Psychiatry as social ordering: Anorexia nervosa, a paradigm. *Social Science and Medicine, 35*(1), 57–71.

Gremillion, H. (1996). In fitness and in health: Crafting bodies, selves, and families in the treatment of anorexia nervosa. Doctoral dissertation, Stanford University.

Janowsky, Z. M., Dickerson, V. C., & Zimmerman, J. L. (1995). Through Susan's eyes: Reflections on a reflecting team experience. In S. Friedman (Ed.), *The reflecting team in action* (pp. 167–183). New York: Guilford.

Kvale, S. (1993). Postmodern psychology: A contradiction in terms? In S. Kvale (Ed.), *Psychology and postmodernism* (pp. 31–57). Newbury Park, CA: Sage.

Lax, W. (1992). Postmodern thinking in a clinical practice. In S. McNamee & K. Gergen (Eds.), *Therapy as social construction* (pp. 69–85). Newbury Park, CA: Sage.

Lowe, R. (1991). Postmodern themes and therapeutic practices: Notes towards the definition of "Family Therapy: Part 2." *Dulwich Centre Newsletter, 3,* 41–51.

Madigan, S. (1994). Body politics. *Family Therapy Networker, 18*(6), 27.

Madigan, S., & Law, I. (Eds.). (1998). *Praxis: Situating discourse, feminism, and politics in narrative therapies.* Vancouver, BC: Yaletown Family Therapy Press.

Monk, G., Winslade, J., Crocket, K., & Epston, D. (Eds.). (1997). *Narrative therapy in practice: The archaeology of hope.* San Francisco: Jossey-Bass.

Myerhoff, B. (1982). Life history among the elderly: Performance, visibility and remembering. In J. Ruby (Ed.), *A crack in the mirror: Reflexive perspectives in anthropology.* Philadelphia: University of Pennsylvania Press.

Neal, J., Zimmerman, J. L., & Dickerson, V. C. (1999). Couples, culture, and discourse: A narrative approach. In J. Donovan (Ed.), *Short-term couple therapy.* New York: Guilford.

O'Hanlon, W. (1994). The third wave. *Family Therapy Networker, 18*(6), 18–26, 28–29.

Smith, C., & Nylund, D. (Eds.). (1997). *Narrative therapies with children and adolescents.* New York: Guilford.

Tamasese, K., & Waldegrave, C. (1993). Cultural and gender accountability in the "just therapy" approach. *Journal of Feminist Family Therapy, 5*(2), 29–45.

Turner, V. (1969). *The ritual process.* Ithaca, NY: Cornell University Press.

van Gennep, A. (1960). *The rites of passage.* Chicago: University of Chicago Press.

Watzlawick, P. (1984). *The invented reality.* New York: Norton.

Waldegrave, C. (1990). Just therapy. *Dulwich Centre Newsletter, 1,* 6–46.

White, M. (1984). Pseudo-encopresis: From avalanche to victory, from vicious to virtuous cycles. *Family Systems Medicine, 2*(2), 150–160.

White, M. (1986). Negative explanation, restraint and double description: A template for family therapy. *Family Process, 25*(2), 169–184.

White, M. (1987). Family therapy and schizophrenia: Addressing the "in-the-corner" lifestyle. *Dulwich Centre Newsletter,* 14–21.

White, M. (1988). The process of questioning: A therapy of literary merit? *Dulwich Centre Newsletter,* 8–14.

White, M. (1989). The externalizing of the problem and the re-authoring of lives and relationships. *Dulwich Centre Newsletter,* 3–21.

White, M. (1995a). *Re-authoring lives: Interviews and essays.* Adelaide, South Australia: Dulwich Centre Publications.

White, M. (1995b). Reflecting teamwork as definitional ceremony. In M. White, *Re-authoring lives: Interviews & essays* (pp. 172–198). Adelaide, South Australia: Dulwich Centre Publications.

White, M. (1997). *Narratives of therapists' lives.* Adelaide, South Australia: Dulwich Centre Publications.

White, M. (1998). Remembering, definitional ceremony, and rich description. A workshop in the Narrative Therapy Series for Bay Area Family Therapy Training Associates, Cupertino, CA.

White, M., & Epston, D. (1990). *Narrative means to therapeutic ends.* New York: Norton.

Zimmerman, J. L., & Dickerson, V. C. (1994a). Tales of the body thief: Externalizing and deconstructing eating problems. In M. Hoyt (Ed.), *Constructive therapies* (pp. 295–318). New York: Guilford.

Zimmerman, J. L., & Dickerson, V. C. (1994b). Using a narrative metaphor. Implications for theory and clinical practice. *Family Process, 33,* 233–246.

Zimmerman, J. L., & Dickerson, V. C. (Eds.). (1996a). Special edition on narrative therapy. *Journal of Systemic Therapies, 15*(1).

Zimmerman, J. L., & Dickerson, V. C. (1996b). *If problems talked: Narrative therapy in action.* New York: Guilford.

Chapter 41

NATURAL HIGH THERAPY

WALTER E. O'CONNELL

Psychotherapy, as practiced and as innovated, undoubtedly reveals the personality of the practitioner/theoretician, and the next account should introduce you to a unique personality of our times, equivalent in many ways (including style of writing) to our mutual hero, Dr. J. L. Moreno.

Undoubtedly, Buzz O'Connell has something very important to say. Heavily influenced by both Alfred Adler and Carl Jung, O'Connell has developed something new, much closer to Adler in terms of common sense, with strong elements of Jung's mysticism but interlaced with Moreno's expansiveness. This chapter and O'Connell's other writings should intrigue individuals who are of a particular complex cast of mind, say those who appreciate the writings of Trigant Burrow. In any event, what follows, though perhaps difficult to understand, is well worth careful reading. I would equate O'Connell in many ways, including importance, to Egon Brunswik, another seminal thinker. Read the next chapter very slowly and very carefully.

Natural High (NH) Therapy is an optimistic, action-oriented approach to living in the here-and-now that stresses the response-ability of each person for the creation of one's own state of self-actualization. This theory and therapy focuses directly upon the sense of humor, in all its ramifications, as the essential criterion of the actualization process. A sense of humor is the end result of self-training for the expansion of one's sense of worth and feelings of universal belonging, plus the development of an appreciation for the basic paradoxes of the human condition. Techniques of inner and outer change, both individual and group, are used in NH Therapy to encourage persons to become active agents in the game-of-games, one's actualization through training and practice of self-esteem (SE) and social interest (SI).

Level 1, *machinations of inner ego constrictions,* is the cornerstone of the whole actualization approach. Level 2, *encouragement,* gives the ideal movements of active social interest. *The transpersonal dimension,* level 3, has as its goal further enhancement of SE and SI by transcending ego-addictions and experiencing the timeless eternal self. The super-natural high is similar to the natural high in feelings of unconditional worth and basic similarity and belonging. Moreover, this numinous state is produced under "marketplace" situations of severe stress and is the affective counterpart of the cognitive-perceptual sense of humor.

HISTORY

Precursors

The salient influence upon NH creation has been the individual psychology of Alfred Adler (Ansbacher & Ansbacher, 1956, 1964), especially as concretized and modeled by Rudolf Dreikurs (1971). The Palo Alto Group, which systematically studied the movements of communication, added greatly to the particulars of level 2, the dyadic-interactional. From their work on the pathologies of communication, the importance of self-disclosure and feedback first became evident. Haley (1963) formulated what has been standard practice for therapeutic interactions of natural high therapists. Symptoms are encouraged; resistance is depicted as expected cooperation; and the therapeutic figure embodies a resolution of opposites, as a gently benevolent person who moves the patient into painful situations. Natural High Therapy received much of its didactic-experiential theme from the National Training Lab (NTL) orientation, especially that of the Bethel group. The psychodramatic techniques of J. L. Moreno, together with his oft-maligned nebulous psychospiritual outlook, made a pronounced contribution to natural high growth (O'Connell, 1976c). The school of analytical psychology of C. G. Jung (1961) has given tremendous support to the theory and practice of level 3, the transcendental humanistic facet of the natural high theory (O'Connell, 1978b). Ram Dass, the former Dr. Richard Alpert of psychedelic fame, has stimulated level 3 development by his use of Meditation to develop the quiet, expansive space-between-thoughts (Ram Dass & Levine, 1977).

Beginnings

Four lifestyle foibles of this writer, buoyed with social interest, have stimulated theoretical biases. The first foible is a concern for the person, especially for the discovery and implementation of the secrets of joyous, socially responsible existence. The second foible is a persistent penchant for synthesizing persons, ideas, and techniques into practical, simple (yet seldom easy) alternatives. A thorough distrust of institutional ways—in schools, homes, and professions—has certainly been most pronounced. And the final foible is a wariness of institutional subtleties for constriction of personal self-esteem and social interest. All these have given birth to Natural High theory and Therapy, a psychospiritual avenue to actualization. Perhaps the most important stimulus for the creation of NH Therapy is my lifelong need to control, honed, by decades of frustration, into the deep and wide belief that only one's self-esteem and social interest are amenable to absolute personal control.

Research by this writer on the sense of humor followed a lifelong curiosity on the "hows" and "whys" of humor—rather than hostility—among the significant figures of childhood. My research and clinical studies were viewed as professional oddities until the recent surge of interest in studying actualizing rather than pathologizing attitudes (O'Connell, 1975, 1976a, 1977, 1979b). Humor was desperately in need of theory building and inferences based upon observed behavior from lived lives, instead of abstract armchair speculation.

Psychodrama was a forerunner of Natural High Therapy. For seven years I employed it at the Waco Veterans Administration Hospital as a treatment method of choice for chronic schizophrenics, as a training device for personnel, as a diagnostic methodology for interpersonal competence, and as a data-gathering therapy for theory building (O'Connell, 1978a). When I transferred to the Houston Veterans Administration Medical Center in 1966, I was introduced to the techniques of the patients' interactional training lab (O'Connell, 1975). As the hospital's research psychologist, operating from a ward oriented toward the methodology of Kurt Lewin, there was ample opportunity to integrate the views of Adler and Moreno with those of the National Training Lab's (NTL) instrumented, trainer-led and development groups (*T*- and *D*-groups).

Following training at the Bethel NTL Center, I felt that the instrumented group approach worked well for those already close to actualization, but failed to deal

adequately with the constriction of the average ego-addicted individual. Cooperation-as-equals could become a fact only after an awareness and appreciation of ego-induced mistakes and foibles, within an optimistic theory of change.

To this writer, much valuable time seemed to be wasted in Action Therapy hoping to have patients discover, completely by themselves, the movements of actualization. Also about that time the particular question on my mind was simply a reiteration of what numerous members of psychodrama groups had broached: "How about showing us the right way?" So in 1971 I launched the first Adlerian encouragement labs, an admixture of Adler-Dreikurs-Lewin-Moreno perspectives.

In 1976 I began Natural High Therapy in earnest, both as a treatment and research method for outpatient addicts and as a way of interacting and program problem solving for the clinic staff (O'Connell, 1976b; O'Connell, Bright, & Grossman, 1978).

CURRENT STATUS

This writer has taught courses and organized workshops throughout the United States. In 1977 I taught in Holland with the International Committee for Adlerian Summer Schools and Institutes (ICASSI). I am on the faculty of the University of St. Thomas, Baylor College of Medicine, the University of Houston, and the C. G. Jung Educational Center. With two former students, Pattye Kennedy and Dayton Salisbury, I founded the Institute for Creative Community Living at the University of St. Thomas. In 1970 I was instrumental in organizing the Texas Society of Adlerian Psychology and a family education center in Houston. Two Adlerian priests, Fathers Maurice Ouellet and Dayton Salisbury, later succeeded me in directing the center.

Death and Transformation Labs have contributed in some measure to the hospice movement in Houston. When institutions become sufficiently instrumental in assisting persons to grieve and die with dignity, such workshops provide the setting for personal bereavement and the training for staff development.

Action Therapy, psychodrama workshops, and natural high labs are also available through the auspices of the Jung Center and other Texas growth centers. All labs are similar in their use of group exercises, active imagination, instrumented procedures, and psychodramatic settings (O'Connell & Bright, 1977).

In the Houston area television viewers received initial exposure to Natural High Therapy during my dozen one-hour interviews on the local *Spotlight* television show during the 1970s. Almost 100 persons have continued their self-education by volunteering to participate as auxiliaries, along with Veterans Administration trainees, in my ongoing groups. I have written over 400 publications, some available from the C. G. Jung Educational Center in Houston, Texas, and from the Alfred Adler Institute in Chicago, Illinois. My books include: *The Odyssey of a Psychologist* (1974), *Action Therapy and Adlerian Theory* (1975), *Psychotherapy: Theoretical and Technical Readings* (1976c), *Natural High Primer* (1977, with M. Bright), *Super-Natural Highs* (1979b), and *Essential Readings in Natural High Actualization* (1981).

THEORY

In Natural High (NH) theory, all life is dyadic: To live is to be able to focus the attention on only one object at any given time. Every interaction at the human dimension involves behavioral movement (or lack of it), perceived by an imperfect perceiver. The perceiver infers meaning, mainly unconsciously, and is always responsible for creating the subjective evaluations that define this meaning. Therefore in every human event, there is the contributor (who cannot not communicate) and the perceiver (who is responsible for generating meaning). In lived life, these actions and reactions go on rapidly and interminably. While each dyadic player in NH is responsible for the interaction, no one is to blame. Each acts and perceives according to the state of self-actualization (amount of self-esteem and degree of social interest). Persons have absolute control over only these two variables: self-esteem (SE) and social interest (SI). Only those who realize this basic NH premise have this control.

A completely actualized person (level 3) feels "as if" he or she is a wonder-full person, regardless of the environment, but has no urge to prove it to anyone (high self-esteem). The actualizer likewise feels belonging in life and experiences overriding similarities with living beings across time and space (wide social interest). Another necessary condition is to have mastered (to understanding, not perfection) the dyadic movements of encouragement (level 2). By loving the mysteries of life (the paradoxes) and being able to make quick perceptual swings between the poles of paradoxes, the actualizer qualifies as a humorist (level 3). NH sees life as a serious, but not grave, game. To become competent in a game means to accept imperfection. Practice is an essential element in games. A worthy opponent (in NH, a discouraged person) is a necessary ingredient for skill development. En route to game competency, one must learn his or her mistakes, mainly from observations and feedback from self and others. To excel, not simply to win over others, some athletes practice mistakes, share, and celebrate them. When one fights mistakes, or hypnotizes the psyche into discouragement, symptoms of mental dis-ease persist.

This narrowing of what one must think, feel, and do

and how one must behave toward others was the start of ego identity. The constrictions can be outgrown only through self-actualization. One needs an ego identity. It is necessary to experience its limitations and pitfalls humorously before going to the inner voyage to experience self-identity (level 3). An ego identity compels attachments to roles, goals, and controls. It motivates the search for differences and separateness, for the *unique* identity. The basic fear of catastrophies, centered in the loss of the ego (as in death and insanity), is the prime panic rumbling beneath ego-identity consciousness. The difficulties of solitary self-help are immense because one of the rules of any ego identity is that one must never be aware of the operation of the grave game.

The "sinister circle" proceeds in this manner: unconscious invidious comparisons constricting SE and SI, followed by cognitive demandments. The latter are readily accessible to consciousness, given the help of a gentle-strong guide who is friendly, firm, and active. Since demandments (Table 41.1) are not usually satisfied unconditionally beyond infancy, frustrations of hidden arbitrary "musturbatory" (Ellis, 1974) wishes are assured. Frustration needs no definition. Everyone has experienced the ego tensions from frustration. From this point

Table 41.1   The Twelve Demandments[a]

1. I MUST be loved and approved of by everyone for everything at all times.

2. I MUST be thoroughly competent, adequate and achieving in *all* possible respects.

3. Some people *are* bad, wicked, or vile and MUST be punished.

4. Things MUST go the way I very much want them to or it would be *awful, catastrophic,* or *terrible!* (awfulizing . . . terriblizing)

5. Unhappiness is externally caused so I MUST control things and others.

6. One MUST remain upset or worried if faced with a dangerous or fearsome reality.

7. I MUST avoid responsibilities and difficulties rather than face them.

8. I MUST have a *right* to be dependent and people MUST be happy to take care of me.

9. My early childhood experiences MUST continue to *control* me and determine my emotions and behavior!

10. I MUST become upset over my and other people's problems or behavior.

11. There MUST be *one* right, precise, and *perfect* solution and it would be *terrible* or *catastrophic* if this perfect solution is not found. (catastrophizing . . .)

12. The world MUST be fair and justice (or mercy) *MUST* triumph.

[a]Adapted from list of common irrational ideas, Ellis (1974). Reprinted with permission from O'Connell and Bright (1977).

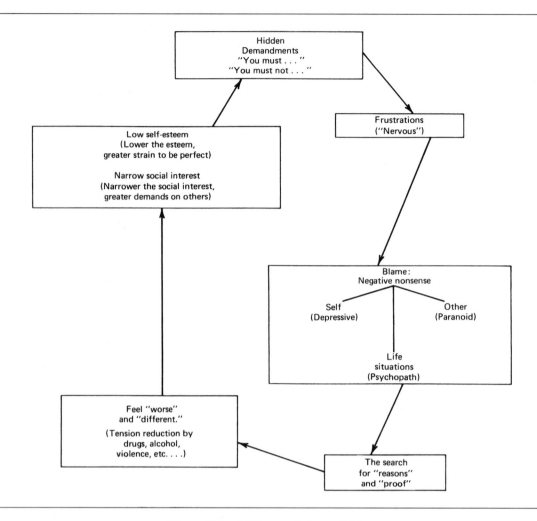

Figure 41.1   EGO constricting activities.

interpretations in NH Therapy proceed back to a focus on the internalized sentences of demandments or forward on the circle to "blame," the gist of negative nonsense. Blame of self can lead to depression. Centering the onus on others culminates in our ever-popular paranoid stances. Taking it out on life is seen in psychopathic games. In this sense, blame is a social plague, and serves no useful purpose except to provide actualizers with intense adversaries. Once blame becomes certain, through inner training, one can find or provoke the proof to maintain the blame object. Creating blame is the opposite of the scientific attitude according to which one tests the null hypothesis of no relationship. In constricting, one assumes the necessity and certainty of the blame, and finds the proof one is looking for. What in descriptive psychiatry is viewed as sickness is regarded as creative (but not actualizing) behavior in NH. After the proof comes the tensions of misery, which are temporarily diminished through drugs, alcohol, promiscuity, and more open forms of violence.

Another basic idea of NH is that one cannot encourage or discourage another. One dyadic partner merely "behaves," even though the hidden motives may be for attention, power, revenge, or display of disabilities (Dreikurs, 1971). Each person is responsible for his or her own perceptual judgment, but the weak (low SE and narrow SI) do not know and/or believe this premise.

Natural High theory differentiates between three concepts often lumped together to the detriment of dynamic understanding. Common usage to the contrary, *power, ego esteem,* and *self-esteem* are not synonymous. Everyone needs and gets power wherever human interaction takes place. Power or influence is therefore communicated or subtly negotiated with every social transaction. To be utterly powerless in human interactions is impossible. When people are called "powerless," the implication is that they are lacking positive influence to the point of being highly creative, with extreme nuisance value (O'Connell, 1975).

Any quest for external signs and symbols of personal and social power is, at best, an overcompensation for undeveloped strength. Those with actualizing attitudes

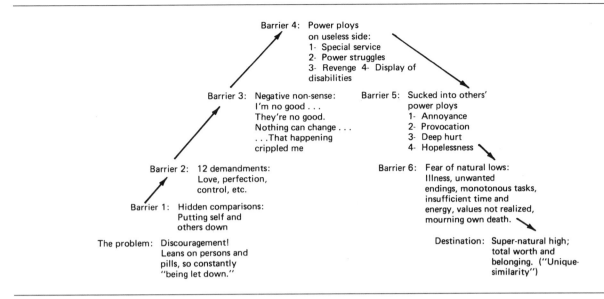

Figure 41.2   Obstacles to natural high actualization.

and a loving community (level 2) are not addicted to power. Strong (SE and SI) persons do get positive power, but without clinging and grasping greedily for attachments.

Ego esteem has similar affective qualities as self-esteem; therefore, one can experience natural highs by receiving signs and symbols of success from the environment. In such instances, though, the psyche is not centered and runs the risk of being addicted to external sources for proof of worth and belonging. Hence the declaration in NH that such circumstances of proof are ego addictions, a risky search for ego esteem outside of the self. The ego addict, lacking the energies of self-identity, needs to "score" on others. Without the external fix, the withdrawal symptoms of anxiety and other psychic pain follows immediately. The pattern is that of attachment to roles, goals, and controls that need subjective proof of the support of significant others (or in extreme cases, assurance from all others, at all times). Self-esteem is a giant's step beyond the ego-imposed limitations of the externalizer. A person cannot shortcut this journey from ego to self any more than levels 1 and 2 can be circumvented for instant SE and SI at level 3, the dimension of self-generated SE and SI.

It is axiomatic to NH that any psychospiritual pilgrim will be prevented from venturing into levels 2 and 3 for long without discouragement by the ego-induced monsters of hyperdependency, competition, and ignorance of the effects of human transactions. Such creative discouragement is not to be shocked, cut, or chemically drowned out of commission. All resistance is "grist for the mill" for the NH therapist. Through alternative perceptions, the patient is shown the tremendous creativity

and power, perhaps for the first time, hidden beneath constrictions and symptom formation.

Level 3 is an introduction to the deep self, the object of curiosity and contentment for generations of mystics, including C. G. Jung. Personkind needs a certain support, beyond the ego, to justify the monotonous struggles toward actualization in a discouragenic world. Yet the ego (level 1) and other (level 2) dimensions cannot be ignored in favor of a hyperdependent, helpless, and hopeless stance toward an utterly externalized God, as in institutionalized religiosity. Ego actualization and encouragenic movements toward others precede the spiritual dimension in time; hence, the re-solution of opposites in the term "psychospiritual," with the psychic (level 1) first. Later comes the attention on the experiencing of the deep self and connections with the universe, a facet now becoming popular through Meditation and contemplation (level 3). When level 3 becomes paramount, there is no diminution of the attention on the preceding psychosocial levels, 1 and 2. They are equally important for the continuation of the actualization process, which is never a static state or encapsulated entity.

We never completely overcome our early constrictions. There is no quick, easy, pain-free authentic human existence. NH is simple; but it is not easy or painless. If there were packaged actualizations for over-the-counter bartering (the implicit goal of the chemically addicted), humans would have no use for humor and little need for self-disclosing, feedback-rendering support groups. These groups can tell us gently and firmly our mistakes when we "con-strict" ourselves into narrow ego traps. They offer psychic nurturance and growth. Yet again paradoxically or ironically, we are responsible for creating and maintaining such groups through our own loving of ego, others, and self, put into inner and outer action.

With the sense of humor, we watch with awe the invidious comparisons, demandments, and negative nonsenses (level 1) develop, from the space-between-thoughts, the disinterested seat of the timeless, universally connected self (level 3). Through Meditation, contemplation, and concentration, persons learn not to collapse before moods. NH people do not solidify discouragements by inner struggles against its constrictions, as the neurotic does, so becoming inseparable from his symptoms.

The humorous attitude evolves from an acceptance of the necessity of an experiential understanding of the movements of the three levels of Natural High theory and practice. With an increase of self-worth and belonging comes a willingness to share and celebrate the mistakes of here-and-now ego constrictions. Well-practiced Meditation contributes to an enlivening distancing from chronic ego attachments to demandments and negative nonsense. Such a "witnessing" of mistakes, then letting the "musturbations" and negative certainties flow on, is not even slightly akin to the pathological depersonalization and derealization emanating from inadequate SE and SI. It is rather a curious disinterested inner-watching that does not degenerate into catastrophizing or fighting untoward ego reactions of any person. Reactive resentments and strenuous struggles of resistance frequently stabilize into symptoms and become part of one's search for power on the useless side of life. A premise of NH theory is that early constrictions are always potential stress reactions. Humor, coming after SE and SI expansion and an appreciation for life's paradoxes, gives a distancing perspective, a "God's-eye view," that nips constrictions in the bud. Humor is the chief coping capacity. Beyond being in the service of the ego addictions, humor is a perspective in the service of the self, the royal road toward actualization.

METHODOLOGY

Private Patients

All private patients are told that individual psychotherapy would be appropriate initially to work out individual expectations and demands and to receive individual instructions in the practice of natural high actualization. Early in therapy, homework is introduced, suggesting (but not demanding) that the client focus on habitual inner reactions that prevent or enlarge on opportunities for expansion of feelings of self-worth and belonging. Since all persons operate by cognitive maps of the world,

even if they cannot read their own, NH therapists are ever concerned about making the inner creative process conscious and acceptable. Beyond this awareness, there is the ever-active effort to specify steps to the client for self-training in actualization in a discouragenic world.

Group Psychotherapy follows after a few individual sessions. As they enter Group Psychotherapy, the patients/students/clients are given the option of discontinuing individual psychotherapy or selecting a schedule less frequent than once a week. It is in Group Therapy that patients practice the steps of level 2 encouragement, especially the search for similarities. Members routinely rehearse self-disclosing present, past, and perhaps even future constrictions. They give feedback to other members about reactive feelings and ask for feedback from peers. Group Therapy, and occasionally psychodrama, offers an opportunity to share projections and be able to reach cooperation-as-equals through honest, open communications. The therapist is an integral part of this disclosure-and-feedback system, modeling attempts at actualization, giving and receiving feedback, and reinforcing encouragenesis, whenever it appears ("Thanks, that effort helped me . . .").

All the steps of level 2 (encouragement) were formed to provide a behavioral prescription for the accepting atmosphere. Level 2 is attuned to the regressive urge of constrictive identity-seeking through shades of psychic isolation and worthlessness (level 1). Level 2 is not verbal pablum, but requires strength (adequate self-esteem and social interest) to risk courageous self-disclosure and feedback.

The therapist will give the patient structured movement of "what to do," not insisting, in a senseless power struggle, that this student will ever perform this dyadic dance. Rather the tutor will *anticipate* what the neophyte will do to avoid these courageous (active SI) acts. With this anticipation is admiration, expressed by the body as well as the words, for the well-practiced creativity of cooperation-as-*unequals*.

In general, those pilgrims who are spoilsports on level 2 are likewise on level 3. Similar dynamics operate. Without the psychic energy of abundant SE and SI, the unactualized will not accept the challenges, homework, and persistent practice of the dyadic and transpersonal dimensions of NH. Anyone ego-trapped into diminishment (of SE and SI) and into nonconscious, reactive one-upmanship (or "pride") will not approach the practice of movements for psychic increase with equanimity. The diminishment process, on the other hand, is in the service of hyperdependency, competition, and ignorance of psychic connectivity, all assumed to be part of the quest for ego identity ("who you must be . . . or not be") and subsequent reactions to this basic condition.

On the other hand, those beings who are motivated to leave the fixations of childhood identifications and experience the possibilities of self-generated alternative perceptions can practice steps of level 2 as well as share and ultimately celebrate life-style constrictions. As continuous practice is part of any serious game, level 2 behaviors can be put into action either overtly or covertly. Using level 3 techniques of contemplation and concentration, the NH student focuses his mind (or attention) on symbols or signs of encouragenic level 2 (or level 3) movements. With contemplation, the mind is blanked by one-pointing (e.g., attention on nostrils, feeling the inhalations and exhalations). Concentration, the opposite of free association, keeps the attention on thoughts of the action in question. As with any focusing of the mind, inner resistance to the task is not catastrophized or otherwise fought. The attention gently but firmly goes back to the task at hand. At the completion, the student learns to stroke the self for effort, never for perfection (which simply cannot be attained).

Workshops and Labs

In encouragement labs, lectures on the topics precede any practice. Participants are then paired and the partners interview each other in turn. For encouragement labs, the question for each interviewer to consider might be "How do you prefer to be encouraged by others?" In a death and transformation workshop with a similar introductory format, the theme for the dyadic interview could be "What do you want to get out of this workshop, and what are you willing to contribute?" "What do you do to prevent natural highs?" is a suitable question for natural high lab interviews. While doing the interviewing, the participants are getting practice on the 12 steps of encouragement: (1) stop, look, and listen; (2) paraphrasing and guessing; (3) searching for similarities; and (4) attempting encouragenic body language. After an allotted period of time, each interviewer self-discloses (step 5) the image formed of the interviewee. The latter then gives nonjudgmental feedback (step 6) on the perceived correctness of the interviewer's task. Dyads are then combined into groups of eight, each member in turning self-disclosing to the group the similarities (step 4) discovered with the partner.

A number of group exercises are distributed, in instrumented group format, for participants to learn the content of encouragement and experience in putting it into practice. A number of self and group rating scales are also available for the process of feedback and self-disclosure. Group exercises are constructed for participants to make rankings of endings and then work together in the stress of trying to arrive at consensus.

One of this writer's favorite procedures is to roleplay with all groups, singly before combined groups. I play a discouraged person of any age, sex, diagnostic category, or presenting problem desired, with members of each group playing encouragenic persons. Afterward they self-disclose their reactions to the problem. Others in the lab share their similar experiences and give feedback about behavior noted. Playing the discouraged person illustrates behaviors not to be engaged in: goals on the useless side of life (step 12). Participants realize, through this type of exercise, how easy it is to reinforce negative goals (step 12). Other behaviors of encouragement include (step 7) acknowledging skills of the other, even when they frustrate our ego drives; telling others how they have encouraged and could do so more (steps 8, 9, and 10); and guesses as to how we encouraged others and could do so even more (step 11).

Close to 5,000 persons have participated in death and transformation labs as they progressed in content and aim from a limited focus on terminality of patients to didactic-experiential means of self-actualization (O'Connell & Bright, 1977). This writer directs an average of six death and transformation labs annually, working whenever possible with music and art therapists. Ideally the lab is a weekend workshop, the participants living together in a retreat setting. As far as is known, there have been no psychological casualties from these labs, despite many grim professional warnings that the death experiences would provoke masochistic, suicidal, and depressive attacks. I believe that the success of the workshops, in which almost all participants have emotional experiences, is due mainly to three factors. First and foremost, the lab structure is one in which crying is expected and regarded as positive involvement. No one is labeled negatively or pampered for crying. Moreover participants are told many times that they do not have to participate and no one should have the effrontery to categorize nonparticipation as "sick." Because, or in spite of, these instructions, very few people ever decline to participate. A second factor is my insistence that groups learn to be open, sharing, and authentic (level 2) before death and dying exercises commence. In this manner, participants, for the most part, have a ready-made support group before facing the issue of the death of significant persons. An essential part of the workshops involves guided imagery of one's own death; psychodramatic involvement in playing one's most significant survivor; and dialoguing with death and with dead persons with whom there is unfinished business. A third vital safeguard is the focus on humor after the emotionally charged experiences, guided imagery, and psychodramatic techniques. Art and music exercises are used to give the participants a sense of competence and purposiveness in facing the certainty of death for all bodies and egos. In humordrama, after empathy is developed for the plight of others, doubles are employed in the psychodramas to stimulate alternative humorous responses to one's death sentence.

Institutional Patients

In seven years at an outpatient drug clinic, this writer never witnessed a discussion, instigated by anyone else, concerned with treatment as a *dyadic* responsibility. In contrast, NH treatment is a serious game in which healers try to contribute behaviors that will assist the client in expanding self-esteem and social interest, and to guess, often aloud, at how the other will resist encouragenic efforts. No negative judgments are made of the patient. In fact he or she is regarded as creative, not sick, in efforts to resist. In institutions concentration upon *dyadic* responsibility is an unpardonable sin. I believe that this one observation—whether staff and patients are allowed to focus upon how each person contributes to discouragement of others—is the prime interaction that separates institutional from instrumental settings. The constant dyadic quality of the interactional human system is totally ignored, suppressed, or repressed by the institutional mind.

Natural High Therapy for addiction has entered another stage, one that the addicts appreciate and practice much more. They learn to meditate and clear the mind of ego noise in groups. At the same time they start to treat themselves gently, perhaps for the first time. When the mind wanders, they bring the mind (the focus of attention) back to breath counting (feeling the breath at the top of the nostrils). When patients can one-point (do one thing at a time, with relaxed alertness), they are ready to concentrate and contemplate. Starting with five-minute periods per day, they concentrate or focus fully on a segment of NH theory (e.g., self-esteem, social interest). Then may come contemplation, letting the symbols unfold without diagnosing, judging, or interpreting. Even if the mind wanders, the addict's reactions or even the contents of the wanderings are a projective test of where one is on the actualization pilgrimage. Any patient may focus on the elements of encouragement and practice (e.g., step 4), looking for similarities with others. Even more important is familiarity and acceptance of the "space between thoughts" that may have commonality with the Jungian self, spirit, or soul, and with right-brain speculation (Watzlawick, 1978). Whenever patients feel level 1 ego constrictions taking place, they can one-point, clear the mind, and so avoid the aftermath of ego-induced frustrations, the chemical fix.

APPLICATIONS

Natural High Therapy applies to all categories of persons; the focus is on a wide base of inner and outer behaviors, from psychopathology to psychospiritual self-actualization. Natural High theory and techniques have been used in individual and group psychotherapy and counseling, didactic-experiential workshops, and in teaching through lectures and television presentations. The limiting boundaries are, as in any learning situation, intelligence and motivation. The emphasis on identifying feelings and movements in the here-and-now, rather than on remote abstractions, lowers the parameters of NH applicability, when compared with orthodox verbal "talking-about" psychotherapies. Age and diagnostic categories are therefore less limiting factors in NH Therapy.

Natural High Therapy began as a therapy for hospitalized psychotics and continued as treatment for hospitalized alcoholics and drug addicts. Currently this writer works with outpatient drug addicts, but the same NH approach is used with individuals, families, and groups in private practice. Although I do not work with children and adolescents outside of the family context, some expressive therapists (art, music, dancing) specialize in their natural high practices with young persons.

An outstanding feature of NH is the democratization of the therapy situation. The same concepts and constrictions apply to everyone. However, with children, as a rule, lifestyle certainties are not so well-practiced over time, so environmental factors carry more weight. This egalitarian atmosphere does not imply sameness. Both therapist and patient are born, exist, and die differently. They have their own lived skills and experience dissimilarities. But similarities in needs, hopes, fears, and constrictions are accepted and often shared in NH learning. Hopefully the NH therapist personally practices and actualizes the steps of levels 2 and 3 and has past and present experience and awareness of level 1 constrictions. The therapist must be the more learned intellectually and behaviorally on the natural high dimension; otherwise there is no need for the learning relationship to exist. Yet this superiority in one facet of life never implies superiority of individuals.

According to Natural High theory, there are no unmotivated persons. Children and patients typically classified as unmotivated are often so highly motivated to be perfect that they will avoid interactions so as not to risk failure of power and esteem (displays of disability). Undoubtedly many such persons are more powerful than the therapist in resisting influence. The therapist does not use this supposition to discourage self or patient. Perhaps at other times, with different supports and perceptions, the patient may change. But even without change, the worth of the person in the ultimate scheme of things is not questioned. Therefore, the NH therapist maintains contact, but does not get involved with power struggles, revenge, or other hyperdependent dyads with the discouraged others. Looking to the therapist's own self-(and other-) encouragenesis makes the therapist perceive the world as a vibrant interacting system in which the tutor is responsible for his own resolution of paradoxes, as well as for actively pursuing here-and-now dynamic interpretations. In all relationships the NH therapist, within and without of the therapy game room, may have certain superior skills, but is no molder of uniquely superior persons.

Because the actualization process applies to all, so does Natural High Therapy and training. Incorporating Adlerian psychology and instrumental religious actions, NH brings schools, homes, and churches into the same serious game as clinics, hospitals, and the rest of the moving, developing community.

NATURAL HIGH THEORY AND PRACTICE IN THE TWENTY-FIRST CENTURY

Artistic and scientific creations usually explode in a blaze of frenetic activity. A long period of sculpting and molding follows until the creator burns out or dies. Over the last score of years there has been no corrections or revisions in what is now termed Natural High Theory and Practice (NHTP). NHTP has persisted in its focus on a mindfulness of inner and outer movements, which both enhance and constrict feelings of unconditional worth (spirit) and compassionate connections with all others (soul). However, the social climate of gullibility regarding simplistic and permanent psychosocial changes has passed. Curiosity about the roles of psyche, spirit, and soul in happiness has receded for the time being. Free-market ethics of downsizing for immediate profit has an obvious expression in inadequate managed health care. These organizations are not primarily for the purpose of health care. Financial health and gain for the investor and quietment for the patient are the hidden rules of the game rather than fulfillment of the democratic ideal of cheap and easy grace and health (O'Connell, 1997a).

During the last decade of my hospital and academic affiliations, I received the annual professional service award for "accomplishments (which) represent the highest example of . . . therapeutic rehabilitation" (O'Connell, 1988), in the development of theory and practice with drug addiction and posttraumatic stress. But this period was also the time of the zenith of the one-sided (and hence tragic) allopathic power coup. Starting with our diverting of mental and financial resources to the Vietnam involvement and ending with arbitrary discharging based on days-per-diagnosis, the therapeutic optimism of 1960 faded away into a search for immediate perfection, without pain and practice. Those who could not reach that glorious impossibility often demanded to be seen as passive victims entitled to interminable compensation. This one-sided, hence discouragenic, climate answered the hidden pleas of burned out

helpers (whose well-practiced discouragement made for "hinderers"). Helpers-turned-hinderers choose the maximizing of interpersonal power (not personal strength) and the minimizing of social responsibility (Mansager, 2000; O'Connell & Gomez, 1990; O'Connell & Hooker, 1996). And so we find that at the end of the century, the culturally acceptable dependency upon pills and professionals overshadows any disciplined dedicated to self-training for soul-making. NHTP psychospirituality is countercultural on that point, being well-grounded in a personalized ritual of inner and outer practice of movements toward goals of mindfulness of the experiences of spirit (self-esteem) and soul (compassionate connections).

Faced with the concept that such allopathic premises, allied with a rampant consumerism, would tether NHTP research ventures for the rest of this life, I retired to the Lost Pines of Texas on Halloween, 1986. But NHTP living, which is grounded in cooperation-as-equals, carried me to a more intense community involvement. I became the health chairman for senior retirement organizations and organized programs with a consistent goal of an active encouragenic aging. With my assistance, the Bastrop Senior Center became a reality. I organized "Senior 4H" groups (health, humor, healing, and happiness). Then came the line dance and the Spiritual Pilgrims group which I led (and co-lead) for ten years. During my "learning-through" experience with cancer (O'Connell, 1992), I wrote a column, "Close to Eternity," for the oldest continuous weekly in Texas. To paraphrase the quote of Carl Jung of ninety years ago, I am forever learning more wisdom from community participation of all sorts here (churches, schools, homes, and prisons) than I ever did from the academic institutions of abstract intellectual studies (O'Connell, 1984).

A goodly portion of my continuing "learning-through" stressors comes from my being the only clinical psychologist practicing in the county. Imagine for the moment having no staff, no consultants, no dialogues with professional peers and no backups. Imagine having no institutional and bureaucratic safeguards, no buffer zones. Here I live in community with all persons who have sought my help in coping with living and dying. This unplanned experience tells me that it is possible to create an instrumental institution able to train a professional to cooperate as equals with ex-clients. NHTP's serious and necessary (but not grave) game orientation is well-suited to play with and teach mischievous clients. The emphasis on teaching with humor can be insightful fun for mischief-makers who are eager to test emotional tutors on their skills in the marketplace. NHTP's solid base in psychodramatic treatment guarantees an ongoing emphasis upon the modeling and rewarding of encouragement in difficult inner and outer circumstances (O'Connell, 1987b).

Fifty years' experience studying and creating positive lifestyle changes has taught me the efficacy of contemplative practice for monitoring images, words, and bodily sensations as the treatment of choice for physical, psychological, spiritual, social, and interpersonal growth (O'Connell, 1987a, 1997b). Life is a continuous decision-making process, which is not the solid, permanent, dead, and determined happening on which hinderers with Newtonian mindsets dwell. In NHTP psychospirituality, one sign of a person enjoying free will is in choosing to practice the inner and outer movements required to love a loving, nonpampering God. Because professionals (religious and secular, medical and nonmedical) are offered no spiritual training, the delusion arises and persists that psychospirituality means regression to religiosity. Nothing could be further from the truth. All institutions and institutional minds harbor the popular superstition that the universe is nothing but dead, determined Newtonian invariance. Competitive warfare is inspired by the institutionalized delusion of a separated and hateful God. NHTP is now often called "Natural High Psychospirituality" for all helpers who want to be guides, coaches, and referees but never stretcher-bearers. All real healers are fellow pilgrims in the dance of awareness-of-opposites. Self-disclosure and feedback about choices is the practice of choice, letting go of resistance and negativity to the reality of what is happening. Psychospiritual pilgrims know that the images, words, sensations, and actions of our grasping and hiding ego-identities must be "learned-through." That is, when they are blamelessly identified and humorously released, the growth experience of awareness of self-esteem (spirit) and belonging (soul) is gracefully and gratuitously at hand.

NHTP psychospirituality is the only free gift you may ever be offered. It may also be the only really free gift you will always refuse.

CASE EXAMPLE

A typical case is that of Frank, a 45-year-old white single male. A former minister, now a counselor in a state alcoholic rehabilitation project, Frank came to therapy with the presenting symptoms or "calling cards" of chronic ennui and depression. He discovered this writer and Natural High watching a local television talk show, coming as a self-referral.

The contract session, for which there is no payment, was to further understanding of the expectations of both participants for an optimal relationship. Goals were articulated and the psychological pitfalls postulated (e.g., identifying possible expectations that, when unvoiced, might become pathological demands). The client was then told to call back if he decided he wanted to "work-play" with the therapist. Frank made the commitment.

At his next session, Frank was interviewed for his family constellation, early recollections, and dreams. He was also given ongoing homework (or "homeplay") assignments as per his agreement during the contract session. The tutoring sessions of individual psychotherapy were not to be used for the teaching of the abstract "psychomaps" of levels 1, 2, and 3. They were rather for helping the client/student to get his own bearings (mistakes, purposes) on his NH pilgrimage. Questions could be asked and answered, but the NH therapist was not there for generalized lectures. Frank, well aware of this interactional structure, on his own volition enrolled for a weekend death and transformation lab and a course also taught by this writer on the sense of humor at a local university.

Individual tutoring discussions on level 1 began with the client's frustration and then followed the "sinister circle" of constriction; to gather information for both therapist and patient; and to watch defensive reactions and discuss them disinterestedly with the patient/pilgrim. Frank experienced frustrations as "unbearable tensions and shakings." The immediate blame-object was himself (depression): "no good shit . . . damned monkey . . . failure, failure." He could find proof for discouragement anywhere. "I can't express anything out in the open . . . either want to run and cry or start to insult others." The unpardonable sin, the ultimate irreversible stigma, was: "I've always been a sissy and queer." Frank rated his demandments from zero to four. Later in therapy, between sessions, he recorded in his journal, without blame and punishment, the instances of demandments. Automatic-appearing invidious comparisons appeared in most human male contacts; females were simply not interesting.

As I anticipated and acknowledged, I was soon cast in the father-figure role. Frank then became silent, nervous, and discouraged about his progress, wanting to stay away after the third session. From the earlier testing, I expected this occurrence. I readily but tentatively gave a genetic interpretation, prefaced by "spitting in the soup" (O'Connell, 1975). "I would like to give you my guess as to how you're constricting yourself and why right now. But if I do, I think you might get yourself more angry and depressed and use your feelings as an excuse to drop out of therapy, as you have in the past. What's your reaction to what I've told you?"

Frank could readily make the perceptual connection between past and present behaviors and did start to express himself more honestly with me. At this point, the time seemed ripe to talk of "how" and "why" miscasting, defining, validating, and invalidating by parental persons and peers are allowed to determine present constrictions. I self-disclosed how my former constrictions were my ego-induced efforts at maintaining early dependencies. Frank reported he felt less isolated. He then related homosexual experiences at the age of five to nine with his oldest stepbrother, his father's favorite. Frank was seen by his nuclear family, he believed, as "no good shit . . . damned monkey . . . failure, failure," especially by his father and three stepbrothers. Frank was the youngest child with two pampering sisters and a pampering mother, all three reinforcing his avoidance and ineffectuality in relating to males.

After six sessions Frank was beginning to understand intellectually the NH theory and his part emotionally in becoming an active agent in creating constrictions. Three more sessions of role playing with the therapist followed. Frank did empty-chair assignments with significant members of his family, experiencing both "as it was" and "how I want it to be now." Although he could express anger and later forgiveness even with the oldest stepbrother, he balked at playing the father in the empty-chair technique. "I'm simply too scared and my mind is blank." I played father, as I saw him through the patient's eyes. Frank moved through 20 minutes of tears, followed by 15 minutes of loud, intense anger. Before the close of that session, Frank was able to finally make his peaceful farewell with the father who had died two years earlier. Frank had not attended the funeral, having given "poor health" as his excuse. Depression had followed and he quit his parish work three months later.

I reframed Frank's faith in "early psychic traumata" and "probable libidinal defects" as the cause of his homosexuality into here-and-now lifestyle constrictions. It was especially important for me to focus Frank on how he constricted himself, by his learned internalized sentences, just before his unwanted homoerotic fantasies. He then became his mother's and sisters' helpless, hopeless little boy, searching for an ideal male to transform him magically into one of his father's manly sons. Even his dreams followed the same pattern: passively incorporating the magic semen of a male who was competent, assertive, and had a profusion of hair on the head and more on the body. (Frank saw himself as ridiculed by his whole family for being a bald monkey, a small manicky creature with grossly misplaced hair.) The passive sexual fantasies were often followed by raping the male ideal in both orifices. In actuality Frank reported that he acted out only two passive homosexual encounters with strangers in adult life. He masturbated over the active fantasies, more to reduce tension over inhibited hostility than the sexual content per se. Frank could understand all this content in the frame of his ego-identity problems: his current ideals and family-induced constrictions.

He practiced haltingly the steps of level 2, giving feedback and self-disclosure assertively yet gently and appropriately to both males and females. In early therapy sessions, I pointed Frank toward expressing hidden feelings of frustration about the discouragenic acts of others. After acknowledgment of and awkward practice in the expression of negative emotions in therapy, Frank

was ready to think and perceive dialectically. In other words, he considered that he saw according to his level of self-esteem and social interest processing. As he actualized, Frank could harbor and share positive emotions. Untoward behaviors of others now became simply reflections of *their* constrictions. Frank then noted that he was either stimulating and/or noticing more the positive respect from others. And above all, the rejections of others became "gifts" from them, a chance to give an encouragenic volley to their provoking serves. Frank was now looking at his life at times from the humorous God's-eye view, becoming a useful player in the game-of-games. The same behavior that stimulated angry frustrations was now evaluated more dispassionately, from the perspective of an evolving interactional system in which he played an important part.

The time was then ripe to place Frank into my group of three males and four females, who were well schooled and practiced on their own constrictions and the theory and techniques of actualization. Frank was able, in 20 sessions, to put in his own words the personal details of his aforementioned dynamics. Early in group sessions, he voiced feelings about perceived pampering by the females and rejection by the males. He self-disclosed his generalized tendencies to compete with males unsuccessfully and seek nurturing females when defeated. After the sixth session, Frank started to share humor. He caught the ridiculous way he diminished himself and foolishly recoiled in passive anger. The group stroked him for his courage in taking this risk of self-disclosure and thereby helping them to share similar reactions.

The last ego-obstacle noted in many incipient actualizers is the fear, in fantasy and dreams, that a catastrophe would overwhelm them, and possibly the world, if they performed well or succeeded. Frank felt it too. To diminish this fear, Frank went beyond his continued sharing with group and put extra hours into creating a ritual of meditation, contemplation, and concentration. At this time he returned for two individual sessions to learn techniques of level 3 for self-expansion of worth and belonging.

At present Frank has been married for over two years in his native Montana. He considers himself quite successful in parish work and counseling. He continues to correspond intermittently with me, sharing novel ways in which he handles with humor any recurrence of his time-honored constrictions. The main-tent for Frank's life is now with others; constrictions are merely an interesting side-show of his former existence. (For another case study, with a female client, see O'Connell, 1979a.)

SUMMARY

Natural High is a broad, holistic therapy, not a minitheory of narrow concepts and techniques. It transcends pop psychology's promise of instant ecstasy in its emphasis on continuous practice within the serious (but not grave) game model. NH is the only therapy that has at its core a well-formulated focus on the sense of humor as a criterion of actualization. Traditional psychopathology finds its place in the ego constrictions and subsequent ego defenses of level 1.

The therapist himself is responsible for his own actualization as well as communication of encouragement (and the knowledgeable awareness of the "hows" and "whys" of discouragement). The active, encouragenic therapist/tutor is the key element of the change process; therefore, the state of actualization is not totally ignored in NH, as it is in contemporary professionalization and institutionalization. NH stands apart from dualisms of persons and professions, centering on overcoming ego-identity defects and the attachments to tentative ego esteem. The process of creating unconditional self-esteem and universal belonging is regarded as paramount for all persons and the most pertinent goal of all human activities. NH is therefore seen as the treatment (or education) of choice, the overt manifestation of the ideals of the perennial philosophy and democracy-in-action. The premises and techniques of all humanistic depth psychologies are incorporated within NH. NH goes beyond conventional therapies in not separating experiential education from the tasks of psychology, psychiatry, education, and religion. NH has a strong Adlerian base, but goes beyond the Adlerian social dimension to symbolic transpersonal catalysts of self-esteem and social interest expansion. NH spells out the steps of encouragement, as well as concretizing and systematizing the nuances of diminishment. The tragic side of life so neglected in Adlerian psychology, as well as by other therapies, is embraced by NH in the appreciation of the presence of natural low states and constricted others, so vital to one's own practice of self-realization.

NH represents a continuation of Jung's emphasis on the inner dialogue between ego and archetypes (behavioral potentials) of the collective unconscious. NH stresses the signs and developmental steps of this strong or actualized ego, a prerequisite to accepting (and not diagnosing, judging, or interpreting) the expansive energies of the collective unconscious. It carries on, through its transcendental courage, Jung's later concern with the human partnership in transforming the divine or cosmic shadow. NH is not phobic about the mystical thrusts (e.g., Teilhard de Chardin) that drastically elevate both the human worth potential and our innate universal belonging. The avoidance of false dichotomies fructifies the latent positive relationship between actualizing psychologies and instrumental humanistic religions. The bedrock of NH is each person's awareness of ego constrictions (level 1) and social obligations (level 2) *before* and basic to transpersonal explorations (level 3). Present

cognitive and behavioral deficiencies of both the unactualized ego and institutionalized social settings cannot be circumvented by demands for an instant magical-egotistical euphoria.

REFERENCES

Ansbacher, H., & Ansbacher, R. (Eds.). (1956). *The individual psychology of Alfred Adler.* New York: Basic.

Ansbacher, H., & Ansbacher, R. (Eds.). (1964). *Superiority and social interest: A collection of later writings.* Evanston, IL.: Northwestern University Press.

Dreikurs, R. (1971). *Social equality: The challenge of today.* Chicago: Regnery.

Ellis, A. (1974). *Humanistic psychotherapy: The rational-emotive approach.* New York: McGraw-Hill.

Haley, J. (1963). *The strategies of psychotherapy.* New York: Grune & Stratton.

Jung, C. (1961). *Memories, dreams, reflections.* New York: Random House.

Mansager, E. (2000). An interview with Walter E. "Buzz" O'Connell on psychospirituality. *Journal of Individual Psychology, 56*(3), 329–342.

O'Connell, W. (1974). *The odyssey of a psychologist.* New York: MSS Information Corporation.

O'Connell, W. (1975). *Action therapy and Adlerian theory.* Chicago: Alfred Adler Institute.

O'Connell, W. (1976a). Freudian humour: The eupsychia of everyday life. In A. Chapman & H. Foot (Eds.), *Humour and laughter: Theory, research, and applications.* London: Wiley.

O'Connell, W. (1976b). The "Friends of Adler" phenomenon. *Journal of Individual Psychology, 32,* 5–18.

O'Connell, W. (Ed.). (1976c). *Psychotherapy: Theoretical and technical readings.* New York: MSS Information Corporation.

O'Connell, W. (1977). The sense of humor: Actualizer of persons and theories. In A. Chapman & H. Foot (Eds.), *It's a funny thing, humour.* London: Pergamon.

O'Connell, W. (1978a). Action therapy. *The Individual Psychologist, 15,* 4–11.

O'Connell, W. (1978b). A re-solution of Adlerian-Jungian opposites. *Journal of Individual Psychology, 34,* 170–181.

O'Connell, W. (1979a). The demystification of Sister Saint Nobody. *Journal of Individual Psychology, 35,* 79–94.

O'Connell, W. (1979b). *Super-natural highs.* Chicago: North American Graphics.

O'Connell, W. (1984). Letting go and hanging on: Confessions of a zen Adlerian. *Individual Psychology, 40,* 71–82.

O'Connell, W. (1987a). Natural high psychospirituality: Stalking shadows with "childlike foolishness." *Individual Psychology, 43,* 502–509.

O'Connell, W. (1987b). Natural high theory and practice: The humorist's game of games. In W. Fry & W. Salameh (Eds.),

Handbook of humor and psychotherapy: Advances in the clinical use of humor (pp. 55–79). Sarasota, FL: Professional Resources Exchange.

O'Connell, W. (1988). Natural high theory and practice: A psychospiritual integration. *Journal of Integrative and Eclectic Psychotherapy, 7,* 441–454.

O'Connell, W. (1992). The public practice of Adlerian wisdom with the elderly. *Individual Psychology, 48,* 441–450.

O'Connell, W. (1997a). Introduction to Natural High Theory and practice. *Canadian Journal of Adlerian Psychology, 27,* 100–122.

O'Connell, W. (1997b). Radical metaphors of Adlerian psychospirituality. *Individual Psychology, 53,* 33–41.

O'Connell, W., & Bright, M. (1977). *Natural high primer.* Houston: Natural High Associates.

O'Connell, W., Bright, M., & Grossman, S. (1978). Negative nonsense and drug addiction. *Rational Living, 13,* 19–24.

O'Connell, W., & Gomez, E. (1990). Dialectics, trances, and the wisdom of encouragement. *Individual Psychology, 46,* 431–442.

O'Connell, W., & Hooker, E. (1996). Anxiety disorders II. In L. Sperry and J. Carlson (Eds.), *Psychopathology and psychotherapy* (pp. 179–220). Washington, DC: Accelerated Development.

Ram Dass, B., & Levine, S. (1977). *Grist for the mill.* Santa Cruz, CA: Unity.

Watzlawick, P. (1978). *The language of change: Elements of therapeutic communication.* New York: Basic.

Chapter 42

THE NEW IDENTITY PROCESS

DANIEL M. CASRIEL

Throughout the centuries there have been voluntary institutions, such as monasteries, and involuntary institutions, such as prisons, dedicated to reforming individuals, changing them in a direction desired either by the person himself or herself or by others. Perhaps the oldest and best known of these was at Epidaurus in Greece, a healing center that existed as such for over 1,000 years.

In recent years, a somewhat different type of treatment center has developed, based more on psychological rationales than on the physiological ones of the watering spas. Examples range from the meditational ashrams of the Orient, to diet-oriented "fat farms" for the wealthy and bored, to Synanon, an organization that has itself spawned a wide variety of other treatment modalities—Daytop Village and Habilitat, for example.

Daniel Casriel, the author of this chapter, was conventionally trained in psychodynamics and psychiatry. After visiting Synanon, he changed his thinking and his life. Eventually he developed the concepts of Synanon into his own system, first called Scream Therapy and now New Identity Process, which is similar in many respects to several other approaches in this volume, especially Integrity Groups and Reevaluation Counseling. As the reader will soon find out, the entire process is well conceived, theoretically consistent, and from all indications is being accepted and is developing at a rapid rate.

The New Identity Process (NIP), also known somewhat less precisely as Scream Therapy, is a comprehensive therapeutic system for reeducating a person's emotional, thinking, and behavioral responses, especially those that have to do with giving and getting love.

The tools of NIP are bonding—physical closeness with emotional openness; screaming for discharging historic emotion and preparing the person to incorporate fresh messages; confrontation of behavior; and new information about the ABC's—affect, behavior, and cognition.

The aim of the process is not simply adjustment—cognitive absence of painful emotion—but happiness—cognitive awareness of a preponderance of pleasure. A happy person is autonomous, successful, fallible, able to put things in perspective, and capable of giving and receiving love, expressing needs, and getting those needs filled in a responsible way.

NIP is effective with all degrees of neurotic and character-disordered personalities, including the delinquent, the addict, and the alcoholic. It is also effective in treating the so-called borderline schizophrenic, provided the disorder is not organic in origin.

HISTORY

The main ingredients that went into the development of the system were: (1) training in Adaptational Psychodynamics; (2) work with drug users and exposure to Synanon in 1962; and (3) work with Synanon techniques at Daytop and with private patients.

Adaptational Psychodynamics

After graduating from the Cincinnati College of Medicine in 1949, this writer attended the Columbia Psychoanalytic Institute for Training and Research, at that time directed by founders Sandor Rado and Abram Kardiner, who formulated Adaptational Psychodynamics. Their theory advanced Freudian tenets by attributing pathology not to instinct alone, but also to the conditioning the individual is subjected to in infancy and childhood by those responsible for meeting his or her needs. Later, spurred by 18 months of exposure to a different culture on Okinawa, I contacted Kardiner, who was well-known for his anthropological approach to the human personality. I was an analysand of Kardiner's for over seven years, and through that experience became convinced that no inborn human feature was without purpose.

The Synanon Experience

Shortly after opening my private practice in 1953, I began working with various government and judicial bodies to apply psychoanalytic techniques to rehabilitating young drug addicts, most of whom were severely character-disordered personalities. I found, as had so many of my colleagues, that the transference integral to successful analysis simply did not develop with addicts, and the program failed. I concluded that there were only two ways to deal with drug addicts: maintain them on their habit or lock them up.

My attitude changed drastically in 1962, as a result of exposure to Synanon, a California drug and alcohol rehabilitation community consisting at that time of about a hundred people. The visit, part of a nationwide survey of drug treatment facilities for the National Institute of Mental Health, was to change radically my approach not only to drug addiction, but to the entire field of applied psychiatry.

Apart from tremendous productive physical activity and a rigidly authoritarian structure, the two ingredients I saw as most critical at Synanon were: (1) people expressing genuine love and concern overtly; and (2) the focus on behavior through highly charged emotional confrontation in groups, known widely today as Synanon games. Their belief was that when one changes one's objectionable behavior *first*—that is, stops taking dope *first*—only then can inner change take place. And addicts *were* changing into productive, responsible, loving human beings.

My Work with Synanon Techniques

Fired with excitement by the possibilities Synanon had suggested, and by the love and insights I had experienced during the confrontation groups I'd participated in, I returned to New York and over the next two years cofounded Daytop Lodge; a Synanon center in Westport, Connecticut; and Daytop Village in New York, which became a model for scores of government-sponsored therapeutic communities that sprang up worldwide over the next 15 years.

I was equally intrigued by the potential that the Synanon type of group might hold for speeding treatment of my more recalcitrant neurotic patients. Using some Synanon-trained people as catalysts, I first introduced the technique in 1963 to a group of eight patients from my private practice. The technique was astoundingly successful, producing breakthroughs that dramatically speeded progress in individual analytic sessions. Soon people were coming asking for group treatment only. At first, I was hesitant, but gradually, as I became more comfortable with the group process and the safety it provided, I dropped the requirement for individual sessions.

Within six years it was necessary to move three times to accommodate the flow of patients. In 1970 I left Daytop to begin my own residential program for middle- and upper-class addicts. By that year almost 600 patients were participating in groups each week.

In the 30 years since then, NIP has evolved considerably. The highly charged emotional group is "an emotional microscope" through which we can see clearly and map for the first time the geography of emotions. The process today has shifted emphasis more toward bonding and toward what we experience as love. "People are starving, and love is the only thing that will feed them."

CURRENT STATUS

The headquarters for NIP treatment and training is in a brownstone building in New York City. There, around the clock, seven days a week, five programs are offered tailored to meet individual needs. These include:

1. AREBA (Accelerated reeducation of emotions, behavior, and attitudes), a residential treatment program that rehabilitates young addicts. The term of residence in the three-phase program ranges from 12 to 24 months, with an average of 15 months. Of those who complete the program, over 90 percent are cured—drug-free, socially functioning, and educationally or vocationally employed.
2. Intensives, a residential program for nonaddicts that consists of three groups a day, six or seven days a week.
3. Outpatient group therapy sessions, which often include residential patients.
4. Individual therapy to deal with special problems or with people who for one reason or another are not available for group work.
5. Various training programs for individuals wanting certification as NIP group leaders, including one-year training internships and less concentrated programs for practicing therapists.

In addition I travel for about four months a year in Europe and another two to three months a year in the United States, giving workshops and training therapists.

As of 1980, there were seven national societies of the New Identity Process in the United States, Sweden, Switzerland, Germany, Holland, France, and Venezuela. An estimated 15,000 people a week are experiencing the process or a modification of it.

The process is explained in more detail in *A Scream Away From Happiness* (Casriel, 1972) and *The Huggers*.

THEORY

In evolving New Identity Process theory, I have blended humanistic, neo-Freudian, and behaviorist thinking with insights arising out of my own experience and observation. The theory can be summarized as follows.

1. *The origin of pathology:* A human being is born with intrinsic value and entitlements. Pathology originates from early conditioning that opposes these basic entitlements by making the process of getting one's needs met painful. On the basis of early conditioning, a person makes decisions regarding the pleasure and pain of getting biological needs met; these decisions constitute the central dynamic of his or her disorder and are what distinguish one category of disorder from another.
2. *The locus of pathological patterns:* The individual acts out these early decisions in relation to bonding, the one biological need for which, even as an adult, he or she must continue looking to others to satisfy.
3. *The keys to change:* To change destructive patterns, we must rectify the current vast ignorance regarding the dynamics and biology of emotion, and apply new understanding of how thinking, feeling, and behavior interrelate and perpetuate pathological patterns.

The Origin of Pathology

In the NIP system, people are born good, having value simply for being alive. As such, they are each entitled to (1) exist as separate beings with an identity of their own, (2) have physical and emotional needs and get them met, (3) be happy, and (4) be imperfect. Pathology originates during our dependent years with conditioning that subverts these basic entitlements by suggesting that we have to earn them or be something we are not in order to have them. This subversion is painful.

All animal behavior is motivated by the pursuit of pleasure and avoidance of pain. Feeling entitled is pleasurable; feeling unentitled is painful. We learn to feel entitled in infancy and early childhood when our caretakers meet our biological needs (physical, mental, and emotional) in a caring, loving way with a minimum of pain. We learn to feel unentitled when we do not get that loving care, when we have to beg; or wait interminably; or manipulate; or do without, with too little, or with too much.

Faced with this dilemma, we eventually make two major decisions, one about dealing with pleasure, the other about dealing with pain. Because the decisions relate to dependency needs, it is only to be expected that as adults we act out our pathology in those areas in which we still feel dependent on others, in personal relationships.

Acceptors and Rejectors

How we decide to deal with pleasure puts us in one of two categories: *acceptor* or *rejector*.

In the acceptor's experience the pleasure of getting needs met exceeds the pain, and they decide "I have to get my needs met no matter what." Later on they accept human relationships even at the price of pain, humiliation, and loss of freedom and identity.

Rejectors experience the pain as greater than the pleasure and say, "To hell with it. I'll suck my own thumb and do it myself, as much as I can." Later on they reject human relationships no matter what price they have to pay in pain, deprivation, and isolation.

Neurotics and Character Disorders

The decision about how to deal with pain is what differentiates neurosis from character disorder.

Neurotics are aware of their pain, but are afraid to express it, and they utilize elaborate defense mechanisms to keep from doing so, especially if there is associated anger. They say something like, "If I let out my pain, I'll never stop," or "Someone (everyone) will reject me, I won't get my needs met, and then I'll die."

By contrast, character-disordered personalities say, "The pain's too great, I won't feel it." They don't opt for "fight or flight," they "freeze," simply detaching from the pain, and keeping it at bay by acting out in ways destructive to self and others. Most addicts—from alcoholics to workaholics—are "on" their habit to blot out pain they don't even know they have.

The Locus of Disordered Patterning: The Continuing Need for Bonding

As we become self-sufficient in meeting our own needs for proper temperature, food, water, and so forth, the attitudes and feelings that were originally conditioned around those needs are uncoupled from them, but reattach themselves to those other needs for which the individual must still depend on others. Ultimately there is only one such need, and that is the need for bonding.

Bonding is physical closeness combined with emotional openness. One without the other does not meet the need. Bonding is not sex, because sex without emotional openness does not meet the need.

From the moment we are born to the moment we die, bonding is essential to human health. This is especially true, of course, in infancy. James W. Prescott, a developmental neuropsychologist with the National Institute of Child Health and Human Development in Washington, D.C., conducted studies whose results suggested that early lack of bonding actually produces brain damage. Specifically, its lack retards or distorts development of the dendrites—nerve-cell branches in the neuronal systems that control affection and violence. Prescott suggests that the inability to experience affection and to control violence will be at levels inversely proportionate to levels of infant affection because of this impaired nerve-cell development. Other recent studies in California and Illinois comparing brain-cell branch development in monkeys reared in colonies or in isolation show similar impairment in isolation-reared animals. Bonding is not precious as diamonds are precious. Bonding is essential, as water is.

Filling one's need for bonding gives rise to pleasure. Failing to fill it creates pain, just as not getting enough food creates hunger, which is painful. The greater the need or desire for bonding, and the higher the quality and quantity of its fulfillment, the more we experience it as love. Without bonding, we don't feel lovable, good enough, or entitled, and we remain "weary, leery, teary, or phobic of emotional intimacy." We lack concentration or wrestle with obsession, our perception narrows, and we feel empty. With sufficient bonding, we feel lovable, potent, loving, and right: Whatever life throws at us, we can cope.

In Western culture, in both the United States and Europe, deprivation of bonding is almost universal. Infantile physical contact varies between 5 and 25 percent of the time, compared with 70 percent of the time for the !Kung bushmen, whose tribal living style approximates that which formed the basis for millions of years of human evolution. The pain that results from this deprivation underlies the vast majority of emotional disorders. The solution isn't pills. Hungry people show symptoms of the biological need for food; they're not sick. We don't prescribe a pill for deadening their feeling of hunger. We feed them to fill their biological need, and the hunger disappears. So it is with the need for bonding.

The Keys to Change

In NIP a person is seen as triangular; a free interplay of thoughts, emotions, and behaviors clustered around a biological organism that is in the process of taking in fuel, converting it to energy, and discharging that energy in various ways. In the healthy human, thinking and emotion help organize perception and experience and guide behavior to maximize sensations of pleasure and minimize sensations of pain.

The Logic of Emotions

All affect is a response to pain, danger (the anticipation of pain), pleasure, or desire (the anticipation of plea-

sure). Emotions arise in response to intense thoughts related to pleasure or pain, to sensations (including biological processes), and nothing else. There are five basic emotions: pain, pleasure, fear, anger, and love.

Although the five emotions are experienced locally in the body (pain in the abdomen, pleasure in the pelvis, fear in the throat, anger in the chest, and love in the heart), they are biochemically a full-body reaction called for by the autonomic nervous system from the glandular system. The autonomic nervous system consists of two parts—the sympathetic and the parasympathetic systems. The combined action of all these systems prepares us physically and psychologically to cope with stimuli of all kinds: Our sense of physical readiness increases confidence while our emotions release energy to power effective action. Clearly, emotions evolved as a crucial part of our survival system.

If pain or danger is the original stimulus, then, neurophysiologists tell us, the sympathetic nervous system is activated to help the body mobilize to *flee* or *fight*. The body's metabolism is increased, sugar floods into the bloodstream for quick energy, blood carrying oxygen and glucose goes to the skeletal muscles for great strength and speed in running or hitting. The body assumes a slightly crouched, self-protective stance. A third option, taken when escape is impossible and fighting dangerous or pointless, is to *"freeze"*—mentally and/or physically to withdraw or detach from others and from one's own body, to immobilize one's body and thus one's emotions. More research is needed to determine the biological operation of the withdrawal or freeze response.

It is natural to hypothesize that a stimulus of pleasure or desire activates the parasympathetic system to prepare the body for taking in pleasure and love. This is a logical extension of what neurophysiologists already tell us: that the parasympathetic is a anabolic agency that assists in taking in and storing energy and repairing the body systems. The body's processes are reversed—blood flows from the extremities, the heart slows, as does the metabolism. The body assumes an open stance, shoulders back and pelvis forward, as in a yawn.

What we experience as psychological preparation is a biochemical change effected throughout the body by the glandular system, sometimes referred to as the third nervous system, which can be equated to emotion itself. Certainly it is experienced as emotion.

Further proof of the biochemical/glandular nature of emotion is emerging from research, which is beginning to discover a whole chemistry of emotions: adrenaline for fear; nor-adrenalins for anger; steroids and fatty acids for pleasure.

Research has also found evidence suggesting that general body preparedness to cope with stress is indicated by the level of eosinophiles in the blood. An alcoholic craving a drink has an eosinophile level of practically nil. After taking a drink—his or her way of coping with stress—the alcoholic feels much better and his or her eosinophile level has risen to between 80 and 100 per cubic millimeter. Blood samples taken before and after screaming show similar changes, more than a 15-fold increase, from 5 per cubic millimeter to between 80 and 100 per cubic millimeter. With an increased eosinophile level, of course, people feel much better, far more prepared to cope.

It is critical to psychological and physical health to be able to mobilize emotions quickly and utilize the energy they provide; otherwise our sense of being able to take in strong pleasure or defend against pain is crippled, and we feel insecure, frightened, tense, unready to face life's tests. When we do feel prepared, we feel better, even if the emotions involved are "negative." Fully expressed, anger can be experienced as potency, fear as excitement, pain as bearable or releasing, and pleasure and love as nourishing.

The blocks to achieving the sense of psychological preparedness lie less in the emotions themselves than in the ways in which specific emotions are associated with decisions and attitudes about emotions, entitlement, survival, and identity.

Attitudes and How They Relate to Emotions

The word "attitude" refers to thought, but as we treat issues closer to the core of a person's identity, the lines between thought and feeling and between one feeling and another become increasingly difficult to draw. This is because such attitudes involve deep-level, preverbal programming, incorporated before the person has developed the skill to discriminate between thought and feeling. There is evidence to suggest that decisions arising from this early conditioning are lodged in an emotional memory in the cortical level on the nondominant side of the brain. If so, these attitudes are unlikely to be accessible for treatment through rational, verbal methods: instead, the therapeutic course must be navigated through emotional seas.

Take the attitude "People can't be trusted." It is often programmed into the person within the first year of life and relates to survival—life and death. Associated with the attitude are repressed emotions of fear, pain, and anger. Until those associated feelings are discharged, there will always be an underlying sense of mistrust, which the person will continually seek to reinforce by the way he or she interacts with the environment. No treatment will quite hold when the heat is on. It's as if the negative attitude were a string of words cut out of cloth and nailed to the personality by deep spikes of negative emotion. Not until the spikes are removed will the negative attitude be released for deep, lasting change that is strong enough to persist through deep crisis, to permit the risk of openness with others.

Table 42.1   Emotions and the Attitudes They Inspire

Emotion	Attitude about Expressing the Emotion
Anger	I will go crazy, destroy others, be destroyed, be a bad person.
Fear	I'll be helpless, crazy, unable to defend myself, unmanly, bad.
Pain	I'll die, fall apart, hurt forever, disappear, go crazy, be ugly.
Pleasure	I'll be bad, childish, irresponsible; someone will be angry, punish me; I'll have to pay it back.
Love	I'll be trapped, hurt, abandoned, scorned, obligated, resented by others, responsible for the loved one (completely).

Before the emotional spikes can be pulled out, a person must overcome attitudes preventing the expression of specific emotions. A most common one is that one or more emotions is "good" or "bad." This attitude can be learned very early; for example, when a baby cries in anger because he isn't getting picked up or fed, and the overworked mother repeatedly responds with disapproval, anger, and rough handling, the baby, responding with fear to her anger, quickly learns that being angry is dangerous. To avoid the danger, the child concludes that whenever he is angry, he is "bad" and liable to be punished; thus he learns to repress his anger.

Such attitudes are numerous. Table 42.1 lists some other common ones.

A special note about love: Our society has distorted, even perverted, the concept of love. So powerful have these attitudes been that it has been necessary to redefine the word "love" in NIP. Eventually each of us comes to our own understanding—love is a personal matter—but in NIP, love is defined as just a feeling—no more, no less—not something one can promise, recall, or sustain, not a commitment or a relationship, just a feeling for now. It is this kind of thinking that enables many people to accept that it is possible to feel love for someone across the room whose name we don't even know, and whom we'll quite likely never see again.

Behavior

NIP focuses considerable attention on behavior. We live in a character-disordered society, very few patients come in without some degree of character disorder, and behavior is the character-disordered personality's primary insulation against having to grapple with feelings. Stripping the person of that insulation is the fastest way to get him or her to deal with emotions.

Demanding that a character-disordered person stop acting out is also the best way to test motivation. Because the person is unaware of his pain, his motivation to change is practically nil. Only when he encounters un-avoidable pain is he likely to show up for treatment, and even then, he tends to stay only as long as the pain lasts. He's woven an elaborate and often brilliant web of be-haviors and ideas about the world and people to defend himself from having to change; he gives up that protec-tive web only as a last resort and will take it up again at the least indication that it might work again, even tem-porarily. His fear of emotional pain is so great that often the faintest taste of it will reactivate his decision to act out rather than to feel.

Knowing this, AREBA staff and participants don't use kid gloves with character-disordered newcomers. When a young addict comes in off the street, they don't ask, "What painful feelings brought you here?" They ask, "Who's on your tail?" and they don't accept the per-son into the program until they've heard a cry for help as genuine on an emotional level.

Behavior is important in treating neurotics too, but on a more subtle level, and primarily at a later phase in treatment. With neurotics NIP focuses on signaling, bringing the language of the body into line with the new attitudes and feelings the person has been acquiring.

What is the person's level of maturity in each functional area? The functional areas include (1) social, sexual, and personal relationships, and (2) vocational and educa-tional pursuits.

The four basic levels of personality maturation are:

	Infant	Child	Adolescent	Adult
Attitude	Helpless Unreal	Dependent Dishonest	Defiant Dishonest	Self-reliant Honest
Transference	Worship Magical Wish, Deity	Seductive, Timid Manipulative	Resentful Provocative	Objective Confrontation
Emotion	Panic	Insecure Fearful	Angry Controlled	Appropriate
Behavior	Impotent	Helpless Irresponsible	Aggressive Irresponsible	Responsible

METHODOLOGY

When a person first arrives at the Casriel Institute, he or she goes through an intake interview and an introduc-tory group before being allowed to participate freely in the general programs. During this time, the therapist be-gins to check off answers to the following questions. They provide a description of pathology that is not symptomatic (e.g., anxiety reaction or depressive reac-tion) but dynamic.

Is the person emotionally open or closed? Emotionally open means one expresses feeling. Pseudo-open refers to the hysteric, who is not in touch with real emotion. Emo-tionally closed means someone who has no experience with emotions or feelings. Pseudo-closed refers to a per-son who never expresses feelings, doesn't know he has

them, but when uncorked, his feelings tumble out in full resonant emotional communication.

Is the person a rejector or an acceptor? Pseudo-rejector or pseudo-acceptor (acting "as if" but relenting eventu-ally) or other possibilities.

What are the person's primary and secondary behavioral defenses against pain (flight, anger, withdrawal, or control) and what attitudes are attached to those behaviors?

Is the person functioning up to potential vocationally and socially? Is he taking advantage of the best options available to him?

Is the person able to deal effectively with all emotions from self and others (accepting and expressing anger, love, fear, pain, and pleasure)?

With the answers to these questions, a NIP therapist can understand symptoms dynamically. For example:

Sadist	Attitude:	A love object is dangerous
	Feeling:	Anger
	Behavior:	Neutralizes the power of the love object until he or she feels safe.
Masochist	Attitude:	I don't deserve pleasure
	Feeling:	Guilt, fear
	Behavior:	Punishes self to pay/atone for having pleasure
Anal-Obsessive	Attitude:	I can't be separate from Mommy
	Feeling:	Fear, anger, guilt, depression
	Behavior:	Acts only for or against authority, never for self.

Once a person is accepted for therapy, the basic sequence of treatment is as follows.

Introduction to NIP

Routinely, the therapist shows a videotape of an NIP process in progress, which includes some basic information on the logic of emotions and the need for bonding, the difference between emotional memory and intellectual memory, and the purpose of the process—to discharge and reeducate emotions as a mandatory step in changing the quality of one's life.

Patients are also introduced to the institute's rules: (a) no violence; (b) no drugs or alcohol; (c) no sexual intercourse on the premises. In group meetings there are three other rules: (d) no smoking; (e) no dishonesty; and (f) no storytelling—the focus must be on feeling, not on facts.

A Positive Experience of Bonding

Since bonding must take place in the context of emotional openness, the first step is to help a new patient get to his or her feelings. This takes place in "emotional" groups.

Generally, a group begins with a "go-round," in which each person shares how he or she is feeling at the moment, and what he or she wants to work on. If there are feelings at the surface, the therapist will deal with them briefly; otherwise the entire group reports, and more extended work takes place later.

Often a person's first feeling is fear about being in group. Let's take Mandy: The therapist has her make eye contact with each person in turn and say, "I'm afraid." The fear seems acute, so the therapist urges her to say it louder and louder until finally she is screaming out the fear full measure. Jane rises and goes to hold her, providing warmth and support. After a minute or so, it is clear that Mandy is less withdrawn and feels better. She says so, states her reasons for being in the group—she is depressed because her fiancé has left her—and the "go-round" continues.

After the "go-round," when a few people have worked, the therapist comes back to Mandy and says, "Look at each person, and say 'I hurt.'" Mandy obediently goes around, tears streaming, crying pitifully. "Now imagine your fiancé on the mat and tell him 'You *hurt* me!'" Mandy begins to say, "You hurt me," and within just a few repetitions, her body comes out of its collapsed attitude, her voice takes on strength, and she begins screaming in rage from deep in her belly, "You *hurt* me, you *bastard!*" She continues screaming for a few minutes, and then turns around and says with her eyes snapping, "I'm *angry!* I think I could kill him." She suddenly looks guilty and draws her arms in. "It's not okay

to do it, but it's sure okay to feel that way," says the therapist. "Go around and tell everybody, 'My anger is not bad.'" Mandy does so, looking less guilty as she gets nods of agreement and support from the group. "Now pick someone and go in the other room to get some more of that anger out and take in some pleasure."

Therapists have different styles of working. Some do all their work in one room; Mandy's current therapist uses two: One room, lined with mats, is exclusively for emotional work (working through feelings while bonding with someone), the other is for attitudinal work. Mandy chooses Jane, and they go to work. Mandy continues screaming while Jane holds her, providing support and encouragement, sharing her own experience and—most of all—just being there, a warm teddy bear to hold on to. Little by little Mandy will learn that anger and pain don't have to be total. One can take in pleasure while going through the pain. She is now being taught specific techniques for doing just that—for example, breathing through her mouth instead of clenching her jaw.

When the overload of emotion has diminished somewhat, Mandy and Jane return to the group for attitudinal work.

Reprogramming Attitudes Through Screaming

This is where the real work of change, lasting change, begins. It is nothing less than the reclamation of basic entitlements—to exist, need, be happy, make mistakes, feel, think clearly, love and be loved, be successful, powerful, weak—to be, in short, what we are.

Basically, the therapist takes attitudes that were uncovered through the emotional work and suggests corrective messages for the individual to work with. The mechanism of screaming is used to reprogram—for what sometimes seems an endless period of time, but in reality is not.

In Mandy's case, much of the anger covers fear that if her fiancé doesn't love her, it proves she isn't lovable, and she won't be able to get her needs filled. So the therapist concentrates on messages that assert Mandy's worth and her need to be loved. First she goes around the circle, saying, "I'm Mandy and I have value." Her voice is toneless, even at volume. "Tell your father. Tell him 'I'm Mandy and I'm *important!*'" the therapist says. Mandy appears to wilt before our eyes. "He wouldn't hear. He thinks I'm a foolish child, and stupid," she quavers. Jane lets out a roar of anger, and another and another. "Don't let him do that to you!" she howls at Mandy. "Stand up and tell the bastard off. Fight for yourself!" Mandy shifts uncomfortably. "What's the point? He wouldn't care." "*You* care!" yells Rick from across the room. "You're doing just what *I* do. *Stop it!* Care for yourself!" "You can do it, Mandy," urges Jane. "Stand up and tell him, like this." Jane stands up, throws her head and shoulders back, and says over and over, full volume, "*Listen* to me, I'm Mandy and I'm *important!*" Mandy watches, her mouth open. She glances at the therapist, who nods a go-ahead. She gets up and, in a fair imitation of Jane, begins to assert herself. As she taps into her anger, her voice strengthens. Jane draws back, cheering her on. Mandy goes around the group three times. By the time she stops, she is flushed and vital looking. Group members are grinning in delight.

This marks the first of many times that Mandy will need to exercise her feelings of self-love. So long dormant, they must be nourished through a new emotional-attitudinal conduit, which can be etched in only by repeated reinforcement.

Hal provides another case in point, the difficulty of accepting one's need for others. A textbook character-disordered personality, Hal chose orthopedic surgery as his first addiction, barbiturates as his second, and came for treatment only after having sacrificed his marriage, children, professional partners, and personal health on the altar of "service to humanity." It has taken cancer to take him out of the operating theater and put him in touch with his pain. He is bewildered and angry, terrified of a life without his work, and in dread of a lonely death.

Even under such pressure, it takes a week of "Intensive" before he can bring himself to admit aloud that he needs anything emotionally. Even then, it is an intellectual conclusion reached during an individual session. Nevertheless, it is enough: He accepts intellectually that getting in touch with his need and his basic entitlement to need is a requisite for getting well. Even though he doesn't feel the need, he commits to doing the necessary work. And work it is.

He spends many hours lying on the mats repeating, "I need," "I need to be loved," and "Love me." And the feelings come up. First the ritual anger, then fear, and finally, after three days, the first cries of anguish for years of deprivation.

Each time a new set of feelings come up and out, Hal moves back to the attitudinal group to report on and deal with the attitudes around needing. He is given new attitude statements, such as "I'm not weak when I need"; "If I show you my need, you won't hurt me"; "I'm not bad when I need"; "I'm a man, and I need."

Two weeks later, one can hear a new note in Hal's voice. At last he begins to be able to say "I need," not as a confession of weakness or an indictment of caretakers, but as a statement of fact and rightness, and an invitation to share. He is beginning to accept that his need can be a pleasure for someone else to fill.

Confrontation of Behavior

The stated purpose of a confrontation group is to increase intimacy through honest expression of feeling and thoughts. Originally patterned after the Synanon model, the NIP confrontation group has some added features.

The formula is: (1) get out the feeling that keeps you from getting close to the other person; (2) say what the feeling is about; and (3) say what you want from the other person. This last component is critical and is what keeps a confrontation from becoming a shooting match, and a group from turning into a firing squad, as often happened at Synanon.

The benefit of confrontation is to the confront**er**, not the confront**ed**. Each person is expected to deal honestly and openly with his or her feelings, and that means expressing them full measure, by screaming.

In fact, there are many benefits of honest confrontation. What typically happens is that the behavior that A objects to in B is what A him- or herself does, and this becomes evident to A as the process proceeds. People learn that honesty on a feeling level doesn't kill anyone, that no one bleeds. In fact, it is common to have the confronters end up in one another's arms. For this reason many married couples having trouble come in to work out their difficulties within the protection of the group. They learn that no matter how unlovely their feelings and attitudes may be by social norms, honest expression is ultimately preferable to a coverup.

APPLICATIONS

New Identity Process is best suited for neurotics and character-disordered persons of all degrees. In order of their frequency and importance, the most common problems dealt with at the Casriel Institute are (1) the inability to accept love, (2) the inability to express anger, (3) the inability to accept anger, and (4) the inability to give love.

The inability to accept love is primary for the rejectors, who have found that pain exceeds pleasure in intimate relationships. The key phrase here is "Am I lovable?" As the person hears and begins to take in answers in the affirmative, he or she experiences first a sense of wonder and then tremendous pain for all the years of deprivation. When the person has shared this pain, and only after, someone who has avoided love can begin to accept it.

This exercise is also helpful for acceptors, who feel entitled to love, but not fully so, or only for a price.

The inability to express anger is primarily an acceptor's problem. Acceptors have repressed their anger as part of the price they believe they have to pay for love. They need anger exercises to help them assert the strength of their personalities.

For rejectors, anger exercises help when expressed at the deepest level, called the Identity level. The statement to elicit is "I've been hurt. It wasn't fair. I'm angry, and I'm not going to allow that to happen again."

Some people cannot separate the expression of anger from physical aggression, or from rejection; they suffer from *the inability to accept anger.* In confrontation, however, within a safe structure, they can learn that they can accept anger without being wrong and without getting hurt, be wrong without being guilty, and make mistakes without being bad or stupid.

The inability to give love afflicts some people who fear that if they love someone, they then become responsible for that person. Others feel so inadequate that they think their love has no value. It is when the fear, pain, and anger are expressed fully that a person can understand and begin to let him- or herself feel love for others.

NIP is also ideal for people who defend themselves by intellectualizing—the kind of people who can spend years increasing their understanding and never change. In NIP, achieving a new level of happiness—good feelings—is the jackpot. Understanding, as always, is the booby prize.

CASE EXAMPLE

Henry, only son of a physician, was youngest of three children. His father was a self-made man, son of a Romanian family; his mother, of German stock, was a housewife. Until age five, Henry was a quiet child, and very bright; he read from the age of three and a half, and later posted an IQ of 148.

As soon as he went to school, Henry became hyperactive, partly because he was so bored, he recalls; but owing to his inability to fit in, he concluded that he was stupid. He was also accident-prone, constantly requiring stitches and bandages from his doctor father. "It was the only time he paid any attention to me," he says.

Starting at age eight, he began to get into trouble—trespassing, vandalism, shoplifting. At the age of 11, he was thrown out of sixth grade for screaming at a teacher. Then, in the summer between sixth and seventh grade, his family moved to another town, and Henry, feeling stupid, out-of-step, accident-prone, and lonely, lost what peer support he had had. Always a voracious reader, Henry began to withdraw even further into books.

At his new school, Henry began tripping on LSD, amphetamines, barbiturates—anything he could get his hands on. He stole sleeping pills from his mother and swigged whiskey on the sly. He devoured food as rapidly as he consumed books and drugs, and gained weight rapidly.

By ninth grade, Henry was high practically all the time, mostly on LSD and barbiturates. Then he began to experiment. He shot "speed" (benzedrine) for the first time, and a little later began to deal in "speed" and marijuana. Before the year was out he'd shot heroin for the

first time. By the end of tenth grade, he was shooting heroin every day and traveling to Harlem to buy and deal. "I hated going up there, and to the Bowery, and all those places. I knew how my life was going—it was going to be bad, and I always figured when it got bad enough I'd kill myself."

All the while, Henry was still reading, developing a philosophy that was negative enough to justify his eventual suicide.

At the age of 16 he did make an effort of sorts to kick heroin. "It was messing up my life, my friends were mad at me." He attended some group therapy sessions for about four months, but there was no change. "I never met a shrink I couldn't corner in those days," says Henry.

It was a rough year. He had sex with a girl for the first time and experienced it as "weird," so became terrified he was homosexual. Also, for the first time, he lost a friend who overdosed on heroin; another friend was sent to prison on a manslaughter charge.

Where were Henry's parents during all this? Oblivious, for the most part: No one had arrested Henry because his father was a doctor, and until the next year he did well enough in school.

Then, in eleventh grade, at the age of 17, he quit high school and withdrew almost totally from everyone. At that time he also stopped eating and became anorexic. He was taking four fixes a day, and he had contracted hepatitis. His parents, finally worried, sent him to a psychiatrist, but he cornered him easily and quit.

In June that year, one of Henry's sisters, a straight-A-student at college, became worried when she began receiving odd letters from him. She went to see him. She found him anorexic, delusional, suicidal, depressed, and immovable. He weighed 95 pounds. He no longer cared what happened to him. She persuaded her parents to send him to the Yale Psychiatric Institute. There he managed to create such chaos in the wards and groups that at the end of August they "threw him out." He remembers feeling so tired—sick of the world, people, himself.

It was then that he heard of the AREBA program for drug addicts. He could have gone back to his old life, but he was weary—it was just too exhausting to think about going back to the rat race and the pressure of getting drugs, going down to Harlem, feeling so wasted. The pain didn't really disappear. There was always time, especially just before getting a fix, when the pain and hatred would become overwhelming.

In this state of mind and body, Henry arrived at the Institute. Once in residence, however, it was another story. He became panicky. It was like going to another planet. "You don't know anything," he was told, "except how to shoot dope. So listen, and do what you're told." He saw people being reprimanded openly on behavior—"pulled up." He saw people screaming at one another. He saw people caring and being physically close. He heard people accepting both the reprimands and the love and making changes.

He focused all his wits on convincing the staff he couldn't be pressured. "For four months I never opened my mouth in group. I feigned illness constantly, and I looked sick enough to get away with it. I spent most of my time reading."

Then one day, Alan, a resident staff member, came in while Henry was reading in bed—he'd convinced them he was too sick to work that day—but was invited to write up a complete list of what was wrong with AREBA. Everything. Recalls Henry:

> I had a ball. I've always been pretty sharp about where people are, and what kind of games they're playing, and I'd done a lot of watching and listening. I didn't leave anybody out. From that point on, they knew I wasn't crazy the way I'd made out I was.
>
> Not that I didn't need help. I had plenty of problems: I related to myself at the time as asexual. And I was anorexic, but they hadn't yet picked that up yet. Male anorexics are incredibly rare, and it was natural to attribute my thinness to heroin. Also, I'd learned in the hospital to eat and then throw up later when no one was watching. It was Dan (Casriel) who caught on finally. It was my way of rejecting of my own unmet needs for love, and it contributed to my inability to take in pleasure.
>
> But it was from that point that I began to turn around attitudinally. I stopped acting out negatively and I began to work emotionally in groups.

The first issues Henry worked on concerned the hostility he felt toward anyone who cared for him. It was, he found, because they represented a barrier to his eventual suicide. He worked actively with both fear and anger, but wasn't able to accept or express his pain.

After being given socializing privileges eight months after arriving, Henry began to run into problems. He had done no work to that time on his sexual identity problems, but they came to torment him. He would go out with the assignment to date girls and be rejected time after time. Then he would come back to the Institute and throw up. It was through this that he first got in touch with his pain, and began working through the historical pain of his mother and father's indifference to him. As he worked, he started gaining weight and stopped throwing up regularly. He had an unhealthy addiction to sugar and coffee, though, and he was not dealing with his fears of homosexuality, or with his pain over problems of impotence and rejection.

In June Henry was promoted to Second Phase, which means living at the institute, attending a group each day, but working and socializing outside. He took a job in a small retail store and was seduced by the 29-year-old manager. He wasn't conscious of being able to take in pleasure, but he adored her. When she dumped and fired

him 10 weeks later, he left AREBA, became severely anorexic, and returned to his old neighborhood to buy some heroin. One day later he was back: He had run into some friends, and they looked like old, old men. He couldn't go back to that.

He was returned to First Phase for a month, and assigned to working in Intensive emotional groups. Most of that time Henry spent working on the mats, learning to take in pleasure and expressing his hostility toward his mother and the pain of rejection by his father. He was also required to eat with a staff member, because he was still partially anorexic and weighed only 105 pounds.

After a month, he was returned to Second-Phase status, and he took another job, this time with an uncle in a retail store. At the Institute, he continued going to groups, and he held a position as house "guru," responsible for individual sessions with First Phasers. This was consistent with the theory that if one "acts as if" one were already well, one will eventually think as if and feel as if.

By Christmas, a little over a year after his arrival, he weighed 130 pounds, and although he was doing well enough, he felt stalled. He still had trouble getting dates, and he was watching friends in AREBA pass him by. That hurt. Then in January his uncle attempted suicide and closed the store, thus cutting off the one family tie he enjoyed. At the same time, the fiancé of one of his sisters died, and as his family gathered around her for support, he experienced tremendous anger and jealousy that a girl was able to get support but that he was not.

His next job was clerking in a bookstore. In four months, he rose to become a buyer and then assistant manager. However, he was still somewhat anorexic and still had trouble taking in pleasure. But he had finally begun to open up the issue of his sexual fears.

Shortly after starting at the bookstore, he started taking courses at Long Island University. In June he moved out into his own apartment for the third phase of AREBA, during which time one continues to hold responsibilities in the AREBA structure while living, working, and socializing outside.

To graduate from the AREBA program, a person must (1) be clean—free of drugs and alcohol; (2) have a solid relationship with a person of the opposite sex; and (3) be either vocationally or educationally occupied. By June of 1974, Henry qualified. He had a nice relationship going that included a sexual relationship; he had become night manager of the bookstore; and he was maintaining straight A's with a full courseload at LIU. His schedule was too heavy to maintain, so he dropped out of the AREBA program, but continued with individual therapy twice weekly at the Institute. The focus of that individual work was mainly on enlarging his self-image. During the ensuing year, he gradually became more comfortable with his sexuality and brought his anorexia under control.

After two years at Long Island University, Henry transferred to Antioch. There, for the first time, he felt truly challenged intellectually. He recalls: "I had a field day. I became very political. There wasn't a rally I didn't attend. I also began doing more creative work—writing, drawing, and photography, and I developed a relationship with a wonderful girl."

Henry graduated from Antioch at the age of 24, with a double major in psychology and communications and almost a year's worth of extra credits. A year later, Henry was living in New York, working part-time as a freelance photographer and also part-time as a Second Phase adviser on the AREBA staff. He is anticipating a full and varied life, possibly but not necessarily including further work with addicts. He is still seeing his girl from LIU and feeling good about his sexuality. He weighs 145 pounds.

SUMMARY

Many people mistakenly confuse the New Identity Process with Primal Therapy. Apart from the fact that they both use screaming to discharge excess emotion, they are very different.

Janov's process focuses primarily on pain, regressing to early experiences repeatedly until the historic emotions are exhausted. The theory is that when the old emotions are exhausted, the personality will then be able to right itself. Primal Therapy uses isolation and other forms of stress, and deals minimally with cognition and behavior.

NIP, by contrast, focuses on pleasure in the here-and-now, and deals with negative emotions only when they block a person's ability to take in pleasure and love. Screaming is used not only for ventilation, but to prepare the body to take in new messages. Cognition and behavior are dealt with as extensively as affect. NIP is primarily reconstructive in focus.

Perhaps the most critical difference between Primal and NIP Therapy is that NIP is a group process. It's hard to improve on a statement made by Richard Beauvais, a member of Casriel's group in 1964:

We are here because there is no refuge, finally, from ourselves.
Until a man confronts himself in the eyes and hearts of his fellows, he is running.
Until he suffers them to share his secret, he has no safety from it.
Afraid to be known, he can know neither himself nor any other—he will be alone.
Where else but in our common grounds can we find such a mirror?
Here, together, a man can at last appear clearly to himself,
    not as the giant of his dreams
    nor the dwarf of his fears,
    but as a man—part of a whole with his share in its purpose.
In this ground we can each take root and grow not alone any more as in death,
but alive, a man among men.

We live in a character-disordered society; that is, a society that has decided not to feel its pain, and that acts out in ways destructive to self and others. Much of our behavioral insulation is socially useful, but because it sustains our estrangement from our feeling selves, it is pathological.

It is therefore destructive, to individuals, to society, and, ultimately, because of the power wielded by Western nations, to the world. How can we appreciate the suffering of others when we are so cut off from our own feelings, our own pain?

REFERENCES

Casriel, D. H. (1963). *So fair a house: The story of Synanon.* Englewood Cliffs, NJ: Prentice-Hall.

Casriel, D. H. (1972). *A scream away from happiness.* New York: Grosset & Dunlap.

Casriel, D. H. & Amen, G. (1971). *Daytop: Three addicts and their cure.* New York: Hill and Wang.

Casriel, D. H. *The huggers.*

Chapter 43

NONDIRECTIVE PSYCHOANALYSIS

I. H. PAUL

I view the field of psychotherapy as a kind of vast struggle, with proponents of the various theories and systems contending in a life-and-death battle for supremacy. These days, as the reader can see, there are many psychotherapeutic contenders for supremacy—at least 300. Even though there are probably as many roads to mental health and enhancement of self as there are roads to salvation, I believe that, in theory, differences among systems of psychotherapy cannot always be tolerated. While individual practitioners can get along despite theoretical and philosophic differences, in the long run some system must take over and all others must become subordinate.

The final emergent system will probably manage, in a resolution of differences, to combine what are currently considered incompatible elements. I. H. Paul's Nondirective Psychoanalysis is an example of the direction I think eclectic psychotherapy will take. Eventually, the brilliant insights of the great pioneers and the many others working in this maddening field of psychotherapy will be gathered together in a system that will be universally accepted. It may take centuries—but I believe it is only a matter of time until we have an allopathic psychotherapy. Nondirective Psychoanalysis may be the final answer.

Nondirective Psychoanalysis is a blending of traditional psychoanalysis and Client-Centered Therapy. It is both interpretive and non-directive. Its format is one to one, its mode is mainly verbal, and its central process is inquiry focusing primarily on the patient's intrapsychic (phenomenal and mental) realm. To sustain a thoroughgoing nondirectiveness, the therapist maintains a stringent neutrality and impersonality, and relies chiefly on the interpretive mode of intervention to supervise the therapeutic process. This, along with its reliance on the principal conceptions of psychoanalysis's clinical theory (resistance, regression, transference, and catharsis), qualifies the method as psychoanalytic. It qualifies as nondirective insofar as the patient is given a maximum feasible role in determining the form and content of the sessions, and the therapist strives for a nonauthoritarian and unique role definition, which entails regard for the patient's individuality and autonomy, as well as self-healing and actualizing potentials, characteristic of nondirective Client-Centered Therapy. Accordingly, this form of therapy can be construed both as Client-Centered Therapy with interpretations and/or as psychoanalysis stripped of directives.

In published writings this writer (1973, 1975, 1979) has chosen to designate the method informally as "psychotherapy." For the purposes of this book, however, it will be given the descriptive title "Nondirective Psychoanalysis."

HISTORY

The evolution and vicissitudes of psychodynamic psychotherapy are Nondirective Psychoanalysis's heritage. More specifically, it shares the same history as psychoanalysis and Client-Centered Therapy.

Insofar as the analyst's principal mode of intervention is interpretation, and fundamental attitude one of neutrality, psychoanalysis is inherently a nondirective form of therapy. However, following Freud, analysts (such as Menninger [1958] and Brenner [1976], to cite only two) have felt that a set of directives and task requirements was necessary to establish and sustain the "analytic process." There was never unanimity on the composition of the set, and some influential analysts (e.g., Fenichel [1941], Singer [1965], and Langs [1974]), out of a conviction that certain directives and task requirements were unnecessary on balance, have advocated flexibility in regard to them. The requirement of daily sessions and the use of the couch, the instructions to free-associate and to report dreams, and the several abstinence proscriptions have variously been modified

451

and softened. To cite an extreme instance, Hellmuth Kaiser (1965) evolved out of psychoanalysis a method that is radically nondirective, in that the only requirement of patients is to appear for sessions. There is no requirement as to what they talk about, and the analyst is limited to interpretations of their defenses against the awareness of feelings, impulses, and motives. Kaiser formulated the analyst's task in a way that placed the greatest emphasis on promoting in patients a sense of responsibility for their thoughts and actions. Similarly, many therapists in the Rogerian tradition have loosened its restrictions on interpreting and moved in a psychoanalytic direction. Levy (1963) and Bone (1968), for example, have argued that the differences between psychoanalytic and client-centered procedures have been overstated and misconstrued, and the two methods have had more in common than was generally recognized. Are interpretations necessarily judgmental? Do they necessarily violate the patient's rate of exploration? Do they "create" resistances and transferences? These are the crucial questions. And Rosalea Schonbar (1968), for one, has concluded that they do not. She describes how she introduced the interpretive mode into the structure of Client-Centered Therapy, and concluded that the act of interpreting does not require any significant change in the basic attitudinal aspects of that therapy—which, she contends, are basic to becoming an effective therapist of any kind.

The specific history of Nondirective Psychoanalysis is twofold: my training first in Client-Centered Therapy and then in psychoanalysis, and my subsequent experience teaching therapists. My training determined its structure and orientation; my teaching experiences are largely responsible for its emphasis on technique. In addition to clinical practice, the method evolved out of pedagogical considerations and experiences, out of the need to articulate explicit and concrete principles and guidelines that could be acquired by appropriate study and training, and that did not rely too heavily on certain kinds of predispositional personality traits and talents. Consequently, conducting psychotherapy came to be regarded as a craft with objective and specifiable technical requirements, minimally dependent on unlearnable traits. A method had to be fashioned that was craft-oriented, that required an exact technique, and whose constraints allowed relatively little latitude with respect to a therapist's personal characteristics.

During the course of 10 years of teaching psychotherapy, my method grew increasingly rigorous and parsimonious. For instance, the interviewing mode—interrogating and probing—was entirely abandoned; the use of confronting and diagnostic interpretations was sharply curtailed; and the distinctive role definition of the therapist was kept consistent throughout the entire therapy. The reasons for these developments are several,

but one is paramount: Clinical experience strongly suggested that therapeutic efficacy was correlated with technical purity and rigor. At any rate, the method that evolved—Nondirective Psychoanalysis—requires study, work, and practice; and the main natural talents the therapist needs are sensitivity, empathy, and clarity. The ability to understand, and to communicate understanding, accounts for the bulk of the variance; and that ability is largely a function of comprehending the special dynamics of the method itself. The technical precepts and principles of Nondirective Psychoanalysis rest upon these specific dynamics.

CURRENT STATUS

Within the broad category of psychoanalytically oriented psychotherapy, but also under the rubric of existential and humanistic therapy, psychotherapy that is both nondirective and psychoanalytic is widely practiced and taught. Nondirective Psychoanalysis is a particular form of that therapy, practiced and taught at the clinical psychology program of the City University of New York's graduate school at City College.

I have described and explained the method in two books and a paper. *Letters to Simon: On the Conduct of Psychotherapy* (1973) is an informal treatise, written in the form of letters to a hypothetical student that discuss and exemplify a wide range of issues pertinent to its theory and practice. "Psychotherapy as a Unique and Unambiguous Event" (1975) is an elucidation of the method's basic orientation and principal conceptions, organized around a paradigmatic clinical situation explored in concrete detail. *The Form and Technique of Psychotherapy* (1979) is a comprehensive explication and discussion of the method's main technical precepts and principles, as well as theoretical rationales. The book examines in detail the interventional modes of psychotherapy, the problem of timing, the structure and formulation of interpretations, and the nature and limits of neutrality, impersonality, and consistency.

THEORY

Nondirective Psychoanalysis does not rest on any single theory of behavior and personality. Because it is a relatively pragmatic method, based largely on procedures and principles that have proven useful in clinical practice, it is compatible with a variety of quite different and even nonpsychoanalytic theories, and draws on a wide range of conceptions pertaining to the structure, functioning, development, and change of personality and behavior.

A theory of unconscious mentation, for instance, is

useful but not indispensable. Perhaps its chief utility is in helping insure that our interpretations remain sufficiently nondiagnostic and nonconfronting. For when we accept the hypothesis that an effective interpretation addresses preconscious derivatives of unconscious mentation, and that its ideal function is to facilitate the emergence of unconscious ideas, memories, and fantasies (i.e., to help patients discover what is in their mind), then we have a practical guideline for ways to formulate and structure, as well as time, our interpretations. The same can be said for the concept of defense; the effective interpretation aims to make contact with a kind of barrier (a threshold, a countercathexis, or a defense) and, in one way or another, weakens it to permit not only the uncovering of unconscious contents but also their reorganization. Another theory that is clinically useful centers around the conception of "ego"; for when it is construed as the personality's executive agency, under pressure from competing and conflicting forces, then our interpretations will take account of ego's intrinsic and often conflicting interests by speaking to its "synthetic function" (Hartmann, 1958).

The psychodynamic point of view, on the other hand, is probably quite indispensable; but it can be limited to the proposition that behavior and experience are both purposeful and goal-directed. Every psychological act is presumed to be either instrumental or consummatory with respect to purposes and goals; all behavior is based on needs, drives, wishes, fantasies, and the like. To be sure, the dynamic point of view can be a more complicated motivational theory; it can construe behavior to be the result of a hierarchy of forces acting in concert and in conflict, and additionally make the assumption that no behavior is the result of a single drive or purpose—there are always two or more at work. When these forces act together, the behavior is conceptualized as overdetermined or multiply functioned (Waelder, 1936); when they act in dissonance, it is conceptualized as conflict. Maladaptive behavior can be understood as the result of conflict, enhanced and magnified and sustained by overdetermination.

While the practice of Nondirective Psychoanalysis does not require or imply a particular psychological theory, it does rely heavily on a particular theory of psychotherapy, as well as on conceptions about the processes that inhere in therapy. Its basic premise is that psychotherapy can be a unique situation, and that, as psychotherapists, we can define ourselves in a distinctive way. Its basic thesis is that psychotherapy can be relatively unstructured without being concomitantly ambiguous; and our nondirectiveness and neutrality do not prevent us from being active and effective.

The short-term or proximate goal is for the patient to have a distinctive psychological experience, an experience that is designated as the *therapeutic process*. The therapeutic process is defined as the core event of Nondirective Psychoanalysis. It is conceptualized as an intrapsychic and mental process, as distinct from interpersonal and behavioral; it is presumed to be based on the act of discovering, as distinct from learning; and it shares many of the theoretical features of psychoanalysis's "relative ego-autonomy" (Rapaport, 1967). In empirical terms, the therapeutic process refers to patients' work, as well as their subjective experience, when they express, examine, and explore their inner and outer realities; when they strive to articulate and to understand their behavior, their self, and their mind. It entails the acts of reflecting and introspecting, reminiscing and recollecting, and reorganizing and reconstructing; it implies a major focus on the inner reality of affects and impulses; of needs and expectations; of attitudes, beliefs, and values; of habits, defenses, and fantasies. A special emphasis is placed on the experiencing of individuality and autonomy, as well as sense of volition. Finally, it is a process that comes down to the complementary acts of "understanding" and of "being understood."

In short, the therapeutic process is an activity of self-inquiry that strives to articulate, to comprehend, and to discover. This is a broader conception than psychoanalysis's "analytic process"; it does not mandate genetic reconstructions, nor does it necessarily require the resolution of experiences and behaviors into component parts and determinants. It relies on the exercising of choice and decision, not on the more passive free-association mode. It shares with the "analytic process" (as well as with corresponding conceptions of Existential Therapy, Humanistic Therapy, and others) the conviction that the actuality of the patient as an individual with volition and responsibility, as an agent active in the direction of his or her life, must be the principal subject of discovery that lays the groundwork and provides the framework for the crucial process of therapy. The patient's essential autonomy is the paramount subject for discovery, and serves as the main context for self-inquiry.

The technical precepts and principles that guide us, as therapists, are fundamentally and intimately linked to the goal of facilitating and optimizing the therapeutic process. Insofar as this process is viewed as the core event of Nondirective Psychoanalysis—and the event that effectuates the long-range alterations and reorganizations that are the goals of the therapy—we as therapists have to protect its integrity by behaving in ways to promote and sustain its full development; and we must strive to avoid behaving in ways that prevent, impede, or interfere with it.

Accordingly—and to the limits of feasibility and good clinical practice—nondirective therapists refrain from directing the patient in any way; we do not interview or counsel; we do not judge or criticize; we provide no reinforcements in the forms of rewards, punishments, and incentives of any kind; and we do not share our personal feelings, attitudes, beliefs, and opinions. Instead, though we are as caring and as tactful as possible, we maintain a position of neutrality and impersonality; we observe without much participation beyond empathy, along with a degree of warmth and enthusiasm; and we bend ourselves entirely to the purpose of understanding the patient, relying principally on the instrumentality of interpretation to share that understanding.

Offering interpretations is our way of "participating" in the therapeutic process. This formulation, however, is potentially misleading, insofar as it portrays therapists as providing understanding or information about patients' inner and outer reality, and doing it for their sake; or it may imply that therapists help patients make discoveries by making interpretations to maximize the occurrence of such discoveries. Instead of that congenial formulation a more awkward one is preferable: Interpreting is the nondirective therapist's way of "supervising" the therapeutic process. This formulation emphasizes that the main purpose in offering interpretations is to promote the ongoing process itself. Because the process is conceptualized as intrapsychic and as entailing autonomous action on the part of patients, and because the overriding goal is for them to be active (actively strive for understanding, actively exercise and strengthen their synthetic function, and thereby maximize their control and freedom), it follows that the therapist's chief goal is not to impart information, not to give understanding and insight; instead, it is to provide the optimal conditions for patients to examine themselves openly and freely, and to experience themselves as fully and as authentically as they can. Accordingly, it is dissonant with the aims and spirit of Nondirective Psychoanalysis for roles to be divided in such a way that the patient provides the facts and therapists the meanings. It is also somewhat dissonant to conceive of therapists as participating as a kind of partner in the uncovering and explaining process. Our function as therapists is chiefly to promote the work of therapy itself, and our promise to speak when we have "something useful to say" (see "Methodology" section) really means "useful for the therapeutic process."

Nondirective Psychoanalysis requires a full faith in the therapeutic efficacy of patients' choosing freely what they will talk about during the sessions. As therapists we must hold in abeyance all convictions about the differential fruitfulness of topics (childhood memories, traumatic experiences, interpersonal relations, fantasies and dreams, etc.). We have to be prepared to work not only from the surface of the patient's consciousness but also from the matrix of the patient's decisional and volitional processes. We must try to keep from using the interpretive mode in a directive way. Whether this is altogether possible is a theoretical question, but it can be examined at the empirical level.

An interpretation, broadly defined, is any attempt to articulate thoughts, wishes, intentions, and feelings—a remark that addresses what is in (and on) the patient's mind, even if the remark doesn't seek to explain why, and even if there is no reason to believe it was obscure or disguised or preconscious. At the very least, an interpretation implies the directive "Am I correctly understanding you?"; at the most, it implies the directive "Pay attention to this!" But when it resonates with the patient's focus of attention, when it addresses what the patient is addressing, even the latter directive becomes inconsequential. Therapists' central timing criterion requires that an interpretation be offered only when its attention-deflecting properties are at a practical minimum, only when it doesn't impose a fresh idea or deflect attention. The effective interpretation explains only when the patient is interested in having something explained, and it tries to explain in ways that are consonant with the patient's mode of explaining and understanding. Furthermore, it is formulated in a way that corresponds directly to the patient's thinking and experience, and does not draw upon theoretical or nomothetic considerations. It is not diagnostic in form, nor is it confronting in nature. Its directive properties can, accordingly, be held to a minimum.

A nondirective psychoanalytic session cannot be construed as an interview, because the interviewing mode is stringently avoided. This means therapists keep from asking questions and probing for feelings, and neither do we confront ("hold up the mirror"). The interviewing mode tends to define us as diagnosticians, troubleshooters; and the same can be true for the confronting mode, which, in addition, defines us as alert observers. Both modes tend to put patients into a passive and objective position. By contrast, the interpretive mode defines us as observers who try to understand and empathize, whose aim is not so much to uncover problems as to apprehend and comprehend them; and insofar as our interpretations embody the act of sharing rather than giving, we allow patients to take a more active and subjective position. To the extent that well-formulated and well-timed interpretations are shared discoveries rather than of one-sided observations, they run less of a risk of defining us as the controlling one, and they maximize a patient's short-term freedom and long-range autonomy.

There are, however, circumstances in which certain directives can support the therapeutic process without impairing it. One relates to unclarity or ambiguity of communication, another to silence. To ask, "What are you thinking?" when a patient falls silent may sometimes be necessary, and an argument can be made for its distinctiveness as a directive. This is especially true for the clarification question ("What do you mean when you say . . . ?"), which has a special position in respect to the therapeutic process. Such directives can be fully consonant with the principles of Nondirective Psychoanalysis; their use—along with other noninterpretive modes of intervention that are commonly used in therapy—depends on context and clinical judgment.

METHODOLOGY

To divide a course of psychotherapy into three stages—the beginning, the middle, and the ending—is more than a didactic tradition; the stages can be a vital aspect of the therapy's dynamics, having significant ramifications for procedure and technique. Though our aim as nondirective therapists is to participate chiefly by offering interpretations, therapy has to be carefully conducted through its developmental stages and their vicissitudes, and we have to be sensitive to a variety of possibilities and exigencies (impasses and crises, for example). It is useful to bear in mind that not everything that transpires in therapy is grist for the interpretive mill; there are issues that need to be dealt with directly. (Being nondirective does not mean being indirect.)

These issues include matters of "business," which can be broadly defined to include the structure and format of the therapy, the schedule and fee, as well as the nature and limits of our expectations and requirements. If, for instance, a patient wants the therapist to take an active role in the sessions, say, by asking leading questions, it can be a mistake to respond with an interpretation seeking to explain the wish. (For one thing, the patient may not be interested in having the wish explained.) But it is entirely consonant with the method's orientation to respond by saying that nondirective therapists prefer not to make such a modification, and to explain the rationale—provided, of course, we choose not to comply with the wish and introduce the modification.

Moreover, Nondirective Psychoanalysis entails no proscription of "manipulation." Any action on the therapist's part, or modification in the procedure, that a patient requires or requests has to be weighed against the state of the therapeutic process. If the patient needs it for the process to work best, then that counts as a salient criterion. Any action or modification is weighed against this further criterion: Will it interfere with the therapist's ability to listen and remain sufficiently neutral, so that he or she can supervise the therapeutic process in a satisfactory way? This can be a function of our flexibility, among other things, and can also depend on the developmental stage of the therapy—what has gone before, and where the therapy stands. It can make a significant difference whether we introduce a modification into a therapy that has only recently begun or into one that is well into its middle stage.

The beginning stage is mainly concerned with defining and clarifying the structure and format of the ther-

apy. The therapists' principal task is to inaugurate and facilitate the therapeutic process. In practice, we have to establish the nature and limits of our nondirectiveness, our neutrality and impersonality, and also our caring; and we have to introduce the patient to the method in a way that minimizes ambiguity even as it maximizes unstructuredness. Consequently, it may be quite unavoidable to give an instruction; but the instruction can be formulated carefully so as to keep its directive properties to a minimum. A succinct formulation, which notifies more than instructs, which conveys the essence of Nondirective Psychoanalysis's format and orientation and provides patients with the widest, most feasible latitude to begin the way they want and deem appropriate, is worded as follows: "*You can talk about the things you want to talk about. It's up to you. I will listen and try to understand. When I have something useful to say I will say it.*" This *basic instruction* informs patients that they are free to speak as openly and self-directedly as they want. It does not request them to share their thoughts or express their feelings, and neither does it suggest they tell about themselves. They can do these things if they choose to and want to.

In addition to issues and problems that commonly accompany the basic instruction and pertain to the method's structure and requirements, the beginning stage is often marked by themes that center around the meanings and implications of being in therapy. There is the frequently encountered fantasy of a passive cure ("Once you have all the facts you will proceed to straighten me out"); there is the conviction that being in therapy is something to be ashamed of, it's a kind of defeat ("I can't do it myself, after all"); there is the expectation of being shocked and hurt, of hearing things that will confirm their most dreaded judgments of themselves, that they are insane or abnormal; and there is the fear that therapy will make them worse off in certain ways. These themes—together with the issue of trust ("Can I really count on you?") and the exposition of presenting problems, life history, significant experiences, current functioning, and the like—are the earmarks of the beginning stage.

In the middle stage—similar to the development section of a sonata—the exposition and themes of the beginning are subjected to repetition, articulation, variation, and development. This is when the major reorganizations and transformations occur, as well as the major discoveries and insights, the major transferences, and the major impasses. This is when the main struggle for and against change takes place. The beginning is often marked by optimism and enthusiasm; the middle, by contrast, is often marked by despair and resistance, because now the patient's basic unwillingness to change becomes manifest and powerful, and pits its strength against the forces of change and development. It is now that long-entrenched patterns of behavior can be weakened and altered; and the transferences reach their full intensity and exert their full force. Therefore, during the middle stage the therapist's technical skill and resourcefulness is usually put to its severest test, for here the art and craft of making effective use of the interpretive mode becomes paramount.

The criteria for well-formulated and well-timed interpretations may change as therapy develops. During the beginning some useful functions can be served by interpretations that become quite unnecessary during later stages. For instance, patients have to learn at first how therapists participate—how we listen both empathically and dispassionately, how we formulate understanding without judging and criticizing—and we may choose to offer interpretations with that goal alone in mind. Furthermore, it is not uncommon (especially early in therapy) for interpretations to be taken as directives and as criticisms, and for patients to react as if they'd been evaluated. Those unintended and unwanted side effects cannot be entirely avoided, but we can take active measures to undo them, both by keeping patients informed of our neutral intentions and by interpreting their reactions. Nevertheless, it is an aspect of good technique not only to listen for a patient's reaction to each interpretation but also to avoid interpretations that carry too strong an implication of evaluation and direction. Two kinds of interpretations are particularly vulnerable to such implications (especially during the beginning): diagnostic and confronting ones. Therefore, such interpretations should be reserved for the later stages, and only used even then when unavoidable. They are difficult to avoid when defense and resistance are the subjects; for it can be difficult, and sometimes not entirely possible, to make sound and responsible interpretations of defense and resistance without being diagnostic and confronting.

Another technical guideline centers around clinical tact: nondirective therapists avoid shocking the patient or generating intense emotions that may elicit defensive measures. Clinical tact cannot be described and characterized in a simple way—it is best illustrated and exemplified—but it plays an important part in Nondirective Psychoanalysis and contributes importantly to its uniqueness. Patients must enter each session free from the apprehension that they are in for rude shocks and intense emotions at our hands; whatever shocks and emotions occur will be of their own doing. Considerations of tact—as well as of effectiveness—can be served when our interpretations are succinct but not curt, and when they are offered in a gradual or stepwise fashion. It is often possible to divide an interpretation into parts that gradually zero in on the issue and allow the patient to participate in its final formulation. (This is quite different from cryptic or allusive interpretations, which are generally ineffective.)

The ending is usually the most problematic and ambiguous of the three stages. Because of its manifold meanings and implications, and because it brings to the forefront the issue of separation, the problem of termination is commonly the main theme. The potential ambiguity centers around two questions: Does Nondirective Psychoanalysis have a natural kind of conclusion? and, What marks the "cure"?

We can accept the proposition—at least, as a strong and useful working hypothesis—that Nondirective Psychoanalysis has a natural developmental course that is relatively independent of "cure," or of change in personality and behavior, or of amelioration of symptoms and problems. Another way of putting it is that the therapeutic process, similar to an organic process, is characterized by naturally occurring stages of maturation. Accordingly, the ending, like the beginning and the middle, is the result of processes indigenous to the therapy itself; and it has defining characteristics.

The ending stage is often as distinctive as the beginning. This is particularly the case when it is substantially taken up with the issue of separation, but it can be distinctive in other ways as well—as, for example, when patients turn their efforts to consolidating the gains they experienced from therapy, when they turn their attention to the future, and the like. Sometimes the transition to the ending can be marked by impasse, sometimes by a burst of intense therapeutic work, sometimes by the appearance of an altogether fresh theme, and sometimes by a regression or the reappearance of an old symptom. And the ending is often strongly resisted—mainly because of its association with termination.

The ending presents therapists with a variety of methodological problems and pitfalls, and it can test our rigor and consistency. Our principal task is to insure that the decision to terminate is substantially the patient's and not ours. Just as the patient took an active role in initiating the therapy, so must the patient take an active role in ending it; optimally, the decision should not be imposed. It is quite typical of patients to experience termination as our decision: and we must try to be in the position to say to them, "It was my interpretation, yes, my formulation; but it was based directly on your experience of therapy; it was based on your thoughts and feelings."

We must also be convinced that termination is an integral part of the process, and that no course of Nondirective Psychoanalysis can be considered complete before it has amply dealt with the conflicts and fantasies associated with it—most notably, of course, the issue of separation. Moreover, since it is central to relative ego autonomy, separation is central to the fundamental dynamics of Nondirective Psychoanalysis. To be autonomous and free is to have come to terms with separation. Nevertheless, just as autonomy is relative, so is separation; and termination can be regarded as a kind of trial period. Just as the beginning of the beginning stage can be viewed as a period of trial, so the ending of the ending can be viewed as not irrevocable.

APPLICATIONS

When we face the task of determining whether a patient is suitable for Nondirective Psychoanalysis, and vice versa, we must rely on clinical judgment along with a grasp of the nature and requirements of the therapeutic process. To begin with, however, the patient has to choose the therapy; to a significant and substantial extent, the kind of experience it offers has to be "wanted." Therefore, the patient must be capable of comprehending the nature of the method and of fulfilling its requirements; and having understood what the methods entails, the patient has to be in a position to exercise choice.

The patient has to be capable of self-inquiry, of reflection and introspection; this rests on the ability to distinguish inner from outer reality, to locate events in the inner realm, and to attribute causality and responsibility to self events. Therefore, a certain amount of reality testing and psychological-mindedness is requisite. Also, a degree of frustration tolerance is necessary; the patient must tolerate the therapist's neutrality and impersonality, which can frustrate the most basic of human needs (for support, for nurturance, dependency, love, and the like).

An important consideration is time and the urgency of the patient's problems. Since a course of Nondirective Psychoanalysis lasts several years (generally, a period of two to four years), and since its beneficial effects may not occur until late in the therapy—and, indeed, may occur only after therapy has been completed—the presenting problems have to be the sort that do not require immediate resolution. Therefore, an estimation of how seriously debilitating they are must enter into our consideration. Finally, a felt need for change is an important requisite. The patient has to want change, and see the benefit of changing: if the problem is located in outer reality, and the patient feels no sense of responsibility for it, then Nondirective Psychoanalysis may not be appropriate.

Do these requirements and criteria lead to the conclusion that a "normal" adult is our only suitable patient? Do they so sharply restrict the range of appropriate patients to only a few? Have we ruled out children, psychotics, and all but a narrow range of neurotics and character disorders? Have we excluded people with serious symptoms and problems? The answer is yes only if we construe the requirements and criteria too stringently, and if we construe Nondirective Psychoanalysis as an inflexible and unmodifiable method. To be sure, its requirements are unfeasible or impractical for some patients, and for others the method could prove detrimen-

tal. A patient suffering an acute depression, for example, can hardly be expected to tolerate most of the requirements, much less benefit from them; similarly, neither can a patient in an acute state of crisis. Patients who show serious impairment of reality testing, who are psychotic or perhaps even borderline psychotic, are generally not suitable. Moreover, there are patients whose chief need is for medication, or for reconditioning, or for an authentic interpersonal encounter, or Group Therapy. A patient who seeks a method that can most directly remove a symptom is best advised not to enter Nondirective Psychoanalysis.

But Nondirective Psychoanalysis is not a rigid system governed by rules. The method's precepts and principles are, at most, ideal standards toward which we strive but can never hope to achieve perfectly; and modifications of one sort or another are generally possible and necessary. Moreover, each of its requirements and criteria has to be measured and weighed; such qualifiers as "a degree of," "a certain amount," and "to a significant and substantial extent," are crucial; and they can only be based on clinical judgment. Furthermore, a person can have sufficient motivation, sufficient reality testing and psychological-mindedness, sufficient frustration tolerance, and the rest, and still suffer from a wide range of psychological problems, including anxiety, depression, inhibitions, symptoms, and the like. Finally, it bears mentioning that an experience of Nondirective Psychoanalysis can be beneficial to someone who is quite "normal."

At the outset of Nondirective Psychoanalysis the therapist's task is to determine whether the patient is suitable for the method and whether modifications may have to be made; therefore, we have to evaluate and assess. Circumstances may call for a series of diagnostic interviews, which can readily be defined for the patient as antecedent to therapy itself. Under certain circumstances we can expect to secure an adequate assessment without the instrumentality of an interview, and instead rely on the initial sessions of the therapy. It is often possible to glean sufficient diagnostic evidence to judge whether any major modifications need to be made, or whether the patient needs an altogether different form of therapy or treatment. We can accept the working hypothesis that Nondirective Psychoanalysis will be the appropriate and suitable treatment, and then use the opening sessions to confirm or reject that hypothesis. The advantage of beginning this way is not only that it is economical; rather, it lies in the fact that every transaction in the therapy—starting from the beginning of the beginning stage—can have significant implications for the course it takes; each detail contributes something to the distinctiveness and uniqueness of the therapy, and details can have a cumulative significance.

To be sure, each patient has to learn whether this is

the right therapy for him or her, and also whether the therapist is the proper one. Therefore, the way the therapy will proceed—its structure and form, its conditions and limits, as well as its probable duration—have to be explained and discussed. This can be construed as "business" and treated as such. Similarly, the therapist's professional credentials and experience must be discussed. Though we strive to maintain a stringent impersonality, we must detail what is directly germane to our ability to conduct therapy for this particular patient. Additionally, the crucial questions "Is this the right treatment for me?" and "Are you the right therapist?" can best be answered by defining the beginning sessions as a trial period.

Whether or not a trial period has been explicitly defined, it is important that we make an effort during the beginning to show patients the full range of our approach and technique. This is true for two reasons: First, we want to be able to judge the quality and nature of their work, to learn whether they are suitable for our method and whether modifications will have to be introduced; second, we want to make these sessions a fair sample of the therapy so that they can best judge for themselves whether it suits them, whether they want it. Nondirective Psychoanalysis requires that patients never be in a passive and submissive position vis-à-vis the therapist, and this has to extend to the decision to enter therapy itself. It is vital that the patient freely choose and actively decide; this places a substantial constraint on our willingness to advise and persuade, or even to advocate and suggest. But even this requirement can be softened—to a degree.

CASE EXAMPLE

The patient was referred by a consultant who had described two options for him. One was a behavioral therapy that would focus on his symptoms—a recurring state of mild but disruptive anxiety and an intermittent but recently more frequent sexual impotency. The patient preferred the second option, a traditional psychoanalytic therapy, and after learning that it would take about six months to see whether the method was helpful, decided to give it a trial. When he called me to arrange an appointment (after I'd heard from the consultant) he offered this contract: If at the end of six months there was no substantial amelioration of his symptoms, he would switch to a behavioral therapy.

The initial session began with his standing in the middle of my office, staring at the couch a few seconds, then asking, "Where do you want me to sit?"—even though there were only two seats, and I was already sitting down in one. His next remark was "What do you want me to tell you?" When I responded with the basic instruction, he looked puzzled. "So I guess you want me

to tell you about myself," he said; and without giving me a chance to respond (i.e., to clarify the first part of the basic instruction), he proceeded to give a full, orderly, and systematic account of his *vita* (omitting only to tell me his age). In a subsequent session he "confessed" to having carefully rehearsed the narrative because he was sure I was going to ask for it, and it was "the right thing to do."

He was a short, somewhat overweight man, who appeared to be about 30; rather stiff and awkward, he spoke quickly and fluently, often with a breathless intensity, and took a down-to-earth, businesslike attitude toward therapy. He told of never having been in psychotherapy, because he was convinced that he could handle his own problems. He spoke of being independent and self-reliant, active and ambitious. He described himself as a bachelor, currently "seriously involved" with a woman who wanted to marry him, but given his sexual problem he felt it would be unfair to her. A pianist and composer by profession, he said he was satisfied with his career, and the only problem was that his anxiety sometimes impaired his ability to practice. He had two older brothers who lived away from the city, which left him to carry the burden of caring for his mother who was needy and often sick. When he was 12 his father had died of cardiovascular disease.

At the outset of the second session he asked for the "rules." (Didn't I expect him to tell about his childhood? Wasn't he supposed to free-associate, to lie on the couch?) When I reiterated the basic instruction and spelled out the extent of my intention to be nondirective, he seemed skeptical and uncomfortable. Nevertheless, in a way that was to be characteristic, he quickly dismissed his feelings and went ahead with a narrative. It didn't take many sessions until it became clear that he needed to avoid decisions and had a number of externalizing strategies to keep from feeling in active control of his life. The main one was to set things up so that others, or the objective situation, would dictate requirements; then he could respond passively and submissively. He habitually returned to the question of whether an action was right or wrong, good or bad, which then became the basis for action and served his need to keep from acting on impulse and wish. Consequently, since my way of doing therapy must be "right" (the consultant had told him I was the "right" therapist for him), he would be "good" and do it. During the beginning stage he regained a memory of early childhood in which his father repeatedly admonished him to be a "good boy." He also acknowledged a sense of shame at being in therapy; as if it were a mark of weakness, as if it meant he was a "bad boy." "I am a bad boy" was a major theme of the therapy and a central feature of his self-image.

Throughout the course of therapy, with only a few significant exceptions, the sessions consisted of a coherent narrative on a single topic (one devoted to his relationship with his mother, another to his girlfriend, one to his career, another his sociopolitical views), each carefully composed to fit the 50 minutes. When he estimated the time wrong and was left with some "free time," he experienced discomfort. So seamless was his talk that I had to interrupt in order to make a remark.

He came to recognize that he was intent on avoiding spontaneous thoughts and memories, as well as keeping me from speaking. One reason was a worry lest I say something wrong (and "dumb"), and then he'd feel disappointed in me—and it was vitally important that he never experience any disappointment at my hands, which had significant transferential ramifications in respect to his father. Another was a worry lest I say something that would hurt him—mainly by confirming his worst fears about himself: that he was "a bad boy." He also grew obsessively concerned over whether he was curing himself in the therapy or whether I was going to do it to him; a passive-submissive fantasy emerged, in which he saw me as the good mother who could save him from death, unlike his bad mother who couldn't save his father. He acknowledged having had, from the outset, the conviction that I was waiting for the propitious moment to give him a thoroughgoing diagnostic evaluation (the "cure"). He also discovered that his punctuality and diligence in attending sessions and paying his bill on time was meant to forestall my indictment of him as bad. The fact that he rarely fell silent, and felt uncomfortable whenever he did, led to the discovery that silence had several meanings, among which was an important identification with the dead father (who frequently had been morosely silent, while his mother was an incessant talker). Keeping me silent had important transference implications, some of which emerged during the ending and were associated with fantasies of my death.

Two transference reactions ushered in the middle stage. One was a growing sense of curiosity about me. He'd been told by the consultant that I was knowledgeable about music; during accounts of his professional experiences he would sometimes speak of technically obscure musical matters in order to see whether I'd ask for clarification. This furtive interest in my music experience led to an equally furtive interest he recollected having had in his father's "business"; not only did the father never talk about his work, he never allowed himself to be seen naked.

The second transference reaction centered on the issue of caring, and occurred first around my remembering what he'd told me. A few remarks of mine early in therapy had impressed him because they indicated that I remembered the details of his narrative, and this made him uncomfortable. It meant I was paying too close attention, I cared too much—and perhaps for "bad" reasons, one of which raised the issue of voyeurism, some-

thing he "confessed" to and was deeply ashamed of. This turned out to be one reason for the remarkable fact that he never spoke about sex in anything but the most general terms. ("I couldn't perform" was the extent of his depiction of an unsuccessful attempt at intercourse.) Despite the fact that after about three months of therapy he enjoyed an almost total remission of his impotency—and it was, after all, a main reason he sought therapy—he scrupulously avoided the subject of sex. ("I performed very well last night," and that was that.) He did, however, explore the reasons for his avoidance; he came to understand that he regarded sex as shameful and secret, and that he had long had exhibitionistic fantasies of a forbidden nature. He couldn't shake off the conviction that I would be disgusted and repelled, as well as fascinated and aroused, were I to hear the details.

My ability to remember had several significant consequences. It became characteristic of him, each time he mentioned someone, to remind me exactly who it was; this reached caricature proportions one session when he caught himself reminding me who his girlfriend was—and he'd been speaking about her a great deal. He then recognized both a need to keep me at a safe distance and to avoid testing my memory for fear that I would fail the test, and then he'd feel outraged and disappointed. My memory did fail me once when I forgot about a pending cancellation that he required. After first trying in vain to take all the blame, he experienced a deep and out-of-proportion discomfort at the possibility that I had simply forgotten. This turned out to have important transference implications, and brought to the foreground his inability to recollect, or to experience even retrospectively, any anger and disappointment toward his father. He discovered how his image of his father was idealized and unrealistic—just as his image of me was—and accepted the likelihood that anger and disappointment had figured importantly in his feelings as a child. It was only later in therapy that he came to experience any of these feelings in a full and genuine way; it was when he faced termination, and the fantasy that if I were perfect I wouldn't abandon him, that he reintegrated the fantasy he'd had that if his father had been perfect (and he himself had been a "good boy"), he would not have died.

The middle stage of therapy was ushered in by an impasse ("I've told you everything there is to know—what now?"); and though he acknowledged that he hadn't been feeling in control of the therapy but was only doing the "right thing," he wanted me to take directive control of the sessions. After several sessions were devoted to exploring how he avoided a sense of control in his everyday life by externalizing responsibility and structuring things according to his value system, he became preoccupied over whether he should lie on the couch, and tried in a variety of ways to get me to give him that directive. ("Tell me, at least, whether in your professional opinion it might be helpful!") Finally, with a remark to the effect that he was feeling tired that day, he took the couch—and delivered an especially well-composed narrative on the politics of the music profession.

During the middle stage the six-month trial period passed by virtually unnoticed. By this time he was feeling a substantial dependency on the therapy, which continued as a major theme until the ending. His sexual problem had abated, but he continued to experience episodes of anxiety. He noticed that the anxiety tended to occur when he was alone and working, especially when at the piano; and he discovered that it was related both to a feeling of being trapped as well as to a temptation to masturbate. (He had a long history of masturbating, which he alluded to but never explored; and he gave up the habit early in the therapy, but it made a brief reappearance during the ending as part of an attempt to forestall termination and evoke disappointment.) He also explored the possibility that his anxiety was associated with feelings in relation to caring for his mother, together with fantasies about taking his father's place. Nevertheless, he continued to feel impotent against the anxiety, and tried to get me to endorse his decision to give up on it and simply learn to live with it. This was part of a larger resistance against any major changes in his personality, and it was formulated in these terms: "The stubborn and disappointed child [in me]—the bad boy—is dead set against changing."

A critical incident occurred during the middle. His mother fell ill and required an operation. When, on the day following the operation, I did not ask him how it went, he reacted with the outraged feeling that I didn't care. For the first time in therapy he experienced feelings of anger toward me, and it was an anger he dimly recalled having had when he was a child. A major discovery then emerged: a fantasy that his mother hadn't sufficiently cared for his father, that she hadn't taken adequate care of him, and therefore he died. What also emerged was the recognition that his own overweening emphasis on independence was based on the conviction that he had to take care of himself because his mother would not. And this theme was soon elaborated by the discovery of an older fantasy: His mother had wanted him to be a girl (and he, alas, was a "bad boy"!); therefore she didn't care for him the way she cared for his brothers. This discovery had profound ramifications in respect to his self-image, and led him to pursue a variety of formulations (about his identity and his defenses) that were based on the wish to be a girl. It was during this period of therapy that he burst out with "This therapy really works!" For the first time the therapeutic process was characterized by some spontaneity and enthusiasm.

The ending stage (late in the second year of therapy) was heralded by the theme of his imminent death, which took the form of a fantasy-cum-conviction that he was

destined to die like his father. This theme was evoked by a vivid dream. The patient rarely told his dreams, and didn't believe they had much significance; this one, however, provoked strong feelings and preoccupied him for several sessions. It involved a funeral ceremony, ostensibly his father's, but the coffin was empty. At first he resisted the suggestion that the funeral in the dream was his own, and he rejected the idea that it had implications for the therapy and meant he was entering the ending stage. Only when I pointed out that the stage didn't have to be brief and precipitous, and also that it could be construed as a trial period, did he accept the fact that he was facing the issue of separation. Most significantly, however, he now faced the problem of mourning, and made the discovery that he had never adequately mourned his father's death. This, in turn, led him to explore the ways in which his habits and traits could be construed as a form of mourning, and also as attempts to avoid the work of mourning.

The ending was taken up mainly by recapitulation. He made a number of attempts to get me to relax my neutrality and impersonality, and tried to induce diagnostic interpretations as well as advice. A brief exacerbation of anxiety occurred, and he experienced a temporary and mild phobia of being in enclosed spaces by himself. The major event was his decision to move in with his girlfriend and set a marriage date. A few weeks before termination (after two and a half years of therapy) he proudly announced that they were expecting a baby.

SUMMARY

Nondirective Psychoanalysis is designed to provide a unique and distinctive kind of therapeutic experience, based principally on free self-inquiry. Its format and orientation stem largely from the premise that psychotherapy is potentially a distinctive and unique event, different from virtually all socially familiar interpersonal and professional paradigms; and psychotherapists can articulate a unique and distinctive role definition, one that doesn't borrow from other professionals who provide human services in our society. A therapist can work in ways that differ significantly from the ways a physician, a social worker, a teacher, an engineer, or a priest works; a therapist can work, and relate to patients, in ways that are uniquely those of a "psychotherapist."

Two fundamental theses underlie the method. The first is that psychotherapy can be relatively unstructured without being concomitantly ambiguous. The second is that a therapist can be nondirective and neutral and, nevertheless, function actively and effectively. In fact, the method rests on the conviction that the efficacy of an average-expectable course of psychotherapy can be profoundly enhanced when a therapist remains as nondirective and as neutral as it is feasible to be, giving the patient little, if any, guidance and counseling, as well as little, if any, evaluation and reinforcement. It is then that the therapist can participate actively in the vital processes of therapy and thereby promote its effectiveness.

REFERENCES

Bone, H. (1968). Two proposed alternatives to psychoanalytic interpretation. In E. F. Hammer (Ed.), *Use of interpretation in treatment*. New York: Grune & Stratton.

Brenner, C. (1976). *Psychoanalytic technique and psychic conflict*. New York: International Universities Press.

Fenichel, O. (1941). *Problems of psychoanalytic technique*. New York: Psychoanalytic Quarterly.

Hartmann, H. (1958). *Ego psychology and the problem of adaptation*. New York: International Universities Press.

Kaiser, H. (1965). *Effective psychotherapy*. New York: Free Press.

Langs, R. (1974). *The technique of psychoanalytic psychotherapy*. New York: Aronson.

Levy, L. (1963). *Psychological interpretation*. New York: Holt.

Menninger, K. (1958). *Theory of psychoanalytic technique*. New York: Basic.

Paul, I. H. (1973). *Letters to Simon: On the conduct of psychotherapy*. New York: International Universities Press.

Paul, I. H. (1975). Psychotherapy as a unique and unambiguous event. *Contemporary Psychoanalysis, 12,* 21–57.

Paul, I. H. (1979). *The form and technique of psychotherapy*. Chicago: University of Chicago Press.

Rapaport, D. (1967). The theory of ego autonomy: A generalization. In M. M. Gill (Ed.), *Collected papers*. New York: Basic.

Schonbar, R. (1968). Confessions of an ex-nondirectivist. In E. F. Hammer (Ed.), *Use of interpretation in treatment*. New York: Grune & Stratton.

Singer, E. (1965). *Key concepts in psychotherapy*. New York: Random House.

Waelder, R. (1936). The principle of multiple function: Observations on overdetermination. *Psychoanalytic Quarterly, 5,* 45–62.

Chapter 44

ORGONE THERAPY

ELSWORTH F. BAKER and ARTHUR NELSON

One of the most fascinating individuals in the history of psychotherapy is Dr. Wilhelm Reich. Conventionally, he is considered a genius during his early years as an orthodox analyst and a madman in his later years, when he developed his own system of psychotherapeutics.

I believe quite a few of my psychological confreres are misinformed about Reich's ideas and procedures, and I am most pleased to be able to present to a wide audience a balanced account of Reich's theory of the orgone and orgone therapy. As many readers probably know, a good many derivatives have emerged from Reich's work. Whether they are advances or not over Reich's original concepts I have no way of knowing, but I feel that in providing readers reliable information about orgone therapy, I am contributing significantly to the field.

A number of the newer methods that employ a wide variety of techniques in a kind of helter-skelter manner frequently use some of the body procedures and concepts originated by Reich, usually without attribution. It is my guess that the final therapy of the future will contain elements of Reich's orgone theory; the reader is fortunate to be able to get the story straight from Elsworth Baker and Arthur Nelson.

Orgone therapy is based on the work of Wilhelm Reich. It involves a concept of health based on the functioning of biological energy ("orgone" as Reich called it, from "organism" and "orgasm") in the body. When this energy flows freely and fully in the body, a condition of health exists. When this energy is blocked, psychopathology and, at times, even functional physical pathology can develop. Orgone therapy per se involves the methodology Reich evolved to bring the patient to a state of health by removing obstacles to the free flow of energy in the organism.

HISTORY

Reich became interested in psychoanalysis as a medical student and was given the unusual privilege of joining the Vienna Psychoanalytic Society in 1920 while still an undergraduate. He rose quickly to importance and became director of the Vienna Seminar for Psychoanalytic Therapy in 1927. Reich became interested in the outcome of analysis; he especially sought the basis for unsatisfactory results. He found that those patients who were successful had all developed a satisfactory genital life, whereas those who failed had not. Reich began to ponder what constituted a satisfactory sexual life. Sexual activity per se did not guarantee this, even when the man

ejaculated and the woman climaxed. He found that a specific type of capacity for sexual gratification was necessary—Reich called this "orgastic potency." It occurred when, through successful therapy, all holding and resistance dissolved.

The orgasm of patients who had achieved orgastic potency showed characteristics far different from those of neurotic individuals. Orgasms of such patients had to be triggered by genital union (in the female, the vagina rather than the clitoris was involved); orgasms from stimulation of pregenital zones did not produce the same effect. Orgasm was far more than a local climax—rather it involved total bodily convulsions of an involuntary nature, that is, involuntary contraction and expansion of the total plasmatic system. There was also complete cessation of psychic activity—there were no conscious fantasies whatsoever, but rather a blurring of consciousness at the moment of acme.

In his book *Character Analysis* (1971), Reich coined the term "character armor" to denote the individual's chronic (defensive) mode of reaction, which has its origins in childhood—the chronic alterations of the ego that it evolves to protect itself from external and internal dangers. As a result, the individual develops characteristic defensive modes of behavior, manifested in the *manner* rather than the *content*—the *how* rather than the *what*. It is these traits—for example, compliance, mistrust, arrogance, and so forth—that function as resistance in analysis. This intuition led Reich to develop his technique of character analysis. The entire neurotic character becomes manifest in treatment as a condensed rigid and inflexible defense mechanism. With successful analysis of these character traits, Reich often elicited strong emotions that he encouraged the patient to express. He noticed, too, that with the thorough release of affect, often locked up since childhood, there occurred changes—at times profound—in bodily attitudes, expressions, posture, and tonus. He became aware and convinced that concomitant with the psychic character armor, there is a somatic muscular armor.

As Raknes (1970), one of Reich's proponents, noted:

> It soon became clear to Reich that the muscular armor, which consists of spasms, cramps, and tensions, is nothing but the bodily expression of the repressed emotions and ideas, and the somatic anchoring of the neuroses. In psychoanalytic circles the question had often been raised as to where the repressed ideas and emotions were located, and the answer was as a rule that they were in the unconscious. Now Reich showed that they were bound as well in the muscular armor, in the spasms, holdings and tensions of which the individual had no consciousness or understanding.
>
> This discovery led to another innovation in psychotherapeutic technique, namely attacking the neurosis from the bodily side, partly by calling the patient's attention to the chronic tensions, partly by making him feel them by direct manipulation. By thus loosening up the holdings and tensions, one could bring into consciousness emotions and memories which had hitherto been completely repressed. (pp. 20–21)

The somatic armor, with its psychic concomitants, binds energy. It interferes with the free flow of energy through the organism. Undischarged energy continues to build up, to produce stasis, and eventually to overflow in the form of symptoms. The goal of therapy is to overcome this stasis by breaking down the armor, reestablishing the free flow of energy, and attaining orgastic potency.

CURRENT STATUS

The educational and training aspects of Orgone Therapy are administered by the American College of Orgonomy in New York City. (This is not a school, but an organization analagous to the American College of Physicians.) It is an organization of dedicated physicians and others who have the proper qualifications and have contributed significantly to the advancement of orgonomy.

Standards for training of orgone therapists are high—an MD degree, together with a medical internship plus residency training in either psychiatry or inter-

nal medicine. Members of the college give technical seminars and supervise therapists/trainees, as well as administer the necessary personal therapy. There are usually several trainees at any given time. The duration of training is dependent mainly on the degree of character restructuring required so that objectivity in treatment of others is insured. The average training period takes a minimum of three years. At present qualified candidates possessing the PhD degree are being trained for competency in orgonomic counseling.

The college also publishes the *Journal of Orgonomy,* a semiannual containing up-to-date clinical and theoretical articles on Orgone Therapy, orgone physics, biosocial problems, and related topics of interest. This journal is now in its thirteenth year.

A thorough exposition of Orgone Therapy is given in Baker's *Man in the Trap* (1967) and in a two-part article in the *Journal of Orgonomy* (Baker, 1978). For the historical and theoretical development of Orgone Therapy, the reader is referred to Reich's books, *The Function of the Orgasm* (1970) and *Character Analysis* (1971). An overview of the many aspects and ramifications of Reich's work can be found in a book by Raknes, *Wilhelm Reich and Orgonomy* (1970).

An ongoing course on the work of Wilhelm Reich for the layman or other professionals is given at New York University School of Continuing Education.

THEORY

Reich's work was based on psychoanalytic precursors that are still considered valid in orgonomy. One, of major importance, is human psychosexual development, which is paired with the vicissitudes of the libido. The ego evolves through various developmental stages, culminating in the Oedipus complex, whose successful resolution leads to the establishment of genital primacy and a state of emotional health. Fixations, or regressions to pregenital stages and/or difficulties in resolving the Oedipal conflict, result in emotional disturbance. This involves binding energy, which makes less energy available for autonomous adult functioning. To Freud, "psychic energy" was a metaphor. To Reich, it had a physical, objective existence, which he was able to demonstrate experimentally, and which he called "orgone."

Individual character development is, then, dependent on the degree of fixation, or armoring, at any particular erogenous zone where the major part of the energy is concentrated. Therefore it is evident that symptoms characteristic of these levels are present whenever there is an increase in energy concentration or block at that level. Blocking or armoring may occur at any zone and implies that the individual has been able to develop beyond that zone, but has not been able to give up that zone completely. Resultant symptoms color the personality and, most important, interfere with complete genital discharge, thus with emotional health. There are two types of blocks: repressed and unsatisfied. The latter is felt constantly as a need, as, for example, the overeating or overtalking of the oral unsatisfied block. The former results in a need to defend against any expression at all from the blocked zone, as manifested, for example, in a lack of interest in food, or in laconic speech.

Blocking is functionally identical with muscular armoring; an oral block, for example, will be manifested by spasm in the muscles of the head and face, such as the submentalis, masseters, and so forth. Character types (see Baker, 1967, and Reich, 1971) are determined by the particular constellation of blocks of the erogenous zones. Blocking in nonerogenous segments determines rigidity of the character type. In orgonomy four major erogenous zones are recognized: ocular, oral, anal, and genital. The ocular zone is a major addition to accepted analytic theory; orgone therapists feel that its blocking accounts for such major pathology as paranoia and schizophrenia. In healthy development each stage fulfills its temporal function, is not blocked, and the individual develops through to genital primacy.

The vast majority of people reach an early genital stage of development (phallic narcissistic, or hysteric), but earlier pregenital blocking may result in regression to a previous libidinal stage. In the case of a phallic with a dominant oral repressed block, for example, the phallic type of functioning is largely given up and behavior is predominantly of an oral type—depression, for example.

Therapy functions to reverse the armoring process. The armor is removed by evoking and discharging repressed emotions in an orderly and consistent fashion. For it is the movement of energy in the body that is felt as emotion; in the muscles as rage, for example; in the skin as pleasure; or inwardly, as anxiety. When armoring is removed, and natural sexuality is reached, one sees a unique physiological event that is an objective criterion of therapeutic success. There occurs a spontaneous tilting forward of the pelvis at the end of complete respiratory expiration, together with a coming forward of the shoulders. This is what Reich called the "orgasm reflex." It signifies that the patient is orgastically potent, has the ability to discharge all excess energy that is normally built up in living, and now has a healthy sex economy. Such an organism can no longer maintain a neurosis, since neuroses exist only on the basis of energy (libido) stasis. The function of the orgasm, then, is to regulate the energy economy of the organism.

As the patient achieves orgastic potency, he or she undergoes fundamental changes. Symptoms are lost. His or her body becomes relaxed, as opposed to previous rigidities caused by muscular contractions holding re-

pressed feelings. This is seen often in a softening of the face, with more expressiveness. The eyes are bright and there is a buoyancy in the whole organism, coupled with a general feeling of "well-being." Many fundamental attitudes change spontaneously.

METHODOLOGY

There are three avenues of approach in the practice of Orgone Therapy—breathing, directly attacking the spastic muscles, and maintaining the patient's cooperation. The priority of each depends upon the individual case, although all three are often necessary tools in every case.

First let us consider breathing, which has several functions. Clinically, the first somatic blocking (or defense) observed in infants is that of the breathing mechanism. The breath is held, and this reduces both anxiety and feeling in general. This breathing inhibition becomes chronic, and the adult is usually seen on the couch with his or her chest in a chronic inspiratory position with little excursion on respiration.

In therapy the patient is asked to breathe as fully and deeply as he or she comfortably can, concentrating on chest movement. This reverses the patient's historical inhibition of breathing. This maneuver often of itself produces considerable emotional release, especially of anger or crying. It helps to reveal and overcome severe blocking in other parts of the organism.

Breathing "charges" the organism energetically. This is often manifested by tingling and streaming sensations felt in the body. The increased charge exerts an inner push on blocks. In analytic terms, deep and full breathing facilitates loosening of repression.

The second avenue of approach consists of directly attacking the spastic muscles to free the contraction. The contraction of the skeletal muscles can be worked on directly, that of the muscles of the organs and tissues only indirectly. To mobilize the skeletal muscles, one must first increase the contraction to a point that cannot be maintained. This is done by direct pressure on the muscle with the thumb or by otherwise irritating it. Best results are obtained by pressure near the insertion of the muscle, which is the most sensitive area. Of course, the muscle will only contract again unless the emotion (or idea) that is being held back is released and expressed. Where muscles cannot be reached by the hands, other methods must be used, such as gagging to open throat muscles or mobilizing the eyes by having the patient follow a moving penlight with his or her eyes.

Third, orgone therapists work to maintain the cooperation of the patient (using character-analytic methods). This is accomplished by bringing the patient's resistances to therapy and the therapist into the open and overcoming them. This is extremely important because the patient will in every way endeavor to maintain his or her immobility, trying desperately not to reveal the self. Behind this is an intense fear of expansion and movement. The patient always begins therapy with distrust and suspicion. This resistance is emotional and cannot remain hidden indefinitely. It must be recognized and brought to the surface. Every defense begins with a negative transference. The patient must discuss this freely. A lack of negative transference is due to its being blocked by the therapist's attitude—being consistently friendly or otherwise preventing the patient from expressing hostile feelings toward the therapist. One must point out the patient's attitudes to him or her repeatedly or mimic his or her behavior. It is necessary to be consistent. The armor protects against stimuli from without and from within. Therapy upsets this equilibrium, which is what the patient resists. The resistance is always attacked from the ego side. The patient understands it better and thus the negative transference is dissolved. We are not concerned with what the patient wards off, but that he or she does ward off and how. Finally, *what* is warded off comes out.

Dissolving the armor renders the patient helpless. His potency breaks down from castration anxiety, and he feels his whole character as sick, not just his symptoms. If potency does not break down, therapy has not touched him.

Anxiety is the basis for all repression and is behind all contractions. The patient is always trying to control anxiety, and cure is effected by forcing him or her to face this anxiety and express forbidden feelings. The most important emotion to elicit is rage, and, until this is released, the patient cannot experience the softer feelings of love and longing. It must be released from every segment.

Through reactions of the body during the process of dissolving the armor, Reich discovered that the body was functionally divided into seven muscular segments, each of which reacts as a unit and is to a certain degree independent of the other segments. The seven segments are the ocular, oral, cervical, thoracic, diaphragmatic, abdominal, and pelvic. One works from the head down, removing the layers of armoring from the superficial to the deep. Any one segment may fail to respond completely until further segments are freed. With each release of a segment, armoring in earlier segments may recur and require further attention because the organism is not used to movement and tries to return to its former immobility. It must gradually become accustomed to free mobility. Treatment requires that the patient lie on the couch with only minimal clothing on, so that the therapist can adequately observe and treat the condition the patient has presented. The patient must understand this.

After working through the three areas of approach, therapists are now prepared to start dissolving the armor in the various segments individually. The chest is usually chosen first. Breathing is the most important aspect of therapy. It raises the energy level and promotes movement of energy. If the chest is not too tightly held, breathing is not too difficult an assignment. If the chest is held high in inspiration and does not move, it is heavily armored; here the therapist steps in and works manually on the muscles of the chest, particularly the intercostals and spinals. The latter cause holding back, "I won't," and spite. The pectorals and trapezii are also loosened. Pressure is exerted on the chest as the patient breathes out. In all cases, the patient is given a chance to breathe for some time before any active attack is made on the armor.

The chest holds rage, bitter sobbing, and longing. When it is freed, there is a feeling of lightness and buoyancy. Rage may be elicited by hitting, choking, twisting, and scratching. We encourage the patient to give in completely by wildly letting go. The chest cannot be rendered completely free until the first three segments are freed, and residuals come out only when one has reached the pelvis. After a moderate loosening of the chest, so the patient can at least breathe adequately, we proceed with the segments in order from above down.

Armoring in the ocular segment is shown by a stiff or immobile forehead. It may appear flat. The patient cannot open his eyes wide, and they may appear dull, vacant, anxious, sad, or defiant. Eye motility is markedly decreased. Schizophrenics appear to be staring into the distance, and the eyes have an empty look. Those few patients whose eyes are free have a trusting look.

The patient is asked to move the forehead; sometimes it may be necessary to start the process by manually moving it. Then the patient is instructed to roll the eyes, focusing on the walls, and open and squeeze them while breathing. The therapist has the patient follow a moving light or a finger with the eyes. One tries to get the eyes wide open. Here again it may be necessary to open them wide with the fingers. We try to elicit emotional expression in the eyes: anger, sorrow, anxiety—the last while screaming with the eyes open. Suspicion is elicited by having the patient look out of the corner of the eyes. Last, flirting, smiling, or longing are elicited by having the patient open his or her eyes wide while breathing out and smiling.

When the eyes are free, one will notice movements and an increase in tension in the lips and jaw. It is now time to proceed to the second, or oral, segment. This is an extremely important segment, for only the oral and genital segments can initiate the orgastic convulsion. They are the only major erogenous zones that provide actual contact and fusion with another organism. The oral zone provides means for the intake of food, fluid, and air, and for vocal communication, emotional expression, and erotic contact. If functioning is inhibited by repression, satisfaction is lost in all these important functions, and the joy of living is replaced by the misery of merely trying to survive and, eventually, by depression. For the rest of his or her life, the unsatisfied individual will try to make up this need through overeating, drinking, talking, and emotional vacillation.

Full expression of the oral segment depends on free mobility of the ocular, or first, segment and sometimes on loosening the lower segments. The jaw usually is tight with clenched teeth, although it may be unnaturally loose. The chin may sag or be drawn, flat, pale, and lifeless. It may be pushed forward in defiance or pride, causing a tightening of the floor of the mouth, which holds back crying. The therapist gently pushes the jaw backward and has the patient breathe, and try to let the jaw be loose. This may bring out crying.

The patient may speak little or talk constantly under pressure. One may observe contempt, a sarcastic smile, or a silly grin. The mouth may be sad or even cruel. The oral segment holds back angry biting, yelling, crying, sucking, and grimacing. The patient almost always needs to bite and is allowed to, on a suitable object such as a towel. When work is done on the submental muscles, or when the patient gags, crying may be brought out. Sometimes screaming does this. If not, the patient may be asked to imitate crying. Suppression of crying is frequently associated with nausea due to tension of the muscles in the floor of the mouth.

The cervical segment mainly holds back anger and crying. The neck is stiff, the muscles are tense, and the neck may balloon in breathing. Anger and crying may be literally swallowed down without the patient's being aware of it. Cervical blocking also gives rise to voice changes, a whining, thin voice, or harsh breathing and coughing.

The gag reflex is important in loosening the throat, but work may have to be done directly on the sternocleidomastoids and deep muscles of the neck, while having the patient scream repeatedly.

The diaphragmatic segment is one of the most difficult to deal with. When this is met, you may be sure you are in for a hard time. This block contains murderous rage. It may be recognized by lordosis and paradoxical respiration. Breathing out is difficult. The therapist repeatedly elicits the gag reflex without interrupting breathing. The patient is encouraged to express rage and to risk feelings of wanting to murder. The first four segments must be free before the diaphragm can be loosened. When this segment is opening, vomiting occurs. Then wavelike movements appear in the upper body, accompanied by a feeling of giving.

The sixth, or abdominal, segment usually causes little difficulty if the upper segments are free.

The pelvis, the seventh segment, is always freed last. If it is opened earlier, the individual cannot handle the sexual impulse, and either confusion and disintegration follow or else earlier problems such as sadistic impulses are carried into the sexual life.

The pelvis contains anxiety and rage. The latter is either anal and crushing, or phallic and piercing. The patient is asked to kick or stamp to discharge the anal rage and to strike with the pelvis to let out the phallic rage. Until anger is released, pleasure in the pelvis is impossible. The various spasms must be released. Spasm in the floor of the pelvis is released by having the patient repeatedly relax and contract the anal and vaginal sphincters. When this is accomplished, the pelvis moves forward spontaneously at the end of each complete expiration. This is the orgasm reflex. The organism is now capable of complete surrender, a capacity that gradually increases during the year or two following the completion of therapy.

APPLICATION

The first step in treatment is the selection of patients. Except for young children and infants, it is advisable to accept only those who request therapy themselves, not those who come because a husband, wife, parent, or friend pushes them to have therapy. It is difficult enough when the patient earnestly desires help—impossible when it is forced on him or her. One should never accept a patient one does not like. Therapy is too difficult to deal objectively with someone you do not like, and it is not fair to either the therapist or the patient. Also, it is advisable to take those one understands the best and can work with the most easily.

The second consideration is whether the candidate is ready for therapy. This may not be determined immediately but should be watched for very carefully. The situation is suspect if the patient cannot grasp what is required of him or her and therapy seems alien and not comprehensible. Those who grasp it immediately and understand what you are trying to do are usually good candidates. Unusual reaction such as blanking out, irrational reactions, turning blue or gray, shock, or extreme weakness make one wary and call for extreme caution. A tendency to develop serious physical symptoms as therapy continues is reason enough to discontinue treatment.

Prior to any therapy, it is essential to obtain both an adequate history and a physical examination. The history itself is relatively meaningless. What is important is the patient's reaction to the events that are anchored physiologically in the character structure. These are the things that therapy stirs up. It is important to estimate the "stuff the patient is made of." Has he or she accomplished a great deal against all odds, or has the patient succumbed to the least frustration? Has he or she been able to socialize, or has contact with people been avoided? Has he or she made a good adjustment to the opposite sex or not? Is the patient willing to make a real effort to get better, or does he or she want it made easy?

Obstacles to success are age, rigidity, severe orthodoxy (religious and/or political), and environment. The last factor may present real circumstances over which the therapist has no control. For example, a woman who has many young children may be married to an impotent man whom she cannot leave for security reasons.

Any physical disease is a complication to therapy and should be corrected if possible. The somatic biopathies—that is, those physical illnesses due primarily to emotional repression—make therapy that much more difficult. In our experience, cancer cases, including those surgically treated with no recurrence even after years, are not candidates for this therapy.

These caveats aside, most psychiatric conditions are amenable to Orgone Therapy, especially the neuroses and schizophrenia.

However, not all cases can be treated; some can only be made worse. It is important to recognize and screen out the individuals who cannot tolerate expansion and movement, react badly to every advance in therapy, or break down into serious somatic illness.

Orgonomic technique is less dependent on verbal communication from the patient than other therapeutic procedures, and therefore can be frequently very effective in attacking pathologic structure not reached by other modalities. It is in part a body-oriented technique, but it also entails consistent character analysis of the patient's resistance. The technique is deceptively simple, but Orgone Therapy is not simply a matter of "working on" muscle spasms or producing dramatic emotional outbursts. One must be able to make an accurate diagnosis, understand character structure and underlying character dynamics, to know when and how to consistently and logically apply orgonomic techniques. In addition, a knowledge of physiology and anatomy is necessary, in order to deal safely with chronic muscular spasm, untoward physical responses, and any biopathic (psychosomatic) conditions. Proper training, experience, and background, therefore, are a necessity—or disaster may ensue. This is especially so because of the profound emotional and physical depths that can be plumbed. The possibility of suicide, psychoses, or serious physical illness as a result of mismanagement is very real. As Reich stated, Orgone Therapy is "no more and no less than bio-psychiatric surgery and can only be done securely by well skilled and well trained hands and structures. . . ."

Many "body" and other cathartic therapies have borrowed from or are derived from the work of Reich. Bioenergetics is one of the few therapies that acknowledges its origins from Reich. Bioenergetics utilizes the concepts of muscular armor and movement of energy. Many of the therapeutic techniques are similar.[1]

CASE EXAMPLE

The following case,[2] conducted by Charles Konia, MD, of Easton, Pennsylvania, represents a clear, uncomplicated picture of Orgone Therapy.

Anamnesis

The patient was a 25-year-old single white school teacher who came to therapy because she wanted to settle down and stop running from herself. The aspect of her behavior that she found most disturbing was her relationships with men. She had a history of repeated unsatisfying, short-lived sexual experiences. In general she chose men who treated her abusively, often to the point of physical punishment. She was entirely unable to protect or extricate herself from these situations, which invariably ended with her being jilted. . . . When I first saw her she was about 25 pounds overweight. Typically she ate when depressed or anxious, following a disappointing love affair. She was unable to be alone for any length of time, requiring the constant reassurance of someone near. She was frigid and was able to have only minimal genital sensations through oral genital foreplay. This was often accompanied by masochistic fantasies of being forced to submit sexually, or imagining that she herself had a penis.

Past History

The patient was an only child. Her memories of her father are few; however, there were two distinct screen memories that she recalled. The first was of being chased under her bed by her father after she cut her mother's dresses with a pair of scissors and then not being punished by him; this left her with a definite feeling of sexual excitement. The second occurred just prior to his death, when she was eight. At that time she had inadvertently seen him naked, and she interpreted his death as a punishment. Immediately following his death she began overeating to the point of becoming obese. In addition, she became spiteful toward her mother until she was to-

---

[1] Bioenergetics has, however, dropped the cornerstone of therapy—the orgasm theory and the goal of orgastic potency. Possibly this is a result of a fatal altering of Reich's theory and technique by removing the pelvic armoring prematurely—thereby insuring that orgastic potency will rarely be achieved.

[2] Excerpted with permission from Konia, C. (1975). Orgone therapy: A case history. *Psychotherapy: Theory, Research and Practice, 12*(2), 192–197.

tally out of her control and had to be restrained by a maternal uncle. She related this behavior to being angry with her mother for not remarrying and bringing another father into the home. At the same time, her behavior produced a fear that her mother would also leave her, and she turned into a "good little girl."

Biophysical Examination

The patient tended to be soft-spoken and seductive. When frightened, her facial expression became indifferent or calm. She was of average height and heavily built. Aside from her obesity, which was mainly centered in her legs, thighs, and abdomen, the most prominent feature was her mouth, which seemed to be stuck with a tremendous emotional charge behind it. The expression varied between a smirk, disgust, indifference, or boredom, depending on her mood. Her face appeared tense and bloated. Her eyes were frightened and slightly bulging, but were lively and expressive.

Treatment

The Ocular and Oral Segments.   I began by focusing on her indifferent facial expression, which I felt concealed her most superficial layer of rage. She admitted that behind her indifference she was afraid of showing her anger and felt that she would get "kicked in the face" if she ever revealed her true feelings. At the same time I worked on her facial tension by having her make faces. This made her frightened, and she recalled her inability to express her anger toward her mother's helplessness and lack of understanding. When she behaved spitefully, her mother's favorite phrase was "What did I ever do to deserve you?" This made the patient feel frustrated and worthless, but she invariably got even with her mother by becoming even more spiteful.

Gradually when her face lost some of its bloated appearance and looked somewhat more expressive, her distrust of men began surfacing. She admitted not knowing how to be herself with someone who was not as bad off and "crazy" as she was. She was afraid that any other kind of man would find out what she was really like and have nothing to do with her. Therefore the surest way to avoid rejection was to submit sexually and become a "receptacle."

Discussion of this material was soon followed by a sneer, and she was able to express a few brief angry shouts. However, her anger soon became stuck in her chest and she became dyspneic. I prodded her trapezius muscle to mobilize this anger, and that produced more angry faces and shouting. She was greatly pleased with this outburst but immediately became frightened and had the urgent feeling of having to do something more. I interpreted this as a fear of incurring my disapproval by not being a good patient, and related it to pleasing men

out of fear. She left with a serious look on her face. In the following sessions she entered feeling angry with me for what I had said last time, but knew that I was correct. As she became somewhat more trusting, she stated that I was the only man that she didn't have to please. I took this declaration with a grain of salt, since I knew that she was still unable to show emotions, especially anger, fully in her eyes. I therefore went back to mobilizing her eyes by having her roll them and express fear. Gradually they became less proptotic. Then with pressure on the masseters, she was able to show anger in her eyes while shouting "Stop it!" She looked as if she could stab me. This was the strongest anger that she had expressed, and following this her face appeared more open. She began asserting herself in her daily life.

When she began to enjoy making angry faces, and became somewhat contactless with herself, I knew that a layer had been worked through and waited to see what would happen next. I didn't have to wait long. In the next session she had a lost look in her eyes, and reported that her weight had been steadily increasing. Her distrust became intensified. Expressing rage in her face beyond a certain threshold produced a great deal of fear; she turned her head away so that I would not see her angry looks. I again mobilized her terror by having her look startled with her eyes. This produced the strongest fear she had ever known. She cried and felt afraid of being alone. When I saw her in the next session her face had regained that typical swollen, bloated appearance that she had when I first saw her, and she reported that she had eaten voraciously all week. She looked intermittently confused, lonely, frightened, and angry. During the session I kept after her tendency to please me, and related it to her fear of being abandoned, pointing out that any display of anger means desertion. Mobilizing fear from her eyes at this time was fairly easy. Rolling her eyes, she would scream in panic for entire sessions at a time. This was often accompanied by crying and an expression of sadness in the lower part of her face. Intensification of her fear made it necessary for her to block off her deeper emotions from her throat. Squeezing a towel (which often helps relieve a spastic throat) partially helped to mobilize the throat block, but then her tongue interfered.

At this time, in spite of her fears, she terminated an unsatisfying relationship with a boyfriend. She began to assert herself with men, and to feel that she had some rights in a relationship. In therapy she became somewhat brazen and decided she was not going to please me by showing feelings, unless she genuinely felt them.

At this time I attempted mobilization of her oral rage, by pressure on the masseters, but this proved to be premature. She became distrustful again, and looked at me as if I were going to leave her. I therefore went back to her eyes and had her express more fear alternating with anger. This brought out murderous thoughts and feelings directed at me, but this made her feel guilty. As she became able to tolerate her fear, her throat spontaneously became mobilized and she began making deep frightened sounds. At this time her fear was so intense that she had to touch me to convince herself that I was still in the room. She recalled that her mother could not tolerate any display of anger, and felt at those times as if she were actually going crazy.

Now her deep oral rage, in the form of biting became accessible. She growled, moved her jaw with a biting motion, and felt like killing. This was the strongest anger that she had felt thus far. It took the form of a blinding rage toward her mother for being so controlling and hypocritical, and this was followed by quivering of her lips for the first time.

The Abdominal Segment.   In the next session she reported the following dream: Her father is sick, and her mother is preventing her from seeing him. She recalled that at the time of her father's death she was never told that her father had died, only that he was sick and went away. This made it possible for her to deny the reality of his death and years afterward she still searched for him. At this time, mobilizing fear from her eyes brought out her deep fear of abandonment. She felt terror and wanted to scream out "Daddy don't leave me," but could not. This gave in to deep sobbing. She began feeling her mourning over her father's death.

In her daily life she began to tolerate being alone for longer periods of time, and in therapy she came in touch with the intense rage in her abdomen (where most of her fat was centered). This rage, in turn, intensified fears of abandonment. She became "scared stiff" and screamed out in panic. This alternated with more abdominal rage, which finally ended in strong abdominal cramps. She recalled the time just prior to her father's death, when she had accidentally seen him naked. She felt somehow responsible for his death since this image was frightening and prohibited. It was immediately after his death that she began to overeat.

Deeper mobilization of her fear of abandonment produced dyspnea accompanied by a fear of dying, and she began to quiver in her arms and chest. She identified this fear as a punishment for having killed her father. Then followed very strong rage toward me which she also felt down to her abdomen. She looked hatefully at me and shouted "I hate you!" She compared me to her father and stated that she loved me, but that I didn't love her, and would leave her just as her father had done. This outburst was followed, during the next week, by a moderate amount of weight loss from her abdominal area. This weight loss intensified her terror, and strong, frightened shouting poured out of her for long periods of time. This resulted in sensations in her pelvis and thighs, although her genital was bypassed.

Then followed deep sadness at her father's death. She felt a deep longing for him, accompanied by an emptiness in her stomach, and described having fantasies of her father being in her abdomen. She felt strong reluctance to face her sadness since this made her feel vulnerable. She also began having genital sensations for the first time in her life, but was afraid to tell me, for fear of being discharged as cured. I reassured her that this was not the case, and that she was only beginning to have genital feelings. There was still a lot of work to be done.

As she began to trust me more, the spasm in her lower abdomen gradually began to yield and she began experiencing an almost unbearable longing for her father. She cried out uncontrollably, "Daddy, why did you leave me, why did you have to die?" Further expression of this longing from her lower abdomen produced strong anxiety in her perineum. At this time she developed a fear of getting appendicitis and dying. She felt this would be a punishment for having sexual feelings for her father. The longing for her father gradually developed into fantasies of swallowing him both through her vagina and orally.

End Stage: The Pelvic Segment.   I then gently massaged her jaw. This produced very strong biting from her mouth, accompanied by squeezing of her pelvic floor. She expressed a very strong rage in her pelvis and thighs, as if she were biting with her vagina. Following this she felt intense genital longing, and felt that her vagina wanted to be filled with a penis. During the session breathing produced a pelvic retraction on expiration (preorgastic sensations).

In the following session jaw mobilization resulted in very powerful clonisms, which terrified her. I knew that once her jaw finally gave, she would quickly develop the orgasm reflex provided that she did not clamp down in another segment. I was not wrong. Within a few minutes the reflex appeared. This at first terrified her, and she cried out of fear. But then very strong surges of sexual excitement overcame her, and she cried "I can feel! It's wonderful!" Her jaw looked open, and her whole face appeared to have completely lost its tension, taking on a seriousness and depth that was not there previously. She felt very alive and sexual.

During the last few sessions I focused on completely eliminating the biting from her mouth and vagina. During one session her pleasurable pelvic sensations became blocked. This led to a violent explosive anger at everyone, including me. She shouted and kicked and hit. "I want to be well! I don't want therapy any more!"

As she gave up her attachment to me, she slowly relinquished her oedipal ties to her father. She became capable of staying open sexually and achieving genital gratification. Correspondingly, her relationships with men changed. She began to select men, not out of neurotic motives or fantasies, but on the basis of whether or not they provided genuine satisfaction of her needs. Therapy lasted 215 sessions.

Discussion

A precise understanding of the structure of the armor, both from a characterological as well as a biophysical standpoint, which presumes an accurate biopsychiatric diagnosis, is essential for the successful treatment of any patient. Since the major armoring of this patient was in the pelvic segment with the secondary source of armor in the oral segment, this patient was a hysteric with an oral unsatisfied block. Her pelvic armoring was manifested by the fact that a primary aspect of her neurotic character was a constant push toward genital contact with simultaneous running from her sexual feelings because of anxiety. . . . (Fenichel, 1945). The end result was that she was left chronically unsatisfied.

Complicating her basic structure was her severe pregenital (oral) block. Her mouth was genitalized and served as a substitute to fulfill her sexual desires. Unlike the simple hysteric who runs at the first sign of a sexual encounter and/or sexual feelings, this patient would cling tenaciously to any man with whom she became involved. During the course of therapy, constant mobilization of her oral block was therefore essential. Prior to loosening up a deeper level of armoring, the therapist repeatedly had to return to the oral segment and release the particular emotion that was being held.

In attempting to understand the treatment of this patient, it will be helpful to follow logically, step by step, the layering of the armor from the most superficial to the deepest expressions.

Psychologically one traces the layering from the patient's most superficial character traits through the deeper emotions which underlie the Freudian unconscious (or, in orgonomic terms, secondary drives) to the successful resolution of the oedipal conflict (Fenichel, 1945). From the biophysical aspect one passes through the segmental layering of the armoring, from the most superficial features in the upper segments (eyes, facial expressions, etc.) down through the cervical, thoracic, diaphragmatic, abdominal, and finally into the pelvic segment where the oedipal conflict is thoroughly dealt with.

The therapist's skill depends on his or her being able to perceive which aspect of the armor is closest to the surface and therefore requires immediate attention. To begin with, this patient's glib, indifferent facial expression covered the most superficial layer of her fear of showing feelings. She would get "kicked in the face" if she did. Expressing this fear brought out her spiteful anger, primarily directed at her mother for controlling her and interfering with her life. Exposing this anger immediately brought out a deeper layer, her present-day distrust of men based on a fear of rejection by them. This fear made her behave like a nice, sweet little girl, and turned her into a "receptacle" to be used by any man. Working through this distrust brought out sneers and other angry faces. This anger, in turn, revealed a deeper fear of abandonment on an oral dependent level directed toward her mother. "Don't leave me the way Daddy did" is what she felt at this point. Until now the primary focus of attention was in her first and second segments (the ocular and oral), but as her emotions became deeper, she began to block in her throat. Facing her fear of maternal abandonment brought out angry biting, expressing her rage at being deserted by the mother. It was at this time that the patient first had fleeting oral-genital sensations with quivering of the lips. This rage was followed by deeper fear of abandonment by the father, which slowly gave way to profound rage toward him, and therefore toward all men. She felt the source of this rage primarily in the upper part of the abdominal segment. Expression of this hatred was followed by a deeper fear of longing (fear of being hurt), which began from her lower abdomen. This fear was based on her feeling that her father would leave her if she expressed any feeling toward him. This was followed by a profound sorrow and longing (localized in the lower part of her abdomen) for her father. Correspondingly, she began to lose weight (gave up the incorporated father in her abdomen), which was followed by sensations in her pelvis and thighs. This gradually produced preorgastic sensations, and the crystallization of the incest wish and castration anxiety (sexual taboo for longing for her father and the revival of her fear of punishment for seeing him naked). This in turn gave way to very powerful biting from her mouth and vagina based on her impulse to bite off and swallow her father's penis. Finally came the total mobilization of her jaw: her organism gave in with clonisms of the jaw and pelvis, which led to the orgasm reflex and orgasm anxiety (fear of dying). Tolerating these feelings soon produced strong feelings of genital excitation and the establishment of genitality.

SUMMARY

Early in his analytic career, in the late 1920s, Wilhelm Reich moved down from behind the couch to sit beside the patient and look at him or her and to allow the patient to see him. He thus made contact with the individual behind the neurosis he was treating. He began to observe patients physically as well as listen to their words and emotions. With release of affect, he noticed changes in bodily attitudes, expressions, posture, and so forth. These accompanied changes in character traits such as arrogance, spite, compliance, and others. He intuitively made a connection between the two—that the neurosis had a somatic concomitant (or was "functionally equivalent," to use his phrase). This led (in the early to mid-1930s) to an important innovation in therapeutic technique, that of attacking neuroses somatically. At the same time he began to question the outcome of psychoanalysis—finding that only successful analysands had developed a satisfactory sex life with a specific type of orgastic response. He further studied orgastic function in conjunction with his new therapeutic techniques. He found that as people got well and lost their character, and physical, armor, they eventually developed a physiological spontaneous reflex of the body, which Reich called the "orgasm reflex" and which signified (and was validated by patient reports) the ability to discharge orgastically in a specific way—the "orgastic potency." Here were physiological criteria for cure. Psychoanalytic theories of psychosexual development and characterology were valid for Reich, as well as the concepts of libido and psychic energy. Orgonomists, however, unlike the Freudians, do not use "psychic energy" as a metaphor. Reich saw indirect evidence for a real energy in terms of tense muscles that became soft after emotional release, of dull eyes that sparkled thereafter.

Reich demonstrated that this energy had a physical, objective existence, and called it "orgone." The orgasm, to Reich, was the great regulator of this energy, and if orgastic potency existed, there was no libido stasis—therefore, no symptoms, and the individual had a healthy sex economy.

Orgonomic psychiatric technique currently uses a combination of physical (breathing and direct work on muscles) together with character-analytic methods. Character is thus specific blocking of the flow of orgone energy and therapy has as its goal the unblocking of this energy so that it might flow freely through the organism, signifying a state of health.

Reich's insights have led us to a new and deeper understanding of human functioning, as well as profound innovations in therapeutic theory and technique.

REFERENCES

Baker, E. F. (1967). *Man in the trap.* New York: Macmillan.

Baker, E. F. (1978). Orgone therapy. *Journal of Orgonomy, 12*(1,2), 41–54, 201–215.

Konia, C. (1975). Orgone therapy: A case history. *Psychotherapy: Theory, Research and Practice, 12*(2), 192–197.

Nelson, A. (1976). Orgone (Reichian) therapy in tension headache. *American Journal of Psychotherapy, 30*(1), 103–111.

Raknes, O. (1970). *Wilhelm Reich and orgonomy.* New York: St. Martin's.

Reich, W. (1970). *The function of the orgasm.* New York: Farrar, Straus.

Reich, W. (1971). *Character analysis.* New York: Farrar, Straus.

Chapter 45

POETRY THERAPY

ARTHUR LERNER

There is something unusual about proponents of various psychological systems and therapies. They tend to become obsessed with the value of their work and frequently are blind to the values of other points of view. My own experience with several dozen therapy innovators and initiators, including some in this book, bears this out. But there are exceptions, and Arthur Lerner is one of these. Modest and unpretentious, a thoroughly well-grounded individual (with, among other things, two doctorates, one in psychology and one in literature), he is an enormously hard worker and strong proponent of Poetry Therapy, but at the same time he is aware of the limitations of this technique, seeing it as an ancillary procedure rather than the method to end all methods.

I believe that the person who wishes to be a truly complete therapist should understand the value of each of the modalities covered herein and should experiment with those that he or she feels comfortable with. Poetry, whether reading it or composing it, should help some individuals to understand themselves better and learn how to fit into the world.

Poetry Therapy is an operational term for the use of poetry in the therapeutic experience. The therapeutic experience may involve a one-to-one relationship, a group process, or both. Poetry in the therapeutic experience is, therefore, an eclectic and adjunctive phenomenon that can be used to complement any prevailing psychotherapy.

HISTORY

Precursors

Song, prayer, and poetry as healing agents have been used by shamans, witch doctors, and medicine men since earliest times. Along with this, the holy books of all societies contain poetic statements and poetry that act as healing/counseling/therapy supports.

In ancient Greek mythology, Apollo was thought of as the god of light, the god of reason, and the god of poetry. His son Asclepius was the god of healing. Thus, in one family, poetry and healing were united. Reason and emotion were the two major life elements with which the Greeks grappled. Their poetic drama addressed itself to deep life forces and the price paid in not attending to emotional blind spots. Their concern was to find an even keel, a balanced view—everything in moderation.

Aristotle (384–322 BC) in his *Poetics* observed literature very much in the fashion of a naturalist or scientist. He believed strongly in the concept of *psychagogia*, the

leading out of the soul through the thrust and power of art, and pointed out that poetry was deeply rooted in two aspects of human nature that he regarded as instincts, imitation and a combining of harmony and rhythm (or meter). It is interesting to note how in contemporary psychological theory cognates of Aristotelian thought can be found in such concepts as modeling, integration, lifestyle, closure, and a host of other terms.

Aristotle also believed that poetry was a form of knowledge, having a positive moral effect on the psyche. He went on to use the term *katharsis,* a purgation of the emotions through pity and fear. It is well to remember that Aristotle's frame of reference in the *Poetics* is Greek tragedy, the form and spirit which are always poetic.

The process involved in Aristotle's concept of *katharsis* includes both a controlling and directing of emotions, reminiscent of William Wordsworth's lines in "Intimations of Immortality":

To me alone there came a thought of grief;
A timely utterance gave that thought relief,
And I again am strong.

Beginnings

At this time of writing there is no definitive history of Poetry Therapy. However, certain events and literary contributions pinpoint the beginnings of the field.

Poetry Therapy has been used at the Pennsylvania Hospital for almost 200 years and is still part of its Milieu Therapy. Jones (1969) indicated that Pennsylvania Hospital began to publish a newspaper, *The Illuminator,* in 1843 in which the mental patients did the writing (including poetry), editing, and hand copying.

In an essay in 1908 entitled "The Relation of the Poet to Day-Dreaming," Sigmund Freud observed that the imaginative writer is close to the daydream and that the poet's work was the daydream or wish. Carl Jung (1933) believed that in a psychoanalytic frame of reference a great work of art is like a dream. He felt a poem touched something in man that dealt with the problem of human existence, not necessarily from a personal point of view.

An essential work, *The Poetic Mind* (1922) by Prescott, was ignored for many years. Eventually it was reprinted in 1959. Prescott, a professor of English, concerned himself with two aspects of poetry, unconscious determinants of inspiration and the phenomenon of dream life with its relevance to poetic expression. He also based some of his thinking on the tenets advanced by an Anglican clergyman, the Reverend John Keble, who 18 years prior to the birth of Freud set off the Oxford movement with his sermon on July 14, 1833 at St. Mary's Church in Oxford. Keble believed that literature was disguised wish fulfillment and that poetry provided an outlet and a catharsis that prevented madness.

Blanton, author of *The Healing Power of Poetry* (1960), indicated the breadth of a psychiatrist's use of poetry in 40 years of practice.

A major thrust in the growth of Poetry Therapy was due to the efforts of Eli Greifer (1902–1966) and Jack Leedy, a psychiatrist. Greifer, trained as a lawyer and pharmacist, found refuge and relief in poetry. He published, filed, and catalogued poems to meet specific ailments in the same fashion as a prescription. In *Poetry Therapy* (1969) Leedy informed us that Greifer was a volunteer in treating the emotionally ill through poetry under psychotherapeutic supervision. Greifer went to the Cumberland Hospital in Brooklyn in 1959 where, along with Samuel Spector and Leedy, poemtherapy evolved into Poetry Therapy. The Association for Poetry Therapy was organized in 1969 and has since sponsored world conferences.

In 1971 Julius Griffin, a psychiatrist, established the Calabasas Neuropsychiatric Center in California. A believer in replacing the custodial care concept with a therapeutic one, Griffin invited Arthur Lerner, a poet and psychologist, to be poet in residence and poetry therapist at the newly formed installation. This was a novel event in psychiatric history at a proprietary mental health setting. Later, under new management, the name of the center was changed to Woodview Calabasas Hospital. Abrams (1978) provides a vivid account of the poetry therapy program at Woodview, making it clear that poetry can easily be incorporated into the treatment program of a psychiatric hospital.

Another event of importance in the development of Poetry Therapy was the founding of the Poetry Therapy Institute in Encino, California, in 1973. The Institute, concerned with education, research, and therapy, offers workshops in cooperation with colleges, universities, hospitals, clinics, schools, and community mental health centers. In the summer of 1979, it cosponsored the First National Conference on Poetry Therapy with Immaculate Heart College in Los Angeles.

CURRENT STATUS

In addition to the Poetry Therapy Institute in Encino, California, other organizations offer courses and/or training programs in Poetry Therapy.

In *The Therapy of Poetry* (1972) Molly Harrower argued that poetry is therapy and is vitally related to normal personality development. She offered many of her poems to point up her rationale. In doing this she has encouraged many individuals to focus on their own poetry as part of their normal developing process.

Leedy, as editor of *Poetry the Healer* (1973), expanded the scope of poetry as a therapeutic modality. In *Psychopoetry* (1976) Schloss reflected the influence of J. L. Moreno, the father of Group Psychotherapy and Psychodrama, and credited Moreno with using the term "psychopoetry" long before the current usage of Poetry Therapy. Schloss and Grundy (1978) also developed this psychodramatic orientation by illustrating diverse psychopoetry techniques.

In *Poetry in the Therapeutic Experience* (1978), Lerner indicated that Poetry Therapy is groping for a basic rationale and is in need of carefully defined and refined research. Though there is evidence of the power of poetry as a healing agent in therapy, Lauer (1978) is of the opinion that Poetry Therapy is not altogether harmless.

Some practitioners have agreed that since Poetry Therapy is an ancillary modality, only specially trained individuals (facilitators and aides) with supervised experience and background in basic courses in psychology and human dynamics should be judged qualified to employ it. Others argue that only the bonafide professional—that is, psychiatrist, psychologist, counselor, and the like—should be involved in Poetry Therapy.

As of this writing, there is no evidence that any accredited college or university offers a specific curriculum with Poetry Therapy as a major, leading toward an undergraduate or graduate degree. Courses in Poetry Therapy are offered at various schools from time to time under diverse headings, such as Creative Arts Therapy or Expressive Arts Therapy. As of now, one "learns" Poetry

Therapy by attending sessions where the process is taking place and then finds volunteer or paid work while under supervision.

In the appendixes of *Using Bibliotherapy: A Guide to Theory and Practice* (1978) Rubin lists points of information regarding certification and training for various programs, including among others Poetry Therapy.

THEORY

One way of looking at Poetry Therapy is as a "merging" of two fields, poetry and therapy. It is important to note that poetry has been around longer than therapy and to remember that the rationale for the two fields is based on different experiences and assumptions. Rothenberg (1973) pointed out the similarities and differences of poetry and therapy in terms of the process of poetic creation and psychotherapy. He is most circumspect in his assumptions and draws conclusions from three sources involved in the creative process, namely, interview studies, manuscript studies, and experimental studies. One of the key points Rothenberg makes is to remind us that the poetic process as such does not involve a helping relationship. Though some poets may view themselves as helpers, their role is not intrinsic to the total therapeutic process.

In spite of difficulties certain guidelines of operation are beginning to emerge that may eventually lead to a refined theory of Poetry Therapy. The following are not all inclusive, not given in any order of importance, and will be familiar to psychologists within their own frame of reference.

1. The use of poetry in a therapy milieu is an ancillary tool and can be employed on a one-to-one basis, group basis, and/or both.
2. The emphasis in using poetry in therapy is upon the reaction of the person; in poetry workshop, the accent is on the poem.
3. The poem may act as (a) a catalyst through which emotions are filtered, (b) an interpretation, (c) a projective instrument, and (d) even be considered as a dream.
4. The basic power charge of the poem is metaphor and simile.
5. A poem is most effective when geared to the level of feeling and understanding of the individual. This, of course, is a tenet of sound education based on proven laws of learning.
6. The same poem that may be meaningful to person A at one point in time may not be at another. Likewise, a poem may be "effective" with person A and not be effective with person B, who may have a similar problem. At present there is no evidence

that one can prescribe poems for specific ailments with assurance that effective healing will result.
7. The use of a poem in therapy may enable the person to facilitate his or her own understanding of feelings, lifestyles, and preferences.

In addition to the interacting and reflecting that accompanies the communication process, the use of poetry in the therapeutic experience involves verbal and nonverbal phenomena. Meerloo (1969) has pointed up the idea that rhythm is essential in life and expresses feelings that were formerly repressed. Each of us is involved in repetition of archaic patterns of behavior. Beginning with our intrauterine life, biological rhythm is a vital part of the human condition. Through rhythm we can bring up forgotten memories. Often the rhyme and rhythm of poetry have a greater effect on our personality than the actual meaning of the words.

Additionally, the way we perceive things does not necessarily provide a "correct" picture of our observations. Ansell (1978) has suggested that we live each day experiencing speech and behavior through a network of illusions. Underneath it all lurks the possibility that Walt Whitman has so poignantly expressed:

Of the terrible doubt of appearances,
Of the uncertainty after all, that we may be deluded
Leaves of Grass

It has also been suggested that, like all the arts, poetry provides an aesthetic experience when it is introduced as part of the healing process. However, in Poetry Therapy, again as in all the healing arts, the aesthetic experience itself is often involved with personality dynamics and unique personal patterns in the development of growth and behavior. Some point to the possibility of a self-hierarchy pattern. Edgar (1978), making use of a Jungian frame of reference in Poetry Therapy, reported an evolutionary and sequential pattern of growth as part of the epiphany of selfhood.

This writer's own experience is that a poem used in therapy enables an individual to enlarge the scope of awareness, retreat from situations, decry, meet a newer concept that has just emerged, or not be affected at all. What is emphasized here is that since all theories of psychotherapy can include poetry in the therapeutic situation, the dynamics of each postulate are operating. Hence, it is to the poetry therapist's interest to have a wide acquaintance with theories of personality and psychotherapy in order to use poetry as an effective ancillary tool.

The use of poetry in therapy often evokes primary processes that go beyond the written and spoken word, and that activate fantasy and archetypal images deeply buried within the psyche. Affects aroused via poetry, primarily through simile, metaphor, and/or rhythm, can in the hands of an able therapist lead to wholesome self-expression and creativity, the raising of personal esteem, and help in developing insight on the part of the patient.

What then may be the goal as the process of Poetry Therapy unfolds? Regardless of the therapist's frame of reference, Stainbrook (1978) clearly indicates the significance of the joining of forces of poetry and therapy when he states:

> Finally, and perhaps most important, there exists the possibility that in its optimum potential the merger of poetry with therapy may result in the revitalizing and re-moralizing of the self by providing a wholeness of consciousness—an integration of emotion, cognition, and imagery—with which to create and maintain personal meaning. (p. 11)

The above statement provides room for the wide variety of processes as reflected in current psychotherapies and for the many elements of theory considered in current personality constructs.

METHODOLOGY

The poetry therapist's goal during the first session, whether individual or group, is to enable the participant to "feel right" about being present. A person coming to therapy for the first time generally has feelings of anxiety and frustration, to say the least. This state is often compounded when poetry becomes the catalyst through which emotions and feelings will be expressed.

The setting in a group session is usually in a fairly large room with people sitting around in a circle. There are no tables or other obstructions to hide members from each other. Poetry books are found on the floor within the circle or copies of poetry may be on the seats as people enter; or copies may be handed out. In addition, group members bring in their own poems. Paper and pencil are also available. There may be a record player and/or a tape recorder in the event music is played and poems are read aloud.

Patients are usually professionally referred in a hospital setting. In other settings, such as clinics, counseling centers, and the like, the selection may be the same or it may be modified to fit the philosophy and schedule of the organization. It is important to let the participants know from the beginning that they are not involved in a poetry workshop. Otherwise, well-meaning individuals, often highly talented, will expect to gain kudos for their own poetry. In addition to being a human need, this expectancy may be vitally tied in with personality factors.

Along with the therapist there are one or two poetry therapy facilitators. Their roles are made clear to the group during the initial session. They assist the therapist in all ways, except that the final therapeutic responsibility rests with the therapist.

The element of applying the arts to therapy, particularly a verbal art such as poetry, often evokes feelings suggestive of a "high." Euphoria may be part of a therapeutic experience, but in and of itself it is not therapy.

Poetry in therapy has been discussed in this chapter with the assumption that a bona fide therapist is involved in the experience. There is no carefully defined ongoing research program at this time concerned with selection, participatory experiences, process, content of poetry therapy sessions, and the like. What we do find is "Poetry Therapy" in hospitals, clinics, private settings, prisons, jails, mental health centers, schools, community centers, gerontology centers, and a host of other places. Included are varied ages, personalities, problems, ethnic groups, and so forth.

In some instances poetry in the settings mentioned above is featured under such headings as "growth through poetry," "communication through poetry," and others. At the other end of the spectrum are therapists and aides or facilitators working under supervision of a trained therapist and engaging in the practice of Poetry Therapy with individuals who have been assigned by their primary therapists. Following each session entries are made in charts and the primary therapist has a chance to review these so as to gain a fuller understanding of an individual's total progress. Facilitators also attend case conferences and thus have an opportunity to discuss mutual professional problems.

It has been this writer's experience that *closure* of each group session is most important. There is a *warmup*, of course, varying all the way from introduction by name and "How do you feel?" to "Let's say anything that comes to our minds." The closure generally involves either sitting or standing up and forming a circle with arms around each other and going around the room stating feelings. Every therapist soon learns that there are some individuals who do not like to be touched or have their arms around each other. While this is to be respected, it is also to be considered in light of the person's individual history and dynamics.

Intuitive experience is a vital part of poetry in the therapy; the therapist soon finds poems to deal not only with the material that has been brought up but finds a host of poems that touch upon questions of personal behavior patterns. Poetry often acts as a "softening up" process for deeper interpretations, and represents a compelling challenge to facilitator, therapist, and participant, who form an important trinity.

APPLICATION

One of the basic ingredients of all poetry therapy sessions, individual or group, is the genuine feelings that poems are able to tap. The atmosphere in Poetry Therapy must, therefore, be honest. What one does not say, the poem does say. Each is revealed as a person who hurts, enjoys, hates, smiles, and feels. The therapist is no exception and cannot hide for long behind knowledge, degrees, status, or whatever. One of the poems that has been used most effectively in uncovering feelings and laying open many defenses is entitled "A Poison Tree" by William Blake. The first four lines seem to do the trick. It reads:

> I was angry with my friend:
> I told my wrath, my wrath did end.
> I was angry with my foe:
> I told it not, my wrath did grow.

The poem opens up many vistas of feelings that touch upon theoretical approaches of psychotherapy and personality.

Groups are either closed or open, depending upon a host of circumstances. They are composed of both sexes as a rule, with a wide range of problems. Sometimes adolescents, young adults, and adults are together. Sometimes they are in separate groups. The addition of poetry to the therapeutic experience does not change the theoretical vantage point of the therapy or the therapist. Questions related to theory and practice still remain.

In general, most individuals, except the acting-out, the medicated and depressed who are "out of it," the extremely disturbed person who can't sit still or won't stop talking (and even they in some instances), can avail themselves of the healing potential inherent in Poetry Therapy. This writer has also conducted poetry therapy sessions, individual and group, with the blind, physically handicapped, mentally handicapped, and illiterate; it has been found to be an effective healing modality.

Because poetry is involved with metaphor and simile, primary processes are easily activated. Thus the skill of the therapist involves not only proficiency in therapy but a wide acquaintance with all kinds of poems—classical, modern, universal, good, and bad. Because the therapist may not have the background in the area of poetry, poetry therapy facilitators can help in the process of effecting a sound program. In this context, therapists can learn a new modality and can also concentrate more fully on the treatment aspect of their concern.

Finally, a word of caution. Poetry in therapy is a most seductive challenge in the nature of things. Each therapist sooner or later learns the importance of being aware of limitations. To illustrate, the poem "Knowing Pains," written after a disturbing group session, enabled the writer of this chapter to cope with his own blind spots.

> I studied parts
> of a flower
>
> to understand
> its flowering.

> I learned much
> about my limits.

> I had forgotten
> Earth and climate.

CASE EXAMPLE

The case example presented is a segment from a group session. This is offered in light of exploratory possibilities. The emphasis is on process and how poetry moves this process within the framework of a therapeutic milieu.

In this example, Martin R. is singled out as the focal point around which the group enters into the poetry therapy situation. Each session was an hour in length. Meetings were held weekly. This was an open group. Each week there was generally one or two new people, while one of the old members was discharged. All the members mentioned had been together from the initial session and had stayed together throughout an eight-session experience. The group was composed of 10 members (only eight for the final session), a facilitator, and the poetry therapist.

Martin R., a 39-year-old male, had been institutionalized off and on for some 12 years. He was married and had a five-year-old son, whom he "dearly loved" and who was a source of ambivalent feelings. Martin was diagnosed as a person who suffered from chronic depression.

Both of Martin's parents were alive. Martin was the eldest of four children (two sisters and a brother). He had dropped out of college in his third year, after realizing that "accounting was not for me." His vocational history included all kinds of odds and ends such as maintenance, tour guide, gardener, truck driver, news vendor, and messenger. He also had spent three years in the military, primarily as a clerk-typist, and received an honorable discharge. As far as could be ascertained, he had had no history of hospitalization while in the military.

Throughout his formative years he was close to both parents and "got along fairly well with others." He claimed his troubles began when "I began to feel too much pain in my head." And that started, as he remembered, when his brother, who was still a high school junior, came home one day and told his parents he had gotten a job as an usher in a theater. Martin, four years older than his brother, felt "like he'd been hit with a ton of bricks." He became consciously aware of feeling inferior to his brother and sisters. "I remember feeling as if the world had caved in. My younger brother had gotten a job and it made me feel like he had pulled me down." In the poetry therapy session, the third he had attended, he wrote these lines:

I remember my brother as a hustling man
Who got a job and made me feel
Like an also-ran.

The group began to question his "also-ran" description, and it became quite evident that he felt hostile toward his brother. This can be seen in the following lines he wrote during the session:

My brother Pete is a good soul
Who knows his place and goal
My brother Pete I love and hate him so
But my hatred steals the show.

Since this session was about to come to an end, it was suggested that Martin think about what he had said and had written and comment upon them at the next session. He agreed to do so. At the beginning of the following session, which was the last, he addressed the group by reading:

This is a brief note to all of you.
I really felt last week
I had been gotten to. So I'll
tell you, it ain't easy to
be true, to reach
inside and get something
out which is new and
you don't know how to
put into words. You're
shaky at first, but then
it all fits
and falls into place.

There were eight people at this session; segments of the interaction process follow.

ALICE (a 48-year-old mother of three, diagnosed as hypochondriacal and depressive): Martin, everytime I hear you talk, it's like I'm hearing myself. We're both playing broken records—like we're losers.

MARTIN: I don't know about that.

FACILITATOR: Martin, what don't you know?

MARTIN: I don't know—maybe.

JIM (a 52-year-old male, father of two, diagnosed as borderline schizophrenic): I agree. Maybe you don't know. But you sound like me and I sound like Alice just said. I sound like both of you. I wrote this over the weekend:

Martin wrote some lines which hurt me
Real bad. I'm glad to hear them
Again and again. I'm no longer sad.
Martin may have planted the truth
Which will help me grow healthy fruit.

POETRY THERAPIST: I hear you saying, Jim, that Martin's lines began to have a big effect upon your feelings, particularly over the weekend. Maybe others in the group felt the same or had other reactions.

JERRY (a 49-year-old widower, father of five, diagnosed as chronic alcoholic): Yes, I felt something too. It seems I hear lots of honesty at times and then run, unless someone says, write, or I read about my situation.

FACILITATOR: What do you feel right now, Martin?

MARTIN: This group does funny things to me. When I'm in the group I learn a lot I don't understand. But I know I'm learning. And it seems to get to me too when I'm on the ward—in my room. It's like the group's fault I'm writing. Here is what I wrote about an hour ago. Here are my lines:

Whenever I'm angry, I feel inferior
Whenever I feel inferior, I'm angry
They both go hand in hand
I often wonder why I'm angry
I haven't learned to be
Totally me and free to be.

FACILITATOR: Martin, have you discussed how you feel with your own therapist? It looks to me that you say some things in here that you find tough to share with others.

JIM: Martin! How does this grab you? I picked it up from somewhere. I thought it was deep stuff, but the more I read it the easier it becomes. It's a line from Shakespeare, so they tell me: "Things growing are not ripe until their season." Maybe you're coming into your own now. What do you say?

MARTIN: This line you've read reminds me of what the Bible says about there being a season to everything—I guess my season is here. I still find it hard to communicate easily.

FACILITATOR: Getting well inside often comes in slow stages.

MARTIN: I guess that's so. Getting well on the outside also comes in slow stages.

POETRY THERAPIST: What do you mean? I'm not quite clear what you're saying.

MARTIN: (hesitatingly) I'm saying—I guess I am—that many times my head and body were telling me to avoid something or say no. I found myself saying yes and not meaning it. What a price to pay. I needed a lot of strength to keep my body from showing I was lying.

TONI (a 25-year-old divorcee diagnosed as chronic depressive): Martin, I know what you mean. I suffer too, like you. We both need psychological tune-ups.

POETRY THERAPIST: Toni! What is a psychological tune-up?

TONI: It's keeping your mind, body, and heart in close—well, I mean all these three should feel right with each other. I wrote these lines and I think they fit. Here:

> When my mind, body, and heart feel right
> I'm at my best with all my might.
> When all three are out of whack
> I feel I'm going to crack.

MARTIN: Right! I agree! It takes time. Like the talking about the seasons before—

POETRY THERAPIST: It seems to me you haven't been able to express this before. Do you feel what you're saying? How do you feel it?

MARTIN: This is the last session. I'll just say I feel what we're talking about will take time. I've just got to learn more patience. By the way, I've kept a notebook and diary—I don't have them with me. But I remember a line I've written goes like this:

> patience is a tough school
> in learning self-rule.

The session ended shortly after and all group members, including Martin, were discharged in a few days.

SUMMARY

Poetry in the therapeutic experience is used as an adjunctive tool. Poetry can be used in therapy on a one-to-one basis and/or group basis. Furthermore, the accent in Poetry Therapy is on the person, unlike a poetry workshop where the accent is on the poem. Poetry Therapy is an eclectic experience. Theories of personality and psychotherapy underlying the field can be found in current psychotherapy and personality constructs.

The use of poetry in therapy is based on an assumption of openness, self-awareness of one's body and feelings, and acceptance of here-and-now life experiences. Inherent in this experience, as in all therapy experiences, are educational and spiritual elements that make for conditions of focusing on personal capacities for growth and creativity. The fact that a poem is saying what a person may be feeling acts like a Greek chorus in moving the drama along.

Poetry in therapy is being introduced in a wide variety of milieus at the present time and is greatly aided in its growth by especially trained facilitators who are knowledgeable in poetry and supervised in therapy. At present there are not many therapists versed in poetry. Thus the facilitator acts as a positive factor in the poetry therapy process.

Because process and psychotherapy movement are closely related, the use of poetry in therapy has carryover affects when individuals are away from their sessions. Often this reflects itself in poetry reading and/or writing by members.

Poetry Therapy can be employed with the young and the old of all sexes, races, beliefs, and educational levels. Illiterates are not excluded, since people will often gesture and utter in their idiosyncratic manner their essential feelings. The same holds true for individuals who do not speak or write the native language of the group but are acquainted with their own.

Poetry Therapy is not a cure-all and makes no claims as such. There are contraindications for its use and for those who are involved in its practice. At present, the evidence for many of the tentative observations and conclusions is in need of further research and data.

Poetry Therapy is involved in developing a central rationale out of its diverse experiences, practical reports, and observations. The field is really at its beginnings, though it may be considered as an old-new discipline.

At present, too, there are psychotherapists who are averse to the use of poetry or any of the arts in therapy. Also there are poets who believe that their field is being bastardized. Nevertheless, while there are numerous questions of a controversial nature that need to be addressed and answered, Poetry Therapy is proceeding at its own pace.

A healthy skepticism, an open mind, and respect on the part of poets and therapists for one another's frame of reference will smooth the road of poetry in therapy. At the same time conclusions drawn here point in the direction of the metaphor and simile as kinfolk in the healing experience.

REFERENCES

Abrams, A. S. (1978). Poetry therapy in the psychiatric hospital. In A. Lerner (Ed.), *Poetry in the therapeutic experience.* Elmsford, NY: Pergamon.

Ansell, C. (1978). Psychoanalysis and poetry. In A. Lerner (Ed.), *Poetry in the therapeutic experience.* Elmsford, NY: Pergamon.

Aristotle. (1941). Poetics. In R. McKeon (Ed.), *The basic works of Aristotle.* New York: Random House.

Blanton, S. (1960). *The healing power of poetry.* New York: Crowell.

Edgar, K. (1978). The epiphany of the self via poetry therapy. In A. Lerner (Ed.), *Poetry in the therapeutic experience.* Elmsford, NY: Pergamon.

Freud, S. (1949). The relation of the poet to day-dreaming. In E. Jones (Ed.), *Collected papers,* vol. 4. London: Hogarth Press and the Institute of Psycho-Analysis.

Harrower, M. (1972). *The therapy of poetry.* Springfield, IL: Thomas.

Jones, R. E. (1969). Treatment of a psychotic patient by poetry therapy. In J. J. Leedy (Ed.), *Poetry therapy.* Philadelphia: Lippincott.

Jung, C. G. (1933). *Modern man in search of a soul.* New York: Harcourt.

Lauer, R. (1978). Abuses of poetry therapy. In A. Lerner (Ed.), *Poetry in the therapeutic experience.* Elmsford, NY: Pergamon.

Leedy, J. J. (Ed.). (1969). *Poetry therapy.* Philadelphia: Lippincott.

Leedy, J. J. (Ed.). (1973). *Poetry the healer.* Philadelphia: Lippincott.

Lerner, A. (Ed.). (1978). *Poetry in the therapeutic experience.* Elmsford, NY: Pergamon.

Meerloo, J. A. M. (1969). The universal language of rhythm. In J. J. Leedy (Ed.), *Poetry therapy.* Philadelphia: Lippincott.

Prescott, F. C. (1959). *The poetic mind.* Ithaca, NY: Cornell University Press. (Original work published 1922)

Rothenberg, A. (1973). Poetry and psychotherapy: Kinships and contrasts. In J. J. Leedy (Ed.), *Poetry the healer.* Philadelphia: Lippincott.

Rubin, R. J. (1978). *Using bibliotherapy: A guide to theory and practice.* Phoenix, AZ: Oryx.

Schloss, G. A. (1976). *Psychopoetry.* New York: Grosset & Dunlap.

Schloss, G. A., & Grundy, D. E. (1978). Action techniques in psychopoetry. In A. Lerner (Ed.), *Poetry in the therapeutic experience.* Elmsford, NY: Pergamon.

Stainbrook, E. (1978). Poetry and behavior in the psychotherapeutic experience. In A. Lerner (Ed.), *Poetry in the therapeutic experience.* Elmsford, NY: Pergamon.

Chapter 46

PRIMAL THERAPY[1]

ROBERT F. A. SCHAEF, DENNIS O. KIRKMAN, and BARBARA UNGASHICK

Perhaps the best known of all the innovative psychotherapeutic approaches is Primal Therapy. I imagine that it is one of the most frequently referred-to systems in this book. After searching for the most qualified person to write this chapter, I was lucky enough to be able to tap the combined experience of Robert Schaef, Dennis Kirkman, and Barbara Ungashick, all of the Denver Primal Center.

Primal Therapy is certainly innovative, even though study of the history of psychotherapy indicates it has close parallels with the first of the modern group psychotherapists, Anton Mesmer, and with the work of the founder of modern group psychotherapy, J. L. Moreno, in both theory and operation. Primal Therapy closely resembles New Identity Process, which is covered within this book.

The reader is in for an intellectual treat in this chapter, which provides a compact authoritative statement of the theory and practice of Primal Therapy.

Primal Therapy is an educative process based on the individual's natural movement toward fulfilling his or her vast potential as a human being. The emphasis is on the experiencing and expression of earlier blocked feelings and on their integration into total life functioning. We believe consciousness and physiology are a product of organism–environment interaction from the moment of conception. Traumatic interactions create a maladaptiveness that continues into adulthood. Therapy consists of guiding the client to the inner body systems (brain/mind, muscular, proprioceptive, etc.), which carry the memory of earlier, usually painful, events or states that were denied full awareness at the time because of their devastating character. These events or states are fully experienced, usually over a series of sessions, and reintegrated into the body and consciousness so that the client may fully function in the present with greatly expanded awareness.

HISTORY

Arthur Janov was a practicing psychotherapist with 17 years of experience when during a session one of his patients told the bizarre story of Ortiz, an entertainer, who wore diapers, drank milk from a bottle, and cried out, "Mommy!" and "Daddy!" until he vomited into a plastic bag. Janov, seeing his patient's fascination with the act, encouraged him to call out "Mommy! Daddy!"

> Suddenly, he was writhing on the floor in agony. His breathing was rapid, spasmodic: "Mommy! Daddy!" came out of his mouth almost involuntarily in loud screeches. He appeared to be in a coma or hypnotic state. The writhing gave way to small convulsions, and finally, he released a piercing, deathlike scream that rattled the walls of my office. The entire episode lasted only a few minutes, and neither Danny nor I had any idea what had happened. All he could say afterwards was: "I made it! I don't know what, but I can *feel!*" (Janov, 1970, pp. 9–10).

Early associates of Janov describe him as being a critical observer whose ideas developed both from what he saw and what his patients told him they were experiencing. Janov did not develop a cognitive, interpretive structure to describe the phenomena but recognized these events as important in and of themselves, allowed them to run their course, and then through feedback from the patient determined what had taken place. Eventually he saw people as reliving old, forgotten, and painful experiences in a pattern that the individual's nervous system demanded, not one that was consciously directed. There appeared to be a neurological sequencing of activity that was not intellectually controlled by the patient.

[1] We wish to acknowledge these people for their contribution toward the development of the concepts contained herein: Jules Roth, Helen Roth, and Warren Baker.

From these surprising beginnings, Janov began formulating a theory that would become known as Primal Therapy and that he would later claim to be "the cure for neurosis." In 1970 he published the first book of his theories and observations, *The Primal Scream,* which possibly was read by more people than any other in its field.

In the early days of his new practice, it has been reported he worked largely with young adult patients. They had experience with drugs and hallucinogens, probably had less intact defense systems, and may have been attracted to an antipsychiatry philosophy that allowed enormous individual freedom of expression and seemed to encourage a certain condemnation of the establishment. (Yoko Ono and John Lennon were two of the early patients of this genre.) So it is possible that these young patients contributed greatly to the early development of the therapy because they were more willing, open, and perhaps adventuresome than the average clinician's clientele.

It is further reported that Janov was very excited by what he was learning and approached his colleagues in the psychological community in California. His ideas were met with rejection and sometimes even ridicule. Janov was challenging some precepts long held sacred among the professionals—he was attempting to overthrow traditional concepts concerning the nature of human beings. He was redefining psychotherapy, and perhaps that was threatening to the traditionalists. (Historically, of course, this is a familiar response when revolutionary ideas are introduced.) His critics claimed that he emphasized the sensational aspects of his success, did not report his failures, and adopted a theatrical approach to treatment.

He later took complete control of Primal Therapy by having the name trademarked so that only he could use it legally. (This has since been challenged in court by the International Primal Association, which won, although Janov appealed the decision.)

Additionally, he states in his writings that only a therapist with his certification may practice Primal Therapy.

Probably as a result of Janov's attitude in *The Primal Scream* toward professionals and the deceptive simplicity of the concepts, many nonprofessionals established themselves as primal therapists. Ill trained and lacking in experience, many outright charlatans and quacks, along with the benevolent ignorant, rode the crest of the primal popularity of the early seventies.

Primal Therapy had become more than an exciting contribution to the body of human knowledge, it had become "the in thing," replacing the encounter movement of the sixties in general public appeal. But aside from the dilettantes and those attempting to establish a new lifestyle away from a world that rewarded nonfeeling, there were many who saw it as legitimately offering hope after a lifetime of suffering.

Janov attempted to define the therapy as being very precise and predictable with techniques that, once learned, could be used on anyone and produce the desired results. For example, he expected the therapeutic process to be naturally chronological. It seemed reasonable that the patient should start with some feeling in the present and work his way backward, into childhood events, and eventually to preverbal, even prenatal occurrences. This linearity did not bear itself out in practice.

Philosophical disagreements erupted from time to time at the Primal Institute. One major schism took place in 1974 when many of the staff and patients left. The Denver Primal Center was formed out of this separation and operates on the premise that the therapy, far from being precise and linear, is actually extremely individualistic. Janov's original belief was that the *method,* once perfected, would help all "neurotics." This is not true. Everyone simply does not fit Janov's model of technique. While there are similarities among patients, the overriding factor is that each person has a peculiar "track" or succession of neurological events; even more particular to the individual is the meaning of those events.

There was a wane of interest in Primal Therapy in the mid-seventies as the fashion died out and most of the psychotherapeutic establishment still staunchly refused to consider the validity of Janov's claims. But now, over twenty-five years since that first "primal," it seems that Primal Therapy has, after all, survived as a radical new way to understand the human process of life.

CURRENT STATUS

The recognized authority and seat on Primal Therapy are Arthur Janov and his institute in Los Angeles, The Primal Institute. Primarily an outpatient clinic, Janov treated patients in his traditional approach to Primal Therapy, which began with a three-week intensive therapy program and included follow-up sessions over a period of one year. There are probably about 200 therapists and/or centers practicing Primal or a Primal-type Therapy around the world. These are concentrated mainly in the New York City area, California, the Great Lakes region, and Toronto. The Denver Primal Center is the second largest center for Primal Therapy and offers a variety of programs for clients.

Primal Therapy has made an impact not only in the United States, but in many other countries as well. There is considerable interest among the lay population in particular in Australia, Canada, northern Europe, and especially Germany, where there are not enough trained therapists to treat those who desire Primal Therapy.

Training is difficult to come by, as Janov trains only people that have been patients at his institute for some time. Once trained, these therapists are defranchised should they leave the Primal Institute to practice on their own (1976). The Denver Primal Center will train the interested professional and encourages such interest. (There are probably many more practicing psychotherapists using some primal techniques than we are aware of who have never had any formal primal training or experience but who are attracted to the philosophy.)

Courses that include the discussion of Primal Therapy are and have been offered at the university and graduate level for several years. Some of these go under unfortunate titles such as "Fad Therapies" (University of Colorado Medical School), and "Pop Psychotherapy" (Metropolitan State College of Denver). Still other universities, particularly those with psychology departments that have a humanistic orientation, include Primal Therapy in their general overview of psychotherapies.

Janov is the only person who wrote anything significant in volume and exposure on the subject. He also published the *Journal of Primal Therapy*. The Denver Primal Center publishes the *Denver Primal Journal*. There have been a limited number of articles in the general literature. Many of these were written from a critical stance as we continued to see the close association of Primal Therapy with Arthur Janov reduce the objectivity of these reports. Most articles reacted negatively to what they considered an oversimplistic and sensational presentation of a rather complex theory in his first book *The Primal Scream* (1970).

From the beginning Janov had made efforts to prove his theories. He had his own research institute—The Primal Foundation. The bulk of his research attempted to show that there are significant and permanent physiological changes that occur as a result of having "primals." Such manifestations of tension reduction as lowered body temperature, lower blood pressures, and alterations in brain-wave patterns were shown to be a direct result of "primaling." Janov published many of these studies in his book, *Primal Man, The New Consciousness* (1975).

Independent research is starting to develop around such areas as the effects of prenatal and natal experiences on later personality development. While not primal per se, they do support some of Janov's basic contentions that very early trauma can be responsible for neurosis and psychosis. One well-known example is Frederick Leboyer (1975), who has been a pioneer in the gentle birthing movement. Preliminary follow-up studies done by Rapoport (1975–76) show that children who had Leboyer births were at age three and four more well adjusted, that is, happier, more tranquil, more relaxed children than their counterparts who had had standard hospital births. In addition, the infant is a far more sensitive organism than the pain-barrier theories of psychoanalysis allow. The exciting research on endorphins and

the recent development of "infant psychiatry" at the Menninger Clinic all fit and support primal theory, however little this work attributes to it.

In 1972 in Montreal, the International Primal Association was formed. It had been active mainly on the East Coast. Some published material is available, and an annual convention is held.

Those interested in finding a psychotherapist who practices Primal Therapy may contact the local psychological association in their city, and the Primal Institute.

THEORY

Primal theory of personality started with observations of the process of psychotherapy and has grown within the pragmatics of the therapist-client interaction. Theory construction of this sort provides a series of assumptions that are intimately tied to and guide therapeutic practice. Such assumptions usually cover the genesis, development, and modification of organismic malfunctioning. However, since therapists have some goal for their clients, a theory of wellness develops alongside the theory of "neurosis."

Some primal assumptions are firmly validated; those more recently generated from the cutting edge of practice are more tenuously held. Others have not held up because new data have proven them false. What follows are general statements of theoretical beliefs and a summary of the basic assumptions of Primal Therapy.

One's notion of reality is based on how he or she selects and processes incoming data (Spinelli & Pribram, 1967). How input is selected and processed is a function of the structure of the individual's nervous system (Festinger, Ono, Burnham, & Bamber, 1967). This, in turn, determines the quality of the individual's consciousness (Sperry, 1951). The structure of the nervous system is a result of genetic determinants evolving over millions of years, in a dialectic relationship with the environment— from the conception of the organism, through ontogeny, and continuing for the life of the organism. An organism is structurally determined by an interaction of what it is and what environment it lives in. In response to a highly acidic or low-oxygen environment, a paramecium will manufacture specific proteins to accommodate and survive. These become actual physical modifications to structure and further affect how the animal will function. This is ever-continuing and is a process of growth for living organisms. The higher up the phylogenetic scale, the more pronounced are the effects of inadequate environments (Simeons, 1960). That is to say, the more advanced the animal, the more profound are the effects of developmental deficiencies.

For many humans the *in utero* environment can be inadequate and stressful. The fetus responds to and is affected by physical and psychobiological events in the mother. The responses range from mild irritation to actual damage, depending upon the amount of deviation from life-supporting norms. Improper nutrition, disease, and the use of drugs, cigarettes, and alcohol obviously will have an effect, but what has not been generally considered is the "psychological" environment—experienced as physical. It makes sense to us, and is backed by research (Ferreira, 1969) that a psychological variable—for example, maternal anxiety, can mediate an excess of adrenal alkaloids to the child and will induce a stress state in the same way a physical variable such as excess smoking can. The infant responds viscerally to all stimuli via the autonomic nervous system, and this may form the child's characteristic style for responding to later stress. As the cortex develops, the capacity for repressing, somaticizing, and symbolizing those early events increases. These traumas will later manifest in dreams, personality structure, and symptomatology. It has been traditional to regard the *in utero* environment as a neutral experience, with the baby emerging as a tabula rasa. But the logic of our biological development and our own clinical observations tell us that often those early times can be truly "at the root" of our problems.

As the infant matures and his or her needs continue to be unfulfilled, the situation begins to compound in seriousness. The infant will pass through a number of important developmental stages for which he or she is inadequately prepared. These are physiologically triggered events meant to correspond, by reason of evolution, with a cumulation of physical and emotional readiness for their occurrence. These stages happen whether or not that individual is prepared for them. If, because of severe trauma, a current hostile environment, or previous assaults on its developing mechanisms, the child is not ready for the next stage, we may find an individual whose behavior and attitudes reflect either an arrest at a certain developmental stage of an incomplete development (Pearce, 1977). For example, a child should be ready at around age 10 months to leave the mother and begin to explore more independently the surrounding world. However, the child will need to return frequently to assure himself that mother is still there and has not left. If past experience has taught the child to doubt that mother will be there when he returns, he may opt to never "leave." This child may eventually become the overdependent adult, unable to make decisions, passive-aggressive, asthmatic, and so forth. On the other hand, another child may have learned as an infant that his or her signals for attention and to have needs met were ignored. Adapting to this limited nourishment, this child formed an attitude of independence—"I can do it myself"—long before the appropriate age. His or her personality is molded with not only independence, but a withdrawal from closeness

and intimacy and an inability to form significant attachments.

In Primal Therapy we feel that it is not enough just to discuss these arrested or inadequate levels of development. In the therapeutic setting it is also necessary for the client to return not only to the memory, but also the feelings associated with it.

Our Western culture encourages the suppression of feelings and praises those who refuse to display their emotions. For example, Jacqueline Kennedy was lauded for her "strength" and "courage" at not weeping during the harrowing events in 1963. Little boys are taught that it's not manly to cry, while aggressive or assertive tendencies in little girls are discouraged in favor of coy and affectionate responses.

This deep cultural behavior goes against what is basically human, and causes conflict in an organism whenever an emotional response is called for but cannot be felt or expressed. The individual who is cut off from his or her feelings loses a basic organic avenue for existence—one which provides the color, texture, pleasure, and appreciation of life—and is condemned to live in a flatness not ever biologically intended. Those who remain connected to their feeling selves may learn to reproach themselves and feel guilty for being incapable of "achieving" a level of functioning that society demands. In losing this connectedness to our central selves, we cannot ever truly be connected to each other, and so we form a world that can incubate violence, cruelty, and terrible insensitivity to life.

In summary, the assumptions of primal therapists are as follows:

1. Experiences are stored in the organism from the moment of conception on. This notion runs counter to most psychological and medical belief that the embryo, fetus, and even the newborn are insensate (Ferreira, 1969). Witness the way circumcision is performed on the neonate.

2. Because the organism is dependent on the environment to have survival needs met and because, gratuitously or otherwise, they are not always met, some of its experiences are traumatic.

3. The earlier in the development of the organism a traumatic experience occurs, the more profound the effect.

4. Experiences of a hostile environment or of events that are life-threatening or traumatic are blocked from full impact or awareness and distort straight-line growth. Cells modify shape or structure, body parts lose sensibility, events are forgotten or not perceived by the senses, and so forth.

5. Fragments of blocked experiences continue into adult life. A seemingly unconnected numbness in

the left hand of an adult may later be associated with repeated slapping of the left hand while learning to write as a child.

6. Experiences stored in the organism are retrievable; that is, they can be felt again.

7. Defenses that interfere with growth are jettisoned by the client at his or her own pace.

8. Feeling and integrating earlier blocked experiences and expressing previously unexpressed feelings is of therapeutic benefit.

9. Our culture supports the suppression of both the expression and memory of negative feelings.

10. Education is necessary to identify feelings and the sensations that signify feelings, especially those that are remnants of early trauma.

11. Feeling *is* the basic material and modus operandi of change.

METHODOLOGY

The application process in Primal Therapy consists of writing an autobiography, giving a history, having a physical examination, and then having a preliminary and final interview. Upon acceptance clients are matched with a therapist at a full staff meeting and given a starting date.

The full program involves a three-week intensive during which the client, who devotes full time to therapy, is seen daily for a session lasting up to three hours. The therapist is on call twenty-four hours a day and additional emergency sessions may be scheduled. Each client is seen twice by a therapist of the opposite sex from the primary therapist and may attend up to six group sessions in addition to the regular sessions. At groups the client becomes familiar with the other therapists. After the three weeks the client has the choice of individual or group sessions with the therapist(s) of his choice.

Others may choose to begin therapy with only one or two weeks of intensive therapy and follow-up sessions. Also, there are those who begin with weekly individual sessions and forego the intensive. We recommend an 8- to 12-month period be committed to therapy.

The setting in which we do our work is somewhat unusual. The center has two group rooms and a number of small individual rooms. There are no windows. The floors and walls are padded and soundproofed. Pillows, blankets, and tissues are the only furnishings. Sessions are usually carried out in dim lighting. The facility is open 24 hours so that clients can "feel" on their own, or with another client who will sit for them, or can meet as a group at any time without a staff member present. Another important modification of usual psychotherapeutic practice is that the rooms are scheduled for three hours per session: Sessions run from one to three hours.

In every session there is an emphasis on feelings never before felt, never before spoken, about things that hurt—words, looks, deeds. Memories are uncovered; neglect is reexperienced in a physical way. Need becomes not just a psychological concept but a gaping wound that has been covered up for survival's sake—a physiological deficit that has required a deviation around the potential development of the organism. These are factors in the client's development that, while they are disintegrating or traumatic in and of themselves, are compounded or "overlaid" by later events, usually within the family. The lack of connection within the organism is increased when the attempts to "run off" the pain or attempts to reintegrate are blocked; what is natural expression to the person is denied. It is this natural expression that therapy attempts to reestablish.

An example of this dynamic is Carl, whose application and interviews provided us with most of the following information. He started drinking when he was 19. Previous to that he had been diagnosed as a catatonic schizophrenic. For three years, from age 16 to 19, he had been unable to find the impetus to get out of a chair. Sitting, he would watch the hands of the clock spin, as time flew by. Although he came from an affluent and well-educated family (mother a biology professor), Carl was unable to work for more than three months at a time, couldn't apply himself in any endeavor, and gravitated toward the lifestyle of a hardcore inner-city wino. Carl came into therapy not because of difficulty in feeling, but because of a great excess of pain occurring beyond his ability to assimilate. He was unable to function and described feelings of imminent dying and blackness. His appearance was unkempt and disheveled, and he vacillated between expressions of apathy and great fear. Carl was accepted for therapy and began with a three-week intensive.

During his intensive he talked predominantly about his mother; particularly that she was constantly undermining and criticizing him. Carl described a scene when he was seven where his mother had made an especially cutting remark (a useful tool in Primal Therapy is developing a scene; this involves helping the client piece together in as full a fashion as possible the details surrounding an earlier, significant event):

T: What would you say to her when she'd hurt you like that, Carl?

C: Oh, I could never say anything. I'd just withdraw farther into myself.

T: Tell her now. Just look right at her and tell her how it feels.

Confronting the feeling so directly, Carl was rarely able to get out more than a few words before he would fall upon the floor, writhing and nearly convulsing, arch his back, with his head against the padded wall, and appear to have great difficulty in breathing. After going through this sequence many times and approaching it from different aspects of his life (how he felt his father had died trying to save him from his mother, losing his ability to play basketball, circumstances around the beginning of his catatonia), he began to piece together what it seemed his body was attempting to resolve.

In these sessions Carl revealed details of an especially traumatic birth and difficulties early in his life. He reported that as a child he always wanted to be active—very active. He wanted, in fact, never to sit still. This behavior represented a way for him to deal with the early pain he had incurred. It served to "run off" the excess, to keep the channels to direct expression open. However, as so often happens in this culture, spontaneity, rambunctiousness, and unorthodox behaviors were not suffered gladly in Carl's family. Directives like "straighten up," "be still," "behave yourself" presented familial and social demands for him to deny primal impulses, however symbolic, and to start jelling into the cultural mold. What opportunity he had for integration was thrown away by the imperative to deny that opening. The care and environment Carl required as a child, *particular* to his *in utero,* trauma, were not there. In fact, as is usually the case, the opposite was true.

Primal therapists assume that there are etiologic components to trends of thought—that language, how it is used and its content, is symbolic of experience. The experience is what we are after, since it is its neglect and its expression that is most often at the roots of disintegrity. The therapist attempts to guide the client underneath the hubris of his or her own symbolization process to the "heart of the matter." This guiding ranges from merely providing safety, to the mechanics of the therapy, to intuitive grasps of what we call "openings." An opening is an opportunity whereby the person, either of his or her own accord or with some help (as with Carl), will begin what looks like a neural sequence. In psychoanalysis, the client may go from thought to thought with occasional affect. The analyst is in the position of knowing what the patterns and content of those meanderings might mean (in conjunction with transference, resistance, dreams, etc.). But primal therapists believe when the client is given the safety to not have to symbolize, or verbally defend, his body will begin to *experience,* the meaning of which is his interpretation alone.

"Tracking" is another word used to describe what looks like an autonomous neural process. Steven Rose in *The Conscious Brain* (1973) describes a neuronal pathway model for memory, learning, and information processing:

> In transversing a particular sequence of memory traces, the brain proceeds from state to state along the different individual traces in an ordered manner. The phenomenon is analogous to synaptic conduction or axonal firing—all of these processes are unidirectional. One state must "fire" another almost irreversibly. So the individual brain states associated with memories must presumably be linked by synaptic logic into a sequence in which one follows almost inevitably from another. It is as if the arrow of time is located at the synapse, at least so far as memories are concerned. (p. 210)

The task of the therapist is to guide the person into ever more *specifics* of what causes what feelings. This is an ideal, whereby the client proceeds in what looks like and sounds like an autonomous neural sequencing. This is the organism healing itself. There are times when not even one word is required from the therapist. On the other hand, there are times when the pain is so great, psychological damage so extensive, defensive structure so tight or intricate that it is not initially possible for one's own natural healing processes to emerge. It is at times like these when it is up to the therapist to become a catalyst, so to speak.

"Sequencing" is an ideal of the healing process aimed for where the organism is healing and integrating itself in a way and at a pace that is intrinsic to it, rather than by taking on additional effluvia of a therapist. It can begin by the therapist picking up on an "opening," that is, where feelings may be ascending. These are exemplified below:

BEN: You know, I'm really scared right now. My arms and legs are tingly.

T: What are you scared of?

B: Oh, I don't know. I guess that I'm not going to do this right, that you're not going to approve.

T: Have you ever known this before?

B: Oh yeah, every time I get up to give a presentation at the office all I can think of is how the other architects are going to respond. You know, really negative. It nearly incapacitates me and my stomach goes into knots like this.

T: Ben, as much as you can now, focus on those sensations and let your body express them in whatever way that matches the feeling.

B: (trembles and sobs for a few minutes) Something just occurred to me about this. I remember being in a school play when I was five and my mother and uncle were in the audience. It seems like I fucked up what I was supposed to do and afterward I was really ashamed and upset. When I saw my mother and uncle coming backstage, I wanted to run to her and cry but I saw this look on her face. She and my uncle were laughing. She thought what had happened was funny! She was laughing at me (begins to sob deeply)! Don't laugh at me, goddamn it! Don't laugh at me! Mommy! Mommy! . . .

From here Ben reexperienced a time even younger when his mother misread or missed what he needed. When he was not appeased he would continue to fret and cry. Out of frustration, she would scold and punish him.

It became apparent in subsequent postsessions[1] that Ben learned from his mother that his feelings and what he needed were not "right," they were something to be ashamed of. He also realized the summation of those hurts became symbolized at the time when he was in the play. In later situations in which he was called on to perform, he would suffer debilitating anxiety because of what the situation provoked and meant to him: that he would not be seen and be made to feel worthless. With the removal of societal inhibitions Ben was able to retrieve a part of himself he had had to disown. His body resolved it in an orderly, sequential fashion. The same feeling was traced from a present situation to a previous situation, to a memory, to a prior memory until the initial causal matrix was discovered. Those memories had an emotional charge to them. Because he could not experience or express those early hurts, he was driven to symbolize and generalize in his attempt to integrate himself.

Group sessions vary in format and structure. One form follows a workshop model in that one therapist might meet with the same four to six clients for several hours on a continuous periodic schedule (daily or weekly). These groups may be directed at a special area such as sexuality or creativity, and the purpose is to focus on problems clients have in those areas. The drop-in group is a regularly scheduled group open to any and all clients. They sign in on arrival, before the group starts. They indicate, from the list posted, which therapist they want to work with and which room they will be in. They go into that room and allow whatever feelings emerge while they are waiting for the therapist to come.

The therapists who are working go over the sign-up sheet and divide the clients about equally, each one taking several clients. (Group size has ranged as high as 50 clients with 10 to 12 therapists. However, they tend to be smaller now, with usually two or three therapists working each group.) Therapists then visit their clients twice during a two-hour period, about 15 minutes each time.

Postgroup[2] is announced in all the rooms, and then clients and therapists assemble in the large group room. Lights that have been dimmed are now brightened. During the hour or two that follows, one or two therapists lead the group; they are the focus toward whom comments, questions, and feelings are directed and from whom the majority of responses come.

Postgroup allows for the clients to: continue feeling what was started in the preceding two hours; talk about what they have been feeling, thus giving cognitive structure to what might otherwise be vague feeling experiences; deal with other persons in the room who have, by their presence or in more direct ways, triggered feelings in them and to work through those feelings; and talk about what is happening in their present life. Clients learn from this that others feel in their own unique way and at their own pace and do get better. This helps them to accept themselves and their own process.

The aim of therapy is to provide the environment for gradual movement toward becoming a person who experiences feelings and expresses them appropriately in everyday life as they are evoked, and who also has a process for dealing with an upsurge of feeling that threatens to disrupt or warp functioning. In moving toward this goal, many clients go through one or both of the following steps:

1. Coming to the center and "feeling" on their own. To this end the center is open 24 hours, and over the years has come to be considered a safe place to lie down and express deep feelings at any time of the day or night.
2. A "buddy" system in which one client will "sit" for another as he or she has feelings. The presence of another can facilitate feeling expression for some who cannot do it alone.

At some point, the client will begin to move out and away from the therapeutic environment—will rely less and less on formal sessions. The need to release or run off strong feelings becomes less frequent and diminishes in intensity. Some clients will terminate therapy for months at a time and return occasionally. Others may continue using the facilities on their own or with "buddies" for several years before they have integrated enough material to completely disengage themselves from the security of the center. It is important to us to respect a client's own special timing and intervene only when growth seems to be impeded. Above all else, we value every individual's sense of rightness and truth within himself and will nourish and encourage that awareness to flower so that eventually he can live from that wonderful place inside himself.

APPLICATIONS

When humans fail to live up to the standards imposed by our culture, they are deemed and often consider themselves maladaptive or pathological. What they

---

[1] The latter portion of a session is given over to what we call a postsession. This time provides an opportunity for the client to integrate what he or she has just experienced into full awareness and present life's functioning.

[2] Postgroups and postsessions have very similar functions.

are actually failing to adapt to is a cultural set that is dehumanizing and of itself maladaptive. Their defenses are inadequate, failing to help them adjust to the rigors of day-to-day life. These people are failing to live in an integral fashion; at the same time, they are caught somewhere between the values and expectations of family and culture, and the long-denied and feared primal impulses and expressions they sense in their bodies. Not being able to go in either direction completely, they suffer "nervous breakdowns" or "anxiety attacks" and are vulnerable to labels and diagnoses such as paranoid schizophrenic or manic-depressive, which are in reality all descriptions of symptoms or an organism's attempts to move toward integration, toward healing itself.

These people are in pain—psychologically and often physically—and worse, they have to deny the experience and its expression. While the organism may be attempting reintegration symptomatically and symbolically, those defenses the body has taken on, out of necessity and acculturation, need to be addressed.

Many people who seek out Primal Therapy are "failures" at other types of therapy. They have not been able to grow and change in the ways they want to—the blocks to a complete and comfortable life seem indissoluble. Many have been functioning effectively when they come to the center but report diffuse dissatisfaction with their lives: They want to become more aware of themselves so they may achieve a more fulfilling existence. Others have specific symptoms such as phobias, depression, or drug dependency. Still others have been institutionalized and seek a more humane, pertinent, and individual counseling than they had known.

The information in this section describes clients who have had the full program, the core of which is the three-week intensive. In 1978/79 we experimented with variations on this program to the extent that we now take some clients on a once- or twice-weekly basis. In time we will have data on this new group.

The typical applicant for our full program has been contemplating entering Primal Therapy for more than a year (some as many as seven years). He or she has usually read *The Primal Scream*[3] (Janov, 1970) or other primal literature and searched out our center, many coming from as far as Australia and Germany. Often a usually nonfeeling person will describe having and experiencing deep feelings while reading primal material. Some describe a deep "inner knowing" that this process will help. They then set about planning their lives so they can take the time out for the commitment the therapy requires. At this time many of our applicants have been referred by former clients.

By the time they apply, they are usually highly motivated to become involved in, if somewhat fearful of, the process. However, since they have only a dim perception of the depth and extent of their pain, it is in the first six months that the 2.5 percent who will have dropped out leave. The bulk of these leave during the first month.

A Further Description of Our Client Population

As a group[4] our clients when contrasted with national norms have:

1. Greater birth traumas (premature and postmature, breech, caesarean section, twin, over 10 pounds at birth, especially long or short labor, birth defect, or injury).
2. More trouble with the law, previous psychotherapy and hospitalizations (mental), suicide attempts, "mental illness" in the family, drug and alcohol dependency or heavy usage.
3. More siblings.
4. Fewer marriages: with an average age of 29 years, in this sample 53 percent have never been married (national norm 18 percent).
5. Greater unemployment: 42 percent (national norm 8 percent) are unemployed. This is colored by the fact that a number of people come from distant places and give up their jobs just to do the therapy.

Of the more recently treated 180 clients of the 250 on whom the data were available, 95 percent had multiple psychophysiological disorders. The highest incidence (range = 21 to 81 percent) were in following systems: muscular/skeletal, gastrointestinal, respiratory, special senses, and cardiovascular.

It is our impression that our clients have had more childhood abuse (psychological, sexual, and physical) than the population of patients seen in clinics and by independent psychotherapy practitioners.

While we do not use clinical diagnostic categories in reference to our clients, it is also our impression that our population has included persons whose primary diagnosis would fall into the psychoses, neuroses, personality disorders, psychophysiologic disorders, and special symptoms as defined in the *Diagnostic and Statistical Manual of Mental Disorders* (DSM-IV, 1994).

In summary, then, we have a multiply handicapped client group who have experienced extreme problems in living and are highly motivated to change their life patterns.

---

[3] Some applicants have been led to have high false expectations that have to be dealt with in the initial enquiring interview.

[4] These data are based on 250 consecutively treated clients.

Who Benefits Most

As with most therapies, a highly motivated client committed to enduring the pain and discomfort of the struggle to be real is likely to change for the better. However, there are several types for whom the process is especially suitable.

Persons who are in touch with their bodies seem to move into the process and benefit more easily from Primal Therapy. This stems from the fact that during the therapy session we focus on the body, facies, gestures, large movements, and sensations. Since we are after the recovery and expression of feeling, and feelings start in the body, it is important to move to that level as soon as practicable.[5] We also think that physical data are more reliable of what is happening in an individual than are cognitive data. This again leads us to consider it more efficient to work with body manifestations.

People who are in touch with their bodies may show it in several ways. One such group are those who somatize their pain. This may range from the severe asthmatic or arthritic to the person who carries tension in parts, or all, of his or her body. When they come to therapy, they already have body manifestations of their underlying pain and are easily directed to these entrances of channels into their feelings.

A second group are in touch with their bodies in another fashion. Even though they have learned, for the most part, to ignore body messages (for example: "You're tired, it's time to stop" in favor of some more pressing internalized environmental message: "Quitters never amount to anything"), they are still aware that the body is saying something. With a little help in focusing they begin to find their own "track" into their past history. Persons in this group are often easier to work with than most.

Another group who benefit are people who "can't get anything done." They seem to combine the traits of neurasthenic neurotic, asthenic, and inadequate personality. They are often on welfare or Medicaid.[6] They spend much of their early therapy dealing with feelings that stem from birth and prebirth trauma. The positive changes that occur in this group are generally slower in coming than the second group mentioned above. There is a long period of slow growth followed by a blooming in which they take a place in the world consistent with their chronological age. One reason for the slowness in movement with these people seems to be that, in addition to feeling their feelings in therapy, they must also learn to do things in the real world they never learned as children—they must develop coping mechanisms that other persons have in their repertoire even though they may not be using them efficiently or at all.

CASE EXAMPLE

This study will be a continuation of Carl, who was described in the previous section on methodology. His is not an unusual case, although it does run counter to a general misconception of what Primal Therapy does—to take away defenses and to regress people into nonfunctional states.

Carl came in in a state of "overload." By way of how he looked, moved, what he said, and how he said it, it could be seen that his nervous system was having to process too much pain. He did not have the internal mechanisms to push the pain down, that is, defend, "pull himself out of it." At the same time, his access to what all this meant was quite remote, he was disconnected, and he could not integrate the whole, great mass of feeling at once. The task, then, was twofold: First was to help him lower the level of pain he was living in so that what was experienced could be integrated a tolerable bit at a time. Second was to help him develop access to the lower levels of his psyche/body in a sequential fashion.

Based on this, an opening was taken that represented the level at which he could integrate; that is, experience a feeling, know it was a feeling, and understand where it came from and what it meant to his life. In this case, he could cry about a Joan Baez song he had heard that day. He was allowed and encouraged to cry as much as possible to drain some of the emotional load he carried. He talked about what she said, what it meant to him, and how it made him feel. From there it went to how rock and roll had affected him as a teenager, how it seemed that music was the one thing he could allow in. He proceeded to go into what he would later describe as a birth sequence, which was described earlier. Almost immediately he began to fragment. At this point the therapist addressed the base he had established for himself from when he was a teenager. They talked more and the therapist gradually moved the focus more toward the present, but always with the base Carl established as a reference point. This was to be the tenor of the rest of our meetings: building on what he was able to integrate, lowering the overall pain level, and allowing him to experience ever further the physical trauma he was born and lived in.

Obviously, from what has been said the task with Carl (and what happens often) was to integrate the meaning of what was already happening and to indeed help him develop some internal "stops." His emerging self-acceptance became evident as he found it within himself to not only face and resolve his internal hell, but that

---

[5] General rules for guiding the therapist are to move from the present to the past; general to the specific; cognitive to physical.

[6] We have been unofficially commended by Medicaid for our record in getting patients off their rolls.

other areas of his life were appearing to be within his capacity to change also.

The therapist continued to meet with Carl after the initial "intensive" on a twice-weekly basis for four months and then once a week for four months. The sessions averaged one and one-half to two hours in length. Integrating what he was feeling into his present life enabled Carl to make simple yet profound changes. His attitude that he only deserved to live at a minimal level began to change to where he moved from the inner city (he lived in a bare room in a flophouse) and took an apartment near a park. This was to be the beginning of his development of "defenses" that enabled him to function but that did not impose on his growing integrity. Of the more significant "breakthroughs" was Carl's anger that for so long had imploded and been directed into self-hatred and immobility. Once the intense rage around his biological birth, and later periods, started to be discharged, he no longer depended on large amounts of caffeine for stimulation; in fact, an aliveness began to glow from within that was nurtured and encouraged in his relationship with the therapist. After one especially explosive session, Carl discovered that he could actually see more clearly and had to have the prescription changed on his glasses.

Since Carl enjoyed working with his hands and being out of doors, he became gainfully employed as a carpenter, whereupon he immediately furnished his apartment with a stereo. ("Long live rock 'n roll," he had said.) Carl's relationship with women was one of great frustration for him, as it contained such strong elements of fear and need. However, once with a woman he was seeing and was attracted to, he revealed to her what he considered his infantile need and told her he was afraid she would reject him because of it. The fact that she was open to Carl's just saying what was true for him and giving him the space to explore the feeling in a real context proved of enormous benefit to Carl's "barrier" to women.

He still drank heavily occasionally when his "depression" recurred, but it manifested more as a function of extreme pain (i.e., he knew it was symptomatic of feelings) and happened periodically rather than as a lifestyle. The last contact with Carl was 10 months after he began therapy. He seemed confident and very encouraged by his breaking his lifelong "failure" syndrome. At that time he was going to live in the foothills to work on and live in a cabin.

SUMMARY

Primal Therapy in its theory and methodology has its roots in the humanistic movement. It is primarily client-centered, yet it attempts to synthesize with the "supportive, human" approach a rigorous methodology based on a developmental psychology and the biology of human existence. Underlying the theoretical structure is an implicit belief in the organismic "rightness" of the individual. Each person carries within his or her own healing process that will emerge given the proper therapeutic environment. Each neurological and biochemical individuality is a variation on the theme: disintegrity wrought by unfelt pain. This theme is given a further dimension by a model of neurological functioning that makes Primal Therapy one of the few, if any, systems to have underpinnings in an operational description of neuropsychology. With the theme as a reference point, each individual's variation provides the guidelines for how his or her growth process will proceed. In this way theory may follow from experience and practice—and not vice versa. Since it is basically an open system, information from other fields of thought such as embryology, anthropology, ethology, and so forth, are readily assimilated, providing for a holistic approach, which seems only proper given the complex and interactive nature of human existence.

Primal theory postulates that very early traumatic events and/or negative environmental influences provide the basis for later neurosis and psychosis; memory of these events and circumstances are stored physically in the organism; later retrieval and integration is possible by allowing and encouraging the individual not only to elicit unconscious material cognitively but to actually *go through* the feelings and physical sensations that could not be fully experienced at the time they happened. Maladaptive behaviors are motivated by earlier trauma. One's present life is influenced by earlier behavior patterns formed throughout childhood and adolescence but also during infancy, perinatal, and prenatal times. Attention is finally given to the first nine months of life in the womb as being significant in the development of the personality of the individual.

It is the particular contribution of Primal Therapy to extend our understanding of human functioning to include the prenatal months as important in the therapeutic process. This extension is not mere theoretical formulation but has come out of practice and observation; it has become clear that early events are not only available to us but are most apparent in the symptomatic behavior of all of us. It is these symptoms that bring people into therapy.

The primal approach has been used successfully with a wide variety of symptoms. For example, the lost abilities to think clearly, read and study effectively, and speak directly have been found again after getting in touch with old feelings. Formerly institutionalized patients start to function again in the outside world. Unavoidable impasses between husband and wife, and parent and child, have found alternative resolution through the choice to feel old feelings rather than act out against them.

Psychophysiological disorders have been highly responsive to this regimen. Persons with bad backs who have been treated with traction, surgery, and prosthetic devices have dramatically improved after deep feelings have been felt and body tension permanently reduced. High blood pressure, constant over many years and through many kinds of "remedy," has lowered significantly and permanently in the same way. Skin conditions, treated for years, have vanished during the course of therapy. Progressively worsening arthritis reversed its trend for the first time in 27 years in the crippled body of a 45-year-old woman.

Reclaiming repressed feelings may be a most difficult alternative, although for some it is the only one with any real promise. From the uncommon experiences of those we have been guiding, including ourselves, we feel urged to say to behavioral scientists, to medical practitioners, to parents, to philosophers and other thinkers, to teachers and lawmakers, "Look at this. See what's happening here."

REFERENCES

Ferreira, A. J. (1969). *Prenatal environment.* Springfield, IL: Thomas.

Festinger, L., Ono, C., Burnham, C. A., & Bamber, D. (1967). Efference and the conscious experience of perception. *Journal of Experimental Psychology, 74,* 1–36.

Janov, A. (1970). *The primal scream.* New York: Vintage.

Janov, A. (1971). *The anatomy of mental illness.* New York: Putnam.

Janov, A. (1972). *The primal revolution.* New York: Simon and Schuster.

Janov, A. (1973). *The feeling child.* New York: Simon and Schuster.

Janov, A. (1975). *Primal man: The new consciousness.* New York: Crowell.

Leboyer, F. (1975). *Birth without violence.* New York: Knopf.

Pearce, J. (1977). *Magical child.* New York: Dutton.

Rapoport, D. (1975/76). The Rapoport Survey. *Bulletin de Psychology* (Paris), *29,* 8–13.

Rose, S. (1973). *The conscious brain.* New York: Knopf.

Simeons, A. T. W. (1960). *Man's presumptuous brain.* New York: Dutton.

Sperry, R. (1951). Neurology and the mind-brain problem. *American Scientist, 40,* 291–312.

Spinelli, D. N., & Pribram, K. H. (1967). Changes in visual recovery functions and unit activity produced by frontal and temporal cortex stimulation. *Electroencephalography and Clinical Neurophysiology, 22,* 143–149.

Chapter 47

PRIMARY RELATIONSHIP THERAPY

GENEVIEVE PAINTER and SALLY VERNON

Robert Postel, the man who developed this form of therapy, was a strange and lonely person. A former student of mine at the Alfred Adler Institute, he was a true original, a person who had a unique view of life. It is indeed a shame, as Genevieve Painter and Sally Vernon state in this chapter, that Postel died before he ever wrote anything about his system. Some years ago, when I was editor of the Journal of Individual Psychology, *I asked Postel to contribute to it. Characteristically, he never even answered—and yet some time later we had a wonderful breakfast meeting at which time he poured out to me his belief that Primary Relationship Therapy was absolutely and fundamentally the most correct way of treating certain kinds of problems: certain deprived people must reexperience their childhood but now in a positive manner with loving "parents."*

It is surprising that so distant and unapproachable a person as Bob Postel could have wrought such a loving and tender type of therapy—and I am most pleased that this is the very first published presentation of this potentially very important mode of psychotherapy.

Primary Relationship Therapy (PRT) is a reparenting form of individual psychotherapy for the person who felt strongly rejected by one or both parents, or who lost parents at an early age. This in-depth therapy was devised in the 1960s by the late Robert Postel and is based upon Adler's theory that both the pampered and neglected child manifest a lifestyle that is not adequate for the solution of social problems.

Of the neglected child, Adler stated: "Such a child has never known what love and cooperation can be. . . . He has found society cold to him and will expect it always to be cold" (1958, p. 11). As an adult he usually is plagued with feelings of loneliness, unworthiness, bitterness, and hostility, and lacks the ability to form prolonged close, meaningful relationships.

PRT is effective with the client who is unable to experience a wide range of emotions because he or she fears facing the ancient hurts of his or her life. A lifelong necessity for covering feelings leads to a developmental lack of emotional recognition.

PRT involves the client in an open, close, personal relationship with a mother therapist and subsequently with a father therapist. An average of 30 sessions with each therapist have been found to be necessary. The therapist acts as a warm, nurturing, teaching parent. In roleplays the client receives cuddling, hugging, play, stories, games, and art activities. Clients also participate in guided fantasies that either change a negative childhood memory to a positive one or give them an experience they wish they had as a child.

As progress is made through "adolescence," the focus is more on real-life issues—sexuality, values, and career plans. In experiencing the parent therapist as an adult model who discloses feelings honestly, the client unscrambles past and current confusions and deprivations and builds the missing foundations he or she never had. Finally, after passing into adulthood and independence, therapy is terminated.

HISTORY

Primary Relationship Therapy was devised in the 1960s by Robert Postel. It is regrettable that when Postel died in 1978 he had not yet written about his innovative therapy. He had been an Adlerian psychologist working in the Chicago practice of the late Rudolf Dreikurs when he was asked by a hospitalized schizophrenic if he would only hold and cradle her. He found that she improved markedly and thus was born a new technique within the Adlerian framework. In continuing his investigation of clients disordered enough to be hospitalized, Postel found that most of them had felt either neglected, rejected, or abused as children and that a form of warm, nurturing, experiential therapy was most effective. He extended this therapy to nonhospitalized clients who had felt early rejection.

In writing of the neglected child, Adler (1958) stated:

Such a child has never known what love and cooperation can be; he makes up an interpretation of life which does not include these friendly forces. It will be understood that when he faces the problems of life he will over-rate their difficulty and under-rate his own capacity to meet them with the aid and good will of others. . . . Especially he will not see that he can win affection and esteem by actions which are useful to others. He will thus be suspicious of others and unable to trust himself. (pp. 17–18)

Adler had written more about the pampered than the neglected child, but he believed that both were ill prepared to function cooperatively in the world:

From the beginning of his life the neurotic manifests the pampered style of life, which is not adequate for the solution of the social problems of life. And the potentially neurotic child later, when confronted by a difficult situation, often becomes the neurotic patient. . . . This style of life can be found occasionally in cases where we cannot speak with any justification of pampering, but where on the contrary, we find neglect.

Adler went further in this direction, stating that:

This pampered style of life is found almost more frequently in neglected children or in those who feel themselves neglected. . . . A person with a pampered style of life is one who wants to be pampered rather than necessarily one who actually has been pampered. (Ansbacher & Ansbacher, 1964, p. 242)

Robert Postel left Dreikurs's practice to further refine his techniques in reparenting. He called his new approach Primary Relationship Therapy and trained others in his own practice. Later he gave classroom instruction for therapists. In these classrooms the senior author of this chapter was trained in Primary Relationship Therapy by Postel.

CURRENT STATUS

Postel trained people working in hospital settings, mental health agencies, and private practices. Psychiatrists, psychologists, social workers, counselors, teachers, and the clergy were represented in his classes. Because this training was done in Chicago, more therapists practice Primary Relationship Therapy in that area than elsewhere. Some of these people moved to other parts of the country and are continuing to do this work; they can be found in the Midwest, in California, Oregon, and Hawaii.

One extension of this work in Honolulu has been in an agency setting with paraprofessionals working with abusive parents. The abusive parent was usually neglected, rejected, or abused as a child and now repeats the pattern with his or her own child. The agency was set up to enable a paraprofessional person to work with a client in a one-to-one supportive relationship. With the addition of Primary Relationship Training, the paraprofessional staff developed new insights into the parents' backgrounds and were able to be more nurturing in their supportive work.

In Hawaii, Primary Relationship Therapy has also reached teachers and school counselors. Teachers and counselors, of course, do not have time to practice extensive individual psychotherapy. But an understanding of the techniques and issues involved helps them to deal more effectively with students who feel rejected or neglected. Essentially, PRT is reconstructive and when applied in schools can help counteract cold or oversolicitous attitudes of adults.

THEORY

Adler and Postel differentiated the pampered from the neglected child, both of whom are unable to cope with the challenges of life as an adult. *Pampered* children grow up believing they deserve a continuation of the special treatment received from the parents. Because not much has been expected from them, as adults these people do not consider the ability to cooperate as an essential part of living. They are unable to carry on the tasks of life and are discontented, usually blaming others for the discontentment. They think they are right and that others are out of step. They are okay; it is others who are wrong. They frequently are willing to please others, but only if they get goodies (things, own way, sex, etc.) in return. They expect others to give to, and take care of, them.

On the other hand, *neglected* (rejected or abused) children also do not cooperate with the world but grow up believing that they themselves are always out of step. They believe that if only they try a little harder to please and become a little more perfect they will be acceptable or loved by others. They always feel poorly about themselves and negatively different from other people. They do not trust self or others and, therefore, do not make close, lasting relationships.

Etiology

The etiology of the neglected person syndrome stems from parents who were neglectful, abusive, or rejecting. The rejection may be true or only perceived by the client, because the parents may have loved the client. The feeling of rejection may be due to the following behavior by the parent: unable to express love in a way that fulfills the child's basic warmth and security needs; unable to give physical touching; love being conditional (I love you only if you are good, get good grades, do what I want); absent from the home so much the child is not able to depend on parent for meeting basic needs; distant and unresponsive; inconsistent in responding to the child, thus producing a lack of security; confusing as a role model (often schizophrenic); being so unhappy that the child is compelled to support the needy parent and thus receives no support for self; or not allowing the client to ever be a child.

Indications for Use

Primary Relationship Therapy is beneficial for the neurotic or psychotic client who is afraid of physical or emotional closeness; has difficulty making lasting intimate relationships; is out of touch with many feelings because they are painful; has deep feelings of inadequacy and low self-esteem; feels unlovable; is depressed, pessimistic, or suicidal; continuously feels sad, hurt, or lonely; has difficulty expressing anger because of fear of rejection; has pervasive anxiety about ability to live up to expectations of self and others; is unable to play and enjoy life; or has physical symptoms (particularly digestive disorders and headaches).

The *rejected* client is seen weekly in a group to work on present adult situations. He or she is assigned to a weekly individual reparenting session to provide a bonding with the therapist and deep nurturing to bridge the gap from a love-barren childhood to present life.

The *pampered-rejected* client was not given unconditional love and nurturing as a child but was instead given material possessions, his or her own way, little order, or overprotection. This client feels rejected because love was denied or was conditional. This person seems to have even more difficulty adjusting to life's demands than the purely rejected person since he or she received a greater distortion of life's requirements and many double messages throughout the growing-up years. This client is seen in a group to work on present life problems and in individual sessions for nurturing.

The *pampered* client does not need much reparenting since he or she was given much nurturing as a child. This client is usually seen only or mostly in a group to learn to cope with present adult problems. However, the reparenting therapy can be useful for a short time to work on understanding a wider range of emotions if the client is limited in emotional awareness.

Primary Relationship Therapy may be applied to anyone who deals with rejection (neglect, abuse), whether neurotic or psychotic, whether adolescent or adult. The outcomes of this process include increased feelings of self-love and self-worth, a significant lowering of anxiety level and depression, feelings of internal strength, and the development of social embeddedness that finally enable close, intimate relationships to develop.

METHODOLOGY

Diagnosis

The following questions are asked to determine if the client felt rejected as a child.

1. When you were four, five, or six years old and went to your mother for affection, how did she respond? Did she cuddle you? Could you climb into her lap? Would she hold you?
2. What kind of a person was your mother? Was she a warm person?
3. Did your mother withhold love if you were not good or if you did not achieve? Was her love conditional? Would she stay angry if you were not good?
4. How does that make you feel?
5. Could you find a way to gain her approval?
6. Ask the same questions for father.
7. How do you feel about your brothers and sisters? Did they receive more approval than you? How do you think they felt?
8. How well did you do in elementary, high school, college? (A rejected person usually did similarly throughout school because of trying to please or to be perfect. The pampered person often does better in elementary school than later when school becomes more difficult.)
9. When your parents fought, did you think it was your fault? How did you feel about their fights? (The rejected person often feels responsible for parental fights. The pampered person may feel unconcerned.)
10. Do you want to be best or perfect? (The rejected person wants to be perfect even if he or she says that no one is perfect. The pampered person wants to be best and outshine others.)
11. Do you ever feel sad and not know why?
12. Did you ever feel that there was something not good enough about you—too clumsy, the wrong sex, and so on? Do you at times feel that there is something unacceptable about you, that you are not as good as others and if someone got close to you they could tell? (The rejected person strongly identifies with this question and usually cries when asked this because of a lifetime of this hurtful situation.)

13. Does it make you feel sad that you did not have mother's (father's) love?

14. Whose love did you want more, mother's or father's? (This question is asked if one parent was warm and nurturing and the other rejecting.)

15. There are six ways one can satisfy childhood needs for approval. Which one applies to you—to be good, to achieve, to become independent, to be sickly, to withdraw from others, to play the clown?

16. Were you a loner? Did you usually hide behind a wall? Did you sometimes hide behind a wall, then get lonely and make friends and then hide again?

The rejected person displays much sadness when asked these questions, feels one or both parents did not provide unconditional love, frequently had been or is a loner, tries to reach perfection and do well in school to gain approval, feels that he or she does not receive enough love as an adult, feels unworthy and unlovable. A parent dying or leaving the home is often felt as rejection.

After the diagnosis is made, the client is assigned to a weekly individual session with a mother or father therapist and to a group meeting weekly. Usually therapy starts with the "mother" since the first natural bonding, even before birth, is with the mother.

Individual Sessions

In working with the mother or father therapist, the client requires the experience of a nurturing, teaching, parenting relationship. The need to be accepted and to build trust and bonding to another human being is the basis of the therapeutic process because the feelings of deprivation and nontrust are the common issue.

The therapist seeks the underlying feelings of anger and sadness to help the client acknowledge and handle these. The process involves the discharge of these feelings while accepting the warmth and nurturing that was missing or not perceived in childhood. The goal is to first establish the client's feelings of childhood dependency, then to move toward coresponsibility in the relationship, and finally to increase independence and decision making. Except in infancy, communication and awareness of feelings predominate as the theme of the therapy. Initially the therapist takes responsibility for acknowledging and communicating feelings for both of them until the client is trained to do it for him- or herself.

The client allows him- or herself to become vulnerable and open to feelings through the holding and cuddling experienced as a very small child; the silliness and fun of the preschooler; the adventure and organized play of the elementary school child; the questioning and

reality seeking of the preadolescent; and the discussions, arguments, and identity search of the adolescent.

Throughout the process the therapist's honesty regarding all feelings (including anger and impatience) gives the client the willingness to accept his or her own feelings and the ability to start trusting self and therapist. The long-standing anger and sadness are gradually replaced by feelings of joy; the helpless behavior is transformed into an ability to cope with life situations.

Table 47.1 gives the picture of the issues, emotional needs, major feelings, and behavior exhibited at each emotional age during the therapy.

When the client completes the process with the mother therapist, regression again occurs with the father therapist. Usually the process with the second parent therapist is not as long-lasting. Occasionally the client goes back again to the mother therapist to complete some issues.

Tools and processes used in this therapy include some of the following:

1. *Ground rules:* In the first session the therapist will say to the client: "The trip you will be taking can be scary but not dangerous and I will be going on the trip with you. My only expectation is that you be honest with your feelings as I will be with mine. All feelings are okay, including sexual feelings; little boys and girls may feel sexual with a parent. If it comes up we will talk about it, but we will not act on it."

2. *Issues of suicide hospitalization:* These issues should be explored at the beginning of therapy. The client may have had these considerations in the past, and the fear and thought will surface in the therapeutic process.

3. *Fantasies:* Give client experiences with a parent that were missed in childhood; change negative memory to positive.

4. *Activities outside of the office:* Go for a walk, play, have a treat, have a meal or picnic.

5. *Phone calls as an assignment:* Give permission to a client who is afraid to phone the therapist or to limit a client who phones too often by setting limits for phone calls.

6. *Stories:* Read to client stories that fill the needs of the appropriate emotional age and that touch a client issue.

7. *Games:* Play impromptu and silly games, and noncompetitive and competitive games; these give the client spontaneity and assertiveness and deepen the relationship with the therapist.

8. *Role playing:* Therapist functions as parent and the client as a child. Client gets in touch with old

Table 47.1 Activity Chart

Emotional Age	Predominant Feelings	Behavior	Client Needs/Wants
Womb, fetal position	Numb, safe	Hiding, withdrawn, out of touch	To be held and rocked as a baby; tactile touch (stroking); given permission to just be there; periods of holding in silence.
1–2 years	anxiety, depression, confusion, pain,	Will put arm around P/T;[a] eyes will show warmth at times; seeks out P/T nonverbally in group; looks to P/T for approval	To feel warmth of P/T; to respond and be accepted by P/T; cuddling and holding; permission to cry; to have P/T feedback feelings of hurt and sadness.
3–4 years	anger, hurt, pain, sadness, bittersweet[b]	Temper tantrums; verbalize hurts; crying, sobbing	Tickling, stories, unorganized spontaneous play; silliness, nursery rhymes; fantasies of P/T being with client on trips to park or beach, playing at home; permission and demonstration to act out anger in therapy.
5–6 years	hurt, sadness, bittersweet	Begins to take self-control; continues to talk about hurts	Organized games and fantasies: go out for walk, buy ice cream cone, have a treat; cooperative art activities; stories including client's participation.
7–8 years	Anger, sadness, warmth	Communicates anger; centers on source of anger (parent, therapist, significant other)	Roleplay (coping with problems, expressing feelings); awareness of identification with parent; fantasies to replace childhood memories, to try out a missing experience.
8–10 years	Curiosity; cooperation enjoyment	Interested in friends; peer dependency; questions about life, values	Increased expression of feelings; sharing and discussing life; planning and doing activities; expressing ideas and opinions.
11–12 years	Emotional ups and downs start again, rebellious anger	Interest in peer group, sports, organizations; talks about activities	Wants P/T to listen; dependency on P/T lessens; expression of feelings toward P/T.
13–14 years, early adolescence	Tells P/T when angry; excitement; belonging unsure	Interested in dating, being with opposite sex; sexual fantasies; wants to cope with authority	Shares enjoyment of adolescence; discussion of religion, sex, philosophy; fun to be with.
15–16 years, middle adolescence	Wide variety of feelings: easily gets angry at P/T; disagrees openly	Knows what he or she wants from session; can handle things on own	Equality between P/T and client; information on sex and roles; money and goal planning; dealing with own children.
17–18 years, late adolescence	Rebellion; independence	Wants to break therapy; no longer needs P/T	What kind of man or woman do I want to be? What are my moral values? How will I structure my life? What kind of lifestyle do I want?

[a]P/T: parent therapist.

[b]Bittersweet: client's sadness mixed with parent therapist's warmth.

situations and feelings, replays alternatives for old situations, adds experiences to childhood, assertively expresses new solutions and feelings in current relationships.

9. *Assignments:* Designed to clarify issues between therapy sessions and practice new behaviors.

10. *Therapist self-disclosure:* Enables the client to understand the surrogate parent emotionally and experientially by contrast, since client's parent was often emotionally closed or continually critical.

11. *Problem solving:* Experiences through role play and communication a variety of choices in child-

hood and adult issues. Earlier client often saw only "either/or" solutions.

12. *Art activities:* Work and play together for encouragement, spontaneity, cooperation, having fun, and deemphasizing perfection and competition.

13. *Significant others:* Have a session with significant person in client's life who can give support and understanding outside of therapy.

14. *Information:* Use available community resources to help client make work and educational decisions, such as vocational rehabilitation and educational institutions.

15. *Library:* Therapist and client build library of books, magazines, and other literature to promote understanding and awareness and to encourage reading (some clients' concentration has been poor since childhood). Books are made available that speak to the appropriate emotional age.

16. *Big You, Little You* (Kirste & Robertiello, 1975): Client separates his or her child from the adult state and dialogues with each, thus enabling him or her to handle hurtful and stressful situations.

17. *The demon:* The repressed devil or evil core the client sees in the self (screaming tiger, vulture, etc.) is acknowledged, named, and enjoyed by talking about it, drawing it, and putting the picture on the wall to admire.

18. *Parent study group:* Client studies *Children: The Challenge* (Dreikurs & Soltz, 1964) and participates in a parent study group as his or her own parent, discussing the behavior of self and siblings, understanding parents' position, and finally discontinuing parental blame.

Group Sessions

The group is used to deal with present life situations—family and work relationships—and to experience the opinions of others. This type of group is honest with feedback, at times confrontive, and always supportive. Because one to four members usually work on in-group assignments, thus limiting their general participation, the group size is rather large—from 12 to 14 people. This allows about 10 people to participate in the general discussion.

Friendship and strong feelings of belonging are encouraged because most clients enter therapy feeling quite isolated and do not know how to make close relationships. Groups are held at noon or in the early evening for one hour, and members have lunch or dinner together to strengthen social ties.

The process of each group session is highly structured and divided into five sections: (1) *reactions* to the last session and weekly happenings; (2) *reports* on out-of-group assignments; (3) *introduction of new member* if a new person comes in (groups are ongoing and clients may enter at any time); (4) *presentation and discussion of problems* by two to four clients consecutively; (5) *end-of-group assignment*—some in-group assignments are done at the end, for example, giving each person a criticism by the client who is overly critical. Sections 1, 2, and 4 are done at each session; section 3 is done if a new person comes in; and section 5 occurs if someone has that form of assignment.

Feedback is given by therapist and group members during presentation and discussion of problems, and an assignment is suggested relating to the issue presented. Assignments help the client desensitize a fear, experience a new behavior, practice a nonfamiliar behavior, or overuse a negative behavior to eliminate it. Assignments are given for in-group or out-of-group practice.

Examples of in-group assignments are: (1) group host/hostess—gives a hug to each member upon arriving and leaving the session to help the client feel he or she belongs to the group; (2) group prince/princess—person is catered to by other members (given candy, gum, footstool, shoulder massage) to overdo his or her wish for pampering; (3) mask—client wears mask and reports feelings as session goes on to get in touch with feelings. The group continues with the discussion, tuning out the persons acting out their assignments.

Examples of out-of-group assignments are: (1) call group members or allow them to call you—for persons who feel isolated; (2) do clumsy and silly things—for the client who tries to be perfect; (3) ask people to do things for you (get you coffee, run an errand)—for the client who fears asking or is unable to receive from others; (4) be friendly but uncooperative—for the client who is nonassertive. Assignments last for six or more sessions, until the client learns the necessary lesson.

Through the use of the individual parenting and the group sessions, the client becomes more positive and optimistic about life, anger and sadness lessen, and coping skills increase.

APPLICATION

A very wide range of behaviors and attitudes develops from being rejected as a child. Depending upon the degree of discouragement or nonadjustment, the client may fall into many categories of diagnosis—from the various neuroses to psychoses to character disorders. All of these can be treated in PRT.

Neurosis

The neurotic client who consults us because of problems with family, work, friendship, or intimate relationships is placed in group and Primary Relationship Therapy if rejection (neglect, abuse) is an issue. The diagnosis may be any neurotic disorder—depressive, anxiety, hysterical, and so forth.

Psychosis

The borderline to the severely psychotic client can be helped with a one-to-one, long-term, warmly nurturing therapy plus group therapy. For example, a 26-year-old female schizophrenic was sent to us by a psychiatrist, who said "Either you take her into PRT or I will have to send her to an institution for the rest of her life." The psychosis had prevailed throughout most of the client's life. Her mother was 45 and father 48 when she was born, and they were unable to accept her disturbance of their couple state. As a young child she had been very much aware of not being wanted. The client improved in this therapy and was able to leave her parents' home.

The less severely disturbed psychotic can also benefit from this therapy. Frequently this client is "borderline" psychotic. The warm, nurturing relationship with a parent therapist is usually the first time this person has been truly accepted by another person. The response finally emerges into the development of trust in the therapist.

The Client Who Needs Hospitalization

In our practice we do not accept clients who are hospitalized. However, occasionally a client (psychotic or neurotic) becomes anxious or severely depressed after entering PRT. With the client's desires to escape present pressures and responsibilities, he or she may decide to go to a hospital for a while. We may or may not encourage this step, but once the client chooses this alternative we support it. As of this writing we have had only two clients (one neurotic and one psychotic) who made this decision; both stayed in the hospital three or four weeks. We were not involved in the hospital treatment but did keep in touch with the psychiatrist in charge and visited each client as a friend. Upon dismissal, the clients discussed their hospital experience with their therapy groups. They seemed to benefit from the experience by realizing that the hospital was only a temporary escape, that it was not the most pleasant place to be (although not unpleasant), and that it was up to them to take care of their responsibilities and to get well. Neither client returned to the hospital.

Adolescents and Children

Although Primary Relationship Therapy is generally considered a psychotherapy for adults, we at times accept adolescents for a full-term therapy and children for a short time. This occurs occasionally when we have a parent in therapy who has been unable to give nurturing or support to his or her child, and the child is withdrawn, acting-out, or extremely rebellious. Because the child does not have a bonding with the parents, a nurturing therapist can lead him or her into learning to trust others and to accept self as a loving person. We generally accept adolescents into a teen group only. In the cases mentioned, though, there was severe depression in the adolescents stemming from feelings of rejection and the group did not suffice.

Marriage and Family Counseling

At times a client who has felt rejected consults us for a marriage or childrearing problem. The client is unable to relate closely to his or her spouse, and the deep anger may lead to child abuse, especially if the client was abused as a child. The need for learning to cope with marriage and childrearing processes must be delayed until the client develops the ego-strength to cope with his or her own life. This is a very difficult situation for the entire family.

If one spouse is better able to handle the children, we ask that he or she do so until the client recovers. In one case a mother was assigned to PRT when she was unable to cope with her two children, one three and one four. She had quite seriously abused them. The father was unable to care for them, so they were sent to live with relatives for a year until the mother was able to handle herself and then the children. At that time (before she finished her own therapy) the mother was helped with problems of marriage and childrearing.

A wide range of behaviors develop from neglect, rejection, or abuse as a child. The degree of disturbance or nonfunctioning varies, and many types of the psychoses and neuroses are helped with Primary Relationship Therapy.

CASE EXAMPLE

Joy, 26, a married woman, working as a tutor of children with learning difficulties, was ridden with anxiety but was a master at covering her feelings. She seemed self-assured, competent, and beautiful. Under the mask she felt shaky, incapable, unlovable, and ugly. She had been in other types of psychotherapy for many years.

Joy's mother was a perfectionist who treated her daughter, when young, as if she were a lovely doll. She dressed her beautifully, curled her hair, made sure she used the best manners. Her mother was also very critical because Joy was to be the perfect child—the child who could elevate the mother's position in life. Joy's mother herself had been raised by a strict mother and was not given warmth by either parent. She had not learned to be loving.

After several sessions in Primary Relationship Therapy and group sessions in which she mostly listened, Joy's facade was gone during one visit.

J: I'm scared, I'm feeling like I'm floating above the ground.

T: That is okay. Come sit close to me on our floor pillow and I'll hold you. (Therapist cradles Joy as if she were a very little child.)

J: My heart is beating fast.

T: It will soon slow down (softly). Close your eyes; we are going on a lovely trip. See these big balloons with heavy ropes—one for you and one for me. Now I'm tying one around your waist and one around my own. And I'm holding on to you so you are perfectly safe. Aren't they lovely? They are Disneyland balloons. We're beginning to take off, here we go, just above the ground, and now a little higher. We're just above the rooftops of the small houses and going higher so we can just fly. Now we have cleared everything in the way, and we are up pretty high and just having a marvelous time. It is so beautiful up here, you and I both love it. Let's stay here for a while and just enjoy the beauty, peace, and quiet. (By now Joy is relaxed in the arms of the therapist silently enjoying it.)

T: We're going to land now, just slowly go down. We are enjoying the descent; it is easy. Coming down slowly, slowly, coming down. Here we are, down on the ground, feeling good. Joy, any time you feel that you are floating you can just remember to put the balloon rope around you and land yourself gently, just as we did now. How do you feel?

J: I feel okay. Not scared, and I'm not floating anymore.

Comment. The therapist joined in Joy's hallucination of floating and gently led her back to reality. It was the first time the therapist knew that Joy had psychotic tendencies. They showed again from time to time in which she either felt things were unreal or she was floating.

Joy remained feeling like a very little girl for some time. The therapist quietly cuddled her much of the time and also did other guided fantasies with Joy's assistance.

T: Come let me hold you. Close your eyes. Can you see yourself as a little girl? How old are you?

J: I'm one year old, just beginning to walk.

T: Yes, you are my beautiful little girl, and you are just waking up this morning. I'm going to dress you.

J: No (with alarm)! I don't want you to dress me in a beautiful dress.

T: No, of course not. You are my beautiful baby girl, beautiful with no clothes on. I'm just going to put a diaper on you so you don't weewee all over the floor. You are lovable just as you are. You don't need a pretty dress.

J: That's better (more relaxed). I think I'm walking along a coffee table, looking at the things on the table.

T: Yes, you can look at those things. You really are curious.

J: Yes, I am. Won't you get mad that I'm touching things?

T: No, little girls can explore. There is nothing that will break anyway.

Comment. Joy is given the opportunity to be appreciated and loved just for being herself—with no clothes on. She is also given permission to be a very little girl and to enjoy her environment with a supportive surrogate mother.

As she began feeling older in therapy (five and six years old), Joy enjoyed doing artwork and showed a great deal of talent.

J: Sometimes I feel very strange, like there is someone or something else inside me that no one knows about.

T: Can you draw me a picture of the something inside of you? Joy, is that something bad, not okay? Would you let me see it? What would it look like?

J: A scary, creepy thing like in a horror movie. It can pounce on you and make you scream. You won't like it.

T: Well, I think I can handle it. I would like to know this something. Maybe it just wants someone to know it exists. Is it really that awful?

J: Well, maybe if I draw it you can see. It chews up my insides sometimes. I feel like it is always feeding on me. Let's see, I think it is like a centipede.

T: With all those legs it would feel strange inside of you.

J: (engrossed in the face of the centipede) The eyes aren't right. She must be vicious.

T: She looks sad to me. I can almost see tears in her eyes.

J: She is sad. She is very sad.

T: If no one knows she is there, then she must also feel very lonely.

J: She isn't really mean, is she? She is lonely and sad. There, now you can see the tears. (Joy added tears to the face of the centipede.)

T: I would like to care about the centipede (putting arms around Joy). Would she let me be her friend?

J: She trusts you but she is scared. Yes, she wants you to be her friend. She's scared you will think she is ugly and awful and that you won't really care.

T: We'll have to be gentle with her so she will learn that she is not ugly and awful. Joy, can you accept the centipede and help me take care of her?

J: I want to.

Comment. The centipede represented to Joy the ugly place in her that was unacceptable. She did not want to see this ugly place and wanted to keep it hidden from the rest of the world. In encouraging her to name and draw her ugly place, we had acknowledged the hidden part of Joy that represented the hurts of rejection and sadness, of feeling unworthy of love. The picture was placed on the therapist's office wall, and Joy and the therapist played with the centipede. The sadness was replaced first by shyness and then a happy feeling.

At one point in her therapy Joy suddenly began sobbing and screaming.

J: I am in a black place and I can't get out. It's a black hole or cave.

T: Hold on to my hand; you are not alone. I am going to be with you.

J: I can't get out; there is no way out (sobbing).

T: I am not going to leave you. We will find the way out together. Let's walk slowly and see what is up ahead. This cave has a tunnel and I will not let go of you. I think I feel a turn coming; yes, the tunnel turns to the left. Hold on, it will be okay. There is a faint light ahead; can you see it?

J: Yes (still clinging to therapist).

T: We will walk toward the light, there will be a way out. Yes, it is getting brighter. Oh, the light comes from the top of the tunnel. There are rocks we can climb on. Here, let me help you up. Are you okay?

J: Yes, I made it (no longer sobbing).

T: Here I come. Can you make it through the hole?

J: Yes, but I'm scared.

T: I feel scared too but I'm not going to give up. Let's find out what is outside.

J: You go first.

T: All right. There, I'm out. Give me your hand. We made it, we are out. See where we are. We are on top of a mountain.

J: It isn't black anymore.

T: Let's sit and rest for a while. We can climb down later.

J: I feel safe (still being held by the therapist).

T: Stay quiet and enjoy being safe. We have time to feel safe.

The following is a letter to the therapist written after five months of therapy:

Dear Genevieve:

I've had so many strong reactions to therapy. I want to connect with you. I don't feel comfortable calling at work as I know you are busy and I feel it unfair to take up your time in that situation. [Joy had been given permission to phone when she wanted to.]

Plus I know you're leaving sometime, and to be honest, I think I'd feel sad if a secretary told me you were out of town. So in a way, I prefer not opening it up too much. I guess I'm a little afraid of being overwhelmed by feelings—by reaching out to you.

After our last session I felt joy. Jumping up and down even. I also realized I was cautious about accepting the joy. Like it was on a deep level, but my conscious mind stayed in control.

I've become aware how constantly I desire acceptance from others. I sense my tension, watch it manifest and know exactly where it's coming from. It's difficult getting involved outside of myself, as I'm always watching other people or guarding myself.

For example, Tom [husband] was telling me about some ideas and I could see him only on the edge of my awareness. I was conscious mainly of desiring his acceptance. Not verbally. In a deeper way, like having my head on his lap. In a state like that I appear irrational, as any seemingly critical remark hurts my feelings or angers me, etc. Actually, it might simply be a statement of fact. I guess I'm watching for disapproval from Tom. Guarding myself is the word!

Also, whenever I feel overwhelmed by anything (mental conflicts, like decisions or even ambivalent feelings) I'm usually sad. I know this because this a.m. I stopped trying to decide what to do today in an anxious way and when I paused I regressed and felt small and sad.

I like knowing all this. It helps me to understand myself. It makes dealing with colleagues and outside acquaintances easier. (I'm not trying for their approval as much.) It's made dealing with closer friends and Tom clearer, but not easier. In fact, more difficult. I'm so aware of my deep desire to be loved and accepted by them that I don't know what to do. Like having a tea party in a thunderstorm.

About you. I feel a consistent warmth. I only feel secure when you are especially sending me your love (focusing on me). When you're thinking about an idea (just being you) I don't feel secure. Then it's like with friends—I desire to have that feeling of closeness, and get your full attention. Rationally, I know that it's absurd to take all your attention. The truth is my hunger is so great I have difficulty focusing on anything else.

As far as therapy goes, I basically feel positive and warm. My only fear is that I can never be filled. Filling a well with a measuring cup is my analogy.

Till Wednesday

Joy

P.S. In a way, it's never been easier living with myself. Now I don't fear what's inside, so I feel less out of balance. My difficulty comes when I fight the sadness, or fear the enormity of it.

Joy remained in therapy for one year. Her therapy had not actually been completed when she left with her husband, who had been transferred. Once she got over the infant stage her therapy went faster. She went up and down in age and emotions. By the time she left she felt comfortable in leaving the therapist, who assured her that she was able to handle her life on her own. Initially Joy had greatly feared pregnancy and motherhood. By the time she was settled in her new home, she was looking forward to motherhood and was determined to become pregnant. She later sent the therapist a picture of her baby and parents, and assured the therapist that she already had a close relationship with her daughter.

SUMMARY

Primary Relationship Therapy (PRT) is a form of psychotherapy for the person who feels strongly rejected by one or both parents. Robert Postel, who evolved the therapy in the 1960s, died before he had written about PRT. Postel's new approach is based on Alfred Adler's theory that the neglected child has never known love and finds society cold, believing that it will always be cold.

The therapy involves the client in a warm, nurturing, supportive relationship with first a mother therapist, and then a father therapist, to work on childhood issues of neglect, hurt, anger, fear, and so forth. The client is also assigned to a therapy group to work on present adult concerns.

The therapy is useful to both neurotic and psychotic clients—anyone who has the issue of rejection (neglect, abuse) to deal with. The outgrowths of this process include increased feelings of self-love, self-worth, a significant lowering of anxiety level and depression, feelings of internal strength and the development of social embeddedness, which finally enable close, intimate relationships to develop.

Since this process is experiential more than verbal or insight oriented, it seems to produce a deep and lasting change in the client.

REFERENCES

Adler, A. (1958). *What life should mean to you.* New York: Capricorn.

Ansbacher, H., & Ansbacher, R. (1964). *The individual psychology of Alfred Adler.* New York: Harper Torchbooks.

Dreikurs, R., & Soltz, V. (1964). *Children: The challenge.* New York: Hawthorn.

Kirsten, G., & Robertiello, R. (1977). *Big you, little you.* New York: Dial.

Montagu, A. (1972). *Touching: The human significance of the skin.* New York: Perennial Library.

Chapter 48

PROBLEM SOLVING GROUP THERAPY

JAMES P. TROTZER

Practically any system of psychotherapy can be converted to group therapy by having two or more clients, but some systems are expressly developed for groups. There is a basic element in these groups that determine their nature: whether they are open or closed. In an open group, new members can enter at any time and older members are expected to leave when they either give up on the group or when they have achieved satisfaction. Problem Solving Group Therapy is of the closed type, in which the group goes through five steps and each member is expected to go through the same steps. The stages are Security, Acceptance, Responsibility, Work, *and* Closing. *Within each stage are four to six substages. James Trotzer gives credit to many whose ideas are inherent in this system.*

Another aspect of this system is its concerns with brief therapy in the world of managed care. An unattributed quote defines managed care quite adequately. This is a complex and exciting system that shows a good deal of thought with clever and unexpected strategies and if one were to attempt group therapy with a consistent group, this is the system of choice.

Problem Solving Group Therapy is an integrated, developmental treatment model that provides a perspective and structure that is adaptable to both therapeutic practice and training. It has particular utility in the current climate of economic efficiency generated by the medical model and managed care that prompts treatment processes that are brief and solution-focused.

The psychological rationale for the model, first published in 1977 (Trotzer, 1977), incorporates an integrative perspective that combines personality dynamics of group members, interpersonal process dynamics of group interaction, and problem-solving purposes of therapeutic initiatives. The rationale provides a conceptual framework for group process and a content focus for problem solving. In addition, the overlay of family theory as a group resource provides process, content, and technical assistance that enhances the therapeutic group process. As a result, the transitional relevance of the therapeutic endeavor is increased via transfer of learning and application of results in the client's world outside the therapeutic setting.

The approach emanates from the integration of the following conceptual frameworks: Maslow's (1943, 1954, 1962) hierarchy of needs; Luft and Ingram's Johari Window interpersonal process model (Luft, 1970; 1984); Trotzer's (1985) generic problem solving agenda; and family systems theory. The resulting group process

model is explicated in five overlapping stages that depict the developmental life of the group. Each process stage is deconstructed in the form of specific developmental tasks that provide structure for the stage and mark its existence dynamically. The stages, labeled sequentially along with their respective developmental tasks, also serve as the agenda for problem solving.

Structured activities designed from a variety of conceptual frameworks and emphasizing developmental and systemic qualities are used to introduce both content (problems) and process (group dynamics). Group members are introduced to the approach via the initiative of identifying and choosing problems they are willing to address and then sharing that information through participation in structured activities reflective of the stages of the group process.

Problem Solving Group Therapy (PSGT) may be implemented in the form of long- or short-term counseling or therapy groups or in a learning/training format such as a workshop, psychoeducational group, or class. Results of the approach are subject to verification because of the purpose (problem solving) and the specificity of focus (each person's problems). In addition, members acquire a secondary benefit of primary importance as they not only learn how to solve their problems but also learn problem solving processes applicable to other aspects of their lives. They contribute as resources to their own and others' well-beings, thus experiencing a general improvement in self-esteem and empowerment. The benefits of PSGT as a microcosm approximating social reality and a social laboratory are also significant, giving the approach validity on both a personal and interpersonal level. The purpose of this chapter is to explicate the theoretical underpinnings and demonstrate the practical utility of Problem Solving Group Therapy.

CONCEPTUAL FRAMEWORK

Definition

Generally, therapeutic groups must meet parameters that provide for both interpersonal stimulation and individual autonomy without intruding on the volitional primacy of the person or abandoning direction to the relational vagaries of group pressure. Such groups must consist of three or more members so that group dynamics materialize, but they must also be small enough to insure that face-to-face communication is preserved (Trotzer, 1989). Consequently, for our purposes, a group of three to 10 members (depending on age and maturity of clients) is considered the appropriate size for a therapy group. For training, a workshop format using subgroups of four to six members also qualifies as Problem Solving Group Therapy.

The following definition will serve as our reference point for this chapter:

> Problem Solving Group Therapy (PSGT) is the development of an interpersonal, therapeutic system characterized by trust, acceptance, respect, warmth, communication and understanding through which a therapist and several clients come in contact for the specific purpose of addressing problems in the clients' lives with the stated objective of discovering, developing and implementing ways of resolving those problems (Trotzer, 1972, 1989).

This definition establishes a process perspective that emphasizes the nature of the therapeutic atmosphere, differentiates the identity of the participants (therapist as leader and clients as members), and cites the objective of the group (personal problem solving). To realize this definition, a psychological framework is necessary that addresses what I have called the "three Ps" of a therapeutic group: Person, Process, and Purpose.

Psychological Rationale

Group therapy has merit because it recognizes the social nature of the human organism. It takes into account that who we are as persons is revealed through, reflected in, and forged by our relationships with others. By the same token, relationships are often focal points of our problems and contribute to them. For example, Yalom (1985) has noted that "without exception patients enter group therapy with a history of highly unsatisfactory experience in their first and most important group—their primary family" (p. 15). However, by the time members appear in group therapy, the impact of relationships has been internalized in such a way that individual traits are initially more critical than their interpersonal derivatives. Consequently, the person of the client is our first concern.

The Person Component

Therapy groups are composed of individual members, each of whom brings a personality and perspective that must be taken into account for the individual to connect with the group and for the group to form. In addition, each person has certain basic needs that motivate them in relating to others, creating dynamics that must be addressed if the group is to develop therapeutically. Maslow's (1943, 1954, 1962) conceptualization of the human needs hierarchy is a useful tool in understanding and addressing the person component in groups. According to Maslow, each person's needs are differentiated hierarchically, with each need having prepotent qualities that influence when and how it will be activated as a motivator of behavior. Consequently, lower-order needs must be addressed before higher-order needs can be called into play. Maslow's hierarchy provides a useful perspective of individual members as they come into and move through the group therapy process.

Maslow postulated five basic needs (in order of priority): physiological needs, safety, love and belonging, esteem, and self-actualization. These needs, embellished with psychological merit for our purposes, give credence to the import of the person component. Fulfilled physiological needs are a prerequisite to effective group participation, because deprivation (e.g., lack of sleep or hunger) or distortion (e.g., use of alcohol or drugs) can only distract or disrupt the group process. In addition, the physical safety of members is necessary as an assurance for participation. Beyond that, the group must provide an atmosphere in which each member experiences a sense of security (safety), acceptance (love and belonging), and respect (esteem), in that order, to fully engage in and commit to involvement that taps the productive energy of the self-actualization need to do therapeutic work in the group. (For detailed discussion of these needs in relation to group process, see Trotzer, 1999, Chapter 3). To meet these needs in group therapy, a relational component is necessary, because it is only in the context of interpersonal connections that the needs for security, acceptance, and respect can be addressed.

The Process Component

In the development of our personhood, individual needs prompt interaction with and response from people in our environment. As a consequence of that interchange over time, we develop our individuality and our sociability. Subsequently, any interventive group process must reflect dynamics of that primary interaction for therapeutic effect to be realized. The Johari Window (Luft, 1984) is a useful model for depicting the nature of the group process that is necessary for groups to have therapeutic effect.

The Johari Window (See Figure 48.1) describes relationship dynamics in the context of the interaction between an information component and a person component. Each component, in turn, is composed of two elements: known and unknown (information) and self and others (person). When these elements are combined and juxtaposed, a matrix of four quadrants is formed that describes the dynamics of a relationship. Quadrant I is the *open* quadrant, which includes information that is known to self and known to others, or held mutually in common. Quadrant II is the *hidden* quadrant, which contains information that is known to self but unknown to others. This is the private domain of the individual who possesses the right to choose whether to reveal the information or not. Quadrant III is the *blind* quadrant, containing information that is known to others but unknown to self. This is data that others know about a person that is unknown to that person until it is disclosed. Quadrant IV is simply called the *unknown* quadrant, and it represents information that is unknown to both self and others. It represents the material that emerges as relationships develop and signals the facts that all relationships have potential and no relationship is completely open.

The boundaries between the quadrants reflect risk and their permeability is determined by the amount of trust present in the relationship. Information passes into the open quadrant from the hidden quadrant via the channel of self-disclosure, and information moves from the blind quadrant to the open quadrant via feedback. The greater the amount of trust and security in the relationship, the more permeable the boundaries and the greater the likelihood of openness. The objective of therapeutic group process is to create an atmosphere where trust grows sufficiently so that self-disclosure and feedback can be mobilized as tools in forming the group and in addressing the problems that individual members bring to the group. Thus the reason for forming therapeutic groups emerges. People have problems that they are not able to resolve on their own or in the context of their environmental and relational resources.

The Purpose Component

Problems result in people's lives when they have difficulty meeting their needs and developing their individuality (intrapersonal problems) or when they have difficulty in relationships or in forming healthy relationships (interpersonal problems; Trotzer, 1985). When either or both of these generic problems emerge in specific form, problem solving becomes necessary. When that enterprise is housed in a group led by trained professionals called therapists, it is group therapy. Therefore the third component of our rationale is that the purpose for forming a therapeutic group is to resolve the problems that have brought the clients to the group in the first place. In that sense a therapy group is an artificial environment (i.e., not a naturally occurring entity in the client's life). Consequently, the ultimate goal of any therapy group is to dissolve the group by resolving the problems of its members (Trotzer, 1999).

To summarize, the psychological rationale for group therapy consists of three interactive components formulated as follows:

$$\underset{\text{Needs}}{\underset{\text{Individual}}{(\text{Person})}} + \underset{\text{Development}}{\underset{\text{Relationship}}{(\text{Process})}} + \underset{\text{Solving}}{\underset{\text{Problem}}{(\text{Purpose})}} = \underset{\text{Group Therapy}}{\overset{\text{(Therapeutic}}{\text{Modality)}}}$$

Individual members motivated by their respective needs interact in a group milieu to develop a relationship in which they work to resolve their problems (Trotzer, 1999).

CURRENT STATUS

The Impetus of Efficiency, Efficacy, and Expedience

The emergence of the "rapid change" phenomenon in therapy, called variously brief therapy or solution-

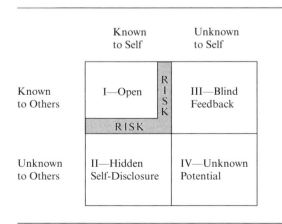

Figure 48.1   The Johari Window

focused therapy, is actually a reframing of a well-known dimension and long-standing fact of the human experience. For human beings, changing quickly when necessary is not only desirable but also preferable, especially in relation to mental health problems and life adjustment issues. When problems arise, we all would like them to be resolved expeditiously and with a minimum of effort. However, in most cases reality teaches us that change takes time and effort. There are exceptions to this general rule, however, in the form of what I have called the "CCE Syndrome." CCE stands for conversion, crisis, and eureka. In the context of these three phenomena, change does occur rapidly. Each term reflects the particular dimension of human nature that predominates when concrete modifications in one's life occur in a short period of time.

Conversion (The Affective Version)

Many people report rapid and permanent changes in their lives as a result of a magical or mystical experience that transforms negative feelings and into positive feelings producing subsequent changes in behavior, lifestyle, and perception. These conversion experiences are often labeled with terms like "born again," "reborn," "new life," or "renewal." The typical scenario is to experience a rapid shift from a sense of hopelessness, guilt, despair, or helplessness to one of uplifting hope and resiliency. I am not referring here to mood swings (depression to euphoria and back again), manic-depressive disorders, bipolar illness, or physiological syndromes like PMS. These conversion events produce actual, verifiable, observable change in the person's life. The person often refers to the conversion as a "turning point" in his or her life, from which time on the person's life is different.

Crisis (The Behavioral Version)

Many people also experience rapid changes in their lives because circumstances over which they have no control or consequences of their own actions produce situations where the person has no choice but to change. These forced changes are called "crises". (Note: When a crisis does not produce change that is constructive and relatively fast or generates destructive change in a person's life, it is called trauma. If such events are not resolved, symptoms emerge which are then diagnosed as Post-traumatic Stress Disorder or PTSD.) Circumstances such as loss of job, accidents, illnesses, death of a spouse or other intimate relation, business failure, and so on prompt unalterable modifications in one's life. When positive results ensue, the crisis is looked upon as a turning point in life, thus qualifying as an example of the "rapid change syndrome."

Eureka (The Cognitive Version)

The mental phenomenon of "Eureka" ("I found it") accounts for another rapid change experience. The impact of insight, the result of a "brainstorm" or mental power surge, produces a clarity of direction and focus that results in action that permanently changes a person's life. Like the previous two examples, resultant changes are evident in the observable portion of the person's life, including his or her outlook and attitude.

All these types of rapid change are common to the human experience and when therapy, regardless of modality, is associated with the process, therapeutic intervention is inevitably brief, concrete, and positive. All this is to simply affirm that the dynamics of rapid change are already inherent in our natures and any approach that attempts to incorporate rapid change is merely piggybacking on what already is. But there is currently a catalytic agent that is prompting such efforts in the mental health arena—the advent of managed care.

Managed Care (The Catalytic Agent for Rapid Change)

Long-term and short-term therapies, regardless of modality, have coexisted and vied with each other for prominence and predominance from the genesis of the helping professions. So why now is there such a fervor about making therapy brief? The simple answer is money. "Managed care in mental health" (an ambiguous phrase if ever there was one) is the driving force behind completing therapy briefly. It is a reality and a primary reason why Problem Solving Group Therapy is appealing and pragmatic. But before moving on to explain the dynamics that make it so, I ask leave to make one quotable quote that captures for me the essence of managed care:

> Managed care is an economic anomaly prompting (read *forcing*) therapists to do brief treatment so that managed care companies can make money for their investors under the guise of saving money for businesses and individuals while playing on the entitlement myth that health insurance is a right for everyone when it is really a business.

A reasonable implication of the above statement is that therapists prompted by managed care must learn to elicit conversions, precipitate crises, and generate insights (Eureka experiences) in their clients so that therapeutic change can be brought about rapidly. That said, let us move on to a consideration of Brief Therapy as it relates to Problem Solving Group Therapy.

A Brief History of Brief Therapy (The Solution-Focused Reframe)

Short-term therapy or doing therapy briefly has always been embedded in the individual therapy approaches.

Behavioral therapy, the cognitive therapies, and crisis intervention therapy have all emphasized change processes that qualify as rapid in terms of both process and product. However, family therapy must be credited with organizing the constructs and creating the language and terminology that has resulted in our current, expedience-oriented, therapeutic climate.

Structural family therapists (Minuchin, 1974) discovered that by making a change in the structure of a system, changes would invariably occur almost immediately in the way the system functioned, thereby producing observable changes in the way individuals in the family behaved. These changes may or may not have directly related to the family's presenting problem, but they often alleviated the need for the family to have the problem.

Strategic family therapists (Haley, 1973, 1976; Madanes, 1981) were more concerned with the symptoms or problems themselves. They posited that the structure of the system was organized around the problem, and that if a strategic intervention could produce a shift in the system's response to the problem, change would eventuate. Subsequently, they devised an approach that encapsulated the family in a kind of inevitable change situation. They created therapeutic parameters that prevailed in such a way that no matter what the family did, change resulted. Their rules were concrete and fairly simple: The family was told that change was guaranteed, that families were not to change too quickly, and that time was limited (i.e., families were given a temporal mandate that change must occur within a limited number of sessions, and whether change occurred or not that's all they would get). Then by using directives, either straight or paradoxical, the family was instructed to do something different. The result was typically change, and symptoms (problems) abated.

Enterprising family therapists, in the interest of expediency, became intrigued by the "directives" aspect of the process and began to question whether the solution portion of the intervention could be developed as an entity in its own right. This gave rise to the solution-focused or brief therapy approach (De Shazer, 1980, 1982, 1985). Instead of spending time on the problem, they concentrated on solutions based on the premise that the solution was the problem and not the problem. In other words, people used outmoded, inappropriate, or ineffective solutions which resulted in the continuation of their problems and increased their distress. So instead of wasting energy muddling through what the problem was and what had not worked, solution-focused therapists jumped right into the problem solving end of the business. The classic intervention became, "If you cannot remember you have this problem, what will your life be like? How will you feel? What will you think? What will you do?" From the responses to these queries, ideas for solutions were formulated, and therapy became a process of implementing them.

Elements of each of the above described family therapy conceptualizations are part of the underpinnings of Problem Solving Group Therapy as will be evident in the remainder of the chapter.

GROUP THEORY

Group theory, research, and practice have all provided evidence to substantiate the premise that therapy groups evolve through a developmental process characterized by identifiable stages that are consistent within and across groups. These stages may vary in number and nomenclature, but they generally describe the same phenomena (Glass, 1978). The process, however, is a basic facilitative element of the therapeutic change experienced by individual group members. An overview of the group therapy process is presented here emphasising the interpersonal dynamics that characterize it. The model described is a summary of more in-depth discussion presented elsewhere (Trotzer, 1999, Chapters 4 & 5).

The process of group therapy is comprised of five stages that reflect characteristics of our basic human needs, qualities of therapeutic relationships, and the dynamics of problem solving. In addition, each stage includes a set of developmental tasks (24 in all; See Figure 48.2) that must be accounted for if the group is to evolve through the various stages in a cogent manner. This process establishes a milieu that accounts for individual needs in a relational context (the group), thereby setting the problem solving process in motion (See Figure 48.3). Group members realize the group is a safe place to talk about their problems (step 1), and understand that even though they have problems they are still accepted by the group as persons. This acceptance enables them to accept their problems as part of themselves (ego-syntonic vs. ego-dystonic; step 2), and prepares them for taking responsibility for their problems (internal locus of control vs. external locus of control; step 3). Once problems have been owned without negative ramifications relative to self esteem, developing and implementing a plan to solve them (step 4) and implementing successful changes into one's life (step 5) follow. Johnson and Johnson (1997) make the point that both the origin and solution to a client's psychological problems can be found in their relationships with other people. Consequently, the group therapy process is a prototype for problem solving by its very nature.

Security Stage

The initial stage of the group process is characterized by feelings of discomfort, anxiety, and resistance common

I: The Security Stage
Objective: Develop a psychologically safe environment in which each member can feel secure and free to engage in self-disclosure about themselves and their problems.

Security Stage Developmental Tasks
1. Getting Acquainted: Develops rapport and begins connecting process
2. Interpersonal Warmup: Eases reconnecting each time the group reconvenes
3. Setting Boundaries: Provides knowledge of expectations and parameters of the group experience
4. Building Trust: Initiated at the beginning of group and continues throughout the process

II: The Acceptance Stage
Objective: Form a milieu in which members experience a sense of belonging and acceptance as a person and as a member with and in spite of problems or issues they are experiencing.

Acceptance Stage Developmental Tasks
1. Personal Sharing: Develops the communication channel of self-disclosure for sharing oneself with the group
2. Giving Feedback: Develops the communication channel of feedback between members and sharing of perceptions of one another
3. Building Cohesiveness and Closeness: Develops a connectedness in the group that secures belonging and generates a sense of caring in community
4. Accepting Self: Generates experiences in which members learn to accept and value themselves as persons
5. Accepting Others: Generates experiences in which members learn to accept and value others and learn to value and respect similarities and differences

III: The Responsibility Stage
Objective: Develop a group atmosphere with a norm that emphasizes differentiation in a group context and an expectation that supports owning responsibility for one's self and one's problems while practicing individuation/differentiation of one's own identity.

Responsibility Stage Developmental Tasks
1. Self-Assessment: Provides opportunity to critically examine oneself without fear of judgment or criticism
2. Recognizing Ownership: Helps members take responsibility for their own lives and realize the inherent empowerment of personal choice
3. Building Responsibility: Provides experiences in which members can differentiate, recognize, and respect diversity and build a sense of responsibility as a person and member of a group
4. Giving Respect: Contributes to the group atmosphere by requiring members to attribute worth and value to others in the group
5. Doing a Fair Share: Engages members in group interactions as contributors and resources

IV: The Work Stage
Objective: Develop a working-together culture in which members can work collaboratively to help each other resolve problems and cope with issues in their lives.

Work Stage Developmental Tasks
1. Problem Solving: Establishes a process for identifying, clarifying, and understanding problems for the purpose of developing a solution-focused plan that incorporates practice, implementation, and evaluation
2. Decision Making: Provides opportunity for members to make decisions in their lives for the purpose of empowerment
3. Learning and Applying Information and Skills to Personal life
4. Mobilizing Group Resources: Promotes the resources of group members as the primary means of help in the group
5. Reality Testing: Ensures that the productivity and impact of the group and choices of individual members are relevant and appropriate

V: The Closing Stage
Objective: Terminate the group experience individually and collectively in a manner that constructively perpetuates the impact of the group experience and enables each member to disconnect as the group disbands or as the individual leaves.

Closing Stage Developmental Tasks
1. Addressing Unfinished Business: Gives members opportunity to address unfinished personal, interpersonal, or interactional group business.
2. Giving Support: Provides reinforcement, accountability, and encouragement as members reintegrate outside the group.
3. Affirming Growth: Uses self-disclosure to promote members' sharing their growth and learning in the group.
4. Confirming Growth: Uses feedback to confirm members' growth and learning in the group.
5. Saying Goodbye: Provides means whereby members can disconnect from the group and disband as a group.
6. Follow-up: Individually tailored efforts to follow up members for evaluation, accountability, and determination of continued growth.

**Figure 48.2   Problem solving group therapy
group stages and developmental tasks.**

Process (Group Dynamics)	Content (Problem Solving)
I. *Security Stage:* Develop a psychologically safe environment in which each member can feel secure and free to talk about themselves and their problems.	1. Find a person and place where it is safe to admit to and talk about problems

Individual Need: Security
Relationship Trait: Trust

II. *Acceptance Stage:* Form a milieu in which members experience a sense of belonging and acceptance as a person and as a member with and in spite of problems or issues they are dealing with.	2. Accept problems as part of one's self.

Individual Need: Love and belonging
Relationship Trait: Acceptance

III. *Responsibility Stage:* Develop an atmosphere that emphasizes individuality in a group context and develop a norm of owning responsibility for one's self and one's problems.	3. Take responsibility for one's own problems and commit to resolving them.

Individual Need: Esteem
Relationship Trait: Differentiation and accountability

IV. *Work Stage:* Develop a working-together culture in which group members work together to help each other deal with their issues and solve their problems.	4. Identify, clarify, understand the problem, and work to resolve it (solution-focused plan, practice, implementation, and evaluation).

Individual Need: Self-actualization
Relationship Trait: Cooperation

V. *Closing Stage:* Formulate closure with an emphasis on transfer of learning, internalization of change, and affirmation.	5. Problem is solved and problem-solving process is learned.

Figure 48.3   Problem solving group therapy.

to forming interpersonal relationships in a new social environment. Group members, regardless of how well they have been orientated, are reluctant to interact because their presence in the group is contingent upon some recognized purpose that involves personal risk. This stage is referred to as the security stage because it must account for each group member's need for psychological safety. The goal of this stage is to develop a psychologically safe environment characterized by trust and confidentiality in which each member can feel secure and free to talk about themselves and their problems.

The basic developmental tasks of the security stage are Getting Acquainted, Interpersonal Warmup, Setting Boundaries, and Building Trust. As these tasks are addressed, members are able to make contact with one another, establishing a basic rapport and connection that facilitates a deeper level of interpersonal relating.

Acceptance Stage

The second stage of the group process is predominantly concerned with the development of group cohesiveness. The acceptance stage is derived from our psychological need to belong. Caring and being cared about are essential therapeutic qualities of this stage because members need to experience acceptance before they are willing to disclose parts of themselves or relational difficulties that require change. As group cohesiveness develops, a supportive milieu is formed which reinforces the norm of personal sharing and where disclosing problems becomes an integral part of a total person perspective.

The developmental tasks of the acceptance stage are Personal Sharing, Giving Feedback, Building Cohesiveness and Closeness, Learning to Accept Self, and Learning to Accept Others. As these tasks are performed, a cohesive and supportive group environment emerges in which members become willing to risk individuation, which prepares them for movement into the next stage of group development.

Responsibility Stage

The responsibility stage of the group process is a transitional phase that reflects our psychological need for respect (esteem), which is acquired through responsible, individual action in relationships in which individuals are perceived as worthwhile. The group moves from an emphasis on acceptance of self and others to evaluating self and others in terms of ownership of and satisfaction with their behavior, feelings, and thoughts. Focus shifts from a group orientation to an individual orientation in which members are helped to explore their uniqueness and to take responsibility for themselves. Group members not only become responsible for themselves but also commit to helping each other work on problems as well.

The developmental tasks of the responsibility stage are Self-Assessment, Recognizing Ownership, Building Responsibility, Giving Respect, and Doing a Fair Share. These tasks form the foundation and impetus for working on personal problems. Members realize their own initiative is necessary to solve problems while recognizing their interdependency within the group and in society. Subsequently, the stage is set for investment of group resources and energies in the problem solving focus of the next stage of the group life cycle.

Work Stage

The work stage is the central core of the group process and focuses on the basic purposes for which the group was formed. The atmosphere and relationships in the group allow individuals to examine their personal concerns without fears of rejection or reprisal, explore alternatives to resolving those problems, experiment with new behaviors in a safe environment before risking changes outside the group, and export potential changes outside the group while maintaining a supportive connection in the group. The leader as expert, guide, and facilitator contributes by encouraging members to be resources to each other when working on problems and by keeping the group in touch with reality. The work stage prepares group members for reentry into the world outside the group, arming them with well-thought-out plans, useful skills and behaviors, and bolstered self-confidence. Implementation and integration are emphasized through the supportive functioning of the group for purposes of acknowledgement, encouragement, and accountability.

The developmental tasks of the work stage are Personal Problem Solving (See Figure 48.4), Decision Making, Learning and Applying Information and Skills to Personal Problems, Mobilizing Group Resources, and Reality Testing. These tasks form the agenda for each session during the work stage. They are applied and recycled as each member addresses the specific concerns that brought him or her into the group. When these concerns are resolved and/or the group approaches its time-limit boundary, the final stage of the group process is imminent.

Closing Stage

The closing stage of the group process serves a valuable transitional function for both the group as a unit and for its individual members. This stage is characterized by members actively pursuing change in their lives outside the group while at the same time preparing for disengagement from the group. Closure brings the group experience to an end by enabling members to be responsible for the work they have done, acknowledging and reinforcing it, and then having them move effectively back into the mainstream of their day-to-day lives without the group.

The developmental tasks of the closing stage are Addressing Unfinished Business, Giving Support, Affirming Change or Growth, Confirming Change or Growth, and Follow-Up. These tasks translate termination into a commencement experience in which group members are

---

I. IDENTIFY THE PROBLEM: Individual indicates the nature and focus of the problem.

II. CLARIFY THE PROBLEM: Group seeks information and asks questions to clarify the problem.

III. UNDERSTAND THE PROBLEM: Group develops a problem statement that represents a consensual understanding of the problem.

IV. GENERATE ALTERNATIVES: Individual and group members brainstorm (without evaluation) alternatives for resolving the problem (divergent thinking process).

V. EVALUATE ALTERNATIVES: Individual and group evaluate the alternatives, citing pros and cons (convergent thinking process).

VI. DECISION MAKING: Individual selects solution from alternatives discussed, derivatives of alternatives discussed, or another option.

VII. PLAN: Group works with the individual to devise a plan for implementing the solution (includes a commitment).

VIII. PRACTICE: In the social laboratory, of the group, the individual tests the solution and develops confidence and competence in the solution prior to implementation.

IX. IMPLEMENTATION: Individual enacts the plan outside the group reports results to group.

X. EVALUATE: Group helps individual evaluate results, revise plan as necessary, affirms or holds individual accountable.

Figure 48.4 PSGT problem solving process.

able to disengage from the group without undermining the work that has been accomplished. They propel members forward in their lives with confidence and assure clarity in the closure experience.

METHODOLOGY

The following section on methodology will be organized in a general-to-specific manner considering generic group therapist skills and functions first and then presenting idiosyncratic techniques endemic to Problem Solving Group Therapy (PSGT). Specific methods reviewed relate to using family theory as a group therapy resource and the use of structured activities in conducting PSGT.

Group Therapist Skills and Functions

Effective group therapists develop skills and engage in functions that relate to the individual member, the group context and the group purpose. They use their expertise to develop, enhance, and control the interaction between individual personalities, group dynamics, and group content as the therapy group unfolds and evolves (Donigian & Malnati, 1997).

Leadership Skills

Leadership skills can be divided into three categories based on their nature and the impetus of their emergence. Reaction skills are responsive in nature and aid the leader in being receptive to individuals and the group as whole. Interaction skills serve a mediating/moderating function in the group. They provide the leader the wherewithal to facilitate, control, guide, and intervene in the group interaction and serve as a catalytic agent relative to therapeutic impact. Action skills enable the leader to be proactive in promoting and directing the group process. They provide the means by which leaders can assert their expertise for the good of individual members or the group (Trotzer, 1999).

Reaction skills are the derivative of the "active listening" expertise of skilled helpers. They include such skills as restatement, reflection (both content and affect), clarification, summarization, tracking (individual members), and scanning (group dynamics). Interaction skills include moderating, interpreting, linking, blocking, supporting, and consensus taking. Action skills include questioning, probing, tone setting, confronting, personal sharing, and modeling. (For a more detailed discussion of each of these skills see Trotzer, 1999, Chapter 6.)

Leadership Functions

Functions are the operationalized use of skills in the group context for purposes of conducting a therapeutic process. While the manner in which each leader uses skills is determined by his or her personality, theoretical orientation, and training and by the nature of the group, the basic functions a leader performs are generic. Leadership functions include initiating and maintaining effective group process, helping members establish and address goals, protecting members from harm, and effecting appropriate termination. Leaders function to promote, facilitate, initiate, and guide group interaction and intervene when necessary. They perform rulekeeping, consolidation, and conflict resolution functions. They act catalytically to enhance communication and mobilize group resources. The combination of skills and functions generates the essence of leadership in a particular therapy group (Trotzer, 1999).

Family Theory as a Resource in Problem Solving Group Therapy

PSGT utilizes an integrated blend of group dynamics methodology and family systems methodology to enhance the relevance of the therapeutic experience and increase the transferability of the learning and change that results. The importance of this relationship has been described by Donigian and Hulse-Killacky (1999).

> Family-centered group therapists see the family as the first group in which individuals learn to interact. It is within the family that individuals initially develop human relations skills, learn the rules that guide individuals in interacting with others, learn how to manage conflict, learn how to deal with authority, learn how to become responsible, and so forth. These skills and knowledge are what individuals bring to group therapy. Family theory helps explain and develop an understanding of how and why individuals behave as they do from the context of their family of origin (p. 26).

Family theory is a resource to Problem Solving Group Therapists in three ways.

Group Process

Both the family and the group rely on interpersonal dynamics to function. Consequently, each group member comes to group therapy with primary group experience in a family that leaves indelible effects relative to interpersonal relating and provides blueprints for relating outside the family. Therefore, the more the group leader knows about family theory and family dynamics, the more understanding and expertise he or she will have in leading groups relative to group process.

Group Content

Second, most client problems relate directly or indirectly to family or intimate relationships. As Satir (1972) has observed, "troubled families produce troubled people" (p. 18). Family background may provide issues of derivative impact or current family interactions may be the prime focus of a group member's problem. Therefore the more cognizant the group leader is of family theory, the more understanding he or she will have of client problems and the more effective the interventions leading to change will be. Grounding in systems thinking, family of origin and intergenerational family dynamics, the family developmental life cycle, the impact of divorce, the dynamics of single-parent and remarried families, and the importance of ethnicity, race, culture, and diversity in families are essential for Problem Solving Group Therapists to be effective.

Group Techniques

Third, family theory is an excellent conceptual base from which to construct group techniques and structured interventions. Group therapists can develop myriad activities that enhance the group process and bring relevant material to the surface for group interaction. Both intrapersonal and interpersonal issues derived from one's family background and current family experience can emerge. The advantages of family based techniques are that they have immediate relevance for each group member (everyone has a family background), they are intrinsically motivating and stimulating (people are naturally curious about other people's families), and they emphasize the expertise of each group member (no one is more knowledgeable or expert about his or her family background than the presenter). Consequently, Problem Solving Group Therapists use family-based techniques in conducting the group process as demonstrated in the case example. (See Trotzer, 1999, Chapter 14, and Donigian & Hulse-Killacky, 1999, Chapter 3, for more detail).

Structured Techniques in Problem Solving Group Therapy

Structured activities are an identifying feature of PSGT because they are the primary means of generating a work-oriented, problem solving, solution-focused perspective into the fabric of the process from its very inception. They are also the means by which the systemic overlay of family theory is integrated into the context. As such, a brief consideration of their nature and use is warranted.

Structured activities are differentiated from other group methods and techniques by three distinguishing characteristics. They involve specific directions and parameters that are communicated to the group, thereby providing a format and focus for group interaction; they often use materials or props to carry out the activity; and

they can be standardized, thus enabling group leaders to use them in the same or adapted form across a wide variety of groups and with diverse clientele (Trotzer, 1999). The three basic ways structured activities are used in PSGT are to initiate, facilitate, and terminate (close or conclude) group interaction.

Initiating Activities

Initiating activities are useful at the beginning of group sessions and early in the group process (Stockton, Rohde, & Haughey, 1994; Hetzel, Barton, & Davenport, 1994) to introduce problem topics; generate a specific, new, or different focus; and provide structure to the interaction. Initiating activities are useful for orienting members to helpful group skills or behaviors and to help them iron out process glitches when they occur. They are also helpful in addressing issues of resistance, because the activity provides a natural target for resistive action.

Facilitating Activities

The main purpose of using structured activities to facilitate is to help the group use its resources to the fullest possible extent. These activities are designed in response to interaction in the group rather than as a stimulant to interaction. As such, they help to clarify problems, present alternatives, alleviate anxiety-producing circumstances, and break through impasses that occur in the group. Use of structured activities in this manner usually results in ready acceptance by group members because their design emanates directly from what is transpiring in the group.

Terminating Activities

Structured activities are helpful when individuals conclude their participation in the group, when individual group sessions end, and when the group as a whole disbands. They bring closure to the group experience and provide a jumping-off place for members. Their impact removes much of the awkwardness of ending and makes for a clear transition between being in the group and out of group. They involve little risk and generally enjoy a cooperative response. The case example that follows uses structured activities in the ways just described.

CASE EXAMPLE

The following material outlines a PSGT group designed for adolescents in an alternative school or inpatient/outpatient psychiatric setting. Six to eight members, ages 15 to 17 including both genders, meet twice a week for two hours over a four-week period with a follow-up session scheduled two to four weeks later if feasible. A short-term condensed format is used because the turnover rate in the population from which members are drawn is typically high. However, group members may be recycled through the process with other groups because the emphasis is on problem solving, not on continuity of group membership.

Group members are identified and referred to PSGT by their primary therapist who, together with the adolescent, completes a referral form that specifies the problem(s) the adolescent intends to work on in group. This form is forwarded to the group therapist prior to a screening interview, during which the problem is reviewed, the ground rules and nature of the group are discussed, and member questions are addressed.

Structured activities in each group session introduce and use family-centered, work-oriented, solution-focused dynamics to make problem solving primary in the group process. Group members are given problem solving notebooks in which to record their ideas spontaneously, as part of a session-ending evaluation activity, or as a journal entry between sessions. Structured activities used reflect dynamics of the group stages and their respective developmental tasks, and serve as the means by which a framework is generated, content is raised, and an agenda is formulated. Additional activities may be introduced and utilized to facilitate progress or conclude sessions. Examples of activities are presented for each session.

Problem Solving Group Therapy Format

Session I (Security Stage)

Will and Won't Cards.   Members are given two 3 × 5 cards on which to write three things they "will not talk about in group" (Won't Cards), and three things they "will talk about in group" (Will Cards). The Won't Cards are disposed of, and the Will Cards are shared in a go-round format (Related task: Setting Boundaries). This activity stresses the volitional autonomy of group membership.

Introductory Dyads.   In Problem-Sharing/Perspective-Taking Dyads, members rotate through four dyads in which they share who they are, what their problem is, and how another party in their life would suggest they resolve it, such as a parent, peer, friend, teacher, Higher Power, and so on. A different perspective is required for each dyad. This activity helps members get acquainted, establishes problem sharing as a norm, and introduces the vital problem solving skill of perspective-taking (Goleman, 1995).

Session II (Acceptance Stage)

Draw Your Family Table.   Following an interpersonal warmup task using a go-round, members are asked to draw the table at which their family eats, placing all members of their household around the table. Words or phrases are added to describe each person around the table and a brief description of their problem is written on the tabletop. Each group member then describes their family members and indicates how each person around the table would suggest that the group member solve his or her problem. Group members are instructed to listen for the family members they most agree with or most disagree with. At the end of the description, each group member is asked to place themselves around the table near the person they most agree with or opposite the person they most disagree with. They are then asked to give feedback explaining their placement (Related tasks: Personal Sharing and Giving Feedback; Trotzer, 1998).

Session III (Acceptance–Responsibility Stage)

Strength Bombardment.   The entire session is devoted to a lab activity designed to accentuate positive dynamics and resources. Elements of the lab include writing a list of accomplishments and achievements as defined by your self (Task: Self-Assessment); writing a self-statement describing only positive traits (Task: Recognizing Ownership); sharing the list of achievements (Task: Building Responsibility); giving and receiving positive feedback using an open-chair go-round in which each person takes the open chair and receives "only positive" feedback from each other group member (Tasks: Giving Respect and Doing a Fair Share); and identifying resources and assets that might relate to solving their problem. Members assist each other in this effort.

Session IV (Responsibility Stage)

Diamond and 4 Activity.   A diagram of a large diamond is given to each group member. Each writes the ideal solution (no limits) to their problem in the middle of the diamond and on each side of the diamond a reason, excuse, or obstacle that prevents that solution from being applied (four in all). One by one, each group member presents his or her ideal solution and its barriers to the group. While the presenter listens in silence, the group discusses the solution and the obstacles and suggests ways of overcoming them. After a period of time the presenter interacts with the group about the group's suggestions and perceptions. This activity is timed so that each member has opportunity to participate.

Sessions V–VII (Work Stage)

Each session is organized via a different problem solving strategy (Tasks: Problem Solving, Mobilizing Group Resources, and Reality Testing).

1. Problem Rating Strategy for Agenda Setting: Each member writes out his or her problem on a 3 × 5 card and passes it to the leader. The leader reads each problem one at a time and asks members to rate the problem on a 1 to 5 scale based on their interest in the problem, identification with the problem, and sense of its seriousness. (This is a rating, not a ranking, process.) When all problems have been read and rated, the ratings are totaled and the problems rank-ordered from highest to lowest, creating an agenda. The Problem Solving Process (Figure 48.4) is handed out and reviewed. The group is then instructed to start with the highest rated problem and work it through using the problem solving schemata. This activity can be done in subgroups to facilitate efficiency.

2. Making Miracles Happen: The solution-focused miracle intervention format is introduced and used in this session. Each member is informed that due to the onset of a unique form of amnesia, they can not remember what their problem is. Discussion is then directed to answering the questions, "If you can't remember what your problem is, how do you feel? What do you think? What will you do?" Each person's responses are reviewed by the group to glean ideas for solutions.

3. Clearness Committee Method: Subgroups of three to four are formed in which one person is the "focus person" and the others are committee members. This strategy is adapted from a Quaker tradition (Palmer, 1998). The focus person supplies the committee with a written description of their problem. The committee members then ask thought-provoking, open-ended questions to get the person to think deeply and critically about his or her problem. No advising, suggestions, or personal sharing is permitted. Only asking questions and listening to answers is involved. One additional limit is confidentiality (i.e., once the questioning period is over, the committee members agree not to initiate discussion of the problem with each other or the focus person). The questioning period is for a significant amount of time (30 minutes to one hour).

Session VIII (Closure Stage)

The Accountability Catapult.   The final session is devoted to concretizing the solution-focused emphasis of the group by engaging in activities that create accountability, acknowledge success, and make provisions for follow-up. Members write personal contracts that are signed and sealed in the group, form accountability partnerships, give commencement addresses, write letters to themselves, and set up a follow-up meeting. (All closure tasks are relevant).

SUMMARY

Problem Solving Group Therapy is a pragmatic approach that is useful in a wide variety of settings with a broad range of clients and client problems. Its adaptability is its calling card. It provides a focus, format, and framework that enables group therapists, regardless of philosophical orientation or theoretical affinity, to use it effectively with a modicum of effort. It demystifies the therapeutic process and gives credence to problem solving as a therapeutic product while maintaining the integrity of group therapy as a professional modality.

REFERENCES

De Shazer, S. (1980). *Clues: Investigating solutions in brief therapy.* New York: Norton.

De Shazer, S. (1982). *Patterns of brief family therapy: An ecosystem approach.* New York: Guilford.

De Shazer, S. (1985). *Keys to solution in brief therapy.* New York: Norton.

Donigian, J., & Hulse-Kilacky, D. (1999). *Critical incidents in group work.* (2nd edition). Pacific Grove, CA: Brooks/Cole.

Donigian, J., & Malnati, R. (1997). *Systemic group therapy: A triadic model.* Pacific Grove, CA: Brooks/Cole.

Glass, S. (March, 1978). Group work in the 80s: What next after encounter groups? Luncheon address at the meeting of the Association for Specialists in Group Work, Washington, D.C.

Goleman, D. (1995). *Emotional intelligence.* New York: Bantam.

Haley, J. (1973). *Uncommon therapy.* New York: Norton.

Haley, J. (1976). *Problem-solving therapy.* San Francisco: Jossey-Bass.

Hetzel, R. D., Barton, D. A., & Davenport, D. S. (1994). Helping men change: A group counseling model for male clients. *Journal for Specialists in Group Work, 19*(2), 52–64.

Johnson, D. W., & Johnson, F. P. (1997). *Joining together: Group theory and group skills* (6th edition). Englewood Cliffs, NJ: Prentice Hall.

Luft, J. (1970). *Group process: An introduction to group dynamics* (2nd edition). Palo Alto, CA: National Press Books.

Luft, J. (1984). *Group process: An introduction to group dynamics* (3rd edition). Palo Alto, CA: National Press Books.

Madanes, C. (1981). *Strategic family therapy.* San Francisco: Jossey-Bass.

Maslow, A. (1943). A theory of human motivation. *Psychological Review, 50,* 370–396.

Maslow, A. (1954). *Motivation and personality.* New York: Harper.

Maslow, A. (1962). *Toward a psychology of being.* Princeton, NJ: Van Nostrand.

Minuchin, S. (1974). *Families and family therapy.* Cambridge, MA: Harvard University Press.

Palmer, P. J. (1998). *The courage to teach: Exploring the inner landscape of a teacher's life.* San Francisco: Jossey-Bass.

Satir, V. (1972). *Peoplemaking.* Palo Alto, CA: Science and Behavior Books.

Stockton, R., Rohde, R. I., & Haughey, J. (1994). The effects of structured group exercises on cohesion, engagement, avoidance, and conflict. *Small Group Research, 23,* 155–168.

Trotzer, J. P. (1972). Group counseling: Process and practice. *Guidelines for Pupil Services, 10,* 105–110. Madison, WI: Department of Public Instruction.

Trotzer, J. P. (1977). *The counselor and the group: Integrating theory, training and practice.* Monterey, CA: Brooks/Cole.

Trotzer, J. P. (1985). Interpersonal problem solving: The group counseling approach. In R. K. Conyne (Ed.), *The group worker's handbook: Varieties in group experience* (pp. 91–112). Springfield, IL: Thomas.

Trotzer, J. P. (1989). *The counselor and the group: Integrating theory, training and practice* (2nd edition). Muncie, IN: Accelerated Development.

Trotzer, J. P. (1998). Draw your family table/family-o-gram. In H. G. Rosenthal (Ed.), *Favorite counseling and therapy techniques: 51 therapists share their most creative strategies* (pp. 179–181). Bristol, PA: Accelerated Development.

Trotzer, J. P. (1999). *The counselor and the group: Integrating theory, training and practice* (3rd edition). Bristol, PA: Accelerated Development.

Yalom, I. D. (1985). *The theory and practice of group psychotherapy* (3rd edition). New York: Basic.

Chapter 49

PROGRAMMED SUCCESS THERAPY

FRANK DUMONT and J. DAVID SMITH

Frank Dumont, the primary author of this system, has fashioned a simple and logical system of therapy by combining the educational wisdom of past ages with what we have learned of human behavior from recent studies. The focus of Programmed Success Therapy is the dysfunctional self that has generalized past failures in one domain of life to pessimistic expectations in similar and even unrelated domains.

The theory, built on a scaffolding of six principles, first requires recognition of the current developmental level of the client. From that perspective the therapist designs a succession of graded experiences in which clients are led from the known to the unknown, promoting a sense of competence as they climb a gradual slope of increasingly demanding tasks. Finally, a process is implemented for reframing apparent setbacks to the therapeutic goals.

Programmed Success Therapy has a wide range of possibilities for use with clients of all ages, whether treated individually or in groups. Based as it is on educational principles, it can be used for helping children as well as adults to overcome discouragement and to take charge of their lives.

DEFINITION

Programmed Success Therapy (PST) is a method of changing the perceptions, behavioral repertoire, attitudes, and self-concept of clients who have learned dysfunctional schemas in all these domains. It is based on a simple theory: Most people who regard themselves as failures have transferred schemas resulting from negative experiences they have endured in one sphere of their life to other spheres, private and social, that are more or less unrelated to them. They have lost awareness of their personal resources and have learned to attend to their deficits and past failures. PST is a program of systematic sensitization to both the positive potential and qualities of the client's personality and the positively toned qualities of their environment. It frames objectives such that the therapist can guarantee success at every step of the process. That means that the therapeutic process begins where the client feels secure and competent, and then proceeds from there in just noticeably more difficult (JNMD) increments to more taxing assignments. This is an educational program and uses the classic principle of psychopedagogy: *Always proceed from the known to the unknown.* It is not an exclusively intrapsychic therapy, because it calls for an interaction with, and a shaping of, the social environment in which client complaints and fears have originated.

CURRENT STATUS

The body of principles that constitute this approach to doing therapy can be found larded, often implicitly, throughout a large number of theoretical systems. The authors make no claim to originality for any single principle articulated here. (Inevitably, psychologists find that their most treasured inventions were articulated, or at least prefigured, by more or less renowned thinkers in past eras.) PST is a newly configured perspective for working with such individuals as Albert Ellis (2000) calls, "Nice Neurotics." It owes much to Alfred Adler and has much in common with the numerous therapies that have been spun off from the work of the exceptionally gifted Milton H. Erickson (e.g., Zeig, 1980). The experiential aspect of PST has much in common with the exposure techniques of behavior therapy, but its closest cousin is the solution-focused approach to working with client dysfunction that one finds in the work of Steve de Shazer (e.g., 1985) and Bill O'Hanlon (e.g., O'Hanlon & Weiner-Davis, 1989).

THEORY

First Principle

The most important principle of sound psychotherapy is the following: Work at the client's developmental level, neurological, emotional, and cognitive, regardless of their chronological age. This of course applies to the education of toddlers and adolescents as much as to adults—and to their education as well as to their therapy. It should go without saying that the fundamental need of infants, children, and even adults is to live among people who are caring, nurturing, loving, and attentive to them (cf. the copious literature on Attachment Theory, e.g., Ainsworth, 1966; Bowlby, 1973). In the domain of education, however, we postulate that the most grievous errors in childrearing are attributing cognitions to children that are beyond their understanding, and that often are appropriate only to mature adults; and exacting behavior from them that requires a level of maturity they have not yet reached. If an individual does not have the neuro-muscular-skeletal capability, nor the experience and practice necessary, to perform certain complex psychomotor activities, (for example, a four-year-old practicing on a grand piano), putting pressure on him or her to do so creates tension, a sense of futility, and an anxiety that if sustained can develop into a dispositional problem that will require therapy in the future. With equal cogency, this reasoning applies to clients who have sought therapy. Developmental psychologists will recognize the signature of Arnold Gesell (Gesell & Ilg, 1943) in these notions.

Second Principle

In collaboration with clients design a series of success experiences. Such successes will slowly erode the constellation of negative self-attributions that have hampered their efforts to make friends, advance their career, free themselves from dysfunctional habits, achieve mature sexual fulfillment, overcome fears and social avoidance patterns, or dissipate crippling self-doubts. These self-attributions not only result from the buffets of a stressful environment, but also from the real and imagined limitations that spring from within. The matrix for any dysfunction is always systemic—in this context, bio-psychosocial. Dysfunctional self-attributions are often found, surprisingly, in relatively competent individuals who are perceived as such by others. They have often become oblivious to the aspects of their personality that are solid grounds for success (in the areas where they have felt unsuccessful) as well as to the availability of other opportunities for success that are fully realizable.

Many clients who seek clinical help from professional helpers are just such individuals. They consider themselves failed members of society, at least in significant domains of their lives. Their anguish, which drives them into the clinic, springs not only from their real and imagined failures but also from their assessment of themselves as inadequate. What we know is that this particular malaise is a continuous variable. It is present at a minimal and innocuous level in individuals who typically cope with life's experiences more effectively than those who seek professional help. At higher levels it becomes increasingly disabling, even though the individuals who suffer from it are able to compensate more or less adaptively by a number of strategies, and by adopting a persona that is intended to communicate mastery, competence, and self-assurance.

Negative self-assessments promote a pattern of behavior that aggravates feelings of incompetence. They move people into a spiral of social avoidance and lost opportunities, of discouragement, self-contempt, and further behavioral failures. The acknowledgement of these is the first step to sanitizing this condition, and programmed successes are designed to reverse such a process.

Third Principle

Those therapies that are most effective utilize a set of principles that have an educational character (and have an ancient philosophical lineage as well). Programmed Success Therapy, proposed here, is just such an educational process. It is founded on the simple Thomistic principle that in order for learning to take place, one must proceed from the known to the unknown. Of course, "the known" is a continuous variable. There are various levels of competence relative to any concept or complex skill one possesses. Those clinical endeavors are most promising that begin at a place where our clients (the agents) have a sense of mastery of the materials and the actions to be performed. *We start where they feel competent.*

That many of our clients have distorted and dysfunctional views of themselves is a conviction springing from one of the authors' experience in the 1960s and 1970s with highly successful professional men and women with whom he participated in human relations workshops. He was stunned to witness the vulnerabilities, fears, self-doubts, vocational confusion, and insecurities that they felt they could safely reveal in the haven of a professional clinic. Some of the most successful appeared to be the most convinced they were fundamentally flawed. When they removed themselves from behind the social ramparts of privilege, titles, institutional rank, and money, their professional persona began to splinter, and in some cases the cracks raced crazily in directions that surprised *them* as well as their fellows. As this happened to a participant, one sensed one was witnessing the death of a noble denizen of the jungle who had wandered onto the savanna. The others, who had their own eroding defenses to attend to, usually felt a keen sense of responsibility to provide to such persons the support, the personal reinforcements, and the small but potent social successes that are essential for leading a productive life.

Fourth Principle

Determine what the client wishes to achieve and build a ramp to it. The slope needs to be gradual and gentle. Those of our clients who have experienced serious failure have a need for nothing so much as the sweet, if modest, taste of success in a domain in which it has eluded them. Motivating clients to risk an activity that has a significant chance of failure is unnecessary and unwise. One of the authors recalls a meeting with an aged Japanese monk in the early 1960s who recounted to him his experience climbing Mt. Fujiyama. Annually, on a national holiday, he joined a throng of people who wished to climb to the summit. He recounted how the youths in the crowd, at a signal, would begin a rapid ascent, at a half run. He, on the other hand, had always proceeded up the slopes taking small steps—slowly placing one foot in front of the other. "My objective," he explained, "was always to reach the next turn in the path, and I was always pleased when I reached it." He stated that after several hours of ascent, he began to meet his fellow climbers, physically spent, sprawled by the wayside. Their run up the mountain had finished prematurely. He slowly plodded on, pleased to be taking one step at a time, and he continued to pass those who had thought to climb the mountain with giant strides. He added that he had always reached the top.

This mystic was not in the excellent physical condition of many of the younger climbers whom he surpassed in his ascent to his goal, but he respected the mountain and the demands it would make on his resources and he measured his own strength. The approach advocated by PST is similar to the philosophy of this monk. Our view has been that clients need to respect the constraints of the social environment in which they choose or are obliged to live. On the other hand, they are never without the resources that would allow them to make small steps toward modest goals. We can sensitize them to this by collaborating with them in programming small successes that can swell into a cascade of behavioral changes that eventually lead to the positive outcomes that have long eluded them. The old saw, "nothing succeeds like success" is especially valid in psychotherapy.

Fifth Principle

Success is a relative matter. For example, in a difficult economic environment, suffering smaller losses than one's fellows can be construed as a relative success. Reframing defeats as successes can enable recovery from disabling mentation and behavior. Milton Erickson recounted that the best teacher he ever had was poliomyelitis, a disease which nevertheless hastened his death. The work of Shelley Taylor (e.g., begin with her 1983 article in *American Psychologist*) demonstrates that those women she studied who managed best following a catastrophic trauma in their personal lives demonstrated a number of adaptive strategies. A pertinent one in this context is their penchant for "downward social comparisons." They passed in review the numerous individuals who had suffered misfortunes similar to their own, but who were more sorely afflicted. In a relativistic, coordinate universe such as the one the physicists describe for us, you can establish a center wherever you please. In a moral universe such as we all equally inhabit, your center can be anywhere that allows you to make a comforting comparison with the rest of the human race.

It has been objected that setbacks in therapy are highly probable. After all, life goes on outside the clinic, and it is filled with unforeseen as well as anticipated hazards. Some defeats are inevitable. Distinctions have to be made here. First, the therapeutic endeavor is not one that attacks on all fronts at once. Calvin Coolidge is reported to have said, "You can't do everything at once, but you can do something at once." The task of the therapist is to bring some common sense to bear on catalyzing the resolve of the client to *do something at once.* Frequently, clients have been so demoralized by the magnitude of the task they have undertaken that they have stopped making reasonably sustained efforts to succeed in it. Secondly, success and failure are not "all or none" variables. It is an ill endeavor that harbors no redeeming qualities. On this continuum, it is rare that one slides so far away from total success that one can find no shred of value in the valiant attempt. The astute therapist will always be able to reframe any apparent failure as an effort that was worthy and noble. Incomplete successes are not setbacks but momentary interruptions in the client's advance.

Consistent with this is the notion that stumbling is not falling. Clients need to be informed that they will encounter difficulty when they undertake activities they have heretofore avoided. They must expect, for example, that their voice will crack when they speak out in class, their palms will be sweaty when they shake the hand of a prospective employer, or that they may experience a memory block (for which they may calmly excuse themselves) when they are speaking before a large audience. These are not signs of failure but signs of success, as the goal always is to face, rather than avoid, an anxiety-arousing experience. In fact, if a programmed experience does not evoke some anxiety, its therapeutic value is very limited, because clients do not have the opportunity to learn that they can cope with the anxiety that the experience elicits.

Sixth Principle

When our clients present a complaint, describe dilemmas they feel powerless to resolve, or express a yearning for a somatic or mental state that is free of pain, they are soliciting resources they already have, but that they are not aware that they have. Therapists (who are not mind readers) are not aware of what those resources are either. They need to rely on the judgments of their client, whose memory is an embodied history of innumerable experiences, many of them extremely painful.

Clients' problems are not simply rooted in cognition. Problems are organismic conditions that implicate every dimension of the *soma*. Damasio (1994), a world-class neurologist, has hypothesized that the body retains memories of bad outcomes, multitudes of them, that are evoked but never reach consciousness when a social situation presents itself. Bad experiences "mark" the body, and Damasio refers to this residue from the past as somatic markers (1994, Chapter 8). These memories are "sedimented" in the neurological substrate that primes our social intelligence. Our clients experience a set of gut reactions when a situation or a response option is proposed to them. This "feedforward mechanism" allows the total organism to respond, but in ways to which the conscious of the thinking person is largely not privy (cf., e.g., Mahoney, 1991, pp. 100–108; 390–435). Troubled clients have become sensitized to intrinsically benign stimuli that have become negatively toned discriminative stimuli. Although their friends and associates may regard their avoidance patterns and fears as irrational, some are in fact eminently reasonable in light of their personal history.

Programmed Success Therapy trusts the fears of the client. Clients know at subliminal levels what they have suffered and also know the social cues that surrounded bad experiences. It is not necessary, nor may it even be possible, for the dyad to bring them all to light, for they would fill an encyclopedia. Consequently, clients must be allowed to choose the tasks they wish to engage in. Let them trust their bodies. The point of departure for therapy is the task they feel certain they can pull off. As the therapy progresses, admix, in minuscule doses, the negatively toned stimuli to which they can become desensitized. The thrust of this approach is sensitization to the positively toned capabilities that reside not only within them but in their present environment.

Thus, clients who feel discouraged about their prospects for succeeding in life can be led by a succession of experiences to feel positive about certain environmental cues. Their view that "things are totally out of control" is modified by the realization (that is, the insight) that some things *are* under their control. Such insight need not be fully conscious. We disagree with the popular notion that insight needs ever to have resided in full awareness. As a Hellenist philosopher said millenia ago, "we know more than we can tell." And more recently Milton Erickson (e.g., Zeig, 1980) has taught (and demonstrated) that the unconscious is a reservoir of creative resources and wisdom. Though we may not have taken conscious thought of them, they need only a propitious set of circumstances to catalyze functional and productive activities (cf., as well, Jaynes, 1990, on the relation of reason to consciousness, pp. 41–47). So, we have defined insight as any realization that guides us in the exercise of the options that are possible for us, no matter how idiosyncratic, or dimly suspected they may be.

Lastly, it is not only memories of the past that help our clients to shape a better life, it is also "memories of the future" (Damasio, 1994, p. 262). These are the scenarios and the scripts that have been written in the clinic, the anticipated successes with which we have filled each others' minds. This is the stuff the theorists have categorized as the potent Common Factor in successful psychotherapy, namely, hope, embodied in plausible and promising planning.

METHODOLOGY

The therapist must gather enough information about the client to begin to form a sense of the level of maturity, both physical and emotional, that he or she has reached. That assessment will determine the appropriateness of the interventions one will make. One vital aspect of the assessment that PST shares with most other psychotherapies is the formulation of end goals, as well as some intermediate ones. The therapist needs to discuss with clients precisely what they wish to get out of therapy, and how they want themselves and their circumstances to be different at the end of therapy. Setting goals, of course, is a collaborative process, and the therapeutic dyad must ensure that they are realistic, concrete, measurable, and syntonic for both the client and the therapist.

In most instances, embryonic goals do not have these qualities. The first step in therapy, then, is to determine what the superordinate goal will be. The next phase is to map out a series of subgoals. This involves a process of negotiation and inevitable ongoing adjustments. Clients know their limits best, and therefore should take the lead in selecting tasks that will help them achieve the subgoals. Their typical means of coping with distress seem invariably to manifest themselves in this task-selection process (e.g., in the form of using subtle avoidance strategies).

We suggest that the first activities should be below the threshold that they can with significant exertion and attentiveness achieve, but taxing enough to be judged as nontrivial and rewarding. This is not to say that one must not stretch clients or acquiesce in activities that go beyond their level of comfort—that assessment will determine the appropriateness of the interventions one will make—but we are suggesting that the first activities should be below the threshold that can only be achieved with significant exertion and attentiveness. Thus begin, in collaboration with the client, to plan a series of useful and valued activities in which it can be virtually guaranteed that there will be success. Let him or her get the feeling with the opening assignments that they are not being sent across a mine field. Let them think, rather, "OK, this I can do."

From this point on, the sensitization that we spoke of above is done in a hierarchical fashion. Progress usually occurs in a succession of just noticeably more difficult (JNMD) and useful success-experiences. Engineering a series of these successes allows clients to gradually build confidence and take control of the social contingencies in their lives. Later experiences can be more ambitious and exceed the JNMD thresholds. Those which are not unqualified successes can be accepted and maturely acknowledged as partially successful; after all, we are not pursuing the holy grail of perfection.

In any event, the client must be instructed that although any activity may not be completely successful, it can never be qualified as an unmitigated failure. Quality of some magnitude can be found in everything that we do. The very fact of having undertaken a task is a success in itself. In PST the focus is always on the successful aspect of the task that was undertaken.

After an exploration of the domain in which they wish to gain confidence as well as competency, one engages in a process that is common to many therapies. The reader will be familiar with this. There are three steps to this process: imaginal, role-played, and in vivo.

- *Imaginal*—Lead the client through the imagined activity; for example, think of making eye contact with a person as one passes him or her in the hallway, and smiling.
- *Role-play*—Act out this activity repeatedly with the client, alternating roles if necessary, until the client feels comfortable, relaxed, and successful in the activity. One may choose to do this in a more ecologically plausible environment outside of one's office or clinic.
- *In vivo*—Program this success-experience in "home turf" circumstances. This can be done with the clinician present and, later, absent.

Progress through a succession of tasks that are gradually distantiated from the initial and successful efforts.

PST can also be implemented in a group, particularly when the members of the group share the same genre of concerns. Indeed, this is an apt forum for this kind of sensitization of clients to their individual strengths. It provides the immediate reinforcement and support of efforts that they are individually making to master a set of social behaviors. The group ambience provides more ecological validity, of course, than rehearsals done in the privacy of a one-to-one setting. Alternatively a therapist with the help of a confederate can provide some of the advantages of a group.

APPLICATIONS

The clients for whom this approach is appropriate are those who are *compos mentis.* Unlike the case for many therapies, this approach does not require that clients be intelligent, articulate, well-educated, highly motivated, or even cooperative. The absence of these qualities has often contributed to the problems that many clients have and comprise some of the factors that have caused them to seek our clinical attention. For example, client resistance to some initiatives that we may be inclined to take may be part of the problem that is brought to us for remediation. Therapist discouragement in the face of that resistance reflects more on the competence of the therapist than it does on the character of the client.

PST is especially suitable for those who have feelings of insecurity in the presence of others, indeed any of the symptomatic behaviors of avoidant personality disorder, poor self-concept, agoraphobia and other phobias of a social kind, feelings of impotence in the face of new tasks, immobilizing intimations of panic when envisioning exams, stage fright, or procrastination in the face of long-term educational projects.

Needless, perhaps, to say, problems with significant neurological or endocrinological involvement require the adjunctive attention of a physician. When the clinician has determined that this is the principal cause of the disorder, it is best to relinquish the overall care of the client to the physician. Correcting hormonal deficiencies like hypothyroidism can often set in motion systemic factors that eventuate in satisfactory psychological adjustment. Psychological counseling as adjunctive treatment is never without its benefits.

There are some disorders in which this therapy has had only limited success. Although it appears to have initially succeeded in therapeutic communities moving drug traffickers (who have been diagnosed as being psychopathic) up a ladder of increasing competence in socially adaptive behaviors and mainstream occupational skills, these offenders usually reach the great divide that separates the domain of the modest moral decision from the domain of the profoundly amoral, antisocial, and remorseless decision.

CASE EXAMPLE

Reason for Referral

Jim, a 39-year-old single man, works as a billing clerk in a large national transport company. Only a few weeks before his first appointment with me (JDS), his employer announced its intention to move the company headquarters to another city. Jim was presented by his supervisor with the choice of relocating along with the company or giving up his position. He had no desire to give up a secure and well-paying job that he had held for 19 years, but the prospect of leaving the familiar environment of his home and workplace caused him tremendous anxiety. After several difficult and anxiety-filled weeks, he sought help from his physician, who in turn referred him for psychotherapy.

History

Such intense anxiety was not new to Jim. In fact, he had been struggling with anxiety problems for all of his adult life. Over the years, he had frequent and regular episodes of anxiety. For the most part, these episodes arose in response to actual or anticipated social events. Typically, the onset and remission of these episodes were gradual. His anxiety manifested itself mainly as gastrointestinal symptoms, including bouts of diarrhea and a feeling of constriction in his stomach that interfered with his eating. At the height of the episodes, he experienced shortness of breath and had ruminative, catastrophic thoughts (e.g., "I'm going crazy!") that aggravated his distress.

The primary source of Jim's anxiety was a fear of losing control of his bowels in a public place. When he was 16 years old, he was driving with a couple of friends on a country road when he suddenly had the urge to have a bowel movement. By the time they stopped at a gas station, he was in desperate need of a toilet. He lost control of his bowels just as he entered these facilities. Although the incident remained his secret, Jim nonetheless experienced, and continued to experience when I saw him, intense humiliation about the event. The constraints that Jim's anxiety placed on his lifestyle were considerable. He would not venture outside the few familiar routes he traveled nearly every day. These included his bus ride to and from work and regular outings to the movie theater in his neighborhood and to a downtown bar. He could tolerate these trips only because he knew where the public toilets were located along his bus routes. He would never take the faster city subway to work, as there were no public restrooms in the subway stations. Additionally, he never left home on any occasion without first emptying his bowels.

Jim was the second of five children born to his parents. He has had a positive relationship with his mother, a homemaker, whom he described as "saintly" and overprotective. His relationship with his father has always been problematic. His father, a retired city maintenance worker, has had lifelong problems with alcoholism. He was largely absent from the home during Jim's youth, as he spent nearly all of his evenings in a neighborhood bar.

Their relationship has been marred by frequent conflict. Jim has a fraternal twin brother with whom he had shared an apartment for the last 10 years. The twin brother is on long-term disability leave from his job because of panic disorder and depression.

According to Jim, his only close friend is his twin brother, although he had had many acquaintances and "drinking buddies" over the years. Jim had married 15 years earlier, but he and his wife separated two years later. His anxiety has prevented him from dating since his divorce. Jim quit high school in grade 11 at 17 years of age. He began working with his current employer at the age of 20 in an entry-level clerical position, and he had since been promoted several times. He has no chronic medical conditions, and, according to his physician, Jim is in very good physical health.

Intervention Plan

Fundamentally, Jim was a person with very low self-esteem. A thin veneer of strength, self-confidence, and masculinity, which he tried to portray in his appearance and behaviors, barely masked pervasive feelings of insecurity, personal incompetence, and self-loathing. These debilitating self-esteem deficits fed the manifold psychological problems that compromised his personal functioning. I implemented Programmed Success Therapy with Jim in order to redress these deficits. PST, while targeting specific syndromes with structured interventions, would inevitably reverberate through the biopsychosocial system in which Jim lived and ultimately impact in a positive way on his dysfunctional self-schemas. Therapy began with a discussion of what particular issue he wanted to tackle first.

THERAPIST: Jim, we've talked over the last couple of sessions of what's been bothering you and the various things you want to improve in your life. I think that your therapy experience will be most beneficial if we select one of these issues and focus our efforts on dealing with it directly. Where do you think that you'd like to start?

JIM: Oh, God, there's so much I want to do: I'd like to reduce my use of alcohol. And after being single for all these years, I'd love to actually go out on a date. Then there's the move. Well, I guess if I don't take care of that, there's little hope these other things will work themselves out.

THERAPIST: So you think the relocation is where we should focus your attention?

JIM: Well, that's the thing that's been really stirring up my guts lately. So, sounds like we should.

Jim and I immediately set ourselves to devising a number of success experiences, hierarchically arranged according to level of difficulty, that would ultimately end with his moving to the new city. The essence of the intervention was to plan and then execute, one at a time, progressively longer trips away from his home. After extensive discussions and some negotiation, we constructed the following list of tasks that we would address in the therapy:

1. Take the subway to his work rather than the bus, which was his practice.
2. Take an afternoon drive to a small town outside the city on a road he had not traveled before.
3. Travel to a neighboring city on a weekend and stay overnight.
4. Spend a weekend in the city where he would be relocating.

The Therapy Process

Before embarking on any trips, I instructed Jim in the use of breathing and progressive muscle relaxation exercises, and our initial meetings focused largely on monitoring Jim's progress with these exercises. The relaxation exercises would assist Jim in dealing with the general anxiety that pervaded his life and with the acute episodes evoked by thoughts related to the impending relocation. The lesson Jim was to extract from these simple, nonthreatening assignments was that he was not a hapless victim of his anxiety and that he could learn to control his negative emotional reactions. Success on these early tasks constituted the first step toward other successes in his life that had heretofore eluded him.

After Jim had established a consistent, positive response to the relaxation techniques, the therapy turned to his fear of traveling on unfamiliar routes without knowledge of the location of restrooms. Only when he had succeeded with each assignment in the hierarchy and felt ready to move on did we start planning the next assignment.

THERAPIST: We've focused our attention on the relaxation exercises over the last couple of weeks. You've been using them regularly, and the practice has paid off.

JIM: Yeah, well, at least my anxiety isn't spinning out of control as it was before. I've noticed, too, that eating is getting easier. I don't feel like my stomach is in a knot all the time.

THERAPIST: So having mastered the relaxation exercises, are you ready to move to the next step, riding the subway?

JIM: (heavy sigh) I guess so.

For each of the trips listed in the hierarchy, the planning comprised the imaginal phase of these therapeutic tasks. Working through all the details associated with these trips (i.e., when, where, how, and with whom he would travel) permitted Jim to visualize successful outcomes to each of them. Considerable effort was given to anticipating all potential obstacles to success and discussing how Jim would deal with these should they arise. Clients, naturally, are often anxious about these therapeutic assignments and express in words and behavior reluctance about following through with them. On these occasions, the therapist should reassure clients that they possess all the tools they needed to succeed as evidenced by their previous successes; they needed only to learn to trust the tools to serve them well.

THERAPIST: You seem apprehensive about taking the subway to work.

JIM: Well, as soon as you said that, I had this picture in my head of me panicking on the subway.

THERAPIST: It's normal for you to be apprehensive. You've avoided this for a long time because it made you anxious, so it's natural for you to feel a bit of that now. But what if you did get anxious, what could you do?

JIM: Well, in the worst case scenario, I guess, I could get off the subway and sit on a bench and calm myself down. I could do my breathing exercise, couldn't I? I mean, no one in the subway is going to care, are they? Who am I kidding? No one will even notice!

Jim had little difficulty completing the task. At our next meeting, he reported that he took the subway to work for all five work days during the previous week. He admitted that the first day was difficult and that he considered turning back after entering the subway station, but he pushed himself and succeeded. The other tasks unfolded in much the same way. At each new step in the process, Jim pushed himself past his initial apprehension and achieved his goal. His confidence was clearly growing, and he became increasingly eager, indeed almost impatient, to move up to the next step in the hierarchy.

Predictably, perhaps, Jim's demeanor changed when we reached the last step on the hierarchy, traveling to the city to which he would relocate. Beyond the long road trip and the challenges it would present, the trip represented accepting a new life in the new city with all of its attendant uncertainties. Discussions during the planning phase of this trip revealed that he was overwhelmed with the magnitude of this task.

JIM: I've been thinking hard about this move over the past week, and I'm starting to think that maybe this isn't the best thing for me. Who knows, the company may decide a month after I move to cut my post. Then all of this time and effort would have been wasted.

THERAPIST: So you're having doubts now. This is new. You never questioned your decision before.

JIM: Yeah, well, everything seemed clear before. Now everything is a mess again in my head, just like before.

THERAPIST: Are you anxious about taking the trip we've planned?

JIM: God, I've barely been able to eat all week.

THERAPIST: Maybe we need to rethink our strategy. Let's look at how we could break this down into a few smaller steps, so you'll be better prepared to make the trip at a later time.

JIM: Sounds like a good idea. Whew! I feel better already. That was really bothering me all week.

We proceeded to identify a number of smaller, more achievable goals as intermediate steps to this superordinate objective. The first of these involved buying the local newspaper from the new city and contacting three individuals who had rental properties advertised in the classified section of the newspaper. We agreed that Jim would simply gather information about the property from the owners and not make any commitment to visiting any of them. After succeeding with this assignment, he would contact a real estate agent in the new city and set up some house visitations for a future date when he would be in the city. Only after succeeding on each of these tasks was a visit to the new city planned and, finally, executed.

PST challenges clients emotionally, cognitively, and behaviorally because it moves them gradually but steadily toward grappling with the situations they have avoided in their lives. Jim encountered numerous challenges over the course of his therapy. His first trip to the new city presented one particularly difficult challenge. He made the trip with his twin brother, who drove the car. Jim felt anxious during the long drive and used his relaxation exercises several times to try to manage his anxiety. Despite his best efforts, his anxiety escalated. He spent one sleepless night in a hotel and insisted on leaving first thing the next day for home. At the next therapy session, Jim appeared clearly shaken by his experience.

JIM: What a disaster! It was hell! I was nervous the whole time. I didn't sleep, I couldn't eat. I don't know what I was thinking about going there.

THERAPIST: So it was difficult, but you went anyway. You toughed it out for a night in the city, and then you came home the next day. Sounds to me like it was a resounding success!

JIM: What do you mean? I was a mess the whole time. By the way, I told my supervisor that there's no way I can move. She told me to get back to her in a week, but as far as I'm concerned, it's off.

THERAPIST: But you made the trip despite the difficulty, and you persevered for a full day. Isn't that what we set as the goal? We both knew that you might get a bit anxious; you did every time previously. Now maybe we underestimated your reaction a bit, but the fact remains that you achieved your goal, you succeeded.

JIM: (long pause) I guess so. . . . Yeah, you're right.

At his session the following week, Jim reported that he had reversed his decision again and had informed his supervisor that he would be relocating with the company after all. At Jim's suggestion, we began planning another trip to the new city to investigate housing arrangements. He made the trip about three weeks later without incident and returned home after a three-day stay with a signed lease for an apartment.

Outcome

Jim had 16 therapy sessions over a period of five months. At the time of our last meeting, he had moved out of his apartment and was living in temporary housing while awaiting his official transfer to the new city, which was to occur two weeks later. He was somewhat apprehensive about the challenges that lay ahead of him, but his anxiety had markedly diminished. He was obviously proud of his newfound ability to exert some control over his anxious reactions to the inevitable vicissitudes of life. Overall, his outlook on the future was positive. Jim aptly summarized his experience in therapy as a process of "learning to trust myself."

SUMMARY

This therapy has reconceptualized systematic desensitization to negatively toned stimuli as systematic sensitization to positively toned stimuli. We have organized it such that therapy always begins at the developmental level to which clients have attained. Further, the initial tasks are carefully gauged to fall within the domain of the competence they have brought into the clinic. From that point on, therapy proceeds in just noticeably more difficult steps.

The process has drawn on the research of Shelley Taylor and her colleagues, who have demonstrated that certain positive, self-enhancing distortions, (call them illusions; the term is used advisedly), are conducive to mental health. Among these constructions are those she characterizes as downward social comparisons. Clients who can, on the one hand, achieve a modicum of success in a domain they value and, on the other hand, can view their achievements as comparable, if not superior, in worth to that of many of their neighbors, colleagues, or schoolmates, are well on the way to mental health.

The therapy relies on the unconscious neurological resources of the client. According to the model of Damasio, through a succession of feedforward mechanisms the encoded, affectively toned traces of our personal history are unconsciously funneled into our decisional processes. Positively valenced options get selected. We build on these in an Ericksonian fashion.

Finally, the Adlerian principle that discouragement is at the heart of the disorders that clients bring to us for help is the principal focus in this therapy. The tasks and homework that the dyad design are such as they are reasonably certain the client can succeed in. No client is counseled to engage in any activity that will possibly eventuate in greater discouragement. Small successes are programmed that will escalate into larger successes. There is nothing more healing than winning in such an endeavor.

REFERENCES

Ainsworth, M. D. S. (1966). The effects of maternal deprivation: A review of findings and controversy in the context of research strategy. In J. Bowlby (Ed.), *Deprivation and maternal care: A reassessment of its effects.* New York: Schocken.

Bowlby, J. (1973). *Attachment and loss* (Vol. 2). London: Hogarth.

Damasio, A. (1994). *Descartes' error: Emotion, reason, and the human brain.* New York: Avon.

de Shazer, S. (1985). *Keys to solutions in brief therapy.* New York: Norton.

Ellis, A. (2000). Rational-Emotive-Behavior Therapy. In F. Dumont & R. Corsini, (Eds.), *Six therapists and one client.* New York: Springer.

Gesell, A., & Ilg, F. L. (1943). *Infant and child in the culture of today.* New York: Harper & Row.

Jaynes, J. (1990). *The origin of consciousness in the breakdown of the bicameral mind.* Boston: Houghton Mifflin.

Mahoney, M. (1991). *Human change processes.* New York: Basic.

O'Hanlon, W. H., & Weiner-Davis, M. (1989). *In search of solutions: A new direction in psychotherapy.* New York: Norton.

Taylor, S. (1983). Adjusting to threatening events: A theory of cognitive adaptation. *American Psychologist, 38,* 1161–1173.

Zeig, J. K. (1980). *Teaching seminar with Milton H. Erickson, M.D.* New York: Brunner/Mazel.

Chapter 50

PROVOCATIVE THERAPY

FRANK FARRELLY and SCOTT MATTHEWS

Undoubtedly this chapter will not only inform the reader about Provocative Therapy but will also provoke him or her to amazement—laughter—disbelief. Certainly, PT is one of the more innovative of psychotherapies in current use, and apparently it violates many of the commonly accepted preconceptions of courtesy and the dignity of the therapist-client professional "relationships."

Developed by Frank Farrelly, PT employs humor as one of its major tools. It also uses the "Leaning Tower of Pisa" approach to exaggerate and make worse various situations, to lead the client to see the humor and nonsense of his or her well-established position. Other forms of humor are found in O'Connell's Natural High Therapy.

I imagine that Farrelly's rationale is that his system works best for him, and that he will employ many forms of humor including exaggeration, mimicry, ridicule, distortion, sarcasm, irony, and just plain jokes for the patient's benefit by deliberately violating the shibboleths of conventional thinking. This leads to the central issue of this book: Should a therapist employ such shock tactics even if they are personally distasteful to him or her? Should one at least know that such an approach can work with some people at some time? Should mordant humor become part of the complete therapist's armamentarium?

Among the interesting elements of this therapy is that it was developed in the context of that most courteous and gentle of all therapies—Carl Rogers' Client-Centered Therapy. This too can be seen as client-centered—with an ironic, humorous twist. PT deserves careful study.

Provocative Therapy is a system of working with clients[1] developed by Frank Farrelly in the early 1960s, primarily while working with psychotic people in a state mental hospital; it has also been used successfully for almost two decades on a wide range of clients in outpatient settings. The therapeutic focus is on clients' false ideas, erroneous assumptions, painful feelings, and self-defeating behaviors. Clients are humorously and perceptively provoked or challenged to continue in their misery-seeking ways to mobilize their own resistances and defenses against themselves for change. To effect this change, a strongly affective experience is deliberately established by the therapist, who uses nonpredictable behavioral responses that place clients in an altered state of consciousness, creates in them the felt experiencing of being deeply understood on multiple levels, irritates and amuses them, and rapidly connects them to their own personal power. The most outstanding characteristic of this system of psychotherapy is its ef-

fective and unusual use of humor to motivate clients to positive and growth-producing actions.

HISTORY

One of Frank Farrelly's early goals was to enter the priesthood to help people. As a member of a devout Irish Catholic family, he grew up listening to the nuns and priests and to his father's Irish folktales and humor, all of which set a stage for what was to come as he began his studies in social work. It was his clients, however, who played the most influential part in the eventual development of Provocative Therapy as a system.

The history of the development of Provocative Therapy centers around a series of client-provoked experiences. Early in his career Farrelly read Carl Rogers's *Client-Centered Therapy* (1951) and was impressed with the verbatim interview samples. As Farrelly remembers: "This is the way it really is, with a broken sentence structure, the 'uhs,' the fractured grammar, the misunderstandings and efforts to correct them, and all" (Farrelly

---

[1] Note: The words "client" and "patient" are used in this chapter. A client is a nonhospitalized person; a patient is a hospitalized person.

& Brandsma, 1974). He especially was impressed with Rogers's attempt to understand his clients from *their* internal state of reference.

The next important client influence was "the case of the malingering nut" (p. 10).[2] One day Farrelly "threw therapy out the window" and became furious at a client for writing obscene and frightening letters to a young hospital secretary. He threatened to "lock him in seclusion and throw away the key." "You can't hold me responsible—I'm mentally ill," replied the patient. Farrelly's conclusion was that the "mentally ill" have not all lost contact with reality, but that they know perfectly well what they are doing in most instances and are, in a sense, clever social systems analysts.

Through the inadvertent development of "open-fly therapy" (Farrelly's pants fly was open and obviously influenced an interview with a woman from whom he had to get a confession of sexual infidelity to her husband), he learned to laugh at himself and to share his "bloopers" with colleagues and clients.

In the "Clem Kadiddlehopper" case, he treated the patient who, indeed, looked and acted like the Red Skelton character, Clem Kadiddlehopper—a man with a shock of red hair standing four inches straight off his head and with his false teeth missing, two squinty little pig eyes, a bulbous tomato nose, and a ludicrous tone of voice. As soon as he saw the man, Farrelly began to laugh until tears streamed down his face. The psychologist cotherapist told him, "That's no way to treat a patient." The patient interrupted, "No, it's okay, that's been the trouble. I try to make people laugh, then they laugh sometimes when I don't want them to, and I get hurt and mad and into trouble." Farrelly learned that "radical congruence, held constant, was very helpful to the patient." Laughter toward the patient's idiotic ideas and behavior did not inevitably demean their dignity (p. 13).

In the "case of the dangerous psychopath," Farrelly, after listening to an obviously well-thought-out speech by a patient about why he should be discharged from the hospital, stated, "Well, I think it's the slickest con job I've ever had pulled on me." After an excited tirade of anger and disjointed emotional behavior, the patient asked Farrelly to be his therapist. When asked why, he replied, "'Cause you don't give me no shit off the wall." Farrelly concluded that confrontation and emotional honesty can quickly build a relationship of trust (p. 14).

In the "case of the slutty virgin," a young woman in group therapy who acted promiscuously but protested she was still a virgin was told, "Well, you talk like a slut; you dress like a slut; you walk like a slut; and you look like a slut. It's not what you are objectively, kid; it's the image you create in other people's minds." The patient

tearfully remarked that she "wasn't that kind of girl." The group helped her develop more appropriate behaviors, she became a model patient, and was soon discharged. Several basic lessons were learned from this case. First, people can change dramatically and maintain their new behaviors and attitudes. Second, they can change in a relatively short period of time. Third, a vicious circle of negative feelings, attitudes, and behaviors can be changed to a beneficial reaction of positive behavior reinforced by praise and positive feedback, which leads to further changed feelings and attitudes. Farrelly concluded that the group is a powerful therapeutic tool and that people react to a person according to the subjective image they have of him or her in their "heads and guts." If this is true, the therapist's task is to aid the patient to attend to and not ignore the feedback that others, including the therapist, are communicating toward the patient and to help the patient act on this feedback (p. 17).

To a young male patient who bellowed, "You sound just like my father," the reply was, "Then your father and I would get along famously, buddy!" Farrelly discovered early that in his "countertransference," or strong reactions toward the patient, he often was highly accurate and learned that expressing these responses was more helpful than if he had suppressed them. In their book *Critical Incidents in Psychotherapy* (1959), Standal and Corsini describe case after case in which the therapist abandoned the standard response patterns and vented some long pent-up feelings toward the patient, with surprisingly consequent patient improvement.

In 1963 a woman being discharged from the mental hospital shared her worry that "my family is going to be watching my every move." Farrelly agreed with that observation and helped her utilize this insight to effect a community adjustment. Often patients' observations and formulations are more accurate than ours are (p. 21).

The specific interview in which Provocative Therapy was discovered occurred in July 1963, while Farrelly was participating in Carl Rogers's research project with chronic schizophrenics at Mendota State Hospital.

In the ninety-first interview with Farrelly, who was using a client-centered approach, the patient was still insisting that he was worthless and hopeless, and averred that he was doomed to be perpetually psychotic. Farrelly had been reiterating that the patient was worthwhile, of value, and could change. Finally tiring of arguing with the patient, suddenly Farrelly humorously began agreeing with the patient's negative self-concept. Almost immediately the patient began to explode with laughter and to protest that he was not *that* bad or *that* hopeless, and to say the therapist had been of great help to him. The therapist disagreed humorously and declared that if he had been of any help to the patient and the patient was

---

[2] From this point forward, all citations are to Farrelly & Brandsma, 1974

showing any kind of progress, he was moving with all the speed of a turtle encased in concrete. Within six interviews, the patient rapidly improved and was discharged (p. 27).

Each of these isolated experiences cemented together an experientially based theory that Farrelly later christened Provocative Therapy. Each therapist reaches his own "moment of discovery". Albert Ellis (1962) discussed the particular interview in which he discovered Rational-Emotive Psychotherapy. Carl Rogers (1961) described the critical interview he had with the mother of a failure case. Blanchard (1970) has stated:

> It is a convention in the scientific world to report the emergence of new theory as though it emerges slowly and inevitably from the analytical throttling of data. The scientist is pictured as plodding through his method, discovering some discrepancy until he stumbles over the doorstep of theory. Actually, far more often than not, the theory springs into the scientist's vision as a wild surmise, and he spends most of his time searching for facts to fit it. (p. 10)

And so it was with the discovery of Provocative Therapy.

CURRENT STATUS

Provocative Therapy now is used in a wide variety of settings in both private and institutional work. Practitioners of psychology, clinical social work, psychiatry, psychiatric nursing, guidance and counseling, and others in the mental health field have been trained in and are currently using Provocative Therapy as their primary identifiable mode of treatment.

Currently the only center for training in Provocative Therapy is through the Madison Psychotherapy Associates in Madison, Wisconsin. Training is available in various forms, including: (1) PT supervision by telephone, (2) PT telephone seminars, (3) in-service training, and (4) individual training in Provocative Therapy.

Farrelly gives workshops throughout the country, which last from one to three days and include a lecture on Provocative Therapy, interviews with workshop members, "therapist-client" feedback session, group discussion, role playing of clients difficult for the therapists, experiential training, and so forth.

In PT supervision by telephone Farrelly is called by therapists across the nation for consultation on specific cases: for help when they are "stuck"; to broaden their perspectives about their work, themselves (both professionally and personally), and the systems within which they operate; as well as to increase their therapeutic response repertoire.

PT telephone seminars are provided to universities,

agencies, and training centers; usually there is a two-hour "live" lecture on Provocative Therapy with case illustrations, comparisons with other psychotherapies, and wide-ranging discussion with embarrassing questions invited.

With in-service training, professionals in a variety of therapeutic settings work with both voluntary and involuntary clients. In-service training provides an opportunity for in-depth discussions on a wide variety of topics, including mental health delivery systems and system maintenance needs; predictable community and psychological pressures with specific client populations; meeting the needs of professionals to obviate "burnout"; you, sex, and the client; and others.

In addition to the above modes of teaching, individual supervised training in Provocative Therapy is offered which has been dubbed "the peripatetic school of Provocative Therapy." This is an intensive experience for one or two mental health professionals or trainees for one week, tailored to their goals and individual schedules. This program includes direct therapeutic encounters in individual, family, and group treatment; PT interviews with trainees; audiotapes; readings; and so forth.

There are several publications, both written and audiotaped. *Provocative Therapy* (Farrelly & Brandsma, 1974), the major text, is a personal and detailed account of the system. The book includes a history and theory of Provocative Therapy as well as chapters on humor and Provocative Therapy, the four languages of Provocative Therapy, and the role of the provocative therapist.

"The Code of Chronicity" (Ludwig and Farrelly, 1966) and "The Weapons of Insanity" (Ludwig and Farrelly, 1967) are papers that develop the theoretical stance that is taken in Provocative Therapy.

"Provocative Therapy" (Farrelly, 1977) is a series of twelve audio cassette tapes in which Farrelly talks about the PT system and then demonstrates it with a series of interviews with patients ranging from the seriously delusional mental hospital patient to a confused college student.

The American Academy of Psychotherapists Tape Library tape number 58 is *Provocative Therapy* (Farrelly, 1971). This tape includes a lecture on Provocative Therapy and a demonstration with a hospitalized suicidal adolescent.

Richard Bandler and John Grindler analyze Frank Farrelly's demonstration of Provocative Therapy in an audio *Digest* tape entitled "Analyzing the Analyst—Identifying Effective Interventions" (Farrelly, 1978).

THEORY

There is an old tale of the five blind Indian fakirs who are led to an elephant—one touched the trunk, another the ear, still another the leg, another the belly, and the last was given the tail to touch. Each, of course, experienced the elephant differently, then came to his own conclusions about his experiencing of this object. Much as the Indian fakirs did, each theory of psychotherapy is based on its own set of assumptions and hypotheses—a mental framework that utilizes specific techniques.

There are 10 assumptions and two hypotheses upon which Provocative Therapy is based (pp. 36–52). The assumptions are:

"People change and grow in response to a challenge." In Provocative Therapy, the client is carefully challenged so that he or she is forced to cope with rather than run from problems and the therapist. The therapist will pursue the client and not tolerate avoidance on the client's part. In contrast to many therapies where the attempt is to maintain the calm, cool, and smooth interview, the provocative therapist is attempting to create a healing energy vortex.

"Clients can change if they choose." In the Old Testament of the Bible, Adam and Eve were given free will. They were not helpless pawns, and neither are today's clients. "Few people other than therapists really believe that man is not responsible for what he does, that he does not choose but is driven." Instead of accepting the client's "I can't change," the provocative therapist firmly believes the client can change but humorously agrees and echoes the helplessly despairing "I'm trapped" messages of psychological determinism that the client asserts, in order to provoke the client into perceiving that his or her nonfunctioning is because he or she will not, rather than cannot, change.

"Clients have far more potential for achieving adaptive, productive, and socialized modes of living than they and most clinicians assume." Although clients believe they are helpless and hopeless, the greatest tragedy occurs when the therapist seriously agrees with the self-evaluation and says, "If I can't cure them, they're incurable." Furthermore, for the therapist to believe this is to perform an inappropriate psychological alchemy whereby the therapist's failure is transformed magically into a *fact* residing in the client.

"The psychological fragility of clients is vastly overrated both by themselves and others." Although most clients and therapists see the client as someone similar to Humpty Dumpty, the ill-fated egg that fell off the wall, who will crack, break, or fall apart at the slightest provocation, the provocative therapist sees the client as having many strong, positive traits that form the basis of the emergence of the new person. For the provocative therapist it is not such a miracle that most people survive growing up and becoming adults without going crazy. The provocative therapist deliberately and humorously overfocuses on what is "wrong" with the client to provoke him or her into offering what is "right" with him or her, to reaffirm strengths, and to actualize operationally personal power.

"The client's maladaptive, unproductive, antisocial attitudes and behaviors can be drastically altered whatever the degree or severity of chronicity." There is ample clinical evidence (cf. research on self-fulfilling prophecy) that supports the contention that people will change and respond to the belief of their significant others. If others believe the client can get well, the client often gets well, not by any miraculous process, but by the multiple ways in which the client is treated by others perceived as important by him or her. Finally, a frequently significant phase in the process is when the client *chooses* to get better.

"Adult or current experiences are as at least if not more significant than childhood or previous experiences in shaping client values, operational attitudes, and behaviors." This is essentially the assumption underlying all views of psychotherapy as a corrective emotional experience capable of reversing years of maladaptation and generalizing to other relationships outside therapy. Every effective therapist operationally believes that the client is capable of changing, and that the experiences the client is having with the therapist are capable of being transferred by the client to life outside the hospital or the therapist's office.

"The client's behavior with the therapist is a relatively accurate reflection of his habitual pattern of social and interpersonal relationships." Even though the client will act and react much as he or she acts outside the therapy room, the therapist presents a much different stimulus configuration. The therapist frequently presents the client with an evaluation as significant others might perceive him or her and react to him or her; negatively models social situations that will humorously demonstrate the negative social consequences that follow with a high degree of probability from the client's attitudes and behaviors; and refers to the behavioral shaping and feedback available to the client from the matrix of his or her social relationship. ([T, leaning forward, places his hand gently on C's forearm, says in a warm, "supportive" voice] "Look, dummy, you have got about the craziest picture of yourself I have ever seen, but then nobody is perfect. Even with your own distorted perception, I bet you can hear what others are telling you. But go ahead and ignore them, then you will really have a reason to be depressed.")

People are relatively easy to understand—especially when we have the relevant data. The provocative therapist, believing firmly in the necessity to obtain this data to achieve depth and breadth of understanding, will immediately approach those areas that the client shows he or she wants to avoid. In effect, the provocative therapist develops "red-green color blindness." When the client signals "Stop!" (blushing, hesitancy, avoidance, or outright resistance to discussing a topic), the therapist charges ahead.

The judicious expression of "therapeutic hate and joyful sadism" toward the client can paradoxically markedly benefit him or her. The reason that the mentally ill often feel rejected and unloved is because they *are* often rejected and unloved—for their rejectable and unlovable behaviors. The provocative therapist would rather offer genuine rejection for a given client behavior than a phony constrained acceptance. Consider this 18-year-old functionally illiterate female patient. Very combative and assaultive, she stabbed three people with pencils and threw a TV at a pregnant woman.[3]

P: (Snarling) I am going to kick your goddamn teeth down your fucking throat.

K: (Looking levelly at the patient) Yeah? And what do you think I am going to be doing while you're kicking my goddamn teeth down my fucking throat?

P: (Taken aback; pauses, muttering sulkily) You'll bite my foot off at the ankle.

T: (Nodding and smiling) You got it, you bitch. (Farrelly & Brandsma, 1974, p. 49)

In another example, a large family came in for therapy. Their house was in a constant state of chaos and the educationally sophisticated mother felt angry, guilty, and ready to collapse. She was asked for one concrete example of how she could be helped by the children in this situation. She decided that things would be measurably easier for her if the children would pack away their own clothes after being laundered.

T: I am going to teach you how to be joyfully sadistic.

C: What's that?

T: How to inflict pain on others and get to love it. (Farrelly & Brandsma, 1974, p. 50)

In front of the children and with much humor and persuasion, the therapist convinced her to offer her children no food until their clothes were put away and to adopt the biblical injunction "If you don't work, you don't eat." With only five meal deprivations scattered among 10 children in two days, each and every child was cooperating beautifully. Often in therapy, distinction must be made between short-term cruelty with long-term kindness versus short-term kindness and long-term detriment.

"The more important messages between people are nonverbal. It is not what is said, it is how it is said that is crucial." Because often the provocative therapist transmits

very negative verbal feedback (to sensitize or desensitize, set limits, provoke reality testing, etc.), he or she must also counterbalance that with highly positive nonverbal messages (for support, to make more palatable the rather bitter pills all of us must swallow at times, etc.). The provocative therapist frequently and deliberately appears to be incongruent by communicating one thing at one level with words, but quite the opposite with body language, tonal inflection, and other significant nonverbal qualifications. The therapist is communicating at different levels simultaneously, thereby creating ambiguity and a consequent altered state of consciousness within the client, a period of heightened suggestibility and receptivity during which the client can receive the nonverbal suggestions far more easily.

T: (Smiling, laughing warmly, leaning forward, gently patting the C.'s knee) Me like you? You have to be kidding. (T leans back, gazes quizzically at far corner of ceiling as though mental vistas are opening to him; slowly, in a puzzled, low tone, as though to himself.) Actually . . . I will confess to a scientific curiosity in *his* (gesturing nonchalantly toward C) case.

C: (Exploding with laughter) Well, I guess you've got poor judgment then, Scott.

T: ("Coming out of trance") Huh?!

There are two central hypotheses upon which Provocative Therapy is based. The first concerns the client's self-concept: If provoked by the therapist (humorously, perceptively, and within the client's own internal frame of reference), the client will tend to move in the opposite direction from the therapist's definition of the client as a person. The second hypothesis focuses on the client's overt behavior: If urged provocatively (humorously and perceptively) by the therapist to continue his or her self-defeating, deviant behavior, the client will tend to engage in self- and other-enhancing behaviors, which more closely approximate the societal norm. These hypotheses are subject to proof and disproof with each new client.

In addition to the assumptions and hypotheses, the four different stages of process for the client in Provocative Therapy merit inclusion here. Although not sharply defined and somewhat impressionistic, they occur with sufficient frequency to be discernable.

First Stage

Typically in the first interview, the client is often left astonished and incredulous, uncertain, and humorously provoked. A typical response might be "I don't understand how you can help people this way; I've never had anybody talk to me like that." Or "I don't know why

---

[3] In the following dialogues, T stands for therapist, P for patient, and C for client.

I'm laughing at what I've said. . . . I can't help it, what I've been doing seems so funny." Almost invariably the client returns for subsequent interviews (more than 90 percent return).

Second Stage

The client begins to realize that the therapist is accurate, and it is the client, not the therapist, who must change. Often there is a transitory sulkiness in the client's responses: "I don't like it, but you are right about me." A reduction and even at times total absence of psychotic defenses (when they have been present) is a mark of this stage.

Third Stage

This stage is characterized by the client becoming more rational and attempting to prove the therapist wrong. The client marshals and displays specific, concrete, and easily observable behaviors as evidence to disprove the therapist's definition and description of him or her.

Fourth Stage

Here the client will refer to his or her former self, or "the way I used to be." Often the client is able to laugh at his or her old self and laugh when he or she "goofs up" with new behaviors. This is an integrative and terminating stage in Provocative Therapy.

APPLICATIONS

Because of the powerful tactics and strategies inherent in this system and the wide variety of behaviors that it allows the therapist to engage in to enhance communication skills in the interview, it has been successfully employed with clients ranging in age from pre-school to geriatrics, with hospitalized and nonhospitalized clients, with psychotics from mute catatonics to manic-depressives in the manic phase, with character disorders and neurotics, with clients ranging in intelligence levels from the mentally retarded (educable level) to genius, as well as with all the major racial and ethnic groups in the United States and with people of other nationalities. Perhaps because of the provocative therapist's determination to and delight in crossing boundaries (class, sex, ethnic, racial, educational, religious, etc.), no major group, either diagnostic (with the exception of organic disorders) or sociological, has been found to date with which Provocative Therapy has not been successful. Additionally, as with other therapeutic orientations it has been especially successful with the YAVIS client (young, attractive, verbal, intelligent, successful) who sees talk-

ing over problems as helpful; has an inner felt disturbance rather than an overt, acting-out behavioral disturbance; and who is willing to engage in extensive self-exploration. Finally, it has been used with different client system sizes: individuals, couples, families, and group therapies.

However, it should be emphasized that therapy systems do not directly help clients. Instead therapy systems help therapists organize the kaleidoscopic ideational, affective, and behavioral phenomena that individuals bring to therapists to treat. Again, therapy systems do not help people; people help people.

And here is perhaps the significant, albeit puzzling, limitation of Provocative Therapy: Why should it aid and facilitate the therapist in helping one client while, with another highly similar client (in diagnosis, age, social background, etc.), the system apparently fails the therapist to be equally helpful? No research study of Provocative Therapy has been made to date to examine questions such as this, but preliminary evidence from provocative therapists across the country suggests that the therapist's energy level and investment with unsuccessful clients were not as high as with the puzzlingly similar clients who enjoyed successful outcomes. Was the decrease in energy investment a function of the specific relationship between the therapist and this particular client, or did the client counterprovoke the therapist to the degree that the therapist's initial energy investment was counterconditioned or extinguished? Is Provocative Therapy—in point of fact, any healing endeavor—basically a transfer to, release of, or increase in energy magnitude? When the therapy was unsuccessful, was this because the energy level of the therapist (healer) was not sufficiently high or was blocked or short-circuited in some undefined way by either the client or the therapist so that the transfer, release, or increase of energy failed to occur?

METHODOLOGY

Provocative Therapy is described as a "broadly based procedure applying many techniques and a wide range of freedom in responding for the therapist" (p. 55). Bandler and Grindler in *Frogs into Princes: Neuro-Linguistic Programming* (1979) state "Frank Farrelly, who wrote *Provocative Therapy,* is a really exquisite example of requisite variety." The intent within the variety afforded the therapist allows the therapist access to the totality of his or her experiences to increase empathic understanding and caring for the client, to employ tactics and strategies counter to those of the client in an effort to help the client change at multiple levels and to have fun and avoid burnout while doing therapy. The therapist's behaviors that distinguish this form of therapy from other approaches are the degree of directness and the use of confrontation, contradictory and equivocal communication style, the systematic use of both verbal and nonverbal cues, the eschewing of professional dignity, and the deliberate use of humor and clowning.

The stated goal is "to provoke the client to engage in five different types of behaviors":

1. To affirm his self-worth, both verbally and behaviorally.
2. To assert himself appropriately both in task performances and relationships.
3. To defend himself realistically.
4. To engage in psychosocial reality testing and learn the necessary discriminations to respond adaptively. Global perceptions lead to global, stereotyped responses; differentiated perceptions lead to adaptive responses.
5. To engage in risk-taking behaviors in personal relationships, especially communicating affection and vulnerability to significant others with immediacy as they are authentically experienced by the client. The most difficult words in relationships are often "I want you, I miss you, I care about you"—to commit oneself to others (p. 56).

In many forms of psychotherapy, the therapist is often expected to play according to the rules of Hoyle, while the client can employ any form of street fighting imaginable. In Provocative Therapy, the therapist can "lie," deny, rationalize, invent phony "research data," "cry," and think and act "crazy." The provocative therapist acts as a devil's advocate and sides with the negative half of the client's ambivalence toward self, significant others, and his or her goals and values. At times the therapist will voice the client's worst thoughts and fears about him- or herself. The therapist will "express the unutterable, feel the unfeelable, and think the unthinkable" (p. 58). He or she often will volunteer idiotic rationalizations for the client's behavior. This has the effect of short-circuiting the client's own excuse-generating mechanisms and often leads clients to laugh at themselves for the rationalizations they have been developing. Often the therapist will overemphasize the negative, thus forcing the client to emphasize the positive aspects of his or her life. Also, there is no such thing as a taboo subject and often feedback is immediate. Example: An obese patient enters the office.

P: May I speak with you, Mr. Farrelly?

T: My God, the Goodyear blimp has slipped its moorings! (p. 61)

There are several techniques that are specifically used to assist the client in reality testing. *Reductio ad absur-dum* (reduction to absurdity) is the carrying of the client's negative statements about him- or herself to the logical extremes until the client rejects them. A typical response to this is "Even *I* don't believe I'm *that* bad." Often the therapist marshals idiotic "instant data or research" to humorously support the client's contentions that he or she is indeed either helpless or bad. The therapist all too readily accepts the contentions that the client is no good and "gives up exhaustedly" with a smiling "What hope is there for someone so bad off as you?" The therapist will directly challenge the client to "prove it." One of the more frequently used tools that the provocative therapist uses to help the client focus specifically on himself is listing. For example:

T: (Sighing laconically) Give me three good reasons, sweetheart, why anyone would want to go out with you. Hell, you're either a ducker, a spitter, or a swallower.

In using negative modeling, the therapist acts like the client. If the client acts in a staring and detached way, he or she may suddenly find the therapist acting just as "crazy." Often the client will laugh at this behavior, and if the client doesn't laugh, he or she at least must try to decode the therapist's "psychosis."

It is important to note here that the therapist and his or her role as well as the client often receives the butt of the joke.

C: (Withdrawn and whining) Well, Scott, I thought you might be able to help me. . . . (Plaintively) Won't you help?

T: (Plaintively protesting loudly) Help!? Who said anything about help? . . . Time I can give you . . . uh . . . I'm not smart enough to work miracles anymore. (Sadly) I lost my magic wand last year. (Puts head in hands as if crying.)

Neither the client nor the therapist's role is immune to lampooning.

The provocative therapist will often send contradictory messages to the client. Even though clinicians agree that this is one outstanding characteristic of schizophrenogenic families, the provocative therapist differs radically from these pathology-inducing familial constellations in that the goal in sending these powerful messages is to provoke independence rather than dependence, and they are also sent within an easily decoded context of caring, warmth, and support for the essential personhood of the client. If double messages have the power to drive people crazy, then they also have the power to drive people sane. The client is forced to choose between either the therapist's verbal messages, which agree with the client's predictions of doom and gloom, or with the strongly supportive, easily decodable, nonverbal messages that the client is lovable and worthwhile, can change, and has the power and knowledge within himself to take charge of and direct his own life. Provocative Therapy *releases* the client from powerlessness and places him or her in touch—often quite rapidly—with his or her own power; hence it is centrally and diametrically opposed to the schizophrenogenic, pathological-dependency-inducing type of messages that *bind.*

The provocative therapist's utilization of humor is central to his or her work. Among the several discernible forms of humor used are exaggeration, mimicry, ridicule, distortion, sarcasm, irony, and jokes.

With *exaggeration* the provocative therapist either over- or understates the client's view of him- or herself. The therapist's artistic hyperbole, done with a twinkle in the eye or a sly smile, provokes the client into a more balanced perspective.

The therapist *mimics* the client in two ways. One way is by role playing the client's self-defeating behaviors. For example, the client who has fits of pique may find the provocative therapist suddenly rising out of a chair "ranting and raving," much as the client does. The impact is immediate. Since behavior is controlled by its perceived consequences, the client perceives quickly with embarrassment and laughter how he or she affects others negatively, which tends to lead to the extinction of the client's self-defeating behaviors.

The provocative therapist does not *ridicule* the client but rather the client's screwball and idiotic behaviors in an effort to extinguish or countercondition them. It should be emphasized that the therapist's role and "professional dignity" are also open to caricature. Since clients do not easily distinguish between themselves and their behaviors ("Love me, love my deviant behaviors"), ridicule is a tactic to be sparingly and skillfully used. As with any powerful tool, it can be used for better or for worse, so the provocative therapist invariably pairs warmth and obvious caring with ridicule of the client's inappropriate ideas and behaviors. Within a given social-psychological context, ridiculous thoughts and action merit ridicule.

In using *humorous distortion,* the therapist deliberately "misunderstands" the client or gives wild or plausibly distorted "psychological explanations" for the client's behavior or others' behavior toward the client. In the same vein, in order to provoke the client's reality testing and self-affirmation, the therapist will lampoon the client's expectations of the therapist's traditional role. For example, a middle-aged, female patient knocked almost inaudibly at the office door; when the therapist opened it:

P: (Querulously) May I see you, Mr. Farrelly?

T: (Loudly) Of course, gorgeous. (He strides back to his desk and sits down.)

P: (Coming into the room timorously) Where do you want me to sit?

T: (Pointing at chair next to his desk; the patient begins to sit down in the chair) Sit right there. (In a gruff tone; loudly) Hold it! (Pointing to a chair at the opposite wall) Sit over there.

P: (Shuffles over to the chair at which the therapist is pointing)

T: (In a commanding tone: looks around the office) No, wait a minute. . . . (He pauses, looks uncertain) I've got it! Sit over there (pointing to a chair near the door).

P: (Suddenly straightening up, frowning; loudly and forcibly) Aw, go to hell! I'll sit where I want! (She plumps herself in a chair.)

T: (Throwing up his arms as though defending himself; plaintively) Okay, okay, you don't have to get violent!

P: (Burst out laughing)(p.181)

Sarcasm must be accompanied by non-verbal warmth, caring, and acceptance if it is to have the humorous and therefore therapeutic effect on the client that the therapist wants. Sarcasm is a powerful communication modality frequently highly effective in sensitizing and desensitizing clients to certain perceptions and behaviors, but it needs to be used with discretion to achieve the desired therapeutic effect. As in the following example:

P: (Promiscuous patient coming into therapist's office, holding her hand out in a "halt" gesture) Now before you say anything, I want you to know I got a job.

T: (Suspiciously) Where did you get it?

P: (Triumphantly) In a laboratory.

T: (Sarcastically) As what, a specimen?

P: (Annoyed but grinning in spite of herself) Oh, you think you're so goddamn funny.

T: (Suspiciously and with a sarcastic tone) Oh yeah, how did you persuade him to hire you, sweetheart?

P: (Flushing) It wasn't like *that.* (p.110)

There are three types of *irony* used in Provocative Therapy:

(1) By using Socratic irony, the therapist is assuming the pretense of ignorance so that by adroit questions, the client's nonuseful conceptions are made conspicuous. (2) Another form involves the use of words to express something other than the literal meaning of those words. (3) Dramatic irony involves making evident the incongruity between the actual situation versus the described situation. (p.110)

Example: A combative female who has just been locked in the hospital seclusion room is standing near the grill in the door shouting obscenities at the hospital staff for putting her there for assaulting a fellow patient.

T: (Sidling up to the grill, in full view of the patient; chortling loudly) Atta girl! You have got 'em on the run! They're scared shitless of you now, the sonuvabitchin' bughousers and that crazy freak! Keep it up, don't let 'em break you (through clenched teeth) *no matter what! No matter how long they keep you in there!*

P: (Laughing in midshout) Aw, go to hell, Frank! You ain't locked up in here. It's easy for you to say that. You try it, if you like it so goddamn much.

T: (Cringing, looking furtively up and down hall, drops his voice to a conspiratorial whisper) Not me! They broke my spirit long ago, but I always have hopes that they'll finally meet somebody they can't break. (Suddenly glaring furiously, raising his voice in a fanatical shout) *No matter what tortures they*—

P: (Laughing: interrupting a conversational tone) Careful, they'll put you in here, next. Aw, piss on it, I'm shapin' up and shippin' outa here. (p.110)

There are many truly funny things that clients say or do that can be used to provoke laughter. There are many more times when the provocative therapist is reminded of an appropriate *joke* that parallels the client's present situation. Laughter has the powerful effect of reversing the context of the conversation or freeing up the client's frame of reference, so that the client can see his or her life in a new, hopeful, and more healthful light.

A final note. In using humor, the provocative therapist speaks four different languages, which are explicated at length in *Provocative Therapy* (1974, p. 74). Space limitations here permit only the enumeration of these. The four languages are: a religious-moral language; locker-room, or a language of the street; a body or kinesthetic language; and professional jargonese. Each of these is used humorously.

CASE EXAMPLE: HERBERT THE VIRGIN

This excerpt is from Herbert's twelfth session. Approximately the first five minutes are presented to demonstrate the continuity and present a flavor for the provocative style. Shorter samples from the same interview follow the first long excerpt to highlight various techniques the provocative therapist uses.

Herbert (pseudonym) is a highly intelligent, good-looking university student. He is in his early twenties, heterosexual, and painfully shy, avoiding women like the plague.

Therapist and client walk into the office and sit down.

C: Too bad Susan can't be here (ruefully).

T: You'd like to have Susan here, huh?

C: Yuh (with a chuckle).

T: So would I (matter-of-factly). Sure would relieve the boredom, I'll say that. (Turns to tape recorder) Let the record show that he is referring to Susan ———, a graduate student of mine. Just a dynamite person and brilliant and also just the mere view of her is enough to make strong men weak (with lustful enthusiasm). (Turning to client) Now which was it, her strength, her brilliance, or the fact that she looked like certified gorgeous?

C: Well, I wouldn't put any of those quite so strongly but it was all of them put together (chuckling). She was very nice . . . gracious.

T: Yeah, she's very gracious to creeps (nonchalantly).

C: (Laughing, and then sighs) Oh, I think she kinda liked me—actually.

T: Oh, yeah, she did have a certain positive attraction to your psychodynamics (puzzled, "disgusted").

C: (Mumbles softly)

T: Oh, yeah, what (challenging)? Are you muttering? Your lips are moving: Either that or my hearing aid battery has run out.

C: Well, I'm not even mumbling this time (defensively, humorously).

T: (Laughing) Well! (To tape recorder) Students, you've heard of counterconditioning. He used to mutter and mumble, now he just moves his lips.

C: You really ought to turn that intimidating tape recorder off (laughing quietly).

T: Agh, what are you talking about (feigned irritation)? The audience—this thing—Christ, nobody is going to listen to *our* tape. Some of them *might* listen. I say, "Here is some boring stuff. You oughta listen to this stuff because you'll find a lot of boring clients in the clinical field. Every once in a while you run across a jazzy one that perks your interest, but you got to learn how to deal with the boring ones too."

C: I bet I was boring last Sunday night (slyly).

T: Uh, what? (fumbling for the right word) Wait a minute, I'll get this question right. . . . I'm supposed to respond by saying. . . . How were? . . . No, wait a minute. . . . Who? . . . to . . . (Gives up) No, that just slipped my mind.

C: (Interjects) Well? . . .

T: I thought there was a response called for there (with a grin).

C: Well, there was (smiling). You were supposed to say something like, "Well, what happened last Sunday night?" (chuckling)

T: Well, not what *happened* Sunday night (laconically). I don't like to say something like that because that means that something fell from out of the sky. I usually prefer to say, "What did you *do*, creep?" . . . or *didn't* do?" Something like that, see? Not "What *happened?*" Should I say, "What did you do Sunday night?" or "What did you *not* do to make you boring?"

C: Something like that. . . . (with a knowing grin).

T: (Overriding and still fumbling for the "right" words) . . . Or "With *whom* were you boring?"

C: Well, I . . .

T: (Comically fumbling) Or "What were you *doing*?" or "What *weren't* you doing?" or . . .

C: Oh, never mind! (smiling, exasperated)

T: (Interrupting again) Well, it's Tuesday morning and . . . I can't seem to . . . Well, I feel a response is called for (professionally).

C: Well, I didn't want to plunge into the tale (grinning knowingly).

T: Well, you want to ease your way into it. That's typical. Okay, with your glacial slowness.

C: I want to be made to know that someone wants to hear me tell this fascinating tale (with insight, grinning).

T: You want to know whether I'm fascinated. (Bored sigh) How do I know, maybe it's going to be a boring story. You've already said you were boring Sunday night.

C: (Laughs)

T: I'm supposed to be fascinated with your boredom.

C: Actually it's kinda dry, but anyway . . . (with wry sense of humor).

T: You are? (Interrupting and acting ignorant) The story is? . . . or . . .

C: Everything, just everything (laughing out loud and giving up procrastinating).

T: Everything is a drag.

C: Anyway, I went up to this concert with this girl.

T: With a real live girl! (sarcastic enthusiasm)

C: And, uh . . .

T: Let the record show that the creep nodded (talking sarcastically to tape recorder). All right, we have to do that (talks to client, explaining). You see, we're going to get videotapes and so we'll be able to see your lips working, nods, and stuff.

C: (Laughs and adds cooperatively) . . . And body writhings.

T: Really! (enthusiastically)

C: (Continuing) Get some closeups and show my perspiration. (Laughing)

T: Yeah. (more enthusiasm and joining in) Head shots and armpit shots to show the sweat. . . . All those non-verbal cues.

C: And my nervous leer.

T: Yeah. (agreeing with a laugh) I like the choice of the word "leer."

C: Instead of merely grimace or something like that (smiling proudly and nodding agreement). Well, anyway, we went up to this concert. She had a boyfriend so I re-

ally didn't expect much and I got even less than what I expected. So did she. It was a boring conversation.

T: Oh, Lord (moaning).

C: It was a good concert, but. . . .

T: Oh, Jesus (still moaning his words).

C: But the conversation before and after was forced labor.

T: Uh? (playing dumb)

C: Awkward.

T: Oh, shit (moaning again).

C: We just couldn't think of much to say.

T: Agonizing, excruciating silences (moaning in agreement).

C: Naw, well, she talks when there are silences, but we sure didn't interrelate much.

T: Interrelate!? (incredulous)

C: Or whatever. We didn't hit it off.

T: I was going to say you were starting to sound like a frigging social worker or therapist (relieved). (Turning his head as though holding a conversation with another person and voicing both responses) "I can't interrelate to ice cream." "Huh?" (Both laugh) I can't relate to that . . . you didn't hit it off . . . like oil and water, you didn't mix. . . . Well, is she a queen? You keep going after those queen types. I've told you to take out other people.

C: Well, let's not get on this again (assertively). As a matter of fact she's not a queen.

T: Is she a frump?

C: What's a frump? Is that a dog?

T: Well, first cousin to a dog, except . . . more disheveled.

C: No, she wasn't a frump either. She's fairly attractive. Actually sorta cute, charming face, a mildly dumpy body but nothing to be offended by.

T: Oh, that Ichabod Crane body of yours (wincing). Hell, you shouldn't be too choosy and picky. Really, you don't look like Baretta.

C: I'm just running up against an insuperable genetic barrier (humorously and with a big grin, agreeing with therapist).

T: All right, I like it (laughing uproariously). You *know*, you're a bright guy. There's no-o-o question about it. . . .

C: Oh, gee, thanks (grinning with gratitude).

T: . . . You just act stupid (finishing sentence).

C: That makes my day (feigning a crest-fallen attitude, laughing) [End of first excerpt]

Second sample: later in the interview they discuss some girls that C met.

T: So you danced with a couple of gals but you didn't get their names or telephone numbers so you could know how to call them or how to get in touch with them.

C: Frank, I don't think that girls like to get hustled (protesting).

T: No, one has to proceed slowly, especially if everything is riding on it (mocking seriousness with a grin). You know these are pretty crucial kinds of maneuvers and, yuh, there's a great deal riding on them. (C laughs) What are you saying there?

C: Well, all right (agreeing calmly). In the long run there isn't much riding on this. Well, I mean I *could* be embarrassed (more seriously).

T: Well, *horrors*! (sarcastically and smiling) 'Course that's your continual state anyhow. What difference would it make? But I can see what you're saying, you know. It continually embarrasses you so that you can barely tolerate it. I mean you are neck deep in embarrassment and acute, kinda self-conscious awareness.

C: Right, I don't want it to become acute (agreeing humorously). It's chronic but I don't want it to become acute so that's where it hurts. And I don't want it to hurt. [End of excerpt two]

Third excerpt: they talk about alternatives to meeting girls.

C: Well, the night before I sat around and fantasized (interrupting).

T: Well, yes, a lot of guys do, and there's no harm in that (agreeing facetiously). A lot of guys fantasize—they're not making a lot of moves, but they are having a whole hell of a lot of good picture-time-shows in their heads. It's a lot safer. You can't get crotch rot from your fantasies; research shows that *conclusively!*

C: Yeah, well, also (explaining) . . .

T: (Interrupting) And you can't get a girl in trouble either, and you avoid risk of embarrassment: *You could be rejected.*

C: As I'm filming the whole show myself I can just . . . you know (humorously playing along with T, smiling).

T: Exactly! (agreeing)

C: I'm the director and producer.

T: Script writer (nodding). . . . You can make it turn out anyway you want.

C: And I do (with a laugh).

T: Fantasies many, many times with interpersonal relationships, especially heterosexual, are infinitely to be preferred than the actual thing, which is frequently a bummer (philosophically and ponderously).

C: You mean you're saying I should just lay in bed all the time. . . .

T: (Interrupting) You just lay there with a smile on your face and beatin' your pud and just singing (Bursts into song) "Dream along with me, I'm on my way to the (T makes obvious mistake) st—uh, girls."

C: (Laughs)

T: Sure, hum a little tune.

C: It doesn't work (thoughtfully).

T: It certainly *does* (protesting with a twinkle in his eye).

C: It does *not* (protesting more loudly).

T: (Giving in a little) Well, it doesn't work to get a lot of embarrassment—or do your fantasies turn out embarrassing too?

C: (Giving in) All right!

T: All right, then, by God, don't tell *me* it doesn't work (loudly). (T and C break up in laughter) And aren't they all dolls and queens in your fantasies?

C: Well, just this morning I was fantasizing about Betty, sweet Betty, from moonlight bay. . . .

T: Did it turn out right this time?

C: Oh, it sure did (enthusiastically).

T: Oh, God, thank God, sweet Jesus, thank the Lord (sarcastically and then with great enthusiasm)! See there? Don't tell me it doesn't work. It works a hell of a lot better than the real thing. (C laughs through this whole sentence) Shit, I know a guy who screwed a gal on moonlight bay—she got sand in her vagina and he was rubbing his cock back and forth and damn near abraided the thing down to a pencil size. (Instructively) See what I mean? The reality is *not* as good as the fantasy.

C: (Laughing in mock agreement) . . . And I know some guys who have been hit by comets from outer space. But I mean that thing doesn't happen very often. [End of excerpt three]

SUMMARY

When clinicians observe or listen to a provocative therapist at work, they are immediately struck by the quality of creative play inherent in the therapist's approach ("My God! Therapy can actually be fun!"), by the amount of energy the therapist invests, and by the concomitant energy response or release from the client. The serious work of therapy is being conducted at multiple levels by both participants in a spontaneous atmosphere of warmth and playfulness and humor, which energizes both. To their astonishment observers also hear the hallmark of provocative therapy: laughter. In spite of themselves, they invariably begin to laugh with the client and therapist. Fisher (1970) caught this flavor of PT interaction when he wrote:

Among the several possible models (e.g., healer) for the psychotherapist, consider the court jester. This figure, we are told, made playful comments about the king, his followers, and affairs of state; he punctured pretensions, took an upside-down look at human events. Now the patient, it might be said, suffers from gravity. To him life is a burden, his personality a riddle; yet viewed from outside, he may seem altogether obvious and his problems nothing much. Indeed, just because he hurts and has a dreadful sense of failure, eventually he must find laughter in the midst of his accustomed tears and glimpse his own absurdity. Without irreverence both he and the therapist stay mired in earnestness.

In psychotherapy the therapist deals with human pain and suffering, problems that often have tragic consequences for the client and his or her significant others. However, the tragic mask alone really does not adequately symbolize the human condition; the provocative therapist holds that the addition of the comic mask is necessary to more completely reflect the entirety of our lives and struggles. Laughter is the sound of victory.

REFERENCES

Bandler, R., and Grindler, J. (1979). *Frogs into princes: Neuro-Linguistic Programming.* Moab, Utah: Real People.

Blanchard, W. H., (1970). Ecstacy without agony is baloney. *Psychology Today, 3*(8), 8–11.

Ellis, A. (1962). *Reason and emotion in psychotherapy.* New York: Lyle Stewart.

Farrelly, F. (1971). Provocative therapy (#58). Philadelphia: American Academy of Psychotherapists Tape Library. (audiotape)

Farrelly, F. (1977). Provocative therapy. Chicago: Human Development Institute. (audiotape)

Farrelly, F. (1973). Analyzing the analyst—identifying effective interventions. *Audio Digest, Psychiatry, 7*(15). (audiotape)

Farrelly, F., and Brandsma, J. (1974). *Provocative therapy.* Cupertino, CA: Meta.

Fisher, K. A. (1970). The iconoclast's notebook. *Psychotherapy: Theory, Research, and Practice, 7,* 54–56.

Ludwig, A. M., and Farrelly, F., (1966). The code of chronicity. *Archives of General Psychiatry, 15,* 562–568.

Ludwig, A. M., and Farrelly, R. (1967). The weapons of insanity. *American Journal of Psychotherapy, 21*(4), 737–749.

Rogers, C. R. (1951). *Client-centered therapy.* Boston: Houghton-Mifflin.

Rogers, C. R. (1961). *On becoming a person.* Boston: Houghton-Mifflin.

Standal, S. W., and Corsini, R. J. (Eds.). (1959). *Critical incidents in psychotherapy.* New York: Prentice Hall.

Chapter 51

PSYCHODRAMA

ADAM BLATNER

I am, of course, familiar with psychodrama, having been on the stage with J. L. Moreno several times, served as president of the American Society of Group Psychotherapy and Psychodrama, and been the author or editor of several books on the subject. I have used Moreno's methods, along with Rogers' and other approaches through most of my working life.

Psychodrama is completely different from all other systems in that it is a method, such as the interview or hypnosis, without really any theory of its own, and consequently can be used by any therapy. As a teacher of psychodrama I have found about one in twenty people that ever really understood it or could use it. In my judgment this system needs a certain type of individual to be a successful user of psychodrama—one who is bold and quick to make decisions.

Adam Blatner, who has written several books on psychodrama, gives a good account of this procedure, summarizing its history, general theory, and the myriad uses of the system. Clear definitions of the various terms in psychodrama are given, as well as its uses in special circumstances. While psychodrama is usually used in groups, single person psychodramas are possible. Special attention is given to the problem of warming up, the usual problem for new users.

DEFINITION

Psychodrama is a method for exploring psychosocial problems using improvised enactments. One person (a "protagonist") plays out a situation in which he or she is seeking more insight and a better solution to a problem. Another person can play a supporting "auxiliary" role, and this process is facilitated by a trained leader ("director").

Psychodrama is generally considered a type of group therapy, but it is also used with families, couples, and individuals (Corey, 2000). Although psychodrama was originally developed as a form of psychotherapy, it has been modified for use in business, education, personal growth, community building, and other non-clinical settings. It should be thought of as both a method and a set of principles which can be integrated with not only many other forms of therapy, but also in other contexts. A more complete discussion of method, applications, and theories as well as extensive updated references may be found in the author's most recent books (Blatner, 1996, 2000a).

Psychodrama and drama therapy overlap somewhat, but are different in the following ways: Psychodrama focuses on persons enacting situations from their own lives, while drama therapy offers clients roles commonly used in theater repertoires (Emunah, 1997). Also, psychodramatists are primarily clinical psychotherapists who pursue further training in this subspecialty. Drama therapists have their primary background in the theater, with specialized training in its therapeutic applications.

Although the term "role playing" has been used as a synonym for psychodrama, it is inaccurate. Psychodrama refers to a method that investigates the deeper experiences, attitudes, and emotions of an individual. Role playing is used for finding or practicing a more effective behavioral response and is thus more widely applied in business and education.

HISTORY

Psychodrama was developed in the mid-1930s by Jacob L. Moreno, M.D. (1889–1974). A fascinating and complex person, Moreno was also a major pioneer of group psychotherapy, social psychology, and improvisational theater. Less well-known was his philosophical vision of the value of and need for creativity and spontaneity in interpersonal and social affairs.

Moreno was born in Romania and raised after the age

of five in Vienna, which, around the turn of the century, had become one of the intellectual centers of Europe. As an adolescent, Moreno felt a sense of near-religious mission to implement creativity in the world—an idea in keeping with those of some philosophers of his day, such as Bergson and Berdyayev. Observing the imaginative play of children around 1908 in the parks around Vienna, and joining them as a storyteller, Moreno was impressed with the way they became even more vital when they were encouraged to add a measure of spontaneity to their play.

Moreno attended the University of Vienna from 1907 to 1917, first as a student of philosophy and then of medicine, the field in which he received his degree. He also fully entered the intellectual ferment of Vienna, and during this period his social activism offered examples of what in retrospect might be some of the first self-help groups.

During World War I, Moreno worked as a medical consultant for a refugee camp, and there he noted that people's morale and function improved when they were given the freedom to choose those with whom they would live, instead of simply being subject to arbitrary administrative assignments. This served as the stimulant to Moreno's later development of the applied social psychological method of *sociometry,* in which people in groups can give feedback about their interpersonal preferences.

Moreno envisaged a social process in which people could become more spontaneous with each other, and as part of this, he developed and expanded on concepts such as the category of the moment, the "here-and-now," and the idea of "encounter" as a direct meeting in which both parties open to the viewpoint of the other. (These ideas became integrated in the phenomenon of the encounter group fifty years later.) Such ideas also may be recognized in retrospect as being part of the emerging philosophical movement known as existentialism.

Moreno's search for a higher degree of spontaneity and authenticity also found expression through a parallel interest in revitalizing the theater, which he felt should be an instrument of social change and healing, not just entertainment. Moreno felt that traditional theater at that time had become decadent, constrained by memorized scripts, the separation of playwright and actor, and the process of rehearsal. In short, the theater lacked spontaneity. To remedy this, in 1921, while serving as a general practitioner in a suburb of Vienna, Moreno gathered together a group of actors with similar ideals and began what may have been the first improvisational acting troupe, which he called the "Theatre of Spontaneity." They would perform scenes based on events noted in the news of the day, and functioned as a "Living Newspaper." During this effort at a combination of social therapy and revitalized art form, Moreno also no-

ticed that the process seemed to be helpful for the personal development of the members of the troupe—an observation which later led to psychodrama as therapy. Moreno saw how the process of role taking, through improvisation, led to an internalization of a wider range of role behaviors and greater mental flexibility, as if the actors using the process could then draw upon a wider repertoire of role components in their own personal lives.

In 1925, Moreno emigrated to the United States. Post-war Central Europe was in a state of economic and political chaos and unable to support his vision of the potential for theater as therapy. In his new country, while learning the language and becoming settled, Moreno continued to develop his ideas about working with groups and impromptu theater. Even though the focus of Moreno's work in subsequent years addressed the more limited applications in treating mental illness, he never lost his dream of helping society as a whole develop more effective forms of practical democracy, interpersonal freedom, and interactive creativity.

Out of his consultations in prisons and other group settings, Moreno began to develop the method of interactive group therapy, and, indeed, introduced the term "group psychotherapy" at a meeting of the American Psychiatric Association in 1932. Thereafter, he continued to be one of the earliest and most vigorous proponents of group psychotherapy, whether or not that would include psychodrama.

Another type of group research emerged in the early 1930s based on his consultation at a home for delinquent girls. This work was a maturing of his method of sociometry and other associated concepts, such as role theory. Role training and the beginnings of psychodrama also were forming.

In 1936, Moreno opened a sanitarium in Beacon, New York, about sixty miles north of New York City. Here he began to use psychodrama as the primary treatment approach, helping patients by allowing them to act out their emotional conflicts, even their delusions and hallucinations, and through this, to gradually modify these distortions in a process of healing. Actually, there had been some psychiatrists in the previous few centuries who had similar ideas, but they were almost certainly unknown to Moreno and furthermore never systematically developed their methods and concepts as he did. Also, Moreno emphasized the need for patients to play their own life experience rather than using scripts of stories about others, and combined this process with what he had developed in the way of group psychotherapy, inviting other patients and staff to participate as important agents of healing.

During this fertile time, Moreno was creating his own ideas about role theory, an idea that was just beginning to catch on also in the fields of sociology. He was one of the first to write about *interpersonal relations* as a focus for therapeutic intervention, a dimension beyond the intrapsychic dynamics of those concerned. He introduced the ideas of co-therapy (implicit in the technique of the "auxiliary"), marital and family therapy, and worked with the phenomenology of the patient, a form of existential psychotherapy (Compernolle, 1981). He published numerous monographs and began the first of several professional journals.

In 1942, he opened an institute in New York City, and offered open sessions in which many professionals enriched their own conceptual frames of reference. That year he started the first professional organization devoted to group psychotherapy, the American Society for Group Psychotherapy and Psychodrama (ASGPP). Unfortunately, he had made an enemy of Samuel Slavson, one of the pioneers of psychoanalytic group psychotherapy, and because psychoanalysis was becoming far and away the dominant force in the field, Moreno's own efforts were largely eclipsed.

Moreno was at his most vigorous in the 1950s, traveling internationally to lecture and demonstrate his methods, fostering the growth of his own and others' organizations. It should be noted that Moreno promoted group psychotherapy in all its forms, including family therapy and the use of the therapeutic community. He encouraged further research in sociometry or microsociology. He was also instrumental in supporting innovations in the creative arts therapies and the applied social sciences. He organized international conferences and wrote prolifically (Fox, 1987).

Moreno was aided immeasurably in his work by his second wife, Zerka Toeman Moreno, who was much younger and has been able to continue to carry on his work. (At the time of this writing, she is in her mid-eighties and continues to travel, teach, and is considered the foremost exponent of the method.) By the mid-1960s, Zerka began to do most of the teaching at Beacon, which had become the main center for learning the method. Nevertheless, they both continued to lecture and travel nationally and internationally.

By around 1970, Moreno was beginning to weaken. Finally, in 1974, at the age of eighty-five, following several small strokes, he chose to stop eating, made his farewells to his old friends, and died.

Moreno was a vibrant and charismatic man, but qualities which in some roles were strengths in other roles were weaknesses. His flair was dramatic, but slightly careless, so that his lectures sometimes rambled into historical reminiscence and reproaches to those whom he felt had appropriated his ideas without giving him credit. His writing lacked precision, cohesion, and systematic development, though his basic ideas were brilliant. In daring to brazenly challenge psychoanalysis he became a maverick. However, in the ensuing years, as new innovations in therapy emerged, many of his ideas were incorporated into a variety of other approaches.

CURRENT STATUS

Although many standard texts seem to be knowledgeable only of Moreno's earliest work, psychodrama as a field has continued to evolve and spread in influence and application. Many excellent books in this field have been published by others since Moreno's death. Current references may be found in the books by Blatner (1996, 2000) and Sacks, Bilaniuk & Gendron (1995).

Following Moreno's death, the ASGPP began to reorganize as a modern professional organization, and established an independent American Board of Examiners in Psychodrama, Sociometry, and Group Psychotherapy to certify those who had achieved full training in this field. Prior to this, rigorous standards had not been required. There are people directing psychodramas who haven't taken the full training, but now one can ask to see proof of certification. The Board keeps records of certified practitioners, offers regular exams, and maintains standards for professional qualifications.

At present, the training required for full certification includes the possession of a Masters' degree in one of the helping professions and over 780 hours of didactic/experiential work and specified supervision—to ensure a level of maturity and competence. The examination requires an understanding of ethical issues, knowledge of theory and practice, and an observation of the candidate's actual directing skills.

There are at present about two hundred certified trainers and another two hundred certified practitioners in the United States. In other countries, increasing professional interest has resulted in the forming of national and multinational organizations, publication of journals, and the holding of international conferences. There are an estimated 10,000 practitioners with over two hundred hours of training in the world today, and half of those have over 700 hours of training. Substantial organizations of psychodramatists have been formed in at least twenty-five countries. A number of these countries now have their own psychodrama journals.

Moreno's journals went through several name changes and, beginning in 1980, the psychodrama journal was titled the *Journal of Group Psychotherapy, Psychodrama, & Sociometry*. In 1997, reflecting an expansion of its scope, it changed its name again to the *International Journal of Action Methods*.

The national psychodrama association, the ASGPP (mentioned earlier in the History section), continues to hold national conferences. The American Group Psychotherapy Association, once a bastion of psychoanalysis, has in the last few decades opened somewhat to other methods, including Gestalt therapy and psychodrama. Moreno helped found the (only) International Association of Group Psychotherapy (IAGP), and in that organization psychodrama also has a significant presence.

While psychodrama has been included in a number of hospital treatment programs, as yet it remains on the periphery of traditional psychiatry and psychology in this country. However, psychodramatic methods have been integrated into many types of therapy, often without most practitioners recognizing this source. Family sculpture is one example, and Fritz Perls' adaptation of the empty chair technique in Gestalt therapy is another. Much of the method of role playing in schools and businesses may also be traced back to Moreno's seminal work.

Modified forms and adaptations of psychodrama also are being used for recreation (Blatner & Blatner, 1997) and as a type of nonscripted "Playback Theatre" (Fox & Dauber 1999). Other people are similarly extending the scope of these approaches, exploring ways of cultivating emotional intelligence in youth, sensitivity and empathy among professionals, and conflict resolution skills in various settings.

THEORY

In the spirit of trends towards integration among the psychotherapies, psychodrama makes no claim to being an approach which should be used in isolation, instead of any other method, but rather it is a powerful adjunct with concepts and techniques that can broaden the repertoire of a therapist or other type of group facilitator. Similarly, Moreno's writings should no longer be considered the only source of theory in the field; many other sources are also useful. Drama has been an element in healing among the ancients and in nontechnologized cultures, and anthropology and related studies of cross-cultural healing are highly suggestive. Developments in psychotherapy itself have transcended the ideologies of specific schools of thought and sought instead to elucidate underlying common elements. Writings in group and family therapy, in the other creative arts therapies, and especially in drama therapy contribute also to an understanding of how psychodrama is effective.

Of course, the main support for psychodrama rests on the concepts written about by Moreno and developed further by others in the field. It should be noted that, quite apart from the actual use of action methods, many of the following ideas also can illuminate aspects of the more general fields of psychology and psychotherapy.

Surplus Reality

This is Moreno's term for the category of activities in which imagination is applied in an intentional and coop-

erative fashion. It integrates the power of subjective experience—phenomenology—in order to help people more fully work with the psychological potentials in any situation. Moreno called psychodrama "the theater of truth" not because what was enacted was objectively accurate, but paradoxically almost the contrary: What needs to be enacted is the heart of human yearning, the deeper psychological truth of what was never said yet needs to be spoken. For example, clients may be helped to have an encounter with an unborn or stillborn infant, a final parting with someone who died before one had a chance to say goodbye, or an opportunity to comfort a still-frightened inner child of the past. Through living out such inner "act hungers"—even though it's only symbolic—the soul is aided in healing.

Surplus reality is close to the natural dimension of play, or what Winnicott (1971) called "the transitional space." Play therapy uses this principle, as do the imagery therapies. The almost archetypal tendency to dramatize, manifested in ritual and ceremonies of all types, implicitly uses surplus reality, but Moreno made the process more explicit and more aimed at therapy.

Catharsis

Healing is linguistically related to the same word root as wholeness, and psychotherapy in general aims at promoting a re-integration of parts of the psyche that have been disowned. At the point when previously non-integrated elements come together, emotional energy is released, which is catharsis. It is not emotion itself that heals, but rather helping clients to become aware of feelings with which they had lost touch (Blatner, 2000a).

The "catharsis of integration," is needed to follow-up on the "catharsis of abreaction" (i.e., simply re-owning the emotions) in order to make the process safe and meaningful. Clients need to discover that feelings or thoughts that were felt to be inimical to a valued or coherent sense of self can instead be sources of strength or attractiveness. Thus, the psychodrama director's task is to help the protagonist learn to find ways to channel previously unacceptable feelings in more socially positive ways. Catharsis involves integrations that may occur at an intrapsychic, interpersonal, social, and existential-religious level, as the client discovers that parts of the self can be integrated with an adaptive lifestyle in relation to others and in the sense of having a deeply meaningful life.

Creativity

Both Moreno and the psychoanalyst Otto Rank (independently) came to a sense that the challenge of healing involves not mere insight or adjustment, but active creativity. Life is ever-changing, and people are complex in their individuality, so life may best be thought of using the metaphor of art as a creative challenge. In psychodrama, people are helped to become the artistic playwrights and co-directors of their own lives, to re-write the scripts, substituting discriminating spontaneity for patterns of habitual or automatic thinking. People like being treated as though they have creative potential: It is open-ended and honors their strengths; it expects the best from them and draws them forward. The goal of creativity also undercuts tendencies to seek the status of being "right," an illusory position with little actual interpersonal effectiveness.

Spontaneity

One of Moreno's greatest insights is that creativity is most commonly generated through active experimentation rather than through quiet contemplation. This applies not only to the composing of music or art, but also in dealing with psychosocial problems of all kinds. It is an invitation to shift the process of planning from mere cognitive calculation to involved action, using simulations and by playing out possibilities. Many sophisticated systems from astronaut training to military war games explore problems thus through trial and error.

Moreno noted also that there is a great deal of vitality, excitement, and enjoyment generated in this process of creative improvisation, and that spontaneity can build on itself gradually until a creative breakthrough occurs (which is also a kind of catharsis). Interpersonally, people feel more rapport and safety when they can be spontaneous together—and that, in turn, also works the other way—the more one feels safe and has rapport with the others in a situation, the more spontaneity comes forth.

In a broader sense, the principle of spontaneity suggests an ongoing process of subjecting whatever has been created in the past—theories, social norms, techniques, and even Moreno's own writings—to reevaluation in light of present circumstances. The present moment, the here-and-now, thus takes on an existential significance, an opportunity to revise and refine any residuals of habitual or automatic thought.

Play as Context

Another aspect of play, aside from its power to generate the magical realm of surplus reality, is its relatively failsafe context. Lion and wolf cubs in play fighting have ways of signaling that the rough-and-tumble isn't really destructive, so do children—and so does the context of drama. In psychodrama, for example, if it seems as if it might be healing for a protagonist to reown his or her own deeply aggressive feelings, there are ways of allowing for vigorously attacking behavior without anyone re-

ally getting hurt, such as beating a mattress with a tennis racket, or using a foam bat.

Similarly, people can enjoy the positive experience of being the center of attention, showing off and being enjoyed by others, without the activity being viewed as unduly narcissistic. Many other experiences can be entertained and experienced in this "pretend" realm which, it is clearly understood, reflects aspects that at the same time are psychologically quite meaningful.

Drama

Drama is the more organized form of imaginative play, conducted in a more focused and grown-up fashion. It is the *vehicle* for the integration of the aforementioned principles. Drama is in turn associated with a variety of techniques, analogous to the stuff in a laboratory, the stage, the director, the techniques, and so on. These elements allow for the portrayal (in more explicit form) of many interpersonal dynamics which in ordinary life occur just under the surface of awareness.

Action

Moreno noted that spontaneity and insight emerged far more readily by integrating physical movement, that is, enacting a situation instead of just talking about it. Rather than explaining to the therapist (or audience), the protagonist is reminded to speak directly to those in the roles of the others in the scene, as if the interaction were happening in the here-and-now. This type of encounter and dialogue evokes more authentic feelings. The insight so gained is experiential rather than intellectual.

In working through, the benefits of actual behavioral practice, affirmed by the behavior therapists (forty years later), also make learning and integration more meaningful. Indeed, what Moreno called "role training" has become a major therapeutic modality, such as used in assertion training or anger management.

Group Dynamics

Psychodrama is most often used in a group context, because the presence of others adds to the vividness of the experience, increases the level of support and encouragement, offers modeling and feedback, and confers other benefits of group therapy (remember, Moreno was one of the pioneers of group psychotherapy, long before it became dominated by psychoanalysis).

Applied Role Theory

Moreno was also one of the pioneers of social role theory, but he gave it a special twist in emphasizing the capacity of people to monitor and modify their own role playing (Blatner, 2000, pp. 150–187). In other words, while the more sociological role theorists used this rich approach for description, Moreno focused on its practical application. In psychodrama, the protagonist plays not only the role of the actor, but also is helped to develop the "meta-roles" of observer, evaluator, and experimenter. In dramaturgical terms, the actor (protagonist) also shifts back and forth with the roles of director, playwright, audience, critic, and other players. The cultivation of this capacity to draw back from the role performance is the essence of psychological mindedness and one of the chief elements in therapeutic transformation.

Drama has also become a metaphor for life, as Shakespeare's line, "All the world's a stage" suggests. Psychodrama builds on this, adding the invitation for all of us to participate as co-creators, improvisors, and artists. As a metaphor, drama and its associated ideas, such as role, actor, scene, and so on are all powerfully evocative, suggesting a number of useful associations.

Because drama has become associated with the arts, and in our culture, the arts in turn have been associated with an implicit invitation to be creative, so the psychodramatic process reinforces that expectation in its language. This language is also familiar in this era of television and other dramatic media. Most people have become familiar with the process of staging dramas and producing plays, so speaking of situations in terms of the roles being played is, as they say in computer lingo, "user-friendly." Clients and non-professionals can participate more effectively when all can easily understand the concepts. This language is also relatively neutral, and does not as strongly imply illness and pathology.

The role concept applies to many levels of human organization, from the different roles within an individual to interpersonal, family, smaller group, larger group, and cultural levels. Psychodrama (in its larger sense) thus functions as a bridge between individual and social psychology.

It opens psychology to every viewpoint that can conceivably be represented dramatically, which includes comedy, spirituality, politics, and other facets which are too often overlooked by more traditional psychotherapies.

Playing a role makes an idea more concrete, yet in being a role that could conceivably be played by many people, it also retains enough of an abstract quality so that generalizations may be drawn and it can be worked with more flexibly.

Applied role theory suggests a pluralistic model of the mind, which invites a more dynamic way to work with intrapsychic conflict: through internal dialogue. Many therapists who do not otherwise use psychodrama have come to use the technique of having the client take first one part and then another, as if each role could directly address the responses and concerns of the other roles.

The natural relationship between role theory and role playing is fortuitous. For example, promoting understanding of others, even to the point of actual empathy, may be accomplished through the exercise of the technique of role reversal, having a client relinquish his or her own habitual egocentric perspectives and, like an actor, imagine what it might be like to be in the predicament of certain others. Taking one role at a time, and warming up to a few known features, gradually a composite picture may be gained.

Because roles are negotiable, the concept itself invites a reconsideration of one's life roles, and functions as a medium within which adjustments may be made without such adjustments having to immediately affect the sense of self in an all-or-nothing fashion. In other words, there is a differentiation between the sense of self and the roles that are played, just as is done by any actor, and this "role distance" makes any self-confrontation less narcissistically threatening. Roles are like large building blocks that can themselves be taken apart into smaller building blocks—roles have role components, and those often have sub-components. Each component can be examined or played psychodramatically, and each can be revised as needed. Thus, applied role theory is, if not psychoanalytic, nevertheless analytic in the scientific sense of being able to clarify and review the parts of the whole.

There are many other theoretical issues which are more extensively discussed in some of the source books (Blatner, 2000a). To note again, many of these concepts may be applied even if no action methods are used.

METHODOLOGY

The basic approach to psychodrama involves the physical and verbal enactment of scenes, improvised and created as situations which (usually) involve dialogue between various players. This basic idea is also capable of extensive modification in order to adapt to the needs of the group and situation.

Terminology

In the setting of scenes, more roles are in play than just therapist and client. So that people can keep track of who is doing what, more terms are needed: director, protagonist, auxiliaries, stage, and audience (Moreno, 1946).

The director is roughly the equivalent of the therapist, if the context is clinical. Alternatively, it is a type of group process facilitator. This role involves not only staging an enactment, but also remaining aware of the overall group process, engaging in a mutual yet astute ongoing diagnostic process as part of helping protagonists to understand themselves.

The protagonist is generally one of the members of the group whose problem is explored, and who enters the enactment as the central figure. Interestingly, the protagonist usually shifts roles during the psychodrama, sometimes taking the role of another person (role reversal), sometimes stepping outside the scene to observe a fragment of interaction (the mirror). Later in the course of a group therapy session, other clients might become the focus of attention, and during their enactment they would become the protagonist.

The auxiliary (plural: auxiliaries, also termed "auxiliary egos") is a person—usually a group member or a trained cotherapist—who plays other roles in a scene. In addition to playing more obvious roles, such as the protagonist's employer or sibling, auxiliaries may portray a figure in a dream, one of the protagonist's subparts or inner voices (by using the "double" technique), or even an abstract entity, such as "the government."

The stage refers to a designated area for the enactment. It is usually beneficial to use a separate area rather than playing the scene in the midst of the group. By providing a separate locus of dramatic action, the protagonist is reminded that the events in the enactment are clearly different from verbal interchanges. Moreno designed and installed special stages at his own institutes, and some hospitals have created stages for psychodramatic work. Generally enactments are conducted in an area cleared of chairs in a group therapy room.

The audience refers to the other people present besides the director, the protagonist, and auxiliaries. In psychodrama, the role of the audience shifts during the course of a session, with some members becoming auxiliaries and others becoming protagonists. Sometimes the audience plays an active role, giving feedback, encouraging, making sound effects, or calling out pertinent evocative phrases at the request of the director. (This technique is termed the "chorus.")

In addition, I would add a sixth element, that of the various psychodramatic techniques, such as role reversal, replay, soliloquy, stopping the scene, the mirror, coaching, asides, and so on.

When a problem comes up, if it seems appropriate to explore it psychodramatically, a scene is set. One of the tendencies in our culture is for the protagonist to talk *about* the situation, to narrate and explain. Instead, the director's task is to circumvent those patterns—which, for the most part are defensive in nature—and to help the protagonist to begin to explore the problem *in action*. The director may interrupt an explanation and say, "Don't tell us, show us." With this phrase, the patient is encouraged to plunge into the situation at a more intense and committed level of experience, acting "as if" instead of talking "about."

The technique of enactment is the most obvious, inviting a setting up and replaying of some event. The director might say, "Show us what happened with your family." The protagonist is helped to set the scene, indicate the layout of the room or other location, and to pick from the group the various auxiliaries who will play the people involved in the situation.

A related technique is multiple parts of self, in which an inner conflict is portrayed as if it were an argument within a group or family (Blatner, 1999). The director suggests, "Show us the conflict you're having within yourself." One aspect of this is the technique of role naming, which is itself therapeutic, bringing into consciousness more discrete themes, where before there had only been emotionally-loaded yet elusive shadows. This is then followed by placing each role into a different location, in chairs, standing on chairs, curled-up under tables, and having each part dialogue. The point here is again not to allow the protagonist to explain each part to the group or director, but to plunge in to the process of playing this or that role, speaking directly to one of the other inner roles. Thus, the inner child might speak to the imagined harsh and blaming inner conscience, and the director then seeks to have the other parts answer, accuse, defend, negotiate, distract, and in other ways express the range of maneuvers which reflect the protagonist's characteristic mental attitudes.

The future projection technique simply enacts a scene which is anticipated rather than remembered. The director may say, "Show us what you'd like to be doing in ten years."

Warming Up

The key to enactment is improvisation, and this requires a fair amount of spontaneity. Most people are inhibited at first, and both the group and individuals who may work as protagonists need to warm up, just as singers and athletes warm up. Spontaneity cannot be generated on demand, it must emerge gradually, as interest in meaningful themes is aroused, a sense of playful involvement is generated, and group support makes the risk-taking of any action modality feel relatively safe.

To this end, a director often begins the group with some structured experiences, which tend to bring issues into sharper awareness. Other functions of the warm-up phase include the development of a sense of rapport among group members. Sometimes other creative arts or expressive techniques may be integrated for this purpose. Theater games and creative dramatics warm-up exercises are also useful.

Interactive Dynamics

One of the concerns about using others to play parts in psychodramas is that they will distort the experience of the protagonist. This is one reason why Gestalt Therapy, which uses the psychodramatic techniques of encounter and empty chair, generally stays with monodrama, with the protagonist playing all the parts. While this often suffices, there are many other times in which protagonists really need and respond better to the stimulus of having another living actual person (albeit in role) saying provoking things, asking penetrating questions, and heating up the protagonist's experience of the predicament.

APPLICATIONS

Classical psychodrama is a powerful method which requires a good deal of special training on the part of the director, sufficient time for preparation and followup, the establishment of group support, and clients who are appropriate for this type of intervention. Used judiciously, it is an especially beneficial approach. More widely applicable are the techniques and theoretical elements derived from psychodrama, which may be integrated into a multimodal or eclectic orientation to therapy.

Group psychotherapy

Many types of group psychotherapy may be enhanced by the integration of psychodramatic methods (Corey, 2000).

- *Self-help groups,* such as ACOA (Adult Children of Alcoholics) and many other groups, offer something less specific than psychotherapy and yet more than a general personal growth group. In such sessions there are occasions in which "telling one's story" in action is even more healing and also generates even greater degrees of group cohesion.
- *Personal development groups,* the inheritors of the "encounter groups" of the 1960s and 1970s, nevertheless carry forth the ideals of the human potential movement along with continuing refinements in the organization of the many varied programs that use this medium. Psychodrama is useful as an adjunct in many of these settings.
- *Other therapies:* Articles have been written about applications of psychodrama in conjunction with Transactional Analysis, Adlerian Individual Psychology, Reality Therapy, Psychosynthesis, various creative arts therapies, and many other approaches.
- *Family therapy* is a natural locus for applying psychodramatic methods. One of these techniques, "family sculpture," expresses perceived relationships in concrete form and has been used extensively, often by those who never realized its origins in psychodrama. Other action techniques may be

added to family sculpture work to make it even more effective.
- *Therapeutic milieu* is a group therapy approach often found in residential treatment centers, in challenging risk-taking or outdoor-life programs, and many other settings. The immediate situations that arise, conflicts, flagging morale, and acting-out behaviors all may be immediately addressed using the technique of replay, followed by exploration of alternative responses.

Education

With modification, emphasizing the commonalities within certain general roles (i.e., sociodrama—which contrasts with psychodrama's examination of the particulars associated with the combined roles of a single individual), a variety of social issues may be examined even more vividly. The personal involvement generated in this process makes the subject relevant. Issues in history, literature, and current events are obvious candidates for this mode of teaching, but even a number of concepts in science, mathematics, and other fields can be brought alive through dramatic representation.

- *Religious education* offers a special case. The stories in the sacred scriptures can be made far more vivid and offer a deeper degree of contemplation when enacted. Class members are further invited to improvise, adding their own unspoken thoughts, were they to find themselves in the predicament of the various figures in the story. Alternative responses may also be explored. This form of "Bibliodrama" may be applied to the myths of other cultures also (Pitzele, 1998).
- *Spiritual dialogue* is another approach, that of encouraging people to play out their unresolved issues, imagining that some sage, saint, or spiritually wise figure could dialogue with them. An individual becomes a protagonist and then role-reverses, playing the wise other, and portrays what the protagonist imagines the other would say. Then, reversing roles again, questions are encouraged. The point is to bring out the tensions, doubts, reservations, accusations, and clarifications generated in an authentic dialogue, a process of making explicit the negotiation that rarely happens in most people's processes of prayer, contemplation, or meditation.
- *Grief work* may be stimulated by having the bereaved engage in an imagined encounter with the lost other, using "two-chair" work, also known as the "empty chair" technique. Shuttling back and forth, playing both the part of oneself and the other, questions are asked and answered: "What espe-

cially memorable experiences have we shared?"; "What did you mean to me?"; "What did I mean to you?" The point is to get past tendencies to offer general or vague responses, and to generate answers specific enough so that everyone listening could imagine the scene vividly (Blatner, 2000b).

Underlying Processes

Approaching the issue of application from a more functional viewpoint, some of the intermediate goals in problem exploration may be considered:

- *Diagnosis* involves more than simply finding a label for a condition. In its essence, it includes helping people to become aware of their own dynamics and those of others in an interpersonal field. Psychodrama, by bringing out the unspoken thoughts and associated implicit attitudes and beliefs, fosters insight. Understanding others, via role reversal, should also be appreciated as a kind of insight, not sufficiently emphasized in many other therapeutic approaches. (For example, at some point in their treatment, perpetrators of violence, sexual abuse, or other crimes may benefit from learning to include the reality of the feelings of others in their field of awareness.)

- *Role training* involves practicing for some future task, such as rehearsing a job interview, saying no if pressured by peers to take drugs, making a graceful apology, and so on. Indeed, many skills are best learned through a process of enactment, with sufficient opportunities for repeated feedback and replay.

- *Role expansion* involves the exploration of unfamiliar roles, in order to experience through drama aspects of living that supplement one's habitual role repertoire. In some ways, this is similar to George Kelly's approach to treatment within his Personal Construct psychological theory.

- *Spontaneity training* itself is a new role dimension, that of learning the skill of improvisation in a variety of roles. This is an incredibly empowering aspect of psychodrama. People discover that they can use their intuitions, feelings, and imaginations as powerful elements in their everyday coping behaviors. The fail-safe context of play (as part of the nature of drama), mixed with the encouragement of a group with a supraordinate goal of creative and expressive action rather than conformity, generates a profound sense of inner freedom.

- *Healing of emotional trauma* requires experiential methods, and psychodrama offers a method that may address the individuality of each person (Hudgins, 1998; Kellermann & Hudgins, 2000).

- People with *developmental disabilities* can be helped by using psychodramatic methods to develop skills in assertion, conflict resolution, and interpersonal awareness (Tomasulo, 1998).

CASE EXAMPLE

Knowing that psychodrama can offer an experience of mastery in place of a memory of humiliation, one group member volunteered to heal an old wound. She was a middle-aged woman with a somewhat timid manner, and she noted that even as a child she was sensitive and sought to please. One painful memory was still vivid, and the director moved right into action: "All right, let's set up the scene."

P [for protagonist, whom we shall call Jane]: We were at a party, and I was about seven years old.

D [for director, whom we shall call Don, making the genders contrast for the purposes of distinguishing pronouns]: Who would be the key players?

P: There would be the children, of course.

D: Pick some group members who will be the children.

P: Let's have Eileen, and Matthew, and you (pointing at another, chooses about five).

D: Anyone else?

P: Oh, yes, my uncle, but he comes later.

D: Where is the scene?

P: In a living room or den, a play space where the children are throwing pillows.

D [to the auxiliaries chosen]: You're kids now, playing rambunctiously. . . . [The auxiliaries throw pillows or pretend to run around yelling.] Was it like this?

P: Yes. . . .

D: You be one of the children.

P: Well, I didn't really join them, I was afraid. . . .

D: Show us what you did.

P: [Goes to the sides of the children's hurly-burly and squeezes her face anxiously, seemingly torn by wanting to join in and feeling a bit worried and overwhelmed by the noise. The auxiliaries are enjoying their rowdy and childish behavior.]

D: What happens next?

P: Uncle comes in.

D [to auxiliaries]: Okay, pause in the action, and stay about where you are, but you can sit down, make yourself comfortable. [to P] Pick someone to be your uncle. [She picks one of the larger males, Joe.] Now [still to P] be the uncle and show us what he does.

P [puffing herself up, acting a bit of a caricature of fierce]: What's going on here? What's all this noise?

D [to Joe as auxiliary]: Okay, now you be the uncle. [To the "children"] Okay, restart the scene in the living room! [The auxiliaries start playing, the protagonist stands at the edge of the activity. D nods head at the Uncle and he enters the stage area as the living room, repeating the given lines.]

JOE [Auxiliary 1]: Hey, what's going on here? What's with all this noise? [Auxiliaries may not get the words just right, but if it's close, the D lets it pass; if there's some possible loss of meaning, the D checks it, turns to the P and asks, "Is that the way he does it?" In this case, the D just lets the action continue. Auxiliaries as children continue to play and P cringes. Uncle restates his command/question much louder.] I said, what's going on here?

P: That's where I didn't really understand the question, you see, he wasn't really asking. . . .

D: Just show us what you did.

P: Oh, Billy and Bobby were playing rough and then they . . . and then he got mad at *me!* (P begins to get a little red-eyed just remembering.)

D: Show us what he did.

P [Takes role of uncle]: Oh, *you're* gonna be a tattletale, huh? That's no way to behave! [Turns on the other kids, but just a touch milder] You kids settle down, now. [Uncle walks out . . . falling out of role and speaking as herself] . . . and, you see, I thought he really wanted to know what was going on! I didn't know I was being a tattletale. . . .

D: How old were you?

P: About six. I thought I was supposed to answer him.

D [to auxiliaries]: Okay, stay in the stage area, but relax, sit down. [to P] So, you didn't get the social cues straight yet, well, that's understandable. How would you like to fix it?

P: I want him . . . not . . . to be so mean.

D: Well, okay, show us how he should be. Pick someone to be little you. [P picks a woman, Judy, to be little Jane, and the auxiliary then goes into the stage area, stands at the side of the group and looks anxious.] Now you be the uncle, only you do it nicer. [This is a variation of the technique of "replay."]

D [To the group on stage]: Action. [They play roughly and noisily again, and "little Jane" cringes. D signals to P as "Uncle"]

P as Uncle: What's going on here?

JUDY [Auxiliary 2, playing Jane as little girl]: They're being rough, Bobby and Billy, and everyone was . . .

P [as "nice Uncle," squats down and puts arm comfortingly around "little Jane's" shoulder, looking at her directly]: Janey, you are trying to be helpful, but it's okay that you don't have to speak up. I won't be cross with you. I was just wanting all the kids to quiet down.

A1 [as Jane]: But Uncle Joe, I thought you wanted to know what was happening! [expressing her vulnerable confusion]

P: Yes, little Jane, I did say that, but I didn't mean it exactly. That confused you, and I'm sorry. I should have just said, "You kids quiet down now."

A1 [whining just a bit]: But I was just *standing* there.

P: It's okay, when I got gruff I scared you too much, but I wasn't angry at you. I wasn't even very angry at the kids, I just wanted to tell them pretty strongly to calm down. I'm sorry I scared you. I like you.

D: Okay, cut. Now, let's replay that again, only let's let Joe play the nice uncle this time, and you be little Jane. [This is the technique of the "reformed auxiliary," and is designed to give the protagonist an even more vivid experience of being treated with gentleness. This also amplifies the nascent role of empowered self who can more consciously ask people to be nicer to her now and in the future. They replay the scene, with Joe behaving the way Jane just played the role while Jane reverses roles and becomes herself as a child. While being held gently by a largish man, she weeps a little, a gentle catharsis in which the protagonist mentally re-owns her more vulnerable "inner child" that had been partially repressed.]

D [sensing that the action has reached its status of "act completion," closes the scene and invites the protagonist to reenter her own role in the group, leaving the enactment; he speaks to the group]: Okay, let's go to sharing. [The director holds out a chair for the P and one for anyone who wants to sit next to the P to share.] A number of people tell the P and the group about times when certain elements of the enactment was true for them.

Joe, the auxiliary playing the uncle, confessed to a time he had unwittingly been too gruff with a sensitive child and how guilty he felt afterwards. He also "deroled," making more explicit the way he is different from the "Uncle": "My name is Joe; I'm not that man." He turned around and made a brushing-down motion, as if sweeping off a skin or gown. Another person noted how they suffered by not being able to understand a parent's mixed messages.

After a few others shared, the director drew the enactment phase to a close. This was not a very extensive psychodrama, as those can go on for over an hour. Still, vignettes such as these are meaningful and can easily be woven into other group therapy or personal growth group activities.

SUMMARY

Psychodrama should be thought of as a powerful combination of techniques and underlying principles, tools which can significantly enhance an integrative approach to psychotherapy and other processes for fostering problem-solving, communications, and self-awareness. The power of this approach is that it integrates imagination and reasoning, intuition and emotion, and action and reflection. Its scope is similarly broad, addressing cultural issues, spiritual concerns, and group dynamics, as well as intrapsychic conflicts. This capacity to bridge individual and social psychology has special relevance for our postmodern era, because questioning cultural norms and becoming intelligently politically active is also a kind of therapy, what Moreno called "sociatry," a kind of psychiatry for a society that may be in need of its own healing. Psychodrama, applied to broader problems in the form of "sociodrama," can help people renegotiate habitual role definitions.

Perhaps the most powerful result of the use of psychodrama is that it fosters a more mentally flexible mode of thinking, more capable of self-reflection, embodying as it does the metaphor of the actor in role. The activity of trying on this role, revising its structure and refining its performance, and then shifting to another, perhaps even an opposite role, creates a mentality that goes beyond Piaget's final stage of formal operational logic, opens the mind to the challenge of ongoing transformation of its own consciousness.

Finally, Moreno's emphasis on creativity and spontaneity involves a complex of associated ideas, opening to the dynamics and flow of the group, granting people the room to maneuver and to experiment without fear of failure, building in a lightness and compassion to human affairs. In short, psychodrama reclaims the innate power of one of the most fundamental (and often neglected) dimensions of human existence: playfulness. It was for this reason Moreno asked to have written as his epitaph, "Here lies the man who brought laughter and joy back into psychiatry."

FURTHER INFORMATION

American Society for Group Psychotherapy and Psychodrama (ASGPP), 301 North Harrison St., Suite 508, Princeton, NJ 08540. email: asgpp@asgpp.org - website: www.asgpp.org

The American Board of Examiners in Psychodrama, Sociometry, and Group Psychotherapy, P.O. Box 15572, Washington, D.C. 20003–0572. Phone: (202) 483-0514. You may write to the American Board of Examiners and ask for a list of certified trainers or practitioners of psychodrama in your area. They will also supply information regarding the requirements for certification.

Website for the International Association of Group Psychotherapy:

http://members.tripod.com/~portaroma/international/psychodrama.htm or www.go.to/internationalpsychodrama

For other articles relating to psychodrama, references, etc., see www.blatner.com/adam/

REFERENCES

Blatner, A. (1996). *Acting-in: Practical applications of psychodramatic methods* (3rd ed.). New York: Springer.

Blatner, A. (2000a). *Foundations of psychodrama: History, theory, and practice* (4th ed.) New York: Springer.

Blatner, A. (2000b). Psychodramatic methods for facilitating bereavement. In P. F. Kellermann & M. K. Hudgins (Eds.), *Acting out your pain: Psychodrama with trauma survivors* (pp. 42–51). London & Philadelphia: Jessica Kingsley-Taylor & Francis.

Blatner, A., & Blatner, A. (1997). *The art of play: Helping adults reclaim spontaneity and imagination.* Philadelphia: Brunner/Mazel—Taylor & Francis.

Blatner, A. (1999). Psychodrama. In D. Wiener (Ed.), *Beyond Talk Therapy.* Washington, DC: American Psychological Association.

Compernolle, T. (1981). J. L. Moreno: An unrecognized pioneer of family therapy. *Family Process, 20,* 331–335.

Corey, G. (2000). Theory and practice of group counseling (5th ed.). Pacific Grove, CA: Brooks/Cole.

Emunah, R. (1997). Drama therapy and psychodrama: An integrated model. *International Journal of Action Methods, 50*(3), 108–134.

Fox, J. (Ed.). (1987). *The essential Moreno: Writings . . . by J. L. Moreno.* New York: Springer.

Fox, J., & Dauber, H. (Ed.). (1999). *Gathering voices: Essays on playback theatre.* New Paltz, NY: Tusitala.

Hudgins, M. Katherine. (1998). Experiential psychodrama with sexual trauma. In L. S. Greenberg, J. C. Watson, & G. Lietaer (Eds.), *Handbook of experiential psychotherapy* (pp. 328–348).New York: Guilford.

Kellermann, P. F., & Hudgins, M. K. (Eds.). (2000). *Acting out your pain: Psychodrama with trauma survivors.* London & Philadelphia: Jessica Kingsley-Taylor & Francis.

Pitzele, P. (1998). *Scripture windows: Toward a practice of bibliodrama.* Los Angeles: Alef Design Group.

Sacks, J. M., Bilaniuk, M. T., & Gendron, J. M. (1995). *Bibliography of psychodrama: Inception to date.* New York: Author.

Tomasulo, D. J. (1998). *Action methods in group psychotherapy: Practical aspects.* Philadelphia: Taylor & Francis/Accelerated Development.

Winnicott, D. W. (1971). *Playing and reality.* London: Tavistock.

Chapter 52

PSYCHO-IMAGINATION THERAPY

JOSEPH E. SHORR

One of the most energetic and successful proponents of the use of imagination in therapy is Joseph Shorr, the author of this chapter, who takes an existential/phenomenological point of view and who uses imagery as his main modality for personality change.

Psycho-Imagination Therapy is one of the purest of systems. It is essentially an autochthonous system unsurpassed in charm and elegance by any of the systems in this book. In my judgment it provides a process that all therapists should understand and be able to use. Like role playing, the interview, and analysis of early recollections, Psycho-Imagination is a technique of general value.

Psycho-Imagination Therapy is a phenomenological and dialogical process with major emphasis on subjective meaning through the use of waking imagination and imagery (Shorr, 1967). Emphasis on the therapeutic interaction itself has to do with the question of one's identifying oneself and separating one's own view of oneself from the attributed self as defined by the significant others in one's childhood.

First developed by this writer, a clinical psychologist, in 1965, the use of Psycho-Imagination Therapy is growing. Theoretically it is related to the interpersonal school of psychoanalysis that stems mainly from the work of Harry Stack Sullivan.

HISTORY

Human beings have always been intrigued by their imagination, although historically it has variously been granted prominence or relegated to insignificance. The concept of imagination has served as an explanation of human behavior; as an agent of causality; and as a source of physical, emotional, and mental disease—even death.

In the history of psychotherapy, imagination has played many roles with diverse implications. Eighteenth-century thought ranged from ascribing the effects of Anton Mesmer's hypnotic technique to imagination, through Italian Lodvico Muratori's concept of imagination being comprised of dreams, visions, delusions, *idées fixes,* and somnabulism.

During the nineteenth century, actions once attributed to imagination were deemed the products of suggestions or auto-suggestion. Sigmund Freud (1959), however, as early as 1892 attempted a "concentration technique" that utilized the patient's imagery:

> I inform the patient that . . . I shall apply pressure to his forehead, and I assure him that all the time the pressure lasts, he will see before him a recollection in the form occurring to him, and I pledge him to communicate this picture or ideal to me, whatever it may be. . . . Having said this, I then leave go and ask quietly, as though there were no question of a disappointment. "What did you see?" or "What occurred to you?"
>
> This procedure has taught me much and has also invariably achieved its aim. Today I can no longer do without it. (Breuer & Freud, 1953, p. 270)
>
> My expectations were fulfilled; I was set free from hypnotism. . . . Hypnosis had screened from view an interplay of force which now came in sight and the understanding of which gave a solid formation to my theory. (Freud, 1959, p. 29)

Despite much enthusiasm, Freud later abandoned the concentration technique for free association. Jerome L. Singer (1971) suggests:

> Freud may have erred in not insisting on imagery alone rather than allowing patients to shift to free verbal association. He might have gotten more powerful uncovering more rapidly from his earlier technique. Undoubtedly individual practitioners have sensed the importance of fostering greater emphasis on concrete imagery by patients and have found themselves impatient with the ap-

parent glibness of defensiveness that often characterizes verbal free association. (p. 9)

One can only imagine what changes would have occurred in the field of psychotherapy if Freud had proceeded with "free imagery." However, Carl Jung's concept of "active imagination" had an important influence on European intellectual thought.

The twentieth century saw a resurgence of interest in imagery in Europe. Carl Jung and Sandor Ferenczi redefined and revitalized imagination and imagery. But in the United States the use of imagination and imagery as psychotherapeutic tools followed a difficult path. Although E. B. Titchener worked with problems related to imagination and introspection, J. B. Watson, America's first major proponent of behaviorism, turned the mainstream of psychological investigation away from a concern with inner images—daydreams, dreams, and fanciful ruminations—toward concepts of conditioning. The psychoanalysts of the period viewed fantasies and dreams as relevant areas of analytic investigation, but the free use of imagination was not encouraged since, to many, it reeked of resistance.

Freud believed fantasy and imagination were essentially limited to the person's defenses. The adaptive function of imagination was largely ignored except by Heinz Hartmann in 1958. Neither Hartmann's work nor an earlier emphasis by Erich Fromm (1955) was given much attention. Fromm voiced a plea for moving beyond the conventional free-association procedure into therapist-initiated situations. He advised analysts to make fullest use of their own imagination and suggested the use of active imagery methods to improve the flow of the patients' free associations.

By and large, however, American psychologists have tended to regard reverie and imagination as unproductive, impractical, and completely unempirical.

The return of the image in American psychology has, oddly enough, been given impetus by the same theoretical framework that delayed its emergence—behaviorism. The behaviorists' emphasis on visual imagery during systematic desensitization provides an example. T. G. Stampfl and D. J. Leavis (1966), for example, used powerful negative imagery in their Implosive Therapy. Although the behaviorists have helped reintroduce imagery in therapy, they do not show a keen interest in the patients' inner experiences or fantasies, and they generally leave unconscious processes uninvestigated.

Gestalt therapists use imagination in conjunction with dreams, but have limited the interpretive value of images and have shown disinterest in the imagination as it relates to past experience.

European psychotherapists draw heavily from the work of Robert Desoille, Hanscarl Leuner, Carl Happich, Robert Assagioli, Andre Virel, Gaston Bachelard, and others, investigators who share an interest in using imagery and imagination in the psychotherapeutic experience.

Desoille stands above all others in the psychotherapeutic use of imagery. His pioneering work was influenced by E. Caslant (1927). From Caslant's original notion, Desoille (1965) developed the *rêve éviellé*, Guided Affective Imagery Technique. This served as a point of reference for nearly all psychotherapeutic developments employing imagery as a prime modality. His method suggests that many problems can be ameliorated by means of the symbolic combat, or transformation, that takes place in imagery.

The philosophical roots of psychoanalysis are uniquely Freud's—the concept of psychic determinism and the matrix of the triplicity of the ego, id, and superego. Jung, too, provided his own philosophical base—the collective unconscious. A comparable philosophical base emphasizing imagination and imagery was offered by a nonpsychotherapist, the phenomenologist Gaston Bachelard. He broke with the more traditional psychological method of introspection by calling attention to man's innate capacity for generating imagery and symbolism.

With the increased awareness of imagination and imagery, the last decade has also seen a growing emphasis on phenomenology—the study of how a person sees his or her world. This writer believes that phenomenology requires that a person use his or her imagination as a vehicle by which to ready the self for all that he or she uniquely perceives, anticipates, defends, and acts upon. The person imagines how things will be, thereby preparing for whatever action may result. The integration of phenomenology with the concept and use of imagination is a palpable necessity. Our world of images reflects and represents our being-in-the-world, and we can only understand man as an individual, and as a part of mankind, when we grasp the imagery of his experience.

R. D. Laing (1965, 1971) helped to formalize and concretize the phenomenology of self-other concepts originally developed by H. S. Sullivan. By integrating this stream of thought with the European studies of imagery through a natural bridge—psychotherapeutic imagery productions—this writer has organized a systematic and comprehensive theoretical framework to provide a viable and innovative psychotherapy.

I find that the intensive use of imagery in psychotherapy heightens therapist motivation and involvement because of the interesting and dramatic nature of the material that is elicited. The probability is high that the vividness and intensity of the patient's imagery productions serve as a catalyst to his or her own therapeutic motivations.

CURRENT STATUS

The Institute for Psycho-Imagination Therapy (IPIT) was founded in Los Angeles in 1972 by this writer. I had already spent close to 10 years developing the theory and methodology of Psycho-Imagination Therapy. Some of the basic work and theoretical structure was presented originally in several journal articles.

My first book, *Psycho-Imagination Therapy,* was published in 1972. My second book, *Psychotherapy Through Imagery* (1974b), contained new material developed during clinical and research work with Psycho-Imagination Therapy. My third book, *Go See the Movie in Your Head* (1977b), added material relating to self-image imagery.

Since its inception the institute has constantly expanded its field of influence. Seminars are held several times a year at the University of California at Los Angeles, Immaculate Heart College, California School of Professional Psychology, and the University of Southern California.

The Shorr Clinic was opened in 1976 to provide affordable therapy to a broad segment of the population. The staff members of the clinic have a minimum of four years training in Psycho-Imagination Therapy.

In 1974 the institute published the *Shorr Imagery Test* (SIT). This projective test using imagery yields both a quantitative conflict score and a qualitative personality analysis. The SIT is individually administered and has been used in numerous educational institutions and hospitals throughout the United States. It is also used in several branches of the Veterans Administration and at the Great Lakes Naval Station. In 1977 the Group Shorr Imagery Test (GSIT) was published. The GSIT makes it possible to administer the SIT to any number of persons simultaneously.

The Supplementary Shorr Imagery Test (SSIT) (1978) is another projective test using imagery, which provides both a quantitative conflict score and an in-depth qualitative personality analysis. It can be used independently or as an adjunct to the SIT to yield additional information.

The *Shorr Parental Imagery Test* (SPIT) (1979b) focuses on conflicts between parents and children and is used for diagnosis and treatment in counseling.

Current research projects have been done with the various Shorr imagery tests in research projects. David Tansey (1979) found confirmation for the thesis that there is a "criminal personality" and researched the ability of the SIT to predict recidivism among felons convicted of violent crimes.

Jack A. Connella (1978) used Psycho-Imagination Therapy with groups of chronic benign intractable pain patients. He used the SIT pre- and posttherapy to evaluate the efficacy of the imagery treatment. Due to Connella's findings, the City of Hope Hospital in Duarte,

California, regularly incorporates Psycho-Imagination Therapy procedures into their treatments and uses the SIT for patient evaluation.

Pennee Robin used the SIT to do in-depth personality analyses of persons interviewed for the book *Sexual Jealousy.*

Gail Sobel (1979) employed the GSIT as a tool in a test-retest situation to measure the degree of conflictual level reduction as a result of participating in a course entitled "Group Dynamics."

Clifford Morgan (1979) has adapted the SIT for use with disabled persons and with the personnel who treat and/or deal with the disabled.

In 1976 the Institute for Psycho-Imagination Therapy was the initiating force in founding the American Association for the Study of Mental Imagery, which held its first annual conference in Los Angeles in 1979. The proceedings of this conference are published by Plenum Press (Shorr et al., 1979).

THEORY

Psycho-Imagination Therapy is a phenomenological and dialogical process with major emphasis on subjective meaning through the modality of waking imagery and imagination.

The basic phenomenological proposition of Psycho-Imagination Therapy recognizes individuals' need to become aware of how they define themselves in relation to others, and how they feel others define them. For example:

> How I see myself
> How I see you
> How I see you seeing me
> How you see me seeing you

This phenomenological "in-viewing" is a synthesis of the self-other personality development theories of R. D. Laing and Harry Stack Sullivan. Sullivan (1953) believed that personality consists of the characteristic ways in which a person deals with others in his or her interpersonal relationships. In order to abolish anxiety—which is always the direct result of interpersonal interactions—a person must develop security operations. When those security operations are maladaptive, they produce the wide variety of interpersonal warps, emotional discomforts, and behavioral maladjustments that constitute psychiatric symptoms and psychiatric illnesses.

The two basic premises of Psycho-Imagination Therapy are: (1) everyone needs to make a difference to someone, and (2) everyone seeks confirmation or acknowledgment of the self. These needs occur contemporaneously.

When not fulfilled, the child develops false positions. If one is not confirmed for one's true self, the person then develops strategies to secure confirmation for a false self. The security operations one involves oneself in serve to maintain one's identity even in the absence of true acknowledgment.

My major emphasis in the therapeutic interaction is on separating one's own view of oneself from the attributed self as defined by the significant others in one's childhood. Ideally, the "true" identity is helped to emerge while the "alien" identity is eliminated.

Interpersonal and intrapersonal interactions, as well as the individual's strategies within the self-other relationships, are best seen through systematic use of waking imagery. A person's imagery can show how he or she organizes the world, his or her style of action, and marked individual differences to which the therapist should be attuned. Imagery provides a primary avenue through which thoughts, wishes, expectations, and feelings can be most effectively reactivated and reexperienced.

Imagery, unlike other modes of communication, ordinarily has not been punished in the past and is, therefore, less susceptible to personal censorship in the present. Thus imagery provides a powerful projective technique resulting in a rapid, highly accurate profile of the individual's personality and conflicts.

Imagination is viewed as the central kernel of consciousness and an important means of access to the uniqueness of the individual's world. The active introduction and conscious use of imaginary situations provides a stimulating investigative tool, an avenue to action possibilities. It allows the patient to explore more safely and openly, to differentiate, to experiment with and to integrate fantasy and reality, all within the context of a cooperative therapeutic alliance and encounter.

Psycho-Imagination Therapy puts the individual, through imagery, into a particular situation that can evoke a set of interactions useful in revealing major problems in the significant areas of life, and that also permit the individual to relive experiences. J. L. Singer (1971) writes: "Shorr uses an almost infinite variety of images geared very much to the specific characteristics of the patient and to specific developments in therapy."

I emphasize subjective meaning by recognizing that the patient's images are uniquely his or hers, coming from each individual's own storehouse of knowledge and experience. In the process of describing his or her image, the imager begins to relate it to something of meaning in his or her life. Hidden meanings of the events, attitudes, feelings, and motivations attached to the image are then used to explore further the interpersonal implications.

I have systematically categorized over 2,000 imaginary situations to reveal specific information about the patient's personality, world view, self-definition, areas of conflict, and style of defenses. Other categories are specifically for focusing on change and for facilitating the process. Responses to the categorized imagery usually elicit hidden or repressed material more efficiently than direct questioning by the therapist. In addition, the imagery bypasses the conscious censor and is less liable to denial by the imager than imprecise verbal statements.

The major categories of imagery employed (Shorr, 1978a), with examples, follow.

Spontaneous Imagery

These images are generated by suggesting that the patient report the flow of imagery as it occurs, or report the next five consecutive images that occur, then another five, and so forth. In either sequence, certain images usually become affect laden and then will serve as the vehicle for dialogue or release of feeling.

Directed Imagery

At times a spontaneous flow of images seems to go on endlessly without theme or apparent coherency. Directed imagery can be then used to control the flow and bring coherency and integration to the production. My experience validates those of Horowitz and Becker (1971), who say that the specificity of instructions for reporting visual images increases the tendency to form, as well as to report, images.

Self-Image Imagery

Each of us has a self system—a set of attitudes about ourselves and by which we define ourselves (Shorr, 1979a). This system is inextricably bound to our perception of how others see us. Imaginary situations that help reveal this self system include:

Imagine there are two of you. Imagine kissing yourself (sitting on your own lap, looking at yourself through a keyhole).

Dual Imagery

Inner conflicts are caused by the opposition of two strong and incompatible forces, neither of which can be satisfied without exacting pain, fear, guilt, or some other emotional penalty (Shorr, 1976).

A remarkable phenomenon occurs when a person is asked to imagine two *different* animals, dolls, forces, impulses, and so forth. In the majority of reported imageries there is some degree of polarization. The contrast becomes more evident when the imager is asked to assign an adjective to each of the two images. The opposition is further enhanced when the patient imagines statements and replies from the two images. The complementary opposites within experience are thus revealed.

These dual images frequently represent two parts of the self in conflict—self vs. self, or conflict between self and another. The dialogue that is a natural outgrowth of this imagery helps the patient become aware of the conflicts and their meanings.

Body Imagery

Empirical evidence indicates that people can sense the body-part core of their identity. They can also identify in which part of the body their anger (fear, guilt, joy) resides. These images provide clues to self-image, body image, and areas of conflict (Shorr, 1973).

Furthermore, introjection of parental figures is evidenced when persons are asked to imagine in what part of their body their parents reside. If, in the developmental process, a person has been falsely defined, the false definition may take on a body locus. The mother or father who "resides" in a part of the patient's body (chest, heart, guts, limbs) and appears hostile is, in reality, the false identity or the neurotic conflict internalized. When the patient "exorcises" the bad parental figure, the way is open to a healthier, more independent identity.

Sexual Imagery

Clinical experience reveals that people who say they do not have images will respond when asked to imagine or recall sexual scenes. Sexual themes are among the most powerful and most frequently occurring images. Many are related to the strategies of interaction between the sexes that anticipate acceptance or rejection.

Imaginary situations that are most productive in revealing attitudes and feelings about sex include:

Imagine an animal that comes out of a penis and an animal that comes out of a vagina. Then imagine that both animals go down a road together.

Parental Imagery

Parental imagery is a highly specialized category of imagery relating to the interactions of parents and children, or individuals and/or significant others. One example is:

Whisper into your mother's (father's) ear. Have her (him) whisper something back to you.

Depth Imagery

Images that reveal depth or unconscious forces almost always elicit profound reactions. These highly emotion-ally charged situations should be employed with caution and with the therapist's awareness of what the patient is ready to face. One example is:

Imagine you are a child and you are crying. Now imagine your mother (father) licking away your tears.

Unconscious Imagery

Although this material can emerge in any imaginary situation, those categorized as unconscious imagery achieve their purpose more readily. One of the most useful is:

Imagine reaching into a cave three times, each time reaching deeper than the last. What do you do, see, and feel?

Task Imagery

Task imagery may reveal the patient's internal conflicts, style and manner of approach, defenses, and fears; it also serves as a vehicle for focusing on a changed self-concept in the "working through" of the imaginary task (Shorr, 1975).

An important ingredient following the initial flow of imagery is to redo or reexperience the imagery in a manner that leads to a healthy conflict resolution. But the patient must be *ready* to focus for change. The elements determining this readiness are the patient's awareness of his or her internal conflicts, the release of feeling connected with contributory traumatic incidents, cognizance of the undermining strategies of behavior of significant others, and recognition of his or her own counterreaction strategies.

Examples of task imagery include:

Imagine building a bridge across a gorge. You are in a tank of the foulest liquid. How does it feel? Imagine getting out of it.

Cathartic Imagery

Imaginary situations in which patients are asked to imagine the "bad" parent in front of them and openly define themselves in a positive manner can substitute for actual face-to-face confrontations. Obviously this kind of focusing procedure requires a supportive therapist aligned on the side of the patient, and, equally important, a readiness on the part of patients to liberate themselves from a false identity.

In addition to the finish-the-sentence approaches such as: *I am not _____; I am _____; Never refer to me as _____;* and so forth, the therapist can suggest general, special, or group therapy imagery.

General Imagery

These images cannot be classified as specifically dual images, task images, or others, yet they plumb a vast area of the imagination and often lead to meaningful dialogue and awareness. They are often the stimulus for focusing and change. Examples include:

Imagine an image of a molecule of you (your conscience, paradise). What do you do and see and feel?
Stare into a fire. What do you do and see and feel?

Special Imagery

These images defy ordinary categorization. They have proven to reveal enormous amounts of information about layers of personality, core conflict, and sexuality. Examples include:

Imagine three boxes, large, medium, and small. Imagine something inside each box.
Imagine three doors (left, center, and right). Open each door. What do you see, do, and feel?

Group Therapy Imagery

Psycho-Imagination Group Therapy emphasizes the patients' self-definition and the degree to which their self-concept permits or constricts behavior vis-à-vis the other group members. Group interaction crystallizes each member's awareness of how others in the group define him or her. In addition, the group becomes an arena for reenactment of old family interactions that molded the patient's false positions and negative self-images.

The overall purpose of interaction within the group is to help each patient become aware of his or her conflicts and then take the risks inherent in focusing for change. While nearly all of the imagery approaches suggested for individual therapy can be utilized in group therapy, several factors must be considered. First, groups involve interaction between men and women. Some patients find it considerably easier to express feelings and imagery to members of the same sex. Difficulties in revealing such material to members of the opposite sex is especially prevalent among persons with problems relating to exposure of sexual inadequacy. Overcoming this kind of reluctance, permitting oneself the free flow of imagery and emotional expression without the feeling that one is weird, is a barometer of the patient's growth.

Second, the factors of peer competition and belonging, while not always evident in one-to-one therapy, may surface in group contact. Disclosing such feelings and coping with them are part of the group process. Also, basic trust of authority figures and basic trust of one's peers are areas that may be subjected to considerable emotion

and conflict within the group setting. Co-patients often afford the conflicted group member a chance to develop and nurture the courage for new alternatives by example, by identification, by stimulating one another, and by giving increasingly free play to their fantasies, dreams, imagination, and unconscious productions.

Group sessions are not so structured that only imagery is involved. Anything may be brought up at any time—a particularly traumatic situation or decision; carryover reactions from previous sessions; thoughts and feelings people have about others in the days between group meetings. Awareness and feelings patients have gleaned from individual sessions may be brought up in group situations. Nothing, certainly, should deter spontaneous behavior unless that behavior is used as a cover-up for some difficult internal conflict. A fine goal for any group therapist is to keep the structure and the spontaneity of the group unfettered.

METHODOLOGY

Psycho-Imagination Therapy uses four techniques, namely: (1) imaginary situation (IS), (2) finish-the-sentence (FTS), (3) self-and-other question (S&O), and (4) most-or-least question (M/L).

The infinitely varied waking imagery elicited through the imaginary situation is the essence of the phenomenological method. This method involves asking patients to relax, close their eyes, and trust their images. The therapist then suggests the appropriate imaginary situation to elicit the desired material. The patient's responses are the basis of the dialogical aspects of the therapeutic process. These responses suggest what patients are opening for examination, what they are willing to face, where they are going, what they are ready for, and what they appear to deny.

It is not wise to push the patient to image if none are forthcoming after a long interval. One may prefer to go either to other imaginary situations or perhaps to discuss current concerns. The patients must be assured that material is always available to them for awareness and meaning whether or not they are involved in imagery.

The patient's responses to certain structured situations often accurately bring into the "here-and-now" states of feeling that have their roots in the past. The therapist then stresses the *situation* and *interpersonal interactions* with patients and encourages them in their *choice of action* within the situation. This ultimately helps them in greater choice of action in their external reality.

Clinical experience demonstrates that the finish-the-sentence technique can uncover the more complex emotional blockages. However, its effectiveness depends on its being woven into the fabric of the therapeutic dialogue at the appropriate moment. Consider the case of a young man who, when asked for the body-part core of his identity, replied: "My hands. . . . I am only what I'm doing. . . . If I am not doing anything, then I have no identity." The therapist can follow through by asking the patient to finish a sentence such as: "But for my father (or mother) I would have been _____." "My identity will suffer if I go toward _____." "I feel most hostility toward _____."

Both therapist and patient may be surprised by the response to the question "I deprive my wife (husband, father, mother, boss, or other significant person) of the satisfaction of _____." A variant of the latter refers to any other two significant persons in the patient's life: "My father deprives my mother of the satisfaction of _____."

Patients who are amnesic about their childhood and who may have difficulty with an imaginative situation often respond well when asked to supply 10 different endings to the sentence: "I strongly resent _____." After the patient selects the item he or she feels most strongly about, the therapist can use dialogue to stimulate awareness.

An important way to elicit the patient's conflict areas is by the use of existential, or self-and-other, questions. An existential question elicits how a person views the self and how he feels others define him. It is an effective tool when used in conjunction with the imaginary situation.

The manner of presenting these questions is of the utmost importance. Timing is critical, and under no circumstances should they be asked routinely or as a series of test items. This weakens the desired therapeutic effect. Nor should they be posed with predetermined answers in mind. Do not try to fit the patient in advance into any dogmatic theory or system of thought.

For example, with one patient it may be appropriate to ask: "How do you make yourself aware to others when in group therapy?" The answer will probably reveal the patient's inner consistency in functioning with others in a way that is unique to his or her self-system. If the therapist is following a pre-conceived theory, he may unwittingly try for a "desired" response and miss the way the patient really sees himself in relation to others.

Furthermore, judgment must be used to decide whether the patient has the ego strength to handle certain questions at a particular time. There is no substitute for the skill that comes from experience. In sessions where the patient requires much therapeutic support, they may have to be eschewed completely.

Following are some examples of self-and-other questions:

To whom are you accounting?

Never refer to me as _____.

Did (Do) you make a difference to anyone?

Did (Does) anyone acknowledge your existence?

How do (did) you make people aware of you?

Were (Are) you ever believed?

What qualities did your parents deny in you?

How would you drive somebody out of their mind?

The most-or-least question sharpens awareness of a person's self-image and the concept of his basic attitudes and values. Typical of this category is "What is the most immoral thing you can think of?" or "What is the least exciting part of your body?"

Often a person will assume a false identity ascribed to him through the unconscious strategy of his parents. This can lead in two directions. The first is what Karen Horney (1945) refers to as "the idealized image" in which the person is constantly trying to live up to his image and needs the world to concur with it. The other direction is when a parent, or significant other, confers a despised image. The person may continuously strive unconsciously to throw off this false self and live up to his true potential.

To assist the patient in becoming aware of his own despised image or the rigid need to sustain the idealized image, and to try to change it, the following questions are helpful:

What is the biggest lie you have ever told?

What was the most unfair demand put on you?

What was the most often repeated statement made to you by your mother (father)?

If the answer to the latter question has been a continual harping on the child's shortcomings, this will become the despised image that may haunt him as intolerable all his life.

The most-or-least question is an excellent tool to reveal a person's guilt. Inevitably either of the aspects of false identity is locked into guilt. If someone identifies with the despised false image, then he or she feels guilty; if someone falls short of the idealized image, the guilt will be compounded.

Questions such as "What did your mother (father) despise in you the most?" and "What is the most distasteful thing about you?" are guides to the dimensions of a patient's guilt. Also important in this context are: "What is the most shameful day of your life?" or "What is the most humiliating thing that ever happened to you?" In a sexual connotation an effective question is "In whose presence would it be most (least) difficult to have sexual thoughts?"

These four techniques enhance each other as they are combined and interwoven. Singly they can be valuable, but in combination the whole can be much greater than each of its parts. The integration of all the specific approaches within the framework of the individual's phenomenology, so that he can achieve greater awareness of himself, opens the door to possible ways of change. Here, for example, are some possible ways that each of the four techniques can be utilized to make the patient aware of a single feeling reaction:

1. Finish-the-Sentence (FTS): Never call me _____.

2. Self-and-Other (S&O): What image of yourself can you not allow?

3. Imaginary Situation (IS):
   (a) Picture yourself on a blank screen in a position in which you detest yourself.
   (b) You are walking down a street and a person your own age accuses you of something. What does he accuse you of, and why?

4. Most-or-Least (M/L): What is the most detestable thing anyone can say about you?

As patients become accustomed to this kind of therapy it is less and less necessary to make interpretations for them. With specific cross-checking of the four modalities, it is possible to help focus patients to greater awareness where they are forced to face the truth *for themselves.*

APPLICATIONS

Psycho-Imagination Therapy is applicable to a wide range of problems and situations. It has been used successfully in treating neuroses, emotional maladjustment, marriage and family problems, sexual dysfunction, psychosomatic problems, extreme jealousy, anxiety, and maladaptive behavior patterns.

Psycho-Imagination Therapy techniques have been useful in breaking impasse situations that arise in conventional therapy. A verbatim transcript of a patient/ therapist interview concerning an impasse situation is included in Shorr (1972).

Clinical experience has shown that obsessive/compulsive patients are helped to cut down on meanderings and repetitive verbalizations when they are attending to their imagery productions. The imagery helps to focus attention on the root causes of the obsessive behavior and to aid in opening up new avenues to behavioral change.

Anxiety, depression, and other neuroses respond favorably to imagery techniques. In addition, the imagery productions accurately reflect the degree of conflict resolution and the changes made in therapy. For example, the imagery productions of depressive patients become more positive—for example, bare trees begin to show leaves, and scenes are more light and pleasant. I have found that psychodramatic confrontation through imagery often leads to conflict resolution and the lifting of anxiety.

When used in conjunction with psychodrama, imagery, especially dual imagery, has been of catalytic value and has had a highly therapeutic effect on institutionized psychotic patients.

One of the most dramatic applications of Psycho-Imagination Therapy is in group therapy, where the interactions of the members through the modality of imagery can be highly therapeutic.

Since sexual conflicts deal with the most vulnerable, the most tender, the most shame-inducing, and the most guilty feelings, they are the most difficult to disclose to oneself and to others. The use of imagery bypasses the censorship and offers a vehicle for dialogue and possible conflict resolution.

The *Shorr Imagery Test* (1974a), the *Group Shorr Imagery Test* (1977a), the *Supplementary Shorr Imagery Test* (1978c), and the *Shorr Parent Imagery Test* (1979b), which have been developed and utilized primarily for diagnostic purposes, are the direct outgrowth of the theoretical structure of Psycho-Imagination Therapy. It must be emphasized that the tests are able to verify the concepts of Psycho-Imagination Therapy. Few systems of psychotherapy can utilize a test for verification.

CASE EXAMPLE

The following is a report of a patient, Jim, in group therapy.[1]

JIM: I don't really remember too well what actually happened. I know that I had been suffering from extreme stomach pains for two days. Everything had been going extremely well in school for three weeks. Karen and I had just had the best two weeks of our relationship. For the first time in my life, I felt productive, social, myself, and in love with Karen at the same time. My fantasy of a "sunshiny winter afternoon" was going very well, except, for some unknown reason, my neck and shoulders were tightening up harder than steel—more than I had ever known.

Back to the stomach pain. At first I thought I had the flu. But I had extreme pains that were very high in my stomach. At the same time, I felt like vomiting, but I couldn't. I even stuck my finger down my throat and I couldn't, I wouldn't vomit.

Tuesday morning, I went to work. I talked to Helen (our friend) before I left and she said it sounded like I

---

[1] In this case example Shorr was the therapist. Other names refer to other group members.

had an ulcer. Right then I got extremely depressed, angry, tearful, and alone. I went home and I was really angry. I felt shitty (guilty) for having an ulcer. I felt shitty that I was still so uptight and fighting and unproductive as to have an ulcer. I was also really mad and untrustful of group and my last two years in it. I went back and forth, between guilt and anger.

Then I called Bill (group member). The one thing I remember from the conversation was him saying, "I care that you are in such pain" and "I really like being around you and Karen when you're happy." When I got off the phone, I was wide open. I cried by myself and for myself without hesitation. For the first time, I let my guts hurt and I cried without any thoughts or judgments. I then felt like I wanted to cry "mommy." I wanted someone to love me and take care of me. I wanted a mother. But I knew I didn't want my mother. And it made me angry to realize I never had a mother.

When Karen came home, I was very aware of not wanting to show her my feelings. But I had called and asked her to come home. That was pretty hard to ask for. If I ever let it out to my mother, she used it for false motherings, and to shrink my cock and consume my balls.

By the time I got to group, my stomach was really hurting and I explained that everything was good but I was dying of pain.

SHORR: What part of you hurts?

JIM: My stomach. Right in the middle of my guts.

SHORR: Can you hand that part to someone?

JIM: When Dr. Shorr asked that, all I could do was cry. He asked me several times and it seemed impossible. It seemed it would be giving the vulnerable and dearest part of me away.

GWEN: No wonder it hurts so much. It always hurt you and you were always alone with it.

JIM: What bothers me is that I never got anything with my pain, and I'm not now.

JOHN: You must have gotten something.

JIM: Yes, I got to stay home. I didn't have to go to school and compulsively achieve. I got protection against my father. I didn't have to feel alone at school with the kids. I felt like I got some love. Even though it was being used to manipulate me into taking care of her. She had a way in, through my pain, and I had a way in with my pain.

SHORR: Who does your stomach belong to? [self-other question]

JIM: To me. It's a good stomach. Good color on the outside. But the inside is all jumbled.

SHORR: Give that part a name. [imaginary situation]

JIM: Me.

JOHN: How does the rest of your body feel?

JIM: Fine. It's all mine.

JOHN: Then your stomach must not be yours.

JIM: No, it's not. It's the shit part of me.

SHORR: In what body part does your mother reside in? [imaginary situation]

JIM: In my stomach.

JOHN: Isn't it true that you still want a mother, and you want to call for her?

JIM: Yes, no—I want a mother, but I don't want mine.

SHORR: Reach in and grab her out.

JIM: She's in there with tentacles. It is all around me of . . . (pause) . . . all through my meat.

SHORR: Rip her out. She's scared of you. [imaginary situation]

JIM: That's really true. That makes a difference. She's goddamned scared of me. I scream at her and she shrinks like a sea urchin. I'm not really the scared one, she is. (I remembered the dream where I jacked off on my mother and then I screamed I was going to kill her.) I pulled her out with my right hand, and held her there and talked about her. She was like a huge, sickly cancer cell. I talked a lot about her, and the more I talked, the more she was back in my stomach and the more my stomach hurt.

SHORR: Rip her out and throw her in the fire (a dream I had about the ending of the world). Scream at her and tell her to get out. [imaginary situation]

JIM: For a long time I didn't feel like I could. I just couldn't reach in and get her out. I decided to stand up and try it. I had to. My stomach hurt so bad. I couldn't let her stay in. Thinking of her as scared of me helped. But I still couldn't do it.

GROUP MEMBERS: You won't be alone—we're all here.

SHORR: I'll be right here.

JIM: I know you all love me and you'll be here. But I'm afraid once I scream, I won't be able to call for you any more when I really need you. (This feeling is the same feeling when I get sick and am scared that I'm all alone and I wouldn't get any help if I really needed it.)

SHORR: You won't have to call for me. I'll be right here with you, anyway. (That did it.)

JIM: AND THEN I SCREAMED. I SCREAMED WITH ALL MY MIGHT. WITH ALL MY PAIN FOR MY WHOLE LIFE. WITH ALL MY ANGER FOR MY WHOLE LIFE. WITH ALL MY GUTS. I SCREAMED FOR HER TO GET OUT. I SCREAMED FROM MY GUTS. WITHOUT ANY HESITATION. I SCREAMED FOR MYSELF. 'CAUSE I WANT TO LIVE FOR ME. 'CAUSE I DESERVE FOR ME, AND SHE GOT OUT. YOU'RE DAMN STRAIGHT SHE GOT OUT. AND SHE CAN NEVER GET BACK IN. SHE'S SCARED. I KNOW NOW. I KNOW IN MY GUTS. I KNOW

WHO I AM. I KNOW MY STRENGTH, AND I KNOW HER WEAK, SADISTIC, INHUMAN GAME. I DON'T NEED IT. I DON'T NEED YOU. I'LL NEVER NEED YOU. SHE'S GONE.

As soon as I screamed, I bent over and clenched my fists. I felt like I was screaming to hell and back. Dr. Shorr straightened me up and told me I didn't have to bend over. She couldn't get back in now. He hugged me and protected my stomach with his belly. It felt good. I really needed the warmth. I don't really remember what happened after that. I was shaking a lot and Dr. Shorr stayed next to me and hugged me and sat down next to me. He really cared. And he was really there. And I didn't have to call for him. And I looked up and people really looked human and warm. And especially the women looked different. I guess not so much like my mother. They looked human and fleshy. My stomach actually felt like it had a wound in it. But it was a clean, fleshy wound. And now it can grow back together with me. It's mine.

Several months have passed since that group session. Jim has shown considerable change; he is much calmer and most of all, there has been a marked decrease in his strong suspiciousness. His own conclusion, verified in time, strongly suggested that he accounted his behavior to his mother according to her standards and felt great guilt if he did not. Since she was "inside" him, the accounting system was acute and ever-present. Just as the paranoid person is defined by nearly everyone he meets, this man on a lesser scale was defined by his mother and mother substitutes.

SUMMARY

Psycho-Imagination Therapy (PIT) believes that any method of psychotherapy should be firmly rooted in a systematic theory of personality. PIT is operationally based on existential concepts and phenomenological foundations blended with the interpersonal developmental theories of Harry Stack Sullivan and R. D. Laing. The therapeutic emphasis is on the integration of imagination with existential phenomenology and the centeredness of the individual—imagination in the service of awareness and of the possibility for change.

While other types of psychotherapy use imagery as a modality, only Psycho-Imagination Therapy uses imagery systematically according to a well-defined theoretical stance. In addition, PIT uses other modalities, such as finish-the-sentence, self-other questions, most-or-least questions, and dialogue within the same interpersonal theoretical framework.

A person's imagery, more than any other mental function, indicates how he or she views the world. The use of systematically categorized imagery opens up the inner world to both patient and therapist. Imagery helps the patient to recognize and cast off the conferred "alien" identity and to redefine himself. It also aids the patient in becoming aware of strategies developed to maintain false positions and then supports him or her in focusing for change, resolving conflicts, and overcoming resistances.

Perhaps the most important factor of imagery is its ability to bypass the usual censorship of the person. Lowenstein (1956) made the point that the patient, through hearing himself vocalize, may control his own reactions to his thoughts. In short, one is verbally editing, and in so doing attempting to control the reactions of the therapist. Because one cannot usually tell in advance what effect or meaning the imagery will have, the patient may reveal in imagery what would not ordinarily be revealed in verbal conversation. Imagery has a prime value in that it can help break resistances usually found in verbal transactions.

The verbal process can be comingled with imagery to yield a cohesive logic and internal consistency to the psychotherapeutic process.

A further function of imagery in psychotherapy is that images can be transformed, reexperienced, and reshaped in line with a healthier self-concept. The patient's growing awareness of internal conflicts is one of the most important products of imagery in therapy.

In the long run it is not enough for a person to be aware of inner conflicts; a change must be made in self-definition. Resolution of a conflict is more important than mere solution. Sleeping pills offer a solution to insomnia, a vacation offers a solution to an unpleasant situation, but in neither case is the actual problem resolved. Superficial solutions are easily conceived and prescribed, but the therapist must ignore such temptations and deal constructively with the problem itself, however difficult it may be to liberate a person from a neurotic conflict resolution.

The focusing approaches of Psycho-Imagination Therapy are designed to free the patient from a deadlocked position in his or her psychological life. Suppression, avoidance, distortion, and withdrawal provide avenues to sustain conflict and escape from resolution. PIT approaches depend upon the patient's self-definition. It is essential that the patient be assisted in changing his self-image, thus combating the inclination to let others define him falsely. Psycho-Imagination Therapy mobilizes the patient's constructive forces to work for liberation from an alien identity. The goal is to be what we are all striving to be—more human, namely, ourselves.

REFERENCES

Breuer, J., & Freud, S. (1953). *Studies in hysteria.* London: Hogarth Press.

Caslant, E. (1927). *Method of development of the supernormal faculties.* Paris: Meyer.

Connella, J. A. (1978). The effects of Psycho-Imagination Therapy on the treatment outcome of chronic benign pain patients. Ph.D. dissertation, CSPP.

Desoille, R. (1965). *The directed daydream.* Monograph No. 8. New York: The Psychsynthesis Research Foundation.

Freud, S. (1959). *An autobiographical study.* In J. Strachey (Ed.), *The standard edition of the complete psychological works of Sigmund Freud,* vol. 12. London: Hogarth Press.

Fromm, E. (1955). Remarks on the problem of free association. *Psychiatric Research Reports 2.* American Psychiatric Association.

Hartmann, H. (1958). *Ego psychology and the problem of adaption.* New York: International Universities Press.

Horowitz, M., & Becker, S. S. (1971). The compulsion to repeat trauma: Experimental study of intrusive thinking after stress. *Journal of Nervous and Mental Disease, 153*(1).

Laing, R. D. (1965). *The divided self.* New York: Penguin Books.

Laing, R. D. (1971). *The self and others.* New York: Pelican Books.

Lowenstein, R. M. (1956). Some remarks on the role of speech in psychoanalytic techniques. *International Journal of Psycho-Analysis, 37,* 460–467.

Morgan, C. O. (1979). Disability through imagery experience. In J. Shorr et al. (Eds.), *Imagery: Its many dimensions.* Proceedings of the First Annual Conference of the American Association for the Study of Mental Imagery. New York: Plenum.

Shorr, J. E. (1967). The existential question and the imaginary situation as therapy. *Existential Psychiatry, 6*(24), 443–462.

Shorr, J. E. (1972). *Psycho-Imagination Therapy: The integration of phenomenology and imagination.* New York: Intercontinental Medical Book Corp.

Shorr, J. E. (1973). In what part of your body does your mother reside? *Psychotherapy: Theory, Research and Practice, 10*(2), 31–34.

Shorr, J. E. (1974a). *Shorr imagery test.* Los Angeles: Institute for Psycho-Imagination Therapy.

Shorr, J. E. (1974b). *Psychotherapy through imagery.* New York: Intercontinental Medical Book Corp.

Shorr, J. E. (1975). The use of task imagery as therapy. *Psychotherapy: Theory, Research and Practice, 12*(2), 207–210.

Shorr, J. E. (1976). Dual imagery. *Psychotherapy: Theory, Research and Practice, 13*(2), 244–248.

Shorr, J. E. (1977a). *Group Shorr imagery test.* Los Angeles: Institute for Psycho-Imagination Therapy.

Shorr, J. E. (1977b). *Go see the movie in your head.* New York: Popular Library.

Shorr, J. E. (1978a). Clinical categories of therapeutic imagery. In J. L. Singer and K. Pope (Eds.), *The power of human imagination.* New York: Plenum.

Shorr, J. E. (1978b). Imagery as a projective device. *Imagery Bulletin of the American Association for the Study of Mental Imagery, 1*(2).

Shorr, J. E. (1978c). *Supplementary Shorr imagery test.* Los Angeles: Institute for Psycho-Imagination Therapy.

Shorr, J. E. (1979a). Imagery as a method of self observation in therapy. *Imagery Bulletin of the American Association for the Study of Mental Imagery, 2*(2).

Shorr, J. E. (1979b). *Shorr parental imagery test.* Los Angeles: Institute for Psycho-Imagination Therapy.

Shorr, J. E. (1979c). Discoveries about the mind's ability to organize and find meaning in imagery. In Shorr, J. E., Connella, J. A., Robin, P., and Sobel, G. (Eds.), *Imagery: Its many dimensions and applications.* Proceedings of the First Annual Conference of the American Association for the Study of Mental Imagery. New York: Plenum.

Singer, J. L. (1971). Imagery and daydream techniques employed in psychotherapy: Some practical and theoretical implications. In C. Spielberger (Ed.), *Current topics in clinical and community psychology,* vol. 3. New York: Academic Press.

Sobel, G. A. (1979). Study of group dynamics at Los Angeles City College. In J. Shorr et al. (Eds.), *Proceedings of the 1st Annual Conference for the Study of Mental Imagery.* New York: Plenum.

Stampfl, T. G., & Leavis, D. J. (1966). Essentials of implosive therapy. *Journal of Abnormal Psychology, 72,* 496–503.

Sullivan, H. S. (1953). *The interpersonal theory of psychiatry.* New York: Norton.

Tansey, D. (1979). The use of the Shorr imagery test with a population of violent offenders. In J. Shorr et al. (Eds.), *Imagery: Its many dimensions and applications.* New York: Plenum.

Shorr, J. E. (1981). The psychologist's imagination and sexual imagery. In E. Klinger and M. Anderson (Eds.), *Imagery: Its many dimensions and applications,* vol. II. New York: Plenum.

Chapter 53

PSYCHOMATERIALISM

GEORGE BOUKLAS and LEONARD SCHWARTZ

Psychomaterialism is a theory that human behavior is fueled by the energy released in the Big Bang. The material generated by this energy follows the principle that all matter seeks to connect to other matter. Human behavior is energized to connect to other humans. Consciousness and the development of the ego skew human perception away from this fundamental relationship, leading to feelings of isolation and the various psychological symptoms of a fragmented self-image. Psychotherapy based on psychomaterialism utilizes the therapist as an agent in reformulating a relationship with patients emphasizing their psychic connectedness.

DEFINITION

Psychomaterialism emphasizes continuity between humanity and the universe, regarding them as an integrated and indivisible whole. It is a cosmology intended to invite the therapist and patient into a larger world of spirit, creativity, acceptance, and tolerance.

Psychomaterial technique is primarily supportive in nature, respecting and honoring resistance as essential to self-esteem and integration. The action of the therapy occurs in the way therapists use themselves as instruments of expansion. Their awareness of their own transpersonal dimensions helps the patient both develop and mature, towards a more healthful and transcendent position.

The therapeutic interest of psychomaterialism is in understanding the foundational issues of human experience and how these impact our patients. Connecting is the key, and patients want us to relate to them in a way that helps them bring more Being into being.

The therapist is able to psychologically join with the patient, understanding that this will pave the way for the patient in turn joining with him, and getting in touch with his own transpersonal dimensions.

HISTORY

Fashion dominates perception. No one ever recognized a human being until an artist captured humanity and presented us to ourselves, as a completed work. An observer of human behavior selects certain stimulus features and emphasizes them over the myriad others that coexist in the manifest world. The style of the resultant theory suits us. It speaks to us and it says something important about us. We engage the theory passionately. We argue its points in academic halls, and we generate a host of technical words to further legitimize this distinct worldview. But it becomes apparent, sooner or later, that we are indulging in fashion. The manner in which we produce characteristic ways of viewing the world, and ourselves, bears a close resemblance to the way early humans' distinct character arose artistically out of a more nondescript, integrated "We."

Science and fashion are inextricable. The way in which we seek "to know" is guided by these subjective processes. At the same time that they superimpose order on a seemingly chaotic field of view, they also confound fuller understanding. Psychoanalysis so dominated our consciousness that it put a veritable lock on psychiatry for years. Behaviorism accentuated phenomena that had been missed or underplayed by psychoanalysts, and so burst forth with a vigor that suggested the too-long repression of principles of learning.

The ground of being does want to be revealed, and through more than just one guise. But the defensive ego commits its forces to camouflaging and obfuscating the wholeness that makes us. We still only get pieces of the picture. The salient features of any theory of humanity move us back and forth on this gradient. There is the will of more Being to come into being. In apposition to this is the structuralizing of experience to reduce to a trace our sense of our being-in-the-universe. Fuller consciousness demands the resolution of this dilemma.

Fashion leads us down one path and places a steep energy cost on a change in direction. New "takes" on the cosmos are greeted with external as well as internal resistance. The fashion of science generates intellectual property that vests a high interest in the status quo. This is natural to human beings, part and parcel of the gestalt hungers built into perception, as well as the cooperation needed to acculturate and be part of something bigger socially. I am who you say I am, and to break the covenant of perceptual agreement is to risk loosing the ties that confirm my identity and help me feel integrated.

Science itself is the larger fashion that overtook religion from the 1700s on. It replaced demonologies with matter, energy, and field. Our psychological theories followed suit, and there is always the hope that one day chemists, biologists, and physicists will accept us as a brother. But physics itself has been undergoing drastic changes in its cosmology. Mathematizing the universe is proving too difficult, not because we do not possess a big enough computer to do the numbers, or lack particle accelerators to smash things into even smaller bits. It is a problem because the quanta of the universe appear to be embedded in non-mathematizable qualia (Burrow, 1996). A quantum would be a speck of matter, measurable and observable. A quale would be an experienced value that defied such direct quantification, such as our subjective experience of a particular color. "Good" and "Bad" are the most elementary qualia of our universe, designated with capital letters because they are at the base of our individual experience of "good" and "bad."

Bohm and Hiley (1993), Goswami (1995), and Capra (1991) describe a very different view of things on the physical level, indeed, one less inimical to a spiritual view. They invite our scientific selves to return to elements of life and being that our religious selves first began studying at the dawn of civilization. If we take their ideas together, the universe has an implicit order to it, which flows in an interconnected way throughout itself. It is a richer and more whole place than its manifest matter, energy, and field would have us believe.

Wilber (1996), Dossey (1993), and Grof (1993) have placed us squarely within this implicate, holographic, connected universe to suggest how we can act more healthfully, feel more joy, and experience more consciousness, as well as solve the immediate and pressing problems we bring to the therapist's office. By respecting the defensive value of fashion but also attending to the ground of being which gives rise to it, psychomaterialism creates an opportunity for people to bring their scientific and spiritual sides together. The ground is just as important as the figures that rise out of it in clear relief, and this is a fruitful direction to take in understanding the elements of psychotherapy. For there must be a basic and universal action, an "UR-therapy," that lies underneath the hundreds of ways therapy is conducted all over the world.

Current Status

Psychomaterialism follows in this tradition, stating the direct link between people and the universe. We may seem separate on the explicate or manifest level, but within the implicate order of the universe, we are all of one piece. Psychomaterialism considers physics to be subsumed by psychology, and not the other way around. Since the scientist is connected to everything around him, he is in the curious position of not being as objective as he says he is. The observer-subject split is occurring on the explicate level of the universe, while within the implicate order there is no such distinction between observer and subject. We have felt intimations of this, shifting in our view from the therapist as neutral figure and observer to participant-observer. At the UR-level (referring to something basic and common to all therapies), the therapist has gone all the way, for he acknowledges that he is subject, observing subject.

Further, the scientist, in different guises of psychotherapy researcher, physicist, or even infant making his first cause-and-effect conclusions, functions wholly within the qualia surrounding the Big Bang (Burrow, 1996). Before this event, the singularity was perfectly spherical and rotating, in a "Good" state. The Big Bang sent the universe into a wobbly and oscillating state of "Bad." Efforts within the universe to create energy out of the void and stabilize the oscillations marked the initiation of a "Good" dynamic. The qualia determine how we will connect on a conscious level to the subject we are "with," or "observing," or seeking to "have" or "control." Higher consciousness avails itself of these qualia, and this is how fashion is created. The various admixtures of "Good" and "Bad" highlight into figural aspects what was once a homogeneous field, creating differentiation. With this higher consciousness, we are in the position to discover our condition of primary consciousness and have thoughts and feelings about it.

The physical world, which includes all observers, is at base qualitative, and thus a psychological entity. It is moving against Entropy to build a consciousness with which to regard itself. Reductionism will simultaneously bring science to psychotherapeutic and physical roots. It will be found that we-as-the-universe experience the "good" and "bad" within us, cognitively, emotionally, spiritually, and morally, and that our emotional and social connections are paramount, both colored and directed by our implicitly intertwined nature.

THEORY

Psychomaterialism arose out of an interest in discovering the foundational aspects of all healing relationships. It posits a direct and full expression of the universe through humanity, and humanity through the universe. The elemental urge to connect is the formative universal theme. It is played out by the material specks coming together after the Big Bang. In our psychological makeup, it penetrates as understanding, relating to, and resonating with the other person. As our defenses are quieted by the removal of threat, it expresses itself in the way we allow ourselves to be taken up by others. In its most integrated form, it is expressed in romantic love (Schwartz & Schwartz, 1986).

The urge to connect in various ways is felt in our higher consciousness, which is continuous with, and indistinguishable from, the higher consciousness of the universe. Underlying the felt urge to bring together parts into a greater whole is the pristine condition of full and uninterrupted connection. All the parts are already together in the implicate universe, as it captures the singularity before the Big Bang. The experience of separateness exists in the explicate universe, as does the felt urge to connect.

The goal of higher consciousness is to grasp, appreciate, and articulate the full connection existing in primary consciousness. All things animate and inanimate are "one thing," undivided by time in its forms as past, present, and future, or by space, in its forms as length, breadth, and depth. Each of us is fully within the integrated "We" of the universe.

In our conscious minds we have a difficult time experiencing this. We have glimpses of such a unity in our dreams, fantasies, and supernatural experiences. During crises that test our egos, we may also take advantage of the instabilities in our self-state to glimpse something entirely different than prosaic observation offers us. Fuller realization is blocked by ego dynamics that sacrifice this larger reality of an integrated "We" for a consistent and reliable "I." We suppress and repress the busyness of the psychomaterial experience in favor of the ego project. This means that even as we are cataloguing our psychomaterial foundations, a series of events conspires to keep this hidden. Fashion directs us away from any direct and prolonged view. The ego fears dissolution and so its defensive dimensions remain observant and suspicious. Language distracts us in its signs and content, each word leaving only a trace of the oceanic out of which it crystallized.

But we will know ourselves more fully. The universe will know itself more fully through us. Thus, fashion is being challenged by data that cry out for explanation. We occasionally know things before they happen. We have a supernatural accuracy in reading another person in a timeless instant of first meeting. We have prescient dreams. The lionization of the ego may be proceeding with renewed vigor throughout the world, but like any resistance, the numbing repetitiveness of its surface use hides an effort of higher integration from within, until

the resistance gives way to a more realistic view of the world. The ego, as a form of resistance, attenuates, and even gets resolved to some degree, allowing glimpses of the integrated "We."

The superflux of language works in tandem with this process. The increasing discriminations of word meanings act in accordance with reaction formation. Words are designed to befuddle any grasp of the integrated "We," but in their sheer profuseness they secretly let on to the "id" of the semioticians, and the "Id" of psychomaterialism. The "id" in lower case belongs to the individual, but the "Id" in upper case is the "Good" and "Bad," or in updated psychoanalytic terms, the Eros and Entropy of the universe. Freud identified the source of the oceanic experience as the amnion, and so the psychoanalytic id remained a local and individual phenomenon. He avoided exploration of Eastern thought, which would have introduced him to an uncontrollable vastness. For the Id is universal, and flows through us, rather than being a local phenomenon created by each person individually. Mother's womb is a representation, on the explicit level, of the implicit Id. It is a representative form of the oceanic, a gateless gate. With a little language, we can understand one another. A lot of language, and we have the confusion at Babel. But even more language, as is occurring around the world as the Internet draws us closer together by eye and ear, moves us beyond Babel to the shared experience of an integrated "We."

METHODOLOGY

The patient's symptoms, complaints and goals are understood as psychomaterial efforts to experience consciousness of the integrated "We" state. The patient achieves the connection he needs with the therapist through his preferred way of operating, which proves to him that this is also possible in his life outside the sessions. Adding a psychomaterial dimension to his work, the therapist silently asks himself:

1. What is preventing the patient from functioning effectively in his various social environments?
2. Why is the patient feeling misunderstood, stressed and incapable of getting the reactions he needs from others?
3. Why is the patient stuck, either fearing the regression that accompanies growth, or acting out regressively as an alternative but ineffective solution?
4. What is blocking the patient's ability to empathize, to relate and to engage in loving relationships?
5. Why does the patient feel foreign, excised, "out of the loop?"

6. How is the patient using his defenses and his consciousness to block the shared experience available in the sessions?

These are silent questions, for the therapist respects the ego project (Becker, 1973). The patient has vested much energy in keeping himself together as an individual "I," and direct challenges in a therapy session are more likely to be experienced as narcissistic hurts, rather than helpful, educational, or insight-provoking. The therapist maintains a complementary attitude, moving with the patient. He sides with the ego's maneuvers to deflect a grasp of oneness and connection. He notes how the patient has connected in the past, and brings out aspects of his personality that help the patient feel understood. The effect might be considered paradoxical to an outside observer. Rather than being helped to avoid the shared experience, the patient is freed to gain access to richer connections.

This dedication to connecting in the right way reduces the patient's stresses, helps him assimilate emotional knowledge more freely, reframes his thoughts and feelings, and releases energy for connections outside the session. The beliefs of psychomaterialism form part of the methodology. They state "I" has emerged out of the ground-of-being, and its frustrations and difficulties are bound up in its defensive nature. "I" needs the connection that therapy provides, in order to access the shared experience that is the elementary facet of the universe. The maturational experiences of connecting in the therapy expand the patient's consciousness, and bring him to his own understanding of his "We" condition. The therapist models the art of connecting. He finds the patient in himself, again and again as the patient brings up various themes or makes requests. A gestalt is engendered. The patient reacts by finding the therapist in himself. Through this process of intermirroring the patient expands his consciousness, his possibilities for connecting and his repertoire of ideas and actions.

To help things along, the therapist evenly holds sentiments that originate with the patient. The weight of feelings is shared, as is responsibility for the way the patient thinks and feels. This is a powerful way for the therapist to communicate psychomaterial connections. There is nothing foreign about the patient, for both people in the room emerge out of the entangled universe as a unity. This empathic sacrifice has a profound effect on the functioning of the patient. He learns that his isolation and loneliness are defenses that he has a right to assert at anytime, but they are not the essential state of things. Through the therapist, the patient learns of his link to others, and this returns him to his maturational path.

The Experience of Living and the Experience of Dying

One of the great transformations in an analysis involves the patient becoming a dual-drive enthusiast. He develops the insight to follow the interplay of libido and mortido in his life. He has needed to do this, because by not giving equal value to the entropy working within him, how could he truly express his eros? He learns how entropy—the death instinct—structuralizes in his defenses and character structure. He understands how it dynamically flows through his character to deaden his experience. He discovers entropy at work in depression (killing off one's feelings), in psychotic dynamics (killing off one's thinking), in paranoia (killing off the object), and in acting out (killing off connections).

Psychomaterialism is comfortable with this process, silently focusing on the Eros and Entropy of the universe as they flow through the patient. The patient wants to feel alive, but we understand that the patient also needs to experience dying more directly. Before transforming it into a fashion of character, defense, or action, he can own his dynamic of dying in a more direct way. This is accomplished by the therapist being in touch with his own experience of dying and living. As the patient talks, there is acknowledgement and support by the therapist that is more than education, or differential reinforcement for certain internal behaviors. Both therapist and patient become brothers, soul mates in this quest to be more open to the foundational energies that inform consciousness, intent, and action.

Modern psychoanalytic training (cf. Spotnitz, 1985) describes this as knowing where the murder is in the room. A famous example involves Freud's conception of student Tausk acting in an uncanny way (Roazen, 1969). This trainee and analysand was making speeches that prefigured ideas Freud was forming in his mind, but was not ready to publicize. Freud became concerned with this uncanny phenomenon, wrote a paper about The Uncanny and sent Tausk from his presence, asking Helene Deutsch to finish the trainee's analysis. At that time he also wrote *Beyond the Pleasure Principle* (1930), where he laid out the idea of the death instinct. Tausk was bereft, and committed suicide. Freud's aggression was intellectualized in his writings, and acted out in a destructive interruption of analysis. Were he more aware of "where the murder was in the room," he might have kept Tausk with him and worked on the young man's resistance, as well as his own counterresistance.

Regression in the Service of Transcendence, and in the Service of Immanence

It is quite apparent that all regressions are not pathological. Furthermore, all regressions seem to possess within them some saving grace. Regression is an effort to deal with the frustration of a stifling character. It allows more Being to come into being. To the early therapists, it seemed wholly problematic. Yet there was a regression implicit in the artistic act. Freud decided this was a special case of regression in the service of the ego. Kris (1952) advanced a new notion, that the ego possessed its own energy above and beyond the primitive drives. This view further depathologized regressive phenomena, which now seemed to have a purpose in helping the ego become more masterful.

Investigations with a large number of elderly patients in their 80s and 90s (Bouklas, 1997) suggested that regression routinely helped, if the emotional communications of the therapist were gauged to control for aggressive or destructive reactions by the environment. This phenomenon showed itself to be a regression in the service of integration, but writings of Wilber (1996) introduced the notion that regression serves transcendence. Wilber's is the more inclusive view of the term, and has been widely adopted. The patient gives in to the experience of "Being." In psychomaterial terminology, the "I" gives way to the integrated "We."

This "We" has dual properties. It can be experienced as a transcendent phenomenon, the person growing beyond himself, and also witnessing higher consciousness in the form of a vision or conception. It can also be experienced as an immanent experience, the integrated "We" of the universe wholly within the person of the patient. The loving relationship is the most obvious place for such connection to unfold, and as the person's work proceeds, he faces the challenge of finding himself in the Other, concluding that he is any Other he knows, and finally that his unity encompasses all things, everywhere in the universe.

APPLICATIONS

Emotional Communication in Psychomaterialism

A 14-year-old Down's Syndrome boy was referred for evaluation and treatment because he was displaying uncontrollable behavior at home. The patient's fixed smile betrayed his angry and self-destructive behavior. He was mute and only occasionally responded to speech directed towards him.

The therapist laid out a set of dolls representing a mother, father, brother, sister and baby. The patient ignored these dolls and picked up a ball which he threw in the direction of the "doll" family. Each time the therapist reconstructed the dolls into a family setting and smiled at the patient. Their "game" of the patient expressing anger at the "family" and the therapist restoring the family structure continued week after week for two months. Finally, the therapist picked up the baby doll, threw it across the room and then "spanked" the mother doll. The young patient immediately picked up the baby, took the mother doll out of the therapist's hands and sat cradling both. Not a word was ever expressed between

them. However, the patient's mother called the next day to say that her son had stopped his angry behavior.

The psychomaterial nature of our relationships is most evident where talk is not an option. In such treatment relationships the therapist is better able to experience the psychomaterial dimension of his unity with the patient. He is more aware of how he and the patient are connecting, and communicates on an emotional level. Such cases are helpful in discovering the "We" quality of the relationship, and building on it.

Deep Connecting

A nine-year-old girl was referred by her family physician because she was failing in her parochial school, rarely spoke and remained in her room most of the time. Her parents reported that this had been going on for most of the school year. After getting a full history from the parents the therapist asked the girl to come into his office alone. The girl looked younger than her years, was extremely thin and appeared frightened to death, her large, dark eyes beseeching a savior. The therapist repeated her parents' worry and helplessness over her behavior. He asked her if her parents' account of her behavior was accurate. She did not respond.

The therapist asked her why she thought she was brought to his office. She remained silent. The doctor said he wanted to help her but needed her cooperation. No response. After about twenty minutes of silence between therapist and patient, the therapist finally said, "I am afraid. I'm afraid that I cannot help you. I don't know what to do." He got up, went to the door of his office leading to the waiting room, shrugged his shoulders and said, "I'm sorry." The girl, looking terrified, said, "Doctor, my teacher says that if I commit a sin I will go to hell. And doctor, I don't know what a sin is."

When her parents took her out of parochial school and reassured her that she was too young to commit a sin, the girl opened up, became more socially and educationally active, and was professionally never heard from again. What might seem antithetical to a good therapeutic relationship was in fact a deep connecting with the patient's helplessness. The therapist experienced the patient in him, and expressed her position in a way that she could lower her defenses and speak freely.

The Shared Experience as an Objectionable

A 15-year-old boy was ordered into treatment by his school. He was fighting, got caught selling drugs, and set fire to the Language Lab after receiving a failing grade. He came to the office, but refused to remain in the therapist's presence without the support of a friend. Exploration ensued concerning who he would like to accompany him. He decided that he would come to sessions if his girlfriend could join him. He instructed the therapist not to read any of his school reports. If the therapy was going to be his, then he wanted to be the one to bring in information that he alone decided was cogent. The family and the school howled over the arrangements made in the therapy, and the boy allowed the therapist to meet with all interested parties to explain how this was going to proceed. The outline for this meeting was carefully worked out beforehand in sessions, and got a final okay from the patient.

The therapist understood the patient's need to rid himself of frustrations through action, and engaged him in talk about even more things he could do. By talking freely, the patient got relief through symbolic and fantasy activity, and at the same time developed a richer repertoire for self-expression. He purchased a beat-up race car to work on, joined a judo school, and spoke up for increased contact with his girlfriend. So far this would resemble any other complementary and non-directive therapy. However, the therapist's behavior was somewhat different, in that he continued to be open to psychomaterial experiences in the session and in himself, as regarded his connection to the integrated "We." At one point in the therapy the girlfriend urged the patient to reveal his private, psychic experience.

PATIENT: I don't think you would understand, if I told you.

THERAPIST: Why would that stop you?

PATIENT: (Laughing) Funny guy, huh? I see things, okay? Apparitions, ghosts, things that go bump in the night. So you think I'm nuts?

THERAPIST: Why would I think you're nuts?

PATIENT: You mean everybody comes in here and says they see things?

THERAPIST: And what if everybody did?

PATIENT: Do you see things like that? Would you say it if you did?

THERAPIST: Suppose I said I also saw things?

PATIENT: I'd believe it. You're kind of wacky, not like the last guy I saw. I didn't tell you about him. I was going there alone. He asked me a lot of questions about starting that fire in the Spanish teacher's office. Then he said that meant some guy raped me. I was so mad I burned down the woods behind the shopping center. I only have sex with women.

THERAPIST: So how come I'm not like him?

PATIENT: He was kind of official, you know? A doctor. I don't know what you are. I bet you even see things.

THERAPIST: And why not?

The therapist sought to avoid overstimulating the patient with too much information, and instead followed

the rule of observing and respecting contact function (Margolis, 1994). The quality and content of a request, along with the feelings, determine what is to be given back. The patient is helped to advance by being given no more and no less contact than he invited. The patient took the therapist's acceptance of him as a loving communication, and felt understood. Discussion of ghosts and apparitions did not dominate the therapy. What happened was that the simple acknowledgement of the verity and value of the patient's experience allowed him to talk in a progressive fashion about his life. The regression was understood in its transcendent proportions, and this helped the therapy proceed successfully through the enriched connection that was achieved.

Confusion and Blame

An 85-year-old woman was referred for therapy in a nursing home. She was paranoid, uncooperative, and suffering over the finality of the placement. She felt betrayed and abandoned by her family, and her frequent and repetitive requests of staff marked her as someone to avoid. Sensitive to such social consequences, she only became more paranoid. The therapist was in a position to spend an appreciable amount of time with her twice a week, and she soon stabilized. She practiced cooperative skills in the session as she might display them with staff, role-played self-control over paranoid regressions, and reported on efforts to be more assertive with her family. As with many nursing home residents, she felt a lot of anger towards her family members. But she so needed their visits, and feared retaliation, that she sought to limit any expression of her true feelings. Her anger and hostility were then displaced on to the caregivers.

Meetings with the caregivers focused on countertransference, and how people in general can get us to do things we ought not do, or block us from doing things we ought to do. Insight about this hidden emotional substrate in all human relationships, along with behavioral training in the salutary use of antecedents and consequences to influence behaviors of concern, gave a transdisciplinary dimension to the treatment. All went smoothly until one afternoon, when the patient was able to bring her paranoia more directly into the treatment relationship.

PATIENT: You scared me out of my wits last night.

THERAPIST: (Feeling the patient-in-him, what it was like to be scared out of his own wits, and being with her in this way without yet responding verbally. Ignoring the fact that he was nowhere near the building last night.)

PATIENT: You know that what you did was horrible. Scaring an old woman like that. What were you thinking?

THERAPIST: What was I thinking, indeed?

PATIENT: You tell me. You think it is all right to barge into my room with a mask on, and growl at me? I didn't laugh. I didn't think it was funny. I could have died from a heart attack. Were you trying to kill me?

THERAPIST: (Not to go so far into the fantasy as admitting, but to stay with the patient emotionally) What should I say?

PATIENT: You should say what is on your mind. Just like you tell me. You should tell me you never liked me from the start.

THERAPIST: (Accepting the paranoia. His "I" was perceived in a way incongruent with her "I," so that he became like the "looming Other" in her history.) If the therapist has feelings that are not helpful to the patient, things won't go well. In that case, he should confess his responsibility.

PATIENT: Don't ever frighten me like that again!

The psychomaterial dimension was reflected in a silent, shared acceptance of the paranoid experience. The patient's ideas were not confirmed outright, and this was out of a special care not to propel her into action. The paranoia was evenly held by both people in the session, so that its destructive properties came under increased control due to the "I" of the therapist. It was an "I" that acknowledged the integrated "We," in a way to share the badness in the room.

The Psychomaterial Dimension of the Psychoanalytic Process

A researcher who was studying laser technology employed a therapist as a consultant. He wanted to establish an environment where he could use his hidden and latent thought processes in conceptualizing his work. He was a very cooperative person who came on time, spoke freely, and paid on time. The therapist took the role of asking a few questions each session, all of which directed attention away from the patient's "I." Such questions reduce the defensive reflexes of the ego. They engage the patient's thought processes and invite primary process to be exposed more openly. Some months into the process, the researcher reported a new experience.

PATIENT: I had a psychotic episode yesterday.

THERAPIST: What happened?

PATIENT: The team was going over some changes in the [laser] project, and I stopped listening to everyone. Suddenly, lights and sparks were dancing all over me.

THERAPIST: What were they?

PATIENT: I don't know. I felt on stage. Nude, maybe. The lights were lighting me up. (Talks out the experience for a bit. Seems to have experienced himself as the molecules he was studying, being in the subject that he was observing.)

THERAPIST: You were like a molecule, then.

PATIENT: Yes! I was like a molecule and a light like the laser was illuminating me. It washed over me. (Shivering) I don't want to have an experience like that again.

THERAPIST: Why not?

PATIENT: It made me sick inside. I saw no value in it.

THERAPIST: Kekule struggled with the structure of organic compounds for months, but could not solve the riddle of how their carbon atoms were situated. One night, he fell into a reverie in front of his fireplace, and "saw" a snake emerge from the flames. It grabbed its own tail and whirled around. He roused himself and drew the vision. Later he correctly decided that the six carbon atoms formed a closed loop, a hexagon, and discovered the structure of organic compounds.

PATIENT: He had to go nuts to find this out?

THERAPIST: Einstein reported that his theory of relativity came as a feeling in his muscles. He "felt" relativity, and then used all his intelligence and wiles to force words on the bodily experience.

PATIENT: So you abandon rational thought?

THERAPIST: Sometimes you do research by regressing. It's called regression in the service of transcendence.

The patient was prepared to awfulize this regression as a journey into the night. He felt dread, with its attendant uneasiness and even shivers (Washburn, 1994). His experience was reframed as a redemptive one, and he was helped to stay with it until he could use his secondary process to sample it more thoroughly, and take from it what he wanted.

"Good" and "Bad" Together

A 67-year-old woman was referred for psychotherapy by her physician because she was not responding to increased dosages of antidepressive medication. Her physical health was good. She was trim, good-looking, and took care to stay well-groomed. Her tailored clothes were immaculately clean, coordinated, and never worn twice to a session.

She articulated well, demonstrating a studied mastery of communication skills. She was forthright in expressing her likes and dislikes, particularly about other people's behavior. She prided herself on always speaking the truth and not pulling her punches.

Her history was one of a highly accomplished individual who was in control of all her relationships. She was generous to a fault, easily hurt when her giving was not reciprocated, and quick to cut off ties with those who did not accept her dominant role. She was highly judgmental, leaving a narrow window of behavior that was acceptable. She described herself as a perfectionist. She had been married 38 years and referred to her husband as "like my grandmother, unconditionally loving of me."

After listing many of her physical symptoms of depression, she stated that she felt bad for her husband, who had to put up with her in this condition.

PATIENT: You have no idea what he does now that I am sick.

THERAPIST: You are right. I can't imagine what he does.

PATIENT: He no longer insists on having sex.

THERAPIST: Do you feel relieved by that?

PATIENT: For some time I have not enjoyed sex and lately find it painful.

THERAPIST: Why do you think so?

PATIENT: I've been having some crazy thoughts. You wouldn't like to hear them.

THERAPIST: What about me makes you think that?

PATIENT: Well, you know, you're a doctor and I'm sure you live a pretty normal life.

THERAPIST: What do you consider normal?

PATIENT: Well, I'm a failure sexually.

THERAPIST: I can see how the perfectionist in you would find that difficult to accept. (This is stated in a straightforward but warm manner.)

PATIENT: It's not so much my need for control and perfection. I've had several affairs during my marriage and you are the only one I've ever told this to.

THERAPIST: How does it feel to let that out?

PATIENT: It is the first time I feel relaxed in months.

In accepting her guilt, the therapist helped the patient's depressive symptoms disappear. That was not a "flight into health," nor a verbal "acting out" by displacing an unacceptable self-image onto the therapist. The patient's basic character structure of rigid rules and perfectionism combined with her history of speaking frankly and truthfully allowed this previously rejected part of her to become incorporated in her expanded self-image. As the "good" therapist accepted her with all her faults, she could let the "good" part of her take in her "bad" part. Such work is essential to therapy, and it therefore must have an ur-element.

CASE EXAMPLE

In Freudian therapy, the patient receives support in altering, or at least dealing more adaptively with, the intrapunitive superego. In Jungian therapy, the patient is becoming more comfortable with his shadow side, as certain elements that cannot find their place in the persona are legitimized as being important and essential to growth. In a humanistic approach, the unconditional positive regard the therapist shows allows the patient to be more self-accepting. In behavioral treatment, the antecedents to the depression are identified through a therapeutic exploration, to fix the point of intervention. Many treatments would point to the cathartic, disclosing, assertive dimensions of the patient's contributions.

As psychomaterial entities, the therapist and patient cited directly above were portraying aspects of the universe. The patient was suffering in a state of increasing dis-ease, the "Bad" of the universe dominating the way tensions played out in her body and mind. The therapist found a way to be with the patient to help her feel understood. By the time she made her revelation, she had already experienced the "Good" within the therapist calming and righting her. With her defenses lowered, she experienced a shift in her perceptions. Now the "Good" and "Bad" flowed through her in a slightly different manner, in updated fashion. This was an engagement of two people through the integrated "We," which is the empathic sacrifice every therapist makes when he attempts to put aside his own fashion, and tries to understand the patient.

The Love Relationship

A woman came into psychotherapy because she felt her life was shattered. She had just learned that her husband had an affair. Besides hurt, anger, and disillusionment, she was perplexed. She thought her marriage was a good one, that she and her husband were well-suited to one another. Both seemed happy and optimistic about a future together. She could not understand how her perception of her marriage could have been so wrong. This shook her self-confidence and spilled over to her questioning all her decisions. She was all but paralyzed into inaction.

Prior to her marriage, 3 years earlier, she was a highly successful account executive in the advertising business. In addition to numerous compliments regarding her work, she regularly received large raises and bonuses. She met her husband at one of her job sites. He was the chief executive officer. He took her to fancy restaurants, night clubs, and resorts throughout the country. She met famous people and movers of industry. She was awed by his power and ability as well as his apparent desire to care for her. When she became pregnant they decided to marry.

The birth of their daughter was rapidly followed by buying a new house, furnishing it, and holding elaborate parties and dinners for friends and business associates. In all of this, she felt secure in her marriage and close to her husband. He made the big plans and supplied the money. She formulated the details and made them a reality. While she was vaguely aware that both the frequency and quality of their sexual encounters were diminishing, she believed that was normal after the birth of a child.

She learned of the affair when she unexpectedly went to the hotel where her husband's company was holding a show for their products. She stumbled in on him and a strange woman—both naked. She ranted and raved at her husband and asked him to leave their home. After several weeks of trying to cope with her pain by herself she called for an appointment.

The initial therapy sessions revolved around the patient's inability to overcome her sense of helplessness and indecisiveness.

PATIENT: I don't know what to say that makes any sense.

THERAPIST: Is it important that you make sense?

PATIENT: I have no direction—no way to resolve where I am.

THERAPIST: I know what you mean. It *is* difficult to find a signpost.

PATIENT: Well, you must have had people in this kind of situation before.

THERAPIST: I have never been in this situation with you before.

PATIENT: Yes, but you have been there with other people. What works?

THERAPIST: What works is you and I finding the answer together.

PATIENT: Okay, how do we begin?

THERAPIST: We just keep talking.

PATIENT: About what?

THERAPIST: What do you think?

PATIENT: I don't know. I would like you to know.

THERAPIST: Okay, how do you feel about my not having immediate answers for you?

PATIENT: I don't like it.

THERAPIST: I don't blame you.

PATIENT: (After a pause) I guess you are trying to show me that if you take over like my husband did, it is going to be bad for me.

With this insight the patient mobilized herself, made several decisions about a lifestyle change, involved her husband in marital therapy, and after six months began to help bring about a change in role in her marriage. The psychomaterial essence of the helping relationship is called forth more forcefully when the therapist seeks to listen, understand, and resonate with the patient. The integrated "We" is used more openly as a pivot, where the therapist sides with the patient's desires for a superior text, and at the same time delays a conclusion.

When taking a psychomaterial stance, the therapist is making it much easier for the patient to realize his own psychomaterial foundations. This stance has to do with the goals listed earlier, their summation occurring in understanding our connection to all things animate and inanimate in the universe. As we resonate with the boundaryless condition of the integrated "We," but at the same time respect the patient's ego-building efforts at the spot where he is placing his greatest energies, we become therapeutic figures.

SUMMARY

The universal role of psychotherapy is to create therapists, and therapeutic action, everywhere. The burgeoning of therapy schools from 200 to 400 or more in the United States alone follows the track of language and communication in general. One or two theoretical fashions were too severely limiting of people's needs to express. The fact that hundreds of schools exist suggests the manner in which all the permutations and combinations of the universe's qualia of "Good" and "Bad" play out in human being. We probably need 4,000 or 40,000 schools before we get a superflux of psychotherapy. At this point, human character will be able to perceive its façade quality, and grow further. Fashion and expression need to be in dynamic resonance with each other, so that there can be enough "takes" on the universe to help the majority bring more of Being into being.

The patient coming to psychotherapy feels separated from the world at large. He also feels separated from an integrated self-image. When joined with the therapist, the patient opens himself up to the possibility of rejoining himself and the environment that nurtured him. To the extent that therapy helps such unities, the patient's symptoms are likely to dissolve. Each therapist is his/her own school of treatment. Whatever focus, orientation, or method employed, the therapist must help the patient become more united in the therapeutic endeavor. By joining with the therapist and allowing the therapist to join with him, the patient takes on self-therapeutic prowess. He accesses the "We" experience—the singular, most important element in therapeutic movement.

REFERENCES

Becker, E. (1973). *The denial of death.* New York: Macmillan.

Bohm, D., & Hiley, B. (1993). *The undivided universe: An ontological interpretation of quantum theory.* London: Routledge.

Bouklas, G. (1997). *Psychotherapy with the elderly: Becoming Methuselah's echo.* Northvale, NJ: Jason Aronson.

Burrow, B. (1996). *First principles.* See http://www.users.dircon.co.uk/~maximus/index.html

Capra, F. (1991). *The Tao of physics.* Boston: Shambala.

Dossey, L. (1993). *Healing words: The power of prayer, the practice of medicine.* San Francisco: Harper.

Freud, S. (1930). *Beyond the pleasure principle, Standard edition. 18:* 7–66.

Goswami, A. with Richard Reed and Maggie Goswami. (1995). *The self-aware universe: How consciousness creates the material world.* Putnam, NY: Jeremy Tarcher.

Grof, S. (1993). *The holotropic mind.* New York: Harper Collins.

Hochman, B. (1985). Lecture for Union Institute, delivered at Lasalle Academy, New York.

Kris, E. (1952). *Psychoanalytic explorations in art.* New York: International Universities Press.

Margolis, B. (1994). The contact function of ego: Its role in the therapy of the narcissistic patient. *Modern Psychoanalysis, 19,* 199–210.

Roazen, P. (1969). *Brother animal: The story of Freud and Tausk.* New York: Knopf.

Schwartz, R., & Schwartz, L. (1986). *Becoming a couple.* Lanham, MD: University Press of America.

Spotnitz, H. (1985). *Modern psychoanalysis of the schizophrenic patient.* New York: Human Sciences Press.

Washburn, M. (1994). *Transpersonal psychology in psychoanalytic perspective.* New York: State University of New York Press.

Watts, A. (1992). *The book: On the taboo of knowing who you are.* New York: Vintage Books.

Wilber, K. (1996). *The Atman project: A transpersonal view of human development.* Wheaton, IL: The Theosophical Publishing House.

Chapter 54

PSYCHOSYNTHESIS

MARTHA CRAMPTON

This chapter was the first one contracted for and the last one received. Between the first author contacted and the final author, no fewer than six other individuals promised—and did not deliver—an account of Psychosynthesis. So from Honolulu to California to Massachusetts I contacted psychosynthesist after psychosynthesist; finally, Martha Crampton delivered. I bring this up because the typical reader may believe all an editor has to do is write and ask—and the chapter comes in. Not at all. But this is an unusual chapter—well worth waiting for and agonizing over.

In my judgment, Dr. Roberto Assagioli, the developer of Psychosynthesis, like Trigant Burrow and many other giants in this field, has not received his full credit. Consequently, it is a pleasure to be able to introduce Psychosynthesis to a larger audience. As I was developing a list of therapies to include in this book, I informally questioned many therapists; it became clear that few knew much about Psychosynthesis. The reason will be evident on reading this complicated chapter, which, due to rigid space limitations, I had to cut considerably. More than most complex systems, Psychosynthesis stresses value; it is therefore similar to Formative Spirituality, Mutual Need Therapy, and others with a strong value orientation. In these respects Psychosynthesis is also similar to Alfred Adler's Individual Psychology. In view of the richness and complexity of Psychosynthesis, it is hoped the typical reader will further explore Assagioli's enormous vision.

Psychosynthesis refers to the theory and practice of a perspective on human development first articulated by Italian psychiatrist Roberto Assagioli.

The approach is based on unifying one's personality expression with a deeper source of purpose in and direction to life, the transpersonal Self, which is seen as the integrating principle of the personality and as a source of wisdom, inspiration, unconditional love, and the will to meaning and service. The term "psychosynthesis" is also applied to the process of personality integration occurring within this framework, either through the individual's own efforts or with the assistance of a psychosynthesis practitioner.

HISTORY

The foundations of Psychosynthesis were laid in the second decade of the twentieth century by Roberto Assagioli, whose work was far ahead of its time. Assagioli was one of those rare persons who can truly be called a sage. His wisdom, his radiant love, his down-to-earth simplicity were appreciated by all who knew him. Psychosynthesis, for him, was not merely an abstract doctrine but a

practical philosophy that he applied in his daily living. Assagioli died in 1974 at the age of 86.

When Psychosynthesis spread to North America in the 1960s, it attracted many people who had a background in the new therapies and growth disciplines such as Gestalt, the abreaction therapies, Transactional Analysis, and so forth. Some aspects of these therapies enriched Psychosynthesis as it is currently practiced in North America. Many people within the human potential movement found in Psychosynthesis a framework that was comprehensive enough to include what they had found of value in other approaches and that provided an orientation for deciding which methods, among the vast spectrum of available ones, were best suited to particular people in particular situations.

Assagioli's thought had its roots in many Western and Eastern traditions. He knew Freud, was active in the early psychoanalytic circles, and was one of the first Italians to introduce psychoanalysis in his country. The Freudian conception of the unconscious was included within his framework, but he felt it was incomplete. He expanded his own conception of the unconscious to include what has since been called by Maslow "the farther reaches of human nature" (1972), and he distinguished between the primitive or lower unconscious—the repository of our basic biological drives and our unresolved complexes—and what he called the superconscious—a realm that he postulated as being above or beyond our normal level of conscious awareness.

Assagioli agreed with the view that an important goal of therapy is to "make the unconscious conscious," to extend the frontiers of our consciousness into areas that were formerly unconscious. He differed from the psychoanalytic position in that he believed we must have a "height" psychology as well as a "depth" psychology—that we must go "up" as well as "down" in the psyche. Therefore, he developed techniques for evocation of the superconscious that helped people to contact directly latent positive and constructive energies within themselves. Contact with the superconscious often gave people the strength and inspiration to deal with disturbing aspects of themselves. At least for those persons who wished to undertake a spiritual Psychosynthesis, he also considered it necessary to look "upward" toward the transpersonal Self as a source of direction and meaning in their lives.

Emphasizing the need to assume conscious responsibility for the contents of the unconscious, he did not agree with the assumption of most depth psychologies that making the unconscious conscious was sufficient to effect change. He believed that awareness was only part of the picture and that awareness had to be balanced with will for the personality to become effectively integrated. Unless his clients established a connection with the source of will within themselves, he found that their insights would tend to get lost and be wasted. There was a need to rouse the person's motivation to take responsibility and to help the person "ground" the insights achieved through active techniques applied in the course of day-to-day living.

Assagioli's insights into the nature and training of the will are perhaps his greatest contribution to modern psychology. His understanding of the will is both profound and radically different from most previous conceptions. Viewing the will as an expression of the I or the Self, depending on its level, he saw the intimate connection between the will and the source of identity. He realized that the will was an unpopular topic in psychology, attributing this in part to the Victorian misconception of the will as a harsh taskmaster that forces us to do things we do not really want to do. Therefore, he endeavored to show that the true will is serene and unstrained, that it enables us to choose what is in harmony with our own deepest needs.

CURRENT STATUS

The various centers and institutes of Psychosynthesis that have emerged in the Western world have all taken their point of departure in Assagioli's teaching. No orthodoxy has been established, however, and each center has interpreted theory and practice in its own way as well as adding to it. It was Assagioli's wish that the institutes remain autonomous and, to use his metaphor, relate to each other as the stars in a constellation rather than as satellites revolving around a central sun. He saw Psychosynthesis as needing to change and evolve with the times, as well as to adapt to the needs of different cultural settings. Founded in this spirit, the movement has avoided more than most therapeutic systems the tendency toward ossification. Psychosynthesis is practiced by an increasing number of human service professionals in North America, Europe, and South America. Areas of application include psychotherapy, counseling, medicine, education, religion, management and organizational development, and creative problem solving in a variety of fields.

Practitioners have generally been trained in one or more of the training centers that have been established in these countries. Training programs in Psychosynthesis vary somewhat from one institute to another, according to the particular emphasis of the center and the needs of the student. In the United States there are several training centers in California and Massachusetts, with other centers in Seattle, Washington; Lexington, Kentucky; Redding, Connecticut; and in Walpole, New Hampshire. The centers in Boston, Massachusetts, and Walpole have a particular emphasis on educational applications of Psychosynthesis, while the others focus more on psychotherapy and personal growth counseling. In addition, individual practitioners are working in most areas of the country and sometimes offer training as well as counseling and consulting services. In Canada the major center is in Montreal.

The basic reference sources on Psychosynthesis are the two books by Assagioli: *Psychosynthesis: A Manual of Principles and Techniques* (1965) and *The Act of Will* (1973). Another reference, *The Realization of the Self: A Psychosynthesis Book,* was written by James Vargiu in 1980.

THEORY

Although Assagioli was a psychiatrist, his model of the human being was not based exclusively on the data of the psychiatric couch. He believed it was necessary to study the functioning of healthy individuals, including the most self-realized members of the human race, to gain a complete understanding of the full range and potentials of human nature. He deplored the tendency of diagnostic psychiatry to equate people with their illness. Instead, Assagioli viewed the person as a whole and considered pathological manifestations to be simply one aspect of

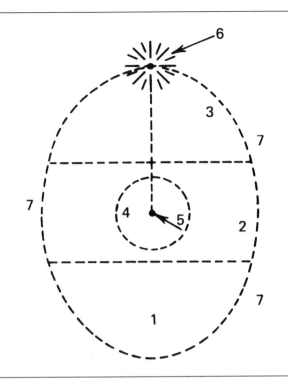

Figure 54.1 The egg diagram. 1. Lower unconscious; 2. middle unconscious; 3. higher unconscious or superconscious; 4. field of consciousness; 5. "I" (center of consciousness or Personal Self); 6. Self (Transpersonal Self or Higher Self); 7. collective unconscious.

the total person. As his perspective was one of growth, he tended to view symptoms not so much as something undesirable to be "gotten rid of" but rather as an indication of an energy blockage that needed to be explored. His emphasis was on releasing the constructive forces, on development of the person's positive resources, which he found would often cause symptoms to fall away.

Assagioli summarized his view of the human psychological constitution in Figure 54.1, which has come to be called the "egg diagram."

The area within the central circle is the field of consciousness, at the center of which is the "I," or personal self. The "I" is the point of pure awareness and will, which is the subject of our field of consciousness and the integrating center of our personality.

In the egg diagram the "I" or personal self is connected by a dotted line to a point above it—the higher or transpersonal Self. This transpersonal Self, like the personal self, is a center of consciousness and of will; however, its domain is more inclusive. The transpersonal Self extends its awareness to include the whole realm of the personal unconscious as well as the more limited field of consciousness. It is the center around which integration takes place at the stage of the transpersonal or spiritual psychosynthesis.

The area of the egg diagram that falls within the oval represents the personal unconscious, or that part of the unconscious that relates specifically to the individual, to his or her life experience, and to the unfolding of his or her inner qualities. The personal unconscious is divided into three levels: the lower unconscious, the middle unconscious, and the superconscious. The middle unconscious contains those elements that are similar to our normal waking state of consciousness.

A variety of "maps" are used in Psychosynthesis to help us understand and describe what is going on in a person. In discussing these, it is important to bear in mind that a map is only useful if it happens to fit the situation. The skillful psychosynthesist will be careful not to impose a preconceived conceptual system on the person he or she is working with, and will attempt to sense the unique reality of a particular individual rather than distorting the person to fit a rigid mold.

The Subpersonality Map

We are all familiar with the many inner voices that clamor for our attention, often bearing messages that contradict one another. There may be a voice, for example, saying, "I am really worn out; I think I will take a week off at Christmas and go to Florida." Another voice will reply, "But it costs too much; I can't afford to go." And yet another will be saying, "I really ought to buckle down during the holiday and finish fixing the kitchen so my wife will stop nagging me." This may be answered by a voice that says, "I don't care what she wants; I'm tired of her always telling me what to do anyway!" This kind of inner dialogue, which occupies so much of our energy, is going on within most of us a good deal of the time.

Psychosynthesis uses the term "subpersonalities" to refer to these "small I's" that speak for the part rather than for the whole. The subpersonalities are generally named. We might say that the person has a "pleaser" subpersonality that wants to ingratiate his wife, a "rebel" subpersonality that resents this, possibly a "striver" subpersonality that causes him to work too hard and become exhausted, and perhaps a "martyr" subpersonality that will not allow him to indulge in the expense of a vacation. Of course, we would have to know the person well to identify the subpersonalities accurately.

We can describe subpersonalities as being structured constellations or agglomerates of attitudes, drives, habit patterns, and belief systems, organized in adaptation to forces in the internal and external environment (Vargiu, 1975). They are similar to the "complexes" of psychoanalysis or the "games" of Transactional Analysis in that they contain crystallized energy that is "split off" from the whole of the personality.

When the child is unable to satisfy his basic needs and drives in a healthy, direct way, because of his own inadequacies or those of "significant others," he develops indirect and covert means to satisfy these needs. These means are the best available to protect his psyche from injury at the time, given his lack of experience, the immaturity of his organism, his internal dynamics, and the limitations of his environment.

An example to illustrate the process of subpersonality formation is the child who becomes the "good boy." Such a child is usually praised for obedient behavior and threatened with loss of love for expressing his own will. To obtain love, he learns to conform to the wishes of his parents. He develops a desire to please, to do what others want him to do, even when this means ignoring his own needs, because it is the only way he knows of gaining acceptance. The same child may later develop a "rebel" or "bad boy" subpersonality, as subpersonalities often develop in pairs of opposites, with the tendencies of one balancing out the tendencies of the opposite pole. The child who is experiencing an inner compulsion to submit to authority will suffer from this restriction and may try to counterbalance this by a provocative and rebellious attitude, or by acting out a tough, daredevil role. One "good boy" I worked with—a man in his thirties—still played an abjectly servile role toward his mother but attempted to create a more "manly" image for himself through "tough" behaviors such as car racing and heavy drinking. Each subpersonality has some valuable qualities that are important to preserve in the process of personality transmutation.

The "Personality Vehicles" Map

The term "personality vehicles" refers to the body, the emotions, and the mind. These three components, which make up the personality, are like "vehicles" for the Self because they are its media of manifestation on the material plane. It is important that each vehicle be adequately developed and coordinated with the others so that the personality expression is balanced and harmonious. Some people are so identified with one of the personality components that they are cut off from other aspects. Such a split is most common between the mind and the emotions. A person who has been rewarded in life primarily for mental performance may be very mistrustful of his or her emotions, thinking that they are dangerous and would completely take over if given a chance. A mentally identified person will need help in accepting and in educating the emotional side of the personality. People who are strongly identified with their emotions, on the other hand, may reject the mind and fear that mental activity would eliminate the vitality of their emotional life. Such people are likely to be flooded with uncontrolled emotionality and will need help in accepting the mental side of their personality.

The "I"–Self Map

Psychosynthesis posits that the process of synthesis requires an integrating center around which the synthesis can take place. Two such centers are postulated within the human psyche: the "I" and the Self. The "I" is considered to be a projection within the field of consciousness of the Self and functions as its deputy at the personality level. Both centers have the dual functions of will and consciousness. They are capable of awareness within their particular domain and of action upon it.

The psychosynthetic process can be considered as involving two stages that are successive but not rigidly separated: the personal Psychosynthesis and the transpersonal Psychosynthesis. In the personal Psychosynthesis, the "I" serves as the integrating center around which the process takes place. During this stage, the subpersonalities and personality vehicles are harmonized and integrated so that the person becomes able to function effectively in the realms of work and personal relationships and develops a relatively well-integrated personality.

During the transpersonal Psychosynthesis, the focus of personality integration gradually shifts from the "I" to the transpersonal Self. The "I" continues to collaborate in the process, but the transpersonal Self increasingly assumes a primary role, becoming the new center around which integration takes place. The "I" is like the mayor of a city who at first believes that he has full power and autonomy in his area of jurisdiction. He happily proceeds in the governing of the "citizens" (the various elements of the personality that require integration) until one day he discovers that many of the laws of his city are determined by the policy of the federal government.

During the transpersonal Psychosynthesis, the "I" has the task of aligning the personality with the more inclusive purpose of the transpersonal Self, with which it has now entered into conscious relationship. The personality sometimes rebels and struggles to maintain its autonomy. It must learn that in cooperating with the greater whole, in harmonizing and blending its energies with those of the transpersonal Self, it will achieve greater fulfillment than in seeking to maintain the illusion of independence. For it is through our connection with the transpersonal Self that we experience real purpose and meaning in life, that we transcend the boundaries of our small ego and discover our deeper relatedness to the universe.

The psychosynthesis guide aims at helping the client experience the reality of the "I" as early as possible, since the "I" plays such a central role in the therapeutic process. It is particularly important to cultivate and reinforce this experience when dealing with issues of will, of inner direction, and of identity to help people gain a sense of their own worth and identity, of their human dignity, and of their capacity to take responsibility for the direction of their own lives. Without this awareness of the "I," we are like a ship adrift upon a stormy sea without a rudder to guide its course.

Once the client's identity with the "I" is firmly established, the personality is gradually harmonized and integrated through the will of this organizing center. In the course of the process, the consciousness of the "I" is expanded, the area in which its will is active is correspondingly increased, and the "I" moves "up" or closer to the transpersonal Self, eventually to reunite with its parent entity. The expansion of the "I's" field of awareness is analogous to what occurs when a mountain climber approaches the top of a mountain. With each step upward, broader vistas appear and one can see the surrounding areas more clearly and comprehensively. To pursue the analogy, we could say that the closer a person's "I" is to the Self, the more full and enlightened will be that person's perspective on the total context of his or her life, with more understanding and acceptance of the past, and more strength and inspiration in approaching the future.

An interesting point is that as the individual's field of consciousness expands more into the "heights," he or she is thereby enabled to descend further into the "depths," when there is a need to do so. As the energies of the superconscious are increasingly contacted, the ability is gained to approach the confusion, the pain, and the distortions of the past with clearer vision and with greater compassion and understanding.

This point is illustrated in the stages one goes through in working out the relationships with the parent figures. As will be discussed later in the section dealing with emotional release, a client will often go through a period of expressing strong primal emotions, such as rage and pain. The field of consciousness at this stage of the work is relatively restricted, as the person is identified with his or her own strong feelings and is unable to see the parents' point of view. Later, when the person is more in touch with transpersonal energies, it becomes possible to disidentify with the "hurt child" attitude, to empathize with the situation of the parents, and to forgive them. At a still higher level of consciousness people can integrate more fully the experiences of their childhood, moving beyond simple forgiveness of and reconciliation with the parents to an understanding of deeper meaning and purpose in the fact that they were born to those particular parents. They become reconciled with their life as a whole. They are then able not merely to accept but actively to embrace their own destiny. They can see how even the most difficult and painful experiences have contributed to the development of cherished qualities and have prepared individuals for the part they are called upon to play in life.

METHODOLOGY

The Personality Assessment

Assessment of the client's personality, needs, and existential situation is the first step in Psychosynthesis after the initial contact has been established. It is an ongoing process that has value not only in terms of guiding the initial direction of the work but also for evaluating the progress and needs at various stages of the Psychosynthesis.

Unlike diagnosis, which is often something "done to" the client by an authority, the psychosynthesis assessment respects the client's perceptions of his or her own needs and goals. It also has a therapeutic value in that the ongoing aspect of the assessment process helps to keep the client's will aligned with the work that needs to be done.

Unfolding of the Process

The real guide of the psychosynthesis process is the client's higher Self that, at any particular time, is directing the person's attention in certain directions. With this in mind, the external guide, whose role is to support the client's inner process, is attentive to what seems to "want to happen" in the session.

The actual sequence in which the issues emerge may come as a surprise. It is important that the guide refrain from imposing preconceived structures on the situation, remaining open to allow the client's process to *unfold from within*. For one client the most urgent need may be to get more in touch with powerful emotions; for another client the need will be to step back from emotional reactions so that he or she can perceive them more clearly and better understand what they are expressing. One client will need to explore intrapsychically a conflicted relationship, while another will need to work this out at the interpersonal level. Sensitivity to timing and to the level at which particular issues can best be resolved at a particular time is crucial.

Identification and Disidentification

The concept of disidentification is a central one in Psychosynthesis, and it is probably one of the most important contributions made by this theory to psychological thought.

Disidentification can be understood best in relationship to its polar opposite: identification. We are identified with something when we are unable to separate ourselves from that thing, when our sense of identity is bound up in it. Some men are so identified with their cars that, should the car be scratched, they experience it as though they had been personally defaced, as though they were diminished by the fact that their car was scratched. A woman who is identified with the appearance of her body may feel that her worth as a human being is lessened if she develops wrinkles on her face or gets gray hairs. It is as though these people believe "I am my car" or "I am my body."

In the work of integrating our subpersonalities, disidentification plays an important role. We must be able to "stand back from" our subpersonalities in order to see them more clearly and to find the vantage point from which we can do something to transmute them. A man who was identified with a manipulative "salesman" subpersonality always aroused defensive reactions in people until he was able to disidentify from the need to sell himself. When he saw what he had been doing, he found it very comical and felt motivated to change his way of relating to others. When he realized that he could now choose not to play this role, he experienced a great sense of relief and inner freedom.

In addition to the various forms of unconscious and blind identification with some partial aspect of the personality, there is a process of voluntary or conscious identification. At certain points in the psychosynthetic process, the guide may encourage a client to voluntarily identify him- or herself with some particular element of experience to achieve a specific purpose.

A basic principle is that we must "own" our experience: We must be aware of what is there and recognize it as part of ourselves before we attempt to disidentify from it. Paradoxically, we are often able to be more in contact with our feelings when we are not identified with them. The ability to step back from our feelings into an observer position makes the feelings less threatening, allowing us to explore them more fully.

Activation of the Will

The will is one of the central themes in Psychosynthesis, and it plays a pivotal role in the psychosynthetic process.

The psychosynthesis guide must patiently seek out and support the will of the "I." The guide presents the client with many choices during the session to determine what issues he or she is ready and willing to explore, and to develop in the client the sense of being able to choose one's own direction.

The process of eliciting and reinforcing the client's experience of intentionality creates vitally important side effects or "incidental learning." The fact that someone is interested in the client's choices and respects them gives the person a sense of being valued as a human being and helps to build feelings of self-worth and dignity.

A client's motivation to work at the beginning of a session often comes from a subpersonality rather than from the "I." This may take many forms. A striver subpersonality may be trying to elicit the guide's support to elimi-

nate a "lazy" subpersonality, or a "superman" subpersonality may be seeking to eliminate the person's "weakness." A dependent client may passively wait for the guide to do something to make things better, or a controlling client will try to push the session in a preset direction, rather than being open to his or her own process or to the guide. The most obvious motive of many clients at the beginning of their work is to get rid of some pain or symptom rather than to explore the meaning of the pain. When the motivation of the client in coming to the session is not in line with what really needs to happen (i.e., the purpose of the Self for that session), the guide must find a way to help the person sort out the various strands of conflicting motivation and find the way back to center. When the fog lifts in the process of coming to center, the person can see more clearly what is happening and is in a better position to make wise choices.

Another important aspect in working with the will is the role of "grounding," or putting into practice the insights that have been achieved. Psychosynthesis utilizes a variety of methods to facilitate the grounding process. Within the session itself, guides often use role playing to help the client practice new attitudes or behaviors. If the work is done in a group setting, group members can provide an opportunity for trying out new ways. Writing is also a useful means of anchoring insights that come in a session. Most important of all is the application in the client's daily life, which the guide will attempt to keep informed of, giving extra grounding help to those persons who have trouble applying their insights in action.

Abreaction or Emotional Release

With many persons, since they bind so much of the person's energy, there is a need early in the therapeutic process to release strong emotions that have never been fully expressed. These emotions are usually related to painful relationships with the parent figures or to other traumatic situations in the person's life. At the stage when strong emotions of pain and anger are being expressed, the work may appear similar to Primal Therapy or other abreaction therapies. The philosophy of emotional release is different in Psychosynthesis, however, as the expression of hatred, pain, and anger is considered just a first step and not the ultimate goal. It may be a necessary step if a person's feelings in these areas are blocked, but one must move beyond the negative feelings so that the energy bound in hatred and resentment can be released for creative purposes. Real healing only occurs when forgiveness and reconciliation take place.

Multiple Techniques

Many techniques are employed in Psychosynthesis, as no one technique fits all purposes or all persons. Some clients may work very well with certain techniques and not at all well with others. This depends both upon the psychological type and the level of development. A therapist who wishes to be fully responsive to the needs of a particular client must therefore be able to use a variety of approaches. It is important to bear in mind as well that new methods and techniques are being developed in Psychosynthesis. Techniques are made to fit the person rather than the person being made to fit the techniques. Often the most effective approach is one that the guide develops on the spur of the moment to meet the needs of a particular situation.

A Holistic Approach

Psychosynthesis can be considered a holistic approach concerned with balanced development of the various aspects of human experience: physical, emotional, mental, and spiritual (related to essence, purpose, values, and will). In choosing techniques the therapist will bear in mind the development of these dimensions, stimulating those that are underdeveloped, using those that are well developed as entry points, and attempting to orchestrate them all in an integrated way.

The Processes of Integration and Synthesis

The process of Psychosynthesis, as the name implies, is one in which the conflicting and disharmonious elements of the personality undergo a process of harmonization, integration, and synthesis. In the course of this process they are brought into alignment with the person's higher Self, so that the personality becomes an instrument or channel through which the Self can become manifest in the physical world.

Many polarities within the personality require integration. The exact nature of these varies from one individual to the next. Most can be related to the polarities the Chinese call *yin* and *yang.*

The entry points for therapeutic intervention can be at physical, emotional, or mental levels. In addition, the "I" or the Self can serve this purpose. This can be summarized in Figure 54.2.

Most current therapies tend to focus on the link between two of the three dimensions on the points of the triangle. Approaches like psychoanalysis, TA, and Rogerian Therapy emphasize the mental–emotional link; methods such as Gestalt, Bioenergetics, and Primal Therapy utilize primarily the link between the body and the emotions; and approaches like the martial arts, the Alexander technique, and the Feldenkrais method are based on the link between the mind and the body. Psychosynthesis recognizes all these links and uses whichever seem most appropriate to the situation. In most cases, there is an attempt to complete the circuit

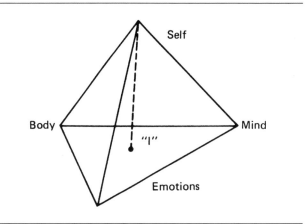

Figure 54.2 Entry points for therapeutic intervention.

and to have the person work through the material at all levels, regardless of the entry point. Psychosynthesis differs from several other current therapies in that it values the role of mental understanding. Though a client may work through an issue primarily in a physical or emotional mode, it is important to understand the patterns and dynamics involved to be able to generalize from this experience and to ground it in daily living.

The Technique of Guided Imagery

The technique of guided imagery consists in having the client utilize visual and auditory imagination to get in contact with an inner world of fantasy. It is assumed that the images encountered in this way are symbolic expressions of dynamic patterns within the client's personality.

The client is instructed to relax and allow the imagery to unfold on its own, just as though watching a film on the mind-screen.

The guide may suggest that the client attempt to do certain things, such as establish communication between different elements in the imagery, identify with a particular person in order to experience his or her emotions more deeply, or explore particular aspects of the imagery in more detail. This method allows one to work directly on the symbolic contents of the psyche, exploring the qualities and interrelationships of the various elements, and attempting to bring a greater degree of harmony and integration among them. The guided imagery technique is able to reveal unconscious material in the same way as night dreams do, while it offers the advantage of permitting the person's consciousness and will to interact with this material. Thus, it creates a bridge between the conscious and unconscious levels of the mind.

The role of the guide in a guided imagery session is to help the traveler maintain contact with the flow of his or her inner process, keep a productive focus, deepen the emotional connections, clarify issues when necessary, and "ground" the experience or relate it to the client's everyday life.

Evocation of Inner Wisdom

Various techniques may be used to help clients get in touch with their inner wisdom. Usually these methods involve dialogue (imagined visually or acted out) with a figure that is designated as a source of wisdom. The figure may be imagined in human form, such as an elder or spiritual teacher, or it may be a sacred animal, an element in nature, or an abstract symbol. The guide will usually suggest that clients allow their own symbol to appear spontaneously. When outer dramatization is used, it has the advantage of "spacializing" the different positions so that the clear place of the client's wisdom figure may be more easily kept separate from the subpersonalities with their distorting lenses. This technique is based on disidentification and often yields amazing results. The wisdom figure is invited to comment on various aspects of the client's life or to respond to particular questions or fears the person may have. It is reassuring and uplifting for clients to discover that they have within themselves sources of wisdom that they can readily tap. The major counterindication to this technique is when clients with a harsh super-ego take on the role of a judge rather than that of a compassionate sage.

Kinesthetic Imagery

A helpful technique is focusing on the kinesthetic sense of what is happening in the psyche, along with the feelings that are associated with the body-sense. Gendlin (1978), in his book, *Focusing,* speaks of contacting a "felt sense." The felt sense, which includes both a feeling and a bodily sensation, is first experienced and then translated into words or imagery. This technique is more effective than guided imagery with clients who tend to intellectualize, and it is a valuable foundation for most inner process work.

The Spirit behind the Methods

The essence of Psychosynthesis lies beyond a particular set of techniques. New methods are evolving with the times, and they differ from one practitioner to the other. Far more important than technical knowledge is the practitioner's own level of consciousness and his or her ability to be with a client from a place of clarity, wisdom, and unconditional love.

APPLICATIONS

Psychosynthesis appears to be an effective approach for relating to a wide variety of human conditions. Its flexi-bility and lack of attachment to particular techniques or terminology allow it to respond to the needs of widely different clients and situations.

Persons trained in Psychosynthesis have applied this perspective to working with most kinds of clients in the mental health field—from "normal neurotics" to persons who are severely disturbed and who demonstrate antisocial behavior. The approach must, of necessity, be adapted to the individuals concerned. The most widespread field of application for Psychosynthesis to date has been in counseling persons who are relatively healthy. Such persons utilize the approach to facilitate their personal and spiritual growth and to enhance their creativity.

Psychosynthesis offers a perspective of particular value to individuals or groups who are seeking to orient their lives around a deeper sense of purpose and meaning, and who experience a need to include a spiritual dimension in their lives. It is also particularly effective in working with persons in "existential crisis" whose distress signals the need for reorientation to new, more inclusive values and/or new forms of life expression. Persons in transition, either in their careers or personal lives, benefit from the contact Psychosynthesis provides with deeper sources of identity and life direction. There is a special need at such times of outer flux for the experience of inner stability and contact with one's own creative process. Persons faced with the need to make life choices may be helped by the psychosynthesis approach to open up a place of inner clarity from which to discern the path of greatest life meaning and growth.

Psychosynthesis has also been applied in the field of education, particularly in teacher training and in the development of curricula, often in such neglected areas as self-understanding, imagination, creativity, intuition, and volition. Educational applications of this kind offer a significant opportunity for preventive mental health work. Other fields of application include religion, management and organizational development, interpersonal relations, and the facilitation of creative process in a variety of fields.

CASE EXAMPLE

Jeanne, a young woman in her late twenties, was referred to me by another therapist who had become discouraged by her refusal to speak in therapy sessions over a period of several months. Heavy-set and overweight at the time, with an expressionless face, Jeanne was a secretary and was functioning well on her job while supporting herself in a bachelor of arts program in psychology, which she had almost finished. She had been married for a short time to an abusive man and was now living alone. She had been raised in an orphanage by nuns since the age of three, when her father had abandoned her mother. Jeanne's mother, later institutionalized as psychotic, was unable to take care of her and saw the girl only a few times while she was in the orphanage. Jeanne never saw or heard from her father again after he left home. She consulted a therapist because of depressive symptoms.

In our first session, Jeanne adopted the same stance as with her previous therapist. She sat in silence throughout, immobile as a statue, staring into space. At first I made some unsuccessful attempts at communication, both verbal and nonverbal, and finally realized that I needed to let go of the place within myself that wanted to "make something happen" in order that our communication could take place at another level. I needed to trust that, in allowing the deeper center within both of us to direct the process, what was needed would happen in its own way. And so I, too, sat in silence and simply chose to open myself to experience Jeanne's presence and to allow her to experience mine. As I did so, I became aware of her higher Self as a very bright light and felt that it was trying to break through in her life at this time. I was also aware of painful memories from the past that needed to come forward into consciousness to be healed. As I sat with Jeanne, I experienced her inner beauty and felt a deep love for her. At the end of our session, I told her that I sensed the presence of a very beautiful person inside her who wanted to emerge and that I believed I would be able to assist in the process. I also told her that I was powerless to do it alone and needed her cooperation for this to happen. I informed her that I did not have the skills to help her unless we could talk and that I felt it would be a waste of our time as well as of her money to continue meeting unless she were willing to speak to me. As she still did not respond verbally, I suggested that she go home and think about it, and that she call me for another appointment if she was willing to meet me halfway. My intuitive sense was that an inner contact had been established and that Jeanne's will was beginning to mobilize for the work, which was shortly confirmed.

At our next appointment, Jeanne's behavior was very much different. She was still stiff and fearful, but willing to communicate. In the interval between sessions, she had done some imagery work by herself, which had gotten her in touch with some previously repressed memories of her early childhood. The fact that she did this on her own suggested that she felt a need to demonstrate her power and autonomy in this way. Though she had consented to speak to me, she maintained her sense of personal control by unlocking the memory bank alone. Jeanne reported the work she had done on her own with a sense of pride and agreed to let me guide her imagery process where she had left off. She immediately went back to the image of herself as a small child huddled in the corner of a room while her father, who had been drinking, was beating up her mother so viciously that he

almost killed her. Jeanne recalled that this was the event that had precipitated her being sent off to spend the rest of her childhood in the orphanage.

She got in touch with the feelings of fear and anger and pain that she had had at that time. She expressed anger to both parents for abandoning her and not caring about her feelings. Having done this, she got in touch with the feelings of love she had for her father and expressed resentment toward her mother for being jealous of this love and trying to keep her away from her father. She felt her father's warmth, but sensed that he was placing impossible demands upon her to fill a vacuum in his own life. She felt the burden of having to meet the strong emotional needs of her father and expressed resentment at having been used in this way. The father figure in her imagery said that he was sorry—that he didn't realize what he was doing to her and that the reason he left home was not that he didn't love her. She started to feel more warmly toward him, but still had some residual anger, the reason for which did not emerge until our next session.

Jeanne came to our next session feeling quite agitated, with a sense that she still had to uncover something more. She was aware of anger toward her father but felt that something was stuck in her throat when she tried to express it. I asked her to let an image come that would help her get in touch with what it was that was blocking her. She then saw an erect penis and recalled having been sexually abused by her father. This released the energy and she was able to complete the expression of anger toward him.

The following session was the turning point for her in terms of the transmutation of her anger. In this session, we took as a starting point a dream she had reported in which she was in a room that had a door covered over with wallpaper. I had her imagine that she was going through this door. She followed a tunnel leading down to a room in which several old men were seated. One of these men, who appeared to be very wise, came over to her and told her that she had a firm foundation now and no longer needed to be angry. She was at first unwilling to accept this, as she still felt resentment at having been pushed around by so many people in her life. He explained to her that it was natural for her to have had these feelings when she was small and powerless, but that she was strong now and it was no longer appropriate. He told her that to continue holding on to her anger would only be a waste of energy. He then showed her some sort of plan or model that demonstrated to her that she really did have a strong foundation. As she opened herself to this realization, she felt that she could love without fear. She felt that she could trust other people now that she was able to trust herself. After that she was able to forgive her father and no longer saw him as a threat. Jeanne's process illustrates the usual progression in working with the parental "images" from expression of negative feelings through to reconciliation and forgiveness. The Self, or integrating center of the personality (symbolized by the wise old man figure in the imagery), seems to know when the stage of expressing anger is completed and can guide the person to the next stage.

After this stage in our work had been completed, Jeanne was a changed person. She was much more warm and open, and her depression lifted. She began to ask herself what she really wanted to do with her own life and developed a much stronger sense of her own worth. We were only able to have a few sessions together after this because unexpected commitments on my own part necessitated transferring Jeanne to another therapist. The work that we did during this period was focused on her own life direction and the exploration of possible alternative futures. She felt that she needed more time to find out what she really wanted to do and took some positive steps to explore various areas of interest. She also changed her job to work for an agency where the values were more in line with her own. After a period of work with another therapist, she decided that she wanted to lose weight and within three months had lost 40 pounds. Shortly thereafter she met a very nice man with whom she fell in love, and at the time of this writing is happily married and waiting for her first child.

Jeanne's case is of particular interest because of the rapid and dramatic changes that occurred. This seems to be a result of several factors: her ripeness for this work, the good contact she was able to establish with her transpersonal Self, and the strength of will she had developed through coping with the challenges of her difficult life alone. Just as she used her powerful will in a distorted way at first to remain mute, she was able to move forward with surprising alacrity when she chose to align her will in a positive direction.

SUMMARY

The psychosynthesis approach is founded on the basic premise that human life has purpose and meaning and that we participate in an orderly universe structured to facilitate the evolution of consciousness. A corollary is that each person's life has purpose and meaning within this broader context and that it is possible for the individual to discover this.

Psychosynthesis postulates that the sense of meaningful relationship to a greater whole is mediated through a transpersonal or spiritual center of identity, called the Self. It asserts that in learning to cooperate consciously with this deeper source of our being, we experience the fulfillment of human life. The Self is seen as having attributes of consciousness and creative, loving will, which seek expression through service in the world.

Thus, the Self finds consummation as we develop our gifts and discover our particular mode of contributing to the needs of the planet—our "calling," or unfolding vocation.

In line with this perspective, much of the work in Psychosynthesis is directed toward experiencing and expressing the life source from which one's most profound sense of identity is derived. Much of a client's therapeutic experience involves learning to discern when one is "coming from" the "source" experience and when one is coming from a false sense of identity with a distorted self-image, or "subpersonality." To facilitate the client's experience of this deeper center, it is important for the guide to stay inwardly connected to the client's essence and to avoid being taken in by the games or facades. A kind of "bifocal" vision is maintained in which the guide is simultaneously aware of the client's creative potentials and of the personality distortions that block their expression. In seeing through the client's outer shell of defenses to the place of inner strength and wisdom, the guide "holds up a mirror" that reflects to the client his or her hidden resources and helps to evoke them. This understanding of the subtler dimensions of the helping relationship is an important feature of Psychosynthesis.

In addition, the many techniques developed to facilitate the source experience represent a significant contribution to the field of therapy. In the early phases of work, the therapist's focus is on helping the client to differentiate the "I" (which is considered to be a "spark" of the Self operating at the personality level) from the various pushes and pulls within the personality and from the environment that the person tends to confuse with the "I." Techniques that are useful at this stage include: inner dialogue to gain understanding of and distance from the subpersonality patterns; healing of memories that have distorted the self-image; learning to attune to one's organismic sense of what is right; and direct evocation of the source experience through suggestions involving the creative imagination and/or the will. Later, when the foundations of personal autonomy have been laid, the person begins to come into conscious relationship with the Self and issues of a different order emerge. The process of alignment with the Self generally stimulates various crises of spiritual awakening, which the therapist must be equipped to handle. The person's illusions at this stage tend to revolve around fears of power or of the lack of power. The client is commonly afraid of such things as visibility, being alone or different, being criticized, making a wrong choice, or losing control, and may project the image of a harsh, judgmental, or controlling parent onto the Self. Work at this level may require the withdrawal of such projections when they exist. The major focus, however, is on helping the client have access to a place of inner knowing where wisdom, healing, and life direction are available. Psychosynthesis is one of relatively few therapies that offer some understanding and practical tools for intervention at this stage of development.

In the long run, it is perhaps for its innovative and profound understanding of the human will that Psychosynthesis will be best remembered in the annals of history. First, it has helped to clarify the nature of the will and to free it from various misconceptions that have given the topic a bad name in modern psychology. It asserts that true will is an expression of the "I," or the Self, and as such is a unifying and enjoyable experience. The imposters of will, such as harsh discipline, self-flagellation, "shoulds," perfectionistic striving, and the bulldozer approach are considered by Psychosynthesis to be subpersonalities—an expression of inner division rather than of creative will.

Second, Psychosynthesis proposes a particularly useful developmental model for understanding the stages of will maturation. It suggests that the first stage in will development is learning to differentiate oneself from "mass consciousness" as a separate individual with an internal locus of valuation and responsibility for one's own life. When this stage of "individual consciousness" has been reached, the person is ready to relate to the collective or more universal dimension without getting lost in it. He or she can then learn to cooperate with others in a common purpose and to cooperate with the transpersonal Self without losing the sense of individual identity. Thus the full flowering of spiritual maturity requires the integration (not the surrender) of one's hard-won individuality within a more inclusive and transcendent pattern. The term "co-creation" is an appropriate one to describe a person's experience at this stage. At first there is a sense of creating one's destiny in partnership with a deeper life source that provides the pattern and direction. Later, as the center of identity shifts from the "I" toward the Self, the person is increasingly in touch with the creative will of the Self and experiences the personality as his or her vehicle of expression.

One feature in the Psychosynthesis approach to the will that deserves special attention is its balanced appreciation of the role of both conscious and unconscious levels of motivation. Psychosynthesis acknowledges, on the one hand, the importance of taking conscious responsibility for one's life and of attempting to actualize one's highest values. It recognizes, on the other hand, that unconscious dynamics exist that a person must come to terms with. These are seen to include both unresolved material from the past and emerging patterns from the superconscious that point to the person's next step. While the value of "positive thinking" and of conscious efforts to reprogram "old tapes" is recognized, Psychosynthesis does not make a simplistic assumption that this approach alone is sufficient. Thus, it avoids the imbalances common to many systems that tend at one extreme to emphasize a passive, receptive attitude toward the unconscious or, at the other extreme, to focus on conscious control while they neglect the role of the unconscious.

In summary, the uniqueness and special contribution of Psychosynthesis might be said to lie in its radically integrative view of the human being. Its unifying perspective offers a theoretical framework and a practical methodology for reconciling many traditional pairs of opposites: conscious/unconscious; individual/collective; inner/outer; awareness/action; spirit/matter. As such, it provides a point of view that can assimilate new findings from diverse sources as we move toward a more inclusive understanding of human nature and destiny.

REFERENCES

Assagioli, R. A. (1965). *Psychosynthesis: A manual of principles and techniques.* New York: Hobbs-Dorman.

Assagioli, R. A. (1973). *The act of will.* New York: Viking.

Bucke, R. M. (1923). *Cosmic consciousness, a study in the evolution of the human mind.* New York: Dutton.

Carter-Haar, B. (1975). Identity and personal freedom. *Synthesis, 2,* 56–91.

Crampton, M. (1969). The use of mental imagery in psychosynthesis. *Journal of Humanistic Psychology, 2,* 139–153.

Crampton, M. (1973). Psychological energy transformations: Developing positive polarization. *Journal of Transpersonal Psychology, 2,* 39–56.

Crampton, M. (1974). *An historical survey of mental imagery techniques in psychotherapy and description of the dialogic imagery method.* Montreal: Canadian Institute of Psychosynthesis.

Crampton, M. (1975). Answers from the unconscious. *Synthesis, 2,* 140–152.

Gendlin, E. (1978). *Focusing.* New York: Everest House.

Haronian, F. (1975). The repression of the sublime. *Synthesis, 1,* 125–136.

Maslow, A. H. (1970). *Religions, values, and peak experiences.* New York: Viking.

Maslow, A. H. (1972). *The farther reaches of human nature.* New York: Viking.

Miller, S. (1975). Dialogue with the higher self. *Synthesis, 2,* 122–139.

Ouspensky, P. D. (1949). *In search of the miraculous.* New York: Harcourt.

Vargiu, J. (1975). Subpersonalities. *Synthesis, 1,* 51–90.

Vargiu, J. (1980). *The realization of the self: A psychosynthesis book.*

Chapter 55

RADICAL PSYCHIATRY

CLAUDE STEINER

By now the reader may be fatigued by my use of the word "innovative," but I daresay that after finishing this chapter every reader will agree that the concepts of Claude Steiner are totally different from those described in any other chapter of this book. Even the title of the chapter indicates the radical approach this bold author and social critic takes.

Steiner's point of view is quite simple: He believes that the emotional disturbance of the so-called maladjusted is largely the result of power abuse—oppression—often sanctioned by the society. Instead of attempting to cure the victims of society, we should change society. Don't we all know that crime is a function of social inequality? That insanity depends on social stresses? While most of us recognize the validity of these arguments, still we do little about the causes: We keep mopping up the floor because the sink is overflowing. But Steiner says we should turn off the water. In other words, he goes to the root of the problem—therefore he takes a radical approach.

Whether one agrees or disagrees with the views presented in this chapter, they are worthy of careful consideration. Were we to generate a factor analysis of the points of view in this book (a good idea for someone) Steiner's chapter would probably lie in a dimension of its own. This is a chapter that will challenge all readers.

Radical Psychiatry holds that all functional psychiatric difficulties are forms of alienation resulting from the mystified oppression of people who are isolated from each other.

People's alienation is the result of power abuse and is therefore a political matter. Any person in the practice of psychiatry (soul healing) becomes involved in the personal politics of those he or she attempts to help, either as an ally or as an oppressor; there is no possibility of neutrality for a person with power in an oppressive situation. In order to be helpful, any person who claims to practice psychiatry needs to become an ally against the oppressive influences in the lives of those he or she is attempting to help.

Radical Psychiatry is a political theory of psychiatric disturbance and a political practice of soul healing.

HISTORY

I first heard the term "Radical Psychiatry" at the 1968 American Psychiatric Association meeting in Miami, Florida, where a group of young residents, outraged by the ways in which the psychiatric profession was aiding

and abetting the Vietnam War, called for a Radical Psychiatry as an alternative to their profession.

At the time, I was a clinical psychologist attending the psychiatric convention with Eric Berne and others to present a panel discussion about Transactional Analysis.

Prompted by a growing awareness of psychiatric power abuse and by some crystallizing, radicalizing experiences in Florida, I returned to Berkeley, California, where I was practicing Transactional Analysis, and began to teach a course called Radical Psychiatry at the Free University at Berkeley. This course resembled in format a number of other courses being taught at the Free University, all of which dealt with the patterns of power abuse in industry, the arts, commerce, the healing sciences, the law, institutions, the media, and so on. The Radical Psychiatry course focused on the oppressiveness of the practices of psychiatry, psychology, psychotherapy, and allied "helping" professions. Over the next year I taught several of these courses to small groups of Berkeley students and residents.

In September 1969 a coalition of women, homosexuals, mental patients, and others who felt oppressed by psychiatric practice organized to disrupt the American Psychiatric Association's conference meeting in San

Francisco. I prepared the Radical Psychiatry Manifesto, which follows, to be distributed at the conference.

MANIFESTO

1. The practice of psychiatry has been usurped by the medical establishment. Political control of its public aspects has been seized by medicine and the language of soul healing (ψυχη+ιαγρεα) has been infiltrated with irrelevant medical concepts and terms.

   Psychiatry must return to its nonmedical origins since most psychiatric conditions are in no way the province of medicine. All persons competent in soul healing should be known as psychiatrists. Psychiatrists should repudiate the use of medically derived words such as "patient," "illness," "diagnosis," "treatment." Medical psychiatrists' unique contribution to psychiatry is as experts on neurology, and, with much needed additional work, on drugs.

2. Extended individual psychotherapy is an elitist, outmoded, as well as nonproductive form of psychiatric help. It concentrates the talents of a few on a few. It silently colludes with the notion that people's difficulties have their sources within them while implying that everything is well with the world. It promotes oppression by shrouding its consequences with shame and secrecy. It further mystifies by attempting to pass as an ideal human relationship when it is, in fact, artificial in the extreme.

   People's troubles have their course not within them but in their alienated relationships, in their exploitation, in polluted environments, in war, and in the profit motive. Psychiatry must be practiced in groups. One-to-one contacts, of great value in crises, should become the exception rather than the rule. The high ideal of I-Thou loving relations should be pursued in the context of groups rather than in the stilted consulting room situation. Psychiatrists not proficient in group work are deficient in their training and should upgrade it. Psychiatrists should encourage bilateral, open discussion and discourage secrecy and shame in relation to deviant behavior and thoughts.

3. By remaining "neutral" in an oppressive situation, psychiatry, especially in the public sector, has become an enforcer of establishment values and laws. Adjustment to prevailing conditions is the avowed goal of most psychiatric treatment. Persons who deviate from the world's madness are given fraudulent diagnostic tests, which generate diagnostic labels that lead to "treatment" that is, in fact, a series of graded repressive procedures such as "drug management," hospitalization, shock therapy, perhaps lobotomy. All these forms of "treatment" are perversions of legitimate medical methods, which have been put at the service of the establishment by the medical profession. Treatment is forced on persons who would, if let alone, not seek it.

   Psychological tests and the diagnostic labels they generate, especially schizophrenia, must be disavowed as meaningless mystifications, the real function of which is to distance psychiatrists from people and to insult people into conformity. Medicine must cease making available drugs, hospitals, and other legitimate medical procedures for the purpose of overt or subtle law enforcement and must examine how drug companies are dictating treatment procedures through their advertising. Psychiatry must cease playing a part in the oppression of women by refusing to promote adjustment to their oppression. All psychiatric help should be by contract; that is, people should choose when, what, and with whom they want to change. Psychiatrists should become advocates of the people, should refuse to participate in the pacification of the oppressed, and should encourage people's struggles for liberation.

- Paranoia is a state of heightened awareness. Most people are persecuted beyond their wildest delusions. Those who are at ease are insensitive.
- Psychiatric mystification is a powerful influence in the maintenance of people's oppression.
- Personal liberation is only possible along with radical social reforms.
- Psychiatry must stop its mystification of the people and get down to work!

During 1969 I joined the Berkeley Free Clinic, an organization started by a group of Vietnam paramedics and antiwar medical professionals to start a psychological counseling section, the Rap Center (Radical Approach to Psychiatry). We offered drug, welfare, and draft counseling services, group psychotherapy, and some individual one-to-one therapy to the young people who were crowding the streets of Berkeley. Many of these "street people" were involved in the student revolt and participated in the riots against the Vietnam war and in support of People's Park that took place in Berkeley during that period.

In the course of 1969 a number of people joined the Rap Center, notably Hogie Wyckoff and Joy Marcus, who soon added their imprint on our work. It can be said that Radical Psychiatry today is a product of my initial impetus plus the many contributions of a large number of people who have practiced and taught Radical Psychiatry in the last decades. Rebecca Jenkins, Darca Nicholson, Beth Roy, and Robert Schwebel deserve special credit for their extensive involvement and contributions.

CURRENT STATUS

Important in the development of Radical Psychiatry was the publication, starting in 1969, of the magazine *The Radical Therapist,* which encouraged our early writings by publishing them. Eventually the workers of *The Radical Therapist* declared their opposition to any psychotherapy practice, which they regarded as inevitably oppressive and in support of the establishment, and repudiated our point of view. Therefore, we started another publication, *Issues in Radical Therapy,* to publish papers that shared with Radical Psychiatry the belief that psychotherapy is a valid political activity.

There are currently about 20 who, by virtue of their training, can legitimately call themselves radical psychiatrists.

A radical psychiatrist is a person who has been personally, intensively trained by another radical psychiatrist. Intensive training is unfortunately almost completely unavailable at this time.

Since 1980 when this chapter first appeared, much of what was pioneered by the Radical Psychiatry movement has become common understanding in modern psychiatry in the US and, to different degrees, around the world. Consequently the radical somewhat incendiary nature of the pronouncements herein may seem outlandish and outdated. Mental patient rights movements, feminism, the movements for healthy food and physical fitness, the improved understanding of the dangers of abusing over the counter and prescription drugs have all improved the performance of the psychiatric profession. In addition the principles of equality and cooperation have penetrated institutions, corporations and the media making the working environment generally more humane and without doubt less alienating.

Still, as I review this chapter there is very little that I would take back, though I feel that much of it is taken for granted and it might seem that I am beating a dead horse to some US and European readers. But world wide, power abuse and oppression continues and psychiatry continues to serve the powerful at the expense of the powerless. Alienation continues apace, depression is becoming epidemic, teenage suicide is at an all time high. Any one who is practicing the art of soul healing whether a physician social worker psychologist, psychiatric nurse, counselor or correctional worker would do well to give these words serious consideration.

THEORY

At the core of Radical Psychiatry is a theory of alienation drawn from the writings of Karl Marx, Wilhelm Reich, Herbert Marcuse, Franz Fanon, and R. D. Laing.

The Theory of Alienation

People are, by their nature, capable of living in harmony with themselves, each other, and their environment. To the extent that they succeed in this ideal, they feel, and are, powerful; to the extent that they fail, they are alienated. People's potentials are realized according to the conditions that they are born into and continue to find during their lives.

Clearly, different people have different innate strengths and weaknesses; however, these do not, by and large, account for the large differences in well-being we find among people. Rather these differences are explained by the material conditions of their lives.

Conditions of oppression directly affect people's power, and since conditions vary immensely for different people across the world, it follows that the development of people's potential will vary greatly as well. To the extent that a person's potential for a harmonious life is not realized, his or her state of being can be considered to be alienation, or powerlessness; to the extent that it is realized, the state is one of power in the world.

Karl Marx used the term "alienation" when he spoke of people being separated from their human nature, especially when they became estranged from a major aspect of their lives: their work and the products of their work.

The term "alienation" is used in a similar manner in Radical Psychiatry. We have observed that alienation tends to affect certain specific sources of individual power: our hearts, our minds, our hands, and our bodies. It also affects collective power, that is, people's capacity to live, love, and work together.

Alienation from Our Hearts, or from Love

We become alienated from our hearts, or from our capacity to relate to each other in a satisfying way. Our natural tendencies to love, appreciate, cooperate, and help each other are thwarted from early on. We are taught the rules of Stroke Economy, which effectively reduces the amount of strokes or positive human interaction and follows a set of rules I call stroking that occurs among people.

The Stroke Economy is a set of rules supported by strong internal and social sanctions that reduce the exchange of "strokes" between people young and old, married and unmarried, men and men, women and women, and so on. In addition the Stroke Economy enjoins people not to give strokes that they want to give, not to ask for or accept strokes they want, not to reject unwanted strokes, and not to give themselves strokes.

As a consequence the exchange of strokes, human affection, and love is severely reduced. We feel unloved and unlovable, incapable of loving, sad, isolated, and depressed. We don't love humankind and fail to act in each other's behalf. We learn that we cannot allow someone else to become close or to trust others with our hearts, and we fail to learn how to deal with the normal ups and downs of our relationships.

Alienation from Our Minds, or from the Capacity to Think

We all have the capacity to understand the facts and workings of our world, to predict the outcome of events, and to solve problems. This capacity has been developed to a large degree by some people but has become unavailable to others who, in their alienation from their minds, are incapable of thinking in an orderly way.

Because of the way people are treated from early childhood on, some grow up unable to use their minds effectively. They cannot keep thoughts fixed in their consciousness long enough to combine them with other thoughts so as to derive logical conclusions. At the same time, they cannot exclude from their minds chaotic thought patterns and emotions. Complete confusion and the utter terror of mental breakdown are the extreme form of this kind of alienation, which tends to be misdiagnosed by the psychiatric establishment as "schizophrenia." Those who suffer from mind alienation are singled out for the harshest and most unjust treatment. Tranquilizing medication, shock therapy, imprisonment, padded cells, straitjackets, hot and cold water treatments, forced feeding, experimentation with dangerous drugs, and brain surgery have all been applied over the last century on people who have shown extreme forms of alienation from their minds. These methods, whose principal effect is to terrorize people into submission causing them to temporarily conform to the expectations of their helpers, have proven, one by one, to be totally ineffectual in anything but sweeping the problem under the rug. Recently, mental patients' rights groups in some parts of the world have succeeded in curbing some of these abuses, but there is no doubt that the mistreatment of the "mentally ill" continues.

Alienation from our minds is a result of systematic, lifelong lies and discounts. A discount occurs when another person denies the content of our experiences. If, in addition to being told that our experiences aren't valid, we are also fed false information in the form of lies, the combined effect is an interference with our thinking functions, which eventually can lead to total mental breakdown.

One particular well-known form of alienation is known as "paranoid schizophrenia"; here the natural intuitive perception of the facts of our persecution, which some become keenly aware of, are systematically discounted by others who also often lie to explain away their oppressive behavior. People's budding perceptions of oppression, persecution, and abuse are most often effectively squelched and ignored; but for others, these perceptions can evolve into large-scale obsessions that develop into systems that, when elaborated, become fantastic and unreal, at which point they are called "paranoid delusions." Radical Psychiatry holds that paranoia, no matter how fantastic, is always based on a kernel of truth, and that is why we say that "paranoia is a state of heightened awareness." Consequently, we encourage the expression of people's "paranoid fantasies" by willingly searching for the grain of truth in them and validating whatever aspect of them that may be realistic.

Alienation from Our Bodies, or from Our Feelings

Our intimate relationship with ourselves, that is, with all parts of our bodies, is interfered with by a number of alienating influences. We are told that our minds or spirits are separate from our body or flesh and that one or the other is, in some manner, the lesser of the two. We are told that those who use their minds rather than their bodies are the ones who really deserve power. We are encouraged to ignore our body's perceptions of dis-ease resulting from abuse, especially at the workplace, and to deal with them through drugs that temporarily eradicate the symptoms of dysfunction. We learn to deny our bodily experiences, including our emotions, whether they be positive or negative. We eat adulterated food without nutritional value and ignore its side effects. Eventually this systematic attack creates an alienation that puts our body's function and its experiences beyond our conscious control. Our bodies, which are the vessel, the matrix of our aliveness, become complete strangers to us and seem to turn on us through illness, addictions to harmful amounts and kinds of foods and drugs, and through unexplained and seemingly perverted needs over which we have no control. We may come to feel that we are dead, or that everyone around us is dead, or that we deserve to die. We commit slow or sudden suicide.

Alienation from Our Hands, or from Our Work

People have a natural desire for and capacity to enjoy productive labor. The pleasures of productive activity are lost in two major ways. People are separated from the products of their labor when they are forced to work at a small, seemingly meaningless portion of the product that they are creating. In addition, many are separated from the value of the product that they are helping to create by those who employ them and who eventually profit disproportionately from their own participation in the product's creation. To add insult to injury, those profits are used to further separate the worker from their products and the means to produce them. This is done through strike breaking, automation, and the creation of multinational corporations that import and exploit third world labor and set worker against worker.

The result is a population-wide hatred of work, lack of productivity, job-related illness and accidents, and a loss of awareness of the joys of work that are people's birthright. Consequently, people resign themselves to being unhappy at work and seek pleasure through recreation, which has in itself been taken over by an exploitative industry. Our labor, or the creative and productive capacity of our hands, is lost to us, and we come to feel that we are unproductive, bored, without goals in life, lazy, and worthless failures.

These four forms of alienation account for most of the expressions of human unhappiness described in the psychiatric texts as "functional" psychopathology. Neurosis, addiction, depression, character disorders, anxiety disorders—a great number of psychoses are forms of alienation. Alienation, as described in the above examples, is always the result of some form of oppression or abuse, combined with a set of lies and mystifications that supposedly legitimize that abuse. Oppression and mystification combine with physical and personal isolation of people from each other to create alienation:

ALIENATION = OPPRESSION + MYSTIFICATION
+ ISOLATION

Oppression

The oppression that is a prime cause of alienation comes in the form of various systems that attack specific subgroups of people: the poor, workers, people of color, women, old people, children, gay people, fat people, short people, and so on. As a rule, oppression, and therefore alienation, is greatest for people who are most dispossessed.

Workers, more often than not, are oppressed by their employers. People of color are oppressed by white people. Women are taken advantage of by men. The rights of young and older people are usurped by and taken away by the middle-aged. The healthy and attractive dismiss the unhealthy and unattractive. We live in a society in which competition and the use of power are taught and valued as ideals. Most people automatically will take advantage of their positions of power, whether based on their wealth, their ownership of land or a business, or whether their power is based on their race, their gender, or their age. People almost unwittingly infringe on the rights of those who are less powerful, with full sanction of those around them.

Oppression is accomplished through a wide variety of manipulative power plays that are taught to people, ranging from the very crude, physical ones to the very subtle, psychological ones. Power play transactions are designed to cause people to do what they would not do of their free will. The study of power and power plays is an essential aspect of understanding oppression and alienation. Power plays can be detected, analyzed, and classified through the application of transactional analysis.

Mystification

The perpetration of abuse and oppression upon others is usually accompanied by some kind of explanation, which supposedly justifies it. Corporations explain the disproportion of their profit by pointing out that the corporation (or its owners) did, after all, invent the process or own the machinery or pay the overhead that is essential for the manufacture of their product and ignore the essential contribution to the process made by the workers. Rich people assert that everyone has equal opportunities in this land of plenty, so that those who don't succeed are responsible for their failures and overlook the advantages that they are privileged to. Landowners mystify peasants by claiming divine or private property rights to the land. White people claim that people of color are less intelligent, less creative, less productive, lazy, and slow, and thereby try to explain their own unequal access to privilege. Men justify their privilege over women with sexist arguments. Children are told that they are not complete human beings, and that they must obey grownups who know best. Old people are mystified with notions of aging and loss of vitality and productivity. Gay people are told they are depraved and sick. Single people are made to feel that their singlehood is neurotic. Each system of oppression has a set of mystifications that justify the power abuse perpetrated on its victims.

Eventually the oppressed actually come to believe the lies used to justify their oppression. When a person has incorporated in his or her own consciousness the arguments that explain and make legitimate his or her oppression, then mystification and alienation are complete. People will no longer rebel against abuse, but instead will blame themselves for their failure, accept it, and assume that they are the source and reason for their own unhappiness. In addition, they will apply their internalized oppression to everyone around them and enforce others' oppression along with their own.

This is where psychiatry has traditionally come into the picture: to reinforce the mystification that is the source of alienation. Again psychiatric attitudes in some parts of the world have improved; any person who holds him- or herself out as a psychiatrist or soul healer and is offered the power of giving counsel to an alienated person has one of two choices: (1) demystifying the real causes of alienation: sexism, racism, class prejudice, and all the other oppressive systems and institutions; or (2) reinforcing mystification of oppression and alienation by ignoring these oppressive influences and looking for the reasons of the alienation *within* the person, whether it be through Psychoanalysis, Transactional Analysis, Gestalt Therapy, Primal Therapy, or any other conventional system of psychotherapy when it is applied in this mystifying manner.

The portion of our mind that accepts the mystifications of our oppression is called, in Radical Psychiatry, the "Pig" or the "Enemy." The Enemy is like a prison warden who stands guard over our actions and feeds us messages to bolster and reinforce our alienation. The Enemy tells us that we are not okay: that we are bad, stupid, ugly, crazy, and sick and that we deserve, and are the cause of, our own unhappiness. The Enemy is an internal obstacle toward the achievement of people's power and the recapturing of our capacities to work, love, think, and be at home in our bodies. It is the internalization of oppression and its mystifications.

Isolation

Being isolated from, and unable to communicate with, each other is essential to alienation. By ourselves, without the aid of others who are in similar circumstances, we are powerless to think through our problems or do anything about them. It is part of the American Dream that people should achieve and do what they must do as individuals in isolation. Only those achievements that we can claim entirely for ourselves are thought of as being worthy. As a consequence, we erect barriers of competition, secrecy, and shame between each other. When we are together we do not trust each other, we do not share our thoughts and feelings with each other, and we go at the tasks of our lives as separate individuals, each one with separate projects, living quarters, transportation, and nuclear families. The cult of individualism is an important source of our isolation and alienation.

METHODOLOGY

The opposite of alienation is being powerful in the world. The task we as radical therapists set for ourselves is to aid people in reclaiming their alienated human powers. This is accomplished by fighting each element of alienation in turn. It is because of this that we say that *power* in the *world* equals *contact* to deal with *isolation, awareness* to deal with *mystification,* and *action* to deal with *oppression:*

POWER = CONTACT + AWARENESS + ACTION

Contact

To combat isolation it is necessary for people to join hands and gain the power of working together and supporting each other in their common goals through cooperation. The concept of cooperation is central to the methodology of Radical Psychiatry. We seek to establish cooperative relationships by establishing a cooperative contract with everyone we live or work with. The cooperative contract specifically defines a relationship in which everyone has equal rights and which is free of power plays in particular, lies and secrets, and Rescues.

By no lies or secrets we mean not only that we do not lie to each other by omission or by commission, but also that we do not keep hidden any of what we feel, or fail to ask for all of what we want. We share our feelings, our wishes, and our paranoid fantasies.

By not using power plays we mean that we do not coerce others into doing what they would not otherwise do.

By not Rescuing each other we mean that we do not give or do more than what is fair and that we do not do anything we don't want to do. Rescue is one of three alienated game roles that people alternate between. The three roles are Rescuer, Persecutor, and Victim, and by remaining in these three constricting roles people never deal with each other as equals in a spontaneous, intimate, or aware manner.

We pursue cooperation for what we need without being Victims, by helping others without being Rescuers, and by expressing our feelings of anger without being Persecutors.

Only when we work cooperatively in an organized, coherent effort is it possible for us to make true progress in the fight against alienation. No one person can accomplish power in the world as long as he or she stands by him- or herself, whether alone or in a crowd. That is why Radical Psychiatry focuses so intensely on group process.

The practice of Radical Psychiatry occurs primarily in three types of groups: problem-solving groups, bodywork groups, and mediations.

A problem-solving group is a group of seven or eight people, all of whom have an individual problem-solving contract and all of whom share a "cooperative contract" as defined above. The group works with a trained radical psychiatrist as a facilitator; additionally, there may be one or two observers in training. The group meets continuously weekly for two hours, and whenever a vacancy occurs it is filled with a new person.

A bodywork group is a group of five or more people, led by a radical psychiatrist trained in bodywork, who come together once or regularly on a weekly, every other week, or monthly basis for two or more hours with one assistant for every two or three people. Bodywork is designed to break down the person's alienation from the body and its feelings. This is accomplished through relaxation exercises, deep breathing, and other techniques designed to bring about emotional release and centering.

A mediation is a meeting of two or more people who have experienced conflict with each other in their working or personal relationships, and who come together with a trained radical psychiatry mediator to explore their difficulties and make agreements aimed at resolving their conflicts.

Awareness

The expansion of consciousness, especially one's understanding of the manner in which oppressive influences operate to diminish our power, is the essence of Awareness. Consciousness raising is the accumulation of information about the world and how it functions, and it is an important continuing task in expanding one's power in the world. Awareness of the function of class oppression, racism, sexism, ageism, heterosexism, coupleism, and so on is an essential aspect of consciousness raising.

Constructive criticism is a vital consciousness-raising technique. In the constructive criticism process, people will offer information to those who want to hear it concerning their behavior and how it affects others. In addition, a person may offer suggestions of how another person's behavior may be changed and corrected for the benefit of all. Constructive criticism is greatly aided by self-criticism and assumes willingness in all who participate to accept and learn from other people's critical analyses.

Action

Action is the process whereby our awareness of things that need to be changed is put into effect. Contact alone, or Contact and Awareness, can lead to strong, increased, subjective feelings of power. However, objective power in the world is different from subjective feelings of power and cannot result from Awareness or Contact alone. Awareness and Contact must be translated into some form of Action that changes the actual conditions in a person's life. Action implies risk, and when a person takes risks, he or she may need protection from the fears and actual dangers that can result from that action. Potent protection in the form of actual alliances for physical or moral support are needed in effective Action and are an essential aspect of Contact. Action, Awareness, and Contact together are the elements that make it possible for people to reclaim their birthright and become powerful in the world.

APPLICATIONS

Radical psychiatry problem groups have been attended by about a thousand people, between the ages of 16 and 70, almost exclusively white and of all social strata except the rich or very rich. This approach has been especially effective with problems of depression and the difficulties that people have in their relationships. People who have problems with alcoholism and drug abuse and those who have been psychotic have benefited from the method as well. On the other hand, Radical Psychiatry seems to have no particular effectiveness with problems of smoking and overeating. In the 30 years that Radical Psychiatry has been practiced, there have not been any cases of suicide or of a serious malpractice allegation or suit. On the other hand, the majority of the people who have worked in problem-solving groups and participated in mediations and bodywork seem to be pleased with the effects and recommend it highly to others. Because practitioners of Radical Psychiatry are politically aware and socially conscious people, the fees charged for problem-solving groups are modest and affordable by most. The majority of the people seeking help from Radical Psychiatry are referred by satisfied users of our services. We rarely have referrals from mental health professionals.

CASE HISTORY

Initially, John and Mary contacted me to do a mediation for their deteriorating marriage of seven years. I made sure that each one of them was interested in the mediation, by speaking to each of them separately. In this conversation I checked the reasons for their interest and asked them to think about any held resentments and paranoid fantasies that each one had for the other as well as any Rescues that they may have been engaged in. We met, and in the process of trading held resentments, paranoid fantasies, and Rescues it became clear that Mary resented how John reacted to her feelings of anger and hurt and that she had been having sex with him when she really didn't want to. She had a suspicion (or paranoia) that he was unfaithful to her; he confirmed that her suspicion had a grain of truth by acknowledging that he had seriously considered having an affair with a neighbor. On the other hand, John was hurt and angry about Mary's lack of desire for sex and felt victimized by her emotional outbursts. We then agreed on a contract for the mediation: we would establish agreements that would reestablish communication between them.

My initial observations of the couple were as follows: John and Mary have two children, 8 and 10. John, a probation officer, smokes, drinks, and eats too much, seems unhappy at home, shows Mary little affection, and is continually harassing her for sex. Mary works part time as a clerk, is depressed, cries a lot, feels guilty about yelling at her children and being "frigid," has trouble sleeping, and often thinks of suicide. She made one suicide attempt with sleeping pills but immediately called

Suicide Prevention afterward. John and Mary spend most of their time in a polite superficial harmony punctuated by violent arguments, which often end up with Mary crying hysterically and John leaving the house and returning drunk. Both of them are concerned and would like to change the situation. They feel that they still love each other, and both of them have tried various methods of psychotherapy including some marriage counseling.

During the initial part of the mediation I observed that John repeatedly interrupted Mary especially when she talks about her feelings and that Mary had outbursts of anger and crying that caused John to become afraid, cold, and parental. Only through strict control of their transactions was I able to prevent their discussion from continually escalating into outbursts, accusations, and subtle insults on both parts.

I explained that I thought the problem between them was that they were deeply immersed in a repetitive of interaction pattern in which John discounts Mary's feelings, tries to dominate her behavior, and is unwilling to react to her emotions with sympathy, and in which Mary terrorizes and tyrannizes John with outbursts, which she sees as the only way she can get the faintest resemblance of what she wants from John. I explained my belief that this behavior on both of their parts is founded on stereotyped sexist roles that cause John to avoid feeling and to abuse power to get what he wants from Mary, especially sex, while Mary finds herself unable to verbalize what she wants, ask for it, and take steps to get it. Instead, Mary adapts to and then lashes out at John with her emotions. I explained that her depression and wishes to commit suicide were probably the result of stroke deficit and that John's abuse of alcohol, cigarettes, and food were all attempts to improve his bodily experience, which was one of emptiness, loss, and fear. I explained how their relationship is a faithful reproduction of society's role expectations of people and how John's lack of feelings, sexual obsession, and substance abuse and Mary's lack of control over her feelings and her depression were all the result of the oppression of men and women. I recommended that Mary join a women's group and that John enter a mixed group with me.

Over the next year and a half John and Mary participated in problem-solving groups, and their situation was discussed at the radical psychiatry collective in which I and Mary's group leader participate. Mary learned how to get John to account for her feelings and how to speak clearly, how to ask for what she wanted, and how to implement her desires. She learned how to deal with John's interruptions, and she stopped adapting sexually. Her participation in the women's group gave her a sense of support and confidence that she was able to bring to the relationship and that gave her a sense of power so that she no longer allowed John to push her around. Soon she was no longer depressed or suicidal.

John slowly came to the realization that he was not able to adequately express his feelings, and that he abused her emotionally with his anger for her emotional outbursts and sexual denial. In bodywork he was able to contact some of his other emotions and to allow himself emotional release of sadness, fear, and joy. He developed a good level of emotional literacy, which made it possible for him to understand and respond to Mary's feelings as well as express his own in the relationship. He learned to stop interrupting and discounting, and he learned to stop imposing himself sexually on Mary. Instead he learned to accept her affection and return it and to wait patiently for her desire for sexual intercourse to develop, and to find satisfying alternatives to intercourse in the meanwhile. He made and kept a contract to stop drinking altogether, eventually stopped smoking, and is currently working on life changes including more physical exercise, a change of job, and a change of diet.

Separately, John and Mary have changed dramatically from how they were when they entered therapy. Their relationship has improved. They had spoken seriously about a separation and a possible divorce but are presently reasonably happy with each other. Mary has allowed John to express his desires for strokes from other women, but this is only in an experimental stage. Mary is fundamentally disinterested in a sexually open marriage at the time. At present they are both considering stopping therapy, as they both feel they have accomplished quite a bit for themselves even though the status of their relationship is still not clear.

Both of them seem happier, more hopeful, healthier, and more alive. They speak very highly of the process of problem-solving groups and have incorporated into their daily lives the principals and guidelines of cooperation, which they use in their relationships with each other, their children, and their friends. They no longer fight, and their relationship is cordial. Though they do not necessarily feel that they are going to remain an intimate couple for the rest of their lives, they love each other and know that they will remain friends and helpmates in raising their children.

SUMMARY

Radical Psychiatry is a theory of human emotional disturbance and a method designed to deal with it. The theory of Radical Psychiatry holds that people's problems are the result of oppressive influences and institutions that are mystified and with which the person colludes, thereby creating a state of alienation and powerlessness. The notion that emotional disturbance is externally caused is not new in psychiatry, but it is certainly not a popular one at this time and is not generally accepted by the psychiatric establishment. Yet many of Radical Psychiatry's precepts have been absorbed by the psychiatric culture across the country and abroad as a theory and practice. Radical Psychiatry is not only a system of psychotherapy; it is also a world view applicable to institutions and communities, and it represents and proposes a cooperative style of life. We feel it is conducive to well-being and power in the world.

REFERENCES

Berne, E. (1961). *Transactional analysis in psychotherapy.* New York: Grove Press.

Berne, E. (1976). *Beyond games and scripts.* New York: Grove Press.

Fanon, F. (1968). *The wretched of the earth.* New York: Grove Press.

Karpman, S. (1968). Script drama analysis. *Transactional Analysis Bulletin, 7,* 26–29.

Laing, R. D. (1967). *The politics of experience.* New York: Ballantine.

Laing, R. D. (1969). *The politics of the family and other essays.* New York: Pantheon.

Marcuse, H. (1962). *Eros and civilization.* New York: Vintage Books.

Marx, K. (1969). *Karl Marx, early writings.* New York: Ballantine.

Reich, W. (1961). *The function of the orgasm.* New York: Farrar, Strauss.

Steiner, C. (1974). *Scripts people live.* New York: Grove Press.

Steiner, C. (1975). *Readings in radical psychiatry.* New York: Grove Press.

Steiner, C. (1997). *Achieving Emotional Literacy.* New York: Avon Books.

Szasz, T. (1968). *Law, liberty and psychiatry.* New York: Collier.

Wolff, R. P., Barrington, M., & Marcuse, H. (1969). *A critique of pure tolerance.* Boston: Beacon Press.

Wyckoff, H. (1974). *Love, therapy and politics.* New York: Grove Press.

Wyckoff, H. (1981). *Solving problems together.* New York: Grove Press.

Chapter 56

REEVALUATION COUNSELING

GEORGE LOCKWOOD

When I first began planning this book, I wrote to my friend Albert Ellis, with whom I generally check out everything that has to do with psychotherapy, since he is probably the single most knowledgeable person I know of in this field. I asked him to tell me what were, in his opinion, the most important innovative systems. To my surprise, one of the systems he mentioned was Reevaluation Counseling, which I had heard of only vaguely.

When I investigated, I realized that this system had quietly spread and had generated a good deal of interest in various communities. Practically everyone I talked with had good things to say about Reevaluation Counseling. However, when I looked for someone to write about it, I ran up against a blank wall. Neither its founder and developer, Harvey Jackins, nor any other well-qualified person was available. And so I turned to my friend George Lockwood to see if he would investigate and report on this important system. In my judgment he has done an outstanding job in explaining this approach.

The reader should prepare to learn about something important and different in the field of psychotherapy.

Reevaluation Counseling, developed by Harvey Jackins in the 1950s, is a growing theory of human behavior and set of procedures for eliminating human irrationality. It views human beings as basically intelligent, happy, loving, and powerful. It assumes, however, that these qualities have, until now, for most people been largely obstructed by the harmful effects of distressing experiences that begin early in life. It is possible for this unfortunate result to be corrected by an inborn recovery mechanism that operates spontaneously under certain conditions in the aftermath of emotional or physical trauma. However, this innate curative capacity is usually blocked by social conditioning processes that encourage children to inhibit the discharge of emotions. The recovery mechanism can be liberated and the repressed intelligence, happiness, love, and power regained through the reestablishment of a special kind of relationship. This relationship can be unidirectional or, more advantageously, it can be a peer relationship that involves two people, each alternately taking on the role of a counselor who is caringly attentive toward the other. This attentiveness triggers a discharge of painful emotion and a subsequent reevaluation of the contents of past distressing experiences on the part of the individual acting as client.

HISTORY

Precursors

Early in the history of Reevaluation Counseling (RC), Jackins made a decision to avoid borrowing from previous theories and to make a fresh start. This was because he felt none of the existing approaches seemed to work well enough to warrant endorsement. RC theory developed, therefore, directly out of the firsthand experiences of Jackins and his associates. Once they had built up a sufficient base of successful practices, a theory was gradually constructed to explain the results. Jackins claims that this process was rigorously scientific and empirical in the sense that no conclusions were accepted unless supported by actual observations and behavioral data. Subjective "studies" and opinions of people based on past experience are said to have been avoided. Development progressed in this inductive fashion until the early 1960s, at which point a parallel structure was created based on deductive logic. This structure consisted of 24 postulates whose intent was to assure logical consistency among the conclusions arrived at earlier, as well as to clarify the basic set of assumptions upon which RC theory was based. In addition, the postulates served as a new source of theorems. Hypotheses derived from and consistent with them were deduced and then checked against reality. As this deductive structure grew, RC practitioners continued to work inductively. Insights arising out of practice and supported by empirical evidence were formulated so as to be consistent with the deductive structure. The two systems worked in a complementary fashion, one ensuring logical consistency and the other guaranteeing empirical validity.

Throughout the development of RC, Jackins has been hostile toward eclectic practices in which well-meaning individuals have attempted to mix RC with other approaches. Even though there may be superficial similarities, Jackins maintains that RC works from an entirely unique set of assumptions. Randomly incorporating such theories and practices without checking to be sure their assumptive base is consistent with RC leads to internal contradictions, which in turn may generate harmful results. Eclecticism is also seen as interfering with the generalizability of outcome. The criterion for selection of a given practice is often based simply on its having worked at one time in a specific setting for a certain group. RC, on the other hand, attempts to develop an approach that works consistently for all people.

Beginnings

After receiving a bachelor of arts degree in mathematics, Jackins spent a number of years as a labor organizer. During this period he was active politically and became known as a poet and inventor.

In the early 1950s accidental circumstances confronted him with the problem of distressed human behavior. Jackins had a friend whose business partner, unbeknownst to Jackins, had been under psychiatric care for months and had deteriorated to the point where he had been consigned to a state institution for life. Jackins's friend asked him to rescue his partner before the authorities arrived. Jackins took the man to his home and, in an effort to interrupt his wild behavior, began to ask him questions. The man began to cry. At first Jackins attempted to get him to stop but, after many attempts to question him always brought tears, he decided that perhaps the man needed to cry. The man cried for many hours as Jackins listened and encouraged him. After two days of this, there was a noticeable improvement in rationality and competence. This improvement continued through a week of crying. Many hours of shaking followed the tears. At the end of two weeks the man was back at work, functioning well, and thinking clearly.

Jackins found the results so startling he tried to duplicate them with others. He experienced enough success within a few months to attempt a generalized explanation. He concluded that humans became less disturbed when they were allowed to discharge accumulated distress. There was no need for interpreting, analyzing, or other such authoritarian tactics. Given the right conditions the mind seemed to have a capacity to heal itself. Apparently all the helper needed to do was pay warm attention in a way that facilitated the individual's discharge; the rest was a spontaneous process.

This seemingly natural capacity for recovering intelligent functioning, capacity for love, and zestful enjoyment of life caused Jackins to hypothesize that these may actually be people's true natures and that only through emotional and physical hurts are they obscured. Environmental factors became the assumed cause of all human dysfunction.

Crucial in the early development of RC was the implementation of what is termed co-counseling. Jackins found that over a period of time counselors would fail to gain in effectiveness unless their own levels of distress were lowered. In addition, they became eager to obtain the results observed in their clients. Their effectiveness was increased and the desired results obtained by having counselor and client regularly reverse roles. This peer or co-counseling relationship proved so effective it has become the main mode of RC.

RC achieved an encouraging degree of success with its permissive approach, yet certain patterns of distress (distress patterns are viewed as the unfortunate results of hurtful experiences responsible for rigid and compulsive behavior) seemed to persist. The underlying difficulty was clarified sometime in 1955 when the difference between chronic and latent distress patterns was first noticed. Latent patterns were triggered in certain settings, while chronic patterns seemed to be engaged continuously, permeating all behavior. In the case of chronic patterns, Jackins found it necessary to go beyond the permissive approach to become much more active and directive.

CURRENT STATUS

In 1952, a research and development organization called Personal Counselors, Inc. was founded in Seattle for the purpose of permitting full-time exploration of Reevaluation Counseling as well as providing teaching and counseling services. For about 20 years it was the main vehicle for the development of RC theory and practice. During this period many series of RC classes were taught to the public in an attempt to train people to become co-counselors. From the students in these classes eventually developed what are now called "RC Communities." These communities are currently established in 28 countries and are distributed widely throughout the U.S. and Canada.

Membership continues to climb. In recent years considerable numbers of clinical psychologists, psychiatrists, and other professional mental health workers have been among the new participants. New members come primarily from Fundamentals Co-Counseling Classes, in which the elementary theory and techniques of RC are taught through 16 weeks of weekly two and one-half hour meetings. Admission to the classes is selective— only those who can be expected to become proficient counselors in a relatively short period are accepted. In some communities, Fundamentals Classes are attended indefinitely and serve as a continued source of theoretical and practical development. Other communities offer advanced classes beyond the Fundamentals Class to serve this function.

The entire network of RC communities is led by an International Reference Person. An Area Reference Person is chosen for each locality and is in charge of its development as well as making decisions regarding policy. There is a Reference Person leading international liberation efforts for each of the following groups as well: Blacks, Asians, Latinos, young persons, elders, Jews, women, physically different, Gays, Native Americans, and the working class. In addition, there are international reference persons for areas of special interest, such as for educational change, university and college faculty, and men.

Rational Island Publishers, the publishing firm of RC, has produced a variety of books, pamphlets, videotapes, and audio cassettes on the theory and practice of RC. Publication began with several forerunners of what is now entitled the *Fundamentals of Co-Counseling Manual* (Jackins, 1962). This contains a description of elementary counseling techniques used in beginning classes. *The Human Side of Human Beings* (Jackins, 1965) was written shortly afterward, and provides a succinct introduction to RC. A collection of essays and articles on RC appearing between 1962 and 1973 appear in *The Human Situation* (Jackins, 1973) and, together with the two publications mentioned above, round out the basic theoretical knowledge necessary to become a functioning member of an RC community. Important theoretical developments that appeared between 1973 and early 1977 are contained in *The Upward Trend* (Jackins, 1978). In addition, separate RC journals and periodicals are published for the following populations: scientists, teachers, college and university workers, teachers of RC, those in health work, wage workers, young RCers, Jews, Asians, Blacks, parents, the handicapped, elders, Native Americans, men, Latinos, priests and nuns, Gays, mental health workers, women, and those interested in social change. Important means of communicating recent developments in theory have been the journals *Present Times,* a quarterly publication read by most all community members, and the *Reevaluation Counseling Teacher,* geared toward those teaching RC classes.

Books, journals, and related materials may be purchased through an RC teacher or may be ordered directly from Rational Island Publishers in Seattle. Theoretical and practical knowledge of RC, outside of beginning classes, is generally spread by means of one-to-one communication. Someone who is experienced discusses it with or offers a session to an interested individual. Sole reliance on written communication is discouraged, because Jackins has found that all too often the message is unwittingly distorted by the receiver. One-to-one communication seems to afford a personal touch that cuts through much of the potential distortion and enables the remaining false conceptions to be cleared up quickly.[1] Theoretical and practical knowledge is also imparted through RC workshops.

Similarities between RC and other approaches to counseling and psychotherapy have been discussed by Somers (1972). Among the approaches dealt with are Psychoanalysis, Gestalt Therapy, Existential Therapy, learning theory, and behavioral therapies. Schiff (1972) has discussed some of the social implications of RC. In particular, he notes that the current problems arising out of dependence on professional experts for psychotherapy, such as high cost and limited accessibility, could be circumvented since RC trains lay people to provide help for one another.

Experimentation in RC has primarily taken the form of action research. RC is characterized by its practicality and direct relevance to the counseling situation as well as its flexibility. Few of the studies have as yet been formally recorded. Furthermore, little in the way of true experimental research has been done since on-the-spot innovations have been favored over rigid controls.

THEORY

Human Nature

Basic to Reevaluation Counseling theory is its definition of human intelligence, which is seen as the ability to create, on the spot, new and rational responses that meet exactly the demands of each situation encountered (Jackins, 1965). This ability is assumed to be the trait that distinguishes humans from all other animals. When a new situation is encountered, the incoming information is compared to the existing store. Memories of successful responses in similar contexts are recalled and modifications are made to allow for differences. These elements are then used to construct the new response. Concomitantly, an evaluation process goes on during which incoming information, including feedback from the results

---

[1] It was partly for these reasons that Jackins refused to write this chapter and hoped I would refrain from doing so as well. In addition, he objects to RC being bracketed with schools of psychotherapy or human growth movements, believing strongly that it is distinctly different from any of these.

of the new response, is broken down into usable bits, categorized, and then filed away in the memory bank to be used in the generation of future responses.

RC makes a number of other assumptions about human nature. It maintains that people are born with a far greater capacity for intelligent behavior than anyone currently demonstrates. RC assumes that individuals considered to be geniuses have simply managed to avoid the damaging circumstances that have obstructed this capacity in others. RC also asserts that successful people innately take a keen pleasure in living and view life, with all its uncertainties and problems, as an exciting and challenging process rather than an anxiety-ridden or depressing struggle. Furthermore, it holds that humans have an inborn desire to cooperate as well as to love and be loved. Thus, conflicts of interest are not seen as inevitable, but rather as events that could be entirely eliminated if people were free to live according to their true nature. Any deviation from this rational, happy, cooperative, and loving mode of functioning is viewed as a distortion of human nature and the result of some harmful experience.

At the core of Reevaluation Counseling's theory and practice is the distinction made by the above set of assumptions between people's intelligent or rational essence and irrational aspects added to it. This distinction rests upon the posited criterion for rational behavior—*flexibility*. Rational behavior is typified by its responsiveness to the environment. It is continually changing and adapting to fit the subtle nuances of each new situation that arises.

Human Dysfunction

Irrational responses seem to be most reliably characterized by their rigid, preset character. A behavior is irrational when it is repeated over and over in the same manner regardless of changes that arise in the environment and regardless of unfortunate results that may ensue. Jackins noted that an activity taking place unawarely is not necessarily indicative of irrationality. A great deal of rational behavior takes place at an unaware level.

RC theory asserts the sole cause of human dysfunction to be the residual rigidity left by an experience of physical or emotional distress generated by a traumatic event. During such times one's ability to think rationally is suspended and incoming information, which is usually analyzed and filed away, remains unevaluated. It becomes lodged in the mind as an undigested mass consisting of a complete literal recording of everything that occurred during the distressing episode. This literal recording is termed a "distress pattern." When part of this pattern is referred to, the entire unit is recalled, and this in turn generates a fixed, predetermined pattern of behavior. Because of this all-or-none process, there is no

way for a relevant bit of information to be combined with others to form an entirely new response. The net result is an overall decrease in intelligence and a predisposition to function inappropriately in certain settings.

This unevaluated or mis-stored unit of information generates rigid behavior whenever a new situation is met that is similar enough to the distressing episode to trigger its recall. Once triggered, it is as if one is compulsively forced to reenact the original experience. A destructive cycle is established because the information from the second situation also goes unevaluated, enlarges the distress pattern, and consequently leaves the individual predisposed to acting even more irrationally in the future.

When a particular set of mis-stored information is restimulated enough times, it becomes chronic and tends to fade from conscious awareness. Chronic distress patterns result in fixed attitudes and emotional tones and become manifest in such features as bodily tensions, tone of voice, posture, or facial expressions. The bulk of the irrational forces that impinge on people are said to be due to these chronic patterns.

The chronic patterns are carefully distinguished from latent patterns, which become evident only under certain conditions. For instance, an individual may exhibit compulsive anger only when confronted with inefficiency in others. On the other hand, an individual may seem to hold a grudge against the world, as would be the case for a person exhibiting a chronic pattern associated with anger. Even though similar in origin and effect, the overcoming of chronic patterns requires a great deal more initiative, skill, and persistence on the part of the counselor.

The loss of human potential due to this repression of flexible intelligence is extensive. Jackins believes that most adults judged "successful" by current cultural standards seldom operate at better than about 10 percent of their inherent capacity for intelligent joyful living. In other words, he believes that about 90 percent of such people's behavior is tied up in nonadaptive patterns of thinking, feeling, and responding. RC theory does not view this as a permanent loss. Flexible intelligence is said to simply retreat and lie dormant in a perfectly preserved state ready to be actualized under more favorable conditions.

As stated earlier, all distress experiences are seen as resulting from some unfavorable aspect of the environment. Society serves as a source of much trauma through irrational practices such as exploitation, prejudice, and war. However, the most significant factor in the transmission of human disturbance is asserted to be the distress well-meaning parents beset upon their children. Healthy behavior on the part of the infant may trigger a distress pattern in the adult, which in turn serves as a source of distress for the child. The human infant is particularly vulnerable to this insult due to a lack of physical and cognitive development and a prolonged dependency upon adults. In addition, dysfunction produced in this way is perpetuated by a social conditioning process in which individuals learn to avoid the discharge necessary for its removal. For instance, children are taught to choke back emotions and to alternatively act "brave" or "grown up." Physical or even chemical force may be resorted to as children are beaten or given drugs to "calm them down."

Recovery

Perhaps the most significant assertion of RC theory is that humans have an inborn capacity to recover their occluded intelligence. This process is available immediately upon the termination of trauma or injury and automatically leads to a complete retrieval if allowed to operate.

Recovery consists of two major processes termed "discharge" and "reevaluation." Discharge consists of a release of tension, characterized by a series of emotions that proceed in a specified order beginning with what is viewed as the most severe of all emotions— grief. The discharge of grief is evidenced by tears and sobbing. After repeated release such discharge will eventually give way to the trembling, shivering, and cold perspiration that typify the release of fear. Intense laughter will follow, and is considered to be a lighter type of fear discharge. The expression of anger then comes to the fore as loud words or sounds, violent movements, and then laughter are exhibited. Following this, reluctant and then interested talking are engaged in to release the painful emotions associated with boredom (Jackins, 1962). Throughout the process of discharge a spontaneous recall and review of mis-stored information takes place. The individual may or may not be aware of this.

Physical hurts are also believed to involve a storing up of tension that seeks discharge. The tension associated with physical discomfort, however, is assumed usually to be surrounded by emotional distress that must be let go of before the underlying physical discomfort is available for release. Discharge of physical distress is outwardly manifested by yawning and sometimes stretching and scratching.

Jackins asserts that a great deal of firsthand experience with RC shows that this exact series of discharges occurs for virtually all humans, with possible exceptions being when the order is obscured or a certain means of release is blocked through conditioned resistance to a particular form of discharge.

During and following discharge an automatic rational evaluation of mis-stored information takes place. This reevaluation entails an analysis of distressing material from a logico-empirical vantage point. As analysis

progresses the mass of unevaluated information is broken into usable bits, categorized, and stored away to be utilized in the creation of rational behavior. Jackins maintains that the degree to which distress patterns can be reevaluated in this manner is directly dependent upon the degree to which the preceding discharge process has been completed.

As a whole, the recovery process can be seen essentially as one of attaining a more and more accurate picture of reality as distorted notions are reevaluated and irrational beliefs given up. With a clearer view of reality it is assumed that one will become more consistently zestful, loving, and intelligent.

Necessary Conditions for Recovery

The necessary and sufficient condition for the initiation of the recovery process is said to be "the division of the client's free attention approximately equally between the distress on which discharge is being sought and material contradictory to the distress" (Jackins, 1973). Throughout both discharge and reevaluation, the mere presence of an attentive counselor is often a significant factor serving to contradict the distress pattern. The effectiveness of the counselor's presence can be enhanced if he or she expresses caring for and validation of the client. This attitude is achieved to the extent that the counselor has discharged his or her own distress, has assimilated RC theory, and has made a decision to wholeheartedly commit him- or herself to the client's reemergence.

RC emphasizes that the attention given by a counselor should establish a special type of relationship. When counselors present themselves as authorities and attempt to analyze, understand, and in other ways do the client's thinking for them, this interferes with the process of recovery. The recovery process must involve a relationship between peers—in which the client is essentially self-directing and has as full a possession of the theory as possible. Such a peer relationship is fostered by the co-counseling mode of RC in which counselor and client regularly reverse roles.

Additional elements are added to the relationship as the counselor begins to confront the client's chronic patterns. He or she becomes more active in identifying problem areas and helping the client achieve a direction of thought and action that will lead to discharge. Jackins discovered that such a direction needs to contradict exactly the contents of the chronic pattern and to be maintained vigilantly both in and out of sessions if the pattern is eventually to lose its grip.

RC contends that basing all of one's actions on reason rather than emotion is another necessary condition for overcoming the influences of past afflictions. That is particularly evident in the case of chronic patterns that, if one is to successfully overcome them, require the experiencing of much discomfort and a sense of continually going against the addictive pull of distress.

METHODOLOGY

The foundation upon which all Reevaluation Counseling methodology is built is the caring and interested attention of the counselor. It is said to make up about 90 percent of good counseling and is transmitted first of all by listening well. This in itself is often enough to produce significant gains in rationality. Asking questions is the second primary mode of paying attention. It is not done for the usual purpose of gathering data but to assure the client of the counselor's interest and to guide his or her awareness back to the appropriate balance between the distress pattern and material contradictory to that pattern.

The techniques discussed below describe the practice of RC in only the most general way. The real essence of its methodology lies in creating, on the spot, a specific technique for each moment with a given client. While the theory and general guidelines for technique are important, they are no substitute for the continual vigilance required to treat each client and moment as totally unique entities.

Spectrum of Techniques

An ever-present danger to the counseling process involves the restimulation of a pattern so significant that it engulfs all the client's free attention, leaving none available to observe the painful material from a secure and objective framework. Even though the client often appears outwardly calm at such a time, no further progress is possible. This danger is avoided by working within what is referred to as a spectrum of techniques. One begins at the end of the spectrum, using methods that demand very little of the client's free attention, and works toward techniques that demand progressively more. If overstimulation seems imminent one retreats to the previously effective method.

One of the first methods in the spectrum involves guiding the client's awareness to various aspects of the environment. It is believed that attention freed up in this way becomes available for rational thought, with a resultant increase in the client's well-being. Next in the hierarchy are a series of remembering techniques also geared toward lighter material. The client is initially asked to recall successful or pleasant memories. He or she is then asked to move quickly through a series of types beginning with ordinary memories and continuing on to those of rational activity and then back to those of successes or pleasant experiences. This change in topics is suggested to avoid too much free attention from being soaked up by deeply distressing events that may be recalled. As more and more free attention is accumulated, the counselor moves on to a procedure in which the client is asked to randomly recall mildly upsetting events in a rapid fashion. This process prompts further releases of tension. When a sufficient accumulation of free attention is gained, it is possible to move on to a technique in which the client is asked to recall the earliest memory of a specific type and to progressively recall later ones of similar content up until the present. This process is repeated many times, during which time the client adds additional experiences to the list as he or she remembers them. A point will be reached when it may prove difficult for the client to remember the series of experiences any longer due to the discharge and reevaluation taking place and progressively freeing the memories from the grips of a particular distress pattern.

Some memories, rather than fading, become more and more vivid. These experiences involve a great deal of tension and necessitate the use of thorough discharge techniques that differ from the above in that discharge usually involves greater amounts of painful emotion and is persisted in for longer periods. To accomplish this, the counselor waits for clues from the client that indicate whether or not emotionally charged material is being discussed. The client's attention is then redirected to this point and discharge is encouraged. Encouragement may be provided simply through the counselor's aware attention and a warm direct gaze, or by holding the client's hands in a warm and relaxed manner. After a time the client's attention will tend to stray. It is up to the counselor to persistently bring it back to the particular thought or phrase that prompts release until no more discharge is left.

A client may compulsively, but unintentionally, block discharge from occurring. These blocks are referred to as *control patterns* and consist, in part, of observable behavior at the time of resistance. Since such blocks are employed in a repetitive and fixed way, one means of breaking through them is to ask the client to act in a manner that interferes with the patterned aspects of their behavior. For instance, if a client is slumped low in a chair and exhibits a deep frown indicative of a depressive control pattern, one might ask him or her to sit upright and look as if he or she were enthusiastic about life. As he or she discusses the experience of doing this, discharge is likely to follow.

The techniques described so far have been those useful in overcoming latent distress patterns, with the counselor guiding part of the client's attention to the distressing material. Chronically restimulated patterns require the counselor to direct enough attention away from such material for the client to establish a rational and secure vantage point from which to work. In addition, chronic patterns necessitate going beyond the permissive methods described above and becoming a good deal more active and directive.

When a pattern becomes chronic an individual may no longer see it as a problem or as an entity separate from him- or herself. Consequently, the counselor needs to take an active role in watching for and identifying them as foreign elements. Identification is accomplished by noticing rigidities such as a monotone voice or fixed facial expression. The next task for the counselor is to develop a counterdirection—a way in which the client can challenge and contradict the pattern at all times. For instance, countering a chronic depressive pattern might involve one forcing the client to become more active, speak in more positive terms, and challenge the negative thoughts that arise. Once such a course of action is established and the counselor is able to get the client to commit him- or herself to it, it must still be implemented.

The chronic pattern persistently pushes the client to forget the proper course of action or creates confusion. Such hindrances derive from the chronic pattern's tendency to soak up the client's free attention and leave none with which to obtain an objective vantage point. The counter to this force, and part of all counterdirections, is an effort to think rationally at all times. The role of the counselor during this phase is to join the client in ruthlessly attacking the pattern while at the same time providing him or her with love and support. The client needs to be reminded often of the direction against the pattern. Special aids may be used, such as written reminders or publicly announcing the chosen course of action. To further counter the pattern's tendency to cause confusion and forgetting, the client is encouraged to draw up a set of clearly spelled-out goals. These goals are designed to guide a course of action affecting all levels (self, family, mankind, etc.) and are both immediate and long-range.

Among the many possible counterdirections are several that have proven to be close to universal directions for countering all patterns of distress. One involves a process of unconditional self-validation. This direction is particularly effective in the battle against a chronic pattern's ability to confuse and distort because it is clearly defined, well mapped out, and can be understood logically prior to a commitment to it. The distinction between the person, wholesome and good in every respect, and the pattern parasitic upon that person clarifies that the real person behind the smokescreen of irrationality is unreproachable.

The details of this ameliorative procedure involve the client expressing unlimited self-approval in word, tone of voice, posture, and facial expression to him- or herself and others. Doubts as to the validity of the statements are inevitably triggered, at which point the client is encouraged to persist in spite of his or her feelings. When actual self-invalidating thoughts are encountered, the client is to force him- or herself to examine them and contradict them aloud. This in itself may effectively challenge the validity of the negative thought; however, the client usually needs to continue on to compute the exact opposite of the statement. For instance, an individual might catch him- or herself thinking he or she is hopelessly slow and inefficient. This thought would then be turned around by declaring oneself to be remarkably efficient and quick. Discharge frequently follows such declarations.

Whether working against a chronic or a latent pattern, the key danger for client as well as counselor is suspension of critical thought. Once thinking stops, RC assumes one is likely to succumb to old patterns. Maintaining the required critical thought demands continual vigilance and the tolerance of much discomfort. Jackins notes, however, that there is satisfaction despite the discomfort in knowing one is approaching a highly valued goal.

The primary method for relieving physical distress is to focus efforts upon discharging the associated emotional tension. Guiding the client's attention directly to the somatic pain is to be avoided, since it may simply increase it. A complete release of emotion will automatically lead to the yawning indicative of physical discharge, at which point the counselor should continue to direct the client's attention to the thought or phrase that triggered the yawning, perhaps for hours, until it has been persisted with as long as possible.

RC makes use of group counseling as an adjunct to co-counseling. Groups function by giving each member an equal amount of time in front of the rest to do whatever brings emotional release. Discharge and reevaluation is accelerated in this context, possibly because the effectiveness of the attention of each member combines with others in an additive fashion.

Co-counseling classes are an integral part of the RC approach as well. Through regular attendance, co-counseling pairs are able to sustain a high level of motivation and an effective direction. Without it, perspective is often lost and distress patterns begin to form the basis for decisions, leading counselor and client into a dead end. It has also been found that these classes, and in turn individual co-counseling sessions, are enhanced when they exist within a strong local RC community organization. The community setting within which RC operates has proven to be an important aspect of its method.

APPLICATIONS

It is the long-range objective of Reevaluation Counseling to reach everyone, including the most distressed individuals. At present, however, resources are insufficient to deal with severe disorders. In an effort to establish the necessary assets, RC communities are limiting membership to those who can become effective co-counselors with a relatively small investment of time and energy. Within this limitation, the effectiveness of RC has transcended national and cultural boundaries.

RC has found an important application in assisting individuals in their fight against social oppression. It does so by helping them emerge from rigid ways of responding and thereby become more effective in their struggle. Jackins was first led to his support of liberation groups when he realized that release from the harmful effects of one's past was not enough. It became clear to him that so much distress was being acquired anew each day due to the irrational ways of society that these forces would have to be faced as well.

The first major inroad for an application of RC principles in this area came when Jackins discovered that the maintenance of all oppression seemed to be rooted in one particular distress pattern. He said its content consists of the view that "situations which oppress us are beyond our powers to change and . . . we must 'adjust' to them" (Jackins, 1978, p. 25). This belief is said to obscure people's natural inclination to take the initiative and seek solutions to life's difficulties. With the discovery of this view, it became clear to Jackins that the route to liberation from socially oppressive forces was through individual liberation from patterned helplessness.

RC theory and techniques have also been successfully applied to the classroom learning situation. Along with assuming a vast untapped amount of intelligence, RC posits an inborn thirst for learning that is also blocked by environmental distress. In most classrooms these qualities remain obscured because no provision is made for discharge. Students arrive in a depressed, anxious, or hostile state and often remain this way with little free attention left to digest new information. Worse yet, many teachers place new distresses upon those already present by failing to recognize the difference between the student, with his or her natural desire to learn, and the pattern that throws up a resistance. Consequently, the externally visible pattern is met with attempts to manipulate and control, while the real student behind them goes unnoticed.

According to RC, the key job of the teacher is to get students to the point where they are relaxed and feeling good. It is believed that this can only be accomplished through effective use of the discharge and reevaluation process. It should be noted that a severely distressed student cannot be handled in the classroom. However, if time is set aside for those who can, students spontaneously will begin to seek out new information.

A good deal can be accomplished in terms of promoting the necessary affect during the learning process itself. For instance, chronic feelings of loneliness can be disputed through a teacher's warm touch and caring gaze. Common sources of distress, such as invalidation, can be avoided by making students feel loved for who they are and by drawing them out on their strong points rather than instructing through criticism. Furthermore, it is recommended that grading systems be significantly revised or, better yet, entirely done away with. Grades are viewed merely as additional sources of invalidation. The message of grades to those who don't excel is that they are defective in some way. Low grades also imply that their recipients are responsible and therefore blameworthy for their shortcomings. RC asserts that motivating students through such a system of honors and demerits is unnecessary since more than enough inducement is provided by the learning situation itself.

Education can be further expedited by having learners teach learners. Just as counseling works best when there is a relationship between peers, learning seems to thrive in a similar context.

RC is also involved in the area of relationship counseling. Initially progress is more difficult with this application due to the complexity of the interaction that may develop. Instead of one distress pattern, there are now two or more to keep track of, which at times set one another off, creating a chain reaction that is difficult to diffuse. It is frequently necessary to employ a neutral party, acting as a buffer against such mutual restimulation. This can be accomplished by enforcing certain rules, such as having participants direct potentially restimulative comments to this neutral person, or by obtaining a commitment from each to hear the partner out. The use of a neutral party is viewed as a temporary phase to be ended as soon as the participants have discharged enough to successfully avoid mutual restimulation in the future. At this point the regular rules of co-counseling are followed. Marital partners who have learned to co-counsel effectively in this manner can begin to include their children. Small group sessions in which members express unlimited appreciation of one another are often effective in this situation.

A further application of RC can be made in relation to chemical dependency. RC assumes the roots of such dependency to be no different from those of any other form of rigid and compulsive behavior. During ingestion of the chemical the body is hurt. As with experiences of emotional trauma, the information coming in at the time remains unevaluated and is stored as a complete literal recording of everything that went on at the time. This recording of distress compels an individual to reenact the distress experience when stimulated by circumstances similar to the original hurtful situation. In this way, the alcoholic or the heroin addict is compulsively forced to continue intake of such substances.

What leads those dependent upon chemicals to begin ingestion in the first place is the same factor that leads to addictions unrelated to chemicals, such as compulsive procrastination or aggressive outbursts. In response to the pain of successive restimulation of distress patterns, one is pushed to seek out anything that can provide an immediate deadening of the painful feelings, regardless of the long-term consequences. Chemicals often provide such a short-term "escape" along with the damage they instill. Since chemical dependency both arises from and is maintained by processes similar to those involved with other types of dysfunction, their treatment is handled in similar ways.

Jackins also discovered that RC may be utilized as a type of first aid for physical injuries. Typically any somatic disturbance acquires a shell of emotional tension that must be discarded prior to the commencement of any physical discharge. This, however, is not the case for a certain period shortly after an injury has been received. Apparently it takes some time for a layer of emotional distress to form. Before this occurs it is possible to focus attention directly on the physical discomfort as well as a review of the actual circumstances of the injury and thereby initiate discharge. If one refocuses upon this material a sufficient number of times and experiences it fully enough, there ensues a total and permanent elimination of pain as well as a hastening of the healing process (Jackins, 1962).

CASE EXAMPLE

The following case history is adapted from a firsthand report. Identifying data are altered.

The client (C) was a young woman whose father (F) had been hospitalized repeatedly for manic depression and for attempted suicide over a period of 13 years. F was first hospitalized when C was seven years of age. At this time C began to feel guilty for not having prevented his "illness." In addition, she grew to hate her father and eventually lost all respect for him. C became increasingly inhibited in her self-expression for fear of releasing painful emotions that had welled up inside. She suspected that if she did so she, too, would be labeled crazy.

When first exposed to Reevaluation Counseling's optimistic view of human nature, C became hopeful of being freed from some of her pain by acquiring a new, more rational view of her father and of her past experiences with him. She started co-counseling and for the first time began to express a great deal of anger and grief over her father's condition. As this process continued she began sharing experiences about F with old friends, which she had previously been afraid to do.

Counseling eventually led to a clarification of a chronic pattern whose content generated in C a sense of powerlessness. Even though she had opened up a great deal, she was continuously worried that at some point her discharges would be so heavy she would be labeled as too "sick" to remain in the RC community. As more and more of her intellect became free for rational thought, C began to understand the roots of this chronic fear and its relationship to her complete rejection of her father. She came to see that her fear of being labeled crazy came out of a reaction to culturally oppressive forces that tend to leave people feeling hopelessly stuck as "sick" individuals once labeled as such. This fear also led her, in an effort to affirm her sanity to herself and others, to maintain a view of her father as a destroyed person.

Through RC group counseling she encountered others who had experienced the "mental breakdown" of a parent and consequently became less ashamed of it and increasingly willing to face the associated distress and to share it with others. During one of these sessions a counterdirection was discovered through which she could contradict her view of her father as a sick man as well as her fear of complete disclosure. It involved validating and accepting so-called "sick" individuals in thought and action and working to view them as essentially good and wholesome humans who have been victimized by deeply distressing experiences.

Shortly after committing to this direction, the client received word that her father had become disruptive in his current place of residence and was being asked to move. This meant a possible return to the hospital and restimulated in C fears of another suicide attempt by F. Furthermore, she desired to be close and at the same time feared being drawn into F's irrationality. With her co-counselor she was able to discharge some of her fear of his failing again, and to plan for an effective means of being supportive of F, while maintaining the previously committed to direction. This meant that C would have to continually look for and validate the real father that lay behind the patterns. Rather than criticize, she would need to draw him out on his strengths as well as act against her desire to take responsibility for his well-being, since this too was seen as a form of invalidation by reinforcing a belief in his inadequacy.

C's counselor decided to offer additional support by going along during her first visit with F. During this meeting the counselor's insights and comments at times disrupted C's tendency to do too much for her father and at other times validated the way in which C was supporting and appreciating her father. Through this process the client came to see her father in a new light. She noticed his genuine interest in people and the environment, how well he had done in managing to survive and get support, and came to believe more in his capacity to free himself from his distress. F, in turn, began to feel safe enough to disclose facts about himself he had not mentioned to his daughter before.

With the support of his daughter, F has managed to avoid rehospitalization and is now living on his own and caring for himself. In the meantime, C has continued to distinguish person from pattern and keep the father she loves in sight. As a result she has been able to maintain an unconditional acceptance of F and his life style; this in turn has left her feeling more accepting of herself. In addition, C has since become socially active in combating oppressive forces associated with mental illness.

SUMMARY

Jackins maintains that Reevaluation Counseling theory is a scientifically rigorous system. It grew inductively, with conclusions being drawn only from the results of firsthand experience. In addition, a deductive structure was developed to ensure logical consistency among the basic assumptions of RC. It takes a dim view of eclecticism through which individuals often gather techniques and theorems without regard for logical consistency, firm empirical checks, and subsequent generalizability. RC is not interested in developing a theory and practice that works for a certain subset of the population. RC is attempting to develop an approach that will be effective with all humans, in all situations, at all times.

One of RC's most important assumptions involves its view of human nature. People are said to be born with vast amounts of intelligence, a feeling of zest, and a desire to love and be loved. Dysfunction is not seen as a bad side, but rather as a foreign element parasitic upon an essentially wholesome being. This foreign element is different in origin and nature from all human qualities. It originates from experiences of emotional or physical hurt that cause the information being received at the time to be deposited in the form of a rigid pattern. The nature of all emotional dysfunction, of every type and degree, consists essentially of the effect produced when one is compulsively forced to meet a new situation with fixed and compulsive behavior generated by this rigid pattern of information. A compulsive reenactment occurs when a new situation is encountered similar to the original one.

RC also maintains that people do not have to turn to "authorities" for cures or answers. The processes necessary for recovery are all part of their innate makeup. The only place for outside assistance is in setting up the proper conditions so that curative powers can spontaneously take over in the form of discharge and reevaluation. The client remains in full control of the process, doing his own thinking and arriving at his own solutions. The counselor relates to the client as a peer. The counselor may be directive only in relation to the dysfunctional entities, never toward the person behind them.

By viewing all forms of irrationality as foreign to human nature and having definite causes and cures, one is led to another important assumption in RC. Dysfunction, in any form or degree, is not something people must learn to accept as part of life. It is believed that such misfortune can be completely and permanently overcome.

RC is distinct in the range of responsibilities it has taken on. Involvement is not limited to personal liberation, and fundamental changes needed in society are not viewed as a distant or impossible goal. It sees personal growth and profound social change as integral parts of the same process, and is actively promoting progress in both arenas. Furthermore, Jackins believes that RC may have the tools to conquer all human irrationality and to bring about one of the most fundamental revolutions that has ever occurred.

REFERENCES

Jackins, H. (1962). *Fundamentals of co-counseling manual.* Seattle: Rational Island Publishers.

Jackins, H. (1965). *The human side of human beings.* Seattle: Rational Island Publishers.

Jackins, H. (1973). *The human situation.* Seattle: Rational Island Publishers.

Jackins, H. (1978). *The upward trend.* Seattle: Rational Island Publishers.

Schiff, T. (1972). Reevaluation counseling: Social implications. *Journal of Humanistic Psychology, 12,* 58–70.

Somers, B. (1972). Reevaluation therapy: Theoretical framework. *Journal of Humanistic Psychology, 12,* 42–57.

Chapter 57

RESPONSIVE THERAPY: AN INVITATIONAL COUNSELING MODEL

STERLING K. GERBER and WILLIAM W. PURKEY

I had a special interest in this therapeutic approach because this system began with students' evaluation of themselves regarding failure or success in school. A reading of my introduction explains my interest. The system as it developed included the ideas of Arthur Combs, who was one of my instructors at Syracuse University.

This system represents the merging of a theoretical system (Invitational Counseling) and a method of therapeutic intervention (Responsive Therapy). What was originally a method for helping students developed, after the merger, into a full-blown therapeutic system. The final product is essentially simple and logical. Special attention is paid to the self. Responsive Therapy is concerned with how clients see themselves. The therapist is to respect this, taking the position that the client is the primary source of information but that the therapist is the expert who deals with the client's self. This calls for careful handling and leads to a conflict which demands resolution and which eventually leads to new understanding on the part of the client.

DEFINITION

Responsive Therapy is a context/content model of professional helping. It combines a theoretical context (Invitational Counseling) with a systematic content (Responsive Therapy) to create an innovative approach to therapy.

Invitational Counseling (Purkey & Schmidt, 1996) is based on four assumptions that give it identity, direction, and purpose: (1) *respect* for the self-directing powers of the client, (2) *trust* in the therapeutic process, (3) *optimism* for the therapeutic outcome, and (4) *intentionality* in allowing the client to provide the material and set the direction.

The client is the partner who is the expert on himself or herself. The therapist is skilled in processes of communication and intervention. Together they cooperatively establish an awareness of client circumstance and style and explore alternative intervention strategies. Together they engage in the intervention process and evaluate the results of their partnership.

Responsive Therapy is a method of therapeutic intervention that is relatively simple in structure. It assumes that the most appropriate problem solving approach is one that accounts for both the unique *circumstances* and the personal perception/problem solving *style* of the client. Once client circumstance and style are determined, Responsive Therapy requires therapist expertise in several divergent theoretical models. *Intervention follows understanding.*

HISTORY

In the Gestalt tradition of meaning coming from context, various approaches to therapy are best understood with reference to their contexts. In the case of the context/method model presented here, two separately conceived and developed approaches to professional helping evolved over several decades at locations a continent apart. Yet their affinity for each other was readily apparent, and their compatibility so compelling, that unification was virtually a foregone conclusion upon their first meeting.

Invitational Counseling

From 1964 until 1976 the second author was a faculty member at the University of Florida. During this period he studied with Sidney Jourard and worked closely with Arthur Combs. Together with Don Avila they authored *Helping Relationships* (1971, 1978) and *The Helping Re-*

lationship Sourcebook (1971, 1977). These books emphasized the utter centrality of individual perceptions in human behavior and the profound significance of how individuals define their own existence.

Purkey's early professional endeavors focused on the student's subjective and personal evaluation of himself or herself as a dominant influence on success or failure in school. Once this connection was made between student self-appraisal and student performance in school, the next step was to propose an approach to enhance student self-concept as learner.

What began as a way to influence what happens to students in school gradually developed into a general invitational framework. This framework provided a context for professional helping that has been described in *The Inviting Relationship* (Purkey & Schmidt, 1987) and *Invitational Counseling* (Purkey & Schmidt, 1996).

Responsive Therapy

The roots of Responsive Therapy go back to the graduate school training of the first author. The training environment of the 1960s was an interesting amalgamation of influences, including Carl Rogers, E. G. Williamson, Frederic Thorne, B. F. Skinner, Rollo May, and Abraham Maslow. International events resulted in a push to identify and prepare the brightest minds as scientists. A priority was to increase the number and quality of school counselors. This placed additional emphasis on the vocational guidance tradition, with heavy emphasis on psychometric methods.

From a curriculum that stressed, somewhat equivalently, human development, learning, therapeutic skills and techniques, psychometrics, and research, the first author emerged a challenged and uncomfortable eclectic. The breadth of the curriculum virtually mandated a heterogeneous orientation, yet the strong model of a major professor who advocated non-directive counseling and the mandate of another influential professor, "Do not be eclectic. Believe in *something!*" produced an inner tension that required resolution.

The result of the tension was awareness that (a) virtually all systems that survive over time have usefulness and are worthwhile, (b) no system is broad enough to meet the needs of every client, and (c) techniques taken out of their theoretical contexts produce disappointing results, particularly when combined with techniques from other models. The answer, in retrospect, seems obvious. The best approach is one that incorporates many extant models, each managed in its appropriate context and according to the dynamics that give it power. This approach includes emphasis on relationship building; assessment of client circumstance and style; selective intervention that matches client considerations and can be used intact within its theoretical

context; and stabilization of new, self-enhancing client behavior.

Responsive Therapy evolved through application of its emerging concepts at counseling centers, in private practices, and in the supervision of graduate student therapists at three Utah universities, the California State University at Chico, and Eastern Washington University. It was in the training environment at Eastern Washington that Responsive Therapy became formalized and applied to the counselor preparation program. Subsequently, Gerber published materials on Responsive Therapy (Gerber 1986, 1999).

Serendipitous Union

During the spring of 1996, the first author was invited to spend a term as the Upsilon Nu Chi (Chi Sigma Iota) Visiting Scholar at the University of North Carolina at Greensboro. Here, as a co-researcher with Purkey, whose graduate classes provided a platform for demonstration and analysis, Responsive Therapy was joined with Invitational Counseling.

During the ensuing years, Gerber found the philosophy of Invitational Counseling to be a well-explicated context for Responsive Therapy. Similarly, Purkey spent time and effort in mastering the method of Responsive Therapy and found that it served as a dependable bridge in connecting theory to practice.

CURRENT STATUS

The principles of Invitational Counseling have been instrumental in many areas, including the creation of the Schools without Fear Project (touching over 150 schools nationwide), the development of *The Journal of Invitational Theory and Practice,* the creation of The Alliance for Invitational Education (which now boasts over 1,000 professional members), and over 70 articles in scholarly journals. There is also an active Invitational Education Special Interest Group in the American School Counseling Association, the American Educational Research Association, and the Association for Supervision and Curriculum Development. Invitational Counseling, combined with Responsive Therapy, is a central ingredient of the counselor education curriculum in the Department of Counseling and Educational Development at the University of North Carolina at Greensboro.

Responsive Therapy has a following, principally among graduates of Eastern Washington University. It has served as the theoretical structure for CACREP programs in Mental Health and School Counseling, and is particularly noted for the intensity and duration of its practica and internship experiences and its emphasis on phenomenological tracking prior to adoption of active intervention strategies. This approach is embodied in Gerber's (1999) book, *Enhancing Counselor Intervention Strategies: An Integrational Viewpoint.* In this text, Gerber elucidates the relationship between a variety of intervention practices with their respective theoretical roots. Further, he strengthens the integrational viewpoint and emphasizes the dynamics of Responsive Therapy in determining client circumstance and style and in selecting specific intervention strategies that have a high probability of success. Responsive Therapy has enjoyed successful application in mental health clinics, private practices, K–12 schools, community colleges, universities, crisis intervention services, substance abuse agencies, and other social service settings.

Articles—in addition to those cited that deal with Responsive Therapy, Invitational Theory, and related topics—have been published by the authors and their students. Presentations have been made at international, national, regional, and state psychology and counseling association conferences.

Topics of publications and presentations include Invitational Theory as it pertains to the classroom and to the larger school context, self-talk and school achievement, self-esteem, counselor education models, personal commitment, affective deficit, spirituality and counseling, computer-mediated training of counseling skills, multiple-channel monitoring, management of the counseling process, perceptual and cognitive processes in education, working from client experiential vignettes, and application of Responsive Therapy skills to military supervision and management. Current bibliographies may be requested from the authors.

THEORY

It is the responsibility of theorists to state their premises. Responsive Therapy and Invitational Counseling embrace the view that humans are different in significant, qualitative ways from other forms of life. That which contributes to the human essence is critical for understanding and professionally intervening in the lives of clients. Such characteristics are cumulatively referred to as the self.

At the present time there seems to be general agreement among therapists that how one views oneself and one's situation has profound effects socially, psychologically, and even biologically. Self-perceptions are pivotal and are in fact a "necessary prerequisite" for psychological well-being. At the same time, a negative, despising self has been associated with a host of physical and psychological problems including alcohol abuse, anorexia nervosa and bulimia, and extreme shyness. Self-identification and personal reflection are active agents in healthy or unhealthy living (Purkey, 1999).

The self is a totality of a complex, dynamic, and organized system of learned beliefs that an individual holds to be true about his or her personal existence. It is this self that provides consistency to the human personality and allows the individual to maintain a reference point for antecedents and consequences of perceptions and behavior (Purkey & Stanley, 1999).

Because of the centrality of the self in human experience and motivation, it is imperative that the individual be respected and honored in the processes of therapy. Responsive Therapy stresses the importance of creating a relationship that is marked by shared responsibility. This requires an orchestrated process in which the cognitive structures and predilections of the therapist are prevented from dominating the interaction and, similarly, the personal strictures of the client are loosened to permit thorough observation by both. Within that context, cooperation in identifying critical components, selecting reasonable and probable goals, and adopting mutually acceptable interventions can be realized.

The client brings to this shared interaction expertise or knowledge of his or her "self." *The client is the primary source of information. The therapist is the expert on communication processes and behavioral change.* Thus, the client generates the content. The counselor manages the process.

For theoretical description, Responsive Therapy can be viewed in three sections: relationship formation, establishment of common understanding of client circumstance(s) and style, and application of an intervention strategy tailored to that circumstance and style. Each section has its own theoretical underpinnings.

A relationship that is invitational includes assumptions about the inherent worth of both client and counselor and the potential inherent in the client for self-direction and self-management. This relationship finds expression only in an interaction that is carefully managed so as to assure shared responsibility between client and therapist for both process and outcome.

Establishment of common understanding is accomplished through adherence to principles of phenomenology. The client's phenomenal world includes information necessary to identify what is not working for the client, the context in which it is occurring, and the approaches already attempted for resolution. The process of Responsive Therapy contributes to a new phenomenal awareness. By experiencing himself or herself in the responses of the therapist and, consequently, revisioning self and circumstance, the client gains understanding. *The therapist and client enter into a dynamic, the outcome of which can be a surprise to both of them, a creation of their interaction.*

This process is a perceptual rather than a cognitive one. It is more of an attempt to see, through progressive variation of perceptual frames, than it is to figure out in a logical way. It is more like insight than deduction. Without assuming the universal client dis-integration basic to Gestalt theory, the principles of varying perceptual frames, changing figure and ground relationships, and increasing and refining awareness are basic to this portion of Responsive Therapy.

Once client circumstance and style have been determined, the focus of therapy is arrived at by a conscious decision to pursue an intervention strategy that fits (is responsive to) the client. Theoretically, if the client has a knowledge problem—either lack of necessary information or the presence of a belief that results in self-defeat—then a cognitive strategy is best. Emotional concerns respond to affective strategies. Behavioral deficits or habit-bound surpluses are efficiently altered by operant techniques. Absent or confusing frames indicate use of a perceptual approach. The theory that underpins the selected approach generates its results. *It is necessary for the Responsive Therapist to be well grounded in at least one behavioral, one affective, one cognitive, and one perceptual approach so as to respond sensitively and effectively to a wide range of clients.*

Responsive Therapy recognizes four stages in the therapeutic process, each managed by the therapist: (1) ventilation, (2) clarification, (3) alteration, and (4) acommodation. Superimposed over these four stages is a skill process involving initiating, tracking, and enhancing skills.

METHODOLOGY

The first few minutes of the therapeutic interaction with a new client are critical in teaching the client how to be an effective partner in the therapeutic endeavor. *Shared responsibility is a critical ingredient in Responsive Therapy.*

Initiating Skills

Shared responsibility is established in the first minutes of the therapeutic session. Each client comes with two universal and unspoken questions: "When do I talk?" and "What do I talk about?" The indirect lead, a declarative statement that carries the message, "Tell me about yourself," employed within the first few seconds, gives answers to those questions. "Talk now, about you." This is an invitation to disclose. Once the client is talking, the therapist relies primarily on appropriate silence and selective paraphrases.

For clients in distress, the invitation to talk results in an emotion-laden flood of words—the expressing of pent-up emotions. This is the opening, *ventilation stage.* It is important for the therapist to honor this process, to avoid giving it direction, to listen carefully for what may

be significant themes (circumstance), and to watch for client style of thought and problem solving attempts (style).

If, instead of ventilating, the client responds with an attempt to cast the therapist in the role of questioner by saying, "What do you want me to talk about?" or "What do you want to know?", the therapist reflects the responsibility back. "You choose." Where there is further difficulty getting started or resistance from the client, the therapist may give a multiple choice lead: "You may start with personal background, major concerns, employment information, goals/dreams/aspirations—you decide." *Getting the client to disclose from his or her phenomenal space and not in response to questions is critical to establishing shared communication.*

The use of initiating skills, primarily indirect leads and paraphrases of content, creates the process wherein the client discloses and the therapist demonstrates acceptance and understanding. This process is facilitated by therapist attentiveness, including eye contact (especially while the therapist is making responses), and by keeping the focus on the client. Therapist self-references, experiences, advice-giving, editorializing, analyzing, and/or small talk are inappropriate and counterproductive. It is also important that the therapist refrains from asking questions, particularly closed or interrogative questions. Questions move the focus away from the experience-rich phenomenal field of the client to the cognitive field of the therapist.

An effective paraphrase of content is a restatement of client disclosure without adding to, subtracting from, or distorting client production. It is restated in more denotative language. Denotative precision demonstrates the serious intent of the therapist to understand.

As soon as the client is disclosing freely, the therapist will want to move from general toward specific disclosure. The direction to "give me a specific example," followed by persistence in getting to a very specific "he said . . . she said . . ." level will clarify previous client disclosures that were of a more general nature.

A skill that is peculiar to Responsive Therapy is called structure of content (Gerber, 1986). This involves the therapist organizing paraphrases in a manner that reflects the *pattern* of client disclosure. Because words can only be uttered one at a time, the client must rely on some form of cognitive or perceptual organization from which to disclose.

As clients survey their phenomenal reality, they perceive and report their self-observations in patterns. Each client may have a unique approach. One approach reflects what is taught in school as proper paragraph construction: topic sentence and elaboration. The client labels his or her focus and proceeds to give data in support of it. "I think maybe I'm losing my mind. Frequently I go into another room for something and when I get there

I've forgotten what it was. Occasionally I have heard my name called out but there is no one around."

A second approach references a time sequence. The client begins by talking about events leading up to the present, then discloses concerns in the present, and goes on to project the outcome—past, present, future structure (see Gerber, 1986, for more examples).

By reflecting the client's structure, the therapist gets an awareness of how various segments fit together and how the client organizes his or her thoughts. Clients indicate their structure very frequently in the first things they say.

Tracking Skills

In the interchange of disclosure and structured paraphrase of content, the therapist begins to gain an awareness of information just below the level of content or "between the lines." The attempt to verbalize this awareness is the therapist's contribution to the tracking process. Tracking skills are most appropriately used in the second or *clarification stage.*

Communication is complex. Clients seldom are able to clearly describe their situation in denotative language. Skills are needed that will provide a knowledge of client circumstance and style.

The Responsive Therapist develops the ability to attend, simultaneously, to expressions or indications of content, feelings, nonverbal cues, structure, messages, and situations. This is called multiple channel monitoring (Gerber, 1986). The following tracking skills are used to accomplish mutual awareness of client circumstance and style.

Reflection of Feeling

This is the mirroring back of the client's attempts to express and to communicate emotional response. Emotions only occur in the present, hence reflections of feelings are stated in the present tense. Recalled instances of emotion are either content or are indications of feelings still present, accessed or recreated from the disclosure. Anticipation of future emotion-laden events usually includes feelings in the present that accompany the anticipation or rehearsal of the future happening.

Formalization of Nonverbal Cues

Another mirroring technique, one that calls the attention of the client to posture, movement, and changes in voice tone or volume, is the *formalization* of nonverbal cues (Gerber, 1986). It is a reversal of figure and ground. Nonverbals and paralanguage usually exist in the background as attempts to modify or strengthen what is being said. *Unlike use of nonverbals in other forms of ther-*

apy, there is no attempt in Responsive Therapy to interpret the meaning of the cues. They are only brought to client attention. The client then has the opportunity to explain what they mean.

Paraphrase of Message

There is an essence of meaning that is incorporated into the totality of client talk and behavior. Because of difficulties inherent in language, and because clients do not always have a clear understanding of just what they are thinking or experiencing, clients frequently do not say what they mean. When the therapist gives a powerful, bottom line version of what the client appears to be communicating, it is called a paraphrase of message. The ability to efficiently and consistently paraphrase client meaning is the hallmark of an excellent therapist. Again, it is important to point out that this is a perceptual skill and not a cognitive or interpretational one. The therapist "sees" or "hears" the message. He or she does not figure it out.

Description of Situation

One additional skill that is useful in the tracking process is called description of situation (Gerber, 1986). As the client progressively provides information, the therapist sees bigger and bigger segments of client reality. Content transforms into structure. Content, feelings, and nonverbals augment or give way to messages. The accumulation of messages provides an opportunity to see yet a larger picture, a contextual frame.

A paraphrase or reflection of something that has not been mentioned by the client is a description of situation response. The therapist provides the client with an awareness of not-quite-apparent or not-yet-disclosed information.

General Enhancing Skills

There are other skills that are useful in the second (clarification) stage and are applicable, to some degree, to all clients. They are termed general enhancing skills. These include:

1. the proper and effective use of silence;
2. pacing—adopting client posture, language speed and emphasis, and/or pause rate to provide increased awareness of client condition;
3. minimum interrogation, necessary to preserve the process of client disclosure from his or her space and to keep the therapist out of an analytical process and in a perceptual one; and
4. perception check, the use of a paraphrase or reflection preceded or followed by a request for vali-

dation—"See if I've got this right. . . ." or, "Is that the way it is for you?" Its uses are slowing the interaction and countering defensiveness and resistance in clients.

The use of general enhancing skills facilitates rapid movement while respecting the client.

The end of the clarification stage is a pivotal time in the therapeutic process. An obvious conclusion regarding client behavior would be, "What you are doing is not working. Unless you do something differently, it will continue to not work." This is a time of transition into the third stage of therapy, which involves the application of specific enhancing skills.

Specific Enhancing Skills

Techniques that are applied to a particular client, selected in response to his or her unique circumstances and style, are specific enhancing skills. Their application comprises the *alteration stage* of therapy.

Gerber (1999) described categories of circumstance and categories of client style. Included in his model are cognitive, affective, behavioral, and perceptual circumstances, each of which contains a surplus and deficit differentiation.

Client styles may be similarly categorized into (a) cognitive—preference for solving problems by analysis and decision, (b) affective—a response set based on what feels right or good, (c) behavioral—responding to external contingencies and from previous conditioning, and (d) perceptual—doing what seems right, what "fits the picture." The required specific nature of the third (alteration) stage of therapy is a function of the unique combination of circumstance and style presented by the client.

The transition to the alteration stage is critical. It provides a redirection away from what hasn't worked in the past toward a strategy that holds promise for increased self-enhancement on the part of the client. Clients who have not recognized a new vision for themselves through the clarification stage can be asked to predict their future. Their plan may be to "try harder," or to "be careful to not make the same mistake." They will often envision great changes without adopting new behavior.

When clients work with the therapist in determining a desirable end, with the realization that the old methods are unlikely to produce new results, an opportune time is presented for re-scripting. The role of the Responsive Therapist is to describe two or more strategies for re-scripting. He or she probably will recommend the strategy that seems to hold the greatest promise. It is at this juncture that the therapist may adopt any of a number of interventions, including (a) operant techniques for effecting change in externally-cued habit behavior, (b) cognitive restructuring for disputing and altering self-defeating beliefs, (c) *in vivo* experiences or observation of models for framing or reframing perceptual deficits or surpluses, or (d) some relationship management approaches for working through affective difficulties. *At this juncture, the Responsive Therapist becomes, essentially, whatever kind of specialist the strategy calls for.*

Tracking and General Enhancing Skills: Reprise

The Responsive Therapist is required to have the ability to support the client in his or her individuation following the third (alteration) stage. It is during the final *accommodation stage* that adaptation and stabilization of the new responses are accomplished. During this concluding stage, the tracking and general process skills again come into play. Clients' experiences are met by an invitational attitude, opportunity to disclose, and nonrestrictive mirroring.

Transition, Termination, Bridging to the Future

Bridging to the future, a time without formal contact with the therapist, is as important as bridging between sessions and across vacation periods. The use of a scheduled "check in" or "check up" about six months from the end of a therapeutic episode provides an expectation that the client will do very well for at least six months and the reassurance that the therapist is caring enough to want feedback. Some statement of optimistic prognosis or of positive expectation lends some perceptual structure to the bridge into the future.

APPLICATIONS

The range of clients and settings for which Responsive Therapy has demonstrated viability is large. The authors have used it in private practice, university counseling centers, training programs, and public schools. Principles of Responsive Therapy have been applied to military supervision and management. Variations of its dynamics demonstrated effectiveness in classroom instruction and student behavioral management. Its usefulness in substance abuse populations has been demonstrated by graduate clinicians. Parallels between the application of Responsive Therapy and art therapy are demonstrable. It has been used to study clients showing obsessive-compulsive disorder and in couples experiencing the dissolution of long-term relationships (see Gerber, 1999, for references and further examples).

Its application with children younger than 10 years of age and with mentally disabled populations is limited, requiring modifications in the communication process. There is a preference for using behavioral and/or play therapy techniques with these special populations.

The necessity for an invitational relationship and shared responsibility in communication requires modification of standard approaches in some settings. For example, the frequently mandated preface to therapy (client rights, procedures and expected outcomes, financial matters, confidentiality, etc.), unless managed properly, can create difficulty in inviting confidence and free disclosure from the client.

Similarly, required and lengthy intake procedures can have a dampening effect on a productive relationship. They communicate the message, "I'm interested in very specific things and your job is to answer my questions. We will conduct this interaction in the phenomenal space of the therapist and the agency." The systematic, form-dominated request for mental status information, suicide ideation, drug use/abuse, and familial history of emotional disorders often sets up an interrogative interaction.

It is advisable to have the routine intake and business activities conducted in a different room and by a person other than the therapist. Separating nontherapeutic interactions from therapeutic ones helps the client to accept and respond positively to both.

Another caveat in the application of Responsive Therapy that may require special accommodation in some settings is the influence of shared responsibility and shared process on forms and records. Therapist note taking and record making are open processes. Diagnostic and descriptive entries are made with concurrence of the client and with a bias toward "least restrictive" labels.

There appear to be no generic restrictions to the application of Responsive Therapy across most settings. There may be situational dynamics that preclude the entirely open, honest, and client-respecting application of this form of therapy.

CASE EXAMPLE

The following is an elaboration of a case vignette taken from Gerber (1999). The client, Virginia, is a university student who was referred by the attending physician at the university clinic. Her presenting symptoms at the clinic were nervousness, nausea, and headaches. The physician prescribed some medication that would temporarily stabilize her physical responses, but would not result in long-term relief.

COUNSELOR: Come in, Virginia, and have a seat. You filled out the intake forms and read over the client rights pamphlet. Do you have any questions about them?

VIRGINIA: No. They were very clear.

C: Let's begin by having you talk about yourself.

V: I'm a student at the university. The doctor at the clinic sent me to see you. I'm not sure why—I guess I'm supposed to figure out what is making me sick. The medicine he gave me is supposed to make me feel better. I'm afraid maybe I'm wasting your time.

Note: Virginia has given several clues about her style and structure of content. "I'm supposed to figure out" strongly suggests a cognitive style wherein understanding is seen either as sufficient to resolve the problem or as a necessary requisite to finding a solution. There is indication of a parallel structure of content—I need to be here but maybe it will be a waste of time. This same content indicates the possibility of another style, behavioral surplus, with an externally-cued response set toward authority.

C: A You're a student and experiencing . . . some . . . physical concerns. The doctor sent you to me, you believe, to find out the cause of your symptoms. You don't want to waste my time.

V: Well, yes. I have been sick to my stomach and nervous at times.

C: At times . . .

V: Not at particular times during the day. More often just before test days . . . and when my fiancé is upset at me.

C: For example . . .

V: I really am having difficulty being around Tom. I love him, yet it's easier sometimes just to be alone.

C: Be more specific. Tell me of the most recent incident.

V: Well, last Sunday as we were getting out of the car to go get lunch, I noticed that his hair was sticking up. I said, "Tom, you just must do something about that cowlick." I thought I said it with a smile. He just glared at me and was cold and distant for the rest of the day.

C: You are feeling put off by his coldness and you're afraid to let him know how you feel.

V: I'm so mixed up. I like it when he is happy and when he pays attention to me. He is attractive and has a really good personality when we're around other people, but it seems like he is so sensitive around me that I can't be free to be myself. I'm constantly having to be careful, to avoid offending him.

C: A part of you likes him. A part doesn't. A part of you wants to be with him. A part doesn't.

Other observations and information that came out of the first session included her being a little overweight, dressed in clean and unfashionable clothing. She was an education major with grades in the mid-"C" range. She expressed having a hard time keeping up with the fast pace of university work. Being a wife and mother were her priorities, yet her parents and high school adviser urged her to pursue a career. She had wanted to talk through her difficulty in school, her career ambivalence, and her difficulties with Tom, but her father on numerous occasions had said, "We don't need to talk to outsiders. Keep your concerns in the family!"

The counselor listened patiently, paraphrased what she said, and reflected her feelings while she expressed her ambivalence about school, her fiancé, her parents, and her goals. Believing that she still needed to ventilate some more before moving to an active intervention, the counselor ended the session at about the 50-minute mark and scheduled her next appointment for two days later.

C: Hi, Virginia. Help me understand where you are today.

V: I feel a little better in my stomach and head, but I'm still confused about what to do. I visited with my older sister, and she told me I should just dump Tom, that he is really a no-good, narcissistic bum. She almost had me convinced, but then I went out with Tom, and he was so nice. Of course, I didn't say anything to offend him.

C: Your sister seemed to take sides with that part of you that doesn't really like Tom. The other part was strengthened by your pleasant date.

V: Yes. It's almost like I don't have any control over myself. I just get tossed back and forth. I was thinking that I respond to my father that way. He'd be shocked to know I'm seeing a counselor, yet he has told me to be responsible.

C: It's almost like you are reacting to Tom the same way you do to your father.

V: And to my sister, and to my roommate. Jenny, my roommate, is constantly rearranging the furniture in our apartment. I really like things to be settled down and sort of samish, you know, but she gets really mad when I ask her why she is changing things again.

The counselor summarized what Virginia had disclosed, using a white board to chart the dynamics of what appeared to be externally-cued, contingent relationships with her parents, fiancé, sister, and roommate, and to a lesser extent the physician at the clinic and the counselor himself. He reflected her need to understand and explain what was going on. As he developed the chart, he checked with her frequently for validation or corrective input. Then, based on the rationale given below, he said:

C: Virginia, it looks to me like there are two approaches we might take to resolve your dilemma. Each holds promise of being effective and both will require about the same amount of time. We need to agree on one of them and pursue it vigorously in order to get this resolved in an efficient and effective manner.

The first approach would be to change your pattern of letting others control your interactions with them. By learning a new set of responses, you will be able to assert your interests and find more stability and comfort in your relationships. This approach will involve your being a member of an assertion training group. It meets twice weekly, at 3 P.M., and runs for about 90 minutes. One major advantage of the group is the opportunity to learn from other group members.

The second approach involves teaching you how to identify, dispute, and replace many of your beliefs that set you up for self-defeating responses. This will require weekly sessions that can be arranged at a mutually acceptable hour. You will need to do some homework between sessions, of the nature of charting situations, thoughts, and responses.

My belief is that the assertion training will produce quicker results and that your desire to explain the problem will become unimportant, so I am recommending you pursue that option.

The cognitive restructuring option will address more quickly your desire to understand, but it will be a little slower in getting to the behavioral responses that seem to be well-practiced habits.

With either approach, we will know within three weeks whether or not you are progressing appropriately. At that juncture we will evaluate your progress and consider any fine tuning or change of procedure.

You need to be aware that the changes you make with either of these approaches may result in Tom's rejection of you and, possibly, some stress to other relationships until people come to accept the "new" you. Unless you accept some risk, and make the change, most likely you will continue to have periodic recurrence of your physical symptoms and continued confusion in your relationships.

Note: The choice is left to the client, thus maximizing shared responsibility and the probability that the feeling of self-efficacy that accompanies choice will be a significant factor in the change process. The therapist adopts the role appropriate to the selected option, saving the alternate option as a "plan B" should problems arise in the chosen approach. Since both options are defensible from analysis of the client circumstance and style, following either of them precisely and thoroughly permits evaluation and accountability.

V: The 3:00 time fits my schedule, so I will try the group approach.

C: We will schedule an evaluation appointment in three weeks.

Note: Given her habitual response to authority figures, it is not surprising that she accepted the counselor's recommendation, which was based on the conclusion that this is a behavioral deficit circumstance, with a client cognitive style.

The circumstance appears to be one of boundary mismanagement. Virginia has adopted a reactive style of letting others take an action to which she tries to respond. This represents an external locus of control. Apparently her father dominated interactions in her family of origin and she is placing her boyfriend in a similar role. Involvement in an assertiveness group would be an appropriate intervention strategy. Through involvement in such a program, she would learn to assert boundaries, to say "no," and to permit others to be different without giving in to their strength. Her cognitive style probably would not be of concern because she would rationalize her new position as she experienced success in boundary setting and maintenance.

The alternative option is based on assumptions of cognitive surplus circumstance, and cognitive style. Fundamental to cognitive restructuring, an approach useful for working with a cognitive surplus circumstance, is the assumption that thought precedes action. All responses are mediated by cognitive assumptions manifested by self-statements. A simple ABC analysis of the client's cognitive structure might look like this:

Activating Event: Boyfriend

Belief(a): Happiness results from getting married and pleasing my husband.

Consequent Response(a): Persisting in face of a punishing relationship

Belief(b): I can't be happy if he's displeased or unhappy.

Consequent Response(b): depression, discouragement

Belief(c): I must make it work.

Consequent Response(c): somatic symptoms

Belief(d): It's my fault he's unhappy, or It's my job to make him happy.

Consequent Response(d): tension

Activating Event: Counselor

Belief: I'm betraying my father. I should do what my father says. Father knows best.

Consequent Response: resistance, uneasiness

Challenging each of the self-statements or defeating beliefs and helping the client to replace them with self-enhancing beliefs would be the therapist's role.

SUMMARY

The name *Responsive Therapy* is intended to reflect the underlying structure of its approach. Clients are first, foremost, and fundamentally individuals. They are the best source of understanding regarding their own circumstances and styles. In order to gain access to that awareness, the therapist must establish an inviting relationship, one that is based on shared responsibility and respect. To accomplish this the therapist relies on the use of sequential initiating, tracking, and enhancing skills to manage mutual exploration of the client's world. This requires a perceptual set and the avoidance of contamination by the therapist's cognitive intercession.

The initial one to four sessions involve ventilation and clarification that result in client and therapist gaining an understanding of client circumstance and problem solving style. From this base of understanding, the emphasis shifts to a focused and theory-sound intervention strategy that is mutually selected by client and therapist and that has a high probability of accomplishing the desired results—a strategy that is *responsive* to client circumstance and style.

To be able to deal with a wide range of clients, the therapist is required to be proficient in at least four modes of therapy: behavioral, affective, perceptual, and cognitive. During the alteration stage of therapy, he or she operates as a specialist in the mode that best fits the client's circumstance and style.

Throughout therapy, including a period of client accommodation to new response patterns following the alteration stage, the therapist maintains a relationship that is optimistic, trustful, respectful, and intentionally inviting. Client and therapist are companions on a journey within the client's world. Their mutual goal is to direct client behavior toward an improved and enhanced future.

REFERENCES

Avila, D. L., Combs, A. W., & Purkey, W. W. (1971). *The helping relationship sourcebook.* Boston: Allyn and Bacon.

Avila, D. L., Combs, A. W., & Purkey, W. W. (1977). *The helping relationship sourcebook* (2nd ed.). Boston: Allyn and Bacon.

Combs, A. W., Avila, D. L., & Purkey, W. W. (1971). *Helping relationships: Basic concepts for the helping professions.* Boston: Allyn and Bacon.

Combs, A. W., Avila, D. L., & Purkey, W. W. (1978). *Helping relationships: Basic concepts for the helping professions.* (2nd ed.). Boston: Allyn and Bacon.

Gerber, S. (1986). *Responsive Therapy: A systematic approach to counseling skills.* New York: Human Sciences Press.

Gerber, S. (1999). *Enhancing counselor intervention strategies: An integrational viewpoint.* Philadelphia, PA: Accelerated Development/Taylor & Francis.

Purkey, W. W. (1999). *The whispering self.* Thousand Oaks, CA: Corwin Press.

Purkey, W. W., & Schmidt, J. J. (1987). *The inviting relationship: An expanded perspective for professional counseling.* Englewood Cliffs, NJ: Prentice Hall.

Purkey, W. W., & Schmidt, J. J. (1996). *Invitational counseling: A self concept approach to professional practice.* Pacific Grove, CA: Brooks/Cole.

Purkey, W. W., & Stanley, P. H. (in press). The self in psychotherapy. In D. Cain (Ed.), *Handbook of research and practice in humanistic psychotherapies.* Washington, DC: American Psychological Association.

Chapter 58

SELF-IMAGE THERAPY

CAMILLA M. ANDERSON

I have a special fondness for this chapter, not only because it was the first one to come in, but because the writer, unknown to me except through her writings and her letters, seems to be a most unusual person. She deals courageously and sensibly with many problems in life, including a retarded daughter, about whom she wrote a book.

The ideas that Camilla Anderson expresses form a complete theory of personality and psychotherapy. The reader will have an opportunity to become immersed in an in-depth system of thought developed over many years.

One can feel Anderson's repressed anger at a world that just doesn't appear to value her contributions, her simple and obvious approach to life, her very logical explanation of the human condition and how distortions can be dealt with. Her ideas seem to follow those of another great woman, Karen Horney, who also, in my judgment, has been unfairly treated by the "psychological establishment." What struck me strongly was Anderson's view that people with so-called feelings of inferiority really are people with grandiosity—a simple truth, but one that I had personally never grasped until I read the following exciting and extremely wise chapter.

Self-Image Therapy is a simple yet comprehensive system of psychodynamics applicable to any person throughout a lifetime. It accounts for the development of the person's self-image and shows the role of the self-image in all behavior and feelings. A person's self-image begins to be developed soon after birth and is the product of surviving despite helplessness. From the beginning, interpersonal operations are paramount and are an integral part of all assumptions developed and, therefore, of all behavior.

The system encompasses the becoming of an individual as well as his or her being. The threat to survival associated with helplessness is the factor that leads to development of one's moral value system, and this, in turn, becomes one's "road map" for living. Surviving is accomplished with the help of others, and the value system is evidence that all assumptions, all actions, all feelings, all values are developed in an interpersonal setting with survival as the goal.

A person's unique psyche is his or her reservoir of moral value judgments set up by experience in the interpersonal world. Psyche and self-image are synonymous and relate to security–insecurity experiences. It is that with which one identifies. Any threat to one's value system is experienced as a threat to survival.

Because the self-image is bigger than life—grandiose—being cut down to size is experienced as a threat to survival, and it sets the stage for anxiety and stress symptoms. Reconstitution—healing—means either removal of the stress or acceptance of the new and deflated, but more realistic, self-image. The business of living encompasses establishing or becoming, living out, protecting, defending, enhancing, and reconstituting one's self-image.

HISTORY

Self-Image theory and Therapy was not developed or written "forthright and out of hand," but took many years aborning.

I came into psychiatry in New York in 1931, a time when there was a near religious fanaticism and fervor in the espousal of Freudian psychodynamics. To deviate from the "true religion" represented a foolhardiness that amounted to defiance of God. In 1934 I moved from New York, the heart of Freudian territory, to Pennsylvania, where there were other gods. Up to that time I had scarcely been aware that there were competing faiths. Gradually I developed a sense of my right to question, to doubt, and to challenge. Before then I had believed that, had I been more competent, I would surely find that my deviant impressions showed lack of maturity, and the Freudian system would be vindicated. No longer, however, did I have to be apologetic over disagreeing.

In 1941 I married, and this was, without doubt, the beginning of my personal growth and emancipation. The stresses I felt and the symptoms I developed as a result did not seem to follow the dynamics I had been taught, and they did not respond to the techniques I had used faithfully on my patients. I became aware that whereas resentment, stemming from frustration of felt entitlements, was an important factor in my case, Freudian literature did not even mention this.

This period marked the beginning of my professional growth, when I dared openly to challenge and disagree with those who had been accepted authorities. I still had no thoughts or expectations of developing any "system," but was content to note whatever I observed. I continued to be amazed at how many of my patients were like me, caught in a web of resentment and frustrated entitlement, and fortunately, this provided a framework for relieving their stresses, but it had nothing to do with developing a system.

My first clear move toward presenting a new framework was in 1950, when I published a paper (Anderson, 1950a) and later the same year a book (1950b) that recognized that assumptions were derived from experiences in a two-party system, and that the foundation of all behavior is interpersonal assumptions. A new concept was emerging that was reflected in all I was seeing clinically and in my psychotherapeutic efforts.

I no longer made any pretense of being Freudian, and I found that I seemed to understand patients as well as or better than most other therapists I knew. I had good results in psychotherapy through using my concepts of structure and function (two-party assumptions) as laid down early in life, and through dealing with entitlements and resentments as they showed up.

Through the years when Self-Image Therapy was growing and developing, I knew of no way that I could hasten the process or steer it in its course. I simply used the insights I developed, with no idea of whether there would be a next step or where it might lie or where it would take me. It was obvious to me that all assumptions regarding behavior had an actor and a reactor component—they were interpersonal phenomena—and that, therefore, disturbances were possible in either the area of the action or the reaction (1950a). Sometimes as I watched myself I would be the actor; other times, I would be the reactor.

It was not until later, in the 1960s, that it dawned on me that while I had accumulated a host of the components of a system or theoretical framework, I had only dealt with the mechanics. The final detail left out was the dynamics, which would hold the components together and make it all into a single piece.

Then I made the discovery—startling to me—that the central core or the dynamic drive in all behavior was simply the drive to survive and to maintain oneself. This was the integrating as well as the dynamic factor in the whole picture. It was involved in the formation of the psyche or self-image; it was the theme in the daily application of the system in real life; it was clearly operative in the occurrence of stress feelings and symptoms, when surviving was threatened; and it related to psychotherapy when a model was needed to help in the face of an unrealistic and malfunctioning self-image. It became a tool to use when there was a need for exploration and understanding, no matter at what stage of development one was or what type of functioning or malfunctioning one had. Understanding the survival drive was as important when dealing with the psyche as when dealing with the soma.

An interesting aspect of this long and leisurely search and exploration was that I had less and less need for what is commonly known as "the eclectic approach," because there was contained within the self-image system itself the basis for guiding and comprehending. It provided me with a North Star. Once seeing this, everything else followed automatically; it eliminated any confusion.

There were, however, areas that clearly had to be omitted from inclusion in its applicability, for there were people who did not develop any comprehensible or dependable psychic structure; they did not behave in a manner compatible with a belief in the overall guiding presence of a psyche or a value system; nor was it possible with them to utilize the schema I had elaborated in doing psychotherapy. But such people were in the minority, and fortunately for me and my continued growth and practical operations, I was familiar with the total picture of MBD (minimal brain damage or dysfunction), an organically determined deficit that is far more common than most people have been led to believe (Anderson, 1963). Those who have suffered this handicap, which shows up in all areas—the physical, the intellectual, and the emotional—do not follow the usual patterns of behavior, and it is impossible in dealing with them to make use of the concepts I had developed for doing psychotherapy.

Fortunately, it is possible to understand the nature of MBD and to make fairly accurate observations and predictions, so one is not at the mercy of guesswork, and one can stand on solid ground even here. Anyone who proposes to work in a therapeutic manner with patients needs to be familiar with MBD—its history of development, its characteristic symptomatology, and its usual nature (Anderson, 1972a)—so as to avoid the frustration of trying to do analytic psychotherapy with a person incapable of carrying out the details of such therapy—that is, integrating.

I have come to view all behavior as either an expression of the psychodynamic self-preservation drive or an expression of the neurologic inadequacies of MBD. One must have different expectations of the two, and the manner of "doing therapy" with the two groups is widely different.

During the 1970s there was little or no change in the nature of the theoretical framework (Anderson, 1971) of the self-image system, but clinical experience has reinforced the validity of my concepts. I feel no need to search further, but rather I use what is already obvious. The system now seems to be completed. Everything one needs for understanding and dealing with behavior is here. Others may add to the mechanics from time to time, but the dynamics are provided.

CURRENT STATUS

As far as I know, no one else is using Self-Image Therapy. This, in my estimation, does not derive from any significant theoretical defect, but from a combination of factors that I will attempt to make clearer. To do this, I must share a number of personal experiences.

During the 1950s I was a member of an active teaching community (University of Utah College of Medicine and University of Utah School of Social Work, 1948–1957). I was making good strides in elaborating my system, trying to develop enough interest in it to promote its use for critical checking. As I began saying openly that my system and Freudian theory differed (Anderson, 1950), I was literally shut out from the Department of Psychiatry and told I could not return until I was willing to concede that my concepts were not unique and that there were no differences between my concepts and the Freudian system. Students were no longer assigned to me, opportunities for teaching were deleted, and in every possible way I was excluded.

Because at that time (1957) the University of Oregon Medical School was looking for a new person to head their Department of Psychiatry, and because Oregon was my school, I placed my name before their faculty appointing committee as a candidate. After waiting for months, I finally called the chairman of the committee (who also happened to be a classmate of mine in medical school), asking when I might expect a response to my letter. He replied, "Camilla, we would not even consider appointing a woman." That ended my hope that I could develop this position into a place for presenting and testing my theory.

After almost 10 years in Salt Lake City, in 1958 I accepted a position as Director of the Outpatient Department of the Oregon State Hospital. It was a very comfortable position. While I continued to explore, write, and publish, it was obvious that to promulgate new ideas one must be tied into a "machine," that is, to a teaching institution that has sufficient clout so that it would be easy to get publishers, and there would be enough momentum in the machine for both push and reinforcement. No matter how good—or bad—ideas are, unless they see the light of day, they haven't much chance to survive.

Oregon State Hospital was a teaching hospital, but it was in the backwater. Few people associated with it were making any great waves, and the new head of the Department of Psychiatry at the University of Oregon Medical School was so involved in his own progress and programs that he had no time either to listen to or to push someone else's ideas. I had a couple of good critics on my staff, but no one was capable of assisting in getting my ideas before the public.

Nine of my papers were published by the *Journal of the American Medical Women's Association,* but it was not a good place to publish if one were looking for acceptance by the national psychiatric community, for it was not expected that this journal would present anything new or significant in the field of psychodynamics.

The emptying of the state hospitals and closing the state's clinics was the direct cause of my leaving Oregon. My next clinical experience was in California, where I had accepted the position of Chief Psychiatrist at the California Institution for Women at Frontera, then the largest prison for women in the world. It was a good place to expand my insights into criminal behavior and to share my concepts with staff, but it was remarkably isolated and this obstructed wider acceptance of my concepts. Nevertheless, I continued to write and to teach wherever there was an opportunity, and it is quite likely that there are still some individuals using my concepts, without being aware that these are new or different.

In 1971 I published a brief summary of my psychodynamic concepts. Since that time most of my published works have dealt with MBD or with the current status and plight of psychiatry (Anderson 1972a, 1972b, 1973a, 1973b, 1974).

In 1966 I wrote a chapter, "Assumption-Centered Psychotherapy," for a book on various systems of psychotherapy (Anderson, 1973b). In 1977 a priest living in San Diego wrote a doctoral thesis entitled "The Self-Esteem Theory of Human Motivation" (Campbell, 1977), and he wrote me that I had arrived at the same conclusions his research had led him to. From time to time individuals have been impressed with the validity and usefulness of my concepts, but no one in a position of influence has made self-image theory a useful tool for teaching or for therapy. Also, psychiatry has had minimal interest in psychodynamics for many years, while it has been busy developing new drugs to change behavior.

In 1978 I requested permission to present a formal course to be titled "An Alternative System of Psychodynamics" to any interested members of the American Psychiatric Association at its annual meeting in Chicago, May 1979. My request was rejected. If my concepts fall by the wayside, "at least" I tried. It could be that my presentation has not been adequately clear, or that my concepts are so different from those psychiatrists are used to that they find it difficult to tie them to anything familiar. The problem of Self-Image Therapy is not its complexity, but rather its simplicity.

THEORY

I am seemingly as oblivious of "personality" in my theoretical formulations as I used to find Freudian theory oblivious of such things as "entitlements" and resulting "resentments." What replaces personality is "self-image," the total construct an individual uses to guide and determine behavior and reactions.

Each person's self-image is as unique, as detailed, and as faceted as the physical self-image. Like the body, the self-image is made up of an endless array of organized parts called assumptions, which relate to both action and reaction; that is, they are always two-party. They concern every conceivable aspect of behavior a person can be involved in (Anderson 1950, 1957).

By the time children start school they have accumulated enough beliefs—assumptions—to have a reasonably complete road map for living. They are the things people take so much for granted that they are unaware of their existence. Nevertheless, these assumptions about self, others, and life guide people in their choices and selections; they determine what will and will not be done, what people anticipate from others, what provides security, and what is seen as dangerous. People acquire these concepts and conclusions out of their own experiences, just because they were there.

Because of self-image each individual operates almost unconsciously or automatically in all familiar settings. A person's total functioning, like his or her assumptions, is organized into consistent and reliable patterns that are so completely identical with self that for all intents and purposes self-image *is* the self. People now can count on the person as well as on his or her behavior to be according to that structure. Part of the therapist's task is to become aware of repetitive patterns (structures) the patient operates according to, and to help him or her see them and thus to see the self.

Whatever concepts the person takes for granted— what he or she believes—was not arbitrarily or even casually laid down or incorporated into his or her self-image; rather it was the product of that person's experiences in his or her particular world. Likewise, every assumption is associated with a value judgment, determined by experiences in a world of significant people, and each experience was given a value depend-

ing on the security/insecurity or danger/well-being factor that resulted. For example, in my world, eating heartily was associated with parental approval—*good;* cleaning my plate—*good;* waste of any kind—*bad;* working hard—*good;* carrying my own weight—*good;* being a nuisance or bother—*bad;* having good posture—*good;* carrying gossip—*bad.*

Assumptions are the building blocks of a person's makeup and therefore of behavior. Included are reactions or responses to everything seen or done. Assumptions guide the individual, determine what he or she will and will not do. They determine what the person expects or anticipates from self and others in any situation. They also establish attitudes.

Every action is associated in the person's mind with some degree of good or bad, right or wrong. One develops a hierarchy of value judgments that derive from experiences. Values tell one that certain behaviors and things are good and others are bad. Behaviors and things, however, are not merely black or white, but more or less good or bad according to one's particular value schema. This is of great importance in determining choices and attitudes and in warding off guilt.

Of major importance in all behavior is a hierarchy of values schema, which determines one's *at least*s. A person may do things ordinarily not acceptable to one's value system *provided* one is sure to do or not to do something worse in one's schema than the prohibited thing; for example, I may have done *this* bad thing, but "at least" I did not do *that.* One feels no guilt as long as one's *at least*s are intact. One may ward off guilt by following a code—by adhering to compulsive *have to*s; by keeping at least's ready and available; by moving from the role of actor to the role of reactor, and thus feeling justified. Preventing guilt is a constant and major occupation of everyone (Anderson, 1950, 1957).

Everything a person experiences is classified into actions and reactions, or the role he or she or others is playing at any moment. If one does a bad thing as an actor, it is occasion for guilt, but when one does the same thing as a reactor—in response to someone else's behavior— it is assessed as justified.

Another way of making classifications, and therefore knowing what to do, is by *role.* Everyone falls into a variety of groups (Anderson, 1957) determined by age, sex, relationship, physical state, occupation, incidental activities, in-group or out-group status, religion, political persuasion, and so forth. There are an infinite number of these possible roles. Every role implies a whole constellation of related assumptions that determine how others must behave and what is expected.

Assumptions regarding role behavior are acquired early and are the basic determinants of behavior in similar situations. Even young children know what is to be done in all manner of interpersonal situations. Autistics are the only people who apparently do not have such a handy reference guide available to them. This deficiency appears to be due to their inability to retain concepts, which makes classification impossible.

Every assumption concerning role behavior is associated with a moral judgment. *Right–wrong, good–bad* labels are attached to every action and reaction, and the degree of rightness or wrongness is fairly clear to the person. People characteristically behave in ways accounted by them as right or justified, because that was the safe way for them to behave as children. It was safe because significant people approved of it—there was no pain or penalty—and they were "good." Past approbation is the basic reason why most people approve of themselves and feel satisfied with their manner of functioning. Attitudes and values do not change readily.

Contrary to common belief, *no person has a poor self-image*! Shedding this assumption is of major importance if we would do psychotherapy. We never need to build up a good self-image, because everyone already has one. It is never a poor self-image that causes people to behave inappropriately. On the contrary, it is our grandiose self-image—our bigger-than-life self-concept—that leads to difficulties. To help the person understand this is part of the goal of the therapist.

We have our grandiose self-image because of several factors: When our self-image was forming—in our infancy, when we were most helpless—we were the center of attention for important people. We were adept at controlling them and we took our power for granted. We cried and they came running. The fact that we survived is evidence of our success. Next we are the beloved children of very important people, and this alone was sufficient to make one believe in one's importance. Third, when our self-image was forming, everything we did was accounted special, both by ourselves and by the people significant to us whose opinions we valued.

Finally, we have still another basis for our private sense of specialness. We have arrived at value judgments remarkably akin to those of our significant people, and accounted *by them* as right values. The more right one's opinions, judgments, and values are, the greater is one's right to high self-esteem. It is the threat of low esteem from significant others that forces children to adopt "right" values and makes them acceptable in their specific interpersonal world. The conclusion from all this is that our self-image inevitably has a high value; it is *never* low.

When people insist that they have low self-esteem, the truth is they really have excessive expectations of themselves. Others may have faults and blemishes, but they do not permit themselves to have any. What looks at first like low self-esteem is actually grandiosity: *I must be perfect—without blame or defect (i.e., God) or I cannot tolerate myself. I may look only at my inadequacies, never at my assets. I must never let myself see that this is what I am doing. I may not see how I am playing God by striving for perfection, but only that I failed.*

It is common for us to attribute to others a low self-esteem because we see them as inferior, and we think they have reason to have low self-esteem. The fact that people attribute to others low self-esteem does not bring about such self-devaluation on their part. Instead it brings resentment. The devaluated person feels he is being short-changed, that he is not getting what he is entitled to, such as appreciation or recognition of quality. Everyone has his or her own private values, and these give each person the "right" to think well of him- or herself. Whenever one finds resentment, there cannot be a poor self-image.

Consequently, people at all levels—socially, intellectually, economically—have a good self-image. This is the basis of all our interpersonal operations. It dictates our functioning, our assertiveness, our self-pity, and our reluctance to be challenged. We hesitate to allow ourselves to be "put on the line." We avoid situations in which we might not show up well; we isolate ourselves from competition, or we find other ways of preserving our *amour propre*. Everything we do is calculated to preserve our pride system intact, to maintain our grandiose self-image. The primary driving force in life is preserving this grandiose self-image.

In the Orient this is called "saving face," and is seen as basic and essential. When pride is threatened and our grandiose self-image is endangered, we feel anxious, and the experience is stressful. Anxiety results whenever one feels a threat to one's self-image. Hurt pride is anxiety provoking, and such tensions frequently result in the occurrence of psychological and physical symptoms. Whenever one finds decompensation symptoms, one can assume that there has been threat to the person's self-image, that is, to his or her pride.

Several well-defined feelings are possible in any situation. If people have been following their code regarding behavior, they will tend to feel comfortable with their behavior. This is the usual way for everyone to feel. If they have followed their code, their value system, but did not get the anticipated interpersonal results, they may feel confused and helpless. Helplessness is the "mother" of rage or depression. They may also feel resentful of those who let them down.

It not infrequently happens that a person's assumptions set him or her up for trouble—for example, smug arrogance, clear assumptions regarding entitlements, when the appropriate attitude would be awareness of "contingent privilege." The therapist needs to be perceptive of such grandiose assumptions and help bring them to the light of day, even before they have given discernible trouble or symptoms. Many comfortable people are, in fact, "sick"—that is, quite unrealistic.

Since neither the patient nor the therapist deals with total pictures at any time, but only with segments or partials, there is never a need or even a possibility to see "the whole." It is sufficient in therapy to see that part with which we are dealing, and this implies only that one discovers—or uncovers—the specific and limited assumptions each person needs to deal with in this particular situation, which lie at the root of the present discomfort. The better one understands one's assumptions, the better able one can be to change behavior and thus avoid trouble.

The self-image therapist deals with the here and now. The therapist is aware that present actions or feelings are always determined by past experiences, when assumptions were first laid down. The whole of this interplay is generally not clearly visible to the patient, so the therapist deals always with less than conscious elements. We may label this past material unconscious, and so it is, but Self-Image Therapy has no need for such device as "an unconscious." Everything not in conscious awareness is unconscious at the moment, but conscious awareness is constantly changing.

There are no specific determinants of what is unconscious, such as the Freudian system postulates. It is not pain, or nonacceptability that determines the status, but rather the age at which the experience occurred, the clarity of the original impressions, the degree or extent to which words were attached to it then—and later—and the frequency or recency of repetition. Words usually help to fix and to clarify an experience, and to make one's status more accessible to conscious and critical awareness.

What makes patients uncomfortable relates to their failure to see the self accurately and the interpersonal situation realistically. The patients need to see how their natural, spontaneous, and semiautomatic behavior in response to what has been perceived is making life difficult for them. Patients must question whether their actions are necessary and realistic or whether they are merely behaving in accordance with habit and in the service of pride. If they assume that to behave in some other fashion would seriously impair their self esteem, the therapist needs to explore this assumption, as well as to see if each patient's self-esteem is as essential as he or she has always assumed. If patients' pride has been injured, they need to understand that loss of self-esteem is truly not tantamount to death, as they may have thought.

Alterations in the patterns of one's behavior are almost always necessary in successful therapy. Such patterns have come about because they provided the best way to remain safe—they protected one's pride, one's grandiose self-image. People routinely assume they "have to" do this or that; that other people "have to" behave in specific ways toward them, or their world "isn't right." When pride no longer is the most important fac-

tor, then it becomes possible to be aware of other factors and other needs and possibilities, and to have fewer *should*s, *must*s, and *have to*s.

Probably the least important thing in the mind of the average person is a realistic regard for and protection of one's own welfare. People are so busy enhancing their self-image—often by inflating or deflating someone else—or doing whatever it is that makes them feel good about themselves that their real welfare never occurs to them. This must change if therapy is to be successful. Nothing good can be accomplished if the therapist not only condones but assists in disregarding the patient's real self and real needs; in one's eagerness to "look good," be accepted, please others, and avoid hurting feelings, one may "go along" with situations detrimental to the patient's real welfare.

What are a person's real needs? Perceiving the extent of one's grandiosity, increasing meaningful communication, taking time to listen to oneself, becoming more realistically independent, being more honest, spending more time working and planning and less time hoping, being more assertive—or less, being less concerned about being "pretty" or perfect in behavior than being practical and realistic, being more caring about one's own welfare, having increasing respect for the selfhood of other people; these are some possibilities to explore.

Whatever changes need to be made should be made in light of the fact that keeping one's pride intact serves no useful purpose. Life must be lived in such fashion as will best foster growth rather than vanity. Growth in a variety of ways is a realistic goal for everyone, and contentment is the usual accompaniment of growing.

Whereas the need for people is indeed realistic, even this must be carefully assessed to see whether it represents a neurotic dependency or a healthy interdependence that can foster growth. Learning that other people's lives and feelings are important must be evaluated against the possibility that acquiescing may mean giving in to the neurotic demands of other immature people. People no longer can be "just blobs," there for the neurotic and narcissistic convenience of the patient, but are individuals to know, to touch, and to let be free.

To be aware of all these possibilities minimizes the tendency to repeat old patterns and removes the tendency to have resentment, because one will have ceased to expect too much. Disappointment will be minimal to nonexistent, and depression will vanish because one no longer insists on doing the impossible, namely, changing the other person or becoming perfect oneself. After all, people are here for their own goals and not for my—or your—narcissistic designs.

Self-Image Therapy clearly relies minimally on predetermined goals and patterns. By constantly giving heed to unrecognized assumptions, the therapist gets into the world of the patient—the patient's orientation and values—and does not foist or project his or her own preconceptions on the patient.

METHODOLOGY

Whereas every patient needs to tell his or her story without too much interruption, in employing Self-Image Therapy, therapists should not plan to have patients carry the sessions or determine their direction or even their content. The sessions are not free-wheeling. The medical model offers the best plan for limited structure and adequate information. The therapist stays on course with the goal of getting a comprehensive history as early as possible. This will include *chief complaint, history of present illness, personal history,* and *family history.*

Several things must be clarified before formal therapy can begin. The therapist must assess whether the patient is capable of analytic therapy, or whether he or she is impaired in the ability to integrate—to make connections and to see relationships. Did the patient come for help for him- or herself, or is the patient primarily interested in changing someone else? Is the patient willing—and able—to give up drugs? Are drugs regarded as preferable and more helpful than psychotherapy, or does the patient want both? Does the patient regard his or her situation as desperate, and is hospitalization required—if so, briefly, or on a longer term basis?

The therapist must be a good listener, but not merely a friendly neighbor. He or she must listen critically and discover how the patient's difficulties arose and how they fit into the patterns of his or her life. When the therapist notes a repetitive pattern, what is heard should be verbalized. The therapist does not attempt to establish rapport, because it is assumed that the patient will behave toward the therapist as he characteristically does toward people whom the therapist represents to him or her—women, older people, people in a position of authority or control, or other categories (transference phenomena). It must also be assumed that not until the relationship is a truly helpful one should the patient trust or have a positive feeling for the therapist. If the patient's reaction is premature, this should be noted and verbalized.

There is no specific time for introducing observations or tentative insights; they are mentioned as the therapist becomes aware of them, always tentatively, but therapists should not wait until they are absolutely sure they are right. Insights may be phrased as: "Do I hear you saying . . . ?" "Am I correct in hearing you say . . . ?" "Are you saying that your opinions are . . . ?" or "Do I hear you have always . . . ?" It is not important to be right, but it is important to listen perceptively. It is also possible to have heard wrong, and the patient's help and cooperation should be enlisted.

The sooner the patient participates, the sooner we walk along together, rather than one of us being higher and the other lower. Equality gets the patient into the role of critical participant rather than merely feeling or reacting. Whereas the therapist should listen attentively, he or she should never worry about having missed something. If it is important, it will come up again.

In addition to looking for repetitive patterns, evidence of stress should be noted: strong feelings such as helplessness, resentment, guilt, rage, depression, hopelessness, anxiety, vindictiveness, or physical symptoms. Evidences of smug self-satisfaction, pride, arrogance, impatience, or contempt should also be noted. These two main types of strong feeling indicate either that threat has already been felt or that the self-image has not yet been in danger. In either case what is noted may be mentioned. When a strong feeling emerges, therapists should assess whether it makes sense to them, given what is known of the patient, their beliefs and assumptions. When it does not make sense to the therapist, it is used as further grist for the mill. Therapists must understand, for otherwise it is doubtful whether the patient will move beyond where the therapist is (Anderson, 1973).

As an increasingly comprehensive picture of the patients in everyday functioning is gained, repetitive patterns as they move in and out of a variety of situations are watched for. These, together with the sense of *must* or *have to,* tell the therapist how each patient functions, what the patient regards as important, and what is seen to be dangerous. All situations that bring anxiety are obviously important and need clarification. *What is the patient fearful of doing, or seeing, or realizing? What is absolutely essential? Are the patient's goals realistic?*

The therapist does not set traps for the patient or play games. In my practice I do not try to be clever or smart; I am more of a prosaic plodder than a hot shot. I don't try to test patients and I don't try to impress them. I just move along, one foot ahead of the other, always ready to go back over material, ready to take time for patients' reactions. I see that we keep in step. We may spend time on dreams, but this is rare, for routinely they take too much time and they can provide too many pitfalls in interpretations.

There is no schedule regarding how often or how long to see patients. In the past I saw patients more often than I do now. Sessions are usually an hour long. Less than once a week is probably too infrequent for most patients needing help. Rarely are patients seen more than twice a week, although when anxiety is high, this may be necessary for a time. When sessions are too close together, it is easy to overemphasize the importance of both therapist and therapy.

Many problems do not require protracted treatment. Sometimes even a single session suffices, but in any such short-term therapy, what goes on must be consistent with the overall design of the system. I do not mix personal and professional activities. I am not clever enough to wear two hats successfully. To remain helpful through being objective, I must protect us both from personal involvements.

Since self-image theory maintains that stress is the result of threat to one's grandiose self-image, we can say that the patient comes for help when threatened with being cut down to size, so the therapist must look for hurt pride. Those things associated with a sense of "inner have to" are noted. Such compulsions are always directed toward maintaining an intact pride system. They are also trustworthy earmarks of a neurotic trait, and are never in the service of reality.

Symptoms are of two general types: either longstanding ways of behaving and of life, or "decompensation" reactions, of shorter duration, in response to current stress. Common symptoms are paranoid thinking, distortion in perception, anxiety, depression, confusion, compulsions, phobias, physical symptoms, hyperreactions, sexual aberrations, or life pattern disturbances without other notable symptomatology.

Symptoms such as perseveration may also be an expression of organic handicap. The therapist needs to keep this possibility in mind to make correct decisions. The therapist ought not to get sucked into trying to do the impossible, or into an "interminable analysis," when what the patient needs is competent diagnosis and perhaps medical attention.

Often in therapy things are noted long before they are understood, but it is useful to mention them "out loud" even though understanding may be far away. The therapist does not need to wait to mention something until he or she is sure of the answer; to do so tends to increase the patient's sense of being in the hands of a superior person. It is acceptable for the therapist to be uncertain or not to have an answer; one can be uncertain without being lost. If the patient finds it hard to accept such uncertainty, this is grist for the mill. Another reason therapists may fail to acknowledge things of some importance is that they are in agreement with the therapists' own frame of reference and with the things *we* take for granted. Doing psychotherapy is a good way to become aware of our own neuroticisms.

Since so much of psychiatric symptomatology is derived from "hostility" (Anderson, 1957), it is essential to understand the term. There are three kinds of feelings covered by this term: First, there is a longstanding feeling derived from the feelings and reactions of other people—almost a character trait, in that it is incorporated early and it stands ready to be utilized or expressed. For lack of a better term, I call it "essential hostility." Second, there is the feeling that results from helplessness to do what must be done. It is related to the here and now, is always rooted in felt helplessness, and is called "rage." The third kind of feeling is "resentment,"

and this is quite different from the other two feelings. It stems from a sense of frustrated entitlement. It is useless to try to treat "hostility" without a clear understanding of the three separate implications of the term.

No matter what the presenting symptoms, the therapist's goal is to see how the patient's assumptions contribute to his or her distress, then see how the assumptions can be challenged and replaced by different assumptions that are more functional or realistic, and finally, to help the patient see how exclusive attention to maintaining his or her self-image is destructive to the need to live peacefully and productively.

Neurotics' felt need is always to preserve their grandiose self-image, whereas their real need is to discover and give attention to their true welfare. With proper concern for their own welfare, they can begin experimenting and growing. They will no longer be hampered by their need to keep "safe" from injury to their pride system. They need to find out that hurt pride is not tantamount to destruction. The danger of failing to grow and to behave realistically is a greater danger than the danger of being cut down to size. When one no longer has to spend energies protecting pride, there will be energy available for experimentation and for growing. A simple rule to follow is that if the best reason one can find for doing something is that it bolsters and enhances one's pride, it is doubtful it should be done.

APPLICATIONS

The people best suited for Self-Image Therapy are those old enough to have established a relatively stable value system or self-image; they will be beyond adolescence, but not be old in the sense of being rigid. They need to be able to entertain the possibility that their value system may need altering. Sometimes old people can see what is going on, but they would rather not be troubled with changing.

Regarding those people who suffer from minimal brain dysfunction, Self-Image Therapy works best with those who are only minimally affected, as therapy calls for the ability to make comparisons, see relationships, and integrate observations and facts. When there are problems with integration, as there are in MBD, progress will be minimal; this lack of progress should be attributed to factors outside the therapeutic system.

Even people who are very comfortable may be candidates for treatment, because the theory is applicable to everyone regardless of whether he or she has decompensated and responded with symptoms to a stressful situation. Stress remains the basic indicator for treatment. We all operate according to the same rules, but whether we are comfortable or we are having some degree of distress, we can all become more aware of our operations.

Anxiety or stress symptoms always are the result of felt threat to one's self-image, and, therefore, if the person has symptoms we need to understand what has threatened him or her and what he or she fears. The patient needs to learn that threat to the pride system is not the same as threat to the self. The self-image is always grandiose and fearful of being cut down to size, whereas the real individual, the true person, is not so easily damaged. Seeing why the self-image is bigger than life and bigger than it needs to be in any situation is part of the therapeutic process.

It is easy to develop the erroneous notion that, once having seen this, this understanding will remain constant in one's mind. Nothing could be further from the truth. We are forever forgetting our humanity and then repetitiously thinking and acting as though we were God, expecting too much of ourselves, demanding too much from others. All in all, we behave as though we have no true limitations—or at least as if we believe we should not have any. There seems to be no end to the *should*s, *ought*s, and *must*s we place on ourselves and on others.

When we finally see our grandiosity, it is a major therapeutic event. Life can never be quite the same again, for we have seen, even momentarily, how ridiculous we are. But we cannot keep our minds focused on this new awareness; we get busy with living and doing and reacting and feeling, and before we know it, we are off and running again. The moment we do this we bring our grandiosity back into the picture and act as though this is a reasonable point of view. Therefore, we have every reason to expect things to be according to the old grandiose pattern. But once having seen the shape of things and experienced the truth—that our grandiosity is always ready to be implemented again—it is easier to make further realistic adjustments without great effort or expenditure of time. Insights are lost again and again, but regaining them is no longer a major undertaking.

True insight is an emotional experience, and therefore it needs to be in the present tense. One may look at events of the past, consider their meaning and their implications, and see for the first time how they are illustrative of the very things one has been talking about. This is insight of a certain kind, but it lacks the emotional factor present when one can see the self performing in the here and now, and it suddenly dawns on one that here one is, doing the same old thing again!

Self-Image Therapy provides a most useful framework for understanding and treating a wide spectrum of psychiatric patients: the usual and normal symptoms deriving from efforts to maintain the status quo, the selective inattentions so familiar to us, the compulsive and obsessive patterns people have carried around with them for years, the rigidities that interfere with easy living and all kinds of pleasurable experiences are all appropriate areas for treatment with this system; so are the decompensation symptoms that indicate there has been more stress than the patient has been able to adjust to.

There is just enough difference in patients with psychotic symptoms that it is not appropriate to expect them to be able to make use of this system. Occasionally they will benefit from Self-Image Therapy, but one ought not expect it. It is customary for therapists to think of people as having their usual patterns and symptomatology, or as having decompensated from their usual way of being. Determinations have to be made in each case regarding whether treatment of a psychological nature is indicated, and when is the appropriate time for such intervention.

Probably the most nearly unique as well as the most useful aspect of Self-Image Therapy is its emphasis on getting into the patient's frame of reference—getting acquainted with, or recognizing, his or her assumptions rather than projecting our own or some authority's assumptions onto the patient. This insight is always important, but it becomes even more important when we consider that travel is normal—movement of cultures and individuals is an everyday occurrence. This system minimizes the use of projection. All of us need some assurance of protection from bias, and this system seems to provide a good starting point.

CASE EXAMPLE

A 52-year-old woman, Mrs. Y, came for help because she was depressed to the point where she felt she might have to go to a mental hospital. She also had gained too much weight because she eats when she is depressed. She had developed a bad memory in the past year, and her husband said she could not remember anything for two minutes; she has to write notes to herself to be sure anything gets done.

Until a year ago, she had never been depressed. At the first signs of depression, she went to a community mental health center in a nearby town and said she thought the problem was her husband. After therapists saw and talked to her, they told her that Mr. Y was not the problem; *she* was the problem. She felt better after she knew it was not her husband and she had been feeling well until recently, when the depression returned.

They are living in this area, some 300 to 400 miles from their home, because the husband wants to be helpful to his son (Mrs. Y's stepson), who lives here and is in some agribusiness venture. He needed a piece of equipment and Mr. Y borrowed $47,000 to get it for him. The son is supposed to pay it back, but Mrs. Y doubts he can; however, she likes him because he is a good worker. She really did not want to come here, but she felt she should be with her husband, and she hates dreadfully to be alone. Before they came, Mr. Y called his son every day on the phone, and Mrs. Y thinks this was an unnecessary expense. However, it seemed to be helpful to the son as well as to Mr. Y.

The only person Mrs. Y seems to express a great deal of hostility toward is her daughter-in-law, whom she sees as conniving, always going through large sums of money quickly, and having too much to do with lawyers, so she cannot help but feel suspicious of her intentions. Besides that, the daughter-in-law is a Mormon, has too clean a house, and is always ready to be critical of others. Mrs. Y fully expects her daughter-in-law to leave her husband within a year or two. The two women avoid one another carefully, having little or nothing to do with each other.

Mrs. Y had been married for 26 years to her first husband, and she remembers nothing but good about this marriage; there were two children, who are now married and doing well, and two grandchildren ages six and three. They live in another state and she sees them only once or twice a year. Her first husband died suddenly of a heart attack nine years ago, and Mrs. Y had a very hard time adjusting to the loss. For two years she practically hid from people; she never went out. Then she began working in a shop, and while there she met her present husband. They were married five years ago. He too had been married before; his wife had become mentally ill and lived in a mental hospital. They were finally divorced and Mr. Y was alone for 15 years before he met and married Mrs. Y. He had always said he would never marry again. His first wife is still living, and she is working in a shop. Mrs. Y maintains she doesn't see the first wife as a threat.

Mrs. Y's first marriage was happy; she and her husband worked hard, but they did it together. She inherited the ranch she and her husband had struggled so hard to buy, and she wants to give it to her children, but Mr. Y does not want that. He likes the ranch and wants to live on it.

When at home, she had many friends with whom she frequently did things. Now, however, so far from home, there is nobody to do things with. Mr. Y used to drink a lot before they were married, and he played cards, but now he has not been drunk for two to three months. She has no complaints about him now; he is "fun," he kids her a lot, teases her, but he does not annoy her about her weight gain even though he does not like it. He says she takes what he says too seriously, and perhaps she does, because she is a very serious-minded person.

She has always had little in the way of outside interests or activities. Her family has been her entire life. She crochets a lot and gets pleasure out of this. She reads little, but enjoys a number of quiet television shows. She sleeps well with the aid of bedtime medication, but she wakes up feeling tired.

Mrs. Y has a number of mild medical problems: She had thyroid trouble and has taken radioactive iodine, and she takes medication for her thyroid gland twice a day; she had a goiter before the iodine treatment; she has not menstruated for 10 years but she still has hot flushes. Her mother had two nervous breakdowns, and then developed Parkinson's disease plus some other nerve disease. Mrs. Y has migraine headaches and she feels she has "bad nerves." Recently she had a blood clot in her leg. Her husband has shingles on his shoulder and was in the hospital for bilateral hernia last year, but he seems to be in good health now. He is 64 years old, and she sees him as too old to be carrying his son's burdens or working so hard.

Mrs. Y's story suggests that despite her relatively good adjustment up until a year ago, she has marginal nervous system stability. Her family history of nervous disorder, plus gradual onset of memory failure, migraine headaches, and emotional instability suggest that there may be both an organic and a psychodynamic factor in her difficulties. I contacted her local physician and learned that he saw her as having an early aging process. However, there were numerous problems that clearly were of psychodynamic origin; I thought we could profitably explore and deal with these.

I suggested that Mrs. Y enumerate all the problems that she was aware of, and she came up with the following list: her daughter-in-law; her husband's kidding her; the money they have borrowed to give to his son; her weight gain, her having to take medication; her memory failure; and the mental health center's assurance that her husband played no part in her depression (therefore the entire weight of her problem rested on her own shoulders). She was also troubled because she had not done what her husband wanted her to do in regard to the property. She objected to the time and money her husband spent on his son, particularly when he interfered with her desire to give money to her own children, money that some people would rightfully say belongs to them anyway.

We talked of the "good old days" when life was quite simple; when she was sure of her husband's love, and there was nothing to figure out or wonder about. We talked of the expectations this created in her—for acceptance of herself and her children, and how difficult it must be to live with someone who does not see eye to eye with her or have the same goals. We talked of her patterns of dependency and what pitfalls this leads one into—for example, letting the mental health center decide for her what role her husband plays in her problem. We talked about the possibility that part of the problem may also well be herself, in the way she was raised to look at things and what she was raised to expect.

We talked about depression and its relation to a sense of helplessness, and I wondered if she could put her finger on the things that caused her to feel helpless. She decided there were many things. Her daughter-in-law was a major problem; Mrs. Y felt totally incapable of understanding, liking, or trusting her. Mrs. Y doesn't like the way the daughter-in-law has tried to shut Mrs. Y out of her life. She has never before had anything to do with a Mormon, and she doesn't know how to deal with her. Added to this is the problem of what to do with her guilt toward her daughter-in-law. She has strong unacknowledged destructive feelings toward her, feelings she cannot recall having toward anyone before. We talked of how hard it is to stand any guilt.

There were other sources of a sense of helplessness—her husband, for one. She doesn't know how to cope with him. She isn't sure he really cares for her, and sometimes she wonders if he will divorce her if she has to go to a mental hospital. She wishes he didn't like her ranch so much. I encouraged her to feel it isn't occasion for too much guilt if she does not comply with his every wish. I thought there might well be some compromise and urged her to think of other possibilities besides those she had mentioned.

I wondered if she had ever thought of consulting a lawyer, to get help in making suggestions and working out details that she alone could not come up with. We talked about her mistrust of people who consulted lawyers. I indicated she might feel better if she were not totally dependent on her husband, but had some clear property rights of her own, particularly if such rights were fair and considerate of all people involved—herself, most of all, her children, and her husband. Things usually are not all one way, but compromises.

I suggested that her memory failure problem made it even more imperative that she be helped to give herself a fair deal, for she could not depend on her own efforts to support herself, and therefore she needed a financial cushion of some kind. I volunteered that the sooner she acted to protect both herself and her children's interests, the sooner she would get over her feeling of helplessness, and this would contribute to her sense of well-being. Uncertainty, confusion, and vacillation are no big help, so eliminate them as soon as possible. At this time I saw no reason why she would resist living on the ranch with her husband, provided ownership was secured for herself and the children.

We talked a good bit about securing a competent attorney, and I offered to put her in touch with someone who would help her select one. I also suggested she bring her husband to meet me; perhaps the openness implicit in such a meeting would help her feel comfortable with the idea. It took several discussions about this before she agreed it was probably best to keep things open, and how much better that might be than suffering from guilt. She mentioned that her husband had been opposed to her seeking help both from the mental health center and from me, because of the expense involved.

We talked about the center and the role it played in her problems. Although it may have contributed to her discomfort, she had to realize that she is not tied to it. She does not have to accept its verdicts, but may come up with some answers of her own. I encouraged her to express her feelings about her husband, and as she talked she had less feeling of being caught, and more belief that it might be possible to work out a number of things that previously she had assumed had to be just one way or another. I also urged her to try standing a little more guilt than she had in the past—in other words, she should experiment with trying to be more fair to herself. She had been afraid Mr. Y would divorce her, and being alone again seems almost unbearable to her. I urged her to consider that things are not all that fragile, and that somehow with her own strength and the help of others she no doubt would weather whatever storms might come; however, I emphasized that I did not expect any notable storms to arise.

We talked about her reaction to her daughter-in-law's Mormon heritage. I had spent 10 years in Salt Lake City and so had abundant impressions and firsthand knowledge of this segment of our population. I reassured Mrs. Y about the Mormon culture and values, and suggested we take it a step at a time with relation to the daughter-in-law. I was hopeful it might work out to be an interesting and broadening experience, and I was ready to stand by and react to her reports, just as I would when she was confronted by any other new or possibly threatening experience.

The biggest step was taken when Mrs. Y agreed she had not only the right but the obligation to do whatever she did for her own welfare, rather than out of a belief about how people should behave. If she suffered a little guilt in moving in that direction, she had to learn to live with it. Her life would never be good so long as she was afraid to stand a little guilt. She would, no doubt, live her life in such a fashion as would largely preclude both resentment and helplessness, but her prime obligation was to maintain her own welfare rather than be concerned about how she looked to others, or what feeling she had at any moment.

The last time I heard from Mrs. Y, a number of months ago, she was functioning rather well.

SUMMARY

Compared to Self-Image Therapy, it would be difficult to imagine a system of psychodynamics more complete or more simple. Learning how to recognize and to think about assumptions seems formidable and foreign to the average therapist—particularly if he or she is accustomed to the usual psychodynamic jargon—until it becomes automatic. Then the therapist wonders why it ever seemed to pose a problem and why he or she was unable to think in this manner. There are essentially no new terms to learn in Self-Image Therapy, certainly none of a complex or "scientific" nature, and the basic concepts and patterns are completely familiar to us; they always have been.

Given the need to survive, with helplessness there from the start, the fact of surviving has to be related to caring and helpful people, and this interpersonal aspect is woven into the fabric of all a person's basic assumptions about functioning. The "will to live," or the survival drive, makes interpersonal operations a natural and a must.

Some systems describe what takes place—they offer the mechanics—but they do not offer any dynamics. Self-Image Therapy offers both. Recognizing that the survival drive is basic in a psychological as well as in a physical framework brings harmony into the entire picture of human functioning. The moment we grasp the fact of the psychological self-image and recognize that grandiosity is an inevitable part of it, we have the means for understanding how and why people behave as they do, both in sickness and in health. Surviving implies living out and maintaining one's grandiose self-image, because that is the only image the person has. It is all he or she has to work with.

The person is not compensating or overcompensating for inferiority feelings; he is just being himself and actualizing his image.

Originally, threat to survival occurred because of helplessness; resolution of the threat occurred through the assistance of others; this fostered the development of assumptions regarding danger and source of help. This in turn brought about the development of the person's value system—which is the result of the threat of nonsurvival and the experience of surviving—in the days, weeks, and months that follow the first and earliest state of danger. "Right" turns out to be that which promotes security, and "wrong" is that which brings insecurity. Moral values turn out to be the techniques for surviving, and they act as a guide as well as determinant of behavior and feelings. People do only what their code permits or dictates.

The goal of living is to continue to survive, and psychological survival implies survival of one's grandiose self-image, with the aid of one's value system.

Minimizing anxiety may be seen as one goal in therapy; feeling safe and surviving comfortably is no small achievement. A higher level goal is to make such realistic alterations in one's assumptions that self-maintenance takes a secondary place to protecting and enhancing one's welfare. This is the way to go if one wishes to promote growth and to experience "the good life." It cannot be done until the person can distinguish between vanity and welfare. The natural goal is enhancement of one's vanity or pride. Good therapy helps one see pride for what it is—a barrier to growth, to necessary relationships, and to realistic living.

The need for eclecticism vanishes, for Self-Image Therapy includes everything one needs—not only a dependable base, but a North Star and a compass. Therapists no longer feel lost, for they know what they are looking for and where they have to go. The greatest problem is with the people who are new to the concepts; because of prior commitments to other beliefs, they commonly find it difficult to see what is there to be seen.

REFERENCES

Anderson, C. M. (1950a). The anatomy, physiology and pathology of the psyche; a new concept of the dynamics of behavior. *American Practitioner and Digest of Treatment, 1,* 400–405.

Anderson, C. M. (1950b). *Saints, sinners and psychiatry.* Philadelphia: Lippincott.

Anderson, C. M. (1952). The self image, a theory of the dynamics of behavior. *Mental Hygiene, 36,* 227–244.

Anderson, C. M. (1957). *Beyond Freud.* New York: Harper.

Anderson, C. M. (1963). *Jan, my brain-damaged daughter.* Portland, Ore.: Durham Press.

Anderson, C. M. (1971). The self-image, a theory of the dynamics of behavior (updated). *Mental Hygiene, 56,* 365–368.

Anderson, C. M. (1972a). *Society pays; the high cost of brain damage in America.* New York: Walker.

Anderson, C. M. (1972b). Minimal brain damage. *Mental Hygiene, 56,* 62–66.

Anderson, C. M. (1973a). Perspective. *Journal of the American Medical Womens' Association, 28,* 402–414.

Anderson, C. M. (1973b). Assumption-centered psychotherapy. In Ratibor-Ray M. Jurjevich (Ed.), *Direct psychotherapy, 28 originals.* Coral Gables, FL: University of Miami Press.

Anderson, C. M. (1974). The brain-injured adult: An overlooked problem. In R. Weber (Ed.), *Handbook on learning disabilities.* Englewood Cliffs, NJ: Prentice-Hall.

Anderson, C. M., & Plymate, H. B. (1962). Management of the brain-damaged adolescent. *American Journal of Orthopsychiatry, 32,* 492–500.

Campbell, R. (1977). Private communications.

Chapter 59

SEX THERAPIES

DIANNE GERARD

Although clinicians have been dealing with sexual problems for many years, recently a number of advances have been made in the direct treatment of such common sexual problems as impotence, frigidity, and premature ejaculation.

Essentially, as Dianne Gerard explains in this chapter, the big difference now is that the problem is dealt with directly on a here-and-now basis, rather than seeing the sexual difficulty as part of the total problem of the total individual. In this way, the systems mentioned in this chapter represent a kind of symptom removal rather than psychotherapy in the inclusive sense.

However, a good rationale would be an analogy: If you go to a doctor's office because you have a bit of sand in your eye or a splinter in your finger, the usual procedures of taking temperature, blood pressure, and a history may not be worthwhile: why not solve the problem as quickly and with as little fuss as possible? So, too, if a short-term solution may work out for, say, premature ejaculation (a problem the new Sex Therapies have good success with), why not proceed immediately with the cure?

Symptom removal may be the equivalent to psychotherapy, and indeed some advocates of some kinds of Behavior Modification (of the Skinnerian variety) do think that this is what psychotherapy is all about.

Sex Therapies are treatments designed to deal with specific barriers to sexual functioning. Sexual dysfunctions are attitudinal, behavioral, or emotional factors that hinder people from engaging in or enjoying sexual activities. The aims of Sex Therapies are to provide accurate sex education, to increase erotic pleasure by overcoming anxiety about sex, to improve communication between sexual partners, and to improve techniques so that maximal satisfaction is attained.

Sex Therapies focus primarily on symptom removal rather than personality changes. Attention is directed generally to the "here and now" and to specific barriers to current sexual functioning. Deeper, more intrapsychic or interpersonal conflicts are addressed only when they interfere with treatment progress.

There are three main types of Sex Therapy: (1) William Masters and Virginia Johnson's two-week intensive Behavioral Sex Therapy, (2) Helen Kaplan's combination of behavioral plus Psychodynamic Sex Therapy, and (3) Group Sex Therapy as employed by McGovern, Kirkpatrick, and LoPiccolo (1978). Couples typically are treated conjointly by one or two therapists; however, some therapists accept individuals without partners.

HISTORY

Sex Therapies have come of age primarily with the publication of *Human Sexual Inadequacy* by William Masters and Virginia Johnson (1970). The authors described explicitly their short-term behavioral model of Sex Therapy plus data regarding its effectiveness. Earlier roots in this area, however, reach back perhaps 200 years. Sir John Hunter, an eighteenth-century British physician, reported a technique for treating impotence that anticipated that of Masters and Johnson (cited in Comfort, 1967). He used paradoxical intention by advising an impotent patient to go to bed with his lover for six nights in succession but not to have intercourse. The patient reported that he was so preoccupied with fears of having too much desire that he no longer was afraid that he could not perform.

Little progress beyond personal attitudes and beliefs about sexuality occurred until the 1940s, with the collection and publication of Alfred Kinsey's data (Kinsey, Pomeroy, & Martin, 1948, 1965) on the sexual behavior of men and women. This was a large-scale collection of sociological data on sexual functioning. Kinsey relied completely on self-reports; thus the subjectivity of the reported findings became a major criticism. The data presented a picture of the variety and frequencies of sexual activities of males and later of females but said little about psychological or physiological aspects of sexual response.

In the 1950s Masters and Johnson began to study scientifically the physiological sexual responses of men and women in a laboratory setting. They reported data on nearly 10,000 sexual acts, such as coitus and masturbation under a variety of conditions. Subjects were all volunteers. Sex therapy clients were not used for this data. However, this experimental process led to theories regarding sexual response and also served to generate ideas for treatment. They published their data and conclusions after following up treated couples for five years.

John Money and Anke Erhardt at Johns Hopkins University furthered knowledge by studying gender-identity formation and the role of hormonal influences on sexuality. Helen Kaplan (1974) added the psychoanalytic/psychodynamic components of Sex Therapy by examining the psychological roots underlying sexual dysfunctions and marital conflict. Behavior therapists identified the ways in which sexual dysfunctions were acquired and reinforced through focusing on factors in the current sexual situation of affected individuals that impair functioning; they also added innovative techniques for treatment such as combining dating sessions with sexual home assignments (Annon, 1974) and maintaining diaries of sexual thoughts and activities (LoPiccolo, 1978).

Sex Therapy with individuals began in the mid 1970s with the realization that not all people with sexual difficulties had current partners. This approach is controversial when surrogate partners are employed. Masters and Johnson have discontinued this practice. Martin Williams (1978) treats sexually dysfunctional men using "body-work therapists" at the Berkeley Sex Therapy Group; no figures are cited regarding treatment success rate. Lonnie Barbach (1975) devised a group treatment plan for what she calls "preorgasmic" (anorgasmic) women based on the Lobitz and LoPiccolo (1972) masturbation program for females. This method proved highly successful (93 percent of women became orgasmic after five weeks of treatment) and gained popularity across the country. Drawbacks centered on problems with transfer of learning; women might become orgasmic with self-stimulation but remain unable to experience orgasm with a partner.

Group treatment is used to reduce costs, provide opportunity for emotional support and a modeling effect among couples, and serve a wider range of clientele. There appears to be promise in this approach, but as in all aspects of Sex Therapies, there is a lack of controlled research. Relative effectiveness of one treatment over another is simply not known.

CURRENT STATUS

An increase in interest in sexuality research and therapy has occurred since the pioneering work of Masters and Johnson. Numerous self-help books are available to improve people's understanding of sexuality and to help them solve their sexual problems (Barbach, 1975; Heiman, LoPiccolo, & LoPiccolo, 1976; McCary, 1973; Pion, 1977). Journals such as the *Journal of Sex & Marital Therapy, Journal of Sex Education and Counseling, Archives of Sexual Behavior, Journal of Sex Research,* and *Medical Aspects of Human Sexuality* also have been started to keep pace with emerging research and theory.

Many graduate programs in medicine, social work, counseling, and psychology now offer courses on human sexuality and many teach sex therapy techniques. A number of postgraduate programs provide intensive training in Sex Therapy and sex education.

Sex Therapies draw professionals from a variety of disciplines. Physicians, ministers, educators, and psychotherapists all use various theories and techniques to help their clientele. This chapter deals with the treatment of sexually dysfunctional clients by professionals who specialize in the field. Because there is insufficient research data to specify which aspects of the treatment are crucial, there is little in the way of standardization. Much more research is needed to clarify the essentials for effective treatment. Douglas Hogan (1978) has made a start by reviewing the literature and recommending outcome studies that consider the interaction of client variables, treatment components, and modes of therapy using factorial designs.

THEORY

To understand the etiology of sexual dysfunction, Kaplan (1974) examined the immediate and remote causes. Immediate causes are those factors that create an "anti-erotic" environment, anything in the present moment that ruins the sexual responsivity between the partners. Kaplan states that sexual response is a "complex series of autonomically mediated visceral reflexes which can only work successfully if the person is in a calm state and if the process is 'left alone,' i.e., not impaired by conscious monitoring processes" (p. 121). The person must be able to abandon him- or herself to the erotic sensations. Kaplan groups the immediate causes of sexual dysfunction into four categories:

1. Sexual ignorance and failure to engage in effective behavior.
2. Performance anxiety and fear of failure. There is often an excessive concern for pleasing the partner, which stems from an underlying fear of rejection.

3. Spectatoring—a term introduced by Masters and Johnson that refers to self-observation of one's sexual performance rather than total participation in it. This is a defense to bind the anxiety that sexual contact elicits. Another defense is a perceptual one in which the person denies or fails to perceive erotic sensations.

4. Failure to communicate openly and without shame about sexual wishes, likes, and dislikes.

Much of the time in Sex Therapy, the above causes of sexual conflict can be addressed and alleviated via experiential rather than cognitive insight methods with a resulting disappearance of the symptom. If this cannot be accomplished, the remote causes of the conflict are explored in the psychotherapeutic sessions. Remote causes may be classified as either intrapsychic or interpersonal. Kaplan (1974) borrowed from psychoanalytic theory especially with the concepts of unconscious motivation of behavior and the importance of childhood experiences in shaping the adult personality.

Psychoanalytic theory explains sexual disorders in terms of repression of oedipal sexual urges and fixation at certain early stages of development (oral, anal, or phallic-oedipal). However, Kaplan states that an unconscious conflict can cause sexual dysfunction "only if it evokes disorganizing anxiety at the moment of lovemaking or mobilizes perceptual and obsessive defenses against arousal" (p. 145).

Childrearing practices that associate guilt and shame with sex are culprits in the etiology of sexual conflict as well. Our culture enforces a discontinuous type of learning about sexuality; that is, we are encouraged to learn as little as possible about sexual functioning until we are culturally sanctioned to express our sexual feelings in marriage. Conflict results from the backlog of suppression and from the notion that sex equals sin. Many children still are taught that masturbation is sinful, that sexual thoughts are as bad as sexual behavior, and that sexual experimentation prior to marriage is forbidden. These are not easy messages to undo. In fact, Kaplan (1974) remarks that "it speaks for the strength of the sex drive and the inherent potential towards mental health that many persons who come from a restrictive background escape sexual problems" (p. 149).

Relationship variables also create deeper sources of sexual conflict. Lack of trust and power struggles create a destructive atmosphere and inhibit the abandonment necessary for full sexual responsivity. It makes sense that satisfying sexual expression often disappears when the couple's interpersonal system is rejecting, dehumanizing, or fraught with hostility. Thus, the sexual system—the relationship—assumes a central role in Sex Therapies.

Research does indicate that concentration on communication difficulties, marital conflict, and psychopathology without specific attention to sexual interaction have much less success in symptom reversal (citations in Marks, 1978). A major difference between Sex Therapies and psychotherapy or Marital Therapy is that they are not comprehensive; their focus is a narrow one. Traditional psychotherapy aims toward personality reconstruction; Marital Therapy attempts to reverse interpersonal conflict, increase harmony, and improve communication and understanding between the couple. Because the scope of Sex Therapies is limited, there are certain prerequisites. The couple needs to be committed to working on their difficulties, to viewing it as a joint problem rather than as involving one partner only, and to be willing to suspend for the duration of treatment (especially in the two-week intensive therapy) any preoccupation with past hurts and angers. A "here and now" orientation is encouraged.

Further assumptions are made. Sex is viewed as a natural function. The urge for orgasmic release is as natural as the other biological needs to breathe, eat, or defecate. However, the sexual urge is the only one that can be suppressed at will without harmful effects. It operates under two separate systems of influence: the biophysical and the psychosocial. Either or both can create sexual dysfunction. Past learning, misconceptions, fears of performance, anxiety regarding rejection, and sexually embarrassing or traumatic incidents constitute usual psychosocial barriers to satisfying sexual functioning. Drug abuse, alcoholism, diabetes, physical injuries, and certain endocrinological imbalances are biophysical causes of sexual dysfunction. Until recently it was assumed that upwards of 90 percent of sexual dysfunction was psychosomatic. More refined instrumentation has permitted study of physiological barriers to erection via use of the nocturnal penile tumescence monitor; this provides information on the diagnosis and prognosis of impotence (Karacan, 1970).

METHODOLOGY

Sex Therapies are behavioral treatments designed to relieve impediments to satisfying sexual relations. As a treatment method, the therapies focus on relief of specific sexual symptoms via analysis of the etiology of the problem and the communication patterns of the couple; specific behavior suggestions in the form of graduated sexual tasks are given to the couple, which they then experience together in privacy before reporting back to their therapist(s). Unlike analytic psychotherapies, Sex Therapies use a directive approach to modify the attitudes and atmosphere in which sex takes place. Communication exerises and graduated sexual experiences confront clients with their sexual anxiety and facilitate its resolution. Therapy establishes the attitudes and erotic atmosphere necessary for the natural physiological sexual responses to occur; these cannot be taught (Brecher, 1969). The rapid-treatment approach initiated by Masters and Johnson (1970) adds an environmental factor in that the couple is removed from their home situation and spends two weeks exclusively focused on their sexual relationship. Research to date, however, has not proved that this is necessary for treatment success. The method developed by Kaplan relies more on psychodynamic intervention than does the Masters and Johnson model, which focuses on the behavioral and communication aspects of the couple's dysfunction.

Masters and Johnson (1970), Hartman and Fithian (1972), and Kaplan (1974) begin with a detailed chronological history including sexual functioning, family-of-origin experiences, dating, and marital adjustment. A thorough physical examination with appropriate lab tests is conducted. Annon (1974) diverges from this approach; he takes a history primarily of the sexual problem (description, onset and course, client's understanding of causation, past treatment, and goals). With completion of the history, the therapist(s) decides on the feasibility of treating the couple with the sex therapy method, then discusses the findings with the couple. This includes reflecting back in a "mirrorlike" manner the background of each partner, how certain variables created the sexual conflict, and aspects of the current sexual system that serve to maintain the dysfunction. Masters and Johnson (1970) refer to this as the "round table" session; goals are promotion of neutrality between the couple, encouragement of open communication (sharing oneself as accurately as possible), and increasing motivation for active participation by the couple in the treatment. Once the couple understands the likely etiology of their difficulty, learns about the methods that will be used to reverse the dysfunction, and commits themselves to ongoing therapy, the first sexual tasks are assigned.

Sensate focus is typically the first assignment. The couple is instructed to choose a time when they are relaxed and receptive to one another; they are to take turns caressing each other in a gentle, nondemanding manner. Genitals, breasts, and intercourse are off limits. The "receiver" of the sensual touch has but one responsibility: to protect the partner from hurting him or her during the touching. Sensate focus is uniquely designed to increase each partner's sensitivity to sensual touch and to eliminate any need to perform or to watch oneself. The experience is discussed in the next psychotherapy session. If both partners report pleasure and are able to suspend their performance fears, they are asked to try the experience again with a modification: the receiving partner places his or her hand on the giver's hand to nonverbally show the kinds of strokes and pressures that are desired.

As Sex Therapy progresses, the couple learns more effective communication about their specific sexual wishes.

Touching of the breasts and genitals in a light, teasing, and nondemanding way is the next step. Caresses that lead to orgasm are encouraged only when the couple feels relaxed, experiences erotic pleasure, and when spectatoring has been eliminated. Variations in the treatment method for different types of dysfunction begin at this point.

A brief description of the major types of sexual dysfunction and treatment strategies is necessary. Each may be classified as primary, when the dysfunction has been present at every sexual opportunity, or secondary, when there was at least one sexual experience without the sexual symptom. Male sexual dysfunctions include impotence, premature ejaculation, and retarded ejaculation. Female sexual disorders include general sexual dysfunction, orgasmic dysfunction, vaginismus, dyspareunia, and sexual anesthesia. As with male dysfunctions, these may be viewed as either vasocongestive disorders (general sexual dysfunction, vaginismus, and perhaps dyspareunia) or orgasmic phase disorders. Kaplan (1974) conceptualizes sexual response as biphasic: vasocongestion and orgasm. This contrasts with the concept of four phases of sexual response developed by Masters and Johnson (1966): excitement, plateau, orgasm, resolution.

Premature and Retarded Ejaculation

Disorders of ejaculation include premature and retarded ejaculation (or ejaculatory incompetence, a term Masters and Johnson prefer). Difficulty arises in defining precisely what constitutes prematurity. Masters and Johnson (1970) generated the following definition: If a man cannot control his ejaculation for a "sufficient length of time during intravaginal containment to satisfy his partner in at least fifty percent of their coital experiences" (p. 92), then he is a premature ejaculator. Rather than pronouncing a specific length of time in which ejaculation is delayed as the criterion, they define it in the context of the sexual system. Of course, if the female never experiences orgasm during vaginal penetration, this definition falls apart. For premature ejaculation, the stop-start or squeeze technique is suggested. The penis is manually stimulated to the point of ejaculatory inevitability; then the partner either ceases stimulation or squeezes the penis directly under the coronal ridge. Both techniques result in a decrease of arousal, loss of the urge to ejaculate, and sometimes partial loss of erection. This is repeated three or four times before ejaculation is permitted; thus, high levels of arousal are experienced without ejaculation. When the male experiences more voluntary control over ejaculation and can focus on his erotic sensations, he attempts penetration without thrusting. Gradually thrusting is initiated with stops to control ejaculation.

Ejaculatory incompetence is the absence of ejaculation during coitus; ejaculation may or may not occur at other times, such as during masturbation. For treatment the male is stimulated to ejaculation with his penis outside the vagina. Next, as he is stimulated to high levels of arousal, rapid penetration is attempted in the female-superior position. Vigorous thrusting until ejaculation occurs then. If this fails, manual stimulation is employed. Certain drugs may affect this phase of sexual response by causing retrograde ejaculation; certain antipsychotic and antihypertensive medications occasionally cause this. Ejaculatory incompetence is a rare sexual dysfunction, while its opposite, premature ejaculation, is very common.

Impotence

In the treatment of impotence, gentle manual caressing of the penis is used in a stop-start manner, too; however, the purpose is to reassure the man that he can attain, lose, and regain his erection. Once confidence is reestablished and he experiences partial or full erections, he penetrates the woman, who is in the female-superior position. She controls the insertion process to avoid distracting him, and slow, nondemanding thrusting is initiated. There appear to be more organic causes of impotence than of any other type of dysfunction. However, this may simply reflect the current state of knowledge and the difficulties inherent in detecting physiological components.

Vaginismus

Vaginismus occurs when the vaginal muscles involuntarily spasm and prevent penile penetration. Arousal and orgasm may be experienced in the presence of the spasm. Graduated dilators (or fingers) are used to treat vaginismus. Dilators are inserted by the woman or her partner and remain in place for several minutes to several hours. Masters and Johnson (1970) report that much of the involuntary spasm can be eliminated in three to five days. Coitus is attempted when the largest dilator can be tolerated without pain. Masters and Johnson suggest that a pelvic exam in which the involuntary spasm of the vagina is demonstrated to both partners is another important factor in symptom resolution; this relieves the belief that vaginismus represents a conscious rejection of the partner.

Dyspareunia

Dyspareunia is painful intercourse. It may be caused by lack of arousal, which impairs or prevents vaginal lubrication. Other causes include gynecological disorders, endometriosis, vaginal infection, or herpes simplex. Usually there is no difficulty with orgasm. In treating dyspareunia, a thorough gynecological exam is vital to rule out physiological factors that cause pain during coitus. If insufficient lubrication is the cause, lack of arousal is suspected and the couple is instructed in sensate focus and genital pleasuring. Sterile vaginal lubricants may facilitate penetration. In older women, hormonal replacement therapy may help senile vaginitis and reduce dyspareunia. Also, the use of the female-superior position in coitus enables the woman to regulate the depth and angle of penetration, thus avoiding pain from deep penetration. This may be the most viable solution when dyspareunia is caused by physiological impediments that cannot be reversed.

General Sexual Dysfunction

General sexual dysfunction is characterized by inhibition of desire and arousal; the woman reports being uninterested in and unexcited by sexual contact. She fails to lubricate although on occasion she may be orgasmic. This is somewhat analogous to sexual anesthesia in which the woman "feels nothing" when her genitals are touched, but may fully enjoy the cuddling in sexual contact. Kaplan (1974) defines this phenomenon as a hysterical conversion symptom rather than a true sexual dysfunction in that it seems more a psychoneurotic defense than a psychosomatic symptom.

For general sexual dysfunction, therapy relies on sensate focus, genital pleasuring, and nondemanding intercourse in which thrusting is controlled by the woman. Throughout the sexual tasks, her desires determine the pace and variety of caresses. This helps her both to focus on her own erotic sensations and to assume responsibility for her sexual pleasure.

Orgasmic Dysfunction

Orgasmic dysfunction, the failure to reach orgasm during a sexual experience, may occur situationally, randomly, or absolutely, in which orgasm is never experienced under any condition. Having dispelled the myth of two kinds of orgasm (vaginal and clitoral) Masters and Johnson (1966), using laboratory data, report that orgasm has both vaginal and clitoral components. The clitoris registers most of the sensory input, and the orgasm is expressed via vaginal muscle contraction. A lack of solid data exists on the incidence of women who experience orgasm during coitus without concurrent clitoral stimulation. Controversy exists in that this has been held as the standard for normal female sexual functioning. Kaplan (1974) and Hite (1976) report differing figures: Kaplan approximates 50 percent of orgasmic women,

Hite suggests 30 percent. An emphasis on sexual pleasure rather than how an orgasm occurs seems more valuable a measure.

In treatment for orgasmic dysfunction, self-stimulation is sometimes suggested to reduce the woman's fears of boring her partner by taking too much time and because masturbation provides a direct sensory feedback system. She immediately knows which types of caresses provide the most intense pleasure; this facilitates high levels of arousal and orgasm. Once orgasm is experienced during genital pleasuring with her partner, coitus with concurrent clitoral stimulation is tried. Kaplan (1974) suggests that this be used as a transition in which the man stimulates his partner's clitoral area until she feels close to orgasm; rapid thrusting is then begun until she reaches orgasm.

A classification of sexual dysfunction is now being addressed: disorders of sexual desire. Because of its psychological complexity, desire-phase dysfunction may require alternative forms of treatment. Kaplan (1977) is publishing in this area.

Masters and Johnson (1970) strongly emphasize that it is the relationship that is being treated rather than one partner or the other. Conjoint therapy is considered an absolute requirement by many sex therapists, although there are no solid data to back up this contention (Marks, 1978). For maximum transfer of learning, it seems important that the untreated partner at least be committed to the relationship and open to modifying sexual techniques and atmosphere.

APPLICATIONS

Sexual therapy techniques are most useful when an intact couple reports having a specific sexual problem, when there is commitment between the partners and motivation to seek help for their sexual relationship, and where there is no severe psychopathology in either partner. Exceptions to this seem to be those couples who experience vaginismus or premature ejaculation. Kaplan (1974) states that the prognosis for treatment outcome for these dysfunctions appears independent of marital or individual pathology.

Contraindications for Sex Therapies include severe marital stress and hostility, severe psychopathology, and, for many therapists, the nonparticipation of one partner. Typically these impediments to treatment cannot be overcome by rapid symptom-removal treatment such as Sex Therapy. Kaplan (1974) lists a number of factors that predict a poorer prognosis when applying this model: excessive vulnerability to stress (such as in some cases of absolute ejaculatory incompetence and primary impotence), drug addiction and alcoholism, severe depression and/or anxiety, lack of commitment by one partner, and the contingency that the success or failure of the relationship depends on the outcome of therapy.

Dysfunctions with the best prognosis using the two-week intensive therapy model are premature ejaculation, vaginismus, primary orgasmic dysfunction, and secondary ejaculatory incompetence; primary and secondary impotence and situational orgasmic dysfunction are more resistant to the rapid-treatment model. Overall, during the two weeks of intensive treatment at the Masters and Johnson Institute (formerly the Reproductive Biology Research Foundation) (Masters & Johnson, 1970), there was only a one-in-five failure rate. In the five-year follow-up, the overall failure rate (a combination of the initial failure rate and reappearance of the symptoms reported on five-year follow-up) remained the same: 20 percent. Premature ejaculation was successfully treated in 97.3 percent ($N = 186$) of cases. No other researchers or therapists currently cite long-term success and failure rates for the treatment of sexual dysfunction. This is not unusual, as there are few statistics to prove the efficacy of any model of psychotherapy.

Basically, either the two-week intensive treatment method or the traditional once or twice a week outpatient method of Sex Therapy is appropriate and very successful in the reversal of sexual dysfunction. Approximately 80 percent of cases can be successfully treated. Of course, the more long-standing the problem, the presence of dysfunction in both partners, and the degree of relationship conflict and psychopathology all affect prognosis.

CASE EXAMPLE

Mr. and Mrs. A were seen by this writer in nine sessions on a weekly basis. Mr. A was 33 years old, had been divorced once, had two young children who lived with his ex-wife, and reportedly had experienced rapid ejaculation since his first coital experience. He was a factory foreman with a high school education. Mr. A appeared shy and embarrassed; he had difficulty verbalizing his feelings, especially the specific details of his sexual life. His wife, on the contrary, was quite open, talkative, and psychologically-minded. She had prior psychotherapy during her divorce proceedings from her first husband. Mrs. A was 35, had custody of two young teenage daughters, and worked part-time as a teacher's aide. She reportedly was regularly orgasmic with clitoral stimulation and had been orgasmic in coitus with other partners. This couple had been married for one and one-half years.

During the initial session it became clear that Mrs. A was quite angry toward her husband because of his premature ejaculation. Their sexual life had developed to the point where there was little kissing or caressing prior to penetration, little thrusting during intercourse, and ejaculation usually occurred in one minute or less. Mrs. A felt so frustrated and resentful that she would not want additional caressing after her husband's orgasms. He felt guilty, believed he was a failure as a lover, and tried to avoid sexual contact and foreplay for fear of becoming stimulated to ejaculation before penetration. This, in fact, had happened several times.

Historically, Mr. A was given little information about sex by his parents. Reared mostly by his mother because of parental divorce when he was 11, he believed he had to learn about sex from peers and personal experience. During his teen years, he dated sporadically and began experimentation with petting at 16. His first coitus occurred at 17 in his girlfriend's living room. The two were interrupted by her father; Mr. A recalled a feeling of panic. This seemed to have had a lasting effect on him and perhaps was his first association between anxiety, guilt, and coitus. In his first marriage, there was infrequent intercourse, allegedly because his wife was unable to enjoy it or to achieve orgasm. I thought it likely that his prematurity was exacerbated by the infrequency of sexual contact. His masturbatory pattern was similar to coitus; he spent as little time as possible to reach orgasm.

Mrs. A grew up in an intact family with a father whom she described as tyrannical and alcoholic. She was frightened of him during childhood because of his temper outbursts and tendency to break things in the home when he was angry. She grew to have a wary attitude toward men; she desired a lot of nurturance and reassurance yet believed angrily that she would never get it. Her first marriage was to a man who helped her fulfill these expectations. She was pregnant at the time of the marriage. Despite the frustrations of her marriage, she was regularly orgasmic with clitoral stimulation and during intercourse. Sex was the major mode for her to feel loved in that relationship.

During courtship and marriage, this couple experienced the frustrations of their sexual problem but attributed it to the stress of forming a "reconstituted family" and believed that the premature ejaculation would diminish once they became better adjusted. After one and one-half years of marriage, they felt more compatible as a couple and with their step-parent roles; however, their sexual life had almost ended and both felt quite dissatisfied with this. At the time of therapy, there was substantial commitment to the marriage, a desire for Sex Therapy, and much half concealed resentment in Mrs. A toward her husband.

A conjoint session occurred initially in which the history of the sexual problem and some history of the relationship was elicited. The following two were individual sessions with Mr. A and Mrs. A; the emphasis was on personal histories, sexual functioning prior to and during this marriage, and feelings toward the spouse. The fourth session was a "round table" session in which the dynamics of the problem and the possible treatment strategies were shared. Mr. A became more aware of his high anxiety level and how that along with infrequent sexual contact increased his chances of premature ejaculation. Also, focusing his mind on nonerotic thoughts during intercourse only alienated him from the erotic experience. Mrs. A began to acknowledge her resentment and feelings of being cheated by men in general and by her husband in particular. These feelings did not disappear at this stage of therapy, but she had more cognitive insight. She was told that the beginning stages of treatment would focus on her husband and that she might find little erotic satisfaction during this time; this was clearly specified in an attempt to ward off her resistance. Sensate focus was assigned.

Both reported erotic arousal with sensate focus. Mrs. A was particularly pleased because she felt given to and loved without the usual frustrations of brief intercourse. Mr. A was surprised that he could touch and be touched without ejaculating. All was not rosy, however. Mr. A's job required a shift change so that he would be working all night. This left little time for sex.

Sensate focus plus the squeeze technique were suggested. Mrs. A was instructed to manually stimulate her husband's penis until he signaled that ejaculation was imminent. She then would squeeze his penis under the coronal ridge for approximately 10 seconds; when he lost some of his erection, stimulation was to begin again. Mr. A was to direct his attention solely to his erotic sensations, to refocus them if he became distracted, and to let his wife know when he felt the sensations of ejaculatory inevitability. He was not to attempt to control his ejaculation in any way. After three or four stimulation-squeeze sequences he could be stimulated to orgasm. This process was to be repeated until he had a clear sense of ejaculatory inevitability.

This phase lasted for three weeks because of unavailability of time to practice (some avoidance was clearly noted) and Mrs. A's resentment during this procedure. She felt bored and used. Mr. A became aware of her resentment and had difficulty keeping his focus on his erotic sensations. At one point Mrs. A was seen individually to further explore her resistances; the anger she felt toward men as well as her hurt about not being loved enough were discussed. It was suggested that they spend additional time alone together so that she could satisfy her needs for love and attention in alternative ways. This seemed helpful. Also, it was suggested that she be caressed by Mr. A at times other than their squeeze-technique sessions.

Coitus was initiated when Mr. A was able to clearly identify his point of ejaculatory inevitability, when he could sustain an erection for 10 minutes (an arbitrary figure) without ejaculation, and when he could rely on the cessation of stimulation rather than the squeeze to delay ejaculation. Mrs. A was instructed to take the female-superior position while Mr. A guided her thrusting with his hands on her hips; this put Mr. A in control of the speed of thrusting. When he reached the point of ejaculatory inevitability, he would signal her and she would stop moving. This technique was successful in enabling Mr. A to delay his ejaculation until he voluntarily chose. With additional intercourse, Mrs. A was able to experience high levels of arousal and orgasm.

Therapy was terminated at this point. The couple was instructed to continue to use the stop-start techniques as needed during coitus, to continue sensate focus and genital pleasuring, and to focus on Mrs. A's specific desires for foreplay and coital thrusting. Follow-up was not done.

SUMMARY

Sex Therapies are treatments of behavioral, attitudinal, or emotional barriers to satisfying sexual functioning. Such barriers include male dysfunctions of impotence, premature ejaculation, and ejaculatory incompetence, and female dysfunctions of vaginimus, orgasmic dysfunction, and general sexual dysfunction. Sexual anesthesia and dyspareunia are sexual disorders that are typically not considered to be psychosomatic and so are classified separately.

Sex Therapies developed out of research on sexual behavior. This began with Kinsey's (Kinsey, Pomeroy, & Martin, 1948, 1965) collection in the 1940s of sociological data on the sexual activities of males and females and continued with Masters and Johnson's collection and publication of their data on the physiological components of sexual response in *Human Sexual Response* (1966). Since then, techniques have been generated to successfully treat sexual dysfunctions. In *Human Sexual Inadequacy* (1970), Masters and Johnson describe a behavioral treatment plan consisting of sexual and communication tasks for couples. In *The New Sex Therapy* (1974), Helen Singer Kaplan added a psychodynamic focus. Group therapy is being used for more cost-effective treatment and for the emotional support it offers clients (McGovern, Kirkpatrick, & LoPiccolo, 1978; Barbach, 1975). Sex education and self-help books for the public as well as research and treatment journals on sexuality have become popular.

Sexual dysfunctions are caused by immediate and remote conflicts that serve to create tension and an "anti-erotic" atmosphere between sexual partners. Such conflicts may be due to misinformation about sex, hostility between the partners, failure to engage in erotically stimulating activities, fears of rejection, fears of performance and failure, and spectatoring (watching one's sexual performance). Anxiety from previous sexual trauma, an overall destructive relationship between the sexual partners, fears of intimacy and abandonment, faulty sexual learning, and unconscious conflicts may underlie the immediate causes of dysfunction.

Treatment usually involves both members of the couple and one or two therapists, although some clinicians work with groups of couples and some with individuals without partners. Therapy occurs in a two-week intensive style (Masters and Johnson) or traditional outpatient format once or twice a week. The immediate rather than remote causes of the dysfunction are emphasized. If the couple can relax, give up their spectatoring, and create a warm, erotic ambience, they are removing the barriers to satisfying sexual responsivity. The deeper roots of sexual conflict are examined when therapy progress becomes blocked. Major emphases are on facilitating open communication between partners and their experiences with a series of graduated sexual tasks (sensate focus, genital pleasuring, and coitus). Couples who are committed to their relationship, have limited marital conflict or psychopathology, and feel motivated to work on their sexual problems have the best prognosis with this treatment.

Sex Therapies are intended for the rapid treatment of sexual dysfunction. They are not a panacea for marital conflict, personal unhappiness, or psychopathology. In terms of overall psychological benefits accrued from successful treatment, the results are mixed. Kaplan (1974) reports that "removal of the sexual symptom which had been plaguing the patient for years usually engenders an initial feeling of euphoria but this response is of relatively brief duration in most cases" (p. 446). It is rather quickly replaced by a "take-it-for-granted" attitude. Some couples report profoundly positive changes in their overall relationship; others report few changes. Negative feelings typically emerge in two areas: when couples expect that successful Sex Therapy will change their lives and when they experience an upsurge of anxiety just prior to symptom reversal. Sex Therapies are designed to expect and to cope with this anxiety and the defenses that emerge to mask it.

REFERENCES

Annon, J. S. (1974). *The behavioral treatment of sexual problems.* Honolulu: Enabling Systems.

Barbach, L. (1975). *For yourself: The fulfillment of female sexuality.* New York: Doubleday.

Brecher, E. M. (1969). *The sex researchers.* Boston: Little, Brown.

Comfort, A. (1967). *The anxiety makers.* London: Thomas Nelson.

Hartman, W. E., & Fithian, M. A. (1972). *Treatment of sexual dysfunction.* Long Beach, CA: Center for Marital and Sexual Studies.

Heiman, J., LoPiccolo, L., & LoPiccolo, J. (1976). *Becoming orgasmic: A sexual growth program for women.* Englewood Cliffs, NJ: Prentice-Hall.

Hite, S. (1976). *The Hite report.* New York: Dell.

Hogan, D. R. (1978). The effectiveness of sex therapy: A review of the literature. In J. LoPiccolo & L. LoPiccolo (Eds.), *Handbook of sex therapy.* New York: Plenum.

Kaplan, H. S. (1974). *The new sex therapy.* New York: Brunner/Mazel.

Kaplan, H. S. (1977). Hypoactive sexual desire. *Journal of Sex and Marital Therapy, 3*(1), 3–9.

Karacan, I. (1970, April). Clinical value of nocturnal erection in the prognosis and diagnosis of impotence. *Medical Aspects of Sexuality,* 27–34.

Kinsey, A. C., Pomeroy, W. B., & Martin C. E. (1948). *Sexual behavior in the human male.* Philadelphia: W. B. Saunders.

Kinsey, A. C., Pomeroy, W. B., Martin, C. E., & Beggard, P. H. (1965). *Sexual behavior in the human female.* New York: Pocket Books. (Originally published 1953.)

Lobitz, W. C., & LoPiccolo, J. (1972). New methods in the behavioral treatment of sexual dysfunction. *Journal of Behavior Therapy and Experimental Psychiatry, 3,* 265–271.

LoPiccolo, J. (1978). Direct treatment of sexual dysfunction. In J. LoPiccolo & L. LoPiccolo (Eds.), *Handbook of sex therapy.* New York: Plenum.

Marks, J. (1978). Behavioral psychotherapy of adult neurosis. In S. Garfield & A. Bergin (Eds.), *Handbook of psychotherapy and behavior change.* New York: Wiley.

Masters, W. H., & Johnson, V. E. (1966). *Human sexual response.* Boston: Little, Brown.

Masters, W. H., & Johnson, V. E. (1970). *Human sexual inadequacy.* Boston: Little, Brown.

McCary, J. L. (1973). *Human sexuality,* 2nd ed. New York: Van Nostrand.

McGovern, K. B., Kirkpatrick, C. C., & LoPiccolo, J. (1978). A behavioral group treatment program for sexually dysfunctional couples. In J. LoPiccolo and L. LoPiccolo (Eds.), *Handbook of sex therapy.* New York: Plenum.

National Register of Certified Health Service Providers in Sex Education and Sex Therapy. Washington, DC: American Association of Sex Educators, Counselors and Therapists.

Pion, R. (1977). *The last sex manual.* New York: Wyden Books.

Williams, M. H. (1978). Individual sex therapy. In J. LoPiccolo & L. LoPiccolo (Eds.), *Handbook of sex therapy.* New York: Plenum.

Chapter 60

SHORT-TERM TARGETED THERAPY

ROBERT E. WUBBOLDING

This system, as its name indicates, is intended for immediate results. Appropriate candidates for this procedure include people likely to come for therapy only once: People who think that one meeting with a mental health professional is sufficient and who would think it an insult to be asked to come a second time. This view is common in certain socioeconomic groups, and consequently this system is a natural candidate for use with such populations. The system is based on the ideas of five people plus the author of this chapter.

The system is based on fundamental motivations and, as Figure 60.1 illustrates, the process goes from injurious behaviors to beneficial behaviors. The therapy proper begins with a relationship with a client, and my guess is this element is extremely important in short-term relations. Wubbolding spells out the position of the therapist in great detail. The next step is identifying areas to target, then self-evaluation, followed by implementation. Hopefully, success will follow this and possibly other meetings.

DEFINITION

Short-Term Targeted Therapy (S3T) provides a theory and a direction for therapy when time is limited and results are paramount. It identifies sources of human motivation which serve as areas for planning. No matter what the presenting issue is, the therapist can focus on one or more of the deficit areas that become evident to all but the naive helper.

Based on the belief that human beings are motivated by current drives or needs, this approach is action-centered. Clients are strongly encouraged to formulate tactical plans regardless of whether they have been gifted with conventional insights. It is also a systematic process for intervention that can be adapted to most client problems and decisions and that is most effectively implemented by the therapist who is creative and inventive in his/her application.

This chapter outlines this genuinely eclectic process, which is based on the work of Applegate (1985), Frankl (1984), Glasser (1998), Jacobs (1994), Maslow (1970), and Wubbolding (1988, 2000). The system is illustrated in a dialogue between a client, Jay, and a therapist who implements the system in several sessions.

HISTORY

S3T is an eclectic model of brief therapy that extracts useful components from several theorists who teach that be-

havior originates in one or more psychological needs. The monumental work of Victor Frankl (1984) is well known. He saw human beings as searching for purpose and meaning in their lives. S3T borrows from Abraham Maslow (1970) the need for knowledge. Self-actualization is seen as the effective fulfillment of all the needs, a goal never fully achieved. William Glasser (1998) sees the needs for power, fun, and freedom as crucial to effective living. Gary Applegate (1985) describes the need for health as part of survival or self-preservation. He also sees faith as a need which is a driving force for human beings. The delivery system is derived from Glasser (1998) and Wubbolding (1988, 2000), who have extended the principle of self-evaluation and developed the levels of commitment. Edward Jacobs (1994) adds credence to the principle that the therapeutic contract occurs early in the relationship and is not separate from rapport-building. He also stresses that the therapist must, early on, have a clear sense of direction.

S3T is thus a useable system that is a synthesis of theory and practice. It provides the practitioner with areas for treatment planning that are specific yet comprehensive.

CURRENT STATUS

Incorporating the techniques of Glasser (1998), Wubbolding (1988, 2000) and Jacobs (1994), S3T provides tools immediately useable. It is best used with individu-

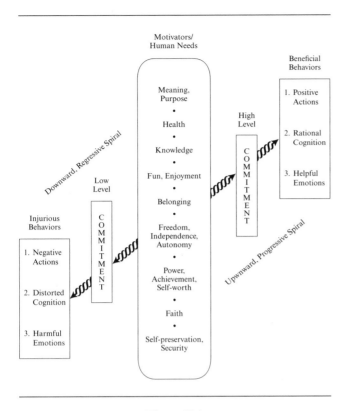

Figure 60.1

als or groups who want to improve their lives. The skilled therapist can often elicit a commitment to change even from clients who are court-ordered, involuntary, or reluctant. This is done by listening carefully to what they want and helping them evaluate whether their life direction is taking them toward their goal.

Because this system is based on universal needs and motivations it is applicable to virtually every culture. It can also be used with personal growth issues, addictions, depression, and even post-traumatic stress. When clients satisfy their needs with effective, upwardly-spiraling actions, thought, and feelings, they relinquish the downward spiral of behavior (Figure 60.1).

THEORY

Therapeutic Alliance

A necessary prerequisite to effective Short-Term Targeted Therapy is the establishment of a relationship with the client. This therapist–client connection is characterized by empathy, respect, firmness, ethics, a sense of direction, hopefulness/optimism, framing problems in solvable terms, and honesty.

Empathy—The ability to enter the clients' inner worlds and see their external worlds as they see them.

Respect—Communicating that no matter how severe the problem is or who caused it, the therapist has regard for the clients. Even more importantly, the therapist respects the clients for what they can become.

Firmness—The therapist is not merely a "nice person." Expectations are clearly defined and explained. This therapy is for clients who are serious about setting goals, want to work, and are willing to take action.

Ethics—The therapist works within his or her limitations, provides professional disclosure, consults when necessary, and explains professional boundaries in unambiguous language.

Sense of Direction—Effective therapy takes place if a rapid assessment of need deficits can be determined and specific strategies formulated for increasing their satisfaction. No attempt is made to resolve every possible issue such as childhood rejection, developmental deficits, and so forth.

Hopefulness/Optimism—The therapist believes that progress can be made with any client and with any problem: Psychosis, depression, domestic violence, incestuous relationships, tumultuous family life, and so forth.

Framing problems in solvable terms—The therapist is skilled in presenting client problems in ways that reflect progress rather than find resolution. "Improve," "increase," and "enhance" are words used to describe treatment plans.

Honesty—The therapist is truthful. Incest is described not as misguided love or a mistake. It is presented as inflicting a spiritual pain on the very soul of the child (Madanes, 1995). Nevertheless, the therapist attempts to adjust the counseling process to the culture of the clients. Some clients require a more indirect mode of communication (Corey, 1998; Wubbolding, 2000), while for others a direct, get-to-the-point approach is more appropriate.

The therapist–client relationship is thus not simply a cozy one. It is warm, friendly, and professional. But assisting clients to define what they want, to exert effort to achieve their wants, and especially to evaluate their wants requires an inner courage on the part of the therapist as well as a willingness to take an occasional risk.

The targets for Short-Term Targeted Therapy have been described as needs (Applegate, 1985; Maslow, 1970) and as genetic instructions (Glasser, 1998). These are the motivational sources of all human behavior. Human beings generate behaviors to fulfill these drives and thus behavior is the result of efforts to gain inner satisfaction from interpersonal relationships, from activities such as work, and from the surrounding world. Treatment plans are geared toward one or more of these needs. Because they are general they overlap. Consequently, treatment plans can satisfy more than one need.

Meaning, Purpose

In S3T the most basic human drive is seen as that articulated by Victor Frankl (1984): People seek a sense of purpose or meaning in life. Nietzsche stated that human beings can endure any "how" if they can see a "why." Homelessness is almost unbearable because it has no purpose or meaning to the sufferer. When some elderly people see that their contributions are no longer valued they are tempted to give up. When partners drift apart with radically diverse interests and lifestyles they see no purpose in staying together. Students give up on their studies when they can see no short-term or long-term purpose to their work and when they have no relationship with the teacher.

Health

People choose behaviors that are healthful or life-giving because they have an innate drive for health. The automatic functions of the body, such as digestion, blood circulation, physical healing, and many others, are "motivated" by the need for health. Conscious choices are often the result of a commitment to health: proper eating habits, exercise, and visits to health professionals can be strategies formulated with the assistance of the therapist.

Knowledge

From infancy on human beings grow in their knowledge of the world around them. A child learns to smile, to crawl, to walk, to run, to speak, to socialize, to read, to compute, to problem solve. These behaviors are derived from the motivation to learn. As individuals develop they often learn behaviors that are destructive to themselves and exploitative of others. Part of the work of the S3T therapist is to help clients try new behaviors with the idea that they will see them as more satisfying than destructive ones. Helping a 17-year-old weigh the merits of a job at McDonald's against the income gained from illegal drug dealing requires ingenuity and skill on the part of the therapist. In the case example, Jay is helped to replace his depression with substitute actions, cognition, and feelings.

Fun, Enjoyment

Rarely do parents tell their toddlers, "It's time to go to work. You get a 15-minute break, one half-hour for lunch, another break, and you can quit work at 5 p.m." Most obvious in children is a high need for fun or enjoy-

ment. Adults, too, are driven to enjoy their lives. "All work and no play makes a dull day" is a profound psychological truth of which the user of S3T is acutely aware. Couples in a dysfunctional relationship are encouraged to spend time together doing enjoyable activities. A depressed person is helped to make a choice to do something that he or she once enjoyed.

Belonging

According to Glasser (1998), most long-term psychological problems are relationship problems. Dysfunctional relationships with other people or things, or dysfunctional ideas regarding one's future, lie at the heart of the downward spiral of behaviors. Relationships improve through the conscious choices of clients when they replace their harmful actions, dysfunctional thoughts, and negative emotions with their opposites: positive actions, effective self-talk, and life-enhancing feelings.

Freedom, Independence, Autonomy

People of all ages, groups of all sizes, and even nations want to write their own destinies. Choice is a theme that underlies all S3T. Regardless of the client's diagnosis, each action is treated "as if" it is a choice. The exact degree of genuine voluntariness in each action is of secondary importance. The amount of responsibility for past actions is equally irrelevant. Clients are seen to be responsible for current and future decisions and choices.

Power, Achievement, Self-worth

Clients enter therapy or are sent to therapists for many reasons. Even though they have many generic needs, such as fun, freedom, purpose, and others, they rarely seek help initially in order to meet such needs. They seem to approach therapists because their lives feel out of control in some way. They feel inadequate as human beings. They lack self-esteem, feel unassertive, or are victimized by obsessive thoughts or compulsive behaviors. They are sent for help because their behavior is seen by others as destructive, such as when they are antisocial, addicted, or engaged in illegal behaviors.

The presenting issue is often connected to ineffective or destructive behaviors related to power. The motivation of power is a persuasive drive underlying many problems. Marital relationships are often successful until the partners are unable or unwilling to resolve power issues. The power need begins to blossom during the adolescent years, creating conflicts with parents who view the child's repertoire of responsible behaviors as lagging behind their own desires. Disruption, aggression, hostility, and passive resistance are expressions of power motivation.

Still, power is more than a motivator of negative behaviors. It includes the drive for excellence, for achievement, and for life-enhancing activities. The word itself is related to the French *pouvoir*, meaning "to be able." Power can be a sense of inner achievement that is noncompetitive. When a person manages time effectively, eats heartily, completes a work project, makes a sale, or achieves a goal, there is the inner satisfaction of the power need.

Faith

It is becoming clear that an underlying motivator of human behavior is a belief in the transcendent. Many people attest to their commitment to a humanitarian cause or their belief in a supreme being. They believe that their families are important or that their jobs add to the quality of human life. They also believe that there is an ultimate purpose behind the laws of the universe, that they are part of an unseen whole, and that their work and lives contribute in some way. Their altruistic motivation can be humanistic, spiritual, or religiously sectarian. They come to therapy to find what they believe is a deeper meaning in life, to learn ways to contribute, and/or to find a place in what they believe is a divine plan.

Self-preservation, Security

The human body generates behaviors to maintain itself: digestion, blood circulation, fevers to fight infection, shivering in cold weather, and perspiring in hot weather. We have a need to survive, and as we develop we learn behaviors designed to protect ourselves. Some human beings have highly developed survival instincts. Others have less sophisticated instincts. Culture and experience circumscribe the effective fulfillment of this need. A street person who can survive on the street might have few skills for Wall Street. On the other hand, the financier would find it difficult to negotiate survival uptown on Central Avenue.

The need for security is part of this general motivator. Individuals feel secure around people who are seen as peers. But when a person's identity is threatened, the results can be discomfort, anxiety, fear, or low self-esteem, accompanied by self-criticism or sometimes hostility and aggressive revenge. Persons whose negative feelings are turned inward seek therapy in order to regain their damaged identity. When a person loses a job more than the power need is attacked. Not only is the sense of control damaged, but the very emotional security and identity of the person can be lessened. Some people see their identity as connected with their careers.

METHODOLOGY

• Get a commitment to therapy.

The first stage of therapy is for the therapist to elicit from the client a firm desire to aim at a target, that is, to improve and to make a change in his/her life. Skilled therapists are able to establish an encouraging atmosphere and present information that make positive change attractive to clients. The reluctant, involuntary, or resistant client often presents with the lowest level of commitment, summarized in such simple phrases as, "I will not change," "I don't want to be here," or "*They* have the problem, not me." Other clients are weakly committed, as evidenced by comments such as, "I might do something" or "I'll try." The therapist's target at this early stage is the formulation of the "I will" level of commitment. This task is described as first in that it is primary. It does not necessarily occur first chronologically. As in the case example below, the therapist helps Jay by gradually leading up to this important task.

• Identify general targets.

The second stage of target formation relates to need-satisfying actions, effective self-talk, and appropriate feelings. These counterbalance the presenting problems described in the *Diagnostic and Statistical Manual of Mental Disorders* (1994), which are destructive and ineffective actions, distorted cognition, and disturbed emotions.

In eliciting a commitment to counseling, the therapist explores the clients' wants, that is, what they hope to gain from the experience of therapy. When clients are referred by courts or pushed into therapy by family, employers, teachers, or others, the initial questioning can center on what others want for them. Frequently there is a wide discrepancy between the wants of the client and the wants of other significant people in the clients' lives. A client might want "to be left alone," "to do as I please," and so forth. Other important people could want the client to get a job, study in school, or cease abusive or neglectful behavior. The discrepancy between these wants can be explored and discussed, along with ways to resolve the differences.

In the case example, Jay is asked to explore what he wants from the therapy, from the therapist, and from himself. He is then asked to make a commitment to the process.

• Conduct self-evaluation and assessment.

The third stage is to help clients conduct a searching inventory of their actions, cognition, and emotions. They are asked to evaluate whether their current actions are effective in getting them what they want in the areas of motivation: meaning, belonging, and other goals. They are encouraged to be both general and specific. Is their life direction satisfactory? Are their specific choices made recently, today, yesterday, in the past week helping them or hurting them in both the short-term and in the long-term? They are helped to assess the attainability of their wants and are asked explicitly, "How realistic is it to get what you say you want?" "What do you think you can realistically achieve in the next week or month?"

Therapists can provide information, facts, and suggestions, but genuine change occurs only after clients decide that their current behavior is ineffective, when they examine their wants and decide to pursue genuinely attainable outcomes.

- Strategy and implementation (Treatment planning).

The fourth stage culminates in implementation outside the therapy sessions. Plans are connected to the nine basic sources of human motivation and involve more than vague insights and nebulous promises to do better. A good plan incorporates the following characteristics:

- Simple—Uncomplicated, clear. Not overwhelming to the client.
- Attainable—Doable and realistically achievable. The degree of repetitiveness depends on the range of effective behaviors which the client brings to the session.
- Measurable—Can be quantified. Answers the question, "when?"
- Immediate—Executed very soon, not at a distant time.
- Controlled by planner—Depends on client. Not contingent on others' choices.
- Committed to—Firm. "I'll try" is not an effective plan. Often a written plan or contract helps to imprint its importance in the mind of the client (Jacobs, 1994).

The importance of planning lies in the value of choosing actions that are alternatives to ineffective or destructive actions, cognition, and feelings. But there is a deeper reason for helping clients make plans even if they fail to follow through. The role of the therapist is to teach clients the theory and practice of this system. This can be done directly, as seen in the case example of Jay, when the therapist explains the levels of commitment as well as the sources of motivation. However, in a deeper and more indirect way, the clients derive an unspoken message: that there is hope, that it is necessary to take action if there is to be any improvement, and that responsibility

for change lies first and foremost with them, not with the world around them.

Among the many techniques in S3T are quality time and the solving circle, used in relationship counseling. These did not apply to Jay, however. Others include "the two roads," "levels of commitment," and paradoxical techniques, which are explained or illustrated in the case transcript.

Quality Time

A major tool used in S3T as it applies to relationships is the strategy of quality time. Relationships are often dysfunctional because clients have unpleasant and even hostile attitudes toward each other. Their storehouse of memories about pleasant experiences is virtually empty. They report that they do not want to spend time together because "we are not getting along," adding, "all we do is argue." S3T is based on the principle that their relationship will improve when their time together is more inwardly satisfying. A therapist can help them make specific plans to be together in ways that are quite different from their previous experience. The more intense their feelings of anger, antagonism, resentment, or alienation, the more urgent is the importance of time spent together that is labelled "quality time." The amount of time spent together is determined by the willingness and ability of the clients to choose an activity that is enjoyable and relationship-building. Such activities have the following characteristics:

1. Effortful. The activity requires expending at least *some* energy. Watching television is not a relationship-building activity because it requires little effort. When parents and children or couples evaluate the content of television, they are more likely to enhance the closeness of the relationship.

2. Mutual Awareness. Choices to spend time together are based on awareness of each other. Watching a son or daughter play Little League has some value as quality time. But playing the game with the child in a non-critical way is even more valuable to the relationship.

3. Non-Critical. The time spent together is devoid of criticism. "Put downs," lecturing, preaching about what the other person *ought* or *should* do is seen as destructive of interpersonal relationships. When such behaviors are chosen by one person, the other is likely to see the time as an attack on his/her needs.

4. Discuss Commonalities. The time together is for building mutual connectedness. This connectedness is accompanied and enhanced by common need-satisfying memories. Consequently, subjects

of conversation are focused on topics that do not involve controversy or pain in any form. Relationships are enhanced when there is common ground in experience, perceptions, wants, hopes, and expectations. Similarly, past misery is not an appropriate focus for conversation.

In selecting topics for discussion during this time, the key question participants ask is, "Does this conversation bring us closer together or further apart?" If the answer is "closer together" or "neutral," it is a legitimate topic.

Solving Circle

In relationship therapy it is useful to teach clients how to state their problems and discuss only solutions (Glasser, 1998). They are asked to imagine themselves sitting in a chalk circle. The rule is that they cannot discuss the problem or its causes. They discuss only what each brings to the relationship and what each will do to make the third entity in the circle better—the relationship. Arguing, blaming, criticizing, and excuse making are omitted from the discussion.

Paradoxical Techniques

The paradoxical technique, prescription, or choosing the symptom are effective tools if used properly and ethically. Loneliness, worry, feelings of depression, and many other behaviors can be addressed with such techniques. Ethical caveats are central to their use. Most importantly, they should never be used with potentially harmful or destructive behavior. Other ethical considerations are detailed by Weeks and L'Abate (1982).

These and other techniques contribute to the effective use of Short-Term Targeted Therapy. However, they need to be geared to helping clients fulfill the nine areas of motivation in ways that are appropriate. With virtually any deficit in healthy behaviors the therapist can begin with and utilize as a theme the enhancement of interpersonal relationships. When clients improve their relationships, they are more likely to relinquish their problems.

APPLICATIONS AND CASE EXAMPLE

Jay, a 46-year-old male, self-employed computer consultant approached a therapist at the urging of a friend. Unmarried until age 41, he was recently divorced after his wife had a two-year affair and suddenly told him the marriage was over. His sense of shock and disappointment has led to further depression. During their marriage his wife had been dissatisfied with his "moodiness,"

which was, in her opinion, more often than not "a negative, pessimistic, dreary outlook on life."

During and after the divorce Jay became listless and, as he said, "immobile." His business deteriorated and he moved into a smaller apartment, an endeavor which required the help of a few loyal friends and an enormous spurt of energy on his part. During this time, in a burst of anger, he smashed the wedding pictures and ripped apart the wedding album. This was followed by feelings of guilt, shame, failure, and self-criticism. The few conversations he does have with friends are punctuated with self-pity and guilt at having lost the one woman in his life.

To add to his problems, one month before his first visit to the therapist, his ex-wife was on vacation with her new lover and was seriously injured in an automobile accident. Jay has repeatedly called her and attempted to see her but she refused to talk to him.

In the last six months he has stopped his minimal exercise program and gained more than 20 pounds on a diet of sweets and starch. His friend called the therapist and told him that Jay was alone on weekends and had alluded to "ending it all if things don't change." The friend persuaded Jay to call the therapist and make an appointment. Jay agreed, saying he would "give it a try."

In the telephone conversation prior to the appointment, the therapist asked Jay to make a short list of five goals he could formulate for the meeting. Jay reluctantly agreed to do this.

A summary of the case is included as it developed from the first session; also included are illustrations of dialogue. Not included are the professional details about informed consent, confidentiality, and duty to warn. Important as these issues are, they apply to all methods of therapy and are not unique to any one.

THERAPIST: Jay, now that we've taken care of several important professional details, we can move on. These are ongoing issues and we will discuss them further as they emerge again.

JAY: Yeah, I guess so.

T: You don't seem to be extremely eager or excited about being here. Am I right or wrong about this?

J: You're right. This seems to be the last straw.

T: At least there's one straw! Let's see if we can find another one. But first, tell me what's going on.

J: My friend called you and talked to you. Then he urged me to come to see you.

T: Since you brought up your friend's call, let's talk about what he thinks. He did have a lot to say. But tell me, from you perspective, what does he think? What did he tell you?

J: He said he was scared that I was not going anywhere, getting fat, sitting around, doing nothing and losing my business.

T: That's about what he told me. In fact, he said a lot more.

J: Yeah. He was afraid I was going to sit in the garage with my car motor on.

T: He was very clear about that. He said he was quite worried about you. He even said that he was willing to drag you here if necessary.

J: I guess he got upset about what I said.

T: I'm wondering about something. What do you think about having such a friend?

J: I've known him a long time.

T: Jay, are you aware of how fortunate you are to have such a friend? Some people abandon their friends when they act down in the dumps for a few months.

J: Well, I never thought of it that way.

T: That's the first thing I'd like to emphasize with you. Your friend said there were other people also who were concerned. They have a hard time getting through to you because of your upsetness but they are concerned about you. We'll come back to this point later, but I wanted you to know that from my point of view this is an important aspect of your life—even if you don't see it right now.

J: That could be.

T: You've been down for a long time. Tell me about it.

J: I just feel rotten.

T: How do you know you feel rotten?

J: I just know it.

T: But your mind tells you you're feeling bad. How does it tell you?

J: I don't have any hope. Everything looks bleak. There's no future.

T: So it's not just feeling bad that leads you to say you're depressed. It's your viewpoint on life. There's a difference.

J: There is?

T: Sure. Feeling bad is one thing but the outlook on life is another. So maybe we could work on one of these.

J: Which one?

T: We'll decide later. I have another question. What is this depression and bleak outlook on life stopping you from doing?

J: What do you mean?

T: If you were not down in the dumps how would your life be going?

J: I'd be happy. I'd be doing things.

T: What else? Name as many things as you can.

J: The main thing is that my business would pick up.

T: Wait. I think we're on to something. If you felt better you'd have more success financially?

J: Yes. But I feel too awful to do anything. I'm immobilized.

T: In other words, when you overcome this sense of depression, you'll feel better, do things, and get the business back in shape?

J: Yes. That's it.

T: What if I said that if we work together there is a good chance that this could happen?

J: I don't know. I just feel that the future is dead.

T: Before we go on I need to ask you about what I believe is not the main issue but is important. OK?

J: Go ahead.

T: You said that the future is dead, the outlook is bleak, and that you don't know if you could go on. Your friend sent you here because he is worried that you might hurt yourself. Would you answer some questions without holding back?

J: Yes. I think so.

T: Are you thinking of killing yourself?

J: Yes. The thought has passed my mind. It couldn't be any worse than things are now.

T: Talk more about it.

J: I just don't see any way out of this rotten mess.

T: You have good reasons for feeling bad right now. Your wife left you and your business is not what it once was. Which of those is easier to handle?

J: I've tried to get her back. I didn't want the divorce. It was her idea. And now she's had the car accident.

T: I want to discuss another point. If your friend were to be in this room, what would he say you *do* have going for you? What would he say are some positive points?

J: He would not find any.

T: I think he would. I've only talked to you a few minutes and I can find some. What would he say?

J: Well, I suppose he'd say that I could find someone else especially if I'd get my weight down again.

T: What else?

J: He'd say that when I'm in good shape I can be fun to be around. He might also add that I have good computer consulting skills. I know how to make things happen in my business.

T: So, he'd find three strengths and you described two negatives . . . more strengths than weaknesses.

J: Yes, but . . .

T: Let's move on. With all these strengths—three or four of them—do you want to end it all?

J: I've thought about putting the hose in my car in the garage.

T: But you haven't done it?

J: No, I don't really want to kill myself. But I have been tempted.

T: If you get a serious urge would you call your friend?

J: I would, but I'm not going to do it.

T: In that case, would you be willing to write down, now, that you will stay alive and not kill yourself accidentally or on purpose?

J: In writing?

T: Yes, in writing.

J: Why in writing?

T: It's just the way we do things in therapy. It makes for a firm commitment.

J: OK.

T: And you add for a specific amount of time.

J: OK. How about three months?

T: That's fine. And this is a firm, no-nonsense commitment to yourself. Right? Agreed?

J: OK. That sounds good to me.

Comment:

In this first segment of the therapy process, the therapist has done the following:

1. Attempted to establish an initial relationship with the client by implying that there is hope.

2. Pointed out that the client has a very good friend. The motivator of belonging will be an important aspect of this session and its unfulfillment has led to the depression.

3. Illustrated to the client that there is more than one side to his current plight. There is the emotional aspect and the perceptual aspect.

4. Pointed out the positive aspects of his life by encouraging him to list two negative ones and then asking him how *his friend* would describe the positives in his life.

5. Asked appropriate questions related to suicide assessment (Wubbolding, 1996).

6. Insisted on a firm, unilateral commitment to himself (not a commitment to the therapist) to remain alive for a specific amount of time. This could be seen as a preliminary step to a commitment to the therapy process.

Second Session: Segment

T: Jay, in the last session we talked about your willingness to remain in therapy and not to hurt yourself for several months. How are you doing now with those decisions?

J: I was feeling terrible. But I'm OK with the decision. I'm definitely not going to kill myself. But I still feel bad.

T: What about the decision to remain in counseling?

J: That's fine with me. I'll give it a try.

T: So you've made two decisions. What effect have these decisions had on you?

J: I feel a little different . . . maybe better.

T: I'd like to ask you to be specific. If 100% equaled total victory over what you called "rotten feelings," how many percentage points would you say you've improved?

J: About 10%. I still feel depressed.

T: 10%!! No kidding! Making two decisions has helped that much!?

J: I still feel terrible about the divorce. It's mostly my fault and then she had a car accident. I've not gotten my business going. Everything looks hopeless.

T: Jay, one thing I've heard today: You definitely take responsibility for what's happened. Some people, probably most people, think that they have no part in how they feel. They believe that outside forces have brought them down. But you seem to be just the opposite. You take *all* the responsibility.

J: I never thought of it that way.

T: I have a hunch you tell yourself, "If only . . ." a lot.

J: Yes, I do. If only I had been different . . .

T: Where is that getting you—to repeatedly sit around and repeat and repeat and repeat that kind of mantra to yourself?

J: It's getting me nowhere.

T: Is it helping you feel any better?

J: Not at all.

T: We'll come back to that point. I want to backtrack and talk about another important point.

J: What's that?

T: It seems to me that you are now at the fork in the road. You can travel down one or two highways: one is downhill and one is uphill. One is dark and one is sunny. One leads to misery. The other, uphill road requires effort and hard work and it's not a straight shot. It's curved and requires attention. To put it another way, you can nurse your bad feelings and let them run your life. You will feel like the perpetual victim of your past decisions and your current rotten feelings. You can slide down the dark road and even lose the 10% you've gained. Or you can choose the other uphill road, to take charge, to let some of the depression behind. This road is made easier when you dump some of the self-blame and self-criticism. This road requires the decision to exert energy and effort. But it is travelled one step at a time. Progress is slow in the beginning, like a car just starting. Sometimes progress is not evident. But before long you can see that the sunlight is much better than the darkness.

J: I see what you mean. But I don't know. I just feel awful, sad, hopeless..

T: Jay, two roads: which one do you want? Which seems better for you even though you aren't sure how to travel or what to take along?

J: There's no doubt the sunny road is a better choice.

T: The question is, do you want to move in that direction? I believe I can help you get started. The journey is not treacherous. It's a matter of choice. The details will become clear as we talk a few times.

J: Yes, I want to make that choice.

T: Actually, I think you already chose that road when you made the two previous decisions. But now you've taken a few major steps.

J: Yeah. I guess so.

T: Let's talk a little about how hard you want to work at this. Whenever I counsel people who are upset and want to get past the upsetness, I explain that there are five levels of commitment to change.

The first level is really no commitment and you are way beyond it. This is when the person wants to make no change and chooses to do nothing. The second level is when someone wants to achieve an outcome but does not want to make an effort. A student who wants to graduate but who refuses to study is at the second level. The third level of commitment is when the person demonstrates an "I'll try" level of willingness. This is equivalent to "I might" or "maybe." The fourth level is that of "I will do my best" and the fifth level is attained when you will do "whatever it takes." I'll give these to you in writing for you to think about. However, it might be a little early to ask you to do anything about this now. Let's talk about how you're doing now and what you've done since we talked last time.

J: I didn't do anything. I feel lousy. I just can't shake this depression. It's like a cloud that follows me everywhere.

T: A cloud? A dark cloud? White cloud? What kind of a cloud?

J: It's the darkest of dark.

T: Then it can only get lighter and brighter.

J: What do you mean?

T: Well, if things are that bad, they can only get better!

J: Yeah.

T: I can see you are not convinced of that yet. Let's talk about the cloud. Would you like to get out from under it? Maybe leave it behind?

J: That doesn't seem possible.

T: Not yet. But maybe there's a way to park it somewhere for at least a while. Maybe you can take a short vacation from your rotten feelings. Who knows? Maybe eventually you can throw away the rotten feelings like you would throw away rotten fruit.

J: I'd like to do that.

T: We'll see if it can happen. First, tell me what you've been thinking about. How about the "if only"?

J: I do that a lot.

T: You keep mulling over in your mind, "if only I did such and such differently." That's called self-talk.

J: That's it. A thousand times a day.

T: Where has that kind of conversation with yourself gotten you?

J: What do you mean?

T: Has it helped you to dump the rotten feelings? Or does it help to maintain them?

J: I don't know.

T: Just take a guess. In your business does it help or hurt you to repeat to yourself that the customer won't want your consulting services?

J: I see what you mean. It will hurt. And you know I've done that a lot.

T: So would it help to replace that kind of self-criticism with something better?

J: It would. But how do I do that?

T: That's what we're going to work on. But I have another question. How have you been spending your time in the last few days?

J: I haven't done anything. Nothing.

T: Nothing? What did you do yesterday that was nothing?

J: Just sat around at home in my bathrobe.

T: Oh!! So you did get up out of bed and sit up. What then?

J: Just watched TV.

T: What did you watch?

J: I didn't pay any attention to it.

T: And you did it all day, most of the day, or part of the day?

J: Part of the day—but a lot of the day. I did get dressed to go to the grocery store.

T: Jay, I want to ask you to think back to when you got dressed and started out to go to the store. How did you feel?

J: I had to pay attention to the details of what I was doing.

T: And did you have to plan what you would do?

J: Yes. It took a lot of effort.

T: Of course. And when you were planning and attending to the details how did you feel?

J: Well . . . I guess I did feel a little better for a while.

T: And what happened to "if only"?

J: I did not think about it.

T: How long were you able to leave the dark cloud behind?

J: Probably an hour or so.

T: Really! That long?

J: But it came back.

T: It will come back. You won't get rid of it because you go grocery shopping once. But there's a lesson here. What do you think it is?

J: I guess doing something helps.

T: Let's put it another way: If you sit around all day, watch TV, don't get dressed, and criticize yourself, will you feel any better, get your life organized better, and rebuild your business?

J: No, but I still want my wife back.

T: Of course you do. And this wish will be part of you for a while. But do you want to put it on hold, put it in the background at least for a while?

J: That would be real good . . . if I could only do it.

T: You did it for a while when you went shopping. You didn't get rid of the problem but you did get away from it for a while. That definitely shows that decision and action help. I'd like to help you extend that hour to longer periods and then to deal with the other issues.

J: That would be helpful.

T: Do you really see how that decision and action can help? And that sitting around maintains the rotten feelings?

J: I see it. But it's so hard to do anything when I feel so lousy.

T: It's also hard to feel rotten when you're doing things that are inwardly satisfying to you.

J: What would be inwardly satisfying is to have my wife back.

T: And how realistic is that?

J: Not very likely.

T: We can talk all about that but it would be good if we could get some "vacation time" going first. In other words, if we can work on some decisions and plans that are inwardly satisfying you can get some good feelings which are the opposite of the rotten ones.

J: One thing builds on another. So if I can get some momentum going I can feel better permanently?

T: Is it worth a try?

J: I guess so.

T: What do you have to lose?

J: Nothing. It's worth a try.

Subsequent session:

T: Jay, I'd like to go back to something we spoke of a while back. How hard do you want to work at this? What is your level of commitment to change?

J: I still have the paper with the description of the levels of commitment. A few weeks ago I was hopeless, then barely willing to make a change. But I really want to get rid of the crap in my life, the grief I've brought on.

T: Don't be hard on yourself. Your unwillingness to blame others can be a strength too.

J: How?

T: I'm not sure yet! But it could have something to do with taking responsibility for the future rather than just blaming yourself for the past. What do you think?

J: Yes, I want to "take charge" as you've said several times.

T: Then I'd like to help you make some plans in some of the categories which are called "human motivators." When these are fulfilled with determined and consistent decisions and plans, the undesirable behaviors such as bad feelings, lack of action, and inner self-criticism become less prominent and certainly less troublesome.

J: What are these inner motivators?

T: There are nine of them. Some apply to you more than others: Survival or security, faith, power or achievement, freedom, belonging, fun or enjoyment, knowledge or learning, health, and a sense of purpose or meaning in life.

J: I think the belonging one is a major problem for me. I feel so alone and rejected.

T: That might be the major one to work on. On the other hand, it is sometimes useful to work on one or the other which is easier and more likely to bring success.

J: Which would be best?

T: I'd like to make a suggestion. What do you think about survival or health—maybe an exercise program?

J: I think that would help.

Comment:

Jay is then helped to formulate a program that is geared to his current level of physical fitness. This is determined in consultation with his physician.

Subsequent Sessions:

In future sessions the therapeutic contract is refined (Jacobs, 1994). Jay is assisted to develop a program of recovery geared to improving his inner sense of satisfaction in the nine motivators. Jay has begun with the target of better health because it seemed to have the most potential success for him. He is also helped to make specific plans to contact clients in order to develop his business. He is asked to pay close attention to how he can provide value-added service, that is, how he can add to the quality of their businesses, thereby gaining an added sense of purpose. As a person who was formerly involved in his church, he makes plans to confer with his minister about matters of faith and spiritual healing related to his ultimate destiny. He also plans to initiate a continuing education program of reading and viewing video tapes about his profession. These have been accumulating for a year, as he receives two per month and he has not yet seen them. In doing this, he also gains a feeling of independence, freedom, and achievement.

His sense of belonging, an important source of behavior, had been seriously damaged. And though the complete satisfaction of this need will take longer to reclaim than the time for therapy allows, Jay makes plans to socialize with friends and stay involved with them, especially on weekends. A specific plan includes turning off radio music that reminds him of his previous relationship.

The therapist helps him plan to wallow in "rotten feelings" for 10 minutes over weekends but to schedule this time between a period of vigorous exercise and another enjoyable activity. If he complies with this plan or defies it by not following through, he wins.

It is crucial to understand that the purpose of planning related to the nine human motivators is to replace the destructive choices, which include the downward regressive behaviors in Figure 60.1. Human behavior is seen as a system of interconnected parts. Changing actions changes feelings and cognition. Additionally, the more weight put on one side, the lighter the other side. Thus, when Jay plans to effectively satisfy his nine internal drives or needs, he thereby chooses to abandon his destructive actions, cognition, and feelings.

SUMMARY

Short-Term Targeted Therapy (S3T) is a systematic and theory-driven series of interventions that are practical and geared to the current world of managed care. In this system human beings are seen as agents of their own behavior, not victims of their history or of their cultural environment. Their behaviors originate from current motives which are specific but connected to nine general needs or genetic instructions.

Therapists utilize the system in stages by helping clients develop a commitment to therapy; identify what they want to accomplish; evaluate their behavior; and implement specific, targeted plans for more effective living. Many techniques can be used, several of which are illustrated in this chapter. Short-Term Targeted Therapy is intended to incorporate a wide range of therapist skills which are less insight-centered and more action-focused.

REFERENCES

Applegate, G. (1985). *Happiness: It's your choice.* Los Angeles: Berringer.

Corey, G. (1998). *Issues and ethics in the helping profession.* Pacific Grove, CA: Brooks Cole.

Diagnostic and statistical manual of mental disorders (4th ed.). Washington, DC: American Psychiatric Association.

Frankl, V. (1984). *Man's search for meaning.* NY: Washington Square Press.

Glasser, W. (1998). *Choice theory.* NY: HarperCollins.

Jacobs, E. (1994). *Impact Therapy.* Odessa, FL: Psychological Assessment Resources, Inc.

Madanes, C. (1995). *The violence of men.* San Francisco: Josey-Bass, Inc.

Maslow, A. (1970). *Motivation and personality* (2nd ed.). NY: Harper and Row.

Weeks, G. and L'Abate, L. (1982). *Paradoxical psychotherapy.* NY: Brunner/Mazel.

Wubbolding, R. (1988). *Using Reality Therapy.* New York: Harper Collins.

Wubbolding, R. (1996). Working with suicidal clients. In B. Herlihy & G. Corey (Eds.), *ACA Ethical Standards Casebook.* (pp. 267–274). Alexandria, VA: American Counseling Association.

Wubbolding, R. (2000). *Reality therapy for the 21st century.* Philadelphia, PA: Brunner Routledge.

Chapter 61 _____

SOCIAL INFLUENCE THERAPY

JOHN S. GILLIS

> *If any readers are partial to humanistic systems of psychotherapy, viewing the client as being worthy of respect and seeing the therapist always dealing with the client on an equal basis, prepare for a surprise. As John Gillis bluntly states, "The approach is forthrightly manipulative."*
>
> *Perhaps we therapists tend to deny the therapeutic influence of matters such as doctoral degrees, diplomas on walls, double doors, soft chairs, attractive receptionists, expensive furniture—but we can be sure that such matters that have nothing to do with a therapist's effectiveness will nevertheless have some effect on the client.*
>
> *Gillis, in my judgment, is correct in his statement that Social Influence Therapy can be applied to all systems of psychotherapy. However, it must be recognized that some practitioners will reject purposefully employing such tactics.*
>
> *This is one of those chapters that actually cuts across all theories—as do the chapters on Feminist Therapy, Crisis Management, and Sex Therapies—and should greatly interest all who practice our arcane arts.*

Social Influence Therapy is an approach to treatment that attempts to change a client's attitudes or perspective by (1) having the therapist establish a position of ascendancy and (2) then using this position to implement attitude-change strategies. The system borrows freely from other disciplines those persuasive techniques of demonstrated or potential value, such strategies deriving mainly from social psychology. Thus the therapist attempting to maximize influence incorporates ideas and methods from such areas as attitude change and interpersonal attraction. The literature on placebo effects in medicine also serves as a frequent source of tactics.

The approach is forthrightly manipulative. Influence attempts are the primary strategies of treatment and are initiated and controlled by the therapist. It is, in fact, the position of those sympathetic to this view that most contemporary therapies involve strong components of influence; social influence therapists simply attempt to identify these and then maximize their efficacy through careful pretherapy planning.

HISTORY

Awareness of the significance of social influence factors in treatment is certainly not new. The importance of influence, placebo effects, and so-called "nonspecific" factors has been recognized in medicine since ancient times.

While acknowledgment of their role in psychotherapeutic practice is more recent, Jerome Frank's classic, *Persuasion and Healing,* summarized a body of speculation and empirical work concerning such factors as early as 1961.

The past several years have witnessed both an increased awareness of influence processes and an exploration of the manner in which they work in therapy. *Psychotherapy and the Psychology of Behavior Change,* by Goldstein, Heller, and Sechrest (1966), has a good deal to say about strategies of influence. So does a series of studies by Strong and his colleagues (Strong, 1968; Schmidt & Strong, 1970; Strong & Matross, 1973) and by other investigators (Harari, 1972; Dell, 1973). It is now not uncommon to view therapy in terms of demand characteristics (McReynolds & Tori, 1972), manipulation (Krainin, 1972), suggestibility (Lang, Lazovik, & Reynolds, 1965), and the intentional manipulation of client expectancies (Klein et al., 1969). Torrey (1972) has pointed out the distressing (to many) similarities between witch doctors and therapists; the bulk of these commonalities involve various means by which influence is exercised.

While many investigators have acknowledged the importance of such processes, few would regard themselves as influence therapists. The difference lies primarily in the readiness of the social influence therapist to elaborate the tactical possibilities of this position. This writer highlighted this pivotal difference in the 1974 *Psychology Today* article that brought the system to public attention. In that paper, I urged that the strategic implications of the influence position be taken seriously. I then described a series of techniques by which this could be accomplished. No claim was made that therapists *should* employ such methods; it *was* argued that they should be aware of their potential efficacy in treatment. I elaborated my theme in my 1979 monograph. Here I attempted to (1) bring together the diverse theoretical and empirical writings concerning influence; (2) identify those areas of literature, both scientific and anecdotal, that might serve as sources of useful therapeutic tactics; and (3) illustrate the means by which such tactics could be generated and implemented.

In my 1974 and 1979 works I outlined a broad framework for conceptualizing influence in therapy. In the years between their publication, a number of specific tenets of the system were assessed empirically. Several of these studies are listed below in the "Current Status" section.

CURRENT STATUS

A number of psychologists, some of whom would not consider themselves "social influence therapists," are acquainted with strategic approaches to maximizing influence. Some who are most familiar with the tactical approaches to be discussed are listed below. None of these individuals necessarily uses the tactics described or necessarily espouses the views presented herein. All, however, are knowledgeable regarding the assumptions, purposes, and applications of Social Influence Therapy. These psychologists include Michael Berren, Ph.D., Phoenix, Arizona; Keith Blevens, Ph.D., Richmond, California; Robert Childress, Ph.D., Tucson, Arizona; James C. Megas, Ph.D., Brownsville, Texas; S. W. Patrick, Ph.D., Houston, Texas; and Michael Sherrod, Ph.D., Knoxville, Tennessee.

Workshops and seminars on Social Influence Therapy, although offered on no regular schedule, have been presented at various locations throughout the country in the past few years. Two workshops were offered in 1979 in the Portland, Oregon area. Any individuals or groups interested in attending or initiating such functions should contact this author.

Several papers outline the social influence position (Gillis, 1974, 1979) or lend empirical support to one of its tenets.

Five works lend empirical support to Social Influence Theory: (1) A 1977 study by Childress and Gillis points up the capacity of pretherapy role-induction interviews to enhance the client's expectations of benefit; (2) a 1976 report by Venzor, Gillis, and Beal shows the diverse range of therapeutic styles that clients accept as helpful; (3) a 1980 paper by Gillis and Patrick demonstrates that this tolerance of therapeutic styles extends even to approaches in which virtually every remark of the client is negated or challenged; (4) a 1977 paper by Friedenberg and Gillis demonstrates the effectiveness of videotaped lectures for enhancing clients' self-esteem; and (5) a 1978 study by Byrd, Osborn, and Gillis demonstrates the therapeutic effects of desensitization, even when the hierarchy employed is not appropriate to the problem.

In addition to evaluating the adequacy of their own propositions regarding therapeutic change, influence therapists refer to the empirical literature in a wide range of areas, particularly social psychology, to generate tactics. An individual attempting to learn to maximize influence might thus be directed to review the work in such areas as interpersonal attraction, placebo effects, coercive persuasion, and hypnosis.

THEORY

Most of the theory underlying Social Influence Therapy concerns the nature of social interactions, particularly those interactions that have as their goal some change on the part of one or all of the participants. In this respect the theoretical base is narrow: Little concern is given to the origins and development of personality. Indeed, there is no explicit theory of maladjustment, other than the position that satisfaction with oneself and one's situation owes little to the objective realities of those situations.

Although Social Influence Therapy offers no detailed theory of personality or psychopathology, it is generally accepted that an individual's attitudes in therapy are critical for success. In this regard, Social Influence Therapy is in agreement with a number of theories—Albert Ellis's rational-emotive approach, the cognitive behavior therapies—that stress the fundamental importance of one's thought processes in adjustment. This being the case, the primary goal of Social Influence Therapy is to alter the client's attitudes or perspective toward him- or herself and his or her situation. Although it is obviously helpful if things change objectively for a client, behavioral changes are neither necessary nor sufficient for the critical cognitive alterations that must take place. Many influence tactics function, in fact, to convince the client that certain desired changes are already beginning to develop, and that he or she can already regard things as having changed for the better. Social influence therapists are certainly not opposed to behavior change, but it is apparent that people who are depressed about their failures or who are concerned about hostility are often no more extreme in these regards than the bulk of individuals who are not at all concerned about them. The task for the influence therapist is thus to alter individuals' view of things and not necessarily the behaviors themselves. This is, of course, precisely what happens when "self-acceptance" is realized by client-centered or other approaches. Empirical evidence on therapeutic outcomes indicates, in any case, that psychotherapy seems best able to achieve the objective of changing the individual's subjective state. To some extent, then, the goals of Social Influence Therapy are simply those that can be most reliably attained.

The probability of these goals being realized is largely dependent on the manner in which the therapist exercises influence. It has been found useful to consider the exercise of influence in therapy as a three-stage process. The first stage involves the enhancement of the client's expectation of benefits; the second, establishment of a position of influence by the therapist; and the third, use of this position to implement change. It is during this third stage that the actual content of treatment, the "healing ritual" as Jerome Frank (1974) calls it, is implemented. It is also possible to speak of a fourth stage, wherein any changes that have occurred are solidified. The tactics appropriate to this last purpose generally overlap those in stage three, however, and the two are treated together here.

The theory of change underlying Social Influence Therapy has some important similarities with Schein's (1971) model of persuasion. Presently held maladaptive beliefs must be "unfrozen"; new views must be inculcated. Clients are seen as seeking treatment because their approaches to the world, particularly the manner in which they conceptualize the social environment and their place in it, are not successful. "Not successful" here means that they do not get from others the responses—affection, recognition, respect—they would like. The number and severity of their objective problems may be no different from those of many persons who are reasonably satisfied with their situations. They are, however, in Frank's (1974) terms, "demoralized." If they are to benefit from treatment, this demoralization must be combated. An altered view of circumstances, a differing way of assessing themselves, or a new framework or belief system must be realized.

Significant change in a basic attitude is not easily accomplished. Nevertheless, such changes are realized in many extratherapeutic situations (religious conversions, advertising, political indoctrinations), and the social-psychological literature has much to say about the variables that are instrumental in these circumstances. It is clear, for example, that an important initial condition has been satisfied simply by the client's present perspective being unsatisfactory ("disconfirmed," in Schein's [1971] terms). Of the remaining factors involved in major alterations of attitude or beliefs, only a few can readily be controlled by the change agent, in this case the

therapist. The best that the therapist can do is to assure that (1) a different and plausible alternative perspective is presented; and (2) the conditions of its presentation are such that they maximize the likelihood of the client adopting it. These conditions are best accomplished by the therapist attending to the possibilities that his or her position allows, that is, attending to the tasks of maximizing expectations of gain, gaining a position of power, and conducting a plausible, persuasive healing ritual. The alternative perspective offered by the therapist can be as complex as a psychoanalytic or behaviorist view of human beings or as simple as the message that "you have positive qualities as well as distressing ones." The most important characteristic of the new perspective is not its objective validity but its usefulness to the client. An explanation of one's current difficulties in terms of the frustrated rage of childhood (and the performance of a therapeutic ritual designed to vent this rage) may be a valuable proposal for a client even if there is little evidence to support it.

The theory underlying Social Influence Therapy might be most succinctly summarized as follows: (1) Clients seek treatment because their view of life and themselves is unsatisfactory; (2) the purpose of psychotherapy is to induce the client to adopt a more benign perspective; (3) this can be accomplished only if the therapist maximizes his or her control over the variables conducive to change; and (4) most of these variables involve the establishment and use of interpersonal influence.

METHODOLOGY

Even a casual perusal of the psychotherapy literature of the past 25 years reveals ample awareness of the role of influence processes. Social Influence Therapy is alone neither in its primary goal—altering the client's perspective—or in its stress on the primacy of cognitive factors in adjustment. What does give the approach some uniqueness is its emphasis on developing specific strategic maneuvers to maximize influence. It is one thing to recognize the contribution of a client's expectations to the eventual outcome of treatment. It is quite another to advocate that the therapist develop an array of tactics specifically intended to raise those expectations and to suggest that appropriate tactics might be borrowed from such nontherapeutic enterprises as advertising and attitude change. Social Influence Therapy, then, to the extent that it offers something unique to the therapy researcher or practitioner, does so by its unabashed advocacy of tactical planning and its willingness to suggest the sorts of maneuvers that might be employed.

The three-stage influence process mentioned in the "Theory" section was developed largely as a framework for generating influence tactics. It can also serve as a convenient scheme for organizing the discussion of these procedures. It should be remembered as these methods are described that Social Influence Therapy is very much an open system as far as tactics are concerned. Indeed, the major contribution of the approach may be to draw attention to some sources of tactics heretofore neglected by therapists. By reviewing such areas—interpersonal attraction and attitude change, for example—with the purpose of identifying items that might generalize to therapy, practitioners will doubtless be able to develop an impressive variety of innovative methods on their own. The suggestions raised by the social influence approach merely serve as examples of the kinds of tactical possibilities that abound in areas seemingly remote from therapy.

With this caveat, several specific procedures that might be employed to maximize influence can be described. These will, as noted, be organized in terms of a three-stage influence process. Due to space limitations, only one or two illustrative strategies will be given for each stage. A more elaborate listing can be found in *Social Influence in Psychotherapy* (Gillis, 1979).

Stage 1. Building Expectations

The first phase of therapy involves enhancing expectations of benefit. (This stage might also be thought of as maximizing placebo effects.) There are two aspects to this: increasing the client's faith in, and commitment to, psychotherapy itself and increasing his or her faith that the therapist is an especially adept practitioner of the art. The first objective might be accomplished in any of several ways.

First, the client's commitment to treatment (or need to believe in therapy) can be enhanced by introducing severe "initiation rites." Many therapy systems and treatment communities already practice this: Drug treatment groups may require prospective members to shave their heads and perform menial tasks for a time prior to receiving full status in the program; candidates for Primal Therapy spend a couple of days isolated in a motel room, refraining from sex, cigarettes, and alcohol. In more typical clinical settings the severity of one's initiation, the price he or she has to pay to gain admission to therapy, might be increased by having the client complete an exhaustive screening routine, perhaps involving repeated administrations of lengthy personality inventories. Inconvenient appointment times might be scheduled for initial sessions; clients might be made to spend some time on a waiting list; the therapist—because of a busy schedule—might have to arrive late for a few weekend appointments that the client made some sacrifices to attend.

Second, forced-compliance studies in social psychology suggest that under certain conditions persons will come to adopt attitudes that they have used to persuade others, even if these attitudes are contrary to their initial positions. Clients who have been in treatment for only a short time might therefore be asked to tell still newer clients, perhaps those awaiting their first contact with the therapist, about the benefits and promise of treatment.

Third, a commitment-enhancing gambit of a different order has been referred to as the "pseudo-free choice" maneuver. Here the therapist, preferably after one or two sessions, informs the client that two alternative forms of treatment are employed. One of these involves rather direct confrontation. While relatively stressful, it often yields strongly positive outcomes for the client who can cope with it. The alternative is more benign and less stressful, but also more superficial. The therapist adds that he doesn't typically give people a choice of treatment strategies, but that the client seemed to be one who could indeed handle the more challenging approach if he or she should choose it. The dice are, of course, loaded; clients invariably choose the more difficult approach (if there are any doubts that the client might not select this procedure the tactic should not be used). By virtue of this maneuver the client makes a commitment to a certain way of proceeding. His or her investment in the treatment's effectiveness, and belief that it will work, is increased. He or she has selected it precisely for these reasons. In presenting the choice to the client in this way the therapist is also sending a clear message: This is a client with obvious strengths who will indeed profit from therapy.

Increasing the client's faith in the personal merits of the therapist can be accomplished with similar maneuvers. The common theme of these practices is giving the client positive information about the therapist but doing so in a manner that is not suspect. To this end the therapist might arrange to have the client overhear certain persons (former clients or possibly confederates) discussing the merits of the therapist. This is most easily accomplished in the clinic waiting room. A second possibility is the "busy schedule" gambit. Here the client is told, most conveniently by the clinic receptionist or by a colleague during a role induction interview, that Dr. X is precisely the therapist he or she needs. Dr. X is in considerable demand, however, a very full schedule being displayed to substantiate this point. After considerable negotiations about scheduling problems the client is eventually assigned to Dr. X.

A variety of additional tactics designed to build expectations have been described (Gillis, 1979). I also consider the *maintenance* of credibility through the use of a series of statements ("no miss" interpretations) that are likely to be viewed as perceptive and insightful by a high proportion of clients. It is perhaps appropriate here to restate the position that "Social Influence Therapy" originated as an attempt to offer an alternative view of treatment. "No-miss" interpretations, for example, were seen as statements that were offered as comments on a client's situation with great frequency. Giving them tactical status therefore amounts to little more than claiming that therapists should recognize what they are doing. If such practices increase the effectiveness of treatment, however, the therapist may wish to use them strategically rather than leave their occurrence to chance.

Stage 2. Gaining Ascendancy

"Ascendancy" in psychotherapy has some overlap with the concept of "power" in social psychology, but the two are not identical. To gain ascendancy in therapy is to achieve a status where one's remarks are "taken account of" by the client. Such status is necessary, we would argue, since the essential messages the therapist delivers are not substantially different from those given the client by others. The therapist's communicating of the message (e.g., "you *can* control your anger"; "you are an adequate person") is often effective where others' doing so was not, however, because the therapist presents it (1) in terms that the client has never before encountered or, more likely, (2) from a uniquely authoritative and powerful position.

Tactics for gaining such a position can be usefully classified under two broad headings: command power and "friendship" (or referent) power. The former can be, and is, achieved with a number of traditional practices. These include the use of powerful arguments in which the therapist clearly has the advantage; the use of esoteric jargon and interpretations in which the client has no choice but to defer; and the "audience-performer" strategy, in which the client's task is essentially to present his or her case while the therapist comments on the meaning and appropriateness of this verbal performance. The research literature suggests a myriad of additional procedures for establishing command power. Schmidt and Strong (1970), for example, have empirically determined a set of characteristics by which clients define "expertness" in therapists; these include such items as hand shaking, sitting postures, and a confident tone of voice. Torrey (1972) advises on the construction of a persuasive "edifice," the foundation of which is the display of the accoutrements of authority and knowledge.

"Friendship" power is perhaps more often sought by present-day practitioners. Effective tactics here induce allegiance of client to therapist, usually because the latter has established himself as an attractive, decent, caring person whose friendship and approval the client wishes to maintain. Cohesive links can often be fashioned (and likely are) in therapy by the use of the "ingratiation" tactics described by Jones (1964). These include

such practices as expressing liking for the client (making it difficult for him to dislike you), flattering him (by commenting on his positive characteristics or his ability to handle confrontation), stressing the similarities between the two of you ("I know what it's like being under those kinds of pressures"), and stating your own strengths in a noncompetitive manner. Even admitting one's weaknesses or regrets about not having sufficiently helped a client can beget cohesion when used at appropriate times. Most therapists employ some or all of these practices unwittingly. Social Influence Therapy points up the possibility of using them strategically. The value of obtaining a positive affective response from the client, one of liking and respect, cannot be overstated. In the extreme, one might argue as I (1979) have, that once one has induced a patient to feel positively about the therapist and therapy itself, *nothing else* need be accomplished in order for the treatment to be regarded as successful.

A range of other strategies can be used to bring about a cohesive relationship between client and therapist. These might include:

1. The disclosure of personal difficulties by the therapist
2. The initiation of unexpected or "disinhibiting" experiences in which both parties participate (George Bach's birth scenarios and constructive aggression exercises probably accomplish this, as do some psychodrama formats)
3. The introduction of an external enemy (e.g., an impersonal society, tyrannical parents, materialistic employers) against whom client and therapist can unite.

Each of these tactics has a basis in social psychological research. Any number of similar strategies can be derived from that literature or from the therapist's experience *outside* of the clinic.

Stage 3. The Healing Ritual

The third segment of treatment involves the carrying out of a therapeutic ritual. If the initial stages—building expectations and establishing ascendancy—have been successfully negotiated, this segment, while it appears to be the focus of therapy, should present few problems. The task of the therapist is to select a set of procedures that the client can accept as plausible. The client, that is, should view the activities of the therapeutic hour—discussing childhood experiences, venting intense emotions, reenacting one's birth, meditating, repeating positive statements about oneself—as being somehow related to the source of his or her disorder and to its alleviation. The concerns of the therapist here are two:

determination of a treatment method that the client will find believable (meditation or exploration of one's dreams may not seem, to a ghetto resident, like the answer to his or her problems) and competent performance of that ritual. An important point here is that the client who expects to benefit will accept a wide range of therapeutic rituals or styles. Part of the therapist's task is thus to simply avoid the totally implausible ritual (such as the meditation–ghetto client combination). If selection is carefully made, however, a ritual likely to have maximum influence power with each specific client can usually be identified.

In addition to encouraging a thoughtful selection of treatment methods, the therapist interested in exerting influence might consider the following two methods: (1) The therapist may provide the client with evidence that he or she is indeed changing as treatment progresses. This can be accomplished with techniques as elaborate as charting response rate changes over time, or as simple as selectively commenting on anything that might be remotely construed as change. Used in this way, such feedback is a vehicle to *induce* change rather than a recognition of change already accomplished. The therapist might also consider adding a description of the altered behavior so that the client will know specifically *how* to change.

(2) The therapist may direct the client to behave differently—that is, *tell* him or her to change. If authority has been effectively established, many clients require nothing more than an order to change and a clear description of what the new responses should be.

These, then, are some of the methods that can be used to enhance the effectiveness of treatment. There are countless others, of course, limited only by the ingenuity (and perhaps the role-playing ability) of the individual therapist. The therapist interested in social influence will consider some such maneuvers as adjuncts to his or her customary, perhaps more traditional, methods.

APPLICATIONS

It is difficult at this juncture to map the limits of influence tactics. It was originally thought that the tactics would be most readily applicable with patients who (1) were not severely ill, (2) were highly susceptible to suggestions, (3) did not have highly circumscribed symptoms, and (4) were somewhat vague about their own desired outcomes from treatment. Neurotics, particularly hysterics, and those with relatively moderate personality disorders were obvious possibilities. These persons would have much in common with the clients whom Frank (1974) labels as "demoralized." Influence maneuvers would thus be most efficacious for those who were anxious and depressed, had lost hope that things might improve, and felt that they didn't measure up to either their own or others' expectations.

Fortunately or not, the greater proportion of clients seeking psychotherapy would seem to qualify as appropriate under these guidelines. What such individuals require is not a major change in situation or behavior but a fresh perspective: A perspective that will give them a feeling of control over their destiny, a feeling that life and they themselves can be understood and enjoyed.

Influence tactics have proven, in fact, to be applicable to a much broader spectrum of patients than these. They have been successfully employed with some psychotic patients. Influence strategies have also been adapted for use in group, marital, and family therapies. The principal patient sample for which they are relevant, however, remains those who are "demoralized." The techniques have thus been most often employed with outpatients and college students having vague complaints of depression, social isolation, and alienation.

CASE EXAMPLE

Social Influence Therapy is most usefully considered as an adjunct to other systems (although it can be maintained that the substantive aspects of these systems have little to do with their effectiveness). Citing a case in which the method was successful, then, is most readily done by identifying a case in which a special conscious effort was made to maximize influence, regardless of which other techniques—the healing rituals—were employed. One case is familiar to this writer, however, in which influence tactics constituted almost the sole approach to treatment. This case was meant to demonstrate the power of providing patients with concrete feedback that they have indeed changed even before this change is fully realized.

The client was a 21-year-old female with a phobia for injections; a phobia of such severity that, a few months previously, she had postponed her wedding in order to avoid a blood test. She was unable to receive an injection without fainting or, at the very least, engaging in considerable histrionics. She came in for treatment when she learned that within the next three weeks she would have to receive a shot for an allergy. After discussing the problem, the therapist assured her that dealing with the phobia would be no problem and that they would be using a behavioral technique that had proven very successful in the past. The "treatment" consisted of handling a toy syringe every evening for 10 minutes. The prospect of this task did not arouse any anxiety in the client and it was decided that she would return in one week for another interview. The therapist then handed the syringe to the client, and wished her good luck (in a manner analogous to Dorothy of the *Wizard of Oz* being sent off to kill the wicked witch).

The client reported back the following week to participate in a 10-minute session with the therapist. This meeting consisted of therapist and client squirting each other with the toy syringes. It was explained that this was a very important aspect of treatment. At the end of the session the client was told once again to handle the syringe every evening and then to report back in one week. At the next session the client was presented with a "certificate of improvement," awarded with no small degree of ceremony.

For the first few minutes, therapist and client again squirted each other with the syringes. The therapist then asked if handling the syringe at home had been upsetting. The client reported that it was not (which was expected, since the toy version of the feared object had aroused little reaction initially). The therapist then announced that treatment was completed and congratulated her on such a speedy recovery. He told the client, that, as good as he thought the method was, he had never seen anyone go through it quite so smoothly and with such dramatic changes. The therapist then reported that his supervisor had been watching the previous week's sessions through a one-way vision screen (this was the case) and that he too was amazed at the rapidity with which the client recovered. Indeed, he was so impressed that he thought it appropriate that she be presented with some formal recognition of the change. The therapist then gave the client an impressive-looking "certificate of change" signed by the supervisor (and identical to that given introductory psychology students for participation in departmental experiments). It was explained that this was very rarely done but, considering the fact that her progress had been exemplary, he and the supervisor thought it appropriate here. The therapist then shook her hand, congratulated her, and told her that she was now ready to receive her injection.

The client immediately made an appointment at the student health center. Unfortunately, her allergy had cleared up and she did not require an injection. She then asked the physician to give her any shot at all because she wanted to prove that it really wouldn't bother her. The physician refused. Acting on the client's request, the therapist made arrangements with the health center for her to return for an injection of a saline solution. The client received the injection and reported only minor fearful anticipation. The certificate, she reported some weeks later, was still hanging on her bedroom wall.

It is not suggested that improvement in this case was traceable solely to the presentation of the "certificate of change." One can argue, for example, that the simple handling of the toy syringe might have served as a form of systematic desensitization for the client. Neither is the case meant to suggest a tactic that is appropriate to a large number of clients. Indeed, such a transparent gambit is likely to evoke suspicion, if not outright derision, in most patients. The therapist must select tactics with the specific client in mind. What the case *is* intended to illustrate is the use of feedback to induce change and to solidify change once it has occurred. The specific procedures by which feedback is implemented to this end will vary with each patient. Such methods can be used as an adjunct to any method of treatment, including a more formalized systematic desensitization. More generally, this case report is meant to serve as a demonstration of the use of influence strategies with a patient who had formerly proven resistant to change. The reader interested in other case reports from influence therapy should consult my 1979 monograph, particularly the accounts of the use of "friendship power" with psychotic patients.

SUMMARY

It has long been recognized that certain aspects of therapeutic interaction, apart from the techniques themselves, may contribute to the effectiveness of treatment. Such non-specific factors are sometimes seen to be common to all effective therapeutic systems. The central tenets of Social Influence Therapy are that (1) within such nonspecific factors are contained the essential curative elements of therapy; and (2) these essential ingredients can be most usefully conceptualized as methods by which the therapist exerts influence over the client. Social Influence Therapy thus attempts to identify and analyze the many ways in which influence operates in therapy.

This approach was originally intended to offer an alternative perspective on existing systems of therapy. The initial goal of the system was to determine whether all forms of therapy could be translated into a common set of terms—most likely those derived from social psychology. Because of a focus on the specific maneuvers used to exert influence, the influence perspective has come to be increasingly viewed as a strategic guide to therapeutic practice. In a broad fashion it may be said to possess the rudiments of a system of therapy: It includes a view of the client and his or her source of distress; a view of the therapist's role and task; a view of the interaction between the two; and suggestions as to the procedures that might make that interaction most efficacious. Because of these characteristics, it is probably possible to use Social Influence Therapy as one's major approach to practical treatment problems. It is this writer's belief, however, that Social Influence Therapy is still best considered an alternative conceptual scheme that can be applied to *all* systems of psychotherapy. So, too, are its tactical possibilities most usefully considered as adjuncts to more traditional systems.

Influence pervades all human interactions, therapy included. It can be enhanced by thoughtful planning, should the therapist decide to do this. It can be ignored, perhaps to the jeopardy of the encounter, only if some of the realities of human interaction are ignored.

REFERENCES

Byrd, G. R., Osborn, S., & Gillis, J. S. (1978). Use of pseudo-desensitization in the treatment of an experimentally produced fear. *Psychological Reports, 43,* 947–952.

Childress, R., & Gillis, J. S. (1977). A study of pretherapy role induction as an influence process. *Journal of Clinical Psychology, 33,* 540–544.

Dell, D. M. (1973). Counselor power base, influence attempts, and behavior. *Journal of Counseling Psychology, 20,* 399–405.

Frank, J. D. (1961). *Persuasion and healing.* Baltimore: Johns Hopkins Press.

Frank, J. D. (1974). Psychotherapy: The restoration of morale. *American Journal of Psychiatry, 131,* 271–274.

Friedenberg, W. P., & Gillis, J. S. (1977). An experimental study of the effectiveness of attitude change techniques for enhancing self-esteem. *Journal of Clinical Psychology, 33,* 1120–1124.

Gillis, J. S. (1974, December). Therapist as manipulator. *Psychology Today,* 90–95.

Gillis, J. S. (1979). *Social influence in psychotherapy: A description of the process and some tactical implications.* Counseling and Psychotherapy Monograph Series, No. 1. Pilgrimage Press.

Gillis, J. S., & Patrick, S. W. (1980). A comparative study of competitive and social reinforcement models of interview behavior. *Journal of Clinical Psychology, 36,* 277–282.

Goldstein, A. P., Heller, K., & Sechrest, L. (1966). *Psychotherapy and the psychology of behavior change.* New York: Wiley.

Harari, H. (1972). Cognitive manipulations with delinquent adolescents in group therapy. *Psychotherapy: Therapy, Research and Practice, 9,* 303–307.

Jones, E. E. (1964). *Ingratiation: A social psychological analysis.* New York: Appleton.

Klein, M. H., Dittman, A. T., Parloff, M. B., & Gill, M. M. (1969). Behavior therapy: Observations and reflections. *Journal of Consulting and Clinical Psychology, 33,* 259–266.

Krainin, J. M. (1972). Psychotherapy by counter-manipulation. *American Journal of Psychiatry, 129,* 749–750.

Lang, P. J., Lazovik, D. J., & Reynolds, D. J. (1965). Desensitization, suggestibility, and pseudotherapy. *Journal of Abnormal Psychology, 70,* 395–402.

McReynolds, W. T., & Tori, C. (1972). A further assessment of attention-placebo effects and demand characteristics in studies of systematic desensitization. *Journal of Consulting and Clinical Psychology, 38,* 261–264.

Schein, E. H. (1971). *Coercive persuasion.* New York: Norton.

Schmidt, L. D., & Strong, S. R. (1970). "Expert" and "inexpert" counselors. *Journal of Counseling Psychology, 17,* 115–118.

Strong, S. R. (1968). Counseling: An interpersonal influence process. *Journal of Counseling Psychology, 15,* 215–224.

Strong, S. R., & Matross, R. (1973). Change process in counseling and psychotherapy. *Journal of Counseling Psychology, 20,* 25–37.

Torrey, E. F. (1972). What western psychotherapists can learn from witch doctors. *American Journal of Orthopsychiatry, 42,* 69–76.

Venzor, E., Gillis, J. S., & Beal, D. G. (1976). Preference for counselor response styles. *Journal of Counseling Psychology, 23,* 538–542.

Chapter 62

SOLUTION FOCUSED THERAPY

LINDA METCALF

The fundamental thinking behind this system changes the role of the therapist from a detective seeking to discover a "major crime" committed in the past to observing the person from the side, as it were, and giving minimal assistance as an interested observer. The patient becomes the therapist.

The group that originally worked on this system developed the "miracle question" that goes as follows: "Suppose that one night, while you were asleep, there was a miracle and this problem was solved. How would you know? What would be different?" This approach is essentially similar to Alfred Adler's question, which asks, "If you did not have this symptom, what would you do?"

The moment of major help seems to be in Solution Focused Therapy, a change from concern with the origin of the problem to discovering solutions to the problem. Insight is not considered essential, nor are details important. Clients' reports are considered complaints, not symptoms, and clients are motivated in the process of determining goals. An apparent minor correction leads to a snowball effect. In essence, the system takes the position that complex problems can have simple solutions. The therapist works with the client, attempting to understand the person and the problems, and eager to be of help—but holding back as much as possible—respecting clients so that the clients cure themselves with minimal help. Finally, and surprisingly, the therapist avers that this system is incomplete and urges others to complete it.

Solution Focused Therapy is a nonpathological approach to working with clients that focuses on their competencies rather than their deficits, their strengths rather than their weaknesses, and their self-identified goals. The model assumes that language is the source of personal and social reality and can be the vehicle for change in the future once personal perceptions are changed. The solution focused therapist converses with clients about the client's goals while complimenting and curiously asking questions about the client's present reality. The therapist proposes through the conversations a time in the future when the problem brought to therapy does not exist nor interfere with the client's life. By creating an environment in which clients can perceive their lives differently, it is believed that change becomes more attractive and more likely to occur.

The task of the solution-focused therapist is to identify a method of cooperating with the client in order to accomplish what the client desires. This is accomplished by asking questions about the problem deemed important by the client, identifying existing and potential resources of the client, and proposing a future in which the problem does not exist. "This conversation shifts the clients' reality toward one that includes both/and thinking and possible new options. It also promotes hope and motivation" (Lipchik & Kubicki, 1996, p. 69). The promotion of hope and possibility is elicited through the discovery of exceptions, or times when the problem is less intrusive in a person's life. The model emphasizes that problems do not continuously occur and it is the job of the therapist to assist the client in recognizing that phenomenon. It is the belief of the solution-focused therapist that if clients realize their abilities and competencies, the impact of a problem on their lives can be lessened.

HISTORY

Traditionally, when clients came to therapy, they did so with a desire to understand how their lives went wrong. They looked to therapists to give them explanations in the hope that understanding the root of the problem, or why the problem occurred in the first place, would tell them what to do differently in order to correct the problem. Thus, therapists oriented themselves in the past instead of the present, searching for *why* problems occurred so those clients would have information. For some action-oriented clients, such explanations motivated them enough to try the strategies handed down to them by their therapists. For other clients, such explanations gave them more reasons to feel and act incompetent. When Milton Erikson began working with clients, he took a new approach to therapy that began instigating new ideas for therapists to consider: "He addressed himself consistently to the fact that individuals have a reservoir of wisdom learned and forgotten but still available. He suggested that his patients explore alternative ways of organizing their experience without exploring the etiology or dynamics or the dysfunction" (Minuchin & Fishman, 1981, pp. 268–269).

With this new approach emerged a new sort of client who could leave therapy with identified tools to solve future problems independently. This was particularly helpful to non-action clients who tended to dwell on reasons why their lives were in shambles. The therapist became someone to help clients access their resources and put them into use. This respectful stance became one of the basic constructs of Solution Focused Brief Therapy. However, the solution focused approach was still years away, even though a briefer approach was emerging on the West Coast at the Mental Research Institute.

At the Mental Research Institute (MRI), John Weakland, Richard Fisch, Paul Watzlawick, and others worked with clients within a time limit of 10 sessions. Their purpose was to reorganize the thinking of clients instead of trying to promote insight. The therapists at MRI viewed problems as occurring when the actions in life were mishandled. The more people tried to solve the problem, the more the problem was perpetuated and the less responsibility the client took to solve it. This problem-focused approach involved thinking that problems were interactional and could be best solved when the clients did something different in response to the problem.

In the 1980s, Solution Focused Therapy took a different turn in reference to how problems were viewed. Steve de Shazer and his team at the Brief Family Therapy Center in Milwaukee began looking at "what has been working in order to identify and amplify these solution sequences" (de Shazer, 1982, 1985). In this approach, the new belief that problems do not occur constantly encouraged the therapist to focus on those problem-absent times as exceptions, and to bring those times forward as solutions to the presenting problem. De Shazer's team studied one particular task, "The First Session Task," and was pleased with the results. They asked the clients to do the following: *"Between now and the next time we meet, we (I) would like you to observe so you can describe to us (me) next time, what happens in our (pick one: family, life, marriage, relationship) that you want to continue to have happen"* (de Shazer, 1985, p. 137).

By identifying the specific interactions, behaviors, and thinking that helped the situation, clients seemed more apt to realize that they were indeed competent, and

could solve their own problems with minimal assistance. Tasks began to develop from these exceptions that the clients presented to the therapist. The therapist's task became one of creating opportunities for the clients to see themselves as competent and resourceful. Sometimes that meant asking a client to leave the therapy session and observe for a few days the times when the problem occurred less often. Other times, it meant carrying out small, specific tasks that the client identified as helpful in dissolving the problem. These new, less intrusive actions of the therapist placed the therapist in a less directive role. By believing that the client was the expert on his or her own life, the solution focused therapist became a sort of facilitator, guide, or assistant to the client, whose purpose was to create opportunities for clients to see themselves as the experts on their own lives.

Creating the opportunity for clients to see their lives without the problem then led the team in Milwaukee to develop the "miracle question." The basic miracle question is: "Suppose that one night while you were asleep, there was a miracle and this problem was solved. How would you know? What would be different?" (de Shazer, 1988, p. 5)

When clients responded to the miracle question, the therapist began gathering new information regarding how clients wanted their lives to evolve. By further expanding on the goals of the client, the Milwaukee team then continued to ask "exception" questions to elicit descriptions of times when the problem occurred less. By talking with clients about the problem-free times, the clients discovered solutions that they had forgotten about or had not noticed before. The team then began to ask exception questions earlier and earlier in therapy to develop solutions quickly and efficiently. They found that identifying and building on the exceptions helped clients to resolve their problems efficiently and with competence.

A great deal has been written about the application of Solution Focused Therapy and its effectiveness with a variety of complaints (Amatea, 1989; Berg, 1991; Berg & Gallagher, 1991; Cox, Chilman, & Nunnally, 1989; de Shazer, 1985, 1988; de Shazer, Berg, Lipchik, Nunnally, Molnar, Gingerich, & Weiner-Davis, 1986; Kral, 1988; Kral & Schaffer, 1989; Molnar & de Shazer, 1987; Molnar & Lindquist, 1990; Dolan, 1991; Walter & Pellar, 1992; Metcalf, 1995, 1997, 1998). This chapter will present information that reflects the progress of the model in its application and theoretical evolution and provides guidelines for its integration into the therapy process.

CURRENT STATUS

The solution focused brief therapy model is currently being utilized by many therapists in many areas, including depression, chemical dependency, sexual abuse, panic disorders, and eating disorders. For example, Eve Lipchik has focused on the interviewing process of therapy as a way to shift clients' perceptions during the initial therapy assessment and follow-up process. By doing so, the assessment becomes part of therapy. Insoo Kim Berg and Scott Miller have worked extensively with substance abuse, with remarkable results. Insoo Kim Berg has also worked with homeless families to show that even the most difficult populations have competencies to see them through hard times. John Walter and Jane Pellar have continued to push the limits of solution focused work and assume that only "solution talk" is necessary in therapy. By focusing on solution construction, Walter and Pellar keep therapy on a course of "goaling" rather than on goals, or "solving" rather than on solutions (Walter & Pellar, 1992, p. 86). Michelle Weiner-Davis has utilized the model's worth with couples. Michael Durrant has applied the principals to residential treatment, Linda Metcalf has taken the approach into the school system and group therapy practice, and Karen Rayter has developed parenting groups for parents of troubled adolescents.

The model continues to grow and expand into all types of contexts, with research being conducted on its effectiveness on long-term change. At the 1995 East Coast Conference on Brief Therapy, the diversity of ideas presented around the model indicated that there was no one clear theory of Solution Focused Therapy. The model has evolved from including the word *brief* in its name (Solution Focused Brief Therapy) to, currently, Solution Focused Therapy. The word *brief* seemed to imply that the model's worth was that of simply having a short duration, whereas it was its effectiveness that resulted in short-term therapy. In the late 1990s the model continued to evolve with a combination of many developments from talented therapists and clients who tested its flexibility and trusted its effectiveness when presented in an atmosphere of hope, respectfulness, and true belief that clients are competent.

THEORY

Many therapists who utilize the ideas of Solution Focused Therapy and believe in its effectiveness have difficulty delineating a single theoretical construct of Solution Focused Therapy. Instead, those therapists would attest that the model consists primarily of a new way of constructing reality and perceptions with clients through thinking differently about the event of therapy. Steve de Shazer has used the analogy of the skeleton key to explain the nature of working with a solution focused approach. "He contends that the therapist does not need to know a great deal about the nature of the problems brought to therapy to solve them. More relevant is the nature of solutions. It is the key that opens the door that matters most, not the nature of the lock. Analyzing and understanding the lock are unnecessary if one has a skeleton key that fits many different locks" (Cade & O'Hanlon, 1993, p. 21).

In theory, the solution focused therapist helps clients to discover the skeleton key so that clients realize their competency to solve their own problems. The model endorses a manner of thinking between client and therapist that is not problem-focused, but solution-focused, and is accomplished through conversations that focus on times when the client was more successful at managing the problem of concern. Those times are defined as *exceptions*. An example of asking a question that focuses on an exception would be: *"Take me back to a time when the depression you are describing was not as intense."*

The solution focused therapist recognizes that there are various types of clients who come to therapy. The following definitions of the types of clients in therapy helps solution focused therapists to understand their role in the helping process. A *visitor* (Fisch et al., 1982) in therapy has been defined as someone who comes to therapy at the request of others. The solution focused therapist simply listens to the visitor and offers no suggestions or tasks. The visitor is respectfully seen as a window shopper who has not come to buy a solution. The *complainant* comes to therapy with a particular problem and is usually prepared to talk, often at length. The solution focused therapist waits to be invited to be helpful to the complainant and offers no advice or suggestions until the complainant tells the therapist how he or she wishes life to be different. The *customer* is a client who comes to therapy with a complaint about his or her life or about someone in his or her life and wishes to do something different to improve the situation. The customer seeks the therapist's help in identifying solutions and the therapist actively assists the customer in identifying exceptions to the times when the problem exists.

Assumptions of Solution Focused Therapy

Over the past several years, postmodern philosophy has emerged as the dominant discussion surrounding Solution Focused Therapy and the assumptions that are referenced serve as constructs of the model. The following assumptions were initially instigated by O'Hanlon and Weiner-Davis and are considered to be the basic ideas of the model. I have modified the following assumptions in my work with group therapy, school issues, parenting issues, and teaching situations. I will attempt here to explain them as they apply to a wide variety of clinical therapy settings.

1. Use a nonpathological approach to open up possibilities.

When the solution focused therapist *redescribes* the problem to a client in a normalizing manner, hope and possibilities emerge, since the problems seem to become more solvable. The therapist can then look for exceptions to when the problem occurs, again implying that solutions exist. For example, a client referred to therapy for being hyperactive may experience the therapist's reframing of the complaint as "very energetic," a non-pathological term. This non-problem approach lessens resistance by replacing it with a notion of normalcy. When the therapist talks to clients about the times when they are controlling the energy instead of it controlling them, clients are challenged to gain control over the problems that seem to be interfering in their lives. As the definition of the problem shifts to one of normalcy, clients perceive the possibility that their problems are solvable, or at least manageable.

2. It is not necessary to promote insight in order to be helpful.

Insight is interesting, but it does not tell us how to change what we do. As previously mentioned, knowing why we are the way we are does little to develop new solutions. In fact, as clients discover why they are sad, angry, or depressed, they often use the information as a symptom and reason for not succeeding. Even in severe cases of past sexual or physical abuse, clients who are complimented on their strength to survive often blossom into competent, confident human beings who can then deal with problems and events more efficiently. It is the job of the therapist to assist them with noticing their competencies. One of the easiest ways of noticing a client's competencies is to *notice if the problem is occurring at the time of intervention or initial interview*. For example, a client who perceives himself as withdrawn may be observed as opening up to the therapist and talking nonstop for 20 minutes. If the therapist asks the client, "how have you managed to talk to me for 20 minutes?" both the therapist and the client may realize that exceptions are occurring. The therapist can then explore what was different during their time that facilitated the change. From that point, other times when the client feels comfortable and less withdrawn can be examined.

3. It is unnecessary to know a great deal about the complaint.

Using a solution focused approach does not necessitate that the therapist knows everything about the problem in order to be helpful to the client. The therapist can refer to the problem as "it" or "the problem," utilizing whatever language the client suggests. This is protective and often less threatening for the client. Helping a client to become more stable in a crisis situation merely by talking about the "situation" will create confidence in the client and will create an atmosphere of trust between therapist and client.

For example, in the case of sexual abuse, traditional therapies have suggested that retelling the story of abuse was necessary to begin absolving oneself from feeling victimized. While some people will benefit from "getting the story out," others fall back into the trap and become part of the story again, reliving the trauma and feeling victimized and helpless. Bill O'Hanlon's work with sexual abuse survivors has suggested the benefits of asking the client whether she wished to explain details or not. He found that most clients were relieved to learn that they could move forward without going backwards. I have found that clients who have experienced sexual abuse benefit when they begin to perceive themselves on a sort of timeline in which they picture themselves as having emerged from the event and as moving with vast momentum toward the future. This new way of working does not de-emphasize the trauma, but rather respects the client's need to remove herself from it.

4. Clients have complaints, not symptoms.

Clients who have been labeled with a diagnosis know how it can change the way they perceive themselves. I recall a young woman who came to therapy and declared that she was manic-depressive, suicidal, bipolar disorder, *and* post-traumatic stress disorder. After receiving this resume of pathology, I acknowledged her descriptions and then asked if we could talk for a short while about what she wanted to be different as a result of our meeting. When the session was over and I asked what we did during our time that might have made a difference, she said: "it was nice to talk about something besides 'the problems,' because now I don't feel as sick . . . I don't feel as hopeless as I did before." Perceiving clients as simply having complaints, not symptoms, and being stuck in the grips of a problem allows the therapist to propose a time in the future when the problem will not be occurring.

For example, an adolescent who begins failing school in the tenth grade after having nine years of success can be referred to as "off track" instead of "having problems." By reverting back to times when school was difficult but successful, the adolescent regains confidence and his or her parents review the positive history. In addition, the review of successful times may suggest more positive family situations and interactions, thereby suggesting a return to what worked before. This systemic approach to including Solution Focused Therapy in family therapy frees the adolescent from the role of the identified patient and instead suggests that change can happen simply by looking backwards to more productive times.

5. Clients are more motivated when they define the goal.

Consider these bizarre statements: "All clients who come from divorced homes are not functional. All clients who wear an earring are in gangs. All college students try drugs and alcohol. His brother was a troublemaker so he must be one as well. She certainly must be promiscuous . . . look how short her skirt is. There is no way he can graduate from high school with that attitude."

Do you see how globally ridiculous and unfair these statements are? Yet for years we have decided what clients needed to do because they exhibited certain problems. There have been tasks designed by therapists and other experts who saw commonalities in behaviors and consequently assigned the same solutions. Many times the suggestions worked, after much labor by the experts. However, the clients became dependent on the therapist. Even worse, the clients got little credit, except for a pat on the back for following directions given by the therapist. Needless to say, the clients must have felt that they must converse with the therapist in order to stay on track.

Some of the most outstanding solutions develop from exceptions defined by the person(s) involved. It seems to be more useful for clients to construct their own strategy. When clients succeed, they earn the credit, thus becoming more confident in their competence. If clients do not succeed at once, they can still be encouraged to see the strategy as an experiment by the therapist, thereby encouraging clients to continue to explore and refine the solution. The key to assisting clients in solving their own problems seems to lie primarily in listening to their definition of "what needs to be different" (the goal); specifying the goal in specific, behavioral terms; and asking about the times when the goal appeared in their life on a small scale.

6. A snowball effect can occur when one person makes a change.

Virginia Satir, an experiential therapist who believed in the "ripple effect," often remarked that when she wrapped a rope around a family, when one person moved the rest of the family would move as well. When families perceive that they must deal with a difficult child without his cooperation, they sometimes avoid doing anything just because it is easier than creating a conflict. However, suppose the family does something slightly different from what the child typically expects. Suppose, for example, a young child with a fear of the dark cries out for his mother, who tends to his anguish. Typically the mother would try to convince the child that there was nothing to be afraid of, or she would scold the child for waking her up. This time, instead of trying to convince the child that there is nothing to be fearful of, she recalls how a week ago, the child calmed himself at the doctor's office when the doctor told him everything he was going to do as he examined him. The boy seemed to feel comfortable when he was reassured. The mother then enters the bedroom, turns on the light, and asks the child to look for monsters with her to make sure that they are all

gone. Afterwards, the child calms himself; the mother kisses him goodnight and tells him to call her again if the monsters return. The child falls asleep, reassured.

In families, adolescents can be asked to "help your parents to not yell this week" and given responsibility for changing their reputations at home. In return, the parents are asked to "watch for changes in your son only for the next week." This way of changing the system by challenging and suggesting different behaviors to family members often results in the system changing many behaviors.

7. Complex problems do not necessitate complex solutions.

An adolescent girl and her mother had difficulties with telephone time, since it often interfered with the daughter's completion of homework. The girl was failing several classes at school and was becoming disrespectful to her parents. The girl was restricted to a 10 p.m. curfew, yet on several nights the mother would get out of bed at midnight to find her daughter on the phone. When I asked them how they had maintained other rules in the past, the mother said she often set limits. For example, she would withhold her daughter's car keys, allowances, or rewards. In viewing these past successes, the mother told the daughter that at 10:00 she was to bring her the phone, which the mother then took to her bedroom upon retiring for bed. The girl agreed and the two developed trust again. When the daughter began completing her homework earlier in the evening and passing classes, the phone time was extended again. While this may not be a terribly complex problem, it is an illustration of how focusing on "what worked before" could have an effect on other related behaviors. Complex problems do not mean that the solutions will need to be complex, too. Such thinking may hamper the process by creating a notion of impossibility. Instead, searching for small successes in similar circumstances can assist people in applying them to even the most trying situations.

8. Fitting with the client's world view lessens resistance and encourages cooperation.

Often therapists encounter clients who felt persecuted by a parent, spouse, or significant other. For example, adolescents often exaggerates their dilemma and appear to dramatize the seriousness of a situation, gaining a reputation for being defiant. Suggesting to adolescents that *they* must change is sometimes a guarantee that they will not cooperate. It is the nature of adolescence! However, aligning with adolescents by stepping into their world view to get their parents off their backs is the quickest way to resolution. Resigned to the fact that the parent may not change, adolescents have no recourse but to come up with ways to just get the parent off their backs. The adolescent then behaves differently and the parent may respond differently.

Earlier in this chapter, the notion of *complainant* was addressed as a client who simply comes to complain. This assumption is quite useful with the adolescent since it recognizes the complaint and places responsibility for resolving the complaint with the complainant. In another example, a high school student who feels the coach just won't get off his back and is full of complaints to the vice principal, can be asked:

VP: "How will you know when things are just slightly better for you, in regard to the coach?"

STUDENT: "He won't hound me as much . . . he'll get off my back."

VP: "When, this year, has he been off your back? . . . I agree, getting him off your back is a good idea."

The vice principal can then explore times when the student felt less taunted by the coach. The student will then feel heard by the administrator, and the goal to "get the coach off my back" will probably develop into the student behaving differently, as he recalls days when the coach picked on him less. Most importantly, the student will solve his own problem by changing *his* behavior.

9. Motivation is a key and can be encouraged by aligning with the client against the problem.

Many times, motivation is not present because people do not know what they want to occur differently. They know what they do not want, yet they do not have a specific goal in mind. Motivation may also be absent is if the client feels that the problem is not her fault, but that it is someone else's fault. One way to find out about motivation is to ask directly: "are you willing to do whatever it takes to make things better for you?" If the answer is "yes," this is a customer. If not, the client can be told that the therapist will be available whenever she is ready to come back and tell the therapist what it is that she wants to be different. The following comments may be helpful:

THERAPIST: "Sandy, it's obvious to me that you have some true concerns about Mr. Smith, your boss. One thing I've learned, however, is that unless you know how you want things to be, it's hard to accomplish anything different. Let's take a break. For the next few days, I'd like you to think about what you want to be different with Mr. Smith. You might try watching times during work when things are better for you. In a week, I'd like you to let me know what you observed about those times and what you would like to happen more often."

It can be tempting for a therapist to try to motivate clients so that their problems are solved. However, doing so can be frustrating to the therapist and disrespectful to the client. The solution focused therapist recognizes the unmotivated client as stuck and sees the therapist's role

as one of helping the client to recognize times when life goes more smoothly. The therapist may say: *"Notice this week, times when you feel slightly better . . . notice where you are, who is there, and what you are doing. I will be anxious to hear about the times when you are less depressed when we meet again."*

10. There is no such thing as resistance . . . when we cooperate.

Steve de Shazer mentions that when we find ways to cooperate with people, there is no such thing as resistance. This does not mean we subscribe to the client's every whim about change, but it does mean that we align, sympathize, empathize, and simply use their language to connect with them. Children and adolescents are quite vulnerable to acceptance and validation. An adolescent who fights constantly may be perceived as wanting some control in his/her life. A parent who overprotects can be perceived as protecting slightly more than necessary. These connecting statements and messages cooperate with whatever the clients need, yet the reframing opens up possibilities instead of perpetuating the problem.

For example, a parent who is overprotective may be told: *"You obviously love your child very much. I wonder if it is working for him that you are at school constantly, to help him grow into an independent young man who can take care of himself? What would he say if he were here?"*

This redescription allows the therapist to offer another perception to the mother so that she can re-evaluate how her strategy is working. In the following dialogue, an adult with an alcohol problem is dealt with differently: *"What does drinking do for you?"*

This is a simple question that respectfully allows the therapist to enter the world of a problem drinker without threatening the client's habit. Often, clients dealing with alcohol or drug issues do not expect this question. Instead, they expect to be told to stop drinking or doing drugs. This raises resistance and causes treatment to fail, since the therapist is not helping the client to cope with life differently. It seems better to continue the dialogue as follows: *"While I am concerned about your drinking, I also realize that, as you said, drinking helps you to relax. Tell me, over the past few years, besides drinking, what else has helped you to relax? What activity, what situation other than drinking has given you some relief from the problems you are describing to me?"*

This dialogue will encourage clients to re-examine other solutions in their lives that might have helped them to cope. By assisting the client in such identification the therapist can then say: *"As you go through your week, what do you see yourself doing when you want to drink but decide to do something else to relax? How often would you suggest doing this?"*

The client is now in charge of strategizing solutions for the week. He has been given respect and confidence by the therapist to do what seems best for him. He is more likely to watch out for his own health when empowered in this way than if he is told that he must never have another drink in his life.

11. If it works, don't fix it; if not, do something different.

The above statement is a logical way of perceiving life. One of the most helpful questions to ask clients who keep trying the same ineffective strategy over and over is, "is this working for you?" At times, it sounds absurd to describe previous strategies that did not work. The session can become more productive by then asking the same client, "what *has* worked for you in other situations similar to this one?" This allows the client to see successful interventions that worked in similar situations and to recognize their usefulness in the present situation. The task for the day, week, or two weeks develops from the past successes, no matter how small and insignificant they once appeared to be.

For example, an adult female who was asked by her mother to absolve her father of sexually abusing her continued to visit the family on Sundays and pretend that she was not bothered. When she became severely depressed, she acknowledged that not only did she dread the visits, she felt ashamed of herself for putting herself and her family through the ordeal. She came to recognize her ability in the past few years to resign from two jobs that "did not fit" who she was becoming as a person. From that recognition, the client decided that visiting her parents did not fit her life currently. She decided to begin keeping a slight distance by visiting only when her father was not present. She eventually told her mother that she would visit her only occasionally, when she felt comfortable. Her depression lifted, as she and her own family began spending more time together on the weekends.

12. Focusing on the possible and changeable lessens frustration.

Many children would like to be Teenage Mutant Ninja Turtles and many adolescents would like to stay out all night. Realistic thinking is of utmost importance while working in a solution focused approach, as it must focus on the visible and specific. For example, a child who wants Tommy to stop teasing him can't change Tommy, but can change where he encounters Tommy on the playground. An adolescent who complains about his mom's yelling can't stop mom from yelling, but can change his responses to those that work at other times with other people, such as his grandfather or coach at school.

The use of scaling questions (de Shazer, 1985) utilizes a scale that is helpful in focusing on small changes, which are more probable and possible to be achieved. For example, if an adult was dealing with anger, a therapist might ask:

THERAPIST: "On a scale of 1–10, 10 where anger is in control of you totally and 1 where anger is being controlled by you, where are you now?"

```
_____x_____
1    2    3    4    5    6    7    8    9    10
(I am in control)              (anger is in control)
```

THERAPIST: "Since you are at a 4.5, where would you like to be by the time I see you again tomorrow?"

These questions create a goal for the client. To be in control of anger has a different meaning from a demand that the anger stop totally. The scaling questions also encourage short-term success, promoting more of the same. Performing a task within this short time period is more achievable than attempting to change forever.

13. Go slowly and focus on tasks that lead to success.

Clients come to therapy to change their lives. They expect that change will happen quickly and expect it to happen completely. While therapists always hope that change can be accomplished quickly, often such expectations inhibit the process. It is more helpful to go slowly and talk about being "less depressed," "less angry," "slightly more in control," or "slightly back on track," so that the client can attempt tasks that are achievable. In actuality, when defeating a problem is the focus, simply returning the next week after not moving backwards into the grip of the problem can be grounds for success and praise. Remind clients that as change occurs, there may be highs and lows, but the gradual climb to success will be more efficient if expectations are not as high.

14. Rapid change is possible when we identify exceptions.

An elementary counselor told the story of a kindergarten student who had temper tantrums at least three times a week, usually before 10 a.m. Tiring from the frequent referral, one morning she went to Scott before he was referred and asked:

COUNSELOR: Would you like to fight off the temper tantrums (since he referred to them as such, as did the teacher) just for today?

Scott looked puzzled at first but then replied that he wasn't sure if he could. The counselor then stated:

COUNSELOR: It's 9:45 and I've just realized that you have not had a tantrum yet this morning. How have you done that?"

SCOTT: "I just did it!"

The counselor then briefly talked with the teacher, asking her to remind Scott when he continued to fight off the tantrums during the morning and to ask him, "How are you doing this?" Scott did not have a tantrum that day and decreased his tantrums to once every two or three weeks. His teacher rewarded him with being line leader more often and his counselor presented him with a certificate stating that he defeated the temper tantrum monster.

I recall one family several years ago that had a history of hitting each other whenever they were angry. While in a family therapy session one day, I asked: "When is it that you talk about things that are important to you without hitting each other?" The nine-year-old sister quickly replied: "When we are in public. You know, when we eat out, or we are outside, we don't hit each other. I guess we don't want other people to see us fight."

While perhaps too simple, the straightforward reply brought on both laughter and the realization that they indeed did experience violence-free times. The mother suggested that future discussions that tended to provoke fighting would be held in the garage or the front yard.

15. Change is constant and inevitable; one cannot not change.

New experiences cause a change of context. When you read a new book, experience a new workshop, or develop a new habit, change occurs. Change can't not occur. The systems we live in change constantly. Change is not always easy, but it is inevitable. When clients express the sad notion that "she will never change," it is more helpful to acknowledge this perception and then cooperate with such a statement by saying:

THERAPIST: "When have you noticed _____ making very small changes in other situations? Did you have a part in that? How did you help that to happen? What did you see her do that told you she was putting forth the effort?"

The therapist can also recognize the client's reality by saying:

THERAPIST: "Suppose the notion that your wife will never change is true. How will you stay in the marriage, as you say you desire, and be content with yourself? What would I see you doing for the next week that would tell me you have resigned yourself to not trying to change your wife and have started working on being happier yourself?"

This cooperative stance challenges the reality of the client, exposes him to the fact that he must stop trying to change someone else, and challenges him to begin making personal changes that will probably lead to systemic ones.

16. Every complaint pattern contains some sort of exception . . . keep looking.

"I'm angry all of the time." "He's hyperactive constantly." "She never stays at home." "I'm totally stressed out with my job." These global statements of complaints are typical from people who feel hopeless and out of control. Yet, no one stays angry 100% of the time, for they would surely be exhausted! When clients talk about their job being awful, ask "when is it not as awful?" Opening up the possibility that to each problem there is an exception, gives people opportunities to see that they are in control more often than they think. Many times counting the minutes, hours, or days when a problem is not happening, makes the problem seem more solvable and less intrusive in one's life. To realize, for example, that of a seven day week, three days are more likely to be depressing for only three hours on each day, means that only 9 out of 168 hours are "depression hours." This minimizing of the effects of the problem lessens the burden and helps the client feel more in control.

17. Looking at problems differently can encourage their resolution.

Normalizing problems through empathy and compassion go a long way towards lessening hopelessness. As mentioned previously, when labels are placed on children, adolescents, and adults, self-perceptions change to that of pathology and feelings that the person is forever altered by the disorder. However, redescribing problems of hyperactivity as energetic, or depression as sadness, or isolated as private changes perceptions and encourages hope.

I once remarked to an adolescent who had been placed in a psychiatric hospital-based school how well he did on a weekend visit with his parents. In the past, he had talked to me about his violent outbursts and angry words, which truly were interfering with his reconciliation with his parents. As he described doing okay but "stuffing my feelings" and feeling negative about that action, I remarked that I saw it a little differently. I saw him at successfully "disciplining" himself around his parents. He stopped for a moment and then agreed that he had disciplined himself and kept control. I challenged the adolescent to continue to be on watch for times when he needed to discipline himself and keep the former destructive habits from interfering with his home life. He agreed that he indeed deserved a home life free of the habit.

This assumptions listed here have been shown to assist clients in using their imagination and desires to set specific behavioral goals. The assumptions offer the therapist opportunities to create chances for the client to imagine life without the problem. The removal of the problem for even a moment presents a clearer picture of life without the problem and allows specific behaviors to be imagined. The ideas of Solution Focused Therapy are centered on opening up possibilities to solutions. When people cannot see past their problems, they fail to see themselves as competent. The solution focused therapist is encouraged to search extensively for competencies in clients, always with the belief that clients can solve their own problems given a different context.

APPLICATIONS

In addition to individual and family therapy, which have been discussed throughout this chapter, the model has been applied to various other treatment situations. The following contributions have been made by therapists who adapted the assumptions of the solution focused model to the needs of their clients and their positions, and who have been successful in instigating change.

Residential Treatment

Michael Durrant has introduced a cooperative, competency-based approach to residential treatment and outpatient agencies. He views such treatment as a *transition stage* that clients need. His model of working with a solution focus centers on the idea of the rite of passage. He also expounds on the idea that it is the *context* of therapy that either perpetuates pathology or leads to competency. He refers to "context" as "the milieu or general situation, which provides some clues or framework for interpreting actions" (Durrant, 1993, p. 7). In his work, he encourages therapists to not try to understand *why* things happen, but instead to try to understand how our clients make sense of what happened to them. Afterwards, he sees the therapist's role as one of helping the client to make sense of his or her experiences differently. By experiencing new possibilities, Durrant says that clients will most likely find new ways of looking at themselves "that will provide new options for relationships and behavior" (Durrant, 1993, p. 11).

Domestic Violence

Lipchick and Kubicki have worked on a program to treat both partners involved in domestic violence with a solution focused approach. The basic assumptions and strategies for working with such cases are:

"Accept both sides of the story and take a collaborative stance."

"Motivate the man to accept responsibility by not making him more defensive."

"Identify positives in the relationship and amplify them in the future."

"Help the couple set goals for themselves that satisfy both their needs" (Lipchik & Kubicki, 1996, p. 91).

Lipchik and Kubicki view each client as unique and the solutions to the problem as unique as well. They listen to the batterer take responsibility for his actions and then move forward to working on mutual, collaborative solutions which may assist the couple in reconciliation without violence. They suggest the use of medication for batterers who have difficulties in identifying triggers to violence. The team also uses questions and statements such as:

"If you were your wife, how would you react if you were accused of lying?"

"When you have the urge to call her, ask yourself which choice will make you feel best about yourself afterwards."

In addition, the team appeals to the male's need to accept the absence of his partner through encouraging him to identify activities that he enjoyed prior to the relationship. The team also encourages the male to identify traits and abilities that he needs to utilize to feel like he is a good father, and so on.

Sexual Abuse

During the past few years, I (Metcalf, 1998) have worked with many clients who had experienced being sexually abused. I refer to them as *survivors* since I view them as such, instead of victims. By thinking of them in this way, my perceptions become contagious to the client. In addition, the following assumptions, initially suggested by Bill O'Hanlon and then modified, are important to consider while working with sexual abuse survivors:

- Find out what the client is seeking in treatment and how she will know when treatment has been successful. Ask her what she wishes to accomplish.

- Ascertain to the best of your ability that the sexual abuse is not current. If it is, take whatever steps are necessary to stop it. If the client is an adult, check out how she was able to step out of the story of abuse.

- Don't assume that the client needs to go back and work through traumatic memories. Some people will and some won't. Remember that everybody is an exception. Most clients will be relieved that they are encouraged to move forward and not retell their story. Allow the tearful client to tell you what she needs to tell you without prodding. She will appreciate the respect.

- Use the natural abilities the client has developed as a result of having to cope with abuse (e.g., disassociating, distracting). Turn the former liability into an asset.

- Normalize the trauma, fear, and anxiety. Help her to see that her mind was helping her to forget the tragic details.

- Look for resources and strengths. Focus on underlining how they made it through the abuse and what they have done to cope, survive, and thrive since then. Look for nurturing and healthy relationships and role models they had in the past or have in the present. Look for current skills in other areas, which indicate strengths.

- Validate and support each part of the person's experience. Help the client to realize that the story has ended and that she has the power now to write the next chapter as she wishes.
- Make provisions for safety (contracts) from suicide, homicide, and other potentially dangerous situations. Help the client to designate a plan to keep her safe based on past experiences.

The therapist can suggest that there are many roads to take in life and whatever road one chooses, and how she thinks about herself as she travels, can influence her experiences. The therapist can ask the client to imagine how she would like her life to be a month from now in specific terms such as actions, not just emotions.

Alcohol/Drug Abuse

In their groundbreaking book, *Working With the Problem Drinker*, (1992), Insoo Berg and Scott Miller present the following ideas about problem drinking: *"Since the popular conceptualization holds that the problem is caused by an irreversible, fatal disease requiring a lifelong commitment to recovery, any individual who experiences a positive response to briefer, less intensive treatments is simply dismissed as not having been a 'real alcoholic'"* (Alcoholics Anonymous, 1939, 1976; Heather & Robinson, 1985). In addition, *"some have suggested that the alternative models are further evidence that mental health professionals, especially those not 'recovering' from alcoholism, do not understand the disease and are, in fact, in 'denial' about the severity of the alcohol problem"* (Berg & Miller, 1992, p. xvi).

The idea of gaining cooperation from clients who are caught in the web of chemical abuse is vital, especially when such clients may be feeling out of control or when employers or significant others in their lives are demanding sobriety. While working in an adolescent inpatient unit for several years, I (Metcalf, 1998) became acutely aware of the torments that behavior modification placed on adolescents who would not cooperate with the program. Placed in treatment for six months at a time, those adolescents were supposed to learn a lesson and stay straight for all the "right reasons." Too many times, relapse occurred with patients who "talked the talk" but did not "walk the walk."

In the past, therapists dealt with alcoholism or drug abuse by confronting group members until they admitted their powerlessness and accepted a label of "addict" or "alcoholic." While many persons achieved positive

and healthy results from such a process, there remained a population of persons who did not respond. It is that population in particular that is often helped more effectively in Solution Focused Therapy. The following ideas and questions (Metcalf, 1998) serve as a guide for therapy for persons who have problems with drugs and/or alcohol.

1. Attempt to understand the group member's need to use the substance. Step into the client's world and become the client's partner against the substance.
2. Assist the client in visualizing life without the problem. Suggest thinking about how others will view and relate to him or her when the problem dissolves. This process will serve to develop goals.
3. Explore past attempts to gain control over the substance. Acknowledge the difficulty of beating a habit that was useful in some ways yet harmful to the client's health, job, family, and relationships.

After the therapist has had an opportunity to utilize these steps, he or she can go through each strategy and verify whether the strategy worked to defeat the drinking or drug problem. The therapist should leave only the "exceptional strategies" that brought even the slightest relief from the problem. These become the first of many solutions for the client to examine.

Solution Focused Group Therapy

Clients enjoy being part of a solution focused process group primarily because it helps them find a comfortable place in the world where their problems do not seem to take over. Such a safe experience offers an oasis to even the most despondent client. Despondent clients are more likely to give up their pathological descriptions when they discover that such descriptions are not going to be discussed. Instead, clients are invited to revisit the past, reminiscing about the times when life was better. This experience often has the same uplifting effect as looking at old photographs of loved ones or remembering former good times. As clients recall more pleasant times, they realize that life has not always been as difficult as they thought, and as they hear other group members make similar discoveries, a kinship develops within the group, creating an atmosphere of hope. As clients realize that they have had successes in their lives, whether those successes are in the current situation or in similar situations in the past, they seem to enjoy the idea that someone else, namely the group, has noticed the success. In such solution focused group therapy sessions, the group helps to define the direction for its members to go, validating and giving permission to each other to try strategies as individual as the group members themselves.

Group therapy suggestions (Metcalf, 1998) have been developed for clients dealing with eating disorders, anxiety, depression, family of origin issues, sexual abuse, panic disorders, alcohol and drug abuse, and relationship issues.

CASE STUDY

Sadly, there will always be some clients who come to therapy with a long list of symptoms, which seem to prolong their unhappiness in life. Lost in a world where victimization is imposed upon them by legal authorities and then scoffed at by those who want them to "just move forward," the survivor sometimes seeks strength and justice, yet is inhibited by discouragement and the need for revenge. When therapists meet such clients, an individual session or two is often helpful before suggesting group therapy. Understanding the client's need to be heard is of the utmost importance in this case, for it begins to give the client what he or she deserves and was denied, namely respect.

Caroline, age 22, was date-raped by an athlete after a fraternity party during the last semester of her senior year. The experience was her first sexual encounter. She was physically as well as emotionally injured. After reporting the incident to police and being examined at the hospital for bruises and abrasions, it was suggested that she seek counseling. Caroline described the visits with one of her first therapists as very depressing and unhelpful:

"He kept asking me each week to tell him about what happened to me, over and over. I never understood why he did that. I always felt much worse later. He also told me that I felt more shameful because I was too religious. He put me on an antidepressant and some antipsychotic drugs, which did nothing. I cried constantly with the medications and was always so angry. He told me it was time to move on, but I never could. Everyone did the same thing. I would tell them that I was not going to give up until Joe (perpetrator) was indicted, but no one seemed to want to help me. Instead, they just kept telling me to stop thinking about it and get on with my life. The more they told me that, the madder I became. Pretty soon all I did was go to work and hate men. I would come home and watch television and argue with my sister. We started to hate each other."

As Caroline began to feel victimized by the legal system and was given more reasons to feel victimized by other professionals, she began to take on the characteristics of a victim. She lived the victim role each day, believing that her life was forever altered and that people looked down upon her. Even worse, she began to think that people did not believe her story. Many of her friends in the fraternities on her former campus had turned against her after the assault, accusing her of wrongful accusations. Some of her close friends questioned her determination to file charges. Her family discouraged further legal action and told her that it was time to move forward. In spite of these pressures, Caroline was able to graduate that semester with an "A" average and tutor other students in English, her major. After graduation she moved 200 miles away to a small city where she obtained a job at another university. As she spoke of her traumatic experience and then of her efforts to move away from the university from which she graduated, her strengths and ability to function in such a horrific situation became obvious to me.

When I asked her about her ability to complete her college career and to move so far from her family after the situation occurred, she said that all of her life she had been a very determined person who rarely let anything stop her. She said that perseverance was a nice distraction for her when she was troubled, so when she was upset with a situation, she often overcommitted herself to other activities. She still struggled daily with frustration with the legal system and from a fear of seeing the perpetrator when she visited her hometown, which was close to the campus. Even though she feared future abuse and suffered from depression, sleeplessness, fatigue, and distractibility, her inexhaustible pursuit of justice taught me that I needed to cooperate with her determination if I were to be helpful.

The story Caroline had constructed with the encouragement of others was that of being a victim. The victim role she took to heart kept her isolated, sad, threatened, and fearful. To make things worse, the people in her life who minimized the severity of the event and attempted to push her into recovery too soon actually encouraged the opposite to occur. Caroline began to pursue being a victim for all to see in order to save face and become more believable. When people take on characteristics in order to make their story more vivid to others, they give up their chance at being successful in order to be more understood.

From her description, Caroline seemed to want desperately to stop living within an unhappy and unsuccessful story, yet she was having a very difficult time writing a more successful one. In order to assist her, I needed to consider the following exceptions she was revealing to me in our first session:

- She was strong and competent enough to finish a semester with high grades in spite of a very traumatic event.
- She would persevere to see justice done in spite of the discouragement of others.
- She was not ready to move forward in her life. Only she would know when she was at that point.

- She desperately wanted others to know what happened to her so her embarrassment would dissolve and the perpetrator's guilt would be revealed.
- She wanted to be helpful to other women as a result of achieving "justice."

Obviously, any attempt to move Caroline forward before she wanted to go would not be well received. She had made that clear. However, I did see her as stuck in the victim role and unable to pursue the justice she desired. As long as she thought of herself as a victim, she would remain isolated and distant.

During Caroline's last semester in college, after the situation occurred, she was active and visible on campus. She said she had distracted herself by staying busy and tutoring students while filing charges against her abuser. As we identified these strategies, Caroline acknowledged them but did not see the relevance in using them in the current situation. With this in mind, before the first session ended I presented an idea to her for consideration. I took a large dry erase board and drew a timeline. I asked her for the exact age that the "bomb" (her externalized description of the sexual assault) went off in her life. I then asked her how long people tended to live in her family. She said many of her relatives lived a long time, to an average age of 80. Looking at Caroline, I took a marker and slowly illustrated that the "x" represented the bomb, and then moved my marker very slowly from the number 22 across the timeline towards 80, while saying:

```
_____×_____
birth     22                                   80
```

"On the scale that I have drawn here, I want you to envision, as we look at it together, how a year has already pushed you away from the 'bomb.' You will never go back, Caroline, to that 'bomb' because now you know too much. You are too educated and cautious now. The bomb is already over 365 days farther away from you than it was on that day. We can see the bomb only at a distance. As I move my marker across the timeline, I want you to realize something . . . that you probably have almost 60 more years to live without that 'bomb' ever going off again in your life."

And then I continued,

"I would like for you to think about your life in this new way. As you do, imagine with me what you will be doing, now that you have stepped away from 'the bomb' and it begins to have less of an impact on your life."

To assist Caroline in beginning to move slowly in her life towards solutions, I then asked her:

"What would you and I see you doing, specifically, in a very small way, just for the next week or two that would tell us both that you were indeed stepping out of this situation?"

At the next session, Caroline told me that she was beginning to have some good days but that she would catch herself and tell herself that she couldn't let that happen.

She was terrified that if a jury saw her feeling better, they would interpret this as evidence that she had not really been hurt. This was dangerous thinking. Her beliefs about how she should appear to others were holding her back from living in the present. As Caroline related her small attempts to go out with friends, when she would "catch" herself feeling better and then drift back into a depressed state in order to maintain her victim role, I thought of how much I wanted for her to appear as strong on the outside as I believed she was on the inside. Apparently, she did not see the advantages in appearing to be strong. I related to her as she sat feeling the need to be weak:

"My kids and I take Tae Kwon Do. At times we have to spar with each other and it gets to be quite interesting. They are obviously better at being fearless than I am, and it truly makes a difference in the outcomes of their matches!

"Once I watched two fighters fight in a tournament. I knew one fighter to be a rather weak fighter. When the strong fighter won, I thought 'well, he really didn't have to put up much of a fight because the other fighter was too weak.'

"Another time, I watched two strong fighters spar. When the winner was declared, I thought 'he really had to be strong and violent to beat the other guy. The loser really had to put up a fight just to stay in the ring.'"

I then said to Caroline:

"I wonder which image the jury might see in you that would convince them that he (abuser) was very violent with you? The strong Caroline or the weak Caroline?"

A week after that session, Caroline reported having a better week. Shortly afterwards, she entered a women's group and continued for a month until she obtained a new job in a large city nearby and moved into an apartment on her own. She called once to tell me that she had enlisted the services of a well-known attorney who had taken her case and was preparing for trial. Caroline was not only filing suit against the abuser, but also the fraternity for having alcohol at a college party, the bar for serving alcohol, and each athlete who harassed her after she filed charges against their peer. Two months later, I received a letter from her describing how her pursuit of justice was being accomplished. She had spoken at a fund raiser for a candidate running against the incumbent District Attorney who had refused to try Caroline's case. She got up and told her story. After struggling with the legal system for several years Caroline was advised to drop her case. Even though her case never went to trial, she told that she had achieved justice for herself. Caroline's new image of herself as a survivor assisted her in stepping back into life slowly, and helped her to begin dealing with a situation she is now choosing to step out of each day. "Just knowing that I have pursued it like I have, and that others know what happened through this process, has already begun to give me some of the relief I have wanted all along. I know he may never go to jail, but doing all I have has at least helped to take me out of this emotional jail, and every day I feel farther and farther away from it."

(This case originally appeared in Solution Focused Group Therapy, *Metcalf, 1998, pp. 93–100.)*

SUMMARY

Solution Focused Therapy offers therapists a new direction and approach to working with clients who desire change but see themselves as powerless against the problem. The focus allows the client to feel superior over the problem and resilient in his/her life. As the model continues to evolve, producing new applications in the future, the premise of the model that will most likely persist is the empowering atmosphere that is created whenever the solution focused therapist collaboratively discovers the strength of the client alongside the client. This approach helps clients reach their goals more quickly while always allowing the client to lead the therapy process.

REFERENCES

Alcoholics Anonymous. (1939). *The story of how more than one hundred men have recovered from alcoholism.* New York: Works.

Amatea, E. S. (1989). *Brief strategic intervention for school behavior problems.* San Francisco: Jossey Bass.

Berg, I. K. (1991). *Family preservation: A brief therapy workbook.* London: Brief Therapy Press.

Berg, I. K., & Gallagher, D. (1991). Solution focused brief treatment with adolescent substance abusers. In T. Todd & M. Selekman (Eds.), *Family therapy approaches with adolescent substance abusers.* Boston: Allyn & Bacon.

Berg, I. K., & Miller, S. (1992). *Working with the problem drinker.* New York: W. W. Norton.

Cade, B., & O'Hanlon, W. (1993). *A brief guide to brief therapy.* New York: W. W. Norton.

Cox, F. M., Chilman, C. S., & Nunnally, E. W. (1989). *Mental illness, delinquency, addictions and neglect.* Newbury Park, CA: Sage.

de Shazer, S. (1982). *Patterns of brief family therapy.* New York: Guilford.

de Shazer, S. (1985). *Keys to solutions in brief therapy.* New York: W. W. Norton.

de Shazer, S. (1988). *Clues: Investigating solutions in brief therapy.* New York: W. W. Norton.

de Shazer, S., Berg, I. K., Lipchik, E., Nunnally, E., Molnar, A., Gingerich, W., & Weiner-Davis, M. (1986). Brief therapy: Focused solution development. *Family Process, 25*(2), 201–211.

Dolan, Y. (1991). *Resolving sexual abuse.* New York: W. W. Norton.

Durrant, M. (1993). *Residential treatment.* New York: W. W. Norton.

Fisch, R., Weakland, J. H., & Segal, L. (1982). *The tactics of change: Doing therapy briefly.* San Francisco: Jossey-Bass.

Heather, N., & Robinson, I. (1985). *Controlled drinking.* London: Methuen.

Kral, R. (1988). *Strategies that work: Techniques for solution in the schools.* Milwaukee, WI: Brief Family Therapy Center.

Kral, R., & Schaffer, J. (1989). *Creating relationships in adoption.* Milwaukee, WI: Milwaukee County Social Services.

Lipchik, E., & Kubicki, A. (1996). Bridges toward a new reality in couples therapy. In S. Miller, M. Hubble, & B. Duncan (Eds.), *Handbook of solution-focused brief therapy.* San Francisco: Jossey-Bass.

Metcalf, L. (1995). *Counseling toward solutions: A solution focused approach for working with students, teachers and parents.* New Jersey: Center for Applied Research in Education.

Metcalf, L. (1997). *Parenting toward solutions: How parents can use skills they already have to raise responsible, loving kids.* New Jersey: Prentice-Hall.

Metcalf, L. (1998). *Solution focused group therapy: Ideas for groups in private practice, schools, agencies and treatment programs.* New York: The Free Press.

Minuchin, S., & Fishman, C. (1981). *Family therapy techniques.* Cambridge, MA: Harvard University Press.

Molnar, A., & de Shazer, S. (1987). Solution-focused therapy: Toward the identification of therapeutic tasks, *Journal of Marital and Family Therapy, 13,* 349–358.

Molnar, A. & Lindquist, B. (1990). *Changing problem behavior in schools.* San Francisco: Jossey-Bass.

O'Hanlon, W. H., & Weiner-Davis, M. (1989). *In search of solutions.* New York: W. W. Norton.

Walter, J., & Peller, J. (1992). *Becoming solution focused in brief therapy.* New York: Brunner-Mazel.

Chapter 63

STRATEGIC SOLUTION FOCUSED THERAPY

ELLEN QUICK

This system has had many parents; it includes the thinking of the Mental Research Group of Palo Alto, the ideas of Milton Erickson, the conclusions of the Brief Family Therapy Center, and the thought of Carl Rogers and others, including Aaron Beck and Fritz Perls. Eventually Strategic Solution Focused Therapy boils down to a three-part theory that is at the same time simple and profound: (1) What is the problem? (2) If it works, do more of it. (3) If it does not work, don't do it any more: do something different.

The therapist is seen as an agent of change in collaboration with the client. Nothing is hidden; the client is to see everything and know everything being done. The process starts with a clarification of the problem, followed by development of a solution scenario, evaluation of attempted solutions, and a suggestion to do more of what works and to change what does not.

DEFINITION

Strategic Solution Focused Therapy is an approach to the treatment of individual and interpersonal problems that combines the principles and techniques of Brief Strategic Therapy and Solution Focused Therapy. It is a constructivist, interpersonal, and collaborative approach; it also emphasizes the importance of the therapeutic alliance. A critical component is clarification of the client's views of both the problem and how the therapist might best help.

A three-part theory—"What's the trouble? If it works, do more of it. If it doesn't work, do something different"—operates at two levels simultaneously. On one level, the therapist attempts to clarify the client's highest priority problem and to assist the client to amplify solutions that "work" and to interrupt those that do not. At the same time, the principles apply to the therapist's process: when techniques and inquiry seem to be "working," the therapist often continues them; when they are not working, the therapist typically shifts the focus and "does something different."

The strategic solution focused approach has four components: problem clarification, solution elaboration, evaluation of attempted solutions, and intervention design. Interventions contain validation, compliment, and suggestion components. Suggestions may encourage continuation or interruption of behavior. Frequently they suggest both, reflecting the fact that the balance between change and stability is central to the approach.

HISTORY

Brief Strategic Therapy

Strategic Solution Focused Therapy has two main "parent" models: Brief Strategic Therapy and Solution Focused Therapy. Chronologically, Brief Strategic Therapy is the "older" of the two. The brief strategic approach was developed at the Mental Research Institute, or MRI, in Palo Alto, California. Gregory Bateson, Don Jackson, Virginia Satir, and Paul Watzlawick were among the original participants. The MRI approach was also shaped by the work of Milton Erickson.

In 1965, some MRI therapists began the Brief Therapy Center project. The purpose of this project was to investigate what could be accomplished therapeutically in a time-limited period (designated as up to 10 sessions) by attempting to resolve the chief complaint. Working "briefly" was a somewhat radical idea at the time. Fisch, Weakland, and Segal (1982) have described the project's techniques and conclusions in the book *The Tactics of Change.*

The MRI therapists emphasized that all people and families experience ordinary difficulties and manage developmental stages and life transitions. In their attempts to resolve those predictable difficulties, people do what makes sense. For example, if A nags, B may try to solve the problem by withdrawing. Sometimes B's approach works, but sometimes it does not. In response to B's withdrawal, A may nag even more; then B withdraws further. For both members of the dyad, the action intended to decrease something ends up increasing it. Although neither person's "attempted solution" is working, both keep doing "more of the same," and the problem-maintaining cycle continues. As John Weakland (1986) said, "Life is one damn thing after another. A problem is the same damn thing over and over again."

If well-intended "attempted solutions" were maintaining problems, then interrupting the problem-maintaining feedback loop should decrease the problem behaviors, the MRI therapists hypothesized. They believed that the therapist needed to: (1) identify the primary problem or complaint, (2) assess what was maintaining it, and (3) interrupt the problem-maintaining behavior. The word "strategic" referred to the therapist's task of developing a strategy or plan to interrupt the unsuccessful attempted solution.

If change could be brought about by simple suggestions, a simple, direct approach was seen as preferable. But sometimes direct, common sense approaches did not work well enough. When this happened, the strategic therapists sometimes made suggestions that seemed to move against the goal rather than toward it. They talked about "taking one's time" and "the dangers of improvement" (Fisch et al., 1982).

Over the years, some clients—and some therapists—have expressed concerns about the MRI approach using "reverse psychology" or manipulation. In response, the MRI therapists have pointed out that influence occurs in all interaction, whether or not it is deliberate. Clients consult therapists when they want to change something, and strategic therapy designs deliberate strategies for producing that change.

Solution Focused Therapy

The other "parent" model, Solution Focused Therapy, began as a variation on the MRI approach. In the 1970s, Steve de Shazer, Insoo Kim Berg, and their colleagues were using the approach at the Brief Family Therapy Center, or BFTC, in Milwaukee, Wisconsin, and they began to modify it. They spent less time clarifying the problem and attempted solution, asserting that these things did not always seem to matter. Instead, they focused on times the complaint did *not* happen. These occasions were called "exceptions." The therapists encouraged clients to notice "how they did it" when exceptions occurred. Encouraging clients to envision a future in which the complaint was resolved, the therapists began to ask "the miracle question" (de Shazer, 1988).

Berg (in Hayes, 1991) has said that she and her colleagues came upon the miracle question almost by chance. They heard clients saying, "It would take a miracle to solve my problem" and decided to find out what the clients really meant. The miracle question is actually a variation of Milton Erickson's crystal ball technique (de Shazer, 1988).

The BFTC therapists also used "scaling questions" (Berg & de Shazer, 1993). These questions asked clients to rate the severity of their problems (e.g., on a 0 to 10 scale, where 0 represented the greatest severity and 10 represented problem resolution). Once a client had picked a number, the therapist could ask how he or she "did it" (e.g., "How did you get to a two?") and what the next sign of change would look like (e.g., "What will be different when you're at a three?")

Other Influences: Client-Centered, Cognitive Behavioral, Gestalt, and Ericksonian Therapy

Although Brief Strategic Therapy and Solution Focused Therapy are clearly the primary "parent" models, several other approaches influenced the development of the strategic solution focused approach. Client-Centered Therapy, as described by Rogers (1961), was one important influence. Rogers emphasized the importance of therapist empathy, genuineness, and unconditional positive regard. When these qualities are present, a bond is formed: the therapeutic alliance. More recently, Miller, Hubble, and Duncan (1995) have pointed out that therapy is most likely to be successful when the client perceives that these qualities are present. The therapists who developed Strategic Solution Focused Therapy were thoroughly trained to recognize the importance of the therapeutic alliance.

Cognitive behavioral principles also shaped Strategic Solution Focused Therapy, because the therapists who developed the present model had a solid grounding in cognitive behavioral treatment. The behavior therapists emphasized the importance of changing observable behaviors. In operant conditioning, the assumption was that behaviors followed by positive reinforcement would increase in frequency. In the treatment of phobia, *in vivo* desensitization became the treatment of choice (Sheehan, 1983). If there were skill deficits, behavior therapists taught social skills, including assertiveness and communication training for couples. Cognitive therapists (Beck & Emery, 1979) emphasized that changing one's cognitions, or views about a situation, a behavior, the self, or others, could have a tremendous impact upon both feelings and behavior. The cognitive behavioral influence can be seen in much of the "homework" assigned in Strategic Solution Focused Therapy.

Gestalt Therapy, as developed by Perls (Wallen, 1970), was another influence. The Gestalt therapists emphasized that different parts of a whole (a person, a system) could emerge into the foreground at different times. Guided by therapist input, clients could learn to see things differently—both literally and figuratively. According to Gestalt Therapy's paradoxical theory of change, "change occurs when one becomes what he is, not when he tries to become what he is not" (Beisser, 1970, p. 77). During the early 1970s, the author of this chapter received training in Gestalt Therapy, as practiced at the Gestalt Institute of Cleveland. Ideas involving polarities and opposites influenced later strategic solution focused techniques such as "the prescription of inconsistency."

Finally, Milton Erickson influenced Strategic Solution Focused Therapy in several different ways. As noted above, Erickson's earlier work influenced the therapists at both the MRI and BFTC, thereby shaping both of the primary parent models. Independently, and before learning much about Strategic or Solution Focused Therapy, I studied Ericksonian hypnosis. In 1978, I briefly received some training directly from Erickson. Later, in the mid-1990s, several therapists associated with the Milton Erickson Institute of San Diego were members of the San Diego Strategic Solution Focused Therapy Interest Group. The Ericksonian emphasis on utilization of client strengths and on tailoring interventions to clients' unique contexts (Erickson, Rossi, & Rossi, 1976) left a clear imprint on Strategic Solution Focused Therapy.

The Influence of Managed Care

During the 1980s and 1990s, my colleagues and I worked in settings where demands for service skyrocketed, while financial resources were dwindling. Practice guidelines implemented by insurance companies frequently limited the number of times clients could be seen. In seminars, professional interest groups, and consultation, therapists who wanted to work more efficiently learned about the strategic and solution focused models.

Gradually it became clear that a number of therapists who were familiar with the two models were integrating them. Was this Strategic Therapy or Solution Focused Therapy? Some of the therapists began to ask themselves (in a kind of "solution scenario elaboration"): What if it didn't matter whether this approach were strategic or solution focused? What if using the two together didn't have to be seen as a problem? In fact, what if using them together could become a *solution*? Thus, Strategic Solution Focused Therapy was born.

CURRENT STATUS

Strategic solution focused therapy is currently practiced primarily in San Diego, California. There has been a San Diego Strategic Solution Focused Interest Group, where therapists have discussed theory and cases. At the group model health maintenance organization where I practice, a number of therapists have learned about and use

the model. It is used flexibly and in combination with other treatment modalities, including medication, psychoeducational classes, and group therapy.

Seminars offering training in Strategic Solution Focused Therapy (sometimes for continuing education credits) have been offered in various locations. Most of the training has been in southern California, but the approach has also been presented at national meetings, such as the American Psychological Association's (APA) annual convention. Training has also been conducted outside the United States, in France and the Netherlands Antilles.

Strategic Solution Focused Therapy is taught as one component of an APA-accredited predoctoral psychology internship. The internship seminar series includes training on the theory and on strategic solution focused approaches with couples, children, and families. In a series of "Applications" seminars, interns conduct Strategic Solution Focused Therapy behind a one-way mirror and receive live supervision. Social work interns also attend several seminars on Strategic Solution Focused Therapy.

The most comprehensive published description of Strategic Solution Focused Therapy is the book *Doing What Works in Brief Therapy: A Strategic Solution Focused Approach* (Quick, 1996). A number of journal articles (Quick, 1994a, 1994b, 1998a, 1998b, and 1998c) provide additional information on the topic. Thomas (1997) and Ardern (1997) have reviewed the approach. Kadushin (1998) discusses the model's problem clarification component, and Hoyt and Berg (1998) refer to its application with couples. So far no research has been published on the efficacy of Strategic Solution Focused Therapy; empirical studies of the approach are clearly needed. However, in a preliminary discussion of the application of the model in a county agency serving an at-risk population, Carter (1998) refers to positive feedback from consumers long labeled "unworkable."

THEORY

Strategic Solution Focused Therapy has a three-part theory that is on one level extremely simple and on another level quite profound:

1. What's the trouble?
2. If it works, do more of it.
3. If it doesn't work, don't do it any more. Do something different.

The first and third components of the theory come primarily (but not completely) from Strategic Therapy, while the second comes primarily (but not completely) from Solution Focused Therapy. As described above, Strategic Therapy can be seen as having the following steps: (1) Clarify the presenting complaint; (2) Identify what is maintaining it; and (3) Interrupt the unsuccessful attempted solution. Solution Focused Therapy can be summed up in these steps: (1) Describe what the solution will look like; (2) Identify parts of that solution that are already happening; (3) Amplify those already-occurring pieces of the solution.

Strategic Solution Focused Therapy, the current model, combines the strategic and solution focused approaches in two important ways. First, Strategic Therapy's *clarification of the problem* is blended with Solution Focused Therapy's *elaboration of the solution.* Second, the solution focused *amplification of what works* is combined with the strategic *interruption of what does not work.* The specific procedures—and the component parts of the theory—are not original. What is different in the current model is the *deliberate plan* to use the components together.

Different components of the model take on more importance with different clients, and at different points in the treatment of any individual client. A central guideline of Strategic Solution Focused Therapy is that treatment must be tailored to specific clinical needs. In fact, the therapist follows the model's own principles in deciding what to do next in any clinical situation. When something the therapist is doing is "working," the therapist frequently will continue it; when something is "not working," the therapist probably will "do something different." Thus the critical elements in Strategic Solution Focused Therapy operate at two levels simultaneously. On one level, the therapist is working to clarify the *client's* problem and to facilitate the client's "doing what works and changing what doesn't." At the same time, the principles apply to the *therapist's* process, as the therapist does what works and shifts stances in response to obstacles that arise. *Clarifying problems, doing what works,* and *changing what does not:* those are the recurring themes of Strategic Solution Focused Therapy.

Strategic Solution Focused Therapy is a constructivist approach. As in Strategic Therapy, the assumption is that how people view and react to things can make a tremendous difference. As in Solution Focused Therapy, the therapist helps clients to "make a difference that makes a difference" (de Shazer, 1991).

Like the MRI approach, Strategic Solution Focused Therapy is an interactional model. Problems are often seen as being maintained by unsuccessful problem-solving efforts. This does not mean that there is any deliberate attempt to produce "secondary gain"; rather, problems are often maintained inadvertently. Reversal of unsuccessful attempted solutions is seen as central. Like Strategic Therapy, Strategic Solution Focused Therapy also assumes that it is helpful to label a primary complaint.

At the same time, Strategic Solution Focused Therapy, like Solution Focused Therapy, assumes that many simple interventions function like "skeleton keys" in a wide variety of situations. Highlighting whatever is happening when the problem is absent (or present, but being handled constructively) is of critical importance. Recognizing such occasions is expected to result in such occasions increasing in frequency.

Strategic Solution Focused Therapy is a collaborative model, and respect for the client is of paramount importance. The therapeutic alliance is seen as a critical variable, and it is addressed in more detail here than in many discussions of the parent models. The therapist can be transparent about the theory, because the assumption is that client cooperation is enhanced when therapist and client are working together to solve the problem.

The therapist is an active agent of change, at times suggesting "restraint from change" or other ideas that may seem to move away from the goal rather than toward it. However, this kind of input is not seen as a "gimmick" generated "behind the client's back." It is never assumed that the success of an intervention depends on the client's lack of awareness of the element of paradox. Rather, paradoxical suggestions are seen as reflecting certain very real dilemmas and existential realities, such as the fact that when people get what they are seeking, sometimes new problems must be addressed.

Another assumption of Strategic Solution Focused Therapy is that there is a balance between stability and change. As Storm (1991) and Lipchik (1992) have pointed out, people want to change; at the same time, they want things to stay the same. Ambivalence is seen as common and normal, and the assumption is that the urge for stability often follows "change spurts," while urges to change often follow periods of stability.

At the same time, Strategic Solution Focused Therapy assumes that because inertia can be a powerful force, people sometimes need a push to shift directions. When this is the case, the strategic solution focused therapist assumes that it is normal to not want to do something out of the ordinary. This is the assumption underlying the common strategic solution focused suggestion to *do* something—while expecting to *not feel like* doing it.

Strategic Solution Focused Therapy assumes that if desired changes can be obtained without medication, that is generally preferable. Strategic solution focused therapists tend to use nonpharmacological approaches first. At the same time, the model's principles—if it works, do more of it; if it doesn't work, do something different—apply to medication as well. If a nonpharmacological approach is not working, medication is a way of "doing something different"—and the opposite is true as well. If an already-prescribed medication is working, it certainly can be continued. When medication is needed, Strategic Solution Focused Therapy incorporates that into the treatment, encouraging *acceptance* of physiological predispositions and "doing what works" to manage them.

METHODOLOGY

The strategic solution focused process has four basic steps: problem clarification, solution elaboration, evaluation of attempted solutions, and intervention design. Generally, the components are used in the order listed, but this is always tailored to specific clinical needs. For example, in some situations, much of a first session might be spent on problem clarification, while on other occasions, the therapist might move to solution elaboration after just a few minutes. As emphasized in the discussion of the model's theory, the basic principles guide the therapist's decision about what technique to utilize. If a procedure seems to be useful ("working"), the therapist may well choose to continue it, while if a procedure is not helpful, the therapist should "do something different."

Problem Clarification

The first step is clarifying the problem, or identifying the client's primary concern. That means determining what the client is "here about," or what he or she hopes the therapy will help to resolve. If there are multiple complaints, the therapist attempts to identify which is primary. He or she may explain the rationale behind this kind of inquiry: therapy is more likely to be effective if the therapist and client narrow in on the primary concern. Deliberately leaving other issues aside will assure that those concerns do not deflect the focus.

The therapist wants to know what happened that precipitated the client's request for an appointment *now* (as opposed to last week, six months ago, etc.). Was there a specific incident? As much as possible, the therapist attempts to elicit specific, behavioral details about the precipitating circumstances. Who said or did what? If the problem is defined as an affect (such as depression), the therapist wants to know what the person is depressed or sad about.

The therapist also wants to know whether the appointment was the client's idea or someone else's. If someone else was the primary "customer," how eager was the client to schedule the appointment? If someone else suggested it, the client may be a "customer" for something other than that for which he or she was referred. For example, a wife may suggest that her husband seek treatment for his "procrastination," while the husband's primary complaint may be that his wife is "on my back."

"In what way is this a problem?" is another important question. The therapist wants to know whether the complaint is resulting in a behavioral excess or deficit. If so, would changing that behavior make a significant difference? Or is something problematic primarily because it is subjectively uncomfortable? If the latter is the case, the therapist may ask whether the client believes that the degree of discomfort is excessive or appropriate to the situation.

Because questions like these stimulate thinking about things in different ways, problem clarification is an intervention as well as an information-gathering tool. Defining an issue as "the place to start" can help to make an overwhelming situation seem more manageable. Similarly, the inquiry about "exactly what happened" implies that even powerful and disturbing affect can be seen as an appropriate reaction to a definable sequence of events.

Solution Elaboration

The next step in the process is identifying what the goal or solution will look like, and the strategic solution focused therapist often uses a variation of the miracle question (de Shazer, 1988) to get this information. The miracle question asks something like this: "Imagine that tonight, while you're sleeping, a miracle happens, and the miracle is that this problem—the one you just told me about—has been solved. What will be different? Who will notice that you're different? What will (s)he notice? And how will (s)he be different as a result of that? What else?"

After the initial miracle has been described, follow-up inquiry asks for amplifying detail. As much as possible, even vague or improbable initial statements of the miracle are "narrowed down" to include specific dialogue, behavior, and interaction in daily life.

The therapist then asks the client whether any pieces of this scenario are already happening. (The likelihood that this is the case is increased if small, achievable, behavioral changes have just been described.) If parts of the solution are already happening, the therapist expresses admiration and enthusiasm. A question like "How did you do that?" communicates both respect and the implication that the *client* made those changes happen. The therapist may also ask a scaling question that asks for a rating of the problem on a 0 to 10 scale. If the client is at a "two" (where 0 means "severe" and 10 means "solved"), the therapist might ask what will be different when the client will be able to say that he or she is at a "three."

There are many variations on the miracle question. The word "miracle" is *not* required and in many situations is deliberately omitted. The therapist can ask how clients will know that they are "on track" (Walter & Peller, 1992) to solving the problem. The miracle may involve insight or understanding. It may be general or highly specific, and the therapist might explore multiple or evolving solution scenarios.

An extremely important variation on the miracle question is the "coping question" (Berg, 1991). When clients are experiencing severe distress, inquiry that recognizes the magnitude of the pain often seems more respectful. A coping question may ask, "With everything that's been happening, how *do* you get through the day?" In response, the client may say, "I don't know. I just do it." The therapist's inquiry again communicates respect for client resilience, and it encourages people to view themselves as actively making choices and taking control.

Miracle and coping question inquiry is not limited to those times the therapist asks a "full" miracle question. "Mini-miracle questions" can be used at *any* point in the interview when future projection would be helpful. "What will she notice about you?" "How will that make a difference?" and "When you get that over with, what will you be telling me about how you did it?" are examples of questions that encourage recognition and implementation of small, specific changes in the near future.

Like problem clarification, solution elaboration has a dual function: it provides information about the goal *and* is an intervention. The inquiry produces reframing and can be extremely powerful, especially when it communicates that the client did not have to wait for "the full miracle" in order to create meaningful change.

Attempted Solutions

The next step is evaluation of what the client has already tried in previous efforts to solve the problem or achieve the goal. The therapist may explain the rationale behind this inquiry, often including an explicit statement of the model's theory: "I'm interested in knowing what *works*, and I'm very interested in knowing what *doesn't* work, so you and I don't 'reinvent the wheel.'" For each attempted solution, the therapist also inquires what happened after the attempt was made (that is, did it "work"?).

As the therapist hears attempted solutions, he or she listens for recurrent themes. For example, a man may say that his attempts to keep his wife from leaving include taking out the garbage, buying concert tickets, and coming for therapy. Although these attempts are behaviorally different, all of them are variations on a theme of "I'm changing what you've complained about, so please don't go." If these things have not worked well enough (and probably they have not, if this man has come for therapy), the therapist may recognize that future interventions might best avoid more variations on that same theme.

During the attempted solution inquiry, the therapist checks to see if this client has used the most commonly used means of solving the problem. Commonsense measures frequently include positive, direct messages, like "Cheer up" and "Don't worry." The messages associated with specific clinical problems are discussed in more detail in the *Applications* section of this chapter. If these direct, commonsense measures have not worked well enough, the therapist may consider whether this client would be a candidate for a "restraint from change" intervention. Caution not to change too quickly or encouragement to consider the disadvantages of change can interrupt straightforward advice that is not working.

Intervention Design

Considering everything known about the problem, goal, and attempted solutions, the therapist next designs an intervention. Planning what to say requires some thinking, and the therapist may tell the client that he or she will take a short "think break." Often without leaving the room, the therapist may review any notes already taken, gather his or her thoughts, and write some brief notes to guide what he or she is about to say. Especially at the end of a first session or at the time of a planned termination, the therapist wants to include three important components in the intervention.

The first component is the *validation*. This communicates this message: "I heard you. I'm listening. I'm trying to understand. I know there's something you want to change—that's why you're here—but I don't blame you for feeling as you do, in light of what you've just told me." The goals are establishment of the therapeutic alliance and normalization of the client's reactions.

A *compliment* of some kind comprises the second part of the intervention. This component expresses admiration, surprise, or respect for something the client has already done or realized. For example, the therapist might say, "I'm impressed that you recognize that when you said that to her, she heard it as criticism. Not everyone I see has the ability to look at their own behavior as honestly as you did."

The third component is the *suggestion*. The suggestion may involve behavioral change or observation. To decide what to suggest, the therapist may consider the client's stance toward therapy. In de Shazer's (1988) terms, the therapist may evaluate whether this client is a "customer," "complainant," or "visitor." "Customers" verbalize motivation to personally take action, and they are therefore appropriate candidates for behavioral homework. "Complainants," who describe problems but do not express motivation to personally change anything, may be better candidates for observational tasks. "Visitors" are clients who have come primarily at someone else's request. With visitors, the therapist takes the role of a cordial host, thanking the person for paying a visit and inviting him or her to return in the future if desired.

Suggestions may be specific or generic. Specific suggestions are generally preferable, if the therapist has one. Some specific suggestions invite continuation or amplification of some particular behavior described in a solution scenario. On other occasions, suggestions encourage the *opposite* of an unsuccessful attempted solution. When no specific suggestion is immediately apparent, generic suggestions can be extremely helpful. Like skeleton keys that open many doors (de Shazer, 1985), generic suggestions are powerful tools. Examples are: "Do what works, and notice how you do it" and "Do something different."

When selecting interventions, the therapist may consider where a client is in his or her individual "stability/change cycle." Suggestions to change behavior and to act "as if" the miracle were happening lean toward change, while messages suggesting restraint from change or acceptance of a symptom lean toward stability. If "change" homework has not been completed, an intervention suggesting "restraint from change" or acceptance might be offered at the next session.

APPLICATIONS

Strategic Solution Focused Therapy is most frequently applied in outpatient psychotherapy with adults. When the primary complaint is depression, the therapist encourages noticing "how the client does it" when the depression is "less deep." The therapist also checks to see if some variation of a "Cheer up" message has become an unsuccessful attempted solution. If so, this might be reversed by permission to experience sadness—and perhaps to do whatever needs to be done even in the presence of the distress.

When anxiety is the primary problem, the therapist might check to see if "Don't worry" is an unsuccessful attempted solution that should be interrupted. Worry might be reframed as legitimate. Clients are often encouraged to acknowledge anxiety openly and to recognize that they can take action—perhaps deliberately "imperfectly"—even in the presence of discomfort and distraction.

In interpersonal situations, clients are encouraged to notice and amplify interactions that "work." The therapist also remains alert for messages such as "I promise I'll change" that are not helping. Clients are often encouraged to recognize—and to announce to significant others—that they may "slip." The goal is *not* to "never do it again"; rather, it is to "get back on track" as soon as possible.

Couples and families are often seen conjointly, and the therapist may elicit separate problem clarification and solution elaboration responses from each individual. After each person has heard the others' responses, the intervention may compliment each individual on being able to describe—and listen to—scenarios that would make a difference. The therapist may encourage everyone to "make pieces of the solution happen" and/or to "do something different." When a couple's situation involves difficulty with trust, fidelity, or commitment, the therapist labels this and then goes on to compliment the partners on their ability to talk openly about the difficult situation. Individual follow-up sessions are recommended at times.

Strategic Solution Focused Therapy is most frequently applied in brief therapy, single session therapy, and intermittent care, and it is extremely useful in crisis situations (Quick, 1998a). However, the principles also apply in longer-term, ongoing therapy. At every session, the client is asked if there is a specific issue to be addressed. If this is primarily a "catch up" session or the client mostly wants to ventilate, that is also completely legitimate—and openly acknowledged.

The model's principles are also applicable in the training of therapists. In strategic solution focused supervision, supervisees are asked to identify specific issues or cases for consultation. During audio/videotape review or case discussion, supervisors and supervisees identify both interventions that have "worked" and places where the supervisee might "do something different."

CASE EXAMPLE

When first seen, Marge was 47, divorced, and in an on-and-off relationship with her friend Brad. She had just purchased a small apartment building; she lived in one of the units and was working as the apartment manager. A tall, heavy set Caucasian woman, Marge had long, dark hair. Her grooming and dress were slightly disheveled. Marge had a significant hearing impairment and wore hearing aids in both ears. Her voice was noticeably louder than average.

Marge said that she had a number of problems: money, work, Brad, not enough friends, not enough confidence. She had called for an appointment after her primary care doctor had cautioned her that she was "taking too much Xanax." After many years of working for other people as an apartment manager, Marge had just purchased her first building (with some inherited money). Owning property and working for herself had been Marge's "dream" for many years, but things were not going well. "It's not what I expected," Marge sighed. Some tenants were probably going to have to be evicted, and Marge was getting "wound up" and irritable, and she was "taking it too personal." What was the piece with which Marge wanted assistance? The "taking it too personal," she said.

"Marge," the therapist began, "imagine that after you and I get done talking today, and you go home tonight, and fall asleep, that while you're sleeping tonight, a miracle happens. And the miracle is that when you wake up, you realize you're starting to have the ability to not take things so personal. The miracle hasn't changed anything else—the mess with the tenants, Brad, all the rest. The miracle hasn't changed your hearing. The one piece that's different is that ability to not take things so personal. You wake up—and I'm being very concrete—tomorrow, Thursday, with whatever's on your calendar for the day. What will be the first thing that will be different, that will let you know: this isn't such a problem anymore?"

Marge thought for a minute. "I wouldn't be so wound up," she said. How would that show? She would open the windows, walk down to the corner for a bagel. She would come back and take a shower, braid her hair, and put on her new red sweat suit. "My power color," Marge said with a wry smile.

"And what will be different," the therapist continued, "about how you'll be dealing with the tenant mess?" Marge sighed, "I'll just do what I gotta do. Tell them that they gotta get their shit together. None of that illegal stuff on my property. And if they don't cut it out, give them a month's notice. And get the ad in the paper again."

"How will doing that make a difference?" the therapist asked. Marge answered that she'd sleep better, knowing that she'd done what she needed to do. And when the difficult tenants ignored her requests, or when they made fun of her loud voice (as they'd done in the past), how would she cope with the pounding heart and the churning in her stomach? Marge wasn't sure, but she knew that somehow she would get through it. "After all," she said with a chuckle, "I'm a pretty tough lady."

Were any pieces of this scenario already happening? Marge said that they were. She had already spoken to the difficult tenants, even though she'd been "a nervous wreck" all through the conversation. When one of the tenants had made fun of her, she "just pretended my hearing aid wasn't working."

What had Marge tried, in her best attempts to "not take things so personal"? Mostly telling herself to "chill out," she said. Brad's advice was a variation of the same theme: "Don't get so uptight. They're not worth it." Xanax worked, sort of, but not well enough. Also, Marge had "used drugs in a big way" years ago, and she didn't want to "go down the overdoing it with drugs road again."

At the end of the session, the therapist said, "Well, Marge, I'm not surprised that you're taking things pretty personal these days. This mess with the tenants was *not* what you expected. And I'm not surprised that you get wound up when you have to deal with those characters.

Actually, I'm impressed that you've already talked to them. And that you see dangers clearly, and you *don't* want to go down the drug road again. I think you're right: you *are* a tough lady. Not everyone I see is that honest with themselves. It also sounds like, on some level, you already know that you *don't* have to wait for the anxiety to totally go away in order to do what you need to do. So, in the spirit of 'If something works, keep doing it,' keep doing what you've got to do. The piece that maybe *isn't* working well enough is telling yourself: 'Chill out. Don't take it personal.' So—what's the *opposite* of 'Don't take it personal'? I think it's: 'I probably *will* take it personal, and I'll get wound up, and I'll be a nervous wreck—and I'll do it anyway.'"

Marge had four more appointments over the next two months. She confronted her tenants and eventually did have to evict them. "How did you do that?" the therapist asked, attempting to convey respect and admiration. "I just knew I had to," Marge answered. Marge also mentioned that she had conducted more thorough background checks on her next tenants.

Five months later Marge returned. Things were going smoothly with the property, but Marge had a new concern. Hoping to earn some extra money, she had bought a computer, and she wanted to start a small word processing business at home. She needed customers, and she realized she needed to "market" herself. For Marge that meant designing a brochure, sending it out, and "networking" at a local business women's breakfast. She wasn't doing these things because of "lack of confidence," and that was the problem she now wanted to solve.

The therapist asked Marge to describe her brochure and her service. Marge did so without hesitation, and the therapist pointed out how clear and articulate her responses had been. But Marge still felt "less than" what she considered to be the "typical" business woman. She had been waiting to feel confident, or "like an equal," to take the marketing and networking steps, and that attempted solution—waiting—wasn't working.

The therapist validated Marge's concerns. The therapist also wondered aloud what would happen if Marge "planned" to feel awkward at one of the networking breakfasts. If she attended, she might do so without an expectation of "making friends" or "feeling confident." She would just be there for the specific purpose of getting some word processing business.

Marge's next appointment was ten months later. Marge now regularly had breakfast with the networking group—and she had discovered that "looks can be deceiving." She said, "Women who look like they have it all together have problems, too." Her concern now was confusion about whether or not to buy a second rental property. The opportunity and the money were available, but there would be more work, and she would probably have to hire some staff. "Me—a boss? Me—the former prostitute, drug user, low life?" Marge said. "I'm not exactly the boss type."

The therapist pointed out that even if Marge *were* the boss type (whatever that might be), extra property would definitely mean more work, more potential for difficult tenants, staffing hassles. There would definitely be more opportunities for "taking things too personal." So whether or not to buy was a genuine dilemma.

Marge did buy the second house, and as predicted, more problems came with it. The property manager she hired didn't work out, and Marge had to fire him and hire another one. She also had to challenge an erroneous tax assessment. How had she managed to do those things, the therapist asked. Marge wasn't sure. She had gotten "wound up," but she had "done it anyway." The therapist wondered aloud whether the history of "having done it all" that Marge *thought* made her "not boss material" gave her a street-smartness that actually was a strength, not a weakness, when it came to dealing with tough people and tough situations. The therapist cautioned Marge that she might not want to rush too quickly into "smoothing out all the rough edges."

Whatever Marge was doing with her property management business, it was working. She sold her first building at a handsome profit and bought two more. There were also changes in Marge's relationships. She had a few new women friends, "not low lifes, but not boring, either." Brad had met someone else, and Marge was "looking," but she hadn't met anyone else yet. She celebrated her fiftieth birthday with a cruise to Mexico.

Around the time of the birthday, Marge came for six sessions at two or three week intervals. The therapist asked if there was a specific issue at this point, and Marge said that there was. She was frustrated. "I run around too much. I'm not satisfied with anything," she said. "I need to settle down and relax. I should be doing yoga, a day at the spa, stuff like that. Especially," Marge added, "now that I'm 50."

Marge's attempted solution to her frustration was a belief that she should relax, and she'd tried to do just that. Yoga "worked" for Marge's friend. But it didn't work for Marge. Yoga was "boring." A facial was "a stupid waste of money." Settling down, relaxing, "acting 50"—none of that fit who Marge was. The therapist told Marge that.

"It's like in business," the therapist said. "You know how there are people who do start-up businesses? The ones who get the venture capital and take the risks and thrive on the excitement? Then it's time to go from 'start up phase' to 'maintenance phase.' And those people get bored. And frustrated. Maintenance isn't their thing. Oh, they do it if they have to. They're responsible; it's not like they're flakes. But it's just not as much fun. And then there are the people who *hate* the change, the start-up

part. They do it when they have to. But they *love* the maintenance part. Doing predictable things, keeping things going—that's when they're in their element."

Marge nodded. "Well, it's a no-brainer which one I am," she said. "Maintenance sucks." The therapist asked Marge if she could imagine a scenario that built upon her thriving-with-change qualities rather than fighting them. Marge's eyes flashed. "Maybe I haven't done it all," she said. "After all, I haven't tried flying lessons. Yet."

"And knowing that you're a start-up lady," the therapist continued, "how will that help you get through the maintenance part?" Marge shrugged. She would "just do it." Over the next two sessions, Marge and the therapist talked about the things that probably would always take more effort for Marge. Batteries for hearing aids. Property taxes. The daily give-and-take of relationships.

Marge was ready to stop for now. She would put up with the maintenance when she had to. Marge and the therapist agreed that, as Weakland (1986) put it, "life is one damn thing after another." But Marge was ready for more than maintenance. More property. Flying lessons. New people—not boring ones, but not low lifes, either. "I haven't done it all," Marge grinned. "Yet."

SUMMARY

"Doing what works and changing what doesn't" is this model's recurring theme. Taking a collaborative and respectful—and simultaneously active—stance, the therapist asks the client to label a problem or goal at most appointments. If there is no specific issue and the goal is "just to talk," that is directly acknowledged—and fully accepted. Which component of the model is emphasized shifts during treatment, in accordance with specific client needs. Sometimes there is a full "miracle question" or solution elaboration scenario; on many other occasions, there is highlighting of pieces of the solution or coping behaviors that are already present.

Strategic Solution Focused Therapy frequently emphasizes that pieces of the solution are happening *even in the presence* of significant distress, uncertainty, and difficult situations. That is, the person did not have to wait for total elimination of difficulty in order to create positive change. Waiting for full problem resolution has often become the unsuccessful attempted solution. This message emerges in many ways in the treatment of specific symptoms, longstanding characteristics (personality disorders), and interpersonal situations.

The model's components—clarifying problems, amplifying solutions, and interrupting what does not work—can be applied in a variety of situations. The principles can also be used by therapists who identify with other therapeutic orientations. Strategic Solution Focused Therapy is a flexible approach that can be combined with many other ways of working. Some therapists use one component of the model more than other components. That is considered a fully legitimate use of Strategic Solution Focused Therapy, because "doing what works and changing what doesn't" is the goal for the client—and for the therapist.

REFERENCES

Ardern, M. (1997). Book review: Doing what works in brief therapy. *International Journal of Geriatric Psychiatry, 12*(12), 1196.

Beck, A., & Emery, G. (1979). *Cognitive therapy of anxiety and behavior disorders.* Philadelphia: Center for Cognitive Therapy.

Beisser, A. (1970). A paradoxical theory of change. In J. Fagen & I. Shepherd (Eds.), *Gestalt therapy now.* Palo Alto: Science and Behavior Books.

Berg, I. (1991). *Family-based services: A solution-focused approach.* Milwaukee: BFTC Press.

Berg, I., & de Shazer, S. (1993). Making numbers talk: Language in therapy. In S. Friedman (Ed.), *The new language of change: Constructive collaboration in psychotherapy.* New York: Guilford.

Berg, I., & Miller, S. (1992). *Working with the problem drinker.* New York: Norton.

Carter, L. (1998). Personal communication.

de Shazer, S. (1985). *Keys to solution in brief therapy.* New York: Norton.

de Shazer, S. (1988). *Clues: Investigating solutions in brief therapy.* New York: Norton.

de Shazer, S. (1991). *Putting difference to work.* New York: Norton.

Erickson, M., Rossi, E., & Rossi, S. (1976). *Hypnotic realities.* New York: Irvington.

Fisch, R., Weakland, J., & Segal, L. (1982). *The tactics of change.* San Francisco: Jossey-Bass.

Hayes, H. (1991). The "Zen lady": An interview with Insoo Kim Berg. *Australian and New Zealand Journal of Family Therapy, 12,* 155–158.

Hoyt, M., & Berg, I. (1998). Solution-focused couple therapy. In M. Hoyt (Ed.), *The handbook of constructive therapies.* San Francisco: Jossey-Bass.

Kadushin, G. (1998). Applications of the traditional interview to the brief-treatment context. *Families in Society: The Journal of Contemporary Human Service, 79*(4), 346–357.

Lipchik, E. (1992). A reflecting interview. *Journal of Strategic and Systemic Therapies, 11,* 59–74.

Miller, S. (1991). Solution-focused therapy. Presentation, San Diego Strategic Solution Focused Therapy Professional Interest Group, San Diego.

Miller, S., Hubble, M., & Duncan, B. (1995). No more bells and whistles. *Family Therapy Networker, 19*(2), 53–63.

O'Hanlon, W., & Weiner-Davis, M. (1989). *In search of solutions.* New York: Norton.

Quick, E. (1994a). Strategic/solution focused therapy: A combined approach. *Journal of Strategic and Systemic Therapies, 13*(1), 74–75.

Quick, E. (1994b). From unattainable goals to achievable solutions. *Journal of Strategic and Systemic Therapies, 13*(2), 59–64.

Quick, E. (1996). *Doing what works in brief therapy: A strategic solution focused approach.* San Diego: Academic Press.

Quick, E. (1998a). Strategic solution focused therapy: Doing what works in crisis intervention. *Crisis Intervention, 4*(2–3), 197–214.

Quick, E. (1998b). Doing what works in brief and intermittent therapy. *Journal of Mental Health, 7*(5), 527–533.

Quick, E. (1998c). Clarifying the problem. *Psychotherapy Book News: A Journal of Essays and Reviews, 33,* 43–44.

Rogers, C. (1961). *On becoming a person: A therapist's view of psychotherapy.* Boston: Houghton Mifflin.

Sheehan, D. (1983). *The anxiety disease.* New York: Charles Scribner's Sons.

Storm, C. (1991). The remaining thread: Matching change and stability signals. *Journal of Strategic and Systemic Therapies, 10,* 114–117.

Thomas, F. (1997). Book review: Doing what works in brief therapy. *Journal of Marital and Family Therapy, 23*(4), 482–483.

Wallen, R. (1970). Gestalt therapy and Gestalt psychology. In J. Fagen & I. Shepherd (Eds.), *Gestalt therapy now.* Palo Alto: Science and Behavior Books.

Walter, J., & Peller, J. (1992). *Becoming solution-focused in brief therapy.* New York: Bruner Mazel.

Weakland, J. (1986). Personal communication.

Chapter 64

STRESS MANAGEMENT

HARRY A. OLSON and JOAN ROBERTS

As Harry Olson and Joan Roberts state in their chapter on Stress Management, theirs is a therapy for the well, used to bring well-functioning people higher up the scale of functioning. This is a well-known approach found in the so-called growth centers such as Esalin, and is dealt with in a number of chapters in this book.

The point that Olson and Roberts make is that most successful people could be even more successful if they would relax and take it easy. In a sense, this is the opposite of the position taken by George Gazda, who stresses the importance of below-par people learning new skills. Olson and Roberts say, in effect, that whatever skills you do have can be better employed if you learn to take it easy. Or, as a business saying goes, "Learn to work smarter, not harder."

Stress Management is aimed at the so-called Type A personality—hard drivers, typically executives who agonize over decisions, who are always pushing forward and are at high risk for a variety of psychosomatic diseases.

It seems highly probable that as time goes on, programs such as the one developed in this chapter will become increasingly common to modern businesses, to help people simultaneously to relax and yet be more successful.

Stress Management is a psychotherapeutic intervention process that draws from a number of well-established techniques, including biofeedback, hypnosis, the behavior therapies, and insight-oriented approaches. Its goal is to alter the individual's subjective experience of both psychological and physiological stress as well as to lower such physiological indices of stress disorders as hypertension, cardiovascular disorders, diabetes, gastrointestinal disorders, and others. The program is multimodal. A variety of techniques are employed, including hypnosis, cognitive restructuring, and an educational component embracing nutrition as well as exercise. In this manner the individual is helped to change his or her physical response pattern and to modify the beliefs and behaviors that produced the stress response in the first place.

HISTORY

Attempts to understand the role of stress and psychological factors in disease date back to Hippocrates. Moving into modern times, nineteenth century scientific methods fostered a specialization and emphasis on organic factors that excluded psychological speculation.

Sigmund Freud, Ivan Pavlov, and Walter B. Cannon were the prime movers of modern Stress Management (Wittkower, 1977). Freud's contribution revolved around his discovery of the unconscious and fundamental psychodynamics. In contrast, Pavlov's introduction of the "conditioned reflex" provided a method both for inducing stress and for measuring the associated emotions. Cannon noted that situations evoking fear or rage in the individual could produce important bodily changes (fight or flight reactions). The concept of "homeostasis" was developed as part of his description of the individual's physiological equilibrium. As a result of these three separate developments, the twentieth century began with both psychological and neurophysiological models available, as well as techniques providing access to unconscious processes.

Psychoanalytic theory played a leading role in early formulations and treatment of stress disorders. In postulating that bodily changes have a symbolic meaning, Freud paved the way for psychoanalytic treatment of psychosomatic disorders. Both Felix Deutsch and Melanie Klein developed theoretical models that provided analytic explanations for the stress diseases. Franz Alexander (1950) explained psychosomatic disorders in terms of three key variables: (1) inherited or acquired organic vulnerability; (2) psychological conflict and defense mechanisms; (3) precipitating life situations. In 1930 he founded the Chicago Psychoanalytic Institute, where systematic psychoanalytic treatment of these disorders was carried out. Specific psychological patterns were found to be related to a number of diseases including ulcerative colitis, bronchial asthma, dermatitis, and duodenal ulcer. In general, early psychoanalysts saw psychosomatic symptoms as regressive physiological responses related to the underlying psychological regression. Psychoanalytic treatment for management of stress disorders became less and less popular, because these disorders were often not amenable to this approach and the treatment was not always cost effective. There has also been a gradual shift from treatment to prevention in Stress Management.

CURRENT STATUS

A number of trends are outstanding when the current literature on Stress Management is reviewed. First, there is a move toward prevention and an openness to experimentation and "creative interventions." Many individuals and firms are providing "stress reduction" programs. However, missing from many of these programs are consistency and ongoing evaluation. As with hypnosis and biofeedback, two important treatment techniques, overexposure and inflated promises have led to negative reactions on the part of many individuals as well as the professional community. "Stress Management" may be in for the same type of experience as other programs that proliferate like "mushrooms after the rain." It remains the responsibility of mental health professionals to control the quality of programs and to evaluate outcome. The techniques utilized in Stress Management run the gamut of practical *how to*'s such as "time management" or "priority setting" to more traditional types of psychotherapeutic interventions, biofeedback, and hypnosis.

Insight-oriented individual or group psychotherapy programs are an outgrowth of the analytic tradition, but often are problem focused. Friedman and Rosenman (1974) have identified a personality (Type A) with a high risk of coronary disease, and have also identified a low-risk personality (Type B). Some of the chief characteristics of the Type A person are considerable aggressiveness, competitiveness, impatience, and an extreme sense of time urgency. Studies show that while the Type B person goes about his or her basic life tasks in a far less driven, more relaxed fashion, he or she often gets more accomplished. Rosenman and Friedman point out that "Type A" behaviors are encouraged by our contemporary Western civilization and that there are even "Type A settings." For these reasons, it is difficult for this

"driven" personality to change even in the face of increased health risks. Responsibility and work pressure play a key role in maintaining this lifestyle. Studies of individuals in especially responsible or demanding positions, such as air traffic controllers, showed a higher risk and earlier onset of hypertension and peptic ulcers than were present for the control group of airmen (Cobb & Rose, 1973). Roskies has conducted groups for postcoronary males focusing on behavioral change in an attempt to modify "Type A" patterns (Roskies et al., 1978). In general, the postcoronary patients have fared well in these group experiences. Additional evaluation and research is ongoing. The techniques focus on increasing the individuals' awareness of "Type A" patterns and changing them with the help of the social support of the group. There are still many questions, however, regarding the meaning of the "Type A" syndrome and the most effective interventions into this constellation of behavior.

Frankel (1973) and Field (1979) are involved in Stress Management of disorders through hypnosis. Frankel distinguishes between "mild hypnosis" or relaxation, symptom removal, and hypnotherapy. The hypnosis literature abounds with single case studies of stress disorders, but there is little discussion of hypnosis in prevention programs or in groups for stress control. Group processes have tended to rely on systematic relaxation as the method for returning individuals to homeostasis.

Biofeedback continues to be an effective technique for Stress Management but is generally tied to a laboratory setting. The problem is one of helping individuals generalize from the calm of the lab to the "chaos" of a busy, demanding work setting. However, a growing number of portable, small-scale instruments provide feedback regarding blood pressure and cardiac function. We prefer to see them used as adjuncts to a program rather than utilized by themselves.

In considering the variety of stress management techniques utilized by management consultants and health care providers, we designed our own multimodal approach to Stress Management.

THEORY

In designing a stress management program suitable for industrial groups or individual clients, we attempted to integrate techniques from the most current approaches to stress. Consideration was given to psychobiological studies, psychological variables, and sociological findings. The resulting program provides three main features: (1) Reduction of physical tension through hypnosis; (2) cognitive restructuring of high-stress situations; (3) education and the learning of improved coping skills.

Research findings and our clinical experience indicated that individuals in high-stress situations would need to learn a method of relaxing themselves that could be applied "as needed." Training in autohypnosis proved most efficient in terms of time and degree of response, in contrast to systematic relaxation or biofeedback. Individuals unable to enter a trance have nevertheless reported deep relaxation. Biofeedback equipment is included in the program more as a demonstration tool than as a clinical intervention. Individuals report that they reach a state of physiological homeostasis rather early in our program; the challenge is for them to maintain this state. For this reason, we offer a cognitive restructuring component to the program and follow-up over a two-year period. Intensive follow-up and ongoing assessment are especially important in view of the limited systematic field research.

The cognitive restructuring techniques range from specific management techniques such as problem solving or setting priorities to raising central philosophical issues and establishing individual life goals. This scope is particularly helpful for the workaholic, or "Type A" individual, who often participates in efficiency-oriented programs to learn how to be a better "Type A." Even in presenting routine concepts such as time management techniques, we point out that the goal is to "work smart" rather than "work hard." By allocating "time to think" rather than jumping into relentless activity, the individual saves considerable effort in the long run. The "hurry syndrome" is discouraged at every turn. For persons who deny the reality that they have a lopsided life style with close interpersonal relationships getting "short shrift," we introduce them to the "wheel of life." The key areas included are: work, friendship, love or intimate ties, religious-philosophical issues, leisure, and self. The emotions associated with each dimension are discussed at length, and it is noted that if even one part is missing, one is probably in for a bumpy ride. Research such as Lynch's (1977) work on cardiovascular disease suggests that the "bumpy ride" eventually results in increased physical vulnerability.

Another important issue raised by our program is humor. Any of the stress carrier's victims (commonly known as associates and employees) will attest to his or her lack of a sense of humor in the face of an absurd task. High-stress people are so competitive that they can't laugh at themselves or the situation when appropriate. In conjunction with humor and keeping life in some reasonable perspective, the program introduces some basic rational-emotive principles from Albert Ellis's theory (1962). Various irrational ideas common to Western society are presented with emphasis on the need to be perfect, have everyone love you, and so forth. It is suggested that while it would be "nice" to be successful at every undertaking with full staff cooperation, it isn't "absolutely necessary" for feeling stress-free. It is not events themselves that make us unhappy, frustrated, or stressed but what each individual tells him- or herself about a given event that produces the dysphoric feeling. Often if you "use it" instead of letting it "use you," it is possible to take advantage of a "failure."

Just as high-stress individuals seek perfection in themselves, they often demand it in others. They exert a degree of controlling behavior at work and home that undermines relationships and productivity. We emphasize that you can only "control yourself," and that imperfectly at best. There is no way to "make" others perform. The effective manager learns how to engage others in creative cooperation. The emphasis is shifted from an ego orientation (will I succeed or fail?) to a task orientation (how can I get this job done?).

Another issue important for "Type A" managers is aggression. Often we find that these persons are not sufficiently assertive in delegating tasks or explaining overall goals to staff. They then become overwhelmed and feel that they "never get any help"; frustration builds, and they "blow up" at staff. For this reason some assertiveness training is built into the program, although these are hardly passive, dependent clients.

In contrast to the cognitive restructuring portion of the program, the educational component involves little discussion. The emphasis here is on holism and health maintenance. Managers are presented with information and statistics geared to get them to reevaluate their own health "probabilities." The data presented includes the incidence of disease as related to recent life changes, and the importance of a balanced life and close personal ties for general health as well as weight reduction, exercise, and smoking control. Since this program involves a variety of personal contracts, these individually designed plans may incorporate the behavior modification plan for each individual. It is not unusual to meet up with a middle-aged, overweight client having one or more stress-aggravated disorders (e.g., hypertension, peptic ulcer, etc.) who also smokes and works over weekends. In this type of situation, one begins the modification plan in the life area which (1) the individual is most willing to work on, and (2) has a high likelihood of success. By the time one has completed the basic program and initial follow-up, both long- and short-term goals are outlined.

The assessment of individual change and program effectiveness is central to the stress program. Firms have frequently complained to us that some management programs come in, share some good concepts, and leave. Positive changes last a few weeks, fading gradually. For this reason, our follow-up extends for a two-year period with confidential contact of participants. Counseling and referral to outside resources are included in the program.

METHODOLOGY

While stress management programs exist in a variety of formats on location for business and industry and for the general public, the intervention process to be described here is the individual program. It is designed for the person who wishes to correct a particular problem or manage life pressures more effectively. Such a person may not require or desire a more traditional psychotherapeutic treatment. The individual program is a time-limited (16 visit) psychoeducational experience designed to train the client in cognitive management skills and in techniques for physiological control. The program as described is flexible enough to reflect clinicians' individual theoretical orientations. The following discussion emphasizes an Adlerian approach.

After opening introductions, the initial interview serves to gather essential background information and to orient the client as to what can be expected during the course of the 16 sessions. A fact sheet is completed with such information as age, occupation, income level, members of the nuclear family, parents' occupations, and place in the family of·origin. A brief medical history is then taken, which also includes the client's own report as to how he or she handles stressful situations. Since appropriate and rapid screening is a necessary part of this program, such information is taken in detail; the therapist immediately processes several questions: *Is the client appropriate for this program? What are major lifestyle issues in the client's background? How functional is this client right now? What goals are likely to arise?* The next area of inquiry focuses upon the client's stated concerns—why he or she is there. As part of the assessment, this information provides useful lifestyle information and often an estimate of the client's level of hope and degree of activity.

At this point clients are usually informed that the "problems" of which they complain are their strategies for coping with life's tasks; that difficulties such as anxiety and depression, for example, are actually creative endeavors turned toward unproductive goals and portray their level of discouragement. The emphasis from the beginning is that each client is an active, creative agent, not a passive victim; and that together we will tap his or her well of creativity and use it to solve problems. This approach reinforces the client's owning of his or her personal responsibility and is explicitly stated.

If the client volunteers a "symptom" as part of the problem, the Dreikurs (1954) question is asked: "If you did not have this symptom, how would your life be different?" If the client is able to give a relatively concrete answer, it is likely that the area indicated in the answer— for example, improved sexual relations—is the very area he or she is trying to avoid by producing the symptom. The reader is referred to Dreikurs (1954) for a full explanation.

The stress battery is administered next. This is a compilation of short scales including a modification of the Holmes life-change inventory, Type-A behavior questionnaire, the FIRO-B, and an exercise called the Wheel of Life. On the Holmes scale, the client is asked to indicate which of the life events on the scale he or she experienced in the past year. Research (Holmes & Rahe, 1967) has found that there is a correlation between the number of life changes and the probability of contracting severe physical illness. While a person cannot alter past life events, he or she can alter reactions to present ones and thus reduce stress. The scale serves as an index of the external stresses the individual is experiencing.

The FIRO-B (Schutz, 1966) is an indicator of the client's preferred behaviors in the areas of social relations, affection/love, and independence/decision making, and thus provides a measure of assertiveness and the degree of social interaction and encouragement.

The Wheel of Life provides the client an opportunity for self-assessment regarding six life tasks: *occupation,* the area of work and productive endeavor; *friendship; intimacy,* the area of sex and love; *leisure,* the area of the use of free time; *spiritual,* the area dealing with religious, moral-ethical issues, and the meaning of life; and *self,* which covers self-esteem and self-development activities. The client is given a paper with a circle on it divided into six equal sectors, one for each life task. The tasks are areas in which life makes demands on us just by the nature of our existence. After the tasks are defined, each client is asked to develop a subjective formula of time times energy that he or she devotes to each task. The client then fills in the portion of each sector that he or she determines best represents the amount of investment placed on each task. Clinicians and philosophers have known for years that for life to be fulfilling and meaningful, it must be relatively balanced among the various tasks. Most of our clients, however, end up with wheels that are quite skewed. A common profile is high investment in occupation with scant investment in intimacy. The Wheel of Life technique shows us areas of overinvestment and deficit.

Life goals are a major emphasis in the program, and they are conceptualized in terms of the six life tasks. While most people set short-term goals for certain activities, relatively few people think in terms of developing goals for their lives apart from the obvious area of occupation. We have found that setting life goals in the other areas as well, even if the goals should change, helps provide cohesiveness and meaning to existence, and a sense of increased control and determination, with a resultant lowering of overall stress. Clients often need reorientation from the outset in this area, which reinforces their own power to determine major aspects of their future. As the first interview draws to a close, the client is instructed to write out some tentative life goals based on the six tasks during the week before the next session. Heart rate, blood pressure, and weight are recorded. The client is then oriented to the process of the remaining sessions. The stress battery and physiological measures are repeated at the end of the program. Heart rate, blood pressure, and weight are monitored more frequently if specific problems in these areas are found.

At the close of the first session, the client is instructed to obtain a physical examination from the family physician. While the primary purpose of the physical is to detect any problems, for the purpose of the program both the client and we must be informed if there are any restrictions or requirements regarding exercise or diet. In addition, the possibility of an organic cause for any physical complaint must be checked.

During the second session, feedback from the stress battery is provided. The client's written life goals are examined, refined, and modified if necessary by mutual discussion. These goals are then formalized and serve as a basis, along with the stress data and physical examination, for the stress management/health maintenance prescription, which is the core of the program. This prescription sets forth the operational goals mutually developed by the client and the therapist toward which the client will direct his or her efforts throughout the program. The prescription is flexible and open to change if the client deems necessary. It is also possible that the client will not complete work on the goals during the program, but in the case of broader goals, this is quite permissable. Life is a process of growth and development that continues from birth to the grave; what is important is that the client develop and incorporate new and effective skills and attitudes into his or her attitudinal/behavioral repertoire. Once a solid foundation is laid, the client can, and is most likely to, continue on his or her own. The prescription organizes an action plan under the following headings: family, interpersonal, occupation, hypnosis, nutrition/exercise, and other, and is set up on a form that also allows for recording a formal progress review every fourth session.

During the second session, if time permits, the client is introduced to hypnosis. First, hypnosis is discussed to clarify any myths. Then the client is given a hypnotic induction and scene visualization and/or other suggestions to induce relaxation. The client is also trained at that time in self-hypnosis. Self-hypnosis is a standard part of the program, and clients are instructed to practice it daily. Deep relaxation is the basis from which all other specialized suggestions are developed, and hypnosis is the primary tool used to teach clients to modify their physiological responses. Later in the program, hypnosis is integrated into specific problem-solving and creativity-tapping techniques. The effects of guided fantasy and covert rehearsal are often magnified via hypnosis. Each week the client usually spends some time in hypnosis, and new suggestions and skills are taught to be practiced at home. Skills and suggestions included depend on the client's needs and goals; no two clients will have the same program of hypnotic interventions.

The importance of self-hypnosis cannot be overstressed. Hypnosis is a powerful tool during and after which people often experience notable, if not profound, results. In addition, in the minds of most laymen, hypnosis has a magical quality. Many, unless instructed otherwise, believe that under hypnosis they are under the therapist's control. Even some knowledgeable clients believe that the hypnosis is somehow "better" if it is done by the therapist rather than self-induced. All of these conceptions can lead to excessive dependence on the therapist when hypnosis is involved. When self-hypnosis is used from the outset, this tendency is minimized. Dependent behaviors toward the therapist must be discouraged as they contradict the basic actor-creator role of the client.

Two other ancillary aspects of the prescription are exercise and nutritional recommendations. These recommendations are negotiated with the client, but the overriding determinant is whether the client's physician has indicated any limitations or requirements. Within the framework of such limitations, if there are any, it is recommended that the client engage in fitness activities that exercise the cardiovascular and respiratory systems. Such exercise will raise heart rate momentarily and lower blood pressure over time. The positive effects of exercise also help to lower stress. The exercise program is tailored to the individual and may consist of jogging, active sports, calisthenics, or other activities that exercise the heart-lung-artery systems.

Nutritional recommendations, if needed, usually revolve around a balanced diet. No weight-reduction emphasis is included unless this becomes a program goal. Then the focus switches to initial calorie counting on a nutritionally balanced, calorie-restricted diet and to specific hypnotic and behavioral suggestions focusing on developing a new body image and altered eating habits. The emphasis here is not only on losing weight, but keeping it off.

While the overall framework of the program is structured, the content agenda for each session depends mainly on the goals and issues determined by the client. The major portion of each session involves cognitive restructuring techniques and consists of instruction by the therapist and discussion and skill practice with the client. The week's progress is checked, and new suggestions and homework assignments are given. Homework assignments vary with client needs but are designed to help inculcate new learnings through hypnosis and direct behavior, reinforce new skills through practice, and help the client move toward his or her goals by successive approximation. Homework is assigned and self-hypnosis is reinforced each session.

Over the course of the program, clients are instructed in the nature of stress and stress reduction, how they can lower or intensify stress via self-indoctrination, and how to spot negative thoughts and mistaken ideas with specific techniques for disputing them or altering one's attention. Particular emphasis is placed upon problem solving, developing creative alternatives, and redefining problems as opportunities. At every turn the client is challenged to create, recreate, and explore, renouncing by action and definition any mistaken perception of his or her victim role. We also encourage the individual to make greater use of, and commitment to, existing sociocultural support systems such as clubs and organizations, and kindle a reawakened interest, where necessary, in spiritual-philosophical issues, religion, and family or ethnic traditions, as well as an increased and more philosophical sense of humor and perspective on life.

APPLICATIONS

As stated in the previous section, the client for whom this particular program is most applicable should be verbal and relatively well-functioning. Since we all suffer from chronic human imperfection, all of us face stress in our daily lives, and we all react both physically and emotionally to those stresses whether we are consciously aware of it or not. Most, if not all, of us could learn to manage our stress more effectively and expand into more meaningful and fulfilled lives. The stress management program, then, is a kind of "therapy for the well."

The approach thus far outlined dovetails very well with traditional American values of self-control and achievement, and thus is consonant with the beliefs of the average American businessperson and worker. Yet in Stress Management those values are reorganized away from their limiting and stress-producing aspects. For example, while "self-control" may mean not showing your emotions, it is healthier to view it as not being a victim, but rather one who can actively plan and coordinate one's own life experiences in a more useful and beneficial light. The attempt is to fine-tune the human engine, working out the rough spots for smoother functioning.

The program, therefore, is best suited for "average people" who feel the pinch of pressure or stress and want to achieve a greater sense of relief or control over their life. These people are usually not experiencing major traumas in their daily life, but the little, everyday stressors build. Most of the people for whom this program was designed identify their major stresses as coming from their jobs, and most of the problems here boil down to strained relationships, with high work demands a close second. Such people can be found in almost all occupational fields and strata. Housewives and especially the dual-career woman (housewife plus work outside the home)

are appropriate candidates for this approach. Since the program is flexible in content, it can reach a great variety of human needs, and do so without the stigma often associated with going to a mental health professional.

The people most likely to benefit from the program also may have mild or circumscribed "hang-ups" that may interfere to a greater or lesser degree with some, but not all, areas of their life. They may also have particular worries or fears that limit their potential in some way but that are not overly debilitating.

Specific symptom populations such as minor arthritics, hypertensives, gastrointestinal patients, cardiac patients, and headache and low-back pain patients, on the other hand, often require more long-term and intensive therapy because of the neurotic underlay usually associated with a chronic pain problem.

Severe neurotics are a special case. Our same procedures work very well with neurotics in the context of longer-term therapy. The severe neurotic experiences the symptom as ego-alien—that is, at a conscious level the person wishes to be rid of the symptom, yet the symptom actually serves such a compelling purpose for him or her that, unconsciously, the person cannot conceive of letting it go so easily. In fact, the neurotic symptoms may be deeply ingrained in the fabric of the lifestyle. These clients, as well as psychotics, would be seen in longer-term therapy and our stress program would be contraindicated.

The greatest hindrance to this program, as in all therapy regardless of client disorder, is the lack or the lag of development of a therapeutic alliance. While the stress program is a highly educational/mutual contract approach, it possesses all the interpersonal dynamics of any brief psychotherapy. Given the short-term nature of the program, rapport must be well established very early.

As time goes on, more and more emphasis nationwide is being placed on prevention and holistic health maintenance, and it is in this area where Stress Management has its greatest utility. There is also a need to move such programs out of the confines of the therapist's office into naturalistic settings where the people are, especially into business and industrial locations. In fact, the program described here had its origin in a small group follow-up for a program the Stress Management Institute carries out for executives. As awareness in the business sector is increasing regarding stress and holistic health maintenance, more and more companies are desirous of effective programs of a preventive nature.

What is needed now, however, is a rapprochement between the work setting and the laboratory. Each is often suspicious of the other. Businesspeople may charge that the scientists' results are irrelevant or do not generalize to the complexities of the work environment, and the scientists seeing the same complexities may argue that it is impossible to isolate necessary variables. The rapproachment can be achieved through long-term research follow-up of participants in training and other kinds of health-maintenance programs. In the final analysis, this is the best way to determine program effectiveness. Analogue studies and the traditional "smiles report" ("Did you like the program?") often obtained as "evaluation" directly after a conference or workshop are equally ineffective at assessing a program's or technique's effectiveness in a naturalistic setting.

CASE EXAMPLE

Ted is a 32-year-old white male assistant accountant in his second marriage. He first married at age 22, but the marriage was stormy. He was tense and uptight most of the time and claimed that his wife constantly had to have her own way and achieved it through hysterics. He put up with it for three-and-a-half years and then divorced her at age 25. At age 30 he remarried. He has two children by his first marriage, who reside with his former wife, and is stepfather for two children, ages 12 and 11, from his present wife's first marriage. He describes his second marriage as good.

Ted is the younger of two children. He claims to have been anxious most of his life, and reports three blackouts due to anxiety in childhood and severe migraine headaches through his teens until the end of his first marriage, after which he had only one migraine. Ted was easily given to guilt and had excessive desires to please others and meet their expectations regardless of his own wants. He became anxious in the face of conflict and was generally nonassertive and became "nervous" (sweating palms, fast heart, tingling in hands, lightness in head) at the slightest provocation. He was also depressed and judged himself as perfectionistic. While in the service (1968) he had very high blood pressure.

Eight months before entering the stress management program, he had a severe anxiety attack, with dangerously elevated blood pressure, chest pains, and pounding in his head. He was hospitalized until his blood pressure was brought under control and then treated by his family physician with Hygroton (50 milligrams a day). At the time Ted entered the program, he was on medical leave from his job because of elevated blood pressure. He was under great strain at work, having just trained his own supervisor, who then dumped most of his (supervisor's) work on Ted. Ted felt helpless to complain because the supervisor was in a favored position.

During the first interview, Ted indicated his goals as being able to cope and manage his anxiety. His average score on the Type A Behavior Questionnaire was 2.8 out of a possible 4, indicating a decidedly Type A personality. His Holmes score was 199.

During the second interview, he was hypnotized for deep relaxation, including scene visualization and dialogue with his inner self for assets discovery. A progressive muscular relaxation exercise was also included. His blood pressure before hypnosis was 167/67; afterward in the same session it was 141/61. Ted was instructed in self-hypnosis.

In the third interview, Ted was shown how he used anxiety to push himself into assertive action, that anxiety was his "old friend," a tool he used to act on his own when he otherwise did not give himself permission to act without having to wait to get anxious. He was instructed in his rights and taught step by step how to develop assertive behavior.

During the sessions that followed, the focus in hypnosis was on deep relaxation, patience, and self-control, and positive assets and assertiveness. Progressive scene visualization and direct suggestion were most commonly employed.

In progressive visualization, the client keeps revisualizing the same scene, making modifications until he is comfortable with the outcome. On one occasion we analyzed a dream hypnotically in which Ted was able to confront his boss on the boss's ineptitude. Cognitive and behavioral work was on specifics of handling stress in the office, positive assets, and analysis of his ultimate purposes behind anxiety. He also discovered his negative self-references and was taught to reprogram himself with positive self-talk. Significant emphasis was placed on the development of assertive behaviors through role play, discussion, scene visualization, and homework contracts; making decisions regarding his vocational growth; and gaining a broader perspective and sense of humor, especially about daily stressors. An exercise program was negotiated, including weight-lifting and the Apollo Exerciser fitness routine.

At one point Ted reported feeling anxious when riding the bus to work. He was instructed to make himself even more anxious when riding the bus, a process that in a week caused his anxiety to diminish considerably.

Ted was seen for 17 sessions. His co-workers, he reported, noted a considerable degree of calm and control in his behavior. He no longer gets anxious in his carpool and has mastered his anxiety on the bus. Occasionally he feels mildly anxious about the bus, and he has been told that this is his way of toying with the past. When he is ready to let go of his former game, he will give up that anxiety. His wife notes a remarkable change at home, first in calmness, but also in assertiveness. Ted can now effectively insist on his rights without undue anxiety or anger, and is able to get proper action. Indeed, Ted is liberated.

At the end of the program, his blood pressure was 138/62, which we attributed to program gains because the medication was held constant over the course of the program. Significantly, Ted's termination average score on the Type A Questionnaire was 1.8, down from the prior 2.8, showing a marked reduction in Type A characteristics. Ted is easier on himself, has lessened his perfectionism, and is imbued with much greater self-confidence. While he uses the self-hypnosis on an as-needed basis, he has incorporated most of the cognitive principles and techniques into his daily life.

Ted's case demonstrates the effectiveness of a short-term, encouragement and goal-directed individual stress-reduction program on both cognitive style and physiological symptom control, in this case hypertension. Anxiety and depression, often treated by much longer therapies, also were significantly reduced. It is important to note, however, that while Ted had chronic problems with anxiety, he was highly motivated for change and not too neurotically entrapped in secondary gain to require a much greater therapeutic time frame. The initial impetus that drove him to seek help was his hypertension, and Ted is typical of many who enter treatment for such a specific symptom disorder.

SUMMARY

While "stress" is becoming a household word, Stress Management itself is not a fad in spite of the fadlike nature of the popular emphasis on stress today. Stress research and programs for stress reduction and control will be with us for some time to come, as quality interventions serve a basic human need. In our view, Stress Management was the missing link on the path to developing a holistic, health maintenance, preventive approach to medicine and mental health. An appreciation for the function and impact of stress and the development of specific stress management techniques allows one to move parsimoniously beyond limiting and partial explanations of the human predicament as originally offered by such theories as the sickness or disease model, traditional psychodynamics, instinctual drives, and conditioning. A holistic approach demands an integration of biological, intrapsychic, social-environmental, and ecological concerns impacting on a socially imbedded individual and mediated by his ability to make choices within limits. Holism and the final authority of individual action and choice are cornerstones of the program described in this chapter.

The continual reference to our interventions as "programs" rather than a "therapy" is highly intentional; we eschew the model of "cure" and the traditional implications that accompany that concept. Another reason for the term "program" is that in this manner the intervention is delivered on a contract basic with individuals or corporations.

Because of the multifarious components of "stress," a multimodal approach is essential. While we cannot claim to do everything, our programs involve the three basic areas of physiological control, experiential cognitive restructuring, and direct educational activities with homework.

Two related areas of concern are of prime importance as we approach stress or any other popular topic. The first is research. Intervention strategies need to be based squarely on sound scientific and clinical findings, and new techniques must be thoroughly tested and evaluated in terms of outcome before one can in clear conscience declare them efficacious for the general populace. Much more research needs to be done in such settings as the home and office. The second area is ethics and protection of the public. With any popular topic there is market demand, and almost any new gimmick will attract attention and provide short-term gains. Although one cannot deny the economic aspects of addressing popular concerns, the first issue should be the production of desired and beneficial long-term changes in the client and the commitment to follow through as much as possible to insure client success. We must be prepared to service what we sell as professionals, and we must maintain high standards of program development and performance.

REFERENCES

Alexander, F. (1950). *Psychosomatic medicine: Its principles and applications.* New York: Norton.

Cobb, S., & Rose, R. (1973). Hypertension, peptic ulcer and diabetes in air traffic controllers. *Journal of the American Medical Association, 224,* 489–492.

Dreikurs, R. (1954). The psychological interview in medicine. *American Journal of Individual Psychology, 10,* 99–122.

Ellis, A. (1962). *Reasons and emotions in psychotherapy.* New York: Lyle Stuart.

Field, P. (1979). Stress reduction in hypnotherapy of chronic headache. Paper presented at the Annual Meeting of the American Psychological Association and the Society for Clinical and Experimental Hypnosis.

Frankel, F. H. (1973). The effects of brief hypnotherapy on a series of psychosomatic problems. *Psychotherapy and Psychosomatics, 22,* 264–275.

Friedman, M., & Rosenman, R. H. (1974). *Type A behavior and your heart.* New York: Fawcett.

Holmes, T. H., & Rahe, R. H. (1967). The social readjustment rating scale. *Journal of Psychosomatic Research, 11,* 213.

Lynch, J. (1977). *The broken heart.* New York: Basic Books.

Roskies, E., Spevack, M., Surkis, A., Cohen, C., & Gilman, S. (1978). Changing the coronary-prone (Type A) behavior pattern in a non-clinical population. *Journal of Behavioral Medicine.*

Schutz, W. C. (1966). *The interpersonal underworld.* Palo Alto, Calif.: Science and Behavior Books.

Wittkower, E. D. (1977). Historical perspective of contemporary psychosomatic medicine. In Z. J. Lipowski, R. Lipsitt, & P. C. Whybrow (Eds.), *Psychosomatic medicine: Current trends and clinical applications.* New York: Oxford University Press.

Chapter 65

STRUCTURED LEARNING

ROBERT P. SPRAFKIN, N. JANE GERSHAW, and ARNOLD P. GOLDSTEIN

The various therapies in this book can be classified in a number of ways. One classification may refer to the complexity of the system. For example, my own system of Immediate Therapy has a single dimension and is relatively easy to understand, but it is seriously limited relative to population. Other systems, such as Functional Psychotherapy or Multimodal Therapy, have very broad aims, wide-ranging theories, and ambitious aspirations. Structured Learning, by Robert Sprafkin, Jane Gershaw, and Arnold Goldstein, is of this latter variety: It is a total, complex, complete system.

The logic of this method seems impeccable, and its genius probably lies in the fact that it is a total system that includes in a rational order four sets of processes. The other system in this book most like this one is Nira Kfir's procedure of Impasse/Priorities.

One of the interesting aspects of Structured Learning is the absence of any cognitive-phenomenological concepts. It is a kind of no-nonsense, engineering, behavioristic, complete system for curing human problems.

I believe that the message these authors provide should be well listened to by all readers. Their concept is grand—and even a bit frightening.

Structured Learning is a behaviorally oriented, psychoeducational skill training approach for teaching a variety of interpersonal, planning, and stress management skills to a wide range of clinical and nonclinical populations. It combines four behavior change procedures in its basic training/treatment sequence: (1) modeling, (2) role playing, (3) performance feedback, and (4) transfer of training. Groups of trainees are: (1) shown numerous, specific, detailed examples (live, on audiotape, videotape, filmstrip, or film) of a person (the model) performing the skill or behaviors to be learned (i.e., modeling); (2) given considerable opportunity and encouragement to practice or rehearse the behaviors that have been modeled (i.e., role playing); (3) provided with positive feedback, social reinforcement, and corrective suggestions regarding their enactment of role plays of the modeled behaviors (i.e., performance feedback); and (4) exposed to procedures that increase the likelihood that the newly learned behaviors will be applied in an effective manner at home, at work, or elsewhere in the person's real-life environment (i.e., transfer of training).

HISTORY

Precursors

Structured Learning, like most behaviorally oriented treatments, owes its philosophical allegiance to the tradition of John Locke and the British empiricists. Within that framework, and consistent with much of academic psychology, behavior is viewed primarily as a product of the organism's experiences, and human behavior is considered to be subject to the laws of learning. Structured Learning shares with other behavioral approaches its affinity for the Lockean notion that concepts develop in a hierarchical fashion from experience, and that effective learning also takes place in an incremental, hierarchical manner (cf. Rychlak, 1973).

Another important philosophical influence on Structured Learning and many other behavioral approaches is American pragmatism. William James, John Dewey, and other pragmatists emphasized empiricism, facts, action, consequences—the practical use value of activities. James characterized this basic point of view of pragmatism, so compatible with later behavioral orientations in psychology:

"The attitude of looking away from first things, principles, 'categories,' supposed necessities; and of looking towards last things, fruits, consequences, facts" (James, 1960, p. 33).

Structured Learning, like most other behavioral forms of treatment or training, developed in the context of American psychology. A primary concern of American psychology since its formal inception in the late nineteenth century has been the understanding and enhancement of the learning process. This readiness to center upon learning processes took major therapeutic form starting in the 1950s, as psychotherapy practitioners and researchers alike came more and more to view treatment in learning terms. This joint learning–clinical focus gave birth to the behavior modification movement, with its emphases on laboratory-derived procedures, specified and specifiable treatment goals, and frequent employment of the change agent or therapist as a teacher/trainer. Behavioral approaches to treatment have clearly presented a major challenge to the more firmly entrenched medical model treatments in a variety of institutional and noninstitutional psychiatric settings.

Another historical challenge to the established medical model of treatments for institutionalized psychiatric patients, which also appears as a spiritual precurser of Structured Learning, was the moral treatment movement that began at the start of the nineteenth century. It was characterized by its humane concern for patients' welfare and its emphasis on the environment in shaping normal and abnormal behavior. The particular aspect of moral treatment that bears the closest affinity to Structured Learning was its use of a variety of formal and informal educational methods for bringing about appropriate "mental discipline" (Sprafkin, 1977).

Yet another movement serves as an important historical antecedent to Structured Learning and other psychoeducational skill training approaches. This movement was called by different names at different times; generally, it sought to influence the development of interpersonal, social, and moral behavior through the use of parenting manuals, self-improvement books, religious tracts, and a variety of other educational methods. Best known among these educational methods were Character Education, popular in the 1920s, and methods that sought to use pedagogic techniques for teaching ethical interpersonal behavior, leadership skills, group decision-making skills, and self-control. Even though that particular movement faded by the 1930s, the formal involvement of professional educators with the development of appropriate or prosocial behaviors has persisted under new forms and titles: moral education, affective education, human relations training, confluent education, and identity education. While their methods and rationales vary considerably, these approaches all share the goals of helping to foster the growth, development, and appropriate behavior of their various trainees.

Beginnings

The developers of the Structured Learning approach, Arnold P. Goldstein, Robert P. Sprafkin, and N. Jane Gershaw, each brought a unique set of interests and experiences to their collaborative effort. Arnold P. Goldstein received his degree in clinical psychology from Pennsylvania State University, where he was most strongly influenced by Donald H. Ford and William U. Snyder and their interest in psychotherapy research. He began to develop his own view of psychotherapy research, which took into account social psychology as well as clinical variables. His first book, *Therapist-Patient Expectancies in Psychotherapy* (1962), written while he was at the University of Pittsburgh Medical School, reflected his growing concern with the importance of social psychological factors in the psychotherapeutic endeavor. Shortly thereafter, he began collaborating with Kenneth Heller and Lee B. Sechrest on their encyclopedic review of social psychological research relevant to the understanding of psychotherapeutic practices. This resulted in the publication of *Psychotherapy and the Psychology of Behavior Change* (1966), which cast psychotherapy research squarely within the mainstream of empirically based investigation, and emerged as a standard text for psychotherapy researchers. Goldstein (1971) has long been concerned with the problem of making psychotherapy more relevant, attractive, and available to those who tend to underutilize such services. This preoccupation culminated in the publication of *Structured Learning Therapy: Toward a Psychotherapy for the Poor* (1973), which presented the theory, research support, and basic components of the structured learning approach.

Robert P. Sprafkin worked on his doctorate in counseling psychology at Ohio State University, where he was attracted to the teaching of Harold B. Pepinsky, then engaged in a series of investigations concerning social influence processes operating in dyadic and group communications, including psychological treatments. After completing his doctoral research (Sprafkin, 1970), he moved to Syracuse University and then to the Syracuse Veterans Administration Hospital as Coordinator of the Day Treatment Center, a day-long treatment facility for chronic psychiatric patients. There he became concerned with providing relevant treatment and training to his clientele, who typically had fared poorly in traditional verbal psychotherapeutic endeavors in the past.

N. Jane Gershaw was a student of Goldstein's at Syracuse University, and through his teaching developed a special interest in methods of group psychotherapy. In her first position after receiving her doctorate, she began supervising psychology interns and psychiatric residents at Hahnemann Medical College and Community Mental Health Center in Philadelphia in directive and skill-training-oriented groups with psychiatric patients.

In 1973 Goldstein obtained a research grant from the National Institute of Mental Health to develop concrete training techniques that paraprofessional and professional mental health workers could use in implementing Structured Learning Therapy with institutionalized psychiatric patients. At the same time, Sprafkin was using some of the behavioral components of Structured Learning Therapy, in a less systematic fashion, in his Day Treatment Center program. In addition, Gershaw was beginning to use some components with her own patients at the VA Mental Hygiene Clinic. The situation was ideal for a collaborative effort aimed at the development of specific, systematic techniques for teaching staff to work with psychiatric patients using the major components of Structured Learning Therapy. Goldstein, Sprafkin, and Gershaw agreed to embark on such a collaborative effort, which culminated in the systematic presentation of the Structured Learning Therapy approach.

CURRENT STATUS

As indicated by the title of Goldstein's book, *Structured Learning Therapy: Toward a Psychotherapy for the Poor* (1973), his aim was to develop a therapeutic approach that would be appropriate for those persons served inadequately by traditional, verbal, insight-oriented psychotherapies, which tend to be middle-class in orientation. The structured learning approach, developed for use primarily with institutionalized psychiatric patients (who tend to come from low-income backgrounds) was presented in a systematic fashion in Goldstein, Sprafkin, and Gershaw's *Skill Training for Community Living: Applying Structured Learning Therapy* (1976). This approach has been adopted widely and is currently in use in several hundred inpatient, transitional, and outpatient psychiatric treatment facilities.

It appears to be the natural history of any psychotherapeutic treatment approach that once it is used successfully with one population and/or problem area, it is rapidly applied to other populations and behavior configurations. Such was certainly the case with the attempts at the application of psychoanalysis to populations never envisioned by Freud; certainly Gestalt Therapy, Transactional Analysis, and numerous other treatment approaches have been applied to all types of persons and problems far beyond the scope of their initial usages.

So, too, appears to be the emerging pattern with Structured Learning Therapy. As the writers presented talks and training workshops to various groups, explaining the appropriateness of Structured Learning with institutionalized, low-income psychiatric patients, questions invariably arose concerning the possible application to other clinical and nonclinical populations. "What about delinquents?" "Why not use it with geriatric patients?" "How

about us 'normals'?" "Can only low-income people benefit from the techniques?" The answer to these kinds of questions is obviously "Yes, try it." But the "yes" must be a qualified one. The specific techniques, methods of presentation, and the like must be prescriptively appropriate to the population with which it is used. Rather than insisting that the therapy "works" regardless of where it is used, and that clients, trainees, or patients should be shoe-horned into the existing therapy, we take the opposite approach. That is, rather than saying, "Make the patient fit the therapy," we have attempted to modify the therapeutic offering to meet the particular characteristics of different populations: "Make the therapy fit the patient." Attempts at modification and application should, in our view, always be tied to empirical investigations (e.g., Goldstein & Stein, 1976; Goldstein et al., 1979).

THEORY

Structured Learning views behaviors as having been learned during the individual's developmental history. Major concern is with the social determinants of behaviors, which have been learned through direct or vicarious experience. As a behavioral approach, Structured Learning is not concerned with positing "inner causes"—needs, drives, or impulses. The behaviors that have been learned by an individual are more or less adaptive in enabling that person to meet life's demands and to achieve personal satisfaction. Thus, Structured Learning, as a therapy, training, or teaching method, seeks to: (1) identify the ways in which behaviors have been and may be learned and areas in which the individual is deficient; (2) identify the behaviors or skills that, if acquired, would enable the individual to achieve personal satisfaction; and (3) systematically apply effective learning principles to the task of teaching desirable behaviors.

Structured Learning views behaviors as skills acquired through learning. An individual may be more or less proficient in using these skills in meeting life's challenges. Thus, the goal of Structured Learning is to help people acquire and perfect skills. The individual's behavioral repertoire is described in terms of skill proficiencies and deficiencies, rather than using more abstract diagnostic categories. As a system concerned with the development of behavioral proficiencies, primary emphasis is placed upon effecting behavior change, rather than bringing about self-attitude change. Many approaches to psychotherapy focus primarily on helping the individual change self-attitudes—self-image, self-concept, and so forth—with the assumption that once one's attitudes about one's self change, then one's behaviors will change. By contrast, Structured Learning sees the goal of treatment or training as bringing about behavior change, which will then affect self-attitudes. Evidence suggests that the latter approach is more rapid and more likely to bring about the desired changes.

The first target population for Structured Learning Therapy was low-income, institutionalized psychiatric patients. Historically such patients have faired poorly in traditional, verbal, psychodynamic psychotherapies whose goals are generally to achieve self-attitude change and insight antecedent to any hopes for behavior change. We have argued (Goldstein, 1973; Goldstein et al., 1976) that the roots of preferences for these differing approaches may be in differing child-rearing practices in middle- versus lower- or working-class homes. Middle-class childrearing and lifestyles, with their emphases on intentions, motivation, self-control, inner states, and the like, provide excellent early training for traditional, verbal psychotherapies, should the person require such treatment in later life. Lower- (and working-) class childrearing practices and lifestyles, with their emphases on action, behavior, consequences rather than intentions, reliance on external authority, and a more restricted verbal code, ill prepare a person for appropriate participation in traditional, verbal, insight-oriented psychotherapy aimed at explorations of self-attitudes. A therapy more responsive to the stylistic characteristics of such lower- or working-class childrearing practices would have to be brief, concrete, behavioral, authoritatively administered, require imitation of specific overt examples, teach role-taking skills, and provide early, frequent, and continuous reinforcement for the performance of appropriate behaviors.

We wished to develop a psychotherapy that capitalized upon the learning style characteristics and preferred channels of accessibility of the abovementioned target population, so that the therapy could prescriptively "fit the patient," instead of vice versa. Thus the four major components of Structured Learning—modeling, role playing, social reinforcement, and transfer of training—were combined in an attempt to meet this prescriptive goal. Structured Learning has also been applied to other populations, with modifications in the treatment and training procedures to meet the particular stylistic requirements of each population.

Modeling, or learning by observation and imitation, has been demonstrated as an effective method for learning new behaviors. Such behaviors as self-assertion, self-disclosure, helping others, empathic behavior, plus literally dozens of others, have been learned through modeling. In addition to being a powerful technique for teaching new behaviors, research has demonstrated that already learned behaviors can be strengthened or weakened through modeling.

Laboratory research has identified a number of characteristics of modeling displays that make it likely that the modeled behavior will be imitated by the observer. These "modeling enhancers" include characteristics of: (1) the model, (2) the display itself, and (3) the observer or learner.

1. Greater modeling has been shown to occur when the model is: highly skilled; of high status; friendly; of the same sex, age, and socioeconomic status as the observer; and rewarded for the behavior in question.

2. Concerning the modeling display, to increase modeling effects, the behaviors to be imitated should be shown clearly, with little irrelevant detail, in order from least to most difficult behaviors, and with several different models performing the behaviors to be learned.

3. The observer or learner characteristics that serve to enhance modeling are complementary to those described under the category of model characteristics. Greater modeling tends to occur when the observer is told to imitate the model, likes the model, is similar to the model in background or other important characteristics, and is rewarded for imitating the modeled behavior.

If modeling is so effective, why go beyond modeling to other training procedures? Albert Bandura (1977) states that the learning effects of modeling can be enhanced through procedures that allow the learner to rehearse or practice what has been observed. In addition, many modeling effects are only short-lived. Perry (1970) and Sutton (1970), among others, have demonstrated that modeling effects that occur immediately after training often disappear in a very short time. For learning to be lasting, the individual must be exposed to procedures that enable him or her to practice what has been modeled, receive feedback on this practice, and, most important, encourage use of the newly learned skills in real-life situations.

Role playing, the second major component of Structured Learning, is defined as practice or behavioral rehearsal of a skill for later real-life use of that skill. Research evidence supports the value of role playing in order to effect behavior as well as attitude change. Several role-play enhancers have been identified that make learning through role playing more likely and make the effects of such learning more lasting. These enhancers include: voluntary participation by the role player, role player commitment to behavior or attitude being enacted, role player improvisation of enactment, and reinforcement of the role player following the enactment.

Research has demonstrated the effectiveness of role playing in training such attitudes and behaviors as assertion (McFall & Marston, 1970), empathy (Staub, 1971), moral judgment (Arbuthnot, 1975), and a variety of interpersonal skills (Rathjen, Heneker, & Rathjen, 1976). However, several studies have added a note of caution to the research on role playing. Lichtenstein, Keutzer, and Himes (1969) found in three studies that the effects of role playing on reducing smoking behavior were only short-lived. Hollander (1970) found no change in a number of patient psychotherapy interview behaviors as a function of role playing. Thus, as with modeling, role playing alone appears to be insufficient to effect lasting behavior change. Role playing provides the learner with practice but does not provide a good example or demonstration of the behavior to be learned prior to such practice. This example can be provided through modeling (e.g., Bandura, 1977). But even these procedures, taken together, do not provide the learner with the motivation or incentive to behave differently. This incentive component is the third major procedure of Structured Learning.

Performance feedback involves providing the learner with information following the role-play enactment of the skill. It may include social or material reinforcement, criticism, reteaching, or other instruction. We have placed heaviest emphasis on social reinforcement as a useful form of feedback. Such reinforcement is provided as the trainee's role-play behavior becomes more similar to the skill behaviors modeled earlier.

Research highlights a number of rules of reinforcement that determine the potency of the effect of reinforcement. We have learned that: the type of reinforcement (material, social, etc.) should be flexible and consistent with the needs and reinforcement history of the trainee; reinforcement should follow immediately after the desired behavior; the contingent relationship between the desired behavior and the reinforcement should be clear to the trainee; generally, the larger the reward the greater the likelihood of a positive effect on performance; the desired behavior should occur with sufficient frequency that opportunity for reinforcement is provided; and reinforcement that is provided intermittently is more resistant to extinction than reinforcement provided every time the desired behavior occurs.

Modeling, role playing, and reinforcement, when taken together, comprise a powerful skill-training program. When one adds to this the fourth component of Structured Learning, transfer of training, a critical element of training is added. This element deals with real-life use of what has been learned in the training setting. Transfer of training consists of a set of procedures designed to encourage such real-life use. These transfer-enhancement procedures or principles include providing the trainee with: sufficient opportunity to practice correct use of the skill so that the new response will be more available or, in effect, overlearned; a training setting having many identical elements or characteristics shared with the application setting; and stimulus variability or a variety of interpersonal stimuli in the training setting that will later serve as cues for the desired behavior outside of the training setting.

These four behavioral techniques—modeling, role playing, performance feed-back, and transfer of training—comprise the structured learning approach.

METHODOLOGY

Generally, a group of 6 to 12 patient/trainees, selected on the basis of shared skill deficits, led by two trainers, are presented first with live or recorded modeling displays of the skill to be learned. Each skill is broken down into a series of behavioral steps, or "learning points." Each modeling display depicts a model successfully performing a skill by enacting various behavioral steps. Content for the modeling displays should be relevant to the trainees' lives, so that they can identify with the situation being modeled. In the modeling displays, repetition is relied upon to maximize learning. Ideally the actors who serve as models are as similar as possible to the patient/trainees in terms of age, sex, apparent socioeconomic status, and other relevant dimensions. In each modeling display the model is depicted as successful in using the skill and receives social reinforcement for such effective skill use.

Once the patients/trainees have been exposed to the modeling displays, the trainers stimulate discussion of the modeled skill. Also, each trainee in the group is given a chance to enact the skill via content relevant to his or her own life. Other trainees in the group will play the roles of significant others in the main actor's life. To maximize transfer of training, a great deal of emphasis is placed upon "setting the stage" in the role play. Here the trainer asks the main actor to describe in detail the persons and places involved in his or her real-life problem situation. In keeping with the transfer principle of identical elements, trainees are encouraged to use any props or equipment to help simulate the application setting. Such setting of the stage is also helpful in assisting trainees who think concretely to begin to engage in the rather difficult activity of role taking. Once the stage is set, the trainees enact the skill. The main actor, co-actor, and observers are given cards on which are written the behavioral steps of the skill being enacted. The observers, usually consisting of the trainees who are not involved in the role play, are asked to attend to how well the main actor follows the steps and performs the skill. The trainers provide any added instruction or prompting required by the actors.

After each role play, the main actor receives for social reinforcement and performance feedback comments from the observing trainees and co-actors on how well he or she executed the role play. The trainers also provide the main actor with feedback on the performance. Trainees are instructed to keep a behavioral focus during this phase of the group. If indicated, a particular scene may be re-role played after corrective feedback is given. In a forthright effort at transfer of training as the last step in each group session, the trainer provides each trainee with an opportunity to practice the newly learned material in his or her real life environment. With the aid of a variety of homework forms, trainees who have role played are asked to sign a written contract to practice the new skill at a particular time and with a particular person before the next group session. Having done this, trainees complete the rest of the form, indicating the outcome of their efforts, and report back to the group at the next meeting. After the assignment of homework, the group session ends.

We recognize that unless there is some real-life reward to the trainee for using his or her new skill—unless the people with whom the trainee tries the skill respond in a positive way—it is unlikely that the new behavior will be sustained. Therefore, it is often helpful to enlist the aid of outside people—family members, ward personnel, teachers—and to instruct them in how to respond when the trainee initiates the new behavior in the real-life situation.

Not all significant others in trainees' lives are willing or able to provide the necessary social reinforcement to help make the trainee's new behavior become established, however. Persons with whom trainees work and live may even actively resist trainees' efforts of behavior change. For these reasons, it has been shown to be use-ful to include in later transfer-of-training procedures a method through which trainees can learn to be their own independent self-rewarders. That is, following initial role play and homework efforts, a program of self-reinforcement can be instituted. Trainees can be instructed in the nature of self-reinforcement and encouraged to "say something and do something nice for yourself" if they practice their new skill well.

Applications

In Structured Learning behaviors are viewed as skills, and individuals may be described as more or less proficient in their use of these skills. In developing a comprehensive set of skills for adult psychiatric patients, an attempt was made to include those skills cited in the professional literature as well as by practitioners and psychiatric patients themselves as important for daily functioning in the community. The final list was thus derived from research findings plus surveys of mental health workers and of psychiatric patients. Subsequent to administration and compilation of these materials, the list of Basic Skills found in Table 65.1 was developed.

Table 65.1 Structured Learning Basic Skills for Adults.

Conversations: Beginning Skills

1. Starting a conversation
2. Carrying on a conversation
3. Ending a conversation
4. Listening

Conversations: Expressing Oneself

5. Expressing a compliment
6. Expressing appreciation
7. Expressing encouragement
8. Asking for help
9. Giving instructions
10. Expressing affection
11. Expressing a complaint
12. Persuading others
13. Expressing anger

Conversations: Responding to Others

14. Responding to praise
15. Responding to the feelings of others (empathy)
16. Apologizing
17. Following instructions
18. Responding to persuasion
19. Responding to failure
20. Responding to contradictory messages
21. Responding to a complaint
22. Responding to anger

Planning Skills

23. Setting a goal
24. Gathering information
25. Concentrating on a task
26. Evaluating your abilities
27. Preparing for a stressful conversation
28. Setting priorities
29. Decision making

Alternatives to Aggression

30. Identifying and labeling your emotions
31. Determining responsibility
32. Making requests
33. Relaxation
34. Self-control
35. Negotiation
36. Helping others
37. Assertiveness

Table 65.2   Typical Behavioral Steps.

Starting a Conversation

Learning points:

1. Choose the right place and time.
2. Greet the other person.
3. Make small talk.
4. Judge if the other person is listening and wants to talk with you.
5. Open the main topic you want to talk about.

Negotiation

Learning points:

1. State your position.
2. State your understanding of the other person's position.
3. Ask if the other person agrees with your statement of his or her position.
4. Listen openly to his or her response.
5. Propose a compromise.

Each skill is broken down into its constituent behavioral steps. These steps are based upon behavioral analysis and experimental evidence from the literature. Trainers and/or trainees can assess (via checklists or behavior observation methods) trainees' observed or felt proficiencies or deficiencies in the various skills. The skills, their behavioral steps, and related information appear in Goldstein, Sprafkin, and Gershaw (1976). Examples of behavioral steps are found in Table 65.2.

Structured Learning has been used to teach a variety of interpersonal, aggression-control, planning, and stress management skills to adolescents in both regular schools and residential treatment settings. While some of the skills developed for adult psychiatric patients were used, a substantial number of new skills had to be added. In some instances the wording and complexity of the behavioral steps were modified. Skills developed for use with adolescents are listed in Table 65.3.

In addition to altering the list of skills to be taught, other procedural modifications were made to prescriptively meet the training needs of adolescents. One such change was in the mode of presentation of the modeling displays. While adult psychiatric patients are typically passive and able to attend to audiotaped modeling displays, youngsters seem to require more action, more vivid examples, including visual as well as auditory cues. Thus, an attempt was made to present active models live, on videotape, or on filmstrip.

Another modification used with teenagers attempts to capitalize on the power and attractiveness of natural peer leaders. Such peer leaders clearly have much more influence and sustained contact than any adult could hope for. It is often possible to take advantage of the peer leader's influence by having the (adult) trainer employ the peer leader as a co-trainer in some structured learning sessions. The peer leader must, of course, be trained, follow the sequence of procedures, and be relatively competent in the particular skill being taught. The specific techniques developed for use with teenagers are described in detail in *Skillstreaming the Adolescent: A Structured Learning Approach to Teaching Prosocial Skills* (Goldstein et al., 1980).

The structured learning approach also has been applied to training police officers. The complexity of police work is only slowly coming to public awareness. With this awareness comes the recognition of the need for training in such difficult interpersonal tasks as handling family disputes, hostage negotiations, and crisis intervention. Structured learning techniques have been used to train police officers in these areas (Goldstein et al., 1977; Miron & Goldstein, 1978). Geriatric patients have been a recent target population for the application of Structured Learning. Sensitized to the interpersonal skill deficits of institutionalized geriatric patients by practitioners working with such patients, Lopez and associates (1980) conducted a series of studies to see how much repetition in role playing was optimal for facilitating skill acquisition. These studies demonstrated the prescriptive application of the structured learning approach, whereby the manner of presentation of the components is modified to meet the needs of the population.

We have also recently modified the manner of presentation of the structured learning components so that general audiences seeking to improve their social skillfulness might do so by using Structured Learning on a self-help basis (Goldstein, Sprafkin, & Gershaw, 1979). In this adaptation, *modeling* is presented through written examples that illustrate effective skill use; *role playing* is self-administered (e.g., tape recorded) or accomplished with the help of a trusted friend; *feedback* is accomplished through self-critique, observed reactions of others, and/or requested evaluations from friends; and *transfer* is effected using a variety of practice assignments, contracts, and self-reward systems.

In addition to the populations listed above, Structured Learning also has been used with child-abusing parents, with the goal of helping them develop self-control, parenting, marital, and peer relationship skills; with managers in industry, with the aim of developing effective supervisory skills (Goldstein & Sorcher, 1973); and, most recently, in teaching interpersonal skills to youngsters with learning disabilities and to youngsters and adults considered to be mildly to moderately retarded.

CASE EXAMPLE

The following case is intended as a composite illustration of the application of the structured learning ap-

Table 65.3 Structured Learning skills for adolescents.

Beginning Social Skills

1. Listening
2. Starting a conversation
3. Having a conversation
4. Asking a question

5. Saying thank you
6. Introducing yourself
7. Introducing other people
8. Giving a compliment

Advanced Social Skills

9. Asking for help
10. Joining in
11. Giving instructions

12. Following instructions
13. Apologizing
14. Convincing others

Skills for Dealing with Feelings

15. Knowing your feelings
16. Expressing your feelings
17. Understanding the feelings of others
18. Dealing with someone else's anger

19. Expressing affection
20. Dealing with fear
21. Rewarding yourself

Skill Alternatives to Aggression

22. Asking permission
23. Sharing something
24. Helping others
25. Negotiation
26. Using self-control

27. Standing up for your rights
28. Responding to teasing
29. Avoiding trouble with others
30. Keeping out of fights

Skills for Dealing with Stress

31. Making a complaint
32. Answering a complaint
33. Sportsmanship after the game
34. Dealing with embarrassment
35. Dealing with being left out
36. Standing up for a friend

37. Responding to persuasion
38. Responding to failure
39. Dealing with contradictory messages
40. Dealing with an accusation
41. Getting ready for a difficult conversation
42. Dealing with group pressure

Planning Skills

43. Deciding on something to do
44. Deciding what caused a problem
45. Setting a goal
46. Deciding on your abilities

47. Gathering information
48. Arranging problems by importance
49. Making a decision
50. Concentrating on a task

proach with an adult psychiatric patient. The person described is fairly typical of those individuals who have developed a "revolving door" career of frequent psychiatric hospitalizations, inpatient stays ranging from a few days or weeks to several months, and only limited success at community tenure.

Frank W. is a 48-year-old single man, the second of three children in a working-class family. He grew up in a medium-sized city in the northeastern part of the United States. Frank's teachers described him as withdrawn and fearful. He quit high school during eleventh grade to go to work. Schoolwork never appealed to him, he had no friends, and money was needed at home. After taking a couple of unskilled jobs, he enlisted in the army. Following an honorable discharge from the service, Frank took

a job on a factory assembly line in another part of the country. He lived in furnished rooms, had no friends and no outside hobbies or interests. He quickly lost contact with his family, except for occasional letters from his older brother.

After two years of fairly steady employment, economic conditions changed and Frank found himself out of work. He became more seclusive and felt confused and overwhelmed by various problems. He was hospitalized for the first time in a state psychiatric facility. In the 20-odd years that have passed since that first hospitalization, Frank seldom spent more than a year outside of a state or Veterans Administration psychiatric hospital. Typically he would become overwhelmed by a variety of environmental stresses—financial problems, conflicts with landlords, run-ins with shop foremen—and he would seek hospitalization. Generally he was given the diagnosis of "schizophrenia, chronic undifferentiated." When hospitalized, Frank would usually receive psychotropic medications and custodial treatments; he had not done well with a few attempts at verbal, insight-oriented psychotherapies.

Frank was seen at a Veterans Administration Day Treatment Center, having been referred upon discharge from an inpatient psychiatric facility. The referral information from the hospital indicated that Frank had been an inpatient for three months, tended toward withdrawal and seclusiveness, but no longer needed inpatient care. Frank was accompanied to the day treatment center by his older brother, with whom he was living until other arrangements could be made. The brother indicated that he was Frank's only remaining family, but that he and his wife could not keep him indefinitely. The brother also stated that he managed Frank's money, and that both he and his wife had come to accept Frank's "illness" and tried not to put too many demands on him.

During the initial interview at the center, Frank's brother did most of the talking. Questions directed at Frank were answered by yes or no. He avoided eye contact with the interviewer. The interviewer explained the day treatment center program to Frank and his brother (e.g., Sprafkin, Gershaw, & Goldstein, 1978). The program was set up using a psychoeducational training model, with a variety of classes in social skills and self-management areas. Frank passively agreed to a schedule of classes, which included several in Structured Learning.

Before Frank and his brother left the center, one of the structured learning trainers met with them to explain what would be going on in the structured learning classes. The trainer asked both Frank and his brother to indicate which skills each thought Frank needed help with. While Frank was shown the rest of the center, the trainer explained further to the brother how he (the brother) and his wife might be helpful in fostering Frank's anticipated progress in the classes. The brother was given some written descriptions of the program and an open invitation to remain in contact with the trainer.

Frank was placed in a structured learning class with seven other trainees who were all, by their own and others' reports, deficient in "Basic Conversational Skills." During the first class session the new members of the class were introduced and were then acquainted with the structured learning procedures. The trainer suggested that the class get right to work on practicing the skill of "Starting a Conversation." He then played several audiotaped modeling vignettes, each depicting actors starting conversations successfully by following a series of behavioral steps, or "learning points." The trainers

then opened up a discussion of the taped examples, and a few members of the class volunteered that a couple of the situations reminded them of when they had had difficulty in initiating conversations. The trainer asked Frank if any of the modeling displays reminded him of situations that were problematic for him, and Frank admitted, reluctantly, that he was very uncomfortable starting conversations with certain clerks in stores. The trainer then proceeded to lead the various trainees in role plays of some of the situations they had described. After the role plays, the trainees were provided with feedback, and, finally, those who had been the main actors were given specific "homework assignments" for real-life practice of the skill.

During the second meeting of the class Frank was given an opportunity to role play. He was extremely hesitant and anxious at first, but with encouragement from the trainer and other trainees he assented. He chose another trainee who reminded him of a clerk in his neighborhood grocery store. With a good deal of coaching from the trainer, he completed the role play and received helpful, favorable feedback from the other trainees. As his homework assignment he agreed to start a conversation with the actual clerk, which he did that very day. Fortunately, the clerk was very helpful, and Frank returned to his next class eager to report on his accomplishment.

After practicing a number of other conversational skills, with increasingly more active participation on Frank's part, the class addressed the skill of "Making Requests." In the discussion following the modeling displays, Frank said that he found it extremely difficult to make requests of others, and in particular to make requests of his brother, who, after all, "took care of him." He stated that he would like to ask his brother to allow him to manage his own money, as he now felt competent to do so. As he was eager to deal with the problem, he was the first to role play this skill. He chose as a co-actor another trainee whom he felt resembled his brother. He proceeded to role play "Making a Request," with the content dealing with his money management. While Frank's performance was quite adequate, he did not yet feel confident enough to try the skill with his brother. Rather, as a homework assignment he agreed to make a request of the secretary of the center, a person and situation he felt to be less threatening. During the next class he reported that his encounter with the secretary had been successful, and that perhaps he was ready to try the skill with his brother. The brother, who had maintained contact with the center and was generally aware of Frank's growing desire for financial independence, responded to Frank's attempt in a guardedly positive way, much to Frank's delight.

Frank continued to attend structured learning classes

at the center for several months following the incident described above. During that time he was able to begin discussing with his brother his desire to live independently and secure employment, at least on a part-time basis. After several months Frank was in fact able to master the skills necessary to find a job and to move into his own small apartment. At that point his contact with the center tapered off to occasional social visits.

SUMMARY

Structured Learning is a psychoeducational, skill-training approach for teaching a range of interpersonal, planning, and stress-management skills to a variety of clinical and nonclinical populations. Its roots lie both in education and psychology, with a clear commitment to the incorporation of sound, empirically based principles of learning into training methods that are readily comprehensible to different types of trainees.

Structured Learning is basically a group technique whose major components are modeling, role playing, performance feedback, and transfer of training. While each of these components individually appears to be necessary for learning to occur, their use in combination has been shown to greatly enhance the likelihood of the acquisition and performance of new behavioral skills.

Structured Learning is not conceived of as a static entity, which once described must remain unchanged. The approach began as a psychotherapy tailored to the treatment needs of chronic, institutionalized, low-income psychiatric patients and, in relatively few years, has been adapted and applied to a number of other groups of trainees. It is the authors' hope that the structured learning approach will be creatively and prescriptively adapted to the particular training needs and learning styles of each target population.

The other major goal that remains in the development of Structured Learning is to increase the likelihood that what is learned in the training setting will in fact transfer effectively to real-life applications. Much research has yet to be done in this regard, although much progress has already been made. The challenge lies, however, in helping a variety of trainees to learn *and to apply* the skills they feel they need in order to live productive, satisfying lives.

REFERENCES

Arbuthnot, J. (1975). Modification of moral judgment through role playing. *Developmental Psychology, 11,* 319–324.

Bandura, A. (1977). *Social learning theory.* Englewood Cliffs, NJ: Prentice-Hall.

Goldstein, A. P. (1962). *Therapist-patient expectancies in psychotherapy.* New York: Pergamon.

Goldstein, A. P. (1971). *Psychotherapeutic attraction.* New York: Pergamon.

Goldstein, A. P. (1973). *Structured learning therapy: Toward a psychotherapy for the poor.* New York: Academic Press.

Goldstein, A. P., Heller, K., & Sechrest, L. B. (1966). *Psychotherapy and the psychology of behavior change.* New York: Wiley.

Goldstein, A. P., Monti, P. J., Sardino, T., & Green, D. (1977). *Police crisis intervention.* New York: Pergamon.

Goldstein, A. P., & Sorcher, M. (1973). *Changing supervisor behavior.* New York: Pergamon.

Goldstein, A. P., Sprafkin, R. P., & Gershaw, N. J. (1976). *Skill training for community living: Applying structured learning therapy.* New York: Pergamon.

Goldstein, A. P., Sprafkin, R. P., & Gershaw, N. J. (1979). *I know what's wrong, but I don't know what to do about it.* Englewood Cliffs, NJ: Prentice-Hall.

Goldstein, A. P., Sprafkin, R. P., Gershaw, N. J., & Klein, P. (1980). *Skillstreaming the adolescent: A structured learning approach to teaching prosocial skills.* Urbana, IL: Research Press.

Goldstein, A. P., & Stein, N. (1976). *Prescriptive psychotherapies.* New York: Pergamon.

Hollander, T. G. (1970). The effects of role playing on attraction, disclosure and attitude change in a psychotherapy analogue. Ph.D. dissertation. Syracuse University.

James, W. (1960). What pragmatism means. In M. R. Konvitz & G. Kennedy (Eds.), *The American pragmatists.* New York: Meridian Books.

Lichtenstein, E., Keutzer, C. S., & Himes, K. H. (1969). Emotional role playing and changes in smoking attitudes and behaviors. *Psychological Reports, 23,* 379–387.

Lopez, M. A., Hoyer, W. J., Goldstein, A. P., Gershaw, N. J., & Sprafkin, R. P. (1980). Effects of overlearning and incentive on the acquisition and transfer of interpersonal skills with institutionalized elderly. *Journal of Gerontology, 35,* 403–409.

McFall, R. M., & Marston, A. R. (1970). An experimental investigation of behavior rehearsal in assertive training. *Journal of Abnormal Psychology, 76,* 295–303.

Miron, M., & Goldstein, A. P. (1978). *Hostage.* New York: Pergamon.

Perry, M. A. (1970). Didactic instructions for and modeling of empathy. Ph.D. dissertation. Syracuse University.

Rathjen, D., Heneker, A., & Rathjen, E. (1976). Incorporation of behavioral techniques in a game format to teach children social skills. Paper presented at the Association for Advancement of Behavior Therapy, New York.

Rychlak, J. F. (1973). *Introduction to personality and psychotherapy.* Boston: Houghton.

Sprafkin, R. P. (1970). Communicator expertness and changes in word meanings in psychological treatment. *Journal of Counseling Psychology, 17*(3), 191–196.

Sprafkin, R. P. (1977). The rebirth of moral treatment. *Professional Psychology, 8*(2), 161–169.

Sprafkin, R. P., Gershaw, N. J., & Goldstein, A. P. (1978). Teaching interpersonal skills to psychiatric outpatients: Using structured learning therapy in a community-based setting. *Journal of Rehabilitation, 44*(2), 26–29.

Staub, E. (1971). The use of role playing and induction in children's learning of helping and sharing behavior. *Child Development, 42,* 805–816.

Sutton, K. (1970). Effects of modeled empathy and structured social class upon level of therapist displayed empathy. Masters thesis. Syracuse University.

Chapter 66

THOUGHT FIELD THERAPY

ROGER J. CALLAHAN and MONICA G. PIGNOTTI

This system is probably the most outlandish in this book. I finally accepted it after two rejections, when at my request Dr. Callahan took on a collaborator. Then I asked for the names of some American Psychological Association members who would support the system. Gale L. Joslin, Ph.D. and Gail Zivin, Ph.D. each wrote attesting to their use of TFT and its value to them. After I had accepted it, in the APA Monitor (December 1999) an item appeared stating that APA's Continuing Professional Education Committee determined that TFT did not meet its definition of an appropriate continuing education curriculum for psychologists—but did not say that TFT could not be offered. I called two psychotherapists in this book and they both laughed in derision when I read some of the claims made for TFT.

The senior author is a member of APA in good standing and has published at least ten items, but none in APA publications. He claims that thousands of therapists all over the world are trying the system and finding it very helpful. His criterion of success is something called Heart Rate Variability. I checked with a physician who replied that she knew of the condition but had no knowledge of its relation to psychotherapy.

What is to be made of TFT? It is either one of the greatest advances in psychotherapy or it is a hoax. If the latter, the prime victim of the system is none other than Dr. Callahan. I can not vote on the subject either way, relying instead on independent, objective evaluations of his claims. I don't doubt his sincerity. My guess is that as in the case of Anton Mesmer and hypnosis, a committee in Paris decided (Benjamin Franklin was on the committee) that the cure was real but the condition imaginary.

DEFINITION

Thought Field Therapy (TFT) is a rapid method of treating psychological problems, usually requiring only a matter of minutes. Immediately following a successful TFT treatment, the client reports that no trace of a previously emotionally distressing issue remains. TFT does not require the painful exposure and reliving of traumatic experiences common in other trauma treatments; it either helps or it does nothing.

TFT proposes and demonstrates, through the results of its procedures, that the ancient acupuncture meridian system provides the basis for the control system for disturbing emotions and more generally, for healing. However, while TFT does utilize the meridians of acupuncture, the resemblance ends there. Unlike acupuncture, TFT employs a diagnostic procedure I (Roger Callahan) have gradually developed, based upon my clinical observations over a period of years. Furthermore, it is critical that the diagnosis and treatment be done while the client is thinking about the specific problem to be addressed.

The diagnostic procedure determines which meridian points are to be stimulated and in precisely what sequence, as well as detecting any blocks in the person's energy system that will prevent a treatment from being effective, which can then be easily corrected. Because we are dealing directly with what we believe to be the control system and thus the root cause for all disturbing emotions, I call my method of diagnosis, *Causal Diagnosis*. Each treatment point in the diagnosed sequence is stimulated (usually by tapping), which results in the client's report that the emotional distress is completely gone. (See Theory section for an elaboration on the principles described here.)

HISTORY

Throughout my long psychotherapy career, I have been searching for faster, more effective procedures. Two decades ago a psychiatrist colleague introduced me to a muscle testing procedure. This procedure originated from a chiropractic specialty called Applied Kinesiology (AK), discovered and developed by George Goodheart, DC (Walther, 1988).

Two decades ago, my colleague asked me to think of something upsetting. Then he asked me to hold out my arm, extending it to the side. He then pressed down on it and asked me to try to hold my arm up while resisting his pressure as well as I could. I found that I could not hold my arm up against his pressure while holding the upsetting thought. Prior to thinking the upsetting thoughts, he pressed even harder on my arm and I had no trouble holding it up. My first reaction to this experience was to recall my days as a professor of psychology. This was the best demonstration of mind/body interaction I had ever seen! I began to wonder if an arm that was strong when thinking of a problem might indicate a reduction of the problem. This thought paved the way for the discoveries to come.

The Discovery of Psychological Reversal (pr)

I began doing the muscle test described above on all my clients' arms (this was in 1979) and soon I observed something very interesting—my *most difficult clients' arms did not get weak* when they thought about their problem, as it did for most people. Instead, their arms got weak when I asked them to think about getting over their problem! Because this was a reversal from the norm, I called this condition of a weak muscle while thinking of getting over the problem *psychological reversal* (Callahan, 1981). The *reversal* part of the name is straightforward, but the *psychological* part indicated that the person must think of a specific problem when being tested in order to show this highly specific reaction. I later found that the reversal blocked an otherwise effective treatment, and when I found a treatment for this condition my success rate increased dramatically.

My First Case Treated with "TFT"

My first case treated with this procedure (Callahan, 1996) was in 1980 with a middle-aged woman, Mary, who had suffered from an extremely severe phobia of water all of her life. I had been treating her with cognitive therapy, systematic desensitization, clinical hypnosis, client-centered therapy, systematic relaxation, and rational-emotive therapy for a year and a half. After a year and a half, Mary was able to sit by the side of the pool and dangle her feet in the water. This was a huge advance because she wouldn't go near the pool prior to this year and a half of work. However, she still suffered horribly when doing this; she still could not look at the water, she had a splitting headache after each session, and the nightmares which she had several times a week (about water getting her) continued.

Mary had stated to me repeatedly that every time she thought about water, she got a horrible feeling in the pit of her stomach. I was experimenting with this muscle testing procedure and the test suggested that I might try tapping under her eye (the eye, according to acupuncture theory, is the end point to the stomach meridian). This was the beginning of my causal diagnostic procedure. I asked her to gently tap under her eye and when she did so, she immediately told me that her problem was gone. I treated her at my home because I had a pool there. I naturally didn't believe her, and asked her to go to the pool. Much to my shock and surprise, she ran to the pool, and this scared me. I shouted at her and she turned, saw my fear, laughed and said, "Dr. Callahan, don't worry, I know I don't know how to swim and I am not going to jump in that pool!" This reassured me and she proved beyond any doubt that her lifelong phobia was gone in that instant. I have followed up on her for two decades and there has been no recurrence of the fear and no more nightmares ever since the moment she did the treatment (Callahan, 1997c).

Naturally, I immediately tried this simple treatment on the rest of my client population and did not get the same overwhelming response. Over the years, I continued adding treatments, through my growing discoveries in causal diagnosis, that gradually increased my success rate.

As I improved upon this treatment so that greater numbers of people with phobias were helped, I wrote a book called *Five Minute Phobia Cure* (Callahan, 1985). Many are surprised to learn that the title, as astonishing as it sounds, was actually a modest title, for many were cured in one minute or less. I had been interested in treating phobias since 1950 (Callahan, 1955) and until I made this discovery, I never used the word "cure." However, by any reasonable definition of the word, cure is precisely what the treatment typically accomplishes.

As a result of using the word "cure," I was investigated for a span of about four years by the California Psychology Board. Finally, they sent a professional investigator to my office and she spent a whole day looking over my records, videos, and audio tapes and interviewing me. She was a professional investigator and not a psychologist.

As she was getting ready to leave, she asked, "You really can cure such problems?" I reminded her of the evidence she had been perusing, and she said, "Can you help me with my driving problem?" She had severe anxiety over driving, and she had to drive hours to get back to her office. I said I would be glad to help her but she would have to let me record and use the result. She agreed and I cured her problem in a few minutes. She had a cell phone and I told her to call me if any problem arose while she was driving. She had no further problem.

Months later, the board sent out two psychologists who informed me that the charges were being dropped but they made a curious request. One of them said, "We now know that you can cure problems, but would you mind not using that word, or downplay it?" I can only surmise that they felt that it would offend "serious" professionals who evidently are sensitive about such matters. The American Psychological Association Scientific Directorate reported that it was impossible to cure problems (Adler, 1993). It surprises me that so many professionals show no interest in learning how to do the cure after they learn that it is for real.

CURRENT STATUS

More and more therapists are trying TFT and finding it very helpful. There are thousands of therapists in the US, the UK, France, Germany, Spain, Norway, Japan, Australia, Canada, Singapore, and many other places who are using TFT. Those who take care to do the procedures correctly typically report to me that they have obtained a rapid and complete response. In fact, it is a clear indicator that correct procedure is not being used if the success rate is low.

A Clinical Study Replicated 10 Years Later

The following are the results of a clinical study (Callahan, 1987; Leonoff, 1995) done using the most advanced form of TFT, known as the Voice Technology (see Theory section for a fuller description). The first study was done by me in 1985–1986 and the results were replicated 10 years later by a student in training (Leonoff, 1995). Because the TFT Voice Technology can be done over the telephone, we were able to treat individuals suffering from phobias and anxiety who called into radio shows asking for help.

To minimize selective bias in the analysis of these results, all people who called in were treated and included in the analysis, including those individuals whose treatments were cut short due to time constraints. Audio tapes of all treatments from both studies were made and are available for review.

The SUD Scale

In our practice of TFT and in this study, we define a "successful" treatment as the client's reporting complete elimination of all traces of emotional distress. To measure this, we use the Subjective Units of Distress scale (SUD), originally developed by psychologist Joseph Wolpe (1969). The person is asked to rate their distress on a scale of 1–10, where 10 is the worst it could possibly be and 1 is no trace of emotional distress. An 11-point scale of 0–10 can also be used; it makes no difference which is used, as long as the therapist clearly establishes this with the client.

For those who may be dubious about SUD, it should be kept in mind that with TFT we have internal checks, such as the fact that clients report big changes in the SUD even when they are not aware that this is what is supposed to happen. We also have the HRV data (see section below), which provides scientific evidence of the deep biological effects of these treatments. Personally, however, I believe that there is no substitute for client's report (as provided by giving an SUD).

We find that due to the fact that such results as reported here are foreign to and unheard of by most professionals, cognitive dissonance appears to take place (see section on "Apex Problem" for a fuller description of this phenomenon). Please view Table 66.1 (Callahan

Table 66.1   Treatment of Individuals Suffering From Phobias and Anxiety on Call-In Radio Shows

	Original (1985–1986)	Replication (1995)
Number of radio shows	23	36
Number treated	68*	68
Successful	66	66
Unsuccessful	2	2
Success Rate	97%	97%
Average SUD (pre-therapy)	8.35 (10 = point scale)	8.19 (11 = point scale)
Average SUD (post-therapy)	2.10 (1 = best possible)	1.58 (0 = best)
Average Time (minutes)	4.34	6.04

[Includes all talk and explanation to the end of treatment.]

*In Callahan's study a breakdown was done to provide a measure of the effect of treatment in an actual exposure situation. In talking on the radio the individuals were engaged in public speaking. Fear of public speaking is the most common fear and 11 subjects treated in this study suffered from this fear. The average SUD before treatment = 8.8; after treatment = 1.9. The average time for this subgroup, including description of the problem, diagnosis, and explaining the unfamiliar treatment, was 5.16 minutes. All 11 of the subjects were helped dramatically in this reality test of the treatment. The high success rate of this small subsample does not imply that the brief treatment will cure everyone of this common phobia; if the N were higher for this subgroup, some failure could be counted upon, especially within the time constraints of radio shows.

& Callahan, 1996; Leonoff, 1995) below carefully and keep in mind that it is very easy for our trainees to reproduce the astonishing results to anyone's satisfaction.

Stephen Daniel, Ph.D. (1998) reports still another clinical study. Using VT, he treated 214 therapists attending TFT trainings who presented problems that did not respond to other therapy procedures, including the ordinarily effective TFT algorithms. This group had an average pre-therapy SUD of 7.74 and an average post-therapy SUD of 1.11 (where 1 indicates no distress or pain at all). The average time for diagnosis and treatment per person was 4.98 minutes. The success rate is comparable to the two previous independent clinical studies reported in Table I above.

Success Rate and Prediction

The total number of individuals included in these three independent success rate reports of people treated in public equals 352, and since that time, additional therapists (Graham, 1998; Pignotti, 1999) have reported nearly identical success rates. It should be kept in mind that the success rate, as shown in this data, takes place in minutes and is a scientific prediction. More than that, it is a prediction that is unexpected, since it goes against all conventional knowledge. This prediction is used with clients *who do not believe in the treatment,* and also with therapists administering the treatments who are skeptical. Our predictions are, therefore, radical predictions. Prediction in science is a test of the relationship of our ideas to reality. When our predictions are correct and reproducible by others, we have good evidence that we are "on line" with reality.

TFT Study in a Major HMO

Sakai, et al (in press) conducted a study that involved 1603 applications of TFT done by seven therapists at Kaiser Behavioral Medicine Services and Behavioral Health Services in Honolulu, Hawaii. Conditions treated included anxiety, adjustment disorder, major depression, addiction, anger, bereavement, chronic pain, eating disorders, OCD, panic disorder, social phobia, PTSD and a wide variety of other psychological problems. Pre and post treatment SUD were analyzed with paired t-tests and the change for each condition analyzed was significant at the .001 level, except for tremors, which was significant at the .01 level. Sakai also notes that their results were supported in individual cases by data showing major changes in the Center for Epidemiological Studies of Depression (CES-D) scale and improved autonomic balance as evidenced by heart rate variability (HRV) (see section below for details on HRV).

Heart Rate Variability (HRV)

Our TFT successes have objective support from the cardiological diagnostic and research system known as Heart Rate Variability (HRV). In 1997, Fuller Royal, MD, chief of a medical clinic in Las Vegas, informed me of some findings while experimenting with one of my simple treatment formulas and measuring the results with a cardiology procedure called Heart Rate Variability (HRV) (Malik & Camm, 1995). Dr. Royal found that my simple TFT treatment immediately put the ANS into balance, more rapidly and powerfully than any other of the numerous treatments he was exploring (Callahan, 1997a, 1997b).

Among other things, this diagnostic instrument provides a measure of the degree of balance in the autonomic nervous system (ANS); stress puts the ANS out of balance. It has been shown that a placebo has no influence on ANS balance (Kleiger, et al., 1991; Vybrial, et al., 1993; De Ferrari, Mantick & Vanoli, 1993; Malik & Camm, 1995; Casadei, et al., 1996; Venkatesh, et al., 1996). Kleiger, et al. (1991) conclude that "HR variables measured in this study are suitable for intervention studies because of their stability over time, lack of placebo effect and marked individual reproducibility" (p. 630). Kautzner (1995) notes that ". . . the reproducibility of HRV indices is far superior to those of other variables . . . Thus HRV might be preferable . . . for evaluation of the efficacy of various interventions" (p. 170).

The HRV started as a clinical and research tool for cardiologists but its influence in psychiatry and general medicine is growing rapidly. Psychologists who are associated with MDs are finding out about this procedure and letting other psychologists know about HRV, so the word about this procedure is gradually spreading throughout the field of psychology. More and more investigators are using HRV in the domain of psychological problems (Carney et al., 1995; Friedman and Thayer, 1998a, 1998b; Fuller, 1992; Kawachi et al., 1995; Komatsu et al., 1992; Langewitz & Ruddel, 1989; Lehofer et al., 1997; McCraty et al., 1995; Yeragani et al., 1991, 1998).

Cohen, et al. (1999) in a paper on the use of HRV in psychiatry, note that: "From the interest it has raised, it may be expected that this method will be in widespread use in clinical practice in the future, providing a useful tool, both for diagnostic and prognostic purposes, as well as serving as a further aid towards monitoring therapeutic interventions" (p. 59).

Furthermore, evidence exists of a significant relationship between the client's self-reported level of anxiety and perceived level of emotional stress and a worsened HRV test result. This relationship was found to exist independently of age, gender, trait anxiety, cardiorespiratory fitness, heart rate, blood pressure and respiration rate (Dishman, et al., 2000). This demonstrates that the use of HRV is a very appropriate measure with which to measure change in the domain of psychotherapy and that a person's level of anxiety and stress has a definite and significant impact on the HRV. Therefore, if a psychotherapy is successful in reducing such anxiety and emotional stress, then this should be reflected by a change for the better in HRV.

In our own experimentation with TFT and HRV, we have repeatedly demonstrated that there is a strong relationship between the client's self-reported decreased level of psychological distress (i.e., a lower SUD) and a robust improvement in HRV (Callahan, in press). Such changes were shown for treatments of psychological problems including anxiety, phobias, depression, stress, anger, post traumatic stress disorder, and a wide variety of other types of emotional problems. As far as we can determine from our literature search, the changes in HRV that we have been able to obtain within minutes between baseline and post TFT treatment are unprecedented for any amount of time. Huikuri et al. (1999) noting the lack of effective therapies to change HRV, stated that ". . . no specific therapy is currently available to improve the prognosis for patients with abnormal HR variability" (p. 1878). The changes we are getting in people with very low HRV, post TFT treatment, however, clearly demonstrate that such improvement is now possible.

We have always used the client's self-report of complete elimination of all subjective units of distress to judge TFT therapy success. Now, however, with the HRV changes we are predictably able to achieve objective validation of these subjective reports which rules out any possibility of placebo effect of demand characteristics. These HRV changes objectively show that TFT is operating at a deep physiological level. Interest in HRV is growing and in the near future, most physicians and especially most psychotherapists will doubtless have equipment used to measure HRV in their offices, since it will give them immediate, objective feedback and evidence as to the power of various treatments they are administering. In my opinion, within the near future all psychotherapies will necessarily be tested with this objective measure (HRV). Since this objective instrument is known to be free of placebo influence, we will see an end to testing psychotherapies with a control group and statistical tests in the attempt to demonstrate that the effects of these approaches are greater than chance.

THEORY

TFT's theory has been constructed purely on the basis of the many observable new facts that have been revealed by TFT. It is easy for anyone who has a desire for direct evidence of this to try the treatment for which I have provided instructions in the next section of this chapter. This treatment provides a reproducible experiment, enabling anyone who carries it out to see the union of TFT theory and practice firsthand.

Described below are the key concepts and principles of TFT theory:

The Thought Field

The *thought field* is a hypothetical construct that serves as a canvas that allows us to localize our causal concepts. My early finding was that it was extremely important what the client thinks about in treatment because each thought field will have different characteristics. I call this "tuning the thought field." The thought field refers to the thought that a person thinks about. Animals and very young children can also be successfully treated, but must be in an actual situation in order to be treated successfully, since they are not able to select their thought field. When the problematic thought field is attuned, the fundamental causal elements in TFT, which I call *perturbations* (see below), are revealed by my causal diagnostic procedures.

John thinks about a trauma that happened 10 years ago. Since the onset of the trauma, every time John merely thinks of this event he becomes upset. The simple TFT treatment recipe for trauma is done. When the treatment is ended, perhaps a minute later, the thought has now lost the capacity to trigger the upset. This was a terrible event, but no matter how hard John tries he can no longer get upset. What happened?

Perturbation

The perturbation (p) is the fundamental concept in TFT. There is obviously an entity, residing in or carried by the thought field, that generates and controls upset. The evidence for this, in the above example, is that when the trauma is thought about, John, who was not at all upset before thinking of the trauma, becomes very upset. A few minutes later, after the effective treatment, John thinks about the same trauma and not only does not get upset, but when challenged, is *unable* to get upset. It seems clear that since the exact same thought can be tuned one time with upset, and the next, after successful treatment, with no upset, that something is different in the thought field after successful therapy. I have known this fact for about 20 years, but I did not have a name for the entity in the thought field that generated and controlled the disturbance until about five years ago. When the word "perturbation" occurred to me, I ran to my dictionary and looked it up. What I read there gave me great excitement!

Definition of Perturbation

One of the dictionary definitions of perturbation is *"a cause of mental disquietude."* I simply changed the adjective "a" to "the" and we have perturbation as *"the cause of mental disquietude."* In the theory I am putting forth, a *perturbation is an isolable aspect of the thought field which contains the necessary active and specific information* (Bohm and Hiley, 1993) *not only to trigger, but more importantly, to control all the factors (brain, amygdala, nervous system, hormones, chemistry, specific cellular activity, cognitive activity, etc.) that go into generating highly specific negative emotions.* "Isolable" is a critical aspect of the definition that accounts for the benevolent fact that only the perturbation is eliminated from the thought field in successful treatment. The rest of the thought field remains perfectly intact. This is unlike, for example, LSD, which temporarily removes the perturbations in a thought field associated with fear of heights, but also removes other critical information such as the valid basis for a fear of heights.

Perturbation is used in physics and astronomy to indicate some kind of disturbance or difference from the norm. It has an implication of an almost random quality in this usage. However, the perturbation in TFT is anything but random, for it is clear that it contains highly precise and specific detailed information. The active information is so precise that it controls and generates all of the consequences and activity of the various disturbing emotions. These consequences include the specific neural pathways used in various emotions, the chemical and hormonal factors released with each emotion, and the cognitive result of each of these. The concept of perturbation bridges and integrates the fields of clinical psychology, physics, and biology.

David Bohm, a theoretical physicist, introduced the term *active information* into quantum physics, and this notion fits well with my concept of the perturbation. Bohm and Hiley (1993) describe their pivotal concept in quantum physics: "we have introduced a concept that is new in the context of physics—a concept that we shall call *active information.* The basic idea of active information is that a form having very little energy enters into and directs a much greater energy. The activity of the latter is in this way given a form similar to that of the smaller energy . . . What is crucial here is that we are calling attention to the literal meaning of the word, i.e. to in-form, which is actively to put form into something or to imbue something with form" (p. 35)

To understand precisely what takes place in successful therapy, one must grasp this notion of the perturbation. My view is that *any* effective therapy, natural heal-

ing, or maturation collapses the perturbation(s) in the thought field. When the perturbation(s) is collapsed, there can be no emotional upset.

Coding

Biological code is relevant to TFT, for I believe that a correct TFT treatment represents a code that nature has devised. DNA, for example, is an objective code existing in nature. This complex DNA code, it has been estimated, is equivalent to 20,000 long books about 500 pages each, or about 10 million pages (Foster, 1985). The complexity of this code is not surprising considering that it is responsible for governing the physical structure of all living organisms. The code governing psychological problems is, fortunately, much simpler.

I contend that the encoded information governing such emotions as fear are a result of hard-won experience (traumas), and if phobias, for example, could be cured by merely thinking nice thoughts, invaluable information would be too easily lost. One of the major functions of a code is to protect such crucial information. Survival would be put into jeopardy, since the purpose of phobias is to protect life.

Codes provide this self-protection in life just as coding protects computer programs from being too easily changed. One must learn the special, more complex coding of programmers in order to change the basic programs in the computer. The code for the disturbed emotions had to be discovered. Nature has provided many blessings that helped me in this discovery.

Causal Diagnosis

For every perturbation, there is a corresponding treatment point on the body. The TFT code of the correct treatment points, in their correct sequence, is provided through TFT's unique system of *causal diagnosis.* This method is called *causal diagnosis* because it reveals perturbations, which are the root cause of all emotional distress, and because it indicates what precise sequence of treatment points needs to be addressed. Diagnosis in psychology and psychiatry is nosological, or classificatory. A patient is placed into a descriptive category that best fits the predominant set of symptoms presented. In my almost half century of practice, I have never heard of causal diagnosis in psychology. Our high success rates and completeness support the notion of *causal.* Our algorithms are all a result of being able to determine the specific deepest causes of emotional disorder. Causal diagnosis allows us to determine the precise order in a disorder—if there were no order in the disorder, help would not be possible.

Three Levels of TFT Performance

As a treatment, TFT consists of three levels of performance:

1. Algorithms

Algorithm is a concept and term that originated in mathematics and refers to a common solution for a problem, such as finding the greatest common divisor. Youngson (1994) defines the more general notion of algorithm as: "A sequence of instructions to be followed with the intention of finding a solution to a problem. Each step must specify what steps are to be taken, and although there may be many alternate routes through the algorithm, there is only one start point and one end point" (p. 232).

The term *algorithm* has been adopted in medicine. Emergency personnel and ambulance drivers, for instance, learn easily applied medical solutions to emergency problems, and these procedures are called algorithms. Most psychotherapy consists of algorithms that various innovators have offered. Since I have developed a unique causal diagnosis procedure, it is necessary to distinguish between my recipes or algorithms and my diagnostically-based treatments. All of my algorithms are for specific types of psychological problems and were discovered and developed by my causal diagnostic procedures. The algorithms were then tested on hundreds of individuals and found to have a success rate of approximately 70 to 80%. This fact has now been confirmed by reports to me by hundreds of therapists throughout the world who have used them.

I have developed specific algorithms for phobias, trauma, addictive urges, anxiety, anger, guilt, depression, physical pain, obsessions, and compulsions. An algorithm I developed for trauma will be described in great detail in the Methodology section of this chapter. This description allows an untrained person to do a scientific experiment that easily tests my procedures.

2. Diagnosis

The level of diagnosis consists of special training and development of skills in the causal diagnostic procedure described earlier. The practice of TFT causal diagnosis enables the therapist to obtain individualized treatment sequences for people who do not respond to algorithms or who have a problem for which no algorithm exists. About 500 therapists are currently trained and certified by Callahan Techniques Ltd. in causal diagnostic procedures.

3. Voice Technology

Voice Technology (VT) is the level of TFT that has the highest rate of success (see Table 1 on the replicated success of VT in the previous section). VT is a more sophisticated form of causal diagnosis, where the therapist is trained to diagnose a sequence of treatment points through an objective and unique voice analysis technology which detects perturbations encoded in the person's voice (Callahan & Callahan, 1996). Because VT depends only on the voice to obtain a diagnosis, it can be done via the telephone from anywhere in the world. My current practice consists of an international clientele, with whom I work with over the telephone. The people who come to me for help are typically people who have very complex problems, which have not responded to any other form of psychotherapy, including TFT's usually effective therapy at the algorithm or diagnostic level. I am usually able to help such people significantly in the first session. In a subsequent series of short sessions, which add up to approximately 5 hours, I can then, in most cases, completely deal with their problem and stabilize the results of the treatments. The therapist training for VT is done with me individually and is a three-year program. As of 1999, I have trained 12 mental health professionals in VT.

The Apex Problem

The term *apex* is borrowed from Arthur Koestler (1967), who referred to the mind operating at the apex, or peak, of its capacity. The apex problem occurs when the mind is not operating at its apex; it is a cognitive device used by the client to attempt to account for a surprising (therapy) experience that cannot be accommodated by previous understandings. The person with an apex problem provides an "explanation" that ignores the facts at hand but allows the person to feel comfortable by fitting in with the person's prior experience.

Anyone who does these treatments must be prepared to encounter what I call the *Apex Problem*. A person with an apex problem reports accurately that his problem is gone but compulsively denies that the treatment had anything to do with the elimination. Despite the skepticism clearly implied in the apex problem, the client nevertheless *accurately* reports positive changes. One might expect that the reported results would be watered down, but although this can happen, it is very rare. Instead of correctly identifying the treatment as being responsible, the person invents an explanation for the problem being gone or, in some cases, completely forgets that there ever was a problem. This is an unanticipated but common response to these treatments.

This response is completely unrelated to intelligence level but could accurately be said to refer to the lack of the application of intelligence to the treatment situation. There is a distinct parallel here between what Gazzaniga (1985, 1992, 1998) calls the *left brain interpreter,* and what Festinger (1957) called *cognitive dissonance.* Gazzaniga describes most interesting actions by patients who have had their brains surgically split and who *compulsively* invent explanations with their left brains for the actions of their right brains. He describes this phenomenon as "probably the most amazing mechanism the human being possesses" (1998, p. 27). Those of us who do TFT find this mechanism to be robust even without brain surgery.

Many TFT trained therapists record therapy sessions because some clients may actually "forget" that they had a problem after the rapidly successful therapy. Other manifestations of the apex problem include statements such as, "The treatment distracted me," "I'm repressing my feelings," "I've been hypnotized by the treatment," and "I'm not able to think about the problem." A more precise formulation would be, "Now, when I think of the problem, after the powerful treatment, I am unable to get upset." Since the client is so accustomed to being upset when thinking of the problem, he or she quite wrongly concludes that the problem is not being thought about since he or she is not upset. It is impossible to say the words, "I can't think about x" without actually thinking about x.

Therapists who observe the result of the treatments also commonly have an apex problem, invoking such notions as suggestion, hypnosis, and placebo effect even though the therapists have never personally witnessed a trauma being immediately eliminated through such means. As these treatments become recognized for their power and predictably high success, the apex problem will simply disappear.

Placebo Effect

Due to the apex problem and the skepticism that results from the strange appearance of our treatments, it is believed that we do not get our fair share of so-called "placebo cures." However, we do quite well without the placebo effect. There is considerable evidence that the so-called placebo effect is illusory (Kienle and Kiene, 1996). In a review of over 800 studies on placebo, "The authors conclude that the literature relating to the magnitude of the placebo effect is unfounded and grossly overrated, if not entirely false" (p. 39). Kienle and Kiene (1996) pose the question of whether the existence of the so-called placebo effect is itself not largely, or indeed totally, illusory. Since my treatment takes only minutes, there is not much time for natural healing to take place.

METHODOLOGY

Seligman (1994), has drawn attention to the need for new treatments for Posttraumatic Stress Disorder (PTSD). He points out that existing PTSD treatments have not been successful in the treatment of this disorder and emphasizes the need for new treatments that will successfully relieve the symptoms of PTSD. In this section, I shall provide such a treatment for you to try on yourself or clients. In doing so, you can decide for yourself if you think TFT fulfills Seligman's request.

Architecture of the Treatments

The architecture or form of the treatment is also a unique discovery that I made some years ago. This recommended structure to the treatment procedures, which will contribute to the success rate, is in three segments, as follows:

1. The Majors
The Majors are the initial sequence of treatment points. For example, in the treatment provided below, the Majors consist of tapping the following points: eyebrow (eb), under the eye (e), under the arm (a), and collarbone (c).

2. The Nine-Gamut Treatments
The eye is an extension of the brain and eye movements were used in Neuro Linguistic Programming (NLP) (Bandler & Grinder, 1975), Applied Kinesiology (Walther, 1988), and Feldenkreis' (1972) functional integration method for some diagnostic (not causal) purposes. My contribution was to confirm that the position of the eyes would *diagnostically* reveal a hidden perturbation in the system. I call my discovery "the nine-gamut treatments" because they run the "gamut" of nine steps, all done while tapping on the "gamut spot" (on the back of the hand). The nine gamut steps consist of six eye positions plus humming, counting and humming again, which activate the right and left brain. This provides an effective treatment that results in an immediate and obvious elimination of a perturbation, which enables this procedure to significantly reduce or eliminate a problem. (See instruction section for the exact steps to the nine gamut sequence.)

3. A Repetition of the Majors (see part 1)
After the nine-gamut sequence, the majors (e.g., eb, e, a, c) are repeated as the third segment of the treatment, which usually bring about a further reduction in the SUD.

We call a complete treatment, using steps 1–3 above, a *holon*. Since the nine-gamut sequence is placed in the middle of two sets of majors, a holon could be thought of as a nine-gamut sandwich.

TFT Trauma Algorithm Instructions

Prior to doing the treatment described below, explain that you are experimenting with a new procedure that is quite different and that will seem a little strange. Here are the step-by-step instructions on how to do the trauma algorithm (Callahan, 1995).

Step 1. Tuning into the Problem and Getting a SUD. First, ask the client to think about the trauma. The first step in the procedure is to determine the degree of pain or discomfort on a 10-point SUD scale with "10" being the worst, and "1" being completely free of all traces of discomfort when the trauma is attuned or thought about. An 11 point scale of 0–10 can also be used. It does not matter which you use, as long as you are clear with the client. Record the SUD rating by writing it down in the client's presence—if you do not write it down, the client may actually *forget* that there was a problem prior to treatment due to the apex problem. The more severe the upset the clearer the demonstration. Each time you get a SUD rating it is important to make sure the client gives you the degree of upset he/she is experiencing *right now,* not how he/she has felt in the past or might feel in the future.

For Steps 2–5 below, ask the client to *tap 5 times* on each treatment point described in the steps below. The client should tap with 2 fingers, firmly enough to put energy into the system but not hard enough to hurt or bruise. The tapping can be done on either the left or the right side—it makes no difference which side is tapped.

Step 2: Ask the client to tap the beginning of the eyebrow above the bridge of the nose.

Step 3: Ask the client to tap under the eye about an inch below the bottom of the eyeball, at the bottom center of the bony orbit, high on the cheek.

Step 4: Ask the client to tap under the arm, about four inches directly below the armpit. This point is even with the nipple in the male and around the center of the bra under the arm in the female.

Step 5: Find the "collar bone point" in the following manner. Take two fingers of either hand and move them down the center of the throat until the top of the center collar bone (clavicle) notch is reached. From this point go straight down one inch and then to the right one inch.

Step 6: At this time, ask for a second SUD rating. If the decrease is two or more points, continue with step 7. If there was no change or it was only one point, correct psychological reversal (see below for psychological reversal correction) and repeat steps 1–6.

Step 7: The Nine Gamut treatments. To locate the gamut spot on the back of the hand make a fist with the nondominant (most people prefer to tap with the dominant) hand. This will cause the knuckles to stand out on the back

of the hand. Place the index finger of the dominant hand in the valley between the little finger and the ring finger knuckles. Move the index finger about one inch toward the wrist. This point is called the *gamut point.* Open fingers and the index finger will be resting on the gamut point.

Ask the client to tap the gamut spot on the back of the hand and continue tapping while going through the nine procedures as follows (tapping 5 or 6 times for each of the nine gamut positions). It is crucial to tap the gamut spot throughout the nine steps.

1. Eyes open
2. Eyes closed
3. Open eyes and point them down and to the left
4. Point eyes down and to the right
5. Whirl eyes around in a circle in one direction
6. Whirl eyes around in opposite direction—rest eyes
7. Hum a few bars of any tune (more than one note)
8. Count to five
9. Hum a few bars of a tune again

Step 8: Repeat steps 2–6. After this repetition the presenting problem will usually not bring any trace of upset and hence the client is typically a 1 (or a 0 depending on whether a 10 or 11 point SUD scale is used). If the SUD rating has decreased, but is not yet a 1, then have the client CORRECT MINI-PR (see instructions below) and repeat steps 1–8.

Floor to Ceiling Eye Roll

The floor to ceiling eye roll is given at the end of a successful series of treatments. The client usually reports a 1 or a 2 on the scale and this treatment serves to solidify a 1 and to bring a 2 to a 1. The client taps the gamut spot on the back of the hand while the head is held *rather* level (many people want to move their head in this exercise instead of the eyes). We use the word *rather* because some deviation from level is acceptable. The eyes are then placed down and rather steadily raised all the way up (taking 6 or 7 seconds) while the gamut spot is tapped. The gamut spot must be tapped while the eyes are moving. This exercise will typically bring a 2 down to a 1.

Psychological Reversal (PR) Correction

As mentioned previously, psychological reversal (pr) can prevent an otherwise successful treatment from working due—I believe—to a literal polarity reversal of the energy flow in the meridians and/or systems involved. The TFT success rate would be about 40% less effective without PR and its simple but very powerful correction.

To correct a pr, tap five times on what we call the *pr*

spot, which is located on the outside edge of the hand about, midway between the wrist and the base of the little finger. The pr spot is at the point of impact if one were to do a karate chop. Pr treatment is not in itself a treatment for a psychological problem, but rather a treatment for a block that prevents a treatment from working—therefore, the treatments for the problem (2–6) must be repeated after the pr is corrected.

Some therapists like to begin with the automatic correction of psychological reversal whether it is needed or not. Although it does no harm if one is not reversed and the pr treatment is done (i.e., it won't create a reversal), it is not recommended for professionals, for this obscures from the therapist's view the observation of the important and fascinating phenomena of psychological reversal. The professional is able to observe that the algorithm, e.g., does nothing for the person. A pr correction is done and the treatment, that a moment earlier did nothing, suddenly works dramatically.

Mini-Psychological Reversal Correction

Since there is no obvious difference between the PR and the mini-pr, I should explain that the name of this one is intimately connected to my causal diagnostic procedures, where the name has meaning and relevance. The mini-pr was not discovered until four years after the usual PR was known. This procedure is carried out when a client shows improvement down to about a 3 or 4 but does not go lower. I call this block a mini-pr. This is a block that kicks in after a major improvement has taken place. To correct, tap the pr spot, as described above.

When a traumatized individual is brought down from a high SUD score, which represents intense suffering, to a low score, the treatment effect typically endures over time.

The ability to eliminate a problem completely and rapidly has led us into a new domain of understanding psychotherapy. When a problem is gone, this allows for the possibility that the problem may return—a problem cannot return, of course, unless it is first gone. This domain goes beyond the scope of this paper and is covered in more detail in the chapter "Cure and Time" from my book, *Stop the Nightmare of Trauma* (Callahan & Callahan, 2000). This will be the subject of a future monograph.

Our clients attempt to resurrect the upset in our presence, and if any degree of upset occurs after they leave, they immediately call for another brief appointment. We are then in a position to identify exactly what caused the return for this individual and then retreat the remaining problem.

APPLICATIONS

There are a wide variety of experiences that come under the heading of trauma. I will give just a few of the many examples of how the TFT trauma treatment can be applied to help people in a wide variety of different types of traumatic situations.

Love Pain

Upsets and losses over romantic rejections and disappointments, while not the most objectively horrible traumas, are often the most acutely painful to the person who suffers from them. Based on my half a century of therapy experience, it is my opinion that there are few more devastating emotional pains than romantic loss or rejection. Many things are objectively more terrible than romantic or love pain, but as far as depth and severity of emotional reaction, love pain is among the top in generating severe pain.

People who have suffered in this way develop what I call Amouraphobia, the fear of being devastated in a romantic relationship. They are afraid to commit to intimate relationships with people because of the pain and hurt they experienced from earlier rejections. The worst part of this phenomenon is that they are usually totally unaware of the role and power of this fear in sabotaging otherwise successful romantic love relationships. I detailed the many manifestations and consequences of Amouraphobia in my earlier book, *It Can Happen to You: The Practical Guide to Romantic Love,* which was a Book-of-the-Month Club selection (Callahan, 1982). However, at the time this book was written, I was just beginning to develop treatments for Amouraphobia and love pain. Use the trauma treatment to help heal yourself and/or your partner from past or present love pains.

Illness or the Illness of a Loved One

Experiencing a serious chronic or terminal illness, or observing a severe illness of a loved one, is a very traumatic and stressful experience. TFT can relieve extreme upset and stress around the illness and thereby greatly enhance the quality of life. The less stress, the better the chance for healing.

Job-related Stress and Trauma

Whether one is a boss or an employee, there are many types of upsets and stresses that occur in connection with conditions at a person's job. The trauma treatment can help someone who is suffering from the trauma of being fired or laid off from a job, as well as heal the many upsets that can occur during the course of a rough working day. One of the psychologists I trained has specialized in consulting with companies that have him treat employees who suffer from job-related upsets and problems, including shootings by disgruntled employees. These treatments are very appealing to the businessperson because people can be helped effectively and quickly. More harmony in the workplace and more productive employees often result from this simple but powerful treatment.

People who have jobs where they have to deal with trauma—police officers, firefighters, paramedics, psychotherapists, news reporters, doctors, nurses, emergency room personnel, and other hospital workers—are often themselves very traumatized by what they witness in their day-to-day work (Freinkel, 1994). The TFT treatment for trauma is very effective in eliminating the effects of such secondary trauma. One therapist I trained has worked in a hospital for 20 years and uses this treatment for herself on a daily basis. She reports that the treatment has helped her tremendously in dealing with the stress and upset from which she used to suffer as a result of what she is exposed to on the job. Our treatments can also help dogs, cats, and horses. The rescue workers in natural disasters who use dogs to help them find people who have been injured or killed report that the dogs are traumatized by the experience.

Crime Victims

This treatment is tremendously effective for people who have been victimized by crimes and has helped many people to eliminate the fear, upset, and nightmares that result from such an experience. One of the many people I have helped was a 14-year-old girl who was shot in the leg as the result of a drive-by shooting. Her therapist was unable to help her and referred her for TFT. For eight months she had been severely emotionally upset and had nightmares due to being shot. She couldn't get the horrible noise of the gunshots and the shattering glass out of her head, and she suffered from nightmares in which she relived the shooting and would awaken terrified and very upset. She came to me for help eight months after the shooting and was not able to think about the shooting without getting very upset. The TFT treatment for trauma took less than 10 minutes and removed all traces of her upset. Even though this shooting was, in reality, a horrible event, she was no longer upset or bothered by it and was free to go on with her life without having to repeatedly relive the event. Five years after this treatment, the client reported that she remained free of all upset and the nightmares were gone.

Child Abuse

People with multiple instances of abuse, such as repeated child abuse, can be helped with TFT. Sometimes, in the case of complex, multiple traumas such as prolonged child abuse, the person will need more than one treatment, in order to treat the different traumas that occurred and the different feelings and disturbances connected with them.

Natural or Man-made Disasters

People who suffer the traumatic after-effects of war, hurricanes, earthquakes, floods, bombings, plane crashes, and the many other possible disasters can benefit tremendously from the TFT treatment for trauma. When there was a major earthquake in the Palm Springs area where I live, I successfully treated several people who were traumatized by this event and were living in constant fear of it happening again.

Dr. Jenny Edwards (1998), a therapist whom I trained, happened to be in Nairobi, Africa at the time of the Embassy bombing that occurred in August 1998. After the bombing, she went to the hospital and helped a number of the victims, using only algorithms, who had been severely traumatized by this horrible event. She was able to completely eliminate, with the appropriate algorithms, not only their emotional pain, but also their physical pain.

As you can see from the above examples, my treatment for trauma is helpful for a variety of different types of traumas and life upsets for which there has previously been no help available.

CASE EXAMPLE

The following case example is presented by my co-author on this chapter, Monica Pignotti, MSW, CSW, who is trained at the most advanced level of TFT (Voice Technology). This case is a good illustration of how different levels of TFT (algorithms and Voice Technology) can be appropriately used.

The client is an 80-year-old woman, "Anna," who came to me six months after her husband's death from Alzheimer's disease. She had just been through a 15-year ordeal of being his care giver and having to watch his long, slow, and painful deterioration, which had culminated in his death. She presented with several different symptoms, which had been getting worse since his death. In addition to a sense of deep loss, she also suffered from depression; a painful skin condition, psoriasis, which had started after his death and which she believed to be aggravated by the stress; feelings of guilt; and phobias about going out alone. She lived in the suburbs of a large city and was afraid to take the train by herself into the city. I (Monica Pignotti) chose this case to present here because it is a good example of how multiple, complex layers of issues can be dealt with by using TFT at the appropriate level.

Anna was first treated with algorithms by one of my algorithm trainees, while I was present, supervising a training session. Since she had initially been afraid of coming into the city to see us, we treated her for this phobia first, using the phobia algorithm. When she thought about this fear, she reported her SUD to be at a "9." This problem was easily treated with the phobia algorithm and in less than five minutes her SUD was reduced to a "1" (no trace of fear left).

In the same session, we also treated her in a general way for the trauma/loss of her husband with the trauma algorithm and her feelings of depression with the depression algorithm. For both, she started out with an SUD of 10, which was quickly reduced to a 1 within minutes. In addition to her reported SUD of 1, there were observable physical changes in her. Before the treatments, she had appeared pale. As her SUD decreased, we could readily observe color coming into her face.

This sort of color change is a common observation among therapists who do TFT and has an interesting explanation (Callahan, 1998). There is a medical term, rouleaux, which is used to describe blood when the red cells stick together. Since red blood cells carry oxygen throughout the body, their clumping together results in a shortage of oxygen supply to the body, resulting in the skin having a pale appearance. As an experiment, Dr. Callahan had pre- and post-treatment tests (the examination of blood cells under a special microscope) done by a qualified lab technician for the presence of rouleaux (clumped blood cells). He found changes in rouleaux to be in direct proportion to the reported SUD level: Beginning SUD of 10 = 100% rouleaux; reduced SUD of 7 = 70% rouleaux; further SUD reduction to 5 = 50% rouleaux, and the final SUD after treatment completion of 1 = 0% rouleaux. Along with the evidence of these tests was an observable color change in the face of the person being treated as greater oxygen supply was restored. If you try the TFT trauma treatment, watch for this color change, since it is quite common.

Anna left the first session looking and feeling considerably better. The next week, when she returned, she reported that she had been able to go home by herself without any trace of anxiety. The results of her treatment had held up, since she reported upon returning a week later that she had been able to take the train into the city with no problem whatsoever. Her main complaint in this session was the pain and itching from the psoriasis, which visibly covered her arms, and her urge to scratch it, which made it worse. We did both the algorithm for physical pain and the algorithm for compulsion to scratch, which completely eliminated the itching, and thus her urge to scratch. A week later, her arm was visibly improved and the sores and swelling had completely gone away.

I did not hear from Anna again until six months later, when the anniversary of her husband's death had come around. This had triggered further emotional responses in her that had not been specifically treated with the algorithms. She reported feeling depression, anger, and guilt. She had gone to several traditional therapists, ask-

ing for help, who told her that it was going to take years of therapy for her to get any relief from her suffering and that she would have to learn to live with these symptoms. Fortunately, TFT provided a better alternative for her.

To deal with these problems, we did one hour of Voice Technology (VT). VT sessions are typically very short (10 minutes or less), but since she had multiple issues, this session took longer than usual. To begin, I asked her what discomfort she was aware of right in that moment. At the moment, she said she was not aware of feeling any negative emotions, although she had recently been in quite a bit of emotional distress.

To get her to focus on a specific issue that might evoke an SUD, I asked her to tell me, briefly, about what she had been experiencing. A person can be successfully treated who has no SUD, but I prefer when possible to get an SUD, since this gives immediate feedback to me about results. I like to begin with whatever issue the client is most aware of at the time of treatment. As treatments are done, layers of complex issues are peeled away and the new ones can then be treated.

She started describing how she had been procrastinating cleaning up her house, since it had gotten into a state of great disorganization over the 15-year-period she had been caring for her husband. I had her rate her degree of procrastination on a scale of 1–10, and she gave it an 8. Then, using the Voice Technology, I diagnosed an individualized sequence of treatment points for her. After the first sequence, she reported still being at an 8. At that time, I tested her for psychological reversal, found she was reversed, had her do the correction (tapping on the side of the hand), and then had her do another diagnosed treatment sequence. After that sequence, her SUD dropped to a 5, which shows how the reversal correction gets a response to treatment that will not work in the presence of the reversal.

With her SUD at a 5, I gave her still another treatment sequence to do in order to get her down to our goal, which is always an SUD of 1. However, after that sequence, she reported a rise in the SUD to an 8. I asked her if she was still thinking about the issue of procrastination or if other thoughts had occurred to her, since when the SUD rises during a treatment, it is usually because the client has become aware of other untreated issues (i.e., other thought fields have become attuned). She told me that she had become aware, during the treatment, of tremendous guilt over the way she felt she had treated her husband at the times when she had become impatient and angry with him. The thought of cleaning the house, which she had been procrastinating doing, entailed going through her husband's things and once that issue was treated, the underlying layers of emotion (anger and guilt) came up. Because the anger and guilt came up immediately, the client reported an increased SUD, which was not based on the original issue being treated (procrastination) but rather on the new layers of feelings.

We began treating the feelings of anger, which resulted in her remembering two specific instances when she had felt very angry at her husband. Her SUD remained at an 8 for several rounds of treatments, as the new memories (thought fields) and emotions arose. After treating her upset, anger, and guilt over these specific memories, her SUD began to decrease, to a 5, then to a 3, and finally to a 1. I then went back and checked how she was doing with the original issue (procrastination) and she reported also being at a "1" on this as well. By the end of the session, she reported a tremendous feeling of relief.

The next step for Anna is to track her results and in order to do so, I made sure that she understood that she is to call me if any other issues surface for her or any trace of the upsets we treated in the session returns. So far (two months later), she has not reported any return of symptoms, but if they do return, this can be easily remedied by finding and dealing with the cause of the return (Callahan & Callahan, 2000). The result we achieved in these three sessions with Anna is what my typical experience has been with TFT, where I am able to help completely eliminate a person's emotional distress about a trauma for which traditional therapists are unable to offer any substantial emotional relief. The therapists who told her she would have to learn to live with her distress would, indeed, be surprised to see her now.

I would like to point out that this client's healing had nothing to do with any special healing powers that I personally possess, but is due to the power of TFT. I have treated people in the past, even using innovative therapies such as NLP, and have never seen the kind of results I am now regularly able to achieve using TFT. Initially, like many therapists, I was highly skeptical of these treatments and thought they sounded too good to be true, so if anyone reading this is skeptical, I completely understand. However, having used TFT and gotten predictable results literally hundreds of times with people, and having taught other therapists to do the same with their clients, I can no longer deny the observable effect that this treatment has.

SUMMARY

We are fully aware that, given the previous track record of psychotherapy treatments (Adler, 1993; Seligman, 1994), the claims we have made in this chapter are very likely going to sound grandiose and too good to be true to the professional reading about this for the first time. We fully expect and understand that discerning people will be skeptical. We acknowledge that when claims are made about TFT, the burden of proof is on us. For this reason, we have, in this chapter, provided you with the tools to test these claims for yourself.

The reader should understand that the experiment in psychotherapy for trauma presented in this chapter is reproducible by the reader. Those who take the trouble to learn the simple TFT algorithm presented for trauma can easily repeat the procedures and obtain highly successful results. Other algorithms are available in my book, *Tap The Healer Within* (Callahan & Trubo, 2000). The success rate, if the procedures are done correctly, will be about the same as is reported for algorithm success, which is about 70–80%. With training in the procedures, the success rate is increased as indicated.

I encourage people to contact me (Roger Callahan) with any questions or comments they might have. Any reports people have of the firsthand experiments you do with TFT are very welcome, as this sort of information is valuable to me in my further development of TFT.

REFERENCES

Adler, T. (1993, November). Studies look at ways to keep fear at bay: Science Directorate report. *American Psychological Association Monitor, 24*(11), 17.

Bandler, R., & Grinder, J. (1975). *The structure of magic,* vol. 1. Palo Alto, CA: Science and Behavior Books.

Bohm, D., & Hiley, B. J. (1993). *The undivided universe: An ontological interpretation of quantum theory.* NY: Routledge.

Callahan, R. (1955). *Unrealistic fears of children as a measure of anxiety.* Doctoral Dissertation, Univ. Microfilms, Ann Arbor, Michigan.

Callahan, R. (1981). Psychological reversal. *Collected Papers of International College of Applied Kinesiology,* Winter, 79–96.

Callahan, R. (1982). *It can happen to you: The practical guide to romantic love.* New York: New American Library.

Callahan, R. (1985). *Five minute phobia cure.* Wilmington: Enterprise.

Callahan, R. (1987). Successful treatment of phobias and anxiety by telephone and radio. *Collected Papers of International College of Applied Kinesiology,* Winter, pp. 73–81.

Callahan, R. (1995). A TFT algorithm for the treatment of trauma. *Electronic Journal of Traumatology, 1*(1).

Callahan, R. (1996). The Case of Mary: The first TFT case. *Electronic Journal of Traumatology, 3*(1).

Callahan, R. (1997a). *TFT and heart rate variability: An interview with Fuller Royal, MD.* Video. LaQuinta, Callahan Techniques®.

Callahan, R. (1997b). TFT and heart rate variability. *The Thought Field, 3*(1).

Callahan, R. (1997c). *Introduction to TFT video.* La Quinta, CA.

Callahan, R. (1998). More scientific support—psychotherapy and deep biological change—Rouleaux and Callahan Techniques TFT. *The Thought Field, 4*(2).

Callahan, R. (in press). The impact of thought field therapy on heart rate variability (HRV), *Journal of Clinical Psychology*.

Callahan, R. & Callahan, J. (2000). *Stop the Nightmares of Trauma*. Chapel Hill, NC: Professional Press.

Callahan, R. & Trubo, R. (2000). *Tap the Healer Within*. NY: Contemporary.

Carney, R. M., Saunders, R., Freedland, K., Stein, P., Rich, M., and Jaffe, A. (1995). Association of depression with reduced heart rate variability in coronary artery disease, *American Journal of Cardiology, 76*, 562–564.

Casadei, B., Conway, J., Forfar, C., & Sleight, P. (1996). Effect of low doses of scopolamine on RR interval variability, baroreflex sensitivity, and exercise performance in patients with chronic heart failure. *Heart, 75*, 274–280.

Cohen, H., Matar, M., Kaplan, Z., & Kotler, M. (1999). Power spectral analysis of heart rate variability in psychiatry. *Psychotherapy Psychosomatic, 68*(2), 59–66.

Daniel, S. (1998, October). Ongoing clinical research with Callahan Techniques Thought Field Therapy Voice Technology. *Thought Field Newsletter*.

De Ferrari, G., Mantick, M., & Vanoli, E. (1993). Scopolamine increases vagal tone and vagal reflexes in patients after myocardial infarction. *Journal of the American College of Cardiology, 22*, 1327–1334.

Dishman, R. K., Nakamura, Y., Garcia, M. E., Thompson, R. W., Dunn, A. L., Blair, S. N. (2000). Heart rate variability, trait anxiety, and perceived stress among physically fit men and women. *International Journal of Psychophysiology, 37*(2), 121–133.

Edwards, J. (1998). The right place at the right time. *The Thought Field, 4*(1).

Feldenkreis, M. (1972). *Awareness through movement: Health exercises for personal growth*. New York: Harper & Row.

Festinger, L. (1957). *A theory of cognitive dissonance*. Stanford: Stanford University Press.

Feynman, R. (1967). *The character of physical law*. Cambridge: MIT Press.

Foster, D. (1985). *The philosophical scientists*. NY: Barnes and Noble.

Friedman, B. H., & Thayer, F. J. (1998a). Anxiety and autonomic flexibility: A cardiovascular approach. *Biological Psychology, 47*(3), 243–263.

Friedman, B. H., & Thayer, F. J. (1998b). Autonomic balance revisited: Panic anxiety and heart rate variability. *Journal of Psychosomatic Research, 44*(1), 133–151.

Freinkel, A. (1994, Sept. 24). Witness to the execution. *Science News, 146*(13), 200w.

Fuller, B. F. (1992). The effects of stress-anxiety and coping styles on heart rate variability. *International Journal of Psychophysiology, 12*(1), 81–86.

Gazzaniga, M. (1985). *The social brain*. NY: Basic Books.

Gazzaniga, M. (1992). *Nature's mind*. NY: Basic Books.

Gazzaniga, M. (1998). *The mind's past*. Berkeley: University of California Press.

Graham, I. (1998). Personal Communication.

Huikuri, H., Makikallio, T., Airaksinen, K., Mitrani, R., Castellanos, A., & Myerburg, R. (1999). Measurement of heart rate variability: A clinical tool or a research toy? *Journal of the American College of Cardiology, 34*(7), 1878–1883.

Kautzner, J. (1995). Reproducibility of heart rate variability measurement. In M. Malik & J. Camm (Eds.), *Heart Rate Variability* (pp. 165–172). Armonk, NY: Futura Publishing Company.

Kawachi, I., Sparrow, D., Vokonas, P. S., & Weiss, S. T. (1995). Decreased heart rate variability in men with phobic anxiety data from the Normative Aging Study. *American Journal of Cardiology, 75*(14), 882–885.

Kienle, G. S., & Kiene, H. (1996). Placebo effect and placebo concept: A critical methodological and conceptual analysis of reports on the magnitude of the placebo effect. *Alternative Therapies, 2*(6), 39–53.

Kleiger, R., Bigger, J., Bosner, M., Chunk, M., Cook, J., Rolnitzky, L., Steinman, R., & Fleiss, J. (1991, Sept). Stability over time of variables measuring heart rate variability in normal subjects. *American Journal of Cardiology, 68*, 626–630.

Koestler, A. (1967). *The ghost in the machine*. NY: Viking-Penguin.

Langewitz, W., & Ruddel, H. (1989). Spectral analysis of heart rate variability under mental stress. *Journal of Hypertension, 7*, 32–33.

Lehofer, M., Moser, M., Hoehn-Saric, R., McLeod, D., Liebmann, P., Drnovsek, B., Egner, S., Hildebrandt, G., & Zapotoczsky, H. G. (1997). Major depression and cardiac autonomic control. *Biological Psychiatry, 42*(10), 914–919.

Leonoff, G. (1995). The successful treatment of phobias and anxiety by telephone and radio: A replication of Callahan's 1985 study. *The Thought Field, 1*(2).

McCraty, R., Atkinson, M., Tiller, W. A., Rein, G., & Watkins, A. D. (1995). The effects of emotions on short term power spectrum analysis of heart rate variability. *American Journal of Cardiology, 76*(14), 1089–1092.

Malik, M., & Camm, A. J. (Eds.). (1995). *Heart rate variability*. Armonk, NY: Futura Publishing.

Pignotti, M. (1999). Personal communication.

Sakai, C., Paperny, D., Matthews, M., Tanida, G., Boyd, G., Simons, A., Yamamoto, C., Mau, C., Nutter, L. (in press). Thought field therapy clinical applications: utilization in an HMO in behavioral medicine and behavioral health services. *Journal of Clinical Psychology*.

Seligman, M. (1994). *What you can change and what you can't*. New York: Knopf.

Venkatesh, G., Fallen, E., Kamath, M., Connolly, S., & Yusuf, S. (1996). Double blind placebo controlled trial of short term transdermal scopolamine on heart rate variability in patients with chronic heart failure. *Heart, 76*, 137–143.

Vybrial, T., Glaeser, D., Morris, G., Hess, K., Yang, K., Francis, M., & Pratt, C. (1993). Effects of low dose transdermal scopolamine on heart rate variability in acute myocardial infarction. *Journal of the American College of Cardiology, 22,* 1320–1326.

Walther, D. (1988). *Applied kinesiology: Synopsis.* Pueblo, CO: Systems DC.

Wolpe, J. (1969). *The practice of behavior therapy,* New York: Pergamon Press Inc.

Yeragani, V. K., Sobolewski, E., Igel, G., Johnson, C., Jampala, V. C., Kay, J., Hillman, N., Yergani, S., & Vemputi, S. (1998). Decreased heart-period variability in patients with panic disorder: a study of Holter ECG records, *Psychiatry Research, 78*(1–2), 89–99.

Yeragani, V. K., Pohl, R., Balon, R., Ramesh, C., Glitz, D., Jung, I., & Sherwood, P. (1991). Heart rate variability in patients with major depression. *Psychiatry Research, 37*(1), 35–46.

Youngson, R. M. (1994). *The Guiness encyclopedia of science.* Middlesex, England: Guiness.

Chapter 67 _____

*TRIAD COUNSELING**

PAUL B. PEDERSEN

How does one train counselors to deal with clients from different cultures? How does one effectively treat clients who not only have the usual resistances, but also special resistances due to the circumstances of different classes or different cultures? A well-intentioned and well-prepared counselor who faces hostile, fearful, resistant, or non-communicative individuals from different-from-himself/herself ethnic, social, cultural, or economic groups, with radically different values and lifestyles, often faces what appears to be insuperable communication and relationship problems. As a former prison psychologist and as one who has worked in various social agencies, I am well aware of the extent of this professional dilemma.

The triad model developed by Paul Pedersen is a genuinely novel approach to this kind of problem, and calls for a re-evaluation of traditional assumptions about and procedures used with such groups. The invention of the "anticounselor" is in my judgment a significant innovation not only for training, but also for treatment with fearful, suspicious, or alienated clients frequently met in various social agencies such as mental hospitals, clinics, student centers, and the like. Prepare for a brand new perspective on counseling and psychotherapy.

The triad model of counseling is specifically designed for effective cross-cultural counseling and is seen as a three-way interaction between the counselor, the client, and the problem. Its special features, which include an "anticounselor," are intended to reduce the well-known problem of client resistance, a problem that is generally stronger when the counselor and client come from different cultural backgrounds, whether they be "caste" or "class" differences. The greater the cultural difference, the less likely it is generally for a counselor to form an effective coalition with the client against the problem. When the social psychological perspectives of coalition formation in a triad are applied properly, the counselor is guided toward adjusting his or her power influence effectively to maintain a "willing coalition" format.

In the training of people to become cross-cultural counselors, the counselor, client, and a third person—the "anticounselor"—interact, with the "anticounselor" providing continuous immediate feedback relative to the power flow, thus sharpening the counselor's perceptions and skills (Pedersen, 2000).

HISTORY

The triad model grew out of a graduate seminar in 1965 at the University of Minnesota conducted by Clyde Parker and Donald Blocher, where the class assignment was to develop an original idea in counseling. Having just returned from three years of counseling in an Indonesian university, this writer was intrigued by how Asian clients generally conceptualized personal problems differently from U.S. clients. Problems were seen as both good and bad, and not as simply bad. Each problem was viewed by clients as having rewarding and valuable as well as undesirable features, thereby presenting a dilemma to the client. A problem was viewed as a complex entity, as a personality is, and not limited to the client's presenting symptom. The problem was viewed as actively changing in an almost "demonic" configuration with a "mind" of its own, not passively accepting client or counselor controls. In the counseling relationship a problem sometimes resembled a personified enemy, having a secret strategy of its own with concrete and specific manifestations of control over the client, much as a malevolent person might control the client against the client's best interests, through implicit threats and promises.

*This chapter was prepared through support from the National Institute of Mental Health Grant No. IT24 MH 15552-01.

To better understand the client's problem in cross-cultural counseling, I (1976b) experimented with using a third person from the client's culture in a simulated cross-cultural counseling interview. The third person was called the "anticounselor" to describe that person's function in the interview, using cultural similarity with the client to sharpen the counselor-client cross-cultural coalition.

The use of three persons in therapy is not new. Bolman (1968) was probably the first to suggest that at least two therapists, one representing each culture, be used in cross-cultural therapy to provide a bridge between the client's culture and the therapist. Triads were also advocated by Slack and Slack (1976) by involving a third person who had already coped effectively with the client's problem in the counseling relationship. Triads have been applied to Family Therapy as examples of pathogenic coalitions (Satir, 1964), with the therapist employing mediation and side-taking judiciously to replace pathogenic relating. Counseling thus becomes a series of negotiations in which all three parties vie for control. Zuk (1971) described this approach as a "go-between" process in which the therapist catalyzes conflict in a crisis situation in which all parties can take an active role.

Historically, it is well accepted that counselors who differ from their clients in race, culture, or social class have difficulty effecting constructive changes, while counselors who are most similar in these respects have a greater facility for appropriate intervention. A common example is that alcoholics apparently are best helped by other alcoholics. Barriers of language, class-bound values, or culture-bound goals have a tendency to weaken the counselor-client coalition and disrupt the counseling relationship. In working with clients from other cultures, there is a great danger of mutual misunderstanding; imperfect understanding of the other culture's unique problems; and an ingrained prejudice that destroys rapport, leading to increased negative transference toward the counselor and presenting the danger of confusing a client's appropriate cultural response with foreign constructs such as "neurotic transference" (Pedersen, 1976a; 2000).

The culturally encapsulated counselor might disregard cultural variations among clients in a dogmatic adherence to some "universal" notion of technique-oriented truth.

The usual system of selecting, training, and certifying counselors reflects and even reinforces culturally encapsulated bias. There is evidence that even well-trained counselors are not generally prepared to deal with individuals who come from racial, ethnic, or socioeconomic groups whose values, attitudes, and general life styles are different from middle-class norms (Pedersen, 1976a).

Therapists unable to adjust their own attitudes, beliefs, and style of behavior to those of another culture are likely to substitute their own criteria of desired social effectiveness for alternative criteria more appropriate to the client's environment.

CURRENT STATUS

Most of the current work on Triad Counseling has been done in a training mode rather than in direct service to clients in therapy situations, but, paradoxically, training of counselors becomes therapy for the trainees.

Research among students using Triad Counseling showed they achieved statistically significantly higher scores on a multiple-choice written test designed to measure counselor effectiveness; they demonstrated a lower discrepancy between real and ideal self-description; and they chose a greater number of positive adjectives in describing themselves as counselors than previous semester students who did not use the triad model. In addition, there were significant increases from pretest to posttest on videotaped cross-cultural interviews rated for empathy, respect, and congruence. Moreover, pretest training videotapes, when rated on the seven-level Gordon scales measuring communication of understanding of affective meaning, showed that students had increased their skill levels significantly (Pedersen, Holwill, & Shapiro, 1978; Pedersen, 2000).

After a one-day in-service training workshop with 39 Asian-American counselors working with transient mainland youth, participants responded to a questionnaire: Did the training help them anticipate client resistance? (28 yes, 4 no, 7 no response) Did it help to articulate the problem? (25 yes, 6 no, 2 somewhat, 6 no response) Did they want additional training with the model? (22 yes, 8 no, 1 maybe, 8 no response) When asked what values they had gained as a result of using the model, 12 emphasized better understanding of cultural differences, 8 emphasized improved in-service training for counselors, and 5 emphasized the value of a third person (anticounselor) in simulated counseling interviews. Responding to a similar questionnaire, 40 other counselors were also positive: Did the training help them anticipate client resistance? (32 yes, 1 no, 1 maybe, 4 somewhat, and 2 no response) Did this training help articulate the problem? (30 yes, 2 no, 5 somewhat, and 3 no response) Did they want additional training in the model? (28 yes, 1 no, 1 maybe, and 10 no response)

In 1977, Fahy Holwill-Bailey (1979) compared a traditional mode of teaching human relations/intercultural skills to counselors with a design similar to Kagan et al.'s (1965) "interpersonal process recall" method and a triad model design. As dependent measures she used Ivey's counselor effectiveness scale, the Revised Truax Accurate Empathy scale, the Revised Carkhuff Respect and Genuineness scale, the Shapiro Adjective Checklist, and the Bender Tolerance and Ambiguity Scale. In a three-way analysis of covariance, all tests were found significant between the control group and the treatment group. In a preliminary analysis of her data no significant differences were found between the measures of the triad and the dyadic training design, however, suggesting that both approaches were approximately equally effective but both seemed superior to the traditional counselor education approaches.

Ivey and Authier (1978) discuss the triad model in "the cultural-environmental-contextual implications" of microcounseling as a training approach. Ivey and Authier (1978) indicated that "The most powerful and direct method for cross-cultural training appears to be that of the cross-cultural triad model of Pedersen" (p. 215). At the same time, they pointed out that the triad model would not be appropriate for all trainees; naive trainees might "wilt" under the pressure of the anticounselor. Ivey suggested further that trainees would benefit most from the triad model after having learned basic microcounseling skills of counseling.

The Institute of Behavioral Sciences in Honolulu, Hawaii, is sponsoring an intercultural mental health training program. The program will provide in-service training on cross-cultural counseling skills, annual conferences on cross-cultural counseling, and an evaluation component to monitor the effectiveness of the training methods. Derald Sue (1979) is collecting data comparing the effectiveness of triads with an anticounselor and triads using a "procounselor."

A procounselor is a resource person from the client's culture whose task is to facilitate the counseling experience, emphasizing the positive aspects of the interaction just as an anticounselor emphasizes the negative aspects. The procounselor needs to help the counselor do a better job without taking over the client or disrupting the counseling process. The procounselor role requires more skill than an anticounselor role, as the resource person must not only identify the mistakes being made but reinterpret and redirect the counselor's intervention to minimize the negative and maximize the positive impact. Having a procounselor ally from the client's culture is often reassuring to the counselor, although an insensitive procounselor may take over the interview and become extremely threatening to the insecure counselor.

Additional experiments with Triad Counseling have resulted in six alternative training designs: (1) the anticounselor, in which the client's partner role-plays the negative feedback; (2) the procounselor, where the client's partner role-plays the positive feedback; (3) the interpreter, where the client's partner facilitates accurate communication between client and counselor with both positive and negative feedback; (4) a third-person-hostile, where the client's partner role-plays a close friend or relative hostile to counseling; (5) a third-

person-friendly, where the client's partner role-plays a close friend or relative friendly to counseling; and (6) a quartet of both the hostile and friendly partner to the client interacting with the counselor.

Further modifications seek to specify the training and therapy skills in greater detail; adapt the triad model design to verbal and nonverbal, confronting and nonconfronting cultures; and collect data on the specific impact of the direct and immediate feedback from a client during the simulated cross-cultural interview. This writer has compiled previously published materials on the triad model in a book, *Basic Intercultural Counseling Skills* (1979a), in connection with further research development and teaching that incorporates the model.

THEORY

Counseling can be described as an interaction of push and pull factors in which the counselor seeks fulfillment in being helpful, the client seeks to reconcile internalized ambiguity, and the problem loses its control over the client. The counseling force field suggests a triad of stress, response to it, and ameliorative intervention, all three of which are potentially subject to being culturally mediated. The counselor-client interaction is basically a social interaction following the same laws and principles as other social interactions. This writer (1968, 1973) has described this force field as a dynamic interaction of contrary forces in the mode of social power theory and in the context of an equilibrium between the counselor seeking coalition with the client against resistance by the problem (Caplow, 1968). The counselor-client coalition requires identification of action in accord with a shared goal. Just as the client has called in a counselor for assistance, the counselor must also depend on the client for knowledge about the problem. Negotiating a coalition between the client and counselor describes the task functions of counseling, subject to frequent maintenance and modification.

Figure 67.1 outlines a schematic for describing the relationships between the counselor, client, and problem as a triadic interaction. This figure describes counseling as competition for influence between a client-counselor coalition on the one hand and the problem on the other. The figure assumes that we are able to estimate differences between high and low levels of power or influence as a general descriptor for measuring client progress. Counseling, then, becomes a process whereby a client's contribution of power or influence is increased and, as an inverse function of this process, the problem's capacity for power or influence is decreased. The client is expected to move up the slope from having less power to having more power as the desired outcome. The desired outcome is that the problem is expected to move down

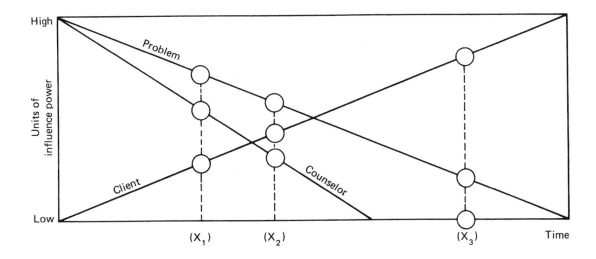

Figure 67.1   A schematic description of the ratio of power influence over time for counselor, client, and problem with three (X_1, X_2, X_3) points in the counseling process indicated.

the slope to having less power. The counselor is expected to intervene to encourage client progress through a client-counselor coalition that isolates and weakens the power of the problem. At any given point along the time dimension, the power of a successful counselor plus the power of the client should be approximately the same as the power of the problem (Co + Cl = P). The unequal and dynamic distribution of power requires the effective counselor to vary the intensity of intervention accordingly. If the counselor assumes too much power, the client will withdraw from counseling, preferring to have the problem, since it will be seen as less threatening or dominating than the counselor. If the counselor assumes too little power, the problem will dominate through a continued coalition with the client.

Three situations (X_1, X_2, X_3) are indicated in Figure 67.1. In X_1, the client has little power and is dominated by the problem. Situation X_2 shows the client able to exert enough power so that the counselor may become the weaker member of the triad, transferring more responsibility to the client. Situation X_3 shows the client able to manage the problem independently, needing little help from the counselor. A "low-power" client statement might be, "I feel bad and I don't know why." This might be matched by a more intense counselor interpretive statement, such as, "Perhaps the reason you feel bad is thus and so." A higher power client statement might be, "But that's not at all how I feel." This might be matched by a less intense counselor reflection, such as, "You don't feel thus and so, and it is a problem for you." Clients who are reasonably effective in dealing with their problem require minimal intervention by the counselor. Good counseling will help clients be more effective.

The units of high- and low-power influence are relative and not absolute points; thus it is necessary to distinguish between a relatively effective client facing a difficult problem and a relatively ineffective client facing a mild problem. Counselors need to coordinate their own intervention according to the variable rate and direction of the client's movement to maintain the client-counselor coalition. Counselor interventions toward the left side of Figure 67.1 tend to be confronting and interpretive, while interventions toward the right side of the figure tend to be reflective and nondirective. The counselor needs to monitor accurately and attend to client feelings, otherwise interventions are likely to be inappropriate. When the client comes from a culture different from that of the counselor, however, it is extremely difficult to interpret client communications accurately.

The "anticounselor" is similar to the alter ego in psychodrama or Gestalt Psychotherapy, except that the anticounselor is not neutral or helpful but is deliberately subversive, attempting to disrupt the counseling interview. The counselor, therefore, is pulling in one direction toward a solution, while the anticounselor is pulling in exactly the opposite direction, attempting to maintain the problem. The client chooses which alternative, the cross-cultural counselor or the same-culture anticounselor, offers the most meaningful ally. A client/counselor coalition against the anticounselor becomes the vehicle of effective counseling, while ineffective counseling results in a client/anticounselor coalition isolating and rendering ineffective the counselor. While the strategies of a counselor and the role expectations for a client are familiar to us, the notion of an active, back-talking anticounselor at first seems bizarre and strange. The problem, represented by the anticounselor, develops its own unique strategies.

The role of the anticounselor is distinguished from the role of a person with a problem. The anticounselor role carries negative function, just as the counselor's role implies positive function in the counseling relationship, thereby polarizing these two roles. The client is "wooed" by both the counselor and the anticounselor. The anticounselor's intention might be to contain counseling at a superficial level; to confuse, distort, distract, discredit, complicate, or otherwise frustrate the counselor. Most anticounselors make themselves attractive to same-culture clients, not being constrained by rules of logical consistency and with private cultural access to the client. The anticounselor provides negative feedback that would not be appropriate coming from the client even in role play, thereby articulating the resistances that would otherwise be symbolically ambiguous.

Triad Counseling combines insights from a wide range of theories. The principles of psychodrama and sociodrama have long advocated the use of role-play to illustrate clearly the otherwise ambiguous elements of a complicated relationship. The role-playing of interviews for counselor training has been standard procedure for many years, although not with the same negative and positive structures described in this chapter. The insights of social psychology are applied in the literature about coalition formation in a triad; the illustrations of force-field theory and analysis of push/pull factors of a relationship are evident in the triad model in the tension between pro- and anticounselor perspectives. Kelley and Thibaut (1978) review the social psychology literature about interdependence in dyads influenced by the social environment. The triad model has adapted theories of social psychology to the counseling dyad partners in their various configurations in their interdependent relationship to one another (Revich & Geertsma 1969; Salomon & McDonald, 1970; Stroller, 1967).

METHODOLOGY

The first step in setting up a triad model is to locate a suitable resource person. He or she must be matched with the client as a team. It is essential that the teams of resource persons be culturally similar to one another and communicate well enough to anticipate what the other would be thinking and feeling. Often, having located one resource person, it is best to let that person select the other. Whether as an anticounselor, interpreter, or procounselor, the client's partner needs to provide accurate insight into what the client is really thinking and feeling for the model to work. The resource team needs to be articulate enough to provide feedback to the counselor that would be understood even by an outsider to

that culture; additionally, the feedback must be authentic to the basic values of the culture. The resource team should also be comfortable giving positive and/or negative feedback to the counselor.

The second step is in training the resource persons to perform in a triadic situation. The resource persons are instructed to give positive feedback exclusively *or* negative feedback exclusively, with the client's partner providing one or the other but *not* both. In this way the counselor working with a culturally different client will enter the interview knowing unambiguously that the resource person is either an "enemy" or a "friend." The counselor gains facility in differentiating positive from negative feedback in a culturally different setting by focusing on them separately without initially having to disentangle them during the interview itself. The triad model can be demonstrated through previously videotaped interviews showing the simulated interaction between a counselor and a client with an anticounselor, procounselor, interpreter, or another adaptation. If videotaped models are not available, simulated role-plays might help the resource persons understand the interaction process. It is important for them to watch a model of the interaction to clarify what will be expected of them later. They will then be able to practice role-playing the triad model, if possible reviewing their interviews on videotape for debriefing. Where resource persons are reluctant to provide negative feedback, it might be useful to involve several persons in the anticounselor role simultaneously to take the pressure off the resource person as an individual. It is important for resource persons to be well trained so that they understand what will be expected of them.

The resource persons should be instructed to give continuous and immediate feedback to the counselor about what is working and what is not working. They may provide this feedback verbally or nonverbally, but the cues should accompany the good or bad counselor interventions as immediately as possible, as unmistakably obvious as possible, and continuously throughout the interview. The counselor, having identified the good or bad intervention, can then recover or correct the intervention immediately. Gradually the counselor is expected to become more sensitive to subtle positive and negative cues from the client/resource person team and take immediate corrective action to anticipate negative feedback even before it is given.

The third step in using the triad model is in selecting the problems to be studied. In an actual setting where the resource person will be used in direct therapy, the problems would be provided by the client. The task of the anticounselor, procounselor, or interpreter would be to accurately reflect and understand the problem from the client's point of view. To perform effectively, the resource person would have to be extremely skilled and sensitive to the client's unique perspective. In a training setting the client/resource person team would be able to identify a series of problems familiar to both of them and likely to be unfamiliar to the counselor trainee. The problems should be selected for their training potential so that they would be complex rather than simple and with no easy solution, reflect the client's cultural values wherever possible, and fairly frequently encountered as serious and meaningful issues in the client's culture. Often the resource team might be helped in selecting the problems for training by asking them to model their problem on the actual problem of someone from their culture. It is extremely important that the resource team *not* use a serious problem in which one of them might themselves be seeking therapy; this would confuse the training situation with direct counseling and could result in the resource person's injury.

Once the resource persons have been selected and trained, and appropriate problems have been selected, the team is ready to work in a direct service, in-service, or preservice setting. While there is some data from using the model for in-service or preservice training, there is no data from using the model in direct service therapy. Extreme caution should therefore be used, especially if an adaptation of the anticounselor is used in direct service therapy.

Direct Service Therapy

The use of a third person in therapy is not new. In many nonWestern cultures the role of the go-between or third person as broker of advice and help has been the standard mode of "counseling." Often the client will bring a third person into the interview who is positively or negatively disposed toward the counseling process. Even when there is only the counselor and the client alone in the interview, however, the triad model hypothesizes that positive and negative advice from the client's environment continue to influence the client's response and is heard much more clearly by the client's "inner ear" than by the counselor as a cultural outsider. Much of counseling is spent articulating these sources of "*anti*counseling."

If the counselor is experiencing an impasse either because of language problems or some other source of client resistance that may be culturally related, the counselor may request an interpreter or third person to assist in the interview. To some extent counseling through a translator resembles an adaptation of the triad model, especially insofar as the culture as well as the language needs to be translated. Even when there is no language problem, however, a third person may be required to help the counselor work more sensitively and effectively in another culture. Such a third person might further reduce the client's anxiety, especially if the client has a role

in selecting the third person, and facilitate the counseling interview. The third person's role would have to be clarified to the client in detail, especially if the third person emphasized negative feedback to the counselor.

Another adaptation of Triad Counseling currently being used in marriage counseling asks the husband and the wife each to bring an advocate to the session who would argue for their point of view. Then a videocamera focuses on the four persons (husband, wife, prohusband, prowife) and the counselor leaves the room while the four persons are videotaped discussing together the disagreements of the husband and the wife. After a period of time the counselor returns to the room and watches the videotape with the husband and wife, and they discuss the issues of disagreement that came out in the earlier quartet. Again, the otherwise ambiguous and obscure positive and negative feedback are made articulate by the resource persons in ways that the client, or in this case clients, were unable to deal with explicitly.

Even in an interview alone with the client, a counselor may wish to "hypothesize" the problem as a third "presence" there in the room working against the counselor, counseling process, and ultimately against the client as well. In helping the client to see the influence of this problem as anticounselor, the client might be helped to articulate many of the otherwise implicit negative feelings about being in counseling.

In-Service Training

Generally in in-service training two teams are trained. Ten to 15 counselors are assembled in a meeting room with a video monitor. Following an introduction and presentation of a video demonstration tape of Triad Counseling, the facilitator answers questions while one of the counselors leaves the room with a client/anticounselor team to make the first videotape. The counselor and team return to the group after having produced a 10-minute videotape of a simulated counseling interview and a 5-minute videotape of the three participants debriefing one another. This 15-minute videotape is then shown to the larger group for comments and discussion. While the first tape is being viewed and discussed, another counselor leaves the room with the second client/anticounselor team to produce a second videotape. Throughout the day there is always one counselor and team making a tape and another videotape being viewed or discussed, until all counselors have had a chance to produce a videotape and receive feedback on their performance. Each counselor thereby misses the viewing and discussing of one colleague's videotape. The advantages of immediate feedback on videotaped counseling interviews are that stimulating discussion on the variety of cultures and presenting problems on counseling relationships is provoked. The videotapes produced during such a workshop can also provide a valuable resource (Pedersen, 1976b). In larger groups the videotaping might be less appropriate than role-played interviews in small groups of about 10 counselors plus a resource team.

Preservice Training

The triad model can also be adapted for use in the classroom. In one trial, 30 graduate counseling students were randomly paired with other classmates from the opposite sex and/or a different ethnic group. Each pair made two videotapes of simulated counseling interviews, switching roles for the second tape, as a premeasure of cross-cultural counseling ability. These tapes and a similar series of posttraining tapes were scored to measure changes in skill resulting from training. The 30 students were then assembled into triads so that each triad contained two subjects of one sex and the third member of the opposite sex. Five of the 10 triads were also cross-cultural in ethnic composition. The objective was to have triads where two persons were much alike and one person was as different as possible, using sex role and ethnicity as indicators of differences. During the first phase of training, one student in each triad was assigned to the counselor role, one to the client role, and one to the anticounselor role. The triads met for three hours in the same roles, simulating and discussing three different cross-cultural interviews. During the second phase of the training one week later, the students rotated roles in the triad and the three-hour procedure was repeated. During the third phase in the third week of the project, students again rotated their roles for a third three-hour session. Afterward, each student had experience in each of the roles, for a total of nine hours, using the triad model with feedback on nine cross-cultural interviews (Pedersen, Holwill, & Shapiro, 1978).

Adaptations of these training designs have been used in a wide variety of workshop or classroom situations. The triad model seems to work best when (1) there is positive as well as negative feedback to the counselor; (2) all three persons interact with one another rather than there being just counselor and client interaction; (3) the client/anticounselor team is highly motivated and feels strongly about the issue under discussion; (4) the anticounselor has a high degree of empathy for and acceptance by the client; (5) the anticounselor is articulate and gives direct, immediate verbal and/or nonverbal feedback to the counselor; (6) the client has *not* selected a real problem from his or her current situation where counseling might be appropriate; (7) the discussion is spontaneous and not scripted; (8) the counselor has a chance to role-play the model and receive feedback three or four times in sequence; (9) the client feels free to reject an inauthentic anticounselor; and (10) the facilitator introducing the model and leading the discussion is well acquainted with how the model operates.

APPLICATIONS

Triad Counseling has been used to train counselors working with welfare clients, alcoholics, the handicapped, foreign students, prisoners, and other identity groups where there is likely to be a difference in values between counselors and clients.

We know that cultural backgrounds influence a counseling relationship, but we do not know how. We know that counselors have a cultural bias, but we are not able to evaluate it. We know that the appropriate matching of problems and solutions differs from one culture to another, but we don't know why.

There are several reasons why a cross-cultural training program for counselors is valuable.

1. Traditional systems of mental health services have a cultural bias favoring dominant social classes, which can be counterproductive to an equitable distribution of services.
2. Various cultural groups have discovered that indigenous modes of coping and treatment that work better for them may also be usefully applied to other groups.
3. Community health services are expensive when they fail, and cross-cultural training might prevent some programs from failing.
4. Training methods that directly include indigenous people as training resource persons have not been widely used in counselor education.
5. The constructs of healthy and normal that guide the delivery of mental health services are not the same for all cultures and might cause the culturally encapsulated counselor to become a tool of a particular political, social, or economic system.
6. Increased interdependence across national, ethnic, and social-cultural boundaries requires direct attention as part of mental health training.
7. Most therapists come from dominant cultures, while most clients do not and are consequently not likely to share the same perspectives.

Triad Counseling seems to offer numerous advantages that complement other training approaches.

1. It provides an opportunity for people of different ethnic groups to role-play critical incidents likely to arise in cross-cultural counseling.
2. The use of an anticounselor makes the cultural problems and value issues specific and concrete to the counselor trainee.
3. Inappropriate counselor intervention is immediately and obviously apparent through feedback from the anticounselor.

4. The counselor trainee becomes very much aware of the unspoken thoughts and feelings of the client from another culture through feedback from the anticounselor.
5. Videotaped simulations between the counselor, client, and anticounselor can be used to analyze specific ways in which cultural differences affect counseling.
6. Counselor trainees can learn to generalize insights from simulated cross-cultural interviews to direct contact with culturally different clients.
7. A careful analysis of the transcripts of simulated interviews with a culturally different client/anticounselor team will identify explicit skills for development with specific cultures.

In their anecdotal comments about the triad model, counselors emphasize the importance of "dealing with feelings" as well as content in the interview, "learning to deal with feelings of helpless frustration" from culturally different clients in a nondefensive mode, learning "how to be in two cultures at the same time," and learning "the cues a client from another culture uses to communicate feelings."

Coached clients report that "the questions you (counselor) ask don't stick in my head as well as what he (anticounselor) says," that "the anticounselor forces me to express myself more totally than I would otherwise," that "having the problem objectified helped lay it out objectively from an outside point of view," and that the problems of working with a counselor from another culture who didn't understand the cues, hints, understatements, or omissions become painfully clear.

Coached anticounselors found that "they could defeat the counselor by carefully attending to feelings," described themselves as "the personalized, hidden self out in the open exposing all the contradictions, value conflicts, fears, expectations that are not supposed to come out," detailed how the model "allows a counselor and client to cut through pretense and the defenses they both have erected against the other," and noted how it can "intensify the client's anxiety and fortify the cultural barriers to communication," which might otherwise escape detection.

CASE EXAMPLE

Four skill areas for counselors have emerged from working with the triad model in simulated cross-cultural interviews. These skill areas are (1) articulating the problem from the client's cultural perspective, (2) recognizing resistance from a culturally different client in specific rather than general terms, (3) diminishing counselor de-

fensiveness when confronted by an anticounselor, and (4) learning recovery skills for getting out of trouble when making mistakes counseling culturally different clients. Excerpts from interviews will demonstrate how the triad model brings to surface otherwise implicit messages from a culturally different client.

Articulation

All of us perceive the world from our own culturally biased points of view. To the extent that a client does not share our cultural background, the client is equally unlikely to share our point of view. In the first example from a simulated counseling interview between a white male counselor, a black female client, and a black male anticounselor, notice how the three-way interaction helps the counselor "articulate the problem."

CLIENT: . . . Like I am a College of Liberal Arts major and a lot of times most of the classes are a lot of white kids, there aren't that many black kids on campus. And not in General College, you know, so the ones I do know I have to go elsewhere to meet, to talk to them and stuff.
COUNSELOR: Is it white gals you have problems relating to and white guys or . . . ?
CLIENT: Well, . . .
ANTICOUNSELOR: Right now, the question is can you relate to *him* (pointing to counselor)? (pause) Yeah, what are you doing here?
CLIENT: Well, umm . . . you got a good question there. I mean . . .
COUNSELOR: Do you have difficulty relating to me now? I'm white, you're black. . . .
ANTICOUNSELOR: Remember all those things that happen when white folks deal with black folks. . . .

There is a clear division of responsibility between the counselor, client, and anticounselor in explicating the problem, with the client acknowledging what the anticounselor says as true but being reluctant to say the same things herself. It is as though the client can rely on the anticounselor to bring out the negative, embarrassing, and critical aspects of the problem, which would otherwise be left implicitly ambiguous. Although those negative aspects might not have been brought out explicitly, they would nonetheless be there and, even unexplained, would have a profound effect on the interview.

Resistance

It is important to recognize resistance in specific rather than general terms as it relates to cultural differences between a counselor and a client. When resistance arises in an interview, it is important to identify and deal with it before proceeding toward controlling the problem dimension of the interview. It is important to listen to the anticounselor and determine whether the client is accepting and thereby validating the anticounselor's statements. The counselor may then modify interventions to accommodate the resistance in specific rather than general terms. An excerpt from the same interview with a white male counselor, a black female client, and a black male anticounselor illustrates this point.

ANTICOUNSELOR: We've been here five or six minutes and how much trust do we have in him? What has he done so far that can make us say that we can trust him to deal with the whole situation? You heard him hesitate. You heard him stumble around, we've heard him take the uniqueness out of the problem. . . .

COUNSELOR: Terry . . .

ANTICOUNSELOR: We've heard him say deal with the jokes. How much trust can we put in this man?

COUNSELOR: Terry, why don't you ah . . . try to, ah . . . eliminate (pause) . . . Not eliminate, certainly not eliminate . . .

ANTICOUNSELOR: I'm beginning to think trust is getting less and less.

COUNSELOR: I asked you a question on . . .

CLIENT: Well, it's like the questions you are asking don't stick in my mind as well as what he is saying to me. It's like he can relate with what I'm, you know, the thing I'm going with and you gave me a lot of stuff about how a lot of black people are approaching the same problem. But the thing is what I want to know is how do I deal with it?

There is a buildup of data where counselor mistakes contribute toward an overall loss of counselor credibility. In all therapy sessions, the client is likely to move toward a conclusion that is either positive or negative. However, the counselor would be less likely to get that explicit feedback in a cross-cultural interview without the anticounselor. Somehow the counselor is going to have to work through the specific resistance before counseling can result in an acceptable outcome for the client; before the counselor can do that, he or she will have to know clearly the mistakes being made.

Defensiveness

The cross-cultural interview is frequently ambiguous for the counselor and can easily cause even a skilled counselor to become less sure of him- or herself, leading to defensive behavior. It is important for the counselor in any interview to avoid the distraction of defensive behavior and focus more directly on the client's message. If the counselor is distracted by becoming defensive, the rapport with a client is likely to diminish. If a counselor is

ever going to be defensive, it is more likely to occur in the presence of an anticounselor, who is seeking to sabotage the interview. The triad model allows counselors to examine their own latent defensiveness and raise their threshold for nondefensive counselor responses. An excerpt from a simulated interview with a U.S. male counselor, a Latin-American female client, and a Latin-American female anticounselor demonstrates how counselor defensiveness can become a distraction.

CLIENT: Yeah, you see this thing, these things for me are very intense for me right now because I just came here. I've been here for only a month.

COUNSELOR: Would you feel better if I got back behind the desk and we sort of had that between us?

CLIENT: No, then you remind me of my father.

COUNSELOR: Okay, I don't want to do that (laugh). . . . Okay, is this more comfortable?

CLIENT: Yeah, it is.

COUNSELOR: Okay (pause).

CLIENT: Then you make me feel like you are rejecting me. You are not rejecting me?

COUNSELOR: I'm in a box here. On the one hand I want to do the things that will make you comfortable, and on the other I don't want to get too distant and make you feel like I'm rejecting you.

ANTICOUNSELOR: He's manipulating you little by little till he gets to a point that he's going to say that you got to be just like American girls. That's the best way.

COUNSELOR: How do you feel now as opposed to when you came in?

CLIENT: Well, I'm kind of feeling uncomfortable. It was okay for a while and now I feel like, I don't know . . . I feel like I want to go.

The counselor is trying to deal with his own discomfort as well as the client's discomfort and is scrambling to establish a comfortable rapport. The harder he struggles to regain the client's confidence, the more anxious the client becomes. As the resistance increases the anticounselor consolidates her position and the counseling intervention is further blocked. Perhaps if the counselor had dealt more with the client's feelings and less with his own defensive responses the rapport could have been restored.

Recovery

Skilled counselors make perhaps as many mistakes as unskilled counselors; however, skilled counselors are able to get out of trouble and recover from mistakes with increased rather than diminished rapport. The function of training is then perhaps not to teach counselors how to avoid making mistakes but rather to help those who make mistakes to recover effectively. If a counselor working with a culturally different client is not making mistakes, then he or she may very well not be taking enough personal risk in the interview. The triad model provides opportunities for the counselor to make mistakes and experiment with various recovery strategies. The counselor who feels confident that he or she can recover from mistakes is likely to be less apprehensive about making mistakes in the first place. Another interview excerpt with the U.S. male counselor, the Latin-American female client, and the Latin-American female anticounselor will illustrate the point.

ANTICOUNSELOR: You know what he is trying to do? He is going to try to get everything out of you and then convince you that you have to be the way Americans do and just screw around. . . .

COUNSELOR: Well, I'm just thinking that you . . . I don't understand much about your country. . . . What you have been used to.

ANTICOUNSELOR: . . . And you know what will happen when you go back home.

COUNSELOR: So I need to find out first of all what you have been used to and what pleases you, and then I can help you learn how to get men to respond to you in that same way here. It is not necessary, you see, that you respond as they demand. It is perfectly possible, and I guess you have to take this kind of on faith. . . . This is, I might say, a problem not just foreign girls have; American girls have this problem too.

CLIENT: No! You know, *they* don't have that problem! They seem to enjoy that type of thing and they don't seem to have a problem with it!

COUNSELOR: I don't want to argue about that. What we want to do is deal with your problem.

CLIENT: That's right.

In the process of exploring the client's problem, the counselor tries to generalize the problem to include American girls as well as foreign girls. Both the client and the anticounselor totally reject that generalization and obviously resent being lumped together with American females in this instance. The counselor could have defended his statement; he could have gotten into a discussion with the client on the topic; he could have argued or apologized; but he did none of these. Instead he brought the focus directly back to the client and the client's problem and very neatly avoided what could have been a serious misunderstanding.

Through simulated cross-cultural counseling interviews the culturally implicit element becomes visible through the interaction of a counselor, client, and anticounselor within the safety of a role play. Separating the roles of client and anticounselor makes the problem less diffuse and abstract to counselor trainees, with the negative feedback being both more direct and specific, appropriate to the role of the anticounselor. Inappropriate counselor intervention is apparent immediately, and the counselor can adjust his or her approach immediately. The members of a client culture become resource persons for learning to counsel persons from those same cultures in a mutualistic exchange of knowledge; consequently, the client culture has more invested in the success of those counselors they have trained. Finally, the triad model illustrates the balance of power between the counselor, the client, and the anticounselor, reminding trainees that ultimately the determination of success or failure lies with the client and not the counselor (Pedersen, 1978).

SUMMARY

Triad Counseling is a conceptual framework for viewing the interaction between a counselor, a client, and the problem that brings them together. The greater the cultural difference between counselor and client, the more ambiguous the problem element and the more difficult the task of appropriate counselor intervention. The triad model therefore is also a training design for developing interculturally skilled counselors by matching the counselor trainee with a coached client/client-partner team from the same other culture. The three-way interaction between the client, counselor, and the client's partner will provide immediate and continuous feedback to the counselor on the otherwise implicit dynamics of the counseling interview. The client's partner may interact as an anticounselor, procounselor, interpreter, third-person-hostile, or third-person-friendly, depending on the appropriate constraints on each training situation.

In each case the culturally different resource persons (anticounselors) become the training authority for helping the counselor learn to articulate the problem from the client's cultural perspective, recognize resistance in specific rather than general terms, diminish counselor defensiveness, and learn recovery skills for getting out of trouble. The counselor learns about counseling in a simulated cross-cultural interview where the otherwise implicit and generalized principles of counseling become explicit and specific. The use of videotape in recording the simulated interviews further enhances the power of the training through detailed debriefing of the interview.

Thus far, little research has been completed on Triad Counseling, although several research studies using the training design are in progress. The triad model is being used in a variety of programs to train counselors to work with culturally different clients. There is interest in using Triad Counseling to train counselors working with clients who are culturally similar but differ from the counselor according to age, sex role, socioeconomic status, physical handicap, life style, or other affiliations important to the client's identity (Pedersen, 1977; 2000).

There is a serious bias among most counselors that favors the cultural assumptions of a very small minority labeled the "dominant culture" in our society. Counseling will need to develop conceptual and training models that will assist counselors to learn a variety of approaches appropriate to our pluralistic society. Triad Counseling is one attempt to suggest an eclectic approach to understanding counseling that might adapt to a variety of cultural environments (Pedersen, 1974; 2000).

REFERENCES

Bolman, W. M. (1968). Cross-cultural psychotherapy. *American Journal of Psychiatry, 124,* 1234–1237.

Caplow, T. (1968). *Two against one: Coalitions in triads.* Englewood Cliffs, N.J.: Prentice-Hall.

Holwill-Bailey, F. (1979). Personal communication.

Ivey, A. E., & Authier, J. (1978). *Microcounseling: Innovations in interviewing training.* Springfield, IL: Charles C. Thomas.

Kagan, N., Krathwohl, D., & Farquhar, W. (1965). *Interpersonal process recall.* East Lansing, MI: Michigan State University.

Kelley, H., & Thibaut, J. (1978). *Interpersonal relations: A theory of interdependence.* New York: Wiley.

Pedersen, P. B. (1968). A proposal: That counseling be viewed as an instance of coalition. *Journal of Pastoral Care, 22,* 139–146.

Pedersen, P. B. (1973). A conceptual system describing the counseling relationship as a coalition against the problem. Paper presented at the meeting of the American Psychological Association, Montreal.

Pedersen, P. B. (1974). Cross-cultural communications training for mental health professionals. *The International and Intercultural Communication Annual, 1,* 53–64.

Pedersen, P. B. (1976a). The field of intercultural counseling. In P. Pedersen, W. Lonner, & J. Draguns (Eds.), *Counseling across cultures.* Honolulu: University Press of Hawaii.

Pedersen, P. B. (1976b). A model for training mental health workers in cross-cultural counseling. In J. Westermeyer & B. Maday (Eds.), *Culture and mental health.* The Hague: Mouton.

Pedersen, P. B. (1977). The triad model of cross-cultural counselor training. *Personnel and Guidance Journal, 56,* 94–100.

Pedersen, P. B. (1978, April). Four dimensions of cross-cultural skill in counselor training. *Personnel and Guidance Journal.*

Pedersen, P. B. (1979a). *Basic intercultural counseling skills.* Honolulu: DISC.

Pedersen, P. B. (1979b). Counseling clients from other cultures: Two training designs. In M. Asante & E. Newmark (Eds.), *Handbook of intercultural communication.* Beverly Hills, CA: Sage.

Pedersen, P. (2000). *Hidden messages in culture-centered counseling: A triad training model.* Thousand Oaks, CA: SAGE.

Pedersen, P. B., Holwill, C. F., & Shapiro, J. L. (1978). A cross-cultural training procedure for classes in counselor education. *Journal of Counselor Education and Supervision, 17,* 233–237.

Revich, R., & Geertsma, R. (1969). Observational media and psychotherapy training. *Journal of Nervous and Mental Disorders, 148,* 310–327.

Salomon, G., & McDonald, F. J. (1970). Pretest and post-test reactions to self-viewing one's teaching performance on videotape. *Journal of Educational Psychology, 61,* 280–286.

Satir, V. (1964). *Conjoint family therapy.* Palo Alto, CA: Science and Behavior Books.

Slack, C. W., & Slack, E. N. (1976, February). It takes three to break a habit. *Psychology Today,* 46–50.

Stroller, F. M. (1967). Group psychotherapy on television: An innovation with hospitalized patients. *American Psychologist, 23,* 158–163.

Sue, D. W. (1979). Preliminary data from the DISC Evaluation Report #1. Hayward, CA: California State University.

Zuk, G. (1971). *Family therapy: A triadic based approach.* New York: Behavioral Publications.

Chapter 68

TWENTY-FOUR–HOUR THERAPY: A PERSONAL RENAISSANCE*

EUGENE E. LANDY and ARNOLD E. DAHLKE

Eugene Landy's Twenty-Four–Hour Therapy well meets the criteria of being theoretically sound and quite innovative. It is, on reflection, a perfectly logical system. When hearing of it for the first time, one is likely to say, "Well, it is common sense. . . ." Unfortunately, common sense is not so common and things look so much clearer on the basis of hindsight.

As is the case with any really effective method that moves in new dimensions, from those readers whose ideas have crystallized and who may object to the complete patient takeover by the therapist—which is indeed a bold and brilliant move—we can expect outraged cries. I am particularly impressed by the apparent internal contradictions involved in this system—a person is led to autonomy through extreme dependency.

This chapter by Eugene Landy and Arnold Dahlke contains many important theoretical elements relating to family life and parenting, proper roles of therapists, and the whole mental health movement. I for one enjoyed reading this stirring account of an unusual and potentially important system.

Twenty-Four–Hour Therapy is a unique, intensive, team approach to therapy developed by Eugene E. Landy in the late 1960s and early 1970s. Unlike traditional therapy, where the patient has limited contact with the therapist in an office setting, or institutional therapy, where the patient is placed in a controlled, artificial environment, Twenty-Four–Hour Therapy maintains total contact with patients, 24 hours a day, in their own environment. The goal of this intensive approach is the patient's attainment of adequacy within the context of his or her natural problem-provoking environment, whether it be home, work, or play.

Twenty-Four–Hour Therapy is based on the central theme that people behave in ways that mask their inadequacies, whether real or imagined, as they function in the world. They do so by creating facades and external support systems, while engaging in interpersonal power games to get what they want. Focusing on those "secret" inadequacies that patients keep hidden from others (and even from themselves), Landy and his associates totally disrupt the privacy of their patient's lives, gaining com-

plete control over every aspect of their physical, personal, social, and sexual environments. Employing a variety of behavioral strategies, Landy and his team confront patients with the secrets of their real and imagined inadequacies and then teach them how to develop a strong sense of self-sufficiency and control over their lives, which Landy defines as adequacy.

HISTORY

Precursors

In the early 1960s, Landy was invited to join Frederick H. Stoller, the father of Marathon Therapy, who had just completed his innovative work with "swing groups" at Camarillo State Hospital (Stoller, 1967). While working with Stoller in marathon groups, Landy was struck by the importance of the time factor in dealing with patients. He became aware of the number of hours it takes for people to drop their facade, or, as T. S. Eliot (1936) says, "to prepare a face to meet the faces you meet. . . ." He concluded that if therapists stay with patients long enough, the patients eventually drop their facades and grow more authentic. Then, dealing more authentically with environmental circumstances, they develop feelings

*The writers express their gratitude to Audrey Levy, Dana Longino, Sara Hardman, Nancy Fuller, and the staff of the F.R.E.E. Foundation for their invaluable critique and assistance in the preparation of this chapter.

of adequacy and confidence about their ability to handle themselves with other people. They begin to make decisions without resorting to their old facades.

Landy noted a significant problem, however, with the marathon approach. When patients left the protective environment of the marathon and returned to their natural environment, authenticity faded and facades reappeared. The relatively short-term marathon experience simply did not allow enough time for sufficient practice of new behaviors. Landy recognized that what was needed was a more prolonged therapeutic experience situated within the patient's normal daily environment. This conclusion was an important precursor to the development of Twenty-Four–Hour Therapy.

Landy further developed methods for application to prolonged therapeutic experiences at the University of Oklahoma in the mid-sixties as a consultant to Job Corps training and Community Action programs funded by the Office of Economic Opportunity (Landy, 1967; Landy, 1970; Landy & Steele, 1967).

He developed close friendships at the university with W. Robert Hood, Director of the University of Oklahoma Institute of Group Relations, from whom he learned the integration of psychopharmacological techniques with traditional therapy and the sociological skills of manipulating contingencies in natural environments (Sherif et al., 1954; Hood & Sherif, 1955), and with Arnold Dahlke, Associate Director of the Institute, who stressed the importance of applying the rigorous thinking of experimental methods to clinical settings (Kelley et al., 1965; LaCharite & Dahlke, 1975; Jones, Dahlke, & LaCharite, 1978).

Beginnings

The initial application of Landy's earlier ideas occurred in 1968, when he was Director of the Adolescent Program at Gateways Hospital and Community Mental Health Center in Los Angeles. During this period he was strongly influenced by the dynamic, interpersonal philosophies of Solon D. Samuels (1971, 1976), an early associate of Eric Berne. Landy considers Samuels to be his most significant influence, both personally and professionally.

Working primarily with drug-addicted adolescents, Landy first attempted to set up a hospital environment similar to the street environment of his patients. His intention was to get at the process that made these adolescents so unable to handle normal circumstances of living that they resorted to substance abuse (including alcohol), which he collectively referred to as "dope." His observations led him to distinguish between dope used for entertainment and dope used to cover up feelings of inadequacy.

Landy further observed three major types of "dopers": those who used "uppers"—amphetamines—appeared to be withdrawn and experiencing difficulties accepting themselves as adequate; those who used "downers"—barbiturates, hypnotics, and sedatives—evidenced a great deal of anger and lack of self-control; and those who used psychedelics were more intellectualizing and existentially despairing.

The more Landy observed the adolescents in the hospital setting, the more he noticed that they tended to separate themselves socially into the uppers, downers, and psychedelic groups. He decided to move them all together into a large house, forcing them into close interaction with one another. In a very short time, arguments and loud physical fights broke out. Landy then brought in staff members to be with them at all times. These staff members continuously provided him with feedback on the daily habits of the adolescents. He became aware of his patients' inabilities to function without the aid of some medicine: The downers adolescents (angry and lacking self-control) were continuously antagonizing everybody; the uppers adolescents (withdrawn and scared) were constantly looking for rescue and approval; and the psychedelic adolescents (intellectual "head-trippers") were bored and depressed. It was this feedback that led him to speculate that they were using drugs to cover their feelings of inadequacy.

From the hospital program, Landy developed a large drug-user, adolescent private practice. He wrote *The Underground Dictionary* (Landy, 1971), a unique compendium of drug and subculture language. The book attracted many parents seeking assistance for their drug-abusing children.

Within the context of this practice, Landy expanded and developed several of the basic notions underlying Twenty-Four–Hour Therapy. Through arrangements with parents, he blocked all of the normal routes that the adolescents had for covering up their inadequacies. They then had to earn their rights and privileges by accomplishments. Their lives were thus organized into the pursuit of adequacy goals.

To facilitate these adolescent accomplishments, Landy established the Center for Adjunctive Therapeutic Activity (CATA). CATA was a unique program that applied principles of occupational therapy to "real-life" settings. The center's program consisted of a wide array of arts and crafts, such as drama classes, leather work, and candle making. The typical patient entered both individual and group therapy and was assigned to a variety of classes. Landy met with his therapists and instructors periodically to assess the progress of his adolescent patients and to structure new experiences for them.

CATA operated on the assumption that one of the dynamics of drug-abusing adolescents is their inability to postpone gratification in the pursuit of long-range success experiences. The classes were therefore structured to give them a variety of immediate success experiences. Operating under the old adage that "nothing succeeds like success," Landy thus created an environment that enabled his patients to develop a generalized sense of confidence in their own adequacy.

Since the early 1970s Landy has applied his total-environment approach to individual patients in his private practice. He continued to refine and expand his methodology in applications with a variety of patients from all walks of life. With the assistance of key staff members, he has trained and continues to train professionals and paraprofessionals in the techniques and strategies of Twenty-Four–Hour Therapy.

CURRENT STATUS

Many patients have benefitted from Landy's full approach focusing on more specific problem areas of their lives, such as weight and substance control, relationships, and career-associated difficulties.

In addition, staff members who trained with Landy on earlier cases currently apply his techniques to cases of their own in various parts of the country, while training still other staff in similar applications. Landy established the F.R.E.E. Clinic (Foundation for the Rechanneling of Emotions and Education), a community counseling center in Beverly Hills. Interns at F.R.E.E. are using his approach on a partial basis with patients plagued by specific areas of inadequacy.

Landy discussed his approach at the 1973 American Psychological Association Convention in Montreal, where he participated in a symposium with Joseph Wolpe and Harold Greenwald (Landy, Wolpe, & Greenwald, 1973) and shared his ideas in conversation hours at the Western Psychological Association meeting in Honolulu, Hawaii (1980a) and the American Psychological Association meeting in Montreal, Canada (1980b). The concept is now used by the state of Hawaii and referred to as "wrap-around therapy".

Landy's patients have come from all over the world and from all walks of life, from adolescent drug abusers and their parents, to executives, to Hollywood superstars. His successful use of this approach with Brian Wilson of The Beach Boys, rock star Alice Cooper, and actors Rod Steiger and Richard Harris (to mention only the few that have publicly acknowledged in print their participation in Twenty-Four–Hour Therapy) made him a controversial psychologist. Landy's approach involved developing complete patient dependency on the therapist and total therapist control of the patient's life such as an infant has on a parent. Most people outside of the patient's immediate circle are fearful of a person upon whom so much dependency is placed and who exercises such extreme control.

THEORY

Adequacy is the central concept of Twenty-Four–Hour Therapy. An adequate person is one who both feels and is capable of getting what he or she wants from the world. People who feel adequate *know* they are capable of accomplishing something, even if they don't have the skills at the moment; those who feel inadequate often say "I could never do that!"

The roots of a person's adequacy (real or imagined) begin in earliest childhood. Landy sees the newborn child basically as a "raw little animal" that brings with itself a quest for life, a continuation, a survival, because it has no knowledge whatsoever. Either it was well nurtured in its intrauterine environment, becoming a healthy newborn, or it is born unhealthy and faces an intense struggle to survive physically.

From the very beginning, the child is socialized. The first thing that it feels is a strange environment. It doesn't know what hunger is—it simply has a physical response. It cries. Someone puts a bottle in its mouth and the life-long learning process begins to take place; the child quickly finds that specific behaviors elicit specific responses.

The most important feature of this life-long learning experience is a person's social environment. First there is the earliest, close family constellation, then the extended family, then peers, and then a variety of other significant figures such as teachers and employers. At each stage along the way, every participant in this social environment is continuously giving "evaluative" feedback (Rogers & Roethlisberger, 1952). The child is praised when it learns how to use eating utensils, when it says its first words, and when it defecates at the right moment in the right place. It meets with disapproval when it throws its food on the floor, when it doesn't speak properly, and when it wets its bed after it has been toilet trained.

Part of this continuous evaluative feedback leads to the development of fears. We fear that we have displeased our parents. We are afraid that we won't be able to pass an exam. We are anxious about doing our job well.

The lifelong learning process shapes our definition of our own adequacy. We all evolve into adulthood with varying levels of self-confidence in our ability to get what we want from the world. Some of us believe we are adequate and can do anything. Others of us feel inadequate and doubt our ability to accomplish even the simplest task.

We continuously compare ourselves to our society's norms. All of us find ourselves "better" on some things and "worse" on others. Thus, each of us ends up with little pockets of inadequacies; these inadequacies become our secrets that we hide as we prepare our face to face the world.

We develop facades to keep others from seeing our secrets and thus avoid the possibility of others evaluating us negatively. We become skilled at manipulative, interpersonal games designed to cover up our feelings that we are basically inadequate. For Landy, the discovery and exorcising of these secret inadequacies is the focal task in all therapy, and especially in Twenty-Four–Hour Therapy.

An important component of adequacy is *emotional control.* Adequate persons are capable of making adaptive decisions to get what they want under the most adverse circumstances. They are capable of making rational decisions even while they are experiencing extreme emotional states such as intense fear.

Inadequate persons, on the other hand, are victims of their emotions. They generally make their decisions out of fear. Whether it is fear of succeeding at a task or fear of the disapproval of significant others, they act out of their emotions rather than from logical thinking. Compared to adequate people who take actions out of conscious choice, inadequate persons are not aware of their capability to choose.

Landy is not arguing that we are capable of doing away with our emotions. Emotions are like perspiration: When the hot sun beats down on us, we will sweat. The question is not whether we can stop ourselves from sweating, but rather what we choose to do about it when it happens. Similarly, we will never stop ourselves from having emotional responses to our environment. But we can train ourselves, as adequate individuals, to choose what is best for us when those emotional situations do occur.

Since our estimate of our own adequacy is a *learned* stance toward our lives, we are capable of reeducating ourselves. Thus therapy can be viewed as a process of reeducation. In therapy we do not *unlearn* the dysfunctional behaviors that grow out of our inadequacies; we simply learn additional, alternative behaviors and, further, we learn that we have the capability to choose an action that serves us best in any specific instance.

METHODOLOGY

The strategies and techniques that make up Twenty-Four–Hour Therapy are all conducted in the service of one central goal: the development of adequacy. To attain that goal, the therapy must be all-encompassing. The therapist, assisted by a team of professional and paraprofessional staff members, disrupts every aspect of the patient's life. The staff size varies at times from three to 30 and always includes a psychiatrist to determine possible medical needs.

All patient contacts with other people are monitored and controlled. Through face-to-face interactions with the patient, extensive use of telephones with staff members, and the use of both video- and audio tapes, the therapist is aware of everything the patient does. In many instances staff members as well as family members are told, verbatim, by the therapist, how to respond to specific actions and verbalizations of the patient. Situations are set up in advance (or on the spot in response to a patient action) to teach the patient some principle or provide him or her with an important experience. The therapist, in effect, choreographs a very complex fabric of activities, 24 hours a day, much like the conductor of a large symphony orchestra; and the music that is played is called *education.*

Each patient is taken through a unique, individually designed program of Twenty-Four–Hour Therapy. Individual programs last anywhere from a week to a year or more. Each program consists of eight major phases: (1) initiation; (2) discovery; (3) inadequacy; (4) preadequacy; (5) self-adequacy; (6) self-functioning; (7) adequacy; and (8) termination. A summary of the activities that occur in the eight phases is shown in Table 68.1.

The length of each phase is a direct function of patient progress at any given point in time. Although the phases are sequential, they do overlap: The therapist, for example, might uncover some inadequacies in phase 4 that call for some of the strategies used in phase 3; and while patients might be in phase 5 in one category, they could be in phase 3 in another simultaneously. The entire process is a fluid, dynamic orchestration of the patient's life directed toward the patient's attainment of adequacy in his or her own environment.

Phase 1: Initiation

Many patients entering Twenty-Four–Hour Therapy are brought in by a family member who has chosen to do so as a last resort because nothing else worked. Others enter because they want to work on some specific problem area but then soon find that their difficulty is tied to a much deeper thread; they decided to totally immerse themselves in the program.

The initial contact with the patient and his or her family is very significant, because the therapist identifies not only what face the patient wants to present to the world but how the family wants the patient to be seen. This provides keys for the therapist in unlocking a picture of the patient's support system.

Three important conditions need to be agreed upon between the patient, family, and therapist. First, the patient must be cut off from all possible financial resources for the duration of the therapy. The success of Twenty-Four–Hour Therapy rests on the extent to which the therapeutic team can exert control over every aspect of the patient's life. When patients have access to any form of financial resources, they can easily use them to engage

Table 68.1   Summary of Phases in Twenty-Four–Hour Therapy.

1. Initiation	Patient and family present themselves; patient cut off from all financial resources; total family cooperation agreed upon; therapist established as absolute authority.
2. Discovery	Delineation of patient inadequacies and total patient support systems; complete therapist takeover of patient support system; creation of total dependency on therapist.
3. Inadequacy	Therapist and team withdraw support, allowing patient to experience total inadequacy; patient sees choice and makes decision to become adequate (get what he or she wants) or continue inadequacy (do without).
4. Preadequacy	Patient learns that there are other ways of getting what he or she wants; therapist sets up contingencies that make learning of new ways easier than doing without; patient learns that he or she is capable of learning.
5. Self-Adequacy	Focus on patient taking care of self and developing sense of self-sufficiency; patient learns the concept of giving to self; therapist begins diminishing patient dependency on therapist/team.
6. Self-Functioning	Expansion of adequacy-learning beyond self-care to function in and getting what he or she wants from the world; increased socializing and sexual functioning; further diminishing of patient dependency.
7. Adequacy	Gradual withdrawal of therapy team and increased one-to-one contact with therapist; patient learns to integrate adequacy functions toward becoming more self-sufficient in the world, living without therapy team.
8. Termination	Patient achieves complete self-sufficiency, lives by self or with nontherapy team roomate; therapist becomes friend and advisor.

in the cover-up of inadequacies that the therapist regards as dysfunctional for their progress.

The second important condition is total cooperation from every member of the patient's support system, usually the family. If cooperation cannot be obtained from some individuals, then they must not be allowed any contact with the patient. An uncooperative family member can easily sabotage the therapy by responding to the patient as being incapable or inadequate, thus retarding the patient's progress.

The third important condition is that the therapist be established as the supreme authority. This means, for example, that if a patient wants something and turns, as usual, to a family member for help, that family member is told to respond with "I'll be happy to help you if the doctor agrees." In this way the family member remains an ally and has not deserted the patient while reinforcing the authority of the therapist.

These three conditions are necessary before Twenty-Four–Hour Therapy can begin, because the therapist must move very quickly to establish patient dependency. It is the dependency that provides the therapist with the necessary authority to reshape the patient's responses to situations that typically elicited the cover-up of inadequacies.

Phase 2: Discovery

The second phase of the therapy begins with a delineation of the patient's inadequacies and the identification of all of the major and minor figures in the patient's support system. Every person identified in that system is contacted and interviewed extensively, to develop a complete "history" of the patient from the viewpoints of each key individual in the patient's life. All interviews are taped and transcribed. The history is then carefully examined for the purpose of uncovering as many of the patient's inadequacies as possible.

Once the key individuals in the patient's support system are identified, the therapist takes over the system. As agreed on in phase 1, the therapist instructs each individual how to respond to specific actions and verbalizations of the patient. In addition, a staff member moves in with the patient; the therapist arranges to have staff members with or observing the patient every moment of the day. The therapist is constantly informed of everything the patient is doing and continually feeds staff responses to the patient.

At this point, then, the therapist has created total patient dependency on the therapeutic team. The therapy cannot proceed to the next phase until this happens.

Phase 3: Inadequacy

During the third phase, a pivotal one, patients are compelled to face their secret inadequacies. They suddenly find themselves without the usual financial or family support systems to help them deal with their inadequacies. Since they are now completely dependent on the therapeutic team, they turn to that team for the assistance that was formerly supplied by family and friends. When they say to a staff member, "Help me, I don't know what to do," the staff member replies only with "Think!" or "I have confidence that you can work it out" or "I know you can deal with this." Then the staff member waits to assist the patient with the logic needed to reach a conclusion or a decision. Previously, family and friends "rescued" the patient in order to expedite action, or out of their own lack of patience; as a result, the patient never learned to do for him- or herself.

Thus, during this phase patients find themselves in a vulnerable position. With all of their normal supports withdrawn, they are faced with either not getting what they want by staying with their inadequacies or getting what they want by learning new, adequate behaviors. Many patients panic at this point. Without the accustomed support of family and friends, they come to recognize that they are really not functionally adequate on their own. With that recognition comes the realization that they have a choice: "I stay inadequate and do not get what I want or I learn new ways of getting what I want."

Landy believes that patients must fully experience inadequacy before the therapy can proceed. He compares this phase to going to the dentist: The dentist must drill to the root of the tooth before reconstruction can begin.

Phase 4: Preadequacy

In the preadequacy phase, patients learn that there are other ways for getting what they want. The therapist sets up contingencies in their environment that literally make the learning of new ways easier than doing without (remaining inadequate).

Patients begin to learn by not being told how to do something. They now must find out for themselves. In the process of finding out for themselves, staff members are available to provide information; staff are instructed by the therapist not to rescue, only to respond to patient questions that ask for specific information—information designed to light up alternative solutions.

The significance of this phase is *not* the information learned by the patients, but rather the concept that they are *capable* of learning. Once they *know* they *can* learn, they also know they have a *choice* to learn. As inadequates, they did not experience that choice. Thus, in this phase they take an important step toward adequacy.

Phase 5: Self-Adequacy

The focus now turns to structuring the patients' environments toward teaching them self-care. Many patients who come into Twenty-Four–Hour Therapy have abandoned themselves; they are so used to being dependent on significant other persons that they have never really learned self-sufficiency. Many of them must be taught how to function by themselves, including such specifics as personal hygiene, taking pride in their appearance, securing and holding a job, planning a budget within which they can survive and get what they want (while

avoiding constant debt), and knowing how to get around the city. They are, in essence, learning a whole new concept of giving to themselves. This is in contrast to their past experience, where they were "psychologically anorexic," working so hard getting someone else to give to them that they never learned how to give to themselves.

Phase 6: Self-Functioning

Once patients evidence the capability of self-care, they are ready to move into the sixth phase of Twenty-Four–Hour Therapy. In this phase they expand their learning beyond themselves to functioning in the world around them. They learn to socialize and then to sexualize, which, in turn, leads them to seek and form relationships. Self-functioning means the ability, in spite of the normal feelings of strangeness that we all experience in a new situation, to walk into strange places, such as a bar, social gathering, or a classroom, not knowing anybody, and yet be able to meet and interact with people.

During this phase patient dependency on the therapist markedly diminishes. Patients learn to increase their ability to function and develop more effective and creative ways of utilizing their talents and skills.

The therapist allows them to become reinvolved with members of their former support system, only now patients act from a place of self-sufficiency rather than dependency. Family and friends, meanwhile, have been educated in the process, either through contact with the therapeutic team or through independent therapy set up for them by the therapist.

An important skill that patients learn during this phase is that of time structuring. In the previous two phases they learned how to develop routines aimed at self-care; now they are dealing with other peoples' schedules besides their own. They learn how to develop a comfortable looseness and flexibility in their interactions with others.

Phase 7: Adequacy

As they move into the seventh phase of therapy, patients have learned methods for making accommodations to the world; they have learned to put themselves first, while still maintaining concern for others. During this phase, the therapist begins to withdraw staff members from the case. Where staff members were previously with the patient 24 hours a day, the patient begins to adequately function alone more often.

At the same time the patient begins to have regular, more traditional individual and group sessions with the therapist. In earlier phases patients interacted primarily with staff members. At that time they felt inadequate in dealing with the therapist with anything other than appeasement or withdrawal. By the time they reach phase 7, however, they have developed enough adequacy to be able to confront the therapist, even in the midst of a disagreement or anger.

Phase 8: Termination

In the final phase of Twenty-Four–Hour Therapy, patients are completely self-sufficient, functioning from a position of a strongly felt sense of adequacy. Their dependency on the therapist is no more than any normal patient-doctor relationship, yet there exists a sense of closeness after having been through so much together.

During this phase, patients live alone or with roommates of their choice. Contact with staff members is minimal, much as a busy person has with friends. Patients are now practicing everything they have learned.

Their contact with the therapist settles down to infrequent meetings, arranged at their own request, to deal with specific problems. The therapist has thus moved from being a strong authority upon whom the patient is dependent to becoming a friend and advisor, a person who can be trusted to be objective.

APPLICATIONS

Landy maintains that Twenty-Four-Hour Therapy is applicable to all diagnostic categories as long as patients can be treated in their natural environments. This is an especially important requirement for mentally retarded patients or for patients with chronic psychotic reactions, who have had long or multiple hospitalizations. The hospital setting provides them with very limited physical and social mobility. More important, almost everyone who interacts with them, from doctors and nurses to relatives, usually treats them as though they are not capable of taking care of themselves and not adequate at functioning in the normal world. Hence, since they are treated as incapable and inadequate, they come to believe and accept that they are. As long as they are in the artificial environment of the hospital, they will continue to be reinforced as inadequate. For Twenty-Four–Hour Therapy to be successfully applied to them, it must be implemented in their natural nonhospital environment.

Age is no limit. Although Twenty-Four–Hour Therapy has been used most often with adults, it has also been very successfully applied to adolescents and some children. In those cases the basic strategies and phasing of the therapy are the same, but the goals and some of the specific procedures differ.

Time is also no limit. Some patients, working in specific problem areas, have gone through Twenty-Four–Hour Therapy in as little as one week; one patient was fully involved for two years. Whether it be one week or two years, patients experience a far more intense and concentrated *renaissance* than in more traditional therapies.

Because of the strong therapist control exerted in Twenty-Four–Hour Therapy, family and friends often react to specific therapeutic moves with angry resistance. Therapists must be strong enough in their convictions and secure enough under intense stress to not personalize such reactions, which should be recognized as fearful responses to the breaking of patients' dependent, manipulative ties with their former support systems. Twenty-Four–Hour therapists, in other words, must not allow these unavoidable encounters to influence their function and decision making with their patients. They must be willing to absorb the inevitable anger that will be directed at them.

Currently, Twenty-Four–Hour Therapy is very costly because of the intensive time commitment required of a large number of professional staff members. Landy and his associates, however, have been experimenting with cutting costs through the utilization of psychological interns who rotate on a part-time basis in various cases as a part of their internship training program at the F.R.E.E. Foundation. Additional attempts at cost reduction in other training institutions and academic settings, supported by grants from federal, state, and local social service agencies, are envisioned.

CASE HISTORY

Robert came into therapy when he was 27 years old. He had been in therapy on and off since the age of 16, first with a psychoanalyst (who had diagnosed him as a chronic undifferentiated schizophrenic) for about four years and then with a psychiatrist for over six years.

After graduating from a public high school, Robert attended one semester of college and then went to work for his father. He entered into a brief marriage at the age of 19, which ended in annulment a few months later. He married again at the age of 21 and fathered two children; his second wife left him when he was 26.

Robert was adopted at the age of one week and raised as an only child by a successful, upper-middle-class businessman, whose wife had not been able to have children. He was desired by both parents and raised as their own son until the age of eight, when his parents told him that he had been adopted.

Phase 1: Initiation

The initial contact with Dr. Landy, the therapist in the case, was made by Robert's father. At the time of presentation, Robert was functioning marginally. He was working as the manager of a store that his father bought for him because of his concern with Robert's inability to function in the world.

Upon meeting Robert's father, Landy informed him of the conditions under which he would be willing to take the case: financial control, complete family cooperation, and the therapist's position as an absolute authority with Robert.

Several days later, as prearranged with Robert's father, Landy visited the store as a customer to observe Robert functioning. He saw him basically "busy keeping himself busy." Robert spent his time talking with employees, but from what Landy could observe, he was not really performing any serious managerial or store function. He would spend periods of 15 to 20 minutes in this kind of activity, walking around briskly, picking up things, looking at them, and then leave the store to go to a local bar, where he would nurse a beer for a half hour or so. Then he would return to the store. Robert thus alternated between his store and the bar throughout the day.

At the bar, observed and taped by Landy (who was unknown to Robert), he lamented to the bartender, telling her how underpaid he was, how busy he was, and what a toll the whole thing was taking on him. Listening to him, one would assume that he had been wronged by his father, who he saw as "the rat-fink of all times." (In fact, since he was unable to provide for himself, his father paid him a salary of $35,000.00 a year, made all the payments on his sports car, and paid all his bills, including rent, utilities, credit cards, and insurance.)

Shortly after the initial observation, Robert's father told him of Landy, and Robert agreed to meet with the therapist in his office. Robert's father agreed to all of Landy's conditions. Landy suggested the conditions be written and the papers be signed in front of Robert.

At the meeting, with Robert's father present, Robert complained about his very difficult life. Landy asked Robert about his feelings concerning his father. Robert looked puzzled and didn't answer. Landy told him what he had heard in the bar. Robert denied everything. Landy played a tape of the bar conversation (in Twenty-Four–Hour Therapy everything is taped). Robert appeared surprised and embarrassed and began to cry. He said he would rather be in therapy with his last therapist, who never made him feel as bad as Landy just had. Landy told Robert it was not his intention to make him feel bad; but if what he was saying was true, Landy would assist Robert by getting his father to stop being such a critical, discounting person. Robert continued to cry.

At that point Robert's father informed him that Landy now had control of any money he would spend on Robert, and that if Robert needed anything he would have to deal through Landy's office and Landy; he then signed a document stating so in the presence of Robert, Landy, and a notary public.

Phase 2: Discovery

Landy immediately formed a therapy team to develop a complete history of Robert and to delineate all of the key figures in Robert's support system. He rented a two-bedroom apartment and a staff member moved in as Robert's roommate. From then on a staff member was either with Robert or in a position to observe him throughout the duration of therapy. Landy also initiated a series of meetings with significant family members and friends, instructing them how to respond to Robert so as not to become hooked into "rescuing" him when they interacted with him. Robert, they were told, was a professional "victim."

Landy told Robert that he was willing to allow him to continue functioning in the store, as long as he did not make any purchase-order decisions without first clearing them with Landy. Robert agreed to the conditions and left his session with Landy, disbelieving that his father was "doing this to him."

Robert tested his father's position and the therapist's authority within three days when he ordered close to $15,000.00 worth of material for his store. Landy (since he had direct lines of communication with everybody associated with Robert, his father, and the store) was immediately informed. He called Robert into his office and told him he was unhappy with the fact that he had broken his agreement. Robert replied that he was sorry. Landy, in turn, said that he too was sorry, but he would now not allow Robert to place any future orders until a complete inventory was taken in the store.

Robert, upset by this turn of events, threatened his father with a knife. When his father attempted to talk to him, he threatened to harm himself. Landy assured Robert's concerned parents that, in his professional opinion, Robert would not harm himself or any others. Landy told Robert that he would close the store if Robert did not start and complete the inventory immediately.

Robert again tested his father and Landy's authority by sending a letter of resignation to his father. Much to his surprise, his father accepted the resignation (at Landy's direction). Robert suddenly found himself no longer employed and penniless. He panicked, complaining that he had "made the business what it was today," in spite of the fact that the business was losing thousands of dollars per month because of mismanagement. Robert had never learned how to read the cash register receipts and employees stole money openly. Robert also had to hire a manager to deal with business affairs he didn't understand. Landy sent a staff member to collect all of his company credit cards and keys for the store.

Phase 3: Inadequacy

Robert was caught off-guard by the suddenness of Landy's actions. In the past, Robert's threats with people had been quite successful, because he convinced them he meant what he said and they didn't know how to deal with him, other than to appease him. He rapidly discovered that Landy would not respond to threats.

Previously, while working in his store, Robert had covered up his inadequacies through his assumed position as manager. This gave him all of the status and social contacts he needed. When Landy withdrew this support, Robert came face to face with the fact that he had no friends or involved relationships in his life. It also became apparent to him that he was no longer able to use his threats as influence with his family or with any of the people who had worked for him.

Because Robert saw Landy's action as punitive, he spent close to four months in the inadequacy phase, demonstrating his inadequacy over and over again. For example, because he did not get a job, he was evicted from his apartment and lost his car.

Landy placed him in a board-and-care home. As Robert began to feel safe in his new environment, he slowly realized that his fellow residents were physically and emotionally handicapped, unable to take care of themselves. After a while, he was given a job in the facility for $5.00 a day, three days a week. This, in effect, was the first real job he had ever held. He worked very hard at it, outperforming everyone else.

He became so comfortable and successful in his new position, the first such success he had ever had, that Landy withdraw all financial support, in order to stimulate his moving beyond this first position. The board-and-care home then refused to keep him. Landy offered him another board-and-care facility in a distant and unfamiliar part of the city, but Robert found that too threatening. Instead, he looked for a job to pay his own way, which signaled his emergence from the inadequacy phase.

Phase 4: Preadequacy

Robert began the preadequacy phase applying for jobs around the city at various locations, but he hesitated to take any of them. Landy expected that he would probably be fired from the first several jobs, and advised Robert that it didn't matter which job he chose, because getting this first job and working was only an "exercise." He used staff members to show Robert how to fill out job applications and how to respond to job interviews.

Since Robert did not have transportation of his own, he had to learn how to use the bus system, which he had never used before. This was a painful experience for him. At one point, stranded several miles from his residence, he sat on a bench for five hours (with a staff member nearby who would not rescue him), before he decided he could help himself by contacting the bus company and getting the information that would tell him how to get home.

Slowly Robert came to accept the reality that no one was going to rescue him at this stage in his life and that his only hope for survival was for him to become self-sufficient.

Phase 5: Self-Adequacy

Robert began to take more care with his appearance and learned how to dress in a suit and tie. He learned how to develop and operate within the limits of a budget.

At this point, Landy assisted him in buying a car with the stipulation that it be a stick shift, which Robert had avoided how to drive. At first Robert felt himself incapable of learning how to drive it, and he regressed into inadequacy: He simply left the car at a curb and eventually it was towed away. After riding buses for a while, however, Robert finally told Landy that he would like to learn how to drive the stick-shift car. Robert made arrangements and slowly and painfully accomplished that task.

Having been through more than a half-dozen different jobs, Robert finally landed a sales job at a major department store. Once he overcame the fear that he would not be able to learn how to handle the computerized cash register, he began to prosper. He increasingly formed new social relationships with people that he encountered at the store. He worked there for almost a full year.

Phase 6: Self-Functioning

Landy moved Robert and a staff member into an apartment located in a very social, singles complex. Again Robert slipped back into some inadequate behaviors, withdrawing and refusing to participate socially; recognizing this pattern of "three steps forward and two steps back," Landy withdrew and waited. Robert then began to socialize, because it was the only way Landy would respond.

Gradually Robert developed new competencies. He came to the realization that spending a great deal of time in getting nothing accomplished and feeling bad about it was not a very effective way for him to deal with the world. He realized increasingly how good he felt after accomplishing something. He began to expand his time horizon, by making more long-range plans.

Phase 7: Adequacy

At this point Robert moved into the adequacy phase. He was able to hold a job successfully; he developed friendships; and gradually he became more comfortable with women.

He determined that he would like to return to school, but could not afford it. Since earning a minimal living and going to night school at the same time appeared to be too great a task, he decided to join the Army for financial support while he obtained an education. He chose to do this to be independent of his family and because, looking to the future, he could put to use his service education after his discharge.

Phase 8: Termination Phase

Robert went off to basic training. When he realized that he was now 28 years old, in with a batch of 18-year-olds, all of whom were in better physical shape than he was, he began to regress again. He was threatened by the possibility of discharge because of his inability to function satisfactorily.

Landy advised Robert's sergeant on how to deal with Robert constructively, suggesting strategies that would facilitate continued development of Robert's adequacy. Even though it took an additional two weeks, Robert successfully completed basic training and was sent off to Korea, skilled in electronics.

Robert is still in the Army. He now relates to women with far less fear. He has formed social and sexual friendships. He is looking forward to returning to university life after military service, supported by the G.I. Bill.

Since Robert had been accustomed to "having," after recognizing his own ability he decided to "get for himself"; he would not settle for a secure, minimal-paying job as a salesman in a department store with little responsibility. He therefore chose the Army as a way of starting to get what he wanted: to have all the good things he had before, but this time he wanted to get them (and more) for himself. He is now aware of the difference in value between "having been given to" for most of his life and the greater enjoyment experienced when he gives to himself.

SUMMARY

Landy compares Twenty-Four–Hour Therapy to a large chess game; the patient makes a move and the therapist responds with a move, which, in turn, elicits still another patient move. The intent in this process is for the patient to learn a lesson from everything that happens; to undercut the patient's manipulative games; and to structure events in the patient's environment that facilitate the occurrence of spontaneous success experiences, continuously and in every aspect of the patient's life.

Landy believes that most traditional therapy is superficial and limited because therapists, in their relatively brief encounters with their patients, are too respectful and courteous of the patient's privacy. This means that therapists rarely get to the bedrock secrets of inadequacy upon which all of their patient's manipulative and acting-out behaviors are based. Only by getting to those se-

crets as quickly as possible can a therapist be a successful facilitator of change for the patient.

An important feature of Twenty-Four–Hour Therapy is its application in the patient's natural environment. As early as the 1920s, J. L. Moreno argued that patients should be treated *in situ* (Moreno, 1927). Lewis Yablonsky, known for his work with psychodrama (Yablonsky, 1976) and an associate of Landy's since the early 1960s, recalls assisting Moreno in his treatment of a female psychotic patient who he had moved into a house where staff members served as "auxiliary egos," entering her fantasy world and then slowly bringing her back to reality (Yablonsky, 1980).

Landy questions why it is that patients don't get the same total treatment as football players: If players break their diet or stay out late, they are fined; they receive special kinds of treatment, special meals, special kinds of rubdowns, special kinds of education, and special kinds of exercises. All of this happens just because they are athletes. Patients are entitled to be given the same good advice, help, and total emotional structure that we afford our gladiators.

Landy's concepts of extreme dependency and total authority are parallel to the "governing principle of direct analysis" developed by John N. Rosen (1953), who specified that the therapist must act as the patient's "omnipotent protector." Twenty-four–hour therapists have as much ethical and professional responsibility to create and exert extreme dependency and authority as they do in preserving patient confidentiality.

Rosen agrees with Landy that patients should be treated in a pleasant therapeutic milieu outside of the hospital setting (Rosen, 1980); Landy, however, goes a step further, proposing that patients are most effectively treated in their own natural environment, those same environments that caused the initial problem. Also, while Rosen and his associates spend a great deal more time with the patient than traditional therapy, Landy extends this concentration to a total twenty-four–hour day involvement.

Jacqui Schiff (1970), in what she calls "reparenting," also extends her involvement to 24 hours. But, as Levy (1978) pointed out, Schiff's reparented patient is still placed in an artificial setting. Further, Schiff's patients are literally spanked and treated as children; Landy emphasizes the facilitation of adequacy through the use of adult choice, logical thinking, and natural consequences rather than punitive parent-therapist responses.

Adequacy, the central concept of Twenty-Four–Hour Therapy, is similar to Albert Bandura's concept of "efficacy expectation," which refers to the extent to which a person expects to be successful at executing behaviors required to produce specific outcomes (Bandura, 1977). The strength of people's efficacy expectations determines whether they will attempt to handle difficult situations. For Landy, self-efficacy is an important ingredient of adequacy: Adequate people hold strong efficacy expectations. He adds, however, that an adequate person knows that he or she has the choice of behaving efficaciously or not; adequate people are willing to attempt an action, even though they might fail. Handling failure is a part of life for successful people. Additionally, they have learned how to be successful at getting what they want, without losing concern for others.

In applications of Bandura's social learning theory, currently being applied to 10-day, intensive workshop settings (Bandura, 1980), therapists model and guide patients through threatening activities, even performing behaviors jointly and with physical assistance, if necessary. Landy, however, does not go for the success experiences until after the patients have fully experienced inadequacy during the third phase of therapy. This experience polarizes the choice between two extreme alternatives: staying inadequate or developing adequacy. In the past that choice was not clear for patients because they were so successful at covering their inadequacy through the facades involved in manipulating members of their support system. This also means that the choice to learn is now theirs and not that of the therapist.

Patients emerge from their intensive, round-the-clock experience with a very clear choice. There are the old facades and interpersonal manipulations that they previously could not live without, because they used them to cover up the secrets of their inadequacies. Now there are the new, self-sufficient behaviors that they, as adequate persons, know they are capable of using to get what they want from the world.

Eugene Landy's Twenty-Four–Hour Therapy thus provides patients with an opportunity to transform their lives into a Personal Renaissance.

REFERENCES

Bandura, A. (1977). *Social learning theory.* Englewood Cliffs, NJ: Prentice-Hall.

Bandura, A. (1980, June). Personal communication.

Eliot, T. S. (1936). *Collected poems, 1909–1935.* New York: Harcourt.

Hood, W. R., & Sherif, M. (1955). Personality oriented approaches to prejudice. *Sociology & Social Research, 40,* 79–85.

Jones, M., Dahlke, A. E., & LaCharite, N. A. (1978). *An empirical examination of the helping relationship in a crisis intervention setting.* Washington, D.C.: American Institutes of Research.

Kelley, H. H., Condry, J. C., Jr., Dahlke, A. E., & Hill, A. H. (1965). Collective behavior in a simulated panic situation. *Journal of Experimental Social Psychology, 1*(1), 20–54.

LaCharite, N., & Dahlke, A. E. (1975). *Improving information gathering for hotlines.* Washington, D.C.: American Institutes for Research.

Landy, E. E. (1967). Sex differences in some aspects of smoking behavior. *Psychological Reports, 20,* 575–580.

Landy, E. E. (1970). Attitude and attitude change toward interaction as a function of participation vs. observation. *Comparative Group Studies, 1,* 128–155.

Landy, E. E. (1971). *The underground dictionary.* New York: Simon & Schuster.

Landy, E. E. (1980a, May). Twenty-four–hour therapy: Return from the land of Oz. Paper presented at the Western Psychological Association, Honolulu.

Landy, E. E., & Dahlke, A. E. (1980b, September). Twenty-four–hour therapy: A personal renaissance. Paper presented at the American Psychological Association, Montreal.

Landy, E. E., & Steele, J. M. (1967). Graffiti. A function of population and building utilization. *Perceptual Motor Skills, 25,* 711–712.

Landy, E. E., Wolpe, J., & Greenwald, H. (1973, September). Directive versus non-directive modes of therapy. Symposium presented at the American Psychological Association, Montreal.

Levy, A. (1978, June). A comparison of reparenting techniques. Paper presented at the F.R.E.E. Seminar.

Moreno, J. L. (1927). *Theatre of spontaneity.* New York: Beacon House.

Rogers, C. R., & Roethlisberger, F. J. (1952). Barriers and gateways to communication. *Harvard Business Review, 30,* 28–35.

Rosen, J. N. (1953). *Direct analysis.* New York: Grune & Stratton.

Rosen, J. N. (1980, June). Personal communication.

Samuels, S. D. (1971). Games therapists play. *Transactional Analysis Journal, 1*(1), 95–99.

Samuels, S. D. (1976). On using our brains again. *Transactional Analysis Journal, 6*(3), 245.

Schiff, J. L. (1970). *All my children.* New York: Evans.

Sherif, M., Harvey, O. J., White, B. J., Hood, W. R., & Sherif, C. W. (1954). *Experimental study of positive and negative intergroup attitudes between experimentally produced groups: Robbers Cave study.* Norman, OK: University of Oklahoma.

Stoller, F. H. (1967). Extending group functions by focused feedback with video tape. In G. Gazda (Ed.), *Basic innovations in group psychotherapy and counseling.* Springfield, IL: Charles C. Thomas.

Yablonsky, L. (1976). *Psychodrama: Resolving emotional problems through role playing.* New York: Basic Books.

Yablonsky, L. (1980, June). Personal communication.

Chapter 69

VERBAL BEHAVIOR THERAPY

HUGH A. STORROW

Some therapies in this book could be classified as unimodal (e.g., Focusing) while others are multimodal, combining two or more approaches (e.g., Non-directive Psychoanalysis and Structured Learning). Going back to the pioneers in the field, we find that both Jung and Freud were essentially unimodal, whereas Adler was a multimodal theorist/therapist.

Which way will therapy go in the long run? My own guess is that the final complete therapist will be truly eclectic. This is in no way intended to disparage any of the unimodal methods. Personally, I would rather go to a capable person using a single method than to one not so capable who combines methods. But in the long run, I believe the final trend will be a combination.

In Hugh Storrow's chapter we find an interesting combination of apparently contradictory theoretical elements: (1) an appeal to the "mind" via words, and (2) an underpinning of behaviorism that denies the importance of cognition. It appears to me that this approach of combining apparently contradictory elements (as in I. H. Paul's Nondirective Psychoanalysis) is a step in the final direction. It is close to the position of such systems as Functional Counseling and Multiple Impact Therapy. Storrow's combination of seemingly contradictory aspects is a well conceived and logical system for dealing with a wide variety of human psychological problems.

Verbal Behavior Therapy is a form of behavioral psychotherapy. Theoretically it rests on the principles of classical and instrumental conditioning expanded and enriched by Bandura's social learning theory (1977) in order to deal more adequately with the complexities of human behavior. It is technically eclectic, drawing interviewing and relationship management methods from traditional insight approaches and many of its specific techniques from Behavior Therapy. From Behavior Therapy also comes its emphasis on precise delineation of target problems and goals as well as careful follow-up of treatment results. Perhaps the most innovative aspect of this approach is its blending of disparate elements into what is hoped will be a harmonious and effective whole.

HISTORY

Precursors

Since Verbal Behavior Therapy is technically eclectic and can incorporate any technique shown to be effective or promising, its ancestors could theoretically include all lines of development in the entire field of psychotherapy. A few streams of influence stand out, however.

The techniques of minimal directiveness that are emphasized in Verbal Behavior Therapy's interviewing are clearly in the psychoanalytic tradition. The history of this movement has been clearly traced many times in the past and will not be covered again here. Carl Rogers (1951) and his many associates have shed light both on interviewing and on methods for fostering therapeutically effective relationships with patients.

John Dollard and Neal Miller, with their seminal *Personality and Psychotherapy* (1950), provided the impetus that began the development of Verbal Behavior Therapy. They helped me to shift from the purely psychoanalytic orientation of my training years into behavioral channels. Their work took psychoanalytic principles and redefined them in terms of Hullian learning theory. Its impact on me was electric; what had been muddy was suddenly clear. I think that what happened illustrates in a minor way what Kuhn (1962) talks about when he discusses paradigm shifts—either for individuals or for entire disciplines. The impact of the new paradigm is often esthetic as well as purely scientific, it feels better as well as seems to explain more. And, at the time it is accepted, there may be no certain proof that it does the latter. The behavioral paradigm certainly feels better to me; it provides me the best peg I've yet found to hang my therapeutic hat on. But I still can't prove that it explains more or predicts more than the theories I was taught earlier.

The behavioral movement from Watson (1913) to Wolpe (1958) stands out as an obvious precursor to the approach of Verbal Behavior Therapy. After a few early—and often successful—attempts to explain and treat mental disturbances along behavioristic lines, the behaviorists retired to the laboratory until Wolpe dragged them back to the clinic. This long-lasting clinical inferiority complex is difficult to explain. It was probably due primarily to the overwhelming but apparently temporary success of psychoanalysis during the first half of the twentieth century.

Another line of influence leading toward Verbal Behavior Therapy comes from the earlier cognitive therapists. They emphasized conscious thought in the form of beliefs, value systems, expectations, and hypotheses about cause and effect as independent variables with important effects on behavior. Furthermore they suggested that efforts to control thinking often led to changes in behavior. Among these cognitive therapists, those with the most impact on me were Kelly (1955), Phillips (1956), Anderson (1957), and Ellis (1962).

When Verbal Behavior Therapy first appeared, its theoretical groundwork and techniques were already available or in the process of development. My contribution was mainly to organize these elements into a systematic treatment approach. In this I think my contribution is not much different from that made by many other "innovative" psychotherapists. But I think I'm more honest than at least some of them.

Beginnings

Verbal Behavior Therapy grew out of personal interests similar to some of the streams of influence described above. First to appear in print was an attempt to apply cognitive reeducation to psychotherapy (Storrow, 1963–64). A year later came an early attempt to put together a psychotherapeutic system, primarily based on learning theory, but already technically eclectic (Storrow, 1965). In this paper the label Verbal Behavior Therapy appeared for the first time. The most complete account of the system was published in book form in 1967 (Storrow, 1967).

The past 25 years or so have, of course, seen further developments in all the precursor areas described above. These changes have brought the methods of many therapists closer to the position advocated here. Garfield and Kurtz (1976) found American psychologists showing increased interest in Behavior Therapy and in eclectic practice. Although these were not the only trends noted,

they were prominent. It seems clear to me that at least two other trends have been gathering adherents among psychotherapists. One of these is increasing interest in the cognitive therapies. Albert Ellis has continued to attract disciples. Other cognitive systems have appeared; they stand on the same basic assumptions but vary from Ellis's to a greater or lesser degree in theory, practice, or both (Beck, 1976; Greenwald, 1973; Mahoney, 1974; Maultsby, 1975; Meichenbaum, 1977).

The other significant trend I have noted among psychotherapists is a tendency toward rapprochement between behavior therapists and those of a cognitive persuasion (Mahoney, 1977). Most of the cognitive therapists cited above use behavioral techniques to some extent. Behavior therapists are also beginning to see the value of cognitive methods (Goldfried & Davison, 1976). At first glance such a joining of forces seems odd. In order to base their work on reliable and repeatable observations, behavior therapists have traditionally avoided inferences about internal processes such as perceptions, thoughts, and affects. Cognitive therapists, on the other hand, begin by violating this sacred behaviorist commandment.

What has happened? Both groups of therapists have had considerable success treating patients suited to their methods. As both groups have tried to handle a broader variety of cases, difficulties have arisen. "Narrow-spectrum" behavior therapists have had trouble handling complex human problems. They have also found simple cases becoming more complex when closely examined. Cognitive therapists have begun to learn the same lessons patients have been trying to teach insight therapists for years: A person can learn all the correct words without changing his or her behavior at all. Because of these troubles, the cognitive and the behavioral points of view have begun to merge. A halfbreed has been spawned: Cognitive-Behavior Therapy.

Verbal Behavior Therapy was one of the first of these cognitive-behavioral blends. As time has passed, it has developed further and now attempts to deal with other facets of behavior as well.

CURRENT STATUS

Verbal Behavior Therapy bears kinship to a number of currently popular active-directive therapies. In line with the convergences described above, most of the "cognitive" therapies and most of the "broad-spectrum" behavior therapies share important basic assumptions and points of view while emphasizing theoretical and technical differences that have not yet been shown to have a great deal of impact on effectiveness. Consequently, training in approaches similar to these can be obtained in a variety of university centers and training institutes.

Some of the elements of Verbal Behavior Therapy—particularly the assessment procedures and forms—have been used by other therapists. These have usually been professionals employing behavioral methods.

Verbal Behavior Therapy as a system has not been extensively taught or promoted. Usually elements of the methods have been presented with clear acknowledgment of their behavioral or cognitive ancestry. For these reasons the system as a whole can still be studied only by reading my publications on it (see references). *Introduction to Scientific Psychiatry* (Storrow, 1967) remains the most complete account; although it is now out of print, a revision is planned. A brief account that covers different ground from this one was published in 1973 (Storrow, 1973).

THEORY

I will begin each paragraph in this section with an assumption, assertion, or hypothesis basic to the theory underlying the system and will amplify it in the sentences that follow. The most fundamental principles are those of behavioristic learning theory: classical and instrumental conditioning. I employ, however, a broader definition of behavior; I also use many of the principles of Bandura's version of social learning theory (1977).

The goal of psychotherapy is behavior change. This notion is, of course, fundamental to all behavioristic psychotherapies. It provides an anchoring point that has been invaluable to the clinician—in choosing and changing treatment tactics—and to the investigator—in trying to learn what tactics work best with which problems.

Behavior can be either overt or covert. Overt behavior—speech, actions, and physiological changes—is, in principle at least, publicly observable, either directly or through instrumentation. Overt behavior is the sole focus of change for the "narrow-spectrum" behavior therapies. It is not, however, the only behavior of interest when one deals with humans. Covert or subjective behavior—perception, imagery, thinking, emotions—is of equal or greater interest as a target of, or an instrument for, change. The two kinds of behavior differ only in accessibility to observation. Overt behavior can be observed and described by anyone with the necessary training; observations can thus be checked for reliability and accuracy. Covert behavior can be observed only by the person behaving; it is not now possible to check such observations in the same fashion: In outpatient practice, however, even this distinction often breaks down; much of the time all we have to work with is the patient's report, whichever kind of behavior is the focus of interest.

Although the human organism always behaves as a whole, for practical purposes it is useful to consider behavior as falling into a number of more or less well-defined categories. We can then check each of these categories as we go about our assessment and treatment planning tasks. The categories I use are:

1. Overt or objective behavior
   a. Actions
   b. Speech
   c. Physiological activity
2. Covert or subjective behavior
   a. Perception
   b. Imagery
   c. Thinking
   d. Emotions

Each of these categories—facets, modalities—of behavior can be, and often is, influenced by one or more of the others. A person's actions, for example, can be a function of speech, physiological activity, perception, imagery, thinking, and/or emotions. Similar equations can be written for the other modalities.

When a given facet of behavior is abnormal or maladaptive, corresponding abnormalities appear in one or more of the other categories. This means that a therapeutic program can be set up to change a given facet of behavior by changing another modality of which it is a function. For example, depressed patients often describe patterns of withdrawal from customary activities coupled with almost obsessional ruminations about personal worthlessness and inability to cope with overwhelming demands. The depressive mood—even when accompanied by the physiological changes we call vegetative signs—may lift in response to a therapeutic attack on the withdrawal (actions) and on the depressive ruminations (thinking).

If a behavioral abnormality is accompanied by corresponding abnormalities in several other facets, a treatment program aimed at multiple facets may produce more lasting change than one aimed at a single facet. This is Lazarus's (1976) multimodal hypothesis. Although I consider it reasonable enough to serve as a general guide for therapeutic planning, it has yet to be proven.

All categories of behavior are strongly influenced by the current environment and can be molded through the well-known processes of simple learning: classical or respondent conditioning and instrumental or operant conditioning. The many successes of behavioral treatment programs based on these principles—for example, token economies—adequately illustrate this point.

In the case of human beings, however, the more complex processes of vicarious learning and cognitive control provide what is usually a safer and more rapid route to new behavior. A child usually doesn't have to experience the aversive experience of being struck by a car in order for the behavior of "running in front of cars" to be suppressed. Often a strongly worded explanation will suffice (cognitive control). Certainly a child's future behavior will be strongly influenced if he or she ever sees another child struck (vicarious learning). A more commonly seen example of vicarious learning is the role-reversal technique in assertiveness training, where the patient takes the role of the menacing authority figure while the therapist stands up to him in the role of the patient. Both these processes—vicarious learning and cognitive control—are discussed extensively by Bandura (1977).

Finally, what about the problem of determinism versus free will? This has plagued psychotherapy system builders for many years—although many system builders have elected to ignore it. The trouble is that a therapist must accept some form of determinism in order to believe that his or her efforts can have an impact on another person; at the same time he or she must accept some form of free will in order to explain why patient improvement so frequently occurs only in the company of patient behaviors labeled as "trying" or "making an effort." Bandura (1977) handles the dilemma in the neatest fashion I have encountered—by advancing the notion of "reciprocal determinism." Behavioral causality is a two-way street. A person is influenced by his or her physical and social environments, but the person's behavior also influences the environments. The obvious fact that a person exerts a considerable degree of control over his or her own acts need not be ignored in order to be "scientific"; it can be explained. Reciprocal determinism also provides a rationale for the "self-control" procedures that have become so important a feature of current behavioral psychotherapies.

METHODOLOGY

Verbal Behavior Therapy—similar to a number of other systems of psychotherapy—can be usefully viewed as divided into three somewhat overlapping phases: opening, middle, and closing.

The opening phase of treatment sets the therapeutic stage by accomplishing a number of preliminary tasks associated with helping the patient become accustomed to his or her role in therapy and familiar with the clinical assessment of the problems. The tasks needing attention—though not necessarily in this order—are: adaptation, diagnostic investigation, and negotiating the therapeutic contract.

Adaptation means giving the patient a chance to become accustomed to the therapeutic setting before demands are made on him or her. It also involves establishing the therapist as a source of reinforcement. As the patient begins to like the therapist and to desire to please him or her, the therapist's approval can begin to be em-

ployed as a reinforcer for effortful activities required of the patient, such as completion of homework assignments. The tasks of the adaptation period are accomplished primarily by establishing an empathic, warm, and authentic therapeutic climate and by making demands on the patient only as he or she is clearly ready to handle them. It is also helpful if the therapist can provide a bit of immediate relief for patient discomfort—by prescribing a minor tranquilizer, for example.

The diagnostic investigation involves a complex set of tasks that are the keystone of the entire treatment. Here's what needs to be done:

1. Inventory symptoms and problems
   a. Personal Data Form
   b. Case Study Form
2. Identify symptoms and problems
3. Identify central symptom or problem
4. Pinpoint therapeutic targets
   a. Central symptom or problem
   b. Other important therapeutic targets
5. Gather baseline data
6. Functionally analyze therapeutic targets
   a. What intensifies problem behavior?
   b. What alleviates problem behavior?
   c. Stimulus antecedents of problem behavior
   d. Consequences of problem behavior
7. Specify goals for each therapeutic target

I continue to label this phase the diagnostic investigation even though I know that diagnosis is a red-flag word for many therapists. I wish to emphasize the notion that here we are attempting a task similar to what confronts the physician in daily practice: the search for functional relationships that will aid our efforts to relieve the patient's complaints. At the outset we don't know whether we are dealing with the symptoms of a disease process or what has been called "problems of living." In many cases we won't know the answer to that question until research yields us more answers.

The inventory of symptoms and problems involves collecting a data base covering the patient's complaints and describing his or her functioning in the various areas of living. I use two forms to aid me in the search. The Personal Data Form is completed by the patient, and the Case Study Form guides and structures the diagnostic interview or interviews. Both may be found in *Introduction to Scientific Psychiatry* (Storrow, 1967).

In spite of the apparent objectivity of behavioral approaches, when treating outpatients we must still depend primarily on the patient's report even in the case of behaviors that, under ideal conditions, could be directly observed. We should therefore try to use interview techniques that inject the least possible bias into what our patient tells us. These seem to be interventions that involve minimal therapist activity, interventions such as those taught generations of insight therapists. These points are dealt with in detail in my book (Storrow, 1967).

Data gathering should aim at discovering all the problems that could possibly merit attention and then winnowing the list to those that will be the focus of treatment. Central symptoms or problems—if they are discovered—always merit attention. These are problems that appear early and appear to be the core around which other problems develop. If they are treated effectively, entire problem complexes often improve with them. Other important therapeutic targets are distressing symptoms or problems that appear to have a life of their own and thus need to be treated separately.

The functional analysis is then focused on the therapeutic targets. It involves looking for environmental antecedents and consequences just as in a strictly behavioristic functional analysis. Beyond this, however, we look for problems in behavioral categories, other than the target, that precede, accompany, or follow the target behavior. These other problems may then be treated along with a direct attack on the target. For example, an anxious patient often thinks frightening thoughts as he or she begins to panic. A good treatment plan may be to couple a direct attempt to reduce the anxiety with relaxation training and an attack on the harmful thought patterns with cognitive reeducation.

We should next try to formulate reasonable goals for each target problem. How will the patient behave when our task is complete? The goal may be complete cure or something short of that. Deciding upon a reasonable goal involves considering a number of different factors, such as how long the problem has been present, the nature of the problem, the accessibility of relevant treatment variables, availability of proven techniques for the problem under consideration, and so forth.

Negotiating a therapeutic contract usually completes the opening phase of treatment. The therapeutic contract expresses the goals and conditions of treatment as well as the rationale for each and asks for the patient's agreement to each point. Each item should be presented and negotiated, not imposed. This helps to insure patient cooperation as treatment proceeds.

Treatment conditions are both general and problem-specific. General conditions are those that seem to favor success regardless of the specific treatment measures being employed. I ask patients to make commitments to be honest with me and to take responsibility for their behavior, both during the interviews and between them. Problem-specific conditions are just that: tailored to specific problems, goals, and treatment plans. For example, many of my treatment plans involve homework assignments to practice relaxation, to ask for a date, to speak up in class. I outline what will be expected and ask

the patient to commit him- or herself to the requirements.

Treatment planning in Verbal Behavior Therapy—as in other behavioristic psychotherapies—is much more difficult than in more traditional approaches. Instead of one treatment for every problem, there are many problem-specific methods. Most of these were devised by behavior therapists, but some—and commonly used ones at that—come from the cognitive therapy tradition. As time goes on, we shall probably employ promising maneuvers from Gestalt and the experiential therapies.

I shall not try here to outline the details of specific therapeutic techniques. The verbal behavior therapist must be catholic in choosing and learning techniques to employ. Most of the common behavioral methods may be found in Goldfried and Davison (1976). Methods for using homework assignments, which I strongly favor, are covered thoroughly in Shelton and Ackerman (1974). For cognitive reeducation, which I find myself using more and more frequently, I prefer Beck (1976) and his Socratic approach to Ellis (1962) and his strident argumentation.

I have one caveat for therapists wishing to move in the directions I advocate. Don't try to incorporate a new technique until you have made every effort to learn it thoroughly. Read about it carefully, try to obtain some competent supervision, and practice it. Otherwise it will probably fail to perform as advertised, and you'll give up on something that could have been useful. The essence of Verbal Behavior Therapy lies in its structure, in its emphasis on a growth-promoting therapeutic climate—rare in the behavioral tradition—and in its approach to assessment. Its essence does *not* lie in a specific bagful of technical tricks.

Selection of therapy tactics depends to a considerable degree on the kind of problem being treated. For "behavior surplus" problems where we wish to decrease the frequency and/or intensity of some behavior—such as anxiety—there are extinction and counterconditioning techniques, such as flooding and desensitization. For "behavior deficit" problems where we wish to increase the frequency and/or intensity of some behavior—such as assertiveness—such techniques as role-playing and positive reinforcement can be employed. Complex methods, such as cognitive reeducation and homework assignments, can be applied to both kinds of problems.

The question of whether specific target problems can be treated effectively and efficiently by concentrating directly on the problem alone or perhaps on one other behavioral category of which the target is a function cannot be settled with data at present. Lazarus (1976) would say we should perhaps treat the entire "BASIC ID," that is, all the behavioral categories where abnormalities can be found corresponding to the target problem. My own solution is to treat central symptoms as intensively as possible and to do the same with other symptoms and problems that prove to be treatment resistant. I'm likely to treat other problems in a simpler and more direct manner.

In the middle phase of treatment, the therapeutic plan is implemented with most of the attention focused on the central symptom or problem, if one has been identified. Progress—or the lack of progress—is monitored by continuing to keep logs of problem frequency or intensity and comparing the new data with baseline findings. If improvement can be demonstrated, its presence serves as a reinforcement for continued effort on the part of both patient and therapist. If no improvement occurs in a reasonable period of time, this serves as a signal to recycle the data to see if there has been an error in assessment, treatment planning, treatment application, and/or patient cooperation. Opportunity is thus available for another try with the error or errors corrected.

As target behavior changes approach the levels specified in the goals, termination should be considered. This brings us to the closing phase of treatment. I like to think of treatment termination as proceeding through four stages: the preclosing stage, the confrontation, the closing stage, and the postclosing stage.

The preclosing stage begins during the middle phase of treatment. As treatment proceeds I try to keep the patient's attention focused on all the hours between treatment sessions. This helps to prevent him or her from valuing the sessions so highly that it will be difficult to give them up. Both of us review events between sessions, focusing on both successes and difficulties. One of the reasons I favor homework assignments so highly is that they help to keep emphasis on those hours of daily life between sessions. I thus strive to prevent my patient from construing our sessions as a way of life. Termination is then much easier when the time comes.

The confrontation comes when I decide that termination may be in order and raise the question with my patient. At this point the notion is "for discussion only." If the patient accepts the notion, we move to the closing stage. If he or she objects, we take time to discuss what our new goals may be, should we decide to continue. I try not to drift aimlessly, although with some patients that's hard to do.

The closing takes a month or so after the patient has accepted—or even first mentioned—the idea. It provides time to discuss what may happen should we actually stop seeing each other. Even patients who at first seem eager to close may have second thoughts later. This stage gives us an opportunity to discuss them.

The postclosing stage continues indefinitely after closing. I make clear to the patient that no known form of treatment for mental disturbance insures against relapse or the development of new problems. I say that I will be happy to communicate with him or her later, should the patient feel it is necessary. We can then decide if further treatment is in order.

APPLICATIONS

When Verbal Behavior Therapy was initially developed during the early 1960s, systematic desensitization stood out as a behavioral treatment effective for phobic patients and applicable in outpatient as well as inpatient settings. Its full range of application was not known, however, and is still not completely known today. At that early time other behavioral therapies were developing—many of them based on the operant model—but they flourished best in inpatient units, where readymade opportunities were available for the careful observation and recording that characterized these procedures.

As a psychiatrist interested in treating neurotic outpatients, I wondered if a system were available to extend behavioral techniques to all such patients, rather than to phobics alone. It seemed at that point that I would have to devise one myself. If patients could be relied upon to make their own behavioral observations and if the biases in self-reports could be minimized through good interview technique, it seemed possible. Thus Verbal Behavior Therapy was born.

As one might expect from this thumbnail sketch, the system seems best suited to neurotic outpatients. It requires a good deal of voluntary cooperation on the part of the patient, though, and works less well with less responsible patients. But then, no form of psychotherapy works particularly well with such individuals; they often won't even take medication as directed. As with other behavioral methods, it seems to handle best those patients whose problems can be precisely defined—such as phobics and obsessive-compulsive persons—and perhaps less well those patients whose problems defy precise definition, such as patients with existential angst. This latter distinction, however, seems less clearcut now that the scope of the method has been extended with increased attention to covert forms of behavior.

Patients with personality disorders respond poorly to all forms of psychotherapy. They are likely to be uncooperative and to drop out prematurely. Although Verbal Behavior Therapy doesn't solve these problems, its nononsense emphasis on present problems and on behavior change probably gives these patients a better shake than do the traditional insight psychotherapies.

My own conviction is that much of the behavior that falls in the psychotic spectrum is not treatable with psychotherapy alone. Some problems that occur in psychotic patients—such as social skills deficiency—can be helped with psychotherapy, however. These difficulties, in my opinion clearly respond better to behavioral interventions than to traditional therapies.

And finally, a clear limitation: the patient who enters treatment expecting to be helped toward insight. This patient is usually widely read along self-help lines and is sometimes familiar with some of the technical psychotherapy literature. To use Verbal Behavior Therapy with this patient requires a careful and ample explanation of its rationale, an explanation that often amounts to salesmanship. Otherwise, he or she is likely to drop out of treatment without announcing that intention. Then he or she goes elsewhere.

CASE EXAMPLE

When Mrs. Morse began her treatment with Verbal Behavior Therapy, she was a 33-year-old married woman with one small child. For the previous five years she had been almost continuously tortured with frightening and guilt-provoking obsessions. She had been hospitalized twice and had received several electroconvulsive treatments about three years previously, during the first period of hospital care. These treatments had altered her clinical condition hardly at all. She had also previously received a great deal of fairly traditional insight-oriented psychotherapy, with little impact on her symptoms.

At the time Verbal Behavior Therapy began, the patient was taking rather large doses of a medication containing both a tricyclic antidepressant and a major tranquilizer. She began therapy about a week after discharge from the hospital for the second time. She stated she was feeling "a bit better," but her clinical condition was essentially unchanged from that illustrated in the brief history given above.

At this point the following diagnostic investigation was recorded, and the problems listed below were identified:

Problem 1. Obsessions. Frightening and guilt-provoking thoughts intrude on the patient's consciousness in spite of almost constant attempts to exclude them.

Problem 2. Agoraphobic syndrome. The patient is frightened of leaving home unless accompanied by her husband or her child. She has not left home alone for two years. Although she has a driver's license, she has not driven a car, either alone or accompanied, for almost three years.

Problem 3. Deficit in assertiveness. Patient describes herself as shy and unable to defend her rights.

The obsessional thoughts were of two kinds clearly distinguished by the patient. First were "bad thoughts,"

thoughts of causing harm to her child, usually by strangling or stabbing him. Second were "fear thoughts," thoughts about being harmed by someone else, about her symptoms becoming worse, about becoming completely incapacitated, and so forth. Both kinds of thought were accompanied by guilt, intense apprehension, and painful muscle tension involving usually the back of the neck, the shoulders, upper back, and upper arms.

The apprehension and the mobility deficit that characterized the agoraphobic syndrome arose out of concern that her fright might increase, at almost any time, to the point that she would lose all control of herself. If such a crisis should occur when she was away from the safety of her home, something disastrous might happen. *What might happen was unknown.*

The deficit in assertiveness was a problem of lesser importance. The patient had found it difficult to stand up for herself "all my life." She did not appear to be greatly disturbed by this problem, and its intensity did not seem to vary in relation to the other two.

Identification of Central Symptom or Problem

Although this patient's deficit in assertiveness was of lengthy duration and meets the central symptom criterion of first appearance, its onset and fluctuation apparently were unrelated to the two problems that bothered Mrs. Morse the most. It was therefore not a central symptom. Since Mrs. Morse was not particularly concerned about this problem, it would not be the focus of treatment efforts at this point.

The obsessional thinking antedated the agoraphobic syndrome. Furthermore, the two problems appeared intertwined. The patient, for example, thought that fear of leaving home could be "punishment" for the "bad thoughts." It appeared that the obsessional thinking was a central symptom and that it should have the top priority for treatment. Note: Even though Mrs. Morse clearly distinguished two kinds of obsessional thoughts, they were treated as one problem because they clearly varied together and because available treatment methods were the same for both.

Pinpointing Therapeutic Targets

Our therapeutic targets were: (1) Obsessions—the central symptom; and (2) agoraphobic syndrome—also very troublesome to the patient.

Gathering Baseline Data

After we had defined the behavior illustrative of the two therapeutic targets as carefully as we could, Mrs. Morse started keeping a frequency log for both. She kept her counts in a pocket spiral notebook that she carried with her at all times. One week of data-keeping showed obsessional thoughts to occur at the rate of 35 to 40 times per day. The behaviors we chose as indices for the intensity of the agoraphobic syndrome occurred at the following rates per day: Leaving house alone—0, Driving car alone—0, Driving car while accompanied by a family member—0.

Note that since the rates of all behaviors of interest were reasonably stable, one week's recording seemed adequate for a baseline. If the rates were more variable from day to day, a two-week recording period would have been employed.

Functional Analysis of Therapeutic Targets

The obsessional thinking was intensified when the patient was alone and "taking it easy." The worst time was when she was sitting at the kitchen table drinking her mid-morning coffee. The problem was alleviated when stimuli for competing responses were present, when she had "something else on my mind," or when she had "something else to do." The stimulus antecedents appeared to be a relative lack of stimuli that might be expected to lead to competing behavior. The immediate consequences were aversive affects such as guilt and apprehension. The only positive consequences I could identify were the conversations she had with her husband about these thoughts. These conversations occurred almost nightly.

Note that obsessions leading to what appear to be aversive affects are difficult to explain in operant terms. I believe that patients subject to these problems are unusually concerned about hostile thoughts. They watch so closely that they attend to thought fragments that most of us ignore.

The agoraphobic syndrome consisted of both aversive affects—primarily fear—and inhibition of action—failure to leave home, to drive, and so forth. The action inhibition was always maximal; the patient never left home alone. The apprehension, however, varied and was intensified whenever an occasion to leave the house arose—for example, when groceries were needed. The feelings were alleviated under the opposite circumstances. The consequences of staying home were obvious; Mrs. Morse's husband helped her shop for groceries and took over many other responsibilities that usually are handled by homemakers.

Behavior in another category was also related to the components of the agoraphobic syndrome. When apprehension was high, the patient was aware of thinking: "I'll get out, and I won't be able to get back. I'll be trapped."

Goals for Each Therapeutic Target

Our goal for the obsessional thoughts was to reduce their frequency to zero. This was probably a bit ambitious, considering the usual prognosis for such problems. The goal for the agoraphobic syndrome was also somewhat grandiose: The patient would be able to go comfortably anywhere she chose.

The treatment plan made the primary focus the obsessional thinking. The first step was to deprive the behavior of the positive reinforcement that might be coming from discussing it with the husband. The patient was asked to discuss these problems only with me. The next step was an effort to reduce the frequency of the problem behavior with self-administered aversive stimulation. Mrs. Morse was instructed to "shout" the word *stop* to herself each time she became aware of either a "fear thought" or a "bad thought." If this measure failed to interrupt the thinking sequence after being employed three times, another measure was to be used. The patient was to go to a preselected place in the home and to think the obsessional thought over and over until she could do so no longer. This procedure is designed to make the symptomatic behavior itself aversive and thus reduce its frequency.

A separate therapeutic plan was designed for the agoraphobic syndrome. This was a graded series of homework assignments. Mrs. Morse was instructed to walk a greater distance from her home each day and to keep a careful log of her performance. A similar series of assignments was later applied to driving the family car. The negative thoughts connected with fear of leaving home were also carefully considered in an effort to alter them. The patient agreed that, in actuality, she was rarely "trapped," that she could almost always return home if panic should occur.

Mrs. Morse agreed to the treatment plan and to the general conditions for treatment. Throughout our work together she completed her assignments faithfully. This was probably one of the primary reasons for the success we attained.

As treatment progressed, the only additional measure employed was relaxation training to counter the muscle tension the patient experienced when she was frightened.

Obsessional Thinking. There was a gradual reduction in this problem behavior over a period of four months. One major interruption in this decline occurred when the patient was called upon to participate in a relative's wedding. At the end of this period Mrs. Morse needed the treatment measures only occasionally, and the obsessional thoughts were noted on an average of once or twice per week. This degree of improvement has been maintained for one year. Medication has been discontinued.

Agoraphobic Syndrome. There was gradual improvement over a period of about five months. At the end of this period Mrs. Morse was able to drive alone for all ordinary household errands. Distance from home was no longer a problem, although she still avoided heavy traffic and crowded shopping center parking lots. She could shop in crowds, however, if someone else drove her to the shopping center. She was satisfied with this degree of improvement and did not wish to work on the problem further. Improvement has been maintained for a follow-up period of one year without medication.

SUMMARY

Since psychoanalysis began to lose its hold—some say stranglehold—on the discipline of psychotherapy in the middle 1950s, the field has become progressively more chaotic and confusing. If there is a single principle of therapeutic importance that has been settled beyond dispute, I'm not aware of it. These are exciting times, but they are also difficult times for both therapists and patients.

Verbal Behavior Therapy represents one therapist's attempt to bring some order to the field. It has several virtues. Although it rests on the firm foundations of a consistent theory, it has the flexibility of technical eclecticism. It has the highly structured qualities of the behavioristic psychotherapies plus the breadth that comes from a broadly conceived definition of "behavior."

Designed for outpatients and tested mainly with them, this approach recognizes the reliance that must be placed on patient reports. It therefore strives to incorporate systematic assessment procedures that reduce the bias often found in such reports.

Today's practitioner of psychotherapy must make choices from a supermarket of competing theories and techniques. He or she must do so with very little hard data to go on. My recommendation would be that he or she look for an approach that is systematic but flexible, and that has room for new developments as they come along. Verbal Behavior Therapy is such a system.

REFERENCES

Anderson, C. M. (1957). *Beyond Freud: A creative approach to mental health.* New York: Harper.

Bandura, A. (1977). *Social learning theory.* Englewood Cliffs, N.J.: Prentice-Hall.

Beck, A. T. (1976). *Cognitive therapy and the emotional disorders.* New York: International Universities Press.

Dollard, J., & Miller, N. E. (1950). *Personality and psychotherapy.* New York: McGraw-Hill.

Ellis, A. (1962). *Reason and emotion in psychotherapy.* New York: Lyle Stuart.

Garfield, S. L., & Kurtz, R. (1976). Clinical psychologists in the 1970s. *American Psychologist, 31,* 1–9.

Goldfried, M. R., & Davison, G. C. (1976). *Clinical behavior therapy.* New York: Holt.

Greenwald, H. (1973). *Decision therapy.* New York: Wyden.

Kelly, G. A. (1955). *The psychology of personal constructs.* New York: Norton.

Kuhn, T. S. (1962). *The structure of scientific revolutions.* Chicago: University of Chicago Press.

Lazarus, A. A. (1976). *Multimodal therapy.* New York: Springer.

Mahoney, M. J. (1974). *Cognition and behavior modification.* Cambridge, MA: Ballinger.

Mahoney, M. J. (1977). Reflections on the cognitive-learning trend in psychotherapy. *American Psychologist, 32,* 5–13.

Maultsby, M. C. (1975). *Help yourself to happiness.* New York: Institute for Rational Living.

Meichenbaum, D. (1977). *Cognitive behavior modification.* New York: Plenum.

Phillips, E. L. (1956). *Psychotherapy: A modern theory and practice.* New York: Prentice-Hall.

Rogers, C. R. (1951). *Client-centered therapy.* Boston: Houghton.

Shelton, J. L., & Ackerman, J. M. (1974). *Homework in counseling and psychotherapy.* Springfield, IL: Charles C. Thomas.

Storrow, H. A. (1963–1964). Learning, labeling, general semantics and psychotherapy. *General Semantics Bulletin, 30, 31,* 84–86.

Storrow, H. A. (1965). Psychotherapy as interpersonal conditioning. In J. H. Masserman (Ed.), *Current psychiatric therapies,* vol. 5. New York: Grune & Stratton.

Storrow, H. A. (1967). *Introduction to scientific psychiatry: A behavioristic approach to diagnosis and treatment.* New York: Appleton.

Storrow, H. A. (1973). Verbal behavior therapy. In Ratibor-Ray M. Jurjevich (Ed.), *Direct psychotherapy.* Coral Gables, FL: University of Miami Press.

Watson, J. B. (1913). Psychology as the behaviorist views it. *Psychological Reviews, 20,* 158.

Wolpe, J. (1958). *Psychotherapy by reciprocal inhibition.* Stanford, CA: Stanford University Press.

Index

Authors listed with last name, first initials.
Biographical references listed with last name, first full name.
Books, etc. referenced in text listed in *italic.*
Chapter subjects listed in **Boldface;** general subjects listed in light face.